GALE ENCYCLOPEDIA OF U.S. ECONOMIC HISTORY

GALE ENCYCLOPEDIA OF U.S. ECONOMIC HISTORY

VOLUME 2 L–Z

THOMAS CARSON, EDITOR
MARY BONK, ASSOCIATE EDITOR

Detroit
San Francisco
London
Boston
Woodbridge, CT

Editor: Thomas Carson
Coeditor: Mary Rose Bonk
Assistant Editors: Talitha A. Jean, Nancy Matuszak, R. David Riddle
Contributing Editors: Pamela A. Dear, Michael Reade
Permissions Team Leader: Maria Franklin
Permissions Specialist: Margaret Chamberlain
Cataloger: Mary K. Grimes
Junior Cataloger: Leitha Etheridge-Sims
Research Manager: Victoria B. Cariappa
Research Specialist: Maureen Richards
Production Director: Mary Beth Trimper
Assistant Production Manager: Evi Seoud
Senior Buyer:Wendy Blurton
Production Design Manager: Cynthia Baldwin
Art Director: Michelle DiMercurio
Graphic Services Manager: Barbara Yarrow
Image Database Supervisor: Randy Bassett
Digital Imaging Specialist: Christine O'Bryan

Library of Congress Catalog
Gale encyclopedia of U.S. economic history / Thomas Carson, editor
cm.
Includes bibliographical references and index.
ISBN 0-7876-3888-9 (set). - ISBN 0-7876-3889-7 (vol. 1)
0-7876-3890-0 (vol.2)
1. United States—Economic conditions Encyclopedias. I. Carson, Thomas. II. Title: Gale encyclopedia of US economic history.
HC102.G35 1999
330.973'003—dc21 99-39623
CIP

27500 Drake Rd.
Farmington Hills, MI 48331-3535

Printed in the United States of America
10 9 8 7 6 5 4 3 2 1

Table of Contents

L'ANSE AUX MEADOWS

L'Anse aux Meadows, on the northeastern tip of Newfoundland, Canada, may have been the first European settlement in North America. In the 1960s Norse ruins were found here, leading scholars to believe this was the site described by Norsemen (Vikings) after they visited a portion of the North American coast around A.D. 1000. The Viking voyages were recorded in a book called the *Greenlanders' Saga* (1200). Norwegian-born Leif Ericsson (c.970–c.1020) is generally credited with having been the first European to set foot on North American soil. Ericsson was the son of navigator Erik the Red who founded a Norse settlement in Greenland, where he moved his family in 985 or 986. About the same time another Norseman, Bjarni Herjolfsson, who was driven off course on his way from Iceland to Greenland, became the first European to see North America, but he did not go ashore. It is believed that Ericsson decided he would follow up on this discovery, and about 1001 he set out from Greenland with a crew of 35 men and probably landed on the southern end of Baffin Island (north of the province of Quebec). The expedition likely reached Labrador, Canada, and later landed on the coast of what is today Nova Scotia or Newfoundland, Canada. This landfall may have been L'Anse aux Meadows. Ericsson and his crew spent the winter of 1001-02 at a place he called Vinland, which was described as well wooded and abounding in fruit, especially grapes. He returned to Greenland in the spring of 1002.

The first authenticated European landing in North America was in 1500 when Portuguese navigator Gaspar de Corte-Real (1450?–1501?) explored the coast of Labrador and Newfoundland.

LABOR MOVEMENT

In the last decades of the nineteenth century it appeared that labor was unable effectively to challenge the combined wealth and power that capitalism in its industrial phase had created. The merger movement brought corporations together into vast concentrations of economic power resting in the hands of relatively few men. These trusts, pools, mergers, "gentlemen's agreements," and other instruments of capital consolidation transformed the structure of whole industries, from oil to coal mining, railroads, iron and steel, and meat packing.

This had a major impact on labor relations. On the one hand, the concentration of capital increased the economic power of the "captains of industry." These vertical and horizontal monopolies brought them the ability, seemingly, to do whatever they liked. Even the growing power of the government seemed unable to contain the power of capital. By the end of the nineteenth century the power among the monopolists seemed to be shifting towards the bankers. An example of this preeminent power of finance capital occurred during Theodore Roosevelt's administration. Roosevelt, who believed that the government must be strong enough to curb the "bad trusts," prosecuted and "busted" the Northern Securities railroad holding company in 1904. J. P. Morgan, who was behind the trust, had pleaded unsuccessfully with Roosevelt that "if we have done something wrong send your man to my man and they can fix it up." In 1904, when the Supreme Court sustained the President's prosecution under the Sherman Anti-trust Act and the Northern Security trust was dissolved, Morgan quietly sustained this challenge to his authority.

Then a few years later, Morgan quietly stepped in to save Roosevelt's political hide when the financial panic of 1907 threatened to scuttle a number of New York banks which might set off a general depression. Working behind the scenes, Morgan constructed a pool of financial support from other banks. Morgan, however, told Roosevelt that the crisis could be avoided only if the government agreed not to prosecute a trust involving U.S. Steel and the Tennessee Coal and Iron

Union density refers to membership in labor unions, proportional to the work force. Between 1930 and 1954 union density increased sharply, with only slight declines.

Company, whose stock was held by one of the threatened banks. Roosevelt had to promise to let the deal go through. To observers it was obvious that the bombastic, trust-busting Roosevelt might make more noise in a confrontation with finance capital, but that the real power was in Morgan's hands.

With this kind of power arrayed against labor, what was the use in trying to organize trade unions? The answer, at least in part, is that by bringing capital together, the merger movement also brought workers together in larger concentrations. One example of this, taken from the 1930s and early 1940s, was the anti-union measures taken by the Ford Motor Company. Henry Ford resisted unionization for decades, but when he built the Dearborn, Michigan Rouge River complex of auto factories and steel mills with a workforce in excess of 80,000, it was only a matter of time before the United Automobile Workers Union (UAW) would successfully organize the plant. It is no coincidence that the first nation-wide strikes in the nineteenth century were called by unions in the railroad industry. The railroads were powerful in their resistance to unions, it is true, but they were also vulnerable. Though they both failed, the ''Rebellion of 1877'' and the Pullman strike in 1894 demonstrated the strategic strength of labor in these new industries.

As for the rest of the economy, labor in the 1880s seemed to be combative, but generally too weak successfully to press its claims for higher wages, shorter hours, and safer working conditions. One of the most interesting workers' associations of the time was the Knights of Labor. This group was less successful in winning strikes than in laying the groundwork for a strong culture which emphasized solidarity among workers. Their mode of labor organizing was to found ''regional assemblies'' which included workers in several nearby industries. This approach stimulated a class-conscious culture, but it was hard to fight strikes when the union was not organized to concentrate on the target industry. Led by a machinist, Terence V. Powderly, the Knights were eclectic in their organizing strategy. They sought to enroll all workers into their lodges: women and African Americans were not excluded; only the ''parasitic'' elements in the communities were not allowed to join—the lawyers, the tavern keepers, bankers and gamblers.

With the Haymarket Riots in Chicago in May 1886, the deteriorating relations with the employers and the government led the labor movement to split in two. One part was the Industrial Workers of the World (IWW). Like the Knights of Labor, the IWW sought to organize all workers in ''One Big Union.'' Also called, affectionately, the ''Wobblies,'' the IWW's roots lay in the unskilled and unruly lumber workers of the northwest, the migrant agricultural workers of the great plains, the Western Federation of Miners, and the textile workers of Lawrence, Massachusetts. They expressed a political culture of American working class radicalism—a political culture that is so complex as to challenge definition. They engaged in free-speech campaigns in southern California during the repressive days of World War I, stepping up to give anti-war speeches on soap-boxes; being dragged away by police; only to be replaced by another speaker. They also most probably murdered mine owners whenever they could get close enough to them. In the exchange of violence, however, they were more often the victims than the perpetrator. They were what political scientists call "Anarcho-Syndicalists," (or anarchist-unionists). They believed that there can only be warfare between labor and capitalism and that either capitalism or socialism would emerge from the battle. They refused to negotiate or sign labor contracts with management because that would signify an accommodation between labor and management. Instead, they simply instigated strikes, something they were very good at. Eventually, as American labor became institutionalized, the Wobblies faded away.

The other side of the split in American labor in the late nineteenth century was the American Federation of Labor. In an era in which the employers seemed to be bent on merger and monopoly, other labor leaders began to think of consolidating the labor movement in a different way—by combining the existing trade unions into a national federation similar to the British Trades Union Congress (TUC). In response to management's monopoly of capital, they set out to monopolize labor, but they did so in a very different way than the Wobblies. This new federation, the American Federation of Labor, was formed in 1886. It did not shrink from the IWW's fear of "legitimizing" normal relationships between labor and capital. That, in fact, was its goal—to become a legitimate voice of labor in a democratic capitalist society (a contradiction in terms, the Wobblies would have argued). It intended to use whatever tools it could to improve the condition and the wages of labor. It would lobby for legislation in Washington and the state capitals. Of it would go on strike. Like the British TUC, it was composed of craft unions and it promised its constituent unions complete autonomy in the operation of their relations with management. Meeting in Pittsburgh in November 1881, the national trades unions formed the Federation of Organized Trades and Labor Unions of the United States and Canada. The federation grew slowly, hindered at first by the economic recession from 1883 to 1885, and also by defeats in a number of labor disputes. Eventually, in 1886 they formed the American Federation of Labor.

The AFL called for solidarity among workers, but they did so through supporting each others' boycotts and refusals to "handle struck goods." They didn't call for the end of the wage labor system. They called for an alliance of labor unions committed to bread-and-butter wage and working conditions, rather than political or social issues and advocacy. At the convention in December 1886, the American Federation of Labor was born. Samuel Gompers of the Cigarmakers' International Union was elected president. Eschewing utopianism and espousing practical objectives, the AFL was able to survive the disastrous strikes of the early 1890s, and emerged in 1897 from the depression of that decade with 265,000 members and uncontested dominance in the American labor movement.

With the revival of traditional conservative probusiness politics after World War I (1914–1918), and the anti-Communism of the first "red scare" (1919–early 1920s) labor evinced a desire to appear "legitimate" and non-controversial. As would happen in the second "red scare" of the early 1950s, the leaders of the AFL denounced the radicals in the labor movement. They stood by as several union leaders accused of instigating the Haymarket Riot in Chicago were indicted, tried, found guilty, and hanged (although the accused were not present at the riot).

Pressing their advantage during the 1920s, the company-sponsored offensive against unions included hard-nosed policies like hiring armed company guards, strikebreakers, and agents provocateurs (hired infiltrators who instigated violence to bring down the repression by the police and the courts), as well as the tactic of founding non-controversial and ineffective "company unions." Capitalizing on anti-labor sentiments in the population at large, employers drew upon local and state authorities to deploy mounted police and militia to harass and arrest union organizers and disrupt picket lines. Yellow-dog contracts, which threatened workers with dismissal should they join a union, became commonplace. Under the auspices of the National Association of Manufacturers, anti-labor propaganda circulated widely, systematically arguing in favor of open shops, which allowed nonunion workers to be employed even though a union may have organized the workplace.

The protective legislation that Gompers and his fellow labor leaders thought they saw in the 1914 Clayton Act's provisions excluding unions from prosecution for being "in restraint of trade" was shredded by a U.S. Supreme Court decision in 1921. In *Duplex Printing Press Company v. Deering*, the Supreme Court interpreted the Sherman and Clayton Acts as protecting employers from labor violence, from secondary boycotts, and from the use of other labor tactics that could be construed as unlawful interference with interstate commerce.

Speaking for a conservative Court, Justice Mahlon Pitney held that certain union tactics constituted unlawful interference with interstate commerce and therefore were subject to antitrust laws. By holding unions accountable under antitrust laws for anything the Court deemed to be other than normal and legitimate union activity, the Court effectively nullified the Clayton

Act's labor provisions, and made it almost impossible for unions to organize workers in nonunion companies.

But under President Franklin D. Roosevelt's administration (1933–1945), things changed for labor. Title 7(a) of the National Industrial Recovery Act (NIRA), gave labor unions the legal right to bargain collectively, and Roosevelt often backed labor in efforts to put forth its side of the story in disputes with management. It was mainly the Congress of Industrial Organizations that benefited from the government's decision not to repress labor. (Under the leadership of United Mineworker President John L. Lewis, the CIO split from the AFL in 1935 and set about organizing the semi-skilled labor in the new mass production industries like auto, steel, and rubber. The CIO demanded that all labor must be organized, not just the skilled trades).

A conservative Supreme Court struck down NIRA, but Congress passed the National Labor Relations Act (the Wagner Act), which upheld the right to bargain collectively, authorized the Fair Labor Standards Act (which continued the 40-hour workweek) and prohibited child labor, and established the National Labor Relations Board to mediate during industrial disputes. When labor unions added the clout of the sit-down strike to government assistance, they secured for themselves living wages and purchasing power.

The 1955 merger that created the American Federation of Labor–Congress of Industrial Organizations (AFL-CIO) healed a serious rift in the American labor movement, but a number of critical problems haunted AFL-CIO leadership during the next 15 years. The nation's political mood following passage of the Taft-Hartley Act in 1947—and the state "right to work" laws that ensued—continued to be generally hostile toward organized labor. Much of this hostility was rooted in public perceptions that many unions were infiltrated and dominated by Communists or, equally menacing to the public welfare, that they were run by corrupt officials in collaboration with organized crime.

The U.S. Secretary of Labor, James P. Mitchell, reflecting the views of President Dwight D. Eisenhower's administration (1953–1961), announced to the 1957 AFL-CIO convention that the president would soon propose legislation to protect union members from "crooks and racketeers." That prediction anticipated passage of the Labor-Management Reporting and Disclosure Act (Landrum-Griffin Act) two years later. When the Senate Permanent Subcommittee on Investigations, led by Senator John L. McClellan (D-Arkansas) and its chief counsel, Robert F. Kennedy, shifted its focus toward union corruption and racketeering, labor leaders began to realize the disruptive potential of union reform. Within months, committee revelations concerning corruption among unions of operating engineers, plumbers, and retail clerks became national news.

Aware that the image of organized labor had become badly tarnished, labor leaders during the 1960s attempted to take the lead in cleansing the unions of communist influences as well as dishonest union officials and mobsters. After the merger, the burden of these efforts fell to the AFL-CIO's first president, George Meany, a New York City plumber by trade and a respected organizer and union leader. In his capacity as the McClellan Committee's chief counsel, Robert F. Kennedy personally presented Meany with damning evidence against the AFL–CIO's largest constituent union, the Teamsters.

The Kennedy-Mollenhoff materials specifically alleged corruption involving, among others, Teamster president Dave Beck. Beck, an AFL-CIO vice president and executive committee member, testified in 1957 before the McClellan Committee about his purported theft of $300,000 of union funds as well as his acceptance of money from employers. Meany was outraged that Beck invoked the Fifth Amendment ninety times. Meany stripped Beck of his AFL-CIO offices and his Teamster presidency and planned to present the Teamsters's 1957 convention with details of Beck's corruption. Under Beck's successor, Jimmy Hoffa, the presentation of the AFL-CIO report on Teamster corruption at the Teamster's 1957 convention was jeered and expunged from the record. Hoffa declared his union ready to "tell the AFL-CIO to go to hell." Thus, in December 1957 the AFL-CIO expelled its largest union, the Teamsters.

Hoffa by that point was standing trial in New York for wiretapping the telephones of Teamsters who were to appear before the McClellan Committee. While under indictment, Hoffa presided over the Teamsters from 1957 until 1967, the year in which appeals from his 1964 conviction on separate charges of jury tampering, fraud, and conspiracy were exhausted and he began serving the remainder of a 13-year sentence in federal prison. In 1971, with his sentence commuted by President Richard Nixon (1961–1974), Hoffa retired from all Teamster offices with his union's thanks and an award of $1.7 million, or about a dollar per member. In 1975, as news reports were circulating that the Teamster leader might be about to reenter active leadership of the union, Hoffa disappeared and was presumed murdered.

Meany's efforts to clean house and refurbish labor's name produced significant changes in the AFL-CIO. The AFL-CIO constitution prohibited union corruption and criminality; it did not, however, prescribe enforcement powers. Meany and his aides and committees expelled errant officials or unions, placed them on probation or under monitors, or gave them dated ultimatums to produce reforms. In initiating these actions, Meany challenged the historic autonomy that many unions, particularly those of the old AFL, had cherished as their right. Although Meany largely abandoned his drive against union corruption and criminality by 1963, leaving further measures to the U.S. Attorney General and Senate investigators, one momentous consequence of his reformism was the centralization of authority in the hands of AFL-CIO leaders. Management found themselves dealing less with a federation of unions than with the federation itself—the world's largest labor organization.

Critics from within the labor movement were quick to observe that a more centralized AFL-CIO was also more conservative and complacent. Some critics attributed a relative decline in nationwide union strength to this complacency. Although no observers lamented the convictions of expelled Teamster officials, least of all Beck and Hoffa, most noted that the Teamsters offered many workers one of few alternatives to the giant federation after the Teamsters' return to political favor during the Nixon administration. The union failed in its efforts between the 1960s and 1987 to reenter the AFL-CIO.

The post-Hoffa Teamsters displayed an interest in organizing almost any workers. This approach to organization, pushed regardless of organizational expense and with great daring, accelerated after 1975. The AFL-CIO avoided trying to unionize companies with only a handful of workers, but the Teamsters, in a spirit that strangely recalled the idealism of the Knights of Labor or the I.W.W., often sought recruits in shops with fewer than a dozen employees. It made no economic sense, but, to many Teamster organizers and rank and file, it was the right thing to do. The overall strength of the union rose only modestly to 1.8 million members by the end of the 1970s. In effect, the Teamsters were the AFL-CIO's only formidable and dynamic competition. This remained true until 1968, when Walter Reuther pulled his United Auto Workers (UAW) out of the AFL-CIO and promptly entered an alliance with the Teamsters. The UAW and the Teamsters each launched vigorous and innovative organizing campaigns that were supposed to put labor on the march again. (Reuther, however, died in a plane crash in 1970.)

After many attempts, the Teamsters were allowed to rejoin the AFL-CIO in 1987. Meany's AFL-CIO tried to maintain its membership during a lengthy relative decline in union membership. By the 1990s the labor scene was businesslike, closely monitored by law and by union leadership. A measure of respectability, if not huge popularity, had returned to a more centralized AFL-CIO.

***See also:* American Federation of Labor, Congress of Industrial Organizations, Industrial Workers of the World, Knights of Labor, Labor Unionism, John Llewellyn Lewis, RICO Act**

FURTHER READING

Brooks, Thomas R. *Toil and Trouble: A History of American Labor.* 2d ed. New York: Delacorte Press, 1971.

Lorwin, Lewis L. *The American Federation of Labor: History, Policies, and Prospects.* Washington, D.C.: The Brookings Institution, 1933.

Mandel, Bernard. *Samuel Gompers, A Biography.* Yellow Springs, Ohio: Antioch College Press, 1963.

Pelling, Henry. *American Labor.* Chicago: University of Chicago Press, 1960.

Taft, Philip. *The A.F. of L. from the Death of Gompers to the Merger.* New York: Harper & Row, 1959.

LABOR UNIONISM *(ISSUE)*

A modern U.S. labor union is an organized body of workers banded together to better their standard of living by seeking higher wages and improved working conditions. Workers authorize their union representatives to negotiate with their employers in a process known as collective bargaining. If negotiation fails, the workmen often attempt to achieve their goals through strikes (withholding their labor) or by persuading others to boycott their employer's products.

Unions first appeared in the 1820s. They were usually small, local, and short-lived. As the factory system grew in the mid-19th century so did the need for workers' organizations. Before the Civil War (1861–65) such groups remained small and localized. But after the war efforts were made to form labor unions on a national scale.

The first such effort began in 1866 when several trade unions sent delegates to a convention in Baltimore. Under the leadership of William H. Sylvis this group formed the National Labor Union. The organization grew rapidly and by 1872 it claimed 600,000 members. Its main issue was the eight-hour day, a demand that was regarded as extremely radical. The National Labor Union experienced success for a short time, but numerous factors combined to destroy it: Sylvis' death in 1869, the union's conversion to a political party in 1872, and the panic of 1873.

The next major effort began in Philadelphia in 1869. Under the leadership of garment maker Uriah S. Stephens six men founded the Noble Order of the Knights of Labor. Their platform called for the eight-hour day, an income tax, and workmen's compensation. Stephens maintained that such tactics as strikes were counter-productive, and advocated "education" as the proper means for workers to achieve their goals.

The Knights were structured on the "one big union" concept; all workers were welcome to join. The membership could include the skilled and unskilled, men and women, and people of all races. This broad inclusion policy was a radical idea at the time and eventually led to serious internal tensions.

Because Stephens feared counter-measures by employers, the organization was secret at first and growth was slow. By 1873 there were only three assemblies, all in Philadelphia. Ten years later the Knights had only 52,000 members. However they expanded rapidly after this initial period. By 1886 membership neared one million. This remarkable change occurred because the union veered away from Stephens' original principles and authorized its members to strike. Its reputation was enhanced when it won several of them, especially against railroad companies in Texas.

The Knights of Labor had no sooner reached their peak of growth than they fell into a rapid decline. Unsuccessful strikes undermined their prestige, which was further damaged by factional differences and financial problems. In addition the Knights faced competition from a new organization known as the American Federation of Labor (AFL).

The origins of the AFL go back to November 1881 when delegates representing the carpenters, cigar makers, printers, merchant seamen, and steelworkers gathered in Pittsburgh. They formed a new organization called The Federation of Organized Trades and Labor Unions. Their purpose was to work for pro-labor legislation. One of the most prominent among the founders was Samuel Gompers of the Cigar Makers Union, who was now beginning his long career as head of the U.S. labor movement. At first, the Federation did not accomplish much, but after it reorganized in 1886, a new era in the history of the labor movement began.

The modern U.S. labor movement started with the reorganization of American Federation that took place in Columbus, Ohio on December 8, 1886. Samuel Gompers was elected as president, and the union was structured according to his wishes. Gompers insisted that the organization represent skilled workers only, that it be built as a federation of autonomous trade unions, that it stay out of politics, that it avoid radical economic themes, and that it devote itself to working for attainable goals. These goals included the eight-hour day, child labor legislation, workplace safety, immigration restriction, and workmen's' compensation.

The AFL grew slowly at first. By 1890 it claimed only 100,000 members, but by 1900 membership had risen to 548,000, and by 1914 it was approaching two million. Along the way the AFL attracted some very large unions such as the United Mine Workers (UMW, founded in 1890). But there were other large organizations that did not affiliate. Most notable among these were the Railroad Brotherhoods: the Engineers formed in 1863 and the Firemen formed in 1869.

During its early years of growth the AFL faced considerable opposition. Employers were not required by law to bargain with unions and some refused to even recognize their existence. Strikes were often met with a violent response and many court decisions went against labor. The public tolerated such actions because unions were successfully portrayed as un-American and the law tended to uphold property rights more often than human rights.

Still led by Samuel Gompers, organized labor in the United States generally cooperated with the government during World War I (1914–18). Union membership continued to grow, reaching nearly four million. After the war however there was a decline of 25 percent, which resulted mainly from a recession between 1921 and 1922 that cost jobs and lowered wages. As the decade of the twenties continued, employers tended to fight the union movement more vigorously. One of their chief weapons was the "company union," an in-house organization that provided benefits but did not allow bargaining. Such "unions" became very popular in the 1920s and contributed to the decline of the labor movement. By 1927 AFL membership had fallen to 2 million, 11.6 percent of the work force.

The Great Depression of the 1930s brought major changes. Between 1929 and 1933 the effects of the economic collapse on labor were catastrophic. But when Franklin Delano Roosevelt (1933–45) became president he inaugurated the New Deal; many New Deal programs were designed to benefit workers. The most important of these was the National Labor Relations Act of 1935, which required employers to bargain collectively with union representatives chosen by the workers. This law triggered a boom in union membership, which by 1941 reached 27 percent of the total work force.

At the same time there were other major changes within the labor movement. Head of the United Mine Workers John L. Lewis demanded that the AFL begin organizing campaigns in the major non-union industries such as steel, automobiles, rubber, glass, textiles, and meat packing. Lewis wanted to organize these industries on the industrial or ''vertical'' basis. This meant that all the workers regardless of skill would be in one union. The majority of AFL leaders presided over craft or ''horizontal'' unions, and they opposed Lewis's views.

In November 1935 Lewis announced the creation of the Committee for Industrial Organization (CIO) to carry on the effort for industrial unions. Lewis and his colleagues were expelled from the AFL in 1936. At this point the CIO became the Congress of Industrial Organizations. They continued their work and successfully organized unions in many mass production industries including steel, autos, rubber, glass, and meatpacking. These successes contributed to the rapid growth of the labor movement. The AFL and the CIO however remained separate and did not reunite until 1955.

World War II (1939–45) caused a labor shortage and strengthened the labor movement once again. During the war union membership rose fifty percent, until it reached 35.3 percent of the total work force, the highest it would ever be. Beginning in the 1950s the labor movement entered a long but gradual period of decline, which was caused by a leadership that no longer recruited aggressively, a loss of interest in social reform, technological and structural unemployment, and growing public animosity. Technological and structural employment were perhaps the most important reasons labor unions became less popular. Because of increased use of machines the number of available jobs declined in many industries. A majority of jobs shifted from the industrial sector to white collar and service sectors. By the 1990s only 16.1 percent of workers worked in factories whereas in the 1970s it was 25.8 percent. Fewer people on corporate payrolls meant fewer people in unions because these are the workers most likely to sign industry-wide contracts.

By the 1990s the labor movement had changed considerably. Only 14.1 percent of the work force belonged to unions. Of these the vast majority held non-industrial jobs: 41.9 percent were in the public sector and only 16.3 percent were in the manufacturing sector. The chances that these trends will reverse again any time soon are very small.

See also: **American Federation of Labor, Brotherhood of Sleeping Car Porters, Congress of Industrial Organizations, Industrial Workers of the World, Knights of Labor, Labor Movement**

FURTHER READING

Aronowitz, Stanley. *From the Ashes of the Old: American Labor and America's Future.* Boston: Houghton Mifflin Company, 1998.

Dubofsky, Melvin, and Van Tine, Warren. *John L. Lewis: A Biography.* New York: Quadrangle/New York Times Book Company, 1977.

Faulkner, Harold U. *American Economic History.* New York: Harper, 1954.

Hirsch, Barry T. and Macpherson, David A. *Union Membership and Earnings: Data Book.* Washington: Bureau of National Affairs, 1998.

Kaufman, Stuart. *Samuel Gompers and the American Federation of Labor, 1848–1896.* Westport, CT: Greenwood Press, 1973.

LAFOLLETTE, ROBERT MARION

Robert LaFollette (1855–1925), known as ''Fighting Bob,'' introduced political and social reforms into his home state of Wisconsin. His practices later served as models for the rest of the United States during the Progressive Era (1900–1914). His legislative efforts to more fairly distribute and diversify wealth and power in the United States helped U.S. politics become more responsive to popular will rather than to special privilege. LaFollette was unrivaled as a radical and was a persistent fighter for democracy. He was known as the enemy of political machines and corrupt corporations and the friend of the farmer and the emerging blue-collar worker.

Robert Marion LaFollette was born in a log cabin in Primrose, Wisconsin, in 1855. His father died eight months after his birth, and his widowed mother worked hard to provide the essentials for her four children.

LaFollette managed to enroll in the state university at Madison, Wisconsin, in 1875. He supported himself by teaching school and by editing a student periodical at the university. He was a gifted speaker, who even considered a career in acting during college. However, he chose to study law, and in 1880 he was admitted as an attorney into the Wisconsin bar.

Since legal work was scarce, LaFollette was attracted to running for the office of district attorney in Wisconsin. Although his opposition had more money and more endorsements, LaFollette's door-to-door campaign among his farmer–neighbors, then an uncommon practice for a politician, won him the election. This experience taught him the importance of speaking directly to voters—a lesson he never forgot.

Two years later, in 1884, LaFollette ran for congressional representative from Wisconsin, and by reminding voters directly of his readiness to represent their interests in Washington, he won the election. At age 29, he was the youngest member of the House of Representatives. However, he failed to be reelected in 1890 and returned to a prosperous legal practice in Madison, Wisconsin.

LAFOLLETTE'S IDEAS IMPACTED THE ENTIRE TWENTIETH CENTURY. THEY LED TO LAWS BENEFITING WORKING PEOPLE AND TO EVEN LARGER GLOBAL SOCIAL CHANGES DURING THE PRESIDENCIES OF MEN LIKE FRANKLIN ROOSEVELT, HARRY TRUMAN, AND LYNDON JOHNSON.

The major turning point in his life came when the fiercely-honest LaFollette discovered that many of his Republican colleagues were stealing public funds. One of these colleagues approached him in an unsuccessful effort to obtain a sympathetic judge. LaFollete was being bribed by his own political allies and he later wrote: ''Nothing else ever came into my life that exerted such powerful influence on me as that affair. It was the turning point, in a way, of my career. . . .''

From that time until the end of his life, LaFollette was a dedicated and principled public servant. It was now he and ''the people'' against the rich and venal politicians. He took his hard facts and preached directly to the people, speaking publicly wherever he could.

His enemies in Wisconsin successfully kept him from becoming governor of the state until he won the election of 1900, promising a reform program to destroy the old party machine. LaFollette was reelected to three terms as governor. Against the will of big business, he created a corporate tax and implemented ''The Wisconsin Idea,'' a plan to use government as an agent of social and political reform. He treated Wisconsin as a progressive political laboratory, with expert commissions attending to taxes, railroads, banking, conservation, insurance, public service, and industrial problems. He next planned to take his ''Wisconsin Idea'' to the United States Congress and try his ideas on a national level.

In 1906 LaFollette became a senator from Wisconsin. He found himself battling with President Theodore Roosevelt (1901–1909), although both of them were Progressive Party members. LaFollette called Roosevelt ''an inconsequential playboy.'' In 1912 he ran against Roosevelt and William Taft (1857–1930) for nomination as the Republican candidate to run against Democrat Woodrow Wilson (1856–1924) for the presidency. LaFollette's passionate run against Teddy Roosevelt split the Republican Party vote and Wilson likely won the election because of this.

President Wilson (1913–1921) gradually adopted many of LaFollette's progressive ideas. Wilson supported LaFollette's programs for public disclosure of campaign contributions and a fairer graduated taxation. LaFollette worked with Wilson indirectly to limit the powers of business, and he helped create the Department of Labor and the Federal Trade Commission. LaFollette fought for higher worker wages and better working conditions for American laborers, and he supported women's right to vote. He also advocated civil rights legislation for ethnic minorities.

LaFollette's ideas impacted the entire twentieth century. They led to laws benefiting working people and to even larger global social changes during the presidencies of men like Franklin Roosevelt (1933–1945), Harry Truman (1945–1953), and Lyndon Johnson (1963–1969).

Robert LaFollette died in 1925 from complications of pneumonia, asthma, and a coronary condition. He spent a lifetime fighting bad business practices and creating laws to protect the rights of ordinary Americans.

FURTHER READING

Case, Belle. *LaFollette.* New York: Harlan Davidson Press, 1983.

Ekirch, Arthur A. *Progressivism in America: A Study of the Era from Theodore Roosevelt to Woodrow Wilson.* New York: New Viewpoints, 1974.

Greenbaum, Fred. *Robert Marion LaFollette.* New York: Twayne Press, 1975.

Link, Arthur. *Progressivism.* New York: Harlan Davidson Press, 1983.

Thelan, David. *Robert M. LaFollette and the Insurgent Spirit.* Boston: Little, Brown, 1976.

LAISSEZ FAIRE

Laissez faire is an economic theory that favors the free market and is suspicious of government intervention in the conduct of business and industry. It encourages private ownership and personal initiative as the best means to enrich individuals and societies. Most laissez-faire economists would admit that there are situations when government intervention is essential, but they would prefer to keep the state's role to a minimum. The term arose in the seventeenth century, when a French merchant responded to royal minister who asked how the government could help him by saying, "Laissez nous faire." The phrase is probably best translated, "Let us be." By the late eighteenth century a group of French economists known as physiocrats popularized the theory as a reaction against a system of state controls over the economy known as mercantilism. They maintained the laws of nature, not state regulation, will foster prosperity. Also the British economist Adam Smith 1723–90), who has been called the "father of modern economics," argued that the market would regulate enterprise more effectively than governments. The theory was most widely accepted in Great Britain and the United States in the nineteenth century, but in the early twentieth century it was in part discredited by the misery that was associated with the Industrial Revolution. In the late twentieth century, however, there was a reaction against intrusive government regulation and high taxation, and the reaction was aided by the failure of socialism in Eastern Europe. Laissez-faire principles were again celebrated in the United States under President Ronald Reagan (1980–1988) and in Great Britain under Prime Minister Margaret Thatcher (1979–1990). Her program of selling of government-owned industries to private investors, which was called privatization, has been adopted by many countries throughout the world.

See also: **Capitalism, Mercantilism, Ronald Reagan, Adam Smith**

LAND-GRANT COLLEGES

Land-grant colleges are those institutions of higher learning which are endowed by funds set up under the Morrill Act of 1862. The legislation, officially called the Land-Grant Act, was sponsored by Vermont Congressman Justin Smith Morrill (1810–1898), who served in the House of Representatives between 1855 and 1867, and in the Senate between 1867 and 1898. The U.S. public was increasingly demanding the establishment of colleges that would specialize in agricultural and manufacturing programs. Farming remained critical to the nation's economy, whose industrial sector was growing. Training in these areas was essential to the country's future. In 1862 this argument convinced Congress to add military programs to the curriculum of the future schools and to vote to grant more than 11.3 million acres (4.6 hectares) of land to states and territories. These lands were to be sold by the states or territories, and the money would be invested in funds used to set up state colleges. Thirty states (primarily in the Midwest and South) used the funds to set up agricultural and mechanical (A&M) colleges; eighteen states gave the funds to already existing colleges to set up new agricultural and mechanical programs; and the rest granted the funds to private institutions of higher learning. In 1890 a second Morrill Act added money grants to the states for use in A&M programs. Michigan State University, founded as Michigan Agricultural College in 1855, became the model for the land-grant colleges, which also include the University of Illinois, Texas A&M, and the University of California. The far-sighted provisions of the land-grant gave the nation many of its foremost universities.

LAND O'LAKES, INC.

On June 7, 1921, hundreds of farmers from all over Minnesota gathered in St. Paul to vote on the organization of a statewide dairy cooperative. With a unanimous vote, the Minnesota Cooperative Creamery Association, Inc., forerunner to Land O'Lakes, Inc., was born.

Unlike investor-owned corporations, cooperatives work for and answer to their member-patrons, who benefit in direct proportion to the amount of business they do each year with the cooperative—how many products they supply for sale to the general public, or how many they buy from the cooperative. Because each member-patron has one vote, cooperatives are democratic enough to have appealed to the independent U.S. farmers who first joined.

Beginning with a meager financial stake of $1,375, the directors of the Minnesota Cooperative Creamery

Association, Inc. launched a statewide membership campaign. Their project was given a boost when in 1922, after a long fight, the U.S. Senate passed the Capper-Volstead bill, which legalized the marketing of farm products through cooperative agencies. The first year's returns showed a slender profit.

John Brandt, one of the original 15 directors elected to run the organization, became president of the association in 1923. He believed that by working together, competing creameries could raise their profits and offer a better product to their patrons. He urged cooperation among farmers, engineered joint shipments of butter, and proposed a common standard of quality. Most importantly, he and the other directors of the cooperative decided to concentrate on the quality production and aggressive marketing of "sweet cream" butter, butter made from cream before it soured. Although more costly to make and not as familiar to the public, sweet butter tasted better and kept longer.

In February 1924, the cooperative announced a contest to capture the public's attention: its high-quality product needed a catchier name than "Minnesota Cooperative Creamery Butter." First prize was $500 in gold. An overwhelming response brought in over 100,000 entries; the contest was tied between two winners who both thought of "Land O'Lakes." Soon thereafter an Indian maiden appeared on the butter's packages, completing a now familiar image. The origins of this Indian maiden, however, remain a mystery.

In April 1924, the cooperative won a contract with the U.S. Navy for 30,000 pounds of the new sweet cream butter, and soon thereafter met with a growing demand from U.S. housewives for its conveniently packaged quarter-pound sticks. Because Land O'Lakes was already becoming a household name, only two years after the contest, the cooperative changed its name to Land O'Lakes Creameries, Inc. in 1926.

Land O'Lakes first ventured outside of the dairy business two years later, in 1928, when it organized egg and poultry divisions. This step toward diversification proved crucial during the Great Depression (1929–1939), when dairy businesses throughout the nation suffered enormous losses. In 1930 dairy production was the lowest it had been in two decades, and by December 1933, butter prices had declined to 15 cents a pound, the lowest figures for that month in 25 years. Excess production and surplus holdings were making it almost impossible for U.S. farmers to get back their cost of production, and dozens of creameries held meetings to decide whether they should continue operating. Although Land O'Lakes suffered setbacks due to these market forces between 1929 and 1940, highly imaginative management and a willingness to fight economic trends cut the cooperative's losses considerably.

Before the Depression Land O'Lakes had dealt mostly with large store chains and other nationwide distributors. But with many of these large accounts cutting back their operations or vanishing altogether, Land O'Lakes began to set up smaller sales branches that could sell directly to groceries and other small outlets. Partly as a result of this marketing strategy, and partly because Land O'Lakes Sweet Cream Butter was being advertised nationally for the first time, Land O'Lakes was able to sell a record 100 million pounds of butter in 1930.

Another Depression era strategy was to diversify the products the cooperative offered both to its member farmers and to the public. Land O'Lakes began an Agricultural Services Division in 1929 to try to reduce member costs for feed, seed, and other farming supplies. In 1934 the cooperative joined three large cheese cooperatives in the operation of 95 cheese factories, and in 1937 Land O'Lakes opened its first milk drying plant, completing a decade of experimentation which pioneered the production of powdered milk. When World War II (1939–1945) called for milk in a form that didn't require refrigeration and had a fraction of its normal bulk, Land O'Lakes was prepared. All of these changes were ultimately successful expansions and contributed to Land O'Lakes' relative prosperity in difficult times.

Following World War II Land O'Lakes diversified further, entering the ice cream and fluid milk markets for the first time. In 1970 the cooperative merged with the Farmers Regional Cooperative, which increased Land O'Lakes capacity to produce and market agricultural production goods (including fertilizers and insecticides) for its member-patrons. That same year, Land O'Lakes Creameries, Inc. changed its name to simply Land O'Lakes, Inc. to better reflect its diverse business. Over the next decade, as Land O'Lakes' butter sales were hurt by the expanding market for margarine, the cooperative diversified further, entering the red meat business in 1978 and launching a soybean processing venture in 1980. But concern about industry overproduction, fluctuating market prices, and increasing operating costs led Land O'Lakes to exit from the poultry and red meat sectors in the late 1980s.

By the late 1990s, through mergers and acquisitions, Land O'Lakes served 300,000 farmers and ranchers in 27 states. In the last years of the twentieth century

Land O'Lakes increasingly sought out growth opportunities outside the United States, and included among its foreign operations feed mills in Taiwan and Poland and marketing functions in Mexico, East Asia, and the Pacific Rim.

FURTHER READING

Cook, James. ''Dreams of Glory.'' *Forbes*, September 12, 1983.

Ruble, Kenneth D. *Men to Remember: How 100,000 Neighbors Made History*. Chicago, IL: Lakeside Press, 1947.

Smith, Rod. ''LOL Getting Members Ready for Major Push to Global Size.''*Feedstuffs*, March 8, 1993.

Stern, William M. ''Land O'Low Returns.'' *Forbes*, August 15, 1994.

''Time Line,'' [cited July 26, 1999] Available on the World Wide Web @ www.landolakesinc.com/OurCompany/CompanyFactsIndex.cfm.

LAND ORDINANCE OF 1785

The Land Ordinance of 1785 was the second of three land ordinances passed by the Confederation Congress after the Revolutionary War (1775–1783). The three ordinances, which included the Ordinance of 1784 and the Northwest Ordinance (1787), were meant to manage the lands of the Old Northwest, ceded by Great Britain at the end of the Revolution. The Treaty of Paris (1783), which established normal diplomatic relations between England and the former colonies after the Revolution, turned the area that is now the states of Ohio, Indiana, Illinois, Michigan, and Wisconsin over to the new U.S. government. In 1784 a committee led by Thomas Jefferson drew up legislation to provide for future statehood for settlers already in the area. The following year, in the Land Ordinance of 1785, Jefferson's committee established the way in which the territory would be measured and divided for sale.

The new nation was governed for the most part by the states. The relationship between the states and with the central government was defined by the Articles of Confederation. The central government was the Confederation Congress, a holdover from the Second Continental Congress which had been convened in the spring of 1775 and had coordinated the revolutionary war effort. The Articles of Confederation, ratified by the states in 1781, summarized the existing relationship between the Congress and the states.

It was an indication of the distrust with which the American people viewed central authority that the Articles of Confederation did not allow the Congress to tax either the states or individuals. As a way of keeping the nation solvent, the states that claimed western lands from the terms of their colonial charters gave up those lands to the Confederation government. The Confederation government expected to use these lands as a way of meeting governmental expenses. In order to attract land buyers, the Congress declared that these lands would be made into new states, which would enter the Union on an equal basis with the original thirteen colonies. This declaration made possible the creation of the modern United States.

The Land Ordinance created the pattern along which American public land would be divided and sold until the passage of the Homestead Act in 1862. The Ordinance of 1785 ruled that the western lands north of the Ohio River would be divided by surveyors into a square grid. Each square (called a township) measured six by six miles and was subdivided into thirty-six one-mile-square sections. Each section (measuring 640 acres) could then be further divided, usually into half, quarter, eighth, or sixteenth-section lots of 320, 160, 80, or 40 acres. Certain sections had restrictions placed on their sales; for instance, money from the sixteenth section of every township was to be set aside to fund public schools in the township. The first territorial survey took place in what is now southeastern Ohio, and it measured land that stretched westward from Little Beaver Creek to the Tuscarawas River and southward to the Ohio River. A total of about 91 townships were created (although some of them were fractional and did not contain a full 36 sections), with about 3,276 sections comprising 2,096,640 acres of land ready for development by U.S. farmers.

Although the Land Ordinance of 1785 was conceived as a way to divide the western territory more evenly than had been the case before the Revolution, in practice it was less than fair. Congress thought that land sales in the territory would help it meet its big debts left over from the war. As a result, land sales were aimed at wealthy purchasers rather than the poorest farmers, who were most in need of land on which to settle. Until 1841 the government also required that public land be offered at auction where syndicates of land speculators usually snatched it up before it could be sold to private individuals. Congress set the minimum amount of land that could be purchased at one section—640 acres—and the purchase price at one dollar per acre. Small purchases on credit were not allowed. The $640 minimum purchase placed the cost of western lands far outside the budget of most U.S.

citizens. Most of the lands went instead to wealthy land speculators, who were also given the option of buying on credit. The speculators bought lands from the government, divided them up, and then resold them to small farmers at a profit.

An interesting sidelight to the Ordinances was the way that they steered the political culture of the nation. The third Ordinance, passed in 1787, stipulated that future inhabitants would be guaranteed a ''bill of rights'' guaranteeing freedom of religion and the right to a jury trial. It also prohibited slavery north of the Ohio River, although this applied to the future and did not contemplate the freeing of slaves that were already held in the Old Northwest Territory. The ordinance also contained provisions for the return of escaped slaves.

See also: **Thomas Jefferson, Old Northwest, Northwest Ordinance**

FURTHER READING

Abernethy, Thomas Perkins. *Western Lands and the American Revolution.* New York: Russell and Russell, Inc., 1959.

Clawson, Marion. *The Federal Lands Revisited.* Baltimore, MD: Johns Hopkins University Press, 1983.

Gates, Paul W. *History of Public Land Law Development.* Washington, DC: Wm. W. Gaunt and Sons, 1968.

Morris, Richard B. *The Forging of the Union, 1781–1789.* New York: Harper and Row, 1987.

Onuf, Peter S. *Statehood and Union: The Northwest Ordinance.* Bloomington, IN: Indiana University Press, 1987.

Rohrbough, Malcolm. *The Trans-Appalachian Frontier: People, Societies, and Institutions, 1775–1850.* New York: Oxford University Press, 1978.

LANE, GERTRUDE BATTLES

At the turn of the twentieth century, when women were making significant legal and political advances that would lead them to obtaining voting rights and a notable say in public governance, Gertrude Battles Lane (1874–1941) was distinguished as the editor of one of the leading U.S. women's magazines, *Woman's Home Companion.* Gertrude Battle used the *Woman's Home Companion* not only as a vehicle focused on women's issues, but she increased the scope of those issues to include political and social matters, as well as to educate women about how to use the vote in their best interests.

Gertrude Lane was born on December 21, 1874, in Saco, Maine, the daughter of Eustace Lane, an organist and piano tuner, and Ella Maud Battles. She initially attended public schools and as the family wealth increased she was able to attend the exclusive private school Thornton Academy, where she edited the school's literary paper.

She graduated from Thornton Academy in 1892, and moved to Boston, Massachusetts, where she took work as a private tutor. In 1895 she completed a year long course in business at Burdett College, and in 1896 she began working for the Cyclopedia Publishing Co. as an assistant editor. She worked there for seven years, developing her editorial skills. During this time she also published essays, poetry, and book reviews in various Boston publications.

GERTRUDE LANE WAS "A GRAND COMBINATION OF MAINE SALTINESS AND LATIN TEMPERAMENT."

Edna Ferber, regarding her friend Gertrude Lane

In 1902 financial problems at Cyclopedia Pub. prompted Lane to search for a new job. In 1903, she accepted the position of ''household editor'' at the popular *Woman's Home Companion*, a monthly women's magazine founded in 1874. Lane stayed with the magazine and its publisher, Crowell Publishing, until her death in 1941.

Lane rose steadily at the *Companion*, becoming the managing editor in 1909 and the editor-in-chief in 1912. She claimed her success was caused simply by hard work, but those who knew her said she also possessed strong editorial skills and a keen business sense. The Pulitzer Prize winning author Edna Ferber (1887–1968), a friend of Lane's, described her as ''a grand combination of Maine saltiness and Latin temperament.''

As editor of the *Companion*, Lane emphasized women and the home, leaving men's issues for the many men's magazines that were being published. She spoke to women as homemakers, but she greatly broadened the scope of what a homemaker was. Her magazine began to provide readers with practical service columns, as well as entertaining fiction and a variety of general interest features. The formula she devised succeeded. Under her leadership circulation grew from 700,000 when she took over in 1912, to one million by

1916, and more than two million by 1923. In 1937 the *Companion* took over the lead in circulation from long-time competitor, *Ladies Home Journal*.

Throughout her career as an editor, Lane ran articles that focused on a variety of social and political issues. Her efforts were aimed at educating her female readers. A year after she took over as editor, Lane established in the magazine what was called *A Better Babies Bureau* to promote improved maternal and infant care. She also ran regular articles related to the ongoing fight against child employment as well as articles about unsanitary conditions in food stores.

Other campaigns she pursued in the *Companion* included a series on educating women about how to use their new voting rights. Articles on international peace issues appeared frequently, as well as informational articles on topics like psychology, careers, politics, and college education. A page written by Eleanor Roosevelt (1884–1962), the wife of President Franklin Roosevelt (1933–1945), appeared regularly in the magazine during the 1930s.

Lane maintained strong service departments. She believed the modern woman wanted a magazine with practical, timesaving advice. Lane said that her image of a housewife was ''. . . the woman who wants to do less housework, so that she will have more time for other things.''

During World War I (1914–1918) Lane served as a member of the U.S. Food Administration under President Herbert Hoover (1929–1933), while continuing to edit the *Companion*. Lane also served as a member of the 1930–1931 White House Conference on Child Health and Protection.

In 1929 Lane was regarded as one of the best magazine editors in the business and she was made a vice president of the *Companion*'s publishers, the Crowell Publishing Co. In 1935, while managing the new *American* magazine for Crowell and editing the *Woman's Home Companion*, Lane began an innovative plan to gain reader support and feedback. She created a ''reader-editor panel'' composed of 1500 unpaid readers nationwide, who provided for the magazine one of the nation's first consumer-opinion panels.

By 1939 Lane was earning $52,000 annually and she was described by the *New York Times* as one of the best paid woman of the day.

Lane never married. She entertained frequently and pursued a passion for antique collecting.

See also: **Publishing Industry**

FURTHER READING

Braithwaite, Brian, and Joan Barrell. *The Business of Women's Magazines: The Agonies and the Ecstasies*. London: Associated Business Press, 1979.

Ferguson, Marjorie. *Forever Feminine: Women's Magazines and the Cult of Femininity*. London Exeter: Heinemann, 1983.

Humphreys, Nancy K. *American Women's Magazines: An Annotated Historical Guide*. New York: Garland, 1989.

Zuckerman, Mary Ellen. *A History of Popular Women's Magazines in the United States, 1792–1995*. Westport, CT: Greenwood Press, 1998.

Zuckerman, Mary Ellen. ''Pathway to Success: Gertrude Battles Lane and the *Woman's Home Companion*,'' *Journalism History*, 16, Spring 1990.

LANGE, DOROTHEA MARGARETTA

Beginning in 1919, Dorothea Lange (1895–1965) began to photograph in detail the people and circumstances of the Great Depression (1929–1939). She later extensively photographed working people of the West, such as poor migrant farm workers. Later, working for *Life* magazine, she photographed Japanese-Americans imprisoned in concentration camps in California and New Mexico during World War II (1939–1945). Through the lens of her camera, Americans began to see for themselves the scope and extent of social injustices in the United States. Lange's seemed to prove the old maxim that a picture could speak a thousand words.

Dorothea Margaretta Nutzhorn was born in Hoboken, New Jersey, on May 26, 1895, the first of several children born to Joanna and Heinrich Nutzhorn. Her father was a lawyer and her mother worked as a librarian. At age seven Lange contracted poliomyelitis (polio) in a time when there was no known vaccine. Her right leg was permanently disabled from the knee down, causing her to walk with a limp. Lange said in later years that the teasing she received in childhood because of this illness was both humiliating and instructive. She became very sensitive to the suffering of fellow human beings.

Lange attended school and lived a relatively normal life under her family's hard economic circumstances. She saw New York at its best and its worst, going to concerts and art museums, but also walking in the immigrant ghettos.

At the time of her high school graduation in 1912, Lange decided to become a professional photographer. She worked in photographic studios and studied photography at Columbia University. At age 21 she began to travel across the United States, selling her photographs along the way to help finance her journey. She ended her trip in San Francisco, California, where she opened a photographic studio and took portrait pictures of wealthy San Francisco families.

Lange married the famous painter, Maynard Dixon (1875–1946), in 1920, and the pair lived a bohemian life. They had two children and moved to Taos, New Mexico, to live for a time at the artist colony presided over by Mabel Dodge Luhan (1879–1962).

When Lange left Taos and returned to California, she saw large numbers of homeless and unemployed people, all victims of the Depression. These images inspired Lange to document through her photographs the social conditions she saw in the United States: the soup kitchens, the breadlines, the tragic scenes of the 1930s. This marked the beginning of her career as a documentary photographer.

Having divorced Maynard Dixon in 1935, Lange married Paul Taylor, an economist who was working closely with migrant farm workers. The two became a team, documenting specific information about the Depression throughout many areas of the United States, particularly the South and Southwest.

Lange's became famous when she produced a volume of pictorial evidence about the plight of the poor in the United States. The photographs revealed the varieties of social injustice experienced by many Americans. They reinforced to the government that social and business reforms were needed quickly. Because her work was so emotionally touching and direct, Lange not only recorded conditions but also helped to change them by sharing her work with those who could and would bring change. Her 1933 photograph called ''White Angel Bread Line'' drew the attention of social, political, and governmental reformers throughout the United States. She photographed the suffering and the social injustices she saw, and let the pictures speak for victims everywhere in the United States.

By 1935 Dorothea Lange was employed by the federal government, helping others to write reports and documenting that writing with her photographs. She continued to work with the government until 1941, when she left to take advantage of a Guggenheim grant offered to her. She then traveled alone to photograph the American war camps, in which Japanese-Americans were imprisoned by the United States government because it feared these people were security risks during World War II (1939–1945).

Lange's photographs provided a vision of her time and many, once seen, were never forgotten. Lange's work touched the heart and put a human face on government statistics. She died in October 1965, just before the opening of her one-woman photographic exhibition at the Museum of Modern Art.

See also: **Great Depression**

FURTHER READING

Becker, Karin. *Dorothea Lange and the Documentary Tradition.* Baton Rouge: Louisiana State University, 1980.

Curtis, James. *Mind's Eye, Mind's Truth: FSA Photography.* Philadelphia: Temple University Press, 1989.

Fisher, Andrea. *Let Us Now Praise Famous Women: Women Photographers for the U.S. Government, 1935–1944.* New York: Pandora Press, 1987.

Guimond, James. *American Photography and the American Dream.* Chapel Hill: North Carolina Press, 1978.

Meltzer, Milton. *Dorothea Lange: A Photographer's Life.* New York: Farrar, Straus and Giroux, 1978.

LASKER, ALBERT DAVID

During the first half of the twentieth century Albert David Lasker (1880–1952) was one of the most important and most creative people in the U.S. advertising industry. His opinions continually influenced the advertising industry in the United States, and his ideas about effective advertising, agency operations, and the place of advertising in U.S. business and society guided the evolution of advertising for years after he left his profession.

Albert David Lasker was born to American parents in Germany in 1880. His mother's poor health after his birth prompted the family move to his father's birthplace, Galveston, Texas, where Albert and his five siblings grew up. From a very young age Lasker was in love with journalism and writing. At age twelve he started his own commercially successful weekly newspaper, the *Galveston Free Press.* At age thirteen he went to work for the *Galveston Morning News* while he attended high school. He was also the editor of his high school's magazine.

Upon graduation Lasker worked for newspapers in New Orleans, Louisiana, and in Dallas, Texas, planning a career in journalism. In 1898, however, his father, who opposed his plans for a career in the newspaper business, intervened by arranging for his son to begin work at the prestigious Chicago advertising firm of Lord and Thomas.

Lasker began as a $10 a week office boy, doing routine general chores around the offices of the firm. His way with words and his experience in writing allowed Lasker to advance rapidly. Within a year he was traveling the Midwest as a top salesman, bringing in major accounts and much income to Lord and Thomas. By 1904, at age twenty-four, Lasker became a full partner and general manager of the agency. His ambition did not end there. In 1910, at age thirty, he bought out the company and became sole proprietor and owner of Lord and Thomas, which had grown to become one of the largest and most successful advertising agencies of its time.

If there was one thing that characterized Lasker's approach to advertising, it was the emphasis on writing and copy writing as the foundation of any good advertisement. He convinced most newspapers and magazines, which were writing their own advertising copy for their advertisers, that good advertising required a specialized and professional approach. Lasker began to offer clients copy writing services. He developed the concept of the account executive, an agency position that served as the central link between the advertiser and all of the agency's creative services. Lord and Thomas became one of the first full-service agencies in the United States.

Lasker's maintained that advertising should be "salesmanship in print." It was an idea quite different from the straight forward, descriptive advertising most common at that time. Lasker wanted an advertisement to sound like a presentation a salesman would make. The advertisement would answer questions that customers might ask.

This approach in strong, persuasive copy led to the original agency copy writing department (a first of its kind). Lasker created his own in-house copy writing classes to train his writers in advertising "salesmanship" techniques. He also began the tradition, well known in advertising agencies, of paying tremendous salaries to proven copywriters. Lasker recognized and appreciated the value of good writers. He almost single-handedly created a profession of copywriters who, if they could produce the profits, could become some of the highest paid writers in the world, earning more than even the most famous journalists of that day.

Lasker's advertising agency became the model for most other agencies. Among his advertising successes was the introduction of products like Kleenex and Kotex to the mass market, and the turning of Pepsodent into a leading brand of toothpaste. His use of radio as an advertising medium was perhaps his greatest innovation.

Albert Lasker led an exciting and creative life during which he created the modern advertising business. He died in 1952, but his on the modern advertising industry remains.

FURTHER READING

Applegate, Edd. *Personalities and Products: A Historical Perspective on Advertising in America.* Westport, CT: Greenwood Press, 1998.

Fox, Stephen R. *The Mirror Makers: A History of American Advertising and its Creators.* New York: Morrow, 1984.

Gunther, John. *Taken at the Flood: The Story of Albert D. Lasker.* New York: Harper, 1960.

Marchand, Roland. *Advertising the American Dream: Making Way for Modernity 1920–1940.* Berkley: University of California Press, 1985.

Ogilvy, David. *Ogilvy on Advertising.* New York: Crown Publishing Co., 1983.

LAUDER, ESTEE

Estee Lauder (c. 1910–) epitomizes the American success story. Born Josephine Esther Mentzer, the daughter of poor Jewish immigrants from Eastern Europe, she built a small line of homemade face creams into a billion-dollar cosmetics business through perseverance, ingenuity, and hard work.

Estee Lauder grew up in the Corona section of Queens, New York, the youngest child in a large family. Her mother's brother was a chemist who specialized in developing skin-care preparations. Lauder's lovely complexion was her uncle's best advertisement for his special face cream. After marrying Joseph Lauder in 1930, she worked on her own kitchen stove to refine and improve her uncle's face cream and other beauty products. Soon she began to sell her creams and lipsticks at upscale beauty salons in Manhattan and resort hotels in the New York area. A perfectionist, Estee Lauder insisted on producing only the highest quality cosmetics. Typical of her attention to detail was her decision to market her products in attractive packaging in a distinctive color she called Lauder blue.

Lauder possessed an intense, single-minded determination to make a success of her cosmetics business.

Grace Mirabella, former editor of *Vogue* and founder of *Mirabella* magazine, writing in *Time* (December 7, 1998), said of the cosmetics tycoon, "She simply outworked everyone else in the cosmetics industry." Her ambition extended to her social life. Lauder cultivated affluent people in influential social positions who could help her in her business. She donated sample products as favors at charity balls and made sure that socialites had her lipsticks in their evening purses. Before long, the elegant Lauder was appearing regularly at fashionable dinner parties and charity benefits and her name had become associated with glamour and celebrity.

SHE SIMPLY OUTWORKED EVERYONE ELSE IN THE COSMETICS INDUSTRY.

Grace Mirabella, *Time*, December 7, 1998

By 1946 Estee Lauder, Inc. was formed with Joseph Lauder handling the financial end of the business and Estee concentrating on product development and marketing. They were the firm's only employees and when the company acquired a coveted sales location at Saks Fifth Avenue in Manhattan in 1948, the couple had to work night and day to produce and package enough face care products to fill the allotted counter space.

The association with Saks opened the door for Estee Lauder products at other prestigious department stores across the country. Lauder traveled to each store and personally trained her handpicked saleswomen in customer service and personal grooming. She pioneered the concept of including free sample gifts with a cosmetics purchase, a practice ensuring the customer would be introduced to a whole range of products she might otherwise never have purchased.

It was the bath oil, "Youth Dew," that launched Estee Lauder, Inc. into the front ranks of the cosmetics industry. The sweet, persistent scent that doubled as a perfume was an affordable luxury for most women. Youth Dew enjoyed phenomenal success in the 1950s and 1960s and it put the company on the map for good. In the mid–1960s Estee Lauder introduced several new product lines, including Clinique, the first line of both hypoallergenic and fashionable cosmetics, and Aramis, a line of colognes for men. Her fragrances, particularly "White Linen," became perennial successes.

By 1998 the Estee Lauder, Cos., still a family-owned business run by the two Lauder sons since their mother's retirement in 1973, was selling cosmetics products in 118 countries and commanded 45 percent of the U.S. cosmetics market. The companies listed $3.6 billion in sales in 1997, and the Lauder family's shares in the business were reported to be worth more than six billion dollars.

Although officially retired for the last 25 years of the twentieth century, Estee Lauder's influence in the family business remained strong, particularly in planning promotional campaigns and creating new fragrances. With more time available, however, she was free to entertain on a grand scale at her townhouse in Manhattan, her villa in the south of France, her flat in London, England, and her oceanfront home in Palm Beach, Florida. After the death of Joseph Lauder in 1983, Estee Lauder carried on the philanthropic work the two had begun two decades earlier. The Lauder Foundation has made significant gifts to many causes including cancer research.

FURTHER READING

Bender, Marylin. *At the Top*. Garden City, NY: Doubleday, 1975.

Duffy, Martha. "Estee Lauder." *Time*, November 11, 1985.

Israel, Lee. *Estee Lauder: Beyond the Magic: An Unauthorized Biography*. New York: Macmillan, 1985.

Lauder, Estee. *Estee: A Success Story*. New York: Random House, 1985.

Mirabella, Grace. "Estee Lauder." *Time*, December 7, 1998.

LEASE, MARY ELIZABETH

Mary Elizabeth Clyens Lease (1853–1933) was an activist, writer, and public speaker for many causes, including farmers' issues and women's suffrage. She was actively involved in the creation of the People's Party in Kansas. She gained national recognition during the Populist crusade for reform in the 1890s.

In 1853 Mary Clyens was born in Ridgeway, Pennsylvania to Irish immigrant parents. After she finished her education, she began teaching in rural schools in New York. In 1870 she moved to Kansas to teach and there she met and married a druggist's clerk, Charles L. Lease.

Lease and her husband tried twice to make a living from farming in Kansas, but were unsuccessful both

Mary "Yellin" Lease.

times, blaming their misfortune on the railroads and loan companies. The couple moved to Texas for several years before returning to Wichita, Kansas in 1883. It was back in Kansas that Lease became involved in public life. On St Patrick's Day, 1885, she delivered her first public speech, "Ireland and Irishmen," on behalf of the Irish National League. In the same year Lease was admitted as a lawyer to the Wichita bar.

RAISE LESS CORN AND MORE HELL.

Mary Lease, Halstead, Kansas, 1890

Lease later became involved in other political issues, particularly those that involved the farming community. In 1888 she spoke before the state convention of the Union Labor Party, a forerunner of the People's Party in Kansas She was the party's candidate for a county office long before women were even eligible to vote. In 1889 Lease became a Farmers' Alliance lecturer and briefly worked as an associate editor for a reform newspaper, the Wichita *Journal.*

In 1890 the People's Party in Kansas, commonly known as the Populist Party, was formed to fight for better conditions for farmers. There was much discontent among the agrarian community at that time because of declining farm prices and the accompanying declines in income. Since farmers blamed corrupt politicians for their plight, Lease and many agricultural laborers became disillusioned with traditional party politics and believed change would only come through a third party.

In the same year Lease took an active role in the successful campaign to unseat United States Senator John J. Ingalls (1873–91), a Kansas Republican. She reportedly made over 160 speeches during the 1890 election. She was often mistakenly called Mary Ellen, and her enemies dubbed her "Mary Yellin'." During a three-hour speech in Halstead, Kansas, Lease encouraged farmers to "raise less corn and more hell."

In 1892 Lease became involved in the creation of the People's Party of America. She campaigned heavily in the south and west for General James B. Weaver (1833–1912), the party's presidential candidate. In 1893, when the Populists gained control of the administration of Kansas, Lease was appointed president of the State Board of Charities, the highest office held by a woman in Kansas at that time.

By 1896 Lease broke with the Populists because the party was merging with the Democrats to support the presidential candidacy of William Jennings Bryan (1860–1925). She then joined the staff at Joseph Pulitzer's *New York World* as a political reporter. Lease moved to New York City and became a public lecturer for several causes, addressing women's suffrage, Prohibition, evolution, and birth control. She died on her farm in New York on October 29, 1933.

See also: **William Jennings Bryan, Farmers' Alliance, Labor Movement, Labor Unionism, Populist Movement, Prohibition, Joseph Pulitzer, Women's Movement**

FURTHER READING

Campbell, Karlyn Kohrs, ed. *Women Public Speakers in the United States, 1800–1925.* Westport, CT: Greenwood Press, 1993.

Hardy, Gayle J. *American Women Civil Rights Activists: Biobibliographies of 68 Leaders, 1825–1992.* Jefferson, NC: McFarland and Co., 1993.

Johnson, Gerald W. *The Lunatic Fringe.* Baltimore, MD: Lippincott, 1957.

La Forte, Robert S. *Leaders of Reform: Progressive Republicans in Kansas, 1900–1916.* Kansas: University Press of Kansas, 1974.

Mayfield, Lydia. "Mary Ellen Lease or 'Yellin' Ellen, the Kansas Tornado." *Texas Quarterly,* Summer, 1975.

LEE, IVY LEDBETTER

Ivy Ledbetter Lee (1877–1934) created the model for professional U.S. public-relations promotions and a giant industry that is generally called the publicity business. Ivy Lee believed that facts themselves could be artfully shaped and placed before the public so that they would be seen in a favorable light. Though he is a largely forgotten figure in U.S. history, his impact on commerce, politics, entertainment, and the general business of the United States cannot be overstated. He was the father of all the modern "spin doctors" and public-relations people who seek to present in a favorable light that which is not always pleasant.

Ivy Ledbetter Lee was born in 1877, in Cedartown, Georgia, the son of a Methodist minister. Lee grew up in Georgia and finished his college training at Princeton University in New Jersey, and later, for a single semester, he attended Harvard Law School in Boston, Massachusetts.

Lee began working for newspapers in 1899, working first for the *New York Journal* and later for the *New York Times*. After marrying in 1903, he quit newspapers and went to work with a fellow journalist, George Parker, in an effort to get Seth Low elected as mayor of New York. Lee and Parker afterwards went on to work for the Democratic National Committee in the 1904 presidential campaign.

In 1904 Ivy Lee and George Parker decided to form a public relations company called Parker and Lee. It was the second public relations firm established in the United States. Lee began to represent the interests of large firms, such as the Pennsylvania Railroad, who wanted public images as good, ethical companies benevolent to public interests.

Lee began to pursue a direct style of press relations to get the company's message across. He described the style in this way: "Shaping their affairs (business) so that when placed before the public they will be approved, and placing them before the public in the most favorable light." Lee ran into many critics by working with the giants of U.S. business and making every possible effort to project their actions as benign and on behalf of the interests of the public. U.S. labor unions were among the first to ridicule Lee for his manipulation of facts. Lee was also attacked by prominent writers of his era. In one of his novels Upton Sinclair (1878–1968) referred to Ivy Lee as "Poison Ivy Lee," and the famous U.S. writer and poet, Carl Sandburg (1878–1967) called Lee "a paid liar." Despite those attacks Lee continued to prosper and became very successful as the Rockefellers' public relations agent.

Working for the Rockefellers and other corporate clients, Lee engaged in what can only be described as the careful management of the press and public opinion. Lee eventually began to oppose granting exclusive interviews to any single member of the press and instead favored controlling the release of any information himself. He was described as a kind of gardener of the press, pruning and clipping, urging the growth of strong stories in one part of the garden and stamping out the poisonous growth of negative stories in another part of the garden.

From 1916 to 1919 the firm Lee, Harris, and Lee grew to become Ivy Lee and Associates, and then Ivy Lee and T.J. Ross. Clients for their public relations management included Anaconda Steel, Chase National Bank, Phelps Dodge, United States Rubber, Armour Meats, United Artists, Chrysler Corp., and Standard Oil.

As early as the 1920s Lee was representing the financial interests of foreign governments in the United States, including Poland, Rumania, and even a brief representation of the Soviet Union. From 1929 Lee also worked for the U.S. subsidiary of the German corporation of I.G. Farben. In 1933–1934 Lee traveled to Germany and met with Adolph Hitler (1889–1945) in a complex effort to improve the Farben Company's public image. In 1934 the House Un-American Activities Committee (HUAC) accused Lee of being Hitler's publicity agent. He was later cleared of that charge. Months later Ivy Lee died as a broken man, leaving an estate of $24,000.

Modern corporations largely follow Lee's approach to public relations, while foreign governments regularly hire public relations firms to represent their interests. In the late 1990s these methods provoked little of the outcry that Lee's work first encountered. Because Lee never published a book on his career in public relations, his work has been largely forgotten.

FURTHER READING

Doob, Leonard W. *Propaganda: Its Psychology and Technique*. New York: H. Holt, 1935.

Garraty, John A., and Mark C. Carnes. *American National Biography*. New York: Oxford University Press, 1999, s.v. "Lee, Ivy Ledbetter."

Hiebert, Ray E. *Courtier to the Crowd: The Story of Ivy Lee and the Development of Public Relations*. Ames: Iowa State University Press, 1966.

Lee, Ivy L. *Human Nature and the Railroads*. Philadelphia: E.S. Nash, 1915.

McGovern, George S., and Leonard F. Guttridge. *The Great Coalfield Wars*. Niwot, CO: University Press of Colorado, 1996.

LEND LEASE ACT

Enacted by Congress in 1941, the Lend Lease Act gave the president the power to sell, transfer, lend, or lease war supplies to U.S. allies during World War II (1939–1945). These supplies included food, tanks, airplanes, weapons, and other equipment.

The lend-lease program was originally developed to provide assistance to Great Britain and China. The legislation also gave the president the authority to extend aid to any nation whose defense he deemed vital to that of the United States. By the end of World War II, 38 nations received aid under the lend-lease program; prominent among them were Great Britain, China, and the Soviet Union.

Repayment for aid given under the lend-lease program could be "in kind or property," as well as by other measures agreed to by the U.S. president. Some of the costs were offset by a reverse kind of lend-lease program, where Allied nations gave U.S. troops abroad about $8 billion in aid.

President Harry Truman (1945–1953) ended the lend-lease program in 1945.

See also: **World War II**

LEONTIEF, WASSILY

In 1973 Wassily Leontief, the Russian-born U.S. economist, received the Nobel Prize in economic sciences "for the development of the input-output method and for its application to important economic problems." Input-output analysis belongs to that branch of economics pioneered by nineteenth century French economist, Leon Walras. This branch of economics is known as general equilibrium theory, focusing on examining the interdependence of economic forces representing the economy as a whole. The first major practical policy applications of Leontief's input-output analysis were made by the U.S. Bureau of Labor Statistics, first in 1939 and then again in 1947. His model was used to predict how total and partial sector employment in the United States would change as the economy of the United States shifted from peace to war and back again.

Wassily Leontief was born in St. Petersburg, Russia, in August of 1906. His father, Wassily Sr., was also an economist. The years of Leontief's childhood were at a time of great social and political upheaval in Russia. He was eight years old when World War I (1914–1918) began and he experienced firsthand the turmoil of the Russian revolution. In 1921 he entered the University of Leningrad (known as St. Petersburg prior to the Russian revolution), where he studied philosophy, sociology, and economics. He graduated in 1925, continuing his education afterwards at the University of Berlin, in Germany. In 1928, at age 22, he received his doctorate in economics.

After graduating he spent a year in Nanking, China, as an economic adviser to the Chinese Ministry of Railroads. In 1931 Leontief emigrated to the United States, coming to America during the Great Depression (1929–1939), where he joined the National Bureau of Economics Research. In 1932 he married the poet Estelle Marks.

In 1931 Leontief began a long tenure as an instructor of economics at prestigious Harvard University. He was promoted to a full professor in 1946. Two years later he founded the Harvard Economic Research Project, a center for what he called "input-output analysis." He directed this project until its closing in 1973.

Leontief had published his first paper on input-output analysis in 1936. His early work was analytical but not mathematical. He criticized attempts to apply advanced mathematical theories to explain world economic problems. Instead, he believed theories were only useful if they could be implemented and observed. He amplified this view with the publication of his first book in 1941, *The Structure of the American Economy, 1919–1929: An Empirical Application of Equilibrium Analysis*. The very basic thinking of this book described his method of analyzing economic input and output, the basis of his reputation as an outstanding economic innovator. Input-output method is now a standard economic projection tool used in countries and corporations around the world.

His system came slowly to a world crippled by a Great Depression, but as World War II (1939–1945) began, there was new interest in testing the applications of Leontief's analysis. It was applied first by the U.S. Bureau of Labor Statistics, which examined the Leontief model for predicting how employment changes in the country would change the overall economy. By 1957, in less than 10 years, Leontief's method had become a basic ingredient in the national accounting systems of most countries in the world, both capitalist and socialist.

The input-output system developed by Leontief focuses on the fact that economic relationships involving complex interdependence came to represent a picture of the economy as a whole. Prior to Leontief, the field of economics studied mainstream economics focusing only on a few variables. For example, an economist might have looked at how a tax on imported oil might effect the demand for gasoline, while ignoring how the same tax might effect the steel industry. A partial analysis led to seriously misleading conclusions, especially if the industry or changes being studied were expansive.

Leontief's brilliant contribution to economics, the heart of his input-output method, involved a multiple transactions table, dividing the economy into many sectors. Essentially, by increasing the number of sectors being scrutinized and by cross-referencing them on a grid, Leontief was able to come up with the ''Leontief inverse,'' revealing what each sector being studied required to produce one additional dollar's worth of output.

The economic significance of Leontief's method was threefold. First, improvements in international data collection had improved enormously in recent decades because Leontief's system required enormous specific data. Thus the examination of this data revealed the workings of any economy in great detail, far more than in the past. Finally, once demands for goods were specified or projected into the future, Leontief's system could be used for policy analysis. Therefore, the Leontief analysis showed both directly and indirectly what each sector of the economy needed in input in order to increase economic output.

The Leontief system improved as data-gathering improved with the use of computers. He was able to increase the number of economic sectors he studied, because the computer had made the sorting of complex data feasible to analyze.

Input-output analysis had become an essential technique in most economic planning and government budgeting, both internationally and nationally. Leontief's success in applying the input-output model of economic analysis resulted largely from his outstanding ability as a general economist. He was interested in several fields: international trade, monopoly issues, and econometrics—the measuring of the specific strength of an economy. Leontief opposed theorizing about economics, and instead said: ''What counts is the relevance of the basic material premises, the capability to exploit effectively all factual data at hand, and to identify promising directions.'' Leontief's practical and empirical approach, causing modern economics to be ever more scientific, had put him clearly in a class as a major contributor to twentieth century economic science.

Wassily Leontief died in February 1999, at the age of 92.

FURTHER READING

Fisher, Franklin M., and Karl Shell. *Economic Analysis of Production Price Indexes.* Cambridge: Cambridge University Press, 1998.

Harmston, Floyd K., and Richard E. Land. *Application of an Input-Output Framework to a Community Economic System.* Columbia: University of Missouri Press, 1967.

Koehler, Gary J., Andrew B. Whinston, and Gordon P. Wright. *Optimization Over Leontief Substitution Systems.* Amsterdam: North Holland Pub., Co., 1975.

Leontief, Wassily. *Input-Output Economics.* New York: Oxford University Press, 1986.

Leontief, Wassily, and Faye Duchin. *The Future Impact of Automation on Workers.* New York: Oxford University Press, 1986.

LEVER FOOD CONTROL ACT

The Lever Food Control Act of 1917 authorized the president to regulate the price, production, transportation, and allocation of feeds, food, fuel, beverages, and distilled spirits for the remainder of World War I (1914–1918). Popularly known as the Lever Act, the law also empowered the president to nationalize certain private factories, and requisition storage facilities for military supplies. Private individuals and proprietors were entitled to be compensated for the fair market value of any property taken by the federal government pursuant to the act. U.S. District Courts were vested with jurisdiction to resolve disputes when agreement on fair market value could not be reached. The president delegated his regulatory powers to the federal Fuel Administrator, who carried out day-to-day operations with the help of regional agents he appointed around the country. Although the Lever Act granted the president extraordinary and sweeping powers, the law was upheld by the U.S. Supreme Court in Highland v. Russell Car & Snow Plow Company (1929). Stressing that the freedom to enter contracts and own property should not be impaired lightly, the Supreme Court nevertheless concluded that the regulatory powers granted by the Lever Act were necessary for successful prosecution of the war. In passing the Lever Act Congress had similarly declared that the food and fuel industries are affected with a public interest essential to the nation's common defense. By its terms the Lever Act became ineffective at the war's end. However, a number of sections were re-enacted on October 22, 1919.

See also: **Council of National Defense, World War I**

LEVITT, WILLIAM JAIRD

William Jaird Levitt (1907–1994) revolutionized the U.S. housing industry. Most construction companies in the United States eventually adopted methods invented by Levitt and his sons to lower the cost of making houses for a mass market of consumers. Levitt's innovations made housing more affordable to everyone. Millions of middle and working class people in the United States became homeowners during the mid-twentieth century due to Levitt's efforts.

William Levitt was born on February 11, 1907, in Brooklyn, New York, the son of a lawyer and building contractor. He attended Brooklyn's public schools and then enrolled at New York University for three years before dropping out.

At the age of 22 Levitt dreamed of becoming a commercial airline pilot. He instead joined his father Abraham and his brother Alfred to create Levitt and Sons, a construction company specializing in single-family home building. The company was founded in 1929. When Levitt became the company's president he occupied himself primarily with management and financial matters. Levitt and Sons did modestly well despite the Great Depression (1929–1939) of the 1930s. Levitt joined the Navy during World War II (1939–1945), serving as a lieutenant with the Seabees, the Navy's "can do" construction team. In the Seabees Levitt gained valuable experience in rapid, safe construction under unsafe conditions.

While he was in the Navy, the family business in the United States made much progress. In 1942 it received a federal war contract to build 1,600 homes for military and civilian personnel near a naval base in Norfolk, Virginia. In the construction of the last 750 homes built there, Levitt's father and brother experimented with building processes, especially with standardization and cost reduction.

After Levitt returned to the family business the company entered its greatest era of success. The Levitt family correctly forecasted the tremendous economic boom that happened in housing construction immediately after World War II. They analyzed the factors that caused single-family houses to be expensive. One major factor was that single homes were largely custom-made and required time consuming custom installations.

The Levitts decided to apply assembly line techniques to their housing construction. They developed one basic floor plan for a two-bedroom, 800-square-foot house, and made as many pre-fabricated parts as possible. They then hired specialized workers who did only one basic job, going from house to house, ahead of one crew, behind another crew, in assembly-line style. With these innovations the Levitts began to make 36 houses a day.

The crews worked so fast that the Levitts created instant suburbs. The houses sold as fast as they could be built. There were plenty of potential home buyers, most of them war veterans who had inexpensive mortgage loans guaranteed them under the G.I. Bill, a provision of the U.S. government to help returning war veterans readjust more quickly to civilian life back home. This included a home mortgage plan.

The first community built completely by the Levitts was called "Levittown." It was located on Long Island, New York; construction began in 1947 and completed in 1951. It included 17,500 Cape Cod-style homes spread over 7.3 square miles of land. What had once been potato fields was turned into homes with small parcels of land for buyers. The features of the homes included up-to-date kitchen equipment, laundry rooms, and television sets. Each house had two bedrooms and an extension attic that could serve as a third bedroom or an office. As the houses were built they were immediately put on the rental market for $65 a month with an option-to-buy clause for just under $7000 and no down payment for veterans.

By 1949 business was going so well that the new houses were no longer rented. They sold immediately, now for $8000. The Levitts also built larger homes for just under $10,000, with four to five bedrooms. By building the houses on winding streets and using different color schemes on their facades, the Levitts created houses that all looked "different," at least from the curbside view.

Levitt and Sons earned a profit of $5 million from the building of "Levittown." The mass production techniques used by the company were clearly the key to its success and future. Later Levittown developments were built in Pennsylvania, New Jersey, New York, and Florida, with the same success.

Levitt understoond his marketing success. The majority of the company's sales were to World War II veterans. Levitt sold to young families who sought

Suburbia flourished in the 1950s pursuant to the vision of house builder William J. Levitt who introduced mass-produced housing.

inexpensive "starter homes." A Levitt home was a family home, and the postwar United States placed great stress on the family unit and of the quality of family life. The Levitt suburban homes also gave families more privacy than was available in city apartments. Living in the suburbs made it possible for young families to have green lawns, small patios, swing sets in a yard, and barbecue grills.

William Levitt and his family company remained successful from the late 1940s to the late 1960s. Levitt's homes, however, were eventually criticized for their conformity and "ticky-tacky" quality. Levitt was also accused of refusing to sell his Levittown homes to African Americans in the 1950s.

William Levitt died in 1994. During his lifetime he created homes for millions of people in the United States. He provided them with a higher standard of living and a better quality of life than previous generations had enjoyed.

See also: **GI Bill, Suburbs (Rise of)**

FURTHER READING

Conrad, Pam. *Our House: The Stories of Levittown.* New York: Scholastic, 1995.

Fishman, Robert. *Bourgeois Utopia: The Rise and Fall of Suburbia.* New York: Basic Books, 1987.

Gans, Herbert J. *The Levittowners: Ways of Life and Politics in a New Suburban Community.* New York: Pantheon Books, 1967.

Popenoe, David. *The Suburban Environment: Sweden and the United States.* Chicago: University of Chicago Press, 1977.

Wetherell, W. D. *Levittown.* Pittsburgh, PA: University of Pittsburgh, 1986.

LEWIS AND CLARK EXPEDITION

The nation's economy diversified and grew during the first decades of the United States' independence from the British Empire. With the vast majority of the population engaged in agriculture, Thomas Jefferson (1801–1809) believed that the health of the republic rested on small independent farms, owned by men he called "Yeoman farmers." Jefferson also favored a strong agrarian economy to counter tendencies of concentrating wealth and power in emerging manufacturing centers of the east.

To find more farming land, Jefferson looked West. Although the Mississippi River formed the western boundary of the United States, Jefferson wanted to explore the region beyond, fearing that if the U.S. did

Lewis and Clark traveled their western expedition with the help of Sacajawea, of the Shoshone tribe, acting as an interpreter.

not expand westward, Britain or other countries might soon colonize the region. The lack of sufficient funding and political support, however, hindered such efforts through the 1790s.

In March of 1801 Jefferson became the third president of the United States (1801–09) and was in a position to further his exploration and land acquisition plans. By the time of his administration, Americans had a clearer understanding of the size of the continent they inhabited. In part, their knowledge was expanded because of the work of Captain James Cook (1728–1779), who measured the longitude along the Pacific Coast in 1780, and later of American Captain Robert Gray (1755–1806), who mapped the precise location of the Columbia River's mouth in 1792.

In 1801, however, Britain, Spain, France, and Russia still held vague claims to western North America, though the territory was in the possession of Native Americans. With water travel essential to commerce, Jefferson favored exploration and development of new water routes. The primary objective of a proposed expedition was, in Jefferson's own words, "to determine the most direct and practicable water communication across the continent, for the purposes of commerce."

Jefferson recruited Meriwether Lewis (1774–1809), a young army captain serving as Jefferson's personal White House secretary, to lead the expedition. Lewis, in turn, identified Lieutenant William Clark (1770–1838), an earlier commander of his, to serve as the expedition's co- leader. With agrarian interests in mind Jefferson directed them to make observations and measurements along the exploration route concerning plants, animals, soils, geography, and climate. Jefferson had Lewis tutored in Philadelphia by experts in these fields to prepare him for the expedition.

With preparations for the journey well under way Jefferson completed the Louisiana Purchase with Napoleon Bonaparte of France in 1803. The acquisition instantly doubled the size of the United States by adding 827,000 square miles of land and, most importantly, control of the Mississippi River for commerce. The expedition's purpose suddenly expanded to include exploration and evaluation of the new lands to determine their settlement and commercial potential.

The party of more than 40 men, called the Corps of Discovery by Jefferson, departed on May 14, 1804, from near the mouth of the Missouri River. Using large canoes and a keelboat for the first part of their journey (up the Missouri River), the party carried provisions to be supplemented along the way with wild game and fish. Lewis was in charge of scientific observations, with Clark directing map making and journal writing. In 1805 after spending their first winter at a Mandan Indian village on the Missouri in North Dakota, the expedition continued to the Missouri's headwaters and through the ranges of the Rocky Mountains. The expedition then journeyed down the Snake and Columbia rivers arriving at the Pacific Coast in the middle of November. They built Fort Clatsop just south of the Columbia River mouth and waited for a supply ship that never arrived. After a miserably wet winter, the expedition roughly retraced its route back eastward in 1806, splitting apart for much of the time to explore as much territory as possible. They arrived safely in St. Louis with great celebration on September 23 after exploring almost 8,000 miles of terrain in 863 days.

Two centuries later the Lewis and Clark Expedition remains remarkable for several reasons. Only one member of the party died, early in the journey, possibly from a ruptured appendix. By treating the Native Americans with respect, the party created a firm basis for trade, peace, and assistance with settlement. Though the expedition showed that the long-sought major waterway for trade did not exist, a wealth of biological, geographic, and cultural information was gathered in the party's eight-volume journal and maps. Included are previously unrecorded descriptions of 122 animals and 178 plants. The information vividly addressed the commercial potential of the newly acquired lands and territories west of the Rocky Mountains to the Pacific shore. Though the crossing was more difficult than anticipated, the Corps demonstrated its feasibility. The maps and detailed journal more immediately aided the U.S. fur trade. The fur trade spread across the region by the 1820s, and provided furs to a demanding European market.

Most importantly the expedition introduced the first United States presence west of the Rocky Mountains. Once the natural resources and potential settlement sites of the Northern Plains and Pacific Northwest were recorded, the agrarian economy envisioned by Jefferson could become a reality. U.S. citizens settled rich farmlands and established ports to ship produce to markets. As an integrated national economy was first emerging, Lewis and Clark opened the way to U.S. expansion from one coast to the other. The stage was set for an agricultural transformation of the west.

See also: **Thomas Jefferson, Louisiana Purchase**

FURTHER READING

Ambrose, Stephen E. *Undaunted Courage: Meriwether Lewis, Thomas Jefferson, and the Opening of the American West.* New York: Simon & Schuster, 1996.

Botkin, Daniel B. *Our Natural History: The Lessons of Lewis and Clark.* New York: Putnam, 1995.

Moulton, Gary E., ed. *The Journals of the Lewis and Clark Expedition.* Lincoln, NB: University of Nebraska Press, 1983.

Nobles, Gregory H. *American Frontiers: Cultural Encounters and Continental Conquest.* New York: Hill & Wang, 1997.

Owsley, Frank L., Jr., and Gene A. Smith. *Filibusters and Expansionists: Jeffersonian Manifest Destiny, 1800–1821.* Tuscaloosa: University of Alabama Press, 1997.

Ronda, James P. *Lewis and Clark Among the Indians.* Lincoln: University of Nebraska Press, 1984.

LEWIS, JOHN LLEWELLYN

John L. Lewis (1880–1969) began his working life as a coal miner, working like his father did for low wages in dangerous situations in an unregulated mining industry. He realized early that organizing his fellow mine workers into a common union of shared self-interest was the only way to fight the business practices that had created the circumstances he and other mine workers faced. Eventually, he became the president of the United Mine Workers (UMW), the national union of miners, and later the first president of the Congress of Industrial Organizations(CIO), the first unionized affiliation of industrial workers in the United States.

John Llewellyn Lewis was born in 1880, one of six children born to Thomas and Ann Lewis, in Lucas, Iowa. His father was a coal miner, a Welsh immigrant to the United States. The family moved often, following the availability of work from one coal-mining community to another. Lewis's childhood was filled with his family's continual struggle for financial security. Only because his father had obtained a steady job as a policeman in Des Moines, Iowa for a few years, was Lewis able to attend high school for three and a half years.

Lewis became involved with the organization of the miner's union in Lucas, Iowa, when he was 17. He continued to work in the mines, but he did not settle

John Lewis (*center*) was a devoted and powerful leader in U.S. organized labor for many years.

into serious union organizing efforts until 1908, at age 28. He moved with his wife to Panama, Illinois, and there became involved in union activities. With the help of his five brothers, Lewis was promoted to spokesman for the UMW.

A year later the UMW, seeking passage of mine safety laws, appointed Lewis as their state lobbyist in Illinois,. In 1910 Lewis was made president of his union local in Panama, Illinois, one of the 10 largest union locals in the state. By the next year he had became a full-time organizer for the national organization of craft and skilled-labor unions known as the American Federation of Labor (AFL). He remained with the AFL for six years. His reputation grew as a fierce and progressive voice speaking powerfully on behalf of those who were then a part of U.S. organized labor.

By 1920 Lewis was elected president of the UMW, and he guided the union of dwindling U.S. mine workers through a long period of decline in the 1920s. He held the union together during a time when U.S. industry moved to prevent further labor organizing. It was an era of cheap labor for industry, which was able to use newly immigrated workers from the southern United States and Europe. The rapid introduction of machinery to business during the 1920s also contributed to the decline of organized labor. The increasing use of machines threatened jobs, and many workers gave up their union activities in favor of preserving their employment. By the end of the 1920s Lewis had obtained absolute control over what was left of the organized mine workers in the United States.

When the United States experienced the Great Depression (1929–1939) after the stock market crash of 1929, Lewis began to fight to keep control of his union. He had to fend off new and aggressive communist labor organizers, as well as union opportunists representing a variety of reactionary labor positions. But, he held the threadbare UMW together.

After Franklin Roosevelt (1933–1945) was elected president of the United States in 1932, Lewis began to regain a large new membership in the UMW, based on Roosevelt's efforts to re-ignite the U.S. economy by mobilizing the industrial forces of the United States back into action with government aid. As part of Roosevelt's National Industrial Recovery Act (NIRA), administered by the National Recovery Administration (NRA), a provision of the NIRA, known as "section 7(a)," guaranteed labor's right to organize unions during this time in an overall effort to not only establish codes of fair competition for business, but also to provide safeguards for labor. Section 7(a) gave the right to all employees to organize and bargain collectively through representatives of their own choosing, without coercion. Labor unions immediately grew in number and size, including the UMW.

By 1933 most UMW miners were working a five-day week, eight hours a day, for the first time in their lives. At that time Lewis was moving in the direction of organizing all U.S. labor by industry, and not by their occupations or skills. By 1935 after the AFL had refused to include industrial laborers into their union, Lewis began to aggressively organize the neglected laborers in the great mass-production industries like steel, automobiles, rubber, oil, lumber, aluminum, and textiles. In conjunction with other labor leaders, Lewis began to put together the Congress of Industrial Organizations (CIO) in 1936. CIO managed victories in the steel and auto industries between 1936 and 1937 led to a massive membership in the CIO. After that a gradual and very difficult affiliation began, eventually joining the AFL with the CIO in an international union known as the AFL-CIO in 1954.

John L. Lewis fought throughout his adult life for the dignity of U.S. labor. On balance, Lewis succeeded in his efforts. By using ''people power'' to fight the raw power of money and business influence, Lewis' creation of an international CIO lead to one of the first example of a consolidation of unions built on the efforts of industrial workers. His achievements in acquiring labor benefits for his union's members were eventually integrated into national policy, as when the Roosevelt administration created legislation to provide social security for the elderly and the disabled. Though this legislation was not due to Lewis' efforts alone, he was one of the first voices at the turn of the twentieth century to advocate for these measures and to see them become a part of life in the United States. John Lewis died in 1969.

See also: **American Federation of Labor, Coal Industry, Congress of Industrial Organizations, Labor Movement, Labor Unionism, National Industrial Recovery Act, National Recovery Administration, United Mine Workers**

FURTHER READING

Alinsky, Saul D. *John L. Lewis, An Unauthorized Biography*. New York: Vintage Book, 1970.

Bernstein, Irving. *The Lean Years*. New York: Houghton Press, 1965.

Brody, Davis. *Workers in Industrial America*. New York: Oxford Press, 1980.

Dubofsky, Melvyn and Warren Van Tine. *John L. Lewis, A Biography*. Chicago, IL: University of Illinois Press, 1986.

Fraser, Steven. *Labor Will Rule: Sidney Hillman and the Rise of American Labor*. New York: Free Press, 1991.

LEWIS, SINCLAIR

Sinclair Lewis (1885–1951) was one of the leading U.S. novelists of the 1920s. He was a social critic of the era who wrote from the political perspective of Progressivism. Lewis wrote some of the most effective mass-market criticism against the business corruption of society. He was a fierce critic of materialism in the United States. In books such as *Babbitt*, *Arrowsmith*, and *Mainstreet*, Lewis attacked the smug provincialism, social conformity, and corrupt business values of the U.S. middle class in the 1920s.

Lewis was born on February 7, 1885 in a prairie village in the most Scandinavian part of the United States—Sauk Center, Minn. He was raised in middle class circumstances and attended the local public schools of his community. Lewis grew up in the midst of the Progressive movement in the United States. Many of his Scandinavian neighbors embraced cooperative and socialist ideas, and had embraced unionization and progressive thinking in various ways. Other neighbors of his were middle-class Protestants who strictly conformed to the social standards they deemed acceptable and who saw financial advancement as the major yardstick of success. Lewis grew up with conflicting feelings about himself. He wanted to be a ''regular guy,'' but he was by nature a non-conformist, an agnostic, a skeptic, and an artist.

Lewis enrolled at Yale University in Connecticut because he hoped to escape Midwestern life. He then began an off-and-on career as a student and world traveler. He graduated from Yale in 1908. Recounting his life to the Nobel Foundation after receiving the Nobel Prize for Literature in 1930 Sinclair wrote: ''I drifted for 2 years after college as a journalist, as a newspaper reporter in Iowa and in San Francisco, and incredibly, as a junior editor of a magazine for teachers of the deaf.''

Lewis wrote five novels between 1914 and 1919, and according to him ''all of them dead before the ink was dry.'' In 1920 at the age of 35 Lewis published the novel *Mainstreet.* It became an instant and scandalous best-seller, largely because he had attacked ''one of the most treasured American myths . . . that all American towns were peculiarly noble and happy,'' as Lewis himself said.

Lewis wrote for mass-audiences and usually criticized class values and virtues. He challenged the smug, narrow-minded, and complacent ''business values'' of mainstreet United States. He became one of the literary voices that indirectly spoke to the issues of Progressive political thinking in the United States. Lewis saw the modernized world of the 1920s change the United States; he saw great problems looming in the near future. He wrote about those people in the United States who had blinded themselves to the perils of smug, small-town thinking.

Lewis' work flourished in the 1920s. It was a perfect era to indict traditional U.S. values, which had become unacceptable in the young, jaded, sophisticated, and cynical urban climate of the so-called ''Jazz Age,'' as the era of the 1920s was called. The generation that had just witnessed the mechanized slaughter and meaninglessness of World War I (1914–1918) was ready for Lewis' books. His writing was welcomed as a refreshing statement of the unvarnished truth—it rejected genteel optimism, blind U.S. nationalism, and traditional religious values.

Lewis continued writing novels after he received the Nobel Prize; his other works included *It Can't Happen Here*, *Cass Timberlane*, and an early civil rights advocacy novel, *Kingsblood Royal* (1947). He never reclaimed the status he achieved in the 1920s as a critic of business-related pomposity.

Lewis' critical faculty was compared to that of Thomas Paine (1737–1809) and Mark Twain (1835–1910). He was regarded as a gadfly of the literary scene in the United States. Lewis both outraged and educated average citizens about their frequently misguided lives as hucksters of U.S. business. His impact on the business world of his era was large, complex, and thoughtful.

FURTHER READING

Dooley, David J. *The Art of Sinclair Lewis.* Lincoln: University of Nebraska Press, 1967.

Hutchinson, James M. *The Rise of Sinclair Lewis, 1920–1930.* University Park, PA: Pennsylvania State University Press, 1996.

Koblas, John J. *Sinclair Lewis, Home at Last.* Bloomington, MN: Voyageur Press, 1981.

Light, Martin. *The Quixotic Vision of Sinclair Lewis.* West Lafayette, IN: Purdue University Press, 1975.

Love, Glen A. *Babbitt: An American Life.* New York: Twayne Publishers, 1993.

LIBERALISM

The term ''liberalism'' has meant different things at different points in the history of the United States. The different meanings of liberalism turn on the changing relationship between the government and the economy. In the nineteenth century liberalism was a critique of the doctrine of mercantilism which had been the reigning theory of economic activity in the eighteenth century. Mercantilism focused on the commercial life of the nation. It asserted that there was only a fixed amount of wealth in the world and viewed economic life as a kind of commercial warfare between nations in which the goal was to accumulate as much as possible of silver and gold. The government played an active role in this commercial competition between the nations. It encouraged specific manufacturing industries, regulated the quality of manufactures, established trading routes and oversaw the relations with the colonies. This doctrine had begun to crumble in the eighteenth century as a result of excessive regulation and poor administration. Also the economies of some European nations, like Spain, had been undermined by the price inflation that accompanied their governments' accumulation of gold and silver. The mercantilist economies also sometimes created obstructions to international trade by erecting high tariff barriers to protect domestic industry from foreign competition.

When Adam Smith wrote his *Inquiry into the Nature and Causes of the Wealth of Nations* in 1776, mercantilism had seen its better days. Smith's was a most elegant critique against the decrepit system, because it was so simple. He argued that all the functions that mercantilism invested in the state could be more efficiently performed by the individual entrepreneur. For instance, rather than have the government dictate prices and quantities of goods for sale, the ''law of supply and demand'' would automatically find the price and the quantity which best accommodated both the buyer and the seller. Secondly, rather than have the government decide what industry to invest in, the individual entrepreneur, spurred by the profit motive, would make that decision. And, rather than have the government organize production, the entrepreneur, again in the effort to maximize his profit, would find the optimum ''division of labor'' that would improve productivity and maximize profits.

It was an age of manifestos and Adam Smith's *Wealth of Nations* became (and remains) the most persuasive manifesto of free market capitalism. The nineteenth century economic liberals believed that property rights were the cornerstone of both political and economic freedom. Underlying Smith's system was an assumption (shared by another Scottish philosopher, John Locke) of the promise of harmonious relations among the members of society. Each individual, endowed with certain natural rights, in seeking personal happiness also enhanced the happiness of all. The economic liberals believed that there was no essential contradiction between the "public good" of all individuals. The economy was not, as the mercantilists held, a "zero sum game." The public good could be most effectively furthered by economic liberalism (or the freedom to invest). Democracy could rid itself of the dead hand of government and increase the benign scope of laissez-faire's "invisible hand."

But the emergence over the next two centuries of industrialization, urbanization, big business, over-production crises, instability, the excesses of competition, and the conspiracy to set prices, and in particular the misfortune of the Great Depression (1929–1939) plus two world wars gradually converted modern liberalism from a crusade against governmental interference in the economy into a movement to protect the weak against the strong and the national economy against the unregulated tendency towards instability. Today, at the beginning of the twentieth century and the dawn of a new millennium, liberalism stands for almost the complete opposite than its nineteenth century meaning.

But did nineteenth century liberalism ever actually exits? Many economic historians argue that during the first three centuries of U.S. history, colonial, state, and federal governments continued to intervene in the economy, in varying degrees, under the more modern definition of liberalism. They argue that during the colonial period government at all levels acted in the public interest and that it could set the "just price" for milling and the price of bread, regulate the purity of beer, establish reasonable ferry charges, and grant monopoly franchises. Colonial governments could set wages and even require work. In the process, many colonial regulations were embedded in common law. To enforce this web of complex rules and regulations, colonial governments used constables and wardens. While many of the colonial regulations had disappeared by the time of the American Revolution (1775–1783), the Revolution itself did little to interrupt institutional continuity.

While some economists assert that the U.S. economy in the nineteenth century followed Smith's vision of laissez faire liberalism, others argue that the government, although undoubtedly supportive of profit-driven economic development, was also beginning to take on the mandate of "twentieth century liberalism"—i.e., the roles of regulator and safety-net. This was the view, clearly present in the Populists and the Progressives, that the profit motive of the individual investor, unless restrained by government, may do damage to the public good.

In addition, the government remained a potent force in the economy, although often in spite of the popular sentiment to limit the role of the federal government in favor of states rights. The federal banking policy illustrates both the resistance to a larger role for the federal government—vented in Andrew Jackson's "bank war" of 1832— and the gradual realization that banks simply needed regulation. Eventually, the national consensus supported President Woodrow Wilson's Federal Reserve Bank which in 1913 created the modern national banking structure.

As the Progressive period unfolded, reforms at the federal level included the lowering of tariffs, the introduction of the income tax, passage of antitrust laws, the Federal Reserve Act of 1913, the direct election of Senators, federal child-labor laws, constitutional amendments prohibiting the consumption of alcoholic beverages, and extending the vote to women. Reforms at the state level brought workmen's compensation laws and pensions for Union Civil War veterans, their widows, and orphans (the nation's first government funded welfare plans). Seeking to break the power of entrenched political interests, reformers also advocated open primaries, initiative, referendum and recall, and promoted governmental regulation of gas, water, and electrical utilities. Urban reformers also sought to weaken political bosses and their machines by implementing commission government and home rule. As the emergence of the modern bureaucratic state continued, various political factions battled for control in a society being transformed by the forces of industrialization, immigration, and urbanization.

Faced with mounting pressure, the federal government also began to regulate the railroad industry as well as break up monopolies. In response to the accumulated demands of the National Grange, Farmers' Alliances, Greenback Party, and eventually the Populist Party, Congress finally passed in 1887 the Interstate Commerce Act, which assigned the federal government the role of market arbiter. On October 15, 1914, Congress passed and President Woodrow Wilson (1913–1921) signed the Clayton Antitrust Act, which was designed to strengthen the Sherman Antitrust Act of

1890 by fully codifying specific illegal antitrust activities. To carry out and enforce the Clayton Act and the Sherman Act, Congress created the Federal Trade Commission in a related measure.

As the country expanded and the population grew, and as the economy became more complex and powerful, some of the underlying structural weaknesses were not apparent to most U.S. citizens. But the Stock Market Crash of 1929 and the subsequent Great Depression changed their views. In 1933 President Franklin D. Roosevelt (1933–1945) formally introduced a new twentieth century liberalism to the United States political and economic landscape. Roosevelt was greatly influenced by the British economist John Maynard Keynes, who proposed the prevention of financial crisis and unemployment by adjusting demand through government control of credit and currency. Roosevelt shifted purchasing power in favor of the poor, the spenders; he provided employment through public works and insurance where it was feasible, and, in other cases, he offered assistance to those injured by economic forces. Essentially through ad hoc measures (measures taken for a specific case or instance), the New Deal unfolded. The objective was to help those in distress, deflate the large interests that had overreached themselves, and improve the functioning of the system.

In the late 1990s, under a more global economy, liberalism was faced with the question of whether the United States and other capitalist countries were prepared to accept a mixed economy—one in which the government, not the market, was responsible for major decisions concerning total savings, investment and spending, which would result, it was hoped, in stable or high levels of employment and output.

See also: **Nicholas Biddle, Federal Reserve Act of 1913, Andrew Jackson, Mercantilism, Adam Smith**

FURTHER READING

Gottfried, Paul. "In Search of a Liberal Essence." *Society*, 39-51, September/October 1995.

Link, Arthur S. *Wilson: The New Freedom*. Princeton, NJ: Princeton University Press, 1956.

Mandle, Jay. "The Lefts' Wrong Turn: Why Economic Nationalism Won't Work." *Dissent*, 45, 1998.

Nuechterlein, James. "The Lure of Social Democracy." *First Things*, May 1998.

Smith, Roger M. "Unfinished Liberalism." *Social Research*, Fall 1994.

LIBERIA

Liberia is a country that lies along the West African coast on the Atlantic Ocean. Sierra Leone borders it on the northwest, Guinea on the north, and the Ivory Coast on the east. The capital of Liberia is Monrovia.

Established in 1821, Liberia was intended as a haven for freed American slaves. Members of the American Colonization Society, which was organized between 1816 and 1817, purchased land from native tribes in Africa, with the goal of transporting freed slaves back to their African homeland. The land was named Liberia, which was derived from a Latin word meaning "freedom."

In 1822 the first returning Africans arrived in Liberia. By 1860, eleven thousand freed slaves from America had settled in Liberia; eventually fifteen thousand made the trans-Atlantic voyage. On July 26, 1847, the country was established as a free and independent republic. But constitutional issues, foreign debt, and territorial disputes soon threatened the new nation. The United States government stepped in with aid to stabilize Liberia.

The plan of the American Colonization Society had always been a controversial one: many abolitionists opposed it, as did some African Americans who believed slavery should simply be eradicated from the United States, and the freed slaves granted all rights of citizenship. The African resettlement movement declined in the mid-1800s.

See also: **Abolition, Slavery**

LIBERTY BONDS

During World War I (1914–1918) the U.S. Treasury sold war bonds (certificates of indebtedness backed by the federal government) to help pay for the high cost of the war effort. Posters advertising the bonds were emblazoned with an image of the Statue of Liberty and the certificates themselves were called Liberty bonds. Patriotism and the motivational messages of Hollywood stars, such as Charlie Chaplin, Mary Pickford, and Douglas Fairbanks, who spoke at bond rallies, encouraged Americans to buy billions of dollars worth of Liberty bonds to help finance the fight in Europe. Towns were even given quotas of bonds to sell. In 1917 alone U.S. citizens bought $18.7 billion worth of the bonds, which would pay a fixed 3.5 percent interest rate compared with railroad bonds, which yielded nearly five percent in fixed interest. The success of the Liberty bond sales enabled the federal government to borrow money from its citizens, promising to pay the sum back (plus 3.5 percent interest). The bond sales served to introduce many U.S. citizens to the practice of investing, which they continued after the war. Some analysts believe this mind-set helped fuel overconfidence in the stock market, which contributed to its escalation during the 1920s and to its crash at the end of the decade (1929). During World War II (1939–45) the government again sold war bonds to help raise funds for the fight for freedom.

See also: **Bonds, World War I, World War II**

LIBERTY SHIPS

Liberty ships were American-made, mass-produced merchant vessels that were used by the Allies to carry freight, troops, and fuel during World War II (1939–1945). A few were converted to other uses, including tank transports, hospitals, and repair shops. A Liberty ship was a modified version of a merchant ship of simple design that was conceived in Great Britain. The original plan called for the vessels to be riveted, but riveting was a time-consuming process. By September 1940, Britain was under siege by German naval and air forces and lacked sufficient time or capital to build such ships for itself. So when production of the merchantmen was turned over to the United States, industrialist Henry J. Kaiser (1882–1967) sped up production by welding the vessels and applying revolutionary prefabrication techniques. Kaiser started with an initial keel-to-deliver time of over 200 hundred days. Within a year, however, Liberty Ships were being launched just 24 days after the laying of the keel. They traveled at a top speed of 11 knots, and came in different sizes and weights, with the largest being almost 450 feet long and over 10,000 tons.

Approximately 250 Liberty Ships were sent to Great Britain and the Soviet Union under the Lend-Lease program, while another 200 were used by American forces. Liberty ships take their name from ''Liberty Fleet Day,'' a day in September 1941 when the first one was launched. Because of the high rate of production, a number of Liberty Ships were defective. But others endured repeated pounding by German surface ships and submarines. One ship even sunk a German auxiliary cruiser with its single four-inch gun.

See also: **Lend-Lease Act, World War II**

LIMITED PARTNERSHIP

A limited partnership is a form of incorporation which involves ownership by two classes of investors known as general partners and limited partners. There can be one or more general partners and one or more limited partners in a limited partnership. Both classes of partners receive income or incur losses of the partnership based on the percentage of ownership each partner has. General partners are responsible for the management of the corporation and assume unlimited liability for any obligations or legal debt. Limited partners are passive owners in that they do not participate in the everyday operation of the corporation. Therefore their financial liability for the partnership is limited to the amount they have invested in the corporation.

See also: **Corporation**

LOBBYING

Lobbying is an attempt to influence the course of government action through persuasion or gifts to legislators. The phrase derives from the advocates' practice of waiting in the lobby of government buildings, such as the U.S. House of Representatives, to talk to lawmakers as they come and go. Lobbying, as an activity, may be as old as democracy, but the phrase itself seems to have originated in the early- to mid-nineteenth century in Washington, D.C.

From its earliest usage, the term lobbying implied activity that was somewhat illegal or unsavory, including bribery of public officials. Even today when laws strictly limit the types of gifts that lobbyists may give legislators, critics of lobbying decry the large campaign contributions that interest groups are able to give to candidates to influence their future actions. Lobbyists themselves defend their profession. They contend that they perform a vital public service by bringing valuable information about public issues to light.

Lobbying is often performed by major law firms on behalf of clients or by nonprofit groups concerned with a single issue. There have been hundreds of well-organized groups that lobby both in Washington, D.C., and in state capitals. These groups represent almost every conceivable special interest, from business and environmental groups to those concerned with abortion, foreign trade, or tax reform. Some of the better known groups that lobby legislators on issues of interest to their members are the National Rifle Association, the American Association of Retired Persons, and the National Association of Realtors. Lobbying has had a profound influence on legislative actions.

See also: **Special Interest Group**

LONG, HUEY PIERCE

Huey Pierce Long (1893–1935) was the seventh of nine children, born in a poor area of Louisiana in 1893. Though he would build his political career on the support of poor whites living largely on farms, Long's family was middle class. In school he excelled as a debater and read widely, particularly from the *Bible*, Shakespeare, and the French writer Victor Hugo.

Long worked briefly as a typesetter and a traveling salesman. He then briefly attended law school, took the Louisiana State bar exam, and passed it in 1915. Long was shrewd, popular, and had a feel for communicating with the ''common man;'' he became an effective attorney almost immediately. Long's political career began in 1918, with his election to the Louisiana railroad commission, which later became the public service commission. There Long made a name for himself by attacking large Louisiana-based corporations, especially Standard Oil, for being concerned only with their profits and as the source of the problems of Louisiana's poor.

EVERY MAN A KING.

Huey Long

Running with the slogan of ''Every Man a King,'' Long was elected governor in 1928. As governor Huey Long continued to blame big business for the financial problems of the poor in Louisiana. He introduced unprecedented programs aimed at helping the poor in exchange for their votes. He initiated a massive highway and toll-free bridge construction project that put masses of people to work, lowered utility and transportation rates, and provided free schoolbooks, school lunches, and hospital care for everyone. He established free public night schools and began a program of dramatically improving the health standards of working people by taxing large Louisiana corporations. At the same time, there were accusations of bribery and corruption against Long. It is certain that Long's control of the Louisiana Democratic Party allowed him to crush most rivals and assume near total control over the state of Louisiana. He was elected to the U.S. Senate in 1930, but stayed on in his post as governor until his term expired in 1932, so as to prevent his lieutenant governor, a political opponent, from taking office.

Huey P. Long.

In Washington, DC, Long allied himself with moderate Republicans, and yet strongly supported President Franklin Roosevelt (1933–1945). But Long quickly became impatient with Roosevelt's efforts to end the Great Depression (1929–1939), and saw the opportunity to further expand his power. In 1933 he broke with Roosevelt and began to plan for his own presidential run, using a ''Share the Wealth'' platform which was aimed at overhauling the tax structure in order to bring about a quick redistribution of wealth.

Under Long's plan the government would limit the income of all people through taxation, and use these funds to ensure that every family would be furnished with a $5000 allowance and an annual income of $2000 plus benefits. This idea was very attractive to millions of Americans who had lost their jobs or much of their wages in the Depression. It was met with horror by wealthier Americans, who decried the plan as communism or facism. Large businesses in particular regarded Long and his ideas as a threat.

Huey Long's dreams of the presidency ended in the Louisiana State Capitol in 1935, when he was assassinated by Carl Weiss, a political enemy. Weiss was immediately shot and killed by Long's bodyguards. The ''Share the Wealth'' plan died with Long. The United States would eventually emerge from the Depression, but at Roosevelt's pace, a pace that left U.S. business intact and arguably stronger after World War II (1939–1945).

See also: **Louisiana, New Deal**

FURTHER READING

Cortner, Richard C. *The Kingfisher and the Constitution: Huey Long, the First Amendment and the Emergence of Modern Press Freedom in America.* Westport, CT: Greenwood Press, 1996.

Dawson, Joseph G., ed. *The Louisiana Governors: From Iberville to Edwards.* Baton Rouge, LA: Louisiana State University Press, 1990.

Long, Huey. *Every Man a King.* New Orleans, LA: National Book Co., 1933.

Martin, Thomas. *Dynasty: The Longs of Louisiana.* New York: G. P. Putnam, 1960.

Williams, Thomas Harry. *Huey P. Long.* New York: Knopf, 1969.

LONGHORN CATTLE

Longhorn are a breed of cattle descended from cows and bulls left by early Spanish settlers in the American Southwest. They are named for their long horns, which span about four feet (over one meter). By the end of the American Civil War (1861–1865) these cattle had multiplied and great numbers of them roamed freely across the open range of the West. Americans found the beef of longhorns stringy and tough. But ranchers in Texas bred the longhorns with other cattle breeds such as Hereford and Angus to produce better quality meat. As beef was in demand in the eastern United States, shrewd businessmen capitalized on the business opportunity, buying cattle for three to five dollars a head and selling them in eastern and northern markets for as much as $25 to $60 a head. Ranchers hired cowboys to round up, sort out, and drive their herds to railheads in places like Abilene and Dodge City, Kansas, which became famous as ''cow towns'' (raucous boom towns where saloons and brothels proliferated.) After the long trail drive, the cattle were loaded onto rail cars and shipped live to local butchers who slaughtered the livestock and prepared the beef. For 20 years the plentiful longhorn cattle sustained a booming livestock industry in the West: at least six million Texas longhorns were driven across Oklahoma to the cow towns of Kansas. However, by 1890 the complexion of the industry changed. Farmers and ranchers in the West used a new material, barbed wire, to fence in their lands, closing the open range. Railroads were extended, bringing an end to the long, hard, and much glorified cattle drives; the role of the cowboy changed, making him little more than a hired hand. Big business took over the industry. Among the entrepreneurs who capitalized on beef's place in the American diet was New England-born Gustavus Swift (1839–1903), who in 1877 began a large-scale slaughterhouse operation in Chicago, shipping ready-packed meat via refrigerated railcars to markets in the East.

See also: **Barbed Wire, Cattle Drives, Cowboy, Cow Towns, Chisholm Trail, Open Range, Prairie**

LOUISIANA

Natural resources and farming hold a significant place in Louisiana's economic history. However, the cultural spice of New Orleans has added to the state's economic base by setting the city apart from any other cities in the world and, over the years, making it a unique tourist attraction.

Indians were the first known inhabitants within Louisiana, living in small pockets. Spanish and French explorers navigated the Gulf of Mexico even before Robert Cavelier, Sieur de la Salle named the land at the mouth of the Mississippi River Louisiana. He did so in honor of King Louis XIV, claiming the land for France in 1682. In the 1700s the French began developing settlements in Louisiana and in 1722 New Orleans was established as Louisiana's capital. These early French settlers started tobacco and indigo farms and brought in slaves from Africa and the West Indies to work them.

Louisiana was not particularly prosperous under French rule, however French culture did take hold. In 1762 France ceded Louisiana to Spain during the French and Indian War (1754–1763). The area fared very well under Spanish rule as American settlers and immigrants from Spain and the Canary Islands relocated to the area. The Spaniards also brought black slaves, but there were also many ''free people of color'' in Louisiana. However the largest number of immigrants were French-speaking Acadian refugees from Nova Scotia who were driven from their homes by the British during the war with France. Their descendants are now known as Cajun. The mixture of these early Spanish, French, and black cultures became the unique and colorful Louisiana of today.

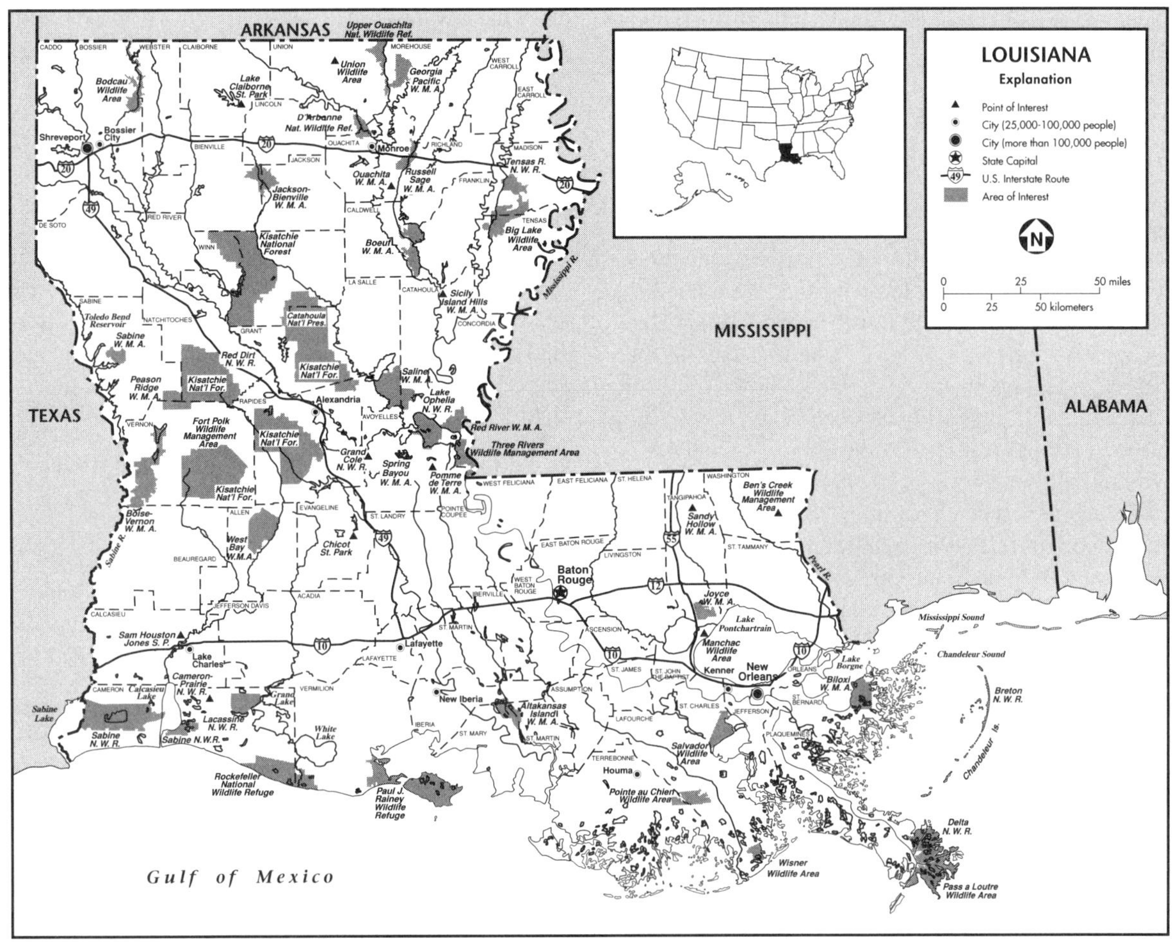

State of Louisiana.

In 1800 Napoleon Bonaparte forced Spain to return Louisiana to France. Three years later Napoleon sold Louisiana to the United States for $15 million. President Thomas Jefferson's (1801–1809) real estate deal doubled the size of the United States with a cash outlay of about 3 cents per acre.

In the early 1800s Louisiana saw an influx of immigrants from surrounding southern states. On April 30, 1812, Congress approved Louisiana's bid for statehood. Between 1815 and 1861 Louisiana's sugar and cotton production made it one of the most prosperous states in the south. The state was also an important location on the inland north and south water route. Steamboats traveling the Mississippi River transported goods such as cotton, grain, and sugarcane to New Orleans, where it was trans-shipped on ocean-going vessels. This assured the city's commercial and strategic importance.

Wealthy planters in Louisiana depended on slave labor. In 1860 there were more than 330,000 black slaves, nearly half of Louisiana's total population. At that time the north no longer allowed slavery and when Abraham Lincoln (1861–1865) became president of the United States in 1861, southerners feared he would outlaw slavery in the south as well. The planters in Louisiana held the majority of economic and political power. Their influence led the state to secede from the union with ten other states and form a separate country called the Confederate States of America, thus beginning the American Civil War (1860–1865). In 1865 the South surrendered having suffered disastrous losses; the war ended, and all slaves were freed. When the Civil War was over, however, opportunities for freed blacks were limited, and former slaves returned as laborers to sugar plantations and cotton fields, which they farmed "for shares," (they rented the land and paid in shares of the crop) along with poor whites.

In the 1880s irrigation systems allowed farmers to plant rice, and midwestern farmers migrated to southwestern Louisiana to become rice farmers. In the meantime, lumber and flour mills were started; oil and natural gas were discovered; and railroads were built.

However, in 1898 a new constitution was drawn up that took voting rights away from blacks as well as many poor whites. Large landowners, businessmen, and politicians controlled the government and resisted social reform, which meant that the small farmers and the urban working class, both white and black, did not share in the general prosperity.

In the late 1920s the Great Depression (1929–1939) caused banks and factories to close around the country and many people lost their jobs. When Huey Long was elected governor of Louisiana in 1928 he based his campaign on the problems in the economy and the growing inequality between the state's citizens. He also campaigned against the Standard Oil Company's high-handed dealings. Although he did not really challenge the racial segregation of the South, he did talk more about class than about race, and he advocated social and economic reforms, such as some improvements in education and health care, for African Americans. Huey Long was an ambitious, talented, and very popular politician who initially supported Franklin D. Roosevelt's New Deal program of governmental aid to victims of the Depression. However, he turned against Roosevelt and would probably have split the Democratic vote in the 1936 election had he not been assassinated in 1935.

The state's economy gradually pulled out of the Depression with the development of offshore drilling, reforesting, and soybean farming. Many residents were put to work building roads and bridges. Louisiana became one of the world's leading petrochemical manufacturing centers with oil drilling in the Gulf of Mexico. After World War II (1939–1945) started, additional jobs were created as ships were built for the Navy in New Orleans.

In the 1970s much of the revenue from the high oil prices was put to work to improve the state's schools and highways. But in the mid-1980s world oil prices dropped, which hurt Louisiana's economy. Energy-related industries, such as machinery manufacturing, also suffered. In 1986 unemployment in the state, especially for women, was the highest in the nation at 13 percent. In the 1990s Louisiana had more people living in poverty than any other state.

In 1992 Louisiana tried to revitalize its economy by legalizing riverboat and casino gambling. This effort created thousands of jobs and also helped attract more than 20 million tourists annually. In the 1990s the service industry was the leading employer. While chemicals were the leading product in Louisiana in 1995, others, such as fertilizer, soap, paint, plastic, ships, airplanes, paper, and praline candy, were also growing. At the same time crops grown in Louisiana included soybeans, rice, cotton, sugarcane, and sweet potatoes. Shipping and transportation was also significant because the Port of South Louisiana, the busiest port in the United States in 1995, handled nearly 400 billion pounds of cargo annually.

While the average household income in 1997 was $34,400, the distribution of that income was skewed. In 1995 nearly 20 percent of Louisiana residents were below the federal poverty level, while eight percent had a disposable income greater than $75,000, including 1.7 percent whose disposable incomes were greater than $125,000.

See also: **Huey Long, New Orleans, Plantations, Petroleum Industry, Sharecropping**

FURTHER READING

Davis, Edwin A. *Louisiana, the Pelican State*. Baton Rouge, LA: State University Press, 1975.

Dryer, Edward, Lyle Saxon, and Robert Tallant. *Gumbo Ya-Ya*. New York: Crown Publishers, Inc, 1984.

Thompson, Kathleen. In ''Louisiana.'' *Portrait of America*. Austin, TX: Steck-Vaughn Publishers, 1996.

Wall, Bennett H. *Louisiana, A History*. Arlington Heights, IL: Forum Press, 1990.

Worldmark Encyclopedia of the States. Detroit, MI: Gale Research, 1998, s.v. ''Louisiana.''

LOUISIANA PURCHASE

In 1801 after a series of secret agreements, French Emperor Napoleon Bonaparte (1769–1821) recovered the territory of Louisiana from Spain, which France had lost in 1763. When the land was handed over, U.S. goods were refused storage at the important international port of New Orleans—a violation of the Pinckney Treaty. Since New Orleans was an integral port to U.S. international trade, unhappy U.S. farmers and merchants grumbled for war.

President Thomas Jefferson (1801–1809) realized that this French acquisition challenged U.S. trade and presented a stumbling block to the United States, should it ever choose to expand its current borders westward. Believing that his decision was in his country's best interests, Jefferson sent Secretary of State James Monroe (1758–1831) to Paris to discuss the possibility of purchasing the Louisiana Territory from

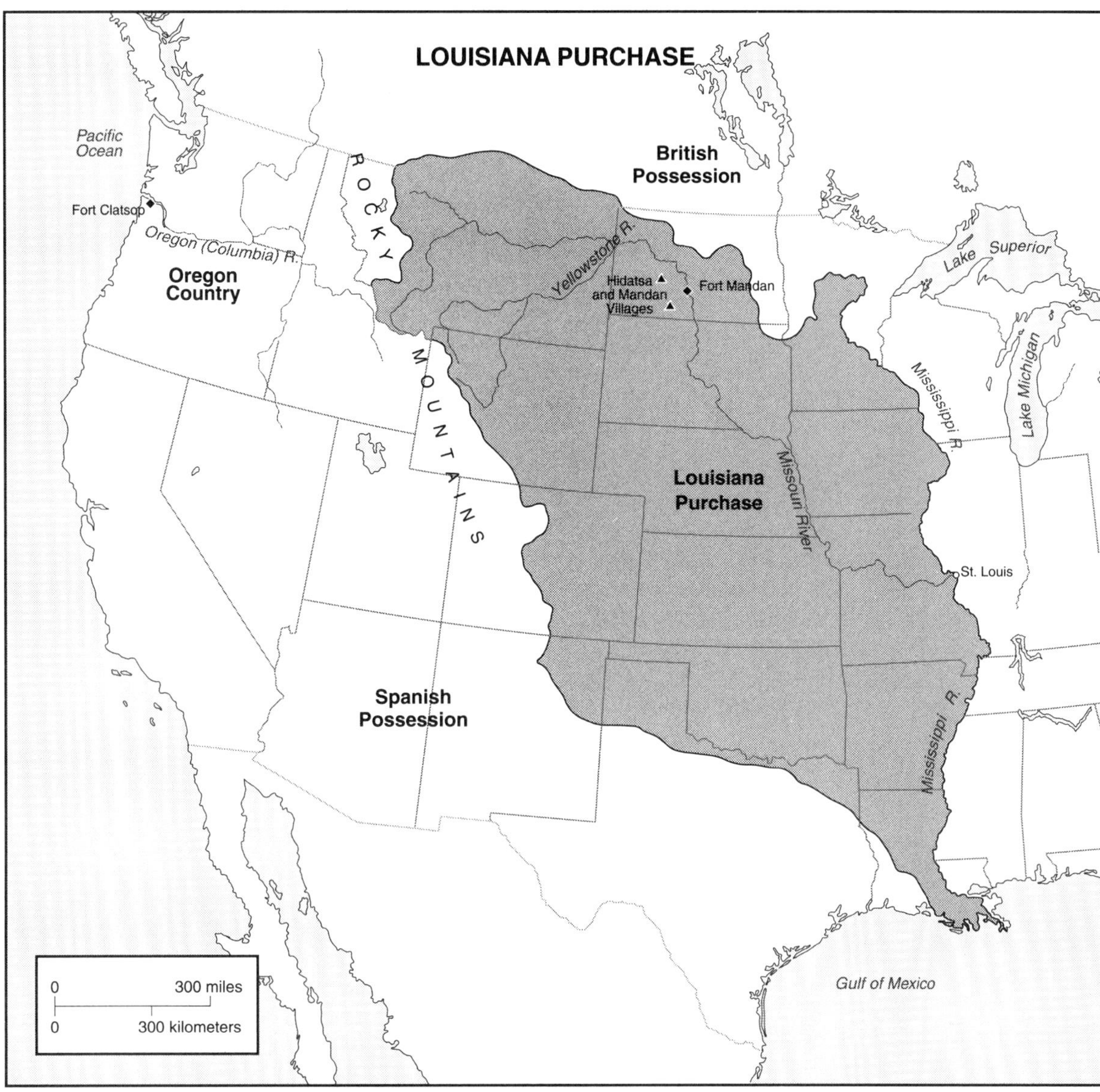

The shaded area indicates the approximate 827,000 square miles of land acquired by the U.S. in 1803 from the Louisiana Purchase.

France. At the same time, Jefferson authorized a gathering of militiamen at home as a show of force against France.

EVERY EYE IN THE UNITED STATES IS NOW FOCUSED ON THE AFFAIRS OF LOUISIANA.

Thomas Jefferson, in a letter to Robert R. Livingston, U.S. minister to Paris, 1802

Napoleon, who was already on unfriendly terms with Britain, did not want to face a British-U.S. alliance. In 1803 he agreed to sell the Louisiana Territory (approximately 827,000 square miles) to the United States for a price of $15 million. The United States doubled its territorial size and extended public lands westward into the Missouri River and the Rocky Mountains.

Although the Louisiana Purchase extended U.S. boundaries and ensured protection of U.S. trade at the port of New Orleans, it presented a dilemma to Jefferson. He had a dream of seeing the United States stretch from the Atlantic to the Pacific Oceans. He also believed the government was invested with only those powers explicitly stated in the Constitution, and the authority to purchase new territory was not among those powers.

In purchasing the Louisiana Territory, Jefferson used implied Constitutional powers, by which he strengthened the national government. His action, however, created a sense of uneasiness among those who feared a return to an authoritarian regime so soon after the American Revolution (1775–1783). A strong central government infringed on states' rights, which Jefferson also ardently supported. At the time he considered proposing a Constitutional amendment to allow explicitly the authority to purchase new territory. But, Secretary of the Treasury, Albert Gelatin, advised Jefferson that the executive office had an inherent right to expand the nation, and Congress had the power to admit newly acquired land into the Union as a state or annex it as territory. Jefferson accepted this position and Congress ratified the land purchase. Regardless of the president's philosophical conflict, the public approved of the purchase. In 1804 Jefferson was reelected to a second term.

Reaching from the Rocky Mountains to the Mississippi River and from Canada to the Gulf of Mexico, the Louisiana Purchase ensured that the U.S. would have ample room for expansion for years to come. Later four whole states (Arkansas, Iowa, Missouri and Nebraska) and parts of nine others (Louisiana, Minnesota, Oklahoma, Kansas, Colorado, Wyoming, Montana, North Dakota, and South Dakota) were made from this vast area. It increased the reach of the agricultural class by securing large amounts of land and transportation networks. With uninhibited access to the Mississippi and Missouri Rivers, goods and services could now be transported over greater distances. The U.S. economy could not help but expand.

Whatever its constitutional implications, the Louisiana Purchase was one of the most important presidential decisions in the nation's history. Through this purchase, the United States became a continental power, controlled the continent's main navigation routes, and became owner of vast new resources. These combined assets promised the young nation greater economic independence from Europe and set a precedent for future territorial expansion.

In order to realize the full potential of this uncharted land, President Jefferson dispatched a 35-member expedition to explore it. Led by U.S. Army officers Meriweather Lewis and William Clark, the expedition was to determine the most direct practicable water communication across the continent for commerce purposes, map the land, gather plant and animal specimens, collect soil and weather data, and record the details of all they saw. It was a large task. Between May 1804 and September 1806, the expedition sighted the Pacific Ocean before returning to St. Louis. The explorers did not find the much sought-after Northwest Passage, but the information they did acquire spurred the nation towards further expansion and settlement.

See also: **Thomas Jefferson, Lewis and Clark Expedition, Napoleonic Wars (Economic Impact of)**

FURTHER READING

Anderson, Michael. "The Public Lands." *Constitution*, Vol. 5, No. 2, Spring Summer 1993.

Balleck, Barry. "When the Ends Justify the Means: Thomas Jefferson and the Louisiana Purchase." *Presidential Quarterly*, Vol. XVII, No. 4, Fall 1992.

Brown, Everett S. *Constitutional History of the Louisiana Purchase 1803–1812*. Berkley, CA: First University of California Press, 1920.

Jefferson, Thomas. *The Limits and Bounds of Louisiana in Documents Relating to the Purchase and Exploration of Louisiana*. Boston: Houghton and Mifflin and American Philosophical Society, 1904.

McDonald, Forest. *The Presidency of Thomas Jefferson*. Lawrence, KS: University of Kansas Press, 1976.

LOWELL, FRANCIS CABOT

Francis Cabot Lowell (1775–1817) was a member of a large aristocratic New England family that came to dominate the business, political, and cultural life of Massachusetts. He was born in Newburyport, Massachusetts, a year before the signing of the United States Constitution. Francis was a U.S. business pioneer who helped bring about in the United States what is now called the Industrial Revolution. By memorizing and bringing to the United States mechanical details of the English power loom used to make cotton fabric, Lowell created with his business partners the first U.S. textile factory. It was a revolutionary facility built in Waltham, Massachusetts. There the new water-powered loom technology was used with all the other processes of spinning and weaving cloth to enable the manufacture of finished cloth from raw cotton under one roof. It was known as the "Waltham-Lowell System."

Francis Lowell grew up in Newburyport, Massachusetts, the son of John Lowell, a prominent judge married to Susanna Cabot, the daughter of an immensely wealthy shipping family. Francis enrolled at Harvard University in 1789, where he excelled in mathematics. After graduating in 1793 he began to work in an import-export company owned by his uncle, William Cabot. Lowell traveled widely and sought to develop trade and business connections. He prospered in his work and, when his father died in 1802, Francis inherited one-third of his father's $80,000 estate, invested for the most part in eight commercial ships.

By 1810 Lowell was, according to most standards, a wealthy man. He was not in the best of health, however, and his wife's health was becoming problematic as well. They decided to travel to Edinburgh, Scotland to improve their health and to observe the power looms that were being used for producing cotton fabric in Manchester, England and other locations.

Lowell had thought of building a textile mill back in Massachusetts believing that New England would only prosper by supplementing its cloth trade with manufacturing facilities. When Lowell returned to Massachusetts in 1812 he was aware that the War of 1812 (1812–1814) would likely cripple his overseas commercial trading business, and so he became intensely active in developing a cloth industry locally, in Massachusetts. The power loom he saw in England was not available in the United States and it was illegal to export the looms for foreign use because the English wanted no competition in their production of power loom finished cloth.

Lowell was determined to bring the power loom to the United States. While he was in England he studied the looms, making sketches and drawings when he could, and memorized mechanical details. Back in Massachusetts, Lowell was able to create his own version of a working power loom with the help of a skilled mechanic, Paul Moody (1779–1831). In 1812 Francis Lowell and other businessmen established what they called the Boston Manufacturing Company. They incorporated it in 1813 and chartered to capitalize it at $400,000.

With the power loom ready, and the business company established, the loom was patented. Land was purchased by Lowell for the Boston Manufacturing Company along the Charles River at Waltham, Massachusetts, and later along the Merrimack River. In 1814 the company erected buildings on the land at Waltham and fitted them with looms and machines based on Lowell's model, powered by water. At the end of 1814 the mills became operational. They were soon recognized to be the world's first mills capable of converting raw cotton into finished fabric under one roof, revolutionizing the entire textile industry.

Lowell and his fellow entrepreneurs, a group of men who were later widely known as the "Boston Associates," transformed the country's textile industry. So great were the profits at Waltham that the Boston Associates soon looked for new sites throughout the state, and found them at East Chelmsford (later renamed Lowell, Massachusetts), at Chicopee, Manchester, and Lawrence. The "Waltham-Lowell System" of producing cotton fabric from raw cotton under one roof in a mill operation succeeded beyond all expectations. It gave the Boston Associates control over one-fifth of cotton fabric production in the United States by 1850. By expanding into other businesses related and unrelated to cotton production their empire expanded. The Lowell and the Boston Associates turned to philanthropy, establishing hospitals, schools, and universities.

Though he died at the early age of 42 in 1817, Francis Lowell clearly took a part of the young United States into the Industrial Revolution era. He pioneered work in mass textile manufacture, making cotton fabric domestically produced by a U.S. work force available to people in the United States at inexpensive prices.

See also: **Rhode Island System of Labor, Samuel Slater Builds First Factory, Samuel Slater**

FURTHER READING

Dublin, Thomas. *Lowell: The Story of an Industrial City*. Washington, DC: U.S. Department of the Interior, 1992.

———. *Women at Work: The Transformation of Work and Community in Lowell, Massachusetts 1826–1860*. New York: Columbia University Press, 1979.

Eno, Arthur L., Jr., ed. *Cotton Was King: A History of Lowell, Massachusetts*. Somersworth, NH: New Hampshire Publishing Co., 1976.

Greenslet, Ferris. *The Lowells and Their Seven Worlds*. Boston, MA: Houghton Mifflin Publications, 1946.

Josephson, Hannah. *The Golden Threads: New England's Mill Girls and Magnates*. New York: Russell and Russell, 1967.

LOWELL SYSTEM OF LABOR

During the early 1800s factories went up throughout New England, where rivers were used to power recently developed manufacturing machinery. One such factory was established between 1812 and 1814 in Waltham, Massachusetts. At this site, on the shores of the Charles River, industrialist Francis Cabot Lowell (1775–1817) built the Boston Manufacturing Company, the first complete cotton spinning and weaving mill in the United States. Here the raw cotton fibers were processed to produce cloth.

To attract the necessary work force to his plant, Lowell established an innovative labor program. He hoped his program would prove an alternative to the system of child labor that had long been in use in Britain and also prevailed in New England textile mills. Called the Lowell System, or the Waltham System, farm girls and young women who came to work at the textile factory were housed in supervised dormitories or boardinghouses and were provided with educational and cultural opportunities. Lowell believed that by providing safety in the workplace, comfortable living conditions, and a socially positive living and working environment he could ensure a steady supply of labor.

Lowell expanded his manufacturing interests, establishing larger mills on the Merrimack River in present-day Lowell, Massachusetts (a town named in his honor). But in the 1830s and 1840s the Lowell System faltered. Increased competition in the textile industry (which was the model for other industries of the day) forced factory owners to cut wages and lengthen hours to stay profitable and meet production demands. In 1834 Lowell cut his workers' wages by 25 percent; the workers responded by staging a strike and organizing the Factory Girls Association, a labor union. But the union's efforts were unsuccessful. Two years later the ''Lowell girls'' struck again when their housing rates were raised; again the strike failed, as workers found themselves unable to make ends meet and were back on the job within a month.

Conditions deteriorated and in 1845 Lowell workers formed the Female Labor Reform Association, which joined forces with other Massachusetts laborers to force government to legislate improved work conditions in the state. The lobby helped to pass laws that limited work hours, but textile mills continued to ignore the legislation. The arrival of the Irish in Lowell, beginning in 1846, also contributed substantially to the demise of the Lowell System of Labor. With unskilled labor available and willing to work for low wages, the system was no longer needed. By the 1850s the Lowell System was a failed experiment. New England farm girls were replaced by immigrant women who were willing to work for longer hours and lower wages.

See also: **Francis Cabot Lowell, Rhode Island System of Labor, Spinning Mills, Textile Industry, Women in the Workplace**

LUKENS, REBECCA

Rebecca Lukens (1794–1854) became a pioneer in U.S. industry largely against her will. With the sudden death of her father and her husband, only a year apart, Lukens inherited one of the first iron manufacturing firms in the United States. She became a successful businesswoman in the iron industry in a time when few women worked outside the home, let alone in industrial manufacturing. Her legacy is her firm, which was renamed Lukens Iron Works (and later Lukens Steel) in 1859, honoring her pioneering life and her industry.

Rebecca Webb Pennock Lukens was born in 1794 in West Marlboro Township, Chester County, Pennsylvania. She was the daughter of iron manufacturer Isaac Pennock. She enjoyed a happy childhood and grew up in a Quaker household that emphasized discipline and learning. She attended two private academies, where she received a good education. Her favorite subjects were French and chemistry. In later years she described her own childhood as ''wild, happy, and joyous.''

While Rebecca was at school, her father Isaac started an iron mill in Chester County known as the Federal Slitting Mill. He extended his interests by purchasing the Brandywine Mill in Coatsville, Pennsylvania. Her father was quite successful at operating both mills.

In 1813 at age 19 Rebecca married 27-year-old Quaker doctor Charles Lukens, and they returned to live at her parents' home. Charles Lukens abandoned medicine to become a partner with his wife's father in the Federal Slitting Mill under the new name of Pennock and Lukens.

Rebecca Lukens and her husband moved their growing family to the Brandywine area and leased the Brandywine ironworks from Pennock. Lukens foresaw the wide use of steam power and was aware of the superior quality of ''charcoal iron'' for withstanding the high pressures of steam boilers. He undertook to adapt the Brandywine mill for the rolling of charcoal iron boilerplates to be used in ships and wood burning locomotives. This was a new departure for the iron industry in the United States. The mill's first big order was for iron plates to gird the first metal hull ship in the United States, the steamship *Codorus*, launched in

1825. But it was also during this year that Lukens' husband suddenly died.

While her husband had requested that his wife carry on the mill, Rebecca Lukens was almost bankrupt from the expenses incurred in expanding the mill for the making of charcoal iron. In addition, her husband died without leaving a clear will and the inheritance of the Brandywine ironworks was legally ambiguous. Compounding her difficult situation, Lukens' father had died the year before and she was without his advice.

Facing these difficulties while she took care of a newborn child, Lukens assumed total responsibility for the ironworks. Through her father and husband she had learned much about the techniques employed in iron manufacturing. While her brother-in-law Solomon took charge of operating the mill Lukens managed and controlled the commercial end. She bought supplies, set prices, made contracts, and studied legislation that might affect her business. She faced all the problems of building a major industrial supply business and supporting a family.

Transportation of the finished iron was difficult. Rough roads and teeming rivers were always a problem. Water was often a difficulty, since the mill was run by waterpower—when the water ran low the mill had to be shut down. Lukens also faced serious litigation related to her ownership of the Brandywine mill at her mother's death in 1844. After several difficult but successful lawsuits there was a final decree that Lukens make heavy payments to the estate. In return she was granted total legal ownership of the Brandywine Iron Works in 1853.

Despite continuing problems and increased competition Rebecca Lukens made a success of her business. The opening of railroads near her mill solved her transportation problems and allowed her to expand her market. Additionally, her iron plates became known throughout the United States because of their high quality and consistency.

By the age of 59 Rebecca Lukens had a net worth of $60,000. She settled her husband's debts, paid the balance due to the Pennock estate, and rebuilt her mill. Three years later she made her son-in-law a partner in the business and went into semi-retirement because of failing health.

The Brandywine Iron Works continued to flourish. After Rebecca's death in 1854 the Iron Works was renamed the Lukens Iron Works in her honor. She was a pioneer of the industry and built the firm nearly from its infancy. The renamed Lukens Iron Works produced steel for over a century. In 1957, 600,000 tons of steel plates were manufactured by Lukens at the same mill site as the one fought for and saved by Rebecca Lukens.

FURTHER READING

American National Biography. New York: Oxford University Press, 1999, s.v. "Lukens, Rebecca Webb Pennock."

Notable American Women, 1607–1950: A Biographical Dictionary. Cambridge, MA: Harvard University Press, 1974, s.v. "Lukens, Rebecca Webb Pennock."

Paskoff, Paul R., ed. *Iron and Steel in the Nineteenth Century*. New York: Facts on File, 1989.

Stern, Madeline B. *We the Women: Career Firsts of Neneteenth Century Women*. New York: B. F. Franklin, 1974.

Stubbles, J. R. *The Original Steelmakers*. Warrendale PA: Iron and Steel Society, 1984.

LUMBER INDUSTRY

Lumber was probably America's first industry. The first sawmill was constructed in 1608 in Jamestown, Virginia, to meet the lumber needs of the colonists. Since an abundant supply was generated in the first year that the sawmill was operational, Captain John Smith managed to export a shipment of lumber and related products to England.

For the early American settlers, lumbering remained essentially a local business. Transporting logs and lumber to another settlement was a difficult and unprofitable undertaking. Trees were cut in the winter when the hard packed, frozen ground provided a hard, smooth surface to transport the logs to nearby springs and lakes. The logs remained there until the spring thaw and then were floated to the sawmill by loggers. This seasonal approach to logging provided winter employment to many farmers, allowing them to cut down the trees that would shade their crops during the spring and summer.

During colonial times, New England was the center of this industry. As the population of the United States grew, so too did the demand for lumber. Soon the industry had expanded to include Pennsylvania and New York. By the second half of the nineteenth century, the lumber industry gradually made a westward and then southward move. White pine was now being cut in Michigan, Wisconsin, and Minnesota. Long timbers for use as masts on ships, originally produced in Maine,

Lumberjacks use the aid of tractors to load these redwood trees onto trucks that will carry them to a sawmill. Technological advancements expanded the logging season and added to the success of the lumber industry.

were now also beginning cut in Oregon and Washington. Southern forests provided oak for warships like "Old Ironsides," and lumber by-products such as tar and turpentine were produced from the pine forests of the Carolinas. The primary use for wood, however, remained as a practical and economical fuel source.

During the Industrial Revolution, immense growth experienced by the United States increased the need for lumber and for a technology that could supply it cheaply and quickly. The steam engine satisfied that need by making the sawmills less dependent on water and weather. The steamboats could transport wood products rapidly and travel against the current. Steam also replaced water wheels as an internal power source for sawmills. Up to this point most of the rivers that were used to transport the logs had also powered the sawmills. During the usually harsh winters these waters were frozen, and the wheels were useless. The steam engine allowed sawmills to operate year-round and gave sawmill owners the freedom to locate their businesses as far as they wished from the flowing rivers on which they were previously dependent. The ability to build a sawmill in any location allowed for expansion into the West.

Since this industry was based solely on the existence of trees, it created a unique situation. Trees provided a renewable resource—unlike oil, coal, or other sources of fuel—as well as useful items such as furniture and building materials. Lumber became the basis for a multidisciplinary and diversified industry that could produce a variety of products. This can best be explained by defining the lumber industry as the "production and harvesting of trees for various uses." The lumber industry mainly refers to the businesses that processed trees into lumber products. This industry promoted the establishment of other industries to convert timber into fuel, chemicals, pulp, paper, and other products.

The development of tools needed to cut and process lumber developed with the growth of the lumber industry. Saws were produced in many types and sizes, from smaller, lighter, hand-held models to large, industrial band saws used in factories. The advent of thinner saws made with high-grade steel that permitted a smaller kerf (cutting groove) reduced the amount of sawdust produced—boosting the efficiency of not only lumberjacks, but of lumber mills as well.

As the lumber industry (aided by technology) grew, it became apparent that the seemingly endless supply of timber could disappear. In 1895 the United States government created the Division of Forestry. One of its first decisions (in 1897) was to authorize forest reserves. By the late 1990s forestland ownership was divided into four different categories.

First, private non-industry lands owned by farmers and other individuals provide living areas, small amounts of food, and sources of private income. Corporations make up a small portion of this category as well. For example, businesses such as power companies "give back" land used in the past, converting these into recreational areas such as privately owned parks designed for public use.

Second, federally owned and protected national forests make up of millions of acres of mostly untouched wilderness and preserves. These massive areas are off-limits to the lumber industry and provide safe habitation for wildlife. Federally owned lands provide other environmental needs as well. Trees provide a majority of the Earth's oxygen and consuming carbon dioxide; this action leads directly to cleaner air and a safer environment.

Third, local governments provide public lands as well. In some cases the land was donated to local governments by philanthropists, giving cities and towns the privilege of having an area of forest wilderness to use for recreational and other purposes.

Fourth, private industrial lands maintain appropriate logging techniques, conservation, and the protection of wildlife while operating commercial lumber business. Enterprises such as the U.S. Timber Company attempt to plan for the years ahead by practicing conservation measures and maintaining tree farms so that harvested forests can be replanted. The Division of Forestry monitors such companies. Between two and three billion trees are reforested in the United States each year thanks to these efforts. This large number is planted so that the amount of trees grown are greater than the number of trees harvested, lost to disease, and consumed by parasites. Technology has evolved to the extent that an estimated 99 percent of all tree byproducts are used.

In the late 1990s the chief lumber producing countries were the United States, Russia, Canada, Japan, Sweden, Germany, Poland, France, Finland, and Brazil. The United States and Russia accounted for more than 40 percent of the world's annual production of lumber at the end of the twentieth century.

See also: **Weyerhauser**

FURTHER READING

Andrews, Ralph W. *Glory Days of Logging/Action in the Big Woods, British Columbia to California.* Atglen, PA: Schiffer Publishing Ltd., 1994.

Bethel, James S., ed. *World Trade in Forest Products.* University of Washington Press, 1993.

Ficken, Robert E. *The Forested Land: A History of Lumbering in Western Washington.* Seattle: University of Washington Press, 1987.

Twining, Charles E. *Downriver: Orrin H. Ingram and the Empire Lumber Company.* State Historical Society of Wisconsin, 1997.

"Wood World," [cited April 18, 1999] available from the World Wide Web @ www.woodfibre.com/wood/.

MAIL-ORDER HOUSE

A mail-order house is a retailer that offers goods for sale through catalogs, which, along with the ordered merchandise, are delivered via the mail service. The mail-order business was pioneered by retailer Montgomery Ward and Company, founded in 1872 in Chicago when American merchant Aaron Montgomery Ward (1843–1913) set up shop over a livery stable and printed a one-sheet ''catalog'' of bargains. Midwestern farmers, hurt by low farm prices and rising costs, were a ready market for the value-priced goods, which were shipped by rail to rural customers. Initially called ''The Original Grange Supply House,'' Montgomery Ward and Company offered 30 dry goods priced at one dollar or less and provided special terms of sale for Grange members. (The National Grange was an association of farmers throughout the United States.) Aaron Ward bought merchandise directly from wholesalers. Since he did not maintain a store building, his overhead was low. By 1876 Ward's catalog had grown to 150 pages; in 1884 it was 240 pages and offered nearly 10,000 products, including household items (such as furniture, cutlery, and writing paper), farm implements (such as harnesses and tools), and fashions (such as ready-made apparel and parasols). Ward offered customers ''satisfaction or your money back.'' In 1886 American Richard W. Sears (1863–1914) entered the mail-order business, opening operations in Minneapolis, Minnesota. He moved the business to Chicago the following year and sold it in 1889. In 1893 he joined with Alvah C. Roebuck (1864–1948) to found Sears, Roebuck and Company. The Sears catalog, which soon consisted of hundreds of pages and thousands of items, became popularly known as the ''Wish Book.''

Montgomery Ward and Sears Roebuck were aided by the U.S. Postal Service's expansion into remote areas: Beginning in 1896, mail could be delivered via the RFD, Rural Free Delivery. In 1913 parcel post was added to the Postal Service's offerings, further benefiting the mail-order houses and their growing lists of customers. Montgomery Ward and Sears Roebuck offered to the rural United States more than merchandise; the mail-order houses were farm families' link to the greater consumer society emerging at the turn of the century. Regardless of geography, rural Americans could purchase ''store-bought'' goods—manufactured goods that were mass-produced in factories. Mail-order houses offered customers convenience because customer purchases no longer had to be deferred for the next trip to a town. They also offered variety, as catalogers catered to a nationwide customer base and on-hand inventory included a multitude of products. Finally, they offered low prices—the mail-order houses bought merchandise at reduced rates from wholesalers. Fashions were no longer restricted to middle- and upper-class city dwellers with access to department stores. Rural customers became aware of new styles each time the Montgomery Ward and Sears Roebuck catalogs were delivered, which, by the early 1900s, was twice a year.

Though both Montgomery Ward and Sears Roebuck exited the mail-order business to concentrate efforts on their chain store retail operations later in the century, they set the standard for modern mail-order houses through their early policies addressing merchandise returns, competitive pricing, flexible payment methods, and shipping terms.

See also: **Chain Store, Department Store, Montgomery Ward, Retail Industry, Sears Roebuck**

MAINE

A look at any map of Maine will confirm that the settlement of the state occurred on the coast and the rivers, with large areas in the center and the north still largely wilderness. Independent and sometimes wary of outsiders, Maine ''down-easters'' first developed their fishing resources and later moved into paper and

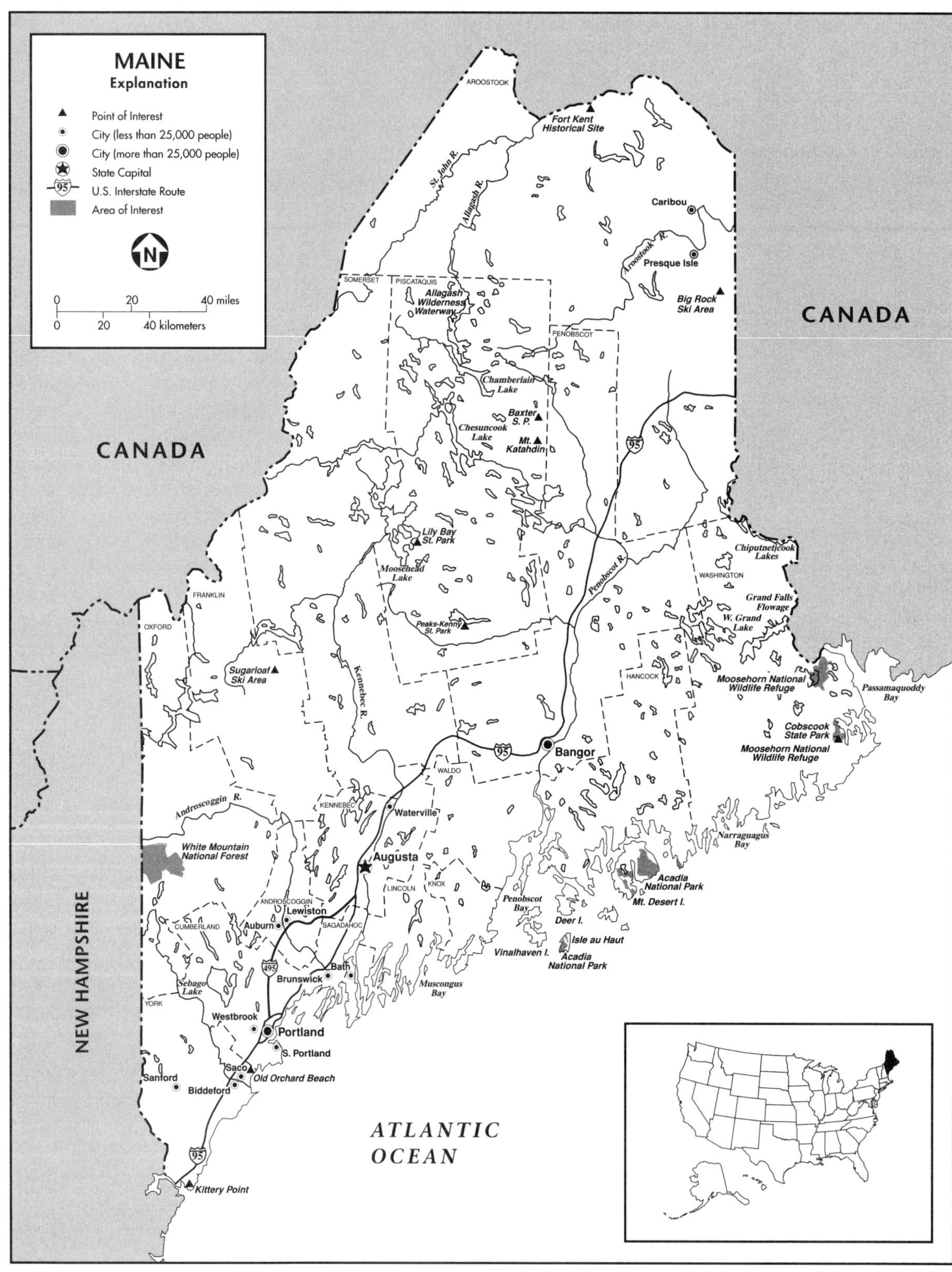

State of Maine.

textile manufacturing. Never among the most prosperous states in the nation, Maine remains a major producer of paper and wood products, an important location for ocean commerce and fisheries, and a popular destination for tourists.

In the early 1600s English expeditions first came to exploit the rich Maine coastal waters. By 1630 about a dozen English settlements existed along the coast and on several islands. An English joint stock company received the first grant of territory between the Merrimack and the Kennebec rivers in 1622. In the late 1640s the Massachusetts Bay Colony began to absorb settlements in the territory, gaining control of the whole area in 1691. The economy of Maine was based almost entirely on fishing, trading, and use of its forests. One major early industry was the preparation of the white pine masts used by the Royal Navy. Maine remained a part of Massachusetts until 1820, when by terms of the Missouri Compromise, it came into the United States as a free, not a slave, state.

Like the rest of New England, Maine began industrialization between 1830 and 1860, as shoe factories and textile mills sprang up on the state's rivers. Many young farm women came to the mill towns to earn additional income for their deprived families during the heyday of the textile mills. Papermaking also grew in importance; by 1900 Maine was one of the nation's leading papermaking states. The first railroad, the Atlantic & St. Lawrence, was completed in 1853 and connected Portland with Montreal, Canada. By 1900 several more railways, among them the Bangor and Aroostook, the Boston and Maine, the Canadian Pacific, and the Maine Central, crisscrossed the state.

[TO A MAINE NATIVE, THE] NONNATIVE SIMPLY COMES FROM OUT-OF-STATE . . . SINCE ANYWHERE THAT ISN'T MAINE IS MUCH OF A MUCHNESS AND A PRETTY POOR EXCUSE OF A PEA PATCH TO BOOT.

Louise Dickinson Rich, *State o' Maine*, 1964

Shipbuilding was another Maine industry which grew rapidly in the mid-nineteenth century. Maine builders provided many of the stately clipper ships, which carried prospectors and settlers around Cape Horn to California. Lumbering was centered on the Penobscot River at Bangor, which was a freewheeling boomtown from the 1830s through the 1850s. Land speculators rushed into the young state during this time, hoping to turn big profits on cheap land and the promise of wealth.

According to historian Charles E. Clark, the economic history of Maine between the 1860s and the 1890s mirrored economic trends in the nation as a whole, with a particular Maine slant. Entrepreneurs, like the "robber barons" who were building industries and railroads after the American Civil War (1861–1865), came to Maine and made the paper industry their domain. Immigrants came down from Quebec, Canada, looking for work and added their own ethnic flavor to the culture. The entrepreneurs soon began to exploit Maine's abundant water and lumber resources. After the discovery that wood pulp could be substituted for rags in paper manufacture, the paper industry grew rapidly. Smaller companies were absorbed into larger ones, notably the International Paper Company and the Great Northern Paper Company. Often owned largely by interests outside the state, these large concerns controlled river traffic, generated their own power, and owned their own tracts of lumber.

Slowly, pioneer farmers began to settle the more northern regions of Maine, following patterns like those in the settlement of the American West. The Maine potato became a staple crop in the state, and by 1880 several starch mills were built to make even more use of this abundant crop.

In spite of its many natural resources, Maine has suffered economically because of its limited access to a national transportation network. In addition, a curious law passed in 1929 forbid Maine from selling its easily accessible waterpower outside the state, and in 1935 Maine refused to cooperate with a proposed federal water reclamation project similar to the one created by the Tennessee Valley Authority. Today Maine ranks only thirty-seventh in personal income among all states, ranking last in New England. In comparison to those in other states, Maine has no truly large cities; Portland, the largest, had a population just over 65,000 in the 1990s.

While Maine at the end of the twentieth century was not highly industrialized or urbanized, it would be difficult to find a state that benefited more from tourism, which yearly generated about 40,000 jobs, added almost $3 million to the economy, and was the state's largest employer. In fact, around 50 percent of Maine's economy in the late 1990s, including the tourist industry, was service-oriented. Some of the first tourists who trekked to Maine established wealthy summer colonies in coastal villages like Ogunquit, York Harbor, Boothbay, and Bar Harbor. In the 1990s Maine offered beaches, sailing, craggy coastlines, fishing, hunting, winter sports, and abundant public lands for all kinds of recreation. Its foremost attraction was Acadia National Park, off its central coast, which attracted nearly three million visitors yearly in the mid- and late 1990s.

A relatively small part of the state's economy is devoted to agriculture. Agriculture and food processing industries, however, contribute over $1 billion annually to the state, and Maine produces more food crops than any other New England state. In addition to ranking first in New England in potato production, Maine leads the world in the production of blueberries, with 25 percent of the total blueberry crop. Milk, apples, and maple syrup are also important Maine products.

Industry occupies less than one-third of Maine's economy but is still a significant sector. In the 1990s, papermaking remained the top industry in the state, followed by transportation equipment manufacture and lumber and wood production. Ninety-five percent of all of Maine's forests are privately owned, primarily by the paper industry. Maine lobster remains the most important fishing product; some of the larger fishing ports are in Portland, Boothbay Harbor, and Rockland. To encourage industrial and recreational projects, the state works through the Finance Authority of Maine to offer such incentives as tax-exempt bonds and loan guarantees for small business. A State Development Office provides assistance for existing and prospective businesses.

See also: **Paper Industry**

FURTHER READING

Bearse, Ray, ed. *Maine: A Guide to the Vacation State*, 2nd ed., rev. Boston: Houghton Mifflin, 1969.

Churchill, Edwin A., et al., eds. *Maine: The Pine Tree State from Prehistory to the Present*. Orono, ME: University of Maine Press, 1995.

Clark, Charles E. *Maine: A Bicentennial History*. New York: Norton, 1977.

Maine, State of. State Development Office. *Maine: A Statistical Summary*. Augusta, ME, 1984.

Rich, Louis Dickinson. *State o' Maine*. New York: Harper & Row, 1964.

MANIFEST DESTINY

The doctrine of Manifest Destiny emerged in the United States in the early 1800s; by the 1840s it had taken firm hold. Manifest Destiny was a rallying cry for expansionism and it prompted rapid U.S. acquisition of territory during the 1800s. Adherents to the doctrine believed that the United States had a God-given duty and right to expand its territory and influence throughout North America.

Territorial acquisitions under the doctrine began in 1803, with the purchase of Louisiana Territory from France. In 1819 Florida and the southern strip of Alabama and Mississippi (collectively called the Old Southwest) were acquired from Spain in the Adams-Onis Treaty. In 1845 Texas was annexed after white settlers fought for and declared freedom from Mexico, then formed the Republic of Texas and petitioned the Union for statehood. In 1846 the western border between Canada and the United States was agreed to lie at 49 degrees north latitude, the northern boundary of what is today Washington state. In 1848, by the Treaty of Guadalupe Hidalgo, the U.S. secured New Mexico and California after winning the Mexican War (1846–1848). In 1853 southern Arizona was acquired from Mexico in the Gadsden Purchase. With the 1853 agreement over Arizona the United States had completed the acquisition of the territory that would eventually become the contiguous United States of America.

FIFTY-FOUR FORTY OR FIGHT!

Expansionist slogan during President James K. Polk's administration, 1845–1849

The fervor of Manifest Destiny was perhaps best illustrated by the expansion into Oregon Country, which was settled by the United States and Canada under the Convention of 1818. The territory began at 42 degrees north latitude (the southern boundary of present-day Oregon) and extended north to 54 degrees 40 minutes north latitude (the recognized southern boundary of Russian America, or what is today Alaska). In the presidential election of 1844 candidate James K. Polk (1845–1849) used the slogan "Fifty-four Forty or Fight" to gain the vote of the expansionists: They insisted U.S. rights to Oregon Country extended north to latitude 54 degrees 40 minutes. Polk promised he would acquire the territory—even if it meant a fight with Britain. After he was elected, Polk settled the dispute with Britain and the boundary was set at 49 degrees north, securing the territory that is today Washington, Oregon, and Idaho, and parts of Montana and Wyoming.

The expansionist doctrine was again invoked as justification for the Spanish-American War (1898), which was fought over the issue of freeing Cuba from Spain. Spain lost the war, and its empire dissolved. Cuba achieved independence (though it was occupied by U.S. troops for three years). By the close of the nineteenth century Manifest Destiny had resulted in U.S. acquisition of the outlying territories of Alaska, the Hawaiian Islands, Midway Islands, the Philippines,

Puerto Rico, Guam, Wake Island, American Samoa, the Panama Canal Zone, and the U.S. Virgin Islands.

See also: **Alaska Purchase, Expansionists, Gadsden Purchase, Louisiana Purchase, Oregon Country Cessation, Texas Annexation, Westward Expansion**

MANN-ELKINS ACT

Congress passed the Mann-Elkins Act in June 1910. It amended the Interstate Commerce Act of 1887, expanding the Interstate Commerce Commission's (ICC) responsibilities to include the regulation of telephone, telegraph, and cable companies. The new law declared such companies to be common carriers subject to ICC regulations.

The 1910 act also strengthened the ICC's enforcement of regulations regarding short-haul versus long-haul rail rates. The legislation was one in a series of laws passed by the federal legislature during the 1900s to broaden the jurisdiction and increase the power of the Interstate Commerce Commission. The laws originally gave the agency control over interstate rail rates and practices. The 1910 bill was partly sponsored by Representative James Robert Mann (1856–1922) of Illinois. Mann had also sponsored earlier legislation (1903) to increase the ICC's authority.

When the bill was brought before Congress in 1910 President William Howard Taft (1909–1913) succeeded in amending it to include a provision for a special court to supervise the activities of the ICC. The Mann-Elkins Act was hotly debated in Congress, but passed as amended. The experiment of the Commerce Court, however, proved a failure. In 1912 both houses of Congress voted to abolish the court, which had tried to interfere in the ICC's investigative powers. The U.S. Supreme Court reversed many rulings of the Commerce Court. Congress therefore felt that the special court had exceeded its jurisdiction. President Taft vetoed the congressional legislation that would have dissolved the judicial body.

In January 1913 judge Robert Archbald was impeached and convicted by the Senate for improprieties committed while holding office at the Commerce Court. Suspicions long-held by lawmakers that U.S. Commerce Court judges could be open to influence by the very companies they were charged with overseeing were borne out. Congress moved again to disband the Commerce Court. In October 1913 newly elected President Woodrow Wilson (1913–1921) signed legislation abolishing the Commerce Court. Other provisions of the Mann-Elkins bill remained intact.

See also: **Interstate Commerce Act, Interstate Commerce: Regulation and Deregulation**

MARCUS, STANLEY HAROLD

Stanley Marcus (1905–) was president of the Neiman Marcus retail department store chain from 1950 to 1975. Involved in the company since 1926, he continued the family tradition of providing high-quality products at reasonable prices. Marcus turned a local Dallas store into an internationally respected retailer with 30 stores nationwide.

Stanley Harold Marcus was born in Dallas, Texas, on April 20, 1905. He was the eldest son of Herbert Marcus, one of the founders of the Neiman Marcus department store, and Minnie Lichenstein Marcus. Stanley Marcus was the eldest of four sons. He was raised in Dallas and attended Forrest Avenue High School. From there, he went East to prestigious Harvard University. He graduated in 1925 and received his Master's in business administration from Harvard's Business School in 1926.

Retailing was a Marcus family affair. In 1907, when Stanley Marcus was only two years old, Herbert Marcus, Sr., along with Stanley's aunt and uncle, Carrie Marcus Neiman and Al Neiman, founded Neiman Marcus. Young Stanley spent his childhood playing among the clothing and display cases of his family's Dallas store.

ONE THING I LEARNED VERY EARLY IS THAT A VALUABLE SALESPERSON IS EASILY WORTH THREE TIMES WHAT YOU PAY THE AVERAGE SCHNOOK.

Stanley Marcus

Upon returning from Harvard in 1926, Marcus went to work at the store. Al Neiman had just retired, and the elder Marcus needed his son's help. Stanley Marcus started work as a floor man in Neiman Marcus' apparel departments. It was not the career he had envisioned for himself; he had wanted to be a book publisher. His father and aunt insisted he join the family business, but promised that his creative energies would not be stifled.

In November 1932, Stanley Marcus married Mary Cantrell. They had three children. After Mary Marcus' death, Stanley Marcus later married his second wife, Linda, in 1979.

During Stanley's first year at Neiman Marcus, his creativity was put to use. He pioneered Neiman Marcus' weekly fashion shows, the first by an American department store. The store became famous for these shows, and it was their first step into the world of high fashion. Stanley Marcus also introduced the Neiman Marcus Fashion Exposition. Under his guidance, Neiman Marcus became the first specialty store to advertise in national magazines. These were the first of many promotional visions that Stanley Marcus brought to life. Over time, his marketing genius became legendary.

By 1928, Stanley Marcus was an executive. He became director, secretary, and treasurer of Neiman Marcus, as well as the sportswear merchandise manager. At this time, the United States was beginning its plunge into the Great Depression (1929–1939). Most of the country saw poverty on previously unknown levels and countless businesses closed. Retail establishments like Neiman Marcus were particularly hard-hit, as Americans struggled to put food on their tables and gave up fashion and decor. Amazingly, Neiman Marcus only had two years of small losses during the Depression, the only losses in the company's history.

In September 1930, oil was discovered in several large oil fields in east Texas. This created wealth for many Dallas families and increased business for Neiman Marcus. During the Depression, Marcus noticed that many of the Southwest's wealthiest continued to travel to New York or Paris to purchase their clothes. This was a market Marcus wanted to catch. He arranged a lunch with the famed publisher Conde Nast (1837–1942). At this meeting, Marcus announced that he wanted to advertise Neiman Marcus in Nast's fashion magazines. He easily convinced Nast, who until then had only accepted advertising from New York stores, and soon Neiman Marcus advertisements were found in *Vogue* and other couture magazines.

In 1938, Stanley developed the Neiman Marcus awards, ''the Oscars of Fashion.'' The awards were presented annually for distinguished service in the field of fashion. Early honorees included Christian Dior in 1947 for ''The Look.'' The same year saw designer Norman Hartnell of London honored for designing Princess Elizabeth's wedding gown.

World War II (1939–1945) involved the entire Marcus family. Stanley Marcus served as director on a three-state regional board of the Smaller War Plants Corporation. He was also chief of the clothing section of the textile, clothing, and leather branch of the War Production Board in early 1942. His brothers joined the armed services. All of the Marcus brothers returned to work for Neiman Marcus at the conclusion of the war.

After the war, Stanley's marketing savvy, combined with Neiman Marcus' legendary quality merchandise and customer service, continued the store's growth. His national advertising campaign continued as Marcus worked to present Neiman Marcus merchandise in an irresistible light. By 1949, the specialty store's charge accounts numbered about 100,000. Neiman Marcus could claim customers throughout the United States and many parts of the world. That same year, French ambassador Henri Bonnet presented Stanley with the Chevalier Award of the Order of the Legion of Honor for his contributions to French industry and commerce by influencing the sale of French fashions.

Patriarch Herbert Marcus Sr. died in 1950. At this time, Carrie Neiman was named chairman of the board, Stanley Marcus became president and chief executive officer, and brother Edward Marcus became executive vice president.

Stanley Marcus was among the most visible of those family members associated with Neiman Marcus, with a strong presence throughout the company's operations. Marcus made the Neiman Marcus catalogues famous. Designed to promote the company's mail order business, the first catalogue appeared in 1915. Stanley Marcus' most famous marketing strategy was his 1960 creation: his and hers gifts in the Neiman Marcus Christmas catalogue. The response was tremendous, stimulating sales and strengthening Neiman Marcus' place as an internationally known retailer. ''His and Hers, the Fantasy World of the Neiman Marcus Catalogue,'' Marcus said, ''did more to establish our catalogue than any other idea. We had His and Hers submarines for $18,700 each. Hot air balloons at $6,850 each. We had His and Hers camels. His and Her airplanes. Matching Chinese junks that we headlined, 'Junk for Christmas, $11,500.' We sold eight.'' This was quite a difference from Neiman Marcus' first Christmas catalogue in 1915, a six-page, five by six inch list of Christmas gift ideas.

Marcus' philosophy was that a successful retailer stays ahead by fighting standardization, ''by selling what he believes in, not just what he thinks can make him money.'' From that point, success becomes a question of high-quality salesmanship. ''One thing I learned very early is that a valuable salesperson is easily worth three times what you pay the average schnook,'' he told *Inc.* magazine. ''Because you never know what that schnook is costing you in lost sales. Why do you think that you have to have so many department stores in a mall these days? It's not because their merchandise is so different. It's because each of them does such a poor selling job that they survive just taking up each other's unsatisfied customers. A store with good sales people wouldn't let that happen.''

Despite the store's purchase by Carter Hawley Hale Stores, Inc. in 1969, Stanley Marcus stayed involved with the day-to-day-operations of Neiman Marcus and remained visible as a business leader in the Dallas community. Marcus was named as executive vice president of the company's specialty store division. He retired in 1974 with the title chairman emeritus.

He continued to be active in his retirement, and served as a consultant in the retail industry. Marcus has written three books, *Minding the Store* (1974), *Quest for the Best* (1979) and *His and Hers* (1983). He also wrote a weekly editorial column for the *Dallas Morning News*, as well as numerous articles on fashion and retailing for well-known publications, including *Atlantic Monthly* and *Fortune* magazines.

Even in the mid-1990s, Marcus, in his nineties, continued to give public lectures around the country. Narrowcasting, the business he co-founded, is a marketing service which gathers information on the shopping habits of America's wealthy. Critics still continued to view his analyses of the current market as cutting edge.

Despite his work responsibilities, Stanley Marcus stayed busy in Dallas' civic and cultural communities. He was a member of the Salvation Army Advisory Board, the American Council for Judaism, the Civic Federation of Dallas, the Greater Dallas Planning Council, the Dallas Health Museum, and the Dallas Historical Society. National organizations to which he belonged included the American Heritage Foundation, the National Commission of Public Schools, and the American Trade Association for British Woollen, Inc., as well as the American Retail Federation. As American Retail Federation chairman, Marcus developed policies for an organization representing over 500,000 U.S. retail stores. He also served as an alumni advisor to Harvard University.

Stanley Marcus is a retailing legend; he lived by the credo ''the customer is always right.'' Customer service and quality were his passion and through that passion, he turned a local Dallas specialty store into an international giant whose name is synonymous with distinction.

***See also:* Department Store, Retail Industry**

FURTHER READING

Haber, Holly. ''Stanley Marcus at 90: The Great Gadfly.'' *WWD*, April 12, 1995.

Raphel, Murray. ''An Interview With Stanley Marcus.'' *Direct Marketing*, October 1995.

Rothe, Anna, ed. *Current Biography Who's News and Why 1949*. New York: H.W. Wilson Co., 1949, s.v. ''Marcus, Stanley.''

Standard & Poor's Register of Corporations, Directors and Executives. New York: Standard & Poor's Corp., 1997.

Tapert, Annette. ''Arbiter of Elegance: Stanley Marcus, at 92, has Observed and Critiqued. . . '' *Town & Country Monthly*, September 1997.

Witchel, Alex. ''So, What Does a Retailing Legend Buy?'' *The New York Times Biographical Service*. Ann Arbor: UMI, Co., 1995.

The Writers Directory. Detroit: St. James Press, 1996.

MARKET

A market exists when a buyer and a seller exchange money for a product or service in a transaction in which neither person is forced into the exchange. Markets can be as simple as children selling lemonade for a nickel or as complex as the international trade in cars, steel, or telecommunications.

The most important question in any market is the setting of the price. Economists since the days of British economist Adam Smith (1723–1790) have noted that prices tend to fluctuate with supply and demand. If, for example, a farmer offers his crop of wheat for sale at a given price and no one buys, she or he will lower the price to try to attract buyers. On the other hand, if there is a scarcity of the product, sellers will be able to charge more for it. In this way prices are set for thousands of products in many markets every day.

The free flow of information is essential to the efficient operation of markets. If a buyer knows that cars are cheaper at one dealership than another, she or he will buy at the less expensive dealership. But if this information is not available, the buyer may spend more money than necessary. This would leave less money to spend on something else, and thus markets would be less efficient. Information, then, is essential, whether passed by word of mouth, newspaper advertisements, or other means. Sellers sometimes try to restrict such information or scheme to keep prices high. Economists refer to such schemes as price-fixing or collusion, and governments generally outlaw such practices.

Economists also believe it is important that governments don't unduly restrict the operation of free markets with burdensome taxes or regulation. Some regulation may be necessary; for example, some regulations protect the health and safety of workers. But when governments restrict the sale of a commodity, such as automobiles, to a single state-controlled brand at an artificial price, then economists say such a market is no longer free. Markets in the former Soviet Union were not free, which is why an illegal market in food and other essential goods and services flourished side by side with official ones. Economists call these illegal markets the underground economy or black markets. Such markets tend to spring into existence in any country whenever government taxes or regulations restrict the sale or supply of a product.

See also: **Price, Supply and Demand**

MARKET REVOLUTION *(ISSUE)*

The market revolution was simply the transition from subsistence economy or barter economy to using money to buy and sell things. This, in turn, transformed the way that people looked at things: from useful objects into commodities with prices attached to them. Except in the case of slavery, among the things that now wore price tags was human labor. The populations of the countryside now included a growing stratum of agricultural laborers who, like their urban counterparts, worked for wages. To the extent that the market revolution penetrated the countryside, however, with cash crops like tobacco and cotton, those who did not own land could often rent it. Those tenant farmers might rent the land by paying the landowner in money or in shares of the crop. But even though the process of production involved various combinations of cash, barter, and sharecropping, the whole system rested on the fact that the crop was eventually sold on the market. Otherwise there would have been no reason to grow crops beyond what was needed to subsist. The market revolution absolutely revolutionized the lives that it touched. The changes that it wrought even extended to the religious sensibilities expressed by the people whose lives were disrupted by the market revolution.

At the beginning of the nineteenth century the United States was still primarily an agrarian nation. Agriculture dominated the lives of people whether they were large planters or small farmers. Most small farmers practiced subsistence farming, making whatever was needed for themselves and their families. Because the shipment of produce was costly and time-consuming, only farmers near ports grew cash crops. The market revolution grew out of this primitive economic regime. Prior to the market revolution, the transportation revolution established the trade corridors that gradually corroded the culture of subsistence farming.

The roads, canals, rivers, and, eventually, the railroad tracks that made up the transportation revolution spurred the market revolution. Self-sufficient farmers became involved in the market little by little: selling eggs, growing cash crops for sale, and relying on industries for the goods—like clothing or the fabric to make clothing—that were formerly produced at home. More people became involved in non-agricultural businesses, which helped to diversify the U.S. economy. By 1860 almost 40 percent of U.S. citizens no longer relied directly on farming for their living. With economic expansion and improvement in transportation the population began to move westward, opening up the interior of the continent. By 1850 almost half of the U.S. population lived outside of the original thirteen states.

The cities grew rapidly. In 1820 only 12 cities had populations over 5,000. By 1850 there were 150. By 1860 over 20 percent of the U.S. population lived in urban centers (towns over 2,500 people), which was up from nine percent in 1820. The Northeast was the most urbanized area in the nation with one-third of its population living in cities. In the South cotton fed a strong, rural agricultural economy. Only one-tenth of the South's population lived in urban areas.

Although some economists see a period of *laissez faire* economics during the market revolution, the federal government nonetheless remained a potent force in the economy. Nowhere was this more clearly seen than in banking. The federal government established the First and Second Banks of the United States as central banks with effective power to regulate commercial banks chartered and licensed by state governments. The existence of a "national" or "central" bank brought relative regularity to the circulation of currency and the funding of enterprise. It also, however, provoked anxiety and skepticism on the part of ordinary citizens as well as politicians like Andrew Jackson, who distrusted concentrations of economic or political power.

Echoing the anxiety of many Americans regarding the financial and speculative aspect of the market revolution was the fear and despair of the slave population of the South in the face of the demand on their labor to feed the cotton-based industrial revolution in

England and the textile producing mill towns of the Northeastern United States. The exploitation of slave labor was based on cotton, rice, and tobacco as cash crops. This required the market revolution and the conversion of subsistence agriculture into cash-crop agriculture.

The market revolution also transformed the culture and the religious life of the United States in the period between the Revolution and the Civil War. What had been a rural, traditional society was now undergoing profound change. The market revolution sped up change. It brought uncertainty and anxiety and it evoked the thinly repressed insecurity of evangelical Protestantism. The question: "What must I do to be saved?" now reverberated in a great many questions of everyday life. People were moving. Jobs were being lost. Slave families were being broken up as the men were being shipped off to new and more fertile plantations along the Mississippi River. Trades were being "degraded" as various forms of capitalist enterprise found cheaper ways to produce the goods that the artisan class had formerly made. Women who had made the candles or the homespun clothes that the family had worn now bought those items in the crossroad store. They were losing their roles and the feeling of equality with men that the shoulder-to-shoulder labor of the subsistence homestead had afforded.

This pervasive and multi-faceted insecurity on the part of displaced populations who were undergoing the trauma of separation from traditional society expressed itself in the religious rhetoric of the age. The camp-meetings of the Second Great Awakening—with the itinerant preachers and the amateurs preaching from tree stumps and the emotional outpouring of sinners all looking for a second chance—served to heal some of the wounds of a population going through the market revolution.

See also: **Bank War, Laissez Faire, Slavery, Subsistence Agriculture**

FURTHER READING

Bruchey, Stuart. *Enterprise: The Dynamic Economy of a Free People.* Cambridge, MA: Harvard University Press, 1990.

Cochran, Thomas. *Frontiers of Change: Early Industrialism in America.* New York: Oxford University Press, 1981.

North, Douglas. *The Economic Growth of the United States, 1790–1860.* Englewood Cliffs, NJ: Prentice-Hall, 1961.

Sellers, Charles. *The Market Revolution: Jacksonian America, 1815–1846.* New York: Oxford University Press, 1991.

Taylor, George Rogers. *The Transportation Revolution, 1815–1860.* New York: Holt, Rinehart, and Winston, 1951.

MARSHALL PLAN

Between 1948 and 1951 the European Recovery Program—or as it is commonly called, the Marshall Plan—restored post-war Western Europe's agricultural and industrial productivity by providing nearly $15 billion in U.S. economic assistance. The plan is named after Secretary of State George C. Marshall, who proposed it in a commencement speech at Harvard University on June 5, 1947.

George C. Marshall (1880–1959) gained military recognition in World War I (1914–1918) as the chief tactical officer of the first American division to go into action in France. He was named chief of staff of the U.S. Army in 1939, making him a four star general and the head of the army throughout World War II (1939–1945). During the war, he planned the amphibious invasions of North Africa and of Normandy, France; his achievements were heralded by the leaders of the United States and its allies. Marshall retired from the army in November 1945, but in 1947 President Harry S. Truman appointed him secretary of state.

IT IS LOGICAL THAT THE UNITED STATES SHOULD DO WHATEVER IT IS ABLE TO DO TO ASSIST IN THE RETURN OF NOMINAL ECONOMIC HEALTH IN THE WORLD, WITHOUT WHICH THERE CAN BE NO POLITICAL STABILITY AND NO ASSURED PEACE.

George C. Marshall, Harvard University commencement speech, *History Today,* June 5, 1947

Shortly after his appointment, Marshall attended a conference in Moscow with British, French, and Soviet leaders to discuss Germany and Austria's future. Europe was physically and economically devastated in the wake of World War II; food, fuel and raw materials for production were in desperately short supply. Businesses had been destroyed through loss of capital, nationalization, or physical obliteration, and confidence in local currencies was badly shaken. Observing the economic collapse of Europe and recognizing the

Soviet Union's intention to take advantage of that collapse to spread communism across Europe, Marshall returned from the conference determined to restore the European economy.

On June 5, 1947, during a commencement address at Harvard University, Marshall stated, "It is logical that the United States should do whatever it is able to do to assist in the return of nominal economic health in the world, without which there can be no political stability and no assured peace. Our policy is directed not against any country or doctrine but against hunger, poverty, desperation and chaos. Its purpose should be the revival of a working economy in the world so as to permit the emergence of political and social conditions in which free institutions can exist." Marshall proposed that European nations determine their needs and suggest a plan for American economic assistance for their recovery.

In response to Marshall's announcement, sixteen Western European countries met in Paris a month later to form the Organization for European Economic Cooperation and to assess and agree on their needs. Although Marshall had claimed that the plan was "not directed against any country or doctrine," from the start the United States attached conditions to their aid that would be unacceptable to the Soviet Union. Thus, while the Soviet Union and the Eastern Europe countries under its control were invited to participate, the Soviet Foreign Minister walked out of the talks. The Western European nations eventually drafted a request for $16 to $22 billion to stimulate economic recovery by 1951.

Back in the United States, the Marshall Plan was debated in Congress. To ensure its passage, Marshall worked closely with congressional committees and made promotional speeches throughout the United States. Congress agreed to Truman's $17 billion request to aid Europe. In April, 1948, Truman signed an act that established the Economic Cooperation Administration (ECA) to administer the program. The ECA's primary goals were to elevate European economic production, support European currency, and assist with international trade. Its other intention was to restrain the spreading Soviet influence in Czechoslovakia, France, and Italy. Paul G. Hoffman (1891–1974) was appointed ECA's chief administrator. Later that year the participating countries—Austria, Belgium, Denmark, France, West Germany, Great Britain, Greece, Iceland, Italy, Luxembourg, the Netherlands, Norway, Sweden, Switzerland, Turkey, and the United States—signed the agreement that instituted the Organization for European Economic Cooperation (later called the Organization for Economic Cooperation and Development) as the head coordinating agency.

The Soviet Union strongly opposed the Marshall Plan and refused to participate; a few other Eastern European countries criticized or ignored it. The Soviets prevented Poland and Czechoslovakia from participating, despite their desire to do so. Stalin accused the United States of trying to use its money to lure Eastern European nations away from Soviet influence. He ordered all Communists to resist U.S. imperialism and established the Cominform, an international Communist information bureau. Stalin's most drastic response to West Germany's participation in the Marshall Plan was the 1948–1949 Berlin blockade, an unsuccessful attempt to force the United States and its allies to evacuate West Berlin.

Completed in 1951, the Marshall Plan greatly contributed to the economic restoration of Europe. At its end, nearly $15 billion in recovery aid had been channeled into Western Europe. Many countries' agricultural and industrial productivity was higher than they had been before World War II. His efforts in preventing famine and political chaos through the Marshall Plan earned George C. Marshall a Nobel Peace Prize in 1953.

Some revisionist historians have contested that the Marshall Plan did not demonstrate American altruism, arguing that assistance to Europe prevented the United States from falling into its own economic decline by providing a market for U.S. capital goods. According to revisionists, the Marshall Plan also let the United States rebuild the Western European economy to mirror the American economy, providing a more compatible environment for U.S. investment.

FURTHER READING

The Columbia Encyclopedia, New York: Columbia University Press, 1993, s.v. "Marshall Plan."

"June 5th, 1947: U.S. announcement of the Marshall Plan." *History Today*, June 1997.

"Marshall Plan Memories." *The New Leader*, June 30, 1997.

"The Marshall Plan,"[cited July 6, 1999] available from the World Wide Web @ www.nara.gov/exhall/featured-document/marshall/marshall.html/.

Morrow, Lance. "George C. Marshall: the Last Great American." *Smithsonian*, August 1997.

The Reader's Companion to American History, Boston: Houghton-Mifflin, 1991, s.v. "Marshall Plan."

MARYLAND

Maryland's natural harbor on Chesapeake Bay, its moderate climate, and its adaptability for agriculture made it a desirable place for settlement in colonial days. The manner of settlement was very different from places like Virginia or Massachusetts. Unlike many other colonies, Maryland was established with an almost feudal system in which the land was considered the property of the English lord who governed it—a proprietary colony. Maryland also had a higher proportion of Catholic settlers than most other colonies and experienced a higher proportion of religious wrangling. Its position as a slaveholding state which did not secede from the Union also set it apart from southern states during the Civil War (1861–65). In modern times, the state has thrived by creating a diversified economy that includes industry, maritime interests, agriculture, and the service sector.

The first Europeans to penetrate into the land which later became Maryland were the Italian Giovanni da Verrazano (1480–1527) and the Spaniard Lucas Vazquez de Ayllon in the sixteenth century. The first explorer of Chesapeake Bay, an area that would become vital to the commerce of Maryland, was Captain John Smith (1580–1631), who was leader of the colony that was established in Jamestown, Virginia. Smith's map of the Chesapeake was used for many years and was an important tool in the settlement of the area. By the time the European explorers arrived, Native Americans had established permanent settlements in Maryland, where they cultivated corn (maize), vegetables, tobacco, and other crops.

The territory was given as a proprietorship by England's King Charles I (1600–1641) to George Calvert (1580–1632), a favorite of the English court. Lord Calvert had resigned his position at the court because his Catholic religion prevented him from holding public office in England. Since the colony of Virginia also wanted the land, it opposed the king's decision, but Calvert prevailed. Later he left the land to his son, Cecilius, who is better known as Lord Baltimore (1605–1675). He named the region Maryland after the queen consort of Charles I, Henrietta Maria of France. This land grant encompassed not only the area that later became Maryland, but also Delaware, part of Pennsylvania, and the valley between the north and south branches of the Potomac River.

As a sole proprietorship, the colony of Maryland was fully under the control of Lord Baltimore, who derived his income from the quitrents, which were money payments that took the place of feudal duties, like military service. The settlers paid them as a kind of rent for the land. Baltimore's financial obligations to the king were minimal. The colony's early years were marked by feuding between Puritans and Roman Catholics. The feuds were settled only when Benedict Leonard Calvert (1606–1647), the fourth Baron of Baltimore, embraced the Protestant faith and was granted proprietary rule.

Maryland was a somewhat reluctant participant in the American Revolution (1775–1783) but finally sent 20,000 soldiers to fight in the war. It was the seventh state to ratify the federal Constitution. Maryland provided the home for the Continental Congress in two cities, Baltimore and Annapolis, before the permanent capital was established in Washington, DC. Maryland's first state constitution favored owners of large rural estates over people who owned no property.

Tidewater and southern Maryland provided the state's main staple crop, tobacco. It was grown with the help of slave labor and indentured servants. German immigrants in western Maryland helped develop the wheat economy. The city of Baltimore was founded in 1729. The city prospered because of its magnificent harbor, which provided access to the import and export trade. Shipbuilding also grew rapidly in the Baltimore area. During the War of 1812 (1812–1814) many naval and military operations took place in the area, and Francis Scott Key wrote the Star-Spangled Banner during the British siege of Fort McHenry in Baltimore harbor

Baltimore harbor provided the first transportation access to Maryland; but other networks developed in due time. The first national highway was known as the National Road (now U.S. Route 40). The highway began at Cumberland in 1811, providing access to Ohio within seven years. The Delaware and Chesapeake Canal opened in 1829, linking Chesapeake Bay and the Delaware River. The Baltimore and Ohio Railroad opened in 1828, soon providing the first passenger train to Washington, DC, and Harpers Ferry, Virginia (now in West Virginia). The line extended to St. Louis by 1857 and precipitated the growth of freight service, which helped Baltimore grow into a metropolis. The Pennsylvania Railroad began providing service to northern cities in the 1850s.

Maryland did not support secession in the Civil War but remained one of the border states that still harbored many southern supporters. In spite of its sympathy to the South, in 1864 the Maryland legislature voted to abolish slavery, which caused a problem

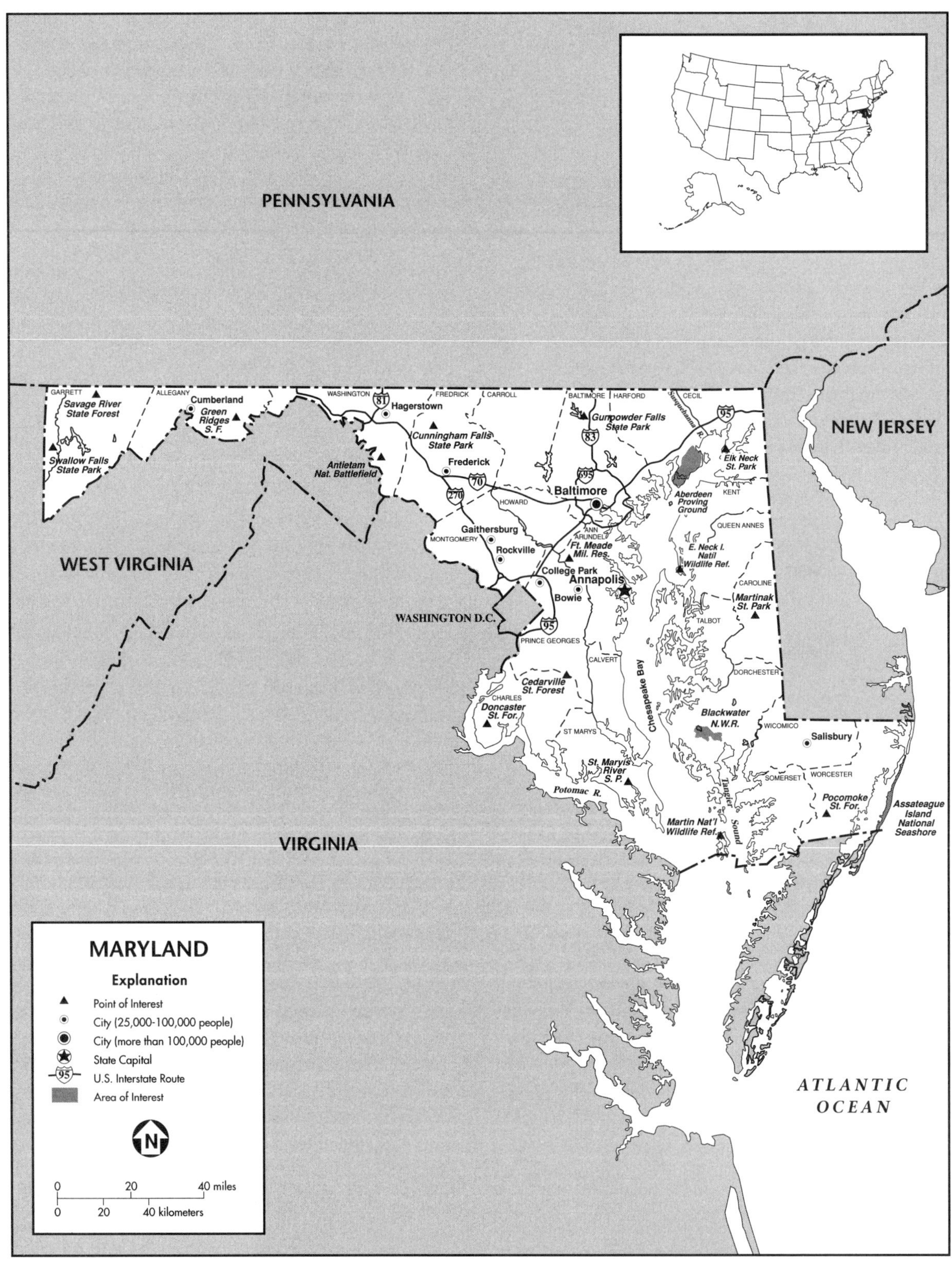

State of Maryland.

after the war, since its economy had been based on slave labor. It was estimated that the value of Maryland's slaves in 1860 approached $35 million. Tobacco plantations in Prince Georges and other southern counties were hit hard by abolition. Tobacco never made a full recovery as a staple crop. Truck farms grew instead, helped by the proximity to water and rail transportation. The Maryland legislature even resorted to an advertising campaign to help economic development. In 1867 it commissioned a pamphlet titled *A Succinct Exposition of the Industrial Resources and Agricultural Advantages of the State of Maryland.*

The economy did recover, and enabled Maryland to participate in the rebuilding of the south. The state's economic base shifted gradually from agriculture to industry, led by shipbuilding, steel-making, clothing manufacturing, and shoemaking. The state's economic success allowed for philanthropy. Millionaires who had made their fortunes between the Civil War and World War I (1914–1918) endowed cultural and educational institutions. Banker and financier Johns Hopkins (1795–1873) founded Johns Hopkins University. Merchant and banker George Peabody (1795–1869) financed the Peabody Conservatory of Music; and Enoch Pratt (1808–1896), a manufacturer and merchant, endowed the Pratt Free Library.

The city of Baltimore was the industrial center of the state. By 1890 its population had grown to 434,000, employing people in manufacturing and mechanical industries, trade, transportation, and personal and professional services. The city attracted a variety of ethnic groups, especially African American descendants of slaves. But there were a large proportion of Germans and Irish as well. Baltimore developed its ethnic neighborhoods likc many other cities during the Gilded Age. The neighborhoods were filled with low-paid factory workers, who often worked in local sweatshops that manufactured men's clothing.

World War I provided another boost to Maryland's economy; but soon the Great Depression of the 1930s brought hardship to many people. The depression spelled the end of the political career of longtime Democratic Governor Albert C. Ritchie (1876–1936). His successor Harry W. Nice was a Republican. However, Nice supported the New Deal program of Democratic President Franklin D. Roosevelt (1933–1945). Like most of the nation, Maryland was only brought out of the economic doldrums by the manufacturing boom created by World War II (1939–1945). The shipyards of Bethlehem–Fairfield and Maryland Drydock in Baltimore had to hire an additional 12,000 employees in 1942 to keep up with war demands. The Martin Company, which manufactured aircraft, added 6,000 employees. People in search of good wages swarmed to the city, not only from Maryland itself, but from Appalachia and the South.

During the latter part of the Depression, Maryland became the site of an experiment in city planning. The experiment resulted in the creation of ''New Towns.'' One of the towns was Greenbelt, Maryland, designed as a conveniently arranged, pleasant place to live, with proportional representation from all kinds of ethnic and religious groups. Later a developer named James Rouse (1914–1996) built the village of Cross Keys in northwest Baltimore along similar lines. He also began to plan for the city of Columbia in Howard County. Columbia, which was begun in the mid-1960s, was planned as a cluster of villages, each with a collection of shops and strategically placed schools. Businesses and industrial parks flanked the village centers. Life in Columbia was never as idyllic as its planner had imagined it, but despite some difficulties during the 1970s the city continued to thrive.

The state of Maryland grew by 13.4 percent during the 1980s, well over the national average of 9.8 percent. The expansion of U.S. government is in part responsible for the growth. Many federal workers have settled in Prince Georges and Montgomery counties, Maryland suburbs of Washington, DC. The headquarters of the Social Security Administration is located in Baltimore. The most significant economic improvements during the 1980s and 1990s, however, were undoubtedly related to the economic redevelopment of Baltimore. The Charles Center development, the renewed Inner Harbor, the World Trade Center, the National Aquarium, and the new Baltimore Oriole Park at Camden Yards created a boom in retailing and hotels. These improvements brought hundreds of thousands of people to the city. The state suffered somewhat from the recession of the 1980s but has increased employment in the service sector. That gave Maryland the fifth highest state income in the country during the mid-1990s. The state ranked sixth in per capita income in 1996.

See also: **Baltimore and Ohio Railroad, Colony (Proprietary), National Road, Tidewater, Tobacco**

FURTHER READING

Bode, Carl. *Maryland: A Bicentennial History.* New York: Norton, 1978.

Council of State Governments. *The Book of the States, 1994–1995 Edition.* Vol. 30. Lexington, KY: The Council of State Governments, 1994.

Dozer, Donald. *Portrait of the Free State: A History of Maryland*. Cambridge, MD: Tidewater, 1976.

Schmittroth, Linda, and Mary Kay Rosteck, eds. *Cities of the United States*. 2nd ed. Detroit: Gale Research, 1994.

Walsh, Richard, and William Lloyd Fox, eds. *Maryland: A History*. Baltimore: Maryland Hall of Records, 1983.

MASS PRODUCTION

Prior to the nineteenth century manufacturing was largely hand-fitted. The artisan worked with the individual product—for instance, a farm wagon—and by using shims or a mallet, he would "make it fit." If production involved machining metal, the machine tolerances would be loose. The system "worked" but the production process was inefficient, repair was chancy, and the price of labor—labor with the right "touch" for making things fit—was high.

In the late eighteenth century, standardized manufacturing transformed production technique. This development was called the American System of Manufactures. First introduced in the firearms industry (especially at the Springfield, Massachusetts federal armory) by inventor Simeon North, the American System was employed in producing pistols for the U.S. government. The parts were machined to set tolerances so that they were interchangeable. Standardization saved time and money in production and made possible the repair of a broken product.

The American System, however, was not yet mass production although the two systems shared the concepts of division of labor and close machining and interchangeability of parts. Mass production also introduced a more efficient organization of the workplace as well as the application of more powerful tools in production. Efficiency in the workplace included the innovation of the assembly line and the time-and-motion studies of Frederick W. Taylor's "Scientific Management." "Taylorism" forced the worker to adopt the most efficient way to do his job. Improved productivity through power tools included the introduction of electric or compressed air power tools and, in more recent times, automated welding robots. All this utterly transformed the factory as a space to work.

Perhaps the most significant difference between mass production and the earlier American System, however, was the enormous production goals of mass production. The best example of this is the Ford Motor Company. The assembly time for a single Model T went from 150 minutes in 1913 to 26 1/2 minutes in 1914. One important difference was the installation of the chain-driven assembly line. Production climbed from 13,380 Model T Fords in 1909 to 585,388 in 1916. The economies of scale associated with such production goals meant that Ford could afford to pay his workers better wages (the five-dollar day) and to cut the price of the car. A Model T dropped in price from 950 dollars in 1909 to only 360 dollars in 1916. In doing this, Henry Ford forever changed the nature of American society.

See also: **American System of Manufactures, Assembly Line, Henry Ford, Frederick W. Taylor**

MASSACHUSETTS

The first Europeans to exploit resources in the state of Massachusetts were fishermen who came from England, France, Portugal, and Spain in the mid-sixteenth century. They went ashore to process their catch; soon a flourishing fur trade was established with Native Americans. Religious persecution later drove a group of English Puritans who wished to separate from the Church of England to the New World in 1620. They settled in a Massachusetts village, which they named Plymouth. In 1630 a non-Separatist Puritan group settled to the north in the Massachusetts Bay Colony. The group was headed by patriarch John Winthrop (1588–1649). Winthrop believed strongly that the material success of the new colony would be a visible sign of God's blessing. Between 1630 and 1640 around 20,000 English people settled in Massachusetts.

Migration of the English to Massachusetts slowed around 1640, because in that year a civil war brought Puritans to power in the mother country and removed religious persecution as a reason for immigration. Towns like Salem, Gloucester, Marblehead, and Boston, however, afterward remained important centers of the fishing industry; but as time went by, fishing and fur trading began to decline. As the supply of valuable beaver skins was being exhausted, the settlers turned to farming the rocky soil as means of sustenance. In the face of white encroachment upon the land, Native American tribes steadily declined, and many were wiped out in King Philip's War (1675–1676). As a sign of European dominance, Plymouth and the Massachusetts Bay Colony were merged in 1692 by royal decree.

Settlements spread across the colony in the eighteenth century. By 1730 Boston reached a population of 15,000. The city soon became a center of shipping and commerce. It also evolved into a hotspot of political

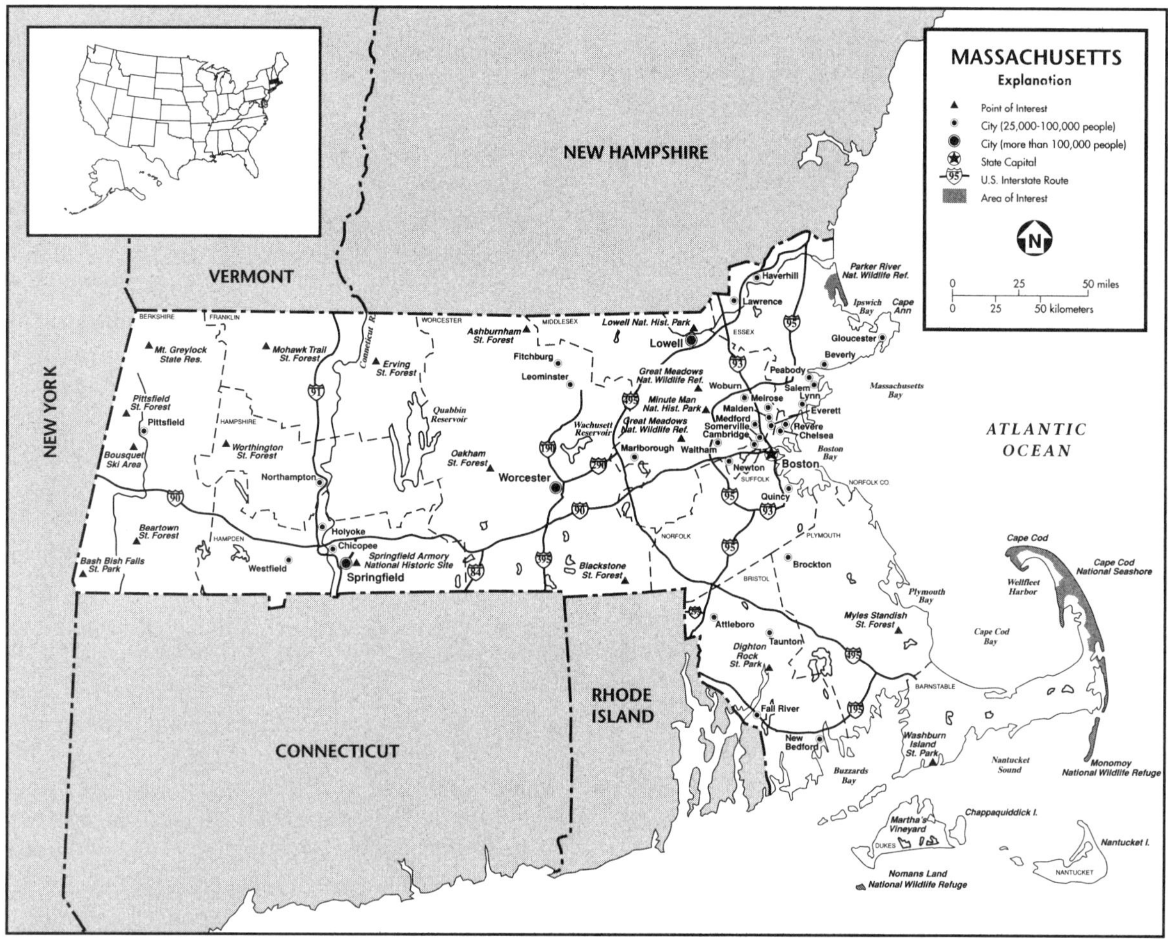

State of Massachusetts.

unrest, since colonists were becoming more and more dissatisfied with tight political and economic controls imposed by the British. The cry of "taxation without representation" accompanied resentment caused by British control of trade and political rights. In 1773 the citizens of Boston expressed their frustration by dumping tea into the harbor. By 1775 the time was ripe for the beginnings of the American Revolution (1775–1783) in Lexington and Concord.

Massachusetts required some adjustments after the defeat of the British. The Shays' Rebellion (1786–1787) occurred when central and western farmers challenged the power of eastern commercial leaders; but the rebellion ultimately failed to change the status quo. Massachusetts went on to become the sixth state of the Union in 1788. The Federalist Party soon became dominant in Massachusetts. They represented the governing commercial interests.

By 1800 it became evident that an agricultural economy was not viable in Massachusetts. In addition to inhospitable, rocky soil, land was depleted of its resources. For years farmers had paid little attention to conservation. More and more farmers moved westward to find better land and better opportunities. The Erie Canal made it easier for western farmers to find markets in the East. Massachusetts began to look toward other economic horizons. For a time the whaling industry in Nantucket and New Bedford was the most profitable in the nation. With the decline of the whaling and fishing industries the state also became a center for the textile industry. That was especially true in the mill towns of Waltham, Lowell, and Lawrence. The mills were originally built because of the unavailability of British textiles during the War of 1812 (1812–1814). Mills flourished since there was ample waterpower available on Massachusetts rivers.

The best-known of the mills was at Lowell. The "Lowell system" included a large capital investment and the concentration of all processes in one plant under a unified management. It specialized in a kind of coarse cloth easily worked by unskilled workers. Most of the workers were young women from surrounding farms who came to supplement their families' meager incomes. They worked from sunup to sunset for very low wages. The well-designed Lowell community provided supervised housing and activities for the girls. Other mill towns copied this paternalistic system. Yet by 1840 Lowell mirrored other mill towns in its overcrowded, dirty conditions.

One positive development in the 1840s was that Massachusetts enacted the nation's first child labor law. It allowed a maximum 10-hour day for children under 10. While this law may seem inadequate by today's standards, it was quite progressive in an era when children were routinely exploited in the workplace.

Other industries that sprouted up in Massachusetts during that period included the manufacture of metal products, leather goods, whale products, and shipbuilding. Shoe factories were particularly prominent. Although most of the shoe factories fled to other states Massachusetts remained the center of shoe workers' unions for a long time to come. By 1850 steam engines were produced in Massachusetts. A network of railroads that was begun in 1826 helped open new areas for industrial expansion. The American Civil War (1861–1865) spurred industrial growth, which was also helped by the many immigrants who flocked to Massachusetts from northern and southern Europe and from French Canada.

As one of Massachusetts' major urban areas, Boston faced a major challenge in the mid-1840s, when a potato famine precipitated a mass migration from Ireland. These desperately poor immigrants were willing to take any menial job in order to survive, but they were greeted in their new country with a widespread disdain that was based upon ethnic and religious bigotry. After 1865, however, the Irish became politically powerful as mainstays of the Democratic Party and economically successful throughout the state. They helped Massachusetts become one of the most industrialized states in the nation by the end of the nineteenth century. The family history of President John F. Kennedy (1917–1963) is a good example of the rags-to-riches stories of some Irish immigrants.

Conflicts between immigrants and their descendants, and the entrenched Republican Yankee conservatives in Massachusetts continued to plague the state into the new century. Class conflicts were largely responsible for a devastating strike of immigrant textile workers in Lawrence in 1912. The various factions eventually learned to accommodate one another. According to historian Richard D. Brown, there was a "pragmatic willingness" to accept diversity and, "haltingly, people adjusted to the multiethnic, urban, industrial character of Massachusetts."

The Great Depression of the 1930s nearly devastated Massachusetts. Unemployment in some localities reached as high as 40 percent. Massachusetts embraced Franklin D. Roosevelt's (1882–1945) efforts to stimulate the economy, but only World War II (1939–1945) brought any real increase in employment. The state's economy began to revive around 1950. While many of the old industries and mill towns were in decline, high-technology businesses began to develop in the suburbs of Boston. Industries oriented toward electronics, computers, and defense systems sprang up. That led to an increase in service sector businesses like banking, insurance, health care, and higher education. White-collar employment in the middle-class suburbs was on the rise.

By 1989 Massachusetts was again in a serious economic decline. It lost 14 percent of its jobs in three years. The general recession of the early 1990s was aggravated by a collapse in the real estate market in the late 1980s. Employment in construction dropped 44 percent between 1988 and 1991. Wholesale and retail trade lost 100,000 jobs. Voters blamed then current governor Michael Dukakis for the state's economic woes. In 1990 they elected Republican William Weld as the new governor. Weld then privatized a number of state operations in an effort to economize. By the mid-1990s the state's economy was improving greatly. Per capita income reached third place in the nation by 1995. Local industries like software and mutual funds led the upturn in the economy. The fishing industry was still the eighth largest in the nation in 1995 though not as important to the state's economy as it once was. Tourism was also important to the state, bringing in well over $8 million annually. Boston, Cape Cod, Martha's Vineyard and Nantucket, and the Berkshire Mountains were popular vacation spots.

At the state level the Department of Economic Development continued making attempts to promote business, increase employment, and generate economic activity. In 1993 the Massachusetts Economic Development Incentive Program (EDIP) was launched to aid existing and new businesses. It provided 34 Economic Target Areas (ETAs) in the state. The Target Areas, along with local initiatives, provided attractive incentives to prospective businesses.

See also: **Boston Massacre, Boston Tea Party, Francis Cabot Lowell, Lowell System of Labor, Shays' Rebellion, Samuel Slater, Spinning Mills, Whaling Industry**

FURTHER READING

Bedford, Henry F., ed. *Their Lives and Numbers: The Condition of Working People in Massachusetts, 1870–1900.* Ithaca, NY: Cornell University Press, 1995.

Brown, Richard D. *Massachusetts: A Bicentennial History.* New York: Norton, 1978.

Handlin, Oscar. *Boston's Immigrants.* Cambridge: Harvard University Press, 1979.

Haskell, John D., Jr., ed. *Massachusetts: A Biography of Its History.* Boston: G.K. Hall, 1976.

Rothenberg, Winifred Barr. *From Market-Places to a Market Economy: The Transformation of Rural Massachusetts.* Chicago: University of Chicago Press, 1992.

MAYA

The Maya were American Indians who settled in southern Mexico and in Central America. Their territory covered Mexico's Yucatan Peninsula, Belize, much of Guatemala, and parts of Honduras and El Salvador. Originating in the region about 1000 B.C., the Maya developed a highly advanced civilization which reached its height during the Classical Period, A.D. 300-900. At its peak, the Mayan population numbered some fourteen million people who lived in agricultural communities and in the city-centers in Honduras (Copan), Mexico (Palenque, Uxmal, and Chichen Itza), and Guatemala (Piedras Negras, Uaxxactan, and Tikal). The capital was at Tikal (population 50,000), which was a center of education, economics, science, and religion. Mayan accomplishments were numerous and many were unparalleled at the time. Engineers produced remarkable architecture including flat-topped pyramids, temples, and towers. Artisans created elegant sculptures, paintings, and murals. Scholars developed an original writing system, which was used to record astronomical observations, chronology, and history. Mathematicians developed a system more advanced than any European system of that time.

The Mayans supported themselves by using slash-and-burn agriculture. The vegetation was cut down and burned to clear the land and provide nutriments for the soil, which was then planted with crops, especially corn, beans and squash. The Mayans also developed advance systems of irrigation and terracing. Terracing involves the construction of horizontal ridges in a hillside as a means of increasing the arable (farming) land. It also hindered soil erosion and evaporation. Though they used no beasts of burden, the Maya established a trade network that linked several Central American Indian groups and eventually extended into central Mexico, where the Maya exchanged goods with the Aztecs.

During the Post-Classic Period, A.D. 900–1546, the Maya were invaded by the Toltecs, whom they eventually absorbed. Rebellions and civil war as well as widespread famine dominated the century preceding the arrival of the Europeans. When the Spaniards arrived in the mid-1500s, the Mayan civilization was in decline. The Maya were conquered by the Spaniards and they became assimilated into the larger Hispanic culture that developed in the region.

See also: **Aztec, Inca, Mesoamerica**

MAYSVILLE ROAD BILL

Following the tumultuous presidential election of 1824 the nation's political factions realigned. The newly formed National Republicans led by John Quincy Adams (1767–1848) and Henry Clay (1771–1852) advocated aggressive federal promotion of national economic development. Internal capital improvements and the use of protective tariffs constituted the core of their policies. Their support came from Northeastern manufacturers, Southern agricultural leaders, and others who stood to benefit from the development of a commerce infrastructure. Many of their advocates were from the cosmopolitan upper class.

In contrast, supporters of Andrew Jackson (1767–1845) and John C. Calhoun (1782–1850) were much more diverse. Jackson was a popular military hero fresh from victories in the War of 1812 (1812–1814). He carried a populist banner, aligning many common citizens and ''plain folk'' behind him. Jackson defeated Adams in the presidential race in 1828.

During this period the United States still suffered from very poor overland transportation systems. A railroad network had not yet been built, and travel was essentially seasonal, since in many areas roads became mud quagmires during the winter months. Many people like Adams and Clay believed that the young nation's economy could not grow to support the emerging capitalist system without substantial improvements to the infrastructure.

At the beginning of his administration, Jackson's policies on transportation and other issues were not well formulated. Calhoun and Martin Van Buren (1782–1862), who both competed to be Jackson's chief advisor, held very different views. When Van Buren finally won, he urged Jackson to oppose federal financing of intrastate public works projects. Van Buren believed a growing trend to fund such projects could deplete the federal treasury by encouraging legislative practices of logrolling and pork barrel projects. (Log rolling was the combining of several distinct project funding bills, each unlikely to pass on their own, into a single piece of legislation to increase their chances of success.) Van Buren feared the fiscal affairs of the federal government would become a mess with numerous improvement projects arising across the country.

Acting on Van Buren's advice, Jackson raised constitutional issues regarding commitment of federal funds for specific internal state improvements in his first annual message to Congress in December, 1829. Jackson proposed providing states with blocks of federal funds when surpluses occurred, and having the states allocate the funds to specific projects themselves. He believed that paying off the national debt took precedence for the federal government. Jackson based his position on the political philosophy of strict constructionism. (Strict constructionism meant that any unclear terms appearing in laws or the Constitution should be given their exact and technical meaning. Individuals must not attempt to expand a law through exploring implied meanings.)

The political battle over funding internal improvements came to the national forefront in 1830, when Congress passed a bill sponsored by Jackson's bitter political foe Henry Clay. The bill authorized a $150,000 federal purchase of stock in the Maysville, Washington, Paris, and Lexington Turnpike Road Company. The company proposed a 60-mile road from Maysville, an inland port on the Ohio River, to Clay's hometown of Lexington. The project lay entirely within the state of Kentucky.

On May 27 Jackson vetoed the bill, maintaining that the road had no connection with any existing improved transport system and that it was fully within a single state. Jackson argued that the proposed bill required an unconstitutional use of federal dollars. The veto decision was highly unpopular with many in the newly established Democratic Party, which Jackson led, including those in the Ohio Valley who supported federal aid for canals and roads.

Jackson's veto was instrumental in establishing long-term federal policy limiting the use of federal transportation funds to interstate projects as well as harbors and river improvements serving foreign trade. No longer did Congress provide sizable federal expenditures for intrastate canals and roads. Jackson's stance on pioneering a sound fiscal policy concerning public works was one of the most important ideological contributions of his presidency. The only large road project funds approved by Jackson while he was president were for continued construction of the interstate Cumberland Road connecting Cumberland, Maryland with Illinois. Jackson approved funds for it four days after the Maysville Road veto.

See also: **Federalism, Andrew Jackson**

FURTHER READING

Cole, Donald B. *The Presidency of Andrew Jackson.* Lawrence, KS: University Press of Kansas, 1993.

Peterson, Merrill D. *The Great Triumvirate: Webster, Clay, and Calhoun.* New York: Oxford University Press, 1987.

Ratner, Lorman A. *Andrew Jackson and His Tennessee Lieutenants: A Study in Political Culture.* Westport, CN: Greenwood Press, 1997.

Remini, Robert V. *Andrew Jackson and the Course of American Freedom, 1822–1832.* New York: Harper and Row, 1981.

Watson, Harry L. *Liberty and Power: The Politics of Jacksonian America.* New York: Hill and Wang, 1990.

MAYTAG CORPORATION

The Maytag Corporation was started in Newton, Iowa by Frederick Louis Maytag and three partners in 1893 to produce threshing machine band-cutters and self-feeder attachments. The company soon began to produce other pieces of farm machinery, not all of it top quality. The Maytag corn husker, called the Success, caused the partners many problems because of its poor quality, and farmers often called Maytag personnel out to their fields to fix the Success. By the time Maytag bought out his partners in 1907 he had learned his lesson; a Maytag product would always be dependable.

Maytag built his first washer in 1907 to bring his agricultural equipment company through the slow-selling season as well as to fill the growing need for home-use washing machines. Home washing machines were already on the market, but Maytag wanted to make them more efficient. His first washer, called the Pastime, revolutionized washing. It had a cypress tub with a hand crank that forced the clothes through the water and against corrugated sides. The washer was a hit, and Maytag continued to improve on it. In 1911 he brought out the first electric washing machine, and in 1914 he introduced the gas-engine Multi-Motor for customers without access to electricity. The first aluminum washer tub was brought out in 1919, and the Gyrofoam entered the marketplace in 1922. This revolutionary washer was the first with an agitator at the bottom of the tub instead of the top. This change allowed for the elimination of friction, making it the first washer to clean with only water action. Sales of this machine pushed Maytag from the 38th largest U.S. washing machine company to first place.

At this juncture the farm implement portion of the business was discontinued. L.B. Maytag, son of the founder, became president of the company in 1920. Under his direction the company began to market nationally. In 1925 Maytag incorporated and was listed on the New York Stock Exchange. By 1927 Maytag had produced one million washers.

During the Great Depression (1929–1939) Maytag held its own; the company even made money. During World War II (1939–1945), Maytag shut down normal operations and devoted itself to producing special components for military equipment. In 1946 the production of washers started up again, and in 1949 the first automatic washers were produced in a new plant built for that purpose. In 1946 Maytag began marketing a line of ranges and refrigerators made by other companies to be sold under the Maytag name.

The appliance industry grew rapidly during the 1950s, fueled by the postwar consumer boom. Maytag first entered the commercial laundry field at this time, manufacturing washers and dryers for commercial self-service laundries and commercial operators. During these years full-line appliance producers began targeting Maytag's market. Full-line operators such as General Electric, Whirlpool, and Frigidaire provided washers and dryers, refrigerators, stoves, and other appliances. Maytag was much smaller than the full-line producers. It limited itself to the manufacture of washers and dryers, which it marketed with ranges and refrigerators built by other companies, and established its reputation as a premium brand.

The ranges and refrigerators Maytag had been marketing with its washers and dryers were dropped in 1955 and 1960 respectively, but the company soon reentered the kitchen appliance field with its own portable dishwasher in 1966 and a line of food waste disposers in 1968. Maytag created a U.S. icon in 1967 when the Maytag "lonely repairman" appeared in advertising for the first time. The character was lonely because Maytag appliances were supposedly so reliable they never needed repairs, and helped to solidify Maytag's reputation for the dependability of its products.

Laundry equipment sales peaked in 1973, and by the late 1970s more than 70 percent of U.S. households owned a washer and dryer. The lifetime of such equipment was 10 to 12 years, often longer for Maytag. A turning point came in 1980 when Maytag decided to become a full-line producer, eventually selling a wide range of major appliances rather than just washers, dryers, and dishwashers. This diversification was achieved through a series of acquisitions. By the late 1990s Maytag sold washers, dryers, ovens, refrigerators, and dishwashers under both premium brands (Maytag and Jenn-Air) and mid-to-lower price value brands (Magic Chef and Admiral). The Maytag brand was also used on coin-operated and commercial laundry equipment. The company also sold Hoover vacuum cleaners and other floor care products in North America; Dixie-Narco vending machines and glass-front coolers; and commercial ovens, fryers, and charbroils for the food service industry under the brand names of Blodgett Ovens, Pitco Frialator, MagiKitch'n, and Blodgett-Combi Ovens.

See also: **Agricultural Equipment Industry**

FURTHER READING

Geisi, Steve. "Spin-Cycle Doctor." *Brandweek*, March 10, 1997.

Hoover, Robert, and John Hoover. *An American Quality Legend: How Maytag Saved Our Moms, Vexed the Competition, and Presaged America's Quality Revolution*. New York: McGraw-Hill, 1993.

Maytag Corporation. *The Spirit of Maytag: 100 Years of Dependability, 1893–1993*. Newton, IA: Maytag Corporation, 1993.

"Maytag: Wizard of White Goods." *Dun's Business Month*, December 1985.

Upbin, Bruce. "Global, Schmobal." *Forbes*, March 10, 1997.

MCCORMICK, CYRUS HALL

Born in Virginia on February 15, 1809, Cyrus McCormick (1805–1884) obtained a grammar school education and assisted his father in the operation of a 1,200-acre grain and livestock farm. While working on

Cyrus H. McCormick.

this farm McCormick invented a mechanical reaping machine that greatly decreased the amount of time it took to harvest wheat. He first developed his reaper in 1831 and spent the next 10 years perfecting it, making only a few, which were used on his father's farm.

By 1843, after bankruptcy and several unsuccessful attempts at a variety of business pursuits, McCormick finally decided to concentrate on making his fortune by producing and selling his reaping machine. In 1847 he moved to Chicago, the heart of U.S. agricultural trade, and opened a factory to manufacture his reaping machine. Though he was having problems renewing the patent on his reaper, he nonetheless organized a mass-production system in his factory, investing heavily in labor-saving machinery to aid his work force.

McCormick offered many incentives to farmers to buy his reaper. He provided deferred payments similar to credit loans and offered money-back guarantees on his product. He advertised everywhere and conducted numerous personal demonstrations of his reaping machine. These demonstrations were usually enough to convince farmers to buy it. On average, a farmer using a McCormick reaper could harvest 10 acres of wheat a day, compared to two acres without the reaper. McCormick also established a research department in his business and hired a staff to systematically improve his products. He paid good wages to his workers, and was one of the first large manufacturers of his era to negotiate with the labor unions.

By 1856 McCormick had accumulated over $1 million in profit from his operations, and continued to earn $300,000 annually. He also began investing heavily in Chicago real estate, increasing and diversifying his personal wealth. McCormick sold 250,000 reapers and mowers in Europe, and with much of his European profits he invested in U.S. railroads and South American mining interests.

McCormick devoted most of his life to work, and did not marry until age 49. His main interests outside of work were his religion and the South. McCormick was a devout Presbyterian, his main relaxation activity was discussing theological issues with Presbyterian clergymen. He lavishly gave to the Presbyterian church from the fortune he made in business. McCormick was a southerner by birth, and supported the cause of the Confederacy throughout the American Civil War (1861–1865).

Cyrus McCormick served as the head of his company until his death in 1884, at the age of 75. In his life he was rewarded with personal fame and awards from many governments for his worldwide contribution to agriculture. After his death, his son Cyrus McCormick, Jr. assumed control of the McCormick Harvesting Machine Company. In 1902 the company merged with four other companies and became the International Harvester Company, which later became Navistar International Corporation.

See also: **Agricultural Equipment Industry, McCormick Reaper**

FURTHER READING

Casson, Herbert N. *Cyrus Hall McCormick, His Life and Work.* Freeport, NY: Books for Libraries Press, 1977.

Hutchinson, William. *Cyrus Hall McCormick.* New York: Century Co., 1930.

International Harvester Co. *The United States as it Appeared in 1831, When Cyrus Hall McCormick Invented the Reaper.* Chicago, IL: International Harvester Co., 1951.

Ozanne, Robert W. *A Century of Labor-Management Relations at McCormick and International Harvester.* Madison, WI: University of Wisconsin Press, 1967.

The McCormick Reaper, invented by Cyrus Hall McCormick in 1834.

———. *Wages in Practice and Theory: McCormick and International Harvester.* Madison, WI: University of Wisconsin Press, 1968.

MCCORMICK REAPER

Reapers were machines developed in the early 1800s to help farmers harvest grain. The first commercially successful reaper was built in 1831 by Virginia-born inventor Cyrus Hall McCormick (1809–1884), who patented it in 1834 and first sold it in 1840 in Virginia. The McCormick reaper was horse-drawn and sharply reduced the amount of manual labor required to harvest grain. It worked in this way: a straight blade (protected by guards) was linked to a drive wheel; as the drive wheel turned, the blade moved back and forth in a sawing motion, cutting through the stalks of grain, which were held straight by rods; the cut grain stalks then fell onto a platform and were collected with a rake by a worker. The device increased average production from two or three acres a day to ten acres a day.

McCormick's reaper was soon in wide use, and the inventor was on his way to becoming an industrialist. In 1847 he moved his business to Chicago, the heart of the expanding Midwestern farm market, where he could transport his machines via the Great Lakes and connected waterways to the East and to the South. Within five years McCormick's business became the largest farm implement factory in the world. As production continued to rise, consumption kept pace: In 1850, for example, U.S. wheat-flour consumption reached 205 pounds per capita, up from 170 pounds in 1830. Sales and distribution of McCormick's equipment increased further during the 1850s as Chicago became a center for the nation's then-expanding rail system.

Because the reaper replaced as many as eight to ten workers, many historians believe the invention played an important role in the outcome of the American Civil War (1861–1865): Farmers in the North had more widely adopted the machinery, allowing more farmhands to go into battle while wheat production continued. The North's superior manpower was critical to Union victory.

In 1879, Cyrus McCormick's business became the McCormick Harvesting Machine Company, with the inventor himself as president (until 1884, when he was succeeded by his son). The reaper was improved over time: in the 1850s a self-raking feature was added, further reducing the amount of labor required to harvest grain; in the 1870s, McCormick introduced a binder, which bound the sheaves of grain and dropped them to the ground to be collected. In the late 1800s the reaper (or harvester) was joined with another invention, the thresher, which separates grains from the stalks. The new reaper-thresher machine was called a combine. Today's combines still use the basic features present in McCormick's revolutionary 1831 invention. His company later became International Harvester (1902) and today is known as Navistar Corporation.

See also: **Agriculture Equipment Industry, John Deere, Cyrus McCormick**

MCGRAW-HILL COMPANIES

The McGraw-Hill Companies encompass educational, financial, business, governmental, and professional publishing and information services. In the late 1990s it was the world's largest educational publisher and its overall revenues were more than three billion dollars annually.

John A. Hill and James H. McGraw were nineteenth century publishers of magazines which served industry and reported on technological progress. As the United States changed from an agrarian to an industrial society, there arose a growing market of technicians interested in the practical application of science to various facets of daily life. In 1909 the heads of the book departments at Hill Publishing Company and McGraw Publishing Company agreed to a merger of the two book departments. A coin toss decided the name of the new company, The McGraw-Hill Book Company, and the new president, John A. Hill. The company was housed in McGraw Publishing's building in New York City.

Although the magazine publishing operations of the two companies remained separate for a while, in 1917 a more complete merger of the McGraw and Hill interests took place when John A. Hill died at age 57. The McGraw-Hill Publishing Company was established as the world's biggest technical publisher, and the book company became its subsidiary.

World War I (1914–1918) brought an increased demand for technical publications, especially engineering books in radio communication, aviation, and other areas directly related to the war effort. In one instance McGraw-Hill supplied 150,000 technical books to the U.S. Army for shipment to France in a matter of days.

McGraw-Hill expanded rapidly during the 1920s, forming a college department in 1927 and entering the field of business books and magazines with the purchase of the A.W. Shaw Company of Chicago in 1928. One of Shaw's monthlies, the *Magazine of Business*, was turned into a weekly that eventually became *Business Week*, one of McGraw-Hill's best-known publications.

In 1930, despite the stock market crash of 1929 and the ensuing Great Depression (1929–1939), McGraw-Hill established four new magazines. That year the company also opened a West Coast office and entered trade book publishing with a new imprint, Whittlesey House, named after James McGraw's father-in-law. A new office building in New York was commissioned and first occupied in 1931. By 1933, however, the company was forced to make deep cuts in personnel and salaries and it had to sell off its printing machinery. The company recovered later in the decade with the help of bestsellers from Whittlesey House, business books, and the establishment of a vocational-education department in 1930. James McGraw, Jr., became president and chairman, and by 1937 profits were more than one million dollars.

During World War II (1939–1945) McGraw-Hill's paper needs received special priority because its technical publications were important to the war effort. Especially important were its special training manuals used in the accelerated training of the men and women joining the armed forces. Many dealt with radio and electronics and continued to be successful after the war. The company also increased its international activities, opening a book-export department and a foreign language-translation office. In 1944 McGraw-Hill acquired the Embassy Book Company Ltd. of Toronto, later renaming it the McGraw-Hill Company of Canada, Ltd. and then McGraw Ryerson. The World News Service was begun in 1945.

After the war Curtis G. Benjamin became president of McGraw-Hill's book company and developed the text-film department, which provided audiovisual materials for educational institutions. The company also published several large multi-volume series in such fields as aviation and radar that grew out of government-financed projects. Another major project begun in the late 1940s was the publication of eighteenth century Scottish author James Boswell's manuscripts, with the first of a projected 40 volumes appearing in 1950. In 1950 the company achieved a major commercial success with *Betty Crocker's Picture Cook Book*.

Building on these successes, McGraw-Hill established several new divisions and added others through acquisitions in the late 1940s and early 1950s. In 1949 it purchased Gregg Publishing Company, which became the business-education department. In 1950 a technical writing division was created to produce specialized materials for government and industry. A medical publishing department was established in 1945, but it was not until McGraw-Hill acquired medical publisher Blakiston Company from Doubleday in 1954 that it would capture a major share of the medical market. The international division, established in 1946, contributed greatly to the company's growth in the 1950s, with book exports trebling and profits coming in from the international sale of text-films, filmstrips, and foreign language rights.

The McGraw family continued to run the company in the 1950s, with John McGraw, Jr.'s brother, Curtis, succeeding him as president. When Curtis died unexpectedly in 1953, another brother, Donald C. McGraw, became president. During the decade McGraw-Hill acquired several companies from Warren C. Platt and began three major encyclopedia projects: *The McGraw-Hill Encyclopedia of Science and Technology*, the *Encyclopedia of World Art*, and the *New Catholic Encyclopedia*. By 1959 revenues exceeded $100 million.

Between 1960 and 1965 overall sales of the book company doubled, contributing 39 percent of the parent company's overall revenue. In 1961 McGraw-Hill acquired the F.W. Dodge Corporation, an information provider to the construction industry. The general book division was created in 1962 by merging the company's industrial, business, and trade book divisions, and in 1963 the book company entered the school textbook market by acquiring Webster Publishing Company.

A major reorganization took place in 1964, when the book company and the F.W. Dodge Corporation merged with the parent company to form McGraw-Hill, Inc. Now there would be a single parent company with three operating divisions: book publishing, magazines and news services, and the Dodge group of construction industry information services. Following the reorganization, McGraw-Hill made several acquisitions, including the California Test Bureau (educational publishing), Shepard's Citations, Inc. (legal publishing), and Standard and Poor's Corporation (financial information services). Internationally the company expanded into Mexico in 1967 and into Japan in 1969.

During the 1970s McGraw-Hill was headed by Shelton Fisher, president and CEO, who had succeeded Donald McGraw in 1968. His goal was to transform McGraw-Hill into a dynamic media giant. He expanded the company internationally into Canada, Brazil, and India; he also bought television stations from Time Inc. and moved the company into a new world headquarters in New York in 1972. Later in the decade he became chairman of the parent company, with Harold McGraw, Jr., becoming president. When Fisher retired in 1974, Harold McGraw, Jr., became chairman in addition to his other positions.

At the end of the 1970s McGraw-Hill was a healthy, well-managed conglomerate. Its several operating divisions included book and publications companies, information systems, Standard and Poor's Corporation, and the McGraw-Hill Broadcasting Company. Overall revenues in 1978 exceeded $761 million. In 1979 American Express attempted a hostile takeover, offering $830 million for the company's stock. Concerned about the integrity of its editorial independence, McGraw-Hill successfully defended itself even when American Express increased the offer to nearly one billion dollars.

The company attempted to strengthen its management by appointing Joseph L. Dionne to the newly created position of vice president of operations. When Harold McGraw, Jr., retired in 1983 as president and CEO, Dionne succeeded him. Harold McGraw, Jr., remained as chairman until 1988. Meanwhile, another generation of McGraws was being groomed to run the company.

During the 1980s McGraw-Hill entered the electronic information marketplace, making available in computerized form much of the information supplied by the company's news service, magazines, Standard and Poor's, Dodge, Platt, and Shepard's. The company entered computer publishing by acquiring three computer magazines, *Byte*, *Unixworld*, and *LAN Times*, and purchasing Osborne Books.

The company also underwent a change in focus under Fisher's direction, switching from a media-based organizational structure to a market-oriented structure consisting of 14 market-focused operating groups. McGraw-Hill acquired Random House's college division for more than $200 million in 1988. Then in 1989 it entered into a joint venture with Macmillan, creating the Macmillan/McGraw-Hill School Publishing Company that combined the elementary, secondary, and vocational education businesses of both companies. McGraw-Hill would buy out Macmillan's interest in the joint venture in 1993. At the end of the 1980s McGraw-Hill's overall revenues were approaching two billion dollars annually.

In 1990 the company introduced the first customized publishing system that allowed professors to design their own textbooks. Later in the decade this electronic textbook publishing system was acknowledged as the leading U.S. custom book publisher with 18.5 percent of the market. By 1993 the company was taking in almost $2.8 billion in revenue, with its Educational/Professional unit accounting for 42 percent and the Financial Services unit accounting for another 48 percent of the company's net income. The company's third unit was Information and Media Services.

McGraw-Hill unveiled a new corporate identity program in 1995 changing its name to The McGraw Hill Companies, Inc. The slogan of the campaign announcing their name change was, "Keeping the world up to speed." It was a remarkable year for the company. Its stock price hit a record high; *Business Week*'s circulation surpassed the one million mark; the company's Web site was launched; and numerous new products and ventures were announced. Revenues topped $2.9 billion and net income rose nearly 12 percent to $227.1 million.

After leading the company for 15 years, Joseph Dionne retired in 1998 as president and CEO; however, he remained as chairman. He was succeeded by Harold (Terry) McGraw III, son of Chairman Emeritus Harold McGraw, Jr. With the company's leadership back in the McGraw family and with more than a century of history, McGraw-Hill could well claim to be one of the premier publishers in the world.

See also: **Publishing Industry**

FURTHER READING

"A Brief History of The McGraw-Hill Companies," [cited May 12, 1999] available from the World Wide Web @ www.mcgraw–hill.com/corporate/news_info/history.html/.

Block, Valerie. "Re-education Plan: Market-Savvy Heir Modernizes Image of McGraw-Hill." *Crain's New York Business*, December 14–20, 1998.

Burlingame, Roger. *Endless Frontiers: The Story of McGraw-Hill*. New York: McGraw-Hill, 1959.

McGraw-Hill Book Company. *Imprint on an Era: The Story of the McGraw-Hill Book Company*. New York: McGraw-Hill, 1959.

Milliot, Jim. "M-H Reorganizes Professional Book Group." *Publishers Weekly*, February 2, 1998.

MEDICAID

Medicaid is a large social welfare program operated jointly by the federal and state governments. A 1965 amendment to the Social Security Act of 1935 created the program, which allows low-income individuals access to medical care.

How does it work? The federal government provides money to the states. The states then add funding of their own to this amount and administer medical programs for the poor in compliance with federally established standards.

Before Medicaid developed, health care for the poor was very limited and came from a variety of sources, including hospitals, charities, and state and local governments.

What type of care can a Medicaid patient receive? A Medicaid recipient may obtain treatment from five different categories of care: inpatient hospital services, outpatient hospital services, laboratory and x-ray services, skilled nursing home services, and physician services.

Initially, Medicaid recipients were able to select their own doctors and hospitals, but because of a large increase in medical expenditures, states now direct Medicaid recipients to certain health plans that attempt to control costs and quality of care. As a result, only approved medical care providers, including physicians, nursing homes, and hospitals are entitled to receive Medicaid payments for their services.

In 1995, there were about 30 million Medicaid recipients.

See also: **Medicare, Social Security Act**

MEDICARE

The Medicare program provides health and hospital insurance to disabled persons and those age 65 and older. It was first proposed by President Harry Truman (1945–1953), but wasn't enacted as policy until President Lyndon Johnson (1963–1969) included it in one of his Great Society proposals in 1965.

Effective since 1966, Medicare was first managed by the Social Security Administration. In 1977, its operations were transferred to the newly created Health Care Financing Administration, where it remains today. Unlike the social welfare program Medicaid, Medicare does not place an income requirement on individuals who receive its services. To be eligible for Medicare, one must be disabled or be age 65 or older.

The Medicare program has two components: a hospital insurance program and a supplementary medical insurance program. The hospital insurance program covers reasonable and medically necessary treatments in a hospital or nursing home. It is funded through a 2.9 percent Social Security tax on employers and workers. The money generated from this tax is placed into a trust fund for use by the Medicare program.

The supplementary medical insurance program is a service offered to individuals who sign up for it with a monthly insurance premium, which, in addition to tax revenue contributions from the federal government, funds the program. Under the supplementary medical insurance program, an individual pays the monthly premium and a small annual deductible fee for medical costs.

While there are limitations as to what Medicare will pay for (no routine physical examinations, for example), most physicians accept Medicare patients. All health care providers accepting Medicare patients must meet state and local licensing laws and standards to qualify for Medicare reimbursements for their services.

Medicare assisted about 37 million people in 1995, spending $178 billion for their care. Under current laws, the year 2002 should see a rise in Medicare spending to $345 billion. Since the 1980s debate about the program has risen. With the quality of medical care increasingly improving, life expectancy also increases. This means Medicare will be taking care of people for a longer period of time.

The program experienced a surplus in the 1980s and 1990s, but its future in the twenty-first century is uncertain. Medicare expenditures are expected to increase more rapidly than tax revenues. As the costs of medical treatment increase and the number of Medicare recipients rise with the 2010 retirement of the post-World War II baby boom generation, the program faces great financial and systemic strain.

See also: **Great Society, Medicaid**

MEDIUM OF EXCHANGE

A medium of exchange is money or any other agreed upon item used in the sale of goods and services. Whether the product being sold is a hamburger, a new car, or a movie ticket, something must be given to transfer value from the buyer to the seller. In modern economies, money serves this purpose. In more primitive economies or in special circumstances other mediums of exchange may develop. In prisoner of war camps, for example, cigarettes have served as a medium of exchange, with inmates trading food or other desired goods for a given number of smokes. For a market to operate efficiently, everyone must agree on the medium of exchange. Early in the history of the United States, banks and not the government issued paper money, and there were endless disagreements over whether one bank's notes would be accepted at another bank or in another state. Finally, to avoid such confusion, the government began to issue the nation's money, which is now used as a medium of exchange for virtually all transactions. It is important to note that credit cards and personal checks are not really a medium of exchange, but merely a stand-in for the real medium of exchange, which is money.

MELLON, ANDREW

In the 1920s Andrew Mellon (1855–1937) was one of the richest men in the United States through his investments in many industries, including aluminum, coke, oil, and steel. In that decade he became an influential member of the government, serving as Secretary of the Treasury for 12 years during the administrations of Warren G. Harding (1921–1923), Calvin Coolidge (1923–1929), and Herbert Hoover (1929–1933).

The fourth son of millionaire Pittsburgh banker Thomas Mellon, Andrew took over his father's business when he was in his twenties and steadily expanded it until the family bank became the leading financial institution for industry in the Pittsburgh area. In 1889 Mellon granted a loan for the manufacture of aluminum to the Pittsburgh Reduction Company, which had acquired the patent for processing aluminum alloys by electrolysis. The process had been discovered by Charles Martin Hill in 1886 and permitted the extraction of aluminum from bauxite at a relatively low cost. Until that time aluminum was expensive to produce and used only for costume jewelry. With this new procedure the price fell dramatically so that commercial aluminum production was now practical. Mellon was able to use his financial leverage to take over Pittsburgh Reduction, and his shrewd business practices enabled him to control all aspects of marketing and production. By 1907, when the Pittsburgh Reduction Company changed its name to the Aluminum Company of America (Alcoa), the corporation had a monopoly in North America and an important share of the world market.

(ANDREW MELLON IS) THE MOST POWERFUL MAN IN THE WORLD TODAY. . . . HE HAS DOMINATED THE FINANCIAL, ECONOMIC AND FISCAL RELATIONS OF THE UNITED STATES FOR THE PAST FIVE YEARS.

John Nance Garner, Vice-President (1933–1941), 1927

In 1901 oil was discovered in quantities that had not been seen before at a salt dome named Spindletop near Beaumont, Texas. The well had been drilled by the J.M. Guffey Petroleum Company of Pittsburgh, which had been financed by a $400,000 loan from the Mellon bank. Because of the size of the find, Guffey soon asked for more money to exploit it properly. Mellon agreed but demanded 40 percent of the stock in return. He was favorably impressed with Spindletop's massive production but not with the waste and rapid depletion of the oil reserves, which were exhausted in only two years. So Mellon bought out Guffey's interest and in 1907 replaced him as president with his nephew William L. Mellon. They renamed the corporation the Gulf Oil Company.

In 1920 Mellon underwrote a $1.5 million deficit in the National Republican Committee's campaign fund, and in compensation President Harding appointed him Secretary of the Treasury. He was considered one of the most important cabinet members in the 1920s, and his unqualified affirmation of capitalism dominated Republican thought. He advocated high tariffs and cuts in government spending and corporate taxes. In his view, low taxes would free up money that could be invested in business and industry to create jobs and improve the economy.

In 1926, after Congress passed the Mellon Plan, a package of legislation that embodied his economic principles, both industrial production and the stock market soared, and his prestige was never higher. He was called "the greatest Secretary of the Treasury since Alexander Hamilton." He became a candidate for president in 1927 but lost the Republican nomination to Herbert Hoover, who kept Mellon as his Secretary of Treasury after his election in 1928.

Mellon's prestige fell dramatically after the Wall Street crash of 1929. He along with Hoover and Coolidge were blamed for the disaster, and Mellon appeared foolish when he predicted that the depression would come to a swift end. Although he overcame an attempt to impeach him in 1932, Mellon resigned his position that year to become ambassador to Great Britain. After the election of President Franklin D. Roosevelt (1933–1944), he became a private citizen, but he continually had to return to Washington to answer questions about his administration of the country's finances. Andrew Mellon died of a stroke, while visiting his daughter in 1937.

Not usually given to philanthropy, he left his art collection and enough money to build an art gallery to the government. Constructed of white Tennessee limestone, the National Gallery of Art, which is sometimes called the Mellon galleries, is one of the most attractive buildings to grace the capital mall in Washington D.C., and it houses one of the nation's most important art collections. It opened in 1941.

Mellon left a mixed reputation. On the one hand, he was a banker with an extraordinary ability to make sound investments and so created a diversified fortune that continued to grow with the country. He was influential in establishing the aluminum industry and in opening the Texas oil fields. His bank was also important in financing heavy industry during an important period of its development. He was one of the three richest men in the country when he entered politics at age 65. During the 12 years that he was Secretary of the Treasury, his influence over the nation's economy was enormous. He represented business interests at a time when their prestige was at their highest. But when the country fell on hard times, the unfettered capitalism that he had advocated was then considered a ruthless economic system, and he became the personification of all the evils associated with it. Opinion of him has subsequently mellowed, so that one may see his faults as also the faults of his age and still appreciate the creativity and enterprise with which he conducted his affairs.

FURTHER READING

Finley, David Edward. *A Standard of Excellence: Andrew W. Mellon Founds the National Gallery of Art.* Washington, D.C.: Smithsonian Institution Press, 1973.

Holbrook, Stewart H. *The Age of the Moguls.* New York: Garden City, 1953.

Koskoff, David E. *The Mellons: The Chronicle of America's Richest Family.* New York: Thomas Y. Crowell, 1978.

Mellon, Andrew. Taxation: *The People's Business.* New York: Macmillan, 1924.

O'Connor, Harvey. *Mellon's Millions, the Biography of a Fortune: The Life and Times of Andrew W. Mellon.* New York: John Day Co., 1933.

MERCANTILISM *(ISSUE)*

Mercantilism was a set of economic ideas followed by many northern and western European countries from the sixteenth to the nineteenth century. These included Portugal, Spain, France, the Netherlands, and England. By the nineteenth century, however, mercantilism was considered discredited as an economic theory. Although it began as a rather vague collection of economic ideas, it was continually refined, elaborated, and modified over time. By the eighteenth century it had shifted from a loosely enforced set of commercial laws to a tightly regulated imperial policy, especially throughout the British Empire.

At the core of mercantilism was the belief that foreign trade could be made to serve the interests of the government and vice versa. The prime objective was the acquisition and retention of as much money (gold and silver) as possible. The state needed gold and silver to wage war. Mercantilism was a form of economic warfare between competing nations. European monarchs realized that in order to secure their political positions and compete with their rival monarchs in other nations they could no longer rely solely on an increase in tax rates. They had to increase their tax base. To do so, many nation-states turned to increased trade and the establishment of colonies.

In the mercantilist system colonies were expected to help the mother country achieve a favorable balance of trade, favorable specie inflow, economic self-sufficiency and an export surplus. Colonies were expected to supply products which would otherwise have to be obtained from non-imperial sources, generate exports by the production and sale of products in high demand outside the empire, and provide a market for the mother country's exports. The mother country would provide the colonies with centralized governmental control of the economy, as well as naval and military protection.

The English laws that systematized these developments for North America were enacted over a century and were built around a series of Navigation Acts beginning in 1651. They were given a comprehensive form in 1696. They confined the transport trade within the Empire to British or colonial ships, required all exports from Europe to the colonies to be shipped via England (and vice versa), and specified a list of goods that could not be shipped to European ports (other than England). These included sugar, cotton, tobacco, indigo, wool, naval stores, rice, furs, and copper. By the mid-seventeenth century, the colonies were prosperous and were encouraged in their prosperity by credits from home. The plantation colonies especially fitted nicely into the mercantilist system because the economies of the South and Britain naturally complemented one another. Britain carried the burden of colonial defense and gave colonial goods and ships protection abroad. From the early eighteenth century until 1763 the colonial policy was on the back burner, as England concentrated on a series of wars with France. The casualness of imperial administration and enforcement soothed points of disagreement and where discord continued, laws were tacitly evaded. Systematic smuggling was confined mainly to tea and molasses. For the most part the mercantile system provided easy credit, assured commercial markets, and brought economic prosperity to colonies and mother countries alike.

English intervention in the economy in order to serve national interests produced financial and strategic advantages to the colonies. By giving the colonies the bulk of the shipping rights on trade with England, British mercantilism benefited the colonies. Mercantilism inevitably brought trade disputes with other countries, which in turn often degenerated into military struggles.

Mercantilism had its critics. In 1776 economist Adam Smith (1723–1790) in his *Wealth of Nations* defined a country's wealth in terms of labor and not money. Smith advocated the free play of individual enterprise and free trade. Historians such as George Bancroft (1800–1891) condemned mercantilism as the source of foreign policy. He concluded that the Navigation Acts and mercantilism in general were the basic causes of the American Revolution (1775–1783).

Many colonists realized that England looked on them purely for their economic role under mercantilism. They also realized that their own prosperity was largely the result of mercantilist policies. As British statesman and political philospher Edmund Burke (1729–1797) declared, "the Act of Navigation attended the colonies from their infancy, grew with their growth and strengthened with their strength. They were confirmed in obedience to it even more by usage than by law."

Twentieth century historians such as Lawrence A. Harper and O. M. Dickerson disagreed with Bancroft that the Navigation Acts presented a great impediment to colonial trade. They argued that the real bitterness among American colonists after 1763 was aimed at British customs and revenue collectors, stamp officials, and enforcement agents. They had a distaste not for mercantilism but for their role in a reorganized empire that emerged after the end of the French and Indian Wars (1754–1763) in 1763. In particular, they objected to the taxation policy. Overzealous officers, racketeering practices, seizures, and new bonding regulations among other things were what brought hostility from colonists.

See also: **Navigation Acts, Adam Smith**

FURTHER READING

Barrow, Thomas C. *Trade and Empire; The British Customs Services in Colonial America: 1660–1775.* New York: Excel, 1999.

Ekelund, Jr. Robert B., and Robert D. Tollison. *Politicized Economies: Monarchy, Monopoly, and Mercantilism.* Texas A&M University Economics Series, No. 14. College Station: Texas A&M University Press, 1997.

Johns, R.A. *Colonial Trade and International Exchange: The Transitions From Autarky to International Trade.* London: Pinter Pub. Ltd., 1989.

Sen, Sudipta. *Empire of Free Trade: The East India Company and the Making of the Colonial Marketplace.* Philadelphia: University of Pennsylvania Press, 1998.

Wallerstein, Immanuel. *Modern World System II: Mercantilism and the Consolidation of the European World-Economy, 175600–1750.* New York: Academic Press, 1980.

MERCENARIES

Mercenaries are soldiers for hire. They differ from a normal army to the extent that mercenaries fight only for money, or for anyone who will hire them, and not out of allegiance to a flag or their homeland. Sometimes ''mercs,'' as they are also known, will sell their services as individual warriors. At other times a government in need has hired entire armies. The use of mercenaries has a long history. The practice dates back at least to ancient times. Ancient Egyptians and Babylonians used mercenaries. Greeks served as mercenary soldiers in Hellenistic states. In the late Roman Empire, emperors hired tribes from the outer regions of the empire to fight their battles. In the decades since World War II (1939–1945) mercenaries have fought post-colonial wars in Africa, cocaine wars in South America, and from the deserts of the Middle East to the jungles of Asia. The typical mercenary is a former soldier who took up fighting for pay after his own army no longer needed him. Defeated German soldiers from World War II served as mercenaries in many small wars around the globe. The collapse of the Soviet Union saw many former Russian soldiers plying their trade as mercenaries. Sometimes dictators with an unruly population may hire mercenaries rather than risk arming their own people. The British army has a long history of loaning out its soldiers to former colonial nations to train and command local armies. Former U.S. Army soldiers have also served as mercenaries. There seems little doubt that mercenaries will continue to see a demand for their services in a world so rife with conflict.

MERGER

A merger is the joining together of two or more companies. The usual goal of a merger is to increase market share, diversify into new products or markets, gain improved efficiency, or eliminate a competitor. Mergers usually take one of three forms: one business may merge with another through purchasing its assets; the merging companies may form a completely new company that acquires the assets of both firms (a ''consolidation''); or the two companies may exchange stock with each other (known as ''a pooling of interests''). When the acquired company resists the merger, it is referred to as a ''hostile takeover.'' Mergers that occur between two companies in the same industry are known as ''horizontal mergers,'' and when one company acquires a customer or supplier it is known as a ''vertical merger.'' When the merging companies are in two different industries, the resulting company is known as a ''conglomerate.''

In U.S. history, mergers have generally occurred in spurts and usually when the stock market is enjoying strong ''bullish'' growth. The first major merger period occurred between 1895 and 1904, when the expansion of the U.S. railroad network made it possible for firms to combine and serve a truly national market for the first time. Between 1892 and 1902 more than 2600 U.S. firms were swallowed up by mergers, and in roughly the same period the 100 largest U.S. companies used mergers to increase in size by a factor of four. In 1901 the American Can Company was formed through the merger of no less than 120 companies. The next big merger period occurred in the late 1920s, when the emergence of radio and the truck presented new opportunities to create national markets through radio advertising and local distribution.

The merger boom of the 1960s peaked in 1968, when the 200 largest U.S. corporations acquired 1.6 percent of the entire manufacturing assets in the U.S. economy. Because of the federal government's successful attempts to prevent companies from forming monopolies many of the mergers of the 1960s took the form of conglomerates. A fourth period of intense merger activity began in the early 1980s and continued into the 1990s. The driving force behind these mergers were technological advances, global competition, and the deregulation of industries, such as the airline industry, that had once been closely supervised by the federal government.

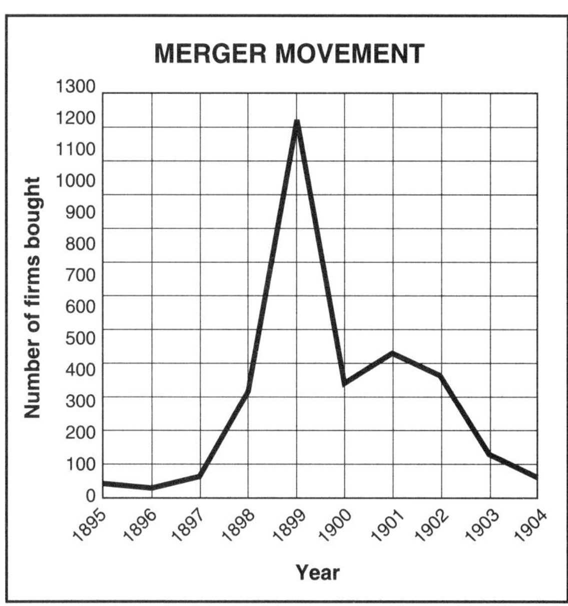

The first major merger period in American history reached a high point in 1899.

MERRILL, CHARLES EDWARD

As cofounder of Merrill, Lynch stockbrokerage firm in 1914, Charles E. Merrill (1885–1956) launched a Wall Street dynasty that would long outlive him. Building on the slogan "Bring Wall Street to Main Street" he designed his business around middle-class investors, not stock exchange insiders. By the time of his death in 1956 his firm had offices in 106 cities across North America; the firm has continued to grow ever since.

Charles E. Merrill was born on October 19, 1885, in Green Cove Springs, Florida, the son of Dr. Charles and Octavia Wilson Merrill. His father, a local physician, also owned a drug store where Merrill worked as a boy in addition to having a paper route. Merrill attended a preparatory school affiliated with Stetson University and was later sent on a partial athletic scholarship to Worcester Academy in Massachusetts. He attended Amherst College in Massachusetts from 1904 to 1906. He left Amherst without graduating and returned to Florida where he dabbled in newspaper journalism at West Palm Beach's *Tropical Sun*. Later in life he commented that the job provided him with "the best training I ever had; I learned human nature."

After one year of law school at the University of Michigan Merrill abandoned plans for a legal career and went to Mississippi to play baseball for a minor league team during the summer of 1907. When the season ended he moved to New York City to look for work and his first job was in the office of the Patchogue Plymouth Mills in Patchogue, New York. Here what Merrill acquired "turned out to be the equivalent of a university course in general and credit finance, cost accounting, and administration, in particular." This training would be invaluable to his future success.

The skills Merrill learned at his early jobs enabled him to become one of the most innovative leaders in the field of financial services. With a sound understanding of business practices, which he obtained during his two years with Patchogue Mills, he went on to a job on Wall Street. Merrill joined George H. Burr and Company in 1909. The company's owner had heard of Merrill's abilities and he wanted the young man to take charge of Burr's newly created bond department. Merrill promptly hired Edmund Lynch, a Johns Hopkins University graduate whom he had met at the 23rd Street YMCA, to handle sales.

Merrill's strategy for attracting new customers was to use direct mail solicitations. He concentrated on informative and accurate information rather than the exaggerated claims and misleading statements that were the norm at the time. This emphasis on honesty was to remain one of Merrill's chief concerns throughout his career. Clear, honest information appealed to a broad customer base, he reasoned, and "having thousands of customers scattered throughout the United States is infinitely preferable to being dependent upon the fluctuating buying power of a smaller and perhaps on the whole wealthier group of investors in any one section."

Under Merrill's leadership Burr's bond department quickly became a success. The company soon expanded into underwriting (guaranteeing) equities. In 1912 the company sponsored a $2 million stock offering in the Kresge chain stores. Chain stores were a new concept at the time, and this project began Merrill's career-long involvement with this retail innovation.

In 1913 Merrill left Burr to become sales manager at Eastman, Dillon and Company and a year later he founded his own small securities firm, Charles E. Merrill and Company. Within six months he had taken on Edmund Lynch as a partner: Merrill, Lynch was born. The partners began by underwriting two chain stores, McCrory Stores and Kresge, the latter being an account Merrill lured away from Burr. With the public receptive to buying stock in this emerging business, Merrill soon made his first fortune. He accepted stock warrants as part of his fee and sold these when they increased in value.

World War I (1914–1918) had began by this time, and Merrill joined the U.S. Army as a first lieutenant in the air corps. After the war Merrill returned to his firm to oversee its period of greatest expansion. The U.S. economy was booming in the 1920s. Many Americans had bought war bonds, familiarizing them with investing; they were now ready to expand to corporate ventures. Merrill's emphasis on straight advice for a broad range of middle-class customers was well-suited to this new business climate. Merrill, Lynch grew rapidly. In 1919 Merrill hired the first bond saleswoman on Wall Street, Annie Grimes, and in 1924 he expanded the company's office hours, opening early and closing late, to better serve customers.

Merrill, Lynch continued to focus on the expanding chain store industry. About half of the company's underwritings in the 1920s were retailers such as J.C. Penney, National Tea, Kresge, and McCrory. In 1921 the company entered the movie business when it took over a studio, Path Exchange. Merrill, Lynch later sold the studio to Cecil B. deMille and Joseph Kennedy (father of the future president). With the profit from the sale of Path Exchange the company acquired the southern California food chain Safeway Stores. Merrill subsequently built up and expanded Safeway, merging it with another western chain. Merrill next founded *Family Circle* magazine, the first magazine distributed through supermarkets.

[H]AVING THOUSANDS OF CUSTOMERS SCATTERED THROUGHOUT THE UNITED STATES IS INFINITELY PREFERABLE TO BEING DEPENDENT UPON THE FLUCTUATING BUYING POWER OF A SMALLER AND PERHAPS ON THE WHOLE WEALTHIER GROUP OF INVESTORS IN ANY ONE SECTION.

Charles Merrill

As the American economy continued to boom through the 1920s, Merrill grew increasingly concerned. In 1928, over a year before the infamous stock market crash that sent the country into the Great Depression, he sent a letter to customers recommending they get out of debt. He persuaded his partner to reduce the company's vulnerability in the event of a sharp decline. When the stock market crashed in October 1929 Merrill, Lynch survived. Merrill became highly respected for his ability to foresee market trends.

In January 1930 Merrill, Lynch left the brokerage business and turned over its accounts to E. A. Pierce and Company. The firm then focused on underwriting and individual banking, specializing in chain stores. By 1931 Merrill had built Safeway up to the third largest food chain in the country; he was also its largest stockholder. The firm's growth continued through the decade, but then, on a vacation trip in 1938, Edmund Lynch died unexpectedly. Without his partner Merrill had to reexamine his business focus and in 1940 he went back into the brokerage business and merged Merrill, Lynch with E. A. Pierce and Company. The next year another merger created Merrill Lynch, Pierce, Fenner, and Beane, the world's largest brokerage house.

New Deal legislation also affected the public perception of Wall Street. During the 1930s the federal government created the Securities and Exchange Commission to monitor the stock brokerage industry. New laws imposed fines and jail terms on those convicted of financial fraud. Merrill wholeheartedly supported these reforms and he was instrumental in influencing other brokerage houses to adopt his firm's direct practices.

During the 1940s Merrill was at the forefront of change in the investment industry. He coined the phrase ''Bring Wall Street to Main Street'' in 1941 to attract small investors to the stock market. He printed ads and pamphlets that contained his characteristically honest information and he insisted on professionalism among his own employees. He provided business education for his employees and paid them a straight salary rather than one based on commissions. These strategies boosted public confidence in the company and enabled Merrill, Lynch to continue its astronomical growth.

After suffering a heart attack in 1944 Merrill withdrew from active management of the firm, but he continued to direct strategy and long-term planning for the company. With partner Win Smith, Merrill instituted additional changes by recruiting younger, better-educated brokers and providing them with training in accounting and commercial banking. He also published the booklets ''Hedging: Insurance Policy or Lottery Ticket'' and ''How to Read a Financial Report,'' and he ran informative ads in the country's leading newspapers.

In 1954 the New York Stock Exchange launched a new plan for moderate-income individuals who wished to make small, regular investments in the stock market. Merrill, Lynch became the largest institutional supporter of this Monthly Investment Plan (MIP). After one year Merrill, Lynch had almost half of all MIP accounts, and within a few years the firm maintained the vast majority of MIP accounts. By the time Merrill died in 1956 his firm had 107 partners in 106 cities, and it employed over 4,600 people and handled almost 300,000 active customer accounts. The firm then became Merrill, Lynch, Pierce, Fenner and Smith; in the late 1990s it continued to be the world's biggest brokerage.

Merrill's innovations in the field of financial services led to far-reaching changes both in the way Americans invested and in the way they spent money. Before Merrill established his brokerage firm, stock market investments were only for the elite or the unscrupulous. Average Americans had no idea of how the stock market worked and they distrusted Wall Street—for a good reason. Many brokerage houses kept the ''best'' information only for their wealthiest customers and they tried to lure others with exaggerated claims and deceptive promises of profits. Merrill, however, provided accurate figures and honest information tailored to the needs of average Americans. One of his first acts when he reentered the brokerage field in the 1940s was to issue a pamphlet that stated ''The interests of our customers MUST come first.''

Merrill, Lynch became a leader in the dissemination of investment information. The company published a bi-weekly magazine, *Investor's Reader*, and it was the first to make full public disclosures of its operations and holdings, as well as the investments of its partners. As Martin Mayer wrote in *Wall Street: Men and Money*, ''Merrill brought in the public [to Wall Street] not as lambs to be fleeced but as partners in the benefits.''

The rapid growth of chain stores, in which Merrill was also instrumental, profoundly affected the U.S. economy. Before the introduction of these giant chains most Americans shopped at small, mom-and-pop style stores that operated with a small volume and charged higher prices. Because chains could operate on an economy of scale they could offer a greater selection of goods at lower prices. The growth of chains became such a threat to smaller retailers that the California legislature passed a tax on chain stores, which would have absorbed about 20 percent of Safeway's net income. Confident that consumers wanted the better prices and selection that chains could offer, Safeway management urged that the issue be put to a popular vote. In a 1936 statewide referendum voters in California repealed the tax. The message was clear: consumers wanted chain stores. Merrill later remarked, ''If ever I get to heaven, it will be because I helped lower the price of milk by a penny a quart in Los Angeles.''

Merrill used a substantial part of his wealth to further the principles by which he had made his fortune. In 1945 he created the Merrill Foundation for the Advancement of Investment Knowledge, which awarded grants to institutions such as Massachusetts Institute of Technology, Brookings Institute, and the Wharton School of Finance. He donated 95 percent of his $25 million estate to churches, hospitals, and colleges. A large portion of this estate supported colleges and universities in the South that served African American populations. In 1951 he donated his 16-acre estate in Southampton, Long Island, to Amherst College which became the Merrill Center of Economics. In 1953 Merrill endowed a chair of medicine at Harvard University in honor of heart specialist Dr. Samuel A. Levine, who had treated Merrill for his heart condition.

In 1947 Merrill was named as the only representative from the securities industry in a poll of 50 outstanding business leaders. He received an honorary M.A. degree from Amherst College in 1933 among other honorary degrees from the University of Michigan in 1945, John B. Stetson University in 1946, Amherst College in 1948, Kenyon College in 1949, and a degree from New York University in 1950.

Charles Merrill married three times: first to Eliza Church in 1912, with whom he had a son and a daughter; to Helen Ingram in 1925, with whom he had a son, (they divorced in 1937); and to Kenta Des More (their marriage lasted from 1939 to their divorce in 1952). Merrill spent his last years at his home on Merrill's Landing in Palm Beach, Florida where he died on October 6, 1956.

***See also:* Chain Stores, Dow Jones Industrial Average, Stock Market, Stock Market Crash of 1929**

FURTHER READING

Ingham, John. *Biographical Dictionary of American Business Leaders*. Westport, CT: Greenwood, 1983, s.v. ''Merrill, Charles.''

Merrill, Charles E., Jr. *The Checkbook: The Politics and Ethics of Foundation Philanthropy*. Boston: Oelgeschlager, Gunn and Hain, 1986.

Perkins, Edwin. *Wall Street to Main Street: Charles Merrill and Middle Class Investors*. Cambridge: Cambridge University Press, 1999.

Regan, Donald. *The Merrill Lynch Story*. New York: Newcomer Society, 1981.

Schweikart, Larry, ed. *Encyclopedia of American Business History and Biography*, New York: Facts on File, 1990, s.v. ''Banking and Finance, 1913–1989.''

MESA VERDE

Mesa Verde, in southwestern Colorado, is the site of well-preserved ancient American Indian ruins. Here in the 1200s A.D. the Anasazi Indians (also called Cliff Dwellers) built their dwellings into the sides of a plateau. The area was named Mesa Verde (which is Spanish meaning "green table") because the stone cities were carved into the sides of the mesas (flat-topped hills) in a region noted for its forests of junipers and pines. The multi-storied dwellings were built for protection from raiding tribes: the inhabitants could retract access ladders in case of attack. The largest and best known of the ruins is the Cliff Palace, which contains more than 200 rooms and was probably inhabited by two to three hundred people at a time. Balcony House and Spruce Tree House are other large, multi-family dwellings.

A National Park since 1906, Mesa Verde provides a historical record of the ancient American Indians who occupied the area for hundreds of years. Nomadic peoples had moved onto the mesa top by the sixth century. As they made the transition from a hunting-gathering life style to an agricultural one, they moved from underground pit houses to the cliff dwellings. Over hundreds of years their culture became increasingly sophisticated. No longer involved in the time-consuming practice of following the herds for sustenance, the Anasazi turned their attention to crafting pottery, making decorative textiles, building kivas (underground ceremonial structures), and carving their homes in the rocky sides of mesas. The settlement at Mesa Verde was empty by 1300. Twenty-four years of low rainfall and increasingly hostile raids wiped out the Anasazi Indians who lived there. The site was first seen by white settlers in 1859.

See also: **Anasazi, Pueblo, Southwestern Indians**

MESOAMERICA

Mesoamerica is a geographic term for the area that extends from northern Mexico through Central America to the Isthmus of Panama. In prehistoric times this area was predominately settled by the Aztec and Maya Indians who built flourishing empires. Spanish explorers arrived on the coast of Mesoamerica in the early 1500s and eventually made their way inland, where they encountered the native peoples. The explorers conquered both the Aztec and the Maya by the mid-1500s. Mesoamerica was brought under the control of the Spanish crown and it formed a substantial portion of the viceroyalty of New Spain. The seat of colonial control was established at Mexico City.

See also: **Aztec, Maya, New Spain (Viceroyalty of)**

MESTIZO

A Mestizo is a person of American Indian and (usually white) European ancestry. The word comes from the Spanish and means "mixed," but it can also refer to a person of French-Indian, Portuguese-Indian, or Dutch-Indian heritage. A race of Mestizos emerged in Latin America by the mid-1500s and changed the character of the region. Historian Arturo Rosales wrote (in *The Hispanic-American Almanac,* 1993) that in central Mexico the "sexual appetite of the Spaniards led to numerous liaisons with the native women. . . . The consequence was a large progeny of children who were half Spaniard and half Indian." By 1821, and the end of colonial rule of Mexico, the possible variations of Mestizo numbered more than 100. Mestizo populations spread northward from Mexico during the colonial era. They also emerged elsewhere, as Europeans arrived in new territories around the world and subjugated native populations. In Latin and North America Mestizos entered the rank-and-file of armies and were wage laborers who worked in mines and in the fields. It was a race that was created and, during colonial times, dominated by European incursion.

See also: **New Spain (Viceroyalty of)**

MEXICAN BAIL-OUT

In December 1994, as Mexicans watched their currency's buying power plummet 40 percent, President Ernesto Zedillo stunned world-wide financial markets by devaluing the peso. Zedillo blamed the crisis on his predecessor, Carlos Salinas, who had attempted to get Mexico out from under mounting foreign debt and national poverty by launching reforms that slashed triple-digit inflation, dismantled trade barriers, and opened the Mexican economy to foreign investment.

Part of Salinas' anti-inflation strategy was to tie the value of the Mexican peso to the U.S. dollar so that the value of the peso would not fall, and investments in Mexico would be safe. Since the beginning of this policy in 1988, investors in the United States and other countries poured $50 billion into Mexico. But with the passing of the North American Free Trade Agreement (NAFTA) in 1994, rising U.S. interest rates lured foreign investors to favor the dollar over the peso. To keep the peso's value on par the Mexican government was forced to use its foreign currency reserves to purchase pesos. Mexico's $30 billion foreign exchange reserves plummeted while the government spent as much as $1 billion a day. By December 19, reserves had dropped below $10 billion, with no end in sight.

By this time Zedillo, the new president, decided that devaluing the peso was the only way to end the situation. This was a drastic step to take, however, sure to cause turmoil in Mexico's economy. Zedillo did not prepare to deal with this impact very well. At first he denied that devaluation was in the works, and then, without unveiling a plan to counter the economic impact, Zedillo announced on December 21 that devaluation would happen. Foreign investors stunned by the news dumped Mexican stock, pushing the peso down even further. The peso's value relative to other currencies plummeted 70 percent.

The number of American investors in Mexico and the amount that they invested prompted U.S. President Bill Clinton (1993–) to attempt to bail out the Mexican government. He originally proposed a plan with $40 billion in U.S. loan guarantees, but Congress refused to authorize that amount. Undaunted, Clinton unveiled an alternate rescue plan that would ''save'' Mexico by letting Zedillo's government take money from the U.S. Treasury Department's Exchange Stabilization Fund, which was designed to help America's ''friends'' out of temporary currency crises. The Exchange Stabilization Fund had traditionally provided assistance for very short periods of time, usually less than a year. But under Clinton's bail-out plan, the White House allowed the Mexican government to withdraw at least $2.5 billion from the fund, with repayment schedules stretching out from 10 months to 10 years.

Clinton's original $40 billion plan consisted only of loan guarantees that might never have been activated. His new plan was a mix of guarantees and immediate loans and was therefore more risky. To minimize the risk, the he required that Mexico agree to divert proceeds from oil exports to the Federal Reserve Bank of New York in the event of a default, and demanded that Mexico pay fees to offset the risks of the loans and guarantees.

Clinton's plan was certainly not without its critics. Some charged that it would benefit only large, rich investors in Mexico, doing little for the Mexicans themselves and nothing for the average American. They questioned why Clinton was willing to lend billions to a foreign government without a vote of Congress, when thousands of investors within the United States lost money and were never offered bail outs. Surely, they claimed, $20 billion in additional loan guarantees to domestic inner-city investors would have provided more benefits to Americans at home. Detractors also focused on the risk involved in the loans. They contended that in order for Mexico to pay back the loans on time it had to succeed at many difficult tasks, including lowering its account deficit, controlling its money supply, privatizing more state companies, suppressing internal rebellion, and insulating its central bank from political interference.

The Clinton plan went into action despite these objections. While supporters conceded that there was no question Clinton took a risk with the loan, they believed that it was justified for two reasons. First, Mexico's problems always had a way of becoming those of the United States, through increased influxes of illegal immigrants, for instance, or through a decline in an otherwise mutually beneficial trade. Second, the Mexican government had been increasingly edging its way toward economically responsible policies, and needed to be encouraged to continue.

Three years before its deadline Mexico repaid its loans from the United States in total with interest. Clinton supporters hailed the achievement and argued that the amount repaid by Mexico amounted to about a half-billion dollars more than the United States would have made if there had been no loan at all.

However economists viewed the situation, most agreed that as of the end of the twentieth century approached, Mexico was still not entirely out of trouble. They felt that more reform along free market lines would be necessary if Mexico was to become a major creator of jobs, products, services and wealth, all of which its growing population badly needed. Still, most acknowledged that the situation had been successfully stabilized, and that recent progress in Mexico was unmistakable.

See also: **General Agreement on Tariffs and Trade, International Monetary Fund, Free Trade**

FURTHER READING

Greenwald, John. ''Mexico: Don't Panic: Here Comes Bail Out Bill With a Recalcitrant Congress.'' *Time*, February 1995.

Koenig, Peter. ''Mexico's Hot Cocktail: If Bill Clinton is Re-elected, He May Find His First Foreign Policy Crisis is in His Own Back Yard.'' *New Statesman*, Vol. 125, September 1996.

Robinson, Edward A. ''Fortune Investor/Emerging Markets: Why You Shouldn't Bank on Mexico.'' *Fortune*, August 1998.

Schnepper, Jeff A. ''Mexico Is Draining the U.S. Treasury.'' *USA Today Magazine*, May 1995.

Seybold, Peter. ''The Politics of Free Trade: The Global Marketplace as a Closet Dictator.'' *Monthly Review*, December 1995.

MEXICAN CESSION (1848)

The Treaty of Guadalupe-Hidalgo was the peace treaty between the United States and Mexico that officially ended the Mexican War (1846–1848). The conflict lasted until the treaty was signed on February 2, 1848, in Guadalupe Hidalgo, a city in south central Mexico near Mexico City. The core of the treaty defined the ''Mexican Cession,'' the territory that Mexico was obliged to cede to the United States as a result of the war.

The Mexican War was the culmination of a series of conflicts between Mexico and the United States. These included the 1836 War of Independence of Texas from Mexico, the 1845 annexation of Texas by the United States, and the claims of United States citizens for monetary damages against the Mexican government. (A group of citizens of the United States claimed they had been injured and their property had been damaged during the civil strife that followed Mexico's 1821 war of national liberation against Spain.) In addition, the Mexican and U.S. governments disagreed over the southern boundary of Texas. The Mexicans contended that the Nueces River was the boundary, while the Texans claimed that the dividing line was further south and west, along the Rio Grande River. Another important source of conflict was the determination of the United States to acquire California. California was a Mexican province where, by 1845, about 700 United States citizens had settled. The United States claimed that if it did not annex California the territory might come under French or British rule.

To this must be added the racial and cultural tensions that developed between these mid-nineteenth century descendants of Spanish and English colonization.

Centuries of subjugation of Indian people by the Spanish had produced the rich cultural and racial amalgamation of the Mexican people. The Spanish influence was communicated through a network of Catholic missions that spanned what is now the southwestern United States. These Catholic missions were also centers of economic life. Gradually, as Mexico developed its own social structure, the Catholic missions were replaced as the focus of economic and social life by large *haciendas*, the seat of a nascent Mexican aristocracy.

This aristocracy of ranchers and farmers led the Mexican Revolution against the Spanish in 1821. After the revolution, in the interest of economic development of its northern, thinly settled provinces, the Mexican government invited settlers to Texas. The Mexican land-owners who were already there engaged in agriculture and ranching until the influx of Anglo-Americans in the 1830s and, in California, especially after the gold rush of 1849. This influx of North Americans turned out to be a disaster, not only for the Mexican nation during the Mexican-American War, but also for the individual Mexican land-owners in Texas and California. Their land was simply taken from them.

Thus it was with some sense of injured pride that Mexico broke off diplomatic relations with the United States when the U.S. annexed Texas in 1845. President James K. Polk (1794–1849) sent General Zachary Taylor (1784–1850) across the Nueces river to enforce U.S. claims on Texas' southern boundary. President Polk dispatched John Slidell, a Louisiana politician and trader, to accompany the invading army with instructions to purchase the land in dispute. He offered $5 million for New Mexico and $25 million for California. The Mexican government refused to discuss this proposal. As a result, General Zachary Taylor advanced to the mouth of the Rio Grande River, 120 miles south. The Mexican government sent troops across the Rio Grande saying that Taylor was engaged in an act of aggression. President Polk proclaimed that the Mexican army had invaded United States soil and, on May 13, 1846, Congress declared war on Mexico.

In a distinct improvement over their record during the War of 1812 (1812–1814), the armed forces of the United States performed well during the war. Contending with rugged terrain and logistical problems, the U.S. force of 14,000 prevailed over the Mexican military force. They occupied Mexico City in September, 1847.

In light of this military success President Polk began to set his sights on annexing all of Mexico. An obscure, low level U.S. agent, Nicolas Trist, scuttled this ambitious goal when he negotiated the treaty of Guadalupe-Hidalgo for the U.S. side. President Polk was outraged when he learned that Trist had secured only the original U.S. demands. Still in the Treaty of Guadalupe-Hidalgo Mexico lost nearly one million square miles of land—almost one-half of its territory. This territory, termed the ''Mexican Cession,'' included land that makes up the states of California, Nevada, New Mexico, Utah, Arizona, Texas, and parts of Colorado and Wyoming. The Mexican government received $15 million and the promise that the United States would settle all claims of its citizens against

Mexico. These claims amounted to more than $3 million. The Mexican citizens in this acquired territory were presumed to be legal U.S. citizens unless they vacated the area or registered as Mexican citizens within a one-year time frame. The treaty also granted the citizens in this area religious freedom, property, and civil rights. Article IX stated that Mexican citizens in this territory ''shall be incorporated into the United States of America, and admitted as soon as possible, according to the principles of the Federal Constitution, to the enjoyment of all the rights of citizens of the United States. In the meantime, they shall be maintained and protected in the enjoyment of their liberty and property, and the civil rights now vested in them according to the Mexican laws.''

In light of the delicate balance in Congress between the slave states and the wage-labor states, the acquisition of this land from Mexico re-kindled the debate in Congress over slavery. Southerners hoped to enlarge the territory that would enter the union as slave states. Anti-slavery northerners feared that very outcome. For that reason many northerners from both parties opposed the war with Mexico. The Mexican cession thus played a part in the nation's drift towards the Civil War.

See also: **Manifest Destiny, Sun Belt, Westward Expansion**

FURTHER READING

Hornblower, Margot. ''Northern Exposure.'' *Time*, March 6, 1995.

O'Rourke, David K. ''Our War with Mexico: Rereading Guadalupe Hidalgo.'' *Commonweal*, March 13, 1998.

Rodriguez, Roberto. ''Treaty of Guadalupe-Hidalgo under New Scrutiny.'' *Black Issues in Higher Education*, April 30, 1998.

Singletary, Otis A. *The Mexican War*. Chicago: University of Chicago Press, 1960.

MICHIGAN

Strategically located on four of the Great Lakes, the state of Michigan was carved out of the old Northwest Territory. Before the advent of good roads and waterways it was known as a remote, wild place full of dense forests. By the mid-1800s, however, when settlers cleared the land and began to make it habitable, Michigan represented what historian Bruce Catton called the ''great American feeling of being en route to the unknown, to something new.'' With a forested, still somewhat undeveloped area in the north, the state now owes much of its economic health to its own industrialized south, particularly to the automobile industry headquartered in Detroit.

In the 1600s the French were the earliest explorers of present-day Michigan, among them Etienne Brul and Jean Nicolet. Father Jacques Marquette established trading posts at Sault Ste. Marie and St. Ignace. Antoine Laumet de la Mothe Cadillac also established the settlement which later became Detroit. In this period Native Americans such as the Hurons, the Miamis, and the Potawatomis were important fur-trading partners with white settlers.

The fur trade, however, did not really encourage the growth of Detroit or Michigan. The area Ottawa chief, Pontiac, led several tribes in an uprising against the British. Pontiac's Conspiracy (1763) succeeded in capturing many British garrisons and the fort at Detroit, but as the Indian tribal alliance weakened the British were able to regain their holdings. The populace in what would later become Michigan sided with the British during the American Revolution (1775–1783), fearing that a massive influx of American settlers would destroy the fur trade as land was cleared for farming. Although Americans had nominal control of Michigan by terms of the Treaty of Paris after 1783, the British continued to occupy the territory for 13 years. A part of the new Northwest Territory, the region came into full U.S. possession in 1796.

IT IS NOT POSSIBLE TO TELL THE STORY OF [MICHIGAN] WITHOUT PUTTING THE INTERNAL COMBUSTION ENGINE, THE RUBBER TIRE, AND THE WHITE DESERT-RIBBONS OF THE CONCRETE HIGHWAY ON TO THE CENTER OF THE STAGE.

Bruce Catton, *Michigan: A Bicentennial History*, 1976

During the War of 1812 (1812–1814) the region became a center of battles between the Americans and British, who refused to accept American sovereignty over the area. The territory was finally in the hands of the United States in 1814. The opening of the Erie Canal in 1825 marked the beginning of a push to settle southern Michigan territory by allowing an inexpensive, convenient route from New York City to Michigan. As the fur trade diminished, so did the value of the Native Americans to the non-indigenous population, and gradually most Indian lands were ceded to the federal government. A few tribes stayed on reservations within the territory. Following the ''Toledo War''

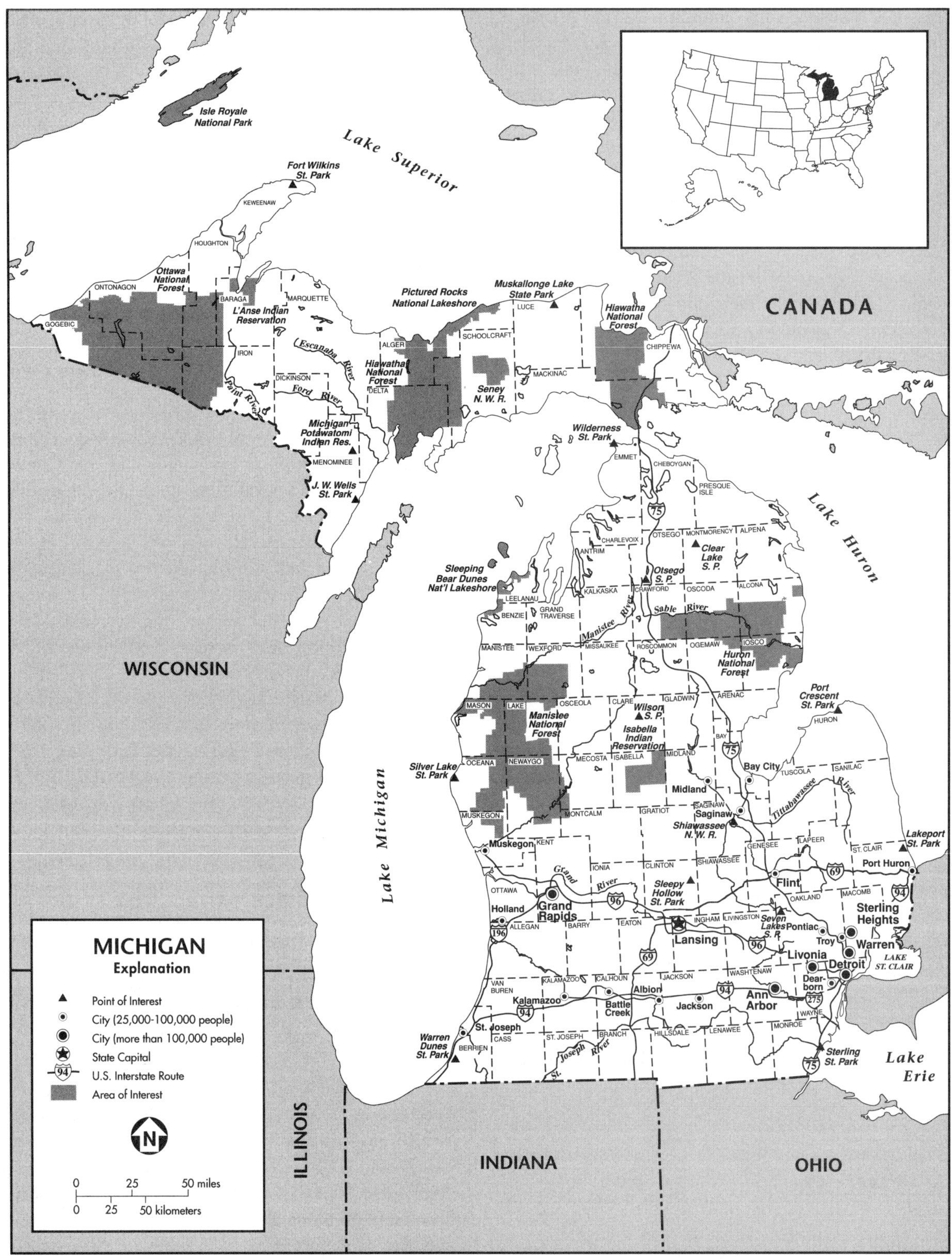

State of Michigan.

of 1835, (which settled the question of whether Toledo would be part of Michigan or Ohio) Michigan territory was granted the upper peninsula in exchange for land that it had claimed in northern Ohio. Michigan was granted statehood in 1837.

As the fur traders had feared, farmers soon began to clear land in Michigan. By 1850, 85 percent of the population in the lower peninsula was dependent on farming in some way. Soon northern areas of Michigan were also being exploited for their vast timber supplies, as well as for their rich mineral deposits. Millions of tons of iron ore were extracted near Marquette and Houghton in the upper peninsula, and copper was mined on the Keweenaw Peninsula. The transportation of iron ore and copper to markets in south Michigan and development of the rest of the country was facilitated by the opening of a canal in 1855 to bypass rapids at Sault Ste. Marie.

At first transportation routes in the state were primarily on Lakes Michigan, Superior, Huron, and Erie, each of which touched Michigan. The first railroad was chartered in Michigan in 1830, but until after the American Civil War (1861–1865), railroad construction was slow in the state compared to other states. Until automobiles came into widespread use in the 1920s, many interurban lines connected cities in southern Michigan. In fact, most mass transportation was decimated by the advent of the automobile until public transit systems began to make a comeback in the 1970s with the help of the federal government. A boon to transportation in the state was the opening of the Mackinac Bridge in 1957, connecting the lower and upper peninsulas. In addition, the St. Lawrence Seaway, opened in 1959, brought many oceangoing ships to Michigan ports.

As timber and minerals began to be depleted in the late nineteenth century, industry took on new importance in the state. The city of Battle Creek became the center of the cereal industry with the establishment of the Post and Kellogg companies. Dow Chemical and Upjohn also became major producers of chemicals and drugs during this period. Grand Rapids produced furniture, and Kalamazoo had paper mills.

However, the automobile industry became the real lifeblood of Michigan. Just after the turn of the century the first ''horseless carriage'' in the state was produced by Ransom E. Olds, followed by the first Cadillac and the first Ford. William Durant made General Motors a success; Henry Ford produced the first Model T in 1908 and introduced the first assembly line several years later. The Chrysler Corporation was established in 1925.

As more and more people bought new automobiles, more concrete highways were being built, producing an even higher demand for automobiles. In the 1930s, however, when the nation's economy collapsed during the Great Depression (1929–1939), over half of Michigan's factory workers were unemployed. This desperate situation, along with ineffective management by Republicans at the state and national levels, helped to precipitate the rise of labor unions in the state. In 1936–1937 the massive sit-down strike staged by the United Auto Workers (UAW), an affiliate of the Congress of Industrial Organizations (CIO), signaled the growing strength of unions in the auto industry. By 1941 the UAW had organized the entire industry and the state, as a whole, had become pro-union. The population of Michigan, moreover, was increasingly centered in its cities, primarily in Detroit and the southern part of the state. As industry took over the economy, the northern two-thirds of the state lost population and became increasingly economically depressed.

Due to the strong influence of unions in Michigan, politics was dominated by the Democratic party, until Republicans captured the state House in 1962. They held on to power until 1982, when Michigan was seized with a serious recession, causing more than 15 percent unemployment in the state. The recession's effect on the auto industry was devastating. American car makers had not foreseen that the public was losing interest in large, gas-hungry vehicles. In addition, Japanese car companies were making serious inroads into the American car market. The Chrysler Corporation was granted a $1.2 billion federal grant to avoid bankruptcy in 1979, thousands of autoworkers left the state, and many auto-related industries closed their doors. The state's tax base was reduced, causing massive reductions in the state budget in 1983.

This downturn, of course, was due to the state's heavy dependence on the auto industry. By the late 1980s, as the industry slowly began to recover, attempts were being made to diversify the economy. The number of factory workers dropped by 30 percent in the ten years after 1970, while new jobs were created in the engineering and technology fields as companies turned to more automation. At the same time, the service and wholesale-retail sectors began to grow. The state government, General Motors, and the UAW all applied significant funds to job retraining programs. Still, by the mid-1990s, the manufacture of transportation equipment was still the most important industry in Michigan; 28 percent of all U.S. automobiles were still being produced in the state, but the unemployment rate was decreasing steadily.

Despite the economic ups and downs that the state had experienced, it remained a favorable location for workers. Strong labor unions, which count over 24 percent of all workers and 34 percent of factory workers as members, have kept wages and benefits high. The per capita income in 1996 was nearly $25,000, ranking Michigan sixteenth among all states. Next to manufacturing, agriculture is the most important sector of the economy, ranking 20th in the nation in income. Attractions such as the Great Lakes, inland lakes and forests, and historic sites such as Dearborn's Henry Ford Museum and Greenfield Village also make tourism very important to the economy of Michigan.

See also: **Automobile Industry, Chrysler Corporation, William Durant, Erie Canal, Henry Ford, General Motors, Model T**

FURTHER READING

Bald, F.C. *Michigan in Four Centuries*, rev. ed. New York: Harper and Row, 1961.

Catton, Bruce. *Michigan: A Bicentennial History*. New York: Norton, 1976.

Dunbar, Willis F., and George S. May. *Michigan: A History of the Wolverine State*, 3rd rev. ed. Grand Rapids, MI: Wm. B. Eerdmans Publishing Co., 1995.

Fuller, George N., ed. *Michigan: A Centennial History of the State*. 5 vols. Chicago: Lewis, 1939.

Rubenstein, Bruce A. *Michigan, A History of the Great Lakes State*. Wheeling, IL: Harlan Davidson, 1995.

MICROSOFT CORPORATION

Microsoft Corporation, the world's largest software developer, began in 1975 as a partnership between two young men, William H. Gates, 19, and Paul Allen, 21. Gates was a sophomore at Harvard University and Allen was employed by Honeywell when they saw a mockup of the Micro Instrumentation and Telemetry Systems (MITS) Altair, the first personal computer, pictured on the cover of *Popular Electronics*. They decided to write a BASIC Interpreter for the Altair and demonstrate it to MITS, which was located in Albuquerque, New Mexico. It was the first computer language program written for a personal computer.

In July 1975 Microsoft signed a contract with MITS that allowed the hardware company to use and market the BASIC software but Microsoft retained ownership of the computer language. It was a contractual relationship between a software developer and a hardware manufacturer that became a model for future software licensing agreements. Allen joined MITS as its director of software development.

By the end of 1976 Gates had dropped out of Harvard and had four programmers working for Microsoft in New Mexico. Allen left MITS in November and in March 1977 Allen and Gates formed an official partnership. Believing that microcomputers would grow in popularity, Gates set about convincing large corporations of the industry's future, licensing BASIC to Fortune 500 companies such as General Electric, NCR, and Citibank, among others. Microsoft licensed BASIC for the newly introduced Apple II, Radio Shack's Tandy computer, and the Commodore PET and TRS-80. It also began selling single copies of BASIC.

Microsoft then developed two other programming languages, FORTRAN (1977) and COBOL (1978), for the control program of microcomputer CP/M, which was one of several operating systems then available. Several hardware firms chose CP/M machines for their new computers and Microsoft became the leading distributor for microcomputer languages. In 1978 Microsoft had revenues of $1.4 million and 13 employees.

On January 1, 1979, Microsoft moved its offices to Bellevue, Washington (Allen and Gates were both Seattle natives), becoming the first microcomputer software company in the Northwest. Having recently established an international sales office in Japan called ASCII Microsoft, the company began working closely with NEC and other international computer manufacturers in the development of their products. By the end of the year Microsoft expanded its service to Europe. International sales would prove to be a significant source of revenue to the company over the years.

In 1980 the company had revenues of $7.5 million and 40 employees. Steve Ballmer, who had formerly worked with Proctor and Gamble, was hired as Gates's first assistant. He had the responsibility of establishing policies and procedures in the financial, organizational, and resource allocation areas. Meanwhile microcomputer technology was growing rapidly and with each new advance Microsoft was there to provide a computer language. It furnished versions of BASIC and FORTRAN for Intel's new 16-bit chip and developed a soft card for the Apple II, the top-selling microcomputer at the time, that enabled it to use CP/M and Microsoft BASIC. This was Microsoft's first hardware product.

In 1980 IBM decided to enter the microcomputer market, and it hired Microsoft to develop a computer

An aerial view of the Microsoft Corporation world headquarters in Redmond, Washington.

language and operating system for its machines, which were introduced to the public in 1981 as the IBM Personal Computer (PC). The operating system used for the IBM-PC was called MS-DOS, short for Disk Operating System. It would become an international industry standard, eventually replacing the CP/M operating system.

In 1981 Microsoft reorganized as a privately held corporation called Microsoft, Inc., with Gates as president and chairman and Allen as executive vice president. After recovering from a lengthy illness Allen would leave Microsoft in 1983. Meanwhile Steve Jobs and Apple had developed a revolutionary new microcomputer, the Macintosh. Microsoft became the first major company to develop products for the Macintosh when it was introduced to the public in 1984.

The microcomputer market began to explode in the early 1980s. The entry of IBM changed the image of microcomputers from that of a hobbyist's toy to a serious business machine. Microsoft's revenues jumped from $24.5 million in 1982 to $50.1 million in 1983 to $97.5 million in 1984, and the growth would continue in the coming years. In 1983 Microsoft introduced its first mouse, its first full-featured word processing program, Word, and Windows. Windows extended the features of MS-DOS by providing users with a graphical user interface (GUI). Although IBM would not adopt Windows for its interface, Gates convinced many manufacturers of IBM-compatible computers to adopt Windows. Retail versions of Windows became available two years later. During that year Gates met Jon Shirley, formerly with Tandy Corporation, and hired him to join Microsoft as president and chief operating officer.

Microsoft went public in 1986 after moving its headquarters to a new corporate campus in Redmond, Washington. With shares introduced at $21, the initial public offering raised $61 million. A year later, Microsoft shares were trading around $85, making Gates a billionaire at age 31. During 1987 Microsoft introduced several new products, including Windows 2.0, Microsoft Bookshelf on CD-ROM, the spreadsheet program Excel for Windows, and a new operating system jointly developed with IBM called MS OS/2. In 1988 Microsoft inched past rival Lotus Development Corporation to become the number one software vendor.

Microsoft's revenues surpassed the one-billion-dollar mark in 1990, with international sales accounting for more than half of that. The company had more than 5,600 employees. During that year Microsoft introduced Windows 3.0 with its largest marketing campaign in the company's history to date. Within a year Microsoft shipped four million copies to 24 countries in 12 languages. By 1993 there were more than 25 million registered users. Microsoft was also branching out into other areas of software, including desktop publishing and network servers, and the Federal Trade Commission (FTC) began investigating the company for possible anti-trust law violations.

In 1992 Microsoft created a three-person office of the president to replace Michael Hallman, who resigned as president after one year. The three members of the office were Mike Maples, head of the Worldwide Product Group; Steve Ballmer, head of Worldwide Sales and Support Group; and Frank Gaudette, head of Worldwide Operations Group. Gates was also recognized this year when he was awarded the National Medal of Technology for Technological Achievement by President George Bush (1989–1993).

Microsoft shipped several new products in 1993, including the network operating system Windows NT, MS-DOS 6.0, Microsoft Mouse 2.0, software for children, and Encarta, the first multimedia encyclopedia designed for a computer. In June the last copyright infringement claims made against Microsoft by Apple were dismissed, settling a lawsuit begun in 1988. *Fortune* magazine named Microsoft the ''1993 Most Innovative Company Operating in the United States.'' Revenues for the year were $3.75 billion, and the company had more than 14,000 employees.

Microsoft celebrated the release of Windows 95 in August 1995 with several special events. More than one million copies were sold to retail customers in the first four days. Toward the end of the year Gates detailed Microsoft's commitment to supporting and enhancing the Internet by integrating it with the PC platform. In November the final version of the Microsoft web browser Internet Explorer 2.0 for Windows 95 was released and made widely available for downloading at no charge to licensed users of Windows 95. Revenues for 1995 were $5.9 billion, and the company had about 17,800 employees.

As the world embarked on the information superhighway in 1996 Microsoft was committed to providing a full range of tools for both Internet and intranet publishing. In January it acquired Vermeer Technologies, Inc., whose main product was FrontPage, a tool for creating and managing Web pages without programming. The company made several organizational changes during that year, creating an interactive media division to focus on interactive entertainment and information products and an executive committee to replace the office of the president. In July 1996 MSNBC, a 24-hour news and information cable network, debuted as the result of a joint venture between Microsoft and NBC News. MSN, the Microsoft Network, was reorganized to offer content on the World Wide Web.

During 1997 Microsoft strengthened its commitment to Internet services by acquiring WebTV Networks for $425 million in stock and cash and releasing Internet Explorer 4.0. WebTV allowed consumers to access the Internet through their television sets. During the year Microsoft also purchased 11.5 percent of the cable company Comcast Corporation for a cost of $1 billion. The company also announced an alliance with struggling Apple Computers and purchased a $150 million stake, giving Apple much-needed financial support. Microsoft's revenues for 1997 were $11.4 billion, and the company had more than 22,000 employees.

Microsoft again came under the scrutiny of the U.S. Department of Justice and in October 1997 the firm was charged with violating a 1994 consent decree. One of the key issues was Microsoft's bundling of its Internet Explorer with Windows, which competitors such as Netscape and Sun Microsystems considered anti-competitive and monopolistic. Informational hearings were held before a congressional committee, and the case went to trial in 1998.

In 1998 Microsoft acquired several Internet-related companies, including Hotmail, a free e-mail service that would become a component of MSN, and Firefly, an Internet start-up that had developed software to give users customized Web site views and protect their privacy. The company's long-awaited reorganization was announced in March 1999. The company was divided into five major groups to better reflect its core customers: 1) a new consumer and commerce group including MSN.com and Internet properties; 2) the business enterprise division; 3) the consumer Windows division; 4) a new business productivity group; and 5) a separate home and retail products division for consumer-targeted products such as games, input devices, and reference products. A new 14-member team to be led by Gates was formed to replace the smaller executive committee.

See also: **Computer Industry, William Gates, Internet**

FURTHER READING

Gates, Bill. *Business and the Speed of Thought.* New York: Warner Books, 1999.

———. *The Road Ahead.* New York: Viking Penguin, 1996.

Gross, Daniel. ''William Gates and the Dominance of Microsoft.'' *Forbes Greatest Business Stories of All Time.* New York: John Wiley and Sons, 1996.

Ichbiah, Daniel, and Susan L. Knepper. *The Making of Microsoft*. Rocklin, CA: Prima, 1991.

''Microsoft Buys Hotmail for MSN,'' *InfoWorld*, January 5, 1998.

Rogers, Danny. ''The World of Gates.'' *Marketing*, August 14, 1997.

Schlender, Brent. ''Bill Gates and Paul Allen Talk.'' *Fortune*, October 2, 1995.

MIDDLE PASSAGE

Middle Passage is a term from the colonial slave trade. It refers to the trans-Atlantic journey millions of black Africans were forced to make from Africa's west coast to the Caribbean, where they were sold to plantation owners. The trip was called the Middle Passage because it was the middle leg of the trade triangles that had developed early during the colonial period. These routes were established in the early 1500s by the Spanish and Portuguese, who imported slaves from Africa to work on sugar plantations in the New World. Early in the next century the English, French, and Dutch also began using slave labor in their American colonies.

The Middle Passage was a brutal trip which often lasted several months. Because the slaves were viewed as little more than a commodity, captains would often carry as many as their ships would hold. Conditions were deplorable: Slaves were transported in chains, cramped quarters, and filth. They were not provided with adequate food or exercise, and many died at sea. How many people endured the atrocities of the Middle Passage is unknown. Most estimates place the number at about 10 million. Of that total, an estimated six percent were shipped to the North American mainland.

In 1833 the great antislavery movement in Great Britain reached culmination in the abolition of slavery throughout the British colonies. In the United States the slave trade was prohibited in 1808, but possessing slaves was still legal—and profitable. Illegal trade in slaves continued until Britain stepped up the enforcement of its antislavery law. Britain conducted naval blockades and surprise raids off the African coast, and effectively closed the trade. Slavery officially came to an end after 1870, when it was outlawed throughout the Americas.

See also: **Abolition, Slavery, Triangular Trade**

MIGRANT WORKERS

Migrant workers are simply persons whose work routine includes relocation across or within national boundaries on a fairly frequent basis. They usually work at temporary jobs. Often they are seasonal workers employed in the agricultural sector of the economy. In that case the demand for their labor is determined by the growing cycles, as in the case of Mexican farm workers. For decades these workers—called *braceros*—moved across national borders in routine violation of laws that authorities largely overlooked because of the need for their labor. Migrant workers may also be non-seasonal, highly paid workers called upon to do highly skilled or particularly dangerous work like putting out oil derrick fires. They may be the combine crews in the Great Plains, moving south to north, harvesting the wheat as it ripens. Or they may be the thousands of tradesmen of various descriptions who follow the building boom from one part of the country to another.

On the other hand, ''Okies,'' people from Oklahoma who left their farms in the dust storms of the 1920s and 1930s and made the trek to California, were workers who were migrating, rather than migrant workers. Immigrant Turkish workers in Germany—living and working for years in the host country without ever breaking from the Turkish culture—are also not migrant workers. Nor are workers in the transportation industry. Airline stewardesses and truck drivers are not migrant workers even though moving about defines the job that they do.

The United States experienced the largest influx of immigrant workers between 1890 and 1914 when 15 million foreign citizens entered the country, mostly from eastern and southern Europe. In the history of American immigration, approximately one-third of these immigrant workers moved back to their home or on to other countries—''birds of passage,'' in the colorful words of one immigration historian. If these workers were seeking permanent employment they were immigrant workers, rather than migrant workers.

Migrant workers, like other workers, stimulate the economy in two ways. First, they take hard, undesirable, low wage jobs, thereby minimizing the employers' costs. Second, they buy things and increase the size of the consumer population, thereby increasing demand. At the same time, jealousy and fear sometimes separates migrant workers from other Americans who objected that jobs were being lost to the newly available cheap labor.

See also: **Cesar Chavez, Anti-Immigration Laws, Immigration, United Farm Workers**

FURTHER READING

Bailyn, Bernard et al. *The Great Republic: A History of the American People*. Lexington, Massachusetts & Toronto: D.C. Heath and Company, 1981.

Johnson, Paul. *A History of the American People*. New York: HarperCollins Publishers, 1997.

Ketchum, Richard M. *The Borrowed Years 1938–1941: America on the Way to War*. New York: Random House, 1989.

Manchester, William. *The Glory and the Dream: A Narrative History of America 1932–1972*. New York: Bantam Books, 1974.

The Oxford Companion to World War II. Oxford and New York: Oxford University Press, 1995.

MILITARY INDUSTRIAL COMPLEX *(ISSUE)*

Is the relationship between the armed forces and the industries that provide them with weapons a safeguard or a threat to world peace and the American democracy? Perhaps no other issue has raised as much concern over the coalescence between economic and political forces as the military-industrial complex, which today has formed a matrix of government spending, foreign initiatives, and ideological commitments.

In 1948 President Harry S. Truman (1945–1953) submitted the second largest peacetime budget in American history to Congress, justifying it as necessary to meet the threat of totalitarianism in the world. The budget came to $39.6 billion, with around $18 billion earmarked for military spending and international affairs. Such spending created a new industry in the United States devoted to the production of weapons for the Pentagon. This industry, which became known as the military-industrial complex, became one of the largest industries in the United States and a crucial part of the economy. In a pattern similar to World War II (1939–1945) mobilization, entire corporations were supported solely by government spending. Unlike World War II, however, there was no end in sight. As long as the Soviet Union continued to exist there was a reason for military spending, even during peacetime.

Within the government, the voices of both private business and the military have only grown stronger since the turn of the century. While on the eve of World War II the relationship between the two was often one-sided and seemed perpetually set against one another, by the 1970s private business and the military developed a formal and comfortable relationship of mutual support. Since the 1950s especially, military calls upon national resources have vastly increased and, for the most part, leading corporations have been the principal beneficiaries of that demand. While payrolls, research grants, and political influence were large enough to ensure a consensus for the system during the mid- to late-twentieth century the whole complex has been underwritten by a popular and almost unassailable anticommunist ideology. But some conservatives fear that the military-industrial complex keeps military spending at a level higher than that dictated by the strict needs of national defense. They claim it leads to economic dislocation at home and dangerous tensions abroad, and that the separate parts of the military-industrial complex will prove to be countervailing forces.

> American makers of plowshares could, with time and as required, make swords as well. But now we can no longer risk emergency improvisation of national defense; we have been compelled to create a permanent armaments industry of vast proportions . . . . Yet we must not fail to comprehend its grave implications. Our toil, resources and livelihood are all involved; so is the very structure of our society.
>
> **President Dwight D. Eisenhower, Farewell Address, January 17, 1961**

While the conjunction between economic and political forces may have been new during the Truman and Eisenhower eras, its roots lay deep in the mandates of Progressive reform which attempted early in the century to rationalize the U.S. economic system and integrate it with public policy. Even so, it was not until World War I that close ties among the military, the civilian government, and businessmen were formalized. Between 1914 to 1916, the federal government's efforts to mobilize people, raw materials, production plants, and transportation proved slow and incompetent. In August 1916, the task of planning mobilization was entrusted to the Council of National Defense (CND), which worked through the National Defense Advisory Commission (NDAC). In 1917, the CND was replaced by the War Industries Board (WIB) and under its auspices American industry was organized into commodity committees. These committees set prices, priorities, allocations, and other controls and mobilized under their own rules. Meanwhile, the military was torn by its own internal conflicts and competition and was in no position to plan the civilian economy. While business was organized along commodity lines, the military was organized along operational lines, and the two proved to be opposing. Answerable to neither a central planning agency within the military nor to the WIB, each military branch entered the market with large orders geared toward its own needs, plus necessary surpluses. In 1918, Bernard Baruch (1870–1965) took over the leadership of the WIB and was given enough authority to force the cooperation of the military. Throughout the rest of World War I, businessmen and military leaders worked closely, and usually harmoniously, to fill the needs of the wartime economy.

During the inter-war years the military and business leaders met regularly to draw up plans for economic mobilization in case of war. Meanwhile, the government facilitated coordination between the two and left military tactics to the military and the economy to business leaders. The result was a series of industrial mobilization plans drawn up between 1930 and 1939. In the end, the military realized the degree to which it was dependent on the cooperation and capacity of business for the materials it needed, while business became more aware of what the present and future needs of the military might be for supplies of all types. In 1933, President Franklin D. Roosevelt's (1933–1945) attempt to plan for economic recovery after the Great Depression adapted the scheme of the WIB for his short- lived New Deal program, the National Industrial Recovery Administration.

In 1940, the coming of actual mobilization after so many years of planning, unleashed a torrent of expenditures that dwarfed those of both World War I and the New Deal. Altogether, some $315.8 billion was spent during the war, with the War Department accounting for $179.9 billion and the Navy Department for $83.9 billion. In the end, a vastly inflated program of government spending and its heavy concentration in a few large corporations, like General Motors, Ford Motor Company, Chrysler Corporation, Bethlehem Steel, General Electric, United States Steel, Du Pont Chemical, and AT&T became the standard policy for the wartime economy.

As World War II was winding down, the alliance between the Soviet Union and the United States, brought together by a common foe, Adolph Hitler (1889–1945), was deteriorating. Tensions between the two nations had existed since the Russian Revolution of 1917, and within a few years after World War II the two powers were engaged in a Cold War. But while the government had been involved in coordinating a mutually supportive relationship between the military and business during World War I and World War II, the Cold War dramatically changed this policy. The policy of "containment" committed the United States to a peacetime military-industrial complex for the first time in American history. For the next 45 years there would continue to be a large standing army with inflated defense expenditures, and large corporations supplying the equipment and supplies.

But with the coming of the Cold War, many leading military and industrial leaders who had previously enjoyed a highly successful and lucrative wartime system of military-civilian cooperation during World War II, sought to preserve these advantages in the demobilization period. During World War II, both groups had kept one eye focused on the postwar period. In the military the desire to keep up budgets and the desire of the Army Air Corps for independent status fueled the arguments that the country should never again find itself unprepared for hostilities, and that the country was bound to honor new and global peacekeeping responsibilities.

Continuing the cooperation that existed between the military and civilian businesses during World War II was considered necessary to meet these new global peacekeeping responsibilities. The nation's new course began with careful consideration to the potential pitfalls. President Dwight D. Eisenhower (1953–1961) cautioned in his farewell address (1961) that though it was important for the country to have a strong national defense in times of peace as in times of war, the development of a military-industrial complex was not without its dangers. "In the councils of government, we must guard against the acquisition of unwarranted influence, whether sought or unsought, by the military-industrial complex. The potential for the disastrous rise of misplaced power exists and will persist."

For the next three decades after World War II, huge military spending and a closely linked program of foreign aid combined to prime the pump of U.S. prosperity as no combination of domestic social programs had ever been able to do. Military expenditures ranged from $37 billion in the mid-1950s to just over $79.1 billion in 1969. The bulk of spending was done directly by the military for research and material and certain large firms were the beneficiaries of the funds. In 1969, Lockheed Aircraft Corporation received the largest single share, more than $2 billion, McDonnell Douglas with $1 billion and General Electric with $1.6 billion.

The Vietnam War (1964–1975) brought orders rolling in as the Air Force and Navy sought to replace planes damaged in combat, marking a peak in aerospace production. The industry had its share of valleys as well. Erratic defense budgets saw sudden buildups during the Korean War (1950–1953) and after the Sputnik launch, but just as sudden drops occurred in the mid-1950s and directly before the Vietnam War (1964–1975).

The scientific component of military technology had also grown significantly since World War II. The closer relationship between the military and business was paralleled by a similar closeness with scientists mostly housed in the big universities. By 1961 some 77 percent of all government spending for research and development was coming from the military.

In the 1990s, contrary to initial expectations, the military-industrial complex survived the end of the Cold War. It reorganized itself with a series of military-industry mergers encouraged and subsidized by the administration of President Bill Clinton (1993–). The "Big Three" weapons makers—Lockheed Martin, Boeing, and Raytheon—aquired a total of $25 to $38 billion in Pentagon contracts in the mid to late 1990s. If they continue to receive federal monies, these new military-industrial companies will earn billions more in the years to come. The Clinton administration's five-year budget plan for the Pentagon calls for a 50 percent increase in weapons procurement, from $40 billion per year in 1989 to over $60 billion per year by 2003.

How best to defend the United States in the post-Cold War period remains a hotly debated topic. Some critics argue that on issue after issue—from expanding NATO, to deploying the Star Wars missile defense system, to rolling back restrictions on arms sales to foreign regimes—the arms industry has launched a concerted lobbying campaign aimed at increasing military spending and arms exports. They argue that these initiatives are driven by profit and pork barrel politics. Others claim that these measures are forward-looking and will create a safer, more democratic world.

***See also:* Cold War, Vietnam War, War Industries Board, World War I, World War II**

FURTHER READING

Koistinen, Paul A. C. "The 'Industrial-Military Complex' in Historical Perspective: World War I," in *Business History Review*, vol. 41 (Winter 1967).

———. "The 'Industrial-Military Complex' in Historical Perspective: The Interwar Years," in *Journal of American History*, vol. 56 (March 1970).

———. "Mobilizing the World War II Economy: Labor and the Industrial-Military Alliance," in *Pacific Historical Review*, vol. 42 (Nov. 1973).

Melman, Seymour. *Pentagon Capitalism*. New York: McGraw-Hill, 1970.

Pursell, Carroll W., Jr., ed. *The Military Industrial Complex*. New York: Harper and Row, 1972.

MINIMUM WAGE LAW

A minimum wage law is a piece of legislation that prevents businesses from hiring workers for hourly wages that fall below a specified level. The first minimum wage laws were passed in Australia and New Zealand in the 1890s. In 1912 Massachusetts became the first U.S. state to pass a minimum wage law, and in 1918 Congress authorized the Wage Board to set minimum wage levels for female workers in the District of Columbia. Five years later, however, the U.S. Supreme Court ruled in *Adkins v. Children's Hospital* (1924) that minimum wage laws violated the Fifth Amendment of the Constitution because they infringed on the freedom of businesses and workers to form contracts as they saw fit. The three dissenting justices claimed that Congress did have the constitutional power to correct social injustices. In 1933 in the depths of the Great Depression (1929–1939), President Franklin D. Roosevelt (1933–1945) convinced Congress to pass the National Industrial Recovery Act (NIRA), which gave the newly formed National Recovery Administration (NRA) the authority to establish national minimum wages. Although several states had passed minimum wage laws by the mid-1930s hope for a lasting federal law seemed doomed when the Supreme Court ruled in 1935 that the NRA was unconstitutional.

Two years later, the Supreme Court unexpectedly reversed its decision and gave states the constitutional right to establish minimum wage laws, setting the stage for the Fair Labor Standards Act (FLSA) of 1938. The FLSA set the national minimum wage at 40 cents an hour, an amount that was increased in 1949, 1956, 1961, 1968, 1974, 1991, 1996, and 1997. The 1997 increase brought the minimum wage to $5.15, which was estimated to affect about 10 million U.S. workers. Some economists have argued that minimum wage laws have an unintended negative effect on the employment rates of the poorest segments of society, many of whom are minorities. These critics argue that raising minimum wage rates encourages businesses to rely more and more on automation to reduce their labor costs, which discourages them from hiring unskilled workers who might otherwise find jobs if the minimum wage were lower.

See also: **Fair Labor Standards Act, National Recovery Administration**

MINNESOTA

The highly publicized 1998 election of Reform Party candidate Jesse Ventura to the governor's seat came as no surprise to those who had studied Minnesota history. With a long tradition of protest politics and a disdain for power monopolies, the state has always steered an independent course. Situated in the heart of the American prairie and supplied with many natural resources, Minnesota was able to parlay its independent spirit into great economic success. From its wheat fields to its iron ore ranges and timber lands to its large industrial belts, Minnesota represented the economic diversity to which most of the country aspired.

Europeans who first came into the territory that is now Minnesota were witness to numerous confrontations between the Dakota and Ojibwa Indians who inhabited the territory. In the mid-1600s French explorers, fur traders, and missionaries sent back the first reports from the region. American and British explorers also came to the area, vying with the French for influence. After the French and Indian War (1754–1763) the part of Minnesota east of the Mississippi was ceded to Great Britain. In 1762 France ceded the land west of the river to Spain. British activity in the region continued until the U.S. Congress banned British fur trade there after the War of 1812 (1812–1814). The American Fur Company headed by John Jacob Astor (1763–1848) replaced a British company at Grand Portage, a center for inland trade.

FROM OUT OF THE PAST OF EXPLORATION AND EXPLOITATION, OUT OF BOOM AND BUST TIMES, OUT OF THE EXPERIENCES OF PIONEERS AND IMMIGRANTS, AND OUT OF THE HERITAGE OF INDUSTRIALIZATION AND THE TRADITION OF PROTEST POLITICS HAS COME THE MINNESOTA THAT IS NOW.

William E. Lass, *Minnesota: A Bicentennial History*, 1977

The eastern part of Minnesota (east of the Mississippi) became part of the Northwest Territory in 1787. Most of the western part of the territory was acquired by the United States through the Louisiana Purchase in 1803. The Red River Valley was ceded by a treaty with England in 1818. The American Fur Company continued to prosper on the upper Mississippi until treaties with the Ojibwa and Dakota Indians transferred large parcels of their land to the federal government in 1837. Unlike pioneer settlers fur traders had developed a profitable partnership with the Indians, one which was threatened by this action. The treaties opened up the territory to lumbering, farming, and settlement. Settlements such as Marine and Stillwater on the St. Croix River and St. Anthony (later Minneapolis) sprang up around the lumbering industry. St. Paul was a trading center at the head of the Mississippi.

In 1849 Minnesota became a territory, and by 1857 it had more than 150,000 inhabitants. It became the 32nd state of the Union in 1858. Minnesota supported the Union in the American Civil War (1861–1865). But during that period the state faced a more serious internal challenge from disgruntled Dakota Indians who waged a war on white settlers in 1862. Following the pattern of white western conquest both the Dakotas and the Ojibwas were eventually moved to reservations.

The first railroad joined St. Paul and St. Anthony, a flour-milling center, in 1862. Later rail routes connected the state with Chicago and the Red River Valley. Immigrants from the east and from northern Europe, especially Scandinavia and Germany, started coming to Minnesota in great numbers. They established farms and grew produce that was carried back east on the trains. Large-scale farming developed along with small farms, particularly for the wheat crop; 70 percent of all farms were planted with wheat by 1870.

Farmers suffered occasional natural disasters such as drought. They felt themselves injured also by high railroad rates and a general deflation. Agrarian discontent became part of the tradition of protest politics in the state. The National Grange of the Patrons of Husbandry was the first national farmers' organization which had its origins in Minnesota beginning in 1867. It had great influence on state politics in the 1880s. In 1890 another farm-oriented activist party called the Populists (or People's Party) helped elect John Lind Governor of Minnesota. Labor organizing was also strong in this period. As the Minnesota Federation of Labor gained power it succeeded in getting a landmark Workmen's Compensation Act passed in 1913. This laid the groundwork for the Farmer-Labor Party.

Aside from third parties the so-called Progressive Movement had other manifestations in Minnesota. Rural residents feared the power of big business, especially the railroad industry. An angry public outcry was heard in 1901 when railroad barons James J. Hill

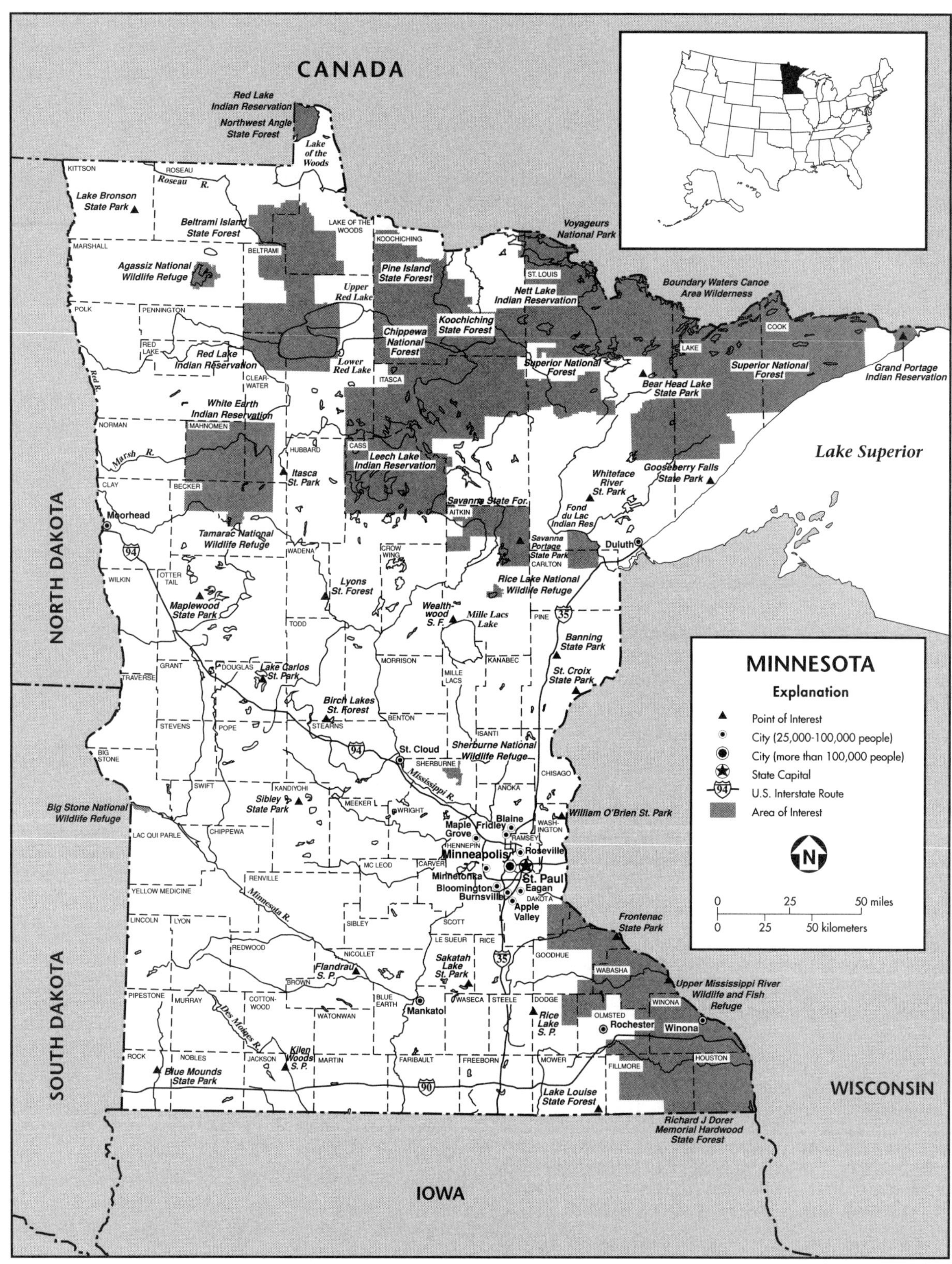

State of Minnesota.

(1838–1916) and Edward Harriman, with help from banker J. P. Morgan (1837–1913), formed the Northern Securities Company. The company merged the Northern Pacific, Great Northern, and Chicago and Burlington railroads, virtually monopolizing railroads in the state. Governor Samuel Van Sant had his attorney general sue the company and led other Midwest governors in condemning the company. When President Theodore Roosevelt (1901–1909) instituted a federal suit against the company in his first action as a "trust-buster," the Northern Securities Company was broken up.

The lumbering industry in Minnesota prospered greatly in the decades following the American Civil War. It reached a peak in 1899. As it shipped some of the logs by rail and even more by water down the Mississippi, Minnesota supplied tons of lumber to the country, particularly the growing areas of the Great Plains states. Minneapolis became a sawmill center. In combination with flour mills and railroads sawmills helped the city's population swell to well over 150,000 by 1890. The combined population of Minneapolis and its "twin city" St. Paul grew to over 250,000. Lumber was also shipped from Duluth, which owed its prosperity to its position at the starting point of the North Pacific Railroad.

Duluth also became a major Lake Superior port after the discovery of iron ore in the northeast Mesabi and Vermilion ranges. After the 1880s eastern cities and industries began to grow. After a short boost to the economy produced by World War I (1914–1918) an economic downturn afflicted the state. Since Minnesota forests had been depleted of their resources lumbering shifted to the Pacific Northwest. An agricultural depression also caused several flour mills to move to Kansas City and Buffalo, New York.

Minnesotans adapted to the changes by planting corn, soybeans, and sugar beets in addition to the traditional wheat crop. Canning and meat packing had become important industries in the early part of the twentieth century; by the late part of the century food processing plants such as Green Giant, Libby, Del Monte, and General Foods shipped more manufactured products than any other industry in the state.

Like the rest of the nation Minnesota was plunged into a depression in the 1930s. The governor during this period was Floyd B. Olson, a reform politician who championed the poor farmers and laborers and supported the policies of President Franklin D. Roosevelt (1933–1945). This period marked the first time that Minnesota departed from a nearly unbroken history of Republican domination. In 1944 the populist Farmer-Labor Party merged with the Democrats and began a new chapter of reform in Minnesota under the leadership of Hubert H. Humphrey (1911–1973). Humphrey would later become Mayor of Minneapolis, U.S. senator, and vice president.

In the ensuing decades other manufactured products like business machines, computers, and electronic components added to the state's economic base. After the high-grade iron ore produced by the state was depleted new processes were instituted to extract iron from low-grade ore. This caused concern about environmental damage to Lake Superior. A sign of the changing demographics in the state was that the urban population of Minnesota exceeded its rural population for the first time in 1950.

Minnesotans experienced some economic challenges in the late 1980s and into the 1990s. An important environmental concern was addressed in 1980 when the Reserve Mining Company was forced to end the dumping of taconite (low-grade iron ore) wastes, thought to be carcinogenic, into Lake Superior. Other companies such as the Minnesota Mining and Manufacturing Company have been forced to clean up hazardous waste sites. Natural disasters also put a strain on Minnesota's economy. A drought plagued the state in 1988 and severe flooding of the Mississippi in 1993 and the Red River in 1997 devastated the lowlands.

The state maintained its economic health through diversification with increasing attention to service industries such as real estate, insurance, and finance. Tourism also became increasingly important to the state as millions of travelers, fishermen, and hunters came to enjoy the state's many scenic and recreational areas. Farming remained important to the state as well; in 1995 Minnesota ranked seventh in the nation by farm income. The state's proximity to the Mississippi River, the Great Lakes, and the St. Lawrence Seaway continued to make Minnesota a major marketing and distribution center for the upper Midwest. The state's per capita personal income in 1996 was over $25,000, ranking it ninth in the nation.

***See also:* Mississippi River, Plains Indians, Populist Movement, Saint Lawrence Seaway**

FURTHER READING

Blegen, Theodore C. *Minnesota: A History of the State*. Minneapolis, MN: University of Minnesota Press, 1975.

Brook, Michael. *Reference Guide to Minnesota History: A Subject Bibliography of Books, Pamphlets, and Articles in English*. St. Paul, MN: Historical Society, 1983.

Chrislock, Carl H. *The Progressive Era in Minnesota, 1829–1914*. St. Paul, MN: Historical Society, 1971.

Folwell, William W. *A History of Minnesota*. 4 vols. Rev. ed. St. Paul, MN: Historical Society, 1956–1959.

Lass, William E. *Minnesota: A Bicentennial History*. New York: Norton, 1977.

MINT ACT

The U. S. Congress passed the Mint Act on April 2, 1792, to establish the country's first mint at Philadelphia, Pennsylvania. The ineffectual Articles of Confederation (1781) had given each state the right to mint its own coins. To ensure the stability of the monetary system, the U.S. Constitution (adopted in 1788) revoked that right, declaring the federal government the sole issuer of currency in the nation (metal or paper money). The Mint Act was the necessary follow-up to the Constitution's proclamation that the federal government alone would "coin Money, regulate the Value thereof, and of foreign Coin, and fix the Standard of Weights and Measures." The Congressional legislation made the dollar the basic unit of money and adopted the bimetallic standard, meaning that both gold and silver became legal tender (an official medium of payment) in the United States. Laws fixed the value of each metal in relation to the other.

American inventor David Rittenhouse (1732–96) was appointed the first director of the U.S. Mint, an office he held from 1792 to 1795. Rittenhouse had been active in state politics and served as treasurer of Pennsylvania (1777–89). The Mint Act authorized coins in three denominations—the copper cent (or penny), the silver dollar, and the gold eagle. The coinage was based on Thomas Jefferson's (1743–1826) decimal system, which he had proposed when he was a member of the Continental Congress (1783–85).

For decades after the Mint Act, U.S. coins circulated along with foreign coins in the states. The federal government determined the exchange rate based on how much precious metal was present in foreign coins. But in 1857 Congress approved a law removing foreign coins from circulation.

For many years the $10 gold eagle was the highest denomination of U.S. coin. In 1933 the government took gold out of circulation; the precious metals present in other coins was also reduced through later Congressional legislation. Today gold and silver coins are minted as commemorative issues for collectors. Silver and gold bullion (bars or ingots) are minted for sale to investors.

A worker at the U.S. Mint in Philadelphia displays freshly minted one dollar coins bearing the likeness of Susan B. Anthony, an early twentieth century suffragist.

***See also:* Bank of the United States (First National Bank), Currency, Thomas Jefferson, Money**

MISSISSIPPI

The words "Mississippi" and "delta" are closely associated in the public's mind with Mississippi history. The delta region indeed dominated the cotton-growing economy that was the mainstay of life in the state for many decades. Contemporary Mississippi, however, has diversified its economy and now has a significant industrial sector. In the late 1990s, the state continued to struggle to bring itself out of a past which

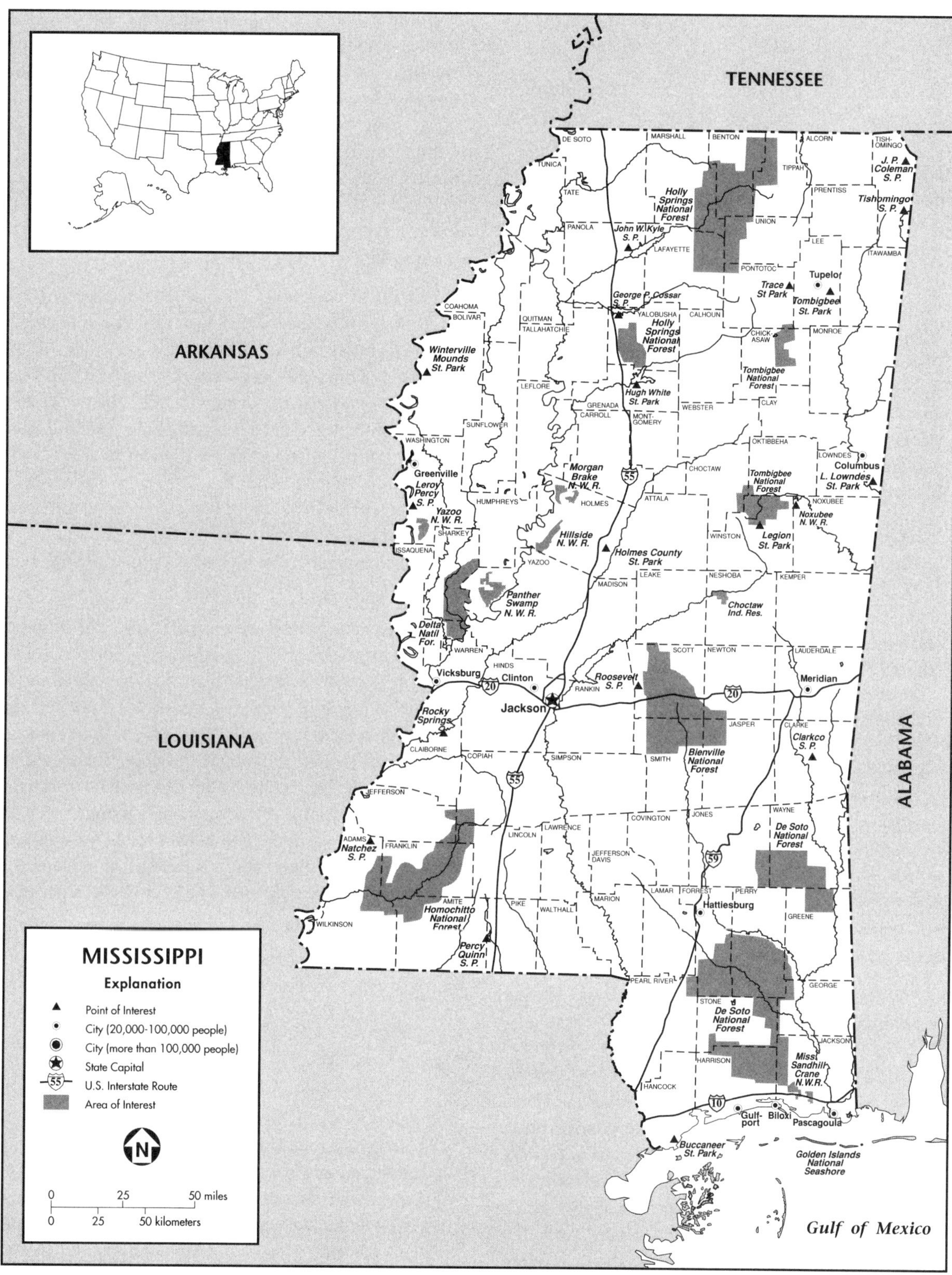

State of Mississippi.

has often placed it last among all states in per capita income.

The Spanish explorers who came to the region of Mississippi with Hernando de Soto in 1540–1541 did not find the wealth they sought and soon lost interest in further exploration. A Frenchman, Robert Cavelier, Sieur de la Salle, explored the lower Mississippi Valley in 1682. He discovered the mouth of the Mississippi River, naming the whole region Louisiana in honor of his king, Louis XIV. The French soon established settlements at Biloxi Bay, Mobile, Natchez, and New Orleans. The area changed hands several times, first from the French to the Spanish in 1762. In 1763 Spain ceded the portion east of the Mississippi to England, but the Spanish recaptured West Florida during the American Revolution (1775–1783). Spain relinquished its hold on the Natchez region, ceding it to the United States in 1795.

The U.S. Congress reorganized the Mississippi Territory in 1798. Alabama, originally part of Mississippi, became a separate territory in 1817. After many settlers from the South, Mid-Atlantic, and New England states had migrated to Mississippi to farm its rich alluvial soil, Congress made it the twentieth state in 1817.

Mississippi was a true frontier territory prior to the American Civil War (1861–1865): It was freewheeling, violent, and full of aggressive adventurers. Joseph G. Baldwin, a Virginia lawyer who came to Mississippi, described the speculative furor of the period: ''Money, or what passed for money, was the only cheap thing to be had. . . . Credit was a thing of course. To refuse it . . . were an insult for which a bowie knife were not a too summary or exemplary means of redress. The State banks were issuing their bills by the sheet. . . .''

When Mississippi became a state, the northern two-thirds of the region was still dominated by Native American tribes. During the presidency of Andrew Jackson (1829–1837), treaties ceded most of this land to the United States and sent Native Americans off to the Oklahoma Territory. Although an aristocratic planter economy grew up around the Natchez area, large plantations did not dominate the whole economy prior to the war. Mississippi society was instead governed by an alliance of large and small landowners. An indication of the importance of slavery to the state's economy was that slaves comprised 52 percent of the population and whites only 48 percent by the end of the 1830s.

The opening of the fertile lands of northern Mississippi caused an inrush of settlers and a flurry of land speculation. The cotton economy, with its slave workforce, came to dominate the state. The land was rich and the cotton economy made many planters wealthy, but the work was hard and life was monotonous in Mississippi. Aside from church and the general store, there was little in the way of recreational or cultural institutions. Jefferson Davis, the President of the Confederacy, came from a family which in one generation had risen from poverty in Kentucky to affluence, social standing and political preeminence in the new land of Mississippi.

After the election of Abraham Lincoln in 1861, Mississippi was the second state to secede from the Union in an attempt to preserve the slave system as the mainstay of the state's economy. During the Civil War, Mississippi was at the center of much of the action. Much political, social, and economic turmoil followed the war under the governance of Reconstruction (1865–1877) Republicans. After the Democrats successfully regained power in 1875, the bitter memories of Reconstruction caused Mississippi whites to institute a system that repressed the rights of former slaves even further.

The prime cotton-growing country in Mississippi was always the fertile Yazoo-Mississippi Delta, located in the northwestern part of the state. Because of persistent flooding problems, this area did not become a plantation economy until after the Civil War. Planters along this section of the Mississippi, according to historian John Ray Skates, ''drained the lands, built the levees, and cleared the forests, [achieving] some of the grandiose style of their prewar Natchez counterparts. Here the plantation system still dominates, in recent times with machines and chemicals rather than sharecroppers.''

Economic stagnation plagued Mississippi from the postwar period into the 1940s. Black sharecroppers on the cotton farms fared nearly as badly as they had under slavery. Many white small farmers were also driven into sharecropping; in 1890, 63 percent of Mississippi farmers were tenants. During this period the practice of leasing convicts to private plantations was also widespread, adding yet another layer of poor and underprivileged workers to the economy. For some of these leased convicts life was possibly harder than it had been under slavery. With a nearly totally agrarian system, the state exported raw materials and had to import most of its manufactured goods. Many former planter-aristocrats dominated state government and all tried to keep the blacks in an inferior position. Fearing a return to Reconstruction and exhibiting deep-set prejudices, whites above all succeeded in maintaining their political and economic domination.

The Great Depression of the 1930s (1929–1939) made things even worse in the state, bringing Mississippi's poor farmers to desperation. Cotton sank to five cents a pound in 1932, while one-fourth of the state's farmland was given up for nonpayment of taxes. Although federal agricultural payments begun during the New Deal helped to hasten the end of tenant farming, had World War II (1939–1945) not brought economic relief to Mississippi, the state might have headed for disaster. Armed forces personnel who came into the state helped to lift it out of its provincialism. Industrial growth and increased mechanization of agriculture finally began to bring Mississippi into the twentieth century. Between 1941 and 1945 the per capita annual income in Mississippi rose from $313 to $627, and more and more citizens began to retire their debts. At the same time many African Americans, encouraged by reports of better economic conditions elsewhere, began to move out of the state to find higher-paying jobs.

The waterways of Mississippi have always been vital to its development. The Mississippi, the largest commercial river in the country, links the Gulf of Mexico to many inland river states. The Tennessee-Tombigbee canal, completed in 1984, links the Tennessee and Ohio rivers with the Gulf. The state has two deepwater ports, Gulfport and Pascagoula; other ports include Biloxi and Port Bienville.

By the 1980s Mississippi was an industrial state, and cotton was no longer the only important agricultural product. Agricultural production was now dominated by cotton, rice, soybeans, and cattle. Mississippi had survived the dark days of segregation and the upheaval of the civil rights movement. Its leaders had finally recognized that the inequalities built into a segregated system did not tend to attract the kind of industries the state sought. By the mid-1960s manufacturing was providing more jobs than agriculture, in part because of a weak labor movement and low wages. In the 1970s many of the low-paying industries such as the garment and wood product trades were de-emphasized in favor of heavy industries manufacturing products like transportation and electronics equipment. In spite of the state's economic strides in the last few decades of the twentieth century, Mississippi remained poor in the late 1990s. In 1996 it ranked 50th among all states in per capita personal income, at only $17,471, and nearly 24 percent of the population fell below the federal poverty level. In 1995–1996, however, the per capita income growth rate was ranked fifteenth in the nation.

***See also:* Civil Rights Movement, Mississippi River, Plantations, Sharecropping**

FURTHER READING

Baldwin, Joseph G. *The Flush Times of Alabama and Mississippi.* New York: D. Appleton and Co., 1853.

Bettersworth, John K. *Your Mississippi.* Austin, TX: Steck-Vaughn, 1975.

Council of State Governments. *The Book of the States, 1994–1995 Edition,* vol. 30. Lexington: KY: The Council of State Governments, 1994.

McLemore, Richard A., ed. *A History of Mississippi.* 2 vols. Hattiesburg, MS: University and College Press of Mississippi, 1973.

Skates, John Ray. *Mississippi: A Bicentennial History.* New York: Norton, 1979.

MISSISSIPPI RIVER

The Mississippi River is a principal United States river. It originates in central Minnesota and flows southeast and then south, eventually reaching Louisiana where it pours into the Gulf of Mexico. States lying west of the Mississippi are Iowa, Missouri, and Arkansas, Louisiana, and Minnesota; to the east are Wisconsin, Illinois, Kentucky, Tennessee, and Mississippi. The river is 2,340 miles (3,765 kilometers) long. With the Missouri River, the Mississippi forms the world's third-longest river system. It is navigable by oceangoing vessels from the Gulf to Baton Rouge, Louisiana. North of that location, it is navigable by barges and towboats as far as Minneapolis, Minnesota.

The mighty Mississippi was first sighted by explorers in 1540–41 when Spaniard Hernando de Soto (1500?–42) ventured through the southern region. In 1672–73 the Mississippi's upper reaches were seen by French-Canadian explorer Louis Jolliet (1645–1700) and French missionary Jacques Marquette(1637–75). In 1682 French explorer Sieur de La Salle (1643–87) investigated the lower part and claimed the entire region for France, naming it Louisiana in honor of King Louis XIV (1638–1715).

After 1763, at the end of the French and Indian War, (1754–63), the river became the boundary between British possessions to the east and Spanish possessions to the west, and the river itself was ceded to Spain. Disputes between Spain and the United States over the waterway were settled in the Pinckney Treaty (1795). With the Louisiana Purchase (1803), the river passed into American control.

In 1811 the steamboat era began on the Mississippi River. Traffic along the Mississippi sped the development of the nation by providing access to the interior territories. St. Louis, Missouri; Memphis, Tennessee; and New Orleans, Louisiana, all flourished as a result of riverboat traffic. In the imagination of most U.S. citizens, the romance of the Mississippi as a steamboat waterway is probably best captured by Missouri-born writer Mark Twain (1835–1910) in his novel, *The Adventures of Huckleberry Finn* (1884).

See also: **Louisiana, Missouri River, Natchez Trace, New Orleans, Pinckney Treaty, Steamboats, Steamboat Act of 1852**

MISSOURI

Access to the Mississippi River and Missouri's central location helped that state's early economic development. The state's fertile land, abundance of lead, and assortment of wild game beckoned thousands of settlers eager to make Missouri the hub of activity in the west. The first inhabitants of what is now known as Missouri were Native American tribes. French fur trader Louis Jolliet and Father Jacques Marquette, a missionary, paddled down the Mississippi River, Missouri's eastern boundary.

The first settlers found the land was rich with deer, beaver, otter, and buffalo; their skins could be traded for other necessary goods. In the 1720s more French people immigrated to the area and established a community near St. Louis, eventually they built the first trading post in 1764. Lead was discovered in the area and a mine was opened near Fredericktown. The French settlers were self-sufficient and grew their own crops, built their own log cabins, and made their own cloth.

In 1762 France ceded its North American land, including Missouri, to Spain during the French and Indian War (1754–1763). When the English were expelled from the Ohio valley area south of Canada as a result of the Revolutionary War, Spain and the United States became neighbors on either side of the Mississippi River. In the 1790s Spain offered free land to Americans who settled in Missouri. People began migrating from eastern states; many brought their slaves with them.

After French leader Napoleon Bonaparte forced Spain to return the Louisiana Territory to France in 1800, the French threatened to exclude the Americans from traveling on the Mississippi River to trade their goods. The issue was pressing and President Thomas Jefferson (1801–1809), who had been one of France's strongest supporters in the United States, now prepared to go to war with France. The right to ship goods on the Mississippi was crucial, in Jefferson's eyes. The Napoleonic wars in Europe, plus a slave rebellion in Haiti, took Napoleon's attention away from the United States, however, and Jefferson offered to purchase the Louisiana territory from the French leader as a way to resolve the crisis. The deal was consummated and Missouri formed part of the newly purchased Louisiana Territory for $15 million. The expanse of land purchased was so large that it was eventually carved up to become Missouri and 14 other states.

Once in 1811, and twice in 1812, earthquakes rocked southeast Missouri. Growth slowed in that area; however, the rest of Missouri flourished. In 1812 a section of the Louisiana Territory was renamed the Missouri Territory. That same year William Clark, of the Lewis and Clark expedition, was elected governor. More people continued to migrate to the fertile and rolling hills of Missouri to establish farms that produced a wide range of crops including corn, wheat, cotton, hay, tobacco, rice, and grapes. As these settlers took over more of the land, Native Americans were eventually pushed out.

Missouri was granted statehood in 1821. During the first half of the 1800s, the development of major transportation routes opened up the west. In 1819 the first steamboat traveled up the Mississippi River carrying flour, whiskey, and sugar. In 1821 the Santa Fe Trail, 800 miles in length, led from Independence, Missouri all the way to Santa Fe, New Mexico. Goods such as wool, tools and mirrors were traded for silver, mules, furs, and horses. In 1841, travelers could follow the Oregon Trail for 2,000 miles from Independence to Oregon. As the transportation system grew, small frontier towns developed along the river and trade routes.

In the mid-1840s, Irish immigrants came to Missouri after suffering failing potato crops in Ireland. These Irish settlers worked the railroads and labored in the towns. A few years later a large number of Germans immigrated to Missouri to make homes in the St. Louis area.

Between 1852 and 1870 the railroad system in Missouri was expanded to meet the demands of the towns. The railroads received grants of federal land along the tracks. It was a profitable acquisition: the railroads sold the land to farmers and the farmers paid to have their goods shipped to markets via the railways. Missouri's railroads opened up new markets in the east for the state's wheat, corn, and other products and also offered easy transportation for easterners who were

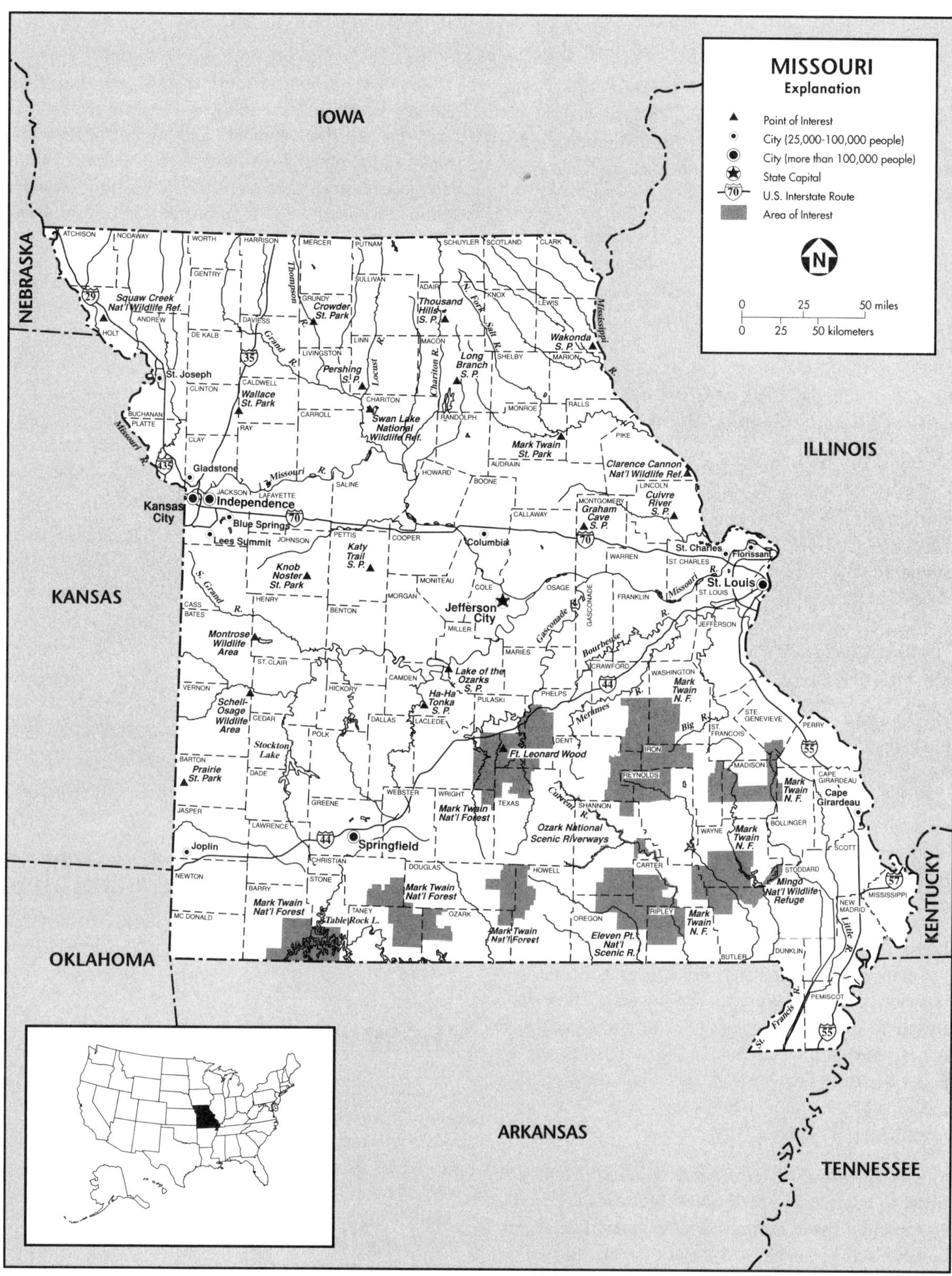

State of Missouri.

moving west. By 1860 more than one million people lived in Missouri. The state's economy flourished.

After the American Civil War (1861–1865) more railroads were laid in Missouri. The railroads transported more settlers to Missouri and continued to open new markets for Missouri's commercial products: crops, iron, and beer.

In the 1870s the fur trade and steamboat traffic declined due to competition from the railroads. The state's economy shifted to industry. Factories drew people from rural areas to the cities. By 1900 St. Louis was the country's fourth-largest city and was called the "Belle of the New World." Urbanization continued—between 1880 and 1970, Missouri's rural population declined from three-fourths to less than one-third of the state's population.

In 1904 about 20 million people attended the world's fair in St. Louis, a celebration to mark the one-hundredth anniversary of the Louisiana Purchase. Fair attendees could feast on the world's first ice-cream cones and the world's first hot dogs. They also had the chance to see the first motion picture, wireless telegraphs, and automatic dishwashers. The Olympic Games also took place in St. Louis that year.

In 1929, The Great Depression (1929–1939) hit the United States. Many farmers and workers lost their jobs. But the start of World War II (1939–1945) helped end the Depression as Missouri produced bombers, landing craft, and explosives. Missouri contributed more than $4 billion worth of supplies to the war effort by the time it was over.

Between 1950 and 1990 the population of St. Louis dropped by more than half. In the 1970s the population of Kansas City also dropped. People and businesses were moving to the suburbs. Those who stayed in the cities were poor. The cities undertook major renewal projects that tackled problems like air pollution, traffic congestion, and crime. In the 1980s millions of government funds were used to renovate apartments and houses.

In 1989 industry was booming as St. Louis was home to many major companies. McDonnell Douglas Corporation made military aircraft, commercial jets, and electronic equipment. Anheuser-Busch, the world's largest brewery, had its headquarters in St. Louis. Chrysler, Ford and General Motors all had assembly plants in or near St. Louis and Kansas City. Missouri was second only to Detroit in automobile production. Other major manufacturers were Monsanto, Hallmark, and Ralston Purina. Each year, more than 60 new companies opened in Missouri and created thousands of jobs.

Missouri produced more than 85 percent of the nation's supply of lead and was a leading producer of lime, barite, zinc, cement, and copper. Missouri's mines added about $1 billion to the state's economy each year. Forestry, another natural resource, was the source for nearly 2,000 industries which produced items such as charcoal, lumber, and barrels.

In 1993 devastating floods required that over half the state be declared a disaster area. Damage to the state was estimated at $3 billion.

In 1998 Missouri's sources of income included manufacturing, farming, trade, tourism, services, government, and mining. While automobiles and aerospace manufacturing were the state's leading industries, soybeans, meat and dairy products were the most important agricultural goods.

In 1995 an estimated 9.4 percent of the state's residents lived below the federal poverty level. Personal income per capita was $22,864 by 1996.

See also: **Missouri Compromise, Missouri River**

FURTHER READING

Nagel, Paul C. *Missouri: A Bicentennial History*. New York: Norton, 1977.

———. *Missouri, A History*. Lawrence, KS: University Press of Kansas, 1988.

Thompson, Kathleen. "Missouri." In *Portrait of America*. Austin, TX: Steck-Vaughn Publishers, 1996.

Worldmark Encyclopedia of the States. Detroit: Gale Research, 1998, s.v. "Missouri."

MISSOURI COMPROMISE

Between 1815 and 1850, the politics of the United States became increasingly sectional. The question of slavery dominated the issues dividing the new republic. An increasing number of northerners viewed slavery as morally wrong and insisted that government abolish the system, while most southerners viewed slave labor as essential to their economic prosperity—and to that of the nation.

Both the North and the South looked to the newly settled western territories to expand their interests. In 1818 when the Territory of Missouri (part of the Louisiana Purchase of 1803) applied for statehood, there were 11 free states and 11 slave states, giving both sides equal representation in the U.S. Senate. (Because of their populations, the free states dominated the U.S. House of Representatives.) Congress began debating the question of whether to admit new states as free or as slave states. In an effort to preserve the delicate North-South political balance, Congress agreed to the Missouri Compromise in 1820.

The Missouri Compromise provided for Maine to be admitted to the Union as a free state, Missouri as a slave state, and designated as free territories north of the Louisiana Purchase (the present-day southern border of Missouri), with the exception of the state of Missouri.

By the 1850s the issue of the extension of slavery had become very controversial. In 1854 the federal legislature again considered the problems of organizing and admitting new states to the Union. This time the Kansas Territory was under consideration. In another compromise, the territory was carved up to form two states, Kansas and Nebraska, and the slavery status of each would be decided by popular sovereignty (the voters in each state). The Kansas-Nebraska Compromise also repealed the anti-slavery clause of the Missouri Compromise, which had pronounced the northern territories free. Violence ensued, especially in Kansas where anti-slavery and pro-slavery adherents squared off in a series of deadly skirmishes, deepening the North-South schism. In 1857 the U.S. Supreme Court's decision in the case of Dred Scott (1795–1858), a slave who had sued for his freedom on the basis of having traveled with his owner in the free territory north of the 36th parallel, declared the Missouri Compromise unconstitutional.

See also: **Abolition, Louisiana Purchase, Dred Scott Case, Slavery, Tallmadge Amendment**

MISSOURI RIVER

The Missouri River is the longest river in the United States. It flows for 2,466 miles (3,968 kilometers). Its source lies in the Rocky Mountains of southwestern Montana; the river is formed by the confluence of the Jefferson, Madison, and Gallatin rivers at Three Forks, Montana. From there the Missouri flows east and southeast, ultimately joining the Mississippi River about 10 miles (16 kilometers) north of St. Louis, Missouri. The Missouri River flows through Montana, North Dakota, South Dakota, Nebraska, Iowa, Kansas, and Missouri. From the Mississippi River, the Missouri is navigable by barges and towboats west and north as far as Sioux City, Iowa. Above Sioux City the water flow is controlled by a series of dams in a project authorized by the U.S. government in 1944. When the water is high the river is navigable to Great Falls (northeast of Helena), Montana.

In 1673 the mouth of the Missouri was passed by French-Canadian adventurer Louis Jolliet (1645–1700) and French missionary Jacques Marquette (1637–75) as they explored the upper part of the Mississippi River. The Lewis and Clark expedition of 1804–06 followed the Missouri for much of the journey to the Pacific Ocean.

During the first two decades of the 1800s, the river provided a chief transportation route for the western fur trade, which relied on keel boats to move goods along the river. In 1819 steamboat traffic began on the waterway, carrying pioneers to the rugged West. Riverboat traffic declined with the expansion of the cross-continental railroads at the end of the nineteenth century. Much of the region through which the Missouri River flows—the interior plains—was the last frontier to be settled in America.

See also: **Fur Trade, Louisiana Purchase, Lewis and Clark Expedition, Mississippi River, Steamboats**

MITCHELL, JOHN

In 1870 John Mitchell (1870–1919) was born in Braidwood, Illinois, a coal-mining village. Orphaned at age six, Mitchell had a difficult childhood. Frustrated and largely penniless, he spent his teenage years laboring as a miner in Colorado and Wyoming. Through this experience, Mitchell came to believe that coal miners, and all working people, could obtain a better and more secure life by organizing labor unions to address their concerns with employers. Mitchell grew up to become one of the most respected yet controversial labor leaders in the United States in the early twentieth century.

In 1890 he was one of the founders of the United Mine Workers of America (UMWA). Later, in 1898, Mitchell won public acclaim as UMWA president. He pursued the organization of labor by using a moderate approach to relations between workers and employers. His conservative style rejected confrontation and class conflict as counterproductive. In his two books, *Organized Labor* (1903), and *The Wage Earner* (1913), Mitchell wrote that the prosperity of workers and employers were inseparably linked together, and harmonious relations between these two groups were best for both.

As more Americans joined labor unions in America, open conflict between unions and employers became more common. Mitchell's theories of harmony between business and labor began to seem naive and unrealistic. American labor was headed in the direction of greater militancy and Mitchell's ongoing associations with businessmen caused a decline in his popularity. He was seen as a pawn of business and a conservative manipulator of union growth. In 1908, despite his reputation as an effective union organizer, the union he founded asked him to step down as president.

Mitchell later tried to pursue his theory of "business-labor harmony" by serving as head of the National Civic Federation (NCF) Trade Agreement Department. (The NCF was an organization comprised mainly of employers and business owners.) But, by 1915, the UMWA insisted he leave the NCF. The UMWA continued to see Mitchell as a collaborator with business and as an unreliable representative of union causes. In 1915 Mitchell became chairman of the New York State Industrial Commission, where he mediated labor issues until his death in 1919.

Arguably, the unions were correct about Mitchell's growing conservatism. He died a millionaire, having grown wealthy through investments in coal mining, the railroad industry, and the steel industry. Many unions came to despise him as a betrayer of union principles, but coal miners remained loyal because of the help he gave them as a labor organizer in the early days of his career. John Mitchell was an inspiration to the early labor movement in the United States, and his policies of mediation and cooperation have, in the long run, triumphed.

***See also:* Labor Movement, Labor Unionism, United Mine Workers**

FURTHER READING

Gluck, Elsie. *John Mitchell, Miner: Labor's Bargain with the Gilded Age*. New York: The John Day Co., 1929.

Green, Marguerite. *The National Civic Federation and the American Labor Movement 1900–1925*. Westport: Greenwood Press, 1973.

Greene, Victor. *The Slavic Community on Strike*. Notre Dame: University of Notre Dame Press, 1968.

Mitchell, John. *Organized Labor: Its Problems, Purposes, and Ideals and the Present and Future of American Wage Earners*. Clifton: A. M. Kelley, 1973.

Phelan, Craig. *Divided Loyalties: The Public and Private Life of Labor Leader John Mitchell*. Albany: State University of New York Press, 1994.

MODEL T

The Model T was an automobile introduced by the Ford Motor Company in 1908 and manufactured until 1927. The automobile's enormous success has been the source of extensive analysis and commentary by historians, sociologists, economists, business writers, and pop culture experts. The Model T has been credited with not only changing the United States but also defining it. When Ford Motor Company founder and president Henry Ford (1863–1947) unveiled the prize Model T in October 1908, he hailed it as "a motor car for the great multitude."

The product lived up to the promise. The internal combustion vehicle had been in production in the United States only since the 1890s; but in the decade preceding the Model T's debut, manufacturers and consumers alike came to regard the "horseless carriage" as a luxury item. It was custom-made for wealthy U.S. citizens. Ford had conceived a different and better idea, as the company would advertise throughout the century: a car that was simple to operate, easy to service, comfortable, and affordable.

The Model T had a wooden body on a steel frame. It had a four-cylinder, twenty horsepower engine, tank capacity of ten gallons (in the "touring sedan") or sixteen gallons (in the "runabout"), and a completely enclosed power plant and transmission. It was also lighter than other models. Through large-scale production based on a system of interchangeable parts the Model T took 728 minutes (just over 12 hours) to build and sold for $850, lower than the price of other automobiles. It was, however, still beyond the reach of the average American consumer.

Nevertheless, in the year the new car was introduced 17,000 Model Ts were purchased by U.S. consumers. Ford improved production methods to increase the number of cars produced and lower the cost; sales steadily rose. The company made an extraordinary offer, when it paid its workers for an eight-hour day a wage of five dollars a day, twice the amount other factory workers were earning. Ford explained that this was merely good business practice. By raising the wages of his factory workers Ford enlarged the potential market for his Model T.

In 1914 Ford implemented the moving assembly line to optimize. Each job had one "best way" of being

A 1921 vintage Model T.

accomplished. The moving assembly line brought unprecedented efficiency to manufacturing. Assembly time per car dropped to just 90 minutes. That year the Ford plant in Highland Park, Michigan produced almost 250,000 Model Ts. To keep up with ever-rising demand operations were sped up and capacity increased to the point when in 1925 Ford produced one Model T every ten seconds. That year the car retailed for just $295, making the so-called "Tin Lizzie" (or the "Flivver") accessible to working class families.

Ford's innovative Model T brought mobility within the reach of the average person in the United States. It was a reliable, no-nonsense, mass-produced automobile, manufactured on a moving assembly line. It changed the consumer mindset to view the car as a necessity. In 1927 Ford retired the Model T so the company could respond to consumer demand for cars with better performance, power, and styling. By then the company had turned out 15 million Model Ts.

See also: **Automobile (Origin of), Automobile Industry, Henry Ford, Ford Motor Company, Mass Production**

MOLASSES ACT OF 1733

In an ongoing effort to control commerce in its North American colonies, the British Parliament passed the Molasses Act in 1733. It imposed heavy duties on any molasses, sugar, or rum imported by the colonies from non-British West Indies (islands in the Caribbean).

The American colonists had a substantial appetite for rum. They consumed it at a rate of nearly four gallons a year for every man, woman, and child. By the time that the act was passed New England distilleries had developed into a successful industry. They bought most of their raw materials (molasses and sugar) from the French islands in the West Indies. The French islands offered cheaper rates than the British islands. Thus Parliament was prompted to pass the Molasses Act to protect its sugar industry.

Smugglers evaded the law by transporting African slaves to Spanish colonies where they were traded for sugar and molasses. These goods were then sold to New England distillers. The smugglers used the profits to buy more African slaves, establishing one of many triangular trade routes that proved lucrative in colonial times.

In 1764 British Parliament passed the Sugar Act to replace the Molasses Act of 1733. The legislation cut by half the per-gallon duty on sugar and molasses imported into British colonies from non-British islands in the West Indies. The Sugar Act also provided for British customs officials to be sent to America where they would work with colonial governors to enforce the law.

See also: **Sugar, Sugar Act, Triangular Trade**

MOLLY MAGUIRES

In 1854 Irish American coal miners in eastern Pennsylvania organized a secret society called the Molly Maguires to wage a campaign of violence against mine owners and operators. The name of the group came from a society in Ireland that used physical force to fight ruthless landlords. The miners were determined to defeat their oppressors at all costs. Their numbers grew and in the decade following the American Civil War (1861–1865) the Molly Maguires were active both as agitators and assassins. In 1875 the group incited a coal miners strike. The strike was broken by the detective work of Irish American James McParlan (1844–1919). McParlan was a Pinkerton guard hired by Philadelphia and Reading Coal and Iron Company to infiltrate the Molly Maguires. He revealed the identities of gunmen responsible for the deaths of nine mine company foremen. Several members of the secret society were arrested, tried, and convicted in 1876. They were hanged for their crimes in 1877.

U.S. sympathies for the plight of the miners were diminished by the headlines proclaiming the terrorist activities of the Molly Maguires. The society dissolved by 1877. Their presence however was long felt in the anthracite coal fields of Pennsylvania, where company police monitored activities in the mines and effectively intimidated many miners from organizing.

See also: **Coal Industry, Pinkerton, United Mine Workers (UMW)**

MONETARY THEORY

Monetary theory holds that a government can manage the level of economic activity by controlling interest rates and the amount of money in circulation. In general, pumping more money into the economy leads to more buying and selling; shrinking the money supply leads to less economic activity, possibly even a recession. A tight monetary policy is one that involves higher interest rates and limits the amount of new money going into circulation. An easy or loose monetary policy involves lower interest rates and more money entering circulation. The government agency responsible for the money supply in the United States is the Federal Reserve Board. The Federal Reserve tries to regulate the nation's economic activity by closely watching over the money supply. It has the power to raise or lower interest rates and to control the money supply. Lowering interest rates tends to stimulate the economy; raising interest rates tend to dampen economic activity. Economists often debate the merits of monetary policy. There is no question that too tight a monetary policy can cause an economy to falter. Some historians say the Great Depression (1929–1939), the worldwide economic crisis of the 1930s, was worsened by the government's tight monetary policy of the era. But too loose a monetary policy can also create problems by leading to inflation.

See also: **Interest, Money**

MONEY

As trade and economies increased, barter—the exchange of goods or services in return for other goods or services—was replaced by money. Money is a convenient social invention used to facilitate the exchange of goods and services. Contemporary money takes the form of paper or coins made from durable metals such as nickel, copper, silver, or gold. The first uses of money, however, took a slightly different form. Early items used as money include shells, stones, cattle, and cigarettes.

What is accepted as money from one time to another may vary according to what the society accepts as its medium of exchange. Ancient agricultural societies may have placed more value in cattle than copper, and thus cattle could become accepted as payment for goods or services. Most modern societies use paper and metal coins as their medium of exchange. At the birth of the United States, when the new nation was governed under the Articles of Confederation, the issuing and printing of money was not centrally controlled. Each state printed its own money and there was no guarantee that money from early Virginia would be accepted in Massachusetts. This created problems in the early republic as the states engaged in interstate commerce. The production of money in the United States was eventually centralized under the federal government.

Internationally, nations use different monetary currencies. As in the early days of the United States, the different currencies affect trade. Rather than convert the world to one monetary system exchange rates are established, for example, to convert U.S. dollars to British pounds. This allows nations engaged in international trade to easily purchase goods and services worldwide.

WHAT IS ACCEPTED AS MONEY FROM ONE TIME TO ANOTHER MAY VARY ACCORDING TO WHAT THE SOCIETY ACCEPTS AS ITS MEDIUM OF EXCHANGE.

At the end of the twentieth century money was not just paper and coin. Money was plastic and consumers could charge items to a credit account, which they then paid for through another form of money, a check. In addition, the advent of computers and electronic communication allowed banks to begin electronic transfers of money, making it possible to move money from a bank account in Los Angeles, California, to a bank account in Zurich, Switzerland, within a matter of hours—all without the hand-to-hand exchange of paper or coin.

See also: **Currency, Exchange Rates, Specie, Wampum**

MONEY SUPPLY

Money supply is the total quantity or volume of money circulating in the economy. Some economists define it narrowly as the total value of coins, paper currency, traveler's checks, and checking account balances at any given time. This definition of the money supply is called "M1." The broader definition of money supply, "M2," adds savings accounts and money market mutual funds. Money supply can also be defined as "M3," which combines M1 and M2 and adds other types of savings deposits and money market funds. At the end of 1998 the total amount of M2 in the United States economy was about $4.4 trillion, while M3 was at $6 trillion.

At about the same time as the United States was being founded, economists were discovering that an economy's money supply had a direct effect on prices and economic growth. The Coinage Act of 1792 defined the value of the U.S. dollar in terms of silver and gold, but after major gold discoveries in the 1830s and in 1849 gold began to replace silver as the standard by which the dollar was defined. The first and second Banks of the United States (1791–1811 and 1816–1836, respectively) tried to control the money supply by making sure that U.S. banks had enough gold on hand to back up the paper bills that they printed and issued. The money supply, however, grew enormously during the American Civil War (1861–1865), when the government began printing "greenbacks" that weren't backed up by gold or silver. By 1879 the dollar was back on the gold standard, and when world gold supplies increased between 1897 and 1914, so did the U.S. money supply.

When the Federal Reserve was created in 1913 it was given the power to control the money supply by increasing or shrinking the amount of currency circulating in the economy. Despite this power, in the early 1930s the Federal Reserve failed to increase the money supply enough to keep the economy from contracting. The resulting Great Depression (1929–1939) led economists who supported the Keynesian economic theory to reject the traditional idea that an economy's health depended on how the money supply was managed. They instead believed that economic growth had to be managed through fiscal policies such as taxation and government spending.

The combined inflation and recession of the 1970s (called "stagflation") convinced a new generation of economists that ineffective government attempts to "fine-tune" the economy through fiscal policy and inconsistent changes in the money supply did not work. Because of these new economic theories in the 1980s, the Federal Reserve began to change the way it reacted to inflation. When inflation rose one percent, the Federal Reserve would raise interest rates 1.5 percent rather than the less aggressive 0.75 percent it would have applied in earlier years. This bolder approach to controlling the money supply was much more effective in controlling inflation. As a result, even though the economy boomed from 1982 through the 1990s inflation remained mild.

See also: **Bank of the United States (First National Bank), Bank of the United States (Second National Bank), Federal Reserve System, Gold Standard, Greenbacks, Money**

MONOPOLIES *(ISSUE)*

The American Civil War (1861–1865) made it possible for men of varying degrees of ability to become wealthy overnight. During the postwar decades these new fortunes were used for the exploitation of natural resources and for industrial development. Men such as Andrew Carnegie (1835–1919) and John

D. Rockefeller (1839–1937) became folk heroes, although in Rockefeller's case, there were also many who feared and despised him. Few laws regulated competition and few taxes were levied on their profits. In time some of these men exerted considerable influence on their state legislatures and on their senators. Even the philosophy of the age was tailored to their needs. Social Darwinism applied the biological concept of survival of the fittest to human society and decreed the successful businessman the fittest of all. Eventually, the Progressive movement confronted some of the more unsavory practices of the business elite and the corrupt politics of the time. The first faint indication that a change in conditions might be close at hand came in 1887 with the passage of the Interstate Commerce Act followed a few years later by the Sherman Antitrust Act in 1890.

Even in a period when business predominated there were certain activities that alarmed the public. The financial manipulations of Rockefeller, for example, indirectly affected the lives of millions who came to fear his company while admiring his personal life. Rockefeller's Standard Oil Company was the first trust or monopoly. It effectively controlled the petroleum refining industry by 1879. Other large combinations followed suit, so that by 1890 large companies controlled the production of such products as whiskey, sugar, and lead, and dominated the nation's railroads. The combinations used their size to exploit markets to the fullest.

In 1889 Kansas became the first state to enact antitrust legislation and the regulatory effort spread across the South and West. Within a year at least 14 other states and territories had enacted similar laws. Pressure mounted for the federal government to take action since individual states were powerless in dealing with the greatest offenders, the trusts and monopolies which were interstate in scope. Both major political parties incorporated antitrust planks in their platforms for 1888, but neither rushed to submit appropriate legislation at the next congressional session. Many Senators may have preferred to ignore the matter, but they were forced to act because of the public clamor and the gentle prodding of President Benjamin Harrison (1889–1893). The result was the passage of the Sherman Antitrust Act in 1890.

The Sherman Antitrust Act had deficiencies that were becoming evident at the turn of the century. One major problem was that the act did not define what a trust or monopoly was. The lack of such a definition left the interpretation of the law up to the judicial branch of the government, and the result was confusion and contradictory court cases. Moreover violation of the Sherman Antitrust Act was only considered a misdemeanor, an offense for which punishment was not serious enough to deter those who saw their interests served by monopolies.

With the accession of Theodore Roosevelt (1933–1945) into the presidency the antitrust movement gained momentum, even though Roosevelt believed it was important to distinguish between good trusts and bad trusts. To Roosevelt good trusts benefited the public with their infusion of capital and products into the economy, while bad trusts consisted of greedy financiers interested only in profits at the general public's expense. Early in his presidency Roosevelt realized that the monopoly situation had reached a critical point and that something had to be done. In 1902 Roosevelt's administration brought suit against the giants of the railroad industry and the "Beef Trust."

The Supreme Court ordered dissolution of the Morgan-Hill-Harriman railroad holding company in the Northern Securities Case (1904), and in the case of Swift and Company vs. United States (1905), the Supreme Court enjoined the "Beef Trust" from engaging in collusive price fixing activities. In 1906 and 1907 Roosevelt had the Justice Department bring suit against the American Tobacco Company, the E.I. Du Pont Chemical Corporation, the New Haven Railroad, and the Standard Oil Company. The Supreme Court ordered the dissolution of the American Tobacco (1910) and Standard Oil (1911) companies. Between 1890 and 1905 the Department of Justice brought 24 antitrust suits while the Roosevelt administration brought suit against 54 companies. The administration of President William Howard Taft (1909–1913) later prosecuted 90 antitrust cases.

Despite many successful prosecutions during his administration Roosevelt realized that the trust problem would not be resolved by judicial review and that a more organized approach was needed. To regulate business Roosevelt specifically advocated a commission similar to the Interstate Commerce Commission, one that had jurisdiction over all businesses engaging in interstate commerce, not just railroads. Big business interpreted this additional governmental regulation as borderline socialism and in response argued for laissez-faire policies. Realizing that big business would invoke any means necessary to avoid regulation, Roosevelt maintained that his idea was not meant to "strangle" business but only regulate trusts, and that legitimate businesses need not be concerned. Roosevelt's proposal was partially implemented in 1913 when the Departments of Commerce and Labor were separated. On October 15, 1914, Congress passed and President Woodrow Wilson (1913–1921) signed the Clayton

Antitrust Act which was designed to strengthen the Sherman Antitrust Act of 1890 by fully codifying specific illegal antitrust activities. The Clayton Act forbade a corporation from purchasing stock in a competitive firm, outlawed contracts based on the condition that the purchaser would do no business with the seller's competitors, and made interlocking stockholdings and directorates illegal. It also contained provisions designed to make corporate officers personally responsible for antitrust violations. The Clayton Act also declared that labor unions were not conspiracies in restraint of trade, thus exempting them from provisions of the bill. This pleased Samuel Gompers, the head of the American Federation of Labor (AFL) so much that he called it "labor's Magna Carta." To carry out and enforce the Clayton Act and the Sherman Act, Congress created the Federal Trade Commission in a related measure.

The Clayton Act proved to be an enduring piece of legislation, and it has been strengthened a number of times since its passage. Just after its passage, however, the antitrust movement began to fade away. Late in 1914 Wilson stated that he believed federal regulation had gone far enough. The president viewed the Clayton Act as the concluding act in the antitrust movement.

The large corporations did not suffer as much from regulation as might be thought. In many ways, the regulatory authority that the government imposed on business made it more difficult for new companies to break into competition with the big companies. Thus, the main thing that they feared and that they formed monopolies to avoid—"ruinous competition"—was killed in its crib by the very regulation that was passed to put a collar on the monopolies.

Many historians have contended that although the antitrust movement reached a natural decline, World War I (1914–1918) further undermined it. War mobilization required coordinated efforts from the leaders of many industries. Economic concentration and collusive efforts were necessary and accepted for the war effort. Some economic historians contend that the Clayton Act actually promoted economic concentration. The Clayton Act clarified illegal actions, thereby helping to eliminate some monopolistic activities, but in so doing it allowed business combinations and trusts to engage in collusive activities not specifically prohibited. By codifying illegal behavior, some historians believe that Congress tacitly sanctioned other collusive activities designed to reduce chaotic competition and ensure stability. Large corporations such as General Motors and the Du Pont Chemical Company grew much larger just immediately after the Clayton Act and especially during the war effort.

Desire for further antitrust reform was rekindled when the Robinson-Patman Act of 1936 and the Miller-Tydings Act of 1937 both supplemented the Clayton Act by attempting to protect small business from wholesalers that practiced price discrimination and by establishing "fair trade" price floors on numerous items. In 1938, Congress created the Temporary National Economic Committee to hold hearings on the issue of antitrust. Attorney General Thurman Arnold reinvigorated federal antitrust prosecution. Arnold brought a number of antitrust suits, notably against General Electric and the Aluminum Company of America. Like the earlier antitrust effort of the Progressive Era, this campaign lost its strength and direction as a result of foreign policy concerns and economic mobilization for a war effort.

There were some important antitrust cases after World War II (1939–1945) as well. In 1945 the Aluminum Company of America was found to be in violation of the Sherman Antitrust Act. In 1948 the federal government forced a number of major U.S. film studios to divest themselves of studio-owned theaters. In 1961 the Supreme Court ordered the Du Pont Company to divest itself of its holdings in General Motors Company. In 1967 the Federal Communications Commission ordered the American Telephone and Telegraph Company (AT&T) to lower its rates. In 1982 after eight years of battling a private antitrust suit in federal court AT&T agreed to be broken up, and a number of rival long-distance communication companies came in to challenge AT&T's control over the market.

In 1950 the Celler-Kefauver Act extended the Clayton Act by tightening prohibitions on business mergers that lessen competition and lead to monopoly. In 1976 Congress passed the Hart-Scott-Rodino Act or Concentrated Industries Act. This was a mild reform law that attempted to strengthen provisions of existing antitrust laws. Monopolistic behavior clearly remained a factor of U.S. economic life while federal prosecution of anti-competitive mergers and acquisitions became rare.

See also: **Clayton Anti-Trust Act, Interstate Commerce Act, Northern Securities Case, Sherman Anti-Trust Act, Tobacco Trust, Trust-Busting**

FURTHER READING

Blum, John Morton. "Woodrow Wilson and the Ambiguities of Reform." *The Progressive Presidents:*

Theodore Roosevelt, Woodrow Wilson, Franklin D. Roosevelt, Lyndon Johnson. New York: W. W. Norton, 1980.

Clark, John D. *The Federal Anti-Trust Policy.* Baltimore: Johns Hopkins University Press, 1931.

Kolko, Gabriel. *The Triumph of Conservatism: A Reinterpretation of American History, 1900–1916.* New York: Free Press of Glencoe, 1963.

Link, Arthur S. *Wilson: The New Freedom.* Princeton, NJ: Princeton University Press, 1956.

Thorelli, Hans B. *The Federal Antitrust Policy: Origination of an American Tradition.* Baltimore: Johns Hopkins University Press, 1955.

MONOPOLY

Monopoly is a market or industry controlled entirely by one seller or firm that produces a product for which no close substitutes exist. The monopolist sets the price of its product and generally produces just enough to ensure plump profits. Although prices are normally higher than in a competitive market, monopolies are still disciplined by market forces. It does not benefit the monopolist to raise the price so high that no one can purchase it or to produce a product that is not in demand. A pure monopolist will examine the different prices and quantities it can sell in terms of the corresponding production costs incurred. Whatever price-quantity combination yields the highest profit will be chosen.

Very few cases in the American economy exist where a single seller enjoys full control of the supply of any one economic product. Few monopolies start off as such unless they own a copyright or patent. A business can become a monopoly by buying up the competition or driving competitors out of business. In addition, a monopoly may develop if production of a product requires specific skills.

The most common and effective barrier preventing monopolies is legal restriction. Nineteenth-century Americans considered competition essential for the democratic way of life. They looked to the legal system to block private accumulation of power or "trusts" which they perceived could threaten democratic government. In 1890 Congress passed the Sherman Antitrust Act "to protect trade and commerce against unlawful restraint and monopoly." To strengthen and complement the 1890 act, Congress passed the Clayton Antitrust Act in 1914 and the Robinson-Patman Act in 1936. The Federal Trade Commission, established in 1914, regulates unfair methods of competition in interstate commerce.

Occasionally a privately owned service is deemed so essential by the U.S. government that it will be shielded from antitrust laws or it will be regulated by the government. These are called natural monopolies. In the United States these primarily include public utilities, such as gas, electricity, natural gas, and water. By 1998 competition was introduced into the electricity and natural gas market through deregulation.

See also: **Clayton Anti-Trust Act, Sherman Anti-Trust Act, Natural Monopoly, Tobacco Trust, Trust-Busting**

MONROE DOCTRINE

The Monroe Doctrine, the foundation for U.S. foreign policy in the western hemisphere throughout most of its history, was declared on December 2, 1823, by President James Monroe (1817–1825) in his annual message to Congress. In the first two decades of the nineteenth century the remarkable success of movements for independence in Spanish America set the foundation for the Doctrine. By the end of 1822 Spain was driven from its major colonies in North and South America by nationalist insurgencies. European powers now remained in control of only Belize, Bolivia, and the Guianas. But, fearing that European powers might move to restore Spain to its colonies, the Monroe administration felt compelled to issue a formal declaration regarding U.S. policy.

Four principles formed the Monroe Doctrine. The Americas were no longer to be considered objects for future colonization or control by any European power. The political systems of the European powers were alien to the United States and any attempt to export it to the Americas would be considered dangerous to American interests. The United States would not interfere with the existing colonies or dependencies of the European powers. Finally, the Monroe Doctrine reaffirmed that the United States would not take part in the wars of the European powers.

Great Britain earlier had prodded the Monroe administration to make a similar but joint declaration on preserving the independence of the new Latin American republics. Under the influence of John Quincy Adams (1767–1848), Monroe rejected the idea, reasoning that the United States would then be cast as the junior partner of Britain, overshadowed by its vastly superior naval power. Furthermore, the motives of the United States diverged significantly from those of Britain. The British were intensely interested in expanding their already valuable trading links with independent Latin America—ties that would be jeopardized if Spain and its mercantilist policies were restored. Although Monroe was certainly aware of the commercial value of Latin America, he placed security and ideological considerations above economic interests when he framed his declaration.

Although the Monroe Doctrine declared unilateral U.S. protection over the entire Western Hemisphere, the United States did not have the military or economic muscle to support such an ambitious policy at that time. Not surprisingly the European powers ignored the Doctrine when it suited them. However, by the end of the American Civil War (1861–1865), the United States had considerable military and economic resources at its disposal. In the first major application of the Monroe Doctrine, U.S. forces massed in 1867 on the Rio Grande River to support U.S. demands that France abandon its puppet regime in Mexico, headed by the Hapsburg prince, Maximilian. France eventually complied, marking a significant victory for U.S. coercive diplomacy.

ALTHOUGH THE MONROE DOCTRINE DECLARED UNILATERAL U.S. PROTECTION OVER THE ENTIRE WESTERN HEMISPHERE, THE UNITED STATES DID NOT HAVE THE MILITARY OR ECONOMIC MUSCLE TO SUPPORT SUCH AN AMBITIOUS POLICY AT THAT TIME. NOT SURPRISINGLY THE EUROPEAN POWERS IGNORED THE DOCTRINE WHEN IT SUITED THEM.

The Maximilian affair demonstrated that the fortunes of the Monroe Doctrine were closely linked to the expansion of U.S. power. Indeed, as American industrial development and trading and investment ties with Latin America grew in the latter half of the nineteenth century, the United States became more willing not only to enforce the Monroe Doctrine, but also to add to its self-assumed rights and responsibilities. Latin America's subservience to the United States was amply demonstrated in 1904, when President Theodore Roosevelt (1901–1909) developed the Roosevelt Corollary to the Monroe Doctrine.

In the late nineteenth and early twentieth centuries political, economic, and social instability plagued much of Latin America. In these perilous conditions, durable and enforceable economic transactions between Latin American and European parties often foundered. Latin American politicians frequently treated European investors capriciously, while European traders and bankers often cheated or exploited their Latin American customers. The European powers increasingly intervened to resolve disputes involving their nations, as when the dictator of Venezuela refused to honor debts owed to European citizens. In response, Germany and Britain blockaded Venezuelan ports and attacked Venezuelan harbor defenses and naval assets. Such incidents were the proximate cause of Roosevelt's decision to revise the Monroe Doctrine, although it is true that the American president was already disposed to expand American power whenever and wherever possible.

The Roosevelt Corollary, which was included in a message to Congress in December 1904, reiterated that the Monroe Doctrine forbade European intervention in Latin American affairs. However, Latin American states had to honor their obligations to foreign nationals and governments. Roosevelt declared that the United States would act as hemispheric policeman, forcing Latin American governments to put their economic houses in order and pay their debts, eliminating the need for European intervention. Over the next three decades, U.S. forces took control of the governments and customs houses of the Dominican Republic, Haiti, and most of Central America. Although this forceful intervention produced a measure of economic and political stability to the region, it aroused increased and intense resentment among the local populace, which viewed the Monroe Doctrine and the Roosevelt Corollary as pretexts for the pursuit of U.S. interests in the region.

The presidential administrations of Herbert Hoover (1929–1933) and Franklin Roosevelt (1933–1945) responded to brewing anti-U.S. nationalism. In 1930 the Hoover administration renounced the Roosevelt Corollary by declaring that the Monroe Doctrine did not justify U.S. intervention in the domestic affairs of Latin America, however turbulent they might be. For his part, Roosevelt withdrew American military forces from Central America and the Caribbean, replacing troops with the "Good Neighbor Policy."

None of these new policies had an immediate and substantive impact on the U.S. tendency for unilateral intervention in Latin America. Rather, they marked a change in U.S. strategies and rhetoric. Thus when the Cold War began the United States moved to combat Soviet subversion in the region, both real and imagined. The United States sponsored a failed invasion of

Cuba (1960); engineered the overthrow of democratically elected governments in Guatemala (1954) and Chile (1973), and trained and armed counter-revolutionary forces in Nicaragua.

When the end Cold War and the collapse of the Soviet Union (1991) removed the strategic rationale for intervention, U.S. policy began to move away its long-standing commitment to unilateralism. As the U.S. contemplated armed intervention in Haiti in 1994 to restore democratic government, it sought formal authorization from the United Nations. This dramatic embrace of multilateralism reflected the increased efforts of the United States during the 1990s to pursue both its ideals and its interests through international institutions, both regional (the North American Free Trade Agreement) and global (the United Nations, the General Agreement on Trade and Tariffs, etc.) The question that remained unanswered at the beginning of the twenty-first century was whether the unilateralism of the Monroe Doctrine will revive—in whole or in part—if multilateralism failed to meet perceived American goals in Latin America.

***See also:* General Agreement on Trade and Tariffs, James Monroe, North American Free Trade Agreement**

FURTHER READING

Cashman, Sean Dennis. *America Ascendant: From Theodore Roosevelt to FDR in the Century of American Power, 1901–1945.* New York: New York University Press, 1998.

Dent, David W. *The Legacy of the Monroe Doctrine: A Reference Guide to U.S. Involvement in Latin America and the Caribbean.* Westport, CT: Greenwood Press, 1999.

Kinzer, Stephen and Stephen Z. Schlesinger. *Bitter Fruit: The Story of the American Coup in Guatemala.* Cambridge: Harvard University Press, 1999.

Lafeber, Walter. *Inevitable Revolutions: The United States in Central America.* New York: W.W. Norton and Company, 1993.

May, Ernest R. *The Making of the Monroe Doctrine.* Cambridge, MA: Harvard University Press, 1992.

Scott, James. *After the End: Making US Foreign Policy in the Post–Cold War World.* Durham: Duke University Press, 1998.

Smith, Gaddis. *The Last Years of the Monroe Doctrine, 1945–1993.* New York: Hill and Wang, 1994.

MONROE, JAMES

James Monroe (1758–1831) came from a family of small planters in Westmoreland County, Virginia. He spent two years pursuing a classical education at William and Mary College (1774–1776) but left before graduation to fight in the American Revolution (1775–1783). He served as a lieutenant in the Third Virginia Regiment, and was wounded in the Battle of Harlem Heights (September 16, 1776). He fought again at White Plains (October 28, 1776), and suffered a serious wound in the battle of Trenton (December 26, 1776). There, General George Washington (1732–1799) promoted him to the rank of captain for "bravery under fire." After recuperating from his injuries he returned to fight in the battles of Brandywine and Germantown, Pennsylvania, in the fall of 1777 and again at Monmouth, New Jersey (June 1778). Because of an oversupply of officers he resigned his commission and returned to Virginia to serve in the lower house of the legislature.

In 1782 Monroe was elected to the Virginia House of Delegates and served as a member of the Continental Congress (1783–1786). He practiced law for a short time but, after the Constitution came into force in 1788, he won election to the U.S. Senate. There, Monroe became a persistent critic of President George Washington's administration (1789–1797). He charged that the federalist leadership of Alexander Hamilton and George Washington was out to enrich commercial and financial interests and was insufficiently sympathetic to farmers. He accused the federalists of passing coercive legislation, such as the Alien and Sedition Acts. In this and in his unabashed support of the French Revolution he found agreement with Thomas Jefferson (1743–1826) and James Madison (1751–1836) and became a member of the Democratic Republican Party.

After the United States fought the British to a standstill in the War of 1812 (1812–1814), the country entered a period of relative tranquility. Monroe was elected fifth president of the United States in 1816 and presided for two terms, during what is now called "the era of good feelings." During this period, President James Monroe's (1817–1825) diplomatically adept Secretary of State, John Quincy Adams, negotiated a number of treaties and agreements with other countries. The Convention of 1818 extended the northern border between the United States and British Canada along the forty-ninth parallel, from the Lake of the Woods in present day Minnesota to the Rocky Mountains in the west. Another important diplomatic accomplishment was the 1817 agreement between the United

States and British Canada to restrict the number of each nation's warships on the Great Lakes. This was called the Rush-Bagot Treaty.

The most reknown diplomatic initiative of the Monroe administration was also suggested by Secretary of State John Quincy Adams. This was the Monroe Doctrine. This declaration, which the president articulated in his annual address to Congress in December 1823, warned European nations to refrain from further colonizing, or exploiting instability which might develop in the new nations in the Western Hemisphere. American "rights and interests," according to the Monroe Doctrine, dictated that newly emerging countries in the Americas were not in the future to be interfered with by any European powers. In exchange for this freedom from European intervention in the Americas (both North and South), the United States promised to not become involved in the internal affairs of Europe. Given the relative weakness of the United States as a military power prior to the American Civil War (1861–1865), this was a promise that was easy to keep.

The Monroe Doctrine addressed not only the relationship between the United States and Europe, it also announced a special relationship between the United States and Latin America. The United States would oversee and protect Latin America against European and other foreign invaders. It would also pursue commerce and capital investment with the less developed nations of Latin and South America. The Monroe Doctrine was used as justification for a U.S. policy of military intervention in the "banana republics" of Central and South America. The United States often intervened when the leaderships of these countries appeared ready to become less accommodating to American foreign investment or military interests.

At the end of Monroe's last term of office, political factions emerged in a four-way presidential race which ended in the election of John Quincy Adams (1825–1829) as the sixth president of the United States. On the occasion of Monroe's death in 1831, Adams credited Monroe with stabilizing the nation.

Monroe died in 1831. He was a courageous soldier and a determined partisan of liberty (although, like his colleagues Madison and Jefferson, he did not extend this principle to freeing his slaves). Monroe is best known for the Monroe Doctrine and for other diplomatic expressions of the new nation's nationalism during his presidency.

See also: **Monroe Doctrine**

FURTHER READING

Dangerfield, George. *The Era of Good Feelings.* New York: Harcourt, Brace & World, 1963.

Elliot, Ian, ed. *James Monroe 1758–1831: Chronology, Documents, Bibliographical Aids.* Dobbs Ferry, N. Y.: Oceana Publishers, 1969.

Levine, Isaac D. *Hands Off the Panama Canal.* Washington: Monticello Books, 1976.

May, Ernest R. *The Making of the Monroe Doctrine.* Cambridge: Belknap Press, 1975.

Perkins, Dexter. *Hands Off.* Boston: Little, Brown, 1955.

MONTANA

Nicknames for Montana reflect the wonder and significance of the state's natural resources—the basis for its growth and prosperity. Familiar references such as "Big Sky" and the "Treasure State" come from appreciation for the state's expansive views and rich supply of minerals.

It is thought that the first white explorers to Montana were French traders and trappers from Canada who migrated in the 1700s. In 1803 when President Thomas Jefferson (1801–1809) orchestrated the Louisiana Purchase, the deal included land west of the Mississippi River which includes land now known as Montana. Jefferson sent the Louis and Clark expedition to explore the new area and record their findings for the rest of the world.

In 1805 Meriwether Lewis and William Clark, along with French trapper Toussaint Charbonneau and his Shoshoni wife, Sacagawea, reached the Yellowstone River near the boundary of North Dakota. They traveled through present-day Idaho, Oregon, and Washington to the Pacific Ocean where they completed their mission. During the trip they encountered a handful of men who were hunting animals and trading furs with the Indians. Their expedition cleared the way for the first American trappers, traders, and settlers to find their way to Montana. In 1807 Manuel Lisa, a Spanish trader, formed the Missouri Fur Company and established the first trading post in Montana, and others rapidly followed. The Pacific Fur Company, the American Fur Company, and the Rocky Mountain Fur Company became important trading companies in the northwest.

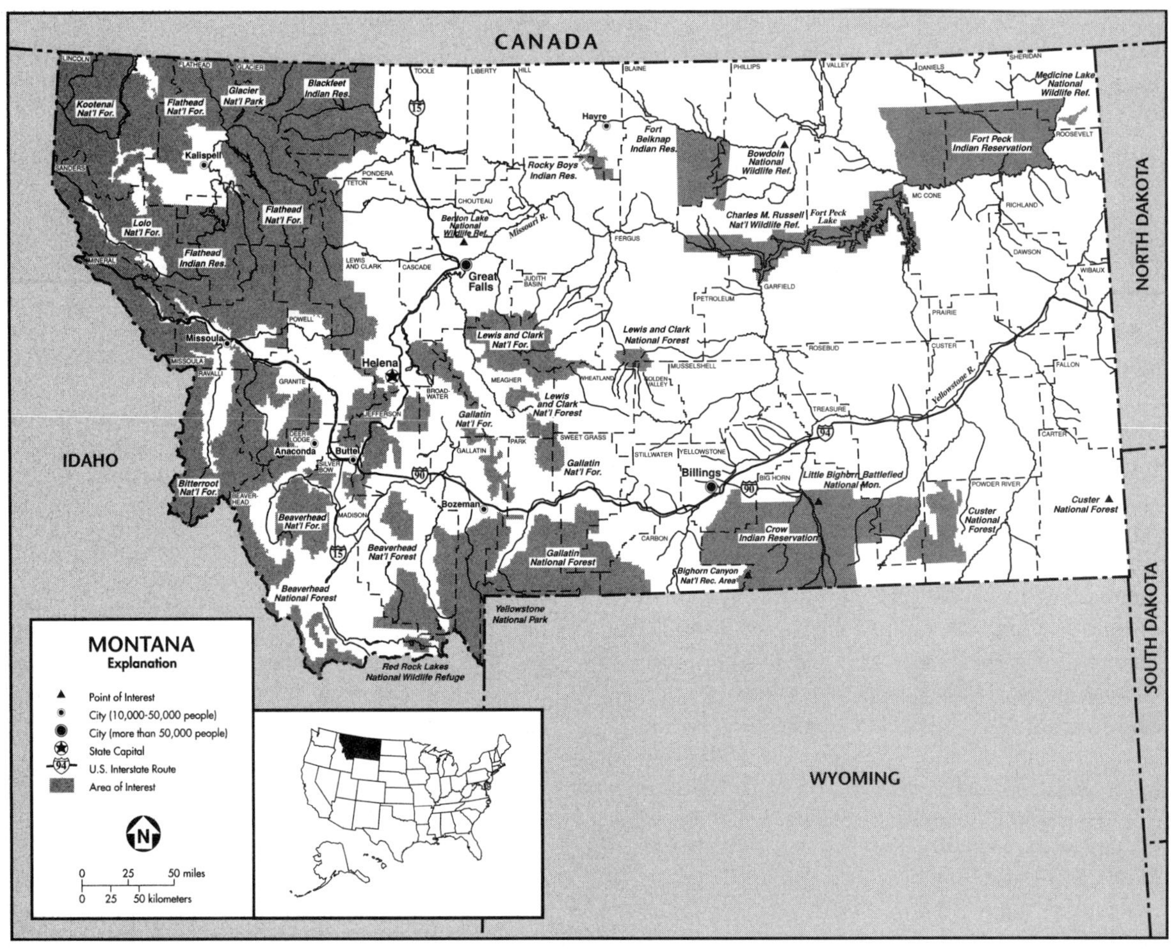

State of Montana.

The fur trade dominated Montana's economy until 1858, when gold was discovered in southwest Montana. By mid-1862, a rush of miners from the gold fields of California, Nevada, Colorado, and Idaho had migrated to the state. The biggest gold discovery was in Alder Gulch near Bannack in 1863. Miners flocked to the gulch, which led to the development of Virginia City and Nevada City. A contemporary newspaper wrote, ''thousands of tenderfeet were wildly filing claims.'' Alder Gulch gave up $10 million worth of gold in one year. Other areas of Montana also proved to be rich in gold and with each gold discovery, a town instantly sprang up. The temporary gold boom brought the state's first substantial white population and an increased demand for government. Bandits robbed and killed miners on the roads. When Montana became a territory in 1864 the legislature was better able to govern the area.

As more settlers migrated westward, they occupied land previously owned by the Indians. Between 1863 and 1876 many battles, most notably the Battle of the Little Bighorn, or Custer's Last Stand, took place. The bloody battles eventually brought about the surrender of several Indian tribes who were subsequently confined to reservations.

In 1864, gold was discovered in the hills around Butte and by 1875 silver was discovered there as well. The Travona Silver Mine was soon opened and Butte became known as ''Silver City'' for the next 10 years. In 1881 one of the richest copper mines was discovered in the hills of Butte—the place became known as ''the richest hill on earth.'' By the 1890s copper was the state's most important mineral and Butte became the industrial center of Montana.

By 1866 the first Long Horn cattle were brought to Montana from Texas and by the mid-1870s sheep also grazed the countryside. In 1886, approximately 664,000 head of cattle and nearly a million sheep grazed Montana's land. Between 1880 and 1909, the state prospered as construction of a railroad system helped open new markets for the livestock and mining industries.

The railroads also allowed farmers to migrate to Montana. Between 1900 and 1920 the population grew from 243,329 to 548,889. In 1889, after several attempts, Montana's bid for statehood was approved by Congress.

Farmers from all over the country as well as Germany and Scandinavia migrated to Montana in the early 1900s planting flax, oats and wheat. Land claims grew from one million acres in 1909 to 93 million acres in 1922. Farmers were able to get good prices for their wheat until a drought ravaged Montana's farm country in 1917. Many could not sustain their farms and left the state for more hospitable soil. In 1920 thousands of grasshoppers descended on the land eating any seeds or grass that were left. Periods of drought and rain over the next 10 years forced the farmers to diversify their crops to suit the climate and use farm machines which helped turn a profit once again.

As the Great Depression (1929–1939) hit the United States the demand for minerals and agricultural products waned. By 1935 mines were closing and farmers were losing their land as one-fourth of Montana residents received financial assistance from the government. However, President Franklin D. Roosevelt's New Deal began to put people back to work in Montana constructing dams and roads and extending power lines.

With the start of World War II (1939–1945), Montana's economy began to thrive again as copper was in demand for use in weapons systems. The government bought wheat and beef from Montana's farmers and ranchers to provide rations for the troops. After the war, Montanans began to movc from farms to cities as businesses grew. In the 1950s as well successful oil wells were developed in eastern Montana.

In the 1970s Montana's petroleum and natural gas were in great demand as a fuel shortage spread across the country. As energy companies started strip mining for coal, environmentalists took action. The Montana Strip Mine Reclamation Act and the Utility Siting Act were passed in 1973, increasing the tax on coal by 30 percent. Half the money was used to restore the land and community by building roads and schools and reviving areas devastated by mining.

In the 1980s the state's economy took a plunge. Copper prices dropped drastically, forcing many of Montana's copper mines to close. At the same time, falling oil prices meant less revenue from petroleum while a drought devastated the farming industry. As a result, Montanans began to leave the state looking elsewhere for better economic opportunities. Between 1985 and 1989, the population decreased by 20,000 people.

The 1990s saw an upswing in the demand for minerals and manufactured goods, which led to a turn around in the state's economy. In 1991 about 26 percent of Montanans worked for the government, the largest employer in the state. Petroleum accounted for half of the mining income as the oil, gas, and coal industries also experienced growth. Gold, silver, copper, lead, and zinc were produced in Montana. Other goods such as aluminum, gemstones, phosphate, limestone, gypsum chromite, barite, clay, sand, and gravel also generate revenue for Montana. As well farmland covered about 25 percent of the state, and wheat—the biggest crop in Montana—was exported to other countries. Revenue from livestock accounted for two-fifths of Montana's farm income. In 1996 per capita personal income was $19,047 and in 1995, only about 15.3 percent of the population lived below the federal poverty level.

See also: **Louis and Clark Expedition**

FURTHER READING

Malone, Michael P., Richard B. Roeder, and William L. Lang. *Montana: A History of Two Centuries.* Seattle: University of Washington Press, 1991.

Small, Lawrence F., ed. *Religion in Montana: Pathways to the Present.* Billings: Rocky Mountain College, 1992.

Thompson, Kathleen. "Montana." In *Portrait of America.* Steck-Vaughn Publishers, 1996.

Toole, Kenneth R. *Montana: An Uncommon Land.* Norman: University of Oklahoma Press, 1984.

Worldbook Encyclopedia of the States. Detroit: Gale Research, 1998, s.v. "Montana."

MONTGOMERY WARD AND CO.

Montgomery Ward and Co., Incorporated had its origins in the 1860s, when young Chicago native Aaron Montgomery Ward saw that he could undercut rural retailers by selling directly to farmers through mail orders and by delivering via the railroad. After a false start in October 1871, when the Great Chicago Fire destroyed his inventory, Ward and two partners sent out their first mailing in the spring of 1872. This was the world's first general merchandise mail-order catalog.

Orders trickled in and Ward soon bought out his partners, who were discouraged by the slow pace of business. Late in 1872 he got a break. The Illinois Grange, a farmers' organization, named Ward its purchasing agent. This gave Ward access to Grange mailing lists and meetings, and greater credibility with farmers. He began subtitling Montgomery Ward price lists with the phrase Original Grange Supply House.

As the business grew Ward needed more capital and more help. Late in 1873 his brother-in-law, George Thorne, put five hundred dollars into the firm and became an equal partner. The two men made an effective team. While Ward had the inspiration for the business, George Thorne was a practical day-to-day manager.

Montgomery Ward's primary customers were farmers who needed new industrial tools and farming equipment that were expensive or hard to find outside of cities. In these early years, his best-selling product was the sewing machine, and the catalog was filled with pumps, feed cutters, cane mills, corn shellers, threshers, saws, grinders, and engines.

As postal rates fell Montgomery Ward stepped up advertising in newly popular magazines. Through publications such as the *Prairie Farmer* he told farmers to query him for catalogs with penny postcards. The spring catalog for 1874 had 32 pages. That fall it was expanded to 100 pages. By the end of 1874 sales topped $100,000.

Increased sales of $300,000 in 1875 allowed Montgomery Ward to increase service. A satisfaction-guaranteed-or-your-money-back policy was instituted in 1875, and the catalogs began rating merchandise as good, better, or best. Montgomery Ward also counseled customers to band together and split fixed freight costs.

During the 1880s competition in the form of major department stores began to enter the catalog field. Jordan Marsh and Co., John Wanamaker, Sears Roebuck and Company, and Carson, Pirie, Scott and Co. all began or resumed mail-order operations. However, Montgomery Ward was still the biggest and most popular. Its 240-page 1883 catalog listed 10,000 items. In 1884 Ward bought the *Farmer's Voice* weekly newspaper to use as an advertising vehicle. In 1886 William C. Thorne, George Thorne's eldest son, increased the size and circulation of the catalog, leading to a boom in orders. By 1888 Montgomery Ward's sales reached $1.8 million. To cap off the decade Aaron Ward and George Thorne turned their partnership into a corporation in 1889.

In 1900 Montgomery Ward built a new office headquarters at Michigan Boulevard and Madison Street in Chicago. Sales that year were $8.7 million, trailing behind Sears's $10 million as competition between the two Chicago firms grew more intense.

The U.S. Postal Service's initiation of a parcel post system in 1913 gave mail-order business a boost. Montgomery Ward made $3.4 million on 1915 sales of $49 million as a boom period began. But in September 1920 a financial panic hit, and prices began to fall. Sales dropped to two-thirds of their 1919 level. Losses for 1920 totaled $10 million.

By 1922 the economy rebounded. The retail market was beginning to displace the mail-order system as the automobile changed the way people in the United States shopped. Montgomery Ward somewhat belatedly entered the retail sector in 1926. That year the company opened its first freestanding retail store in Plymouth, Indiana. The success of this store and the continuing weakness of the mail-order sector led Montgomery Ward to announce that it would open stores in rural towns with populations of 10,000 to 15,000. Ward had 531 stores operating by the end of 1929, but the stock market crash in October of that year, followed by the Great Depression (1929–1939) curtailed further expansion plans and led to the closure of 147 poorly performing stores.

The early years of the Depression were difficult for Montgomery Ward but by 1934 the company turned the corner and returned to profitability. That year the company also began taking telephone orders. In 1939 Montgomery Ward made a public relations coup when a Ward copywriter wrote a booklet about a little red-nosed reindeer named Rudolph, which became a Christmas classic. The booklet was included in millions of catalogs.

From the 1950s onward Montgomery Ward was in an almost constant struggle for survival. By the mid-1950s Montgomery Ward had already fallen well behind Sears Roebuck, whose sales were three times greater. Traditional retailers such as Montgomery Ward and Sears Roebuck also saw competition grow fiercer with the entrance of discount chains such as Wal-Mart into the marketplace. Ownership of the flagging retailer eventually fell into the hands of Mobil Corporation in 1976. Twelve years later, however, the largest management-led leveraged buyout in U.S. history at the time ($3.8 billion) transformed Montgomery Ward into a privately held company. Declining profitability led the company to file for Chapter 11 bankruptcy protection in mid-1997 and placed its future in serious doubt.

See also: **Chain Store, Department Store, Mail-Order House, Retail Industry, Sears Roebuck and Company**

FURTHER READING

Balu, Rekha. "Crunch Time at Montgomery Ward." *Crain's Chicago Business*, March 17, 1997.

Hoge, Cecil C., Sr. *The First Hundred Years Are the Toughest: What We Can Learn from the Century of Competition between Sears and Wards*. Berkeley, CA: Ten Speed Press, 1988.

Latham, Frank Brown. *A Century of Serving Consumers: The Story of Montgomery Ward, 1872–1972*. Chicago: Montgomery Ward and Co., Incorporated, 1972.

Morrell, Lisa. "Ward's Is Changing Everything—Well, Almost: Bright Strategy Faces Huge Obstacles." *Crain's Chicago Business*, February 1, 1999.

Steinhauer, Jennifer. "Ward, Down and Struggling, Plans to Follow Revived Rivals." *New York Times*, May 3, 1997.

MORGAN, JOHN PIERPONT

John Pierpont Morgan (1837–1913) was probably the most important and powerful business investment banker in U.S. history. Morgan played a major role in the rescue of the U.S. government in 1893 and 1907, when the United States experienced major economic downturns. However, Morgan's most enduring achievement was probably the crucial role he played in the creation of the United States Steel Corporation.

Morgan was the son of international banker Junius Morgan. He graduated from the famous English High School in Boston and then studied for two years at the University of Gottingen, Germany. He later graduated from Harvard University.

In many ways John walked in his father's footsteps, succeeding his father in most of the senior Morgan's business enterprises. Like his father Morgan made large gifts to educational institutions and to the arts. He became a great collector of art and books, and later in life donated many of his valuable art collections to U.S. libraries and museums. He also was famous as a yachtsman, defending the America's Cup in international yacht races on several occasions.

John entered his father's banking house, The George Peabody Co., in London. A year later his father secured a position for him in New York with Duncan, Sherman and Co., the U.S. agents for the George Peabody firm. Then, at the age of 23, Morgan founded his own company, the J. Pierpont Morgan and Co., to serve as a special agent for the London Peabody Company. And by age 26 Morgan became a member of a firm struggling for financial control of the Albany and Susquehanna Railroad. After his success in this enterprise Morgan grew significantly in personal status within the banking community. He became known as a voice for stabilization in an age noted for its wild and fiery business sectors.

J. P. Morgan.

Morgan's motive was to guarantee high profits by stunting competition. His first major effort to create business monopolies during this time was his financial supervision of the reorganization of the railroad industry on the East Coast of the United States. This effort was often dubbed "Morganization." By the beginning of the 20th century Morgan made U.S. railways into a vast inter-related empire.

Morgan financed General Electric and consolidated the railroad industry. Toward the end of his career he negotiated with Carnegie Steel in his greatest economic achievement, the creation of the world's largest steel company, United States Steel. It was the first billion-dollar corporation in the United States.

Though the steel industry became the backbone of business growth in the 20th century its growth did not come easily. Internal conflicts emerged between individual steel manufacturers, and the ups and downs of the U.S. economy almost crushed the industry. In 1911 the presidential administration of William Howard Taft (1909–1913) filed suit against U.S. Steel for possible monopoly practices and illegal business manipulation. Federal committee investigations in 1912 revealed that Morgan's partners held 72 directorships in 47 major corporations in the United States. This may have been admirable as a business achievement, but it was also illegal.

Morgan was one of the few truly vital people of his time. He brought together the financial economics of Europe and the United States. He linked those who had money with those who needed it for the enormous industrial development of the United States that began during the middle of the 19th century. As a result of having so much power and money, he was frequently seen as either a force of great good or the source of great evil in the business world. A few months after his appearance as a defendant in the federal business trial, J. P. Morgan died in Rome, Italy, a broken revolutionary force in U.S. industry.

FURTHER READING

Allen, Frederick Lewis. *The Great Pierpont Morgan.* New York: Harper and Row, 1949.

Carosso, Vincent P. *The Morgans: Private International Bankers.* Cambridge, MA: Harvard University Press, 1987.

Cotter, Arundel. *The Authentic History of United States Steel Corp.* New York: Moody, 1916.

Studenski, Paul and Herman E. Krooss. *Financial History of the United States.* New York: McGraw-Hill, 1952.

Winkler, John K. *Morgan the Magnificent: The Life of J. Pierpont Morgan.* New York: Garden City Publishing Co., Inc., 1930.

MORITA, AKIO

Akio Morita (1921–), as a co-founder and later chairman of the Sony Corporation, gave to the general public a revolutionary array of inventive electronic products during the last half of the twentieth century. Worldwide, he introduced consumers to products like the hand-held transistor radio, the video cassette recorder (VCR), the Walkman portable cassette player, and the Diskman portable CD disk player. He not only became one of the most influential businessmen in the world, he also helped to establish Japan's reputation after World War II (1939–1945) as a source for high quality, innovative, and reliable products.

Morita was born in 1921, the first son of Kyusaemon and Shuko Morita, in the small Japanese village of Kosugaya. If Morita had followed in the traditional family occupation of his father and his ancestors, he would have been the fifteenth generation heir to his family's 300 year-old *sake* brewing business, manufacturing an alcoholic beverage made from fermented rice and widely used by the Japanese.

The young Morita, however, was not interested in the family business. He instead developed a passion for improving electronics and sound reproduction. Presumably he was influenced early in his life by his mother's love for Western classical music, which she imported into the household with American-made RCA Victrola records. Recordings were then made out of heavy, clumsy, and easily-broken 12-inch diameter discs, imprinted with fine grooves that had to be tracked by a tiny needle as the discs revolved at 78 revolutions per minute. The sound quality was crude, and the music was often mixed with the sounds of scratches which inevitably accumulated on the discs after use.

Morita became so interested in new electronics, and with improving the qualities of sound, that he almost flunked out of school because of his disinterest in anything other than electronics. His family convinced him to persist in his studies, and he later entered the prestigious Eighth Higher School as a physics major.

Rather than be drafted into World War II (1939–1945), Morita entered Osaka Imperial University, agreeing to serve in the navy after graduation. In 1944 he was commissioned as a lieutenant in the engineering corps of the Japanese Imperial Navy. He worked on projects involving guided weapons and night-vision gun sights. There he met with Masura Ibuka, a brilliant electronics engineer 13 years his senior. They became best friends and together eventually co-founded Sony Corporation.

After World War II, Morita and Ibuka created the Tokyo Telecommunications Engineering Corporation with only $500. Begun with 20 employees and a shared rented office in a burned-out Tokyo department store, the company made electronic equipment—amplifiers, voltage-measuring devices, and communication devices—for the Japanese Post Office. It was the beginning of an electronics revolution, and an electronics empire.

The business grew slowly, but in 1953, Morita decided to buy the rights to the transistor, a miniature electronics circuit that had been developed by the American company Bell Laboratories. The patent was owned by another American company, Western Electric. At that time, transistors were thought to be impractical for most consumer products, except for use in hearing aids. Morita's purchase of the patent would prove to be the basis for a revolution in modern consumer electronics. With this patent, Morita and Ibuka began to use the transistor in ways that transformed the world of electronics, sound, and television. Within two years, the partners created for commercial consumer use the AM transistor radio. In another two years, they began to produce the pocket-sized transistor radio, the AM-FM transistor radio, the first all-transistor television set, the all-transistor video tape recorder, and the small-screen portable battery-operated television set.

In 1958 Morita changed his company's name to Sony Corporation, because it was easy to pronounce, and Morita himself moved to New York City to set up an office for United States operations. Sony became the first foreign-owned business to offer stock for sale in the United States; in 1970, Sony became the first Japanese company to be listed on the New York Stock Exchange.

During the 1960s and 1970s the Sony Corporation continued to introduce to the public several new transistorized inventions: the first inexpensively priced home video recorder, the color video tape recorder, video tape for color video recording, and the first battery-operated portable video recorder and camera. All of these inventions came to the marketplace produced with extremely high quality. Morita's business helped changed the reputation of Japanese businesses for making cheap, poor-quality consumer items. The Sony brand name stood for the creation of transistorized innovations of all kinds, for high quality, and for reliable consumer products. Morita felt he had, among other things, taken the shame out of the label "Made in Japan."

Morita had indeed realized his childhood dream to improve the quality of sound reproduction. The use of CD digital technology eliminated the old-fashioned records his mother used and replaced the scratchy-sounding vinyl discs with a CD technology that reproduced sound almost flawlessly. The Sony Corporation, with Morita's genius for innovation and selling, created an entirely new electronics environment during the last half of the twentieth century.

During the 1980s and early 1990s, Morita wrote two books dealing with careers in business and international business trade: *Made in Japan* (1986) and *The Japan That Can Say No* (1991). In 1994, Morita retired from the Sony Corporation at age 73, after suffering a debilitating stroke which had confined him to a wheel chair.

See also: **Sony Corporation**

FURTHER READING

Ishihara, Shintaru, and Akio Morita. *The Japan That Can Say No*. New York: Simon and Schuster, 1991.

Johnstone, Bob. *We Were Burning: Japanese Entrepreneurs and the Electronic Age*. New York: Basic Books, 1999.

Lyons, Nick. *The Sony Vision*. New York: Crown Pub., 1976.

Morita, Akio, and Edwin M. Reingold, and Mitsuko Shimomura. *Made in Japan: Akio Morita and Sony*. New York: Dutton, 1986.

MORRIS, ROBERT

Robert Morris (1734–1806), possibly America's wealthiest man in the earliest years of the Republic, died penniless and in disgrace. Known as the "financier of the American Revolution," Morris played a role in the highest circles of the new American government, but he spent three years near the end of his life in debtor's prison.

Born in Liverpool, England, on January 31, 1734, Morris emigrated to the American colonies at age twelve. His father, a British tobacco merchant and a part-time resident of Maryland, died from a cannon misfire in a shipboard accident, leaving his son, a teenager, with a small estate.

Morris came under the care of a Philadelphia merchant, Charles Willing. When he also died, Morris and Willing's son, Thomas, formed Willing, Morris and Company, a trading company with three ships and contacts in Spain, Portugal and the West Indies. In the years immediately preceding the American Revolution (1775–1783), the firm traded wheat, flour, tobacco, and other products in a triangular route between Europe, the West Indies, and America.

Through Willing, Morris, and Company, Morris became one of the wealthiest men—if not *the* wealthiest man—in the American colonies. He did not immediately support the revolutionary cause against the British, though he had opposed Britain's levying of additional taxes under the Stamp Act of 1765 and had signed the Non-Importation Agreement opposing it. In June 1774 he became a member of the Pennsylvania Committee of Safety and a delegate to the Continental Congress, where he was named a member of the Select Committee on Trade. Hoping that a way would be found to avoid war with Britain, he did not sign the Declaration of Independence immediately but waited until several weeks after the historic document had been adopted.

KNOWN AS THE "FINANCIER OF THE AMERICAN REVOLUTION," MORRIS PLAYED A ROLE IN THE HIGHEST CIRCLES OF THE NEW AMERICAN GOVERNMENT, BUT HE SPENT THREE YEARS NEAR THE END OF HIS LIFE IN DEBTOR'S PRISON.

In his capacity as chairman or member of several trade-related congressional committees, Morris was in charge of provisioning the Revolutionary Army. He blatantly used the office to his own advantage, selling to the new government material from companies he formed himself. Morris stayed on in Philadelphia when the war forced the Congress to vacate the city in December of 1776 and, during that time, acted with some courage in his role as the army's provisioner. He became banker for the Committee of Commerce in 1777, signed the Articles of Confederation as a Pennsylvania delegate the next year, and became chairman of the Congressional Committee on Finance. Morris left the Continental Congress in November of 1778 to attend to his private business affairs but remained in the Pennsylvania Assembly.

As a member of the Continental Congress, Morris became even wealthier. He used inside information and his network of international connections to profit himself. As a key part of his income, he maintained a very lucrative privateering operation: a state-sanctioned commercial venture wherein pirates seized the ships of enemies. Between 1775 and 1777, the Secret Committees on Trade and Commerce, headed by Morris, spent $3.3 million. Of this amount Morris and his associates pocketed $846,000.

Yet, historians differ about whether Morris was a scoundrel or a hero. In 1781 George Washington (1732–1799) urged Morris to reenter the national government as superintendent of finance. The war was still underway and the new nation's money was virtually worthless, but Morris had the nation operating on a hard-money basis before the end of the war, a formidable accomplishment. Funds that Morris was able to borrow from France, supplemented with money from his own pocket, made it possible for Washington to move his armies from New York to Yorktown, where the British general, Cornwallis, surrendered.

Morris resigned his position as superintendent of finance when the states refused to agree to his taxation policy and blocked the national financial system he advocated. He turned his attention to land speculation and such ventures as turnpikes, iron works, and trade with China. Acting on credit, he bought huge sections of western New York and Virginia. He spent $1 million on the first stage of building an ostentatious mansion in Philadelphia. Suddenly, the bottom fell out of the land speculation business. Many individual investors and land companies failed. Morris, whose fortune was vastly overextended, was never able to recover. He was confined in debtors prison for three years until his release in 1801 and died, five years later, still destitute.

See also: **American Revolution, Stamp Act, Triangular Trade**

FURTHER READING

Chernow, Barbara Ann. *Robert Morris, Land Speculator, 1790–1801.* New York: Arno, 1978.

Ferguson, James E., ed. *The Papers of Robert Morris, 1781–1784.* Pittsburgh: University of Pittsburgh Press, 1973.

Ingham, John. *Biographical Dictionary of American Business Leaders H-M.* Westport, CT: Greenwood, 1983, s.v. "Morris, Robert."

Van Steeg, Clarence Lester. *Robert Morris, Revolutionary Financier.* New York: Octagon, 1972.

Wagner, Frederick. *Robert Morris, Audacious Patriot.* New York: Dodd, Mead, 1976.

Willoughby, Jack. "What Your Country Can Do for You." *Forbes*, October 23, 1989.

MORSE, SAMUEL FINLEY BREESE

Samuel F. B. Morse (1791–1872) is best known as the inventor of the telegraph and the code used to

Samuel Morse with his telegraph.

transmit messages on it. On May 24, 1844, he sent the very first telegraph message—''What hath God wrought?'' His invention revolutionized communications, making it possible to transmit messages across long distances with almost no delay. The telegraph facilitated westward expansion and the development of industry across the continent and it helped to forge a sense of unity in a young nation.

Samuel Finley Breese Morse was born in Charlestown, Massachusetts, on April 27, 1791, to Jedidiah Morse, a clergyman, and his wife, Elizabeth Breese Morse. The oldest of three boys, he grew up being called ''Finley.'' Morse's grandfather had been president of Princeton College and his father was known throughout New England as a fervent Calvinist preacher.

At age seven Morse was enrolled at Phillips Academy in Andover, Massachusetts. Like his father before him, he went on to attend Yale College. While there, he began painting miniatures on ivory. He enjoyed it so much that he considered pursuing a career in art. But his parents were very religious and did not approve. Thus, after graduating from Yale in 1810, Morse found a job in a bookstore in his native Charlestown.

Morse continued to paint, however, and eventually his work came to the attention of two of the country's most respected artists, Gilbert Stuart and Washington Allston. Impressed by the admiration of his son's work, Jedidiah Morse finally allowed the young man to accompany Allston on a trip to England to study painting at the Royal Academy in London. Samuel Morse returned to the United States in 1815 with dreams of painting grand murals of heroic scenes. But there was no market for that kind of art at the time, so Morse had to settle for a career as a portrait painter, in which he enjoyed a fair amount of success. Of all his works, two in particular stand out. Both are portraits of France's Marquis de Lafayette that were painted in 1825 in Washington, DC. In 1826 Morse helped establish the National Academy of the Arts of Design, an organization aimed at helping artists obtain commissions and at improving the public's taste in art. He served as its first president from its founding until 1842.

Having garnered a fair share of praise and recognition by the early 1820s, Morse settled in New York City and married a young woman named Lucretia Walker. But tragedy struck in quick succession. He lost his wife in 1825, his father in 1826 and his mother in 1828. Grief over their deaths ultimately propelled him in a new direction.

To aid in his recovery from a profound state of grief, he sailed to England in 1829 for an extended stay in Europe. During his return voyage to the United States in 1832, he became acquainted with an eccentric inventor named Charles Thomas Jackson. The two men passed the time aboard ship discussing Jackson's ideas regarding electromagnetism, a subject Morse had first heard about while a student at Yale.

WHAT HATH GOD WROUGHT?

Samuel Morse's first telegraph message, May 24, 1844

According to Jackson, electrical impulses could be carried great distances along wires. Morse reasoned that if this were true, ''and the presence of electricity can be made visible in any desired part of the circuit, I see no reason why intelligence might not be instantaneously transmitted by electricity to any distance.'' He soon began sketching plans for a device that might be able to perform such a task.

Upon his return to the United States, Morse resumed his painting career and began teaching painting and sculpture at the University of the City of New York. However, he continued to mull over the question of how to send and receive electromagnetic signals by wire. Not only did he need to come up with an appropriate transmitter and receiver, he also had to devise the code that would enable users to create and then decipher messages. He invented a system in which the long and short impulses could stand for letters and numbers.

Morse worked on his invention for a number of years without making much progress. Part of his problem stemmed from the fact that he was not a scientist and did not have the skill to implement his ideas. But then he met two men at the University of the City of New York who helped him tremendously. Leonard Gale, a chemistry professor, showed Morse how he could improve the electromagnet and battery for the working model of his telegraph. Gale's friend, Joseph Henry, offered additional assistance in the area of electromagnetism. Morse also received valuable help from Alfred Vail, whom he took on as a partner in 1837. Vail suggested several practical refinements to the telegraph device itself as well as to the code it used to transmit and receive messages.

In order to minimize the number of transmission lines per message, Morse had invented a code consisting of combinations of dots and dashes, each representing a single letter, number, or punctuation mark. A visit to a typesetting shop had helped him determine which letters were used most often, and to these he assigned the simplest code symbols. Complex codes were reserved for little-used characters. This marked the development of what would come to be known as Morse Code, the universal standard for communicating by telegraph.

Morse, who had abandoned his art career at this point, was aware that European inventors were also working on a telegraph device, and he was anxious to establish himself at the head of the line. By 1837 he was ready to conduct a public demonstration. Appearing before a select audience at New York University on September 2 of that year, Morse successfully presented his telegraph device. He then contacted federal government officials and suggested that further development work be supervised by the Post Office. But nothing came of his recommendation.

That same year Morse and Vail applied for a patent for the telegraph in both the United States and England. Morse also approached Congress for a grant to fund the construction of an experimental line from Washington, DC, to Baltimore. The American patent was approved in 1840 (the English one was rejected because a similar device had been introduced there earlier), but Morse could not convince Congress to appropriate any money for a telegraph line.

After a few years of frustration, Morse finally obtained a federal grant of $30,000 to lay a telegraph line from Washington to Baltimore. On May 24, 1844, he tapped out the first message, ''What hath God wrought?'' and thus launched a new era in communications. Morse then tried to interest the government in buying the rights to the telegraph for $100,000, but Congress opted to leave it up to the private sector to finance and develop a system.

Morse and several partners formed the Magnetic Telegraph Company to lay telegraph lines themselves. Making money on the new technology proved difficult, however. According to Rosa Harris-Adler's article in *Canadian Geographic*, the company made only one cent in revenue during its first four days of operation and only $193.56 during the first three months. Operating expenses for this same period were $1,859.05.

Additional problems soon surfaced. Morse faced prolonged litigation over his patent rights as Charles Jackson and other scientists who had given the inventor advice demanded the recognition they felt they deserved. Neither side came out looking very good in court. While Morse stubbornly refused to give credit to the many people who had indeed contributed in some way to the development of the telegraph, a few scientists were strictly out to profit from his years of hard work. In 1854 the U.S. Supreme Court upheld Morse's patent rights.

Competitors were also quick to exploit the potential of the new invention. They soon began to establish rival telegraph companies throughout the country. Eventually, several small companies merged into the Western Union Corporation, which finally was able to make a profit on the telegraph. Morse's own company did not stand much of a chance in the face of such a rival, so in 1866 the Magnetic Telegraph Company also merged with Western Union.

In his later years Morse left the business world behind and turned his attention instead to politics and philanthropy. He even ran unsuccessfully for the United States Congress in 1854. His interest in scientific matters never waned, however, and in 1857 he teamed with Cyrus Field in a project to lay a transatlantic telegraph cable.

It is nearly impossible to determine the full extent to which the telegraph changed the way people lived. It was not so much because ordinary citizens made use of it on a regular basis; in fact, it was a rather expensive means of communication that mostly appealed to big business and government. But telegraph lines followed the westward expansion of the railroad across North America. They made it possible to communicate quickly over vast distances and they linked far-flung settlements with population centers back east. This helped foster a stronger sense of national identity and underscored the need for more standardization and uniformity.

One significant consequence of the introduction of the telegraph was the creation of time zones in the United States and Canada. Before the invention of the telegraph, most cities kept their own time based on the position of the sun at noon. A standardized time schedule presented less confusion and less accidents.

Surveying and cartography also underwent some changes as a result of the introduction of the telegraph. Before the telegraph was invented, surveyors calculated longitude by chronometers that were shipped to key geographic points. Though chronometers were fairly accurate instruments at the time, the jostling involved in moving them could affect their precision by as much as 20 seconds a day. In 1849 astronomer William Bond of Boston invented a machine that attached chronometers to the telegraph. With this device astronomers could hit a telegraph key when they saw a star cross the meridian, passing the data along to other astronomers and thus improving longitude precision. As a result, maps showing boundaries and borders became more accurate.

By making distant communities feel less isolated from each other and the rest of the country, the telegraph also prompted greater political and social cohesion. People were better informed about what was happening at a national level and, consequently, they became more involved in influencing policy, mostly because they heard about events in a more timely fashion.

While the telegraph represented the first major breakthrough in mass communications technology, it was rapidly followed by the telephone (patented in 1876), television (first demonstrated in 1927), and eventually computers. Telecommunications has become a multi-billion-dollar global industry that connects people not only by telephone and television but also by cable, satellite, and the Internet.

Morse married for a second time in 1848 and had several children. He ran for Congress in 1854 but was not elected. Morse spent the last years of his life on his estate in Poughkeepsie, New York, surrounded by his large family. Many European nations honored him for his invention; in 1871 American telegraph operators erected a bronze statue of him in New York's Central Park. Morse was elected to the Hall of Fame in 1900, 28 years after his death.

See also: **Standard Time, Telegraph**

FURTHER READING

Coe, Lewis. *The Telegraph: A History of Morse's Invention and Its Predecessors in the United States.* Jefferson, NC: McFarland, 1993.

Harris-Adler, Rosa. ''Creation of the e-nation,'' *Canadian Geographic*, November-December 1995.

Kloss, William. *Samuel F. B. Morse.* New York: H. N. Abrams, 1988.

Mabee, Carleton. *The American Leonardo: A Life of Samuel F.B. Morse.* New York: Knopf, 1944.

Morse, Samuel F.B. *Samuel F.B. Morse: His Letters and Journals.* New York: Da Capo, 1973.

Staiti, Paul J. *Samuel F. B. Morse.* New York: Cambridge University Press, 1989.

MORTGAGE

The purchase price of a home is clearly more than what most individuals can pay with their available savings. Therefore they seek a home loan to finance the purchase. This home loan is called a mortgage. Home mortgage loans generally require a down payment of between five percent and 20 percent of the total purchase price. The remaining money needed for the purchase is the mortgage amount, usually borrowed from a lending institution. To purchase a $125,000 home with a 20 percent down payment would require $25,000 down and a $100,000 mortgage loan. The borrower secures the mortgage with the real estate purchased. That is, the borrower promises to pay back the loan with interest; if she or he does not, the lender can foreclose or take possession of the house.

A mortgage loan is a long-term loan usually established for repayment in 15, 20, 25, or 30 years. Because the mortgage is over a long period of time, small changes in the interest rate (the percentage a borrower pays to a lender for using the funds) make a big difference in monthly payments and the total amount of payback. For example a typical 30-year $100,000 mortgage would require monthly payments of $878 at a fixed interest rate of 10 percent but only $665 at seven percent. The total payback after 360 months (30 years) at 10 percent would be $316,080. The total payback after 360 months at seven percent would be $239,000.

Lenders basically offer three types of mortgages: fixed rate, variable rate, and graduated payment. For a fixed rate loan the interest and monthly payment remain the same for the length of the loan. For variable rate loans the interest rate varies annually according to the prevailing market rates, and monthly payments vary accordingly. The graduated payment option assumes young people generally have low incomes but high earning potential. The interest rate remains the same but monthly payments are adjusted to start out smaller and increase as earning increases.

Mortgage interest rates in the United States remained near five percent after World War II (1939–1945) into the 1950s. Rates began to rise in the 1960s, reaching 8.5 percent in 1970, 12 percent in 1980, and peaking in 1982 at 15 percent. As the national economy began to expand, rates dropped to 10 percent by 1991 and with continued expansion were quoted as low as 6.5 percent in 1998.

MOUND BUILDERS

Mound Builders were prehistoric American Indians, named for their practice of burying their dead in large mounds. Beginning about three thousand years ago, they built extensive earthworks from the Great Lakes down through the Mississippi River Valley and into the Gulf of Mexico region. These mounds, many of which survive today, consisted of several hundred tons of dirt, clay, and stone, and were built on a large scale in spite of the fact that the builders had no beasts of burden and did not use the wheel. The Adena people were one group of Mound Builders. They arose in the Ohio River Valley around 400 B.C. They were hunters and gatherers, and also fished. They settled in villages scattered over a wide area. The largest Adena mound is the Grave Creek Mound at Moundsville, West Virginia; it measures 900 feet (270 meters) in circumference and 70 feet (21 meters) in height. Scholars believe that as the Adena traded with other groups of American Indians, the practice of mound-building spread.

Other Mound Builders were the Hopewell and the Mississippian people. The Hopewell were hunters and gatherers but they also cultivated corn and squash. They settled in the Midwestern United States, where their burial mounds can still be found; the largest site is in Newark, Ohio. Objects such as shells, shark teeth, and volcanic glass discovered in the Hopewell earthworks reveal that they traded with distant tribes. This trade network collapsed about A.D. 500 and the Hopewell died out. The Mississippians, who settled in the Mississippi valley and in what is today the southern United States, were the only Mound Builders to have contact with the Europeans. Their culture emerged about A.D. 700 and lasted into the 1700s. The Mississippians were farmers and raised livestock. In addition to their mounds, the largest of which is found at Cahokia, Illinois, they built cities, which were among the earliest in North America. Since many of their earthworks (c. 1200–1500) include temples atop the mounds, the Mississippians may have traded with the Indians of Mexico (such as the Aztec or Maya), and were influenced by them.

See also: **Great Serpent Mound**

MOVIES

Movies (short for moving pictures) are also called motion pictures or films. They were introduced in the United States in 1896 at a New York screening made possible by American inventor Thomas Alva Edison's (1847–1931) kinetoscope. The kinetoscope was a device for viewing a sequence of pictures on an endless band of film using a projector invented by Thomas Armat. It was not until the early 1900s that the technology was used for entertainment.

In 1903 American director-photographer Edwin S. Porter (1870–1941) made *The Great Train Robbery*, the first motion picture to tell a complete story. (Porter had earlier worked as a cameraman with Edison.) Produced by Edison Studios, the twelve-minute "epic" established a pattern of suspense drama that was followed by subsequent moviemakers. The age of the silent film was launched.

BY 1930 MOVIE HOUSES WERE ATTRACTING 100 MILLION VIEWERS A WEEK AT A TIME WHEN THE TOTAL POPULATION OF THE UNITED STATES WAS ONLY 120 MILLION AND WEEKLY CHURCH ATTENDANCE WAS LESS THAN 60 MILLION.

The popularity of movies escalated during the 1920s. Innovations in movie-making technology broadened the audience. In 1927 the first full-length talking picture was released, *The Jazz Singer*, starring vaudevillian Al Jolson (1886–1950).

The ever-improving technology of motion pictures and the advent of radio combined to spell the demise of vaudeville during the 1930s. By 1930 movie houses were attracting 100 million viewers a week at a time when the total population of the United States was only 120 million and weekly church attendance was less than 60 million. By 1932 all movies were talkies,

This artist's rendering attempts to capture the lure of the silent movie theatre when the only sound accompaniment was an orchestra pit.

and by the end of the decade all movies used technicolor, a trademarked method for making motion pictures in color.

With a theater in almost every town people in the United States flocked to the ''picture shows.'' Hollywood images provided an escape from everyday life. As measured in total capital investment, motion pictures became one of the nation's leading industries. Like sports, amusement parks, and radio programs, movies were meant to appeal to everyone.

An increase in leisure time and a willingness by U.S. audiences to spend money on entertainment guaranteed movie houses would be well attended. Entertainment was no longer a singular experience; Hollywood movies shown in theaters throughout the country provided entertainment for a mass consumer audience.

See also: **Amusement Parks, Baseball, Thomas Alva Edison, Radio, Vaudeville**

MUCKRAKERS

Muckrakers emerged on the U.S. journalism scene around the turn of the nineteenth century. They were journalists who sought out and exposed the misconduct of prominent people or high profile organizations. As crusaders for social change, muckraking journalists wrote articles not about news events, but about injustices or abuses, and corruption in the world of business and politics. Their aim was to bring such information to the attention of the U.S. public.

Politician Theodore Roosevelt (1858–1919) was the first to call controversial journalists ''muckrakers.'' [This was a reference to a character in the then well-known book *Pilgrim's Progress*, by English preacher John Bunyan (1628–1688).] A muckraker was a person who rejected a crown for a muckrake, a tool used to rake dung.

Magazines such as *McClure's*, *Cosmopolitan*, and *Everybody's* published articles revealing abuses of power or negligent practices. These included the use of tainted meat by the meat packing industry, prostitution rings, fraudulent insurance, and corruption among city politicians. Proponents of this progressive journalism included magazine editor Lincoln Steffens (1866–1936), whose collected articles in *McClure's* were published as the book *Shame of the Cities* (1904). Writer and social reformer Upton Sinclair (1878–1968) also incorporated pointed criticisms of business and government into such topical novels as *The Jungle* (1906), *The Money Changers* (1908), and *King Coal* (1917). Author Ida M. Tarbell (1857–1944) penned a *History of the Standard Oil Company* (1904) which was then a scathing indictment of the U.S. petroleum business.

While the muckrakers were derided in their own time, their work succeeded in raising widespread awareness of social, economic, and political ills. This prompted a number of reforms, including passage of pure food laws and anti-trust legislation.

See also: **Upton Sinclair, Social Gospel, Ida Tarbell**

MULTI-NATIONAL ENTERPRISE

A multi-national enterprise is typically a business corporation whose operations literally straddle the globe. An example is PepsiCo. PepsiCo does not ship its famous product around the world directly from the United States. Instead, it produces Pepsi Cola in over 600 plants in 148 countries around the world. A multinational enterprise typically has substantial portions of its total wealth invested in production facilities outside of its country of origin. Because of the expanded activities of these corporations, international banks have grown, allowing the monies of international enterprises to pass quickly over national frontiers to take advantage of favorable interest rate changes in multinational banking operations. A multi-national enterprise considers the entire world to be its potential market, not merely for shipping its home-produced goods, but a market within which it may actually manufacture its product.

By selling products to world markets a multinational enterprise is able to profitably take advantage of different business situations in various countries such as lower wages, lower tax and tariff rates, less business regulation, and other business-friendly incentives. In this way, a multi-national enterprise is able to produce its products in countries where the wages are lower, and to sell their products in countries where people can often afford to pay higher prices for it. The multi-national enterprise meets the international demand for products, resulting in business profitability and consumer satisfaction at the same time.

See also: **General Agreement on Tariffs and Trade (GATT), Free Trade**

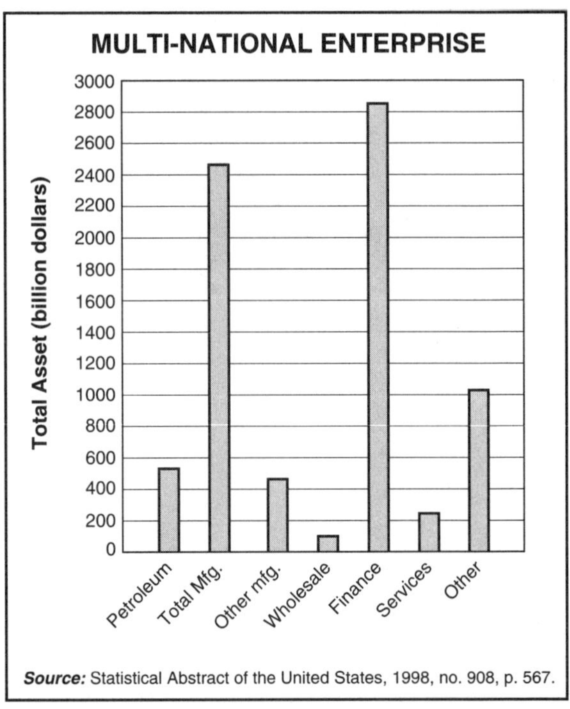

The total assets of various U.S. multi-national companies. A U.S. multi-national enterprise owns production facilities and produces and sells products in countries outside the U.S.

MULTIPLIER

The multiplier is a conceptual tool used to capture the complicated process by which changes in spending affect a nation's income. It is based on the idea that a small change in spending can bring about a much larger change in income. Consider the following example as an illustration of how the multiplier works. Suppose an individual pays a gardener $100 for a spring cleanup. The gardener saves $10 of those $100 but spends $90 at the local hardware store for new tools. Of the $90, the hardware storeowner saves nine dollars and spends $81 on a golf club. The golf storeowner spends 90 percent of the $81 ($73) to take his family out to dinner. The $100 that was originally spent was re-spent three more times and, in the process, was turned into $344 of income to others. This process continues and ultimately $100 of spending could lead to as much as $1000 of income. In that case, the multiplier would be 10. The product of that computation is known as the multiplier effect.

The multiplier effect occurs throughout the economy on an immense scale. Suppose the economy is at less than full employment. Several large firms invest in new plants, workers are hired, new wages are paid, and new profits flow to the companies. The recipients of this income will save some income and spend a portion of it on goods and services. More income is thus created for the suppliers of the goods and services. This process goes on *ad infinitum* and the total increase in national income ends up being many times larger than the initial investment.

The multiplier is a cornerstone of Keynesian economics, based on the theories of John Maynard Keynes (1883–1946). Developed at the time of the Great Depression (1929–1939), Keynesian economics deals with the need to stimulate aggregate, total demand to lower unemployment. The multiplier is used to estimate the impact new private investment, government spending, or tax cuts will have on national income.

The multiplier can work in both directions. For every dollar decrease in investment or spending, the level of national income will fall by much greater than one dollar. The Great Depression is an example of the multiplier in a downward cycle. By the late 1930s investment increased and the Depression ended with the mobilization of resources for World War II (1939–1945), which resulted in increased demand for goods and significant government spending. Thus, the multiplier works in a cumulative pattern, both expanding and contracting economic activity.

See also: **Aggregate Demand, Keynesian Economic Theory, Supply and Demand, Unemployment**

MUNN V. ILLINOIS (1877)

In *Munn v. Illinois* (1877) the U.S. Supreme Court upheld an Illinois law which regulated the owners of grain elevators, declaring that government interference was constitutional in areas ''affected with a public interest'' (*Munn vs. Illinois* 94 US 113). The Court created a confusing void, however, with a later decision in *Wabash, St. Louis and Pacific Railway Company v. Illinois* (1886). It declared state laws regulating interstate railroads were unconstitutional because they violated the Commerce Clause, which gives Congress exclusive regulatory power ''with foreign nations, the several states, and with the Indian tribes'' (Article I, Sec. 8). This decision eventually led to the establishment of the Interstate Commerce Commission in 1887.

Long before the creation of the federal regulatory body, the business practices of the railroads had given rise to a movement led by the National Grange. The Grange was a powerful association of farmers who protested railroad rate structures, citing them as discriminatory and unfair. They pressured state lawmakers into taking action. Midwestern legislatures yielded to the outcry, passing laws that established regulatory commissions to monitor the practices of the railroads. In Illinois and Minnesota these commissions prohibited discrimination in rates and services, fixed maximum freight rates, and established standards of service. The bodies were also given the authority to enforce their standards.

When *Munn vs. Illinois* came before the Supreme Court in 1877, the issue of state regulation was raised. The Supreme Court upheld the power of the state to impose standards on businesses ''clothed with a public interest.'' This decision was often later cited in support of other Granger laws that were passed, primarily in Midwestern states, to curb unfair business practices of the railroads. Ultimately the states found it difficult to enforce their laws on carriers that moved between states. The creation of the Interstate Commerce Commission in 1887 resolved these problems, placing responsibility for the regulation of interstate business transportation firmly in the hands of the federal government.

See also: **Interstate Commerce Act, Interstate Commerce: Regulation and Deregulation, National Grange, Wabash, St. Louis and Pacific Railway Company vs. Illinois**

MUTUAL FUND

A mutual fund is a large, diverse group of stocks and/or bonds in which an individual may invest. There are three basic types of mutual funds. Money market funds invest in certificates of deposit, U.S. Treasury bills, and other low-risk, short-term securities that provide a safe, low-return alternative to checking accounts. The medium-risk bond and income funds invest in both stocks and corporate and government debt, with the goal of invest exclusively in the stock of corporations. The higher risk equity fund invests in the stocks of corporations and comes in all shapes and sizes. Mutual funds are also classified as ''closed-end'' (a fixed number of shares are sold to the public) and ''open-end'' (shares are sold to as many people as want them).

Low, medium, and high risk mutual funds each have many options for investment. One class of higher-risk funds is the aggressive growth equity fund, which may be suitable for an individual looking for a quick return on an investment. A less risky kind of mutual fund, the index equity fund, takes the process of picking stocks out of the hands of mutual fund managers and instead invests in companies listed in such stock market indices as the Standard and Poor's

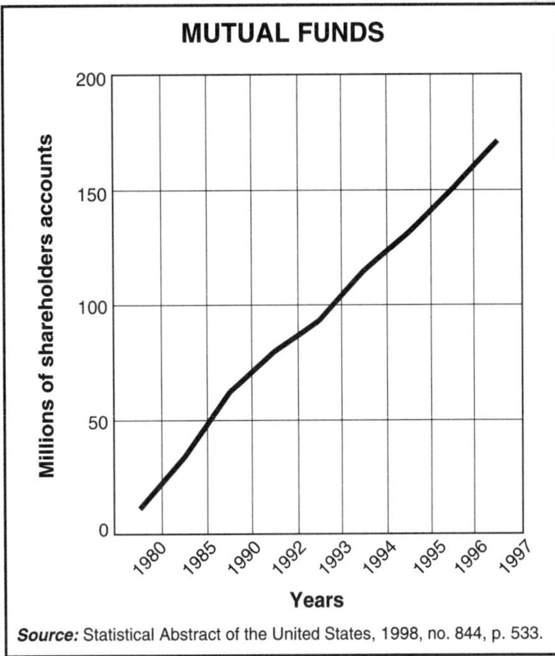

Mutual funds pool the investor's funds into portfolios based upon the desired type of investment and level of risk. This popular form of investment provides Americans with an alternate way to put money into the stock market.

500. Sector equity funds specialize in specific segments of the economy, such as telecommunications, biotechnology, or Internet stocks. While many opportunities exist for domestic investment, an individual can also look to the foreign markets as a place to invest money. International equity funds focus on the stocks of non-U.S. companies and may be region specific, such as an Asia or Latin America fund.

Mutual funds first appeared in Europe in the nineteenth century and were well established in the United States by 1900. Not until 1924, however, did the first modern open-end mutual fund appear—it boasted forty-five stocks and $50,000 in assets. The stock market crash of 1929 soured an entire generation on stock investing, however, and it took new government safeguards and the post-World War II (1939–1945) economic boom to convince U.S. citizens to return to stock investing. In the 1940s there were only about 80 mutual funds with assets of $500 million. In 1948 one of the first sector funds, Television Funds, Inc., was launched; it was followed in 1953 by the first international mutual fund. The number of funds edged up to 100 in the 1950s, but by 1952 still only one-quarter of one percent of the U.S. population owned stocks. The first aggressive growth mutual fund appeared in the 1960s, and in the 1970s money market funds and bond and income funds became more common. Fueled by the beginning of one of the longest bull markets in U.S. history in 1982, the number of funds grew fivefold in the 1980s. By the late 1990s, the nation's 6,700 mutual funds owned 22 percent of the entire U.S. stock market and held assets of more than $4.5 trillion.

See also: **Bond, Investment, Standard and Poor's, Stock, Stock Market**

NABISCO FOODS GROUP

In 1898 decades of amalgamation in the biscuit industry culminated in the merging of the mid-western American Biscuit Company, the eastern New York Biscuit Company, and the United States Baking Company to form the National Biscuit Company (NBC). The merger, comprised one hundred and fourteen bakeries, and was capitalized at $55 million. The Chicago-based National Biscuit Company launched by lawyer Adolphus Green held the monopoly on cookie and biscuit production in the United States.

Adolphus Green began the process of standardization of every company product that could be nationally identified with Nabisco. Exact recipes and uniform standards were developed and used by all of the NBC bakeries. Green also initiated novel and unusual packaging in special protective containers for crackers. He commissioned an advertising agency to assist in promoting the company's products with illustrations. One of the world's best-recognized illustrated trademarks showed a rosy-cheeked boy dressed in a raincoat and galoshes clutching a box of biscuits. As a pioneer in advertising NBC spent seven million dollars in the early 1900s promoting and marketing company products.

In the early years of the twentieth century NBC expanded its line of cookies and crackers. Introduced in 1902, Barnum's Animal Crackers were colorfully packaged in a box resembling a circus cage filled with animals. In 1912 the company introduced Lorna Doone and Oreo, the latter eventually becoming the world's best-selling cookie.

The 1920s were a very prosperous period for NBC. In 1925, with the addition of several new bakeries, the company established its first foreign subsidiary in Canada. NBC expanded its product line to include pretzels, breakfast cereal, and ice cream cones. Diversification came about through acquisitions of other companies, including the purchase of the Shredded Wheat Company (in 1928) and the Mclaren Consolidated Cone Company, the world's largest manufacturer of ice cream cones.

The depression years (1929–1939) slowed company growth until 1931 when NBC took over the Bennett Biscuit Company. NBC concentrated on Bennett's most popular product line, Milk-Bone Dog Biscuits. Advertising ''a dog's dessert'' and its breath-sweetening properties boosted NBC's sales. In 1934 Ritz Crackers was launched as a new prestige product and was a huge success. Throughout the 1930s the company relied heavily on radio advertisements to promote NBC's products. Partly to reduce confusion, NBC changed its official trademark company name to ''Nabisco.''

Nabisco experienced troubled times in the years immediately following World War II (1939–1945). Many of the company's bakeries were outdated and required drastic renovating. With the rise of an energetic George Coppers as president in 1945, inertia gave way to an expansive new attitude. Within ten years $150 million had been spent on renovations to Nabisco's antiquated bakeries. In 1958 the renovation and reconstruction culminated in the grand opening of an ultra-modern bakery and research center in Fair Lawn, New Jersey. The 1950s also marked the beginning of Nabisco's expansion overseas. Forming a manufacturing partnership with La Favorita Bakery in Venezuela and the Formosa Bakery in Mexico gave Nabisco a foothold in South America.

With Lee S. Bickmore at the helm in 1960, Nabisco accelerated acquisitions and overseas expansion. In 1961 and 1962 Nabisco acquired the Cream of Wheat Corporation, the French firm Biscuits Gondolo, the English bakery Frears, and New Zealand's largest biscuit firm, Griffen and Sons. In 1963 and 1964 Nabisco acquired Oxford Biscuit Fabrik of Denmark, the James O. Welch Company, makers of Junior Mints and Sugar Babies, and one of West Germany's largest confectioneries, Harry Trueller. Overseas acquisitions continued and, by the end of the 1960s, Nabisco was the leading manufacturer of crackers and cookies in the United States, Canada, France, and Scandinavia. Nabisco was also a major supplier to other European and South American countries.

The growth of Nabisco continued through the 1970s. Sales reached the one-billion-dollar mark in 1971, and by 1976, sales surpassed $2 billion. The company made the first Asian investment by establishing a joint venture with Yamazaki Baking Company of Japan in 1970. In 1975 construction of a modern flour mill in Toledo, Ohio, and a computerized bakery in Richmond, Virginia coincided with the building of new company headquarters in East Hanover, New Jersey.

Inflation and soaring energy costs in the 1970s led Nabisco to consider a merger with another large food manufacturer. Early in 1981 Nabisco and Standard Brands announced plans to merge. By the end of 1981 the newly named Nabisco Brands, Inc. demonstrated its potential for growth by purchasing the LifeSavers Company for $250 million. It also purchased a controlling interest in Mexican cookie firm Gamesa for $45 million.

R.J. Reynolds, a worldwide manufacturer and distributor of tobacco, food, and beverage products, purchased Nabisco Brands, Inc. in 1985 for $4.9 billion. This created the world's largest consumer-products company, with annual sales of more than $19 billion. Later in 1985 R.J. Reynolds changed its name to R.J.R. Nabisco, Inc. In 1988 Kohlberg Kravis Roberts won a bidding war for Nabisco with a record $24.5 billion in cash and debt securities. Kohlberg Kravis Roberts, along with the current president of Nabisco, Louis V. Gerstner, Jr., pledged to manage the company for the long run. Through the 1990s the Nabisco Foods Group (formerly Nabisco Brands, Inc.) experienced reorganization and downsizing, but the company still continued to acquire other food and snack-related firms.

See also: **Advertising, Merger**

FURTHER READING

Cahn, William. *Out of the Cracker Barrel: The Nabisco Story from Animal Crackers to Zuzus.* New York: Simon and Schuster, 1969.

International Directory of Company Histories, vol. 2. Farmington Hills, MI: The Gale Group, 1990, s.v. ''Nabisco Brands, Inc.''

International Directory of Company Histories, vol. 7. Farmington Hills, MI: The Gale Group, 1993, s.v. ''Nabisco Foods Group.''

Lampert, Hope. *True Greed: What Really Happened in the Battle for RJR Nabisco.* New York: New American Library, 1990.

NADER, RALPH

By the 1960s Ralph Nader (1934–), a lawyer and social crusader, had become a symbol of the public's concern about corporate honesty and consumer safety. Largely beginning with the publication of his first book in 1965, *Unsafe At Any Speed: The Designed In Dangers of the American Automobile*, Nader started to aggressively attack the design problems of consumer products. His documentation linked faulty car designs to a staggering number of automobile accidents and legislation was enacted to protect consumers. This inspired Nader to continue his investigations and efforts at legislation, which eventually led to increased safety standards in mines, federal regulations to control environmentally hazardous oil and gas pipes, and a more intense regulation of meat quality.

Ralph Nader was born in 1934 in Winsted, Connecticut, the son of immigrant Lebanese parents. He graduated with highest honors from Princeton University in 1955, and then went to Harvard Law School, where he received his degree in 1958. After briefly serving in the U.S. Army, and following a period of personal travel, Nader opened a law office in Hartford, Connecticut. There he also joined the University of Hartford faculty, teaching history and government while pursuing his law practice.

YOU'VE GOT TO KEEP THE PRESSURE ON, EVEN IF YOU LOSE. THE ESSENCE OF THE CITIZEN'S MOVEMENT IS PERSISTENCE!

Ralph Nader

Nader became intensely interested in defective auto design largely through his law practice, where he dealt with auto injury cases. He became convinced that it was generally faulty design of automobiles, rather than driver incompetence, that led to the majority of automobile accidents. Certain that he had convincing statistics on his side, Nader began testifying before state legislative committees, and he frequently wrote magazine articles on the subject.

In 1964, when Nader was appointed as a consultant to the U.S. Department of Labor, he undertook a major study of automobile safety. Having all the data he needed, he left the Department of Labor in 1965 to write his first book, *Unsafe At Any Speed.* In March

1966, General Motors president James Roche admitted that his firm had Nader under surveillance in an effort to smear Nader with possible scandal. The admission received national television coverage and Nader became a public figure. Nader's book went on to become a national bestseller and prompted legislation proposals to regulate car safety, which ultimately became federal law in September 1965.

The mood of the country during the mid-1960s was dominated by progressive ideas and politics, and it was not long after the publication of his first book that Ralph Nader came to be known as the country's leading consumer advocate. Nader had made it his life's work to defend the public's well being. His relationship to business was often adversarial and critical. He often condemned businesses as overly profit-motivated and lacking in real concern for the safety of the consumer.

Nader's industry studies, including the coal mining, meat, poultry, and natural gas industries, all resulted in stricter health and safety laws. Nader also investigated hazards in the pesticide industry and alerted the public to the dangers of food additives, radiation from color television sets, and the excessive use of x-rays.

In 1996 Nader ran for the U.S. presidency as the Green Party candidate, winning support in popular polls. While running for president, Nader often summarized his philosophy, insisting: "You've got to keep the pressure on, even if you lose. The essence of the citizen's movement is persistence!" Nader was not elected president, and he continued to work for the consumer in the Progressive tradition. Though he remained a controversial figure, generally disliked by business, he was trusted by many consumers, and he persisted in his work for consumer advocacy and corporate accountability.

FURTHER READING

Buckhorn, Robert F. *Nader: The People's Lawyer.* Englewood Cliffs, NJ: Prentice-Hall, 1972.

Burt, Dan M. *Abuse of Treat: A Report on Ralph Nader's Network.* Chicago: Regency Gateway, 1982.

Griffin, Kelley. *Ralph Nader Presents More Action for a Change.* New York: Dembner Books, 1987.

McCarey, Charles. *Citizen Nader.* New York: Saturday Review Press, 1972.

Turner, James S. *The Chemical Feast: The Ralph Nader Study Group Report on Food Protection and the Food and Drug Administration.* New York: Grossman Publishing, 1970.

NAPOLEONIC WARS, IMPACT ON THE U.S. ECONOMY *(ISSUE)*

The French Revolution (1789–1793) was a watershed in European history. It destroyed the French monarchy and established a republic, but it also divided France and threw much of Europe into turmoil. From the chaos of the Revolution, a general, Napoleon Bonaparte (1769–1821) emerged to lead the nation, first as a republican magistrate and finally as an emperor. He brought domestic tranquility to France, but his ambition and military genius embroiled Europe in a long and bloody conflict, the Napoleonic Wars (1803–1815), which only ended with Napoleon's defeat at Waterloo in 1815.

The strife disrupted both French and European trade, and even the economic position of the newly formed United States began to change drastically. As the Napoleonic Wars drained the energies of Britain, France, and the rest of Europe, America was free to develop its own economic potential. From roughly 1789 till the beginning of the War of 1812 (1812–1814), the United States went through two economic phases that were linked directly to the political factors associated with the wars in Europe.

As a result of the American declaration of neutrality during the French Revolutionary and Napoleonic Wars, the United States experienced a period of rapid growth in foreign trade. The declaration itself reflected domestic political divisions, since the United States was divided on whom to support. The Federalists tended to favor Britain while the Republicans favored France. This indecision was salutary for the nation's commerce, however, since the declaration established free trade, and overnight the restrictions of the old mercantilist system evaporated. As a neutral country the United States could claim unfettered trade with all countries, including Britain and France, and for the most part American ships were welcomed with open arms. American ships carried commodities from all over the world and distributed European manufactures in ports worldwide. Freight earnings boomed. In 1792, American shippers earned an estimated $7.2 million. By 1796 these earnings had tripled to $21.6 million and eventually peaked at $42.1 million in 1807.

As income from the trade boom diffused throughout the economy, the United States experienced dramatic export-led growth. Between 1792 and 1795, U.S. exports doubled; they doubled again in 1801, and by 1807 were five times what they had been fifteen years earlier. Moreover, the rate of growth in foreign trade far outstripped that of population. Per capita income from exports, shipping services, and ship sales averaged $6.77 in 1792. In 1807, the per capita figure was $22.76. This boom in American export trade reflected heavy European demand for re-exports (foreign goods repackaged in American ports), American cotton, (used to supply the British textile industry), and American food to meet European shortages. The growth did hit several temporary slumps: between 1797 and 1798 when an undeclared sea war with France produced a brief dip in export earnings, and also between 1801 and 1803 when the Peace of Amiens allowed European countries to resume peacetime trade activities. After 1803, the United States again experienced another period of rapidly expanding trade. But while scholars agree that the United States experienced increased prosperity during this period, they disagree over the role that export trade played in its growth.

Supporters of the position that an export-led economy led to significant increases in U.S. growth and prosperity also believe this prosperity laid strong foundations for further economic growth after 1815. Critics challenge this position, claiming that the costs associated with neutrality and export-driven expansion have been understated, and the benefits overstated. In addition to all the shipbuilding and freight rates involved in re-exports, critics also argue that the benefits realized by industries such as banking, insurance, and shipbuilding may have been smaller than previously assumed and concentrated only in northeastern ports.

The second U.S. economic phase linked with European affairs began in December 1807 with President Thomas Jefferson's (1801–1809) embargo on all trade with warring nations. This embargo caused America's foreign trade to collapse. In 1805, Napoleon's victories over Austria and Russia at Austerlitz made him temporary master over much of the European continent. Meanwhile, Britain's defeat of the French and Spanish fleets at the Battle of Trafalgar gave it control of the high seas. At the same time both Britain and France ceased to show much respect for neutral countries or the legitimacy of international laws, and both nations reaped havoc on American shipping interests.

In 1805, a British court ruled that goods from the French West Indies bound for Europe on American vessels, even though shipped by way of the United States, were subject to seizure. When the commercial provisions of Jay's Treaty of 1794 expired in 1807 and American diplomats were unable to negotiate a new agreement to President Jefferson's satisfaction, British interference with American shipping increased. Meanwhile, Napoleon challenged British policy with the Berlin Decree of 1806 and Milan Decree of 1807, which closed European ports under his control to British goods and declared that neutral ships complying with British trade regulations would be confiscated. The United States was caught in the middle.

President Jefferson's solution was to resort to "peaceable coercion" with an embargo that banned all trade with Great Britain and continental Europe. Jefferson argued that Europeans, especially the British, were more dependent on U.S. exports, especially grain and cotton, than the United States was on European imports. As a result, U.S. foreign trade fell precipitously. Although trade did recover somewhat in the years following the embargo, it would not reach its former levels until the late 1840s.

During the War of 1812 (1812–1814), the British blockade of U.S. ports almost completely stifled export trade. The blockade followed a general worsening of American commerce, which had declined by almost one-fifth between 1807 and 1809. The embargo was repealed in March 1809, without achieving its goal of forcing the British to reverse their policies, but it may have been a blessing in disguise. While the unemployment and economic distress (especially in U.S. coastal areas) were undeniable, domestic industry did begin to grow. The nation realized if it were to continue to consume the products to which it had become accustomed during the recent period of heightened prosperity, the best course of action was to produce them itself. In 1807, seven new factories were opened in New England states. The next year twenty-six were chartered, eighteen of which were textile factories. The number increased steadily and accelerated during the War of 1812. The pace, however, slowed down after the war, and many of the mills went bankrupt in the following years. As a result both industrial labor and capital sought relief from the government through tariffs on imports.

Although its influence is more difficult to quantify than foreign trade and export growth, another important and perhaps more significant economic impact of the Napoleonic Wars was the Louisiana Purchase (1802). There were several reasons for Napoleon's sudden decision to abandon his imperial ambitions in America and concentrate instead on Europe. He suffered a major disaster in the French colony of San Domingo when his troops failed to suppress a slave insurrection there, and realized the 1802 Peace of Amiens, the treaty that he had hoped would end the European war, had settled nothing. A renewal of war between France and Britain was inevitable. Because of the sustained economic drain of war, Napoleon needed money. In a wise move, he realized that selling the

Louisiana Territory would raise capital for the war and avoid a concerted Anglo-American alliance between Britain and the United States.

As the beneficiary of Napoleon's strategy, the United States acquired the whole of the Mississippi River and its Western tributaries, some 828,000 square miles of territory, millions of acres of farmland, and a vast wealth of natural resources.

See also: **Embargo, Jay's Treaty, Thomas Jefferson, Louisiana Purchase, War of 1812**

FURTHER READING

Adams, Donald R. "American Neutrality and Prosperity, 1793–1808: A Reconsideration." *Journal of Economic History* 40 (1980).

Frankel, Jeffrey A. "The 1807–1809 Embargo Against Great Britain." *Journal of Economic History* 42 (1982).

Goldin, Claudia and Lewis, Frank. "The Role of Exports in American Economic Growth during the Napoleonic Wars, 1793–1807." *Explorations in Economic History* 17 (1980).

North, Douglass C. "The United States Balance of Payments, 1790–1860." In National Bureau of Economic Research, *Trends in the American Economy in the 19th Century*. Studies in Income and Wealth, (24). Princeton: Princeton University Press, 1960: 573-627.

Shephard, James, and Walton, Gary. "Economic Change after the American Revolution: Pre and Post War Comparisons of Maritime Shipping and Trade." *Explorations in Economic History* 13 (1976).

NAT TURNER'S REBELLION

Nat Turner was an American slave who led the only sustained slave revolt in U.S. history (August 1831). Turner was born on a large plantation in Southampton County, Virginia, on October 2, 1800. Through his mother, who had been born free in Africa, he acquired a passionate hatred of slavery. One of his master's sons taught him to read, and he became fanatically devoted to religious self-instruction. His loathing of slavery blended with his religious training to produce a heady and violent brew. Turner came to see himself as divinely ordained to lead his fellow slaves out of bondage, and he launched his uprising after an eclipse of the sun convinced him that the time to strike had arrived.

The revolt had a profound impact on Southern attitudes towards the "peculiar institution" of slavery. For many southerners it exploded the myth that the slave population was either content or at least congenitally unable to rebel against their inferior status. For other southerners the revolt confirmed in their mind the discontent of slaves and the ever-present menace of rebellion that could topple the southern socio-economic system.

On the night of August 21, 1831, Turner and seven other slaves attacked the local white population, and over the next two days 51 whites were killed during a vengeful march to reach the Dismal Swamp, where Turner's group intended to hide, regroup their forces, and attract supporters. En route the insurgents intended to capture the arsenal located in the county seat of Jerusalem.

The rebellion had little chance for success: only 75 African Americans (who were divided by dissent) joined Turner's cause. Virginia responded swiftly, and 3,000 militiamen combined with strong assistance from the local white population led to a swift end to the insurgency. Turner's supporters were soon killed or captured, as was Turner himself after a dramatic manhunt lasting six weeks. Shortly thereafter Turner was tried and hanged at the county seat of Jerusalem, which became a symbolic location for northern abolitionists.

The revolt had a profound impact on Southern attitudes towards the "peculiar institution" of slavery. For many southerners it exploded the myth that the slave population was either content or at least congenitally unable to rebel against their inferior status. For other southerners the revolt confirmed in their mind the discontent of slaves and the ever-present menace of rebellion that could topple the southern socio-economic system. Not surprisingly, the revolt led to a harsh tightening of controls over the slave population, particularly in the form of legislation that prohibited the education and other activities of slaves. The rebellion also strengthened Southern pro-slavery sentiments.

Nat Turner's rebellion hardened sectional animosities, making secession and the American Civil War (1861–1865) more likely. Galvanized by the Turner uprising, Southern congressmen sought to enact or strengthen existing national legislation supporting slavery, particularly the Fugitive Slave Act of 1796. In 1836 the House of Representatives enacted a gag rule preventing the debate of anti-slavery petitions. It was later repealed after a long and acrimonious debate between northern and southern representatives. Southern congressmen also repeatedly demanded that free states restrict the activities of abolitionist societies. For their part abolitionist societies in the North stepped up their activities, and northern politicians felt increasingly vulnerable to abolitionist demands that they adopt strong anti-slavery stands.

See also: **Civil War (Economic Causes of), Fugitive Slave Act, Slavery**

FURTHER READING

Duff, John B. and Peter M. Mitchell. *The Nat Turner Rebellion; The Historical Event and the Modern Controversy*. New York: Harper and Row, 1971.

Freehling, A.G. *Drift toward Dissolution: The Virginia Slavery Debate of 1831–1832*. Baton Rouge, LA: Louisiana State University Press, 1982.

Greenberg, Kenneth S., ed. *The Confessions of Nat Turner and Related Documents*. New York: St. Martin's Press, 1997.

Oates, Stephen B. *The Fires of Jubilee: Nat Turner's Fierce Rebellion*. New York: HarperCollins, 1990.

Styron, William. *The Confessions of Nat Turner*. 1966. Reprint. New York: Vintage, 1993.

NATCHEZ TRACE

Natchez Trace was an old road, measuring more than 500 miles long (800 kilometers); it ran between Natchez, Mississippi, and Nashville, Tennessee. "Natchez" is derived from an Indian tribe, which lived in Mississippi during colonial times, and "trace" is another word for trail often used in the South. The trace was carved out during the mid-1700s by pioneers who followed old Indian trails from Natchez, situated on the bluffs above the Mississippi River, through present-day Mississippi and northwestern Alabama to Nashville, in north-central Tennessee. Traders would float goods on flatboats (barges) down the Mississippi River, later returning north via the trace. The city of Natchez became an important trade center and between 1798 and 1802, when it was the capital of the Mississippi Territory. In 1806 Congress authorized construction of a road to follow the trace, widening it to accommodate wagons, and making it a post road, which was used to transport mail. During the early 1800s Natchez Trace was of great military and commercial importance. In 1938 it was made into a National Parkway.

NATIONAL ASSOCIATION OF SECURITIES DEALERS AUTOMATED QUOTATIONS (SYSTEM) (NASDAQ)

The National Association of Securities Dealers Automated Quotations system (NASDAQ) is a computerized communication system that provides the bid and asked prices of more than 5,000 over-the-counter (OTC) stocks that have met NASDAQ's registration requirements. Introduced in 1971 by the National Association of Securities Dealers (NASD), NASDAQ achieved a listing of more than 4,000 companies and an annual trading volume of over $1 billion by the early 1990s. It is the second largest securities market in the United States in terms of share and dollar volume, but it is the largest in terms of the number of companies listed.

By late 1997, NASDAQ listed approximately 5,500 companies, compared to some 3,000 listed on the New York Stock Exchange. Even though NASDAQ has many more listed firms than the NYSE, market capitalization of NYSE-listed firms was greater, around $8.7 trillion compared to $1.95 trillion for NASDAQ-listed firms. NASDAQ is known as the market for smaller companies, and especially for technology firms. A large percentage of NASDAQ's market capitalization comes from technology companies.

See also: **New York Stock Exchange, Over the Counter Market, Stock, Stock Market**

NATIONAL BANK ACT OF 1863

The National Bank Act of 1863 was designed to create a national banking system, float federal war loans, and establish a national currency. Congress passed the act to help resolve the financial crisis that emerged during the early days of the American Civil War (1861–1865). The fight with the South was expensive and no effective tax program had been drawn up to finance it. In December 1861 banks suspended specie payments (payments in gold or silver coins for paper currency called notes or bills). People could no longer convert bank notes into coins. Government responded by passing the Legal Tender Act (1862), issuing $150 million in national notes called greenbacks. However, bank notes (paper bills issued by state banks) accounted for most of the currency in circulation.

In order to bring financial stability to the nation and fund the war effort, the National Bank Act of 1863 was introduced in the Senate in January of that year. Republican congressman from Pennsylvania Thaddeus Stevens (1792–1868) opposed the act; Secretary of the Treasury Salmon Chase (1808–73), aided by Senator John Sherman (1823–1900) of Ohio, promoted it. The bill was approved in the Senate by a close vote of 23 to 21, and the House passed the legislation in February. National banks that were organized under the act were required to purchase government bonds as a condition of start-up. As soon as those bonds were deposited with the federal government, the bank could issue its own notes up to 90 percent of the market value of the bonds on deposit.

The National Bank Act improved but did not solve the nation's financial problems—some of the 1500 state banks, which had all been issuing bank notes, were converted to national banks by additional legislation (that amended the original Bank Act and was passed June 1864). Other state banks were driven out of business or ceased to issue notes after the 1865 passage of a 10 percent federal tax on notes they issued (which made it unprofitable for them to print money). The legislation created $300 million in national currency in the form of notes issued by the national banks. But because most of this money was distributed in the East, the money supply in other parts of the country remained precarious; the West demanded more money. This issue would dominate American politics in the years after the Civil War. Nevertheless, the nation's banking system stayed largely the same—despite the Panic of 1873—until the passage of the Federal Reserve Act in 1913.

See also: **Federal Reserve Act, Greenbacks**

NATIONAL BROADCASTING COMPANY INC. (NBC)

The National Broadcasting Company (NBC) debuted as a radio broadcast network on November 15, 1926, with a four-and-a-half hour music and comedy presentation. The show was broadcast from New York City over a network of 25 stations, and nearly half of the country's five million radio homes tuned in. NBC was jointly owned by RCA, General Electric, and Westinghouse until 1932, when RCA bought out the other two owners.

It is hard to overestimate the importance of the first coast-to-coast radio broadcasts. The very first one took place on New Year's Day, 1927, when NBC broadcast the Rose Bowl football game. Other early highlights of NBC Radio included the first special events broadcast, when aviator Charles Lindbergh arrived in Washington, DC, on June 11, 1927; the radio coverage of national political conventions in 1928; the presidential inaugurations in 1929 and 1933; and President Franklin Roosevelt's (1933–1945) first soothing "Fireside Chat" to a worried nation, on a cold night in 1933.

Radio also unified the national culture and advanced the assimilation process of millions of immigrants who up to that point had existed within the bounds of their own national cultures. For the first time in the nation's history millions of people hundreds of miles apart had the simultaneous experience of listening to the new sounds of swing music, as "dance shows" brought this powerful music genre to the radio-listening public. Benny Goodman, Paul Whiteman, Tommy Dorsey, and, way down in Texas, Bob Wills and his Texas Playboys all became the pulse of the nation, which, thanks to radio, was now beating as one.

From the beginning, the demand among local radio stations for NBC's network service was high and the company split its programming into two separate networks, called the "red" and the "blue." In 1941 the Federal Communications Commission (FCC) ruled that no organization could own more than one network, and NBC sold the blue network, which became the American Broadcasting Company (ABC).

In 1939 NBC demonstrated television, a new invention, at the Chicago World's Fair, and began regular television programming from New York City. Television was made possible by the invention of the cathode ray tube in 1906. NBC founder David Sarnoff spearheaded RCA's research into "the art of distant seeing" through the 1920s and 1930s. In 1941 NBC obtained a commercial television license from the FCC for WNBT-TV, which became the world's first commercial television station.

World War II (1939–1945) slowed the growth of television, and programming was limited to a few hours a day during the war. NBC Radio broadcast on-the-scene reports from military bases and battle zones, and on D-Day, June 6, 1944, it provided continuous news coverage of the European invasion.

Color City, the control room of NBC's television studio in Burbank, CA.

Television began to expand rapidly after the war: the number of homes with television sets grew from 14,000 in 1947 to nearly a million in less than two years. Television networks began to expand news coverage. New weekly variety and drama programs were created, and popular radio shows were adapted for television. *Meet the Press*, beginning on radio in 1945, switched to television in 1947 and became the longest running show on television.

WHEN NBC ORGANIZED AND BROADCAST THE FIRST PRESIDENTIAL DEBATES IN 1960 BETWEEN JOHN F. KENNEDY AND RICHARD M. NIXON, THE FULL IMPACT OF TELEVISION ON POLITICS WAS FELT. THE WAY KENNEDY LOOKED ON TELEVISION WAS THOUGHT TO HAVE STRONGLY INFLUENCED THE OUTCOME OF THE DEBATES AND THE SUBSEQUENT ELECTION.

NBC started its television network with four stations and by 1951 it had installed regular coast-to-coast network service. Two programming mainstays were introduced in the 1950s: *Today* (1952), an early-morning news and talk show, and *The Tonight Show* with Steve Allen (1954). In 1953 NBC introduced color television, presenting the first coast-to-coast color transmission. Later that year the FCC approved an RCA-backed standard for color compatibility, making it possible for people with black-and-white sets to receive network programs even if they were broadcast in color.

When NBC organized and broadcast the first presidential debates in 1960 between John F. Kennedy and Richard M. Nixon, the full impact of television on politics was felt. The way Kennedy looked on television was thought to have strongly influenced the outcome of the debates and the subsequent election. When Kennedy was assassinated in 1963, NBC provided an unprecedented 71 hours of coverage in which the whole nation once again participated in a national experience together and gave full vent to their grief. In 1964 NBC presented the first made-for-television movie, thus establishing a new genre of television program. During the 1960s NBC expanded its programming, launching popular shows such as *I Spy*, which featured Bill Cosby as the first African American lead in a television series, *The Man from U.N.C.L.E*, and *Rowan and Martin's Laugh-In*, among others.

During the 1970s NBC's most popular programming included blockbuster movies, family series such as *Little House on the Prairie*, the comedy series *Saturday Night Live*, and several popular miniseries.

NBC Television suffered a drop in ratings during the early 1980s. By replacing low-rated programming it managed to climb back to the number one spot in 1985. Popular shows introduced by programming chief Brandon Tartikoff included *Cheers, Hill Street Blues*, and *St. Elsewhere*. *Miami Vice* (1985) and *The Late Show with David Letterman* (1982) also helped lift NBC's ratings.

In 1986 General Electric Co. (GE) acquired RCA for $6.4 billion and became NBC's parent company. Robert C. Wright was named to succeed Grant Tinker as NBC's president and chief executive officer (CEO). In 1988 NBC decided to leave their radio business, which had been struggling, and the company sold seven of its eight radio stations. In 1991 Tartikoff left NBC to head Paramount Pictures.

From NBC's early days as a radio broadcast network, sports programming had been an important component of its broadcasts. NBC dominated coverage of the Olympics in 1988 with its broadcast from Seoul, South Korea. It acquired the rights to the 1992 and 1996 summer Olympics and every summer and winter venue (except Nagano 1998) through 2008.

With cable television making more of an impact on television viewing habits, NBC began aggressively marketing the Consumer News and Business Channel (CNBC), to cable systems in 1988. CNBC began with a base of 10 to 13 million subscribers. It was originally conceived as a 24-hour all-business news channel, but consumer news was added to the mix before the channel launched in April 1989.

CNBC competed directly with Turner Broadcasting System's Financial News Network (FNN). In 1991 NBC acquired the bankrupt FNN for $154 million, increasing CNBC's subscriber base to 40 million households. Political consultant Roger Ailes was named president of CNBC in 1993. Under his direction CNBC underwent a makeover with better graphics and interviews during the day and a variety of talk shows during prime time in the evening. New talk show hosts added in 1993 and 1994 included Charles Grodin, Tim Russert, and Geraldo Rivera.

By 1997 CNBC had become a cash cow for NBC, generating about $120 million in revenues, a 33 percent increase over 1996. CNBC reached about 64 million households, or 90 percent of all cable subscribers. In 1998 CNBC's Wall Street coverage enabled CNBC to surpass CNN's viewership among 25– to 54–year–olds for the first time, even though CNBC reached 12 percent fewer households than CNN.

In 1996 NBC-TV and Microsoft joined forces to create MSNBC, an all-news cable channel designed to compete with CNN. When it debuted in July 1996, MSNBC enjoyed immediate distribution into nearly 20 million homes, with a goal of 35 million homes by 2000. It was distributed in Europe on NBC's Super Channel and CNBC, as well as in Latin America and Asia. As part of the joint venture, MSNBC Online would be launched via the Microsoft Network.

During nearly every season of the 1990s, including three consecutive seasons starting in 1995-96, the NBC television network was most-watched network in the United States. Comedy shows such as *Seinfeld, Frasier*, and *3rd Rock from the Sun* were complemented by popular drama and prime-time news programs. From 1993 through 1998 NBC reported double–digit gains in earnings annually, achieving $5.2 billion in revenue and pretax operating profits of about $1.15 billion in 1997.

NBC had also become stronger during the 1990s through strategic acquisitions and alliances. It owned 12 television stations reaching 26 percent of U.S. households. In 1993 it became an international broadcaster by purchasing a minority interest in Superchannel, a London-based pan-European satellite television service. In 1997 CNBC and Dow Jones entered into an alliance that was finalized in 1998 to share news–gathering and programming. In 1998 the company sold its one-third interest in the money-losing Court TV cable network to partners Time Warner and Liberty Media.

Throughout the decade other companies sought to purchase NBC from GE, but GE chairman John F. (Jack) Welch, Jr., turned them all down. Paramount offered $4.5 billion for NBC in 1992, and then Walt Disney Co. made a bid of $6 billion in 1994. Even media mogul Ted Turner attempted to negotiate an offer. After *Seinfeld* ended its nine-year run in May 1998 and NBC lost the network auction to televise National Football League games, reports began to surface that NBC was again up for sale. Possible buyers included Viacom, headed by Sumner Redstone, and USA Networks Inc., headed by Barry Diller.

In spite of such setbacks NBC was in a strong position at the end of the 1990s. It was the number one broadcast network. CNBC was a leader in business television, and the fledgling MSNBC was on track to break even by 2001. At the end of 1997 NBC president Robert Wright estimated NBC was worth about $17 billion overall, with its cable assets worth about four billion dollars and NBC-owned television stations worth about $7.5 billion. Following setbacks in 1998 outside analysts predicted NBC's earnings growth would flatten for the near-term future.

See also: **Radio**

FURTHER READING

Bilby, Kenneth. *The General: David Sarnoff and the Rise of the Communications Industry.* New York: HarperCollins, 1986.

Carsey, Marcy, and Tom Werner. ''Father of Broadcasting: David Sarnoff.'' *Time,* December 7, 1998, 88.

''CNBC: Newest Initials in Cable.'' *Broadcasting,* July 25, 1988, 34.

Furman, Phyllis. ''General Electric Reportedly Has NBC up for Sale.'' *Knight-Ridder/Tribune Business News,* July 16, 1998.

Goldblatt, Henry. ''Viewers are Bullish on CNBC.'' *Fortune,* December 29, 1997.

Lewis, Tom. *Empire of the Air: The Creation of Radio.* New York: HarperCollins, 1991.

Marin, Rick. ''Rebooting the News.'' *Newsweek,* July 29, 1996.

NATIONAL DEBT *(ISSUE)*

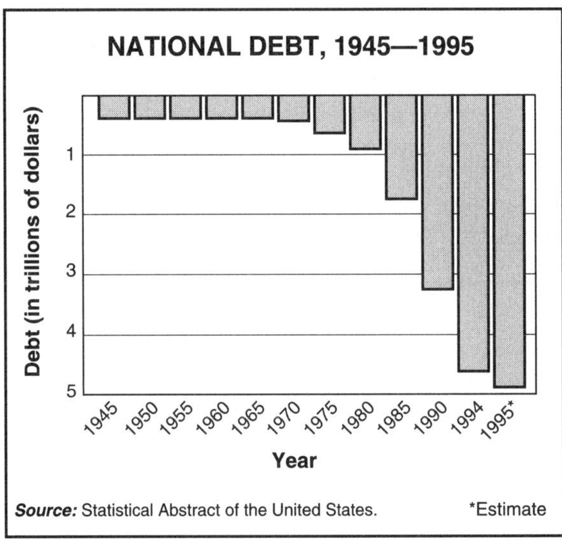

The National Debt remained fairly constant until 1975. In 1980 it began to grow at an alarming rate, and became a major economic and political concern.

The national debt is the amount of money owed by the U.S. government to its creditors, which may include private individuals, corporations, banks and other financial institutions, as well as foreign governments. As a result of better communications technology, improved information processing, and cheaper enforcement costs the ability of the federal government to collect taxes improved over the years. This made lenders more willing to fund the national debt and enabled the government to borrow at favorable interest rates.

The United States began its existence with a large (for the time) national debt of $75 million. This debt was the result of a deliberate policy of the first Secretary of the Treasury, Alexander Hamilton (1755–1804). Hamilton wanted to secure the confidence of wealthy citizens in the new federal government, establish the government as a good credit risk, and provide a compelling rationale for constructing as effective federal tax system. With this in mind he convinced the U.S. Congress in 1790 to assume the debts incurred by the individual states during and after the American Revolution (1775–1783).

According to Hamilton, the funding and assumption of this debt served several purposes. One was to establish the credit of the United States among other nations. If the U.S. federal government voluntarily undertook to retire its debt the credit of the nation would be restored at home and abroad. With the repayment of the loans interest rates would be lowered. With lower interest rates investments in land, commerce, and industry would increase, and capital would multiply along with wages and jobs. Hamilton believed that, with responsible fiscal leadership, the day would not be long before economic dominance would soon pass from Great Britain to the United States—as indeed it did, but not for another one hundred and twenty years.

The South was especially hostile to Hamilton's vision of refunding and assuming the national debt. This was because many of the southern states had made substantial progress in meeting their financial obligations under the Articles of Confederation. New England states on the other hand favored funding and assumption because those states owed the largest portion of the states' collective debt.

Today we understand that the federal government has the ability to expand its own income through borrowing money, printing money, and tax increases. Since the 1930s, however, the economic theories of John Maynard Keynes (1883–1946) brought the realization that retiring the debt should not be an automatic reflex. That is because the debt can help in the fight against depression. If, during a depression, the government borrowed money and invested it in government projects that created jobs and produced a ripple effect and stimulating secondary investment and employment (such as a restaurant near a factory), the economy might regenerate itself and pay off the debt. Keynes believed that government attempts to increase revenues and decrease expenditures during a depression worsened, rather than cured, the problem of widespread unemployment and underutilized industrial capacity. Keynes argued that government spending should be counter-cyclical, that it should move in the opposite direction to private consumption and investment. Keynes believed that during an economic downturn the government should increase its expenditure to compensate for the decline in private demand for goods and services. Conversely, during an economic upturn the government should decrease its expenditure to make room for productive investment and consumption. Thus, governments should increase the national debt during economic downturns and retire the debt during business cycle upturns.

Since the founding of the republic the main source of increasing the national debt has been war. Initially, the war debt was easily retired. Within twenty years of the War of 1812 (1812–1814) the United States government paid off its war debt of $128 million. In World War I (1914–1918) the national debt underwent the first of several huge increases that would last through the end of the century. By 1990 the U.S. national debt soared to $3.2 trillion. In the late 1990s some economists believed that the anti-Keynesian tactics of President Ronald Reagan's (1981–1989) administration only made matters worse. They point to for the fact that his economic recovery program combined tax cuts with increases in government spending, thereby increasing the U.S. national debt by almost $1.9 trillion during his term. Proponents of Reagan's economics defend the administration's plan and the ensuing national debt on the grounds that a Congress controlled by the Democrats would not follow the president's wishes and dramatically cut domestic spending. They also argue that a high level of military spending was necessary to bring the Cold War to an end, and the tax cuts successfully stimulated the economy, as the stock market rose to record levels.

See also: **Alexander Hamilton, John Maynard Keynes, Keynesian Economic Theory**

FURTHER READING

Campagna, Anthony S. *U.S. National Economic Policy, 1917–1985.* New York: Praeger, 1987.

Frazer, William. *The Friedman System.* New York: Praeger, 1997.

Galbraith, John K. *A Life in Our Times.* Boston: Houghton Mifflin, 1981.

Keynes, John Maynard. *The General Theory of Employment, Interest and Money.* New York: Harcourt Brace, 1936.

———. *Treatise on Money.* New York: Harcourt Brace, 1930.

NATIONAL GRANGE

The National Grange of the Patrons of Husbandry (the Grange) was a fraternal society founded in Washington, D.C., in 1867. Its aim was to advance the political, economic, and social interests of the nation's farmers. The Grange was established by U.S. agriculturist Oliver Hudson Kelley (1826–1913). As a clerk for the Bureau of Agriculture, Kelley had toured southern farms and talked to farmers. The trip gave him a clear understanding of the problems faced by U.S. growers. When he returned to Washington he resolved to set up an organization to assist farmers by providing a forum for discussion and the dissemination of knowledge regarding new agricultural methods. Six of Kelley's associates joined him in forming the group, and the following year he traveled to his native Minnesota to set up the first local grange.

Granges were organized at the state, county, and local levels, with membership open to all farmers and their families. After suffering through deteriorating economic conditions during the 1860s, the severe downturn of the 1870s hit the nation's farmers even harder—agricultural prices dropped while operating costs increased. Farmers took action by setting up or joining granges. The groups set up cooperative stores, consolidated purchasing (to get the lowest possible price on agricultural equipment and supplies), and even established factories where farm machinery was produced. The number of granges reached their peak in 1875, by which time there were more than 21,000 granges and national membership climbed to 860,000.

Granges lobbied their state legislators to pass laws favorable to farmers, including the imposition of maximum limits on rail freight and warehousing rates. The so-called "Granger laws" were later overturned by the

U.S. Supreme Court, which ruled that any interference with interstate commerce was unconstitutional. The ruling helped pave the way for the government to establish the Interstate Commerce Commission (ICC) in 1887.

By the end of the 1870s the granges were in decline. Mismanagement of their interests and the pressure of competition forced most of their business initiatives to fold. Nevertheless the group did not completely disappear. Members of the Grange movement and other agrarians (including members of the Farmers' Alliances) joined the People's (or Populist) Party. Members of the national political party pursued initiatives favorable to farmers' interests. These included free coinage of silver, government issue of more greenbacks (paper currency that was first issued to finance the American Civil War, 1861–1865), a graduated income tax, direct popular election of U.S. senators, and passage of stringent anti-trust laws. Though the party itself was short-lived (it formed in 1891 and disbanded by 1908) its influence on U.S. politics was lasting. Many of its Populist initiatives were later made into law.

In the late-1990s the Grange had a total membership of about 300,000 organized in some four thousand local groups in 37 states. The Grange worked toward changing economic and political conditions to favor the nation's farmers and agricultural regions.

See also: **Agricultural Industry, Farmers' Alliance, Munn v. Illinois, Wabash (St. Louis and Pacific Railway) vs. Illinois**

NATIONAL INDUSTRIAL RECOVERY ACT

National Industrial Recovery Act (NIRA) was the centerpiece of President Franklin D. Roosevelt's (1933–1945) initial New Deal programs that were aimed at reversing the economic collapse of the Great Depression. Enacted by Congress in 1933 during the president's First Hundred Days in office, the NIRA was designed to improve standards of labor, promote competition, reduce unemployment, and increase consumer's purchasing power. As the legislation went through Congress, it met with much debate and passed by a slim margin of seven votes.

Title I of the act attempted to accomplish the goals of the NIRA by creating the National Recovery Administration (NRA) to establish codes of fair competition, which were rules governing the wages, prices, and business practices of each industry. Representatives of firms in various industries joined NRA officials in drafting the codes. Although the codes were not intended to foster monopolies or discriminate against small business, applicable antitrust laws were temporarily suspended to prevent the NIRA from being challenged on grounds that it engendered unfair competition. Initially, the codes received wide public support, but over time that support diminished. Enforcement of the codes was limited, and the successes it did achieve, like the end of child labor in the textile industry, were eventually overshadowed by higher prices and limited production.

Title II of the act created the Public Works Administration (PWA) to award $3.3 billion in construction contracts for public projects. The PWA oversaw an enormous number of such projects, including the construction of schools, hospitals, post offices, courthouses, water systems, roads, bridges, and dams. The NIRA also included provisions for increasing minimum wages, limiting the hours in a workweek, and recognizing the right of labor to unionize and collectively bargain with management. Among the PWA's biggest successes are the construction of the Tirborough Bridge in New York City and the Hoover Dam in Arizona. Overall, the Public Works Administration completed 34,000 projects nationwide.

Three weeks before the NIRA's two-year expiration date in 1935, the U.S. Supreme Court unanimously declared the act unconstitutional. In the case of *Schechter Poultry Corporation vs. the United States,* the Supreme Court ruled that Congress had impermissibly delegated its legislative power to the National Recovery Administration. The NIRA ceased operations.

See also: **Great Depression, National Recovery Administration, New Deal**

FURTHER READING

Bailyn, Bernard, David Brion Davis, David Herbert Donald, John L. Thomas, Robert H. Wiebe, and Gordon S. Wood. *The Great Republic: A History of the American People.* Lexington, MA: D.C. Heath and Co., 1977.

Johnson, Paul. *A History of the American People.* New York: Harper Collins Publishers, 1997.

Kennedy, David M. *Freedom from Fear: The American People in Depression and War, 1929–1945.* London: Oxford University Press, 1998.

Ketchum, Richard M. *The Borrowed Years 1938–1941: America on the Way to War.* New York: Random House, 1989.

Manchester, William. *The Glory and the Dream: A Narrative History of America 1932–1972*. New York: Bantam Books, 1974.

NATIONAL LABOR RELATIONS BOARD

The industrialization of the United States created new labor issues for the young nation. Mistreated and dissatisfied workers found ways to work together in an attempt to negotiate better arrangements for themselves with employers. The increased activism of workers, mainly in the form of unions, and the negative reaction by businesses to the union movement led the federal government to develop regulations for fair employment practices.

The National Labor Relations Act of 1935 (NLRA) is the core from which much of present day U.S. labor law stems. The NLRA has its roots in the Railway Labor Act of 1926 and the National Industrial Recovery Act. Until the Railway Labor Act of 1926 (RLA) workers were largely unprotected in the workplace. The RLA, as applied to the railroad industry, was enacted with the intent to avoid work stoppages by employees and lockouts by employers. It provided an alternative to these measures by way of negotiation, mediation, or arbitration.

The standards first devised by the RLA were expanded in 1933 under the National Industrial Recovery Act (NIRA). The NIRA was friendly to unions and employees. Under the NIRA, employees were granted the right to organize and bargain collectively through unions. Before the NIRA employees involved in union activity were treated harshly by employers and often faced firing for their union association.

Building on the standards set by the RLA and the NIRA, the National Labor Relations Act of 1935 established the National Labor Relations Board (NLRB). The board is an independent federal agency created with the primary purpose of enforcing labor law in the United States. It set regulations to prevent unfair labor practices by private sector employees and unions, who had taken advantage of previous federal protection under the National Industrial Recovery Act. It also maintained and extended protection of employees' rights to organize and to use union representation in negotiations with employers. Provisions were made for a secret ballot to determine whether employees wanted to maintain union representation.

Although the National Labor Relations Board is an independent federal agency that regulates U.S. labor, it can only act when officially requested in ''petitions'' (usually for an election) or ''charges'' (regarding unfair labor practices). The NLRB limits its involvement to cases that have a significant effect on commerce.

The National Labor Relations Act was an attempt to deal equitably with labor and management. Until it took effect, the laws shifted uncertainly from pro-business to pro-worker and pro-union, giving employers and workers at times too little protection or too few guidelines. The NLRA set a solid foundation on which industrial relations could be built.

See also: **National Industrial Recovery Act, National Labor Relations Act, Railroad Industry**

NATIONAL RECOVERY ADMINISTRATION

The National Recovery Administration (NRA) developed out of President Franklin D. Roosevelt's (1933–1945) New Deal initiative. The NRA was created under the National Industrial Recovery Act (NIRA) in 1933. The chief provision of the act was the creation of the National Recovery Administration. Modeled after the War Industries Board, the NRA oversaw the implementation of several core initiatives set out in the Recovery Act.

Among the initiatives was the establishment of business codes of fair competition, which were standards accepted by businesses and industries. The codes included provisions for minimum wages, voluntary union participation (neither encouraging nor discouraging union membership), and shorter work hours. The business codes regarding union participation resulted in a sharp increase in union membership. For instance, the United Mine Workers experienced a jump in membership from 100,000 to 400,000 less than a year after the NIRA became law. Businesses who followed the codes displayed a blue eagle and the motto ''We do our part'' to advertise their participation to the public.

WE DO OUR PART.

Motto announcing adherence to the NRA's business codes

Despite its strong start, the NRA began to lose public support. The business codes sometimes conflicted with one another and were difficult to comply with. They tended to raise prices and limit production, which, during the hard times of the Great Depression (1929–1939), was the opposite of what the public wanted. In addition enforcement of the business codes was limited.

In 1936 the National Recovery Administration ceased to exist. It ended activity after the United States Supreme Court ruled that the National Industrial Recovery Act, which gave it birth, was unconstitutional on the grounds that the act overstepped the legislative and commercial powers of the federal government.

See also: **Great Depression, National Industrial Recovery Act, New Deal, Franklin D. Roosevelt, War Industries Board**

NATIONAL ROAD, BUILDING OF THE

The National Road, also known as the Cumberland Road, was the first great turnpike to run across the Appalachian Mountains and into the territory that was known as the Old Northwest (the modern states of Ohio, Indiana, Illinois, Michigan, and Wisconsin). The National Road was built with the intention of creating closer economic ties between the American west and the original thirteen colonies. At the time it was considered a state-of-the-art roadway. Its surfaces were graded to limit water damage and it was surfaced with gravel. Streams, rivers, and gullies were crossed with stone bridges, not the more common and less expensive wooden ones. Thousands of migrants moving westward to take advantage of new land and new economic opportunities used the National Road to move westward. It was the first major road to be built with federal funds and the largest single road-building project until the construction of the modern interstate highway system after World War II (1939–1945).

THE NATIONAL ROAD, ALSO KNOWN AS THE CUMBERLAND ROAD, WAS THE FIRST GREAT TURNPIKE TO RUN ACROSS THE APPALACHIAN MOUNTAINS AND INTO THE TERRITORY THAT WAS KNOWN AS THE OLD NORTHWEST (THE MODERN STATES OF OHIO, INDIANA, ILLINOIS, MICHIGAN, AND WISCONSIN).

Although different sections of the country (particularly in New England) had developed their own turnpike systems in the late eighteenth century, most of the country was not well served by roads. The roads that existed were funded and built mostly by private corporations, who ran them as profit-making toll roads. Construction on the National Road itself did not begin until immediately after the War of 1812 (1812–1814). The road began at Cumberland, Maryland, but it was linked to the earlier Frederick Pike, which led to Baltimore on the coast. Construction continued steadily until 1818, when the road crossed the Cumberland Gap over the Appalachians and reached Wheeling, West Virginia. By 1838 the road stretched all the way to Vandalia, Illinois, and about mid-century it reached St. Louis, Missouri. Construction on the National Road was neglected after the American Civil War (1861–1865) in part because of the boom in railroad construction. It was revived as part of Route 40 in the early twentieth century, when increased automobile traffic highlighted the need for improved roads.

The National Road was a controversial project for several reasons. First, many people questioned whether the federal government was permitted by the Constitution to use its money on internal improvements. Most such internal improvements (such as the Erie Canal, which was built by the state of New York) were undertaken by local or state authorities. Congress had appropriated money to build a trans-national highway as early as 1802. In 1808 Albert Gallatin proposed a series of internal improvements including a number of roads. Even then, several presidents—notably James Madison (1809–1817) and James Monroe (1817–1825)—vetoed the road's funding on the grounds that using federal money for internal improvements was not specifically allowed in the Constitution. Secondly, roads at the time were far less efficient for transport than canals or river traffic. Most of the profits that could be made were for shipping goods over short distances, usually at a rate of about 15 cents a mile per ton. Riverboats and canals, and in later decades railroads, were more cost-effective ways of moving bulky farm produce to markets. Third, the National Road was very expensive to build. At the peak of construction in the early 1820s, it cost more than $13,000 per mile to build and maintain.

Despite its inefficiencies and expense, the National Road helped draw the young United States closer together. Farmers in the Great Lakes and Ohio River valley were able to ship their produce to markets in Atlantic ports rather than sending their goods down the Ohio and Mississippi Rivers to French or Spanish markets. Northern political support for western improvements also helped draw the two sections of the country closer together.

See also: **Cumberland Gap, Economic Development (Federal Involvement in), Maysville Road**

FURTHER READING

Bruchey, Stuart. *The Roots of American Economic Growth, 1607–1861: An Essay in Social Causation.* New York: Harper and Row, 1965.

Haeger, John Denis. *The Investment Frontier: New York Businessmen and the Economic Development of the Old Northwest.* Albany, NY: State University of New York Press, 1981.

Jordan, Philip. *The National Road.* Indianapolis, IN: Bobbs-Merrill, 1948.

Rautz, Karl, ed. *The National Road.* Baltimore, MD: Johns Hopkins University Press, 1996.

Taylor, George Rogers. *The Transportation Revolution, 1815–1860.* New York: Rinehart, 1951.

NATIONALISM

Nationalism is a movement in which the citizens of a nation-state demonstrate a clear loyalty and devotion to the specific social, economic, and cultural interests of their nation, often to the exclusion of international interests. The predominant characteristic of nationalism is a sense of community among citizens of a nation based on a shared descent, language, and religion. Nationalism is also closely associated with the desire for national independence in a country that is under foreign domination. It was not until the eighteenth century that nationalism emerged as a distinctive movement. Before then, loyalty was usually pledged to either a ruling family or a religion.

Nationalism evolved through advances in technology, culture, politics, and economic circumstances. An increase in the education of the lower classes provided them with knowledge of their common history and culture beyond their villages and enabled them to identify themselves as members of a larger nation. With the development of industry and trade, cities and provinces were able to extend their economies outside of previous local geographic boundaries. By the nineteenth century, the Industrial Revolution helped spread economic development, which increased the middle class and lead to a desire for representative government at the national level. Nationalistic symbols such as holidays commemorating national events of historical significance also arose. In the United States, nationalism is essentially based on representative government and the concept of individual liberty as put forth in the *Declaration of Independence*.

See also: **American Revolution, Imperialism**

NATIVE AMERICAN POLICY

Federal Native American policy is considered by many to be an aberration in the U.S. legal system. By the 1990s more than two percent of U.S. lands were actually governed by Native American tribal governments. In the seventeenth century British and Spanish colonies began negotiating treaties with the New World's indigenous groups as sovereign (independent) political entities. The treaties served to acknowledge and affirm Native American ownership of lands used and occupied. The United States, as a successor of Great Britain, inherited this centuries–old European international policy. Thus, tribal sovereignty, recognized well before birth of the United States, became the basis for future U.S.–Native American relations.

With victory complete over Britain in the American Revolution (1775–1783), establishment of Native American policy was one of the first orders of business of the new fledgling government. A formative period of U.S. Indian policy lasted until 1871. The 1787 Northwest Ordinance, enacted by Congress, recognized existing Indian possession of the newly gained lands and established that only the federal government could negotiate treaties with tribes and acquire Indian lands. Sovereignty of tribes was explicitly recognized in the U.S. Constitution and authority for the federal government's legal relationship with tribes was identified in the Commerce Clause. One of the first acts passed by the first U.S. Congress was the Indian Trade and Intercourse Act of 1790 which reaffirmed the treaty policy and brought all interactions between Indians and non-Indians under federal control.

THE FEDERAL-INDIAN RELATIONSHIP IS LIKE NO OTHER IN THE WORLD. INDIAN TRIBES APPEAR TO HAVE THE SAME POLITICAL STATUS AS INDEPENDENT STATES; YET THEY SEEM TO BE FOREVER MIRED IN A STATE OF POLITICAL AND ECONOMIC PUPILAGE.

Vine Deloria, Jr., *American Indian Policy in the Twentieth Century*, 1985

Three Supreme Court decisions between 1823 and 1832, known as the Marshall Trilogy, reasserted the

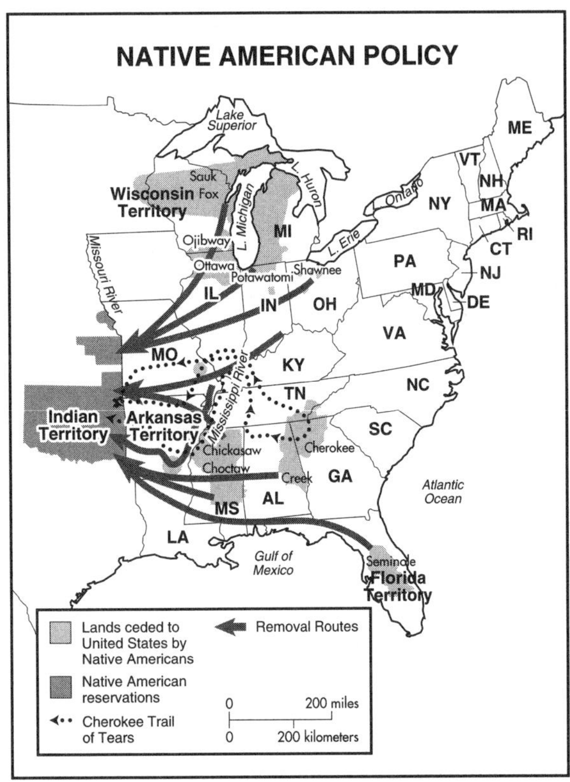

This map shows the lands ceded to the U.S. by Native Americans, and the routes of removal to the western Indian Territories. U.S. Native American policy has vacillated between supporting Indian self-determination and forced assimilation.

tribal right of land possession and tribal sovereignty (meaning no state held legal jurisdiction within Indian reservation boundaries) and defined a moral trust responsibility of the United States toward the tribes. This trust relationship recognized tribes as "domestic dependent nations" yet held the Unites States responsible for their health and welfare. Later deliberation of Indian policy by the Court produced a reserved rights doctrine which recognized inherent tribal rights, but the Court also allocated "plenary" power to the United States. Plenary power meant that the United States held ultimate authority to unilaterally alter U.S.–Native American policy and terminate specific Indian rights. However, the trust relationship compelled a reasoned exercise of this power, to be used only to benefit Indian peoples. For resolving disputes over treaty interpretation, the "canons of construction" established that treaties should only be interpreted from the tribal perspective and, if ambiguous, judicial rulings should be in favor of the tribes.

Despite a seemingly favorable attitude on the part of the judiciary, in actuality Indian peoples suffered catastrophic loss of economies, lands, and life in the persistent push of white settlements westward. The most grievous example was the 1830s removal policy under which the Five Civilized Tribes were forcibly removed from the Southeast to the newly created Indian Territory in what later became Oklahoma. The removal policy persisted with treaty-making in the West in the 1850s and 1860s. The western treaties created a reservation system in which the inherent rights of Native Americans would presumably persist. However, these treaties underscored the long standing tension between trust, responsibility, and a stronger force promoting white settlement and economic development. Some treaties also recognized aboriginal hunting, fishing, and gathering rights outside reservation boundaries to help perpetuate traditional economies. The treaties also implicitly established a unique system of water rights later recognized by federal courts. In 1871 Congress acted to end the treaty-making era, thus closing a chapter on the use of treaties to define U.S.-Indian relations.

An era of forced cultural assimilation followed from 1871 to 1930 in which U.S. Indian policy attempted to blend Native Americans into the dominant society. Believing the tradition of communally held property was a major barrier to Indian assimilation, Congress passed the General Allotment Act of 1887. The act authorized the Bureau of Indian Affairs (BIA) to divide up all Indian lands, allotting parcels of 160 acres to families and 80 acres to single individuals over 18 years of age. Individuals receiving the allotments became U.S. citizens. The hope was that when Indian people held their own property they would become farmers embracing an agrarian lifestyle. Tribal lands left over after the allotment process were considered "surplus" and sold to non-Indians. Much land went into forfeiture when many Indians could not pay taxes on their properties. In all, the policy was a further economic disaster reducing the tribal land base in the United States from 138 million acres in 1887 to 48 million acres in 1934. Much of the most agriculturally productive lands passed out of tribal control. In another assimilationist effort, all Indians became U.S. citizens through the Indian Citizenship Act of 1924, but the Bill of Rights did not apply to Indians because of tribal sovereignty.

By the 1930s, realizing the calamity of the allotment policy, U.S. policy swung back again to the recognition of sovereignty. The Indian Reorganization Act of 1934 ended the allotment process, stabilized tribal holdings, and promoted tribal self–government by encouraging tribes to adopt Western-style constitutions and form federally chartered corporations. Though many tribes rejected developing constitutions, they did organize various governmental institutions during this period.

By 1953 U.S. policy began a significant move back to assimilation with termination policies. Through a House resolution, Congress voted to terminate recognition of a select group of tribes, ending the special trust relationship. Some reservations were terminated and the lands sold to non-Indians, thus taking away the economic base for the Indian communities. In addition, Public Law 280, also passed in 1953, expanded state jurisdiction onto tribal lands in selected states, diminishing tribal sovereignty in those areas.

With little sustained congressional support for termination policies, in the 1970s U.S. policy again took a dramatic shift back to a tribal government, self-determination era. The Indian Civil Rights Act of 1968 extended most of the Bill of Rights to Indian peoples and pared back some of the states' authorities granted in P.L. 280. Most importantly, the Indian Self-Determination and Education Assistance Act of 1975 encouraged tribes to assume administrative responsibility for federal programs benefiting Indian peoples, many of which were in health and education. Congress continued to pass acts empowering tribes including the American Indian Religious Freedom Act (1978), Indian Mineral Development Act (1982), Indian Gaming Regulatory Act (1988), and Native American Graves Protection and Repatriation Act (1990). Tribes could form their own governments, determine tribal membership, regulate individual property, manage natural resources, develop gaming businesses, collect taxes, maintain law enforcement, and regulate commerce on tribal lands.

Tracing the history of U.S.–Indian relations re veals that Native American policy is not actually a coherent body of principles, but an aggregate of policies derived from many sources over time. For more than 200 years, U.S.-Indian policy vacillated between periods of supporting tribal self-government and economic self-sufficiency and periods of forced Indian socio-economic assimilation into the dominant Western culture.

***See also:* Five Civilized Tribes, Trail of Tears**

FURTHER READING

Burton, Lloyd. *American Indian Water Rights and the Limits of Law*. Lawrence: University of Kansas, 1991.

Cohen, Felix S. *Felix S. Cohen's Handbook of Federal Indian Law*. Albuquerque: University of New Mexico Press, 1971.

Prucha, Francis P. *The Great Father: The United States Government and the American Indians*. Lincoln: University of Nebraska Press, 1986.

———. *American Indian Treaties: The History of a Political Anomaly*. Berkeley and Los Angeles: University of California Press, 1994.

Washburn, Wilcomb E., ed. *Handbook of North American Indians: History of Indian–White Relations*, Vol. 4, Washington, DC: Smithsonian Institution Press, 1988.

Wilkinson, Charles F. *American Indians, Time, and the Law: Native Societies in a Modern Constitutional Democracy*. New Haven: Yale University Press, 1987.

NATIVE AMERICANS, TREATMENT OF (SPAIN VS. ENGLAND) *(ISSUE)*

When Christopher Columbus landed on the island of Hispaniola in 1492, he met natives there. When this was reported to Queen Isabella of Spain, she immediately decreed that the natives (Indians as the Spanish would call them) were her subjects and were morally equal to all her other subjects including the Spaniards themselves. They were to be treated humanely and not to be enslaved, and they were to be Christianized and Europeanized.

Columbus violated these decrees from the beginning and thus he created a tension between Crown policy and behavior in the field that endured throughout the colonial period. Columbus' first illegal act was to ship five hundred Indians back to Spain as slaves. When Queen Isabella heard of this, she immediately ordered that the Indians be freed and sent back to Hispaniola. Meanwhile, Columbus' men on the island had continued their practice initiated from the outset—of brutalizing Indians, who eventually rebelled. Those who survived the repression of the rebellion were treated as prisoners of war and were forced to work. For all practical purposes these Indians were slaves.

In addition to the enslavement of rebellious natives, Columbus initiated the practice of tribute. Under this system each Indian male was required to gather and turn in a certain amount of gold every ninety days. If he failed, the Indian was subject to a death penalty. Many ran away and even more died from exposure to the microbes of European diseases for which they had no immunity. The subjugation of native peoples was also employed during the next twenty years on Puerto Rico, Cuba, and Jamaica and the results were the same. Indians virtually disappeared from the Caribbean Islands.

Indians who survived the initial invasion were required to work and to accept Christianity. If they refused, they could be forced to comply. Many did resist and a system was devised to deal with them. It was known as the *encomienda.* Under this system Indians were regarded as part of the land: When land grants were made to settlers, the native inhabitants became a part of the grant. As property of the landowners, they could be forced to work without being technically enslaved. At the same time they were to be converted to Christianity by the local priests.

Spanish churchmen took very seriously their obligation to Christianize the Indians. Some of them were appalled by the harsh treatment meted out to the Indians by many *encomenderos* and they demanded reform. One of these was a Dominican Friar, Antonio de Montesinos. As a result of his demands, the Crown promulgated the Laws of Burgos in 1512. These required that Indians were to be put into villages where they would live under supervision. They were to be baptized, given religious instruction, and encouraged to marry. They were to work for the Spaniards no more than nine months per year, and they were to be free and not mistreated.

The Crown also issued a document known as the *Requerimiento,* which was to be read to all Indians before the Spaniards could declare war on them. Written in Spanish or Latin, and thus unintelligible to the natives, *Requerimiento* was intended to inform them that they were about to become subjects of the Spanish Crown. If they submitted peacefully, all would be well, but if not, they would be attacked and enslaved.

Another priest who took the side of the Indians was Bartolome de Las Casas. He believed the Laws of Burgos were too weak and the *Requerimiento* was a travesty. He persuaded the government to appoint him Protector of the Indians and for a few years (1514–1517) he sought to employ a milder regime for the Indians. This did not work. The settlers obstructed Las Casas' efforts at every stage and the Indians continued to die. Facing a critical labor shortage, the Spaniards began to import African slaves in 1517.

Another important element of Spanish policy in the New World was the mission system. Beginning in the middle years of the sixteenth century, Spanish priests, with the support of the Crown, began to establish supervised communities in frontier areas. A few priests would go into an area, learn the local Indian dialect, and begin to preach the gospel. They would persuade the Indians to build a village, accept Christianity, and settle into a sedentary life. The process was extremely dangerous and sometimes the friars lost their lives; however, they often succeeded.

The pattern established in the sixteenth century was essentially repeated again and again throughout the 300 years of the Spanish colonial period. One major feature of this policy was that it brought the whites and Indians together; it did not separate them. This, of course, led to intermingling and intermarrying and it soon produced a new class of people—the mestizos. Today, mestizos are the majority in most Latin American countries.

The English did not establish permanent settlements in the New World until more than a century after the Spaniards. The first two were Jamestown (Virginia) in 1607 and Plymouth (Massachusetts) in 1620. In both cases the Englishmen faced a problem that the Spaniards also encountered a century earlier: they had to determine how to evaluate the natives and how to deal with them.

The English lived in proximity to the Indians for some years. This intermingling, however, did not produce the same results as that of the Spaniards. The North American Indians did not die out as rapidly as their native peoples of the Caribbean and the English, who came in families, did not inter-marry with the Indians as frequently as the Spaniards. Like the Spanish priests who were appalled at the treatment of the Indians, some English observers also spoke out. Roger Williams, a Separatist Puritan who came to Massachusetts Bay in 1631, charged that the English had no right to occupy land that the Indians were already living on. For the most part, however, especially in New England, the colonists tried to recreate the villages that they had known in England and did not try to bring the Indians into their society or convert them to Christianity.

On the other hand, there were some similarities between the two experiences. Like the Spaniards, the British sought to enslave Indians without much success, and they also sought to Christianize them, although not nearly as diligently as the Spanish had. Under the auspices of the Society for the Propagation of the Gospel in New England, founded in 1649, and the Society for the Propagation of the Gospel in Foreign Parts, founded in 1701, the Puritans in New England attempted to persuade the Indians to accept

Christianity. Settlements known as "praying Indian" towns were established beginning in 1651. Eventually, there were as many as fourteen of these, with a population of around 1100 in Massachusetts alone. It is believed that there had been more of these settlements in other colonies.

However, the overall relationship between the British and Indians was a bad one. The two elements which it was based upon could not sustain cordiality: trade and land occupancy. In most cases the trade relation was based upon an exchange of furs for trinkets, firearms, and blankets. When the furbearing animals were depleted the Indians had nothing to exchange and they became embittered. As for land, the British frequently attempted to buy land from the natives, but the Indian concept of ownership and exchange of title was nothing like that of the Europeans. This difference led to misunderstandings which often resulted in conflict.

As in the case of the Spaniards and the Indians, so in the case of the British and the Indians, the pattern was essentially repeated again and again as the whites moved inexorably to the West. However, the pattern itself was different. Here it was a succession of trade, attempts to secure land, misunderstanding, and conflict. The result was that the Indians were generally in retreat after the first few decades of the colonial period, especially as the Indians learned that close association with the colonists was likely to result in sickness and death from European disease, like smallpox. Efforts to enslave the Indians were given up fairly early and the effort to Christianize them, although part of the agenda of the early period of colonization, never developed as extensively as it did in Latin America. The most important difference, however, was the absence of intermarriage.

See also: **Native American Policy**

FURTHER READING

Craven, Wesley Frank. *The Colonies in Transition, 1660–1713.* New York: Harper and Row, 1968.

Croton, Michael. *Sinews of Empire: A Short History of British Slavery.* London: Temple Smith, 1974.

Haring, Clarence H. *The Spanish Empire in America.* San Diego: Harcourt Brace Jovanovich, 1985.

Klein, Herbert S. *African Slavery in Latin America and the Caribbean.* New York: Oxford, 1986.

Lockhart, James and Schwartz, Stuart. *Early Latin America: A History of Colonial Spanish America and Brazil.* New York: Cambridge University Press, 1983.

Pyson, John. *Columbus—For God and Glory.* New York: Simon and Schuster, 1991.

NATURAL MONOPOLY

Natural monopolies exist where control of an industry by one company is considered more efficient than having many small companies producing the same good or service. One large firm can produce goods or services at a lower per-unit cost, passing the savings on to the consumer. These savings in production costs are called economies of scale.

Examples of natural monopolies with economies of scale are electricity and natural gas utilities, (formerly) telephone companies, and transit companies supplying bus service to a locality. Resources would be duplicated and wasted if several electric companies supplied a city's energy needs. Each firm would have to lay its own cables, repair its own lines, and have separate workers and offices. Similar difficulties would exist with gas and transit companies. To avoid such problems, the U.S. government allows natural or legal monopolies to operate by giving them the right to do business in a certain area free from the competition of other firms in the same industry. Although natural monopolies are often privately owned in the United States, they must accept government regulation. Generally, the government assumes the responsibility of setting prices and establishing quality of service by any monopoly that is allowed to operate. The regulatory activities are carried out at all levels, local, state, and federal. In other countries, many natural monopolies are nationalized, government-owned, and government-operated.

See also: **Economies of Scale, Monopoly**

NAVAL STORES

Naval stores are products used in the construction and maintenance of wooden ships, such as timber, tar, pitch, and resin. These materials are derived from conifers (evergreens) which early American settlers found to be plentiful in the colonies. Pine timbers were also used for masts. The abundance of pine in the forests of New England and the Carolinas fostered a thriving colonial export business as well as a shipbuilding industry. Naval stores were a commodity of the triangular trade routes, since sea captains exchanged them for black slaves on the West African coast. Naval stores were also exported to England, a country that had exhausted much of its own forests and therefore relied on the colonial timber to maintain and sustain its fleets. Although England severely limited American imports after the American Revolution (1775–1783), naval stores remained among the few commodities that were exempt from the policy.

See also: **American Revolution, Lumber, North Carolina, Slavery, South Carolina, Triangular Trade**

NAVIGATION ACTS

Between 1645 and 1761 British Parliament passed a series of 29 laws intended to tightly control colonial trade, shipping, and industry to the benefit of English interests. The American colonists largely ignored these acts, which were intended to ensure that the British colonies in North America remained subservient to the mother country. The initial act of 1645 forbade the import of whale oil into England unless it was transported aboard English ships with English crews. Subsequent laws passed in 1651, 1660, and 1663 provided the basis of the Navigation Acts. The First Navigation Act (1651) resembled the legislation of 1645 but was more far-reaching. It stipulated that goods could only enter England, Ireland, or the colonies aboard English (or English colonial) ships. Furthermore colonial coastal trade was to be conducted entirely aboard English ships.

The Second Navigation Act (1660) reaffirmed that goods could only be transported aboard English ships and established a list of "enumerated articles" that had to be shipped directly to England. The intent was to prevent the colonies from trading directly with any other European country. England required the colonies to sell their materials directly to English merchants or pay duties on goods sold to other countries. The list of articles included sugar, cotton, tobacco, indigo, rice, molasses, apples, and wool. In 1663 Parliament passed the Staple Act, making it illegal for colonies to buy products directly from foreign countries; European countries would first have to ship their products to England or pay customs fees. Through the Navigation Acts England tried to establish itself as the gatekeeper of colonial imports and exports. But the laws were difficult to enforce and the colonists easily circumvented them. Smuggling was rampant: In 1684 Parliament annulled the 1629 charter of the Massachusetts Bay Company. It charged that the colonists had violated English law by exporting tobacco and sugar directly to Europe and had thereby shown disrespect to the king. The laws nevertheless had little effect on the colonial economy, which grew at twice the rate of England's during the period. The acts continued to be passed until the eve of the American Revolution (1775–1783).

See also: **Indigo, Molasses Act, Rice, Sugar, Tobacco, Triangular Trade**

NAVIGATION ACTS, ECONOMIC BURDEN ON THE AMERICAN COLONIES *(ISSUE)*

The economic burden of the Navigation Acts on the American colonies has been a subject of debate both among the eighteenth century colonists and among scholars in the twentieth century. The debate has mostly been over whether the economic burden of the Navigation Acts was sufficient to warrant the American Revolution (1775–1783).

The most important Navigation Acts were enacted in 1651, 1660, 1663, 1673 and 1696. They were expressions of the economic doctrine of mercantilism. This doctrine asserted that foreign trade was a form of economic warfare with other trading nations and that the winner in this war would be the nation that accumulated the most gold and silver. The role of colonies in the mercantilist system was subordinate to the "mother country." They were to furnish staple foodstuffs and raw materials to the mother country as well as a market for the finished goods of the mother country. The most important Navigation Acts of seventeenth century England decreed that only colonial or English ships could trade with the colonies; that certain "enumerated" colonial products could be shipped only to England; that American exports to Europe had to pass through English ports, to be taxed; and that colonial goods shipped to England could not compete with English goods.

Some of these acts hurt colonial trade. Especially in the grain-growing middle colonies and the Chesapeake, there was consternation at the fact that the colonies could trade their main export staples only with England. They would have preferred broader market opportunities. And, given the many coves and inlets on the eastern seaboard, American merchants took the opportunity to smuggle goods and to trade with whomever would give the best price.

Thus the Navigation Acts presented both benefits and burdens to the American colonies. New England benefited from the monopoly in the shipbuilding and shipping industries. Because of the proximity to the forests of upper New England, Massachusetts shipyards already enjoyed lower costs than those in Britain and produced many ships for British merchants. Once built and on the water, the colonial ships fared well in the imperial trade, especially on routes between New England and the West Indies. American crews could be paid and dismissed at home ports while British ships at the same ports were forced to bear the expense of frequently idle deck hands.

The early decades of the eighteenth century were a period of "benign neglect" of colonial trade by Great Britain. The English government was preoccupied with a series of wars with France that grew out of commercial competition. Only after the conclusion of the expensive and exhausting "Seven Years' War" (1756–1763) , known in the colonies as the "French and Indian Wars" (1754–1763) did the English Parliament begin to re-examine the trading policy with its colonies.

After 1763 the English Parliament decided to force the colonies to pay their share of maintaining the British fleet which, in their view, spent much of its time defending the colonies. After the war British policy shifted from a loose commercial system to a tightly regulated imperial one. The new taxes that they attempted to impose—the sugar tax, the stamp tax, and the tax on tea—became the focus of contention between the colonies and the British authorities.

Whig historians such as George Bancroft (1800–1891) and Progressive historians such as Charles Beard argued that the economic burden of the Navigation Acts was considerable. These historians point to the central problem of indebtedness. Because of the chronic imbalance in colonial trade stemming from the Navigation Acts, they chafed under the colonial regime. Even wealthy colonies like Virginia and Maryland masked huge debts. Lesser planters borrowed from larger ones, who in turn were perpetually indebted to British "factors" (brokers). The Progressive historian Charles Beard concluded that it is "generally known the debts due to British merchants and other private citizens constituted one of the powerful causes leading to Revolution."

More recent historians have re-examined the data and concluded that things were not all that bad. Robert Paul Thomas estimated that the gross burden of the administrative empire and the Navigation Acts on imports and exports was $3.1 million in 1770 but that the figure had to be weighed in light of the benefits of membership in the empire. Thomas estimated that the burden was approximately $1.24 per person or two percent of colonial per capita income. But when this was set against the benefits and especially military and naval protection ($1.775 million overall, and a little less than $1 per person) the net costs were less than one million dollars, or about 41 cents per person in 1770. For Thomas as well as a growing number of scholars after him the Navigation Acts posed no serious financial hardship to the colonists. These scholars considered that if these were considered burdens they had been placed on political and ideological, not economic, scales.

Other colonies benefited also from the British policy of subsidizing the production of some colonial staples. The 1748 sixpence per pound bounty on indigo was decisive in boosting the indigo industry in South Carolina. But when the bounty disappeared after the American Revolution so did the industry. Likewise in North Carolina bounties on lumber and naval stores such as tar, pitch, and turpentine yielded cash payments somewhat greater than those on indigo. The general protection that the British markets offered also benefited all the colonies, even those who exported unsubsidized goods. Colonial exports received higher prices in Britain because competing non-imperial products bore special high tariffs.

But the Navigation Acts bore many burdens as well. Most imports and exports within and outside the empire were required to be routed through England first. For this reason colonists had to pay higher prices for most goods imported from the European continent and other non-imperial sources. The Navigation Acts required that roughly three quarters of all colonial exports be shipped through Britain first. The result was that almost two-thirds of all colonial exports were subject to laws that reduced both export volume and price. Americans were forced to pay premium prices for protected English manufactures like lace and linen because they could not buy them from lower-cost continental sources. Meanwhile southern planters had to bear the costs of re-exportation, shipping, and lower prices when their tobacco and rice which was first shipped to England demanded higher prices on the international markets. Because other foreign vessels were excluded from imperial trade, colonists bore higher shipping costs as well. In the long run colonists paid higher prices and earned smaller incomes than they would have earned without the restrictions of the Navigation Acts.

***See also:* French and Indian War, Mercantilism, Navigation Acts, Stamp Act, Sugar Act**

FURTHER READING

McClelland, Peter D. "The Cost to America of British Imperial Policy." *American Economic Review*, LIX, 1969.

McCusker, J., and R. Menard. *The Economy of British America, 1607–1789*. Chapel Hill, NC, University of North Carolina Press, 1985.

Thomas, Robert Paul. "A Quantitative Approach to the Study of the Effects of British Imperial Policy upon Colonial Welfare: Some Preliminary Findings." *Journal of Economic History*, XXV, 1965.

Walton, Gary M. "The Economic History and the Burdens of the Navigation Acts." *Economic History Review*, 2d Ser., XXIV.

NEBRASKA

Admitted to the Union as the thirty-seventh state on March 1, 1867, Nebraska is located in the western north-central United States, midway between the Atlantic and Pacific Oceans. Nebraska shares boundaries with South Dakota in the north, Kansas in the south, Iowa, Missouri, and the Missouri River in the east, and Wyoming and Colorado in the west. Nebraska is spread across 77,335 square miles, making it the sixteenth largest state. Its population of approximately 1.6 million people ranks thirty-sixth among the fifty states. Omaha is the state's most populous city, while Lincoln is its capital.

Nebraska was acquired by the United States in 1803 as part of the Louisiana Purchase. In 1804 the federal government commissioned Meriwether Lewis and William Clark to map the newly acquired territory, catalog its wildlife, and establish relations with local inhabitants. Lewis and Clark's expedition took them along Nebraska's eastern border. Two years later Zebulon Pike crossed southern Nebraska during his own expedition. These expeditions stimulated fur trade in the region, and the U.S. Army built a fort in Nebraska to protect traders from hostile Native Americans.

Native Americans grew more hostile as white settlers began encroaching upon their lands. The Indian Removal Act of 1830 opened land for white settlement in the Atlantic states by authorizing federal troops to relocate Native Americans from the southeastern United States to the so-called Indian Territory comprised of land in Nebraska, Kansas, and Oklahoma. Thousands of Native Americans suffered great hardships as they were forcibly uprooted from their homelands and driven westward in what has become known as the Trail of Tears.

Native Americans were next forced to cede land for white settlement within the Indian Territory. In 1854 most Native Americans were excluded from eastern Nebraska, while the Sioux and the Cheyenne peoples remained in the western half. Skirmishes between the two tribes and federal troops broke out when the U.S. Army opened a trail to Montana that crossed Sioux and Cheyenne hunting grounds in the west. In 1869 Congress ratified a treaty agreeing to abandon the trail in exchange for the Sioux's promise to leave Nebraska and relocate their peoples to a reservation in what is now South Dakota.

But many Sioux refused to move, arguing that the federal government had deceived them into signing the treaty. Fighting resumed between U.S. troops and the two tribes. On June 25, 1876, General George Armstrong Custer (1839–1876) led a Seventh Cavalry attack against the Sioux camps of Sitting Bull and Crazy Horse on the banks of Little Bighorn in Montana. Custer and most of his cavalry were killed during the attack. However the army chased down Crazy Horse in northwestern Nebraska, where the Sioux leader surrendered. All but approximately 12,000 Native Americans were ultimately removed from Nebraska, with small numbers of Santee Sioux, Omaha, and Winnebago tribes remaining.

Nebraska also played a role in the events preceeding the American Civil War (1861–1865). The 1854 Kansas-Nebraska Act created the territories of Kansas and Nebraska, and allowed the residents of each territory to decide for themselves whether to permit slavery. The act repealed the Missouri Compromise of 1820, which had outlawed slavery in the North. But following the act's passage Nebraska showed little interest in establishing slavery. However violence erupted in Kansas between slavery proponents and abolitionists. The slavery debate eventually divided the nation as a whole, leading eleven southern states to secede from the Union.

Nebraska voters rejected statehood during the Civil War, but narrowly approved a state constitution in 1866. In 1867 Congress admitted Nebraska to the Union over the veto of President Andrew Johnson (1829–1837), who contended that the state's admission process was unconstitutional. Two federal laws attracted settlers to the new state. The Homestead Act of 1862 gave 160 acres of land to families that resided in the

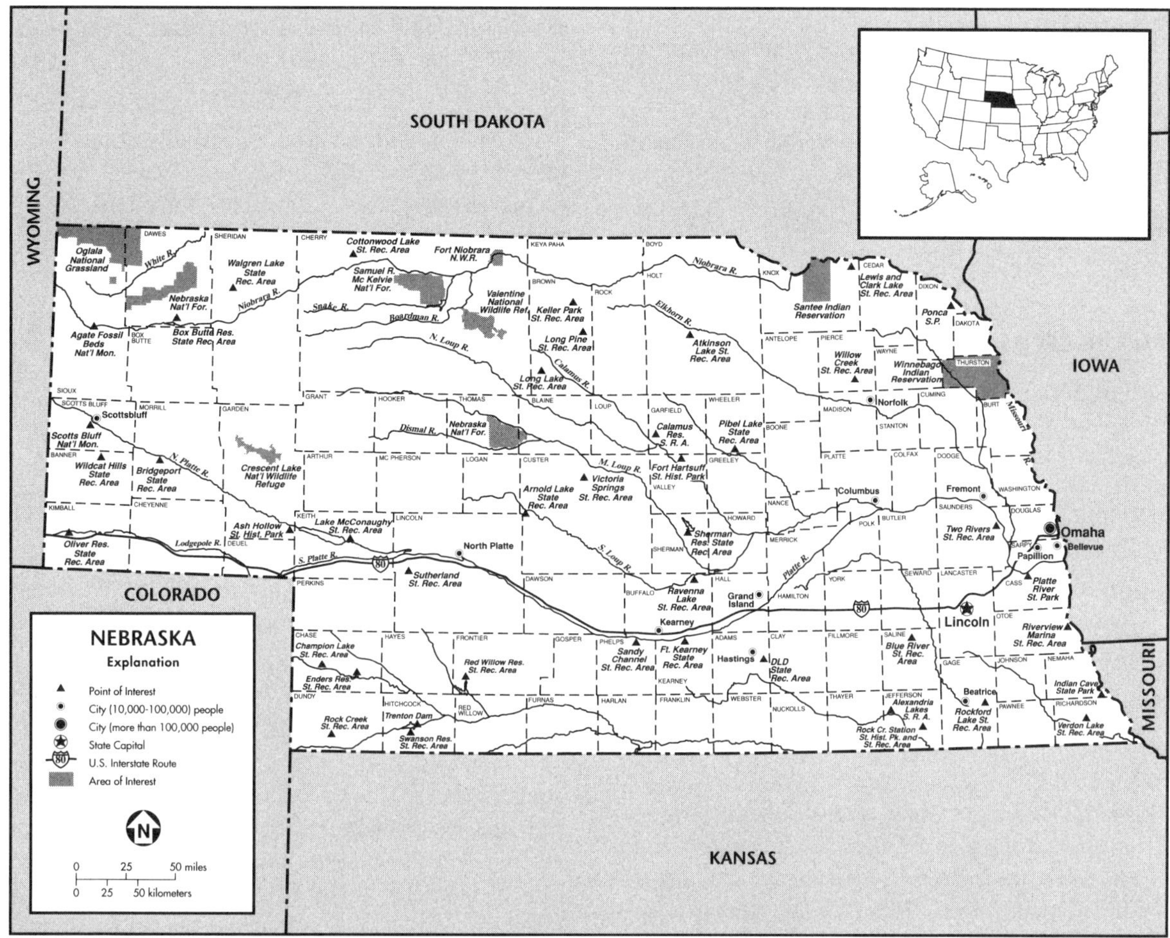

State of Nebraska.

state for five years and paid a nominal fee. The 1862 Pacific Railroad Act authorized construction of a transcontinental railroad passing through Nebraska. Huge tracts of land along the proposed railway were sold to settlers. The Union Pacific Railroad debuted in 1869 with an eastern terminus at Omaha. Nebraska's population swelled from 30,000 in 1860 to almost a million by 1890.

Most of the families that settled in Nebraska during this period were of European descent. Throngs of immigrants from Germany, Czechoslovakia, Ireland, and Italy made Nebraska their home in the late 1800s. A century later little had changed in the state's demographics. The 1990 census revealed that approximately 90 percent of Nebraska residents identified themselves as white persons descending from German, Irish, Czech, Swedish, or Danish ancestry. For the most part these ethnic groups have acclimated well within the state; they have formed closely-knit, thriving communities. However, during World War I (1914–1918) a number of German Americans in Nebraska had their loyalty and patriotism questioned by state officials who feared they might be spies or saboteurs.

Once primarily a rural state, nearly two-thirds of Nebraska residents now live in urban areas. Yet 95 percent of the state's land is used for agricultural purposes, and close to one-half of the state's labor force work in farm-related fields. Known as the Cornhusker State, Nebraska produces 4 billion bushels of corn each year, second only to Iowa. It is also a leading cattle-raising state. But Nebraska's strong economy is bolstered by non-agricultural businesses as well. The state's tourism industry generates about $2 billion a year in gross revenue, while the insurance, telecommunications, real-estate, and healthcare sectors help keep Nebraska's unemployment rate among the nation's lowest.

In terms of political institutions, the Cornhusker State's most distinctive feature may be the government's unicameral legislature, the only one of its kind in the United States. The single house has 49 senators who are elected in even-numbered years to serve four-year terms without designation of political party. The state maintained a bicameral legislature for 68 years before amending its constitution in 1934. Voters hoped the amendment would rein in governmental spending during the Great Depression (1929–1939).

See also: **Kansas-Nebraska Act, Missouri Compromise, Railroad Industry**

FURTHER READING

Federal Writer's Project. 1993. *Nebraska: A Guide to the Cornhusker State*, Reprint, New York: Somerset, n.d.

Luebke, Frederick C. *Nebraska: An Illustrated History*. Lincoln: University of Nebraska Press, 1995.

Olson, James C., and Ronald C. Naugle. *History of Nebraska*, 3d ed. Lincoln: University of Nebraska Press, 1997.

State of Nebraska. Department of Economic Development. *Nebraska Statistical Handbook, 1993-1994*. Lincoln, 1994.

Wishart, Davis J. *An Unspeakable Sadness: The Disposition of the Nebraska Indians*. Lincoln: University of Nebraska Press, 1994.

NETSCAPE COMMUNICATIONS CORPORATION

Netscape Communications Corporation was founded in 1994 as Mosaic Communications Corporation by James H. Clark (b. 1944) and Marc Andreessen (b. 1972). Clark, a former Stanford University professor who studied three-dimensional graphics, had started Silicon Graphics Inc. in 1982 (the company became famous for animating the dinosaurs in the movie *Jurassic Park*). Clark resigned from Silicon Graphics in February 1994.

Andreessen grew up with computers and wrote his first basic program when he was eight. As a 21-year-old undergraduate he was assigned to work on three-dimensional visualization software for the prestigious National Center for Supercomputing Applications at the University of Illinois at Champaign-Urbana. Together with six other computer specialists, he created a graphical user interface (GUI) for finding Internet sites. The GUI, called Mosaic, enabled users to find sites without having knowledge of specialized programming languages. Mosaic was credited with making the Internet much more accessible. It was released on the Internet in January 1993; during its first 18 months of availability, the number of Internet users tripled and the number of sites grew a hundredfold.

> A lot of us were rooting for Netscape. We didn't want to see it get downsized, restructured or swallowed up. Netscape wasn't just another Silicon Valley software company, any more than Apple is just another computer maker. Netscape stood for something grand, something transcendental and empowering. It gave people the tools to communicate their ideas cheaply or sell their stuff to anyone on the planet without going through middlemen, censors, gatekeepers, or even the IRS.
>
> **Joshua Quittner and Marc Andreessen, *Time*, December 7, 1998**

Andreessen and Clark met when Clark sent Andreessen an E-mail message on the same day he resigned from Silicon Graphics. Clark was interested in using the Internet to carry interactive video. Two months later, in April 1994, Clark and Andreessen formed Mosaic Communications Corporation. Andreessen proposed creating a super program known as ''Mozilla.'' While Clark provided four million dollars to set up headquarters in Mountain View, California, Andreessen led the development effort. After the University of Illinois objected to the use of the name ''Mosaic,'' the company became Netscape Communications Corporation in November 1994.

In December 1994 the company shipped its new Web browser, Netscape Navigator. Jim Barksdale, formerly with AT&T's McCaw Cellular division and Federal Express, was hired in January 1995 to be the chief executive officer. Andreessen served as vice president of technology with the primary responsibility of overseeing product development.

In a somewhat controversial move, Netscape chose to give away its browser for free, perhaps following the model established by the University of Illinois with Mosaic. Interested users simply downloaded the software from the Internet via modem. The easy availability of Navigator created a lot of goodwill for the company among the Internet community, and it also established a base of users. Within four months an estimated 75 percent of all Internet users were using Navigator.

Netscape was making money from the sale of its web servers, supplying them to companies for $1,500 to $50,000. The high-priced systems enabled companies to create online or ''virtual'' stores where customers could view products and purchase them online with credit cards. It was a time when electronic commerce over the Internet was in its infancy, and Netscape was providing a key element that would help it achieve explosive growth in the coming years.

While one version of Navigator was available for free, an improved version with more features was offered for $40. Netscape signed up resale partners, including Apple, AT&T, Hewlett-Packard, IBM, and others, and by 1996 the company was selling products in 29 countries. By early 1996 it had signed up more than 1,000 Internet service providers to distribute Navigator to their customers. Netscape Navigator featured an open architecture that enabled it to work with all kinds of computers and operating systems. The open architecture concept, known as TCP/IP (Transmission Control Protocol/Internet Protocol), was the same concept upon which the Internet was based.

Major companies also found that Netscape's web servers could communicate easily with outside networks. These became servers of choice in corporate intranets. Netscape gained a 70 percent market share among the Global *Fortune* 100 companies in the lucrative intranet market.

Following the introduction of Netscape Navigator, the company was almost out of money. It received much-needed equity capitalization when it sold an 11 percent interest to a consortium of media and computer companies that included Adobe Systems, International Data Group (IDG), Knight-Ridder, TCI, and Times Mirror. Without having turned a profit, Netscape went public in August 1995. Its initial public offering (IPO) was one of the hottest of the 1990s, perhaps foreshadowing the skyrocketing prices of Internet stocks that would take place later in the decade. Netscape stock was first offered at $28 a share; it was worth $75 after one day of trading, and it peaked at $171 on December 5, 1995. The company's first-day market capitalization was $2.2 billion.

Microsoft Corporation provided the first serious competition to Netscape Navigator when it introduced Microsoft Internet Explorer 2.0 in 1995. Earlier that year Microsoft had licensed Mosaic from Spyglass, Inc., which had obtained the rights to the Internet browser from the University of Illinois. Microsoft offered free downloads of Internet Explorer and bundled it with Windows 95. Over the next three years Netscape's share of the browser market would decline from a high of 80 percent to 40–50 percent. Barksdale would later accuse Microsoft of ''unfair competition,'' and he was the first witness called by the Department of Justice in its 1998 antitrust suit against Microsoft.

During 1995 the development of electronic commerce was hampered by the lack of a secure payment system that would enable customers to make credit card payments over the Internet. Netscape teamed with MasterCard to develop the Secure Courier encryption standard, while Microsoft and Visa joined forces to develop the Secure Transaction Technology. In January 1996 Netscape teamed with Verifone, the largest credit card transaction processor, to develop a credit card payment system for the Internet using the Secure Courier technology. In September 1995 Netscape suffered a security breach when two hackers at the University of California at Berkeley cracked the security code in Netscape Navigator. Netscape corrected the problem and posted warnings on the Internet. It also established a ''Bugs Bounty'' program, giving prizes to users who identified flaws and potential security problems with the software.

Netscape entered into several strategic alliances in 1995 and 1996. America On-Line (AOL), the nation's largest provider of on-line services, agreed to offer improved Internet access for the users of Netscape Navigator. Both Netscape and Microsoft worked with Hewlett-Packard to develop a Hypertext Markup Language (HTML) that could be printed as seen on screen. Netscape also worked with Sun Microsystems Inc. on the development of JavaScript language, which allowed programs to be imbedded in web pages.

Netscape acquired software developer Callabra Software Inc. in January 1996 for $108.7 million. Callabra's main product was Share, a system that enabled simultaneous E-mail discussions and document sharing among network users. In February Netscape acquired Paper Software Inc. and its 3-D programs for the Internet. Since its founding in 1994, Netscape had enjoyed phenomenal growth, with sales rising from one million dollars in 1994 to $81 million in 1995 and $346 million in 1996. After reporting losses in 1994 and 1995, the company turned a $21 million profit in 1996.

Netscape continued to form joint ventures in 1996 and 1997. Netscape and GE Information Services joined to develop electronic commerce software, with Netscape acquiring full ownership in November 1997 for $56.1 million created Actra Business Systems. Together with Novell it established Novonyx, and

Netscape and Oracle formed the joint venture Navio Communications Inc. to produce consumer-oriented Internet software. Oracle purchased Navio from Netscape for $60 million in May 1997.

In January 1997 Netscape joined an alliance with Oracle, IBM, and Sun Microsystems to develop common standards for all of the company's software products. The NOIS alliance, as it came to be known, was seen as a response to Microsoft's growing dominance in several key sectors of the software market. Netscape also released Communicator, the successor to Netscape Navigator. During the year Netscape improved its position in the business software market by acquiring Digital-Style, which made Web graphics tools, and Portola Communications, which made messaging systems.

Although Netcape's annual revenues reached $534 million in 1997, the company reported a surprising $88 million loss. It laid off 300 workers. Almost immediately thereafter, reports began to appear that the company was for sale. The value of Netscape's stock had fallen dramatically. With $261 million in the bank and no debt, it appeared to be a desirable takeover target. IBM, Oracle, Sun Microsystems, and AOL were all reported to be potential suitors.

In April 1998 Netscape acquired Kiva Software, strengthening its position in the web server market. Later in the year it acquired AtWeb, which provided automated Web site management and marketing services, and NewHoo, a directory-based search service. These acquisitions would enhance Netcenter, Netscape's portal to the Internet.

After nine months of takeover rumors, AOL announced in November 1998 that it would acquire Netscape for $4.2 billion in a stock-for-stock transaction. After passing regulatory approval in March 1999, the transaction was completed, creating what *The Economist* called the "world's most powerful Internet company." As part of the deal Sun Microsystems would pay $350 million to license AOL/Netscape software and sell $500 million worth of servers to AOL/Netscape. With the acquisition, AOL now had two competing Internet sites, America Online and Netscape's Netcenter, both of which enjoyed extremely high traffic.

FURTHER READING

"Acquisition: Netscape Purchases AtWeb for Netcenter." *InfoWorld*, November 16, 1998, 28.

"AOL/Netscape Questions Linger Following Merger." *PC Week*, March 29, 1999, N13.

David, Elliot, and Wilson, Zaret L. "Netscape CEO Lambasts Microsoft in Antitrust Trial." *Knight-Ridder/Tribune Business News*, October 19, 1998.

Green, Heather, and Catherine Yang. "Not So Odd a Couple After All." *Business Week*, December 21, 1998.

Hickman, Angela. "E-Commerce: The Missing Link." *PC Magazine*, April 7, 1998.

"Internet Riders." *The Economist*, November 28, 1998.

Li-Ron, Yael. "AOL Gobbles Netscape, Readies New Version of Communicator." *PC World*, March 1999.

NEVADA

Nevada was one of the last areas of the United States to be explored because with it's vast, dry deserts it was not thought to be worth anything. However, when gold and silver were discovered in the rich earth miners flocked to the area, cities were built, and the state flourished.

Explorers moving westward didn't reach Nevada until 1826 when Nevada was still a part of Mexico. Until then the land was largely ignored by Mexico and Spain, the owners before Mexico. In 1846 the United States went to war with Mexico to take over Nevada and other southwestern land. The United States won the Mexican War in 1848. The first town in Nevada, Genoa, was built up in 1851 around a trading post that was developed as a stop over for gold miners on their way to California.

The first detailed reports about Nevada came from John Frémont, who, with his famous guide, Kit Carson, explored Nevada from 1843–1844. Carson City, the state capital, and the Carson River are named for Kit Carson.

In 1859 miners flocked to Nevada after gold and silver were discovered there. Virginia City was developed near what was to become one of the biggest silver mines in the world, the Comstock Lode. The town had a reputation of lawlessness as bandits robbed stagecoaches, and gamblers tried to win miners' silver and gold. The state's development throughout the rest of the century was dependent on the Comstock Lode. When the silver and gold dwindled in the mine in the 1870s a 20-year depression hit the state. An effort to revive the economy called for encouraging mining by increasing the value of silver. Nevadans supported the movement for free silver coinage during the 1890s, and the Silver Party dominated state politics over the next ten years.

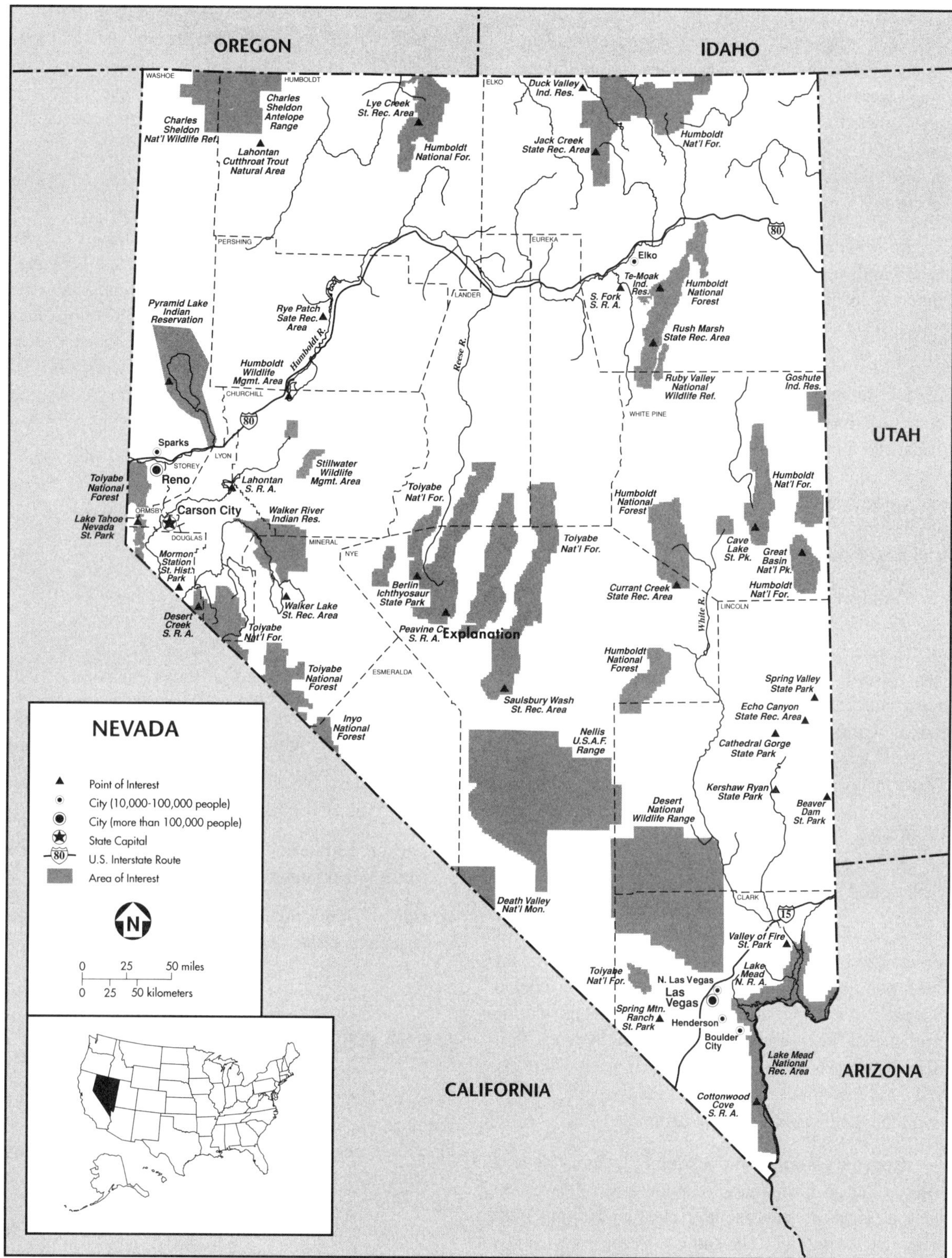

State of Nevada.

Nevada was admitted to the union on October 31, 1864 and enlarged to its current size in 1866. Towns sprang up near gold and silver mines around the state, which were so plentiful that the United States government opened a mint in Carson City, which operated from 1870 to 1893. By 1880 many of the mines were cleaned out, so Nevadans began cattle ranching as a substitute.

In 1900 the economy was revived as another silver mine was discovered in Tonopah and in 1902, two gold miners were founded and the town of Goldfield was built. Also, copper mines were discovered in eastern Nevada.

During the early 1900s settlers attempting to farm in Nevada had a difficult time trying to get water to irrigate their lands. In 1902 the Newlands Reclamation Act set aside federal funds for irrigation and by 1907 the project was finished. The irrigation project allowed farmers to grow crops in Nevada's western desert which previously was sand.

During World War I Nevada's beef industry provided rations for the troops. Then the Great Depression hit the country in 1929 causing banks, farms, mines, and factories to fail. However, in 1931 Nevada's economic health began to turn around as a federal public works project supported construction of the Hoover Dam, the Davis Dam and the Southern Nevada Water Project. These projects provided jobs, water and hydroelectric power for the state. Gambling also was legalized in the state. As a result, Las Vegas and Reno became major entertainment centers in the country as casinos and hotels were built.

After World War II started in 1941 Nellis Air Force Base was built near Las Vegas and a navy air base was built at Fallon. During the war the United States started manufacturing nuclear weapons and the first nuclear tests were conducted at the Nevada Test Site, just northwest of Las Vegas, in 1951. Nuclear tests have continued over the years however, since 1963 they are conducted underground.

Revenues from casino gambling grew as Nevada allowed large businesses to own casinos. Investors such as airplane manufacturer Howard Hughes built hotels and casinos in Reno and Las Vegas. In the 1950s gaming became the state's leading industry. New federal and state regulations were imposed on the casinos when it was revealed during the 1950s and 1960s that organized crime had gradually moved into the gaming industry, using casino money to finance narcotics and other illegal activity on the east coast.

As the number of casinos grew, the populations of Las Vegas and Reno exploded between 1970 and 1994 as the census in Las Vegas tripled and Reno's population doubled. As businesses and people moved to Nevada, larger amounts of water were needed. The drought between 1988 and 1992 did not help matters. Nevada continues to examine new ways of supplying water to areas around the state.

In the 1990s the largest industries in Nevada included gambling and tourism, which together generated more than 50 percent of the state's income. Mining in Nevada produces more than 350,000 pounds of gold and 1.4 million pounds of silver each year. Computers and electrical equipment were also the leading products; beef cattle, sheep, dairy cows, and hogs were the major farm products, along with hay, grapes, and onions.

In 1995 Nevada's per capita income was $24,390 and 11.1 percent of all Nevadans lived below the federal poverty level.

FURTHER READING

Aylesworth, Thomas G. *The West: Arizona, Nevada, Utah.* New York: Chelsea House Publishing, 1992.

Elliot, Russel R. *History of Nevada.* Lincoln, NE: University of Nebraska Press, 1973.

Laxalt, Robert. "Nevada." In *States of the Nation.* New York: Coward-McCann, Inc., 1970.

Thompson, Kathleen. "Nevada." *Portrait of America.* Texas: Steck-Vaughn Publishers, 1996.

Worldmark Encyclopedia of the States. Detroit: Gale Research, 1998, s.v. "Nevada."

NEW DEAL

The New Deal (1933–1939) was a series of programs intended to alleviate the suffering caused by the Great Depression (1929–1939), an abrupt economic collapse that began in 1929 and resulted in massive unemployment throughout the 1930s. The New Deal began with the inauguration of Franklin Roosevelt (1933–1945) as President of the United States in 1933.

To restore confidence in the American financial system Roosevelt declared a "bank holiday," closing all banks for four days until Congress met to pass bank reform legislation. The immediate banking crisis ended soon after when Congress passed the Emergency

NEW DEAL PROGRAMS

Year Instituted	Program	Description
1933	Agricultural Adjustment Administration (AAA)	Farmers were paid to stop growing specific crops. Consequently, the demand for and the value of the crops rose.
1933	Civilian Conservation Corps (CCC)	Provided jobs for urban youth in work such as planting trees, maintaining fire lines, and improving hiking trails.
1933	Federal Deposit Insurance Corporation (FDIC)	Insured individual savings held in banks and other institutions across the country. Monitored and defined standards for the banking industry.
1933	Federal Emergency Relief Administration (FERA)	Provided food and shelter to those most affected by the Great Depression. Distributed cash grants to the states for disbursements to individuals and families on the "dole."
1933	National Recovery Administration (NRA)	Set standards for wages, prices and production to encourage business recovery and investment.
1933	Public Works Administration (PWA)	To stimulate demand in the construction industry, the PWA initiated large building projects such as dams, aircraft carriers, schools, and government buildings.
1933	Tennessee Valley Authority (TVA)	Constructed a series of dams on the Tennessee River to provide electricity and flood control for seven southern states. The program also established health centers and schools.
1935	Rural Electrification Administration (REA)	Encouraged the growth of rural electrification cooperatives, spreading electricity throughout the country's rural areas.
1935	Social Security Act (SSA)	A government-run pension program, designed to provide financial assistance to the elderly, the disabled, and the unemployed.
1935	Works Progress Administration (WPA)	Created urban work projects, such as repairing streetcar tracks and cleaning streets.
1937	Farm Security Administration (FSA)	Loaned money to struggling sharecroppers. Helped relocate farmers to more productive land and provided shelter for migrant workers.
1938	Fair Labor Standards Act (FLSA)	Established a minimum wage and set a maximum of work hours for unskilled laborers employed by business associated with interstate commerce.

Franklin D. Roosevelt's "New Deal" programs attempted to alleviate the financial hardships brought on by the Depression in the 1930s.

Banking Act, which required the Treasury Department to inspect all banks before they could reopen. Three-fourths of the Federal Reserve system banks reopened within three days.

Even though these measures stemmed the immediate crisis, more comprehensive measures were needed. Congress passed the first program, the Agricultural Adjustment Act, in May 1933. The most important aspect of the act was its establishment of the Agricultural Adjustment Administration, which provided subsidies to farmers who were told to reduce crop production by leaving part of their land idle. In 1936 the Supreme Court ruled that it was unconstitutional for the government to require farmers to limit production and the act became inoperable. However, within weeks Congress passed the Soil Conservation and Domestic Allotment Act, which allowed the government to pay farmers to reduce production. In addition, the Roosevelt administration helped poor farmers by setting up the Resettlement Administration in 1935, succeeded by the Farm Security Administration in 1937, which helped farmers on marginal lands relocate to better land by providing loans.

Saving the industrial economy was the most significant challenge facing the Roosevelt administration. On the one hand, businesspeople wanted to stop rapid deflation by relaxing antitrust laws to allow the cooperation of trade associations and stabilize prices. On the other hand, New Dealers wanted business to recognize the rights of workers to organize and bargain collectively in unions, which would allow workers' wages to rise with prices. The resulting compromise was the National Industrial Recovery Act (NIRA), passed in June 1933, which established a new federal agency, the National Recovery Administration (NRA). The NRA called for every business to abide by a temporary ''blanket code,'' with a minimum wage of between 30 and 40 cents an hour, a maximum work-week of 35 to 40 hours a week, and the abolition of child labor. Those employers who followed the code displayed the NRA symbol of the Blue Eagle in their windows.

The NRA also set up codes for most of the country's major industries to establish price and wage floors, below which the specific industry could not go. However, the hastily devised codes would fail. Most importantly, federal officials, inexperienced in running such a large program, did not have the capacity to administer it. In addition, Section 7(a) of the NIRA gave workers the right to form unions, but had no mechanism for enforcement. Thus, the program failed to raise workers' wages and increase consumer purchasing power. In 1935 the Supreme Court nullified NRA legislation when it ruled in the *Schechter* case that in giving the president the power to shape the NRA codes, the Congress had acted unconstitutionally. Consequently, the failing program was abolished.

THOUGH THE PROGRAMS DEVISED FOR THE EARLY YEARS OF THE NEW DEAL WERE INTENDED TO BE TEMPORARY, THEY PROVIDED A BASIS FOR LATER SOCIAL MEASURES THAT BECAME PART OF A PERMANENT WELFARE STATE.

One of the most successful New Deal programs was legislation enacted in 1933 to create the Tennessee Valley Authority (TVA), a project for building a dam at Muscle Shoals and for the comprehensive redevelopment of the region. By building dams and waterways in the region, the TVA nearly eliminated flooding in the area and provided electricity to thousands of people. But the Roosevelt administration also initiated major financial reforms. On April 18, 1933, Roosevelt made an inflationary move by signing an executive order, which took U.S. currency off the gold standard. Enabling the government to manipulate the value of the dollar, government management of currency set a significant precedent in federal policy and changed the relationship between the government and business. The New Deal also gave the government authority in areas of the economy that previously were weakly regulated. The Glass-Steagall Act of June 1933 allowed the government to regulate irresponsible speculation by banks. The act also established the Federal Deposit Insurance Corporation (FDIC), which guaranteed all bank deposits up to $2,500. In 1935 Congress passed a banking act which transferred the authority of the regional Federal Reserve to the Federal Reserve Board in Washington, D.C. Congress sought to protect stock market investors by passing the Truth in Securities Act of 1933, which required corporations to provide accurate and complete information to the public. In addition, in June 1934, the Securities and Exchange Commission (SEC) was established as a stock market watchdog.

The expansion of federal relief provided to millions of unemployed Americans was an enormous undertaking. One of President Roosevelt's first programs was the Federal Emergency Relief Administration (FERA), which gave grants to states in which relief agencies had run out of money. However, the FERA relief would not be enough. The second program, the Civil Works Administration (CWA), provided work relief to more than four million people between November and April during the president's first year in office. But both FERA and CWA were intended as only relief measures, not as long-term programs meant to save the country's economy. By 1934, Roosevelt began to dismantle the CWA. His administration also established the Civilian Conservation Corps (CCC), which employed millions of young men, mostly urban, to work in camps at national parks and forests on conservation and reforestation projects. Though the programs devised for the early years of the New Deal were intended to be temporary, they provided a basis for later social measures that became part of a permanent welfare state.

In 1935 Roosevelt began a new set of programs called the "Second New Deal." Noted for its shift to a decidedly anti-corporate stance, the president proposed one of the most progressive tax systems in American history. Called a "soak the rich" plan by conservatives, the system had taxes reach as high as 75 percent on income for the richest of Americans.

Another significant development during the New Deal was the growth of labor militancy. When the Supreme Court nullified the NIRA in 1935, Senator Robert F. Wagner of New York introduced the National Labor Relations Act (also called the Wagner Act) in Congress. The new law gave workers more federal protection than Section 7(a) provided by including an enforcement mechanism in the National Labor Relations Board (NLRB), which was given the power to require employers to recognize unions. While showing few signs of challenging employers in the 1920s, union leaders and workers, encouraged by the Wagner Act in 1935, stepped up organizing efforts. John L. Lewis of the United Mine Workers helped start the Committee on Industrial Organization to begin organizing unskilled factory workers, a group that the more conservative American Federation of Labor ignored because of their commitment to organizing only skilled workers. The number of workers in recognized unions jumped from three million in 1932 to eight million in 1937, and to 10 million in 1941.

In 1935 Congress passed the Social Security Act (SSA), one of the most important pieces of social welfare legislation in American history. The act established several programs. First, it provided for federal assistance to the elderly in poverty, who could receive $15 a month. The act started a pension system, in which workers and their employers would pay a payroll tax, beginning in 1940, to provide an old age pension of $10 to $85 a month for many workers, though it excluded domestic servants and agricultural workers. The SSA also set up an unemployment insurance system, and provided aid to handicapped people and dependent children.

In addition, the Roosevelt administration set up the Works Progress Administration (WPA) in 1935, a much larger work relief program than the CWA. Between 1935 and 1941, the WPA employed about 2.1 million workers. WPA workers built 110,000 public buildings, 600 airports, and over 500,000 miles of roads, and over 100,000 bridges.

Though President Roosevelt won a landslide victory in 1936, he faced a conservative backlash during the following years. Although the economy had improved by the summer of 1937, a recession struck the economy that year. In 1938, the president asked for emergency funds for public works and relief programs, and as the government's spending saturated the economy, a recovery seemed possible. The American economy, however, would not recover from the Great Depression until World War II. Only the massive federal spending needed to produce the men and material to fight the war brought the depression to an end and laid the ground work for the postwar economic boom. Even though New Dealers failed to meet their goal of rejuvenating the American economy, they had remade the federal government and its relationship to the corporate world.

See also: **Glass-Steagall Act, Hoovervilles, National Industrial Recovery Act, Securities and Exchange Commission, Tennessee Valley Authority, Works Progress Administration**

FURTHER READING

Badger, Anthony J. *The New Deal: The Depression Years, 1933–1940.* New York: The Noonday Press, 1989.

Brinkley, Alan. *The End of Reform: New Deal Liberalism in Recession and War.* New York: Vintage Books, 1995.

Burns, James MacGregor. *Roosevelt: The Lion and the Fox.* New York: Harcourt, Brace and World, Inc., 1956.

Fraser, Steven, and Gary Gerstle. *The Rise and Fall of the New Deal Order, 1930–1980.* Princeton: Princeton University Press, 1989.

Leuchtenburg, William E. *Franklin D. Roosevelt and the New Deal.* New York: Harper and Row, 1963.

NEW DEAL: REFORM OR REVOLUTION *(ISSUE)*

In 1933 the New Deal was initiated after the inauguration of Franklin Delano Roosevelt (1882–1945) as President of the United States. The New Deal represented a set of extensive legislative programs intended to alleviate human suffering that resulted from the Great Depression. In 1929 the Depression had brought about a collapse of the national economy.

Historians have drawn various conclusions about the legacy of the New Deal and its effect on the U.S. economy and society. At the time, critics of the New Deal came from both the political right and left. Conservatives attacked Roosevelt's programs as "socialist" reforms. They argued that he had intervened too deeply in the affairs of business and the economy. Groups such as the American Liberty League, led by the Du Pont family, publicly opposed the "dictatorial" course of the New Deal. By 1935 many New Dealers had given up trying to reconcile their agenda with business interests. Feeling forced by growing Conservative opposition to Roosevelt's liberal programs, New Dealers advocated programs of a more strident, anti-corporate nature. As part of the "Second New Deal" in 1935, for example, the administration proposed to increase taxes on the wealthy, whose income tax could reach as high as 75 percent under this scheme. It was the highest rate ever proposed in U.S. history and was branded a "soak the rich" plan by conservatives, although in practice very few Americans were rich enough to be placed in the highest income bracket.

The liberal policies of the New Deal were for the most part supported by socialists, communists and other radicals. At times, however, critics on the left claimed that New Dealers had not gone far enough in redistributing economic and political power to marginalized groups which included the labor movement, farmers, women, and minorities. The Social Security Act (SSA) was one of the most important pieces of social welfare legislation in U.S. history. Congress passed it in 1935. The act provided federal assistance for the destitute elderly, set up an unemployment insurance system, aided the handicapped and dependent children, and started a pension system. It was a pension system, however, that excluded domestic servants and agricultural workers from coverage. Since both categories contained a large number of African Americans and women, many needy people were denied security in their old age.

NEW DEAL REFORMS OF THE NATIONAL ECONOMY AND SOCIETY OPERATED WITHIN THE CONFINES OF THE POLITICAL AND IDEOLOGICAL REALITIES OF THE CAPITALIST SYSTEM.

Despite the contemporary criticism from the right and left, the widespread popularity of President Roosevelt's policies was evidenced by his landslide presidential victory in 1936 and his reelection in 1940 and again in 1944. He held his office for four terms, longer than any other president in U.S. history.

After World War II (1939–1945) liberal historical interpretations of New Deal policies dominated. Historian Arthur M. Schlesinger argued in the *The Age of Roosevelt* (1957) that the New Deal created a reformed capitalism. He maintained that the power of businesses had finally been constrained by the regulation of public interests. Other liberal historians such as Carl Degler in *Out of Our Past* (1959) took the argument a step further. Degler claimed that in addition to American Revolution (1775–1783) and the American Civil War (1861–1865), the Roosevelt administration brought on a "Third American Revolution."

Other historians were more critical. In *The Age of Reform* (1955) Richard Hofstadter found a break with the past in the New Deal programs. Hofstadter was critical of the New Deal for lacking an overall philosophy in shifting from policies favoring the Progressive reform of the corporate world to a New Deal liberalism with a "social democratic tinge that had never before been present in U.S. reform movements."

William Leuchtenburg was the first historian to provide a systematic, sympathetic critique of the period in *Franklin D. Roosevelt and the New Deal* (1963). He called the New Deal only a "halfway revolution." Leuchtenburg argued that New Deal reforms were limited because of the ideological and political opposition faced by the Roosevelt administration. According to Leuchtenburg little more could have been achieved given the realities of the time. Ellis Hawley, meanwhile, challenged the liberal assumption that the New Dealers worked against corporate interests. He further argued in *The New Deal and the Problem of Monopoly* (1966) that New Deal programs in many cases were meant to promote private business interests.

In the 1960s historians of the New Left were much more critical. Ronald Radosh argued that the New Deal helped enhance the power of capitalism. Radical historians such as Colin Gordon in *New Deals* (1994) also provided evidence that there were close associations between New Dealers, industrialists, and financiers.

But by the 1970s and 1980s most historians agreed with the interpretation that the New Deal was historically significant and positive in its reforms. Nevertheless they ceded the New Deal was severely limited by the political and ideological realities of the time. Later research was concerned less with the "conservative" or "revolutionary" nature of the Roosevelt administration's policies. Contemporary scholars such as Theda Skocpol, James T. Patterson, Barry Karl, Mark Leff, and others focused more on the ideological and political limits with which the New Dealers had to contend. Allen Brinkley in *The End of Reform* (1995) provides an analysis of the New Deal that explores these ideological constraints. The New Deal, he emphasizes, underwent a transition from a government that promoted regulation to one that, for the most part, wished to stay out of the affairs of the business world.

Debate about the efficacy and impact of the New Deal still continued at the end of the twentieth century, almost 80 years later. Conservatives continued to criticize the Roosevelt administration programs for controlling the economy too extensively. Liberal and radical historians, conversely, maintained the reforms were beneficial to society in spite of the constraints that the New Dealers confronted. Although historians somewhat disagreed about the radical implications of the New Deal programs, they came to two similar conclusions. The first was that the New Deal legislation raised federal spending and regulation to the highest levels in U.S. history. The second was that New Deal reforms of the national economy and society operated within the confines of the political and ideological realities of the capitalist system.

See also: **Harry Lloyd Hopkins, Hoovervilles, National Labor Relations Act, National Recovery Act, Franklin D. Roosevelt, Social Security Act, Works Progress Adminstration**

FURTHER READING

Badger, Anthony J. *The New Deal: The Depression Years, 1933–1940*. New York: The Noonday Press, 1989.

Brinkley, Alan. *The End of Reform: New Deal Liberalism in Recession and War*. New York: Vintage Books, 1995.

Burns, James MacGregor. *Roosevelt: The Lion and the Fox*. New York: Harcourt, Brace and World, Inc., 1956.

Fraser, Steven, and Gary Gerstle. *The Rise and Fall of the New Deal Order, 1930–1980*. Princeton, NJ: Princeton University Press, 1989.

Leuchtenburg, William E. *Franklin D. Roosevelt and the New Deal*. New York: Harper and Row, 1963.

NEW FRANCE

New France refers to the collective holdings of France in North America during colonial times. At its height New France consisted of the colonies of Canada, Acadia, and Louisiana. The first land claims were made in 1534 by French explorer Jacques Cartier (1491–1557) as he sailed the St. Lawrence River in eastern Canada. In 1604 Sieur de Monts (c. 1568–c. 1630) established a settlement at Acadia (in present-day Nova Scotia, Canada). French claims later extended the region to include present-day New Brunswick, Canada, and eastern Maine. Explorer Samuel de Champlain (c. 1567–1635) founded Quebec in 1608. He then penetrated the interior (present-day Ontario) as far as Georgian Bay on Lake Huron. In this way he extended French land claims westward. In 1672 French-Canadian explorer Louis Jolliet (1645–1700) and French missionary Jacques Marquette (1637–1675) became the first Europeans to reach the upper part of the Mississippi River. Ten years later French explorer Robert Cavelier (1643–1687) followed the Mississippi to the Gulf of Mexico. He claimed the river valley for France and named it Louisiana. The majority of French settlers lived in the colony of Canada during the time when the French were expanding their North American claims. The fur trade was the major industry. The French called the colony a *comptoir*, a warehouse for animal pelts. It was never very successful in attracting colonists. France lost the colony to Great Britain in the French and Indian War (1754–1763). Louisiana changed hands numerous times before it was finally sold to the United States in 1803 as part of the Louisiana Purchase; it was France's last claim on the North American mainland. French culture remained prevalent in the former colonies of New France during modern times.

***See also:* Louisiana, Louisiana Purchase, Maine**

NEW HAMPSHIRE

Dutch, English, and French explorers navigated the coast of New England before the first English settlement in New Hampshire was established along the Piscataqua River in 1623. At this time New Hampshire was still a province of Massachusetts (it did not separate until 1740). White settlers began to move up the Merrimack and Connecticut river valleys in the 1700s, virtually eliminating the Native American population of the area.

During this period the province's economy was based on fishing, farming, timber harvests, and shipping. Portsmouth became the capital and a busy commercial port. Transportation from Portsmouth to the inland areas was difficult, however, because all travel had to go north or south around the mountains. Thus Boston, not Portsmouth, became New England's busiest trading center. In 1776 New Hampshire was the first of the original 13 colonies to establish an independent government, doing so even before the Declaration of Independence was proclaimed.

During the nineteenth century the textile industry became the most prominent industry in the state. Textile mills were especially plentiful along the Merrimack River. The first workers were generally young "mill girls" who came from neighboring farms to supplement their families' meager incomes. A huge demand for textiles later brought European immigrants to do mill work. Around 1860 French Canadian workers also began flocking south to find work. Meanwhile, farming in the state declined, mostly because of poor soil and rocky terrain.

The growth of what later became the city of Manchester is an interesting case study in how the mill towns developed. The Amoskeag Manufacturing Company was started in 1837 by manufacturers who had worked at the famous Lowell, Massachusetts, mills. In addition to several mills, a whole town was laid out with town squares, schools, churches, parks, and cemeteries, and six block of tenements for the workers and their families. Within eight years the city which grew there increased in population from 50 to 10,000 and the mills were producing the equivalent of 22 miles of yard goods a day for worldwide distribution.

Railroads were making headway during this period as well, despite ambivalence among the populace about how this new mode of transportation would alter New Hampshire life. Railroad companies were granted

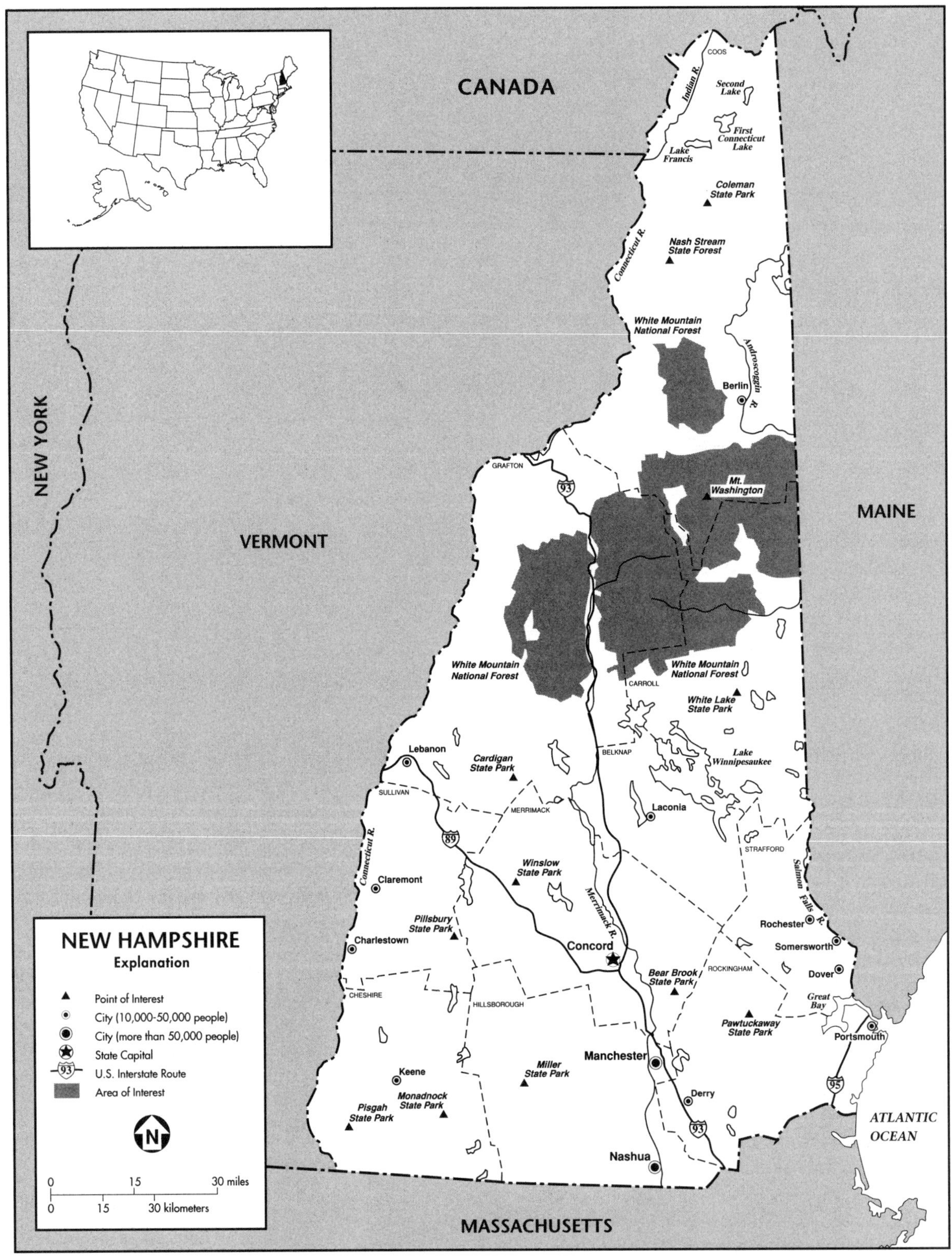

State of New Hampshire.

123 charters in 1846 and 1847, and soon New Hampshire had more miles of track than most other New England states. Regulations on the railroads and on industry passed by the state legislature, however, limited capital growth in the state in the 20 years before the American Civil War (1861–65).

NEW HAMPSHIRE WAS THE FIRST OF THE ORIGINAL 13 COLONIES TO ESTABLISH AN INDEPENDENT GOVERNMENT. IT DID SO IN 1776, EVEN BEFORE THE DECLARATION OF INDEPENDENCE WAS PROCLAIMED.

Ten years after the war people were employed in manufacturing and farming in approximately equal numbers. Like other New England states, however, New Hampshire was experiencing a loss of population as many citizens left the state for newly opened western territories. Farming the rocky soil of New Hampshire was an unattractive option compared to the possibility of a large plot of good farm land in Ohio or Iowa. In 1839 about half the land in the state was agricultural, but by 1870 that percentage had dropped to 39, with more decreases in succeeding decades.

In the southern section of the state mill towns developed where farm land and small villages had been. Elizabeth and Elting Morison observed in their history of the state that on the Merrimack River, ''the continuous line of red brick along the water was, in fact, the west wall of a dense and complicated network of mill structures that, threaded by narrow and tortuous passages, extended well inland.'' These large factories were full of modern machinery, and some began to turn themselves to the production of other industrial products, such as steam engines and rifles.

Besides textile mills, lumbering continued to be an important industry in New Hampshire. The city of Berlin in north-central New Hampshire was the center for lumbering activity. Firms like the Brown Company sent workers out to cut logs, transport them to the Androscoggin River, and float them down river to the mills in massive log drives. This demanding work was done mostly by immigrants from French Canada, Norway, Germany, and Russia.

Taking advantage of its mountains and its rural appeal, New Hampshire developed a thriving tourist business in the later half of the nineteenth century. Throughout the White Mountains large resort hotels such as the Glen House and the Mount Washington Hotel sprang up, and ''summer places'' built by well-to-do easterners began to dot the landscape. Other mountain and lake resorts and cottages were built for the less wealthy. Musicians and artists began to establish colonies in towns like North Conway. By the turn of the century it was estimated that the state was earning $700,000 annually from the ''summer people.'' New Hampshire continued to promote tourism in the twentieth century; it ranked second only to manufacturing in the state's economy in the 1990s.

The last decade of the nineteenth century in New Hampshire was marked by an increase in the power of the railroads, primarily the Boston and Maine. Railroad influence penetrated the state government and it was not curbed until 1911, when a progressively oriented governor and legislature enacted laws to regulate private corporations and public utilities. These reforms preceded similar ones which would be enacted throughout the nation in the coming two decades.

By the early 1920s the New Hampshire textile industry was beginning to decline. A strike at the Amoskeag mills in 1922 only served to highlight the inevitable fact that mills in the South, where much of the raw materials for New Hampshire's mills was produced, were slowly eroding the profitability of those in the New England. Between 1880 and 1925 the number of mill spindles doubled in New England, but in the South this number increased thirty-fold. In 1950 one New Hampshire town which once had six working mills was reduced to one mill—this scenario was repeated throughout the state.

The Great Depression added to an already declining economy, and the post–World War II drop-off in demand for textiles brought severe recession to many New Hampshire towns. Only logging and paper manufacture in the northern part of the state were moderately prosperous. The state's population and employment levels both dropped substantially.

In the 1970s and 1980s, however, the southern part of the state began to make a comeback. Interstate highways, the proximity of Boston, and low state taxes helped to encourage people and new high-technology industry to move into the state. Between 1960 and 1988 the state's population doubled, straining government services and increasing local taxes. Most of the newcomers were relatively more affluent and better educated than the natives of the state. A recession in the early 1990s slowed, but did not stop, this progress.

Modern New Hampshire is one of the most industrialized states in the nation. The state's per capita income in 1996 was over $26,000, ranked eighth in the nation. Only 5.3 percent of its citizens were below the federal poverty level in that year.

FURTHER READING

Clark, Charles E. *The Eastern Frontier: The Settlement of Northern New England, 1610–1763.* New York: Knopf, 1970.

Federal Writers' Project. *New Hampshire: A Guide to the Granite State.* 1938. Reprint. New York: Somerset, n.d.

Morison, Elizabeth Forbes, and Elting E. Morison. *New Hampshire: A Bicentennial History.* New York: Norton, 1976.

Squires, J. Duane. *The Granite State of the United States: A History of New Hampshire from 1623 to the Present.* 4 vols. New York: American Historical Co., 1956.

Stacker, Ann P. and Nancy C. Hefferman. *Short History of New Hampshire.* Grantham, NH: Thompson and Rutter, 1985.

NEW JERSEY

The history of New Jersey is a study in conflicts—geographical, political, social, and economic. One end of the state often seems like a part of New York City; the other end has close ties to Philadelphia, Pennsylvania. Although the state retains a healthy agricultural sector, it is better known as a place where industry developed early and then went into decline for a period of time. High unemployment and urban decay have plagued the cities in New Jersey for several decades. In the 1980s and 1990s, however, better times seemed to be on the horizon for the "Garden State."

In 1524 Italian explorer Giovanni di Verrazano sailed into Newark Bay and became the first known European to reach New Jersey. English Captain Henry Hudson also sailed along the New Jersey shore and established a claim for the Dutch, under whose flag he sailed. Dutch traders founded New Jersey's first town, and Swedish settlers began to settle east of the Delaware River. By the mid-1770s the indigenous Leni-Lanape Indians (whom the English called the Delaware) had exchanged most of their valuable lands for trinkets, guns, and alcohol and had almost disappeared from the area.

England took control in 1664 after King Charles II granted a region from the Connecticut River to the Delaware River to his brother James, Duke of York. The Duke deeded part of the land to his friends Baron John Berkeley and Sir George Carteret, making New Jersey a proprietorship (New Jersey was named for one of the British channel islands). The country was later divided into two separate parts, East Jersey and West Jersey, only to be reunited in 1702 by Queen Anne. A royal governor was appointed in 1738. To this day the two areas of New Jersey have quite different characters, with the northeastern section closely identified with New York and the southwestern section looking toward Philadelphia.

CONTEMPORARY NEW JERSEY IS STILL WHAT GOVERNOR [JONATHAN] BELCHER CALLED IT IN 1745—"THE BEST COUNTRY FOR MIDDLING FORTUNES, AND FOR PEOPLE WHO HAVE TO LIVE BY THE SWEAT OF THEIR BROWS."

Thomas Fleming, *New Jersey: A Bicentennial History,* 1977.

New Jersey played an important role in the American Revolution (1775–1783), but it experienced an economic decline in the aftermath of the war. Its trade with New York was interrupted; its towns were left in ruins; and its profitable iron works were shut down. After New Jersey entered the Union in 1787, however, the state began to recover economically; the town of Paterson, for example, developed as a center of silk manufacturing.

In the 1830s railroads and canals helped to set New Jersey on a course toward urbanization and industrialization. One of the greatest engineering feats of its time, the Morris Canal, connected northern New Jersey with the coal fields of Pennsylvania. The canal benefited many businesses along its route, from iron mines to dyeing and weaving mills. A second canal, the Delaware and Raritan, crossed flat land in the middle of the state. The most important town along the Morris Canal was Newark, the first in the state to be incorporated; it developed around breweries, hat factories, and paper manufacturers. Other towns grew with industries as well: Trenton was noted for its iron and paper plants and Jersey City was noted for its steel and soap operations.

Railroads spelled the end of profitability for the canals, which went into decline after the American Civil War (1861–1865). The first railroad, the Camden and Amboy, opened in 1834; it soon began to monopolize the New York-Philadelphia corridor. Coal brought by the railroad provided a new source of power other than water, and industries sprang up along the railroad's route. After the Camden and Amboy was leased to the Pennsylvania Railroad, numerous other rail lines opened up other areas to development.

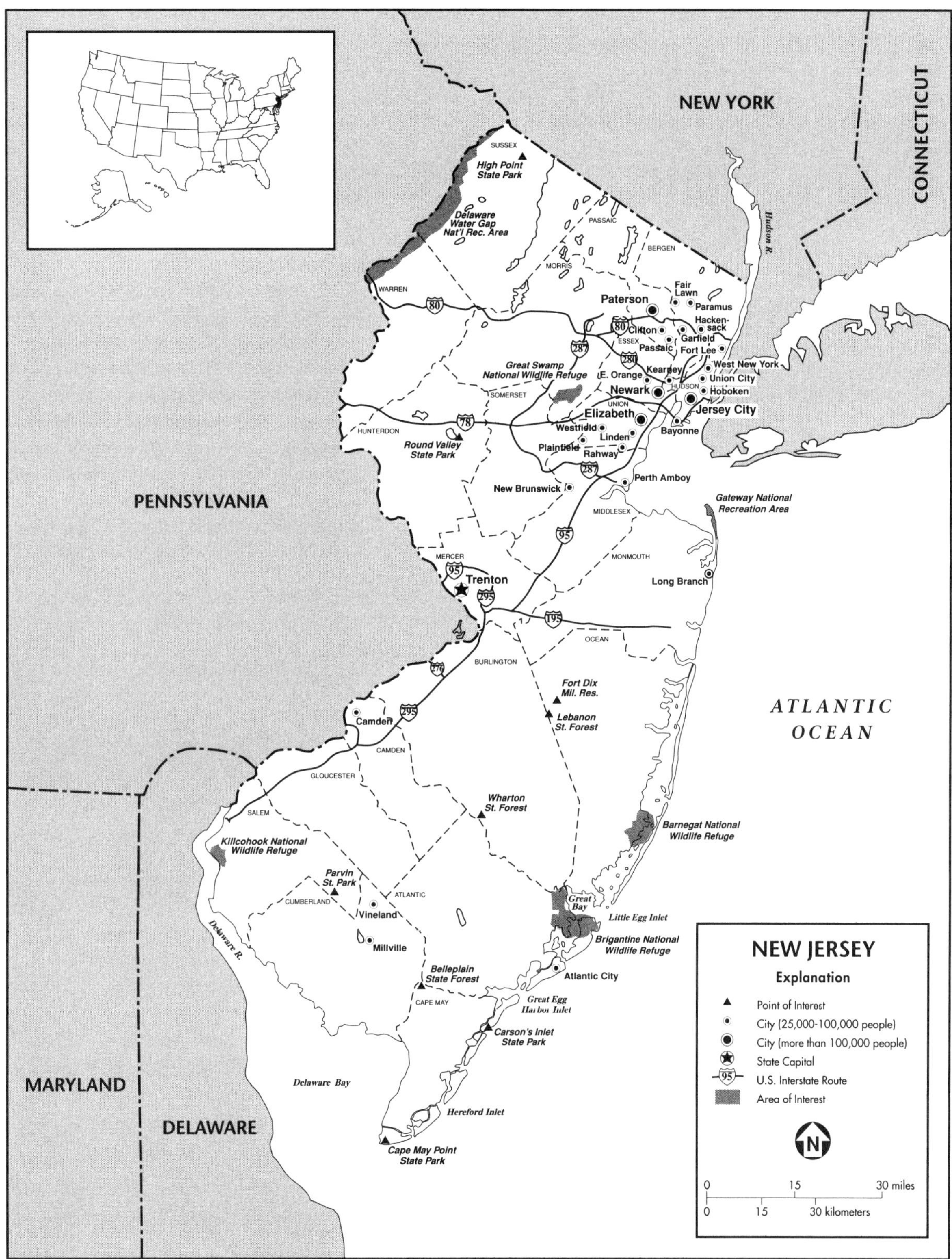

State of New Jersey.

Despite much political wrangling over the Civil War in New Jersey, the state benefited economically from the war by providing tons of ammunition and equipment for the Union army. After the war factories continued to make many components used by other manufacturers. In 1873 Isaac Singer (1811–1875) opened a sewing machine plant at Elizabeth; oil refineries grew along the Hudson County waterfront; and pottery manufacturers thrived in Trenton. Newark had a diversified base of manufacturing and a large number of nationally known insurance companies.

New Jersey became the nation's top shipbuilding state during World War I (1914–1918). In addition, New Jersey refined 75 percent of the copper in the country and loaded an equal percentage of U.S. shells. The war, however, did not substantially hinder labor unrest, which had been a part of New Jersey's history since the 1880s. In 1915, at Carteret, a walkout at a fertilizer factory led to the killing of six strikers by guards. In the postwar era, Passaic textile workers stayed off the job for a year in 1926, and in 1933 Paterson silk workers finally gained union recognition and higher wages after another strike.

By that time, however, many other New Jersey workers were experiencing reduced work weeks or unemployment. As the Great Depression (1929–1939) worsened, many expected to take advantage of President Franklin D. Roosevelt's (1933–1945) New Deal programs to provide a measure of relief. Unfortunately for many, these government jobs were almost entirely under the control of Frank Hague, Mayor of Jersey City, a corrupt politician with many ties to the Roosevelt administration. According to Thomas Fleming's history of New Jersey, *New Jersey: A Bicentennial History*, Harry Hopkins, head of the Works Progress Administration, "ignored stacks of testimony and sworn affidavits from men and women who said that they were forced to vote for Hague's candidates and pay 3 percent of their salaries to the [political] machine in return for their jobs." Fleming painted a sorry picture of the relationship between New Jersey politicians and their constituents during this time: "For the first time politicians had access to huge amounts of *legal* money and jobs. No longer did they have to rely on padded loyal payrolls and money from illegal gambling and phony real estate deals." The power of Hague's political machine in the state was formidable, lasting until his defeat as mayor in 1947.

World War II (1939–1945) brought a revival of industry in New Jersey, especially in shipbuilding and munitions. Chemical and pharmaceutical companies also thrived, while Paterson became the nation's leading aircraft engine manufacturing center. After the war many people left the older cities to build homes in suburbs like Cherry Hill, Woodbridge, and Middletown Township. Between 1940 and 1950 the population of the state burgeoned by 1.2 million, stretching highway use and housing availability to the limit. New Jersey rapidly became the center for many research laboratories during this time, which helped creation of a number of affluent areas such as Bergen County.

For many in the inner cities, however, postwar hopes of economic opportunity had been crushed. According to Fleming, the many African Americans who had come to Newark seeking jobs after the war "virtually guaranteed tragedy." Only half found employment in the declining industries, and "[s]ome 40 percent of them had to travel to work outside the city every morning while 300,000 suburban workers poured into the central district to work in giant insurance company offices or in the remaining industrial jobs." In 1967 the city of Newark erupted into four days of rioting, looting, and burning, which left the city in shambles, both economically and psychologically.

In the next five years Newark lost 23,000 private jobs. In the 1970s and 1980s, 270,000 people left New Jersey as cities lost manufacturing jobs and retailing moved to suburbia. Unemployment reached nearly 10 percent. By the mid-1980s, however, recovery was on the horizon. With the loss of manufacturing jobs came a resurgence of jobs in the service industries. After another recession in the early 1990s, the state rebounded again. The unemployment rate fell to six percent in 1996 for the first time in six years. The recovery was due at least in part to the presence of a highly skilled workforce, which attracted pharmaceutical, biotechnology, electronics, and other high-technology industries to the state. Along with business incentive programs administered by the state Department of Commerce and Economic Development, the relatively low tax burden in New Jersey has helped to encourage new businesses to come into the state. Per capita personal income in the state in 1996 was over $31,000 and ranked second among all states.

Vitally important to New Jersey's economy are the ports which line New York Harbor. Ports at Elizabeth, with three miles of berthing space, and Newark, with four miles, handle more cargo than New York City ports, benefiting the local economy greatly. Privately owned piers in Jersey City and Bayonne also handle significant cargo. Northern New Jersey port facilities taken together form the largest port in the eastern United States and the second largest in the whole country.

See also: **Isaac Singer**

FURTHER READING

Amick, George. *The American Way of Graft.* 5 vols. Princeton, NJ: Center for Analysis of Public Issues, 1987.

Cunningham, John T. *This is New Jersey*, 4th ed. New Brunswick, NJ: Rutgers University Press, 1994.

Fleming, Thomas. *New Jersey: A Bicentennial History.* New York: Norton, 1977.

A New Jersey Anthology. Newark: New Jersey Historical Society, 1994.

New Jersey, State of Economic Policy Council and Office of Economic Policy. *1985 Economic Outlook for New Jersey.* Trenton, 1984.

NEW MEXICO

In 1803 when President Thomas Jefferson (1801–1809) purchased the Louisiana Territory from France, New Mexico had been under Spanish rule for nearly 250 years. After the real estate deal with Napoleon Bonaparte was completed, New Mexico had a new U.S. neighbor.

In 1821 Mexico won its independence from Spain and New Mexico became a province of Mexico. Until then, the Spanish had been very careful about allowing foreigners into Mexican territory. But the new Mexican government was eager to allow New Mexico to deal with U.S. traders. Missourian William Becknell entered Santa Fe and sold U.S. goods such as cloth, pans, and tools to residents there. In exchange he received furs, gold, and silver. He made such a profit that his success created a rush of other businessmen to Mexico who traveled along an 800-mile pathway between Independence, Missouri and Santa Fe, known as the Santa Fe Trail.

America's bid to extend its boundaries to the Pacific Ocean involved the conquest of New Mexico. In 1846 war broke out between the United States and Mexico. When the war ended in 1848, the red, white and blue American flag flew over Santa Fe. Mexico was forced to give up California and New Mexico to the United States. Soon after settlers from eastern and southern states began migrating to New Mexico in the early 1850s to ranch or search for gold and silver.

In 1862 the United States began a campaign against the Native Americans in New Mexico to drive them to a reservation on the Pecos River. Christopher ''Kit'' Carson, a mountain man and military officer, led the charge against the Apaches and Navajos. As the Native Americans resisted, Carson and his men burned the Native Americans' cornfields and pumpkin patches. Two million pounds of grain were destroyed the first year, causing starvation among the Navajos.

At the same time settlers were fighting among themselves. Cattle ranchers fought against merchants for control of Lincoln County. The Lincoln County War, as it came to be known, involved William H. Bonney, or Billy the Kid, and helped give the territory the image of lawlessness.

In the late 1870s the development of railroad lines across the landscape of New Mexico changed the territory forever. Railroads connected cities in the west and the Southern Pacific line became the first transcontinental track to cross southern New Mexico. Prospectors and equipment for mining were brought to New Mexico by train. Several silver mines were established and towns sprang up. Cattle ranching spread to New Mexico from the southeast region of Texas.

In 1876 statehood for New Mexico was opposed by mining companies, railroads and cattle ranchers who anticipated higher taxes as a result. In addition, New Mexico's diverse population, which included Native American, Spanish, and Mexican cultures, rather than bringing about cultural interchange and amalgamation, fueled the fires of bigotry and racism. However, in 1912 Congress proclaimed New Mexico a state.

Soon after, New Mexico became a haven for talented artists attracting painters, poets and novelists from the East and Midwest. In 1930 a scientist and visionary named Robert Goddard moved to New Mexico to test rocket models. Eventually aerospace became one of New Mexico's major industries.

As the Great Depression rocked the country in the 1930s, New Mexico was devastated as mines closed and railroads and cattle ranches laid off workers. Economic recovery in the state began after the start of World War II (1939–1945). A steady stream of newcomers were going to a New Mexican ranch called Los Alamos. The ranch had been turned into a secret laboratory for the Manhattan Project, a plan to build the most dangerous war weapon ever.

In 1945 the first atomic bomb test took place in a desert near Alamogordo, New Mexico. Subsequently, the war ended shortly after atomic bombs were dropped on Hiroshima and Nagasaki, Japan. New Mexico was instrumental in bringing the war to an end and the world into the nuclear age.

After the war the federal government turned Los Alamos into a huge nuclear laboratory. Nuclear research was conducted at Sandia National Laboratories

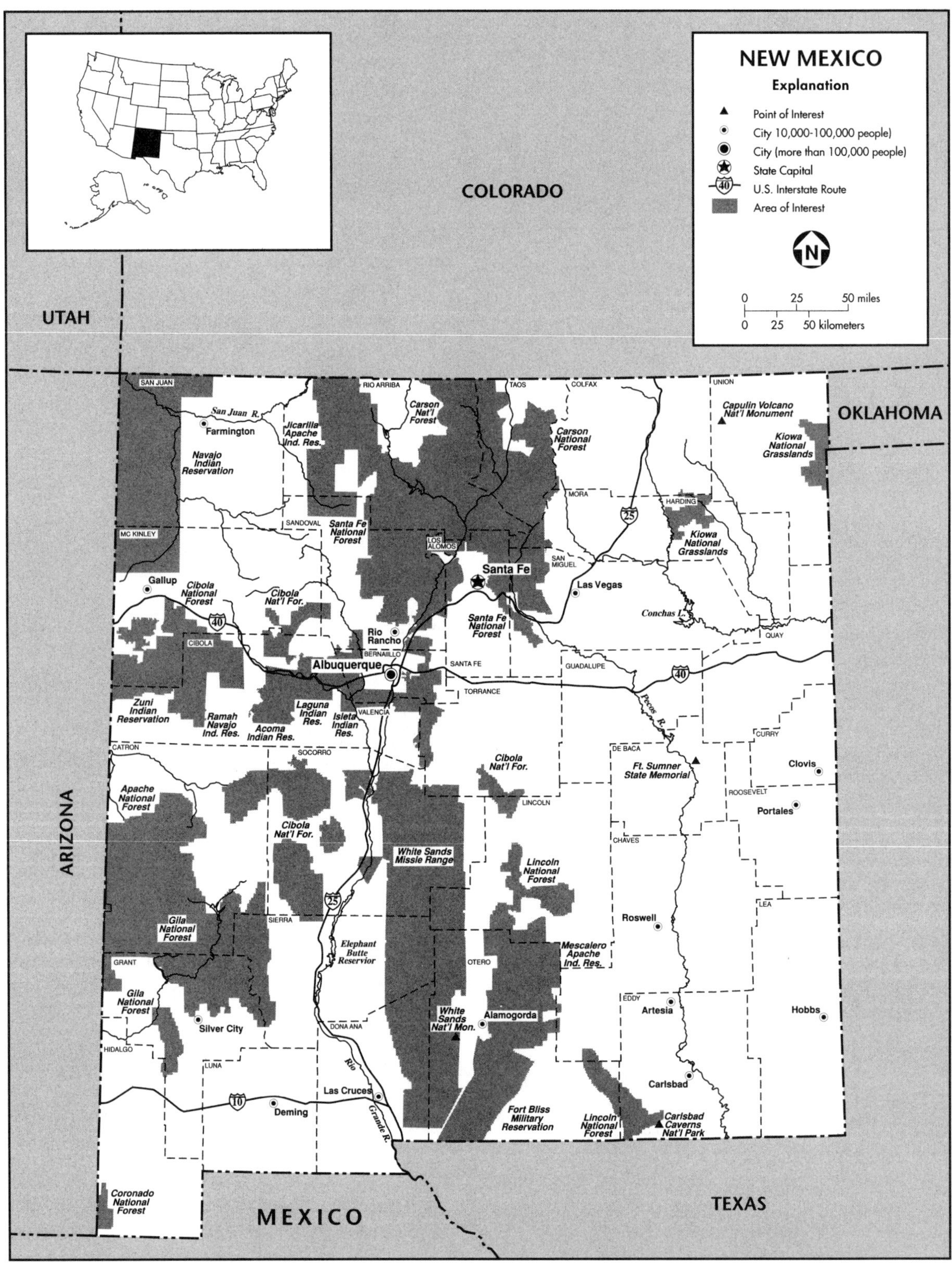

State of New Mexico.

in Albuquerque. The government created the White Sands Missile Range in New Mexico, a test site for rockets. In addition, in 1950 uranium, a metal used in nuclear bombs and nuclear power plants, was discovered in northwest New Mexico. Thus New Mexico became a leading uranium-mining state.

Many scientists, researchers, engineers and their families moved to New Mexico to work at the sites. The state's population doubled in size between 1950 and 1960 and Albuquerque's population quadrupled. So many people were coming from other parts of the country that Spanish-speaking New Mexicans, who once were the majority, became a minority. In the 1990 census, Hispanics accounted for 38 percent of the state's population.

Over the next three decades the state's nuclear and high–tech industries flourished. In 1987 New Mexican companies were awarded $1.8 million to build the SDI or ''Star Wars'' missile defense system. Even though the government reduced military spending and income from the nuclear industry decreased in the 1990s, New Mexico's high tech industry offset those losses with Intel's Rio Rancho plant which was the world's largest computer chip factory in the mid-1990s.

Tourism played a major role in the state's economy in the mid–1990s and the state continued to be a leader in space and nuclear research. However, poverty affects a significant number of New Mexico's residents. In the early 1990s the government instituted job training programs to address unemployment issues. In addition, in 1993 a border crossing opened across from Juarez, Mexico to encourage trade between New Mexico and Mexico. In 1995 the median household income was $25,991 and 25.3 percent of New Mexicans lived below the poverty level.

See also: **Santa Fe, Santa Fe Trial**

FURTHER READING

Early, Theresa S. *New Mexico*, Minneapolis: Lerner Publications Company, 1993.

Jenkins, Myra E. *A Brief History of New Mexico*, Albuquerque: University of New Mexico Press, 1974.

Simmons, Marc. *New Mexico: A Bicentennial History*, New York: W. W. Norton and Company, 1977.

Thompson, Kathleen. New Mexico. In *Portrait of America*. Austin, Texas: Steck–Vaughn Publishers, 1996.

Worldmark Encyclopedia of the States. Detroit: Gale Research, 1998, s.v. ''New Mexico.''

NEW NETHERLANDS

New Netherlands was the only Dutch colony on the North American mainland. The area consisted of lands surrounding the Hudson River (in the present-day state of New York) and later the lower Delaware River (in New Jersey and Delaware). Explorers from the Netherlands (Holland) first settled the area in about 1610. In 1624 the colony of New Netherlands was officially founded by the Dutch West India Company. In 1626 on behalf of the company Dutch colonial official Peter Minuit (1580–1638) purchased the island of Manhattan from the Native Americans for an estimated $24 in trinkets. The colonial capital of New Amsterdam (present-day New York City) was established there.

The Dutch settlement was never very big, consisting mostly of single males who were either fur trappers or traders. The seal of the colony was a beaver surrounded by wampum. The Dutch pioneered the use of wampum as a form of money that could be exchanged with Native Americans for beaver pelts. The Dutch tried several devices to attract new settlers, including the patroon system. Investors would be given a large tract of land, if they could populate it with farmers. Eventually land was distributed more liberally. By 1640, 200 acres would be given free to any family of five, including servants. Larger numbers did come before the Dutch lost the colony in 1664, when it was conquered by the English under the direction of the Duke of York, brother of king James II (1633–1701). The English had sought the territory since New Netherlands had separated its American holdings. Under British control the area was divided into two colonies—New Jersey and New York.

During the colonial period the Netherlands also claimed the West Indies islands of Aruba, Bonaire, and Curacao (called the Netherlands Antilles). The islands were administered separately from New Netherlands on the North American mainland.

See also: **Delaware, New Jersey, New York, Wampum**

NEW ORLEANS, LOUISIANA

The city of New Orleans, Louisiana, is situated on the Mississippi River. It is about 100 miles (160 kilometers) north the Gulf of Mexico, making it a strategic port of entry to the North American mainland.

Before the arrival of Europeans in the 1500s Louisiana was home to the Chickasaw, Choctaw, and Natchez Indians who had lived there for thousands of years. French explorer Robert Cavelier (1643–1687) sailed down the Mississippi River in 1682 in search of a westward route from Canada into the interior. He claimed the entire river basin for France. The claim consisted of roughly the central third of the present-day United States. La Salle named it Louisiana in honor of French king Louis XIV (1638–1715). In 1701 the territory was made a province of France; it was one of three French colonies on the North American mainland (the other two were Acadia and Canada; together the three colonies were known as New France). It was not until 1714 that the French began settling Louisiana. In 1718 colonist Sieur de Bienville (1626–1685) established a settlement at New Orleans. He named it after French regent Philippe II (1674–1723), Duke of Orleans. Philippe II ruled France after the death of Louis XIV on behalf of King Louis XV (1710–1774) who was only a youth at the time. To encourage development Scottish financier John Law (1671–1729) was named controller-general in 1720. This gave him authority over Louisiana. While Law succeeded in increasing shipping between New Orleans and France, his Compagnie d'Occident failed later that year. The city was made the capital of Louisiana in 1722 but under Law's scheme it attracted few reputable emigrants. In 1731 France reclaimed Louisiana as a royal province, but the colony still did not thrive economically.

In 1762 King Louis XV ceded Louisiana to Spain (ruled by his cousin, King Charles III; 1716–1788). He was on the verge of losing the rest of New France to Great Britain in the French and Indian Wars (1754–1763). Under Spanish rule the colony grew more prosperous, attracting French, American, and Spanish settlers. However New Orleans was still beset by problems, including two fires that destroyed more than a thousand buildings during the late 1700s.

In 1800 the economic and strategic importance of New Orleans became clear as French ruler Napoleon Bonaparte (1769–1821) exhibited an interest in reacquiring Louisiana. Spain, which had bought Louisiana and New Orleans from France in 1763 at the end of the French and Indian Wars with Great Britain, was no match for the French militarily, and Napoleon secretly pressured Spain to return Louisiana to France. Under U.S. envoy Thomas Pinkney's 1795 Treaty with Spain the Spanish had been allowing the Americans to traffic on the Mississippi River and to store their river freight in the warehouses of New Orleans' prior to transshipping it onto ocean going ships. In 1800 and 1802 Spain secretly sold Louisiana back to the French. At about the same time Spain began to renege on the privileges that it had accorded the Americans. In March 1803 the transfer became publicly known.

President Thomas Jefferson, who had been a supporter of the French Revolution and a critic of France's enemy, Great Britain, feared that Napoleon would establish a French presence along the Mississippi River and eventually obstruct westward settlement by the United States' farming population. Jefferson wrote to his diplomatic minister to France, Robert Livingston, that although he had always looked on France as the "natural friend" of the United States, now he had to reassess matters. He observed that there was "one spot" on the face of the earth the possessor of which automatically became "our natural . . . enemy." That spot was New Orleans because of its chokehold on U.S. western river traffic. (Brinkley, 211) Accordingly, Jefferson ordered the rebuilding of the United States Navy and prepared for war with France. Rather than go to war with the United States when he was already engaged in hostilities with the British, Napoleon then agreed to sell the Louisiana territory to the United States. For only $15 million in the Louisiana Purchase the United States doubled its size.

The city of New Orleans continued to grow and prosper as the agricultural economy of the Ohio Valley and of the "new" southwest of the country (along the Mississippi River) expanded. During the War of 1812 (1812–1814) New Orleans was the site of the most fortunate military engagement of the war (from the standpoint of the U.S.) The city had already been incorporated in 1805. In the Battle of New Orleans the U.S. troops under the command of Andrew Jackson "whipped" the British in what turned out to be the last armed hostilities between the United States and Great Britain.

After the War of 1812 New Orleans continued to serve in its familiar role of warehousing and shipping agricultural goods as the South's sugarcane and cotton plantations were thriving. As a result New Orleans river trade flourished. During the succeeding years it became a major U.S. seaport. Ten dollar bills issued by the Bank of Louisiana were used to pay riverboat men when they unloaded their cargo in New Orleans. The notes were called "dixies" because the French word for ten, *dix*, was prominently displayed on the bill. So successful was this trade that "dixie" soon began to mean the entire south.

Once again, the strategic importance of New Orleans and of the traffic along the Mississippi River shaped military calculations during the Civil War (1861–1865). Early in the war the Union forces established a blockade of southern ports and, under the command of David Farragut, captured New Orleans on April 25, 1862. Throughout the war the Union forces controlled New Orleans, thus preventing the Confederates from receiving provisions and military hardware from its largest port. The Union Army then proceeded to attack other cities along the Mississippi. They bombarded Vicksburg in June 1862. Over a year later, in July 1863 Vicksburg fell after a six-week siege conducted by Union General Ulysses Grant finally wore down its defenders.

In the modern age New Orleans has continued to prosper not only for its continued economically importance in transshipping agricultural commodities, but also for its tropic climate and its rich cultural resources.

See also: **Civil War, Colonies (Proprietary), Louisiana, Louisiana Purchase**

NEW SPAIN, VICEROYALTY OF

New Spain refers to Spanish possessions in the New World during the colonial period. At its height New Spain included what are today the southwestern United States, all of Mexico, Central America to the Isthmus of Panama, Florida, much of the West Indies (islands in the Caribbean), as well as the Philippines in the Pacific Ocean. The viceroyalty (a province governed by a representative of the monarch) of New Spain was governed from the capital at Mexico City beginning in 1535.

The era of Spanish colonization began with the radical de-population of portions of the Western Hemisphere caused by the slaughter of the indigenous people by the Conquistadores and the mass deaths caused by epidemic disease, mostly measles and small pox. This traumatic de-population produced mortality rates as high as 90 percent. It was a catastrophe which disorganized the culture in ways which may only compare to the trauma of Middle Passage voyage below decks for the newly enslaved Africans.

More than anything, the Spanish conquerors were intent on locating and removing precious metals—gold and silver—from the Aztec and Inca empires that they encountered. The mining of silver was accomplished by the enslaving of the native people, later supplemented by importing African slaves. The mines at Potosí (in modern Bolivia) yielded great quantities of silver.

This lust for gold and silver resulted in a ruinous inflation in Spain as the imported bullion suffused throughout the Spanish economy. The initial impact of the inflation was to raise the price of Spanish exports. This helped to destroy Spain's economy, especially its textile industry. Over several decades during the sixteenth century this inflation spread out to the rest of Europe. Since the economies of Europe were mostly experiencing healthy expansion, this somewhat milder wave of inflation did not have the same destructive impact on the rest of Europe as it did in Spain.

Since the Spanish did not bring women with them they intermarried with the native peoples. The resulting mixture of parentage, plus the missionary efforts of the Catholic Church, produced a complex caste system and a creolized culture further complicated by the addition of African slaves to the population. The leaders of the Spanish forces of occupation sometimes installed themselves in almost feudal splendor based on the *encomienda* system of tribute (in precious metal) levied on the local villages.

In 1821 a Mexican rebellion ended Spanish rule there and the colonial empire of New Spain was dissolved. By 1898 Spain had relinquished all its possessions in North America. Its last holdings were the islands of Cuba, Puerto Rico, Guam, and the Philippines, which were ceded to the United States after Spain lost the Spanish-American War (1898).

During the colonial period Spain claimed other territories in the New World—in northern and western South America. Most of these holdings fell under the viceroyalty of Peru, which was administered separately from the viceroyalty of New Spain. Spain lost these possessions as well by the end of the 1800s.

See also: **Mesoamerica, Middle Passage, Spanish-American War**

NEW SWEDEN

New Sweden was a small Swedish colony established in 1638 at Fort Christina (present-day Wilmington, Delaware). The Swedes gradually extended the settlement from the mouth of Delaware Bay (south of Wilmington) northward along the Delaware River as far as present-day Trenton, New Jersey. The settlers were mostly fur traders; the Swedes often acted as middlemen between Native American trappers and the English. But there was farming in the colony as well. In

1655 the territory was taken by the Dutch in a military expedition led by director general of New Netherlands Peter Stuyvesant (c. 1610–72). For nine years the territory was part of the Dutch colonial claims called New Netherlands. In 1664 the English claimed it along with the rest of New Netherlands. Delaware was set up as a British proprietary colony, which it remained until the outbreak of the American Revolution (1775–83). New Sweden was the only Swedish colony in America.

See also: **Colonies (Proprietary), Delaware, New Netherlands, New Jersey**

NEW YORK

The state of New York was for a long time a leader in industry and economic prosperity. Particularly interesting is how the specific forms of New York's industry and economy have changed over the years, beginning with its days as a Dutch territory in the early 1600s.

The Dutch-employed English explorer Henry Hudson journeyed up much of the length of the present day Hudson River in 1609, giving the Netherlands the right to claim the land. The Dutch soon began to set up outposts in order to carry on the lucrative trading of animal furs with the Native Americans. More settlers arrived and founded settlements that would later become known as Albany, Schenectady, and New York City. The Dutch continued to prosper in New Netherlands until 1664 when English King Charles II gave the land to his brother, the Duke of York (later King James II). York then seized the land and placed it under English control. This was how the name New York was derived. Even under English control fur trading continued to be a major industry, as well as agriculture and lumber.

With the formation of the United States of America New York's first governor George Clinton established policies of protectionism which allowed commerce to expand. New York soon became a leading commercial power with strong dairy and textile industries. Economic expansion in New York continued in the early 1800's, attracting migrants from the surrounding states. By 1810 New York became the most populated state in the union.

Geography always played a vital role in the economy of New York. New York's many lakes and waterways helped in the transportation of goods to and from the various settlements throughout the state. In 1817 Governor De Witt Clinton (nephew of George Clinton) set about to further expand the transport system of the state with the construction of a canal. When the canal was finished in 1825 New York had an all water route from New York City to the Great Lakes. By 1831 fifty percent of U.S. imports and 27 percent of exports traveled on the canal. This led to further development and increased business in the towns along the canal and rivers such as Rochester and Utica.

Engineering projects like the Erie canal and later the railroads provided work for the large numbers of immigrants arriving from Europe. The increased labor force and improved transportation and development allowed New York to become the national leader in manufacturing.

During the period of the early Republic the guild-inspired, artisan production system of apprentice, journeyman, and master craftsman began to be circumvented by the reorganization of capital investment. The system of production in the garment trades, for one example, was transformed by a new system of subcontracting, where the employer used one experienced and well-paid "cutter" who created the cutting pattern which was simply reproduced and sewn together by women working on a piece-work basis. The result was cheap "off the rack" clothing in which productivity was very high, but wages were low and job security was minimal. In this system the apprentices and journeymen eventually lost their status and became wage-workers, while a few of the master craftsmen became entrepreneurs. This result of this was bitter class conflict within the trades which was reflected in the rise of the "Workingman's Party" in the 1830s.

This process of class differentiation was reflected in the rise of a working class culture in New York City among the children and the "factory girls" who worked in the garment district and in other quarters of the city. On the job, they were subject to the "sweating system" of piecework production. They had few rights and little job security. They did, however, evolve a sort of assertive class-defined public culture, as in the ritual promenades along the streets, especially along the bowery. The factory girl was assertive in her manner and in her "fancy" dress. As one women's historian, professor Stansell comments: "The real sin of the factory girl lay not in premarital sex, but in advertising, with her fancy clothes and assertive ways, the possibilities of a life for women outside the household. . ."

The latter half of the nineteenth century saw the rise of several industry giants. They were entrepreneurs such as John D. Rockerfeller (1839–1937), who

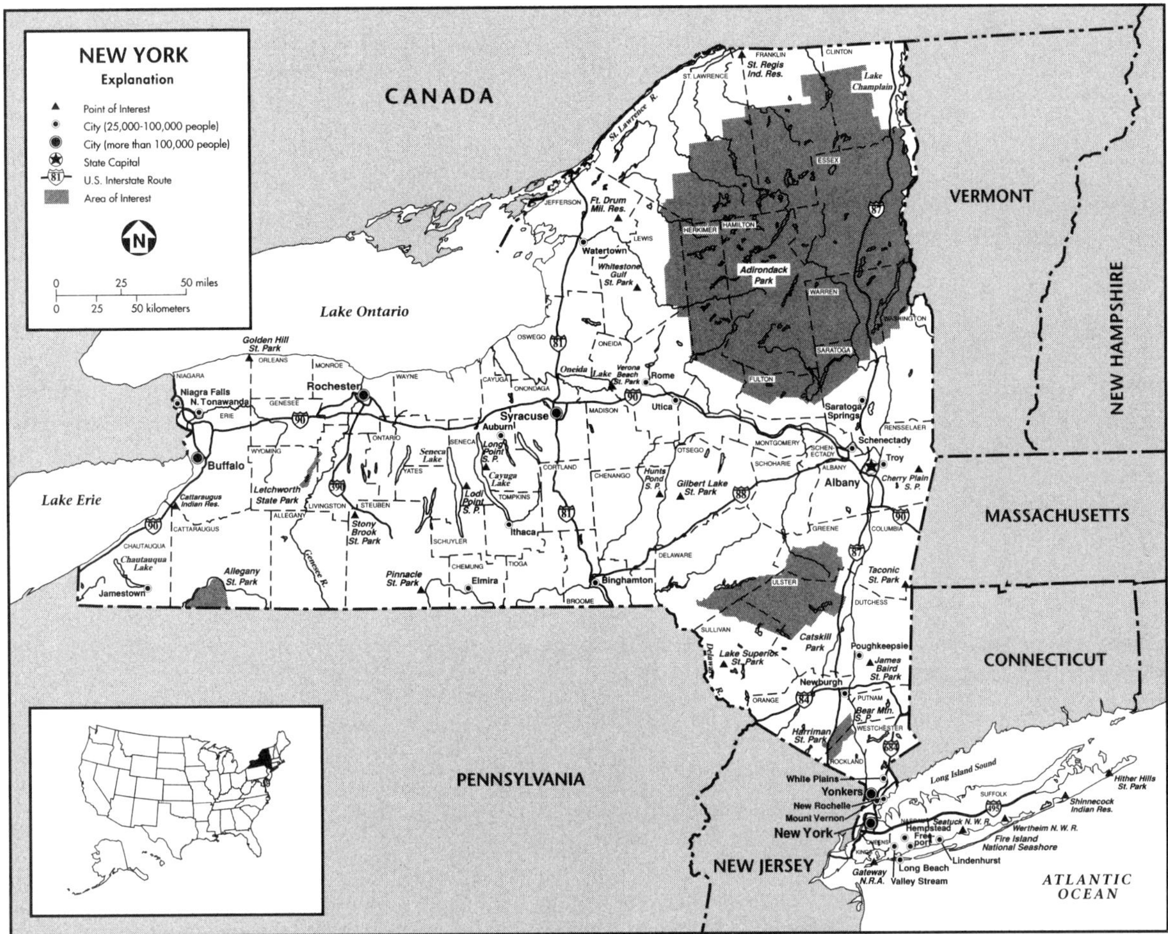

State of New York.

created the Standard Oil Trust, and inventors like Thomas Edison, (1847–1931), founder of Edison Electric (later General Electric). Russell Sage was a prominent investor whose legacy lives on through the New York university that bears his name. Companies such as Westinghouse Electric and Rochester's Eastman Kodak also arose during this time period.

As the twentieth century began New York began to shift increasingly from a highly agricultural state to a manufacturing one. Industry in the second half of the nineteenth century focused around flour, sugar, and lumber. While these industries were still present in the early 1900s there was a rise in the production of machinery, metal, chemicals, and electrical equipment during this period. The fabric and garment industries also grew quickly making the factories unsafe and crowded.

New York's economic rise came to a halt in the late 1920s and early 1930s with the Great Depression (1929–1939). Despite legislation promoted by Franklin D. Roosevelt (1882–1945) while he served as New York's governor (1929–1932), and later U.S. president (1933–1945) the state did not fully recover until World War II (1939–1945).

During World War II New York was a major force in the nation's military industry. Huge amounts of materials important to the war effort flowed out of the state's major cities. Manufacturing centers like Buffalo, New York City, and Schenectady all contributed to the war effort, not to mention the help of many smaller communities. New York's role as a center of the defense industry would be repeated in the Korean War (1950–1975), and the Vietnam War (1959–1975).

New York went through an economic recession in the early 1980s. The state's top industries shifted again, moving from manufacturing to services. Financial services were growing rapidly as New York City banks rose among the state's largest employers. Approximately one million jobs were added to the state's economy between 1980 and 1990 and New York's per capita income hit $21,073 in 1990, at the time, fifth highest in the nation.

In 1994 Republican George Pataki became the governor of New York and began to foster policies with the goal of improving the state's economy. Tax breaks were offered as a means of encouraging businesses to move into the state. In 1996 per capita income rose to fourth place out of the fifty states, and the total personal non-farm income reached $520 billion, second only to California.

New York's economy has varied greatly, centering around agriculture and lumber in its early years, moving into manufacturing and machinery during the Industrial Revolution, and then changing over to services and retail. Regardless of what the major industry might have been the state's economic growth and success earned New York its nickname as the *Empire State*.

See also: **Erie Canal, New Netherlands, Standard Oil, Tenements**

FURTHER READING

Berrol, Selma Cantor. *The Empire City: New York and Its People, 1624–1996*. Westport, CN: Praeger, 1997.

Galie, Peter J. *Ordered Liberty: A Constitutional History of New York*. New York: Fordham University Press, 1996.

Homberger, Eric *The Historical Atlas of New York City: A Visual Celebration of Nearly 400 Years of New York City's History*. New York: H. Holt and Co., 1996.

League of Women Voters of New York State. *A Guide to the New York State Government*. Edited by Mary Jo Fairbanks. Croton-on-Hudson, N.Y.: Policy Studies Association, 1995.

Torres, Andreas. *Between Melting Pot and Mosaic: African Americans and Puerto Ricans in the New York Political Economy*. Philadelphia: Temple University Press, 1995.

NEW YORK CENTRAL RAILROAD

The New York Central Railroad was established from several different railway lines that were joined together to consolidate railway lines throughout the state of New York. George W. Featherstonhaugh applied to the New York state legislature to incorporate the Mohawk & Hudson Railroad Company (M&H) on December 28, 1825. Four months later, on April 17, 1826, Featherstonhaugh appointed Stephen Van Rensselaer III as the first president of M&H. Other key players in the inception of the railroad line were Lynde Catlin (president of the Merchant's Bank of New York City), James Renwick (a mathematics professor at Columbia University), and John Jacob Astor (fur trader and merchant).

Oddly enough, M&H remained essentially inactive until January 1829, when construction began on a line running from Albany to Schenectady, New York, to augment the flourishing cargo business conducted on the Erie Canal. Engineer Peter Fleming was hired to construct this 16-mile stretch of track. Fleming, however, relinquished this position in 1830 and was replaced by John B. Jervis. The railroad finally opened for business in August 1831, at twice the estimated cost. Both horses and the line's only locomotive were used to pull cars during its initial operating phase, although more locomotives were purchased shortly thereafter.

The next link in the line, connecting Utica and Schenectady, began service in 1836. However, since these tracks paralleled the cargo-laden Erie Canal, state legislature proclaimed it illegal to transport freight until 1844. Even then, freight could only be shipped by this railway during the winter months.

During this time other railroads were expanding across the state of New York. Cross-state lines thrived, although the Hudson River proved to be a significant barrier due to the high speed and relatively low cost at which it could be used to transport freight. In 1849 this obstacle was overcome by the construction of a line running from Poughkeepsie to New York. This track was lengthened to East Greenbush, and it soon became apparent that a consolidation of the cross-state lines was in order. The tracks were finally linked in 1853, and the New York Central Railroad (NYC) was formed.

Famous railway magnate Cornelius Vanderbilt (1794–1877) gained control of the New York Central in 1868, and combined it with the Hudson River Railroad. Acting as president of both lines, Vanderbilt set about expanding the reach of these railroads to Chicago, Illinois. He began a series of acquisitions, starting with the purchase of the Lake Shore & Michigan Southern. Vanderbilt's son, William, continued to expand the empire through the acquisition of the Nickel Plate Road (1883) and the West Shore (1885). The Vanderbilt influence continued to hold sway even after William H. Vanderbilt's death in 1885. More railroads were acquired under the leadership of Chauncey Depew, and soon the line reached as far west as the Mississippi River. In 1900 the company leased the Boston &

Albany line, creating one of the most powerful corporations in the United States and a far-reaching railway that spread north from New York to Canada and west from Boston, through Chicago to St. Louis, Missouri.

The New York Central Railroad made many contributions to the railroad industry. These included the American-type No. 999 steam engine, the invention of the dynamometer (an apparatus used to gauge the force exerted by locomotives when hauling trains), and the opening of the first railroad apprentice school. The New York Central was also the first line to adopt the use of high-powered brakes designed specifically for heavy steel passenger equipment.

Unfortunately, troubled times lay ahead. In 1954 Robert R. Young gained control of the New York Central. Alfred E. Perlman was appointed president of the railroad, the last person to ever hold this title. Automotive and airline travel had begun to draw passengers away from the rails. In 1962 the directors of the New York Central and the Pennsylvania Central decided the merge both systems in an effort to eliminate overlapping rail facilities and develop a single powerful railway. Various legal issues held up the merger until 1968, but by then it was too late. The combined railroads, dubbed the New Penn Central, went bankrupt in 1970. What started in 1825 as the Mohawk & Hudson Railroad Company and thrived for years as the New York Central, became a portion of the government-operated Consolidated Rail Corporation (ConRail) in 1976.

See also: **John Jacob Astor, Baltimore and Ohio, Erie Canal, Railroad Industry**

FURTHER READING

Cavanaugh, H.F. *New York Central System, Gone But Not Forgotten*. New Jersey: International, 1983.

"Federal Railroad Administration: United States Department of Transportation," [cited March 22, 1998] available from the World Wide Web @ www.fra.dot.gov/site/index.htm.

Klein, Aaron E. *History of the New York Central System*. New York: Bonanza Books, 1985.

———. *Encyclopedia of North American Railroads*. Bookthrift, 1985.

"The New York Central Railroad Homepage," [cited March 22, 1998] available from the World Wide Web @ www.railroad.net/nyc/index.html.

"NJ, NY, & CT Railroad Page," [cited March 22, 1998] available from the World Wide Web @ haviland.org/rail/.

NEW YORK STOCK EXCHANGE

The New York Stock Exchange (NYSE), is the country's oldest and largest securities exchange. It dates from May 17, 1792 when local brokers agreed to formalize their business transactions. The brokers had, until then, been buying and selling securities under a designated tree.

In 1825 the NYSE opened for business at 11 Wall Street, New York City. At that time most shares traded were in canal, turnpike, mining, and gaslight companies. Though some industrial securities were traded on the NYSE as early as 1831, it would be 40 years before industries began to dominate the trading floor. As the nation became increasingly oriented toward manufacturing, the companies listed on the exchange reflected this economic shift.

Corporations applying to list their stock on the NYSE must have a minimum of two thousand shareholders. Each original shareholder must have one hundred or more shares, the corporation must be able to issue at least one million shares of stock, and it must also provide a record of earnings for the previous three-year period. The board of the stock exchange may make exceptions to these guidelines.

Corporations may be listed with other stock exchanges (such as the American Stock Exchange) or they may allow stock in their company to be traded as unlisted stocks, which are bought and sold in over-the-counter (OTC) trading. Companies that do not allow shares to be publicly traded are called private corporations.

See also: **Stock, Stock Market**

NEW YORK YANKEES

The Baltimore Orioles baseball franchise formed in 1901. In 1903 Bill Devery and Frank Farrell purchased it for $18,000, moving the team to New York. Originally called the Highlanders, the team changed its name in 1913 to the New York Yankees. In 1915 Colonel Jacob Ruppert and Tillinghast L'Hommedieu Huston purchased the Yankees from the original owners for $460,000. Ruppert bought out Huston in 1922.

The first years of this American League franchise team were mediocre and filled with frustration. But after the shift of ownership in 1915, the Yankees began to improve. Miller Huggins was hired to manage the baseball team, and he did an excellent job of assembling a line-up of good players. The team acquired its

A New Year's Eve party, December 31, 1997, held on the floor of the New York Stock Exchange. Traders gathered to celebrate the coming year together.

star from the Boston Red Sox after the 1919 season. His name was George Herman ''Babe'' Ruth, and his contract was obtained for $125,000, plus a loan of approximately $300,000. The year before this trade, Ruth hit 29 home runs and was considered the best and most exciting player in the game of baseball. His yearly salary was a then-unheard of $20,000 per year.

In 1921 the team played in its first World Series, losing to the New York Giants. But in 1923, after winning three American league pennants in a row, the Yankees finally won a World Series, beating the Giants 4 games to 2. Nineteen twenty-three was also the year the team moved into Yankee Stadium, the nation's first triple-deck stadium and acquired one of its greatest stars, Lou Gehrig. In the following years, the Yankees continued to build a dynasty, adding players like Joe DiMaggio (1936) and a host of others. The team won fourteen American League pennants and ten World Series titles by 1943.

In 1945 Larry MacPhail, Del Webb, and Dan Topping bought the team. The final purchase price was almost $3 million. The Yankees had a successful farm team program which continually supplied the major league team with new talent. Throughout the 1950s, 1960s, and 1970s the Yankees continued to win championship titles and increase their market value. By 1964 CBS owned 80 percent of the team, having purchased this share for approximately $11 million.

A colorful millionaire named George M. Steinbrenner III, who was a Cleveland shipbuilder by trade, headed a group of investors who purchased the Yankees from CBS in 1973 for $10 million. Steinbrenner had been an assistant college football coach at Purdue and Northwestern Universities and was part owner of the Chicago Bulls basketball team. He also owned the American Shipbuilding Company, located in Tampa, Florida. Steinbrenner's ownership marked the beginning of the most exciting and volatile era of Yankee baseball.

In the late 1970s, the Yankees won three consecutive pennants. During the 1980s Steinbrenner repeatedly hired and fired many managers. Billy Martin was the most famous of all these managers—Steinbrenner fired him and hired him on a total of five separate occasions until Martin's death in 1989.

In the late 1990s George Steinbrenner became the Yankee's Chief Executive Officer, and Joseph P. Torre acted as the team's manager. Main major league competitors included the Baltimore Orioles, Boston Red Sox, Tampa Bay Devil Rays, and the Toronto Blue Jays. The Yankees won the World Series in 1996 and 1998. They achieved an American League record in 1998 for most wins (114) in a regular season.

THE GAME ISN'T OVER TILL ITS OVER.

Lawrence (Yogi) Berra, Former Yankee catcher

Throughout its history, the Yankees retained its status of a private company. In 1997 the team achieved $144.7 million in sales. Player payroll exceeded $63 million per year. Because of the team's phenomenal success, the Yankees would have no trouble increasing the price of their tickets, concessions, media rights, and sponsorships. Such a sure turn of profits for the Yankees would give the team ample opportunity to attract and sign more star players in the future.

See also: **Baseball**

FURTHER READING

Blatt, Howard. *This Championship Season: The Incredible Story of the 1998 New York Yankees.* New York: Pocket Books, 1999.

Frommer, Harvey. *The New York Yankee Encyclopedia.* Indianapolis, IN: MacMillan General Reference, 1997.

Sullivan, George and John Powers, eds. *The Yankees: An Illustrated History (Baseball in America).* Philadelphia, PA: Temple University Press, 1997.

''Yankees.com,'' [cited April 22, 1999] available from the World Wide Web @ www.yankees.com/.

NIELSEN, ARTHUR CHARLES

Perhaps no other single man contributed as much to the development of professionalism in marketing as Arthur C. Nielsen (1897–1980). Nielsen accomplished far more than developing his famous market researching system, the Nielsen Ratings, for radio and television. He also created services that reduced the costs of product distribution—marketing, sales, and advertising—involved in moving goods from the factory to the consumer. His services made it possible to price essential goods at lower costs, resulting in a higher standard of living throughout the world.

Arthur Nielsen was born in Chicago, Illinois in 1897, the son of Danish immigrant Rasmus Nielsen, a

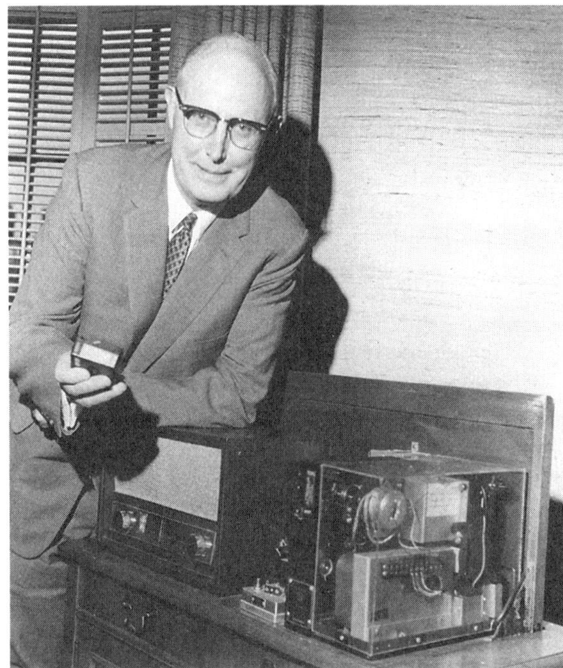

A. C. Nielsen Sr. stands next to his Audiometer.

business executive, and his wife, Harriet, a teacher. After graduating high school, Nielsen attended the University of Wisconsin where he obtained a Bachelor of Science in electrical engineering. Nielsen returned to Chicago in 1919 and worked in a number of companies as an electrical engineer.

For several years Nielsen had been anxious to open his own business, and in 1923 after borrowing $45,000 from his college fraternity brothers, he opened the A.C. Nielsen Company. The company conducted performance surveys of industrial equipment, and provided manufacturers with evaluation reports. By 1930 The company's sales increased to $200,000 annually, but the Great Depression (1929–1939) caused a massive industrial slump in the United States and nearly bankrupted Nielsen. He turned to other research services, creating the Nielsen Food and Drug Index, a research service that recorded the retail flow of grocery and drug brands by regular audits of carefully selected samples of stores. Using this information, food and drug manufacturers could measure the sales of their products against their competitors.

In 1936 Nielsen learned of the existence of the Audiometer, a mechanical device that made a minute-by-minute record of when a radio was on, and where its dial was set. Nielsen bought the invention from its creators, two professors on the faculty of the Massachusetts Institute of Technology. He made some changes to the device, and in 1938 patented the Audiometer under his own company name. Slowly Nielsen began installing Audiometers in a number of U.S. homes in the early 1940s and began to offer to radio stations and advertisers what he called a "Nielsen Radio Index" (NRI). The NRI provided for advertisers a specific reading of their "share" of the market in percentages. The broadcaster and advertiser could be told accurately how many people (by percentile) were listening to their advertisements and programming every 15 minutes throughout the day.

Though Nielsen's rating system was slow to start and his competition, who used phone calls and door-to-door interviews, were often more successful in selling their data to advertisers, Nielsen's system gradually caught on. By 1950 Nielsen had installed 1500 Audiometers across the country, representing 97 percent of the United States, and in ratings surveys the Nielsen Co. had emerged on top. In order to produce his reports faster, more cheaply, and more comprehensively to his clients, Nielsen was one of the first to purchase a business computer. In 1955 the world's first electronic computer, the Univac I, was delivered to the Nielsen Co.

During the 1950s Nielsen adapted his Audiometer methodology to television and abandoned radio ratings in 1964. Nielsen and his son, Arthur, Jr., continued to refine their consumer analysis system before Arthur Nielsen, Sr. retired in 1957. His son succeeded him as CEO of the company. In his free time Nielsen turned to philanthropic activities, which included support for hospitals, medical research, and organizations devoted to conservative economics and political economy.

Arthur C. Nielsen died in 1980. The Nielsen family sold the company for $1.3 billion in 1984 to Dun and Bradstreet. The ratings service Arthur Nielsen pioneered had earned a position as the premier TV ratings service.

FURTHER READING

Honomichl, Jack J. *Marketing Research People*. Chicago: Crain Books, 1984.

Nielsen, Arthur C. *Marketing Research—Past Present Future*. Philadelphia, PA: Philadelphia Chapter, American Marketing Association, 1963.

Nielsen Marketing Research. *Nielsen Review of Retail Grocery Store Trends*. Northbrook, IL: A.C. Nielsen Co., 1980.

———. *Testing Techniques: A Nielsen Marketing Research Newsletter on Test Marketing*. Northbrook, IL: Nielsen Marketing Research, 1986.

Nielsen Media Research. *Nielsen Report on Television*. Northbrook, IL: A.C. Nielsen Co., 1979.

NINETEENTH AMENDMENT

Proposed in Congress on June 4, 1919, and ratified by the states August 18, 1920, the Nineteenth Amendment to the U.S. Constitution gives women the right to vote. After four decades of struggle, the women's movement in the United States had finally secured the vote.

The woman's suffrage movement had its roots in the 1840s, when women who sought social reforms, including abolition of slavery, instituting a national policy of temperance (abstinence from alcoholic beverages), and securing better work opportunities and better pay, organized. These reformers soon realized that in order to effect change, they needed the power of the vote. An early leader of the suffragist movement was feminist and reformer Elizabeth Cady Stanton (1815–1902). She joined anti-slavery activist Lucretia Mott (1793–1880) to establish the first women's-rights convention in 1848 in Seneca Falls, New York. In 1869 Stanton teamed with Susan B. Anthony (1820–1906) to organize the National Woman Suffrage Association. That same year, another group was formed—the American Woman Suffrage Association, led by women's rights and anti-slavery activist Lucy Stone (1818–1893) and her husband Henry Brown Blackwell (1825–1909). In 1870 the common cause of the two groups was strengthened by the passage of the Fifteenth Amendment, which gave all men—regardless of race—the right to vote. When the two organizations joined forces in 1890, they formed the National American Woman Suffrage Association (NAWSA). The suffragists appealed to middle class and working class women alike, as well as to students and radicals. They waged campaigns at the state level, distributed literature, organized meetings, made speeches, marched in parades, picketed, lobbied in Washington, DC, and even chained themselves to the White House fence. If jailed, many resorted to hunger strikes.

From 1878 to 1917, woman suffrage amendments were introduced during every session of Congress; all failed. In 1918, the required support for the amendment was finally mustered in the House of Representatives—the result of years of activism and of the role women played during World War I (1914–1918). Having demonstrated their position as involved and intelligent citizens, members of the House passed the proposal in 1918. It then went to the Senate where it was defeated. Voting again the next year, the amendment passed in the Senate and was duly sent to the states, which ratified it in 1920. The amendment states that the "right of citizens of the United States to vote shall not be denied or abridged by the United States or by any state on account of sex."

See also: **Henry Brown Blackwell, Women's Movement**

NIXON, RICHARD MILHOUS

Richard M. Nixon (1913–1994) took office as the thirty-seventh President of the United States on January 20, 1969. He campaigned on promises to end the Vietnam War (1959–1975), reduce racial divisions in the United States, and decrease the nation's high inflation rate. Despite his ambitious plans, Nixon's accomplishments are often overshadowed by the scandal for which his presidency is best known. Nixon's personal anger and suspicions manifested themselves in the Watergate criminal and political scandal, first revealed to the public through the news of an interrupted burglary at the offices of the Democratic National Committee in Washington, D.C. As evidence of his wrongdoings mounted, Nixon resigned rather than face impeachment by Congress.

Nixon was born in 1913 on a modest farm in California and was raised in the Quaker faith. He was an aggressive and successful student from an early age, graduating in 1934 from Duke University Law School on a full scholarship. After graduation he worked for the federal government and later as a military attorney during World War II (1939–1945). Nixon's humble but aggressive style caught the attention of others, who encouraged him to enter political life.

His active political career resembled a roller coaster ride. He served as President Dwight Eisenhower's (1953–1961) vice president, and was unusually active in the role. But Nixon lost his campaign to succeed Eisenhower in 1961 when he was defeated by John F. Kennedy (1961–1963). In 1962, Nixon again lost a bid for public office, failing to gain the governor's seat of his native state, California. This series of defeats ended his political career for a time and Nixon returned to practicing law. But when the political climate in the United States shifted in the late 1960s, Nixon saw new opportunities and prepared a presidential campaign.

During his campaign, Nixon promised a quick end to the Vietnam War, which was the source of much

Richard Nixon leaving office.

social unrest at home, but once in office he actually expanded the war before decreasing American involvement in the region. Though Nixon did not follow through on his Vietnam promises, he did achieve an arms treaty with the Soviet Union in 1972. Relations with that country were quite strained at the time, and the arms treaty, limiting strategic nuclear weapons, was a timely foreign policy success.

War was not the only item on Nixon's foreign policy agenda. It also included economics. Nixon reopened trade and economic relations with China, which were severed in the early 1950s due to China's involvement with North Korea during the Korean War (1950–1953). Renewed relations between the two countries opened up a wealth of new business opportunities. The vast Chinese market appealed to many U.S. businesses and trade was quickly established. He also proposed a steep tax on imported goods and a freeze on all wage and price increases for ninety days. Nixon's efforts to stabilize the inflation-ridden U.S. economy helped reduce the national debt and the rate of inflation. It also asserted the primacy of business vitality over the artificial economic ties to the value of gold.

Tying the U.S. dollar to the value of gold was seen by Nixon as an economic restriction. By ending the U.S. dollar's attachment to the gold standard, Nixon asserted he had done something long overdue, claiming, "The strength of a nation's currency is based on the strength of that nation's economy.'' With his action the Gold Standard Act of 1900 ended. The nation's currency became subject to the floating exchange rates of the marketplace and endured well.

Nixon's accomplishments as president are often overshadowed by the events that consumed his second term in office, beginning in 1972. Known collectively as the Watergate scandal, these events include criminal acts against Nixon's perceived enemies. Watergate first came to national attention when a break-in of the Democratic National Committee offices in the Watergate building was interrupted. The culprits eventually revealed ties to the White House and Congress ordered an investigation. Nixon was very uncooperative and denied personal involvement in the affair. However, Congress' determination to get to the bottom of the scandal revealed that Nixon was indeed involved. Rather than face almost certain impeachment and removal from office, Nixon resigned on August 4, 1974, leaving the presidency in disgrace.

Nixon went into seclusion for a time and later regained a kind of elder statesman status. He wrote several books on foreign policy and politics, including a personal memoir of his life. Nixon died of a stroke in 1994, at the age of eighty-one.

See also: **Gold Standard, Gold Standard Act, Vietnam War**

FURTHER READING

Commire, Anne, ed. *North and South America M-Z,* vol. 5 of *Historic World Leaders.* Detroit: Gale Research, 1994, s.v. ''Nixon, Richard.''

Mazo, Earl, and Stephen Hess. *Nixon: A Political Portrait.* New York: Harper & Row, 1968.

Miller, Roger LeRoy, and Raburn M. Williams. *The New Economics of Richard Nixon: Freezes, Floats, and Fiscal Policy.* New York: Harper's Magazine Press, 1972.

Nixon, Richard. *The Memoirs of Richard Nixon.* New York: Grosset & Dunlap, 1978.

Nixon, Richard M. *A New Road For America: Major Policy Statements March 1970 to October 1971.* Garden City, NY: Doubleday, 1972.

NORMALCY

Normalcy was the term used by Republican candidate Warren G. Harding (1865–1923) during the 1920 presidential campaign to describe the condition of the United States prior to its entry into World War I (1914–1918). It was also the condition to which the nation would return, Harding promised, if he were sent to the White House. Voters liked the idea of returning to normalcy too, giving Harding the biggest plurality victory ever, 16,152,200 votes for Harding to 9,147,353 votes for Democratic nominee James Cox (1870–1957).

Once in office (1921–1923) Harding's efforts to normalize American political, social, and economic conditions met with mixed results. Part of the president's problem was defining the term ''normalcy.'' Harding's call for ''normalcy'' meant a foreign policy of isolationism and a domestic policy of increased economic freedom. To meet these ends, Harding supported a repeal of the wartime tax on excess profits, a reduction of income taxes on the wealthy, a high tariff on imports, and anti-immigration laws limiting the annual number of aliens who could come to the United States. Harding also opposed U.S. membership in the League of Nations. In contrast, his Democratic predecessor, President Woodrow Wilson (1913–1921) helped establish that international body and urged the country to join it. Although America was prosperous during his years in office, Harding's administration is primarily remembered for its corrupt practices, which represented politics as usual to his opponents and a return to ''normalcy'' of a different kind. Harding has been credited by some with inventing the term ''normalcy.'' The word, however, first appeared in American lexicon during 1857 as slang for the word ''normality.'' In any event, Harding did help popularize the use of ''normalcy'' in everyday speech.

See also: **Anti-Immigration Laws, Isolationism, Andrew Mellon**

NORRIS-LAGUARDIA ACT OF 1932

The Norris-LaGuardia Act outlawed yellow-dog contracts (pledges by workers not to join a labor union) and further restricted the use of court injunctions in labor disputes against strikes, picketing, and boycotts. Imposing strict procedural limitations on issuing injunctions against strike activity, the act pointed the direction towards a more even-handed relationship between the judiciary and the nation's labor relations systems. Although it had few enforcement powers, the act was one of the first federal labor laws supporting organized labor and it marked a significant victory in labor reform. Its passage fostered a trend toward more favorable government labor policies.

Industrialization of the late nineteenth century brought unsafe factory conditions, low wages, repetitious work over long hours, little job security, no benefits: these conditions led workers to favor unions. But the very legality of labor unions was in dispute for much of the nineteenth century. At the anti-union end of the spectrum, many nineteenth century judges considered unions to be in restraint of trade, because they called strikes. Later the courts began to recognize the validity of workers seeking shorter workdays and higher wages. But, injunctions requiring unions to refrain from certain activities (like picketing on company property or otherwise trying to persuade workers from entering company property during a strike) became a major weapon of employers beginning in the 1840s. Later antitrust laws added further legal authority to such orders by prohibiting organizations from restraining free market competition through cooperative relationships. During this period, the Sherman Anti-Trust Act was more often used against unions than against the companies.

PASSED IN 1932, THE NORRIS-LAGUARDIA ACT MARKED A PROFOUND CHANGE IN U.S. GOVERNMENT OVERSIGHT OVER LABOR RELATIONS. IT WAS THE MOST FAVORABLE LEGISLATION TO DATE FOR A U.S. LABOR MOVEMENT THAT HAD ALWAYS HAD TO FIGHT FOR ITS VERY EXISTENCE.

In 1877 and again in 1894 the federal government used troops to end major strikes, actions that radicalized some in the labor movement. In 1905 the Industrial Workers of the World (IWW) was formed, espousing the goal of replacing the capitalist system with socialism. After some successful early strikes, however, it was smothered by government repression.

During the labor shortage of World War I, the Clayton Anti-Trust Act of 1914 Congress finally acted to exempt unions from antitrust laws. Employers turned to other means. Forcing employees to sign "yellow-dog contracts" became a condition of employment. The contracts pledged employees to refrain from joining a union, or to renounce membership if they already belonged to one. Some state legislatures moved to prohibit these agreements but the Supreme Court ruled in 1915 that such state prohibitions unconstitutionally violated freedom to contract.

But, after the crash of the stock market in 1929 and the long stagnation in investment that characterized the 1930s, the high unemployment of the Great Depression made it difficult for workers to express their unified preference for union representation. By the third year of the Depression, however, workers with jobs began to push for unionization anyway. Labor solidarity was borne of desperation. The formation of the Congress of Industrial Organizations (CIO) with the specific purpose of "organizing the unorganized" unskilled and semi-skilled workers in basic industry, sparked an explosion in the size of the union movement. In spite of the high unemployment during the Great Depression, the union movement grew by more than 300 percent. In 1933 national union membership had fallen to less than three million. By 1941 it stood at over ten million.

The Norris-LaGuardia Act was part of this change in labor relations. Even before the New Deal began, Senator George William Norris from Nebraska and Congressman Fiorello H. LaGuardia from New York City, both progressive Republicans, introduced new labor reform legislation, the Norris-LaGuardia Act. With passage of the act, the groundwork was laid for an even more important labor bill, the National Labor Relations Act of 1935, called the Wagner Act. The Wagner Act continued the mission of reforming labor relations. It set out to regulate the nation's labor relations. It granted unions fundamental rights and powers, including the right of collective bargaining, defined unfair labor practices, and established penalties for violating them. Passed in 1932, the Norris-LaGuardia Act marked a profound change in U.S. government oversight over labor relations. It was the most favorable legislation to date for a U.S. labor movement that had always had to fight for its very existence.

See also: **Clayton Anti-Trust Act, Labor Unionism, Sherman Anti-Trust Act, Yellow Dog Contracts**

FURTHER READING

Barkin, Solomon. *Worker Militancy and Its Consequences: The Changing Climate of Western Industrial Relations*. New York: Praeger, 1983.

Cox, Robert W. *Production, Power, and World Order: Social Forces and the Making of History*. New York: Columbia University Press, 1987.

Dubofsky, Melvyn, ed. *Technological Change and Workers' Movements*. Beverly Hills, CA: Sage Publications, 1985.

Dunlop, John, and Walter Galenson, ed. *Labor in the Twentieth Century*. New York: Academic Press, 1978.

Goldfield, Michael. *The Decline of Organized Labor in the United States.* Chicago: The University of Chicago Press, 1987.

Lorwin, Lewis L. *The American Federation of Labor: History, Policies, and Prospects.* Washington, DC: The Brookings Institution, 1933.

NORTH AMERICAN FREE TRADE AGREEMENT *(ISSUE)*

Formal negotiations for the North American Free Trade Agreement (NAFTA) began in 1991. Within three years the United States, Canada, and Mexico signed the trilateral free trade agreement and it went into effect in 1994. Pushed through by both the administrations of Presidents George Bush (1989–1993) and Bill Clinton (1993–) amidst much domestic controversy, this historic agreement established a formal trading bloc with 364 million consumers and a combined economic output of six trillion dollars in North America.

The agreement established what was called the world's largest free trade zone, and included a 15-year gradual phase-in of the elimination of tariffs and traditional non-tariff barriers on trade for all goods and services among the three countries. The accord is a 2,000-page text that contains detailed rules for hemispheric trade liberalization and two side agreements. The rules cover such areas as rules of origin (the country where the product was produced) to qualify for free trade, protection of intellectual property rights, and dispute settlement procedures.

NAFTA originated in negotiations begun in the mid-1980s between Canada and the United States to establish a bilateral agreement to guarantee market access between the two countries. The subsequent U.S.-Canada Free Trade Agreement was implemented in 1989. Canada then wanted to expand the agreement into a trilateral arrangement when the United States and Mexico initiated negotiations on a bilateral agreement of their own in 1990.

In the 1980s Mexican President Carlos Salinas de Gortari (1988–1994) decided to expand economic reforms through international agreements when the protectionist, state-dominated economy was in crisis and unable to pay off its debts to commercial banks. Moving to a market-based economy, the Salinas administration implemented accelerated trade-barrier reductions to encourage foreign investment. Having removed or reduced most of the tariffs between the United States and Mexico since Mexico joined the General Agreement on Tariffs and Trade (GATT) in 1986, the hope for Mexico was that a free trade agreement between the two countries would continue to stimulate foreign investment and economic growth.

The Bush administration had support from most large U.S. industrial corporations that would be able to take advantage of lower Mexican wages. Thus the administration requested "fast-track" negotiating status for NAFTA, which permits a president to negotiate international trade treaties and submit them to Congress for approval without amendments. In 1991 Congress gave NAFTA fast-track status.

NAFTA became a hotly debated issue in the 1992 U.S. presidential elections. Differentiating himself from the incumbent, presidential candidate Ross Perot opposed NAFTA, calling for the public to hear the "giant sucking sound" of jobs being pulled from this country and going South to Mexico. Meanwhile as a compromise in support of NAFTA, candidate Bill Clinton promised that NAFTA would include guarantees for the trading countries to abide by environmental and labor standards. Clinton was the target of mounting pressure from environmental groups and organized labor that NAFTA would amount to a "green light" for environmental "dumping" and human rights abuses in Mexico. After Clinton was elected as president and NAFTA was ratified in 1993 along with the two labor and environmental side agreements, the same groups criticized NAFTA for not having any effective enforcement mechanisms.

Opponents of NAFTA, such as labor leaders, were especially concerned that the agreement would result in massive losses in U.S. manufacturing jobs after Mexico began to attract foreign investment. Critics and supporters drew contradictory conclusions about the long-term consequences of NAFTA after the agreement was implemented in 1994. On one hand, opponents conducted studies such as the one by the Economic Policy Institute (EPI). The EPI authors, Jesse Rothstein and Robert E. Scott, concluded in their report, *NAFTA and the States,* that "an exploding deficit in net exports with Mexico and Canada has eliminated 394,835 U.S. jobs since NAFTA took effect in 1994." On the other hand, supporters such as Nora Claudia Lustig, a senior fellow at the Brookings Institute, claimed that "there is evidence that NAFTA has created more jobs than it destroyed."

Critical studies such as the EPI report contended that NAFTA resulted in the net export deficit growing from $16.1 billion in 1993 to $48.3 billion in 1996. Consequently jobs created with increased exports were offset by jobs lost with increased imports. The EPI argued that the implementation of NAFTA had affected all 50 states, with job losses ranging from 621 in Vermont to 38,406 in California. The states hardest hit were those with the greatest production facility relocation, industries such as automotive manufacturing, textiles, apparel, computers, and electrical appliances. In addition, wages fell four percent between 1993 and 1996 and real median wages fell in at least 25 states.

Meanwhile NAFTA proponents at the Brookings Institute, such as Lustig, claimed that the agreement "has resulted in an increase in U.S.-Mexican trade, business partnerships, specialization in production processes and direct investment flows into Mexico. At the same time, the agreement has protected U.S. exporters from the brunt of the Mexican crisis [peso crisis of 1994], especially in comparison to exporters from Japan and the European Union." The report's author claimed that "there is even some evidence that NAFTA has created more jobs than it destroyed." Lustig contended that a net job gain may be the end result because a strong Mexican economy makes a strong market for U.S. exports.

Despite the absence of follow-up initiative on Capitol Hill to push for fast-track negotiations that would include other countries such as Chile and Brazil in the free trade bloc, President Clinton remained sanguine concerning the outcome of NAFTA in its early years. In a letter to Congress, Clinton noted that "NAFTA is an integral part of a broader growth strategy that has produced the strongest U.S. economy in a generation."

Thus the history of the negotiations over and implementation of the landmark agreement further complicated a centuries-old debate over the economic impact of free trade policies. Departing from traditional trade liberalization agreements, NAFTA became part of a public controversy that resulted in the unique inclusion of labor and environmental standards as an element in a trilateral free-trade bloc in North America.

***See also:* Free Trade**

FURTHER READING

Baer, M. Delal, and Sidney Weintraub, eds. *The NAFTA Debate: Grappling with Unconventional Trade Issues*. Boulder, CO: Lynne Rienner Publishers, 1994.

Bognanno, Mario F., and Kathryn J. Ready, eds. *The North American Free Trade Agreement: Labor, Industry, and Government Perspectives*. Westport, CT: Quorum Books, 1993.

Cohen, Stephen D., Joel R. Paul, and Robert A. Blecker. *Fundamentals of U.S. Foreign Trade Policy: Economics, Politics, Laws, and Issues*. Boulder, CO: Westview Press, 1996.

Ensign, David. "NAFTA: Two Sides of the Coin." *Spectrum*, Fall 1997.

Lustig, Nora C. "NAFTA: Setting the Record Straight." *The World Economy*, August 1997.

Mayer, Frederick W. *Interpreting NAFTA: The Science and Art of Political Analysis*. New York: Columbia University Press, 1998.

NORTH ATLANTIC TREATY ORGANIZATION (NATO)

In 1949, in the aftermath of World War II (1939–1945), sixteen nations in Europe and North America developed the North Atlantic Treaty. It was a measure designed to block the threat of military aggression in Europe by the Soviet Union. The North Atlantic Treaty Organization (NATO) united Western Europe and North America in a mutual security and self-defense agreement. If one of the sixteen members was attacked, they would all fight in defense.

The agreement, at first intended solely to discourage the Soviet Union, created a framework for further cooperation between the members on military, political, economic, and social matters. The members of NATO at the time of its inception were Belgium, Canada, Denmark, France, Germany, Greece, Iceland, Italy, Luxembourg, the Netherlands, Norway, Portu gal, Spain, Turkey, the United Kingdom, and the United States.

While the North Atlantic treaty calls for the peaceful resolution of disputes, the organization is prepared for self-defense. NATO's military forces are comprised of units volunteered from each of its members. The forces are based under three main commands: the Atlantic Command, the Channel Command, and the Allied Command Europe. The supreme Allied commander heads the three commands and directs units in exercising NATO military forces. In times of peace, the three commands plan the defense of their regions.

NATO also has a policy wing, called the North Atlantic Council, a nonmilitary policy group comprised of permanent delegates from all NATO members. The North Atlantic Council is led by a secretary-general and is responsible for general policy, budget issues, and administrative actions. A Military Committee, comprised of the chiefs of staff of member nations' armed forces, meets twice a year to advise the Council.

NATO headquarters was initially established in Paris, France, but in the 1960s French President Charles DeGaulle (1890–1970) complained the United States had too much control over NATO and, in fact, dominated the organization. In 1966, France expelled NATO troops from the country. As a result NATO headquarters moved from Paris to Brussels, Belgium, where it remains today.

With the collapse of the Soviet Union in 1991, NATO expanded its membership to include Poland, Hungary, and the Czech Republic. This raised concerns from Russia about NATO intentions. Russia sees NATO expansion as a threat to its sphere of influence in eastern Europe. Since the 1991 collapse of NATO's main foe, questions have also been raised regarding the continued need for the organization.

In the late 1990s, those questions were quieted by NATO involvement in Yugoslavia. In 1999, NATO launched a military campaign against Serbian leader Slobodan Milosevic in response to his brutal repression of ethnic Albanians in the region of Kosovo. This marked the first time in NATO's history that it became the aggressor in a regional matter outside the boundaries of its member states.

See also: **World War II**

NORTH CAROLINA

North Carolina was slow to develop, abundant in resources and natural beauty, and traditionally tied to the tobacco empire. It is a study in contrasts. Once thought by Virginia settlers to be backward and wild, North Carolina has become an important player in the nation's industrial development and a major producer of agricultural products. It is also an attractive destination for tourists. Though thought to be unfriendly to labor, the state continued to employ hundreds of thousands of workers in its manufacturing and services industries as the twentieth century closed.

Italian explorer Giovanni di Verrazano discovered the North Carolina coast in 1524. Other explorers from Spain later attempted unsuccessfully to settle in the North Carolina wilderness. English courtier Sir Walter Raleigh sponsored the famous ''lost colony'' at Roanoke, and in 1629 Charles I began settlement in earnest of the colony he called, after himself, ''Carolana''. It was set up as a proprietorship and it extended its boundaries from the Atlantic to the Pacific Oceans and from northern Florida to the present boundary between North Carolina and Virginia. The colony of South Carolina split off from North Carolina in 1719.

Less accessible and wilder in geography than neighboring Virginia, the North Carolina country grew slowly. Wealthy landowner William Byrd of Virginia undertook a surveying expedition to settle a boundary dispute between Virginia and North Carolina in 1728. In his *History of the Dividing Line*, he expressed his low opinion of the North Carolina ''backwoodsmen'' he found there (an opinion which was shared by many of his contemporaries). ''Both cattle and hogs ramble into the neighboring marshes and swamps . . . and are not fetched home till the spring. Thus these indolent wretches, during one half of the year, lose advantage of the milk of their cattle . . . and many of the poor creatures perish in the mire . . . by this bad management.''

After North Carolina became a royal colony in 1731, thousands of new settlers came to the colony; the population reached 345,000 by 1775. From the beginning the colony was beset by geographical divisions. While western backcountry farmers were self-sufficient but poor, the wealthy eastern plantation owners used slave labor to cultivate their tobacco and rice fields. Although the colony harbored a number of Loyalists, most North Carolinians were united in opposition to colonial controls from Great Britain—they supported independence in 1776.

After the American Revolution (1775–1783) North Carolina was sometimes known as the ''Rip Van Winkle'' state because of its slowness to develop. It was among the last states to ratify the new U.S. Constitution, in 1789. In addition to widespread illiteracy, the state's transportation routes were substandard, making it difficult to expand commercial agriculture. The western part of the state was the least developed, and eastern interests refused to be taxed to support the westerners. In 1835, however, reforms in the state constitution brought state aid to railroads and other badly needed public works, as well as the first common schools.

North Carolina fought for the Confederacy during the American Civil War (1861–1865). Politics in that war's aftermath was very divisive. Republicans—the party of Lincoln—wrangled with states' rights Democrats, who finally took over state government in 1876. Democrats then slashed public services and solidified the power of landlords over tenants and sharecroppers. They also saw to it that cotton mills were built in the piedmont area and that railroads were consolidated. By

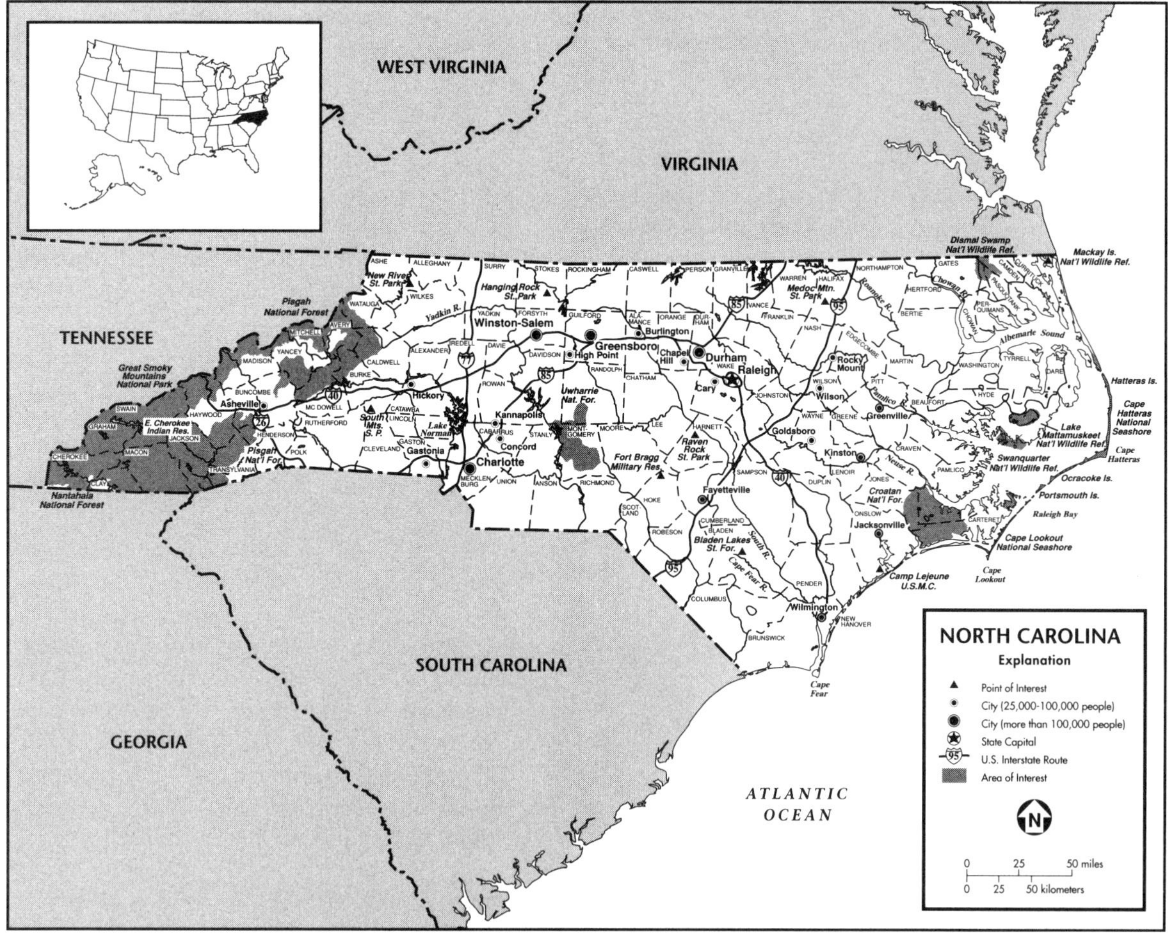

State of North Carolina.

1880 industry in North Carolina had made a big recovery. The plight of African Americans in the state did not improve, however, leaving a legacy of poverty and inequality which persisted into the civil rights struggles of the 1960s and beyond.

The development of the railroads was very important to the rise of big tobacco in the state. In 1875 young R. J. Reynolds saw that railroad access to the city of Winston (now Winston-Salem) would be an important asset to tobacco manufacture and distribution. He established his own plant and by 1920 he had absorbed most of the other small tobacco companies in Winston. Around the turn of the century Reynolds Tobacco (which then manufactured only chewing tobacco) was part of James B. Duke's tobacco trust but it became independent again in 1911. By 1913 Reynolds had expanded into the cigarette market and he was producing the nation's best-selling cigarettes.

Small farmers in the state continued to protest against their depressed economic condition. They were overshadowed by the textile, furniture, and tobacco producers, who, along with banks and insurance companies, dominated the state by 1900. Both World War I (1914–1918) and World War II (1939–1945) deeply affected the state. For one thing, many industrial plants were built in North Carolina to produce war materials, many of them expanding and continuing to provide employment after the war. In addition, returning veterans came home with new ideas. According to historian William S. Powell, after World War II, "Veterans who were no longer content to farm or to work in cotton mills set about to improve themselves by taking advantage of the G.I. Bill of Rights. . . . Military service gave many of these people new skills and broadened their perspectives. . . . "

A good example of postwar economic development in North Carolina was the Research Triangle Park, which began in 1957 in an area equidistant from Raleigh, Durham, and Chapel Hill. The park was constructed to provide research facilities and high-technology industrial sites; it soon became home to many government offices, private research concerns, and cultural agencies. The Research Triangle Park was also ideally situated, close to the University of Carolina, Duke University, and other colleges.

North Carolina has advanced in many areas, but not in its relationship to organized labor. The many "company towns" which grew up around the textile mills left their legacy of fear and dependence. The American Federation of Labor attempted to organize workers in the textile industry at the turn of the century but it failed to produce lasting unions. A number of failed strikes in the first four decades of the twentieth century left a generally anti-union sentiment among North Carolina workers. Repeated charges of unfair labor practices against textile giant J. P. Stevens and Company during the 1970s and 1980s reinforced the anti-labor reputation of the state. By 1970 the percentage of workers belonging to unions in the state was only 7.8, compared to 27.9 percent nationwide. By 1995 the percentage of union members had decreased to 4.2 percent, the second-lowest in the nation. In the late 1990s North Carolina held the dubious distinction of having the largest percentage of manufacturing jobs in the nation but the lowest manufacturing wages. In 1990 30 percent of jobs in the state paid wages below the poverty line.

THE ONLY BUSINESS [IN NORTH CAROLINA] IS RAISING OF HOGS, WHICH IS MANAGED WITH THE LEAST TROUBLE, AND AFFORDS THE DIET THEY ARE MOST FOND OF.

William Byrd, Virginian landowner, 1728

The continuing story of tobacco in North Carolina has also had its vicissitudes. For the last three decades tobacco manufacturers have been under fire from the federal government for causing health problems for large numbers of Americans. Cigarette advertising was banned from radio and television after 1971, and the federal cigarette tax was doubled in 1983. As the public perception of smoking steadily declined, an heir to the Reynolds Tobacco fortune, Patrick Reynolds, shocked his state and the nation in 1986 when he appeared before a congressional committee to call attention to the detrimental effects of tobacco. However, Reynolds Tobacco (now owned by RJR Nabisco), along with other tobacco firms, has survived by diversifying its interests and increasing overseas sales. In the late 1990s North Carolina was still the producer of 38 percent of the U.S. supply of tobacco and shipments of tobacco were second only to those of textile manufacturers in the state.

In the late 1980s and early 1990s North Carolina experienced a shift in job patterns. Traditional industries like furniture, textiles, and tobacco lost ground to high-tech industries and financial concerns. In 1997 the state was home to seven Fortune 500 companies, none of which was connected to the kinds of industries which historically developed the state.

In modern North Carolina agriculture and industry coexist and they are mutually dependent. Although the actual number of tobacco farms has decreased significantly, perhaps one-third of the jobs in the state are directly related to agriculture. North Carolina remains the largest manufacturer of textiles, cigarettes, and furniture in the United States. In addition to J. P. Stevens, some of the important textile manufacturers are Blue Bell Inc., Cannon Mills, and Burlington Industries. The furniture industry is centered in the High Point-Thomasville and Hickory-Statesville areas. Although per capita income has increased faster than the national average since 1986, it still ranks only 32nd among all states. Alternate sources of income in the service industry are increasingly important to the state. Tourism and retirement living were major sectors of North Carolina's economy in the 1990s, with many people flocking to the state's historic sites, recreation areas, and scenic mountains.

See also: **Furniture Industry, Tobacco, Tobacco Industry**

FURTHER READING

Clay, James W., et al., eds. *North Carolina Atlas: Portrait of a Changing Southern State*. Chapel Hill: University of North Carolina Press, 1975.

Jones, H.G. *North Carolina History: An Annotated Bibliography*. Westport, CN: Greenwood Press, 1995.

Kruman, Marc W. *Parties and Politics in North Carolina: 1836–1865*. Baton Rouge: Louisiana State University Press, 1983.

Lefler, Hugh T. and Albert Ray Newsome. *North Carolina: The History of a Southern State*, 3rd ed. Chapel Hill, NC: North Carolina University Press, 1973.

Powell, William S. *North Carolina: A Bicentennial History*. New York: Norton, 1977.

Reynolds, Patrick, and Tom Schactman. *The Gilded Leaf: Triumph, Tragedy, and Tobacco: Three Generations of the R. J. Reynolds Family and Fortune*. Boston: Little, Brown, 1989.

NORTH DAKOTA

As a surveyor for the North West Company (Canada) in 1797, David Thompson was the first to describe part of what is presently North Dakota. Thompson completed the task of mapping the main travel routes through Canadian and United States territory. He also recorded details of the land and described Indians he encountered along the way.

In 1801 the first long-term trading post was set up at Pembina, and it became the center for the first white settlers in the state. Locally, trading furs provided the economic base for early settlers. It also became big business abroad as American trading companies competed with British-Canadian companies for control of the fur trade business. After the Lewis and Clark Expedition was completed, the fur business soared in North Dakota. Because trading furs became more lucrative as more companies were established, John Jacob Astor (1763–1848), founder of one of the biggest fur trading companies in the United States, convinced the American government to pass a law prohibiting other countries from trading with the Indians.

In the 1800s demand for furs was great and traders in the west could answer the call. Fur trading flourished into the 1850s as Astor built the first steamboat to run on the upper Missouri River. (It could carry 144 tons of goods.) Soon after, more trade routes were established including a major trade route that was opened for cart caravans between St. Paul, Minnesota, and what is now Walhalla, North Dakota. St. Paul merchants offered $1,000 to the man who would open more trade markets by putting a steamboat on the Red River. In 1859 Anson Northrup received $2,000 for dismantling a small boat he had launched on the Crow River; using 32 teams of oxen, he hauled it to the Red River and successfully launched it there.

Dakota became a territory in 1861. Some settlers traveled west to Dakota to take advantage of the Homestead Act, which was passed by Congress in 1862. This bill gave free land to those who would work on the land for five years and plant crops. In 1864 Congress gave Northern Pacific Railroad 50 million acres in Dakota to lay tracks from Minnesota to the West Coast. Unfortunately, funds ran out after a few years and the project was not completed until 1881. In the 1870s and 1880s the development of other modes of transportation made it easier for settlers to move west. Steamboats, stagecoaches, and ox-drawn wagons brought hundreds of thousands of people to Dakota in the ten-year period between 1880 and 1890. European immigrants also began to settle in Dakota. However, life on the plains was not easy. The dry summers, forest fires, spring floods, and winter blizzards made every day life extremely difficult.

In 1870 wheat became a major source of revenue in the state. A new milling process was developed for spring wheat, a northern crop that was planted in the spring and harvested in the fall. When the wheat was ground the bran was separated from the flour. Also the railroad companies started up "bonanza farms" that covered thousands of acres of land and produced tons of wheat. A land agent for the Northern Pacific persuaded railroad president George W. Cass and a director, Benjamin Cheney, to purchase more than 13,000 acres for a bonanza farm. This enterprise, and more than 90 others like it, became very successful. The farms were owned by businessmen and were managed by foremen or superintendents. New settlers took advantage of the opportunity to work the farms or to start their own, smaller farms.

Though bonanza farming was successful, it also caused land prices to increase. To turn a substantial profit, many owners sold the farms when they knew they could get the highest price. However, in 1890 a depression caused wheat prices to fall drastically; most of the larger farms had to be broken up and sold in smaller parcels.

While farmers were tending wheat, cattle ranching started to take hold in the 1880s. Among the first was a business built by the Marquis de Mores, a Frenchman trying to make his fortune in Dakota. Instead of shipping live herds to markets in the East, the marquis devised a plan to slaughter his cattle on the range and send the beef to market. In the first year, the marquis was very successful, but he overextended himself and had to go back to France, leaving a $1 million debt behind. Other ranchers in the area had difficulties as well—grasshoppers and fire destroyed the grass in 1886. As a result many ranchers pulled out of the area.

During the late 1880s, Dakota's territorial governor, Nehemiah Ordway, and his friend, Alexander McKenzie, were major political bosses who protected the financial interests of the railroad, banks, lumber and insurance companies ahead of the interests of the people. Along with special interest groups, they were opposed to Dakota's bid for statehood. However, after a new (state) constitution was approved, North Dakota and South Dakota became states on November 2, 1889.

The first action taken by the state's new government was to pass laws regulating railroads and grain businesses. For the next two decades Dakota worked hard to establish a stable economy. More railroad lines were built to serve more towns because the price paid

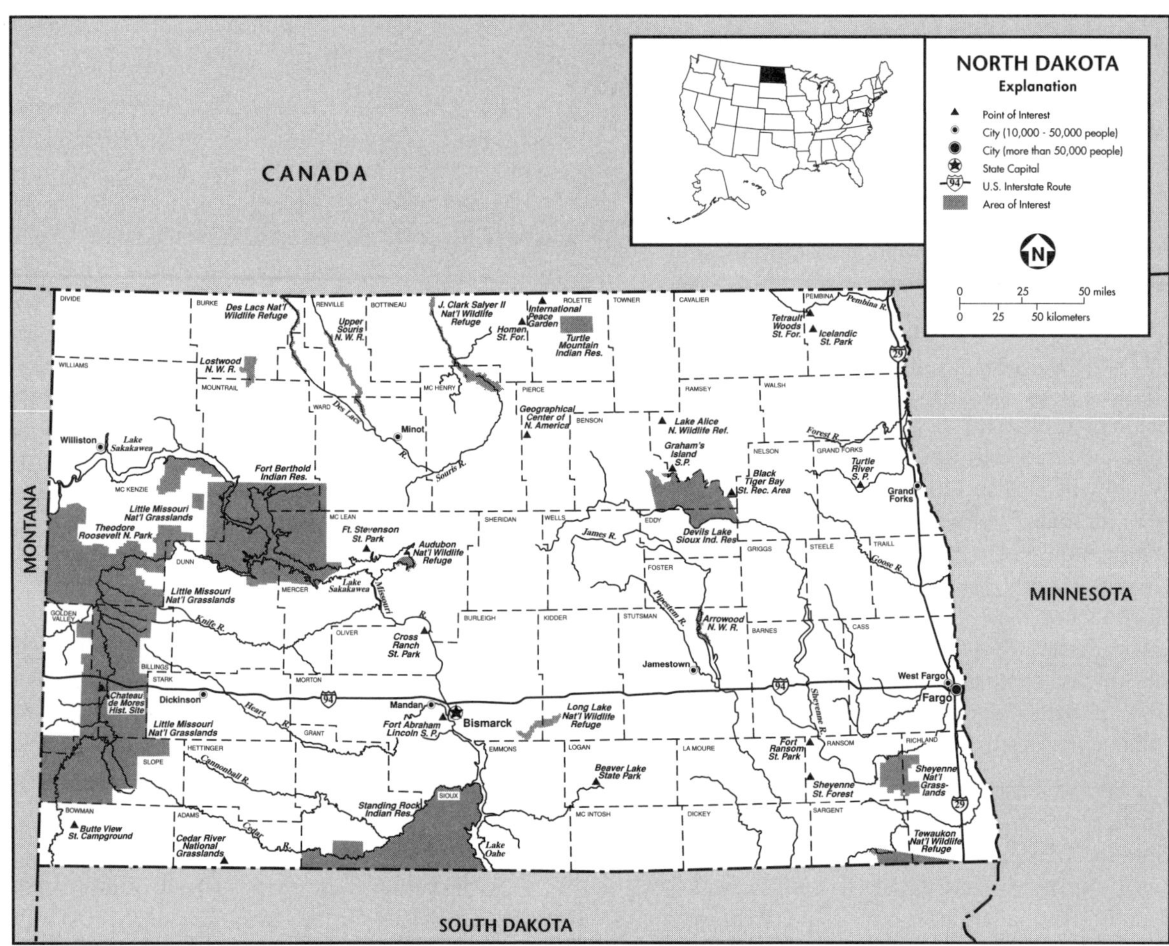

State of North Dakota.

for crops was good. In order to gain more control over wheat marketing, farmers formed cooperatives. These groups of farmers, who worked together to try to reduce the costs of transportation and storage costs and to get fair market prices for their wheat had little success.

Another attempt at fair trade was made by Arthur C. Townley, who developed a powerful farmer's organization called the Nonpartisan League (NPL). A popular organization, it became 40,000 members strong in one year. The NPL called for state-owned businesses such as banks to offer low-interest loans to assist farmers; they also favored grain inspectors to maintain consistent standards. Many voters opposed what they called ''state socialism,'' but in 1918 NPL candidates took over state leadership. The League continued in state politics through the 1950s. Reforms that were achieved under the NPL included tax breaks for farmers, funds for schools, and a better process for grading grain. However, despite NPL reforms, the Great Depression (1929–1939) caused banks to close, farmers to lose their land, and widespread unemployment in the late 1920s and early 1930s.

In the 1940s the economy began to pick up again with the construction of the Garrison Dam. The project relieved flooding along the Missouri, produced hydroelectricity, and provided irrigation for farms. In 1951 another major event took place that would bring new money to the state. Oil was discovered on the Clarence Iverson farm. An oil boom brought oil companies and prospectors flocking to the area. Although production from these wells declined in the 1960s and 1970s, new oil wells were discovered in the late 1970s. The OPEC oil embargo of 1973 and the rise of oil prices throughout the decade encouraged additional drilling and supported another oil boom. However, the state's economy suffered in the 1980s when oil prices dropped and a drought that started in 1987, continued into the 1990s—more than 5.3 million acres of land were damaged. While the agricultural production was strong in the 1980s and early 1990s, more than $600 million in crops were damaged from severe storms and flooding in 1994.

The 1995 median household income in North Dakota was $29,089; twelve percent of all North Dakotans lived below the federal poverty level.

See also: **John Jacob Astor, Bonanza Farming, Homestead Act, Lewis and Clark Expedition**

FURTHER READING

Berg, Francie M. *North Dakota: Land of Changing Seasons*. Hettinger, ND: Flying Diamond Books, 1977.

Grabowski, John F. *The Great Plains: Montana, Nebraska, North Dakota, South Dakota, Wyoming*. New York: Chelsea House Publishers, 1992.

Krummer, Patricia K. *North Dakota*. Mankato, MN: Capstone Press, 1999.

Norris, Kathleen. *Dakota: A Spiritual Biography*. New York: Ticker and Fields, 1993.

Worldmark Encyclopedia of the States. Detroit: Gale Research, 1998, s.v. ''North Dakota.''

NORTHERN SECURITIES CASE

The American economy changed substantially following the American Civil War (1861–1865). Cottage industries, artisan production, and small-scale manufacturing declined, and a new, larger, factory-based manufacturing sector grew. Operating under relatively relaxed state business laws, financiers and manufacturing moguls became rich, often by suppressing the competition.

This led to a concentration of capital in just a few huge corporations, especially in transportation and heavy industry. The giant manufacturing and mining companies that survived the period of cutthroat competition soon folded into nationwide monopolies known as trusts. In a trust, the companies transferred their properties and stocks to a board of trustees who ran the companies in a way that avoided competition—for instance, by dividing the markets up to protect regional monopoly. Such business arrangements substantially restricted the opportunities for new competitors.

During the 1870s the rapidly expanding railroads required long-term capitalization to meet their high fixed costs on a scale never before seen in U.S. business. The railroad companies sought cooperative pooling arrangements to stabilize markets and profits. Despite the ideology of free enterprise so prevalent during these years, the railroads, the steel industry, and the oil industry feared cutthroat competition much more than they feared government intervention. When the passage of the Interstate Commerce Act in 1887 prohibited pooling, railroads turned to other forms of consolidation. Workers, consumers, farmers, and small independent businessmen often faced high transport costs due to the lack of rail competition. Their reaction was frequently to demand antitrust laws.

Embracing the economic philosophy that public interest is best served by free competition in trade and industry, Congress passed the Sherman Antitrust Act in 1890 to guard against ''combination(s) in restraint of trade.'' Congress sought to prevent unreasonable concentrations of economic power. However, vagueness in the terms ''restraint'' and ''monopolization'' placed the burden on the president and judiciary to determine how to enforce and interpret the act.

Existing monopolistic business trends continued through the 1890s. Between 1897 and 1904 more than four thousand companies melded together to form not quite 300 corporations. Meanwhile, the Sherman Antitrust Act was of little use, as the courts initially interpreted the Act as applying mainly to labor union activities ''in restraint of trade.'' The courts held that manufacturing was not commerce and that consolidation was considered a viable means to stabilize costs. In addition, the courts ruled that the Act did not apply to stock transfers.

Under President Theodore Roosevelt (1901–1909), the Sherman Antitrust Act began to be used against corporate mergers. Roosevelt, who was concerned that the blatant favoritism that the government had displayed towards the corporations might result in the radicalization of labor, argued that the federal government should have the power to control big businesses through regulatory boards. Soon after Roosevelt assumed office, a case emerged involving four rail lines serving the northern plains.

Three of the four railroads were owned by prominent New York financiers. J. P. Morgan (1837–1913) owned the Northern Pacific which ran from Minneapolis to the Pacific Ocean. James J. Hill (1838–1916) owned the Great Northern with a similar route. Edward H. Harriman (1848–1909) owned the Union Pacific running from Omaha to Ogden, Utah. All three of them wished to control the Burlington railroad which ran across Illinois and provided ready entry into Chicago.

In 1901 Morgan and Hill cooperated to purchase the Burlington and plotted to drive Harriman out of business. Harriman quickly maneuvered, purchasing the majority of Great Northern stock. To salvage his ownership Hill began buying back the shares which, in turn, led to a sudden escalation in Great Northern's stock. Other investors did not understand what was the driving force behind the price escalation, so they began rapidly dumping other stocks to purchase Great Northern stocks. A panic on Wall Street followed, bankrupting thousands of unsuspecting investors.

A standoff between the three financiers led to a negotiated agreement. To prevent hostile takeovers the agreement established the Northern Securities Company, a holding company to control stocks of the Northern Pacific, Great Northern, and Burlington. The new company in which Morgan and Hill held controlling interest was worth approximately $400 million. Such a merger, through a holding company, was thought to be a viable means of cooperation without violating interstate commerce or antitrust laws.

Roosevelt became keenly interested in the developments pertaining to the agreement between Morgan, Hill and Harriman. Attorney General Philander Knox was assigned to look into the arrangement. In March 1902 the United States filed suit against the holding company in a federal district court in St. Paul, Minnesota, charging violation of the Sherman Antitrust Act. Lawyers for the railroads argued that the intent of the company was not to restrain trade but to prevent hostile takeovers. They asserted that the railroads rarely competed for the same business despite running parallel tracks. Furthermore the Northern Securities Company did not actually run the railroads, but merely held stock in the companies that did. Hence the company was not actually involved in interstate commerce. They argued that the act should not be applied to situations that only involved transfer of ownership.

Accustomed to a more cordial relationship with presidents, as soon as Morgan learned of Roosevelt's intention to prosecute the case, he and two conservative senators hurried over to the White House and declared to the president, "If we have done anything wrong, send your man to my man and they can fix it up." (Brinkley, 642) Despite these pleadings, Roosevelt held firm and the district court ruled that the company essentially eliminated any motive for competition as far as the public was concerned. The court ordered the Northern Securities Company dissolved.

In appeal to the Supreme Court, the railroads claimed forced dissolution would essentially deprive them of their Fifth Amendment property rights. The government countered that the holding company essentially concentrated control of transportation trade over a vast area of the nation under a single entity. In March 1904, the Supreme Court sided with the government's argument and affirmed the lower court's ruling in a 5-4 decision. The holding company constituted an unreasonable restraint of trade as prohibited by the act. Only Justice Oliver Wendell Holmes dissented from the decision. Holmes asserted that essentially all railroads are monopolies since only a single company runs on a particular set of lines. Therefore he could find nothing unreasonable concerning the holding company. These disagreements simply reflected an economic trend toward larger corporations with greater powers. Critics of the ruling complained that mere possession of great power should not automatically make someone suspect and some forms of price fixing may actually be reasonable.

The Supreme Court decision demonstrated to the business world that the Sherman Antitrust Act could be an effective tool used to combat business activities that restrain trade, including monopolies and trusts. The Act thus became not only the first, but also the most important antitrust legislation in the United States. The character of industrial business organizations and particularly railroads changed. Roosevelt became known as the "Trustbuster." With large corporations becoming a fixture in the American economy, this episode inaugurated a lengthy history of government oversight through antitrust enforcement.

See also: **Monopoly, Sherman Anti-Trust Act**

FURTHER READING

Asch, Peter. *Industrial Organization and Antitrust Policy*. New York: Wiley, 1983.

Audretsch, David B. *The Effectiveness of Antitrust Policy Towards Horizontal Mergers*. Ann Arbor, MI: UMI Research Press, 1983.

Brinkley, Alan *et al. American History: A Survey*, 8th ed. New York: McGraw Hill, 1991.

Brozen, Yale. *Concentration, Mergers, and Public Policy*. New York: Macmillan Publishing Co., 1982.

Kolko, Gabriel. *Railroads and Regulation, 1877–1916*. Princeton, NJ: Princeton University Press, 1965.

Martin, Albro. *Enterprise Denied: Origins of the Decline of American Railroads, 1897–1917*. New York: Columbia University Press, 1971.

NORTHWEST ORDINANCE

The Northwest Ordinance was the third of three major land ordinances passed by the Congress convened under the *Articles of Confederation* (before the ratification of the U.S. *Constitution*). The three ordinances also included the Ordinance of 1784 and the Land Ordinance of 1785.) These laws were passed to help manage the lands of the Old Northwest, which were awarded to the United States at the end of the American Revolution (1775–1783)—the modern states of Ohio, Indiana, Illinois, Michigan, and Wisconsin. The Ordinance of 1784 was drawn up by a committee headed by Thomas Jefferson (1743–1826). It created a system of government for the territory and guaranteed settlers the right to organize themselves into new states. The Land Ordinance of 1785 established the way in which the territory would be measured and divided up for sale to prospective settlers and land speculators. The Northwest Ordinance of 1787 (one of the final acts passed by the Confederation Congress before it dissolved) set up the process through which settlers could bring their new states into the Union. The ordinance guaranteed settlers the rights of U.S. citizens; established procedures for dealing with Native Americans in the area; allocated money from the sale of land in the territory to be set aside for public schools; and banned slavery north of the Ohio River. It also established that the territory would eventually be divided into no less than three and no more than five states.

Under the terms of the Northwest Ordinance, the Northwest Territory was divided into a number of districts, each of which was to be administered by a governor and by judges appointed by Congress. When the white male population of a district reached 5000, the district became a territory. It could then form its own territorial legislature, but its executive and judicial officials were still appointed by Congress. When the population of a territory reached 60,000, it could apply for admission as a state. The Northwest Ordinance established that territory brought into the Union would enter on an equal basis with the original 13 colonies, thus, recently-settled areas were prevented from being treated as inferior to more established regions. Settlers in the new areas were also guaranteed certain rights, such as freedom of religion, which the original colonies did not promise to their citizens. Although he took no steps to free the few slaves already living in the territory, Jefferson added a provision specifically banning slavery from being introduced into the territory.

The Northwest Ordinance also tried to establish the government's official policy toward Native Americans living in the area. It required the government to use its ''utmost good faith'' toward the Indians, and it promised that ''their lands and their property shall never be taken from them without their consent; and in their property, rights, and liberty, they shall never be invaded or disturbed, unless in just and lawful wars authorized by Congress.'' The ''just and lawful wars'' clause was ignored more often than it was honored. In a series of wars ranging over 40 years, from Little Turtle's War (1791–1794) to the Black Hawk War (1832), Native Americans were driven from the Old Northwest and their lands were seized and sold to white settlers.

IN PROVIDING FOR ORDERLY DEVELOPMENT AND EVENTUAL STATEHOOD, THE LAND ORDINANCES MAY WELL HAVE BEEN THE MOST SIGNIFICANT LEGISLATION OF THE CONFEDERATION-PERIOD CONGRESS.

James Kirby Martin, Professor of History, University of Houston

The economic impact of the Northwest Ordinance was very broad. By making the process of statehood relatively easy, settlers in the Old Northwest were encouraged to ship their produce to American ports rather than to more accessible British, French, and Spanish ports on the Great Lakes or lower Mississippi River. By banning slavery, the area was reserved for free labor. Finally, by allowing Native Americans to be deprived of their lands through warfare, the Northwest Ordinance set a precedent for settler-Native American conflict that lasted over a century.

See also: **Black Hawk War, Land Ordinance of 1785, Native American Policy, Old Northwest**

FURTHER READING

Abernethy, Thomas Perkins. *Western Lands and the American Revolution.* New York: Russell and Russell, Inc., 1959.

Clawson, Marion. *The Federal Lands Revisited.* Baltimore, MD: Johns Hopkins University Press, 1983.

Gates, Paul W. *History of Public Land Law Development.* Washington, DC: Wm. W. Gaunt and Sons, 1968.

Morris, Richard B. *The Forging of the Union, 1781–1789.* New York: Harper and Row, 1987.

Onuf, Peter S. *Statehood and Union: The Northwest Ordinance.* Bloomington, IN: Indiana University Press, 1987.

Rohrbough, Malcolm. *The Trans-Appalachian Frontier: People, Societies, and Institutions, 1775–1850.* New York: Oxford University Press, 1978.

NORTHWEST PASSAGE

The Northwest Passage is the circuitous sea passage, long sought by explorers, between the Atlantic and the Pacific Oceans. Though it was eventually found through a series of discoveries, it was not completely navigated until Norwegian explorer Roald Amundsen (1872–1928) explored it between 1903 and 1906. Numerous navigators, convinced of the existence of such a passage, attempted to find it during the early years of European westward sea exploration. Though unsuccessful, their determination led to the discovery of other important locations. French sailor and explorer Jacques Cartier found the St. Lawrence River, dividing Canada and the United States, between 1534 and 1535. English commander Sir Martin Frobisher discovered Frobisher Bay off the coast of Baffin Island and north of Quebec in 1576. English navigator John Davis discovered Davis Strait between Baffin Island and Greenland in 1587. English navigator Henry Hudson found the Hudson River in eastern New York State, and Hudson Bay, the inland-sea of central Canada, between 1609 and 1611. Following centuries of efforts Amundsen finally completed the first successful navigation of the Northwest Passage in September 1906, during a journey that lasted more than three years. The hash climate, however, makes the route impractical for commercial navigation.

NORTHWESTERN COAST INDIANS

Northwest Coast Indian tribes occupied the region bounded by the Rocky Mountains to the east and north, the High Sierras to the southwest, and the Pacific Ocean to the northwest. The area roughly corresponds to present-day northern Utah, northern Nevada, northeastern California, Oregon, Washington, Idaho, British Columbia, and southern Alaska. Beginning at the end of the ice age (about 10,000 B.C.) three distinctive cultures emerged in the region as tribes adapted to the varying environments of the Northwest.

The first culture was that of the Great Basin, which is an elevated terrain walled in by the Rockies and the High Sierras. Here tribes including the Shoshone, Bannock, Paiute, and Ute lived simply to survive the rugged region comprised of desert, brush lands, and pine forests. The climate ranged from dry, hot summers to cold, harsh winters. Bands living here hunted small game and foraged for wild grains, nuts, and vegetables; pine nuts were their most important food. Those living near rivers and streams also fished. Dwellings varied by season. During warm months, brush windbreaks served as shelters; in the winter, conical shelters were made of pine poles covered with sod, bark, grass, or skins. The Indians had few possessions, and those they had, such as baskets, were strictly utilitarian.

The second culture lived on the plateaus west of the Great Basin. The inland region tended to be dry but was forged by rivers, principally the Columbia (forming the border between Oregon and Washington) and the Fraser in central British Columbia. Tribes including the Yakima, Walla Walla, Coer d'Alene, and Nez Perce lived off the plentiful seafood, including mussels and salmon. Prime fishing spots were actively protected. These tribes were sophisticated hunters, and their diet was also rich in meat. They foraged for wild bulbs and roots, as well as berries. Dwellings varied by season: in the winter they lived mostly in pit houses (semi-subterranean, circular shelters); in the warm months they made brush or mat-covered windbreaks.

The third Northwestern culture comprised tribes living along the coast of Alaska, British Columbia, and Washington, such as the Aleut, Kwakiutl, and Chinook. From their plentiful environment, which was rich in wildlife and teeming with fish and seafood, these tribes developed a sophisticated culture. Living off salmon, seals, whales, bear, caribou, deer, elk, and moose, some families grew very wealthy in this region. Wealth was measured by possessions such as canoes, blankets, and slaves (captured enemies). Multi-family dwellings were made out of posts and beams, with planked sides and gabled roofs. Armor and elaborate face masks were used in battle. Decorative objects included wooden boxes and totem poles, which displayed a family's genealogy and social standing.

Europeans brought horses, tools, weapons, and diseases to the region. They came to the area to mine minerals, and white settlements gradually pushed Northwestern Indians off their lands. Major conflicts between the Indians and the settlers included the Modoc War (1872–1873) and the Nez Perce War (1877).

See also: **Alaska, California, Idaho, Nevada, Oregon, Washington, Utah**

NUCLEAR ENERGY *(ISSUE)*

In 1954 the U.S. government authorized private ownership of nuclear reactors as part of President Dwight D. Eisenhower's (1953–1961) Atoms for Peace initiative, paving the way for utility companies to build nuclear power plants. By the mid-1960s many utility companies had ''gone nuclear,'' though building reactors proved far more costly than the early hopes; reactor energy did not meet expectations that they could provide power for pennies a day.

Most U.S. citizens' sole experience with the power of the atom was the devastating bombing of Hiroshima and Nagasaki in 1945; accordingly, some opposed the whole issue of nuclear energy. In California, after an earthquake disrupted construction, residents demanded the cancellation of the planned Bodega Bay reactor which was sited on a geological fault. Inhabitants of New York City resisted the siting of a plant within its borders because of the dense population.

Regardless of fears about nuclear weaponry, most people liked the idea of building atomic energy plants. The country was using increasing amounts of electrical energy (produced by burning fossil fuels which created air pollution. Nuclear power promised to be cheaper and cleaner. Moreover, nuclear power had the aura of a neat, high-tech solution to the complicated problems that people had come to expect from politics and business. When an oil embargo by countries in the Middle East hit in 1973–1974, the United States faced shortages of electricity, gasoline, and heating oil. Factories and schools were shut down. There were also cancellations of commercial airline flights, electrical brownouts, and increased lines at gasoline service stations. Blackouts plagued cities and industries, most spectacularly in New York City on July 13 and 14, 1977. High fuel prices reduced the productivity of U.S. industry. To all of these complaints the supporters of nuclear energy claimed a solution. They also argued that nuclear energy would solve the balance of payments problem and neutralize the damage to the international monetary system that was being done by the heavy U.S. imports of fuel.

To some U.S. citizens, atomic energy seemed to offer a way for the nation to achieve energy independence. Support for nuclear power steadily increased. Meanwhile the anti-nuclear movement carried forward the traditions of the anti-Vietnam War movement and many opponents initiated demonstrations at nuclear power plants. At Seabrook Station in New Hampshire, opponents staged sit-ins, civil disobedience, celebrity concerts, and rallies. Supporters of nuclear energy ridiculed the protesters' fear of technology and charged the anti-nuclear movement with a vaguely un-American variety of consumer elitism. One writer caricatured the protesters as ''vegetarians in leather jackets who drive imported cars to Seabrook listening to the Grateful Dead on their Japanese tape decks amid a marijuana haze.''

Regardless of this culture clash, the United States' energy crisis was real and was caused by several factors. One was that in the 1950s and 1960s strategic geopolitical concerns led the government to promote the import of fuel from overseas, especially from the Middle East. Another was that President Richard Nixon's (1969–1974) 1971 attempt to halt inflation (called the New Economic Policy) had imposed price controls on the entire economy. But when the other restrictions were lifted, oil remained regulated, keeping the price artificially low to consumers and increasing demand. The United States was extravagant in its use of energy—few U.S.-made cars got better than 10 miles to the gallon, and homes and businesses were poorly insulated and inefficiently designed. Diverse special interests had skewed portions of the government's oversight and regulation of the oil industry toward their particular interests, and passing general legislation regarding energy became a political nightmare. Accordingly, efforts to develop a consistent energy policy throughout the 1970s were diluted and diverted. The decade ended much as it began, with the United States wastefully consuming inordinate amounts of energy, subject, once again, to an oil crisis.

During the 1960s utility companies were aware of the coming energy shortage. One of their methods to prepare for the shortfall was to construct nuclear reactors. In January 1973 there were 27 functioning reactors in the United States, providing only five percent of the power generated. Fifty-five plants were under construction, and an additional 78 were in the planning stages. The majority, however, were never built. Security expenses, nuclear-waste disposal costs, and construction overruns made the return on investment slim in nuclear-power plants.

In 1974, seeking to assist the nuclear industry, the administration of President Gerald R. Ford (1974–1977) disbanded the Atomic Energy Commission (AEC), which had overseen U.S. nuclear development for 28 years. In its place were constructed two more industry-friendly commissions: the Nuclear Regulatory Commission (NRC) and the Energy Research and

The nuclear era was ushered in as the United States claimed victory over the Japanese in 1945. Soon more benevolent uses were developed for this enormous source of energy, such as the Davis-Besse Nuclear Power Plant in Harbor, Ohio.

Development Administration (ERDA). The latter agency was empowered to develop new energy sources and market U.S. nuclear industry abroad. The NRC streamlined the licensing and commission of reactor projects, but many of the old problems remained. Safety was a pressing issue: fires underscored the potential for a catastrophic accident at nuclear plants (at the Indian Point Two reactor in New York in 1971, the Zion reactor in Illinois in 1974, the Trojan reactor in Oregon in 1974, and the Brown's Ferry reactor in Alabama in 1975). In 1975 the Union of Concerned Scientists presented the White House with a petition signed by 2,000 scientists which called for a reduction in nuclear construction. Public opinion followed that of the scientists. Environmental groups increasingly challenged the construction of nuclear projects in the NRC and in the courts, delaying the deployment of projects and driving up the start-up costs. The 1978–1979 protests at the Seabrook nuclear power plant in New Hampshire were particularly vocal and drew national attention to the issue. Then, in the spring of 1979, an accident at the Harrisburg, Pennsylvania, Three Mile Island nuclear power plant resulted in a partial core meltdown. Although no one was injured, the accident terrified the public and placed the future of the nuclear industry in jeopardy.

On April 26, 1986, near the town of Pripyat in the Soviet Union, attention was again focused on the issue of safety in the nuclear power industry. One of four nuclear reactors at the Chernobyl Nuclear Power Station in the Ukraine exploded with such force that the roof of the building was completely blown off. Eight tons of radioactive materials were scattered about the region immediately surrounding the plant. Airborne radioactivity from the blast rained down on northern Europe and Scandinavia. Fallout contaminating farm produce was measured as far away as Scotland. Engineers at Chernobyl had accidentally initiated an uncontrolled chain reaction in the reactor's core during an unauthorized test in which they unlawfully incapacitated the reactor's emergency systems. In the immediate aftermath of the catastrophe, more than 30 people lost their lives. Moreover, one estimate placed the number at 20,000 who would eventually live shortened lives as a result of the effects of their exposure to radiation from the accident.

In the United States experts argued that the disaster at Chernobyl was not pertinent to the domestic nuclear industry. They noted that the technology employed at Chernobyl was not being used in the United States. The Soviets, they pointed out, were using a weapons-material production reactor to generate electricity for their domestic market—something not done in the United States. Furthermore, the Chernobyl reactor lacked a containment building—a required safety component mandated for all U.S. reactors. Nevertheless, many in the United States drew uneasy parallels between Chernobyl and Three Mile Island, among them, that operator error and equipment failure was possible in the nuclear industry. The consequences of a single major mistake could be catastrophic.

During the 1980s scores of ''anti-nuke'' organizations warned of the hazards of nuclear energy and protested plant construction and operation. In Seabrook, New Hampshire, protesters rallied around the citizens' action group, the Clamshell Alliance, to oppose the building of two nuclear reactors. By 1987 the utility that owned Seabrook was near bankruptcy, in part due to the increased vigilance of oversight safety committees insisted upon by the Clamshell Alliance. At Long Island's Shoreham nuclear facility the story was much the same. Besieged by civic-group opposition and having far exceeded initial cost estimates of $241 million (its actual cost to the utility had surpassed $5 billion), the Shoreham ''nuke'' was closed by the state government in 1988. The utility that owned Shoreham had failed to develop an adequate evacuation plan for the region of Long Island that would be affected in the event of a meltdown. Sold to the state government for one dollar, the completed plant was to be dismantled even before it opened.

Cost overruns and construction problems continued to plague the industry. Florida's St. Lucie Two plant cost about four times its original estimate of $360 million. This price, as it would turn out, was a relative bargain. By mid-decade Michigan's Midland nuclear power plant (initial cost estimate: $267 million) had cost the utility constructing it $4.4 billion, and it was nine years behind schedule. In the West, at the Diablo Canyon Plant, earthquake supports were installed backwards.

Another problem the industry faced was the disposal of irradiated fuel rods. During the 1980s utility companies stored these rods on site at the power plants, in large vats resembling swimming pools, but this was only considered a temporary solution. In 1982 Congress passed the Nuclear Waste Policy Act. The act called upon the Department of Energy (DOE) to find a suitable site to bury radioactive waste. DOE, however, was unsuccessful in locating a site that included both the necessary stable rock formation (free of groundwater) and the requisite local public support. By the end of the 1980s, no solution to the problem of nuclear waste had been found.

FURTHER READING

Glasstone, Samuel. *Sourcebook on Atomic Energy.* Princeton, NJ: D. Van Nostrand, 1967.

Inglis, David R. *Nuclear Energy: Its Physics and Its Social Challenge.* Reading, MA: Addison-Wesley, 1973.

Marion, Jerry B., and Roush, Marvin L. *Energy in Perspective*, 2d ed. New York: Academic Press, 1982.

Stobaugh, Robert, Daniel Yergin, eds. *Energy Future: Report of the Energy Project at the Harvard Business School.* New York: Random House, 1979.

Williams, Robert C., Philip L. Cantelon, eds. *The American Atom: A Documentary History of Nuclear Policies from the Discovery of Fission to the Present, 1939–1984.* Philadelphia: University of Pennsylvania Press, September, 1984.

OFFICE OF EMERGENCY MANAGEMENT

Office of Emergency Management (OEM) was an executive branch office that coordinated defense activities for all government agencies except the War and Navy Departments. It was established by an administrative order on May 25, 1940, in accordance with an executive decree issued by President Franklin D. Roosevelt (1933–1945). OEM created a number of federal agencies that played a critical role on the American home front during World War II (1939–1945). Three of the most important such agencies were the War Production Board, (WPB) the Office of Civilian Defense (OCD), and the Office of War Information (OWI). WPB mobilized the domestic economy, encouraged industrial expansion, and developed policies to regulate nearly every facet of military and civilian production. OCD was in charge of integrating federal, state, local, and territorial efforts aimed at boosting morale and reducing the risks presented by internal and external enemies of the United States. OWI disseminated information to the media about the government's wartime policies and closely monitored the content of Hollywood films to screen for unpatriotic material that might be harmful to the Allied cause. Although OEM is presently listed as inactive by the United States Government Manual, its responsibilities have been largely assumed by the Federal Emergency Management Agency (FEMA), which was established in 1979.

See also: **War Production Board, World War II**

OFFICE OF PRICE ADMINISTRATION

During World War II (1939–1945), the federal government became the major consumer of production for the war period. Accordingly, Congress instituted a price fixing authority on all goods and wages with the creation of the Office of Price Administration (OPA), and the "General Maximum Price Regulation" (General Max), which froze all retail prices at their highest price levels as of March 1942.

On April 27, 1942, President Franklin Roosevelt outlined another aspect of price administration, to be known as "rationing" (which Roosevelt described as a "democratic, equitable solution" to the issue of providing goods for Americans that had become scarce because of the war). Items that were rationed in some way included gasoline, rubber tires, leather shoes, butter, and products with nylon content.

The rationing of goods to U.S. consumers during World War II was one of the many functions of the OPA. Perhaps the major problem of the OPA, functionally, was keeping economic inflation in strict control domestically, while providing military forces overseas with what they needed to fight the war.

See also: **Rationing, World War II**

OHIO

Some historians have said that the history of the state of Ohio is, in some ways, a microcosm of the history of middle America. Ohio has seen Native American revolts, pioneer migrations, and the gradual transformation of its wilderness into farms, towns, and cities. The transportation systems that eventually traversed the state brought rapid economic growth. The immigrants who peopled Ohio's cities helped make them industrial giants. They brought with them a wealth of skills and experiences that enriched society and made Ohio the prosperous, culturally diverse place it is today. The industrial pollution and urban decay plaguing the state have mirrored problems in the nation as a whole. But Ohio's efforts to keep up with changing economic times have been largely successful in spite of periodic setbacks.

The first European visitors to Ohio were game hunters of French and English extraction. When they

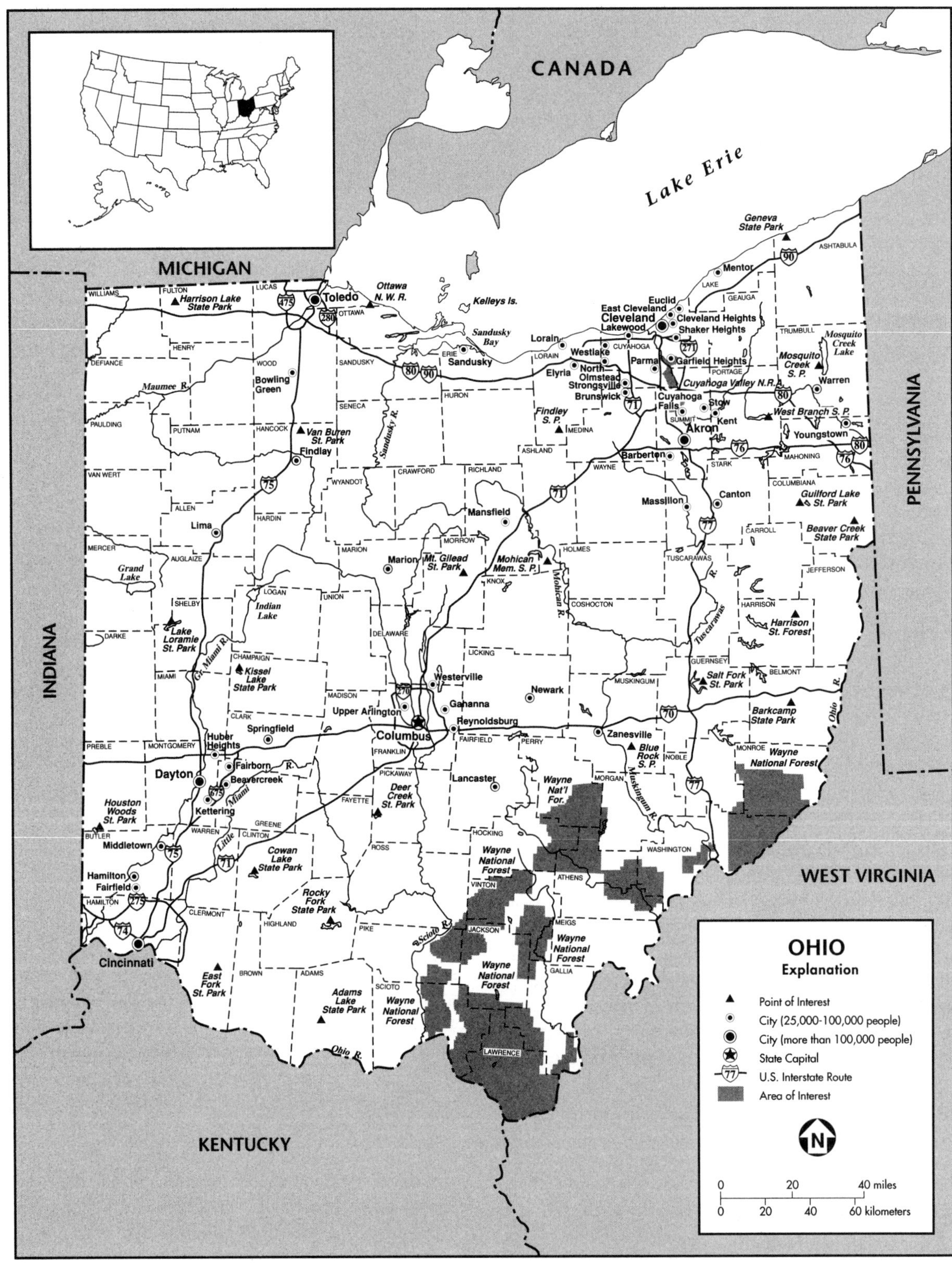

State of Ohio.

began to settle in Ohio in the seventeenth century, they found a number of Native American tribes there, including the Wyandots, the Delawares, the Miamis, and the Shawnees. The hunters soon started bringing in such goods as knives, hatchets, tobacco, and brandy. They exchanged these for the natives' beaver pelts and deerskins. The French and the English competed for the territory of Ohio until the middle of the eighteenth century, when as a result of the French and Indian War (1754–1763), the British became the predominant power in northern North America, gaining control over a vast area that included Ohio. They lost some of this territory in the American Revolution (1775–1783).

After the Revolution, Ohio belonged to the United States, becoming part of the Northwest Territory. Future land development in the new Northwest Territory was regulated by the Ordinance of 1785 and the Northwest Ordinance of 1787. The new territory was defined as the area between western Pennsylvania and the Mississippi River, bounded on the south by the Ohio River and on the north by Canada. When settlers began making their way to the Ohio area, many went by keelboat down the Ohio River. They sought fertile lands and new economic opportunities. The new American nation came into being in 1789, and this set the stage for Ohio's prosperity. The Treaty of Greenville in 1795 pushed Native American tribes out of the territory and further encouraged white settlement in the area. More settlers came from the older eastern colonies after Connecticut ceded the Western Reserve, a tract of land along the southern coast of Lake Erie that now comprises part of northeastern Ohio. By 1803 the area had enough residents to become the seventeenth state of the Union.

EXCEPT ON THE BROADEST LEVELS . . . ONE CANNOT GENERALIZE ABOUT THE PEOPLE OF OHIO . . . [THE STATE] HAS A REPRESENTATIVE QUALITY[, WITH] AN UNUSUAL BALANCE BETWEEN NORTHERN AND SOUTHERN INFLUENCES, BETWEEN AGRICULTURE AND INDUSTRY, BETWEEN RURAL AND URBAN.

George W. Knepper, *Ohio and Its People*, 1989

A final challenge from the British came with the War of 1812 (1812–1814). Commodore Oliver Hazard Perry (1785–1819) won a decisive battle in the war on Lake Erie, making Great Lakes commerce safe for Americans. Gen. William Henry Harrison (1773–1841) repulsed Indian encroachment at the Battle of Tippecanoe in the Indiana Territory. Large numbers of people migrated to Ohio thereafter, both from the eastern colonies and from abroad. Encouraged by low prices for land, new settlers moved quickly to establish farms and begin towns across the new state.

Ohio needed a better system of ground and water transportation to help its economy grow. The first significant route to cross the breadth of Ohio in the 1830s was the National Road (later to become U.S. route 40). The route stretched from Cumberland, Maryland, to Vandalia, Illinois. A canal system was created at about the same time, connecting the northern and southern portions of the state. The Ohio and Erie Canal ran from Portsmouth on the Ohio River to Cleveland. The Miami–Erie Canal ran from Cincinnati to Toledo. The canals were not profitable for their owners but proved successful at opening new markets to many farmers.

By the 1840s railroads were beginning to radiate from the population centers, effectively bringing the canal era to an end. The number of railroad tracks in Ohio increased tenfold between 1850 and 1860, though canals were still being constructed in the state. The railroad was crucial to Ohio's economic growth, connecting small towns and urban centers with other cities across the young nation.

Although the railroad brought unprecedented change to Ohio, the state was still primarily agricultural in the mid-nineteenth century. The American Civil War (1861–65), however, increased industrial development, which continued to grow during the rest of the century and beyond. John D. Rockefeller's (1839–1937) Standard Oil Company in Cleveland quickly took control of most of the oil refining and distribution in the nation. The city of Akron became the "rubber capital" after B.F. Goodrich (1841–1888) began manufacturing fire hose. Cincinnati and Dayton also became major manufacturing centers during this time. There was a new wave of immigrants, mostly from southern and eastern Europe, in the 1880s and another in the 1910s. This influx of population brought many potential factory workers to Ohio cities. The advent of labor unions in the 1880s brought some protection to workers against unfair labor practices.

By 1900 Ohio ranked number four in manufacturing. The coal mines in the southeastern part of the state and Great Lakes access to Michigan and later, Minnesota iron ore helped the iron and steel industry to grow in the Cleveland-Youngstown area. By this time Ohio led the nation in the manufacture of machine tools. It ranked second in steel production.

The state's farm population steadily declined after 1900 and cities began to grow, and World War I (1914–1918) greatly contributed to Ohio's industrial growth.

The automobile industry stimulated Ohio's rubber, oil, and glass industries in the 1920s.

The Great Depression of the 1930s hit Ohio hard. It caused widespread unemployment and stifled the economy in many ways. Labor unions became stronger during this time, as workers hoped to protect their standard of living by organizing. The United Rubber Workers in Akron grew to a membership of around 70,000 after a series of sit-down strikes at the rubber plants. The United Steelworkers also struck at seven steel plants in Youngstown and greatly increased their membership.

Like much of the nation, Ohio benefited economically from the outbreak of World War II (1939–1945), though the state prospered in part because of its healthy industrial base. The state's economy especially grew through war-time production of trucks, tractors, and airplanes. Highway building and airport construction also increased during this time.

In 1959 the St. Lawrence Seaway provided a major economic boost to Ohio. This important waterway connected Toledo and Cleveland with transatlantic commerce. This period unfortunately also brought widespread pollution of the waters, especially Lake Erie, from the dumping of industrial wastes. The rural population continued to decline, and many middle-class people fled to the suburbs from city centers. They left a legacy of urban ruin that would plague the state for years to come.

In the 1970s Ohio's economy began to lag. By the early 1980s it entered a difficult phase. The state's unemployment rate rose to 14 percent by 1983. Manufacturing jobs were on the decline—down from 39 percent in 1970 to 27 percent in 1982. The high sulfur content in most of Ohio's abundant coal supply made the coal largely unusable because it contributed to atmospheric pollution. The state was eventually forced to borrow from the federal government to pay for the high costs of unemployment benefits.

A boost to Ohio's economy was the Thomas Edison Program, initiated in 1983. The project provided venture capital funds for new companies. It also helped establish conservancy districts for the Miami and Muskingum rivers, and began programs that eventually reversed the pollution of Lake Erie. Another major achievement for the state was the establishment of a new Honda Motor Company auto plant at Marysville near Columbus.

Unemployment in Ohio rose again during the recession of 1992, despite considerable economic progress in the mid-1980s. In 1995 there was a major strike at two General Motors plants in Dayton. This added to the state's economic uncertainty. But manufacturing remained the major economic pillar in Ohio throughout the 1990s. The state manufactured mostly durable goods like motor vehicles and other equipment, and steel. The service industry also became significant in the state. Tourism became one of the important segments of the service market. Ohio farms maintained high levels of production in cattle, pigs, and poultry, as well as tomatoes, soybeans, wheat, and oats. The state ranked fifteenth in net farm income in 1995. Ohio's mineral production was also healthy: coal provided more than one third of the state's energy needs, and Ohio was a national leader in the production of sand and gravel. In 1995 Ohio led the nation in lime production.

See also: **Automobile Industry, Keelboats, Northwest Ordinance, Petroleum Industry, John D. Rockefeller, Standard Oil**

FURTHER READING

Galbreath, Charles B. *History of Ohio.* 5 vols. Chicago and New York: American Historical Society, 1925.

Havighurst, Walter. *Ohio: A Bicentennial History.* New York: Norton, 1976.

Knepper, George W. *Ohio and Its People.* Kent, OH: Kent State University Press, 1989.

Raitz, Karl, ed. *The National Road.* Baltimore, MD: Johns Hopkins University Press, 1996.

Roseboom, Eugene Holloway, and Francis P. Weisenburger. *A History of Ohio.* New York: Prentice-Hall, 1934.

OHIO VALLEY

The Ohio River drains into a fertile basin that measures 203,000 square miles (528,101 square kilometers)—stretching across Ohio, West Virginia, Indiana, Illinois, and Kentucky. The river is formed by the confluence of the Allegheny and Monongahela rivers at Pittsburgh, Pennsylvania. From there the Ohio flows southwest, forming the border between Ohio and West Virginia. The river then turns west-northwest to form the border between Ohio and Kentucky before turning southwest again between Indiana and Kentucky, and between Illinois and Kentucky. Navigable by barges its entire length of 975 miles (1,569 kilometers), the Ohio River empties into the Mississippi River at Cairo,

Illinois. The region surrounding the Ohio River is rich farmland. Commercial cities—trade centers that grew as transportation along the principal waterway increased—also dot the region.

The Ohio was first seen in 1669 by a European, French explorer Sieur de La Salle (1643–1687). In the first half of the 1700s, traders traveled the Ohio River, finding the surrounding valley a plentiful hunting ground. The fur trade flourished, making the region a coveted possession for both the French and the British. Numerous battles were fought in the valley, including the French and Indian War (1754–1763), the last major conflict in North America before the American Revolution (1775–1783).

The Ohio River Valley passed to British control (from the French) in 1763. In 1783 it became part of the new republic of the United States. Four years later the U.S. government established the Northwest Territory (the present-day states of Ohio, Michigan, Indiana, Illinois, Wisconsin, and part of Minnesota). Soon many settlers traveled the Ohio River westward. By 1820, more than 60 steamboats plied the Ohio, which remained the main westward route into the region until 1825. Settlement of the Ohio River Valley was aided by the federally built National Road (completed 1852), New York's Erie Canal (1825), and by Pennsylvania's Main Line Canal (1837).

Two companies also helped develop the region. The first was the Ohio River Valley Company (sometimes called the Ohio Company of Virginia), formed in 1747 when England's King George II granted London merchants and landed Virginians 200,000 acres (81,000 hectares) west of the Allegheny Mountains. But conflicts with the French stymied British efforts to settle the region and the company failed. The Ohio Company of Associates was organized in 1786 in Boston, Massachusetts. Shares were sold to raise enough money to petition the Congress of the Confederation to purchase land beyond the Ohio River. Congress sold the company 750,000 acres (304,000 hectares) in what is today southeastern Ohio. In 1787 Congress passed the Northwest Ordinance, which set guidelines by which territories became states. The first settlement founded under the Northwest Ordinance was Marietta, Ohio, which was named the capital of the Northwest Territory in 1788. Within a year three more settlements were made in the territory. Ohio was admitted to the Union in 1803.

See also: **Erie Canal, Illinois, Indiana, Kentucky, Massachusetts, National Road, Northwest Ordinance, Ohio, Old Northwest, Pennsylvania, Pennsylvania Main Line Canal, Steamboats, West Virginia**

OIL DEPLETION ALLOWANCE

Oil depletion allowance refers to deductions allowed in petroleum industry taxation. Mineral resources, including oil and gas, are finite and may become exhausted from area to area. Although difficult to estimate the amount of the deposit left, the allowance takes into account that production of a crude oil uses up the asset. Depletion deductions provide incentives to stimulate investment in oil discovery in hazardous or financially risky areas. The deduction, a fixed percentage of sales, is subtracted from a business' gross income, thus lowering its taxable income.

The oil depletion allowance has been an integral part of the U.S. taxation system applied to oil since the end of World War I (1916–1918). First called the "discovery depletion," the allowance evolved to the "percentage depletion" in 1926 when, regardless the amount invested, corporations deducted a specific percentage of total sales. Long set at 27.5 percent, the deduction came under fire as being overly favorable to the extractive industries. Congress lowered the percentage to 22 in 1969.

In 1975 there were approximately 35 major oil producers but roughly 10,000 smaller independent producers. The oil depletion allowance again entered the political arena with opponents arguing that it constituted a special treatment gift to the oil and gas industry. Fear of losing the allowance completely lead independents to break with the majors and fight to retain it for themselves. Congress agreed that the independents indeed were America's hazardous oil-finders. Congress voted to eliminate the allowance for the majors but, although gradually reducing it to 15 percent by 1984, retain it for the independents and royalty owners. For the first time in U.S. history, a definition for an "independent producer" appeared in the basic U.S. tax code. The explicit legal definition allowed independents to be considered separately from major oil producers in legislation and saved the independents millions of dollars in the last quarter of the twentieth century. Attempts to eliminate the 15 percent tax shelter in 1985–1986 failed when sinking world oil prices alone sent the oil industry into decline.

See also: **Petroleum Industry**

OKLAHOMA

Oklahoma was admitted to the Union as the forty-sixth state on November 16, 1907. Its location in the western south central United States makes it a geographic melting pot. Sharing borders with Texas and

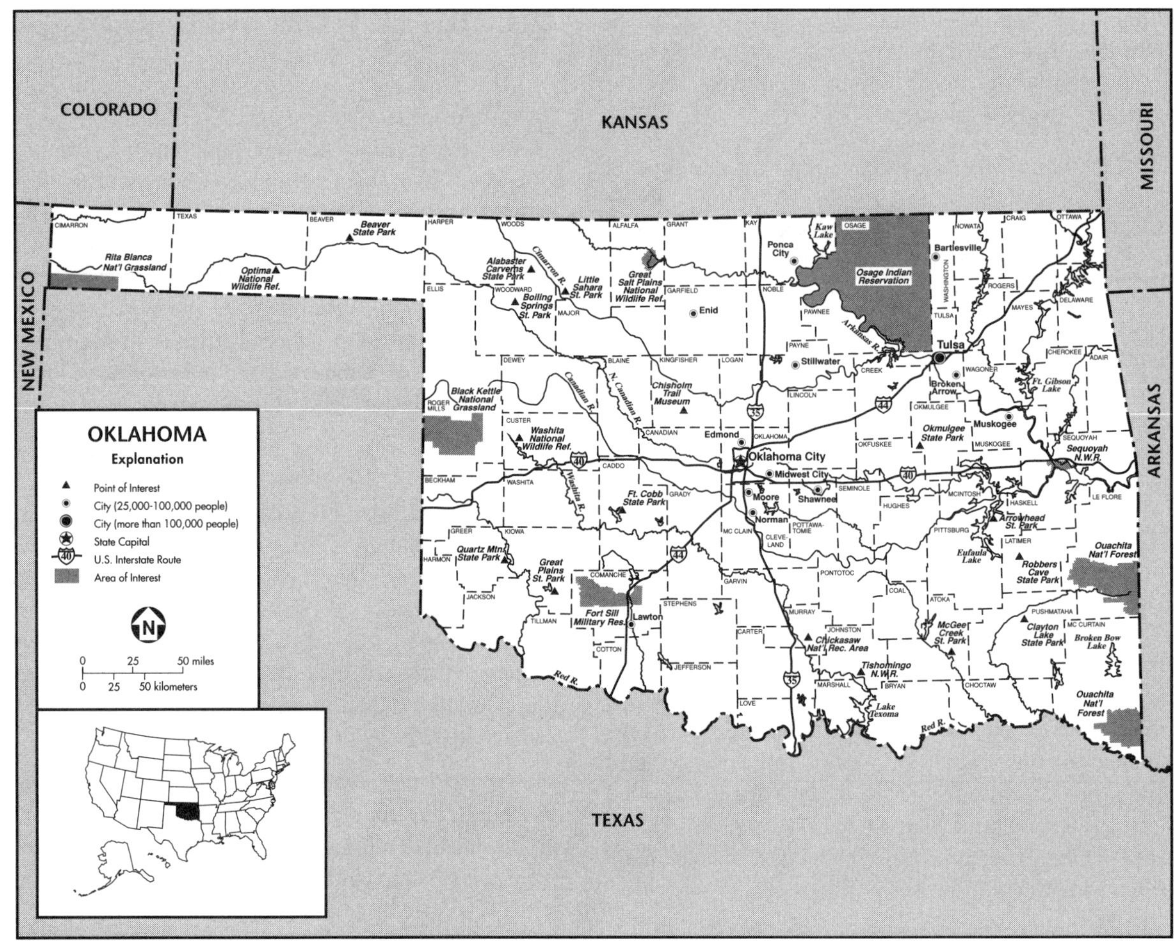

State of Oklahoma.

Arkansas, Oklahoma is part of the South. But its common borders with Missouri and Kansas place Oklahoma in the central United States, and its borders with Colorado and New Mexico give the state a western flavor. Oklahoma is the nation's eighteenth largest state with over 69,000 square miles. Its population of 3.3 million people ranks 30th among the fifty states. Oklahoma City is the state's capital and its most populous city.

The state enjoys a diverse topography, climate, and economy. The humid eastern region of Oklahoma is graced by seven million acres of forests and 2,600-foot mountainous peaks where mining and lumbering are the chief economic activities. The east is also home to hundreds of swift-running rivers, many of which are damned to provide hydroelectric power in neighboring communities. Wheat is grown and cattle raised in the more temperate, low-rolling prairies to the west. Most of Oklahoma's cotton is grown in the drier, heavily irrigated southwestern counties. Petroleum and natural gas are produced throughout the state—Oklahoma is one of the country's five leading producers of both mineral fuels.

Oklahoma winters are relatively mild, with temperatures in January averaging about 38 degrees Fahrenheit. Spring brings dozens of tornadoes that twist through the state annually, usually leaving measurable damage. Summers tend to be long and hot, and periodic droughts can turn the semi-arid western region of Oklahoma into a dust bowl. But the state's sometimes challenging climate does not stop yearly visits from 16 million tourists, who generate over $3 billion in gross revenue for the state. Popular Oklahoma tourist attractions include plentiful state parks, rodeos, Old West shows, and Native American exhibits.

Native Americans played an integral role in Oklahoma's early history. The name "Oklahoma" itself is derived from two Choctaw words: "okla" meaning people and "humma" meaning red. Oklahoma has been inhabited by Native Americans since at least 1200 AD. Explored by the Spanish in the sixteenth century and settled by the French in the seventeenth century,

Oklahoma was acquired by the United States in 1803 as part of the Louisiana Purchase. To open land for white settlers in the Atlantic states during the 1820s the federal government began relocating Native Americans from their homelands in the southeastern United States to the new Louisiana Territory west of the Mississippi. The most populous tribes inhabiting this area were the Choctaw, Chickasaw, Creek, Seminole, and Cherokee. Many of these Native Americans adopted European dress styles, farming methods, and political practices.

In the 1830s the federal government seized more land from Native Americans and created what was then called the Indian Territory, which included all of present-day Oklahoma as well as parts of Nebraska and Kansas. Tens of thousands of Native Americans were forcibly uprooted from their communities and driven into this newly created territory. Two-fifths of the uprooted Native Americans died along the way, while others suffered great hardship in what became known as the Trail of Tears.

During the American Civil War (1861–1865) the five tribes indigenous to Oklahoma signed treaties committing their support to the Confederate states. But the war left Oklahoma in ruins. Homes, land, and personal property were destroyed, creating widespread poverty and lawlessness. From the disorder, outlaws and bandits emerged, including the notorious Frank and Jesse James. In response to complaints about the growing tumult, the federal government built a district courthouse in Arkansas and appointed hundreds of U.S. marshals to quell the chaos.

The federal government also built a number of military posts that were designed to keep Native Americans on their reservations. (The Indian Territory had been reduced to the area of present-day Oklahoma after various tribes surrendered land as a condition for rejoining the Union.) Beginning in 1866 native peoples from several western states were relocated to reservations on the western half of the Indian Territory, while the five tribes were cramped into reservations on the eastern half. Skirmishes soon erupted when Native Americans left their reservations to hunt for food on white settlements in Texas and Kansas. U.S. troops were ordered to chase after the wayward Native Americans, beat them back to the reservations, and disarm them. During one particularly cruel military campaign in the winter of 1868, Colonel George Armstrong Custer led a Seventh Cavalry attack on an unsuspecting Cheyenne village near the banks of Oklahoma's Washita River. Custer's troops killed more than one hundred men, women, and children.

Treaties and federal laws further encroached upon the Indian Territory. In 1889 Congress opened 800,000 acres for settlement in the central Indian Territory known as "the Unassigned Lands." Promoters (called "Boomers") organized the settlers (called "Sooners") into communities of home seekers. On April 22, 1889, 50,000 Sooners lined up on the border of the Unassigned Lands, awaiting their signal to race across the unclaimed lots in search of property they wanted to settle. By nightfall nearly all of the available land was taken, and Oklahoma had a new nickname, the Sooner State. "Boomer Sooner," the University of Oklahoma's fight song, was also named after this page in the state's history.

The Native American population in Oklahoma was decimated by the influx of Sooners during the late nineteenth and early twentieth centuries. Native Americans comprised only 9 percent of Oklahoma's population at the time it was granted statehood in 1907, a stark contrast to their 27 percent of the pre-statehood population of 1890. African Americans, many of whom had been lured from other southern states by the promise of unsettled land in Oklahoma, comprised 10 percent of the state's population. They established more all-black towns in Oklahoma than the rest of the country combined.

Although African Americans were discriminated against in Oklahoma, as they were elsewhere in the country, the Oklahoma African American community served as a bellwether for the Civil Rights Movement. For example, African Americans in Oklahoma were among the first to successfully file lawsuits challenging the system of racial segregation in the South. These lawsuits, brought to court during the 1940s, foreshadowed the U.S. Supreme Court's groundbreaking 1954 decision in *Brown v. Board of Education*, which declared racial segregation in all public schools unconstitutional.

Oklahoma continued to act as a kind of national political and economic barometer for the remainder of the twentieth century. Relations between Native Americans in Oklahoma and the federal government seesawed during this time. The federal government teetered between periods when local tribes were encouraged to exercise greater authority over their internal affairs and periods when the federal government interfered with that authority. Oklahoma farmers enjoyed a boom in wheat prices that resulted from massive grain sales to the Soviet Union in the 1970s, but suffered a swoon when the prices began to fall in the 1980s. The Oklahoma petroleum industry also mirrored that pattern as it watched gas prices skyrocket during the OPEC oil embargo of the 1970s, but then saw oil-industry jobs disappear as prices dropped a decade later.

Near the end of the century Oklahoma became the site of the most deadly terrorist act in U.S. history. On April 19, 1995, 168 people died in Oklahoma City when a bomb exploded inside a rental truck parked outside the Alfred P. Murrah Federal Building. Timothy McVeigh was convicted of 11 counts of conspiracy and murder for his part in the bombing, while Terry Nichols was found guilty of conspiracy and involuntary manslaughter. Prosecutors portrayed the defendants as right wing, anti-government extremists who sought revenge for the federal government's destruction of the Branch Davidian compound in Waco, Texas. McVeigh was sentenced to death and Nichols to life in prison.

See also: **Native American Policy**

FURTHER READING

''Oklahoma Government Information Server,'' [cited May 25, 1999] available from the World Wide Web @ www.state.ok.us/.

''Oklahoma Is Home Of Indian.'' *Daily Oklahoman*, April 25, 1993.

Schumacher, Krista. ''Exhibit Leads Tour of Oklahoma's Indian History.'' *Tulsa World*, September 21, 1994.

''State of Oklahoma,'' [cited May 25, 1999] available from the World Wide Web @ www.surfinok.com/okhistor.htm/.

Worldmark Encyclopedia of the States. Detroit: Gale Research, 1998, s.v. ''Oklahoma.''

OLD NORTHWEST

The Old Northwest is another name for the Northwest Territory—the region around the Great Lakes and between the Ohio and Mississippi rivers. Consisting of about 248,000 square miles (642,000 square kilometers), the territory was acquired by the United States after its victory in the American Revolution (1775–1783). Britain ceded the region in the Treaty of Paris of 1783, which ended the fighting, and the region officially became known as the Territory Northwest of the River Ohio. (Eastern seaboard states also claimed parts of the territory, but those claims were settled by the late 1700s.)

Development of territory was helped by the completion of New York's Erie Canal in 1825. The east-west waterway ran from Albany to Buffalo, connecting the Hudson River (which flows into the Atlantic Ocean) to Lake Erie (one of the Great Lakes). The canal linked the Old Northwest with the established states to the east and promoted the settlement of the territory, mostly by farmers.

Steamboats (invented in 1807) and railroads (introduced to the United States in 1831) also encouraged development of the region. Pittsburgh, Cincinnati, Louisville, Detroit, and Chicago became commercial centers. Out of the Old Northwest the states of Ohio (admitted as a state 1803), Indiana (1816), Illinois (1818), Michigan (1837), and Wisconsin (1848) were created, and part of the former territory was used to form present-day Minnesota (1858).

See also: **Erie Canal, Expansionists, Illinois, Indiana, Michigan, Minnesota, Ohio, Railroads, Steamboats, Wisconsin**

OLD SOUTHWEST

The Old Southwest was the early name for the territories that were acquired by the United States from Spain in the Adams-Onis Treaty (also called the Transcontinental Treaty) of 1819. The region included present–day Florida and the southern parts of Alabama and Mississippi.

The Spanish who first colonized the Old Southwest referred to the region simply as East and West Florida. Unfortunately, the Spanish monarch had only a weak hold on the Floridas and many Americans had settled there. In 1811 U.S. settlers in West Florida rebelled and declared their independence. President James Madison (1809–1817) ordered the Governor of Orleans Territory (gained in the Louisiana Purchase of 1803) to take possession of West Florida. This action provided impetus for the U.S. government to claim the East Florida territory, which would allow the country to organize all its territory east of the Mississippi River.

Negotiations between Spain and the United States were led by John Quincy Adams (1767–1848), the U.S. Secretary of State, and Luis de Onis (1762–1827), Spain's Minister to the United States. Though the United States gained the Old Southwest, it also made some concessions to Spain in establishing the boundary between Spanish and American claims from Texas to the Pacific Ocean. The treaty was signed in Washington, D.C., in 1819 and was approved by the governments of both countries two years later. Plantation owners largely settled the Old Southwest during the 1800s. Later the region became the state of Florida (admitted to the Union in 1845) and formed parts of what would become Alabama (1819) and Mississippi (1817).

See also: **Adams-Onis Treaty, Alabama, Florida, Louisiana Purchase, Mississippi, Mississippi River**

OLIGOPOLY

Oligopoly is a type of market structure where a few large suppliers dominate an industry. Oligopolies are neither purely competitive (with many producers) nor monopolistic (with one producer), but fall somewhere in between. In the United States there are plenty of examples of oligopolist industries (in which only a small number of firms dominate). Heading the list are the following industries: automobile, steel, rubber, copper, aluminum, tobacco, and breakfast cereal. Oligopolist industry products may be differentiated, as with cereals, or homogeneous, as with steel.

In some oligopolies one firm tends to be the price leader, such as U.S. Steel Company in the steel industry. In others, all firms may have similar power. It is generally very difficult for a new firm to break into an oligopoly market because of the huge initial investments required. When only a few large firms dominate the market they cannot act independently without causing a change in output, sales, and prices in the industry as a whole. Where only a few large competitive rivals exist, their interdependence is recognized. They strategize to better anticipate each other's decisions. Competition among oligopolies usually does not include price wars (which would damage potential for generating profit). While price fixing is outlawed, oligopolistic firms keep their prices close together and instead compete with advertising and product variation. Advertising is a means to gain a competitive advantage. By making the product's availability better known, demand for the product is increased along with sales. Product variation results in continuous expansion and redefinition of products. Oligopolists are always seeking the best-selling new model. The automobile industry is a classic example.

The United States economy has traditionally consisted of four industry types: purely competitive, oligopolies, monopolistic competitors, and monopolies. Monopolistic competitors compete for essentially the same customers with slightly differing products. Between the four industry types, in 1939 oligopolies contributed a 36 percent share of the national income while purely competitive firms accounted for 52 percent. By 1958 oligopolies still contributed a 35 percent share but by 1980 they accounted for only an 18 percent share of the national income with purely competitive firms accounting for a 76 percent share. The U.S. economy became more competitive over the years due to increased competition from imports, deregulation, and enforcement of antimonopoly laws.

OPEC OIL EMBARGO

On October 17, 1973, Arab oil producers declared an embargo that drastically limited the shipment of oil to the United States. These producers, members of a cartel known as the Organization of Petroleum Exporting Countries (OPEC), enforced the embargo in response to the Yom Kippur War between Egypt and Israel. In a gesture of support for Egypt OPEC curtailed oil exportation to countries that supported the Israelis. The cartel later extended the embargo to other countries and oil prices soared worldwide. Accustomed to the influx of ample, inexpensive petroleum from OPEC member countries such as Saudi Arabia, Iraq, Iran, and Kuwait, many nations remained at the mercy of these producers of the valuable natural resource.

In the United States the embargo brought on a crisis of unequaled proportions. Daily shipments of oil from the Middle East dropped from 1.2 million barrels to a scant 19,000 barrels. Motor vehicle owners faced long lines at the service stations, and were forced to pay dearly for gasoline when they finally took their turn at the pump. Between May 1973 and June 1974 the average price of gasoline increased by 43 percent. Perhaps the most dangerous effect of the embargo however was the fear and panic it aroused. U.S. citizens were suddenly faced with the shortage of a resource indispensable to every industrialized nation. The shortage was mainly a matter of perception, since OPEC simply withheld oil and had not run out of it. In fact at the time the United States imported only about a third of the oil it used, relying on domestic production for the majority of its supply. But the embargo proved that every drop counted and that a powerful cartel could bring the world to its knees. Daily hardships such as rising oil prices and rates of inflation made the perceived scarcity of the resource seem very real.

Indeed the United States was consuming resources faster and more voraciously than most other countries. Although it represented only six percent of the world's population in 1973, the United States regularly consumed 33 percent of the world's energy supply. Station

Faced with a gasoline shortage during the oil embargo, many gas stations closed, leading to lines at functioning stations that sometimes stretched for blocks.

wagons and other gas-guzzlers were enjoying their heyday. A positive effect of the embargo was that it prompted conservation efforts throughout the country. President Jimmy Carter (1977–1981) declared a national speed limit of 55 miles per hour in order to cut back on gasoline consumption (meanwhile, the number of traffic-related deaths dropped considerably during that period). Between September 1973 and February 1974 the average daily use of petroleum dropped by more than six percent. The U.S. government adopted an energy conservation policy that remained in effect until President Ronald Reagan's (1981–1989) administration discarded it two decades later. The embargo served as a reminder that the world's oil supply was finite and encouraged consumers to use it responsibly, at least for the time being.

OPEC exercised an enormous amount of power during the embargo, which lasted well into 1974. But eventually the crisis hurt the cartel as much as the countries outside of it. The skyrocketing prices and the perceived shortage led to a drop in the overall demand for oil. Countries looked to alternative energy sources such as natural gas, nuclear energy, and coal. Oil-producing countries outside of the Middle East stepped up their pace of production and relied more heavily on their domestic supply.

Unfortunately many of the positive effects of the 1973 crisis, the attempts at energy conservation and the move toward relying more heavily on domestic resources, did not last long enough after the embargo was lifted. Conservation efforts dropped off as memories of long waits at the gas station and inflated prices faded. A new breed of larger, less gas-efficient cars took to the roads in the 1990s when sport-utility vehicles and small trucks gained popularity. In the 20 years following the crisis U.S. dependence on imported oil increased rather than decreased, reaching the 50 percent mark in 1993. In 1998 on the twenty-fifth anniversary of the embargo many analysts pointed to such statistics as indications that a crisis like that of 1973 could happen again. They claimed that the low, stable price of oil was misleading people in the United States into believing that the world's supply of the natural resource was unlimited. Meanwhile the nation continues

OPEC exercised an enormous amount of power during the embargo, which lasted well into 1974. But eventually the crisis hurt the cartel as much as the countries outside of it. The skyrocketing prices and the perceived shortage led to a drop in the overall demand for oil. Countries looked to alternative energy sources such as natural gas, nuclear energy, and coal.

to consume energy at an extraordinary rate. Whether or not it will take another economic crisis to change such ingrained behavior remains to be seen.

See also: **Embargo, Petroleum Industry**

FURTHER READING

Bode, Denise. "Twenty Years After OPEC Oil Embargo, United States at More Risk Than Ever." *The Oil Daily*, October 18, 1993.

Chalabi, Fadhil J. "OPEC: An Obituary." *Foreign Policy*, Winter 1997–1998.

Crow, Patrick. "Remembering the 1973 Oil Embargo." *The Oil and Gas Journal*, October 18, 1993.

"The Energy Embargo of 1973," [cited May 25, 1999] available from the World Wide Web @ www.nettally.com/palmk/nrgopec.html/.

Feldman, David Lewis. "Revisiting the Energy Crisis: How Far Have We Come." *Environment*, May 1995.

Foner, Eric, and John A. Garraty, eds. *The Reader's Companion to American History*. Boston: Houghton Mifflin Co., 1991.

OPEN DOOR POLICY

In 1890 the U.S. Bureau of the Census announced that the western frontier, as a continuous geographical line of settlement, had ceased to exist. This marked a monumental change in the way that Americans thought about their country. What had been an inexhaustible reservoir of natural resource and opportunity was now revealed to be finite and limited. The railroad system had been in the process of unifying the country since even before 1869, when construction was completed on the first transcontinental line. The miners and cattlemen and farmers followed. Now it was declared that the continental frontier had been pushed all the way to the western coast.

One of the first writers to discuss this event was the historian, Frederick Jackson Turner. Turner wrote that the significance of the frontier was immense. It had provided the natural framework for the American experiment with democracy. It had been a "safety valve" for discontent whenever times got too hard and class conflict emerged in the increasingly crowded eastern part of the country. The loss of this safety valve might portend a crisis as profound as the struggle over slavery.

In addition, the increasing power and productivity of the American economy, which up to this point had been a source of pride and optimism, now seemed to increase the feeling of anxiety. The economy had become so productive at the same time that the polarization of wealth had become so marked that the domestic market was no longer sufficient to soak up all the goods that the economy was producing.

Another historian, Alfred Thayer Mahan, (who was also an admiral in the U.S. Navy), held onto the optimistic notion of frontier. He wrote that beyond the Pacific shores lay another maritime frontier. Mahan wrote in *The Influence of Sea-power upon History, 1660-1783* (1890) that all the great nations were sea-powers. In 1890, the United States was the third most powerful sea-power in the world.

By the late 1800s Japan and several powerful western European nations had divided most of China into separate "spheres of influence," each having economic control over a section of the vast eastern Asian country. A latecomer to imperialism, the United States also wanted its piece of the pie. In 1899 U.S. President McKinley's Secretary of State, John Hay, proposed an "Open Door" Policy with France, Germany, Great Britain, Italy, Japan, and Russia that would allow all participating nations to have equal tariff, trading, and commercial development rights in China.

IN 1899 U.S. SECRETARY OF STATE JOHN HAY PROPOSED AN OPEN DOOR POLICY TO FRANCE, GERMANY, GREAT BRITAIN, ITALY, JAPAN, AND RUSSIA THAT WOULD ALLOW ALL NATIONS TO HAVE EQUAL TARIFF, TRADING, AND COMMERCIAL DEVELOPMENT RIGHTS IN CHINA.

The United States declared that it intended to support China's political and territorial independence, while at the same time preserving and protecting foreign interests. Behind this claim was an administrative tactic to strengthen the U.S. position in China. The European powers agreed to the idea based on mutual consent between European nations but with the actual intent of protecting their own interests. Japan, however, objected to the proposal.

The machinations of the European powers over the Chinese trade offended many Chinese people. In 1900 an anti-European rebellion broke out in China fomented by a secret society called the "Boxers." It was directed against all foreigners in China. The foreign diplomatic corps of the European powers sought refuge in the British embassy in Peking. The Boxers surrounded the embassy and threatened to overwhelm the defenders. In August 1900 the U.S. sent in a rescue force of 2,500 troops and the diplomats were saved.

Secretary of State Hay sent a note to the European powers requesting an Open Door Policy for all European and U.S. powers in the whole of China. It turned out, however, that few countries, including the United States, would adhere to the policy in practice. Within a year economic issues turned political and the Open Door Policy would remain virtually ignored.

In the early twentieth century the United States became involved in an international rivalry for Manchuria and China proper. In order to secure railroad, mining, and commercial rights in those locations, the United States had to come to grips with its relationship to Japan and, to a lesser extent, to certain western European powers, particularly Russia. The Taft-Katsura Agreement and the Root-Takahira Agreement of 1908 demonstrated that the United States recognized Japan's increasing influence in the Far East. In return, the United States wanted Japan to respect Open Door principles and allow legitimate U.S. territorial rights within Asia. In 1915, in an attempt to protect its Far Eastern stakes, the United States opposed Japan's Twenty-one Demands on China; but with the Lansing-Ishii Agreement of 1917, the United States consented to Japanese ambitions in Manchuria.

In response to continuing violations of China's territory, an international Conference on the Limitations of Armament was held in Washington, D.C., and the Open Door Policy was reaffirmed as part of the 1922 Nine-Power Treaty. Ten years later, however, when Japan overtly defied the Open Door agreement by conquering Manchuria and establishing it as a puppet state, the United States was the only power to object.

Secretary of State Henry L. Stimson's doctrine of non-recognition, which was supported by the League of Nations, persuaded Japan to withdraw from Shanghai, its next target. The Japanese soon resumed their invasions and in November 1938 they declared that the Open Door was no longer valid. The onset of World War II (1939–1945) essentially ended the debate over the Open Door Policy, and after the war China's de facto position acknowledged it as an independent sovereign state. Thus the Open Door Policy ceased to exist.

See also: **Imperialism, Japan (Opening of)**

FURTHER READING

Dictionary of American History. New York: Charles Scribner's Sons, 1976, s.v. "Open Door Policy."

Foner, Eric, ed. and John A. Garraty, ed. *The Reader's Companion to American History.* Boston: Houghton Mifflin Company, 1991.

Johnson, Thomas H. *The Oxford Companion to American History.* New York: Oxford University Press, 1966.

Pomfret, Richard. *Investing in China: Ten Years of the Open Door Policy.* Ames, IA: Iowa State University Press, 1991.

Sung, Yun Wing. *The China-Hong Kong Connection: The Key to China's Open Door Policy.* Cambridge: Cambridge University Press, 1991.

OPEN RANGE

The open range consisted of the unfenced public lands of the West. When the cattle industry boomed following the American Civil War (1861–1865), ranchers in Texas, Colorado, Wyoming, South Dakota, North Dakota, and Montana allowed their cattle to roam freely across the vast range. Livestock were branded with a rancher's symbol. At the end of the grazing season cowboys sorted the cattle by brand (calves instinctively followed their mothers), rounded them up, and began the long trail drives which ended at the nearest railhead (as far as 1,000 miles or 1,600 kilometers away).

Passage of the Homestead Act in 1862 and the expansion of the railroad brought an ever–increasing number of settlers West after the war. Many of them set up farms on the prairies because provisions of the Homestead Act allowed each up to 160 acres (64 hectares). As the natural landscape lacked trees, fencing the farmlands was not practical and the policy of the open range continued despite the fact that the range was, in fact, being divided up and settled at an increasing rate. When barbed wire was invented in 1874, farmers across the West used the new material to fence in their lands over the two decades which followed.

Ranchers, who were accustomed to the open range, often conflicted with settlers, who tried to protect their farmlands from the cattle herds and drives. Soon ranchers, too, used barbed wire to cordon off their land, limiting where their cattle and sheep could graze. Cowboys were reduced to cowhands—hired hands who made a practice of ''riding the fence'' to maintain the ranch boundaries. By the end of the 1880s the innovation of barbed wire and increased settlement had closed the open range and tamed the wild West.

See also: **Barbed Wire, Chisholm Trail, Cowboy, Cow Town, Longhorn Cattle, Prairie**

OPPORTUNITY COST

An opportunity cost is a way of analyzing an economic decision to determine its real cost. For an accountant or for a consumer in the grocery store the cost of an item is the amount actually paid for the item—that is, its price. In economics, however, determining the real cost of an item or of an economic decision means taking into account the alternative uses that could be made of one's money. For example, a manager making $40,000 a year is considering whether the increase in salary she will get by earning a law degree will justify the cost of tuition, housing, and all her other living expenses at school. In making her decision, however, she must also include the $40,000 in salary per year she will not be able to earn while attending school. The lost salary together with the costs of tuition and living expenses is the real cost—the opportunity cost—of her law school decision. Similarly, suppose someone invests $10,000 in a stock that falls in value over a six-month period and then sells the stock as soon as it climbs back to the price he initially paid. The investor may feel like congratulating himself for being patient enough to wait until the stock regained its initial price before selling; after all, he ''broke even.'' In reality, however, since the investor could have invested the $10,000 in a stock that grew 20 percent over that same six-month period, he did not in fact ''break even''—he incurred an opportunity cost of $2,000.

THERE'S NO SUCH THING AS A FREE LUNCH.

Milton Friedman, Economist

The idea of opportunity costs was first defined by the neoclassicist economists of the nineteenth century, and today it finds application in the economic decision making of individual consumers, companies, and entire economies. In evaluating whether to make a particular investment, for example, a company will first determine what use of its available capital will provide the best return. For various reasons, the company may in the end decide not to invest its money in the option that offers the lowest opportunity cost. However, it will always know what the opportunity cost of each of its options is and whether that cost is growing or decreasing. The expression ''There's no such thing as a free lunch,'' popularized by American economist Milton Friedman (1912–), is another way of saying that every economic decision has hidden opportunity costs that must be taken into account to put money to its best use.

See also: **Milton Friedman, Price**

OREGON

The first European to sight Oregon may have been Sir Francis Drake (1540–1596), while he was on a British raiding expedition against the Spanish during the 1500s. Little contact was made during the next 200 years because mariners considered the Oregon coast too treacherous. In 1778, the Englishman Capt. James Cook (1728–1779) explored the Northwest. He named several of the Oregon capes. Explorers seeking sea otter and other furs soon followed. American Robert Gray (1755–1806) discovered the Columbia River in 1792.

The Lewis and Clark Expedition was the first overland exploration of Oregon, reaching the mouth of the Columbia in the winter of 1805. Fur traders employed by New York magnate John Jacob Astor (1763–1848) built a trading post at the mouth of the Columbia and called it Astoria.

The early history of Oregon was marked by competition between Great Britain and the United States for a foothold in the territory. The two countries signed a joint agreement of occupation in 1818. However from 1824 through the early 1840s John McLoughlin (1784–1857), chief official at Vancouver for the British Hudson's Bay Company, was governor in all but name. Protestant missionaries to the Native Americans, however, established a base for future U.S. settlement. The first of these came by wagon train over the famous Oregon Trail during the early 1840s. In 1843 a provisional government was formed, and in 1846 a treaty with Great Britain firmly established the boundary between the United States and Canada. The

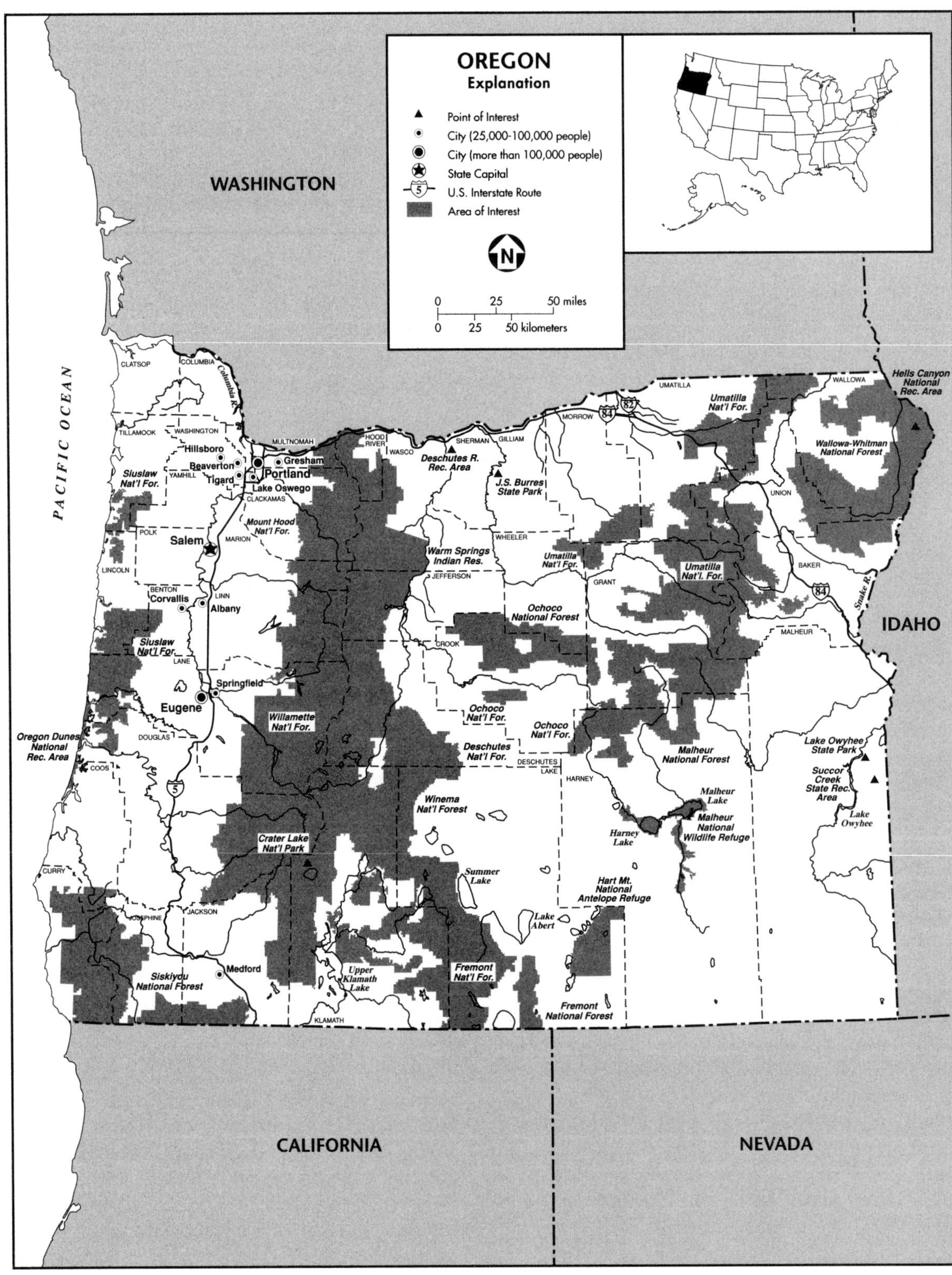

State of Oregon.

Oregon Territory was organized in 1848. It was originally much larger than the state as it exists today. Oregon became the 33rd state of the union in 1859.

[OREGON] HAS NO HISTORY OF ITS OWN, ONLY ENDS OF HISTORIES FROM OTHER PLACES; IT HAS NO COMPLETE LIVES, ONLY BEGINNINGS.

H.L. Davis, *Kettle of Fire*, 1959

Oregon's economic progress was slow until the first transcontinental railroad reached the state in 1883. The fur trade dominated the region up until that time. When the railroad was built, fur traders, who were tired of the rigors of their difficult trade, began to settle on farms. They settled particularly in the Tualatin Valley and in a region near present-day Salem. Most were French-Canadians who were married to Indian women. Others came north from the gold fields of California, including a number of Chinese who continued to seek gold in eastern Oregon. They also worked as salmon packers and farmhands but were best known for their role in completing the Oregon Central Railroad and other railroads.

The California Gold Rush of the 1850s provided the first real impetus to economic growth in the Northwest. The city of Portland grew rapidly as gold miners demanded lumber, flour, wheat, and beef. Portland provided easy access for ship captains, and the city built a rudimentary road to the wheat fields of the Tualatin Valley. Oregon's mountains together with the Columbia River blocked any rivals from providing this wheat through other means. Thus an important export market developed, along with the Northwest's first reliable currency, gold dust. Another gold rush in eastern Oregon brought even more prosperity. Sailing vessel and steamship companies prospered during this time.

Oregon also found ready markets for the salmon taken out of the Columbia River. Lumber and paper industries as well as textile mills began to develop along the Columbia and the Willamette rivers.

Much of the economy remained agricultural because railroads and improved roads were slow in coming to Oregon. Wheat was the most important crop, followed by oats and potatoes. Cattle, horses, pigs, and sheep were the most important livestock. Towns such as The Dalles, Princeville, Klamath Falls, and Pendleton arose to serve the farm market. Before the coming of the Pacific Northwest railroad Oregon was essentially a purveyor of raw materials, with few finished goods being produced there.

By the 1890s several railroads crisscrossed Oregon. Raw materials could now flow to the ocean more efficiently and immigration to the region increased. Consumer goods, farm machinery, and construction materials were now readily available from the East to supply the growing farms and cities. Lumbermen and farmers could compete with those in other sections of the country. The Northern Pacific Railroad and the Great Northern Railroad also had vast publicity bureaus that sent pamphlets to the East, encouraging emigration. The railroad also changed economic patterns. The tracks broke up large cattle ranges and helped to destroy the cattle industry. Because wool was easier to transport by rail than beef, local residents soon preferred to raise sheep.

Waterways were also improved during this time, including canals along the Columbia to bypass falls and rapids. Lumbermen benefited from better water transit, from technological developments in their industry, and from the destruction of forests in the Great Lakes region.

During the 1920s Oregonians had to make adjustments as demand for certain materials declined after World War I (1914–1918). Lumber mills also suffered from a lack of supply because wartime cutting had decimated the forests. Congress acted quickly to pass the Clarke-McNary and McSweeney-McNary acts. The acts provided a model for future federal efforts to conserve forests.

Other changes during the 1920s were related to transportation improvements. Shipping continued to increase because of the Panama Canal. The railroads began to lose business as better roads were built. Oregon had created its first highway department in 1913 and built the Columbia River Highway along the river's south bank.

The 1930s saw a downturn in the economy as a depression rocked the country. After the 1929 stock market crash, lumber companies lost most of their markets but slowly regained strength. However the fishing industry never quite recovered from the market collapses which sent many fishermen to the relief rolls. President Franklin D. Roosevelt's (1933–45) New Deal programs, especially the Wagner Act, encouraged union organizing. Portland experienced a crippling strike by the International Longshoremen's Association in 1934. In the spring of 1935 the Sawmill and Timber Workers practically shut down the lumber industry in the Northwest. On a more positive note, the federal government's water conservation efforts during this period resulted in the construction of the Grand

Coulee and the Bonneville dams along the Columbia River.

World War II (1939–1945) brought much-needed relief to Oregon's failing economy. Portland shipbuilding in particular was a major beneficiary of wartime contracts. Construction entrepreneur Henry J. Kaiser (1882–1967) was the genius behind Portland's shipbuilding renaissance. He was the primary contractor on the Bonneville Dam project. Kaiser used his many contacts in Washington and with other construction interests to gain government contracts for the so-called Liberty ships. The ships were 441-foot long freighters that kept the Allies supplied throughout the war. Kaiser also built escort aircraft carriers, tankers, and Victory merchant ships.

The postwar years in Oregon were quite prosperous, with manufacturing and service industries expanding. Government was also heavily involved in water and forest conservation in the state. Farming changed drastically with the number of farms declining from 63,125 in 1945 to 36,000 in 1982. Large corporate farms using high technology methods began to dominate the economy. Oregon fisheries declined as the salmon supply became depleted, causing most of the state's canneries to be closed; the federal government rushed to supply fish eggs to hatcheries. The 1980s and 1990s were marked by a continuing debate between loggers and environmentalists over logging in Oregon's rainforests. A 1993 federal law helped prevent commercial exploitation of older forests, home of the threatened spotted owl. Despite attempts to diversify the state's economic base employment in manufacturing outside Portland was still mostly in the lumber and wood products field in the 1980s. This made the state increasingly vulnerable to fluctuations in the housing construction market.

In addition the trend toward conservation of the forests from commercial development continued into the 1990s. The total commercial land base decreased by more than 24 percent since 1945. While federal lands were increasingly being removed from timber-harvesting, private forests took on a more important role. The reforesting required since 1941 and the Forest Practices Act of 1971 helped replenish the timber supply. Timber still provided the largest percentage of shipments by manufacturers in the state.

The principal economic changes in Oregon since World War II have been in the development of the aluminum and electronics industries, as well as in tourism and the services industry. In 1994 unemployment stood at a 25-year low of five percent. Per capita income was over $22,000 in 1997, putting the state's ranking at 27 in the nation.

See also: **John Jacob Astor, Environmentalism, Liberty Ships, Lumber Industry, Henry J. Kaiser, Shipbuilding Industry**

FURTHER READING

Corning, Howard. *Dictionary of Oregon History*. Portland: Binfords and Morts, 1956.

Dodds, Gordon B. *The American Northwest: A History of Oregon and Washington*. Arlington Heights, IL: Forum Press, 1986.

———. *Oregon: A Bicentennial History*. New York: Norton, 1977.

Johansen, Dorothy, and Charles Gates. *Empire of the Columbia: A History of the Pacific Northwest*. 2nd ed. New York: Harper & Row, 1967.

Vaughan, Thomas, and Terrence O'Donnell. *Portland: A Historical Sketch and Guide*. Portland: Oregon Historical Society, 1976.

OREGON COUNTRY CESSATION

For thousands of years native peoples lived in the rich lands of North America's Pacific Northwest. The first known European presence in the region was in the sixteenth century as Spanish and English ships ventured northward from Mexico, looking for the mythical Northwest Passage. Not until the late eighteenth century, however, did European expansion in the region truly begin. In the mid-1770s Spanish ships sailed north from Lower California to determine the extent of Russian penetration in the region as they had moved along the southern Pacific Coast of modern Alaska and British Columbia. The British arrived with the voyages of captains James Cook in 1788 and George Vancouver shortly afterwards; U.S. Captain Robert Gray marked the first American presence in the West in 1788 as well. A lucrative fur trade began with furs acquired from the indigenous population and sold in the Orient for substantial profit.

By 1790 several European nations, Russia, Spain, Great Britain, and the United States asserted claims to the region. Following a dispute over fur-trapping rights along the Vancouver Island coast, Spain was the first to begin a withdrawal through the Nootka Sound Convention of 1790 with Britain. The settlement sought to open the region to British colonization.

> By January and February (of 1846) a new slogan, "Fifty-Four Forty or Fight," had stamped its irresistible alliteration on the public mind. The principal themes of extremist argument sprang from both the natural expansionist pride of the people and the more artificial fury of the Democratic press. One theme was defiance of England, the traditional enemy . . . The second theme was that of manifest destiny . . . A third theme was suspicion of . . . the plantation aristocracy (over the slavery issue).
>
> **David M. Pletcher, historian, 1973**

The coast was substantially charted starting in 1792, with Gray's important discovery—the mouth of the Columbia River. Having this information in hand, President Thomas Jefferson (1801–1809) dispatched the Lewis and Clark Expedition to explore the Pacific Northwest over land. They wintered near the mouth of the Columbia River in 1805–1806. The Expedition and Captain Gray's voyages provided a strong U.S. claim to the Oregon country. In 1811 Boston fur entrepreneur John Jacob Astor (1763–1848) established an American trading post at the mouth of the Columbia. However, the post traded hands to the British during the War of 1812 (1812–1814).

Vying for a crucial Pacific coast commercial position, the United States wanted to extend its northern boundary with Britain east of the Rocky Mountains along the 49th parallel, westward to the Pacific Ocean. The British demanded the Columbia River be the boundary. With these continuing rival claims, the Convention of 1818 uniquely arranged for joint-use between the United States and Britain. The joint-use region extended north of the 42nd parallel to near the 54 degree-40 minute parallel (54–40) and eastward to the Rocky Mountains crest, including modern-day Oregon, Washington, Idaho, British Columbia, and western Montana. Spain then relinquished any remaining claims north of the 42nd parallel to the United States through the Transcontinental Treaty of 1819. The treaty resolved all claims between the two nations from Florida westward across the continent. Russia, holding the weakest rights, was the next to bow out of its claim to the area south of the 54-40 line through separate treaties with the United States in 1824, and Great Britain in 1825. However, despite all the diplomacy, Britain held a monopoly over commerce in the entire region through most of the early nineteenth century. Americans attempted to penetrate that market but without success.

American-funded military exploration in the Northwest resumed in 1841. Lt. Charles Wilkes' naval party extensively explored the region, reporting on the great port promise of Puget Sound in western Washington. Lt. John C. Fremont (1813–1890) led an expedition over land in 1842–1843. Those few American settlers who had trickled into the region formed a Provisional Government in 1843, further creating antagonism between U.S. and British citizens in the region. Finally, with restlessness and feelings of manifest destiny (a popular notion of the day that supported U.S. expansion from the Atlantic to the Pacific coasts) quickly growing in the United States, the great migration began across the Oregon Trail in 1843, and "Oregon fever" swept the United States.

U.S. expansionism was a key issue in 1844 presidential election, in which James K. Polk (1845–1849) won, after exhorting desires for a unified continental nation. Though overall American attitudes were split over the question of Oregon, and extremists threatened force in the Oregon boundary dispute, adopting the slogan "Fifty-four forty or fight" in pressing for U.S. control of the entire region.

Following his election to the presidency Polk approached Britain in early 1845 with a compromise to finally split the two nations' claims by setting the boundary at the 49th parallel. Britain, however, balked, still demanding the Columbia River serve as the boundary. Polk hardened his stance, adopting the 54–40 position. Little progress in negotiations occurred through the remainder of 1845, but in 1846 Polk took the offensive again, threatening to terminate the 1818 joint-use agreement. Despite few U.S. citizens residing north of the Columbia River, Polk's assertion of new settlements south of the Columbia that contained over 5000 U.S. citizens by 1845 further validated U.S. claims. Britain, suffering domestic problems and also having moved their Northwest base to Vancouver Island, became more conciliatory to settlement. Anticipating war with Mexico, however, Polk backed off from the 54–40 claim despite bitter political opposition. Both parties finally agreed to the original compromise dividing the Oregon country along the 49th parallel, and they signed the Oregon Treaty in 1846. Britain retained navigation rights to the Columbia River, though, and its Fort Vancouver property. Not until 1872 was the boundary around the south end of Vancouver Island firmly resolved.

Assertion of national ownership of the Pacific Northwest by the United States, while largely ignoring

Native American claims, represented a major step in U.S. expansionism. The United States also annexed the Texas Republic in 1845 and together, with the Oregon cessation, extended the U.S. western boundary both to the south and to the Pacific Ocean establishing the nation's northern boundary. Heavy traffic over the Oregon Trail continued through the late 1840s and 1850s, totaling 53,000 people, leading to a strong agrarian economy. Statehood was granted to Oregon in 1859 and for Washington in 1889.

See also: **Lewis and Clark Expedition, Manifest Destiny, Oregon, Oregon Trail**

FURTHER READING

Fisher, Robin. *Vancouver's Voyage: Charting the Northwest Coast.* Seattle, WA: University of Washington Press, 1992.

Gibson, James R. *Farming the Frontier: The Agricultural Opening of the Oregon Country, 1786–1846.* Seattle, WA: University of Washington Press, 1986.

McCabe, James O. *The San Juan Boundary Question.* Toronto: University of Toronto Press, 1964.

Schwantes, Carlos A. *Pacific Northwest: An Interpretive History.* Lincoln, NB: University of Nebraska Press, 1996.

———, ed. *Encounters with a Distant Land: Exploration and the Great Northwest.* Moscow, ID: University of Idaho Press, 1994.

OREGON TRAIL

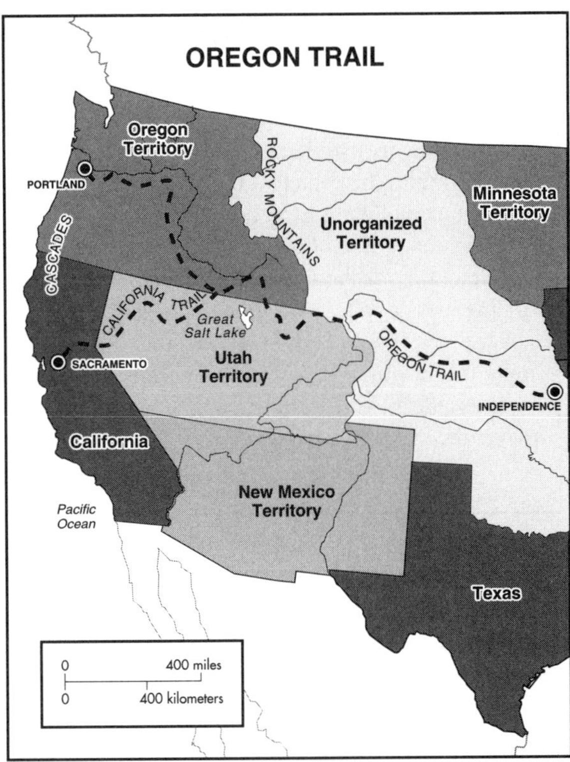

The Oregon Trail originated in Independence, Missouri, and terminated in Portland, Oregon. This 2000 mile trail was the primary passage of settlers from late 1840s through 1870s.

The Oregon Trail was a route used primarily from the late 1840s through the 1870s to reach Oregon Territory—lands that were ceded to the United States by the British in 1846. (The territory comprised present-day Oregon, Idaho, Washington, and parts of Montana and Wyoming.) Measuring 2,000 miles (3,200 kilometers), the trail was one of the great overland routes used in westward expansion. Wagon trains began at Independence, Missouri (today an eastern suburb of Kansas City, Missouri), and traveled northwest to Fort Kearny (near present-day Kearney), Nebraska. From there wagons followed the Platte and North Platte rivers west and northwest to Fort Laramie in southeast Wyoming. Continuing westward along the North Platte, travelers arrived at South Pass, located on the southeastern end of the Rocky Mountains' Wind River Range. Nearby South Pass City became a boomtown during the 1800s. The Oregon Trail then ran southwest to Fort Bridger, Wyoming—where the Mormon Trail diverged to the southwest (into Utah). Travelers bound for the Pacific Northwest continued along the Oregon Trail, following the Snake River through Idaho. The route turned northwest to Fort Boise, Idaho. From there settlers made the difficult crossing through the Blue Mountains to Walla Walla (then the site of a mission) in Washington. The last leg of the journey followed the Columbia River west to Fort Vancouver and into the Willamette Valley of Oregon. The road could be traversed in six months' time, but it was a rigorous journey that took travelers across prairie, through desert, over mountains, and across flooded rivers.

Explorers and fur traders are credited with first forging the route. The western portion of the trail was covered by explorers Meriwether Lewis (1774–1809) and William Clark (1770–1838) in their 1804–1806 expedition to the Pacific. But it did not become heavily used by wagons until about 1842, the same year that military officer and future politician John C. Fremont (1813–1890) surveyed a portion of the route for the U.S. Army. After the Territory of Oregon was set up by the U.S. government in 1848, an increasing number of settlers made their way westward across the winding Oregon Trail. The route was heavily used through the

1860s. However, at the completion of transcontinental railroads its importance diminished by the end of the century.

See also: **John Fremont, Idaho, Lewis and Clark Expedition, Montana, Missouri, Nebraska, Oregon, Santa Fe Trail, Transcontinental Railroad, Utah, Washington, Wyoming**

OTIS ELEVATOR COMPANY, INC.

By 1852 vertical hoisting devices had long been in use. However these had been proven hazardous if the supporting cable snapped. That year Elisha Graves Otis, a mechanic from Yonkers, New York, invented a safety hoist that would change the future of such devices. With two orders for elevators Otis started his own factory in September 1853. By the end of 1856 he had filled more than 40 orders for freight elevators. Within the next year Otis installed his first passenger elevator in a multi-storied retail building in New York. Otis died in 1861, severely in debt.

Otis' sons Charles and Norton took over their father's business, renaming it Otis Brothers and Co. Their collective work produced 53 patents for elevator design and safety features. By 1872 the company produced more than 2,000 steam-powered elevators and grossed over one million dollars in sales. In 1878 Otis produced a faster, cheaper hydraulic elevator. The electric-powered elevator replaced this model in 1889. At the same time Otis first exhibited the escalator at the 1900 Paris Exposition. The early 1900s saw the production of the first gearless-traction elevator. This design remained essentially unchanged even at the end of the twentieth century.

The merger of Otis Brothers and Company with 14 other elevator companies resulted in the creation of the Otis Elevator Company. This incorporation proved so successful that in 1902 the company purchased overseas firms and strengthened its monopoly of the market. By 1912 Otis had seven factories within the United States, and by 1924 it owned subsidiaries in Canada, Belgium, Italy, and Germany. In order to compensate for the lost revenues suffered during the recessions, Otis started selling service and maintenance contracts for all its installations. The company's net income rose to $8.4 million in 1929, falling sharply with the advent of the Great Depression (1929–1939).

Constant improvements in design marked the first third of the twentieth century. Features such as a self-leveling device allowing the platform to stop exactly at each floor and a push-button system increased the sales and reputation of the Company. World War II (1939–1945) generated further business for Otis, not only with orders for elevators but for range finders and tank and aircraft engine components as well. These military contracts continued to be profitable during the Korean War, accounting for approximately one-quarter of its business in 1953.

In 1948 Otis introduced the Autotronic System for commercial contracts. These systems utilized electronic controls to operate the cars while a computer directed and handled the traffic accordingly. These systems became popular because of their speed and efficiency. By 1956 the job of elevator attendant had become obsolete as more and more companies were converting from manual to automatic systems.

In spite of these developments the decade following World War II proved to be a period of stagnation for the company. The trend in architectural design towards single-story shopping centers and ranch-style homes changed the sales environment. To compensate Otis turned to diversification in order to generate income. Purchasing outside acquisitions such as electronic pilot trainers, automatic bowling pin-setters, and forklift trucks generated little profit. Between 1955 and 1968 Otis' net sales quadrupled to $481 million, but its net income rose only from $11.9 million to $22.1 million.

In 1968 Otis installed 255 elevators and 71 escalators in New York's new World Trade Center. At this time the company controlled half of the U.S. elevator market. Refusing to accept a deteriorating sales picture, Otis acquired five companies involved in materials handling. In 1969 the company created its Diversified Systems Division to apply elevator and escalator technology to warehouses, automobile parking, and container handling systems. Further advances in design and manufacturing of horizontal moving systems produced the "Trav-O-Lator" and Odyssey models for transporting people quickly and comfortably.

By 1973 Otis surpassed $800 million in sales while maintaining plants in 17 countries. Its overseas operations accounted for 37 percent of its annual income. Overall Otis' share of the elevator market increased from 19 percent to 30 percent. The backlog of orders in March 1973 reached an all time high totaling $1.1 billion.

In October 1975 United Technologies Corporation (UTC) purchased 55 percent of Otis' stock in order to reduce its dependence on military contracts. This agreement did not hinder Otis' growth as a UTC subsidiary, with sales continuing to grow during the last decades of the twentieth century. The unveiling of the Elevonic 101 system in 1979 brought design and engineering break-throughs. This system boasted the first control system using microprocessors to control every aspect of the elevator operation. The Elevonic 401, produced in 1981, utilized synthesized speech, information display, and advanced security systems. These elevator systems benefited from the continued development of computer technology in the late twentieth century.

By the mid-1990s Otis' major manufacturing plants included facilities in the United States, Mexico, Brazil, Great Britain, France, Germany, Italy, Spain, the Czech Republic, Russia, Japan, China, India, Taiwan, Malaysia, and Australia. Otis revenue of $4.64 billion accounted for 22 percent of UTC's total revenue. Otis also held 23 percent of the world market in 1994 and was selling approximately 39,000 elevators and escalators per year. Two-thirds of its 66,000 employees had averaged 15 years of company experience and typically held the position of field installer and mechanic. With a vision for future development and growth in the world of transportation technology Otis invested more than $100 million in engineering, research, and development in 1994.

FURTHER READING

Drain, Sharon Cramer. ''A Mechanic Gave the World a Lift.'' *American History Illustrated*, November 1987.

International Directory of Company Histories, vol. 13. Farmington Hills, MI: The Gale Group, 1996, s.v. ''Otis Elevator Company, Inc.''

Jackson, Donald Dale. ''Elevating Thoughts from Elisha Otis and Fellow Uplifters.'' *Smithsonian*, November 1989.

Pinder, Jeanne B., ''Fuzzy Thinking Has Merits When It Comes to Elevators.'' *New York Times*, September 22, 1993.

Smart, Tim. ''UTC Gets a Lift from Its Smaller Engines.'' *Business Week*, December 20, 1993.

OVER-THE-COUNTER SECURITIES MARKET

An over-the-counter (OTC) securities market is a secondary market through which buyers and sellers of securities (or their agents or brokers) consummate transactions. Secondary markets (securities markets where previously issued securities are re-traded) are mainly organized in two ways. One is to form an organized exchange, where buyers and sellers of securities (mostly represented by their agents or brokers) meet at a central place to conduct their transactions. The New York Stock Exchange (NYSE), the American Stock Exchange (ASE, located in New York) and the Chicago Board of Trade for Commodities are examples of major organized exchanges in the United States.

An over-the-counter securities market provides an alternative way of organizing a secondary market—in this, dealers with inventories of securities at different geographical locations are in contact with each other through a computer network. In other words, these dealers of securities are ready to buy or sell securities over the counter to anyone who contacts them and accepts their quoted price. One may thus describe an over-the-counter securities market as an electronic market. The National Association of Securities Dealers Automated Quotations System (NASDAQ) is an example of an over-the-counter securities market in the United States.

***See also:* NASDAQ, New York Stock Exchange, Stock Market**

OVERMAN ACT

In 1918 the Overman Act was passed by Congress, in the midst of World War I (1914–1918). It gave President Woodrow Wilson (1913–1921) power to coordinate government agencies for the war effort. The legislation was sponsored by Democratic Senator Lee Slater Overman (1854–1930) of North Carolina.

The emergency powers of the executive office have, at times, been a controversial issue in the political life of the nation. A 1973 Senate report on the subject explained that ''American political theory of emergency government was derived . . . from John Locke (1632–1704), the English political–philosopher whose thought influenced the authors of the Constitution (who) argued that the threat of national crisis unforeseen, sudden, and potentially catastrophic required the creation of broad executive emergency powers.'' Locke reasoned that since the lawmaking power (Congress) is not always assembled and it is ''too numerous, and so too slow'' in dispatching procedures and remedies, latitude must be given to the executive power during times of national emergency. The Senate report described Wilson as the ''model for future Presidents and their advisors.'' While the urgent and pressing matters of the war required Wilson to expand his authority, he also sought congressional approval for his actions.

President Wilson was reluctant to become involved in the war in Europe. However, after German attacks on the American merchant marine in 1917, he resigned himself to U.S. engagement in the conflict. On April 2 Wilson made a special trip to the Capitol where he addressed Congress. He asked them to declare war, saying, "the world must be made safe for democracy." Congress met the pronouncement with applause and on April 6 it passed a joint resolution declaring war on Germany. Wilson immediately mobilized for the fight, organizing a variety of defense and war agencies. In 1917 he set up the War Industries Board but Republicans in Congress pressed for the establishment of a war cabinet instead. Wilson pressed back by asking the lawmakers to grant him comprehensive economic power. These powers were conferred upon the president by the Overman Act, passed April 1918. By that time Wilson had already given the War Industries Board broad authority, but congressional approval was, nevertheless, critical in unifying government during wartime. When the fighting was over (Germany surrendered to the Allies in November 1918), President Wilson promptly relinquished his emergency powers and asked Congress to repeal the wartime emergency statutes, which it did.

OZONE LAYER

Ozone is a poisonous colorless gas with an acrid odor. Chemically, it is a variant of normal oxygen, except that ozone has three oxygen atoms per molecule rather than the two found in normal oxygen. There exists a layer of ozone occurring naturally six to thirty-one miles above the earth. This layer of ozone gas surrounding the earth protects living organisms at the earth's surface from the dangerous ultraviolet radiation of the sun. The ozone layer normally absorbs about 98 percent of the ultraviolet rays that continually shower the earth. In small amounts, ozone can be useful as a water disinfectant and a purifier. If, however, ultraviolet rays came to ground level through the shield of the ozone layer, there would be massive lethal consequences for wildlife, crops, vegetation, and profound life-threatening problems for human beings, including cancer and immune system damage.

In 1974 chemists F. Sherwood Rowland and Marle Molina found that chlorine from chlorofluorocarbon (CFC) molecules was capable of breaking down ozone in the ozone layer above the earth. There was evidence that industrial chemicals and chemical exhaust from jet airplanes, as well as large volcanic eruptions, severely threatened the upper atmosphere and the ozone layer. In 1974, when damage to the ozone layer first became apparent, the propellants in common aerosol spray cans were a major source of CFC emissions. CFC aerosols were banned in the United States by 1978, but CFC chemicals remained in widespread use as coolant agents in refrigerators and in air-conditioners as well as in cleaning solvents. During the last decades of the twentieth century there was only a gradual move to ban CFC chemicals from all refrigerant systems, forcing modern industry to deal with alternative systems to stabilize the ozone layer. The question of how much protection is necessary has continued to be a controversial political issue because necessary changes in industrial systems proved to be profoundly expensive. At some level, however, such expenditure is crucial to the existence of human life.

See also: **Environmentalism**

PACKERS AND STOCKYARDS ACT

In 1921, the result of an investigation by the Federal Trade Commission (FTC), Congress responded to gross abuses within the meat industry by passing the Packers and Stockyards Act. The legislation made the meat-packing industry and any related industry subject to federal regulation and gave the Secretary of Agriculture purview over stockyard markets and operators. The act prohibited price fixing (the practice of pricing below cost to eliminate a competitive product), price discrimination (the practice of setting different prices for different markets), and the apportionment of markets (the practice of dividing up markets). The legislation helped eliminate monopolies in the meat industry (combined with the 1905 prosecution of the ''Beef Trust'' in the case of *Swift and Company v. United States*). However, critics have charged that, like the tobacco industry, government regulation led to industry control by a handful of businesses.

See also: **Trust, Trust-Busting**

PALEO-INDIANS

Paleo-Indians were the first inhabitants of North America (''paleo means old in Greek). They were also known as Lithic Indians; the word ''lithic'' is derived from the Greek ''lithos'' meaning stone, a reference to the material from which they made their tools. They migrated from Asia across the Bering Strait, the waterway that separates Asia (Russia) from North America (Alaska). Scholars believe that during the Late Ice Age (known as the Pleistocene glacial epoch, which ended about 10,000 B.C.) land masses were exposed by a drop in sea level or that ice covered the strait, forming a natural bridge. As large game traveled across this bridge the Asian hunters followed in pursuit, arriving in North America as early as 50,000 B.C.. During the thousands of years that followed they continued their migration, spreading out across the Western Hemisphere. By 25,000 B.C. Paleo-Indians had begun crafting stone into spear points to be used as weapons. Archaeologists have therefore named Paleo-Indian groups for the different types of spear point they used such as Clovis or Folsom. When the number of large game, such as mammoth and mastodon, diminished and finally became extinct, the hunters turned to smaller prey such as deer and rabbits.

Paleo-Indians eventually settled in various post–Ice Age environments, including coastal regions, forests, mountains, and swamps. They adapted their lifestyles to their physical surroundings. Groups along the East Coast, for example, began to rely on the sea as a food source (in Virginia, ruins indicate that early peoples consumed a large amount of oysters). By about 2000 B.C. they began to cultivate plants, marking the transition to agricultural-based societies. Settlements became increasingly permanent. Between the years 500 and 1600 they developed ceramics, jewelry, and the bow and arrow, and began to focus on their spirituality.

When Europeans arrived in North and South America the native inhabitants they encountered were descendants of the Paleo-Indians. Ice Age nomads had settled as far east as Nova Scotia by 10,000 B.C.. There they were succeeded by the Micmac Indians, who in the early 1500s traded with French, Spanish, and Portuguese explorers.

See also: **Beringia, Clovis Point**

PANAMAL CANAL, BUILDING OF THE

After ten years of intensive construction, the Panama Canal was officially opened to shipping on August 14, 1914. In addition to a multitude of engineering challenges, the building of the Panama Canal survived

Foot Gate of Gatun Locks during the construction of the Panama Canal which reached completion August 14, 1914.

political turmoil and environment hazards. It is considered by many historians to be one of the world's greatest engineering accomplishments. Led by a group of American engineers, the completion of the canal fulfilled the dream of a shorter shipping lane between the Atlantic and Pacific oceans.

In 1534 King Charles I of Spain introduced the concept of a Central American canal. The Spanish government was eager to find a sea route between the two oceans that would allow them to ship the gold and silver mined along the Pacific coast of their South American colonies. Land travel to the Atlantic seaports was significantly hampered by the mountainous terrain and muddy jungle trails. The king commissioned a study of the Isthmus of Panama region to determine the feasibility of constructing a water passageway. The local Spanish governor, however, dismissed the survey, and nothing was done.

The discovery of gold in California in the late 1840s revived interest in a canal between the Atlantic and Pacific oceans. The Gold Rush of 1849 stimulated a massive migration of settlers from the eastern and Midwest regions of the United States to California. Many of these settlers traveled by sea along the Atlantic coast, crossed the Isthmus of Panama on foot, and completed their journey to California by ship along the Pacific coast. The momentum for a canal was intensified when the American government finished a railroad across the Isthmus of Panama in 1855.

By then the United States and England had already began surveying routes for a canal in Nicaragua and Panama. In 1850 the two countries signed the Clayton-Bulwer Treaty, which stated the canal would not fall under the control of either country upon its completion. During the Spanish-American War (1898) the United States recognized the need for a sea lane that would allow its fleet to pass from the Pacific to Atlantic Oceans. The United States focused its efforts on gaining full control of the proposed canal and convinced England to waive their claim by signing the Hay-Pauncefote Treaty in 1901.

CONSTRUCTION OF THE 40-MILE LONG CANAL LASTED 10 YEARS. TWO HUNDRED AND FORTY MILLION CUBIC YARDS OF EARTH WERE DUG UP—THE EQUIVALENT AMOUNT OF EARTH NEEDED TO CONSTRUCT 70 EGYPTIAN PYRAMIDS.

The Hay-Herran Treaty of 1903 between Colombia and the United States gave the United States a 10-mile wide strip of land across the Isthmus of Panama. In exchange, the United States would pay $10 million and an annual payment of $250,000 to the Colombian government. Although Congress ratified the treaty, the Colombian government rejected it in hopes of receiving a higher payment.

Its recalcitrance angered many Panamanian business owners, and the local canal supporters began a successful revolution against Colombia. The United States, which had indirectly supported the revolution, immediately recognized the new government and signed the Hay-Bunau-Varilla Treaty with the Republic of Panama in 1904. This treaty included all the provisions that the initial treaty offered to Columbia, but it also provided the United States with a renewable 99-year lease.

The construction of the canal was actually begun in 1882 by a French company led by Ferdinand de Lesseps, who in 1869 had successfully constructed the Suez Canal. After a disastrous seven years of work, the company went bankrupt. Diseases such as yellow fever and malaria took the lives of 22,000 workers.

Twenty years later the United States was determined not to repeat Lesseps' failures. Although the United States was granted ownership of the canal zone in 1904, actual construction did not begin for another two and a half years.

In this interval, Colonel William Gorgas (1854–1920) made a significant contributions to the future construction effort by improving disease prevention. In 1891 Dr. Ronald Ross, a British army surgeon, found that certain types of mosquitoes transmitted malaria through their bites. A similar discovery was made by Dr. Walter Reed, an American army surgeon, who traced the source of yellow fever to the bite of a specific type of mosquito. Colonel Gorgas, who was chief sanitary officer in Havana, used these new medical discoveries to develop detailed sanitary procedures that greatly enhanced resistance to tropical diseases. Gorgas ordered breeding grounds for mosquitoes, like ponds, swamps, and lakes, to be drained or covered with oil to prevent the mosquito's eggs from hatching. Screened windows and doors were installed on all buildings. By the time the canal's construction began in 1906, yellow fever had been eliminated from Panama. Gorgas' methods were also successful at combating malaria, although the process was much slower compared to the conquest of yellow fever. By 1914 only seven workers had died from disease. Colonel Gorgas' guidelines and the medical research on which they were based saved the lives of countless workers and helped ensure the success of the canal's engineering efforts.

President Theodore Roosevelt (1901–1909) established the Isthmian Canal Commission to lead the construction project and he appointed John F. Stevens as the Commission's chief engineer. The project's organizational efforts were extremely demanding because of the scope and size of the construction efforts. The Commission recruited qualified workers from all over the world. Buildings were erected to house the workers; facilities were built to store heavy-duty earth moving equipment, which was shipped to the area from all corners of the globe. The ten-mile wide canal zone established a government with jurisdiction over its own police force and court system. When chief engineer Stevens resigned from the project in 1907, President Roosevelt appointed Colonel G.W. Goethals (1858–1928). Under Colonel Goethals the leadership of the construction efforts shifted from independent contractors to the United States Army Corp of Engineers.

Construction of the 40-mile long canal lasted ten years. Two hundred and forty million cubic yards of earth were dug up—the equivalent amount of earth needed to construct 70 Egyptian pyramids. More than 100 steam shovels were used and thousands of workers survived landslides, heavy rains, and an earthquake. The construction of the canal was completed on October 10, 1913, at a cost of $380 million. The canal was officially opened on August 15, 1914.

By 1964 Congress went on record in favor of establishing a new treaty to govern control of the canal. Relations between the United States and Panama were shaken during the 1960s, when Panamanians voiced their anger at the initial terms of Panama's treaty with the United States. Riots occurred and anti-American resentment continued to fester throughout Panama. In 1977 President Jimmy Carter (1977–1981) signed two treaties with the government of Panama. On October 1, 1979, the Canal Zone ceased to exist as a formal U.S. entity, and the area was returned to Panamanian civil authorities. The United States and Panama share control over the canal itself until December 31, 1999, when Panama becomes the sole proprietor.

See also: **Spanish-American War**

FURTHER READING

Forner, Eric and John A. Garraty. *The Reader's Companion to American History*. Boston: Houghton Mifflin Company, 1991.

Luxner, Larry. ''A Canal Makes History.'' *Americas (English Edition)*, August 1998.

Posey, Carl A. "The Bittersweet Memory that was the Canal Zone." *Smithsonian*, November 1991.

———. *Compton's Encyclopedia and Fact-Index.* Chicago, IL: Compton's Learning Company, 1997.

Panama Canal Commission. "Panama Canal History Overview; History of the Canal" [cited April 22, 1999] available from the World Wide Web @ www.pancanal.com/.

PANAMA CANAL TREATY

On November 18, 1903, the United States and the then new Republic of Panama signed the Hay-Bunau-Varilla Treaty, granting the United States exclusive control over a 10-mile strip across the Isthmus of Panama. This gave the United States control of the Panama Canal, a lock-type man-made channel connecting the Atlantic and Pacific Oceans across the isthmus. The canal is about 51 miles long, from the deep water of the Atlantic to the deep water of the Pacific. The United States paid $10 million and agreed to pay an annuity of $250,000 to Panama, which became a virtual protectorate of the United States. Because Panama had been a part of Colombia prior to its becoming a protectorate of the United States, the United States compensated Colombia for its loss with the signing of the Thomson-Urrutia Treaty in 1914. In 1921 Colombia was paid $25 million when this treaty was finally ratified in Congress. The Hay-Bunau-Varilla Treaty of 1903 gave the United States the right to build and operate the canal, and it awarded the United States sovereign rights of over five miles of territory on either side of the waterway and area known as the Canal Zone. In 1936 the original treaty was voided by the Hull-Alfaro Treaty, which ended the eminent domain provisions of the original treaty and raised the annual annuity to Panama to $430,000. In 1955 the Eisenhower-Remon Treaty further modified the original treaty to increase the annuity once again and to include building of a bridge over the Canal (finished in 1962). In 1977, because of ongoing rioting in Panama, a final treaty amendment was signed between the United States and Panama. The treaty now stated that control of the canal would revert to the Panamanians by the year 2000, giving Panama exclusive control of all the international ship-traffic passing through the canal yearly, including commercial vessels loaded with cargo.

See also: **Panama Canal (Building of)**

PANIC OF 1819

Financial panics have been known since the introduction of modern capitalism in the eighteenth century. Excessive speculation in the stock of a European colonizing company in 1720 led to a panic in France and England. In North America the newly formed United States quickly began experiencing the financial business cycles of booms and crises. A business boom driven by optimism over the nation's future immediately followed victory in the American Revolution (1775–1783), however, economic crises soon followed. Business over-expansion, personal extravagance in spending, the end of military contracts that had inflated prices, and an inability of the United States to establish a treaty regulating trade with Britain, led to widespread debt in the aftermath of the war. British textile products flooded the U.S. market causing domestic agricultural and industrial prices to substantially drop.

Distrust for any form of centralized government activity also pervaded the largely agrarian society. Yet the lack of a centralized government allowed an unsound money system to come into existence which destabilized foreign trade. The stage was set for the financial panic in 1785.

The establishment of a centralized federal government in the 1787 Constitutional Convention brought back optimism for economic prosperity. To institutionalize economic stability in the young country, Congress created the Bank of the United States in 1791. The Bank instantly became not only the largest bank in the nation, but the largest corporation at the time. Functioning as both a commercial and central bank, its chief political objective was to regulate lending practices of state banks. The state banks were issuing their own paper money in the form of bank notes with the promise they could be exchanged for gold or silver coins upon request. The central bank, though effective in achieving its goals, attracted substantial opposition. Western agrarian communities demanded an inflated money system, opposed by the National Bank, to keep agricultural prices high and to pay off debts with cheap money. Responding to public dissatisfaction over the centralized power of the Bank, Congress allowed its charter to expire in 1811. With the National Bank gone, state banks expanded quickly and returned to the practice of issuing paper notes.

The problems associated with the national debt from the War of 1812 (1812–1814) led to chartering of a Second Bank of the United States in 1816. This again attracted the ire of the small farmers. Following victory in the War of 1812 western land speculation rose sharply. State banks and even some branches of the

> Nicholas) Biddle inherited a bank (Second Bank of the United States) whose previous leaders had proved incapable of their tasks. William Jones, the first president, had . . . been a political choice; he was a man who knew nothing of banking, and to make things worse, was venal as well. During his years as president, the bank caused distress in all parts of the country through speculation on the part of its leaders . . . and unwise loan policies. After a Congressional investigation, Jones resigned, and was replaced in 1819 by Langdon Cheves . . . (who) was determined to put the (Bank's) affairs in order, and to do so called in many loans and advances. The result was . . . the abrupt end of a period of wildcatting.
>
> **Robert Sobel, Historian, 1969**

U.S. Bank encouraged the wave of speculation. However, fewer gold coins and silver dollars were in circulation, and currency speculators were hoarding the specie (gold or silver). As a consequence such coin was used primarily for large transactions, bank reserves, and foreign payments. Domestic land and commodity speculation was commonly in the form of paper bank notes printed by wildcat (unregulated) banks. In the South, following invention of the cotton gin in 1793, cotton plantations and exports expanded rapidly, reaping huge profits. The new cotton aristocracy engaged in "conspicuous consumption" and proceeded to spend money lavishly.

The managers of the Second Bank of the United States feared a shortfall in the specie backing up the bank notes, given the unchecked speculation and growth based on a nondescript system of currency. In 1819 the Second Bank decided to initiate a sharp contraction of credit by refusing to make loans. There were "bank runs" where depositors rushed in a panic to banks to have their notes converted to coin. Lacking suitable reserves, many state banks failed. With the banks closing their doors, millions of dollars owed to the federal government for sale of public lands went uncollected. The Second Bank's action led to a severe depression, particularly in the South and West. Prices, such as on the commodity market for cotton, declined sharply. With cotton income down, the South decreased their purchases of manufactured goods from Northern industry. Also, the South was sending much less cotton north to the Northern mills (which had been ultimately exported overseas by Northern shipping companies). The North lost both its Southern and foreign markets.

In the aftermath of the panic, Congress conducted investigations of alleged mismanagement of the federal banking system which, most people thought, had derailed an otherwise booming economy. Manufacturers also lobbied for better protection through tariffs and excise taxes. To the rescue of individual debtors who were victims of the panic, several states passed legislation relieving them of their debts. The depression lasted until 1823 when commodity prices and the economy in general began picking up again and public confidence in the banking system was restored. However, the Panic of 1819 presaged many other financial panics throughout the nineteenth century as the nation sought ways of balancing free market capitalism with economic stability.

See also: **Panic of 1837, Panic of 1907, Panics of the Late Nineteenth Century**

FURTHER READING

Cohen, Bernice. *The Edge of Chaos: Financial Booms, Bubbles, Crashes, and Chaos.* New York: John Wiley and Sons, 1997.

Gilbart, James William. *The History of Banking in America.* New York: A. M. Kelley, 1967.

Rothbard, Murray N. *The Panic of 1819: Reactions and Policies.* New York: Columbia University Press, 1962.

Sobel, Robert. *The Money Manias: The Eras of Great Speculation in America, 1770–1970.* New York: Weybright and Talley, 1974.

White, Eugene N. *Crashes and Panics: The Lessons from History.* Homewood, IL: Dow Jones-Irwin, 1990.

PANIC OF 1837

In the early nineteenth century an unstable currency and a new shaky banking system supported the nation's economic foundation. Construction of the nation's transportation system, which consisted of railroads and canals, led to accumulation of large debts by investors in the early 1830s. In addition speculation was rampant in western lands as states became settled,

> The economy and the securities markets did not recover fully from the 1837 panic until 1844, when trade revived, the effects of the liquidations had been absorbed, and expansion into the West accelerated once more. The Mexican War and gold discoveries in California gave a further fillip (boost) to the economy, as did the banking and tariff reforms of the Polk Administration.
>
> **Robert Sobel, Historian, 1968**

and new banks were chartered. In the 1832 elections President Andrew Jackson (1829–1837) ran on a populist platform marked by an anti-Eastern establishment philosophy including opposition to the Second Bank of the United States (created in 1816). Jackson charged that the Second Bank did not fairly treat the common citizen and that it only served the wealthy.

Following his assumption of office Jackson proceeded to dismantle the central banking system. In 1833 Jackson began transferring federal funds from the U.S. Bank to selected state banks, often owned by friends of Jackson. He also stopped depositing government money in the Second Bank, instead placing new proceeds from land sales and revenue from taxes in various state banks, which he called his ''pet banks.'' With more money the state banks increasingly expanded their issuance of credit, giving out too many loans and printing almost worthless paper money, as banks had been allowed to issue their own paper currency. Confidence in the currency declined, especially within the Eastern business establishment. So much available paper money led to a spiraling inflation rate. The price of land available from the government also rose. Since this did not stem the number of speculators, they borrowed more heavily. In 1832 the government sold less than $3 million in land and by 1836 the amount increased to almost $25 million. To make economic matters worse, in addition to the high inflation, imports began exceeding exports creating a foreign trade deficit.

With land speculation continuing rampantly Jackson issued the ''Specie Circular'' in 1836, which required that all public lands be bought with specie (coin), rather than private script (paper money) issued by individual banks. Also in 1836 Congress passed an act distributing the surplus federal revenues from the U.S. Treasury to the states. In reaction to the tightening of federal monetary policies, banks reduced credit available. With fewer loans available for domestic investment, reliance on British investors grew. Unfortunately, this coincided with an internal financial crisis in England, leading British creditors to collect on their loans abroad. Three British banking houses failed and a trade imbalance for the United States grew as Britain could afford fewer U.S. exports. Gold began an increased flow to Europe. With the U.S. economy already in decline, another financial blow occurred with widespread crop failures in 1835 and 1837. A financial crisis loomed.

In May 1837 New York banks ceased specie payments to investors, leading other banks across the nation to do the same. With no coin to back it paper currency lost its value, triggering the Panic of 1837. During a brief ensuing time span many companies crashed and fortunes were lost. Unemployment skyrocketed, especially in the West and South with a loss of agricultural exports and crop failures. Public calls for banking reform increased as a six-year depression followed.

The Panic of 1837 brought about changes in banking and monetary policy. President Martin Van Buren (1837–1841) moved to establish an independent U.S. treasury system in 1840 to hold and disburse government funds. Though initially defeated, the federal system became permanent in 1846. From that point onward, to help stabilize the nation's economy, public funds were held in the U.S. Treasury and its branches in various cities, rather than in the nation's private banking and financial system.

State governments had also invested heavily in enterprises such as canal and railroad construction with hopes of ultimately boosting their economies. Many of the existing 26 state governments went bankrupt or came close to it. New York state government became a leader in reform with adoption of a new constitution in 1846, instilling a philosophy of state governmental fiscal restraint. To address economic displacement of the states' citizens, a key part of various state legislative reform measures was protection for families who fell into debt. State laws were passed to alleviate the effects of the panic on an individual basis. Texas was the first state to pass a homestead exemption law following the panic. These laws aimed at shielding private individuals from free market fluctuations and provided some state protection for families during the transition to an industrial economy in many sections of the country.

On the national level Congress passed a federal bankruptcy law removing about $450 million in debt from a million creditors. However, by bailing out investors the credit system itself was substantially undermined. Creditors were more hesitant to hand out loans unsure if they could enforce repayment. The numerous bankruptcies resulting from the panic and associated debt relief similarly discouraged foreign investors. The Panic of 1837 had cost British investors almost $130 million.

Difficult economic times contributed to the rush of emigrants that began flooding across the Oregon Trail, beginning in 1843, seeking a fresh economic start. Thousands of emigrants had been displaced by the depression resulting from the Panic of 1837. Ironically, the depression drove U.S. expansionism and spurred new economic hope by the late 1840s.

See also: **Nicolas Biddle, Panic of 1819, Panic of 1907, Panics of the Late Nineteenth Century**

FURTHER READING

Cohen, Bernice. *The Edge of Chaos: Financial Booms, Bubbles, Crashes, and Chaos*. New York: John Wiley and Sons, 1997.

Collman, Charles A. *Our Mysterious Panics, 1830–1930: A Story of Events and the Men Involved*. New York: Greenwood Press, 1968.

Kindleberger, Charles Poor. *Manias, Panics, and Crashes: A History of Financial Crises*. New York: Basic Books, 1989.

McGrane, Reginald C. *The Panic of 1837: Some Financial Problems of the Jacksonian Era*. Chicago: The University of Chicago Press, 1924.

Sobel, Robert. *The Money Manias: The Eras of Great Speculation in America, 1770–1970*. New York: Weybright and Talley, 1974.

PANIC OF 1907

Economic prosperity during the first several years of the twentieth century led to expanded bank credit and rampant speculation in railroad consolidations, western mining ventures, and the coastal shipping industry. With President William McKinley's (1897–1901) administration favoring business interests, powerful business trusts remained poorly regulated and competed with banks. Between 1897 and 1907 imports and exports almost doubled along with the volume of money in circulation, from $1.5 billion in 1896 to $2.7 billion in 1907. Deposits in the national banks (created in the 1860s) more than doubled from $1.6 billion to $4.3 billion. U.S. economic prosperity was shared with many other nations.

Despite economic well-being gold production was lagging behind as demands for investment funds were increasing. A capital shortage was beginning to appear and money was becoming tighter. To help avoid the periodic financial panics of the late nineteenth century, governmental business reforms were introduced. Congress created the Interstate Commerce Commission through the Interstate Commerce Act of 1887. The courts proceeded to weaken the act, but in 1906 the Hepburn Act reasserted the power of the federal government to regulate railroad rates. These regulatory efforts, however, did not save the economy from periodic panics. In 1907 the economy again ran out of steam and fell into depression.

However, business financial troubles began appearing early in 1907. In February the business giant, Standard Oil Company, suddenly faced financial difficulties which caused a sharp drop in the stock market. Then a shipping conglomerate failed in the summer, followed in October by the failure of the United Copper Company. This caused a run on banks as depositors fought to withdraw their funds. Later in October closure of the Westinghouse Electric Company and the Knickerbocker Trust Company accompanied with the suicide of Knickerbocker's president finally triggered a panic in the stock market and suspensions or failures of several banks.

The government turned to New York City's J.P. Morgan and fellow financiers to implement an emergency strategy by loaning $40 million to rescue selected banks and businesses. With President Theodore Roosevelt's (1901–1909) approval, Morgan had United States Steel Corporation purchase holdings of its major rival, Tennessee Coal, Iron and Railroad Company. However, Roosevelt did not initially appreciate what Morgan and others stood to gain personally out of this arrangement—the action strengthened the existing steel trust. This outcome was not well accepted by Roosevelt, known to his public as the "trustbuster."

The panic was limited in scope, not causing extensive unemployment, bank and business failures, or disruption to the agricultural economy. However, the recovery tactics affected the image of big financiers as the public, fearing the power of J.P. Morgan and others, saw the need for banking and monetary reform. Foreign investors also lost confidence, perceiving continued U.S. financial instability from the previous century. (Since the charter of the Second Bank of the United

States had expired in 1836, the nation had been operating for over 70 years without a central banking organization.) In response Congress passed the Aldrich-Vreeland Currency Act in 1908 which, during future crises, provided for issuance of emergency bank currency by groups of national banks. Other congressional actions included the creation of the Postal Savings System in 1910 to protect the savings of the poor, and in particular immigrants. The Aldrich-Vreeland Act also created the National Monetary Commission (NMC) to determine needed banking reforms.

Clearly the historic requirements of banks maintaining certain levels of reserves to help insure liquidity of bank notes and deposits were not sufficient measures to blunt financial crises. The NMC studied banking practices in the United States and Europe, which resulted in a 38-volume report in 1911. Congressional examination and debate over the report's findings indicated that the nation needed greater flexibility in lending power in addition to elasticity of currency. As a result Congress passed the Federal Reserve Act in 1913 creating the modern reserve bank system, the Federal Reserve System. The Federal Reserve became the lender of last resort, designed to meet liquidity demands of the entire banking system. This new system placed Federal Reserve Banks throughout the United States, thus eliminating the concentration of banking in New York City. Lastly, the Federal Reserve would also standardize the currency through issuing federal reserve notes.

See also: **Federal Reserve System**

FURTHER READING

Cowing, Cedric B. *Populists, Plungers, and Progressives: A Social History of Stock and Commodity Speculation, 1890–1936*. Princeton, NJ: Princeton University Press, 1965.

Fuhrer, Jeffrey C., and Scott Schuh, eds. *Beyond Shocks: What Causes Business Cycles*. Boston: Federal Reserve Bank of Boston, 1998.

Moen, Jon R., and Ellis W. Tallman. *The Bank Panic of 1907: The Role of Trust Companies*. Atlanta: Federal Reserve Bank of Atlanta, 1990.

Moen, Jon R., and Ellis W. Tallman. *Clearinghouse Access and Bank Runs: Comparing New York and Chicago During the Panic of 1907*. Atlanta, GA: Federal Reserve Bank of Atlanta, 1995.

Wicker, Elmus. *The Banking Panics of the Great Depression*. New York: Cambridge University Press, 1996.

PANICS OF THE LATE NINETEENTH CENTURY

During the late nineteenth century the largely unregulated and unstable U.S. economy witnessed a series of financial panics between 1857 and 1893. Financial panics are socioeconomic events, often psychologically driven, in which a more or less irrational fear and sense of futility sweeps through investors or some other group. Usually occurring during periods of economic optimism and over-expansion the actual panic-driven activity varies depending on the nature of the sudden crisis that spurred the fear. (For example depositors could start a run on banks by demanding their money back out of fear the bank has insufficient capital reserves to cover its deposits.) Often, but not always, panics lead to economic depressions characterized by high unemployment and lower living standards.

Prior to 1863 U.S. banking in the nineteenth century was characterized by widespread recklessness. The money supply used to finance industrial expansion fluctuated markedly. With demise of the Second Bank of the United States in 1836 state banks would periodically print and lend money, or often make loans with insufficient capital on hand while at other times they would greatly restrict credit. Under this relatively unpredictable system commodity prices fluctuated greatly as did the level of business activity.

The period began optimistically with victory in the Mexican War (1846–1848) which resulted in the acquisition of California and the American Southwest followed by the discovery of gold in California. An economic boom period followed. Speculation was rampant in railroad construction, manufacturing, and the newly gained western lands. The first major sign of financial over-extension was the failure of the Ohio Life Insurance Company of Cincinnati in August of 1857. The Panic of 1857 quickly spread through the developing Eastern industrial centers and Western wheat belt resulting in high unemployment. Yet the South's cotton trade with Great Britain, sustained through low tariffs, continued to prosper. By winter squabbling between the North and South intensified. Suffering numerous bank failures, the North and West turned to the newly formed Republican political party. Economics as well as slavery became the key issues of the 1860 presidential election.

The American Civil War (1861–1865) devastated the Southern economy and financing the war left the U.S. government in debt. Congress created a national

> The ultimate bailout of the Treasury came from Europeans and their best-known agents in New York. Despite eighty years of progress, the situation appeared to have changed little since the War of 1812. This was annoying to many advocates of central banking because two private bankers managed to perform central banking operations for the United States, charging a fee in the process.
>
> **Charles R. Geisst, *Wall Street: A History*, 1997**

banking system in 1863 to stabilize the economy. The National Banks Act created a system of privately owned banks that issued notes backed by U.S. bonds driving previously issued state bank notes out of circulation. However, the new ''national'' banks still failed to take actions to increase the money supply in order to escape the clutches of the threatened depression.

In the 1870s speculators ignored, once again, the problems of the increasing trade deficit. Instead, they loaned more money to the railroad companies. Almost all activity on Wall Street and investment capital was singularly focused on the railroad industry. Unable to raise sufficient loan capital, over four thousand U.S. businesses failed in 1872. In the fall of 1873 a panic ensued as several major New York financial firms failed, including the most noted banking house, Jay Cooke and Company. Wall Street closed for ten days as many other companies and citizens faced bankruptcy. The subsequent severe depression left half a million people unemployed by 1875. Another 18,000 businesses failed in 1876 and 1877 including most railroad companies and iron mills in the United States. With the lack of organized relief programs, hunger and destitution spread. For those still employed, wages declined leading to numerous strikes, including a violent railroad strike in 1877. Finally, by 1878 the economy began to improve and with increasing gold reserves, the U.S. government in 1879 placed the economy on a gold standard.

Nevertheless, economic instability persisted. Capital investments in railroads, the mining of newly found silver deposits in the West, industrialization, and foreign enterprises exceeded possible economic returns in the 1880s. Prices for goods declined and by 1883 an economic depression commenced. Overproducing wheat farmers and silver miners of the West pushed for increased currency circulation through unlimited silver coinage to combat declining wheat prices. Meanwhile Eastern industrial growth outpaced the nation's gold production leaving banks without sufficient gold reserves to adequately back loans for capital investments.

After a mild economic recovery in the late 1880s, the British economy suddenly declined sharply in 1890s leading to failure of the prominent Baring Brothers and Company banking house. Impacts on the U.S. economy were direct and investment of foreign capital, particularly British, into U.S. business dropped dramatically. The sale of American securities by foreign investors led to a Wall Street collapse that year and substantial exporting of gold. In addition, under political pressure from the West, President Benjamin Harrison (1889–1893) promised to relieve the suffering of silver producers from the declining price of silver. Congress passed the Sherman Silver Purchase Act of 1890 which obliged the United States to purchase large amounts of silver on a continuing basis.

By early 1893 the gold reserves dropped below the set $100 million baseline minimum. The amount was considered the minimum to assure redemption of government obligations. With the price of commodities, gold, and silver continuing downward, the Philadelphia and Reading Railroad failed, then the National Cordage Company. The Panic of 1893 had begun. This panic hit banks in the South and West particularly hard as investors rushed to banks to convert their holdings into gold. Almost 600 banks suspended operation and by the close of 1893 4,000 banks and 14,000 businesses had failed and four million people were unemployed.

In an effort to bring relief newly elected President, Grover Cleveland (1893–1897), then in his second term, repealed the Silver Purchase Act. This caused silver prices to drop dramatically and brought economic devastation to parts of the West. A depression with widespread unemployment lasted from late 1893 through much of 1894. Violent strikes erupted, including the Pullman Strike in 1894. Jacob Coxey, a small businessman, led his ''army'' of unemployed on a march from Ohio to Washington, D.C. to present Congress with a demand for creating jobs, mostly on road repair.

Cleveland arranged for Eastern bankers including J. P. Morgan to purchase specially issued U.S. bonds to help replenish the gold reserves. This action raised public fears over the increasing influence of East financiers.

Due to poor European agricultural harvests in 1897, the export of American produce significantly increased the circulation of gold. In addition, the domestic production of gold increased steadily through the 1890s with gold discoveries in the Klondike region of Alaska. The economy rebounded by 1898.

While the recurrent business cycles left many Americans bankrupt foreign investors also lost millions in each panic episode. The pattern constantly repeated itself. Foreign investors would avoid investment in U.S. securities immediately following a economic downturn and contraction. Then as domestic investors began making fortunes with securities at lowered prices and economic expansion growing, the foreign investors would be lured back only to suffer another panic and downturn.

Such financial business cycles of recurrent panics through the late 19th century established a public mood for substantial economic reform. A major factor behind the dramatic financial swings during this period was a lack of public confidence in the largely unregulated economic system, particularly given extensive political and business corruption. Reformers sought increased protection against concentrations of economic power in the hands of a few private financiers and enhanced stability for foreign as well as domestic investors.

See also: **Jacob Coxey, Pullman Strike**

FURTHER READING

Cowing, Cedric B. *Populists, Plungers, and Progressives: A Social History of Stock and Commodity Speculation, 1890–1936*. Princeton, NJ: Princeton University Press, 1965.

Gordon, John S. *The Scarlet Woman of Wall Street: Jay Gould, Jim Fisk, Cornelius Vanderbilt, the Erie Railway Wars, and the Birth of Wall Street.* New York: Weidenfeld and Nicolson, 1988.

Huston, James L. *The Panic of 1857 and the Coming of the Civil War.* Baton Rouge: Louisiana State University Press, 1987.

Sobel, Robert. *Panic on Wall Street: A History of America's Financial Disasters*. New York: Macmillan, 1968.

Van Vleck, George W. *The Panic of 1857: An Analytical Study*. New York: Columbia University Press, 1943.

PAPER INDUSTRY

According to ancient writings paper was first made by a eunuch in the court of the Chinese emperor Ho Ti. He is thought to have used the bark from a mulberry tree. The earliest known paper that still exists was made from rags in about A.D. 150. China was the only area where paper was made until the technique surfaced in Japan and then in Central Asia. The Egyptians did not make paper until A.D. 900. Around 1150 a papermaking mill was built in Spain and the art of papermaking spread throughout Europe. The English built their first mill in 1495; it was 200 years after this that paper was first manufactured in America.

In 1690 the fist paper mill in the American colonies was constructed in Germantown, Pennsylvania. It was built on the banks of the Monoshone Creek by William Rittenhouse, a papermaker trained in Germany and one of the first Germans to settle in the New World. His ambition was to make fine white paper from the raw material of rags. During the American Revolution (1775–1783) the Rittenhouse mill donated paper for pamphlets and newspapers. Paper was also used to make gun wadding and cartridges used in the war.

Papermills sprang up to meet the demands of a growing market. New mills thrived that were near cities and towns and that had a plentiful supply of rags for the basic raw material. A new job title emerged for those seeking employment in the paper industry. For lack of any more sophisticated name, the word "ragpicker" was coined for those that scurried around the cities collecting rags for the papermakers. There were approximately 185 paper mills in the United States by 1810. The supply of rags used to make paper was running low and papermakers began looking for alternative materials. On January 14, 1863, the *Boston Weekly Journal* became the first U.S. newspaper to be printed on paper made from ground wood pulp.

As the United States grew in size so did the paper industry. Technology kept up with the need for faster production. The first practical machine for papermaking was invented in 1798 by Frenchman Nicholas Louis Robert. An improved machine constructed by British brothers Henry and Sealy Fourdrinier appeared in 1803. The first machine that produced paper in a continuous sheet was installed by Thomas Gilpin in Wilmington, Delaware in 1817. Straw and wood were being used as raw materials and machine speeds were greatly increasing. Paper was now being made in longer and wider dimensions.

By the late 1990s the United States and Canada were the largest producers of pulp, paper, and paper products in the world. The U.S. paper industry was accountable for approximately one percent of the U.S. national income. In the 1990s the United States employed 750,000 workers in the paper industry alone.

Towards the end of the twentieth century conservationists became concerned with the impact of paper production on the environment. Paper mills had the unfortunate tendency to foul the water supply and destroy wildlife. The industry set a goal to recover 50 percent of all used paper via recycling by the end of the twentieth century. By 1999 it appeared that this estimate was low; twice as much paper was recovered for recycling as was sent to landfills. Another economic and social issue affecting the paper industry at the turn of the century was the promise of a "paperless" world by those who believed that technology and commerce would shape every facet of society. Instead of this outcome, technological growth seemed to be followed by an increase in the demand for paper. This growth appeared to be based on the premise that paper is universal and relatively inexpensive; replacing it with electronic apparatus makes communication exclusive and, in some cases, too expensive.

FURTHER READING

1995 Lockwood-Post's Directory of the Pulp, Paper and Allied Trades/122nd Year. San Francisco: Miller Freeman Books, 1994.

Carrere, Ricard and Larry Lohmann. *Pulping the South: Industrial Tree Plantations and the World Paper Economy.* London, UK: Zed Books, 1996.

"The National Council of the Paper Industry for Air and Stream Improvement (NCASI)," [cited April 18, 1999] available from the World Wide Web @ www.ncasi.org/.

Smith, Maureen. *The U.S. Paper Industry and Sustainable Production: An Argument for Restructuring (Urban and Industrial Environments).* Cambridge, MA: MIT Press, 1997.

Toale, Bernard. *The Art of Papermaking.* Worcester, MA: Davis Publications, 1983.

PARTNERSHIP

A partnership is a legal organization in which two or more individuals own and operate the business. Partnerships are not limited as to the number of possible partners or the number of employees. Generally, however, partnerships are small in size. Partnerships are a common form of organization in the professions (businesses such as retail shops and service trades like car repair shops) and in wholesale firms (which buy from producers and sell to retailers).

Businesses organized as partnerships are advantageous for several reasons. No formal legal process is required to start a partnership, but most are based on signed agreements between partners as to how the costs and profits will be divided. Although certain licenses or permits may be required, few fees are to be paid or papers filed with government agencies. Owners may have a great deal of flexibility and freedom in decision making. Also, instead of working for someone else and receiving a salary, the owners may keep all the profits to do with as they see fit. The talents and abilities of more than one person will be available to the business, and, with several individuals backing the firm, bank loans may be easier to obtain.

The largest economic disadvantage of partnerships is unlimited liability. The owners are personally responsible to the full extent of whatever wealth they own for all the debts of the business, both jointly and separately. This means that if one individual owns 1/4 of a firm and the firm goes out of business with debts of $400,000, the individual is liable for $100,000. However, if the other three partners disappear, the one remaining would be liable for the entire $400,000 (and even personal possessions may be taken to satisfy creditors). The actions of any one partner are the legal, unlimited responsibility of all partners. Another disadvantage is the limited ability to raise enough capital for the business to grow, be efficient, and highly profitable. In most cases raising sufficient investment capital is problematic.

In the United States during the 1980s and the 1990s, the percentage of total firms organized under partnerships and their sales remained relatively constant. In 1993 partnerships made up 6.9 percent of all U.S. firms and represented 1,467,000 businesses; they received 4.8 percent of total sales, about $627 billion.

PATENT

A patent is a legal document issued by a government granting exclusive authority to an inventor for making, using, and selling an invention. The invention must have a sufficient degree of newness, usefulness, or novelty to distinguish it from items with existing patents. To qualify for a patent, an invention may not merely be a substitution, change, or combination of items. In the United States inventions may include

These two children study the original patent granted by the United States government. The document was presumed lost until it was recovered in a trunk of papers in 1954, and preserved by the Chicago Historical Society.

products, machines, methods, new uses, and even new forms of life as genetically engineered bacteria.

The exclusive authority granted is considered a barrier to entry, that is, something that prevents anyone else from copying or producing the invention without permission. By doing so, government hopes to encourage creative innovations by providing sufficient time for the innovator to recoup his research costs and realize profits. The inventor may manufacture, use, or sell his invention in a monopolistic atmosphere.

Each country has its own system of patents. In the United States, applications are made to the U.S. Patent and Trademark Office (PTO), and it takes up to two years to process. The patent is granted to the first inventor rather than the first person to make application, so inventors must document when they first came up with the idea. The PTO exhaustively checks previous patents to make sure of no duplications. If none exist, PTO sends a notice of allowance to the inventor. Upon paying fees, the patent is issued. The patent protects the invention for 17 years. A design patent, which covers only the appearance of an item, is issued for 14 years. A patent owner may sue on grounds of infringement to stop any copying of the invention.

The U.S. *Constitution* first empowered Congress to secure exclusive rights for inventors. At the beginning of the twentieth century, 82 percent of patents issued in the United States went to individuals and 17 percent to U.S. corporations. By 1962 about 28 percent of the patents went to individuals while 59 percent went to U.S. corporations, 12 percent to foreign entities, and two percent to the U.S. government. The sharp decline in individual patents could partially be explained by large increases in corporate research and development expenditures funded by both the federal government and private industry.

In 1992 the North American Free Trade Agreement (NAFTA) highlighted the continued importance of patents by requiring each member country to provide both product and process patents for all kinds of inventions.

See also: **North American Free Trade Agreement**

PAY EQUITY

Pay equity concerns an aspect of the growth of capitalism involving the fairness with which the system distributes its expanding wealth and how it shares its recurring hardships. An example of the disparity of pay equity is the following: in 1986, in the United States, the lowest 20 percent of all families received only 4.6 percent of the total income, whereas the top 20 percent of all families received 43.7 percent. This disparity, or lack of pay equity, clearly results from the concentration of assets in the upper economic brackets. According to the *Encyclopedia Britannica*, "the disparity is the consequence of highly skewed patterns of corporate rewards that typically give, say, chief executive officers of large companies 50 to 100 times more income than those of ordinary office or factory employees." Advocates of market-determined distribution of capital assets declare that in a society like the United States, with certain exceptions, people tend to be paid what they are worth—their incomes reflecting the economic value of their contributions to production. Critics of this point of view contend that labor, under capitalism, is paid less than its value because of the superior bargaining power of employers; in their view the claim of capital efficiency might easily mask an underlying condition of exploitation. Pay equity (achieving a fair sharing of wealth at all levels of any capitalist society), seems an ongoing dilemma of the capitalist system, a system that generates capital but does not pay heed, necessarily, to the moral or social implications of the creation of wealth. The pursuit of pay equity is ongoing and involves struggles within the capital economy in constant efforts by many groups to achieve justice.

See also: **Capitalism**

PENNEY, JAMES CASH

James Cash Penney (1875–1971) was born on his father's farm in Hamilton, Missouri, the seventh of 12 children. He grew up in a stern, joyless family. His father, a farmer, served as an unpaid preacher for a fundamentalist sect known as Primitive Baptists. By age eight James Penney was forced to earn money to buy his own clothes. This was his parents' way of teaching him the value of money and self-reliance.

Penney's childhood and early adult life appeared quite ordinary. He finished high school and worked mostly in store clerk positions. Penney moved to Colorado for health reasons and his life changed. He was quickly employed by T.M. Callahan, the owner of the Golden Rule Mercantile Company Chain—a company Penney would later buy-out and make into his own.

THE ETHICAL MEANS BY WHICH MY BUSINESS ASSOCIATES AND I HAVE MADE MONEY IS MORE IMPORTANT THAN THE FACT THAT WE HAVE ACHIEVED BUSINESS SUCCESS.

J.C. Penney

Working in the Callahan store, Penney began to dream of operating his own chain of stores, based on the idea of having partner-owners who would share in all the profits. Additionally, he married and found living in a healthier environment stimulated his goals, ambitions, and imagination. In 1902 Penney became owner of his first store, one of the Golden Rule chain stores; he worked night and day for the success of this Kemmerer, Wyoming, store, which opened at 7 AM and closed it between 9 and 10 P.M.. Penney worked six days a week and half a day on Sundays.

His work and his sense of constantly expanding business—with more stores and mail-order catalogues—led to monumental national expansion throughout the 1920s. By 1927 J.C. Penney had opened 1000 stores throughout the United States. Penney knew he could not control the daily operations of many stores with such wide expansion. He decided that his success potential could only come true if he delegated responsibility to others and if he put his faith in the people he hired. This faith and his financial arrangements with store managers worked profoundly well. Individual store managers shared in one-third of the store profits. Sharing profits with store managers was, in Penney's own estimation, was the motivating factor for success in business.

Because of this profit-sharing arrangement with his store managers, J.C. Penney was called "the Man with a Thousand Partners,'' a phrase Penney used in his autobiography. In his book Penney wrote: ''The ethical means by which my business associates and I have made money is more important than the fact that we have achieved business success.''

In later life Penney, who now had the financial means to do what he pleased, operated cattle farms, became involved with charitable and religious endeavors, and pursued frequent public speaking engagements. His rise to fame and fortune crashed with the stock market crash of 1929—at age 56 he was $7 million in debt. Yet the highly motivated Penney, still vigorous and determined, borrowed money and soon regained control of his retail empire. He wrote in his autobiography that all of his business success was based ''in adherence to the Golden Rule, faith in God and the country.''

Despite early health problems, J.C. Penney lived to the age of 95. He died in 1971.

See also: **Chain Store, Mail-Order House, Retail Industry**

FURTHER READING

Beasley, Norman. *Main Street Merchant: The Story of the J.C. Penney Company*. New York: Whittlesey House, 1948.

Curry, Mary E. *Creating an American Institution: The Merchandising Genius of J.C. Penney*. New York: Garland Publishing, 1993.

Encyclopedia of World Biography. Detroit: The Gale Group, 1998, s.v. ''J.C. Penney.''

Penney, James Cash. *Fifty Years With The Golden Rule*. New York: Harper Bros, 1950.

Plumb, Beatrice. *J.C. Penney: Merchant Prince*. Minneapolis, MN: TS Dennison, 1963.

PENNSYLVANIA

In Charles Andrews' *The Colonial Period of American History*, Pennsylvania's founder, William Penn (1644–1718), is quoted as saying, ''I abhor contention, niceties, doubtful disputation, divisions, etc., and am for patience, forbearance, long suffering and all true moderation.'' While Pennsylvania did not fulfill all of William Penn's high ideals as a ''holy experiment'' in tolerance and diversity, it certainly developed in very diverse ways. Its urban areas soon became some of the most influential in the nation, while its rural areas and vast forests remained unspoiled. Its unmatched transportation network and abundant natural resources helped the state to become an industrial powerhouse in the late nineteenth century. Nonetheless, Pennsylvania retained its agricultural base. It weathered declines in manufacturing after World War II (1939–1945) but managed to retain much of its economic health in the 1990s by diversifying its economic base.

In 1614 Cornelis Jacobssen, sailing for the Dutch fur trade, was probably the first European to reach Pennsylvania. Swedes also settled there, surrendering to the English in 1664. The colony was granted by King Charles II in 1681 as a proprietorship to William Penn.

Penn, a Quaker who espoused pacifism, tolerance, and equality, was given broad powers to make laws and run the colony as he saw fit. Penn however gave up his lawmaking powers and set up a form of representative government. Many immigrants came to this tolerant colony. The *Declaration of Independence* was declared from Philadelphia, the state house in 1776, and the new Congress continued to meet there. Philadelphia would serve as the U.S. capital following the American Revolution (1775–1783) until 1783, and again from 1790 to 1800. Pennsylvania was the second state to join the Union, in 1780.

Pennsylvania's destiny as an industrial powerhouse was sealed when iron was discovered there. The first iron furnace was built in 1792, and coal began to be exploited as an energy resource. The early nineteenth century also saw the completion of the Main Line of Public Works, a canal and railroad system, which connected Philadelphia with Pittsburgh. Another aid to economic development was the stock company, which Pennsylvania encouraged to promote local enterprise. Pennsylvania chartered the Insurance Company of North America (INA) and the Insurance Company of the State of Pennsylvania in 1794, both of which profited mostly from marine and fire casualty policies. The Philadelphia and Lancaster Turnpike was also chartered and was completed in 1794, cutting the cost of moving goods from Lancaster to Philadelphia by about two-thirds.

Meanwhile Philadelphia was becoming the commercial center of the state. According to historian Thomas C. Cochran, political and economic business could be conducted there very conveniently: ''Such compactness, possible for a city of less than 75,000 people, meant that business could be conducted reasonably expeditiously without telephone, telegraph, or a clearing house for the four banks.'' By the time President Thomas Jefferson (1801–1809) declared an embargo on foreign imports in 1807, Pennsylvania's

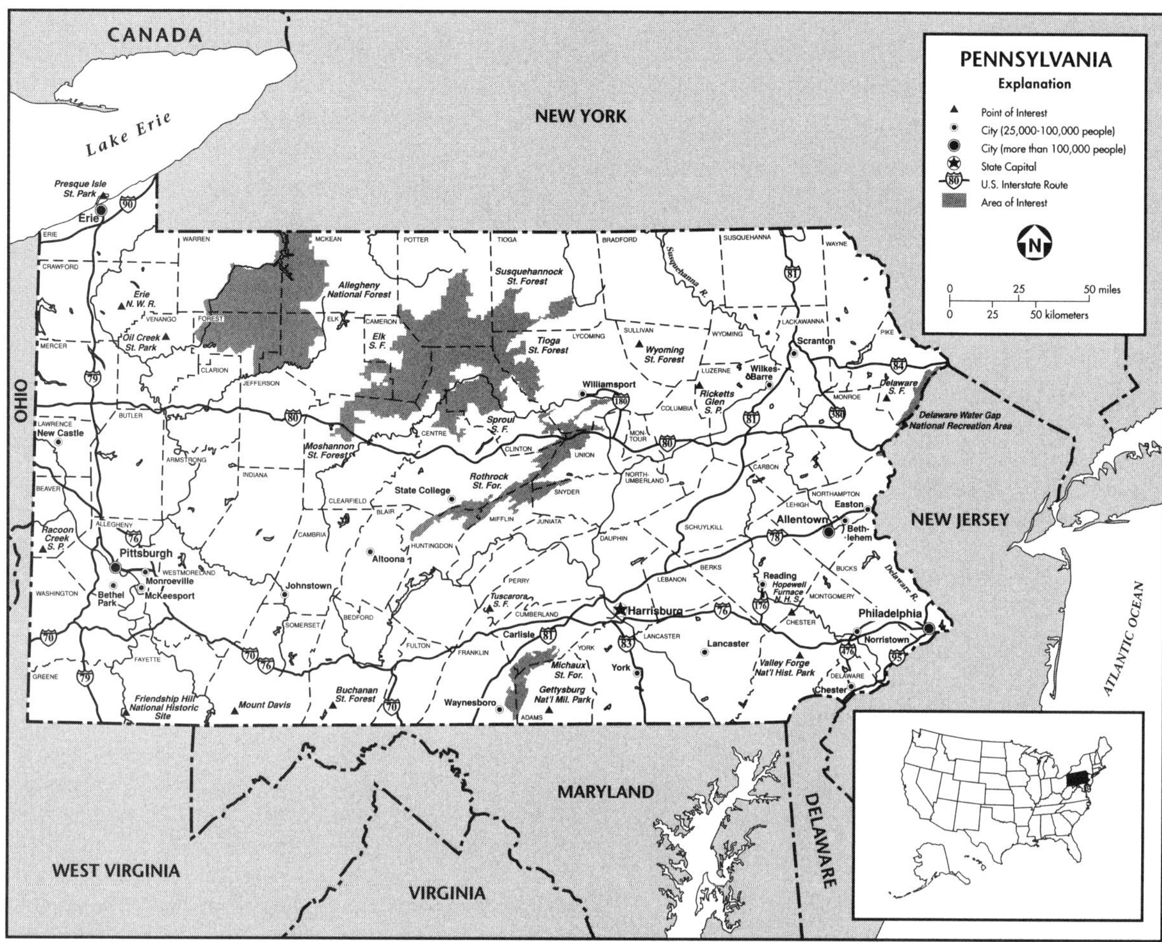

State of Pennsylvania.

financial institutions and insurance companies were ready to meet the challenge, as were local industries, including Philadelphia's many shipbuilders.

By the early 1800s Philadelphia had become the nation's financial center. It was the home of the nation's first stock exchange (1790), the First Bank of the United States (1791), the Second Bank of the United States (1816), and a number of other financial institutions. Under its powerful director Nicholas Biddle (1786–1844), the Second Bank became the only important rival to New York's financial institutions. Philadelphia, however, lost its preeminence as a financial center when President Andrew Jackson (1829–1837) vetoed the Second Bank's re-charter in 1831.

In the mid-nineteenth century Pennsylvania continued to tap its abundant natural resources, creating a center for the iron industry and other manufacturers and developing a transportation network which was matched by no other state by 1840. Both Philadelphia and Pittsburgh became major commercial centers. Several more roads were built, and Pennsylvania also benefited from a section of the old National Road, which passed south of Pittsburgh. By the 1840s the improvements to canals and other waterways in the state also exceeded anything which had been done elsewhere.

It was in railroad building however, that Pennsylvania really excelled. By the 1850s lines connected Philadelphia with Germantown; Trenton, New Jersey; the Lehigh Valley; and New York City. In 1852 the Pennsylvania Central connected Philadelphia and Pittsburgh, solidifying these two cities as transportation meccas. In 1857 the powerful Pennsylvania Railroad purchased the State Works, virtually eliminating state competition and tolls. Following the American Civil War (1861–1865), the Pennsylvania Railroad dominated economic life in the state and held sway over most Republican Party politicians. By 1880 it was the world's largest corporation, with more than 30,000 employees and $400 million in capital.

For the next two decades Pennsylvania was the chief producer of coal, iron, and steel and a major supplier of petroleum and lumber. Immigrants from other states and from abroad came in droves to the coal regions and urban centers to find work in mines, mills, and factories.

No story of the development of Pennsylvania industries would be complete without mention of Andrew Carnegie (1835–1919). A Scottish immigrant, he worked various jobs before being employed by the Pennsylvania Railroad. There he advanced rapidly, laying the foundations for his future fortune by investing wisely. After serving in the Civil War, he formed a company that produced iron railroad bridges and then founded a steel mill. One of the first to use the Bessemer process, Carnegie succeeded quickly, buying up several other steel companies and soon controlling a quarter of the steel production in the United States. In 1901 he sold his Carnegie Steel Company to United States Steel Corporation for $250 million. After his retirement Carnegie was well-known for his philanthropy, endowing many educational and cultural institutions. He is best known to the general public for his gifts to nearly 1,700 public libraries across the nation and in Great Britain.

With Carnegie Steel, and with the financial expertise of banker Andrew Mellon (1855–1937), Pittsburgh retained its position as the preeminent industrial city in the region. The city and the state, however, were not without labor problems. Over a period of years many violent strikes occurred in both the coal and the steel industries. In 1892 a lockout at the Carnegie-owned Homestead Steel plant caused a bloody clash between workers and the Pinkerton guards hired to keep them out. Another strike in 1919, involving 50 percent of U.S. steelworkers, shut down the industry for more than three months.

During the 1920s Pennsylvania barely held its own economically, with a low growth rate and industrial products selling below normal levels. The Great Depression (1929–1939) brought even more economic grief to the state. Democratic Governor George H. Earle, breaking the longtime hold of the Republican party over the state, initiated a "Little New Deal," following the policies of President Franklin D. Roosevelt (1933–1945) in supporting labor and farmers, regulating utilities, and building public works. Industrial workers came out of this period with a renewed ability to challenge industry. During World War II (1939–1945) Pennsylvania returned to a high level of prosperity as it turned out large volumes of munitions, ships, steel, and other materials for the war effort.

Republican and Democratic governors following the war continued efforts to support and encourage industry in the state. Not until the governorship of William W. Scranton (1963–1967), however, did Pennsylvania return to full economic health. Through increased taxes for state services, more federal aid for economic programs, and steady increases in support for economic development, the state was able to bring its high unemployment rate to below the national average by 1966.

By the mid-1980s, Pennsylvania found itself in the throes of converting from an industrial to a service economy. Pittsburgh, long known for its iron and steel (not to mention its dirty air), became a prototype of a city which made the transition successfully, even converting the sites of its former steel plants and railroad yards to parkland, retail shopping, hotels, and other service-oriented industries. Areas such as Wilkes-Barre which remained depressed were helped in the late 1980s by Governor Robert Casey's attempts to assist ailing industries. In the 1990s steel had been replaced as a major industry by food processing and chemicals, particularly pharmaceuticals. Pittsburgh became a center for corporate headquarters, and Philadelphia, a Mecca for high-technology industries.

By 1996 Pennsylvania ranked eighteenth in per capita personal income in the nation. Nearly 27 percent of the state's workers belonged to labor unions, the sixth highest percentage in the United States. Though primarily known for its industries, Pennsylvania also remains an important agricultural state, producing large quantities of staple crops in addition to livestock. Another important economic sector is forestry. Pennsylvania's numerous historic sites and natural recreation areas have also made tourism the second-largest employer in the state.

See also: **Bank of the United State (First National Bank), Bank of the United States (Second National Bank), Andrew Carnegie, Homestead Steel Strike, Steel Industry**

FURTHER READING

Billinger, Robert D. *Pennsylvania's Coal Industry.* Gettysburg, PA: Pennsylvania Historical Association, 1954.

Bremer, Francis J. and Dennis B. Downey, eds. *A Guide to the History of Pennsylvania.* Westport, CN: Greenwood, 1994.

Cochran, Thomas. *Pennsylvania: A Bicentennial History.* New York: Norton, 1978.

Klein, Philip S. and Ari Hoogenboom. *A History of Pennsylvania*, rev. ed. University Park, PA: Pennsylvania State University Press, 1980.

Pennsylvania, Commonwealth of. Department of General Services. *The Pennsylvania Manual, 1995*, vol. 112. Harrisburg, PA: 1995.

PENNSYLVANIA MAIN LINE CANAL

Partly in response to the federally funded National Road project, which began at Cumberland, Maryland, in 1806 and continued westward to eventually reach Illinois, the state of Pennsylvania launched its own program of transportation improvements in 1826 to link East with West. Philadelphia leaders initiated the program because they did not want their city to be eclipsed by Baltimore (which prospered at least in part because of the National Road) or New York City (which flourished after the completion of the Erie Canal in 1832). Pennsylvania developed the Main Line of Public Works—a comprehensive network of canals and railroads to connect Philadelphia with Pittsburgh. The project was approved by the state legislature in February 1826 and work began at Harrisburg in July of that year. In 1837, the project, whose centerpiece was the Pennsylvania Main Line Canal, was completed. Unlike New York's highly successful Erie Canal, the Pennsylvania Main Line Canal was never profitable. The project, built at an enormous cost to the state, never even broke even. One source described it as a "curious and cumbersome combination of railroads and canals." The Main Line Canal did connect the state's major cities, which emerged as thriving commercial centers by the end of the century. Pittsburgh, home to the iron and glass industries, became known as the Gateway to the West.

See also: **Baltimore and Ohio, Erie Canal, National Road**

PENNSYLVANIA RAILROAD

The building of the Erie Canal in 1825 and the emergence of the Baltimore and Ohio Railroad threatened Philadelphia's traditional position as a center of commerce. These modern, accessible transportation networks made New York and Baltimore major trade centers. In an effort to maintain Philadelphia as an important market hub, Pennsylvania merchants secured a legislative charter for the Pennsylvania Railroad (PRR) in 1846.

Construction on the railroad began at Harrisburg, where it would connect to the state-owned Philadelphia and Columbia Railroad, and then advance westward to Pittsburgh. The 245-mile segment between Harrisburg and Pittsburgh was open for service in 1854. Three years later, the PRR purchased the state-owned railroad east to Philadelphia. For much of the 1850s the railroad developers were occupied with upgrading the railroad's physical plant, buying new equipment, and experimenting with coal-burning fireboxes. By the beginning of the American Civil War (1861–1865), the PRR controlled a crucial segment of the nation's rail system. Despite the inflated economy and the railroad's deteriorating equipment, the PRR doubled its net profits during the war. By war's end, the Pennsylvania Railroad was the largest corporation in the world. Free of debt, it was poised for further expansion.

Expansion continued well into the 1870s, providing rail service throughout the state and beyond. Main rail lines emanated from Harrisburg to Erie, Buffalo, Baltimore, Washington, D.C., Jersey City, and New York harbor. Additional lines were leased to provide connections to Midwest cities and extend PRR rails to the Mississippi River. By the end of the nineteenth century the railroad had ceased to expand, and it began to concentrate on consolidating the leased lines and making improvements in service.

BY 1910 THE PENNSYLVANIA RAILROAD OPERATED 10,000 ROUTE-MILES IN 13 STATES, OWNED MORE THAN 260,000 PASSENGER AND FREIGHT CARS, AND EMPLOYED MORE THAN 215,000 PEOPLE. THE PRR HAD BECOME A U.S. CONGLOMERATE—A CORPORATE GIANT THAT REFERRED TO ITSELF AS "THE STANDARD RAILROAD OF THE WORLD."

Between 1899 and 1906 the passenger traffic on the main line between Harrisburg and Pittsburgh was the highest in the nation. To accommodate service demands, the railroad expanded by constructing four additional tracks and several new tunnels. In 1905 the PRR's premier passenger train, the Broadway, began running between New York and Chicago in eighteen-hour trips. In 1907 newly constructed tunnels under the Hudson River allowed passenger trains access to the newly constructed Pennsylvania Station in Manhattan, New York. By 1910 the Pennsylvania Railroad operated 10,000 route-miles in 13 states, owned more than 260,000 passenger and freight cars, and employed more than 215,000 people. The PRR had become a U.S. conglomerate—a corporate giant that referred to itself as "The Standard Railroad of the World."

Throughout this period the Pennsylvania Railroad carefully researched and implemented technological innovations. In the late nineteenth century the PRR pioneered the use of the air brake, steel rails, and automatic block signals. By 1908 the railroad was poised to introduce an all-steel passenger car. The PRR also began to use electric power, first in New York and then later in Philadelphia. The use of electric power reached full maturity in 1935 and completed the largest modernization process attempted by a U.S. railroad. In addition the PRR secured interests in Trans World Airlines, Greyhound Bus Lines, and numerous trucking companies in order to provide consumers with multi-modal transportation options.

The Pennsylvania Railroad did well enough in the first part of the century to survive financially through the Great Depression (1929–1939), but it began running into difficulties soon after. World War II (1939–1945) and the increasing cost of modernization placed a severe financial burden on the entire railroad industry. In 1946 the combination of large capital expenditures and postwar inflation produced the company's first annual net loss.

The need to replace its obsolete fleet of steam locomotives quickly became the company's most pressing issue. In spite of its deep ties and loyalty to the coal industry, the railroad replaced steam with diesel-electric power. This change offered many of the benefits of electric traction without the high initial cost. The completion of the transfer from steam to diesel, a $400 million investment, took place in 1957.

During the 1950s and 1960s the Pennsylvania Railroad continued to experience a drop in revenue and service. The company felt the impact of heavy industry's decline in the Northeast, as well as stiff competition from other emerging means of transportation. In the late 1940s the railroad's average annual ton-miles totaled 54 billion, but by 1960 the total annual ton-miles had fallen to 43 billion.

In 1968 after many years of negotiation to prevent further loss, it merged with the New York Central (NYC) and eliminated duplicate routes and facilities. Unfortunately the new company, Pennsylvania Central, proved to be unable to withstand the declining rail traffic or cope with the soaring labor costs and declared bankruptcy only two years later. In 1976 Conrail and Amtrak purchased most of Penn Central's rail holdings. This allowed Penn Central to return to financial solvency as a real estate development firm.

See also: **Railroad Industry**

FURTHER READING

Alexander, Edwin P. *On the Main Line; the Pennsylvania Railroad in the Nineteenth Centruy.* New York: C.N. Potter, 1971.

Bezilla, Michael. *Electric Traction on the Pennsylvania Railroad, 1895–1968.* University Park, PA: Pennsylvania State University Press, 1980.

Salsbury, Stephen. *No Way to Run a Railroad.* Philadelphia: Pennsylvania Railroad, 1949.

Ward, James A. *Railroads and the Character of America, 1820–1887.* Knoxville, TN: University of Tennessee Press, 1986.

PENNY AUCTIONS

Penny auctions were part of the militant tactics adopted by many Midwestern farmers before and during the Great Depression (1929–1939). The hard times that began in the mid-1920s led to what was arguably the most violent agricultural movement in U.S. history—the Farmer's Holiday Association. As farm foreclosures skyrocketed in the 1920s, with no relief from the government forthcoming, many Midwestern farmers began to cease all buying and selling of commodities. Dairy farmers blockaded roads into Sioux City, Iowa, attempting to increase the price of milk. Violence increased; milk-dumpings were common; and railroad service was interrupted. Fights broke out between the police and farmers. As part of this struggle—a struggle of farmers trying to survive—farmers began to threaten bank officers with physical harm at the auctions of farms claimed in bankruptcy settlements. The penny auctions involved farmers bidding a few cents for a neighbor's farm to re-purchase it, and if a few cents (pennies) did not clear the bank debt, then the bank officers were physically threatened. With the beginning of the Franklin D. Roosevelt (1933–1945) presidency in 1933, creditors and debtors began to work together to arrange re-financing of farms and to resolve payment of delinquent debts.

See also: **Great Depression**

PENSIONS

Pension is a benefit, generally monetary, paid to employees or their supervisors as retirement income or as compensation for disablement. A pension is a regular allowance intended to provide income security.

Pension plan benefits usually depend on the employee's age, years of service, and average salary. Plans may be contributed to jointly by the employer and employee, the employer only, or the employee only. Contributed funds are subsequently invested in a wide variety of financial markets.

Pension plans are available to workers in private industry, in local, state, or national government, or who actively served in a uniformed branch of the military. Private employers are not required to establish pension plans, but in the 1990s approximately half of private employees were covered by plans. Those private employees not covered and self-employed individuals may establish their own individual pension plans. The largest retirement plan, the U.S. government's Social Security system, provides retirement benefits to approximately 95 percent of U.S. workers when they retire. Enacted into law in 1935, the Social Security system requires both employees and employers to pay a percentage of salaries to social security through the Federal Insurance Contribution Act (FICA) payroll taxes.

In addition to Social Security, federal government pension plans include federal civilian retirement systems, military pensions, and railroad pensions. Federal government employees are covered under the Civil Service Retirement System (CSRS) if hired before January 1, 1984 and under the Federal Employee's Retirement System (FERS) if hired after that date. Both CSRS and FERS are funded by automatic payroll deductions from the employees and by contributions made by the particular federal agency for which the employee works. Many Americans are eligible for benefits based on their active military service. The first military pension was granted for the War of 1812 (1812–1814). The Veterans Administration administers the veterans pensions. Railroad pensions provide benefits for railroad workers. Although a private industry pension, a government agency, the Railroad Retirement Board, manages the funds.

Private pensions can be basically considered in two categories: defined benefit plans where an employee receives a definite pre-determined amount of money at retirement or if disabled; and, defined contribution plans where the employer pays a certain amount into the fund in certain time increments but does not guarantee any particular pension amount upon retirement. Examples of private programs include trust-fund plans, annuity plans, profit sharing plans, and thrift or savings plans including a 401(k) plan. Individual pension plans include individual retirement accounts (IRAs) and Keogh plans.

See also: **Social Security Act**

PER CAPITA INCOME

Per capita income is calculated by taking the total income, mostly wages, of a group of individuals, often a nation or a population of a specific geographic area, and dividing it by the number of individuals in the group. The resulting number is the per capita income, or income per person. Per capita income does not account for the uneven distribution of income, or wealth, among the individuals in the group. Per capita income is also usually stated in monetary units that do not reflect the effects of inflation or deflation. Per capita income can, however, be adjusted to account for changes in purchasing power and prices during a specific period of time. The adjusted per capita income is referred to as per capita real income.

PERKINS, FRANCES

Frances Perkins (1882–1963) changed her baptismal name from Fannie to Frances at the age of 25, as part of her religious conversion from Congregational to Episcopalian. Ms. Perkins also changed many other things during her 60-year long career as a social activist, social worker, social reformer, and feminist. Frances Perkins was best known for her appointment as the first female Cabinet officer in the United States government.

Frances Perkins was born in 1882, in Boston, Massachusetts, the eldest of two daughters born to Frederick and Susan Perkins, who were members of an old Maine farming family. She attended Mt. Holyoke College, where she studied physics and chemistry, subjects unusual for a girl in her day. While at Mt. Holyoke, Perkins was inspired by Florence Kelly, secretary of the National Consumers' League. Kelly was an advocate for the elimination of child labor and sweatshops (small businesses that crowded people into miserable working conditions for six or seven days a week, 12 to 16 hours a day). These conditions were quite common as the nation industrialized through the end of the nineteenth and into the twentieth century. Through Florence Kelly, Frances Perkins found her calling, and she devoted herself to a lifelong mission to help the poor and needy of the United States, especially children, women, and immigrants.

In 1905 Perkins joined the resident staff of what was to become a very famous and pioneering settlement house in Chicago, Illinois, known as the Hull House. Working there, she saw the affects of poverty and its daily issues firsthand. Though there was satisfaction to be had in providing direct services to the

Frances Perkins.

poor, Perkins began to understand that until certain laws were changed or created in the United States, no real change in the circumstances of the poor would be possible.

In Philadelphia in 1907 Perkins became a professional social worker. She began to advocate local legislation to stop the exploitation of young immigrant women and African Americans who had recently moved North from the former slave states of the South. She took courses in sociology and economics, and her social consciousness brought her closely in line with existing socialist thought of the time. She earned a degree in political science and moved to New York, where, in 1910 at the age of 30, she was offered the job of secretary of the New York City Consumers' League. As secretary she focused on changing laws to improve sanitary conditions in businesses, creating legislation for fire prevention in factories, and passing a 54-hour-week maximum labor law that would limit work hours of women and children under the age of eighteen. In 1918 she became a leader in the U.S. women's suffrage movement.

Perkins successfully supported many New York laws that regulated business practices with respect to the abuses of the workforce. She developed many political contacts in New York, and she took on various social and legislative projects on behalf of women and children. Among her contacts was the governor of New York, Franklin D. Roosevelt (1882–1945), who later became President of the United States in 1933. Roosevelt was impressed with Perkins' skills and after his election to the presidency (1933–1945), he appointed her to his Cabinet as his Secretary of Labor. Frances Perkins became the first female member of a presidential Cabinet in U.S. history.

The pressure she felt to succeed at this post was immense. Many labor and business leaders were outraged at her appointment. Despite enormous pressures and controversy, she re-organized the Department of Labor during the Great Depression (1929–1939) and restored the integrity of the Bureau of Immigration and Naturalization, which was then considered to be an agency of bribe taking and illegal deportations. She also became an important advisor to President Roosevelt, and she brought in many important members to Roosevelt's administration. Her sympathies for the unemployed during the Depression and her efforts to support organized labor gained her the reputation as a communist sympathizer, though she clearly distrusted the Communist Party in the United States.

Perkins survived an unsuccessful impeachment attempt in 1938, when the House Un-American Activities Committee (HUAC) accused her of being a communist. She remained in government service until 1953, when she retired. The legacy of her work was enormous, not only as a lifelong political and social activist on behalf of women and children, but as a pioneer in social legislation. The pioneering role she undertook as a woman made her arguably one of the most revered feminist role models in the twentieth century, alongside Eleanor Roosevelt; much of her work led to massive federal programs, including the Social Security program.

After her retirement, Perkins spent the rest of her life as a college lecturer, encouraging others to enter the work of social activism. She became a visiting professor at Cornell University, a post she held until her death in 1965, at age 85.

See also: **New Deal, Franklin Delano Roosevelt, Women's Movement**

FURTHER READING

Colman, Penny. *A Woman Unafraid: The Achievements of Frances Perkins*. New York: Atheneum, 1993.

Josephson, Matthew. *Al Smith: Hero of the Cities; a Political Portrait Drawing on the Papers of Frances Perkins*. Boston: Houghton Mifflin, 1969.

Martin, George W. *Madam Secretary, Frances Perkins.* Boston: Houghton Mifflin, 1976.

Milton, David. *The Politics of U. S. Labor: From the Great Depression to the New Deal.* New York: Monthly Review Press, 1982.

Mohr, Lillian H. *Frances Perkins, That Woman in FDR's Cabinet.* Croton-on-Hudson: North River Press, 1979.

PERRY, MATTHEW CALBRAITH

Matthew C. Perry's (1794–1858) primary occupation was that of a naval officer, yet he is perhaps best remembered as a diplomat entrusted by the U.S. government to negotiate a treaty with Japan. Since the early 1600s Japan isolated itself from Western countries. In 1854 Perry successfully arranged a treaty between Japan and the United States. The treaty provided the United States with two Japanese sea ports, enabling the two countries could begin to engage in commercial trade with one another. This was Japan's first modern treaty with a Western nation. It marked the beginning of Japan's involvement in world affairs.

Born in 1794, Matthew Perry entered the Navy at age 16, serving as a midshipman. His first duty was aboard a vessel commanded by his older brother, Oliver Perry. His career in the Navy led him into combat during the War of 1812 (1812–1814); he later battled pirates in the West Indies, carried freed slaves to the newly founded African colony of Liberia, and transported American minister John Randolph to Russia. It was in Russia that Perry was offered a captain's position with the czarist government, but he firmly declined, preferring his commission with the U.S. Navy as a Master Commandant.

In 1833 Perry was appointed Second Officer of the New York Navy Yard, and began notable service on shore. Residing in New York City, he began to aggressively pursue his ideas for naval development. He created a naval apprentice system, which was adopted by Congress in 1837. In 1845 Perry and other examiners prepared the first course of instruction for the Naval Academy at Annapolis, Maryland. He went on to advocate and pioneer the use of steam-powered vessels in the Navy. He organized the first Naval Engineer Corps, and his work on the naval board was used by Congress to help enact federal legislation creating federal lighthouses. Beginning in 1843 Perry was once again actively at sea. He first commanded the African Squadron, and later led a squadron of ships in the Gulf of Mexico during the Mexican War (1846–1848).

In January 1852 Perry was selected for a highly important diplomatic mission—the negotiation of a treaty with Japan, a country which had sealed itself against dealings with Western powers since the early 1600s. His main mission in Japan was to ensure the protection of U.S. seamen and property and to open one or more Japanese ports to U.S. vessels for the procurement of supplies and commercial trade. Perry agreed to undertake the mission, provided that he could go to Japan with a large and imposing naval fleet. He hoped the sheer size of the fleet would facilitate negotiations with Japan. Perry was instructed to use any vigorous and intimidating means necessary in his negotiations with the Japanese, though with the understanding that President James Monroe (1817–1825) had no power to declare war in this situation.

In an effort to achieve his goals without resorting to military action, Perry adopted a strategy of surrounding himself and his mission with an air of mystery. His combination of boldness and mystery succeeded. He met with representatives of Japan's emperor and left the country nine days after arriving in 1853, stating he would return one year later to learn Japan's decision. He returned in seven months and, on March 31, 1854, a treaty of peace, friendship, and commerce between Japan and the United States was signed. It was a diplomatic event filled with much pageantry, and several U.S. naval vessels stood offshore.

Federal politics had changed during Perry's absence from the United States, and little notice was paid to his achievement in Japan. The ''Old Bruin,'' as sailors called Perry, died in New York on March 4, 1858, a year after his return from Japan. He died while preparing a report of his expedition.

***See also:* Japan (Opening of)**

FURTHER READING

Blumberg, Rhoda. *Commodore Perry in the Land of the Shogun.* New York: Lothrop, Lee and Shepard Books, 1985.

Houchins, Chang-su. *Artifacts of Diplomacy: Smithsonian Collections from Commodore Matthew Perry's Japan Expedition (1853–1854).* Washington, DC: Smithsonian Institution Press, 1995.

Morison, Samuel Eliot. *Old Bruin: Commodore Matthew C. Perry, (1794–1858).* Boston, MA: Little Brown, 1967.

Walworth, Arthur. *Black Ships Off Japan, The Story of Commodore Perry's Expedition.* New York: A.A. Knopf, 1946.

Wiley, Peter B. *Yankees in the Land of the Gods: Commodore Perry and the Opening of Japan.* New York: Viking, 1990.

PERSONAL COMPUTERS

Personal computers (PC) were developed during the 1970s and were intended for use by small businesses and in the home. No established industrial computer company, like IBM, Burroughs, or Honeywell believed in 1975 that there would be any market for a PC. The earliest commercial PCs were credited to the efforts of Stephen Jobs (1955—) and Stephen Wozniak (1950—), who began their own PC company, Apple Computers, in 1976, building a microchip-based computer for small businesses and particularly for home use. These computers represented simplicity of design and function, and they were easily used by non-professionals. By 1977 the personal computer industry moved quickly, with Apple, Commodore, and Radio Shack aggressively entering the "home computer market."

The PC was made possible largely because of the miniaturization of electronic parts and the ability to reliably mass produce many parts of the computer, such as the silicon chip, the integrated circuit board, and the microprocessor. The personal computer evolved (in the 1960s and 1970s) from large single-function devices like industrial data processors to smaller single-function devices like pocket calculators. With smaller hardware and more diverse software, the PC of the late 1970s became consolidated into desktop sized, multi-function devices. They now provide international communications, word-processing capabilities, as well as the other educational, recreational, and personal functions associated with modern computers in homes and businesses.

See also: **Computer Industry, Stephen Jobs, Stephen Wozniak**

PETROLEUM INDUSTRY

Crude oil seeps from the earth's crevices and fissures, and accumulates in pools on surface rocks; it has been used as a fuel source since approximately 3500 B.C.. In the early nineteenth century, crude oil was collected from rock pools and primitively refined for commercial use. Dr. Abraham Gesner of Pittsburgh, inventor of kerosene lamp oil, formed the Pennsylvania Rock Oil Company in 1854. In 1859 Edwin Drake and W.A. Smith drilled the first U.S. well, specifically to find petroleum, in Titusville, (Oil Creek) Pennsylvania. Because crude oil was unsuitable for direct use, it had to be refined and converted into such products as kerosene, gasoline, and motor oil. In 1860 D.S. Stombs and Julius Brace of Virginia introduced and patented a semi-continuous refining system. In 1861 the first full-fledged petroleum refinery in the United States opened; it churned out mostly kerosene.

The legendary oil tycoon, John D. Rockefeller (1839–1937), began oil operations in 1863. Based in Cleveland, Ohio, Rockefeller founded the Standard Oil Company on June 10, 1870. Skillfully using the laws of incorporation and assembling trusts, Rockefeller eventually acquired competing companies across the country and established a very effective monopoly. By 1879 the 30 companies that belonged to the Standard Oil trust controlled 80 percent of the refineries and 90 percent of the pipelines in the U.S. petroleum industry. This giant trust leveraged its clout with the railroads to negotiate favorable freight rates.

Rockefeller was the biggest, but not the only, oil entrepreneur. In 1897 Joseph S. Cullinan organized the first pipeline and refinery in Corsicana in Texas. Cullinan also successfully pioneered the use of petroleum as a diesel fuel for locomotives and as a dust settler for streets.

The main reason for increased public demand for petroleum was the proliferation of the gasoline-powered automobile, various renditions of which sprang up in the late nineteenth century. Machinist and inventor Henry Ford employed assembly line techniques to lower the cost of each unit of production, making automobiles available to more consumers, and thus increasing the demand for gasoline.

Advancements in technology during World War I (1914–1918) escalated demand for petroleum. Farmers were able to increase productivity with gas powered tractors; new asphalt highways carried diesel-powered trucks delivering goods across the nation. New products derived from refined petroleum included plastics, synthetic fiber and rubber. Increasing demand for new products promoted a steadily increasing supply of new crude oil.

By 1992 the Chevron Oil Company was the largest petroleum refiner in the United States and was a huge producer of oil in terms of profits and sales. Chevron began in 1882 as Standard Oil of California, and quickly developed internationally. The second largest capacity refiner in the United States was Exxon Corporatoin. Exxon came about through the 1934 merger of Standard Oil Company of New Jersey and the Anglo American Oil Company Ltd. Exxon grew remarkably throughout the twentieth century. By 1993 it was the industry leader with profits totaling $5.28 billion. Profits of the Mobile Corporation ranked second at $2.08 billion from sales of $56.6 billion. Other industry leaders included Texaco Inc., Shell Oil Co., Chevron Corp., Atlantic Richfield Co., Conoco Inc., Amoco Corp., and BP America Inc.

Since the early 1950s natural gas was the refineries' largest end-product. Residential and commercial users consumed the largest proportion of natural gas. Industry consumed the next largest amount with power generation a distant third in natural gas consumption. (Food, paper, chemical, and petroleum refining industries all consume vast amounts of natural gas.)

In 1997 U.S. refineries produced an average of 14.63 million barrels of refined petroleum products each day. The United States supplied over one-fifth of the world's refined petroleum—roughly equal to the production of all the European countries combined. The U.S. refineries employed approximately 93,000 people in 1998.

During the first four decades of the twentieth century, the heyday of internal combustion in the United States, U.S. oil reserves were gradually depleted. Accordingly the oil industry became among the first to undergo "globalization." The Standard Oil Company anticipated this development back in 1888 when it established its first foreign affiliate, the Anglo American Oil Company Limited, headquartered in London. Although U.S. and European companies continued to reap most of the profits of petroleum production, by the mid-1950s much of the world's petroleum was being pumped in a small group of oil-producing countries, most of them in the Persian Gulf. In an effort to gain control of its petroleum reserves, these countries founded the Organization of Petroleum Exporting Countries (OPEC) in 1960. OPEC set a standard cost for producing a barrel of oil in all member countries. The minimum price per barrel was based on the tax-paid cost per barrel plus a profit margin. New petroleum companies could not undermine OPEC's dominant market by offering lower prices. In OPEC's early years, other petroleum producing countries used the organization more as a defensive instrument to stabilize the market. But plagued with oil shortages and political disruptions in the Middle East during the 1970s, non-OPEC refineries and suppliers began to rely more heavily on their own private inventories.

Beginning in the 1970s, many developments led to a sharp decline in world demand for OPEC oil. Several major factors, including environmental concerns, brought about changes; most changes were not in OPEC's favor. Revolutionary innovations in the oil industry drastically reduced the risk and expense of finding and developing oil and expanded output among non-OPEC producers. For example major U.S. oil companies owned and operated exploration and drilling sites around the world. Exploration, production, and transportation of petroleum in the United States was handled by private companies under the regulation of federal, state, and local commissions. Strategies such as this helped to boost the world's oil supplies at the expense of OPEC's market share. By the 1980s OPEC was a shadow of its former self.

Refining and production of oil and gas has become an exacting engineering science. The United States was a pioneer in petroleum refining, exploration, and perfected most techniques and procedures before other nations. U.S. petroleum refiners have been regarded as the world leaders. However, it remains to be seen as to whether shifting political boundaries will allow U.S. refiners to compete directly with foreign companies for a larger market share.

See also: **Exxon Corporation, OPEC Oil Embargo, John D. Rockefeller, Standard Oil Company, Texas Company**

FURTHER READING

Chernow, Ron. "The Monopoly That Went Too Far." *Business Week*, May 18, 1998.

Hast, Adele, ed. *International Directory of Company Histories*. Chicago: St. James Press, 1991, s.v. "Exxon."

Hillstrom, Kevin, ed. *Encyclopedia of American Industries*. Farmington Hills, MI: The Gale Group, 1994, s.v. "Petroleum Refining and Related Areas."

Mack, Toni, James R. Norman, Howard Rudnitski, and Andrew Tanzer. "History is Full of Giants That Failed to Adapt." *Forbes*, February 28, 1994.

Monthly Labor Review. Washington, DC: U.S. Bureau of the Census, July 1993.

PHARMACEUTICAL INDUSTRY

The pharmaceutical industry in the United States dates back to the early 1800s. Opium was routinely prescribed in the United States as far back as the eighteenth century; however, concoctions known as "patent medicines" did not make an appearance until the nineteenth century. Patent medicines became very popular; they bore names such as "Carter's Little Liver

Pills.'' During this time many pharmaceutical companies were founded in the Midwest, including Parke Davis, Eli Lilly, and Upjohn Company.

As the industry developed, New York City was an important center of trade in drugs; Philadelphia also emerged as a home for about six pharmaceutical manufacturers. Pharmacy schools, which began to open in several states between 1821 to 1859, probably contributed to the growth of the pharmaceuticals industry. (The *American Journal of Pharmacy* began publication in 1825.) Another probable factor in the growth of the industry was the prodigious amount of drugs used during the American Civil War (1861–1865). By 1870 there were almost 300 pharmaceutical manufacturers in existence.

During the early nineteenth century, several new drugs quickly came into common use. Some of these were opiates, which were later greatly restricted during the twentieth century. Morphine was first commercially produced in the 1830s. After the invention of the hypodermic needle in the 1860s, morphine use became more widespread as it could be easily injected into the patient. Another (subsequently) restricted drug, cocaine, was first commercially produced in the 1880s. When it was first introduced, it became very popular—physicians thought that it was harmless. (Until it was found to be addictive, cocaine was even used as an ingredient in the soft drink Coca-Cola.) In 1898, another opiate, heroin, was commercially available from the Bayer Company.

The dangers of opiates were not acknowledged until the 1900s, in part because there were no laws regulating the drug industry until the 1870s and 1880s. The Pure Food and Drug Act of 1906, the Shanghai Opium Convention of 1909, The Hague Opium Treaty, and the Harrison Narcotic Act (both in 1912) were all early attempts by the U.S. government to regulate drug manufacturing and distribution.

Several advancements in drug production were developed during the late nineteenth century which furthered development of the industry. Pharmaceutical manufacturers attempted to standardize batches of medicines between the various companies. In 1888 another improvement came in the form of a machine that produced pills of uniform dose and purity. Later, during the early twentieth century over-the-counter drugs were developed and marketed. Products, such as aspirin and laxatives, greatly increased the availability of medicines to the general public.

Following World War I (1914–1918) demand influenced the rapid commercial expansion of the pharmaceuticals industry. The number of chain drugstores increased during the 1920s and, as the industry grew, it consolidated; several drug companies merged. By the 1930s, market research became important in the industry; consumers wanted new medicines that could help two or more symptoms at a time. Sulfa drugs, designed to fight bacteria, were also developed during this period and became the choice for treatment of infections until the mid-1940s, when penicillin was commercially developed and marketed.

In 1937 over 100 Americans were killed when treated with a drug that had a toxic solvent in it. This resulted in stricter governmental regulations to improve drug testing. Changes included passing the Food, Drug, and Cosmetic Act of 1938, which was enforced by the Food and Drug Administration (FDA).

World War II (1939–1945) caused an upsurge in demand for the new antibiotic drug, penicillin, which was first marketed in 1946. (The major producer of penicillin was the Pfizer Company.) New medicines continued to appear after the war. Almost 500 new drugs entered the market between 1950 and 1959. With this expansion came advanced marketing tactics—pharmaceutical companies began to advertise drugs on television. As the pharmaceutical market grew, so increased the level of government regulation. In the 1950s and 1960s several new FDA laws were passed to further regulate the testing, certification, and prescription of drugs.

In the mid-1980s, the FDA was reorganized due to allegations of deficient practices. One issue examined by the reorganized FDA was the use of generic drugs, which, according to ''The American Druggist,'' accounted for almost 45 percent of all prescriptions by the mid-1990s.

In the 1990s the pharmaceutical industry focused on the research and development of new drugs, especially drugs for treating diseases common to an elderly population, as well as cancer and AIDS. Biotechnology began to make an impact in the drug industry, as companies such as Amgen, Inc., and Chiron Corporation were founded. Competition resulted in the merging, restructuring, and downsizing of many pharmaceutical companies.

***See also:* Pure Food and Drug Act**

FURTHER READING

Cray, William C. *The Pharmaceutical Manufacturers Association: the First 30 Years*. Washington, DC: Pharmaceuticals Manufacturers Association, 1989.

Foner, Eric, and John A. Garraty, eds. *The Reader's Companion to American History*. Boston, MA: Houghton Mifflin Co., 1991, s.v. ''Drug.''

McConnell, Stacy A., and Linda D. Hall, eds. *Dun & Bradstreet/Gale Industry Reference Handbooks: Pharmaceuticals*. Detroit: The Gale Group, 1998.

Mez-Mangold, Lydia. *A History of Drugs*. Totowa, NJ: Barnes & Noble, 1986.

''Phrma: Publications: Industry Profile 1998, Chapter 1,'' [cited January 31, 1999] available from the World Wide Web @ www.phrma.org/publications/industry/profile98/chap1.html#improved/.

PHILIPPINES

An archipelago (island chain) consisting of some 7100 islands in southeast Asia, the Philippines became a territory of the United States by the Treaty of Paris (1898). Signed on December 10, the agreement ended the Spanish-American War (1898), which marked a determined U.S. interest in participating more fully in international affairs. One issue during the war was the matter of an independent Cuba. The peace treaty signed between Spain and the United States provided for Cuba's autonomy and granted the United States control of Puerto Rico, Guam, and the Philippine Islands. Spain surrendered the last vestiges of its colonial empire; in exchange, the European country received $20 million in payment from the United States.

U.S. imperialists viewed the Philippines as ''stepping stones'' to mainland Asia, and they stressed the islands' strategic importance for the United States. Anti-imperialists argued that the annexation constituted the conquering of people against their will. While Americans debated the motives and the outcome of the expansion, soon after the Treaty of Paris was signed, the Philippines were embroiled in conflict. Filipinos, determined to achieve independence, revolted in an uprising lasting from 1899 to 1901. A civil government was established on the islands in 1901, and in November 1935, the Commonwealth of the Philippines was officially established. The islands, however, continued to be the site of conflict in the following decade.

The United States struggled with Japan for control of the Philippines during World War II (1939–1945). Under General Douglas MacArthur (1880–1964), the United States established practical control of the islands during the last days of the war (July 1945). After the Japanese surrender, an independent government was established in the Philippines (July 1946), but the United States was granted a ninety-nine year lease of several Philippine military facilities. In the 1980s political upheaval in the island nation resulted in the revocation of the military leases. The United States withdrew its troops from the Philippines in the 1990s.

See also: **Imperialism, Spanish-American War**

PHYSICAL CAPITAL

Physical capital consists of man-made tangible assets, such as factories, buildings, machinery and equipment, that are used to actually convert raw materials into usable products for consumer purchase. Physical capital is considered to be secondary to primary resources such as money, raw materials, and land. Since it is used to produce goods or services over time, the wear and tear on physical capital makes it subject to depreciation, or loss of value, and requires replacement periodically. The more physical capital a nation or company possesses, the greater its capacity to produce goods or services. Physical capital may also be referred to as capital goods.

See also: **Capital Goods**

PICKENS, THOMAS BOONE, JR.

One of the best known and most skillful deal makers ever to emerge on the American scene, T. Boone Pickens (1928–) rose to prominence during the 1980s as one of the decade's premier corporate raiders. Colorful and outspoken, he combined uncanny business skill with the daring of a gambler as he launched one takeover attempt after another and shook up the oil industry in the process.

Thomas Boone Pickens, Jr., was born in the small town of Holdenville, Oklahoma on May 22, 1928. He was the only child of Thomas Boone Pickens, Sr., a distant relative of frontiersman Daniel Boone, and Gracee (Molonson) Pickens. Pickens' father was an attorney employed in the land acquisitions department of Phillips Petroleum Company when his son was born. ''I was very fortunate in my gene (genetic) mix,'' T. Boone noted in a 1985 *Time* magazine interview. ''The gambling instincts I inherited from my father were matched by my mother's gift for analysis.''

Around the mid 1940s, the family moved to Amarillo, Texas, where Pickens excelled in basketball at Amarillo High School. He then attended Texas A&M University on an athletic scholarship but transferred to Oklahoma State University after a broken elbow caused him to lose his financial support. Pickens received his bachelor's degree in geology from Oklahoma State in 1951 and subsequently went to work in the petroleum industry.

Not long after he earned his college degree, Pickens took a job as an oil geologist for Phillips Petroleum. He left in 1955 however, because he found the work boring and felt stifled by the company's conservative style. Pickens then started his own company, Petroleum Exploration Co., with $2500 in cash, a $100,000 line of credit, and "an uncanny ability to find oil and gas," in the words of reporter Lydia Chavez of the *New York Times*.

Pickens focused his efforts on locating oil and supplying it to others. He managed to do this while avoiding the temptation to become involved with often-costly sideline businesses such as pipelines, refineries, and service stations. By 1964 he had become successful enough to diversify some of his operations and incorporate. Thus was born Mesa Corporation, Inc., with headquarters in Amarillo, Texas.

By 1969 profits had reached the point where Pickens could afford to start buying out other companies. His first acquisition was Hugoton Production Co. and its vast natural gas field in Texas. The following year he was rebuffed when he made a bid to take over Southland Royalty. In 1973 however, he added Pubco Petroleum to Mesa's holdings. In 1974 an ill-fated attempt to diversify into cattle cost him $19 million.

Pickens fared much better during the 1980s thanks to a combination of his astute business skills, his love of gambling, and sheer luck. Using a variety of techniques, including some that were not entirely aboveboard, he managed to accumulate a massive amount of cash by selling off some of his assets at just the right time and by buying and trading stock in other petroleum companies in a series of hostile takeover bids. Pickens also profited handsomely from the booming oil market during this decade. His shrewd deal-making netted him the Wall Street Transcripts "gold award" for the top executive in the oil industry in both 1981 and 1982.

Pickens' specialty was "greenmailing," which involved buying huge blocks of a company's stock as if preparing for a takeover, then selling them back at an inflated price so that the company can thwart the apparent buyout attempt. He first used this strategy in May 1982, when he tried to buy a controlling interest in a medium-sized oil firm called Cities Service Company. His efforts touched off a fierce bidding war among several oil industry rivals that drove up the company's stock price. Occidental Petroleum ultimately made the best purchase offer for Cities Service Company, but Pickens and Mesa shareholders still won big. By losing the bidding war, Pickens had strategically positioned Mesa to realize over $31 million in profit on the merger deal.

PICKENS SUPPORTED THE THEN-REVOLUTIONARY VIEW THAT A CEO'S MAJOR RESPONSIBILITY WAS TO CREATE WEALTH FOR HIS SHAREHOLDERS AND THAT THE FAILURE TO DO SO MIGHT WELL RESULT IN THE LOSS OF HIS OR HER JOB.

From that moment on, Pickens became a so-called "corporate raider," pursuing what many believed were authentic bids to assume control of large oil companies, especially ones that he felt were being mismanaged and therefore less able to fight off a takeover. Time and again, he lost bidding wars only to win at the stock manipulation game. In 1984 for example, after a highly competitive struggle involving some of the oil industry's biggest names, Gulf Oil finally allowed itself to be purchased by Standard Oil Company of California to avoid being taken over by Pickens. The transaction resulted in the creation of a new oil company, Chevron; and Pickens and his partners walked away with a profit of $760 million.

In the mid-1980s, Pickens was reported to be the highest paid corporate executive in the United States, earning more than $20 million in salary and deferred compensations that year from his newly renamed Mesa Limited Partnership, Inc. His personal wealth was estimated at over $100 million.

Pickens' reign as the "king of the corporate raiders" was short-lived. In 1985 he went after Unocal Corporation, which responded by offering a unique stock buy-back plan that was open to all shareholders except Pickens and his Mesa partners. Pickens sued in the Delaware courts to block the plan and received a favorable ruling. Then the Delaware Supreme Court reversed the lower court's decision and ruled that a company did indeed have the right to single out corporate raiders and treat them differently than other shareholders. Even though this decision was eventually overturned by the Securities and Exchange Commission, it marked the beginning of the end of Pickens' career.

In 1989 after becoming embroiled in a series of nasty political squabbles in Amarillo, Pickens moved Mesa's headquarters to Dallas. His fortunes took a sustained tumble. The biggest blow came in 1996 when Pickens was forced to resign as head of Mesa after running up one billion dollars in debt, a result of overly generous payments to his shareholders. Pickens had bet that the price of natural gas would rise and bail his company out. But for once his gamble did not pay off, and Mesa suddenly found itself the target of raiders organized by a former Pickens protégé named David Batchelder. Pickens officially stepped down as head of Mesa on December 31, 1996, but stayed on as a commodity market consultant for the company until late 1997 and then served as a member of the board of directors.

Pickens provided considerable time and money through the years to Oklahoma State University, the University of Texas Cancer Center, and a variety of public service organizations. He also served as chairman of the board of the M.D. Anderson Medical Center in Houston, Texas, as chairman of the executive committee of the Texas Research League, and as chairman of the board of regents of West Texas State University.

A key part of Pickens' strategy during the 1980s was his vocal, and often quite colorful, criticism of the U.S. corporate system. He found many of the CEOs and managers he came in contact with to be greedy, careless, and ignorant about important aspects of their companies or their industries in general. He denounced the cushy perks these executives received and questioned their real value to the companies they headed. Instead Pickens supported the then-revolutionary view that a CEO's major responsibility is to create wealth for his shareholders and that the failure to do so might well result in the loss of his or her job. It also infuriated him that a number of corporate leaders did not even own stock in the businesses they ran, meaning that they had little incentive to improve performance and thus increase stock values. And even those who did own stock in their companies, noted Pickens in a 1985 *Forbes* magazine article, ''have no more feeling for the average stockholder than they do for baboons in Africa.''

Such outspoken corporate-bashing made Pickens a hero to those ''average stockholders.'' They applauded his efforts to shed light on inept management practices and were thrilled by the hefty returns they received on their investments as a result of his raids. In the end, Pickens opened more than a few eyes to the flaws in U.S. corporate culture and in no small way changed the way business was done in the United States.

See also: **Petroleum Industry**

FURTHER READING

Current Biography Yearbook. New York: H.W. Wilson, 1986, s.v. ''Pickens, Thomas Boone.''

Nocera, Joseph. ''T. Boone Pickens Gets the Boot at Mesa.'' *Fortune*, July 22, 1996.

Pickens, T. Boone, Jr. *Boone*. Boston: Houghton Mifflin, 1987.

Thorpe, Helen. ''Reversal of Fortune.'' *Texas Monthly*, October 1995.

Willoughby, Jack. ''Interview with T. Boone Pickens.'' *Forbes*, April 22, 1985.

PIECES OF EIGHT

Pieces of eight were Spanish silver coins (pesos) that circulated along with other hard currency in the American colonies. Since the settlements in the New World were all possessions of their mother countries (England, Spain, France, Portugal, and the Netherlands), they did not have monetary systems of their own. England forbade its American colonies to issue money. Colonists used whatever foreign currency they could get their hands on. Pieces of eight (from Spain), reals (from Spain and Portugal), and shillings (from England) were in circulation; the pieces of eight were most common. The Spanish silver coin was so named because it was worth eight reals and at one time had an eight stamped on it. To make change, the coin was cut up to resemble pieces of a pie. Two pieces, or ''two bits,'' of the silver coin made up a quarter, which is why Americans still may refer to a quarter (of a dollar) as two bits.

In 1652 the Massachusetts Bay Company became the first colony to mint its own coins, since because of the English Civil War there was no monarch on the throne of England. The issue of coinage by colonists was strictly prohibited by England, but the Puritans of Massachusetts continued to make their own coins for some thirty years thereafter, stamping the year 1652 on them as a way to circumvent the law.

There were frequent money shortages in the colonies, which usually ran a trade deficit with Europe: the colonies supplied raw goods to Europe, but finished goods, including manufactured items were mostly imported, resulting in an imbalance of trade. Coinage scarce, most colonists conducted trade as barter, exchanging goods and services for the same. The monetary situation on the North American mainland remained tenuous even after the American Revolution (1775–1783). It was not stabilized until after 1785 when Congress established the dollar as the official currency of the new United States.

PIKE'S EXPEDITION

Zebulon Pike (1779–1813) was born in Lamberton, New Jersey in January 1779. He followed his father, a U.S. Army major of the same name, into a military career. The younger Pike was commissioned first lieutenant in 1799. While he was serving on the western frontier in St. Louis, President Thomas Jefferson (1801–1809) completed the Louisiana Purchase with France. The acquisition added 828,000 square miles of land lying between the Mississippi River and the Rocky Mountains, northward to the source of the river. The United States needed to explore and assert legal claim to the newly gained lands as well as to establish friendly relations with the Native American tribes in the region. General James Wilkinson selected Pike to lead an exploratory expedition in search of the Mississippi River's source in the northern part of the Purchase area. (Wilkinson may have also intended to test British reactions to a U.S. military exploration venturing into traditional fur-trapping country.)

Pike assembled a 20-man party and departed northward from St. Louis in early August 1805. At this time, the famous Lewis and Clark Expedition had followed the Missouri River to its source and was crossing the northern Rocky Mountains en route to winter at the mouth of the Columbia River. When winter arrived, the Pike party had journeyed as far as 100 miles north of the Falls of St. Anthony in present-day Minnesota. Taking a smaller party and hauling supplies on sleds, Pike continued onward to Lake Leech, which he mistakenly proclaimed the source of the Mississippi River.

Upon the party's return to St. Louis, Pike received orders from Wilkinson for another venture. This time, Wilkinson requested that Pike explore the headwaters of the Arkansas and Red rivers in the southwest corner of the Louisiana Purchase area and, curiously, to inconspicuously assess Spain's New Mexico settlements. Relations at the time between the United States and Spain were not good and, in the historical record, the purposes of Pike's orders were unclear, especially when it became known that Wilkinson was a secret agent for Spain.

Pike's expedition set out westward in April 1806, to the Arkansas River in modern central Colorado. Apparently, word of Pike's "secret" mission reached the Spanish headquarters for the northern provinces of New Spain in Chihuahua, Mexico. A Spanish military force was dispatched to intercept Pike. Meanwhile, Pike reached the present-day area of Pueblo, Colorado. En route in November 1806, he attempted to ascend a summit located in the Front Range of the Rocky Mountains near modern Colorado Springs, what later became known as Pike's Peak. He had to turn back, however, as his party was not prepared for the snow and cold weather on the 14,110 foot peak.

> (Pike) was completely lost among the great tossing peaks of the Colorado Rockies, some of the highest mountains on earth, lost in the middle of winter, half-starved, frozen, and admittedly "at a loss which course to pursue" . . . Going in a circular route, they passed through South Park, where a few years later the great rendezvous of the fur traders and mountain men would be held.
>
> **John Upton Terrell, *Zebulon Pike; the Life and Times of an Adventurer*, 1968**

After exploring the Arkansas River's headwaters in the Rocky Mountains, Pike then turned south, supposedly to find the Red River's source. However, he crossed the Sangre de Cristo Mountains to the Rio Grande River's Conejos fork, where he constructed a cottonwood log outpost. At that location a Spanish detachment finally found him. The Spaniards requested Pike and his men accompany them to Santa Fe. Pike, claiming he meant to be on the Red River, departed as requested, and wound up in Chihuahua as a prisoner charged with illegal entry into Spanish territory. A year later the Spaniards escorted Pike and his party back northward to the United States territory at Natchitoches, Louisiana, where he was released in July 1807.

After his return Pike was dispatched to the Secretary of War to answer for his actions and his relationship to Wilkinson. Wilkinson, along with Aaron Burr (1756–1836), was accused of plotting to illegally seize the Southwest from Spain. Absolved of wrongdoing, Pike resumed his military career. With the outbreak of the War of 1812 (1812–1814) Pike, who had a series of promotions after 1808, was promoted to brigadier general. In 1813 he lead U.S. troops in a successful attack against the British on York (now Toronto) in Canada. Pike was gravely wounded when a British powder magazine exploded, instantly killing over 90 soldiers from both sides and wounding 180. Pike sustained a broken spine and died a few hours later from wounds.

Pike's official expeditions report, *Account of Expeditions to the Sources of the Mississippi and through the Western Parts of Louisiana*, provided the first description of the broad region lying between the Plains and the upper Rio Grande River region. Though his expeditions charted new expanses of the United

Pike's Peak, part of the Rocky Mountain range near Colorado Springs, was named for Zebulon Pike, who unsuccessfully attempted an ascent of the 14,110 foot summit in 1806.

States—the expeditions were some of the first sponsored by the U.S. government—Pike's journals were not of the same caliber of Lewis and Clark's. Regarding the headwaters of the Mississippi, Pike had misidentified the actual source (Lake Itasca), but he did learn much about the upper Mississippi region. Pike reported on the military weakness of Santa Fe, and he commented on the potential for lucrative overland trade with Mexico. The report fanned American curiosity about the expanding western frontier of the young nation and, in part, stimulated future U.S. expansion to Texas.

See also: **Lewis and Clark Expedition, Louisiana Purchase, Westward Expansion**

FURTHER READING

Hollon, W. Eugene. *The Lost Pathfinder: Zebulon Montgomery Pike.* Norman, OK: University of Oklahoma Press, 1949.

Jackson, Donald Dean, ed. *The Journals of Zebulon M. Pike, with Letters and Related Documents.* Norman, OK: University of Oklahoma Press, 1966.

Merk, Frederick. *History of the Westward Movement.* New York: Knopf, 1978.

Nobles, Gregory H. *American Frontiers: Cultural Encounters and Continental Conquest.* New York: Hill and Wang, 1997.

Owsley, Frank L., Jr., and Gene A. Smith. *Filibusters and Expansionists: Jeffersonian Manifest Destiny, 1800–1821.* Tuscaloosa, AL: University of Alabama Press, 1997.

PILGRIMS

The Pilgrims were Separatists (Protestants who separated from the Anglican Church to set up their own church). In 1609 they fled their home in Scrooby, England, in search of religious freedom, which they found in Holland. Fearing their children would lose contact with English culture, the group decided to voyage to the New World to establish their own community. In 1620 they arrived on the rocky western shore of Cape Cod Bay, Massachusetts. Their trans-Atlantic crossing had taken 66 days aboard the *Mayflower*. Two babies were born during the passage, bringing the number of settlers to 102—only about 35 were Pilgrims, the rest were merchants.

On November 21 the Pilgrims drafted the Mayflower Compact, an agreement by which the 41 signatories (the men aboard the *Mayflower*) formed a body politic that was authorized to enact and enforce laws. Religious leader John Carver (1576–1621) was voted governor. Though their colonial patent from the London Company specified they were to settle in Virginia, they decided to establish their colony at Cape Cod, well outside the company's jurisdiction. By December 25 the Pilgrims had chosen the site for their settlement and began building at New Plymouth.

The first year was difficult and the Pilgrims faced many hardships: Thirty-five more colonists arrived aboard the *Fortune*, and thereby put a strain on already limited resources. Sicknesses such as pneumonia, tuberculosis, and scurvy claimed many lives, including that of Governor Carver; and the merchants in the group challenged the purity of the settlement.

Having secured a new patent from the Council of New England in June 1621, the lands of the New Plymouth Colony were held in common by both the Pilgrims and the merchants. But this communal system of agriculture proved unsuccessful and in 1624, William Bradford (1590–1657), who had succeeded Carver as governor, granted each family its own parcel of land. The Wampanoag Indians, who had previously occupied the land settled by the Pilgrims, proved friendly and were helpful advisers in agricultural matters. In 1626 the Pilgrims bought the merchants' shares, and claimed the colony for themselves. Though they were inexperienced at government before arriving in America and had not been formally educated, the Pilgrims successfully governed themselves according to their religious beliefs; Plymouth Colony remained independent until 1691, when it became part of the Massachusetts Bay Colony.

***See also:* Agriculture, Colonies (Proprietary), Massachusetts, Puritans, Virginia**

PINCHOT, GIFFORD

Gifford Pinchot (1865–1946), first head of the U.S. Forest Service, was a pioneer in forest management. He promoted forest conservation as an effective way to provide a steady source of timber. Pinchot was a close advisor to fellow conservationist President Theodore Roosevelt (1901–1909), and he twice served as governor of Pennsylvania. Pinchot's zeal for conservation earned him loyal friends and bitter enemies. His legacy was the millions of acres of national forests that were preserved as a result of his activism.

Gifford Pinchot was born on August 11, 1865 to an affluent family in Simsbury, Connecticut. His boyhood was divided between his family's vastly wooded Pennsylvania estate and at their stylish home in New York City. He often traveled abroad, but he loved to go camping and to hike wilderness trails. Since there wasn't a U.S. college that taught forestry at that time he formulated his own course of study at Yale to provide him with the background he needed. He graduated from Yale University in 1889, and went on to do postgraduate forestry study in Austria, France, Germany, and Switzerland. In Europe forests were under the management of expert woodsmen; these men were Pinchot's teachers. Pinchot learned that European forests were safeguarded from extinction: lumbering was controlled under strict rules, waste was kept to a minimum, and tremendous precautions were taken to prevent fire and blight.

WANTING A SINGLE, MEMORABLE WORD TO DESCRIBE THE GREAT NEED TO PROTECT EARTH'S RESOURCES, PINCHOT COINED THE TERM "CONSERVATION" IN 1907.

Pinchot returned to the United States with the realization that lumbering needed to be regulated in his own country. A bill was passed in 1891 that allowed the federal government to reserve 13 million wooded acres from lumbering. A year later Pinchot initiated the nation's first organized forestry management program at the Vanderbilt estate in Baltimore, North Carolina. He then became a member of the National Forest Commission and in 1898 Pinchot was appointed the Department of Agriculture's first Chief of Forest Service. He would serve in this position for the next 12 years.

In 1902 Pinchot designed a preservation program for the Philippine Islands. The following year he became a professor of forestry at Yale University, a position he would hold for the next 33 years. Wanting a single, memorable word to describe the great need to protect earth's resources, Pinchot coined the term "conservation" in 1907.

After Pinchot publicly criticized Secretary of the Interior Richard A. Ballinger's policies regarding the administration of coal lands in Alaska, President William Howard Taft (1909–1913) fired Pinchot for insubordination. The dismissal widened a Republican Party rift between Taft and the party's progressive wing, which was led by Theodore Roosevelt. Two years later, when Roosevelt won the presidency, Pinchot played an important role in Roosevelt's revolutionary conservation program. It was a period that became known as the "golden era of conservation."

Although Pinchot lost the Republican nomination for the Pennsylvania governor's seat in 1914 he eventually served two non-consecutive terms as governor of that state. During his first term (1923–1927) he directed the reorganization of the state government and enforced Prohibition. During his second term (1931–1935) he fought for stricter regulation of public utilities. In 1926 William S. Vare defeated Pinchot in a three-candidate race for Pennsylvania's Republican senate nomination. However, the Senate declined Vare after Pinchot announced that the nomination was "partly bought and partly stolen."

Pinchot remained active in conservation affairs throughout his political career and in 1910 he became president of the National Conservation Association. He served on the Inland Waterways Commission, the Commission on Country Life, the United States Food Administration (1917–1918), and was a member of the Commission for Relief in Belgium (1914–1915). From 1920 to 1922 he was the Pennsylvania Commissioner of Forestry and acted as federal mediator in the anthracite coal strike in 1923. The author of several books on forestry and timber, he also published an autobiography called *Breaking New Ground* (1947), which told of his commitment to conservation. Gifford Pinchot died on October 4, 1946 in New York, New York.

See also: **Environmentalism, William Howard Taft**

FURTHER READING

Anderson, Peter. *Gifford Pinchot: American Forester.* New York: Franklin Watts, 1995.

Fausold, Martin L. *Gifford Pinchot, Bull Moose Progressive.* New York: Viking, 1989.

Hirsh, S. Carl. *Guardians of Tomorrow: Pioneers in Ecology.* New York: Viking Press, 1971.

Peterson, Robert W. "Gifford Pinchot: The First American Forester." *Boys' Life,* May 1994.

Pinchot, Gifford. *Breaking New Ground.* 1947. Reprint. New York: Island Press, 1998.

PINCKNEY TREATY

The Pinckney Treaty, officially called the Treaty of San Lorenzo, was signed by the United States and Spain on October 27, 1795, to end a dispute between the two countries over land settlement and Mississippi River trade. The agreement was brokered by American statesman Thomas Pinckney (1750–1828), then U.S. Special Commissioner to Spain. The treaty specified that Spain would recognize the 31st parallel (the northern border of present-day Florida) as the southern boundary of the United States, that Spain would allow American goods to land at New Orleans tax-free for a period of three years (with an option to renew), and that both countries would be allowed to use the Mississippi River freely.

The Pinckney Treaty represented significant gains for the United States during the administration of its first president, George Washington (1789–1797); lingering questions were settled between the two countries which had arisen since the United States won the American Revolution (1775–1783). These disputes had their roots in French concessions of the Louisiana Territory in 1762 and 1763. At that time, the Mississippi River became the western boundary of British colonies in the East and Spanish possessions in the West. When the United States won independence (1783), the Mississippi River became the new nation's western boundary. The Treaty of Paris (1783) granted transport rights along the Mississippi to the United States; but Spain, which had not been party to the treaty, later denied Americans the right to use the water route. Further, during the American Revolution, Spain had claimed—by right of conquest—territory along the Gulf of Mexico and along the eastern shore of the Mississippi, in the present-day states of Alabama, Mississippi, and Tennessee.

As American settlers moved onto Spanish lands, they found themselves in conflict with American Indians who had been incited by the Spanish. Meanwhile, the Spanish also tried gaining the confidence of frontiersmen in the West, who were increasingly dissatisfied with the U.S. federal government. Eventually Spain opened up the Mississippi to American traders in exchange for a 15 percent commission. Pressure thus mounted on Washington's administration to quell the insurgent frontiersmen, settle the boundary disputes, and negotiate free use of the Mississippi. Pinckney was dispatched to Madrid in 1794.

By the time Pinckney arrived to negotiate with Spain on behalf of the United States, in 1795, the diplomatic tides had turned in his favor. Spain's military was so weakened that Pinckney was not forced to make any concessions in exchange for those yielded by Spain to the United States. The treaty was a substantial victory for the new republic, and greatly contributed to westward settlement.

See also: **Alabama, American Revolution, Louisiana Purchase, Mississippi, Tennessee, George Washington**

PINKERTON NATIONAL DETECTIVE AGENCY

In 1842 Allan Pinkerton (1819–1884), a political activist wanted for arrest, fled from Scotland with his bride and set course for the United States. Settling in Chicago, Pinkerton eventually established his own cooperage (the manufacture of barrels and kegs for the storage of beer and wine) in the town of Dundee. In 1847 an event occurred which would change the course of his life. Noticing some suspicious activity on a nearby island, Pinkerton investigated and exposed a gang of counterfeiters. Word spread quickly, and soon Pinkerton found himself employed by local bankers and shopkeepers to help track thieves. This led to his appointment by Kane County as deputy sheriff. In addition, his concern for social justice led him to become involved in the abolitionist movement, helping escaped slaves cross the U.S. border into Canada.

Pinkerton was soon appointed as the first detective in Chicago. A crucial step in the evolution of what became known as Pinkerton Security occurred in the late 1840s. After a rash of thefts in Chicago Post Offices, Pinkerton found himself appointed Special United States Mail Agent. He went undercover and eventually captured one man stealing envelopes. This case made Pinkerton a household name.

THE EYE THAT NEVER SLEEPS

Slogan of the Pinkerton National Detective Agency

Corruption, lack of organization, and the common use of bounty hunters led Pinkerton to realize that existing police forces needed to be augmented. In 1850 he opened Pinkerton's National Detective Agency, described by biographer Frank Horan as "a private police force that could move across local, county, and even state boundaries in the pursuit of criminals." Pinkerton instigated a strict set of rules for his company, stating that it would in no way accept cases involving divorce, public officials, jurors, political parties, or scandal. A code of ethics for Pinkerton employees was also established, forbidding them from accepting rewards or other gratuities. At its inception the company employed five agents and various support personnel. Each agent was trained in crime-solving techniques, undercover operations, and other areas according to standards set by Pinkerton himself. (Pinkerton's National Detective Agency was the first in the country to hire a female detective—Kate Warne.)

Throughout the 1850s, Pinkerton's prospered and adopted the slogan "The Eye That Never Sleeps." The company soon contained a national database of criminal activity, and by the 1870s Pinkerton's had gathered the largest compilation of mug shots in the world. Branch offices sprung up in every state as Pinkerton expanded the agency's territorial coverage.

During the American Civil War (1861–1865) Pinkerton and his agents infiltrated the Confederate Army in search of conspiracy and espionage plots against the Union. The Pinkerton Agency was even credited with saving President Abraham Lincoln (1861–1865) from assassination prior to his 1865 death—though there remains some question as to whether an assassination plot ever existed in the first place.

The postwar period saw no decrease in crime. In fact, technology inadvertently led to new types of crime as inventions opened new avenues for criminal behavior. With the creation of the telegraph, wiretapping became a serious issue. Bank and train robberies were still committed, but had become much more daring. Butch Cassidy and the Wild Bunch, Frank and Jesse James, and the Younger brothers were among the many notorious outlaws captured by the Pinkerton Agency during this time. It was also during this period that the famous Molly Maguires staged violent demonstrations in an attempt to acquire safer working conditions. The Pinkerton Agency was hired to infiltrate this group. After three years of investigation under extremely dangerous circumstances, enough information had been gathered to convict the group's leaders of arson and murder.

William and Robert Pinkerton took over the agency after the death of Allan Pinkerton in 1884. The agency focused increasingly on property protection and labor disputes. Improved police departments and other private agencies had begun to encroach on Pinkerton's business. William and Robert Pinkerton continued the company's expansion, investigating Mafia activity, unions, robberies, and insurance claims as well as providing protection to various public events. Allan Pinkerton II gained control of the company in

1923. He continued the expansion, with business growing due to the number of bank robberies increasingly facilitated by the automobile. In 1930 Allan Pinkerton II died and Robert Pinkerton II took control of the agency. The passing of the Wagner Act by Congress in 1937 made the investigation of labor activities illegal. To offset this loss of business the Pinkerton Agency focused more on the investigation of gambling, particularly the horse racing circuit.

The 1940s through the 1960s saw a change in focus for the Pinkerton National Detective Agency. The guarding of property became the agency's primary service. This was due in part to the services provided by the agency during World War II (1939–1945): the guarding of war supply plants. In 1965 the company was renamed Pinkerton's Incorporated to reflect this shift away from investigative services. In 1967 Edward J. Bednarz became the first non-family member to become president of the agency.

Pinkerton's was purchased by American Brands in 1983 for $162 million. Although it was chairperson and CEO Robert McGuire's objective to improve the agency's service and increase revenues, his efforts resulted in a loss of $11 million in sales by 1987. Part of this loss could be blamed on the competition provided by over 10,000 other security agencies that had sprung up over the years.

Thomas Wathen purchased Pinkerton's from American Brands for $95 million in 1988. Having had great success with revitalizing an ailing security guard firm, California Plant Protection, his goal was to revitalize Pinkerton's back to its former position as a multipurpose investigation firm. Wathen actively sought growth for the company through acquisitions. Within two years Pinkerton's Inc. had a combined revenue of $605 million. Wathen also expanded the agency's reach to other countries, including Canada, Mexico, and Portugal. In 1991, Pinkerton acquired Business Risk International (BRI), a respected investigation, consulting, and business agency. This move brought Pinkerton back into business as a full service security provider. Pinkerton continued to expand throughout the late 1990s, and solidified its position as the world's largest security solutions firm.

See also: **Molly Maguires**

FURTHER READING

Brooks, Cleath, and Harriet H. Wood, eds. *The Correspondence of Thomas Percy and John Pinkerton*. New Haven, CT: Yale University Press, 1985.

Josephson, Judith Pinkerton. *Allan Pinkerton: The Original Private Eye*. Minneapolis, MN: Lerner Publications Co., 1996.

"Pinkertons, Inc. Enterprise Security Solutions for the 21st Century," [cited March 30, 1999] available on the World Wide Web @ www.pinkertons.com/.

"The Evolution of Pinkerton," [cited April 4, 1999] available on the World Wide Web @ web4.insitepro.com/.

Wormser, Richard. *Pinkerton: America's First Private Eye*. New York: Walker and Co., 1990.

PINKHAM, LYDIA ESTES

Lydia Estes Pinkham (1819–1883) was a life-long resident of Lynn, Massachusetts. In 1875 she became a successful businesswoman by marketing a homemade herbal remedy known as *Lydia E. Pinkham's Vegetable Compound*. By spiking a combination of two herbs with a generous dose of alcohol, Lydia Pinkham produced a bottled remedy for women. Promoting it was a cure for "female complaints," she took advantage of the advertising media available to her. Her remedy was an immediate success and one of the earliest products made for female consumers. At the time of her death the business was grossing $300,000 per year, a large sum for her day. The business continued to thrive, and Pinkham's remedy was purchased by generations of American women.

Lydia was the tenth child in a Quaker family of twelve. Born into middle class circumstances, she graduated from Lynn Academy and became a schoolteacher. Taking after her parents, champions of the anti-slavery movement and other reform, Lydia was a passionate social crusader. As a young student she was involved in the women's suffrage movement and was a member of the Lynn Female Anti-Slavery Society. She never gave up her support for women's right to obtain a medical education.

At one point her family ran into financial problems because of her husband's failed business ventures. Pinkham began to market the homemade herbal remedies for women that she had privately produced for years, several of which were based on Native American lore. One of her remedies was very popular among neighbors, and was in demand. She aggressively labeled her product "A Sure Cure for PROLAPSIS UTERI or Falling of the Womb, and all FEMALE

Lydia Pinkham.

WEAKNESSES, including Leucorrhea, Painful Menstruation, Inflammation, and Ulceration of the Womb, Irregularities, Floodings, etc.'' Her product was patented in 1876, and included false unicorn root, true unicorn root, life root, black cohosh, pleurisy root, and alcohol. By the 1890s it was the most widely advertised over-the-counter patent medicine in America.

Pinkham was an ardent believer in the powers of her remedy and made many promises to her customers in her advertising. She marketed directly to women because she believed only women could understand female health problems.

Pinkham's desire to become a businesswoman involved more than just the need to make money for supporting her family. She also hoped to reform medicine and reduce the needless suffering she felt male doctors often caused their female patients. Pinkham believed her remedy, in addition to diet and exercise, was an effective alternative to medical treatment.

Focusing on women's needs and pursuing a massive advertising campaign including church newspapers, the front pages of commercial newspapers, leafleting in theaters and parks, and a smiling picture of the maternal Pinkham on every label, Lydia Pinkham marketed one of the most successful women's products ever created. She became one of the first role models for American businesswomen—she was successful, she embraced the model of motherhood, and she showed how social reform and business could work successfully together. Lydia Pinkham died in 1883.

See also: **Advertising**

FURTHER READING

Burton, Jean. *Lydia Pinkham is Humane.* New York: Farrar, Straus, 1949.

Dictionary of American Medical Biography, s.v. ''Pinkham, Lydia Estes.''

Encyclopedia of American Biography, 2nd ed., s.v. ''Pinkham, Lydia Estes.''

Pinkham, Lydia E. *Lydia E. Pinkham's Private Textbook.* Lynn: Lydia E. Pinkham Medicine, n.d.

Stage, Sarah. *Female Complaints: Lydia Pinkham and the Business of Women's Medicine.* New York: Norton, 1979.

PIRACY

At the end of the twentieth century the term piracy held two distinct meanings. The first, the more historical meaning, refers to acts of plundering on the high seas. The second, the more modern meaning, refers to the theft of intellectual property, specifically copyright infringements against producers of computer software and entertainment programs such music CDs, movie videocassettes, and books.

Piracy on the high seas were acts committed by criminals against a shipping vessel, including hijacking the ship, stealing its cargo, or taking violent action against the crew. Acts of piracy along the U.S. Atlantic and Gulf coasts were prevalent from the seventeenth century into the nineteenth century. The U.S. Constitution made piracy a crime in Article 1, Section 8, and Congress in 1790 first enacted an anti-piracy law. The act banned murder and robbery at sea under the threat of the death penalty. Acts of piracy against U.S. ships off the coasts of Britain and continental Europe from 1803 to 1812 was a major factor leading to the War of 1812 (1812–1814). Piracy legislation from 1818 to 1847 laid the framework for modern anti-piracy law found predominantly in Title 18, Chapter 18, of the U.S. legal code. Twentieth-century international cooperation shaped unique jurisdictional agreement allowing pirates to be apprehended on the oceans by the officials of any nation and punished under that nation's law.

The second meaning of piracy is copyright violations, both in the United States and abroad. The Copyright Act of 1976 gives to the author the exclusive right to reproduce, display, distribute, and sell his original work. The International Intellectual Property Alliance's annual review of illegal copying of works estimated U.S. losses due to copyright piracy totaled approximately $12 billion in 1998. Computer software businesses suffered the highest loss. The People's Republic of China was a major offender. The Business Software Alliance and the Software and Information Industry Association estimated 40 percent of business applications in use worldwide in 1997 were pirated.

The growth of computer network communications, especially the global Internet, made illegal copying of expensive software easy and nearly untraceable. The Software Publishers Association, from its offices in Washington, D.C. and Paris, France, fights copyright infringement. Also, to combat such piracy, the 1990s saw increased international cooperation through meetings, diplomatic initiatives, and treaties.

See also: **Barbary States**

PITTSBURGH PLATE GLASS COMPANY

In 1883 Captain John B. Ford and John Pitcairn created the Pittsburgh Plate Glass Company (PPG), which became the first financially successful U.S. plate glass manufacturer. Originally located in Creighton, Pennsylvania, northeast of Pittsburgh, the company moved its headquarters to Pittsburgh in 1895. Prior to the 1880s more than a dozen plate glass makers had tried unsuccessfully to compete with their European counterparts. Despite U.S. technical ability in the field, plate glass for growing U.S. cities continued to be imported from Belgium, England, France, and Germany.

Ford left the company in 1896, leaving Pitcairn firmly in control. PPG began diversifying around the turn of the century with the construction of a plant in Barberton, Ohio, that produced soda ash, a major raw material used in making glass. This endeavor formed the foundation for the company's chemicals business. In 1900 PPG acquired a Milwaukee paint company that became the foundation of its coatings business. Because paints were distributed through the same channels as glass, they were a logical extension for the company. PPG also diversified into the production of window glass through a factory in Mount Vernon, Ohio, which opened in 1907. Pitcairn died in 1916, having built PPG over a 33-year period into the largest plate glass manufacturer in the United States as well as diversifying its product line and developing sources of raw material.

The 1920s were prosperous for PPG. As steel-cage and concrete-reinforced construction became the standard for building, architects were able to design structures with larger window units, and glass consumption reached record levels in the United States. During this decade, the automobile industry also began consuming more glass. The switch from the open touring car to the sedan caused an expanded need for glass, and PPG met the demand.

PPG also made several technological innovations during the 1920s. In 1924 the company switched from the batch method of making plate glass to the ribbon method. Molten glass from a constantly replenished melting furnace flowed through water-cooled shaping rollers. The glass was then cooled and cut into large plates. In 1928 PPG first mass-produced sheet glass, using the Pittsburgh Process, which improved quality and sped production. For the first time PPG was a major supplier of window glass. The Pittsburgh Process, invented by PPG, involves drawing a continuous sheet of molten glass from a tank vertically up a four-story forming and cooling line. In 1928 the Creighton Process was developed. An economical process for laminating glass for automobile windshields, PPG introduced Duplate laminated safety glass through a glass-plastic unit.

During the 1950s car production and construction of new homes and glass and steel buildings exploded. PPG stepped up production to meet demand, and continued to diversify. Fiberglass had been a laboratory novelty until the 1930s; by 1950, however, it was being used in decorative fabrics and for insulation. In 1952 PPG opened its fiberglass business, making both textiles and reinforcements. In succeeding years fiberglass was found to be useful for more and more applications, with PPG being one of the leading developers of new fiberglass products and processes.

In 1955 PPG's sales topped $500 million. PPG employed 33,000 people in seven glass plants, three glass-fabricating plants, two specialty plants, two fiberglass plants, 17 coating and resins plants, and five chemical plants. In the early 1960s PPG produced materials for the building, transportation, appliance, container, boating, textile, paper, television, and chemical industries. In 1963 PPG became the first U.S. company to manufacture float glass, used in place of plate glass by architects.

During the early part of the 1960s a heavy capital-investment program moved the company toward $1 billion in sales, a goal it reached in 1968. Also that year, the company changed its name to PPG Industries, Inc. to reflect its size, diversification, and global presence. By the late 1990s PPG Industries was a global producer of flat glass, fiberglass, fabricated glass products, coatings, resins, and industrial and specialty chemicals.

FURTHER READING

Baker, Stephen. ''A New Paint Job at PPG.'' *Business Week*, November 13, 1995.

Berss, Marcia. ''Leveraged for Takeoff.'' *Forbes*, November 22, 1993.

Byrne, Harlan S. ''PPG Industries Inc.: It Tops the Goals Set in Its Ambitious 'Blueprint.''' *Barron's*, February 26, 1990.

PPG Industries, Inc. *A Concern for the Future: A History of PPG Industries, Inc.* Pittsburgh: PPG Industries, Inc., 1976.

''PPG Industries: Now into Its Second Century.'' *Paint and Coatings Journal*, September 5, 1983.

Sheeline, William E. ''Managing a Clan Worth $1 Billion.'' *Fortune*, June 4, 1990.

Storck, William J. ''PPG Belies Its Age: The 115-Year-Old Company Is Trying to Shed Its Image as a Staid Old Company while It Moves Quickly and Grows Fast.'' *Chemical and Engineering News*, January 26, 1998.

PLAINS INDIANS

Plains Indians were those tribes that lived in the grassland region extending from the Mississippi River in the east, to the front range of the Rocky Mountains in the west, and from Canada in the north, to Mexico in the south. Algonquian, Aztec-Tanoan, and Iroquoian languages were spoken; eventually a mutually understandable sign language developed among the various tribes. Before European incursion Plains tribes included the Blackfoot, Sioux (or Dakota), Cheyenne, Omaha, Pawnee, Arapaho, Apache, and Comanche.

From 8000 B.C. to 1500 B.C. these tribes were nomadic, moving as many as 100 times a year in pursuit of the buffalo (bison). This large animal provided meat for food, skins for clothing and housing, bones for tools, and manure for fuel. Plants and other animals, such as deer, elk, and rabbits, were also used. The tepee was the typical dwelling: the conical tent was made by stretching skins over a wood frame. Tepees were durable, easily moved, and could be assembled quickly. Tribes traveled mostly on foot; there were no beasts of burden (horses or mules) until the arrival of the Europeans.

After about 250 B.C. some Plains tribes turned to agriculture, settling in river valleys where they cultivated corn, beans, squash, and tobacco. The Omaha and Pawnee were among the tribes that became settled farmers, establishing walled villages of earth lodges. The sustenance of other tribes remained tied to buffalo hunting, which was aided by the development of the bow and arrow (allowing a hunter to remain hidden while he took aim on his prey). Hunting was also a group activity when the large animals were killed by herding them over cliffs. After A.D. 900, Plains Indians began trading with the Eastern Woodlands Indians to the east, particularly the Mississippian tribes. Plains tribes adopted some of their practices and ceremonies.

The arrival of Europeans in the continental interior introduced horses and guns to the Indians and these were readily adopted for use in hunting and warfare. The Plains Indians were warriors, who fought between clans and tribes, and against the white settlers who increasingly encroached on their territory.

By 1890 the buffalo herds of the Plains were virtually extinct—the result of over-hunting by both the Indians and the whites. Diminishing buffalo herds resulted in significant changes in the lifestyle of the Plains Indians. That same year saw the last major conflict between the U.S. Army and the Sioux (who had fiercely resisted white settlement of their lands); federal troops killed as many as 300 men, women, and children at Wounded Knee, South Dakota.

See also: **Buffalo (Extermination of the), Iowa, Kansas, Minnesota, Missouri, Montana, Nebraska, North Carolina, Oklahoma, South Carolina, Texas, Wyoming**

PLANTATIONS

The term plantation originally referred to a colony or new settlement with a planned system of planting. Plantation in American culture gradually evolved to refer to an extensive agricultural enterprise based on slave labor. It would have been similar to a very large, often self-suffcient, farm.

The first plantations appeared in Virginia in the seventeenth century. Settlers began growing tobacco in the rich coastal plains where ocean tides swept up the rivers. Quickly, they realized bigger profits were possible by cultivating tobacco on a large scale. White indentured servants first provided the labor but soon gave way to black slavery. The great tobacco plantations became the hallmark of colonies in Virginia, Maryland, and the Upper South colony of North Carolina. By the 1720s, plantations appeared in South Carolina and Georgia. George Washington (1732–1799), Patrick Henry (1736–1799), Thomas Jefferson (1743–1826), and James Madison (1751–1836) were among the planters.

The greatest expansion of the plantation system occurred between 1790 and 1860. It was spurred by a more efficient textile industry in New England and Britain's increased the demand for cotton. Eli Whitney's invention of the cotton gin enabled cotton to be cleaned and readied for market at a rapid pace. Cotton became so valuable that large areas of the "New South," including western Georgia, Alabama, Mississippi, Louisiana, Arkansas, and Texas, were planted. By 1830 cotton accounted for half of all U.S. exports. Although small family farms worked by the owners grew most of the cotton, the great cotton plantation became the ideal of Southern society. The richest 10 percent of planters owned almost 65 percent of the farm wealth and dominated Southern political and social life as well. A planter was defined by the number of slaves owned rather than by acres owned. Only three percent of planters owned more than 20 slaves, but over 100 slaves worked the grandest plantations.

Typical Southern plantations were self sufficient communities with a mansion for the owner and his family, stables, kitchen, blacksmith shop, extensive gardens, and slave quarters. They encompassed thousands of acres of fertile land with access to waterways for shipping.

While most planters managed the plantation themselves, some hired overseers to help direct the slave workforce. Planters' wives were generally second in command supervising the entire household operation. Slaves worked dawn to dusk in the fields. The more slaves a planter had the more productive his plantation. Emancipation of slaves at the conclusion of the American Civil War (1861–1865) brought the plantation era to a close.

See also: **Cotton Gin, King Cotton**

PLESSY V. FERGUSON

The landmark Supreme Court decision in 1896 of *Plessy v. Ferguson* strengthened the constitutionality of segregation laws in the United States. The ruling would not be reversed for over fifty years, until the Supreme Court finally recognized the inequality inherent in "separate but equal" legislation in 1954 with the *Brown v. Board of Education of Topeka* (1954) case.

During the period of Reconstruction (1865–1877) federal troops were stationed in the South to protect former slaves from their former masters and to insure that the civil rights that had been accorded to African Americans—the Thirteenth, Fourteenth, and Fifteenth Amendments as well as numerous federal laws—were not violated. But the long and stubborn resistance against the federal presence waged by southern whites eventually wore down the patience of the northern public. When the troops were withdrawn the political order in the South reverted to something similar to the pre-Civil War South with the exception that slavery was replaced with sharecropping (blacks—and poor whites—renting land for "shares" of the crop) and violence against blacks came in the form of terrorism committed by groups of "night-riders" (Ku Klux Klan, "Mississippi Red-Shirts," Knights of the White Camellia or a half dozen other groups) rather than by the slave owner himself or his delegates.

PLESSY WAS ARRESTED UNDER THE LOUISIANA SEPARATE CAR ACT OF 1890, WHICH REQUIRED THAT RAILROADS PROVIDE "EQUAL BUT SEPARATE ACCOMMODATIONS FOR THE WHITE AND COLORED RACES," AND WHICH PROHIBITED A PERSON FROM USING A RAIL CAR TO WHICH THEIR RACE HAD NOT BEEN ASSIGNED.

After 1877, southern legislatures set about reversing the civil rights gains made during the Reconstruction period by passing Jim Crow laws, which segregated whites and blacks. ("Jim Crow" was a shuffling, subservient, and stupid black character in minstrel

This sign's placement in front of the Illinois Central Railroad depot is an example of the segregation that resulted from the 1896 Supreme Court decision in the Plessy v. Ferguson case. The laws remained in effect for more than 50 years.

shows.) In June 1892, in the midst of this social counter-revolution, Homer Plessy, a 30-year old shoemaker who was one-eighth African American, purposely challenged such a segregation law in Louisiana. Plessy boarded a train, informed the conductor that he, Plessy, was not 100 percent white, refused to vacate a first class seat, and would not move to a separate "colored" car. Plessy was arrested under the Louisiana Separate Car Act of 1890, which required that railroads provide "equal but separate accommodations for the white and colored races," and which prohibited a person from using a rail car to which their race had not been assigned.

In the 1890s the Comité des Citoyens formed in Louisiana to oppose the Separate Car Act. The committee's members were mostly descendants of "free persons of color," an elite class of African Americans that included writers, musicians, and community leaders, most of whose ancestors probably were never slaves. Some were "Creole," connected by blood ties to families of the white gentry.

In 1892 the Comité des Citoyens tried unsuccessfully to challenge the Separate Car Act when the light-skinned Daniel Desdunes bought a rail ticket to travel out of state, and sat in a car for whites only. But after his arrest, the prosecution dropped the case when the Louisiana Supreme Court ruled in another decision that the state legislature had no jurisdiction over interstate travel. Thus, as part of the continued legal battle, the Comité des Citoyens also challenged the statute within the state of Louisiana with Homer Plessy in 1892. Plessy was released from jail the day after he was arrested. The plan of Plessy's attorney, James E. Walker, was to invalidate the segregation law by invoking the Thirteenth and Fourteenth Amendments. The Thirteenth Amendment abolished slavery and the Fourteenth Amendment gave all naturalized citizens equal protection under the law by state and federal governments.

Plessy appeared before Judge John H. Ferguson of the Criminal Court of New Orleans, who upheld the constitutionality of the state law. Plessy then decided to take the case to the United States Supreme Court, again challenging the law on the basis that it violated the Thirteenth and Fourteenth Amendments. The U.S. Supreme Court found Plessy guilty again. Justice Henry Brown, speaker for the eight-person court, argued that the state law did not contradict the Thirteenth Amendment abolishing involuntary servitude because the statute "merely implies a legal distinction between the white and colored races." With regard to the Fourteenth Amendment, the Court argued, the amendment's purpose was "to enforce the absolute equality of the two races before the law .... Laws ... requiring their separation . . . do not necessarily imply the inferiority of either race." The lone dissenter in the decision was former slave owner Justice John Marshall Harlan. He wrote, "Our Constitution is color-blind ... In respect of civil rights all citizens are equal before the law." He argued that the majority opinion of the Court ceded power to the states, which would "place in a condition of legal inferiority a large body of American citizens."

The test case had failed to undermine the constitutionality of the segregation laws. In 1897 Plessy returned to Court in New Orleans. He pled guilty and was fined $25 for violating the 1890 law. The Supreme Court decision of *Plessy v. Ferguson* subsequently permitted the expansion of Jim Crow legislation until the middle of the twentieth century.

***See also:* Affirmative Action, Civil Rights Movement, Jim Crow Laws**

FURTHER READING

Higgs, Robert. *Competition and Coercion: Blacks in the American Economy, 1865–1914.* Cambridge: Cambridge University Press, 1977.

Rabinowitz, Howard N. *Race Relations in the Urban South, 1865–1890.* Urbana: University of Illinois Press, 1980.

Thomas, Brook, ed. *Plessy v. Ferguson: A Brief History with Documents* Boston: Bedford Books, 1997.

Williamson, Joel. *A Rage for Order: Black/White Relations in the American South since Emancipation.* New York: Oxford University Press, 1986.

Woodward, C. Vann. *The Strange Career of Jim Crow.* New York: Oxford University Press, 1974.

Wright, Gavin. *Old South, New South: Revolutions in the Southern Economy Since the Civil War.* New York: Basic Books, 1986.

POLK, JAMES KNOX

James Polk (1795–1849) was one of the most successful presidents of the United States, and one of the least known. He was elected president in 1844 and carried out every item on his political program. The period roughly corresponding to his presidency (1845–1849) became known as the Fabulous 40s. The country was, at the time, full of excitement, prosperity, and business energy. Polk was responsible for expanding that nation with thc addition of land that today comprises nine western States. He was also largely responsible for admitting the state of Texas to the Union.

Polk was born in 1795, on a small farm near Pineville, North Carolina, in a family of Irish background. He was the oldest of ten children. Because of his sickly childhood, he did little physical labor but helped his father survey and manage large local farms. He later graduated from the University of North Carolina at the top of his class at age twenty-three. Two years later he became a lawyer and soon began his political career with the Democratic Party of Tennessee. His friendship with another great politician and president, Andrew Jackson (1829–1837), allowed Polk to move up quickly in politics. He was soon elected governor of Tennessee. From there he sprang to national political prominence when the issue of acquiring more western land for the United States gained popularity.

Running as a ''dark horse'' (a political unknown), Polk narrowly defeated Henry Clay in the election of 1844 to become President of the United States. During the campaign Polk forcefully asserted that it was the manifest destiny of the United States to expand its borders both west and south. On the other hand, Clay feared a war with Mexico or England might be the price of this expansion and projected an ambivalent, unsure image to the voting public, which may have cost him the election. Once in office, Polk was able to acquire peaceably a large section of the northwest known as the Oregon Territory from England in 1846, although the northern border of this new land was far to the south of what Polk had originally envisaged

Mexico refused to sell the land, which included parts of Texas, New Mexico, and California to the United States. Consequently the U.S. Congress declared war on Mexico in 1846. The United States won the conflict and acquired the territory of Texas and much of the territory of present-day Arizona, California, Colorado, Nevada, New Mexico, Utah, and Wyoming.

During Polk's single term as president, the size of the United States increased by about fifty percent, providing need land for farming, homesteading, and mining development. It was a watershed for U.S. westward expansion and encouraged one of the greatest population movements in U.S. history.

Polk died in 1848, in Nashville, Tennessee.

***See also:* Manifest Destiny, Mexican Cession, Oregon County Cession, Westward Expansion**

FURTHER READING

Bergeron, Paul H. *The Presidency of James K. Polk.* Lawrence: University of Kansas Press, 1987.

Bowers, Claude G. *Making Democracy a Reality: Jefferson, Jackson and Polk.* Memphis: Memphis State College Press, 1954.

Haynes, Sam W. *James K. Polk and the Expansionist Impulse.* New York: Longman, 1997.

Sellers, Charles G. *James K. Polk.* 2 vols. Princeton: Princeton University Press, 1957–1966.

Walton, Brian G. *James K. Polk and the Democratic Party in the Aftermath of the Wilmot Provisio.* Ann Arbor: University Microfilms, 1975.

POLL TAX

A poll tax is a tax levied as a prerequisite for voting. After Reconstruction (1865–1877), the twelve-year period of rebuilding that followed the American Civil War (1861–1865), many southern states passed poll taxes in an effort to keep African Americans from voting. As a result many African Americans (and other impoverished citizens) who could not afford to pay the poll tax were disenfranchised (deprived of their rights as citizens).

In 1870 the Fifteenth Amendment was adopted, stipulating that an individual's right to vote cannot be denied by any state on the basis of race or color. But southern state legislators soon looked for other ways to keep the vote from African Americans, as well as some white Americans. Some states adopted literacy tests: In order to vote, a person had to first pass a strict test; those who failed were denied the right to vote. But in addition to excluding poorly educated African Americans from voting, the measure also affected many others who were also poorly educated, regardless of ethnicity. In response, many state legislatures drew up "grandfather clauses" to ensure non-African American constituents were included in the voting process. For example, Louisiana's grandfather clause granted voting rights only to citizens who were eligible to vote, or whose direct ancestors were eligible to vote, on January 1, 1867, a period when few of the state's African Americans could vote. By the early 1900s, most southern states had adopted this method of keeping former slaves and other African Americans from getting involved in government.

The U.S. Supreme Court declared grandfather clauses unconstitutional in 1915 and again in 1939. But the poll taxes had greater longevity and remained in effect into the Civil Rights Movement. In 1964 poll taxes in U.S. federal elections were finally made illegal; two years later they were prohibited in all government elections held in the United States, including state and local elections.

See also: **Discrimination, Fifteenth Amendment**

POLLOCK V. FARMERS' LOAN AND TRUST COMPANY

In 1898 the U.S. Supreme Court declared the income tax unconstitutional. It had been levied as part of the Wilson–Gorman Tariff Act (1894) and taxed all incomes over $4,000 at two percent. The ruling came in the case of *Pollock v. Farmers' Loan and Trust Company*. Massachusetts resident Charles Pollock was a stockholder in the loan and trust company. In 1895 Pollock sued on behalf of himself and other shareholders, challenging the payment of taxes on the interest and dividends on deposit in the bank during the previous year. In this case, the justices had to decide fundamental questions: (1) whether the federal government could apply "income duty" to the bank deposits of U.S. citizens; (2) whether it could levy an income tax at all. A bare majority of five judges agreed that the Constitution prohibited direct taxation and that, instead, the tax burden had to be apportioned to each state (based on their population). The high court's decision stated that the tax was "repugnant to the Constitution . . . income tax is invariably classified as a direct tax." But the need for an income tax did not abate, and after the turn of the century the graduated tax began receiving bipartisan political support. Eventually the states ratified the Sixteenth Amendment (1913), which authorizes the U.S. Congress to levy and collect income tax without regard to a census (apportionment).

See also: **Sixteenth Amendment**

PONY EXPRESS

Pony Express was a short-lived but emblematic mail and small package carrier service that operated during the mid-1800s. It still remains a symbol of American westward expansion. The service began in 1860 as a means to move messages and parcels from St. Joseph, Missouri (then the western terminus of the nation's rail system), to Sacramento, California, and all points between. The Pony Express trail was 2,000 miles (just over 3,200 kilometers) long and could be traveled in eight to 10 days by a series of riders.

The service was backed by businessman William Hepburn Russell (1812–72), who hired 80 riders and kept 400 horses and ponies to make the relay journey around the clock. Each rider traveled about 75 miles (120 kilometers) per day. Riders followed a trail that ran along Nebraska's Platte River to present day Wyoming, then turned south toward Great Salt Lake (in present day Utah), and south of there turned west to cross the Great Salt Lake Desert to the Sierra Nevada Mountains (in present-day western Nevada), which were crossed into California. Along the route, there were nearly 200 Pony Express stations where riders would change horses or end their day's journey, handing off the specially designed leather mailbag to the next rider. These changes usually took less than two minutes.

Pony Express service was the fastest way to get messages across the frontier at the time; the only alternatives were transport by stagecoach or boat. But when the first transcontinental telegraph line was completed on October 24, 1861, the Pony Express folded only two days later. Its fastest run had been made in March of that year when a transcript of President Abraham Lincoln's (1809–65) first address to Congress arrived in Sacramento in seven days and 17 hours.

See also: **California, Missouri, Telegraph, Utah, Wyoming**

POPULAR SOVEREIGNTY

In the mid-1800s the U.S. Congress struggled with how to organize western territories—in terms of whether they would be free or slave regions—without upsetting the tenuous political balance between North and South. Congress settled on the idea of popular sovereignty, relying on the vote of the people in the territory to decide the question for themselves.

The biggest proponent of popular sovereignty (and the person who coined the term) was Senator Stephen A. Douglas (1813–1861) of Illinois. An ardent expansionist, Douglas viewed popular sovereignty as a way for the nation to get on with the business of organizing new territories. But policy of popular sovereignty had ramifications that even its strongest supporters did not foresee.

Under the Kansas-Nebraska Act (1854), two new territories were established, and the voters in each territory were charged with deciding the question of slavery for themselves. Many lawmakers assumed Nebraska residents would vote in favor of a free territory and Kansas residents would vote in favor of slavery. Instead, advocates from both sides sent people to settle Kansas, which became the backdrop for violent conflicts between anti-slavery and pro-slavery forces, earning it the nicknamc ''Bleeding Kansas.''

The practice of sending people into a territory, sometimes only temporarily, to swing the vote prompted critics of popular sovereignty to dub it ''squatter sovereignty.'' The tragic conflict in Kansas was evidence that the policy had failed. With the failure of popular sovereignty, federal lawmakers had exhausted their abilities to address the nation's political and ideological problems, which would only be resolved by the outcome of the American Civil War (1861–1865).

See also: **Bleeding Kansas, Kansas-Nebraska Act**

POPULIST MOVEMENT

The Populist Movement is the name given to an important movement of agrarian reformists in the United States during the late nineteenth century. In the 1870s and 1880s U.S. society was generally secure and prosperous. Overall economic growth was steady, and no foreign power threatened U.S. interests. One important area excluded from these positive conditions and developments was agriculture. In the decades after the American Civil War (1861–1865), the U.S. farmer suffered a precipitous decline in wealth and status.

Prices for key agricultural products such as wheat and cotton experienced dramatic declines as productivity rose and foreign competition increased. Cotton, the backbone of the Southern economy, sold for over 30 cents a pound in 1866. By the early 1890s, however, the price per pound plummeted to six cents. Not surprisingly, farmers in newer settled regions such as Kansas, Nebraska, and the Dakotas were hardest hit because they had recently borrowed start-up money at fixed interest charges. These obligations were increasingly burdensome as agricultural prices continued to drop. The South was hit hardest of all the regions, not having fully recovered from the economic and social dislocations brought on by the Civil War. The basic problem was that the mechanization of agriculture had created an ''overproduction crisis.'' The domestic market could not absorb the increased productivity of the farm. Wheat had sold for $1.60 per bushel in 1865 was going at 49 cents per bushel in 1890.

The decline in the status of the farmer was equally harsh. At the advent of the American republic, Jeffersonian Republicans lauded the farmer as the wellspring of American virtue and prosperity. This idealization of rural life steadily eroded with the growth of U.S. industrialization and urbanization. Cultural and intellectual currents in the city and in the countryside increasingly diverged, and city dwellers began to view the farmer as uneducated, prejudiced, and superstitious.

Before the 1890s rural distress had generated demands for social and economic experiments that would help shield the farmer from the harsh blasts of the market. For example, the Granger Movement of the 1870s produced legislation regulating warehouses, grain elevators, and railroads. It also led to important cooperative experiments in the marketing of farm products and in the purchase of farm machinery, fertilizer, and the like.

The next important wave of populist reformism emerged in the 1890s. Various regional farm groups, known as Farmers' Alliances, took root and grew rapidly. These included the Southern Alliance and the Agricultural Wheel in the south, and the Northwestern Alliance in northern regions. Although these groups found it difficult to unite due to regional differences based on political preferences and economic interests, they shared the belief that agricultural prices were too low, transportation costs were too high, and that the nation's financial system was in need of serious reform. These and other agricultural groups threw themselves into rural politics in 1890 with spectacular results. In the South alone Alliance-sponsored gubernatorial candidates won elections in four states. The Alliance also captured eight southern legislatures. In the West Alliance candidates dominated elections in Kansas and Nebraska and secured important power bases in the legislatures of Minnesota and South Dakota.

Spurred by these victories and by the failure of the Republican and Democratic parties to seriously address their concerns, the rural reformers, along with representatives of industrial labor and professional reformers, organized the People's Party in St. Louis in 1892 and called for a national convention to convene in Omaha in July. The convention was noteworthy for drafting one of the most comprehensive reform programs ever advanced by a major U.S. political party. The platform called for a number of important measures, including the direct election of senators, the adoption of initiative and referendum procedures, civil service reform, nationalization of transportation and communication networks, and a graduated income tax. To combat deflation, the scourge of the rural economy, the platform advocated the free coinage of silver and the liberal printing of paper money. A "subtreasury" plan was also advocated to protect the farmer from downturns in agricultural prices. Under this scheme farmers could hold crops off the market when prices were low and then receive loans from the government secured by crops in storage. To attract support among industrial workers, the platform also advocated an eight-hour workday, pensions, and the restriction of immigration. Indeed, the strategic political goal of the Populist Party was to displace the Democratic Party by forging an alliance between farmers and industrial workers. Equally important, the Populists, at least in principle, attempted to bridge the social gulf between Southern blacks and whites, arguing that shared economic interests were more important than racial differences.

Despite the excitement it generated in the election of 1892, the Populist Party fell painfully short of its political goals. In the election Democrat Grover Cleveland (1893–1897) garnered 277 votes in the Electoral College to defeat his Republican opponent, Benjamin Harrison (1889–1893), who received 145 electoral votes. James B. Weaver, the Populist candidate, attracted only 22 electoral votes. Although the Populist Party received over 1,470,000 popular votes in the congressional elections of 1894, it suffered a rapid decline soon after. Part of the reason was that the party was never able to construct a cohesive coalition between its constituent rural components. Nor was it able to forge a significant alliance with industrial labor interests. During their presidential convention in 1896, the Democrats adopted the Populist plank of the free coinage of silver, allowing the Democratic candidate, the firebrand William Jennings Bryan, to appeal to Populist voters. At their own convention in July, 1896, the Populist Party also nominated Bryan, all but fusing with the larger and more influential Democratic Party. A period of rapidly rising agricultural prices also helped seal the fate of the Populist Party.

See also: **Farm Policy, Farmers' Alliance, Free Silver, Industrial Revolution, Urbanization**

FURTHER READING

Argersinger, Peter. *Populism and Politics: William Alfred Peffer and the People's Party.* Lexington: University Press of Kentucky, 1974.

Hicks, John D. *The Populist Revolt: A History of the Farmers' Alliance and the People's Party.* Minneapolis: University of Minnesota Press, 1931.

McMath, Jr., Robert C. *American Populism: A Social History, 1877–1898.* New York: Hill and Wang, 1993.

Ostler, Jeffrey. *Prairie Populism: The Fate of Agrarian Radicalism in Kansas, Nebraska, and Iowa, 1880–1892.* Lawrence: University Press of Kansas, 1993.

Pollock, Norman. *The Humane Economy: Populism, Capitalism and Democracy.* New Brunswick, NJ: Rutgers University Press, 1990.

PORKOPOLIS

Porkopolis is an old nickname for the city of Cincinnati, Ohio. In 1788 the area was marked out along the shores of the Ohio River as the village of Losantville. Over the next two decades numerous settlers made their way west in flatboats along the Ohio River. In 1811 steamboat service began on the Ohio River. By 1819 river trade had transformed the territory into a bustling center and the city was officially chartered as Cincinnati.

Cincinnati was perfectly situated on one of the region's major waterways, where it could readily receive raw materials and ship out finished goods. The construction of canals across the region connected natural waterways and made the city accessible from great distances. At its eastern end, the Ohio River extended to Pittsburgh, Pennsylvania. Its western end ran into the Mississippi River, which extended to the busy port of New Orleans and, by ship, to the Atlantic coastal states.

Many farmers transported their livestock (particularly hogs) to Cincinnati for processing. As early as 1818 meat processors in Cincinnati had begun packing pork in brine-filled barrels. By the 1840s the city was home to numerous slaughterhouses and pork-packing plants. By 1850 Cincinnati had become the country's leading center for pork processing. The city's factories also made steamboat boilers, machine tools, railroad cars, and soap, but it became known as Porkopolis because of its most popular product of the time.

See also: **Ohio**

POST, WILLIAM CHARLES

Charles William Post (1854–1914) was a trailblazer in the manufacture and marketing of breakfast cereal products. During the early twentieth century he used his wealth to influence a variety of campaigns that held his interest, including anti-union activism.

Charles William "C.W." Post was born on October 26, 1854 in Springfield, Illinois, the son of Charles Rollin and Caroline Lathrop Post. His mother was a poet whose work was published in magazines, and his father, who joined the California gold rush as a forty-niner, held a variety of jobs and finally settled as a grain and farm equipment dealer.

Post, who preferred to be called "C.W.," was educated in public schools and briefly attended the Illinois Industrial College (later to become the University of Illinois), but he dropped out at age 15. He worked for his father's business before moving to Chicago to work as a salesman for a farm equipment firm. In 1876 he returned home, borrowed $500 from his mother, and opened a general store in Independence, Kansas. Less than a year later Post sold his store and again returned to Springfield. He married Ella Merriweather, and in 1880 established the Springfield Plow Works, a business engaged in the design and manufacture of farm equipment. After four years, both the business and Post's emotional health failed. He spent recuperation time in Texas, where he became interested in real estate, specifically near Fort Worth. By 1891 Post was so ill that he was confined to a wheelchair. He sought help at a well-known sanitarium in Battle Creek, Michigan, run by Dr. John Harvey Kellogg. At the sanitarium Post was fed Dr. Kellogg's

C. W. Post.

high-grain vegetarian diet that consisted of natural food and beverage products.

Post recovered his health at the sanitarium after only a few months, and remained in Battle Creek to open the La Vita Inn, an institute for healing through mental suggestion. He published *I Am Well!*, a book promoting the fashionable belief that the mind could cure physical ailments; the institute, however, never achieved real success.

In 1895 Post formulated a cereal beverage coffee substitute based on a drink similar to one he was served at Kellogg's sanitarium. Post named his beverage Postum. The following year he began to manufacture Grape Nuts, a cereal based on another Kellogg product. With only $50,000 in capital, Post incorporated his company in 1896 under the name Postum, Ltd. Over the next few years he introduced several products, including a corn flakes product he called Post Toasties, followed by other cereals: Post's Bran Flakes, Instant Postum, and Post's Wheat Meal.

Post saw advertising as the most crucial part of his business. Through ads in newspapers and magazines that Post wrote himself, the company achieved nationwide distribution by the early 1900s. Post's marketing strategies appealed to consumers' health concerns by claiming that Postum products would put them on the "road to Wellville" by strengthening "red blood."

The success of his company made Post a millionaire. Five years after its establishment, Postum Ltd.'s capital had risen to $5 million. Post's business, which began in a barn, now employed 2,500 people in factories that covered 20 acres of his Battle Creek farm. It was the largest plant of its kind in the world. Post nonetheless grew bored with his company, hired a team of professional managers to oversee its operation, and used his newfound wealth to turn his attentions elsewhere.

In 1902 Post designed a type of mail currency he called the "Post Check," which was similar to contemporary money orders. He met strong opposition in his attempt to get congressional support for the Post Check. The greatest objection came from New York Senator Thomas C. Platt, president of the U.S. Express Company, which sold its own form of postal currency. The Post Check also upset small merchants, who feared the new currency would promote mail-order business. Realizing that these merchants carried his cereal products, Post eventually gave up on the Post Check.

C.W. POST BECAME FAMOUS FOR CLAIMING THAT HIS HEALTHY BREAKFAST FOODS WOULD PUT CONSUMERS ON THE "ROAD TO WELLVILLE."

Shortly after, Post began purchasing what would total more than 200,000 acres of land in western Texas. He built a community called Post City, which ultimately suffered from the region's arid climate. To combat drought, Post had large amounts of dynamite set off in several experiments to blast rain out of the sky.

Throughout this time Post was a dedicated leader of entrepreneurs against labor unions. He lectured throughout the country and published full-page anti-union denunciations in several newspapers. He even established a magazine called *Square Deal* to disseminate his labor views. Labor unions responded by organizing boycotts against Post's cereal products. To prevent unions in his own factory, Post paid the highest wages in the industry, gave bonuses, and provided welfare, accident, and health benefits. He also had model homes built near Battle Creek that were sold to employees on accommodating terms. Post helped establish, and later served as president of, the anti-union group Citizen's Industrial Alliance. In 1910 the National Trades and Workers Association succeeded this organization. Post offered Theodore Roosevelt (1858–1919) $100,000 to serve as its president, but the former U.S. president (1901–1909) declined.

Post committed suicide on May 9, 1914, at his home in Santa Barbara, California. He was survived by his second wife Leila D. Young, and his daughter, Marjorie Merriweather Post—the sole inheritor of Postum Ltd. At the time of his death, C.W. Post's fortune was estimated at $20 million. Marjorie Post's second husband, stockbroker Edward F. Hutton, led Postum in an aggressive crusade to acquire other grocery brands. In 1929, Postum Ltd. became the General Foods Corporation.

See also: **W.K. Kellogg, Postum Company**

FURTHER READING

Biographical Dictionary of American Business Leaders. Westport, CT: Greenwood Publishing Group, 1983, s.v. "Post, Charles William."

Butler, Mary. *Walking the Road to Wellville: C.W. Post and the Postum Cereal Company.* Battle Creek, MI: Heritage Publications, 1995.

Carlson, Gerald. "Cornflake Crusade: A History of the Food Reformers and Cereal Kings Who Made Battle Creek the Center of a Revolution in America's Eating Habits." *American Heritage*, June 1957.

Encyclopedia of World Biography. Detroit: The Gale Group, 1998, s.v. "Post, Charles William."

Hencey, Robert E. *Empires.* Battle Creek, MI: Miller Foundation, 1996.

Major, Nettie Leitch. *C.W. Post: The Hour and the Man; a Biography with Genealogical Supplement.* Washington, DC: Press of Judd and Detweiler, 1963.

POSTUM CEREAL COMPANY

"Health First—Happiness Follows, POSTUM instead of coffee, 'There's a Reason.'" This 1895 marketing slogan was created by Charles William Post (1854—1914), the man who, in a small white barn in Battle Creek, Michigan, made the first batch of Postum, a cereal beverage. Sales were slow initially: Post lost $800 on Postum in the first year. In writing advertisements for his product, Post brazenly blamed caffeinated beverages for any ailment, including heart disease, rheumatism, blindness, cowardliness, and diminished mental capacity. He literally scared thousands of caffeinated beverage drinkers into switching to Postum. By the end of 1896 Postum sales reached $3000 per month. The same year Postum Cereal Company Ltd. was incorporated.

''Grape Nuts,'' a pre-cooked cereal made of malted barley and whole wheat, was introduced in 1897. It was a commercial success. Post advertised Grape Nuts as a builder of red blood cells and stated that it steadied the nerves and prevented malaria, consumption, and appendicitis. He became well known for outlandish and flamboyant advertising and marketing practices. Post used coupons, samples, and product demonstrations to encourage people to by his products. The stage was set for the company that would become General Foods.

By the early 1900s Postum Cereal Company's Battle Creek plant was the largest of its kind in the world, with 2,500 employees and a net worth of $5 million. Charles W. Post amassed a personal fortune. Though Post crusaded against labor unions, he was not against employee benefits. Post was an active member in the National Association of Manufacturers and he founded many organizations designed to substitute labor unions. Because of Post's genuine concern for employees, Postum Cereal Company did not have any labor problems in its own factories. Post's generosity toward his employees was evident as they were paid the highest wages in the industry. The company placed a high emphasis on safe working conditions and implemented a sickness and accident benefit program. It also assisted some workers with the purchase of company built homes.

HEALTH FIRST—HAPPINESS FOLLOWS, POSTUM INSTEAD OF COFFEE, THERE'S A REASON.

Charles William Post, 1895

Upon the death of Charles W. Post in 1914, his daughter Marjorie Merriweather Post took over company operations. In 1923 Marjorie's husband, Edward F. Hutton, became chairman and Colby M. Chester became president the following year. Marjorie remained active in the company affairs and she was involved in the business strategy related to the acquisition of General Foods. Postum Cereal Company acquired Jell-O in 1925, followed by Swans Down cake flour, Minute Tapioca, Baker's Chocolate, and Log Cabin syrup in 1927. That same year the company also shortened its name to the Postum Company. With the acquisition of Maxwell House coffee in 1928, President Theodore Roosevelt's (1901–1909) 1907 statement ''Good to the last drop'' became a household phrase.

In 1929 Postum paid $22 million for controlling interest in the General Foods Company, which was owned by Clarence Birdseye. The Postum Company then adopted the General Foods title. Birdseye became head of the new General Foods laboratory and continued his research on frozen foods. After record $19.4 million profits in 1929, earnings dropped to $10.3 million in 1932 when the company acquired the remaining 49 percent of General Foods. E.F. Hutton resigned as chairman in 1935 and Colby M. Chester took over. Marjorie Post returned as director in 1936 and remained until 1958.

In 1932 the company added six new plants and offered one hundred different frozen food products. In the same year Sanka Coffee Corporation was purchased from European owners who, since 1927, had an agreement with Postum Company to distribute their coffee. By 1943 General Food sales had more than doubled those of 1929. One of the first postwar products introduced to the market was Instant Maxwell House coffee (1945). Adding to the General Foods beverage line was the acquisition of Perkins Products Company in 1953. Fruit flavored drink mixes, such as Kool-Aid, Tang, Country Time, and sugar free Crystal Light, were added to the beverage division of General Foods. Through the 1950s and 1960s General Foods expanded in the international market: it had controlling interest in La India chocolate Company in Venezuela, acquired Hostess snack food company of Canada, the Kibon ice cream company of Brazil, and numerous others. By the end of the 1960s General Foods was a giant in the industry.

The international acquisitions continued throughout the 1970s. On the domestic front the Bird's Eye brand enjoyed increased sales as frozen foods became more popular. But the Jell-O brands suffered in the dessert market. In 1980 General Foods was not performing as expected and was dependent on its various coffee brands which accounted for thirty-nine percent of entire revenues. In 1981 General Foods merged with Oscar Mayer, the largest national brand of lunchmeats. With coffee and Post Cereal sales sliding in 1984, General Foods sold its Gaines Pet Food division for $157 million. In 1985 Phillip Morris purchased General Foods for $5.6 billion. Phillip Morris chairman Hamish Maxwell had plans to diminish the company's reliance on tobacco products. A massive reorganization of General Foods began in 1987 as coffee, meats, and groceries were split into separate divisions. In October 1988 Phillip Morris purchased Kraft. In 1989, with Michael A. Miles at the helm, General Foods and Kraft merged to become an industry giant named Kraft General Foods Incorporated. The company's name was changed in January 1995 to Kraft Foods Incorporated and the company was reorganized into eleven different international divisions.

See also: **Charles Post**

FURTHER READING

Dudley, Charles Eaves. *Kraft Inc.—Through the Years.* Glenview, IL: Kraft Inc., 1988.

———. *Post City, Texas.* Austin, TX: State Historical Association, 1952.

Fucini, Joseph J. and Suzy Fucini. "The Men and Women Behind Famous Brand Names and How They Made It." *Entrepreneurs*, Boston: G. K. Hall and Co., 1985.

Postum Company, Incorporated. *A Trip Through Postumville Where Postum Cereal, Grape Nuts, Post Toasties, etc., Are Made.* Battle Creek, MI.: Postum Cereal Company Incorporated, 1920.

Van Doren, Charles, ed. *Webster's American Biographies.* Springfield, MA: G. and C. Merriam Co., 1979, s.v. "Post, Charles William."

POSTWAR BOOM

During the 1940s U.S. business was dominated by preparation for World War II (1939–1945), by the war itself, and in the late years of the decade by the Cold War. By the end of the decade Americans saw the positive effect the war had on the U.S. economy and realized that they had never had it so good.

President Franklin D. Roosevelt's (1933–1945) combination of private capitalism and public stimulus accomplished exactly what the government intended: it made the United States the largest arms manufacturer in world history. At the end of World War II, U.S. business and the economy were radically different than they were before the Japanese attack on Pearl Harbor (1941). Americans enjoyed unprecedented prosperity. Corporate profits were astounding. In 1943 alone earnings jumped $2.1 million over the prewar level. Workers' wages on average doubled, increasing from almost $25 a week to $50 a week, and many people earned hefty overtime bonuses. Even farm income increased an incredible 250 percent, despite the loss of nearly 800,000 agricultural workers during the war.

The character of corporate and working America also changed. Despite administration attempts to distribute the benefits of government contracts broadly, 71 percent of all contracts went to the 100 largest U.S. corporations. By the end of 1942 there were 300,000 fewer small companies than there had been before the war. Small farmers lost out as labor got bigger. The total labor force increased by 22 percent during the war, which, along with the draft, eliminated unemployment. Labor unions grew from 10.5 million members in 1939 to 14.75 million members in 1945. An acknowledged power in the U.S. marketplace, big labor insured that many of the wage and benefit gains of the war years would continue into the next decades. Because of wartime labor shortages, moreover, the workforce was more diverse than before. Almost 60 percent of women in the United States were employed during the war. Industry, which for so long had closed its doors to African Americans, now employed 1.2 million. Sixty thousand African Americans migrated to Detroit, Michigan, alone during the war. Even teenagers worked during the war, and their earnings opened up a new consumer market after the war—one geared toward music and automobiles and other status symbols of adolescence. The one problem with all this prosperity was that it was purchased with government deficits justified by the pressure of war. With victory, the new administration under President Harry S. Truman (1943–1953) faced one significant economic problem: how to maintain wartime prosperity without a war.

BY THE END OF THE DECADE PROSPERITY WAS INSURED BY THE TWIN FORCES OF EXPANSIVE U.S. TRADE AND THE GROWTH OF WHAT GENERAL DWIGHT D. EISENHOWER (LATER PRESIDENT, 1953–1961) WOULD TERM "THE MILITARY-INDUSTRIAL COMPLEX."

The Truman administration sought to reconvert U.S. industry to its nonmilitary bases as quickly and as painlessly as the Roosevelt administration had converted it to war production. One way of accomplishing this goal was to use some of the government agencies overseeing war production to supervise the peacetime conversion of U.S. industry. The Office of War Mobilization, retitled in 1944 to the Office of War Mobilization and Reconversion, continued to coordinate manpower, production, and resources after the war. Rations on scarce goods remained in place long after armistices were signed. These wartime agencies and restrictions came under political pressure during peacetime. Truman hoped that the Office of Price Administration and Civilian Supply (OPA), for example, would continue to regulate production and prices in order to check runaway inflation. The OPA, however, faced criticism from businessmen who wanted to raise prices and from individuals who chafed at its limitations on consumer items. In June 1946, Congress extended the life of the OPA but stripped it of much of its power. Truman vetoed the bill, and when price controls expired on July 1, 1946, prices skyrocketed, and the cost of living index rose six percent in one month. By 1947 the cost of living index had risen 24 points—20 more than it had risen in the previous year. The rise reflected not only the artificial depression of prices the government had maintained during the war, but also the enormous consumer demand spiked by high wartime wages and wartime product shortages. This demand ultimately evened out the economic dislocations of reconversion. The postwar period was notable, in fact, for an unprecedented consumer revolution, as Americans rushed to buy houses, cars, appliances, and luxuries in record numbers.

The biggest single economic problem the Truman administration faced was the demobilization of its 17 million troops. Administration officials feared a rapid demobilization of the military would plunge the nation back into depression, yet the political pressure from American families for rapid demobilization was enormous, especially after 1946. The problem was partially solved by the Serviceman's Readjustment Act of 1944, commonly known as the GI Bill, which funneled many returning veterans into college, thus delaying their entry into the labor force and improving their working skills. Government, business, and labor-union policies, furthermore, favored the hiring of returning vets, forcing tens of thousands of working women and teenagers out of the labor market.

There was also an enormous increase in the number of new industries in the United States following the war. Often sparked by wartime government research, industries such as television, aviation, and chemical and metallurgical processing absorbed many of the demobilized troops. Finally, the government maintained a larger military force after the war than it had ever maintained in U.S. history during peacetime. Troops were needed as occupying forces in Europe and Asia, and U.S. naval and air fleets remained enormous. The large standing army, the GI Bill, and new industries nonetheless failed to prevent widespread labor dislocations following the war. From 1946 to 1948, as unemployment rose and the U.S economy slowed, strikes became commonplace, and the Truman administration struggled with popular discontent with its economic policies.

U.S. economic planners also hoped that a revival in U.S. international trade and the reconstruction of European economies would increase U.S. production and absorb the veteran labor force. Even before Pearl Harbor international bankers and interventionists viewed the war as an opportunity to prevent the creation of world economic blocs closed to U.S. trade. With the end of the war they constructed international institutions to accomplish this goal.

The World Bank, the International Monetary Fund (IMF), and the General Agreement on Tariffs and Trade (GATT) were designed to insure U.S. access to colonial markets formerly closed to U.S. trade. These agreements were also designed to help Europe rebuild and resume trade with the United States. This goal was even more explicit in the 1947 Marshall Plan, whose guidelines specified the terms of renewed trade on a basis favorable to U.S. corporations—often accompanied by a surprising degree of U.S. interference in the domestic economies of European states.

The Europeans, devastated and bankrupted by the war, rarely objected to the conditions of Marshall Plan assistance, and by 1950 they had resumed domestic production and trade with the United States on a greater basis than before the war. The Soviet Union, however, committed itself to a policy of economic self-sufficiency and independence. Twice spurned in its requests for less restrictive loans by the United States, it rejected Marshall Plan funds and chose to reconstitute its economy by integrating it, rather poorly, to that of Eastern Europe. The Soviets in effect created an economic bloc and closed it to U.S. trade—it was an anathema to U.S. internationalists.

The actions of the Soviets, as well as the economic restrictions of U.S. assistance, formed the economic backdrop to the Cold War. The political, cultural, and military repercussions of this economic confrontation, in turn, transformed the U.S. domestic economy and by 1949 resolved the problems plaguing postwar industry. The potential military confrontation with the Soviet Union not only cemented U.S. economic ties with Western Europe and increased U.S. trade but also provided a viable rationale for increased military expenditures. By the end of the decade prosperity was insured by the twin forces of expansive U.S. trade and the growth of what General Dwight D. Eisenhower (later President, 1953–1961) would term "the military-industrial complex."

See also: **Cold War, Cost of Living Index, General Agreement on Tariffs and Trade, GI Bill, International Monetary Fund, Marshall Plan, Military-Industrial Complex, Office of Price Administration, Postwar Prosperity, War and the Economy, World War II**

FURTHER READING

Fearon, Peter. *War, Prosperity and Depression: The U.S. Economy 1917–1945.* Lawrence: University Press of Kansas, 1987.

Higgs, Robert., ed. *Arms, Politics, and the Economy: Historical and Contemporary Perspectives.* New York: Holmes and Meier, 1990.

Kennedy, David M. *Over Here: The First World War and American Society.* New York: Oxford University Press, 1980.

Nelson, Donald. *Arsenal of Democracy: The Story of American War Production.* New York: Harcourt, Brace, 1946.

Vatter, Harold G. *The U.S. Economy in World War II.* New York: Columbia University Press, 1985.

POSTWAR PROSPERITY, 1946-1973 *(OVERVIEW)*

The economic acceleration sparked by the war production of World War II (1939–45) ended the Great Depression (1929–1939) and brought prosperity to the United States. But the war's end brought fear of economic stagnation. Many people remembered the downturn following World War I (1914–18) and they were concerned that it might happen again. At first such fears seemed justified, but then Americans went on a buying spree. They used their wartime savings to purchase products such as refrigerators and automobiles that had not been available during the war. This caused inflation because prices rose when supply did not keep up with demand. Also, during the war the inflation increased faster than the wage increases. The unions had been talked into limiting their wartime wage increases to 15 percent per year, considerably less than the actual inflation rate. The government contributed to the problem by removing all wartime price controls in late 1946.

Workers responded to the uncertain economic conditions by going on strike to demand higher wages. In late 1945 and 1946 more than five million workers in major industries were involved in more than 5,000 work stoppages. Most of these strikes were settled to the benefit of the workers who received wage increases; the inflationary trend continued well into the Fifties.

Meanwhile, the Truman administration (1945–53) proposed major government spending programs including an increased minimum wage, price supports for farmers, and support for small businesses. There was also a proposal for a very controversial measure called the Full Employment Bill, which called for the government to guarantee jobs to all workers whenever unemployment rose above a certain level.

President Truman's (1945–53) program met with vigorous opposition from conservatives who called it "creeping socialism." However, some of these proposals, including a modified version of the Employment Act, passed Congress before the end of 1946. Truman proposed a more sweeping program, which came to be known as the "Fair Deal." This included farm supports and other government measures to strengthen growth as well as expansion of Social Security, public housing, national medical insurance, aid to education, and civil rights legislation for blacks. Some of these proposals became law even though there was considerable opposition.

Meanwhile, U.S. farmers experienced many changes after World War II just as they had after World War I. Farming became more mechanized and scientific than ever and output increased at a faster rate than ever. Overproduction once again became a problem. After major increases during the war, prices leveled off and generally showed no gains until the 1970s. At the same time costs increased. The result was that only large commercial farms could be profitably operated. They began to increase in number while the smaller "family farm" declined.

Dwight D. Eisenhower (1953–61), a Republican, succeeded Truman as president in 1953. Generally, he opposed new, large government spending programs, but he favored one project that was profoundly significant: the Interstate Highway System. This was a thirteen–year, $26 billion program to assist the states to build an interstate highway system according to a national plan. This program generated a number of spin–offs. The construction industry boomed; gas stations and motels profited; the trucking industry flourished; the railroad industry declined; and the American people became more devoted to the automobile than ever.

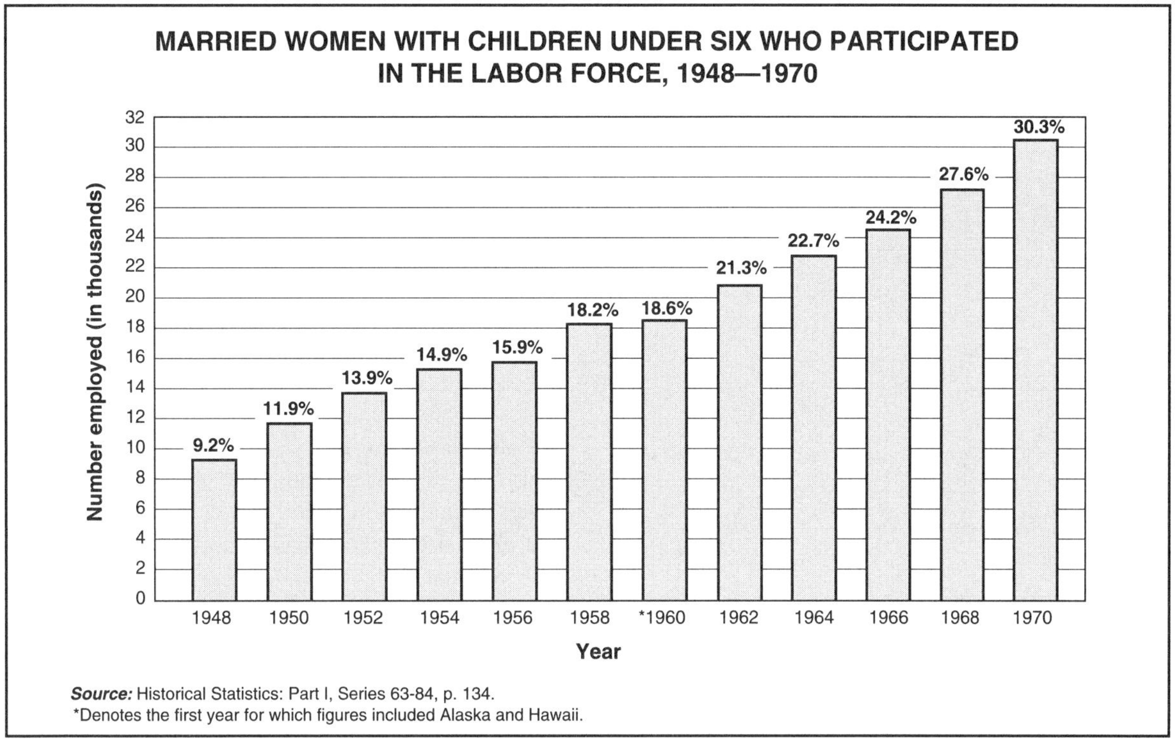

Source: Historical Statistics: Part I, Series 63-84, p. 134.
*Denotes the first year for which figures included Alaska and Hawaii.

Shown is the steady increase of married women, with children under 6-years-old, who participated in the workforce between 1940 and 1970.

Otherwise, Eisenhower kept public spending down and the national economy grew slowly. Moreover, the administration did little to stimulate the economy during recessions. Twice, in 1954 and again in 1957, there were economic downturns, but Eisenhower did nothing. Even when the unemployment rate reached 7.5 percent in 1958, he opposed both tax cuts and increased spending.

Meanwhile, there were numerous social problems associated with the economy. The population grew rapidly—the increase was largely attributable to the ''Baby Boom.'' After the war people tended to marry younger and have larger families. Between 1948 and 1955 the number of children born each year increased by 50 percent, the greatest increase ever. This was a direct result of the prosperity of that period. Jobs were plentiful; incomes were rising; and credit was easily available.

The conditions of that period also exerted a significant effect on the status of women. During the war there was an increase in the number of women in the workforce as they came out of their homes to replace the men who went into the service. Immediately after the war many women left their jobs as the men returned, but in the 1950s the trend reversed again and by 1960, 33 percent of the women of working age had jobs. Most of these jobs were part-time; the pay was low; and the female workers were often over 35 years of age, having gone to work after their children entered school.

During the period of postwar prosperity many people fled the city for the suburbs. They believed that here they would find peace and avoid urban problems such as crime and social tensions. In fact, they frequently traded one set of problems for another. In the suburbs they often found as much congestion as they had hoped to leave behind. In addition, people often went deep into debt for new homes and cars, and they found the long commute to work a burden they had not anticipated.

Despite the flight to the suburbs, the urban population grew dramatically during the late 1940s and 1950s and many of those who flocked to the cities after World War II were black and poor. They came seeking jobs and a better life, but they were often disappointed. They were met with overcrowding, discrimination, and, not infrequently, violence. Still they came. Seventy-seven percent of the African American population lived in the South in 1940. By 1960 nearly 50 percent lived in the North and most of them in cities. They continued to move because, in spite of problems, many actually improved their standard of living. Between

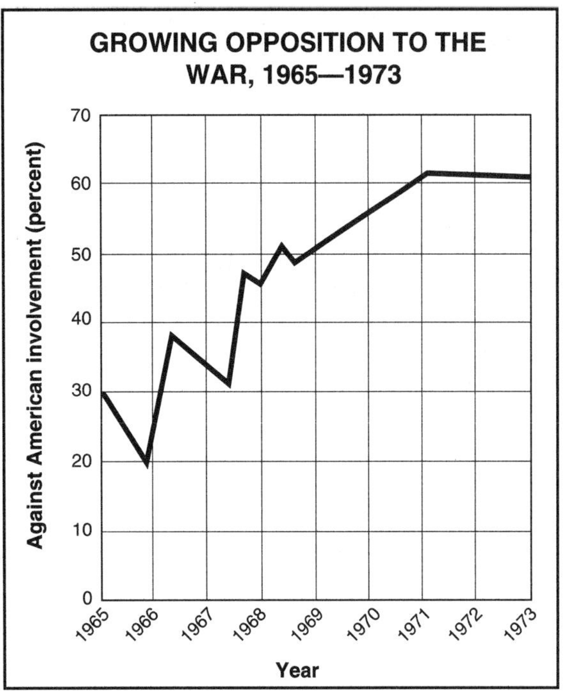

Opposition to the Vietnam War began to rise steadily from 1969 until the United States withdrew involvement.

1941 and 1952 the median annual income of African Americans increased from $1,614 to $2,338. Moreover, those employed in unskilled jobs dropped from 80 percent to 63 percent between 1940 and 1950.

Economic growth slowed down somewhat in the late 1950s; John F. Kennedy (1961–63) used the sluggish economy as an issue during the campaign of 1960. Kennedy promised recovery and long–term growth and he gathered a distinguished group of economic advisers to help him produce results. These included John Kenneth Galbraith of Harvard and Walter Heller of the University of Minnesota. These men advocated what came to be known as the ''New Economy.'' By this they meant that the federal government should use its power over expenditures and monetary policy to promote growth. They convinced Kennedy to push for massive expenditures on social welfare programs and a large tax cut. Kennedy also found himself under increasing pressure to do more in the civil rights arena. However, the conservatives in Congress blocked all such efforts. Thus, Kennedy had achieved little by the time of his death in November 1963.

Kennedy's program, and much more, was realized by his successor Lyndon Baines Johnson (1963–68). The events of the next five years had an enormous impact on the U.S. economy and society. First, Johnson moved to promote rapid economic growth. He precipitated an economic boom by reducing taxes through the Tax Act of 1964 and increasing federal spending (mostly on the war in Vietnam). Between 1960 and 1964 the gross national product (GNP) increased 24 percent and corporate profits rose by 37 percent. In 1965 the GNP climbed another seven percent; profits increased 20 percent; and unemployment fell to four percent. These ''boom'' conditions lasted until near the end of the decade of the Sixties. The GNP increased at a rate of around five percent per year; unemployment never exceeded four percent; and the median family income rose from $8,543 to $10,768.

Some economists cautioned that Johnson's policies could trigger inflation, but the President never deviated from his course. He continued to spend, especially on the war, throughout his tenure. Eventually the economists' predictions were borne out. By the end of the 1960s the nation was experiencing a runaway inflation.

Meanwhile, Johnson launched his grand plan for what he called the ''Great Society.'' The idea was to ''fix'' all of society's problems by means of federal legislation. In the first year of his administration alone, Congress passed the Tax Act and a new and powerful Civil Rights Act. Congress also approved the Economic Opportunity Act that marked the beginning of Johnson's ''war on poverty.'' This consisted of a series of programs designed to provide education, training, housing, and jobs for the less fortunate. It represented the greatest outpouring of liberal legislation in the nation's history.

After his smashing victory over Senator Barry Goldwater of Arizona in the election of 1964, Johnson shifted the Great Society and War on Poverty programs into high gear. Congress passed Medicare and Medicaid to provide health care for the elderly and the poor. There was legislation passed to provide federal aid to education at all levels. The Voting Rights Act of 1965 guaranteed blacks the right to vote in the South. In addition, federal money was appropriated for housing and urban development and two new Cabinet level departments were created. These were the Department of Housing and Urban Development (HUD) and the Department of Transportation (DOT).

War on Poverty legislation included the Job Corps to train young people who lacked marketable skills; Work–Study, to supplement the income of college students; Head Start, to help pre–school children from ''disadvantaged'' families; Volunteers in Service to Americans (VISTA), to send volunteers into impoverished areas; federally funded public works projects, and others. However, nothing was done to redistribute wealth, the distribution of which remained much as it had been since the turn of the century, that is, about 20 percent of the population owned about 80 percent of the wealth.

Lyndon Johnson was forced from office because of the public outcry against his failed policy in Vietnam. His successor, Richard M. Nixon (1969–1974), then had to deal with the major financial and economic difficulties that had been generated by Johnson's policies. He did so by curtailing the money supply. He hoped this would induce high interest rates and consequently business cutbacks.

Nixon's policies did not work. Inflation continued but business activity slowed down more rapidly than expected. This caused government revenues to decline and increased the size of the deficit. It also produced an increase in unemployment. The nation fell into recession.

By 1971 Nixon was ready to try a new, more drastic approach. He froze wages and prices for 90 days, ordered Congress to repeal certain excise taxes, and took the United States off the gold standard by suspending the traditional practice of converting dollars into gold. This had the effect of devaluing the dollar and making U.S. goods cheaper on the international market. Nixon also placed a 10 percent surtax on imports.

This policy worked. By early 1972 the recession was over and industrial production had increased by 5.3 percent over the previous year. Corporate income increased by an average of 11.7 percent over 1971. These changes helped Nixon to win re-election in 1972, but shortly after his triumph the United States faced another economic crisis of significant proportions.

In October, 1973, war broke out between Israel and her Arab enemies, notably Syria and Egypt. The United States supported and aided Israel. In retaliation the Arab states, led by Saudi Arabia, embargoed oil shipments. At that time Middle East imports accounted for about 11 per cent of America's total consumption. Prices shot up and there were shortages. The embargo ended in March 1974 and supplies returned to normal, but prices remained high. The American people now found themselves facing an ''energy crisis.''

There was a mistaken widespread belief that the price increase in petroleum and petroleum products was caused by the embargo. Price increases were fueled by increased demand that had been developing for several years. In any case, Americans now found themselves paying more—a lot more—to drive their cars, heat their homes, and buy the goods produced by farms and industries that were driven by high–priced oil. The nation had entered a new era.

See also: **Great Society, Inflation, Raymond Kroc, Richard Nixon, OPEC Oil Embargo, Suburbs (Rise of), Vietnam War**

FURTHER READING

Ambrose, Stephen E. *Eisenhower.* 2 vols. New York: Simon and Schuster, 1983–84.

Conkin, Paul K. *Big Daddy From the Pedernales: Lyndon Baines Johnson.* Boston: Twayne Publishers, 1986.

Ferrell, Robert H. *Harry S. Truman and the Modern American Presidency.* Boston: Little, Brown, 1983.

Galbraith, John Kenneth. *The Affluent Society.* Boston: Houghton Mifflin, 1984.

Giglio, James N. *The Presidency of John F. Kennedy.* Lawrence: University Press of Kansas, 1991.

Matusow, Allen J. *Nixon's Economy: Booms, Busts, Dollars, and Votes.* Lawrence: University Press of Kansas, 1998.

Patterson, James T. *America's Struggle Against Poverty, 1900–80.* Cambridge, MA: Harvard University Press, 1981.

Rostow, Walt W. *The Stages of Economic Growth, A Non-Communist Manifesto.* Cambridge: Cambridge University Press, 1960.

POTATOES

The potato, an herb of the nightshade family, originated in the Andes Mountain region of South America about 3000 B.C.. Thousands of years later the Inca Indians cultivated it as a vegetable crop. Because the plant is able to withstand heavy frost, the potato was suitable for the Andean region's high elevations—as high as 15,000 feet (4,500 meters). From the potato the Inca produced a flour-like substance called *chuno,* which was used to make bread. When Spanish explorer Gonzalo Jiminez de Quesada (c. 1495–1579) arrived in the Andes in 1530, he found the people growing and eating the tubers. On returning to Europe, the Spaniards took samples with them, introducing it there in the 1539. In 1586 when English admiral Sir Francis Drake (1540 or 1543–96) returned to England from an expedition to North and South America, he carried with him potatoes he had picked up in Cartagena (present-day Colombia), thus introducing the potato in the British Isles. The potato became a major crop in Ireland and Scotland where it was readily grown. (The edible, starchy tuber of the potato is often called the Irish potato.) Since it is also cheap to cultivate, the potato soon became a dietary staple and is credited with spurring a population growth in those countries. The potato did not arrive in North America until 1718, when Irish immigrants landing in Boston brought it with them. They began growing potatoes the following year in Londonderry, New Hampshire. The potato did not become a popular American food until the 1800s.

See also: **Columbian Exchange, Inca, New Hampshire**

POVERTY

Poverty can be defined either in terms of a definite income level or as a relative condition that changes as society redefines it. Most economists agree that a safe definition of poverty is the inability, through lack of income or wealth, to provide decent housing, clothing, health care, nutrition, or education for oneself or one's family. In 1999 the federal government defined the "poverty line"—the arbitrary dividing line between the poor and the non-poor—as $16,700 for a family of four in the contiguous United States. According to the U.S. Census Bureau, the number of U.S. citizens living below the poverty line in 1992 was about 36 million, including 14 million children. Sixty-five percent of this number were women (many unmarried mothers), and in 1990 one quarter of all adult African American males lived below the poverty line.

According to economic historians, roughly seven to 10 percent of the populations of New York, Boston, and Philadelphia were poor in the years before the American Revolution (1775–1783). Between 1790 and 1860 the percentage of U.S. citizens living in poverty probably remained about the same; by 1860 there were approximately 2.7 million poor males in the United States. Since 1870 the percentage of U.S. citizens living in poverty has been cut in half, primarily because of the rapid economic growth between 1880 and 1910 and in the years following World War II (1939–1945). The first efforts by the federal government to cope with poverty began in the 1930s. President Franklin D. Roosevelt (1933–1945) established the Social Security Administration in 1935 to provide minimum retirement benefits to U.S. citizens, and the government began to make federal funds available to the states for programs like Aid to Dependent Children.

By 1960 the U.S. government estimated that 40 million U.S. citizens lived below the poverty line. In 1964 President Lyndon B. Johnson (1963–1969) declared an "unconditional war" on poverty that led to the creation of programs like Head Start and the Neighborhood Youth Corps. Because of these efforts and the billions of dollars donated every year by private citizens and foundations, by 1973 the percentage of the population living in poverty reached its lowest level in U.S. history—11.1 percent, or 20 million U.S. citizens. The Census Bureau estimated that in 1997 about 13.3 percent of the total U.S. population still lived in poverty.

See also: **Social Security Act**

POWDERLY, TERENCE VINCENT

Terence Powderly (1849–1924) was born in Pennsylvania in 1849 to a family of poor Irish immigrants. He rose to become one of the major leaders of U.S. industrial workers during the late nineteenth century. Becoming the leader of the Knights of Labor Union in 1879, his idealism created the first industrial union to admit all workers regardless of race or sex and enabled the birth and development of 135 worker and consumer cooperatives in the United States.

Born in 1849, Powderly did not begin his career as a labor leader. He started out in public office, serving three terms as mayor of Scranton, Pennsylvania. He entered into union work seeking to abolish the capitalist wage system and institute a society where people would live by cooperation, rather than by seeking to gain from exploiting one another.

Powderly sought to lead laborers collectively towards this goal. He preferred to negotiate labor matters in a non-confrontational manner. Powderly hoped to bring harmony to industrial relations, stressing cooperation between workers and industries. With these ideals in mind, Powderly became leader of the Knights of Labor in 1879. Since the labor movement at that time was not open to conciliation and negotiation, Powderly found himself taking the union in a different direction.

Powderly led the Knights of Labor through a series of dramatically successful strikes in the 1880s, among them a victory against the U.S. railroad industry. The 1880s were the early days of the labor movement, and Powderly's victories encouraged union growth. Membership in the Knights of Labor rose from 100,000 to 700,000 in one year. Powderly continued to meet with success as a labor leader, establishing labor

Terence V. Powderly.

bureaus in several states and supporting contract-labor laws.

As time passed the popular union boss became ambivalent about leading a confrontational union, but despite his best attempts, the Knights of Labor continued to be more aggressive. Powderly, who saw himself as a man of peace, became uncomfortable with his position, and as a result, he began to distance himself from union involvement.

Powderly turned more of his attention to pursuits outside the labor movement. While still serving as head of the union, he studied law and served as a county health officer. He partly owned and managed a grocery store and served as vice president of the Irish Land League. He also sought a presidential appointment as the first U.S. Commissioner of Labor. Several times he threatened to resign from the union.

Resignation came in 1893, when a rural wing of the Knights of Labor moved aggressively to oust Powderly from the union leadership. This movement was supported by socialists, who sought open conflict with industrial owners and disagreed completely with Powderly's insistence on negotiation. By this time the union's strength was failing; its membership had dwindled to seventy-five.

Powderly was relieved to leave the union. He resigned at the age of forty-four and soon started a new career as a lawyer and civil servant. Putting his union leadership days behind him, he worked in several capacities as a civil servant with the U.S. Immigration Commission and the Department of Labor.

Terence Powderly died in 1924. His efforts as a labor leader, though often against his personal philosophy, encouraged workers to organize and change the workplace status quo. He continued to serve the public in his work outside the union until his death.

See also: **Knights of Labor, Labor Movement, Labor Unionism, Trade Unions**

FURTHER READING

Encyclopedia of American Biography, 2nd ed. New York: HarperCollins, 1996, s.v. "Powderly, Terence Vincent."

Encyclopedia of World Biography. Detroit: Gale Research, 1998, s.v. "Powderly, Terence Vincent (1849–1924)."

Falzone, Vincent J. *Terence V. Powderly, Middle Class Reformer*. Washington: University Press of America, 1978.

Powderly, Terence Vincent. *The Path I Trod; the Autobiography of Terence V. Powderly*. New York: Columbia University Press, 1940.

Voss, Kim. *The Making of American Exceptionalism: The Knights of Labor and Class Formation in the Nineteenth Century*. Ithaca: Cornell University Press, 1993.

PRAIRIE

The prairie consists of the flat or moderately hilly lands of the nation's middle section, also called the Great Plains. Oklahoma, Kansas, Nebraska, South Dakota, and North Dakota are mostly prairie. Midwestern states of Illinois and Iowa also contain some prairie lands. Primarily covered with tall grasses (which the pioneers described as a sea of grass), the prairie receives low to moderate rainfall each year. Summers in prairie regions are generally very hot and winters harshly cold. These climatic conditions combined to delay settlement of the region. Though ranchers found grasses suitable for grazing livestock, inadequate rainfall did and does make farming difficult. Further, because the region lacked trees, building on the prairie was limited.

Passage of the Homestead Act in 1862 granted settlers up to 160 acres (64 hectares) of frontier land in exchange for building on or cultivating prairie land. Thus many farmers moved their families onto the Great Plains. In the 1870s Russian Mennonites, who introduced a variety of winter wheat, settled Kansas.

A common crop used by early settlers was turkey red wheat, which could be planted in the fall and harvested in the early summer. The crop, which can withstand cold temperatures, received the benefit of the moisture caused by spring snowmelt and was harvested before the scorching summer. Cultivation of the grain spread, and in 1894 wheat became Kansas' principal crop, earning the state the nickname "Breadbasket of America."

In other parts of the Great Plains farmers adopted dry farming techniques. (A technique by which some fields are allowed to lie fallow every other season so that soil can store up enough moisture and nutrients to support the next year's crops.) Wheat was found to be well suited to dry farming, but it was not used exclusively. Some farmers also grew corn. The end of the nineteenth century saw the invention of the steel plow and the improvement of the McCormick reaper; subsequently, these machines were a great boon to farm production.

The introduction of winter wheat, the development of dry farming methods, and innovations in agricultural machinery combined to make possible the settlement of the American prairie. As a result, between 1863 and 1900 about half a million families became homesteaders in the West. Most of them settled on the Plains, which became one of the world's leading wheat-producing regions by the early 1900s.

See also: **Dry Farming, Homestead Act, Homesteaders, Westward Expansion**

PRICE

Price is the monetary value of a good or service for sale. There are several different kinds of price. Those with the most dominant roles in the marketplace include market price and equilibrium price. Both are tied to the laws of supply and demand.

The market price is the price consumers pay for goods or services in the marketplace. The equilibrium price is an economic ideal. It is the point where the supply of goods is matched equally by consumer demand. For example, if there are more bicycles on the market than there are consumers to buy them, it will create a surplus on the market and the market price of bicycles will go down. If there are more people wanting to buy bicycles than there are bicycles available for purchase, the market price will go up because of the higher demand. When the number of bicycles produced equals the demand from consumers, that is the equilibrium price.

Market price is thus affected by consumer demand and the production rates and availability of a good or service. Ideally, the market price will not be far off from the equilibrium price. Prices for goods or services are subject to change according to consumer demand and producer supply. Price can not be permanently set in a free market system where supply and demand are constantly changing.

See also: **Money, Supply and Demand**

PRICE/EARNINGS (P/E) RATIO

The price/earnings ratio (P/E ratio) provides a comparison of the current market price of a share of stock and that stock's earnings per share, or EPS, (which is figured by dividing a company's net income by its number of shares of common stock outstanding). The P/E ratio tells us what a investor will pay for a dollar of earnings. For example, if a company's stock sold for $30 per share and it posted earnings per share of $1.50, that company would have a P/E ratio of 20. A company's P/E ratio typically rises as a result of increases in its stock price, an indicator of the stock's popularity.

See also: **Stock**

PRIME RATE

The prime rate is the rate of interest, reported as a percentage, charged by commercial banks on short-term loans to the nation's largest, most credit-worthy corporations. Relatively few U.S. corporations may borrow at this rate. Occasionally banks lend slightly below the prime rate to very low risk corporations. A firm will frequently be quoted a rate slightly higher than prime. As an example, the quote might be prime plus one-half, i.e., if the prime was six percent, the firm might be quoted 6.5 percent. The prime is an important indicator of short-term credit conditions.

The prime rate also serves as a basis for interest rate quotes to individual customers. Mortgage rates rise and fall as the prime rate moves up and down. Individuals might receive a home equity loan or line of credit at a rate of "prime plus three percent."

The prime rate depends on the cost of funds loaned to the commercial bank by the regional Federal Reserve Bank. This cost of funds is the discount rate. When the discount rate lowers, the savings are passed on within a few days to commercial banks and reflected in their prime and all other consumer loan rates. An increase in the discount rate, in contrast, results in an increase in the prime and other consumer loan rates.

Between 1934 and 1950 the prime rate remained in the 1.50 to 2.25 percent range. The 1950s and 1960s witnessed four to eight percent rates. In September of 1973 the prime climbed to 11 percent on its way to an all time high of 21.5 percent in December of 1980. Rates in the 1990s ranged from six to 10 percent.

See also: **Federal Reserve System, Interest**

PRIVATE PROPERTY RIGHTS

One of the most important characteristics of the U.S. market economy is the private ownership of the means of producing goods and services. Buildings, natural resources, machinery, equipment, and labor are, for the most part, owned privately, not by the government. Under this system of private ownership, known as a system of private property rights, private individuals have certain privileges or legal rights. Producers are largely free to produce what they wish, to decide how to manage the property, and to sell to whomever they choose and under what terms. Laborers are free to work where they choose. This type of system is referred to as a capitalist system. In contrast, a socialist system allows for private property rights regarding labor and personal items but government owns the major productive resources. In a communist system, theoretically, no private property rights exist because the people own everything in common.

Two types of property are recognized, real property and personal property. Real property is land and anything attached to it such as buildings and crops. In modern terms real property also includes the natural resources found over and under the land, such as oil, minerals, and gases. Personal property is anything other than land that can be owned, including money, stocks, machinery, and equipment. Personal property can be tangible or intangible, such as a famous individual's image.

In the United States a system of property law protects private property rights associated with both real and personal property. This system has its roots in English common law. Property law, with principles, policies, and rules, attempts to resolve disputes. It is a unique law in that the disputes are between the rights of individuals with respect to "things," not with respect to other individuals.

Historically, the more confidence is placed in a nation's private property rights, the more private investment will flow to that nation's economy. People are more willing to invest in endeavors that will increase their private wealth in future years. Throughout the history of the United States and especially in the twentieth century, capital from around the world has been invested in the United States because of its well-defined and enforced private property rights.

See also: **Capitalism, Socialism**

PRIVATE SECTOR

Private individuals and organizations in the United States generate most economic activity involving the production of goods and services. Independent ownership and control define the private sector. Independently owned firms, ranging from large corporations to single individuals within a household, manage their privately owned capital resources to make a profit. Examples include all Fortune 500 corporations such as General Motors and IBM, the local flower shop and a small retail clothing store, the vineyard owner and peanut farmer, the consultant working from a home office and the neighborhood babysitter. Also included in the private sector are non-profit organizations including private colleges and universities and the Catholic Church. In contrast, the public sector includes all governmental activities and local, state, and federal government employees such as postal workers and public school teachers.

In the United States the private sector firms produce, for profit, the majority of goods and services. A business for profit may be organized as a proprietorship, a partnership, or a corporation. In a proprietorship one person owns all the assets and liabilities of the firm. A partnership has two or more owners, both responsible jointly and separately for all assets and liabilities. A corporation is a chartered legal entity with shareholders who are liable only for what they have invested in the firm. In 1993 proprietorships accounted for only six percent of total sales, although they accounted for 75 percent of the total firms. Corporations accounted for 19 percent of total firms but 90 percent of total sales.

Interaction among private sector firms depends on the organization of their entire industry. Industry is defined as firms producing similar products. Types of industry organization generally fall into four categories: competitive firms, monopolistic competitors, oligopolies, and monopolies. Their numbers, product differentiation, price setting power, ease of entry into the industry, and specific distinguishing characteristics differentiate the four.

The U.S. economy, from 1939 to 1980, shifted toward competitive firms. Approximately 77 percent of the firms by 1980 were effectively competitive businesses, 18 percent were oligopolies, and only 5 percent were of the monopolistic organizational type.

From 1970 to 1997 private sector firms experienced a major shift in industry type. Judged by number of employees, manufacturing continuously shrunk, while the service sector greatly expanded.

See also: **Public Sector**

PROCLAMATION OF 1763

The British government intended the Proclamation of 1763 partly as a war measure and partly as a means of administering the new territory taken from France under the terms of the Treaty of Paris. It had two main provisions that affected the colonists. First, the British government drew a line along the watershed of the Appalachian Mountains—the point at which waters run downhill either to the Atlantic Ocean in the east or to the Mississippi River drainage system in the west—separating colonial territory from that of the Native Americans. All lands west of the line were reserved exclusively for Indians, and any settlers living in Indian territory were required to leave. Secondly, in order to make certain that peace was maintained on the American frontier, the British government arranged for the garrisoning of up to 10,000 soldiers in the colonies. The cost of their upkeep, British Prime Minister George Grenville decided, would be borne by the colonists—an estimated 250,000 pounds sterling per year.

WE DO FURTHER STRICTLY ENJOIN AND REQUIRE ALL PERSONS WHATEVER WHO HAVE EITHER WILLFULLY OR INADVERTENTLY SEATED THEMSELVES UPON ANY LANDS . . . RESERVED TO THE SAID INDIANS . . . FORTHWITH TO REMOVE THEMSELVES FROM SUCH SETTLEMENTS.

Text of the Proclamation of 1763

Although some members of the British government may have had a sincere desire to protect the land rights of Native Americans, their main intention was to evade more expensive Indian wars. By limiting white settlement to areas east of the Appalachian watershed, the government hoped to minimize conflict between Indians and colonists. However, Grenville's government also wanted to tie the American colonies closer to England. The British worried that settlers who moved to lands across the Appalachians and lost direct contact

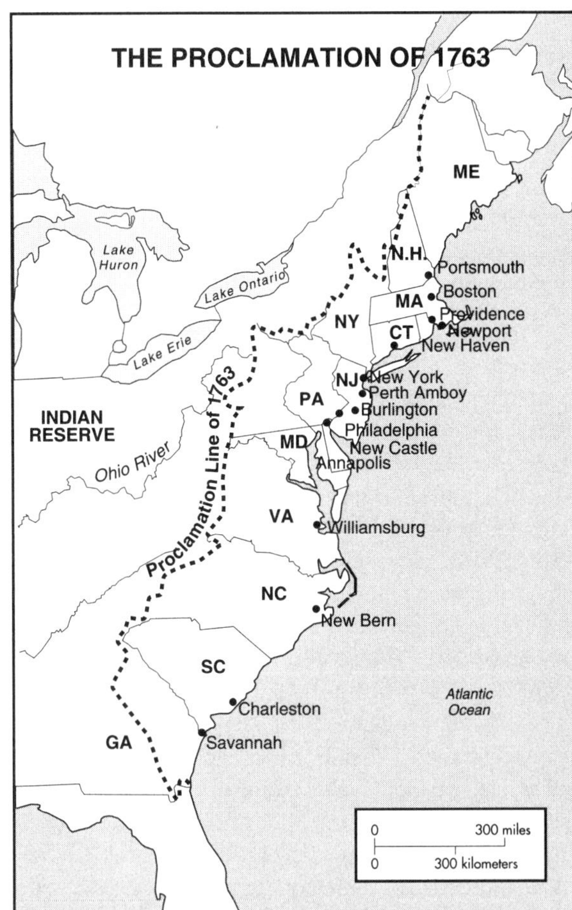

The Proclamation of 1763 was issued by the British to segregate colonists and Indians. The colonists were to stay east of the Appalachian Mountains, and Indians to the west, thus avoiding Indian conflicts, and continued British control of the colonists.

with the British Empire would form economic ties with the Mississippi Valley, then under Spanish control. They also realized that these settlers would need to manufacture some goods for themselves, rather than importing them from England. The British feared that in time such local industries would undercut imperial trade. The simplest way to prevent these things from happening was to forbid settlement west of the Appalachians. This would also keep colonial settlers from drifting away from a market economy. A settler who went far into the interior and began to live in a subsistent economy without using money, would soon lose contact with other colonists and, eventually, also his allegiance to the British crown.

The second part of the Proclamation also threatened American economic prosperity. Grenville's government had inherited a national debt of 137 million pounds sterling, almost twice what it had been before the beginning of the war with France. The costs of administering the North American empire, Grenville concluded, could well be borne by the colonists, whose debt amounted to only 2.6 million pounds sterling. But the colonies were suffering from a severe post-war depression, and hard cash, or specie (minted gold and silver), was in short supply because of the colonial trade deficit with Great Britain. Most colonial specie was used to pay English or Scottish merchants for goods the colonists had imported.

In order to raise the 250,000 pounds sterling needed to fund the frontier troops, Grenville's government put together a series of direct and indirect taxes on colonial goods and services, including the Sugar Act, the Currency Act, and the Stamp Act. These taxes led to conflict between the American colonies and England, eventually culminating in the American Revolution (1775–1783).

See also: **Stamp Act, Sugar Act**

FURTHER READING

Jennings, Francis. *Empire of Fortune: Crown, Colonies, and Tribes in the Seven Years' War.* New York: W. W. Norton, 1988.

Leach, Douglas E. *Roots of Conflict: British Armed Forces and Colonial Americans, 1677–1763.* Chapel Hill, NC: University of North Carolina Press, 1986.

Middleton, Richard. *The Bells of Victory: The Pitt-Newcastle Ministry and the Conduct of the Seven Years' War.* New York: Cambridge University Press, 1985.

Schwartz, Seymour I. *The French and Indian War, 1754–1763: The Imperial Struggle for North America.* New York: Simon and Schuster, 1994.

Walton, Gary M., and James F. Shepherd. *The Economic Rise of Early America.* New York: Cambridge University Press, 1979.

PROCTER AND GAMBLE COMPANY

In 1837 William Procter and James Gamble formed Procter and Gamble (P&G), a partnership in Cincinnati, Ohio, to manufacture and sell candles and soap. Both men had emigrated from the United Kingdom. William Procter emigrated in 1832 after fire and burglary destroyed his woolens shop in London; Gamble came from Ireland as a boy in 1819 when famine struck his homeland. Both men settled in Cincinnati, then nicknamed ''Porkopolis'' for its booming hog-butchering trade. The suggestion for the partnership apparently came from their mutual father-in-law, Alexander Norris, who pointed out that Gamble's trade—soap making—and Procter's trade—candle making—both required use of lye, which was made from animal fat and wood ashes.

Procter and Gamble first operated their business out of a storeroom at Main and Sixth streets in Cincinnati. Procter ran the store while Gamble ran the manufacturing operation, which at that time consisted of a wooden kettle with a cast-iron bottom set up behind the shop. Early each morning Gamble visited houses, hotels, and steamboats collecting ash and meat scraps; he bartered soap cakes for the raw materials. Candles were Procter and Gamble's most important product at that time.

Procter and Gamble were in competition with at least 14 other manufacturers in its early years, but the enterprising partners soon expanded their operations throughout neighboring Hamilton and Butler counties. Cincinnati's location on the Ohio River proved advantageous as the company began sending its goods down river. In 1848 Cincinnati was also linked to the major cities of the East via railroad.

Around 1851, when P&G shipments were moving up and down the river and across the country by rail, the company's famous moon-and-stars symbol was created. Because most people were illiterate at this time, trademarks were used to distinguish one company's products from another's. Company lore asserts that the symbol was first drawn as a simple cross on boxes of Procter and Gamble's Star brand candles by dockhands so that they would be easily identifiable when they arrived at their destinations. Another shipper later replaced the cross with an encircled star, and eventually William Procter added the familiar 13 stars, representing the original 13 U.S. colonies, and the man in the moon. The moon-and-stars trademark became a symbol of quality to Procter and Gamble's base of loyal customers.

By 1859, the company's annual sales exceeded $1 million, and Procter and Gamble employed about 80 people. Following the American Civil War (1861–1865), the transcontinental railroad, completed in 1869, linked the two coasts and opened still more markets to Procter and Gamble. In 1875 the company hired its first full-time chemist to work on new products, including a soap that was equal in quality to expensive castile soaps, but that could be produced less expensively. In 1878 Procter and Gamble's White Soap hit the market and catapulted P&G to the forefront of its industry.

The most distinctive characteristic of the product, soon renamed Ivory soap, was developed by accident. A worker accidentally left a soap mixer on during his lunch break, causing more air than usual to be mixed in. Before long Procter and Gamble was receiving orders for ''the floating soap.'' Although the office was at first perplexed, the confusion was soon cleared up, and P&G's formula for White Soap changed permanently.

Harley Procter, William Procter's son, developed the new soap's potential. Harley Procter was inspired to rename the soap by Psalm 45: ''all thy garments smell of myrrh, and aloes, and cassia, out of the ivory palaces whereby they have made thee glad.'' Procter devoted himself to the success of the new product and convinced the board of directors to advertise Ivory. Advertising was risky at the time; disreputable manufacturers placed most advertisements. Nevertheless, in 1882 the company approved an $11,000 annual advertising budget. The slogan ''99 and 44/100 percent pure'' was a welcome dose of sobriety amidst the generally outlandish advertising claims of the day. Procter, committed to the excellence of the company's products, had them analyzed and improved even before they went to market. This practice was the origin of P&G's superior product development. Procter believed that ''advertising alone couldn't make a product successful—it was merely evidence of a manufacturer's faith in the merit of the article.''

During the 1880s there was much labor unrest at many U.S. companies, including Procter and Gamble, which experienced a number of strikes and demonstrations. Thereafter, the company sought to avert labor problems before they became significant. In 1885 the company began giving workers Saturday afternoons off. In 1887 Procter and Gamble implemented a profit-sharing plan in order to intertwine the employees' interests with those of the company. Although the semiannual dividends were received enthusiastically by employees, that enthusiasm rarely found its way back into the workplace. The next year bonuses were tied to employee performance, which produced better results.

In 1890 the Procter and Gamble Company was incorporated; by that time it was selling more than 30 different types of soap. Two years later, in 1903, the company implemented an employee stock-purchase program, which was tied to the profit sharing plan. By 1915 about 61 percent of the company's employees were participating. The company introduced a revolutionary sickness-disability program for its workers in 1915 and implemented an eight-hour workday in 1918.

Procter and Gamble has been recognized as a leader in employee benefit programs ever since.

Experimenting with a hydrogenation process that combined liquid cottonseed oil with solid cottonseed oil led to the development of another well-known brand. After several years of research Procter and Gamble patented the procedure; in 1911 Crisco, the first all-vegetable shortening, was introduced to the public. Backed by a strong advertising budget, Crisco sales took off.

During the 1920s and 1930s the company introduced a flurry of new products. In 1926 Camay debuted, a perfumed beauty soap; Oxydol joined the P&G line of cleaning products three years later. In 1933 Dreft was introduced as the first synthetic detergent for home use. In 1937 the company celebrated its 100th anniversary, with sales having reached $230 million.

After World War II (1939–1945), the availability of raw materials and new consumer attitudes set the stage for unprecedented growth. Procter and Gamble's postwar miracle was Tide, a synthetic detergent that, together with home automatic washing machines, revolutionized the way people washed their clothes. The company was not ready for the consumer demand for heavy-duty detergent when it introduced the product in 1947; within two years Tide, backed by a $21 million advertising budget, was the number one laundry detergent. Despite its premium price, Tide remained the number one laundry detergent into the 1990s.

Tide helped to fund P&G's rapid growth into new products lines, both through acquisitions and new product introductions. By the end of the twentieth century, Procter and Gamble were the largest maker of household products in the United States, with annual sales in excess of $37 billion. The company boasted of 300 brands in several areas: baby care, beauty care, fabric and home care, feminine protection, food and beverages, health care, and tissue and towels.

See also: **Porkopolis, William Procter**

FURTHER READING

Advertising Age. *Procter and Gamble: The House that Ivory Built.* Lincolnwood, IL: NTC Business Books, 1988.

Decker, Charles L. *Winning with the P&G 99: 99 Principles and Practices of Proctor and Gamble's Success.* New York: Pocket Books, 1998.

Lief, Alfred. *It Floats: The Story of Procter and Gamble.* New York: Reinhart and Company, 1958.

Procter and Gamble Company. *Procter and Gamble History.* Cincinnati, OH: Procter and Gamble Company, 1996.

Schisgall, Oscar. *Eyes on Tomorrow: Evolution of Procter and Gamble.* Chicago: J. G. Ferguson Publishing, 1981.

Swasy, Alecia. *Soap Opera: The Inside Story of Procter and Gamble.* New York: Times Books, 1993.

PROCTER, WILLIAM COOPER

William Cooper Procter (1862–1934) spent his entire professional life from 1883 to his death in 1934 with Procter and Gamble, the soap and household products company founded by his grandfather. For half a century, Procter worked to improve conditions for workers, transforming his company from a hotbed of union dissent to a leading example of outstanding employee-management relations. He was known to have a very strong social consciousness and perhaps could be described best as a philanthropic capitalist.

William Cooper Procter was born on August 25, 1862,, in Glendale a suburb of Cincinnati, Ohio. His parents, William Alexander and Charlotte Jackson Procter, had five children—William Cooper was their only son. Procter attended Hughes High School in Cincinnati and graduated from Princeton University in 1883. On January 1, 1889, he married Jane Eliza Johnston of Glendale. The couple had no children. Procter was active in the Christ Episcopal Church, where he served as a senior warden, becoming one of the most noteworthy laymen in the Episcopal Diocese of Southern Ohio. While serving as a commanding officer for the 1st Regiment of the Ohio National Guard, Procter established a rifle range, Camp Procter, property that he later gave to the Girl Scouts of America.

In addition to his work with Procter and Gamble, Procter sat on the board of the New York Central Railroad and the National City Bank of New York. He was active in politics with the Republican Party, and managed the unsuccessful campaign of General Leonard Wood for the 1920 presidential nomination. (Fellow Ohioan Warren G. Harding, 1865–1923, got the nomination, and went on to the White House.) Procter also served on many relief committees during the Hoover administration. Procter was extremely generous to his alma mater, Princeton University, and was a major donor to the Graduate School. His greatest philanthropic act in his hometown was the amount of time and money that he bestowed upon the Children's Hospital at Cincinnati.

Procter was an unselfish man, a fact borne out by his efforts on behalf of his employees, as well as the contributions he made to numerous charities. He was a sportsman and athlete, active in his church, active in politics, and he received numerous awards and honors, which reflect his many philanthropic endeavors.

A description of William C. Procter is not complete without mentioning his ancestors, James Gamble and William Procter. Gamble and Procter were immigrants from Ireland and England, respectively. Heading West both men stayed in Cincinnati, and married two sisters, Olivia and Elizabeth Norris. William Procter was a candle maker and James Gamble was a soap maker. Their father-in-law suggested that James Gamble and William Procter merge businesses. One essential ingredient for both candles and soap was animal fat at the time, Cincinnati was a major hog-slaughtering center. The men peddled their products along the Ohio River. They became very successful and the company was the largest business in Cincinnati by the time the Civil War started they supplied all the soap and candles for the Union army. In 1890, W.C. Procter's father, William A. Procter, was named the company's first president. William C. Procter was a child when Procter and Gamble's trademark, a man in the moon and 13 stars within a circle, was first used. It was developed by wharf workers who would stamp the symbol on the wooden shipping crates of "Starlight Candles" to identify the manufacturer.

As the grandson of William Procter, William Cooper Procter's future was set. Once he finished his schooling at Princeton University in 1883, he returned to Cincinnati to work for Procter and Gamble. Procter worked in every aspect of the business, both in the factory and office, and as a salesperson. In doing so, he became very much aware of the working and living conditions of the workers. By that time it was an enormous company with large nationwide sales of products such as Ivory Soap. It had developed what was then a model factory called Ivorydale near Cincinnati. But it had a number of problems in the area of worker relations. Procter helped to change the face of employee relations in his family's company and, because of his firm's size and influence, U.S. industry itself. In an era when most business leaders seemed to believe that there was nothing wrong with their workers that pay cuts and the threat of job loss would not cure, his views were extremely progressive, and he set an example for other companies.

When Procter went to work for the family business in 1883, the Knights of Labor, at that time a prominent labor union, were leading a strike at the Ivorydale plant. Whereas the older generation might have taken a hard-line stance that could have caused the strike to go on longer, young William C. Procter talked his father and uncle into letting him use a very different approach. He gave the workers half the day off on Saturdays, an unheard-of concession, and instituted a new profit-sharing plan. He even worked with leaders among the employees to modify the profit-sharing package so it suited their needs.

By his skillful handling of workers' grievances—motivated by what was a genuine concern for his employees' well-being—Procter was able to continue building a successful business in an era when labor unrest was sweeping U.S. industry. Instead of trying to head off the Knights of Labor with billy clubs and rifles, as many of his counterparts in other businesses practiced, Procter dampened their efforts with kindness. The union never gained a foothold in his company's plant.

When the company became incorporated in 1890, Procter became general manager. By then Procter and Gamble was selling more than thirty types of soap and the company was placing large, color advertisements in national magazines. To meet the demand of the consumer, the company opened a second factory. In 1907 his father, William A. Procter, stepped down as company president, and William C. took his place. Once he became company president, Procter went even further. He revised the pension and benefit plans for his employees, and even gave them a voice on the board of directors. In 1918 he instituted a conference committee so that workers had a forum in which to present complaints to management, and in 1923 he guaranteed his employees that they would have work for at least 48 weeks out of every year. That is they would not be laid off for more than four weeks in any 12-month period.

When William C. Procter became president of the company, Procter and Gamble had two plants, the original factory at Ivorydale in Cincinnati and one at Kansas City, Kansas (1905). By the time of Procter's death in 1934, several other plants were built: Staten Island, New York (1908), Macon, Georgia (1910), Hamilton, Ontario (1915), Dallas Texas (1919), Baltimore, Maryland (1930), and Long Beach, California (1931). Procter and Gamble also bought out several other companies, including the William Waltke Company, the Globe Soap Company, and entered the foreign market with its purchase of the James S. Kirk & Company in England and a soap and candle factory in Cuba. Just before Procter joined the family firm, Procter and Gamble had already became well known for its Ivory soap—the soap that "floats and is 99 44/100 pure." Under his leadership, the company introduced several products, most notably Crisco Shortening in 1911. Crisco was the first vegetable shortening. It is made from cottonseed oil, also an ingredient used in making soap. Vegetable shortening was healthier than using animal fats and much less expensive than butter, so Crisco became very popular and the product eventually sponsored cooking shows on the radio. Procter and Gamble expanded its factory holdings to include cotton mills with facilities to crush the cottonseed for the production of oil and to process the seed waste to be used for the manufacture of cellulose materials. William C. Procter had created an expansive industrial empire. Procter developed research laboratories to make new products and he also developed one of the first market research departments to study consumer preferences and buying habits. A product was marketed according to its particular use or a specific need of the consumer. In 1932 Procter and Gamble sponsored "The Puddle Family" and in 1934 developed "Ma Perkins", a serial program sponsored by Oxydol soap—soap operas! In 1930 William C. Procter stepped down as company president. But he remained chairman of the board until his death in 1934.

William C. Procter was a nationally known manufacturer of household products. Perhaps more importantly, he was known for his innovative business management techniques. Elements of Procter's employee benefits package remained in effect two generations after his death, by which time much of U.S. industry had more or less adapted to his view of employee management. Procter changed the American workplace as well as the American marketplace. He was a model citizen in that he sought to better the conditions of workers and shared his wealth with his community. In the wake of his impressive leadership, Procter and Gamble became the leading seller of household products and the nation's most dominant advertiser. The company went on to revolutionize the washday with the laundry soap, Tide. Procter and Gamble eventually entered the food and paper markets. By the mid 1990s Procter and Gamble sold over three hundred brands of products in over 140 countries, and had employed over one hundred thousand employees.

See also: **Procter and Gamble**

FURTHER READING

Dupree, Richard Redwood. *William Cooper Procter (1862–1934) Industrial Statesman.* New York: Newcomen Society, 1951.

Ingham, John, ed. *Biographical Dictionary of American Business Leaders.* Westport, Conn.: Greenwood, 1983, s.v. "Procter, William C."

Lief, Alfred. *It Floats: The Story of Procter & Gamble.* New York: Rinehart, 1958.

The National Encyclopedia of American Biography. Vol. 25. New York: James T. White, 1936, s.v. "Procter, William C."

Procter and Gamble Company. *Into a Second Century With Procter & Gamble.* Cincinnati: Procter and Gamble, 1944.

PROCTOR, BARBARA GARDNER

Barbara Gardner Proctor (1933–) rose from dire poverty to the head of the second-largest African-American-owned advertising business in America. Her fearlessness and determination in facing obstacles originated from her own harsh beginnings. She was unique in the advertising industry for using her values to guide her work, and she was not afraid to turn away accounts that she found objectionable, such as those that demeaned African Americans or women.

Barbara Gardner Proctor was born in 1933 in Black Mountain, North Carolina, to a single mother, Bernice Gardner. Raised by a grandmother and an uncle, she lived in extreme poverty with no electricity or running water. Her grandmother instilled early determination in Proctor, telling her, "You're not cute, but you're smart, and one day you'll amount to something." Proctor never forgot the advice and it turned out to be true.

Proctor's academic ability earned her a scholarship to Talladega College in Alabama, and she went on to earn a B.A. in English and another B.A. in psychology and social science. She graduated with both degrees in 1954. She also was awarded the Armstrong Creative Writing Award from the college in 1954. Later she attended law school.

In 1960 Gardner married Carl Proctor, road manager for jazz singer Sarah Vaughn. But they divorced in 1963. She had one child named Morgan who later worked for her business. She claimed that the 15-hour days that she worked were the best relaxation for her.

Proctor was involved in the business community and received many awards for her work. She served on a number of boards, including the Illinois Bell Telephone Company, the 1988 Illinois Olympic Committee, the Better Business Bureau, the Illinois State Bar

Association Institute for Public Affairs, and the White House Conference on Small Business. She was involved in efforts for the advancement of women and African Americans and worked with such groups as the League of Black Women (served as president from 1978-1982), the National Association for the Advancement of Colored People (lifetime member), and Handicapped Organized Women (served on honorary board). Proctor won a number of awards for her contributions to the fields of writing and advertising. Some of these included the Small Business of the Year Award (1978) and the Black Media Award for Outstanding Professional (1980).

Proctor began her career by using her writing skills in the music field. In 1958 she began working as a jazz music critic and contributing editor to *Downbeat* magazine. From 1961 to 1964 she worked for Vee-Jay Records International in Chicago, creating copy for jazz record covers and later serving as international director.

After her divorce from Carl Proctor, Barbara Gardner Proctor shifted to the advertising industry. Between 1965 and 1970 she worked for three different advertising firms: Post-Keys-Gardner Advertising, Chicago, 1965-1968; Gene Taylor Associates, Chicago, 1969; and North Advertising Agency, Chicago, 1969-1970. Eventually, she served as copy supervisor at North Advertising Agency. She decided to launch her own business when she was fired from North Advertising Agency for refusing to work on an ad campaign to which she objected. The ad, which she found demeaning to women and African Americans, parodied the Civil Rights Movement and featured protesting women running down the street and demanding that their hairdressers foam their hair.

In 1971 Proctor launched her own business, Proctor and Gardner Advertising. To go into business she applied for a small business loan, which she was denied for lack of collateral. Armed with data (three advertising agencies statements of what they would pay her as an employee), she convinced the lender to give her an $80,000 loan using herself as collateral.

She faced a number of societal obstacles that did not deter her. As she explained in *Ebony*, "I happen to be born female and black, but I am much more than that. To view one's self in terms of those two small biological characteristics is very self-limiting." In a time when not many women or African Americans ran businesses, Proctor purposefully named the business using both "Proctor" and "Gardner," so that potential clients would assume that "Gardner" was a male partner behind the scenes.

After six months in business Proctor had her first client. At the end of four years in business, Proctor needed more working capital and applied for another loan from the Small Business Administration (SBA). But the SBA refused. Undaunted, she looked inward, refusing to blame any external situations. In the April 30, 1984, edition of the *New Orleans Time-Picayune*, Proctor explained, "In every case where something would have been an obstacle, I've found a way to turn it to an advantage. I cannot buy the concept that anyone outside is responsible." She credited her impoverished upbringing with giving her the ability to take risks, since she had already been exposed to adversity in her life and had little fear of the unknown.

I HAPPEN TO BE BORN FEMALE AND BLACK, BUT I AM MUCH MORE THAN THAT. TO VIEW ONE'S SELF IN TERMS OF THOSE TWO SMALL BIOLOGICAL CHARACTERISTICS IS VERY SELF-LIMITING.

Barbara Gardner Proctor

Proctor brought to her business a firm belief that advertising should encompass quality and equality. According to *Contemporary Newsmakers*, the timing was right for minority business to succeed. In the advertising arena, the African American market was just beginning to be understood, giving Proctor's company a virtually untapped market. Proctor was able to focus on this niche and maximize profits, as well as present a positive picture of the African American community.

Proctor maintained a diverse staff with many women and minorities, and in a 1982 *Ebony* article she called her staff one of the best in the world. She described herself as a non-boss who did not believe in telling professionals how to do their jobs. On the other hand, she held employees accountable, specifying that if they challenged any directions that she had given, that they had "damn well better deliver" to the client. Her son Morgan served on her staff and expressed an interest in taking over the company in the future.

By the mid-1990s sales had slowed, however, and in 1995 Proctor & Gardner Advertising filed Chapter 11 bankruptcy, a protective measure that offered a chance to restructure the firm's finances and pay off debt. At the time of bankruptcy the company was more than $1.8 million in debt and reported assets of $361,000. The company had more than $5 million in account billings. In 1996 Proctor dissolved the advertising agency. Honing in on the increase in Internet use, she started a new company, Proctor Communications Network, which offered Internet marketing expertise and web site design. The business was later renamed Proctor Information Network, Inc.

Proctor was able to rise from extreme poverty and create a business that became the second-largest African American advertising agency in America. In 1983 the company had $12 million in billing. Some of Proctor & Gardner's long-standing clients included Kraft Foods, Sears, Roebuck and Co., and Alberto-Culver. Another long-term client, Jewel Foods of Chicago, credited Proctor & Gardner Advertising with rescuing Jewel's generic food line, which suffered poor sales. Proctor & Gardner redesigned the food campaign, giving it a stronger and more positive tone.

Noteworthy of Proctor's work in the advertising field was her adherence to her values. She refused to take work that degraded women, blacks, or that she found morally unacceptable. For example, Proctor & Gardner did no work for cigarette or liquor accounts. Proctor was wary of what she called ''ethnically dubious advertising pitches'' that were aimed at women and minorities. She maintained, ''Advertising is the single most important way of reaching everyone in America and I feel a deep responsibility to my work.''

See also: **Advertising Industry**

FURTHER READING

Ball, Millie. ''Ad Whiz Was On Her Way With Her First SBA Loan.'' *New Orleans Time-Picayune*, April 30, 1984.

''Black Woman Advertising Entrepreneur Files for Chapter 11 Bankruptcy.'' *Jet*, October 9, 1995.

Brown, Michelle. *Contemporary Newsmakers*, 1985 Cumulation. Detroit: Gale Research, 1986, s.v. ''Barbara Gardner Proctor.''

The Ebony Success Library. Nashville: Southwestern Co., 1973.

Francke, Richie L. ''Proctor Takes a Gamble and Hits the Jackpot.''*Working Woman*, August 1979.

PRODUCTIVITY

Productivity is the quantitative relationship between the number of inputs employed and the number of outputs produced. For example, productivity on a farm involves the inputs (or resources) of land, labor, tractors, feed, etc., and the outputs (outcomes) of crops and livestock. An increase in productivity means that more outputs (crops and livestock) can be produced from the same or fewer inputs. For instance, crop productivity on a farm may increase because the farmer planted a new, genetically engineered crop designed to be more resistant to insects and disease. The crop is planted on the same amount of land the farmer used the year before, however, the sturdiness of the genetically engineered plant allows more of the crop to survive the growing season and be harvested, increasing the farmer's productivity.

An increase in crop yield is a single-factor productivity indicator. A single-factor productivity indicator defines itself as one factor, rather than many, contributing to increased productivity. Another single-factor productivity indicator may be output per man-hours worked. Several factors combined can also contribute to increased productivity. They are called multi-factor productivity indicators. Total farm output per unit of input is a multi-factor measure.

Productivity plays a vital role in the economy. Increased productivity in national industries can raise the standard of living and the quality of life. It can also improve production efficiency and enhance competition. Technological advances have played a large role in increasing industrial productivity in the twentieth century. However, growth through improved technology may also work against an economy, creating unemployment, as the number of workers needed to produce the same output declines. For instance, with the advent of the multi-purpose tractor in the agricultural industry many tasks previously done by manual laborers were mechanized. The laborers who could not adjust their skills to meet the changes in the industry saw their jobs disappear. Unemployment brought on by changing technology and worker inability to meet those needs is called structural unemployment.

Though productivity and growth clearly affect a nation's economy there is no single way to measure it. Inputs and outputs involve numerous variables and no method has developed to accurately capture all the factors involved.

See also: **Structural Unemployment**

PROFIT

Profit is the money that remains after the cost of manufacturing, marketing, taxes, interest, depreciation, and any other expenses incurred in the production of a product or service have been deducted from the price subsequently received for the product or service. In a market economy profit is the key element that drives buying and selling decisions. A profit is most easily made when the demand for a product or service far exceeds the supply. In such a situation a higher price can be exacted regardless of the production costs of the product or service. Profit may also be referred to as net earnings, net income, or bottom line.

PROGRESSIVE TAX

A progressive tax system is one which assesses a higher percentage rate of taxation as income levels or income brackets increase. The U.S. federal income tax system is a progressive tax system. (For the following examples consider all the taxpayers to be filing their income tax returns as single individuals.) In 1999 the person making from 0 to $25,350 would pay 15 percent on all of their income. Therefore, a low-income person pays 15 percent on their total income. The person making up to $61,400 pays 15 percent on the first $25,350, but then pays 28 percent on the income between $25,350 and $61,400. To illustrate, if a middle income individual makes $50,000, 15 percent or $3,802.50 would be paid on the first $25,350. On the next $24,650 ($50,000 minus $25,350), 28 percent or $6,902 is added to the $3,802.50 for a total tax payment of $10,704.50. That amount is 21 percent of the total income of the middle-income person. This tax rate is an increase of six percent over the 15 percent the lower-income person would pay on his or her total income. Because higher income groups pay a higher percentage of their total income in taxes, this tax structure is considered progressive. Using tax rates for 1999, income in the range of $61,400 to $128,100 is taxed at 31 percent, $128,100 to $278,450 at 36 percent, and over $278,450 at 39.6 percent. In 1982 the top income bracket was taxed at 50 percent and 14 tax brackets existed. The Tax Reform Act of 1986 reduced the number of income brackets to three (15 percent, 28 percent, and 31 percent). The Clinton Tax Package of 1993 increased the brackets to the five used in the 1999 illustration (15 percent, 28 percent, 31 percent, 36 percent, and 39.6 percent).

See also: **Proportional Tax, Regressive Tax**

PROHIBITION *(ISSUE)*

During the colonial period in America alcohol consumption was more common than it was at the end of the twentieth century. Some estimate per capita consumption of alcohol during colonial times at double the rate it was in the 1990s. Puritans brewed beer and ordinary citizens consumed prodigious amounts of hard cider. Part of the reason for so much alcohol consumption was the uncertainty of potable water. Cholera epidemics in the 1830s and 1840s resulted in part from drinking unclean water. Although the abuse of alcohol was more common then, there is also considerable evidence that it was frowned upon. For example in Virginia as early as 1629, ministers were prohibited by law from excess in drinking, and in Massachusetts a 1633 law limited the amount of alcohol that could be purchased while another statute in 1637 limited the amount of time anyone could spend in a tavern. Later, many colonies imposed fines for excessive behavior as well as taxes and license fees.

The last half of the eighteenth century witnessed the beginnings of the temperance movement as religious leaders began to denounce not only excessive drinking but all consumption of alcohol. Technically, temperance meant moderation, but in fact people meant abstinence. In 1773 John Wesley, one of the founders of the Methodist Church, declared that drinking was a sin and Anthony Benezet, a leading member of the Society of Friends, the Quakers, wrote a pamphlet in which he argued that drinking tended to make a man behave foolishly and even dangerously.

The medical community was also concerned. In 1785, Dr. Benjamin Rush, the leading physician of the day, published a pamphlet entitled "Inquiry into the Effects of Ardent Spirits Upon the Human Body and Mind," wherein he listed various diseases thought to plague those who consumed alcohol. At about this time temperance organizations began to appear. Among the first were the Organization of Brethren and the Litchfield Connecticut Association.

In the early nineteenth century, those who opposed alcohol became more strident because many people saw drinking as an impediment to the growth of democracy and U.S. nationalism. This period saw the first experiments with statewide prohibition. Maine passed the first prohibition law in 1843. During the next few years Ohio, Illinois, Rhode Island, Minnesota, Massachusetts, Connecticut, Pennsylvania, and New York followed suit. But most of these efforts were short-lived. They were vetoed, soon repealed or stricken down by the courts. There was also, of course, considerable opposition from the public. State prohibition laws were widely ignored while they were in effect and in some cases there was violence, as in 1850 when people rioted against Sunday closing laws in Chicago. Still, the advocates of prohibition persisted. The American Temperance Society was founded in 1826, followed by the Washington Movement in 1840 and the

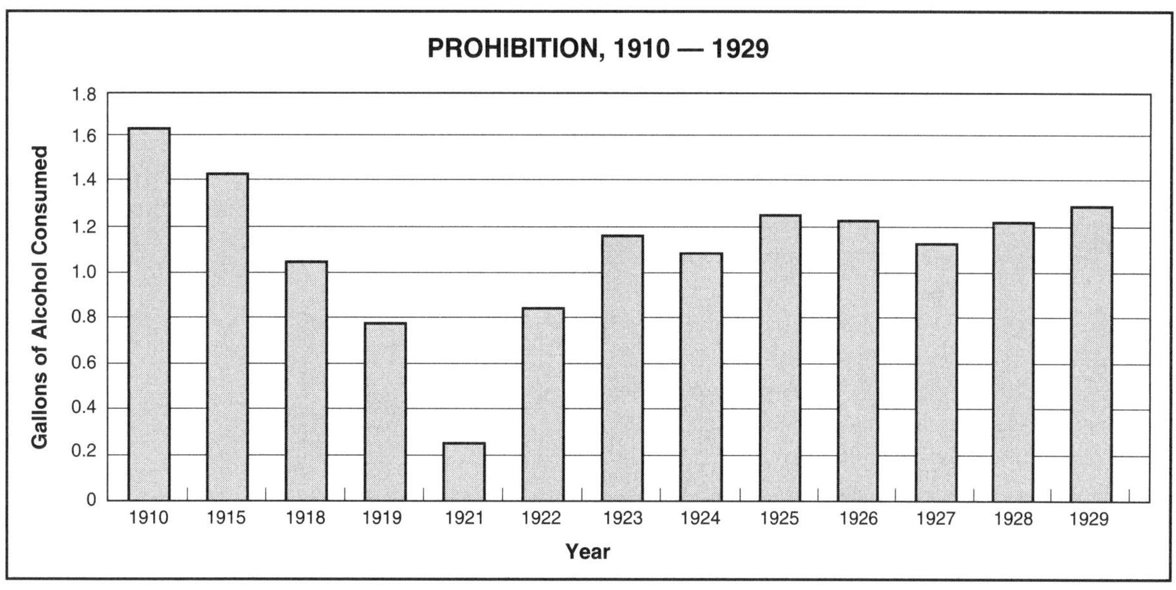

The passage of the Eighteenth Amendment in 1921 outlawed alcoholic beverages nationwide. Although a marked decrease in consumption was seen that year, the law was generally considered a "disastrous failure" because of the rapid growth in illegal consumption and crime in the following years.

Sons of Temperance in 1842. All these organizations advocated total abstinence.

By the late nineteenth century the prohibition movement, like other reform movements, was lobbying Congress. The National Prohibition Party was founded in 1869, and ran its first candidate for president, James Black, in 1872. The Women's' Christian Temperance Union was established in 1874. The organization was led by Frances Willard who was also an advocate of women's rights and suffrage. By 1884 the issue was clearly affecting the national parties. James G. Blaine, the Republican candidate for president in that year, lost to Democrat Grover Cleveland (1885–1889), partly as a result of his ineffective handling of the temperance question. He succeeded only in alienating people on both sides of the debate.

In 1895 the Anti-Saloon League was founded. Over the next decade-and-a-half the Anti-Saloon League was to become the most powerful lobby for prohibition advocates. Supported mostly by rural, middle-class, white Protestants, the League conducted an aggressive campaign. The Anti-Saloon League argued that liquor was destructive to society because it contributed to divorce, poverty, pauperism, crime, child abuse and insanity. During the early twentieth century, the so-called Progressive Era when social and political reforms were in vogue, the League portrayed prohibition as one of the leading reform movements of the day, and the results were impressive. By 1913 nine states had adopted statewide prohibition, and 31 had chosen the "local option" which allowed cities or counties to go dry by referendum. As a result, 75 percent of the population lived under some form of prohibition. While this was regarded as a dangerous trend by wets (people in opposition to prohibition) and their leading organizations such as the National Brewers Association, the prohibitionists would not be satisfied until prohibition covered the entire country.

Between 1913 and 1915 prohibition resolutions were twice introduced in Congress by Congressmen Joseph B. Thompson of Oklahoma and Senator Morris Sheppard of Texas. These both failed, but when the United States entered World War I in 1917, things changed. Prohibitionists could argue that the liquor industry was unpatriotic because it drained resources like grain that should be used for food, that the use of alcohol undermined the effectiveness of soldiers, and that many of the families who owned breweries and distilleries were ethnic Germans.

The resolution to prohibit the manufacture, sale, transportation, and importation of alcoholic beverages passed Congress in early 1918. Just a year later it was ratified as the Eighteenth Amendment when on January 16, 1919, Nebraska became the thirty-sixth state to approve it. The enforcement law, commonly known as the Volstead Act, passed Congress on October 29, 1919, and prohibition officially went into effect on January 17, 1920.

The national prohibition experiment was in effect for 13 years from 1920 to 1933. It was a disastrous failure in most parts of the country although in certain sections like the rural South it more or less worked because it had popular support. Generally however the results were not good. Smuggling increased during the early years followed by a rapid increase in crime as "bootleggers"'—the manufacturers of illegal liquor—sought to meet the overwhelming demand.

It is estimated that by 1930 the illegal manufacturing establishments numbered over 280,000, and illegal saloons—known as Speakeasies—numbered between 200,000 and 500,000. Moreover, people manufactured "home brew" in vast but unknown quantities and doctors issued prescriptions for equally vast quantities of whiskey to be used for "medical purposes." Contemporary estimates believe that doctors earned $40 million in 1928 alone by writing such prescriptions.

Because Congress never appropriated sufficient funds, the Volstead Act could not be effectively enforced and probably would have been repealed eventually under any conditions, but it was the coming of the Great Depression that hastened its demise. This was because the Depression triggered demands for increased employment and tax revenues.

By 1929 it was clear that prohibition was a failure and President Hoover (1929–1933) appointed a special commission to study the issue. Chaired by George W. Wickersham, a former Attorney General, the commission issued its report in 1931. Oddly enough, even though the commission recognized all the problems with prohibition, they nevertheless recommended that it be continued. This however was not to be.

At their 1932 national convention the Democrats advocated for the repeal of the Eighteenth Amendment and their presidential candidate, Governor Franklin Delano Roosevelt (1933–1945) of New York, agreed. Roosevelt was easily elected and the repeal amendment was introduced in Congress on February 14, 1933, before the inauguration. It was approved by both Houses within a few days and submitted to the states for ratification. It was quickly approved and adopted by Congress on December 5, 1933.

Even though the national prohibition experiment failed, there remained millions of people in this country who thought alcohol and its use were sinful, wasteful and dangerous. Thus prohibition in one form or another persisted. The Prohibition Party, though minuscule, continued to campaign, certain churches demanded that their members practice abstinence from alcohol, and 40 states continued to permit the local option.

See also: **Black Market, Great Depression, Illegal Drugs**

FURTHER READING

Cherrington, E. H. *The Evolution of Prohibition in the United States of America.* Westerville, OH: American Issue Press, 1920.

Clark, Norman H. *Deliver Us From Evil: An Interpretation of American Prohibition.* New York: Norton, 1976.

Dobyns, F. *The Amazing Story of Repeal.* Chicago: Willett, Clark and Company, 1940.

Furnas, J.C. *The Life and Times of the Late Demon Rum.* New York: Putnam, 1965.

Krout, J. A. *Pressure Politics: The Story of the Anti-Saloon League.* New York: Columbia University Press, 1928.

Sinclair, Andrew. *The Era of Excess.* Boston: Little, Brown, 1962.

Thornton, Mark. *The Economics of Prohibition.* Salt Lake City: University of Utah Press, 1991.

PROPORTIONAL TAX

A proportional tax system, also called the flat-rate tax, assesses the same percentage rate of taxation on everyone, regardless of income. If the proportional tax rate were set at 20 percent, an individual making $10,000 would pay $2000 in taxes; a person with an income of $50,000 would pay $10,000; and a person making $100,000 would pay $20,000. Even as the income goes up or down, the percent of total income paid in taxes does not change. It is the same percentage at all income tax brackets.

Many state income tax systems are very close to being proportional tax systems. High-income individuals, under a proportional tax scheme do pay more than lower-income people. However, public debate centers on the idea that high-income persons can better afford to pay their taxes while low-income persons need all their income to meet basic needs and are, therefore, hurt by a proportional tax. In the 1990s the flat-rate tax was touted as a way to greatly simplify a complex tax system and, for many people, as an overall tax savings in comparison to the progressive tax system.

See also: **Progressive Tax, Regressive Tax**

THE PROSPERITY DECADE, 1921–1928 (OVERVIEW)

The period of U.S. history between 1921 and 1929, known as the Era of Prosperity, was dominated by the Republicans in the national government. The three Republican presidents who served during that time were: Warren G. Harding (1921–1923), Calvin Coolidge (1923–1929), and Herbert C. Hoover (1929–1933). Harding was incompetent and his administration was corrupt. He died in office (August 2, 1923) and was succeeded by Calvin Coolidge who served for nearly six years. Coolidge came into office with a reputation for honesty that he maintained throughout his administration. Very popular, he was re–elected to his own term of office in 1924; he could probably have run again successfully in 1928, however, he chose to step down. He was succeeded by Hoover who, since 1921, served as Secretary of Commerce in both Harding's and Coolidge's administrations. At first Hoover was very popular but the financial collapse of 1929 destroyed his reputation.

Businessmen wanted lower taxes and higher tariffs and the Republicans tried to accommodate them. In 1921 the new Secretary of the Treasury, Andrew W. Mellon, recommended a tax plan that included repeal of the wartime excess profits tax and an income tax reduction of nearly 40 percent. However, he had to compromise with Congress; the bill that finally passed reduced the maximum tax rate by 17 percent and raised corporate taxes by 2.5 percent. Mellon served all three administrations. By the end of the decade he had reduced the income tax rate by approximately 30 percent.

On May 11, 1924, Congress enacted a law known as the Emergency Tariff. It raised rates on meat and farm products. Then, in September 1922, Congress passed the Fordney-McCumber Tariff. This measure again raised tariff rates on farm products and also protected chemicals, silk and rayon textiles, toys, china, cutlery, and guns. This law remained in effect until 1930 when it was replaced by the Smoot-Hawley Tariff (which, again, raised rates substantially). By then the average on all imports was 40 percent.

The years following World War I (1914–1918) were marked by a declining birthrate in America. The number of children born fell from 23.7 per thousand in 1920, to 18.9 in 1930. Declining birthrates coupled with immigrant restriction led to an overall decline in population growth. However, this was not the only significant demographic feature of the period. Rural population declined and cities grew. Between 1920 and 1930 some six million people migrated from the farm to the city. By the end of the decade only 44 percent of Americans lived in rural areas (farms and small towns). Among those who moved to the cities were large numbers of African Americans. Eighty-nine percent of all African Americans lived in the South in 1910 but by 1930 the number had been reduced by 10 percent.

The overall economy during this period featured erratic shifts in profits and employment. During the World War I and immediately after it there was a production boom triggered by accelerated demand. Beginning in 1920, however, inflation gave way to a decline driven by the collapse of farm prices. Farmers had indulged in significant production increases during the war and now their markets were melting away. By the spring of 1921 the nation was in the throes of a full-fledged depression. Foreign trade was cut nearly in half, wholesale prices fell 24 percent, and unemployment neared 5,000,000. However recovery began in 1922 for most sectors of the economy (except agriculture); economic improvement continued with few reversals until 1929. It is mainly in comparison to the subsequent Great Depression that this decade is called the ''Prosperity Decade.''

Per capita income in the United States during the prosperous twenties rose from $620 in 1919 to $681 in 1929 (9 percent), while at the same time earnings increased by 26 percent. This trend was driven by large expansion in the construction industry and manufacturing; widespread confidence about the period seemed justified. However there were other indicators that suggested general trends were deceiving. These indicators revealed, among other things, a significant maldistribution of wealth. For example, corporate profits increased nearly 62 percent between 1923 and 1929, but workers' real income increased only 11 percent. Despite perceptions about the ''Prosperity Decade,'' many people were not prosperous at all. A decent standard of living during that period required an annual income of $2,500, but 71 percent of all families had incomes below that figure.

Several industries which were barely in their infancy at the end of the war grew dramatically during the next decade. These included automobile, electric power, machinery and appliances, radio, aviation, and motion pictures industries. Measured by its social and economic impact, the automobile industry was easily the most important industry of the era. Automobile industry magnate Henry Ford (1863–1947) was the dominant leader of the industry. He perfected the Model T, a vehicle that practically anybody could afford. More importantly, he developed the moving assembly line which made production cheap and fast.

During the 1920s automobile production expanded dramatically from 1.5 million at the beginning of the decade to 4.8 million by the end. By 1929 the industry utilized 15 percent of all the steel and 80 percent of all the rubber production in the United States. Car manufacturers employed 7.1 percent of all the wage earners in the country and produced 12.7 percent of the value of all manufactured goods.

Electric power became the second most important economic interest in the country during the Era of Prosperity. By 1929 seventy percent of all homes had electric power. Widespread availability of electricity spurred the invention of new appliances such as irons, washing machines, vacuum cleaners and refrigerators.

Closely related to electric power was the radio industry. Until 1919 the federal government banned the private use of radio sets, but once the ban was lifted, the radio industry began its rapid growth. By 1929 forty percent of all American families had radio sets in their homes.

The aviation industry grew slowly in the first, few post–war years. Congress passed the Air Commerce Act in 1926, which gave control of commercial aviation to the Commerce Department; thus, the age of the aviation industry began. Secretary of Commerce Herbert Hoover (1874–1964) did all he could to promote the industry. Scheduled air service began in 1926 and by 1930 there were 122 airline companies in operation.

In 1896 the motion picture machine was invented by Thomas A. Edison (1847–1931); only seven years elapsed before production of the first "movie" with a story, *The Great Train Robbery* (1903). However, the motion picture industry really began in 1905 when admission to a projection house (5 cents) was first charged in Pittsburgh. The first theaters, called nickelodeons, were very popular. By 1907 there were 5,000 of them in all parts of the country. Over the next few years the technology improved dramatically and by World War I the large, ornate movie theater appeared. Sound and color were added by the end of the 1920s. By 1930 there were 23,000 theaters in the country with annual admissions revenue of $1.5 billion. The industry employed 325,000 people with a capital inventory of two billion dollars.

The 1920s (the Prosperity Decade) are often called the Age of Big Business. This is true not only because of the rapid expansion of industry but also because of numerous mergers which produced very large business entities. By 1929 two hundred corporations controlled 49 percent of all corporate wealth in the country and received 43 percent of all corporate income. There were only two monopolies by 1929—in the sulfur and aluminum industries—but there were many near monopolies or oligopolies (an oligopoly is an industry controlled by a very small number of participants).

When Congress passed the Clayton Anti-Trust Act in 1913 and simultaneously created the Federal Trade Commission (FTC), they had sought to end destructive competitive practices that had characterized business since the late nineteenth century. These practices had been largely abandoned by business in the 1920s; the rise of oligopolies had actually enhanced competition. Hence the goal of the government during this period was to encourage healthy competition. If that meant competition among a few, very large businesses which provided high quality goods and services to the people, so much the better. Critics, of course, charged that government had become the handmaid of business, but this was true only in a limited sense.

The American farmer suffered most from the depression of 1921–1922, and never fully recovered as did most other sectors of the economy. In 1919 farmers received 16 percent of the total national income. In 1929 they received only 8.8 percent.

Between 1921 and 1924 a non-partisan group in Congress known as the Farm Bloc worked aggressively on behalf of the farmers. They passed laws regulating the meat packers, the stockyards, and the grain exchanges, and they also created a system of government–backed credit for farmers. However, they did not address the real problem—overproduction. Congress tired to deal with this problem, but their efforts failed. Known as McNar-Haugen Bill, Congress approved a proposal to buy the surplus and sell it abroad. Farmers would then pay a tax on the part of the surplus they produced in order to finance the program. Although complicated, the plan might have worked, but it never became law because it was vetoed by President Coolidge.

Just before the Depression (1929–39) the Hoover administration passed the Agricultural Marketing Act (June 20, 1929). This law created the Federal Farm Board with a revolving fund of $500 million to be loaned to agricultural cooperatives so they could build warehouses and hold their members' products in case of a price decline. The Board was also authorized to stabilize prices through direct intervention in the market. The program was the most important effort yet attempted by the American government to stabilize and support agriculture. However, the Agricultural Marketing Act proved ineffective in the wake of the catastrophic economic collapse which began in 1929.

The country experienced a period of inflation just before the depression of 1921–22. This was the key factor in setting off a wave of strikes by means of which the American Federation of Labor (AFL) hoped to preserve wartime gains and expand the union movement. Some of these strikes succeeded, but there were others that failed and caused long–term damage to the labor movement. Among these were the great steel strike and the Boston Police Strike of 1919. In cases such as these, strike leaders were branded as radicals and public opinion turned against them.

Organized labor, contrary to the hopes of its leaders, did not grow during the 1920s-membership declined. The reasons for this include the absence of aggressive leadership in many of the unions coupled with the rise of a new concept called ''welfare capitalism,'' which became popular in some industries. First promoted by Henry Ford, the idea was to seek cooperation rather than conflict between labor and management. This was to be accomplished by paying good wages, providing benefits like vacations, insurance, and retirement packages, and by listening to the workers' ideas. That this plan worked is reflected in the fact that AFL membership declined nearly 30 percent between 1920 and 1930.

The banking business and the stock market were practically unregulated during the 1920s and this led to considerable fluctuation in the world of finance. Many banks failed, particularly in rural areas dependent upon agriculture; conversely, numerous mergers occurred. Thus, while the number of banks declined by more than 5,700 between 1919 and 1929, their total resources increased spectacularly from $47.6 billion to $72 billion.

The way banks did business also changed. Before the war a commercial bank's chief function was to make short term loans to business and industry. But during the twenties most businesses were so profitable that they relied upon their own resources for expansion and current operating expenses. Hence the banks had large sums to invest in other ways. They increased their investments in stocks and bonds, increased loans against real estate, and loaned vast sums to stock brokers for speculative purposes. Bank loans to brokers against stocks and bonds totaled more than $8.5 billion by the fall of 1929. In addition, banks established their own investment affiliates and did their own speculating in the stock market. This progression continued as long as the market continued to boom as it did between 1926 and 1929, but the collapse, which came in the latter part of the year, took many banks with it. This was the dawn of the Great Depression and a new era in American economic history.

See also: **Thomas Edison, Henry Ford, Andrew Mellon**

FURTHER READING

Bernstein, Irving. *The Lean Years: A History of the American Worker, 1920–1933.* Boston: Houghton, Mifflin, 1960.

Chandler, Alfred Dupont. *Strategy and Structure: Chapters in the History of the American Enterprise.* Cambridge: M.I.T. Press, 1962.

Link, Arthur Stanley. *American Epoch: A History of the United States Since the 1890s.* New York: Knopf, 1955.

Saloutos, Theodore, and John D. Hicks. *Twentieth Century Populism: Agricultural Discontent in The Middle West, 1900–1939.* Madison: University of Wisconsin Press, 1951.

Soule, George Henry. *Prosperity Decade: From War to Depression: 1917–1929.* New York: Rinehart, 1947.

Susman, Warren. *Culture as History: The Transformation of American Society in the Twentieth Century.* New York: Pantheon Books, 1984.

PROTECTIONISM

Protectionism is a set a policies by which a government seeks to shelter its industries from foreign competition and or help them increase exports to international markets. The most common form of protectionism is a tariff, which is a duty or tax imposed on goods based on their value or size. Subsidies are direct payments or credit given by the government to a protected industry to encourage it to export its products. Quotas set upper limits on the amount of imports that can enter the protected country, and governments can also set limits on investments by foreign companies in domestic businesses. A more recent protectionist policy is the ''voluntary export restraint'' in which a foreign country is strongly ''encouraged'' to refrain from importing certain goods under the threat of some more severe action such as quotas. Protectionism can also take the form of preferential purchasing policies, such as the U.S. government's requirement that its agencies ''buy American.''

Throughout its history, the United States has been a protectionist country. A series of tariff laws throughout the nineteenth century steadily raised barriers to foreign trade to encourage the growth of U.S. industry. Beginning in the mid-1870s, however, the United States began exporting more than it imported and it became much more integrated in the global marketplace. Strong protectionist trade policies returned with a vengeance around the world in the 1920s, and the high tariffs the United States imposed through the Smoot-Hawley Tariff of 1930 were later credited with contributing to the United States' shrinking foreign markets during the Great Depression (1929–1939). After World War II (1939–1945) it was clear that strong protectionist policies had contributed to the destruction of the world order in the 1940s. The launching of the General Agreement on Tariffs and Trade (GATT) in 1948 represented a mostly effective attempt to reduce protectionism and create a positive climate for free trade worldwide.

Under GATT, tariff rates were cut and member nations agreed to drop discriminatory trade policies and adopt the same "most favored nation" trade practices for all other members. Under the so-called Kennedy Round (1964–1967) of GATT negotiations, the United States took a further step away from its protectionist history, and GATT members agreed to include agricultural products under GATT guidelines while adopting an "anti-dumping" code to prevent countries from flooding another's markets with cheap goods. The Tokyo Round (1973–1979) brought further tariff reductions, guidelines for outlawing unfair subsidy practices, and policies for encouraging trade with less developed countries. In 1995 GATT was replaced by a permanent free trade organization, the World Trade Organization, but protectionism was far from dead.

See also: **General Agreement on Tariffs and Trade, Quota, Smoot-Hawley Tariff, Tariff**

PROTECTORATE

The term protectorate evolved in the nineteenth century. It refers to a relationship in which a weaker state relinquishes the control of a portion or all of its international relations to a stronger state in return for protection. This relationship is a form of guardianship and the reciprocal rights and duties between the two states generally are delineated by treaty. The protected state is considered the "protectorate." In international law the protectorate still retains recognition as a state by other nations and may retain some of its state rights such as a right to diplomatic representation. The protectorate usually maintains control over its domestic affairs.

In the nineteenth century, protectorate relationships often preceded colonial expansion or, as in the case of the United States and Caribbean, aimed at preventing foreign rivals from gaining a foothold in certain areas and upsetting a delicate balance of power. U.S. foreign policy toward the Caribbean from 1898 to 1933 is known as the protectorate era. The United States feared regional instability would lead to non-U.S. foreign intervention. The United States repeatedly used military force, dollars, and custom's controls to safeguard countries such as Puerto Rico, Haiti, Cuba, and Latin American nations, keeping them solvent and stable.

PUBLIC SECTOR

A "public sector" is comprised of local, state, and federal government agencies, as opposed to the "private sector," which is made up of households and businesses. Economists generally speak of the government and the public sector as the same thing. The public sector employs about one-sixth of the labor force, purchases about one-fifth of the total output of the economy, and accounts for about one-quarter of all personal incomes. Because the public sector includes all government activities, not just the federal government, it includes all forms of public employment. It includes teachers, many scientists, the military, police and fire services, and all other areas of public service employment.

PUBLISHING INDUSTRY

Book publishing began to flourish in the American colonies during the eighteenth century. Printing began in 1639 in Cambridge, Massachusetts, and expanded geographically to Boston in 1674, Philadelphia in 1685, and New York City in 1693. Almanacs, primers, and law books were published; theology being the most popular subject. Books were sold in various ways: through subscription, by the printer, in the streets by hawkers, and in shops by booksellers. Hezekiah Usher, who added books to his general merchandise inventory around 1647, may have been the first American bookseller.

The availability of reading matter after 1650 contributed to the spread of literacy and an educated middle class. During the eighteenth century prose novels grew in popularity, while among those of modest means almanacs and chapbooks were more common. Benjamin Franklin's (1706–1790) *Poor Richard's Almanack* (sic), which contained a variety of information as well as religious and moral sayings, was published in Philadelphia in several editions from 1732 to 1764. Chapbooks typically contained a popular story illustrated with woodcuts.

In 1800 the Library of Congress was established. The growth of book publishing led to the establishment of commercial lending libraries in the eighteenth century and, in the nineteenth century, free public libraries. The nineteenth century marked a new era in book publishing brought on by technological innovations that significantly reduced the cost of printing and publishing books. These innovations included stereotyping, the iron press, steam power, mechanical typecasting and typesetting, and new methods of reproducing illustrations. Paper and bindings became less expensive. After 1820 cloth cases began replacing leather bindings, and publishers that had previously issued their works unbound began to publish them already bound.

The nineteenth century book trade was marked by expansion and competition, both in Europe and in the United States. Populations were rapidly growing, communications were improving, and there was a strong desire both for self-improvement and for entertainment, all of which contributed to a strong book trade. In the United States publishing gradually became concentrated in a few major cities: Philadelphia, Boston, and New York City. In addition to publishing American authors such as Washington Irving, James Fenimore Cooper, Ralph Waldo Emerson, U.S. publishers competed fiercely to publish reprint editions of British works by Charles Dickens, Sir Walter Scott, Thomas Macaulay, and others. U.S. publishers would wait at the dockside for a new British title and have a reprint edition ready within hours. Many of these editions were pirated, with no royalties paid to the authors.

WHAT CAN BE SAID OF THE PAST 25 YEARS IN PUBLISHING, OTHER THAN THAT THEY MAKE THE PREVIOUS 100 SEEM SLOW IN COMPARISON?

***Publishers Weekly*, July 1997**

Comprehensive catalogs of books began as early as the book fairs held in Frankfurt, Germany, in 1564, and in Leipzig, Germany, in 1594. During the nineteenth century several such lists were published in England and France and became national lists, with the first U.S. *Cumulative Book List* appearing in 1898.

Many small publishing houses were started in the United States in the 1890s and in the early part of the twentieth century. Start-up costs were low, and it was relatively inexpensive to publish an edition of 1,000 copies of a new book. Public education created a need for textbooks, and publishers began to specialize. In 1912 the Authors' League was formed in the United States to help standardize relations between authors and publishers, especially regarding contracts and the payment of royalties.

Following World War I (1914–1918), booming economic conditions produced an even more prosperous middle class who demanded even more books. The number of publishing houses grew. U.S. authors, such as Ernest Hemingway and Sinclair Lewis, found a world market. New York City became a source of talent for publishers everywhere. Universities grew in number and college textbooks became an important part of the publishing industry.

Book clubs that offered books by mail began to appear following World War I, with the Book-of-the-Month Club starting in 1926; its rival was The Literary Guild. Book clubs experienced a decline in popularity in the 1950s with the advent of cheap paperbound books.

The Great Depression (1929–1939) caused a trade slump in book publishing beginning in October 1929. In 1935 British publisher Allen Lane launched the Penguin series of paperbacks, and it immediately caught on. Shortly before the outbreak of World War II (1939–1945) Penguin paperbacks became available in the United States through Ian Ballantine, who later founded both Bantam Books and Ballantine Books. U.S. distribution was later taken over by Victor Weybright, who in 1948 founded the New American Library, another successful paperback venture.

The most successful U.S. publisher of mass paperbound books was Pocket Books, founded in June 1939 by Robert F. de Graff. Partnering with Richard Simon and M. Lincoln Schuster, founders of publishing house Simon and Schuster, de Graff began with a modest list of 10 titles, all reprints. Their success was immediate and unprecedented, and the company continued to dominate mass-market paperback publishing for decades. Several magazine publishers decided to launch paperback imprints, including Avon Books in 1941, Popular Library in 1942, and Dell Books in 1943.

World War II disrupted publishing but brought hidden benefits. Nazi persecution of the Jews resulted in the emigration of publishing talent to England and the United States, among other countries. Paper shortages caused publishers to print fewer new titles and fewer copies, but many of these smaller editions sold out to a public that had more time to read. There were also fewer consumer goods to compete with books, because of wartime rationing. As a result a new reading public emerged, and social and economic conditions favored publishing in the postwar period.

Technological developments after World War II spurred the publication of many new technical books, including college textbooks. There was also a major advance in printing, with photo composition replacing the labor-intensive methods of the traditional letterpress system. Large print runs of 100,000 or more copies could now be economically printed, although the problem of printing economical short runs of a few thousand copies remained.

By the 1950s paperback books were more than just a novelty, with paperback sales reaching 200 million copies and paperback revenues an estimated $46 million in 1950. In fact, a paperback revolution took place in the 1950s in the United States and throughout the world. It converted book borrowers into book buyers and created a large population of book buyers. For the first time books fell into the area of impulse buying. They were offered for sale in a variety of new locations from drugstores to airports. Scholarly paperbacks, aimed at university students, began appearing in the United States in the 1950s and soon spread to England and the European continent.

By the 1960s paperbacks had become a fixture of U.S. life. They reflected the social change of the decade, and in some cases helped bring it about. Paperback publishers perfected the ''instant book'' during the 1960s, providing in-depth treatment of major news stories within days of the event. Bestsellers were emphasized, with many authors benefiting from the wide exposure they received through paperbacks.

The tremendous profits generated by paperbacks in the 1960s and 1970s brought another change to publishing. Large corporations began to look at publishing as an area for investment. During the late 1960s and early 1970s many independent paperback firms came under the control of giant corporations such as Gulf & Western, CBS, RCA, and Warner Communications. These parent corporations made large amounts of cash available to their paperback subsidiaries, resulting in new levels of bidding among publishers for bestsellers. By the mid-1970s, million-dollar auctions for paperback rights were commonplace. Unfortunately, this resulted in higher prices for consumers; paperback sales, which had climbed steadily since their introduction, began to level off. During the late 1970s and early 1980s several paperback houses went out of business. It became more common for publishers to issue both hardcover and paperback editions, rather than selling the paperback rights to a separate firm.

Consolidation affected the rest of the book publishing industry as well. Fifteen major corporations dominated the industry by the early 1970s. This consolidation continued through the 1990s, when seven giant publishers accounted for 80 percent of all bestsellers in 1992. Concentration of power raised concerns about the quality and diversity of books being published, and some looked to small presses to fill the need for less popular but higher quality titles that catered to a variety of special interests.

Book publishing experienced tremendous growth during the 1970s, 1980s, and 1990s. From sales of $1.68 billion in 1963, annual book sales doubled by 1973 then reached $8.6 billion in 1983. They nearly doubled again to reach $17.2 billion in 1993.

During the 1990s book publishers became more concerned with cutting costs, maximizing profits, and effective management techniques as a result of corporate ownership. For too long publishers had lagged behind other industries in achieving efficiencies in production, distribution, and marketing. Many challenges faced the book publishing industry in the 1990s, ranging from huge cash advances required to capture best-selling authors to competition from computers and VCRs for the leisure time of traditional book customers.

The fortunes of the publishing industry have been closely related to existing social, economic, and demographic conditions and trends. During the second half of the 1980s, children's publishing experienced tremendous growth, from $336 million in sales in 1985 to $1.1 billion in 1992, as the ''baby boomlet'' market developed. Suddenly, though, sales dropped by one-half, and publishers were forced to rethink their strategies. Trends favorable to publishing in the 1990s and beyond included higher enrollments in schools and colleges as well as an aging population that's interested in a variety of issues.

See also: **Blanche Wolfe Knopf, McGraw-Hill Companies**

FURTHER READING

Davis, Kenneth C. *American Literary Publishing Houses, 1900–1980: Trade and Paperback.* Detroit, MI: Gale Research, 1986.

Hilts, Paul. ''The American Revolution in Book Production.'' *Publishers Weekly*, September 14, 1992.

Holland, Steve. *The Mushroom Jungle: A History of Postwar Paperback Publishing.* San Bernardino, CA: Borgo Press, 1994.

Marmaduke, John. ''Why Publishers are Losing Market Share.'' *Publishers Weekly*, November 10, 1997.

Maryles, Daisy. ''They're the Tops.'' *Publishers Weekly*, January 4, 1999.

PUEBLO INDIANS

The Pueblo are American Indians of the Southwest. Their ancestors were the prehistoric Anasazi Indians. Beginning in about A.D. 700–1000, the Anasazi, who had settled in Utah, Colorado, Arizona, New Mexico, and northern Mexico, began building aboveground dwellings made of stone or adobe blocks. The more permanent shelters reflect a change in lifestyle: as they became increasingly dependent on agriculture (cultivating corn or maize), they also became more stationary. By A.D. 1000 the structures were more sophisticated; the Anasazi had begun to build multistoried houses in the rocky sides of mesas (flat-topped hills) and in canyon walls. For this reason they are sometimes called Cliff Dwellers. The Anasazi continued to farm the lands below their dwellings, which could easily be defended in case of raids. Their descendants, the Pueblo, were living in these areas when the Spaniards arrived in 1540. (Observing the settlements, the European explorers gave the natives the name ''Pueblo,'' which means ''village.'')

During the next 100 years missionaries in the Southwest converted about 60,000 Pueblo Indians to Christianity. In August 1680 Popeé;, a Pueblo Indian, led an attack on Santa Fe, New Mexico, killing almost 500 Spaniards and driving the rest out. In what is known as the Pueblo Revolt, the Southwestern Indian group had reclaimed their territory, eradicating all Spanish-Christian influences and restoring their own culture in the region. This period of reclamation lasted 12 years: Upon Popé's death in 1692, the Spanish recaptured New Mexico and reestablished colonial rule. A band of Pueblos escaped to the west, remained free, and came to be called Western Pueblos. Few traditional (pre-Spanish) Pueblo villages remain today.

See also: **Anasazi, Arizona, Colorado, New Mexico, Santa Fe, Southwestern Indians, Utah**

PUERTO RICO

A territory of the United States granted under the Treaty of Paris of 1898, Puerto Rico is an island in the West Indies, 70 miles (113 kilometers) east of Hispaniola (Haiti and the Dominican Republic). The agreement, signed December 10 of that year, ended the Spanish-American War (1898) and provided for Cuba's full independence from Spain. The United States was also granted control of Puerto Rico, Guam, and the Philippine Islands in exchange for $20 million.

The conflict leading up to the Spanish-American War began during the 1870s, when Cubans rebelled against Spanish rule of the tiny island (which measures 3,435 square miles, or 8,897 square kilometers). Once the insurrection was put down, peace on the Caribbean island did not hold: worsening economic conditions prompted revolution in 1895. U.S. President William McKinley (1897–1901) made several diplomatic attempts to pressure Spain to grant Cuba full independence, but to no avail. On April 19, 1898, the U.S. Congress passed a joint resolution recognizing an independent Cuba, disclaiming American intentions to acquire the island, and authorizing the use of the American Army and Navy to force Spanish withdrawal. On April 25, the United States formally declared itself at war with Spain. In the months that followed American forces battled the Spanish and Spanish loyalists in Cuba and the Spanish-controlled Philippines. There was also military activity on Puerto Rico, but American forces met little resistance. Once Santiago, Cuba, was surrendered by the Spanish after the battle at San Juan Hill (July, 1898), it was only a matter of weeks before a cease-fire was called and the armistice signed (on August 12), ending the brief war.

The war dissolved the Spanish empire that had once included vast territories on the North American mainland and in Mexico, Central America, South America, and the West Indies. Fulfilling the doctrine of Manifest Destiny, the United States gained long-coveted possessions in the Pacific and in the West Indies. Puerto Rico, which then had a population of about one million people, provided Americans with a base in the Caribbean. In 1917 Puerto Ricans were granted U.S. citizenship. In 1952, upon adoption of a constitution, the island became a commonwealth, in union with the United States. As such, Puerto Rico has autonomy in international affairs. The commonwealth status was reproved by the Puerto Rican government in 1967 and again by the people in 1993. The 1993 population was more than 3.6 million. The island's chief products include sugar, tobacco, fruit, livestock, textiles, pharmaceuticals, and tourism. Spanish is the principal language, but some English is spoken as well. The U.S. dollar is the official exchange.

See also: **Manifest Destiny, Spanish-American War**

PULITZER, JOSEPH

The modern newspaper was virtually created by Joseph Pulitzer (1847–1911) during the latter half of the nineteenth century. It was a newspaper that seemed to meet the needs of the modern industrial world.

Joseph Pulitzer.

Boasting headlines, sensationalism with social conscience, a sports page, a business page, and the comic strips, it was a paper the average person could use to learn about the world and be entertained. This was largely the social invention of Joseph Pulitzer.

Joseph Pulitzer was born in Mako, Hungary, on April 10, 1848, one of three children born to Philip and Louise (Berger) Pulitzer. (*Politzer* was the Hungarian spelling of their last name.) As a young child, Pulitzer was considered sickly. He was very thin, his lungs were weak, and his vision was poor. His father was a wealthy grain dealer, wealthy enough to retire early and be with his family. When Joseph Pulitzer was six years old, the family moved to a quiet estate in Budapest, Hungary, where the boy was educated by private tutors, along with his brother and sister. Pulitzer was raised fluent speaking Hungarian, German, and French.

The young Joseph Pulitzer was perhaps overly energetic, and was wild about seeking fame. He was brilliant, very independent, and intensely ambitious. There were early signs, extremes in his behavior as a young man, of the emotional problems that would later hurt him as a grown man.

At the age of 17 he left home and sought to join the Austrian Army, the British armed forces, and the French Foreign Legion. He was rejected from each army because of his poor eyesight. At one point during the American Civil War (1861–1865), a recruiter of the Union army approached Pulitzer. In September 1864 he came alone to the United States to join the Lincoln Cavalry of the Union Army. In Boston, Massachusetts, Pulitzer jumped ship. He then went to New York where he enlisted on his own behalf, thereby collecting his own enlistment bounty. On September 30, 1864, Pulitzer joined a cavalry regiment organized by Carl Schurz, with whom Pulitzer would work after the war.

IN THE *ST. LOUIS POST-DISPATCH* AND THE *NEW YORK WORLD* PULITZER CREATED THE MODERN NEWSPAPER, ONE THAT CAUGHT THE DEMOCRATIC AND POPULIST SPIRIT OF THE UNITED STATES AT THAT TIME AND INSTITUTED CHANGES NEVER BEEN BEFORE SEEN IN U.S. NEWSPAPERS.

Pulitzer was discharged from the Union Army in July 1865. He had little money and no prospects for work. He settled in St. Louis, Missouri, where there was a large German community. In St. Louis Pulitzer found familiar customs that reminded him of his European origins. He worked a variety of jobs including a mule tender, waiter, and hack driver. He also worked for several lawyers and, while doing so, studied law books and was admitted to the bar. In 1867 Pulitzer became a U.S. citizen.

Carl Schurz, whom Pulitzer met during his military service, hired Pulitzer as a reporter for the *Westliche Post*, an influential German-language newspaper in St. Louis. The paper specialized in political articles and was very much committed to social reform in a young United States, which at the time appeared rife with corruption. Pulitzer became very interested in local politics and public affairs, and was an exceptional reporter in these areas. As a result he was nominated for the state legislature by the Republicans in 1869; he won the election.

While serving his term as a representative, Pulitzer also worked as a correspondent for the *Westliche Post*. In 1872 he became very involved in the Liberal Republican movement, which had nominated Horace Greely for president. After the defeat of Greely, Pulitzer became a Democrat.

In 1872 Joseph Pulitzer bought his first newspaper, the *St. Louis Post* for about $3 million. He also bought a German newspaper that had an Associated Press membership, which he quickly sold for a profit. In 1878 Pulitzer purchased the *St. Louis Dispatch*, which he combined with the *St. Louis Post*; the newspaper then became the *St. Louis Post-Dispatch*.

As publisher and editor of his newspaper, Pulitzer declared immediately that it would be devoted to issues of social reform. He vowed to his readers that the paper would be independent of political influence, and would instead be "the organ of truth," as he put it in an early editorial. Along with his editor-in-chief, John A. Cockerill, Pulitzer printed verbal crusades against wealthy tax dodgers and corrupt gambling practices. For example, the newspaper published the tax returns of local citizens, wealthy and poor, in parallel columns. Pulitzer and Cockerill editorialized in favor of the building and maintaining of streets and other public structures and were instrumental in starting a city park system. They made the *St. Louis Post-Dispatch* a very successful civic minded newspaper.

Pulitzer edited the *Post-Dispatch* from 1878 to 1883. From the start he was involved in all aspects of the publication. By 1881 the newspaper had achieved high profits, gained wide readership, and moved to a new building where two Hoe presses were installed. When Pulitzer's health weakened, however, he gave more responsibility to Cockerill.

In 1882 Cockerill shot and killed Alonzo W. Slayback, a local lawyer running for Congress. Slayback, whom Cockerill openly opposed and insulted, had confronted Cockerill and was murdered. Afterward Pulitzer asked John A. Dillon, founder of the *Post*, to take over the management of the paper. During the aftermath of the scandal, Pulitzer's health deteriorated further and he was advised by his physician to take a long rest. On his way to Europe, via New York, Pulitzer met with an opportunity he could not refuse: the *New York World* was for sale.

In 1883, when he was 36 years old, Pulitzer bought the failing *New York World* newspaper, and he applied the same principles that led to success with his St. Louis paper. In 1883 the paper sold 15,000 copies daily. With Pulitzer's genius for sensing what the public wanted, he built a newspaper which, by 1898, was selling 15 million copies a day.

In the *St. Louis Post-Dispatch* and the *New York World* Pulitzer created the modern newspaper, one that caught the democratic and populist spirit of the United States at that time and instituted changes that had never been seen in U.S. papers before. Pulitzer changed the form of how readers received their news, and he created a format and prototype that countless other papers came to imitate.

Pulitzer carefully picked his talent and encouraged them. He paid high salaries to his reporters and demanded hard work from them. He also started the first two-week paid vacation for newspaper staff. Pulitzer's newspapers used illustrations and political cartoons to attract readers and initiated features such as greatly expanded sports coverage. He also began to include line drawings in the newspaper to give variety to the look of different sections of the paper. Pulitzer's newspapers started printing colored cartoon strips known as the "Sunday Funnies," and in doing so captured a new readership for newspapers—children.

Perhaps Pulitzer was able to do so much in changing the form of the newspaper because his own idealistic, crusading, flamboyant, up-and-down character mirrored much of the sentiments of the mixed character of the United States at that time. He remained an idealist, but he also learned how to sensationalize and exaggerate real issues to get public attention. Pulitzer became the master of detailing lurid stories of crime, sex, and disaster. He had his reporters use bold headlines, and illustrations and diagrams for murder scenes. He was one of the first to understand that a successful newspaper had to entertain as well as provide the truth. This was a revolution in newspaper style which became a model for newspapers of that era—sensationalism with a social conscience.

Pulitzer used his newspapers' editorials to speak out against corruption, and his papers uncovered several scandals such as the insurance fraud and corruption in the construction of the Panama Canal. He also crusaded against unsafe working conditions, the Bell telephone monopoly, the Pacific Railroad Lobbyists of 1887, unpleasant conditions in mental hospitals, police corruption and inefficiency, and police brutality. Pulitzer used his power to rally public support around various causes. In one editorial, for example, he urged the completion of the pedestal for Bartholdi's Statue of Liberty.

Pulitzer had married Kate Davis in 1878. The Pulitzers had seven children during their reportedly difficult marriage. When Joseph Pulitzer was in his mid-thirties, his health began to deteriorate. He spent much of his time away from his family, traveling widely. In later years he lived aboard his yacht, called the *Liberty*, where annoyances and distractions were kept to a minimum. Pulitzer continued to be in constant poor health. He had several ailments including asthma, diabetes, insomnia, chronic exhaustion, and manic depression; by 1889 he had become blind. On October

29, 1911, at the age of 64, Joseph Pulitzer died of an apparent heart attack while aboard his yacht in a New York harbor.

In the years leading up to his death Pulitzer had turned his focus toward a plan to endow Columbia University with a large sum of money for the establishment of a school of journalism. In 1902 Pulitzer had drawn up a memorandum in which he compared the preparation of journalists to that of lawyers and doctors. In 1912, a year after his death, an endowment of $2 million was made to Columbia University, which accepted its first class in the School of Journalism. The 1902 memorandum also stipulated that a portion of the endowment be used for annual prizes to journalists and writers. The first Pulitzer Prize was awarded in 1917.

See also: **Muckrakers, Publishing Industry**

FURTHER READING

Ashley, Perry J, ed. *Dictionary of Literary Biography: American Newspaper Journalists, 1873–1900.* Detroit: Gale Research, 1983, ''Pulitzer, Joseph.''

Juergens, George. *Joseph Pulitzer and the ''New York World.''* Princeton, NJ: Princeton University Press, 1966.

Rammelkamp, Julian S. *Pulitzer's ''Post-Dispatch'' 1878–1883.* Princeton, NJ: Princeton University Press, 1966.

Seitz, Dan C. *Joseph Pulitzer: His Life and Letters.* New York: Simon and Schuster, 1924.

Swanberg, W.A. *Pulitzer.* New York: Scribner's Sons, 1967.

Wittke, Carl. *The German Language Press in America.* Lexington, KY: University Press of Kentucky, 1957.

PULLMAN PALACE CAR COMPANY

One of the last industrialists to operate a company town, George Mortimer Pullman (1831–1897) entered adulthood fueled by ideas and ambition. Pullman stepped into his deceased father's business of raising the foundations of dwellings that were built in the low lying flood areas of Chicago. In 1858 Pullman faced the challenge of lifting and rotating the stylish Tremont Hotel. He successfully supervised this tremendous feat, which involved the simultaneous turning of five thousand jackscrews by twelve hundred men. With a $20,000 stake made from the elevation business, Pullman turned his hand to more luxurious ideas.

George Pullman's first overnight train ride was as memorable as it was uncomfortable. Travelling from Boston to Westfield, Massachusetts, in 1851, he attempted to rest on a rough mattress. Sharing the discomfort with fellow travelers and unable to sleep, Pullman decided there had to be a better way to travel. Although sleeping cars on railroads were not new, passengers were accustomed to little more than cots or mattresses and little privacy. Many who sat up all night suffered back-jarring rides on stiff benches in cars filled with dust in the summer and wood smoke in winter. With the growing number of businessmen traveling between cities, Pullman realized there was a market for comfort.

Pullman formed a partnership with Benjamin Field, who had the rights to operate sleepers on the Chicago and Alton, and the Galena and Union railroads. Pullman rebuilt two oversized coach cars, dividing the space into 10 sleeper sections with curtains. He hinged the upper berths so they could be opened at night and did the same with the chairs, so that they could swing back up out of the way. For extra convenience, linen closets and toilets were built at both ends of the car. Most importantly Pullman paid enormous attention to details. Lining the berths with rich cherry wood, and upholstering the seats in plush fabrics, all basking in the soft glow of oil lamps. Such luxury in George Pullman's sleepers was met with modest success in 1858. Business grew slowly but steadily as the country headed into the American Civil War (1861–1865).

In 1862 while running a trading store in Colorado, Pullman continued to develop plans to build an even more luxurious sleeper. His idea to raise travel to an unimagined level began in a shed near Chicago's Union Station. The ''Pioneer'' sleeper would be 54 feet long and 10 feet wide, with accommodations for 50 passengers. Each car would contain thick Bussel's carpeting, heavy curtains, French plate mirrors, black walnut woodwork, oil chandeliers, and fine linens that would be changed daily. Porters would carry baggage and attend to the riders needs. The cost to build one car totaled $18,000, four times more than any other competitive sleeper did. The two-dollar fares for an overnighter in Pullman's Pioneer soon emptied the conventional sleepers of other producers, which charged $1.50. Within a year, Pullman owned 48 sleepers. Within 10 years, Pullman held a virtual monopoly on luxury train travel in the United States.

The assassination of President Abraham Lincoln (1861–1865) on April 15, 1865, prompted arrangements for his body to be transported back to Springfield, Illinois. Part of the funeral procession was by rail from Chicago. The Pioneer, touted ''the wonder of the age,'' was chosen to carry Lincoln home. The size of the Pioneer would not fit on some tracks; nor could it be used in some railroad stations. Rail lines had to modify the tracks to accommodate the Pioneer to complete the last leg of the presidential journey. The Pioneer secured its reputation as the pearl of railroad cars because of this event.

The Pullman Palace Car Company was incorporated in 1867. The addition of a kitchen and tables from which to order delicacies such as oysters and rum omelets, led to the unveiling of the first dining car (known as the ''Delmonico'') in 1868. In 1875, the first parlor car was introduced, sporting upholstered swivel reclining seats. Each new unveiling of an even better or more novel idea in the next Pullman car was met with greater fanfare. Accepted by the inner circle of U.S. corporate barons by 1880, George Pullman had become a rich, powerful, and respected man. Yet he viewed his power through the filter of Old World values.

When it came time to expand, Pullman decided to build a state-of-the-art factory and a town to go with it, at the cost of five million dollars. His idea was to build a community for the factory workers, about 15 miles outside of Chicago. He wanted a special place, workers' utopia, to be built with the same attention to detail as his cars. Pullman envisioned his town as a model of efficiency and healthfulness. A company brochure promoting the town of Pullman stated, ''all that is ugly and discordant and demoralizing is eliminated, and all that inspires self-respect is generously provided.'' In 1884 families began moving into Pullman, Illinois.

By the winter of 1893, recoiling from plummeting orders and economic pressures, George Pullman had laid off more than half the workers living in his town. The wages of the rest were cut by more than 25 percent. However, rent was not cut. Moving to a cheaper neighborhood was not an option for Pullman tenants—if they moved they weren't likely to remain Pullman employees. In desperation many workers joined the American Railway Union (ARU), an organization created by a young labor leader named Eugene Debs (1855–1926). The workers organized a boycott to which Pullman responded by having all the shops in his town cut off credit to all the workers. At the request of the Pullman workers, the ARU took the strike national. Within a week, 125,000 railroad workers refused to work on a train carrying a Pullman sleeper. Very soon after, rail traffic in the West and Midwest shut down.

The railroad strike of 1894 turned very ugly. The strike stopped mail delivery, freight and passenger traffic plummeted, and the stockyards were at a standstill. Hundreds of rail cars were set ablaze. President Grover Cleveland (1885–1889) sent almost 2000 federal soldiers to the Chicago area, at the request of the U.S. marshals. When National Guardsmen fired upon a mob trying to block a train, four people were killed and another 20 were injured. Before the strike ceased, 20 people were dead and 60 were injured. This, the last major strike in the United States in the nineteenth century, ended in September 1894. The boycott was lost, and the ARU was broken.

George Pullman tried to hold on to his model town fantasy. He never evicted any workers from his community, as he hoped to be remembered for what he thought was his greatest contribution to U.S. life—the town of Pullman—but he never recovered from the strike. Three years later at the age of 66, George Pullman died of a heart attack. The community of Pullman was dismantled by the state of Illinois in 1898, with the state pointing out that the corporation's charter did not give it the right to run a town in the first place. What had started as a dream of travel in comfort ended in violence, unemployment, and despair.

***See also:* Labor Movement, Pullman Strike, Railroad Industry**

FURTHER READING

Buder, Stanley. *Pullman: An Experience in Industrial Order and Community Planning 1880–1930.* New York: Oxford University Press, 1970.

Husband, Joseph. *The Story of the Pullman Car.* North Stratford, NH: Ayer Co. Publishers, Inc., 1972.

Jacobs Altman, Linda. *The Pullman Strike of 1894: Turning Point for American Labor.* Brookfield, CT: Millbrook Press, 1994.

Maiken, Peter T. *Night Trains: The Pullman System in the Golden Years of American Rail Travel.* Chicago: Lakme Press, 1989.

''Pullman Today,'' [cited May 26, 1999] available from the World Wide Web @ www.discovery.com/area/history/.

PULLMAN STRIKE OF 1894

The last third of the nineteenth century was characterized by an atmosphere of bitter conflict between labor and management in the United States. One reason for this was that the economy had not performed very well since the early 1870s. Instead of a secure job, American workers were faced with a steady diet of financial panics and wage cuts. The most severe panic took place in 1893. The depression in 1893 deepened

Railway workers pulling spikes from switches in the Western Indiana Railroad yards, 1894.

the unrest and dissatisfaction of the working class. In the winter of 1893–1894 the Pullman Palace Car Company, which built and repaired Pullman's railroad coaches, announced a 25 percent wage cut. Pullman was a "company town" surrounded by Chicago. Most of the Pullman workers lived in company-owned housing. Even though he cut the wages, George M. Pullman, the Chief Executive Officer of the company, refused to reduce the rent payments on the company housing.

The Pullman workers went on strike in early June 1894 and requested other unions to honor their picket lines. The American Railway Union (ARU), led by Eugene V. Debs, announced that its members would refuse to work on trains that included any Pullman railroad coaches. Within a few days the strike spread to the entire Western and Southern sections of the county. Twenty-seven states and territories were affected.

Another thing that contributed to labor unrest during this period was the perception that the government was not neutral in most disagreements between workers and management. In the ARU strike, for instance, rather than allowing labor and management to settle their disagreement by allowing the strike to take its course, many officials in the affected states called out the militia to repress the strike. The most notable exception to this was John Peter Altgeld, the first-term Democratic Governor of Illinois who had already shown his pro-union sympathies by pardoning three union organizers accused of instigating the Haymarket Riot in 1886. Altgelt refused to call out the Illinois militia to break the Pullman strike. He said that public order was not threatened by the strike and that he intended to do nothing to alter the disposition of forces on either side of the struggle.

The railroad company lawyers, with the support of President Grover Cleveland's Attorney General Richard Olney appealed to a federal court for an injunction against the strikers. They put forward two arguments. One was that the strike was "in restraint of trade" and therefore violated the Sherman Anti-trust Act. (This act was passed by Congress in 1890 and ruled illegal "every contract, combination in the form of trust or otherwise, or conspiracy in restrain of trade or commerce. . ." The Sherman Anti-trust Act had been passed to break up monopolies rather than unions, but was invoked mainly against unions.) The second argument was that the strike interfered in the delivery of the federal mails. On July 3 the court ruled in favor of both charges and granted injunctions forbidding the ARU from continuing the strike. The injunction even prohibited Debs from communicating with the union's locals.

The ARU refused to honor the injunction and Debs was sentenced to six months in jail along with his fellow union officers. The U.S. Supreme Court upheld the conviction of the ARU. leaders when it declared the injunction issued against the union was a legitimate device for the protection of interstate commerce and the mails. For thirty years after the Debs case, the injunction was a powerful weapon in the hands of employers threatened with a strike. It would not be until the Norris La Guardia Anti-Injunction Act of 1932 that labor gained some protection against strike-breaking injunctions issued by federal judges.

See also: **American Railway Union, Eugene Victor Debs, Pullman Palace Car Company, Railroad Industry, Sherman Anti-Trust Act**

FURTHER READING

Cleveland, Grover. *Presidential Problems.* New York: The Century Co., 1904.

Nevins, Allen. *Grover Cleveland.* New York: Dodd, Mead & Co., 1934.

Rich,Bernard. *The President and Civil Disturbances.* Washington, D.C.: Brookings Institute, 1941.

Salvatore, Nick. *Eugene V. Debs: Citizen and Socialist.* Urbana: University of Illinois Press, 1982.

Wright, Louis, ed. *The Democratic Experience.* Glenview, Illinois: Scott Forseman and Co., 1968.

Yeller, Samuel. *American Labor Struggles.* New York: Harcourt Brace and Co., 1936.

PURDUE, JOHN

During the mid-nineteenth century John Purdue (1802–1876) became a very successful dry-goods merchant and businessman in Lafayette, Indiana. He accumulated a fortune by beginning a newspaper, *The Lafayette Journal*, in his adopted hometown of Lafayette. Toward the end of his business career, in 1869, Purdue was the primary benefactor in the founding of Purdue University. He endowed the school with $150,000 and a mandate to maintain a college within the university to teach agriculture and ''mechanic arts.''

John Purdue was born on October 31, 1802, in Huntingdon County, Pennsylvania, the son of Charles and Mary Purdue. Purdue was the only son in a family of nine children born to this Scottish immigrant and his wife. The family moved to Ohio during Purdue's boyhood. In his twenties Purdue taught school for four years in the schools of Pickaway County, Ohio.

Not satisfied with teaching, however, John Purdue sought new opportunities farther west. He visited Lafayette, Indiana, and found it to be a flourishing trade center. He settled there in 1839. With his characteristic energy Purdue soon became one of the commercial leaders of the region. He conducted wholesale and retail dry-goods/grocery business for over 25 years. In addition, during the 1850s he and a partner operated a profitable ''commission house'' in New York City. Purdue made a great deal of money, but his unsuccessful political ambitions and unprofitable investments in local manufacturing and railway enterprises caused him to lose money in far-sighted endeavors with the civic development of Indiana.

Influenced by his long-ago work in public schools, Purdue continued to promote all educational enterprises in Indiana. After Congress passed the Land-Grant College Act in 1862, the Indiana legislature gave legal status to the Indiana Agricultural College in 1865. To secure a location for the college in Tippecanoe county, near Lafayette, Illinois, Purdue donated $150,000 in 1869. These funds supplemented certain lands and buildings already accrued by the citizens of the county with their $50,000 donation. With his large donation, Purdue was able to specify that the institution bear his name, which it does.

John Purdue died in on September 12, 1876, at age 73. He was buried, as he requested, on the campus of the university. An unmarked stone was placed at the head of his grave. Purdue never married; Purdue University was his legacy to the future.

See also: **Land Grant College**

FURTHER READING

Cambridge Dictionary of American Biography. New York: Cambridge University Press, 1995, s.v. ''Purdue, John.''

''History,'' [cited July 26, 1999] Available on the World Wide Web @ www.purdue.edu/OOP/facts/facts_history.html.

National Association of State Universities and Land-Grant Colleges. *The Land-Grant Tradition.* Washington DC: National Association of State Universities and Land-Grant Colleges, 1995.

Topping, Robert W. *A Century and Beyond-The History of Purdue University.* West Lafayette: Purdue University Press, 1988.

Wilson, William E. *Indiana History.* Bloomington: Indiana University Press, 1966.

PURE FOOD AND DRUG ACT

June 30, 1906, was a red-letter day for those who sought progressive reform and consumer protection in the United States. On that date the U.S. government passed the Pure Food and Drug Act, the first in a series of legislation designed to regulate the quality of food and pharmaceutical products. The act banned manufacturers from selling mislabeled products, from adulterating food with unacceptable ingredients, and from misleading consumers with false claims. The passage of the act marked a victory both over certain manufacturers who wished to avoid regulation, as well as some politicians who questioned the constitutionality of the act. Those who fought for consumer protection found that their battle was only just beginning, however, and that effective reform would take place only with a series of acts passed over many years. Government regulation of this kind strongly affected the ways in which foods and drugs were prepared, packaged, labeled, sold, and advertised in the United States.

FOOD SCAMS, SUCH AS APPLE SCRAPS AND HAYSEEDS SOLD AS "STRAWBERRY JAM," CORRUPTED THE MARKETPLACE IN THE NINETEENTH CENTURY UNITED STATES. THE TIME WAS RIPE FOR REFORM.

Prior to 1906 the regulation of food production and commerce fell mainly on the state and local authorities. In the colonial period, the colonies followed the British precedent of establishing laws to ensure standards of decency for such mainstays as bread and butter, while coastal colonies called for mandatory inspection of fish and other seafood. The laws did not extend to drugs, however, and their production remained largely unregulated. State laws scarcely differed from the colonial legislation, which was often loosely enforced. Since food and drug consumption was for the most part safe, there was little reason to push for more stringent regulation.

It was not until the middle of the nineteenth century, with the rise of industrialization and increasing urban populations, that fraudulent practices in the manufacturing of food and drugs became all too common. Food processors often added fillers to extend and cheapen their products: Water thinned out milk, sawdust bulked up flour, and sand stretched sugar. The development of new chemicals that enhanced the color, flavor, and texture of food made it easier for manufacturers to mask their manipulations. Unbeknownst to consumers, dyed and jarred apple scraps and hayseeds sometimes sold as "strawberry jam." With these practices corrupting the marketplace, consumers found it difficult to judge the "truth in labeling" of commodities. Health risks increased, and state laws seemed insufficient to protecting the vulnerable public. The time was ripe for reform.

Harvey Washington Wiley (1844–1930), professor of chemistry at Purdue University and evangelical Christian, led a campaign to stop wayward manufacturers from selling elixirs and bottled medicine which was often no more than alcohol-laden placebo. Wiley was appointed chief chemist of the U.S. Department of Agriculture in 1883. He led a campaign for federal regulation of food production and commerce. He was not alone in his efforts: many upstanding, reputable manufacturers wished for regulations that would outlaw the shady practices of their dishonest competitors. Meanwhile state food and drug officials asked for the federal support necessary to effect such sweeping change. Wiley enlisted scientists to analyze the ingredients in adulterated foods and to conduct tests on harmful preservatives, food colorings, and other chemicals, effectively amassing evidence to present to legislators. Interested as much in the moral as in the medical implications of ingesting tainted foods, the chemist did everything possible to dramatize the issue and to galvanize the public.

Two events gave Wiley's efforts a much-needed boost. The first event was the 1898 "embalmed beef" scandal, which highlighted the quality of food served to soldiers in the Spanish-American War (1898). The second event was the January 1906 publication of Upton Sinclair's *The Jungle*, a deeply disturbing novel about unsanitary conditions in the Chicago meatpacking industry. Sinclair's best-selling novel—with its grotesque descriptions of rats, filth, and even human body parts that found their way into goods sold as "pickled meats"—was the final straw. President Theodore Roosevelt (1933–1945), who did not always respond to Wiley's sensationalist style of lobbying, reportedly read *The Jungle* with interest. It is no coincidence that the Pure Food and Drug Act was passed only five months after the book's publication.

The bill was not as thorough as Wiley hoped it would be, but it did represent a triumph for consumer protection in the United States. It forbade the adulteration of food, the addition of harmful ingredients, and the use of erroneous or misleading labels. Interstate and foreign commerce of both food and drugs were to be diligently monitored, and drug manufacturing was to comply with purity standards listed in two authoritative pharmaceutical reference books. Critics of the bill noted the absence of a specific list of purity standards for food manufacturing, which made the law difficult to enforce in certain cases. A Bureau of Chemistry, operating under Wiley, was established to propose a system of enforcement, but the bureau (which was renamed the Food and Drug Administration [FDA] in 1927) often met with opposition from manufacturers and farmers who resisted regulation.

Amendments to the Pure Food and Drug Act—such as one that required manufacturers to list net weight on products' labels (1923) and another that specifically defined the quality standards of canned foods (1930)—helped to plug certain loopholes and ultimately made the bill more effective. The need for certain reforms required new legislation, though, such as the Food, Drug, and Cosmetic Act of 1938, which extended regulatory laws to cover the cosmetics and therapeutic device industries. The FDA gained power to set certain standards and to inflict penalties on those who failed to comply. Ultimately, the Pure Food and Drug Act and subsequent legislation effectively altered the ways in which manufacturing and commerce were conducted in the United States. The events of 1906 set into motion a trend toward consumer protection that persisted throughout the remainder of the twentieth century.

See also: **Food Processing, Lever Food Control Act, Pharmaceutical Industry, Regulation**

FURTHER READING

Dictionary of American History. New York: Charles Scribner's Sons, 1976, s.v. "Pure Food and Drug Movement."

Henkel, John. "A Colorful History." *FDA Consumer*, December 1993.

Hunter, Beatrice Trum. "Detecting Adulterated Food." *Consumers' Research Magazine*, December 1995.

The Reader's Companion to American History. Boston: Houghton Mifflin Co., 1991, s.v. "Pure Food and Drug Act."

Weisberger, Bernard A. "Doctor Wiley and His Poison Squad." *American Heritage*, February/March 1996.

PURITANS

The Puritans were members of a religious movement that began in England during the 1500s and lasted into the first half of the 1600s, when it spread to America. Influenced by the teachings of religious reformer John Calvin (1509–1564), the Puritans were so named because they wanted to purify the Anglican Church (also called the Church of England). They believed that too much power rested with the church hierarchy (its priests, bishops, and cardinals), and that the people (called the laity or lay members) should have more involvement in church matters. Ceremonies should, the Puritans believed, be simplified to stress Bible reading and individual prayer. They defied the authority of the Archbishop of Canterbury, head of the Anglican Church, believing that each church congregation should control its own affairs through a council (called a presbytery) of lay members. The Puritans also had strong feelings about government. They maintained that people can only be governed by contract (such as a constitution), which limits the power of a ruler.

When King James I (1566–1625; ruled 1603–1625) ascended the throne of England in 1603, he was the first ruler of the house (royal family) of Stuart. The Stuart monarchs were Anglican or Catholic, but faced with the challenge of radical Puritanism, they tried to enforce national adherence to the Anglican Church, which stressed the ceremonial and traditional elements of worship. Further, the Stuart kings viewed the Puritan agitators as a threat to their authority.

Persecuted by the throne, groups of Puritans fled England for the New World. One group was granted a corporate charter for the Massachusetts Bay Company (1629). Unlike other such contracts, which provided the framework for establishing colonies in America, this one did not require the stockholders to hold their meetings in England. What is striking about the organization of the Puritan colony is the fact that their organization combined economic, political, and religious levels of meaning. Stockholders who made the voyage across the Atlantic would become voting citizens in their own settlements; the board of directors would form the legislative assembly; and the company president, Puritan leader John Winthrop (1588–1649) would become the governor. In 1630 the group settled in what is today Boston and Salem, Massachusetts, establishing a Puritan Commonwealth. By 1643, more than 20,000 Puritans had arrived in Massachusetts, in what is called the Great Migration. Puritans also settled Rhode Island, Connecticut, and Virginia during this period.

Puritans founded the Congregational Church. They also established grammar schools and colleges (including Harvard, Yale, and Dartmouth) in New England.

See also: **Connecticut, Colonies (Corporate), Massachusetts, Rhode Island, Virginia**

PUTTING-OUT SYSTEM

The putting-out system was a production method that was used in New England from the mid-1700s to the early 1800s. Under the system, merchants supplied raw materials (cotton, for example) to families, especially women and young girls, who would make partially finished goods (yarn) or fully finished goods (cloth) for the merchant. These manufactured goods were then sold by the merchant. Homeworkers who "put out" goods provided the needed manufacturing labor of the day. But the factory system of manufacturing was on the horizon.

In 1813 the Boston Manufacturing Company opened the first textile factory, in Waltham, Massachusetts, in which laborers operated spinning and weaving machines to produce woven cloth from start to finish. The advent of machinery had given rise to the factory system, and laborers were shifted from working in their homes to working in factories. While native New Englanders continued to provide the labor for the textile industry for the next two decades, an influx of immigrants in the mid-1800s provided the hungry manufacturers with a steady supply of laborers who were willing to work for lower wages and longer hours.

See also: **Andrew Jackson, Lowell System, Samuel Slater, Samuel Slater Builds First Factory, Spinning Mills, Textiles**

PYRAMIDING RESERVES

Pyramiding reserves refers to the practice of concentrating many small bank reserves in certain big city banks. The National Banking Acts of 1863 and 1864 established the requirement that banks maintain money reserves. Reserves are the portion of each deposit placed into the bank that is set aside in the form of vault cash or held deposits. The tempting high interest rates on inter-bank deposit balances offered by the larger banks led small rural banks to keep their reserves at large urban national banks. This practice led to the pyramiding of reserves in central cities, especially New York City.

In the nineteenth century the need for liquidity (cash on hand) of the rural banks were driven by the needs of farmers. In the planting season farmers required currency to purchase farming implements and seed. At harvest cash deposited into banks increased as farmers sold crops. As a result rural banks withdrew their reserves from the urban banks in the spring to meet farmers' demands for cash and deposited money back into the urban banks in the fall. The withdrawal of the inter-bank balances in peak agricultural season put seasonal pressures on the banking system. Consequently short-term interest rates varied seasonally by as much as six percentage points through the course of a year. Large urban banks could anticipate this demand most of the time and provide rural banks with all the cash they needed. The mere rumor, however, that a bank could not meet the needs of credit-hungry farmers and businessmen in the rural areas led to runs on banks by depositors demanding their money. Financial panics resulted in 1873, 1884, 1893, and 1904.

In an effort to end the recurring panics Congress passed the Federal Reserve Act of 1913. One of the Federal Reserve Act's main purposes was to alleviate the liquidity crises and interest rate seasonal swings exacerbated by reserve pyramiding. The act established 12 Federal Reserve Banks around the country as depositories for required reserves that previously had been held predominantly in New York City banks. This regionalization eliminated reserve pyramiding and eased the seasonal strain. The central banking system could create additional reserves in a period of high liquidity demands.

See also: **Federal Reserve Act of 1913, Federal Reserve System, Financial Panic, National Bank Act of 1863**

QUANTITY THEORY OF MONEY

According to the quantity theory of money there is a direct relationship between prices, income, and the amount of money circulating in the economy. The quantity theory was first propounded in its most basic form by French philosopher Jean Bodin (1530–1596), who observed that the large amounts of gold and silver being brought back from the New World were driving up prices across Europe. Later two British philosophers, John Locke (1632–1704) and David Hume (1711–1776), noted that when the quantity of money grew, so did purchasing power and economic activity. Thus, if a government wanted to lower prices to combat inflation, according to the quantity theory, all it had to do was decrease the amount of money in circulation. Consumers would have less money to spend, demand would fall, and prices would drop. Over the next two centuries other economists elaborated on this basic interconnection between the quantity of money, income, and prices, and until the 1930s it remained the dominant theory for explaining inflation, deflation, and the nature of business cycles.

During the 1930s the quantity theory came under attack because its opponents argued that government attempts to increase the amount of money in circulation during the early years of the Great Depression (1929–1939) had almost no affect on consumer demand. The primary opponent of the quantity theory was British economist John Maynard Keynes (1883–1946). He claimed that increasing the money supply alone would never be enough to stimulate a contracting economy. Only high levels of employment could resuscitate demand and that meant the government had to create jobs for unemployed workers if the private economy could not.

Keynes's ''fiscal policy'' approach to economic growth ruled the world of economics until the 1960s when a new quantity theory of money arose to take its place. Led by U.S. economist Milton Friedman (1911–), the new quantity-of-money theorists agreed with Keynes that government fiscal policy had an important role to play in stimulating the economy. However, they showed that during the Great Depression government officials had not really expanded the money supply fast enough or in large enough quantities to get the economy growing, so the Depression did not really disprove the quantity theory of money after all. Moreover, using new tools of economic research, the Friedman school of economists showed that increasing and decreasing the money supply did in fact have a direct effect on inflation and deflation.

See also: **John Maynard Keynes, Milton Friedman**

QUEBEC ACT OF 1774

The Quebec Act was passed by the British Parliament on June 22, 1774, on the eve of the American Revolution (1775–1783). The legislation extended the province of Quebec south and west to the Ohio and Mississippi rivers, ignoring the western land claims of colonial Massachusetts, Connecticut, and Virginia. It also guaranteed that French civil law would be used in the enlarged Quebec, then a British colony that had been largely settled by the French. English criminal law would apply in the enlarged province. It also stipulated that the French could practice Roman Catholicism and that the Roman Catholic Church could collect taxes from its members. Historians believe the legislation was largely damage control on the part of the British, who faced the imminent revolt of their thirteen American colonies to the south. By passing the Quebec Act Britain intended to prevent the French colonists from joining the struggle of the American patriots and also to possibly gain their support should fighting break out. The Quebec Act was one of the five so-called Intolerable Acts (also called the Coercive Acts). British Parliament passed these acts the same year in an effort to assert its authority in the Massachusetts colony following the rebellion of the Boston Tea

Party (December, 1773). These laws were severely resented by the American colonists and in many ways they precipitated the revolution. Shortly after fighting began in 1775, American colonists invaded Quebec but they were turned back. The province and its settlers, which included many loyalists who had fled the American colonies, remained neutral during the American Revolution.

See also: **American Revolution, Boston Massacre, Boston Tea Party, Connecticut, Intolerable Acts, Massachusetts, Virginia**

QUOTAS

Quotas, a form of trade barrier, are limits on the quantity of a commodity that can be imported or exported. Import quotas limit the amount of particular foreign goods that can be brought or imported into the country. Import quotas protect domestic production of those goods and keep prices high. Export quotas limit the production of certain primary goods in short supply in the rest of the world. Restricting production limits the amount that can be exported and keeps prices high. Export quotas stabilize export earnings. A prime example of the use of export quotas are oil producing nations agreeing to limit oil production, thus keeping world prices high.

Import quotas specify the maximum amount of a foreign good that can be imported. They may be legislated or negotiated with the foreign country. Import quotas are generally more effective at reducing imports than are protective tariffs, another form of trade barrier which is a tax on imports. Tariffs only interfere with trade. If a foreign producer can lower his cost of production he could lower prices and increase imports into the country despite the tariff. Quotas either eliminate import of the product altogether or allow only so much in, after which consumers must buy the domestic product.

Major arguments for import quotas are: (1) protection of infant or emerging domestic industries allowing them to gain strength before having to compete against foreign firms; (2) protection of U.S. jobs against foreign firms; (3) stabilizing the balance of payments, the difference between money paid to and received from other nations; and (4) protection of national security by not allowing the United States to become too reliant on another country for a certain product, the supply of which could be cut off in time of war. On the other hand those opposed to trade barriers point out that a relatively small number of individuals, those domestically making the product, reap large benefits from quota restrictions while all individuals purchasing the item incur higher prices.

Goods for which the United States has enforced import quotas include sugar, meat, textiles, motorcycles, and color television sets. A classic example of restraints was applied to Japanese auto imports. In 1981 the United States negotiated with Japan to limit its auto imports to 7.7 percent below the 1980 level. The agreement saved approximately 44,000 U.S. auto industry jobs, but the price of U.S. cars rose by an average of $660.

See also: **Trade**

RACKETEER INFLUENCED AND CORRUPT ORGANIZATIONS ACT (RICO)

The Racketeer Influenced and Corrupt Organizations Act (RICO) was an article of federal legislation enacted as Title IX of the Organized Crime Control Act of 1970, designed to combat organized crime in the United States. The Supreme Court ruled that RICO was not limited to organized crime, but could also be applied to legitimate businesses. RICO prohibits any person from using income received from a crime or a racketeering activity, and also applies to any unlawful, direct or indirect, racketeering activity. The purpose of RICO was to remove organized crime from the legitimate business community.

The RICO statute has been increasingly used in the context of organized labor prosecutions. One such case was the federal indictment of the International Brotherhood of Teamsters, where the Second Circuit Court found sufficient evidence to support a finding under RICO that a Teamster employee was associated with an organized crime figure and was subject to discipline. In another labor-related case, the *United States vs. Carson*, the government brought action against a former union officer under RICO, alleging that the officer committed racketeering acts that benefited organized crime. This charge was dismissed by the Second Circuit Court because the action allegedly occurred too far in the past to prosecute.

All RICO convictions require the government to prove that the defendant, based on two or more acts of racketeering activity, directly invested in, maintained an interest in, or participated in a criminal enterprise that affected either interstate or foreign commerce.

RADICAL UNIONS *(ISSUE)*

Anti-labor commentators in the nineteenth century would have argued that all unions are by their very nature radical because they make ''unreasonable'' demands upon the owners of property. But in the era of the domestication of most labor organizations we can more closely define ''radical'' labor unions as those unions that espoused the goal of working towards the final collapse of the capitalist system.

One important precursor to radical unions was the Knights of Labor, led by Terrence Powderly and dedicated to the abolition of ''wage slavery.'' The Knights of Labor organized on a geographic basis, forming ''local assemblies'' that included workers from different employers (or even different sectors of industry) within the same organization. This furthered the cause of labor solidarity, but it complicated the process of winning strikes and securing contracts.

The most famous of these radical unions was the Industrial Workers of the World (IWW) whose members were generally known as the ''Wobblies.'' This union was organized in 1905 in direct opposition to the American Federation of Labor (AFL), an association of skilled trades unions organized in 1886. Whereas the AFL was a business union, the IWW was a revolutionary union. IWW leaders wanted to organize all the workers of the world to take control of all the means of production and abolish the wage system.

Among the founders of the IWW were Daniel DeLeon, leader of the Socialist Labor Party, Eugene V. Debs, leader of the Socialist Party of America, and William D. ''Big Bill'' Haywood, head of the Western Federation of Miners. The latter group was formed in Colorado in 1898 to oppose the hard conditions experienced by miners in all the western states. At first Haywood had hoped to redress the grievances of his followers through the law and the courts, but he soon became disillusioned and concluded that direct action would be the only feasible approach.

IWW strategy was to organize its members into 13 departments representing the 13 major industries of the country. When the moment was ripe, the ''Wobblies'' intended to call ''one big strike'' and seize control of

Jimmy Hoffa, the leader of the Teamster's Union, with his attorney, George Fitzgerald, as they are being questioned by the U.S. Senate Committee regarding racketeering activities.

all the industries. The nation's economy would then be in the hands of the workers, and socialism would replace capitalism.

The IWW opened its membership to those workers in the most oppressed industries. These included lumberjacks, textile workers, agricultural workers, longshoremen, construction workers, and meat packers. It also welcomed women workers, the unskilled as well as the skilled, and workers of all races. However, its main strength was among the immigrant workers of the East, the mine workers, and the migratory farm workers in the West.

The IWW never had a membership of more than 60,000 because it did not emphasize the building of permanent unions. It did not even believe in negotiating contracts with management. They said that a contract signified labor peace, and that there could be no peace between workers and capitalists. Instead, the IWW sought to attract people to its philosophy by means of winning strikes. The ''Wobblies'' would step into a dangerous situation, help win a strike against an oppressive employer, and then withdraw hoping that the workers had been won over to their socialist views.

A number of the ''Wobblies'' strikes were very successful. In 1906 they won wage increases for sawmill workers in Portland, Oregon, and in 1907, they similarly aided the textile workers in Skowhegan, Maine. However, their most famous effort was the strike of textile mills in Lawrence, Massachusetts in 1912. Thousands of workers walked off the job in response to pay cuts. Joseph J. Ettor, an IWW organizer from New York, came to Lawrence to lead the strike. He worked effectively and called for peace, but violence broke out anyway. Many strikers were arrested. Then a worker was killed in a riot and Ettor along with Arturo M. Giovannitti, an Italian newspaper editor who was assisting him, were arrested. There was no evidence against them but they were freed only after massive demonstrations orchestrated by the IWW.

Because of its openly radical agenda the IWW was constantly under attack and its leaders were mercilessly persecuted, but it survived until World War I (1914–1918). When the United States entered the war in 1917, Wobblie leaders called upon the workers to oppose it and to refuse to serve in the military. Imperialists and profiteers, they said, were conducting the war. In response the government cracked down on the union and arrested many of its leaders. Haywood was one of them. He jumped bail and fled to Russia.

By the end of the war the IWW was nearly defunct. Many of its leaders had fled or were in jail and many of its members joined the newly formed Communist

Party of America (CPA). The IWW never ceased to exist, but its active period was over after the Lawrence strike.

The IWW had many weaknesses. It neglected to undertake political action, it failed to build stable unions, and its extremist philosophy left it vulnerable to attack. Nevertheless it was important. It influenced the thinking of many workers and won gains for thousands who had no other advocate. It also forced the AFL to be somewhat more progressive by focusing attention on the needs of the unskilled workers.

In 1920 the CPA formed the Trade Union Education League (TUEL) to be used as a vehicle for infiltrating main line (conservative) unions. The TUEL had relatively little success although for a time they were active in the International Ladies' Garment Workers Union (ILGWU), the furriers' union, and a few others.

Meanwhile, the Socialist Party of American (SPA) had for years been working to establish control of such unions as the Brewery Workers, the Boot and Shoe Workers, the International Ladies' Garment Workers, the International Association of Machinists, and the United Mine Workers (UMW). For varying periods between the 1890s and the 1920s, the Socialists experienced some successes, but never gained permanent control of these organizations.

The Great Depression (1929–1939) initially seemed like a catastrophe for labor. How could you organize unions when a high percentage of the workers are unemployed? After the labor movement began to recover from the seemingly hopeless obstacles associated with the high unemployment during the 1930s, the attitude of existing labor organizations seemed to toughen and unions began to confront their situation and to organize in a more aggressive manner.

The more combative union leadership (like John L. Lewis of the United Mine Workers) broke from the conservative trade unions associated with the AFL and in 1936 formed the Congress of Industrial Organizations (CIO). As the labor movement confronted the problem of organizing unions when the demand for labor is low, some of the most gifted organizers came from the ranks of the radicals. For one thing, they understood that organizing had to take place in the communities as well as on the job. Members of the Socialist Party and of the Communist Party understood the need to coordinate organizing among the employed and the unemployed workers. In Toledo, Ohio in 1934 a strike at an automobile parts plant won a contract when the Lucas County Unemployed League walked on the picket lines with the strikers. For a decade or more, a portion of the labor movement was led by members of the CPA. These unions included the International Fur and Leather Workers Union (IFLWU); the International Longshoremen's and Warehousemen's Union (ILWU); the United Electrical, Radio and Machine Workers of America (UE); the International Union of Mine, Mill, and Smelter Workers (IUMUSW); the United Packinghouse Workers of America (UPWA); the Food, Tobacco, Agricultural and Allied Workers (FTA); the Farm Equipment Workers (FE); the United Office and Professional and Workers of America (UOPWA); the United Public Workers (UPW); the American Communications Association (ACA); the International Fishermen and Allied Workers of America (IFAWA); and the National Union of Marine Cooks and Stewards (NUMCS).

The left-led unions frequently advocated racial integration in their unions and in their strikes. As one historian writes, this effort to build labor solidarity across race lines could have significant outcomes for organizing—even as early as the 1930s: "Black workers—once their initial doubts about white-dominated unions had been overcome—especially in the South, were the first to join, were the most steadfast of members, and were the most militant. . . ."

In 1947 the Taft-Hartley Law stipulated that unions whose officers refused to sign an affadavit that they were not members of the Communist Party would not have recourse to the National Labor Relations machinery. This law was a severe blow to the radical unions, which were expelled from the CIO in 1949 and 1950, in spite of an estimated membership of 750,000-900,000. Thus, the CIO lost somewhere between 17 and 20 percent of its total membership. Eventually some of those expelled unions merged with others, passed out of existence, or, in a few cases, re-affiliated with the AFL-CIO. Their separation, however, brought an end to any significant influence of the U.S. labor movement's left wing.

See also: **Eugene Debs, Industrial Workers of the World, Knights of Labor, Labor Movement, Labor Unionism, John Lewis**

FURTHER READING

Austin, Aleine. *The Labor Story: A Popular History of American Labor, 1786–1949.* New York: Coward-McCann, 1949.

Dubofsky, Melvyn. *We Shall Be All: A History of the Industrial Workers of the World.* Chicago: Quadrangle Books, 1969.

Goldfield, Michael. *The Color of Politics: Race and the Mainsprings of American Politics.* New York: The New Press, 1997.

Laslett, John H. M. *Labor and the Left: A Study of Socialist and Radical Influences in the American Labor Movement, 1881–1924.* New York: Basic Books, 1970.

Livesay, Harold C. *Samuel Gompers and Organized Labor in America.* Boston, MA: Little Brown, 1978.

Oestreicher, Richard Jules. *Solidarity and Fragmentation: Working People and Class Consciousness in Detroit, 1875–1900.* Urbana, Illinois: University of Illinois Press, 1986.

Rosswurm, Steve, ed. *The CIO's Left Led Unions.* New Brunswick, NJ: Rutgers University Press, 1992.

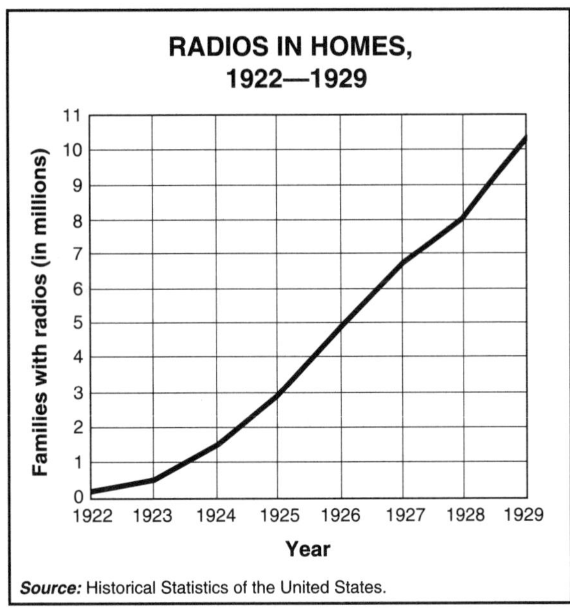

Radios in the home steadily increased from 1922–1929, due to families having more leisure time and discretionary income.

RADIO

The radio, or "wireless," was born in 1895, when Italian physicist and inventor Guglielmo Marconi (1874–1937) experimented with wireless telegraphy. The following year Marconi transmitted telegraph signals through the air from Italy to England. By 1897 Marconi founded his own company in London, Marconi's Wireless Telegraph Company, Ltd., which began setting up communication lines across the English Channel to France and completed the project in 1898. In 1900 Marconi established the American Marconi Company. He continued making improvements, including sending out signals on different wavelengths so that multiple messages could be transmitted at one time without interfering with each other. The first trans-Atlantic message, from Cornwall, England, to Newfoundland, Canada, was sent and received in 1901.

At first radio technology was regarded as a novelty and few understood how it could work. But in January 1901 a Marconi wireless station at South Wellfleet, Massachusetts (on Cape Cod), received Morse code messages from Europe as well as faint music and voices. That event changed the perception of radio. Before long, Americans had become accustomed to receiving "radiograms"—messages transmitted via the wireless. In 1906 the first radio broadcast of voice and music was made. Ships within a radius of several hundred miles picked up the event, which originated at Brant Rock, Massachusetts, on Christmas Eve. That accomplishment resulted from the invention of another radio pioneer, U.S. engineer Reginald Fessenden (1866–1932), who patented a high-frequency alternator (1901) capable of generating continuous waves rather than intermittent impulses; his invention became the first successful radio transmitter.

In 1910 U.S. inventor Lee De Forest (1873–1961), "the father of radio," broadcast the tenor voice of opera singer Enrico Caruso over the airwaves. In 1916 De Forest transmitted the first radio news broadcast. Within three years of the first commercial radio broadcast, there were more than five hundred radio stations in the United States. National networks were organized, including the National Broadcast Company (NBC), the Columbia Broadcasting System (CBS), and the Mutual Broadcasting System (MBS). Congress tried to keep pace with the growth of the communications industry by passing the Radio Acts of 1912 and 1927 and setting up the Federal Communications Commission (FCC) to regulate the airwaves.

During the trying times of the Great Depression (1929–1939), President Franklin Roosevelt (1933–1945) spoke directly to the U.S. public using the new medium which broadcast his "fireside chats" from the White House. By the end of the decade radio was woven into the fabric of everyday American life. People across the country, in cities, suburbs, and on farms, tuned in for news and entertainment; they listened to broadcasts of baseball games and other sporting events as well as comedy and variety shows, dramas, and live music programs. Between the 1920s and the 1950s gathering around the radio in the evenings was as common to Americans as watching television is today. Networks offered advertisers national audiences and corporate America eagerly seized the opportunity to speak directly to people in their own homes. The advent of television in the 1950s and its growing popularity over the next two decades changed the role of radio in American life. Having lost their audience to TV, radio programmers seized rock music as a way to reach a wide, albeit a very young, audience. Many argue that the rise of the musical genre kept radio alive. In the decades since, radio programming became increasingly music-oriented; talk and news programming were also popular.

See also: **Radio Act, RCA-Victor**

RADIO ACT

The advent of radio, first as a mode for sending wireless telegraphs (called radiograms) via Morse code and later as a broadcast medium, necessitated government regulation of the airwaves. Congress first stepped in to establish guidelines for radio in 1912, in the wake of the *Titanic* disaster. The legislation of the Radio Act of 1912 stipulated that ship radios be manned day and night, that they have an alternate energy source (other than the ship's engine), and that they have a range of at least one hundred miles (161 kilometers). Further, Congress required that all radio operators, including broadcasters, be licensed and adhere to certain bandwidths. The Secretary of Commerce was given authority to assign frequencies to new radio stations, thereby eliminating competition among operators for the same frequency.

As radio stations proliferated, the airwaves were jumbled; interference prevented the transmission of clear signals, particularly when a listener was located more than twenty miles (thirty-two kilometers) from the transmitter. Further, the distribution of radio stations was uneven: Eastern and Midwestern cities were well served by broadcasters, while people in the South and West had few stations to choose from. Congress responded by passing the Radio Act of 1927, setting up the Federal Radio Commission (FRC) as the licensing authority for broadcasters. The legislation tried to bring about the equalization of service throughout the United States. It stated that when applications for licenses or license renewals were considered, the licensing authority (the Federal Radio Commission) "shall make such distribution of licenses, bands of frequencies or wave lengths, periods of time for operation, and of power among the different States and communities as to give fair, efficient and equitable radio service." When the FRC's authorization came up for renewal in Congress the following year, the Radio Act was amended (in the Davis Amendment). The amendment clarified the commission's objective to provide "equality of radio broadcasting service, both of transmission and reception" to all regions of the United States.

The Communications Act of 1934 provided comprehensive legislation for the government regulation of the radio broadcasting, telephone, and telegraph industries, which Franklin Roosevelt (1933–1945) classified, along with transportation and power, as public utilities. The act reformulated the Federal Radio Commission (FRC) to create the Federal Communications Commission (FCC), an agency charged with the broad authority to regulate interstate and foreign communications. Its purview includes all types of radio transmissions as well as television, wire, and cable transmissions. The agency assigns broadcast frequencies and issues broadcast licenses. It is empowered to modify or revoke licenses as well.

See also: **Radio, RCA Victor**

RAG MONEY

Rag money is a derisive term for paper currency. The name comes from the early days of paper money, when paper itself was predominately made from the cotton and linen fibers of rags. Since valued currency was issued in silver or gold coins by the established governments of Europe, it is not surprising that Americans greeted with skepticism paper currency that was little more than a promise of future payment in silver. The first bills that were issued by the U.S. government became worthless shortly after the Declaration of Independence (1776). In its effort to fund the American Revolution (1775–1783), the Second Continental Congress printed so many bills, called Continentals, that there was not enough silver to back them up. The expression, "that's not worth a continental" reflected that reality. The financial crisis that emerged did nothing to inspire American confidence in paper currency. So-called rag money continued to have its detractors even after the Revolution had been financed by European loans and the U.S. government had established the dollar as its unit of currency (1785).

See also: **American Revolution, Continental Congress (Second), Continentals, Currency**

RAILROAD GAUGES, STANDARDIZATION OF

As railroads proliferated in the United States, rail companies guarded their areas of service by using various widths of road gauges (gauge is the distance between the inner sides of the heads of the two rails as measured 5/8 inch, or 16 millimeters, below the top of the rail heads). Companies would use their own rail gauge width to prevent competitors' cars from passing to their line. By 1840 there were more than three hundred American railroad companies in operation and their tracks varied in gauge from four feet 8.5 inches (1.4 meters) to six feet (1.8 meters).

The practice of employing different-sized gauges, sometimes called the "battle of the gauges," interrupted transportation. A similar situation had unfolded in England and in 1846 British Parliament decided to set the standard at four feet 8.5 inches (1.4 meters); the Gauge Act of 1846 abolished all other gauges. In the United States, the completion of the first transcontinental railroad (1869) forced the issue of rail standardization. Freight shipped long distances had to be unpacked from one rail car and packed to another at junctions where rail gauge variances required a train transfer. The high cost of handling combined with the practicality of the narrower gauge (it required less clearance on either side and allowed for sharper turns in tracks) encouraged American railroads to adopt the standard gauge of four feet 8.5 inches (1.4 meters). This made rail lines accessible to any car or locomotive. By 1886 most rail companies had worked out agreements to handle the "rolling stock" (cargo shipped long distances) of other companies.

See also: **Transcontinental Railroad**

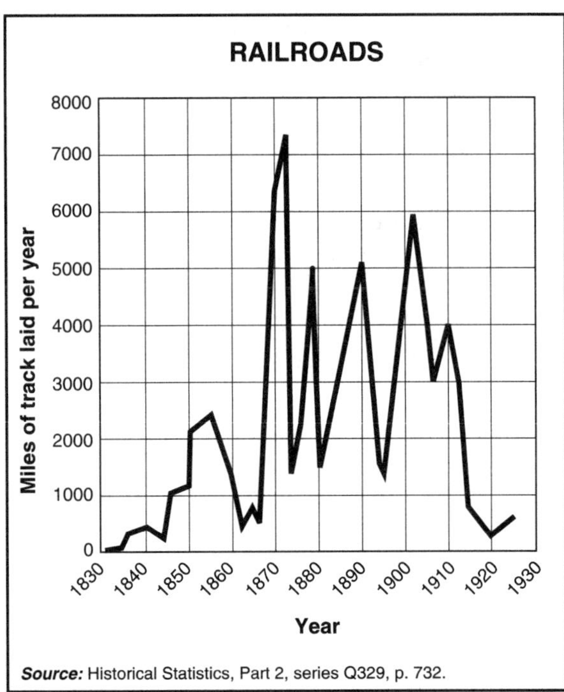

According to the miles of track laid each year, the railroad's greatest decades of expansion followed the Civil War until 1910.

RAILROAD INDUSTRY

The U.S. railroad industry began with the founding of the Baltimore and Ohio Railroad Company in 1827. The Baltimore and Ohio was the first U.S. railroad chartered as a common carrier of freight and passengers. It was only two years earlier that John Stephens from Hoboken, New Jersey built the first steam locomotive in the United States. The railroad itself had originated some years before in Great Britain. Railroads achieved great significance later on when the western part of the North American continent was being settled. They enabled transport and expanded the possibilities of the agricultural industry. They also played an important role during the American Civil War (1861–1865).

The first operating line on the Baltimore and Ohio Railroad carried passengers from Baltimore to Ellicott's Mills (later renamed Ellicott City). The line was only 13 miles long. In the 1830s railroad companies began to spring up in other parts of the country. By 1834 the tracks of the Baltimore and Ohio Railroad reached West Virginia.

Several other railroads came into being at around the same time as the Baltimore and Ohio. The South Carolina Canal and Rail Road Company completed construction of its gauge line from Charleston to Hamburg in 1833. It was the first railroad line in the United States that used a steam locomotive to run scheduled passenger operations. It was also the longest then operating in the United States. Eventually it became part of the 10,000 mile Southern Railway System.

The Galena and Chicago Union Railroad began operation in 1848 with the first locomotive in Chicago. The first line to run from Chicago to points along the Mississippi River started in 1854. As the railway industry expanded westward, many towns and cities came into being as railroad "division points." There eventually were nine major routes going from the Midwest or South to the West Coast. Cities and manufacturing centers were no longer dependent on water transportation after the onslaught of railroads. They could therefore be located away from rivers and canals.

In the early years of the railroad industry, state governments significantly aided railroad construction in the United States. The federal government gave land grants for building railroads after the American Civil War. The country had 30,000 miles of track on the eve of the war.

U.S. railroad companies were mainly based in the north of the country. This gave the Union (Federal) effort in the American Civil War an important advantage. The railway was used to transport troops and supplies. Construction of railroads was slowed down during the war, but resumed on a high level immediately following the war. The American Civil War was the first war in which railroads played a major role.

THE RAILROADS WERE THE FIRST TRULY BIG BUSINESS IN THE UNITED STATES.

The railroads became an essential means of transport during the era of industrialization in the United States. In the 1880s railroad construction reached a peak with 70,000 miles of track being built during that decade. The first transcontinental railway route had been completed shortly after the war. In 1969 the Union Pacific tracks met the tracks of the Central Pacific Railroad at Promontory Point, Utah.

The evolution of the railroad industry was strongly linked to other industries. In the late nineteenth century a decrease in the price of coal was brought about by an increase in anthracite coal mining. That lowered the price of coal-fueled steam engines as well. Innovations in the steel-making process introduced by Scottish-born U.S. industrialist Andrew Carnegie (1835–1919) made possible the production of more durable rails. Steel rails were first introduced in 1857 in England. Captain James B. Eads built the first steel bridge was built between 1867 and 1873, over the Mississippi River at St. Louis. Another type of bridge called the timber-truss was adapted to support trains shipping heavy loads. It had originally been developed by a number of U.S. inventors in the early nineteenth century.

The railroads were the first truly big business in the United States. As such, they were at the center of many protests and conflicts. During the 1870s a farmers' group called the Grange protested the high rates that the railroad charged for shipping. The Supreme Court eventually ruled that states would have the power to regulate businesses with a strong public aspect. However, no regulation was imposed on the national level. In 1877 railroad workers organized the first nationwide strike. Between 1881 and 1905 there were 36,757 strikes throughout the country. As an outcome, the emergence of railroads resulted in the forming of the most prominent labor unions in the United States. The railroads were regulated by the Interstate Commerce Act of 1887. Yet rival companies in many industries, including the railroads, formed huge trusts despite the legal obstacles. This knocked out competition coming from smaller companies. In 1902 a suit was filed against the railroad monopoly founded by James J. Hill (1838–1916) and J.P. Morgan (1813–1890). The suit was directed by President Theodore Roosevelt (1901–1909).

The railroad industry continued to grow in the decades that followed despite all the setbacks. But by the 1950s and 1960s it started to decline as air travel and air shipping became less costly. By that time, railroads were used mostly for transporting materials such as coal, grain, and lumber. In the 1980s an increasing reliance on the trucking industry for transport represented another setback to the U.S. railroads. But by the end of the decade the industry had for the most part recovered due to technological innovations and industry deregulation. It was at its highest since it began to decline in the 1950s.

There were 535 registered railway companies in the United States in 1992. The 13 companies dominating the freight railroad industry employed around 200,000 workers. The largest of these was Union Pacific Railroad, with sales exceeding $7 billion, with Amtrak (the National Railroad Passenger Corporation) dominating the passenger railroad industry. In the 1990s rail employees were overall the best paid segment of the working population.

The railroads continued to be linked to the development of other industries. The technological innovations that helped the resurgence of railroads in the 1980s mostly had to with the telecommunications and computer industries. They also involved the development of high-speed trains using magnetic levitation systems along with the traditional wheel-on-rail trains. The railroad industry thus continued to play a significant role in economic development and on the transport service market.

See also: **Baltimore and Ohio Railroad, Central Pacific Railroad, Great Railroad Strike of 1877, New York Central Railroad, Pennsylvania Railroad, Pullman Palace Car Company, Pullman Strike, Railroad Gauges (Standardization of), Railroad War Board, Railroads (Federal Land Grants to), Santa Clara County v. Southern Pacific Railroad, Transcontinental Railroad, Union Pacific Railroad Company**

FURTHER READING

Encyclopedia of American Industries. Detroit: The Gale Group, 1997.

"Forbes Annual Report on American Industry." *Forbes*, January, 4, 1993.

Holbrook, Stewart. *The Story of American Railroads.* New York: American Legacy Press, 1981.

Nash, Gary B., et. al., eds. *The American People: Creating A Nation and a Society.* New York: Harper and Row, 1986.

Welty, Gus. "Rebuilding America's Railroads: The Information Evolution." *Railway Age*, February 1993.

RAILROAD WAR BOARD

On April 11, 1917, five days after Congress declared war on Germany, and the United States entered into World War I (1914–1918), the president of the Baltimore and Ohio Railroad, Daniel Willard called a meeting of railroad executives in Washington, DC. The executives signed a resolution agreeing to support the war effort by running their lines in a coordinated manner to create a "continental railway system." The conference set up a five-person Railroad War Board to oversee the plan. The plan's objectives were to maximize use of all railroad potentials and speed up transport. Pools were organized; load weights were increased to utilize the full capacity of cars; the loading and unloading of freight were expedited. Shipping times of war-related goods (such as coal and iron) were speeded by prohibiting transport of non-related items during certain hours. Use of all in-service equipment was maximized and some passenger lines were eliminated in order to conserve coal.

The Railroad War Board and the companies it coordinated faced numerous obstacles in reaching their goals. One of them was a labor shortage that resulted from the draft: the passage of the Selective Service Act (May 1917) required men between the ages of twenty-one and thirty (later eighteen to forty-five) to register for military service. Some 70,000 of the draftees were rail workers. Shortages of equipment, parts, and capital also hampered the wartime effort. Nevertheless, the actions directed by the Railroad War Board and carried out by the railroads allowed carriers to operate as a unit. During World War I anti-trust laws were suspended because of the national emergency; corporations set aside their private interests to run a nationwide rail service in support of the fight for democracy.

See also: **Railroad Industry, World War I (Economic Impact of)**

RAILROADS, FEDERAL LAND GRANTS TO *(ISSUE)*

Between 1850 and 1871 the United States government used a portion of the public domain (federally owned land) to assist and encourage the building of railroads. In all, during that twenty-one year period approximately 1.31 million acres of land were transferred to private ownership. This represented 9.5 percent of the public domain as it stood in 1850 (1.39 billion acres). The land was located in twenty-seven states, but the largest grants were made in California (11.5 million acres), Kansas (8.2 million acres), Minnesota (9.9 million acres), Montana (14.7 million acres), North Dakota (10.6 million acres), and Washington (9.5 million acres). Although the program began in 1850, most of the grants were made under the terms of the Pacific Railway Act of 1862. This law was in effect from 1862 to 1871 and its purpose was to encourage the construction of the transcontinental railroads.

The law provided that companies agreeing to undertake the construction of transcontinental railroad lines would be eligible for loans ranging from $16,000 to $48,000 per mile of track laid. The precise amount of the loan was determined by the difficulty of the terrain through which the construction passed. The government loaned a total of $64,623,512 to the transcontinental companies. These loans were for the most part paid back at six percent interest. The law also provided that a company could be given up to twenty sections (a section is a square mile) of land for every mile of track put down. This land would be granted in alternate sections (a kind of checkerboard pattern) within an area lying forty miles on either side of the proposed right of way. To qualify for the subsidies a company had to agree to actually build track or forfeit the grant, and carry mail, government passengers, and freight at reduced rates.

Most of the loans and land grants distributed under the Pacific Railway Act went to the first five companies that built transcontinental lines. These were: the Union Pacific, the Central Pacific, the Northern Pacific, the Southern Pacific, and the Santa Fe. They received a total of 130 million acres of land, with the largest single grant (of 44 million acres) going to the Northern Pacific line. The states added another 50 million acres of land grants. Local communities also subsidized railroad companies by giving them land for depots and rights of way and tax exemptions. The state governments granted a total of around 50 million acres of land. Whereas the federal and state land grant programs were designed to promote the building of trunk lines, these local subsidies were designed to facilitate the building of connecting lines. Even though not all lines were built in this way, the effect was to stimulate railroad building in general. Hence the national railroad system expanded from 9,000 miles in 1850 to 87,000 in 1885.

The total of public land grants given to the railroads by states and the federal government was about 180 million acres. At the time, the value of this land was about one dollar per acre, which was the average price realized by the government for sales in the land grant states during that period. Hence the total value of the land granted to these companies was approximately $180 million. Later, much of the land was sold by the railroad companies at an average price of $2.81 per acre. (Proximity to the rails increased the value of the land.) These sales offset a portion of the construction costs, which have been estimated at approximately $168 million.

Although these figures are immense and would appear to suggest that the American railroad system was built largely on the basis of government aid, this is actually not the case. In fact, only 18,738 miles of railroad line were built as a direct result of these land grants and loans. This figure represents only eight percent of the total railroad mileage built in the United States between 1860 and 1920. The government program was important because the building of these lines opened up the trans-Mississippi West and stimulated settlement, but most of the railroads were built by private enterprise—in some cases with state and local support.

Not everyone applauded the subsidies. For example, the land grant–loan system under the Pacific Railway Act was subjected to harsh criticism by reformers who argued that it represented a vast give–away of money and public property to assist businessmen who made vast fortunes. As a result, the program of federal aid was discontinued in 1871. However, the arguments of the reformers were not entirely correct. The loans were, for the most part, repaid and the railroad companies did not reap vast fortunes from the re–sale of their land grants. Moreover, the country benefited immensely from the rapid construction of the railroads, which produced a viable transportation system connecting all portions of this vast nation. The railroads literally bound the states together thus contributing significantly to national unity.

See also: **Transcontinental Railroad**

FURTHER READING

Chandler, Alfred D., Jr. *The Railroads: The Nation's First Big Business; Sources and Readings.* New York: Harcourt, Brace and World, 1965.

Henry, R. S. ''The Railroad Landgrant Myth.'' *Mississippi Valley Historical Review*, September 1945.

Howard, Robert West. *The Great Iron Trail: The Story of the First Transcontinental Railroad.* New York: Putnam, 1962.

Riegel, Robert R. *The Story of Western Railroads.* Lincoln, NE: University of Nebraska Press, 1964.

Taylor, George R., and Irene D. Neu. *The American Railroad Network, 1861–1890.* Cambridge: Harvard University Press, 1956.

Winther, Oscar O. *The Transportation Frontier: Trans-Mississippi West, 1865–1890.* New York: Holt, Rinehart and Winston, 1964.

RAND, AYN

Ayn Rand (1905–1982) used her novels as a vehicle for her objectivist philosophy, which endorsed individualism by stressing ''rational self-interest'' over charity and the welfare state. Her best-known novels include *The Fountainhead* (1943) and *Atlas Shrugged* (1957).

Ayn Rand was born Allisa Rosenbaum on February 2, 1905 in St. Petersburg, Russia, the first of Fronz and Anna Rosenbaum's three daughters. Her father was a self-made Jewish merchant. Rand taught herself to read and write by age four and had decided to become a writer by age nine. Her greatest hero was author Victor Hugo (1802–1885). Rand's family barely survived the siege of St. Petersburg during World War I (1914–1918), and they later lost their possessions in the Russian Revolution. As a teenager, Rand learned to hate her country's new communist doctrine and vowed to make it her life's work to use the written word to prove that doctrine wrong.

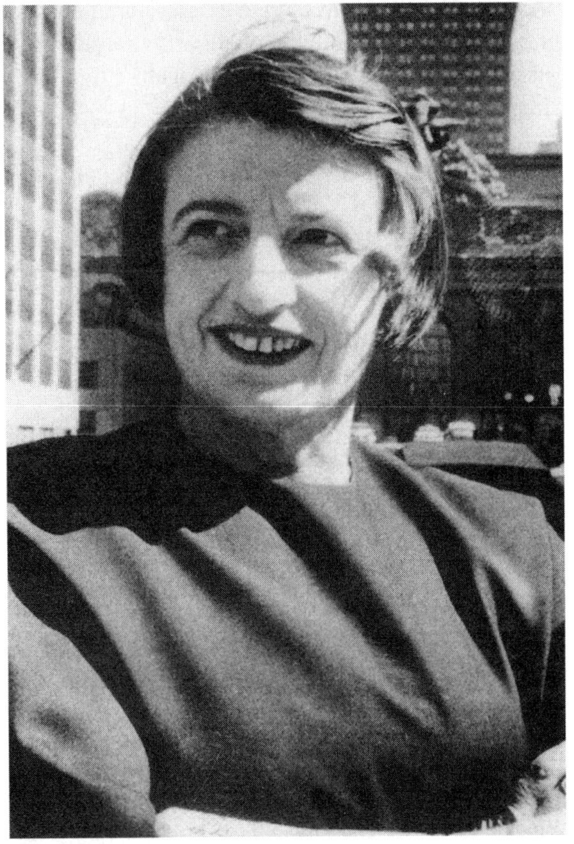

Ayn Rand.

After graduating with a degree in history from the University of Leningrad in 1926, Rand immigrated to the United States. In her new country, she changed her name to Ayn Rand. She lived with relatives in Chicago, Illinois, for a few months before moving to Hollywood to work as a screenwriter and movie extra. There, she met actor Frank O'Connor, and the two were married in 1929. Rand became a U.S. citizen in 1931.

CIVILIZATION IS THE PROGRESS TOWARD A SOCIETY OF PRIVACY. THE SAVAGE'S WHOLE EXISTENCE IS PUBLIC, RULED BY THE LAWS OF HIS TRIBE. CIVILIZATION IS THE PROCESS OF SETTING MAN FREE FROM MEN.

Ayn Rand, *The Fountainhead*, 1943

Penthouse Legend, Rand's first play, was produced on Broadway in 1934. Two years later she published her first novel, *We the Living* (1936). It was set during the Russian Revolution and condemned communism and those who would follow its principle of sacrificing self for the state. Her next novel, *Anthem* was published in 1938. *The Fountainhead* (1943), Rand's most famous work, was initially turned down by several publishers for being considered too intellectual for a mass market. The novel took four years to complete, but became the medium through which Rand defended her philosophical beliefs. Her hero, brilliant architect Howard Roark, blows up his own building when the architectural establishment alters its design. Using a classic metaphor, Roark symbolizes "good" while the establishment is "evil." The book was highly praised by critics and hit the national bestseller list several times during 1945. Hollywood even hired her to write the screenplay.

Rand's later works include *Atlas Shrugged* (1957), *For the New Intellectual* (1961), *The Virtue of Selfishness* (1965), *The Romantic Manifesto* (1969), and *Philosophy—Who Needs It?* (1982). *Atlas Shrugged*, concerned with the philosophical faults of collective societies, became her second most popular novel.

Rand spent a large part of her career defending her philosophy of objectivism. During the 1960s and 1970s, she was a visiting lecturer at the Nathaniel Branden Institute and other American university campuses, including Harvard and Yale. *The Ayn Rand Letter* and *Objectivist Bulletin* were circulated to promote her philosophy. Rand's pro-capitalist views are considered by some to have helped influence the collapse of the Berlin Wall. Ayn Rand died on March 6, 1982 in New York City.

See also: **Capitalism, Laissez Faire**

FURTHER READING

Harriman, David. *Journals of Ayn Rand*. New York: Dutton, 1997.

Landrum, Gene N., Ph.D. *Profiles of Female Genius: Thirteen Creative Women Who Changed the World*. Amherst, NY: Prometheus Books, 1994.

Peikoff, Leonard. *Objectivism: The Philosophy of Ayn Rand*. New York: Meridian, 1993.

Rand, Ayn. *The Letters of Ayn Rand*. New York: Dutton, 1995.

Sciabarra, Chris Matthew. *Ayn Rand: The Russian Radical*. University Park, PA: Pennsylvania State University Press, 1995.

RANDOLPH, ASA PHILIP

Asa Philip Randolph (1889–1979) was an American labor and civil rights leader. During the first half of the twentieth century he was considered one of the most prominent of all African American trade unionists as well as one of the major figures in the African American struggle for civil rights. He maintained that African Americans could never be politically free until they were economically secure, and so Randolph became the foremost advocate of the full integration of black workers into the American trade union movement. In 1925 he organized the Brotherhood of Sleeping Car Porters (BSCP), which was the first African-American union in the country to sign a labor contract with a white employer.

In 1889 Asa Philip Randolph was born in Crescent City, Florida, the son of an African Methodist Episcopal minister. Randolph graduated from the Cookman Institute in Florida in 1907, at the top of his class.

Randolph was a good singer and actor. The idea of becoming a professional performer led him to New York, where he found himself working as a delivery driver, sales clerk, and a laborer on the railroad. In 1911 he moved to Harlem, where most African Americans in New York lived during that era. Harlem was the nation's capital of black intellectual life at that time and the center of what would later be called the Harlem Renaissance.

DURING THE FIRST HALF OF THE TWENTIETH CENTURY HE WAS CONSIDERED ONE OF THE MOST PROMINENT OF ALL AFRICAN AMERICAN TRADE UNIONISTS AS WELL AS ONE OF THE MAJOR FIGURES IN THE AFRICAN AMERICAN STRUGGLE FOR CIVIL RIGHTS.

In Harlem Randolph turned to politics instead of the stage. He began attending City College of New York (CCNY), studying history, philosophy, and economics. In college he made friends with political radicals and founded the Independent Political Council in 1913, a radical current affairs group. He also worked on the campaign of socialist John Royal who was running for city council.

By 1914 Randolph met Ernest Welcome and began working for Welcome's Brotherhood of Labor, an organization that brought workers from the South and helped them find jobs in New York. Randolph also married Lucille Campbell that year. She supported Randolph economically as he pursued his political activism. In 1915 Randolph began to emerge as a dominant voice in the "New Negro movement." In 1917 he co-produced the first issue of *The Messenger*, a journal that became what Randolph called "the first voice of radical, revolutionary, economic, and political action among Negroes in America." *The Messenger* has been regarded by scholars as among the most brilliantly edited magazines in African-American publishing.

In 1925 Randolph became the leader of a campaign to organize the African American men who employed as porters aboard most trains in the United States. In 1937, after years of continuous work, the first contract was signed between a white employer and the Brotherhood of Sleeping Car Porters. This was a milestone for African American workers and the labor movement.

By 1940 Randolph was deeply involved in the black civil rights movement. During World War II (1939–1945) he planned a massive march on Washington, D.C. to protest the exclusion of African Americans from working jobs in defense industries. He agreed to call off the march only after President Franklin Roosevelt (1933–1945) issued Executive Order 8802, which banned discrimination in defense plants and created the nation's first Fair Employment Practices Committee.

In 1948 Randolph once again initiated strategic efforts to enhance civil rights for African Americans. He warned President Harry Truman, (1945–1953) that if segregation in the armed forces was not abolished, then masses of African Americans would refuse military induction. Truman soon issued Executive Order 9981, establishing "equality of treatment" in the armed forces.

Randolph continued his civil rights work on behalf of African Americans. In the 1950s he organized youth marches to integrate schools. It was Randolph who organized the famous march on Washington in 1963, when Martin Luther King, Jr. (1929–1968) gave his now famous "I Have a Dream" speech to a quarter million people who came to the nation's capital.

Randolph's career reads like a history of struggles for unionization, worker equity, and civil rights in the twentieth century. His efforts focused on securing political freedom for African Americans by creating greater economic security. He created unions and organized millions of people in the Civil Rights Movement. Randolph died in 1979, having realized many of his goals for African Americans and civil rights.

See also: **Brotherhood of Sleeping Car Porters, Civil Rights Movement, Labor Movement**

FURTHER READING

Anderson, Jervis. *A. Philip Randolph; a Biographical Portrait.* New York: Harcourt Brace Jovanovich, 1986.

Branch, Taylor. *Parting the Waters: America in the King Years, 1954–1963*. New York: Simon and Schuster, 1988.

Davis, Daniel S. *Mr. Black Labor; the Story of A. Philip Randolph, Father of the Civil Rights Movement*. New York: E.P. Dutton, 1972.

Harris, William H. *Keeping the Faith: A. Philip Randolph, Milton P. Webster, and the Brotherhood of Sleeping Car Porters, 1925–1937*. Urbana, IL: University of Illinois Press, 1977.

Pfeffer, Paula F. *A. Philip Randolph, Pioneer of the Civil Rights Movement*. Baton Rouge, LA: Louisiana State University Press, 1990.

RATIONING

Rationing refers to the equitable allocation of scarce or valuable resources among competing consumers who have varying degrees of demand or need. Resources can be rationed informally at the local level on a merchant-by-merchant basis, as was done by many U.S. businesses during the Great Depression. Resources can also be rationed systematically by the government. During World War II (1939–1945), President Franklin D. Roosevelt (1933–1945) and Congress, in an effort to eliminate from the economy every ounce of excess and waste, enacted legislation (1942) authorizing the president to establish the War Production Board (WPB) and the Office of Price Administration (OPA).

WPB was assigned the task of dividing scarce resources between the military and civilian production sectors, while the OPA was responsible for administering rationing plans. Both agencies had regional and state branches of enforcement. More than 100 million Americans were issued ration cards, coupons, and certificates, which restricted the quantity of goods that could be purchased and the uses to which they could be put. Windshields were stamped to indicate how much gasoline car owners could buy during a given week. Civilians working outside the defense industry, for example, could buy no more than three gallons per week. Horses, trolley cars, and walking quickly became popular modes of transportation. Rubber, gasoline, and sugar were rationed in 1942, meat and shoes in 1943. By the end of the war the list of items rationed in the United States included typewriters, bicycles, stoves, tea, coffee, canned and processed foods, fats, coal, and an assortment of leather items. Manufacturing stopped altogether for other items deemed unnecessary to the war effort and daily subsistence, such as curlers, electric toasters, waffle irons, cocktail shakers, and lobster forks.

Most Americans understood that it was their patriotic duty to make ends meet within the rationing system, but violations did occur and black markets sprang up around the country. Some amusing blunders befell the system as well: a Pennsylvania rationing office had to close because it failed to ration enough fuel for itself. Nonetheless, domestic rationing played a significant role in increasing the resources available to Allied cause.

See also: **Black Market, Office of Price Administration, War Production Board, World War II**

RCA-VICTOR COMPANY

> One of the most outstanding trademarks ever marketed was . . . the image of a dog (named Nipper) staring at an old phonograph with the caption "His Master's Voice." Nipper, along with the selling techniques of the newly formed company, helped this new invention of a "radio music box," priced at approximately $75, become one of the most popular inventions of its time.

RCA-Victor Company merged from two earlier companies—Victor Talking Machine Company and the Radio Corporation of America (RCA). The Victor Talking Machine Company was founded in 1901 after the development of the cylinder phonograph. It went into the business of producing phonographs, providing people with recorded sounds and music. The Radio Corporation of America was formed in 1919 by General Electric Company (GE), and spawned several supporting businesses, like RCA-Victor, to better manage its growing interests.

General Electric formed the Radio Corporation of America in 1919 in order to acquire the assets of the British-owned American Marconi. It was the only company operating in the United States equipped to handle transatlantic radio and telegraph communications. Franklin D. Roosevelt (1882–1945), then undersecretary of the Navy, strongly supported GE's bid to acquire American Marconi. He spearheaded efforts to facilitate the purchase because Roosevelt believed that

This famous painting by Francis Barraud entitled "His Master's Voice" became one of the most famous trademarks for RCA.

Americans should own the only company in the nation able to handle transatlantic radio and telegraph communications.

General Electric succeeded and RCA went into business. Though GE was the main stockholder in RCA, American Telephone & Telegraph Company (AT&T) and Westinghouse Corporation also owned significant shares of the company. Between 1919 and 1921, AT&T and GE licensed their patents for long distance transmission. Westinghouse granted RCA access to all of its patents and offered its radio equipment to the public.

Under the combined resources of these companies, RCA flourished. In 1924, RCA transmitted the first radiophoto from New York to London. This photo-transmission paved the way for the development of television. At the same time, RCA was still heavily invested in radio, and it wanted to maintain control over the radio stations it owned. To better manage their operations, RCA formed the National Broadcasting Company in 1926.

Most phonograph companies during the 1920s did not express enthusiasm over the introduction of radio. However, David Sarnoff (1891–1971), a leader at RCA, had an idea to market a radio and a phonograph together in one unit. The best way for RCA to do this was to acquire a phonograph company. In 1929, RCA purchased the Victor Talking Machine Company for $154 million. The RCA-Victor Company was formed, with David Sarnoff serving as its president. The company began manufacturing radios and phonographs in Camden, New Jersey. Sarnoff became known as the "father of broadcasting."

One of the most outstanding trademarks ever marketed was purchased along with the Victor Talking Machine Company. It was the image of a dog (named Nipper) staring at an old phonograph with the caption "His Master's Voice." Nipper, along with the selling techniques of the newly formed company, helped this new invention of a "radio music box," priced at approximately $75, become one of the most popular inventions of its time.

RCA also created two spin-off companies to manufacture key components in the RCA-Victor phonograph production. Shortly afterwards, the Radio Corporation of America's increasingly complex operations caught the attention of the federal government. The company became embroiled in legal issues regarding its near-monopoly status. Under federal pressure, General Electric, AT&T, and Westinghouse sold their interest in RCA in 1932. The company, renamed RCA

Corporation, became independent and was led by David Sarnoff.

RCA, still the parent company of RCA-Victor, introduced a new invention—the television—at the 1939 World's Fair. However, the company quickly turned to more basic matters as the United States entered World War II (1939–1945). RCA factories manufactured a variety of items to help with the war effort, including bomb fuses and radio tubes. A month after the war ended, RCA-Victor's television products found their way back to the market and were produced at a rapid rate. The television age had begun, and RCA-Victor was in the lead.

Under Sarnoff's continued leadership the Radio Corporation of America involved itself in a range of interests, including education, broadcasting, and sound system design. This trend set by Sarnoff continued through the end of the twentieth century, when RCA became an industry leader in digital high-definition television (HDTV) development.

See also: **Radio, National Broadcasting Corporation, Telegraph**

FURTHER READING

Cowie, Jefferson R. *Capital Moves: RCA's Seventy-Year Quest for Cheap Labor.* Cornell University Press, 1999.

Curtis, Philip J. *The Fall of the U.S. Consumer Electronics Industry.* Greenwood Publishing Group, 1994.

RCA Receiving Tube Manual. Antique Electronic Supply, 1994.

Sherman, Michael W., William R. Moran, and Kurt R. Nauck. *A Collector's Guide to Victor Records.* Monarch Record Enterprises, 1992.

"The Web's Home for Home Entertainment," [cited April 21, 1999] available from the World Wide Web @ www.nipper.com/nipper.asp.

REAGAN, RONALD WILSON

Folk wisdom holds that the burden of politics is much like the burden of fame. If that is true then no one knows that as well as Ronald Reagan. Born in Tampico, Illinois, on February 6, 1911, Ronald Wilson Reagan (1911–) grew up to become the fortieth president of the United States. Reagan was raised in several towns in the rural areas of northern Illinois. His family finally settled down in Dixon when he was nine. Reagan graduated from Eureka College in 1932. After graduating, he began working in Davenport, Iowa, as a radio sports announcer. He also authored a sports column on a weekly basis for a Des Moines newspaper.

Ronald W. Reagan.

While covering a sports story on Catalina Island, near Los Angeles, Reagan caught the attention of a agent from the Warner Brothers movie studio. After doing a screen test for Warner Brothers, Reagan was signed to a movie contract with the studio. His first film was *Love Is on the Air* (1937). In the several years following, he was seen in a number of forgettable films. There were a few, however, that were exceptions, such as *Brother Rat* (1938), *Dark Victory* (1939), and *Kings Row* (1941). His most notable film was made in 1940, *Knute Rockne—All American*, in which he portrayed football legend George Gipp. With the onset of World War II Reagan found himself making air force training films.

He continued to act after the conclusion of the war but he also found himself becoming extensively involved in politics. During his early political years, Reagan was an active member of several liberal organizations, including the Americans for Democratic Action. Eventually he began to grow fearful of communist subversion and his political attitudes made a turn to the right. In 1947 he testified to the House Un-American

Activities Committee regarding the influence the communists had in the movie industry.

It was during the 1950s that Reagan's movie career faltered and he began working for the General Electric Company as a traveling spokesman and as the host of *General Electric Theater* (on television from 1954 to 1962). It was also during this period that he shifted from being a liberal and a Democrat to a conservative Republican.

Leadership was not unfamiliar to Reagan when he began to work in politics. By the time he co-chaired the Citizens for Goldwater-Miller Committee in 1964, he had already served on the board of directors of the Screen Actors Guild, serving as president from 1949 to 1952, and again in 1959. He had also served as chairman of the Motion Picture Industry Council in 1949. Two years after the Barry Goldwater campaign, Reagan successfully ran for governor of California against Democratic incumbent Edmund G. Brown.

Reagan's first term agenda as California's governor was to enact a freeze in state hiring, consequently restraining the growth rate of the state's bureaucracy. He also increased taxes to eliminate the state deficit and reduced social services. Welfare reform, reducing the caseload while increasing the payments to families with dependent children, was on the agenda for his second term. Reagan only had moderate success in promoting his programs.

In 1976 he made his first serious run for the U.S. presidency. His long-fought campaign against Gerald Ford was a lost battle and the Republican nomination went to Ford. Reagan was not deterred, and in 1980 he easily won his party's nomination and defeated the Democratic incumbent, Jimmy Carter, for the presidency.

Reagan's presidency was filled with substantial tax cuts. He reduced spending on domestic programs, increased military expenditures, and doubled the national debt. His moves are credited with decreasing the inflation rate, which had seen rapid growth in the 1970s, down to 3.5 percent during his tenure. On March 30, 1981, a 25-year old drifter named John Hinckley shot Reagan. His wounds were serious, but he recovered and the stories of his good humor while in the hospital added to his popularity.

In 1986 it was learned that the Reagan administration had participated in the shipping of arms to the radical Islamic fundamentalist government of Iran. This was apparently an effort to gain the release of American hostages who were being held by Iranian terrorists in Beirut, Lebanon. During investigations it became clear that high-ranking officials in the National Security Council, an agency that advises the president, had covertly moved money from the Iranian arms deals to aid the U.S.-supported insurrectionists against the (Marxist) Sandinista government in Nicaragua. While others resigned or were prosecuted for their involvement, Reagan himself was left relatively unscathed by the scandal.

Reagan's foreign affairs policies may be the legacy which will stand the test of time. During Reagan's tenure he pushed for the largest peacetime military buildup in American history. In 1983 he unveiled a proposal for the Strategic Defense Initiative. His strong military build up lead to the 1988 summit meeting with Soviet leader Mikhail S. Gorbachev where they signed the Intermediate-Range Nuclear Forces Treaty (INF Treaty) limiting the use of intermediate-range nuclear weapons. Arguably, this marked the beginning of the end of communist Russia. Many credit Reagan's policies with the end of communism in Europe and its reduction as a political alternative in much of the world.

Ronald Reagan retired to Santa Monica, California, with his second wife Nancy Davis Reagan (born Anne Frances Robbins). His last public act was to have President William Clinton inform the country of his Alzheimer's Disease.

***See also:* Laissez Faire, Supply-Side Economics**

FURTHER READING

Carter, Hodding. *The Reagan Years*. New York: G. Braziller, 1988.

D'Souza, Dinesh. *Ronald Reagan: How an Ordinary Man Became an Extraordinary Leader*. New York: Free Press, 1997.

Morris, Edmund. *Dutch: A Memoir of Ronald Reagan*. New York: Random House, 1999.

Reagan, Michael. *The City on a Hill: Fulfilling Ronald Reagan's Vision for America*. Nashville: Thomas Nelson Publishers, 1997.

Reagan, Ronald. *The Common Sense of an Uncommon Man: The Wit, Wisdom and Eternal Optimism of Ronald Reagan*. Nashville: Thomas Nelson, 1998.

REAGANOMICS

There was a story that circulated within the Washington Beltway during the 1980s that "Reaganomics" began as a doodle on a cocktail napkin as two economists employed by the Reagan administration sat whiling away happy hour in a Washington, D.C. cocktail lounge. The story may or may not be true, but at least it has the ring of truth. The term ''Reaganomics'' was derived from the name of its best-known supporter, fortieth U.S. President Ronald Reagan (1981–1989). Reagan, however, did not originate the theory. Reaganomics, also called supply-side economics or trickle-down economics, is based on a thing called the ''Laffer Curve.''(It was the Laffer Curve that was supposed to be the subject of the doodle.) The economist Arthur B. Laffer is the true creator of the supply-side theory. He asserts that high marginal tax rates and government regulation of industries discourage private investment in areas that stimulate economic growth, and that if the taxes and the regulation go away, the additional capital available to the private sector will ''trickle down'' to the rest of the population. Supply-side theory gained popularity during the late 1970s, when tax rates were at an all-time high, inflation hovered around 15 percent, oil shortages brought high energy costs, foreign competition took profits from domestic operations, and the business community complained about confining government regulations.

The theories of Milton Friedman, the founder of monetarism and economic adviser to Reagan in the 1970s, also influenced Reagan's economic policies. Monetarism claims that the level and direction of spending on the federal budget is more important than the amount of the deficit, and that a stable monetary policy allows borrowing to finance an unbalanced budget.

RONALD REAGAN HIMSELF ONCE REMARKED THAT "THE BEST SIGN THAT OUR ECONOMIC PROGRAM IS WORKING IS THAT THEY DON'T CALL IT REAGANOMICS ANY MORE."

Although supply-side economics and monetarism are rival conservative theories, Reagan more or less combined the two when he administered a plan that relied on faith in free enterprise, not in government, as the basis for economic expansion. Reaganomics consisted of four main initiatives: (1) tax reductions that would encourage investment and production, (2) spending cuts that would reduce the size of government, (3) elimination of federal regulations that were constricting business growth, and (4) a stable monetary policy that would keep inflation under control.

In 1982 as a nation in recession witnessed tax cuts, defense weaponry buildup, and a reduction in services for school lunch programs, the *New York Times* named Ronald Reagan's economic agenda ''Reaganomics.'' By 1984 however, the economy had turned and inflation and unemployment dropped dramatically. The United States maintained an economic boom that lasted for the remainder of the Reagan administration.

The president's policies have continued to be an issue of critical debate. Supporters of Reaganomics claimed that by adopting supply-side economics, the Reagan administration conquered the inflation that plagued the economy during the 1970s and set the economy on the tracks of the longest peacetime economic recovery in U.S. history. Opponents of Reaganomics argue that huge tax cuts were simply a gift to Reagan's political constituency among the rich even though it brought a doubling of the federal deficit.

True to his agenda, Reagan brought some of the largest tax cuts in history. According to Reaganomics, lower taxes prompted corporations to invest, leading U.S. consumers to buy more. As the economy grew, thanks to increased consumer spending, they would indirectly raise government tax revenues. The trend would ''trickle down'' to benefit even the poorest U.S. citizens. An initial shock to these new policies led to a recession in the early 1980s, but by 1984 the economy began to surge, inflation leveled and unemployment dropped.

Still many experts believed that the middle class and the poor did not benefit from Reaganomics. It was widely reported that the share of income going to the wealthiest 20 percent of the nation's population nearly doubled during the Reagan era, while the share going to the remaining 80 percent fell to its lowest level since the mid-1940s. Yet almost everybody but the very poor were better-off.

Reaganomics also encouraged many industries to deregulate during the early 1980s. At first, deregulation led to greater competition and lower prices for consumers. Diminished government supervision, however, also brought about problems. By the mid-1980s, the savings and loan industry collapsed amidst fraud and mismanagement. In the airline industry, deregulation led to the failure of many airlines, while others were bought out by rival airlines; the ultimate outcome was less competition and higher ticket prices.

The Reagan era also produced a large increase in the federal budget deficit (the difference between money the government spends and the amount it earns through taxes and other sources). When Reagan's policies were put in effect in the early 1980s, tax cuts did stimulate the economy, but Federal spending continued to grow, because of the refusal of a Democratic

Congress to cut domestic spending as dramatically as Reagan wanted. There was also an increase in borrowed money to fund the creation of defense weaponry at the climax of the Cold War and.

Ronald Reagan served two terms as U.S. president. Reaganomics contributed to the creation of more than 20 million jobs and a $1 trillion federal deficit. Some economists say that Reagan's policies were ultimately a failure that should never be repeated, although others argue that Reagan's polices have been clearly vindicated over time by our increasingly prosperous society. Regardless of opinion, the effects of Reaganomics were felt well past the end of Reagan's terms of office. Ronald Reagan himself once remarked that ''the best sign that our economic program is working is that they don't call it Reaganomics any more.''

See also: **Milton Friedman, Alan Greenspan, Andrew Mellon, Monetary Theory, Ronald Reagan, Supply-Side Economics**

FURTHER READING

Bartley, Robert L. ''How Reaganomics Made the World Work.'' *National Review*, April 21, 1989.

Evans, Michael K. *The Truth About Supply-Side Economics*. New York: Basic Books, Inc., 1983.

Hage, David and Robert F. Black. ''The Repackaging of Reaganomics: Republican Tax Cuts Could Well Boost The Deficit.'' *U.S. News and World Report*, December 12, 1994.

Lekachman, Robert. *Greed is Not Enough: Reaganomics*. New York: Pantheon Books, 1982.

Lind, Michael. ''Reaganomics, RIP.'' *New Republic*, November 13, 1995.

Lowe, Carl. *Reaganomics: The New Federalism*. New York: H.W. Wilson Co., 1984.

''As the Reagan Era Ends-And Appraisal and An Appreciation.'' *Nations's Business*, December, 1988.

Rich, Thomas. ''The Magic of Reaganomics.'' *Newsweek*, December 26, 1988. 112:40-1.

Tarshis, Lauren. ''The Legacy of Reaganomics.'' *Scholastic Update*, March 6, 1992.

REAL WAGES

Real wages are wages adjusted for inflation, which reflect the actual purchasing power of goods and services. Suppose an individual was paid $10 per hour in 1997 and $11 per hour in 1998. This increase in the nominal wage rate, wage in current dollars, is $1 per hour. This represents a 10 percent raise. If the cost of goods and services also increased by 10 percent in the same time period, the purchasing power of an hour's wages or the real wage rate did not increase. The worker could buy the same amount of goods in 1998 for $11 that he bought for $10 in 1997. On the other hand, if the cost of goods and services did not increase, the workers' purchasing power or real wage rate would have increased by 10 percent. An hour of work in 1998 then buys 10 percent more than an hour's work in 1997.

Workers are more concerned with their real wages than with their nominal or money wages. To calculate the real wage rate the nominal wage rate is divided by a price index. The price index used might be the consumer price index or the gross domestic product (GDP). Using the above example, say the price index rose 5 percent between 1997 and 1998. Using 1997 as the base year the price index would be 1.00 in 1997 and 1.05 in 1998. The real wage rate is W divided by P, where W is the nominal wage rate and P is price index. In 1997 $10 divided by 1 is $10, so the real wage rate is $10. In 1998 $11 divided by 1.05 is $10.48, so the real wage is $10.48. These calculations demonstrate adjustments for inflation yielding the real wage rate in constant dollars. Research indicates that the higher the real wage rates the larger the labor supply, house wealth, and consumption of goods and services. Economic indicators tied to consumption expenditures will be positive.

In the United States real wages in manufacturing doubled between 1910 and 1940, only to double again between 1940 and 1970. Although nominal wages rose steadily, beginning in 1973 real wages for manufacturing non-supervisory workers began a downward trend that continued into the 1990s.

REBATES

Rebates are an extension of the coupon promotion. Also known as refunds, rebates reimburse a customer for part of the purchase price of an item after the sale. They differ from coupons in that coupons offer a discount in price at the time of sale. Rebates developed after the broad success of coupons in the latter half of the twentieth century.

The word ''rebate'' is derived from the Middle English word *rebaten*, which means ''to deduct.'' The rebate is an attractive marketing tool to consumers because its offer of partial reimbursement for a purchase is tax-free. The Internal Revenue Service considers rebates a reduction in the price paid for a product and not as income.

How do consumers learn about rebates? Manufacturers typically offer a rebate to all purchasers of a product for a limited time offer. At the time of purchase, the consumer receives a form, which must be completed and mailed with proper proof of purchase to a specified address. This address usually belongs to a large clearinghouse that processes rebate claims, not the manufacturer. The clearinghouse processes the rebate and issues a check in the name of the manufacturer.

Who offers rebates? A wide range of businesses offer rebates to consumers who purchase their products. Rebates may be offered for household appliances, like a refrigerator, for auto parts, and for health and beauty products, among others. The amount of money offered in a rebate varies from product to product and manufacturer to manufacturer.

During the twentieth century, the enticement of the rebate has played an appealing role in wooing customers in a competitive marketplace.

RECESSION

A recession is a downturn in the business cycle that occurs when the real gross national product (GNP)—the total output of goods and services produced by the U.S. population—declines for two consecutive quarters, or six months. Recessions are usually characterized by a general decrease in output, income, employment, and trade lasting from six months to a year. A more severe and long-lasting economic crisis is known as a depression.

Virtually all advanced world economies that are not controlled centrally have experienced recurring cycles of slump and recovery in business activity since the Industrial Revolution. The United States suffered through four severe depressions in the 1800s, as well as the Great Depression in the 1930s. These crises cost a great deal in terms of national wealth and personal hardship. Since then, however, sophisticated analysis of economic trends has combined with increased government intervention to prevent such extreme fluctuations in economic activity. In fact, no depressions have occurred in industrialized nations since World War II (1939–1945), although there have been many recessions. Governments monitor the business cycle closely and take various steps to stabilize the economy before it reaches extreme peaks and troughs. Formerly, the typical stages in the business cycle were depression, recovery, prosperity, and recession. Today, the phases are usually defined using the more moderate terms, upswing, peak, recession, and trough.

See also: **Business Cycle, Gross National Product**

RECONSTRUCTION

Reconstruction (1865–1877) was one of our most controversial political eras. It followed the American Civil War (1861–1865), the bloodiest war in U.S. history, and saw the South's transformation from a slave to a free society. The U.S. government had to decide how to reintegrate the Confederate states into the union and how to assimilate almost four million freed slaves into the war-torn and hostile society of the South. Its economy was in shambles at the end of the Civil War, with manufacturing and transportation systems in disarray, banks insolvent, and Confederate currency worthless. The agricultural labor pool of slaves, who represented the most valuable asset that the South had possessed prior to the war—more valuable even than all the land in the South, was no longer legally available and the planters had little on-hand cash to pay wages. The freed slaves faced destitution.

President Abraham Lincoln (1861–1865) was anxious to get the Confederate states back into the union. As early as December 1863 he had issued a ''Proclamation of Amnesty and Reconstruction'' which detailed a lenient approach that he felt would receive wide acceptance in the South and hasten reunion of the eleven Confederate states. Prompted by considerations of how to smooth over the process of reunification of the nation, as well as by long-term political considerations for himself and the newly founded Republican Party, Lincoln's Reconstruction plan was called the ''10 percent plan.'' Only ten percent of a state's electorate who had voted in 1860 had to take an oath of allegiance to the United States before its citizens could be granted pardons, their property restored, and their state governments recognized. Lincoln's plan did not include much in the way of provisions for post-war recovery of the South or safe-guards to protect the newly freed slaves from their former masters.

In July of 1864 Congress adopted a compromise Reconstruction plan which increased the requirements for reentry of the Southern states into the Union. Lincoln, however, vetoed this Wade-Davis bill, which proposed raising the 10 percent voter oath requirement to 50 percent and limiting participation of former Southern leaders in state constitutional conventions.

Realizing that few safeguards existed to protect the new found liberty of former slaves, Congress also established the Freedmen's Bureau in 1865 to help feed, protect, and educate them.

Fearing that rebel leaders would regain control of the South, some "Radical Republicans" in Congress (Congressmen who advocated strong measures against the former Confederacy) sought to grant voting rights to former slaves and even spoke of confiscating the wealthy Southern planters' property. A precedent existed for this land reform idea: in a few cases during the war union troops had allowed former slaves to occupy and farm the plantations of rebel planters, including the President of the Confederacy, Jefferson Davis. A rumor arose among the former slaves that the federal government was going to redistribute the land and give each slave family "forty acres and a mule."

But after the surrender of the southern armies and in the wake of the uncertainty that accompanied Lincoln's assassination in April 1865, a dispute arose between Lincoln's successor, former Vice President Andrew Johnson, and the Radical Republicans in Congress. Johnson, a small farmer and slave owner from Tennessee, believed blacks were inferior and envisioned a South economically dominated by white farmers holding property redistributed from wealthy planter's land. He seemed to believe that a conspiracy existed between the large plantation owners and the slaves against the small white farmers. Johnson adopted contradictory policies—on the one hand formally declaring that the Confederate military leadership would be executed and that slave holders would be denied the vote, and on the other, pardoning an unending line of petitioners from the southern planter class who flattered him and received full exoneration.

IN THE END . . . THE VAST MAJORITY OF SOUTHERN BLACKS REMAINED PROPERTYLESS AND POOR. BUT EXACTLY WHY THE SOUTH, AND ESPECIALLY ITS BLACK POPULATION, SUFFERED FROM DIRE POVERTY AND ECONOMIC RETARDATION IN THE DECADES FOLLOWING THE CIVIL WAR IS A MATTER OF MUCH DISPUTE.

Eric Foner, *American Heritage*, October/November 1983

During this period of confusion, the southern political elite adopted make-shift constitutions that abolished slavery and elected the surviving members of the pre-war political elite to Congress. At the same time, however, in their own state legislatures the former planter aristocracy was passing "black codes" that re-subjugated the former slaves to conditions that approximated slavery. Ex-slaves could were restricted to farming jobs, they could be rounded up, charged with vagrancy, and put to work without compensation. They had to carry passes. They lived under curfew laws. Major race riots instigated by whites broke out in 1866 in Memphis and New Orleans with blacks receiving little protection from local law authorities. As these conditions became known in the first months after the southern surrender, the Radical Republicans successfully led a movement to exclude the southern congressmen who were being elected and sent to serve in Congress. A prolonged struggle erupted between the executive and legislative branches of the federal government pitting the president and his conservative program of restoring pre-Civil War conditions in the South against the Radical demands for extensive social and political change in the South.

Angered by the South's persistent and violent resistance to restructuring and disappointed with Johnson's views, Congress adopted a Radical Reconstruction strategy. First, over Johnson's veto, Congress passed the Civil Rights Act of 1866 which recognized blacks as citizens and guaranteed equal protection under the law. Congress included the Act's key provisions in the Fourteenth Amendment, which was approved in 1866 despite rejection by most Southern states. The amendment granted citizenship to all persons born or naturalized in the United States and directed that states could not deprive citizens of due process of law and equal protection of the laws. Next came the Reconstruction Acts between 1866 and 1868, also over Johnson's veto. The acts firmly established military control over the South with the eleven Southern states divided into five military districts. State governments that were recognized under Lincoln and Johnson were thrown out and the black codes eliminated. A Major General controlled each district by holding extensive authority over state officials. Between 1868 and 1870 all states were readmitted to the Union with new governments that were controlled by blacks, carpetbaggers (Northerners who came to the South to carry out Reconstruction programs), and scalawags (Southern collaborators). Though violence temporarily ceased and a number of postwar recovery measures were instituted (including a lasting public school system for both races), most Southerners viewed the governments as artificially contrived.

In 1870 the Fifteenth Amendment prohibited states from restricting voting rights on the basis of race. Congress followed with a series of enforcement acts until 1871. However, Northern support for Reconstruction measures began to fade in the 1870s as a national economic recession captured attention. President Rutherford B. Hayes (1877–1881) withdrew the last federal troops in 1877 and Southern states once again assumed full control. Racism flourished. State Jim Crow laws established a racial caste system in the South during the last years of the nineteenth century. Some historians attributed the failure of Reconstruction to the failure to redistribute southern lands to poor farmers, both black and white. In any case, a new labor system involving sharecropping and crop liens replaced slavery. Black families farmed assigned portions of plantations in return for a share of the crop and necessary food and supplies. The new system, in which the new Southern ruling class of planters and merchants were subservient to Northern financiers, did not reestablish the prosperity seen before the war.

See also: **Civil War (Economic Impact of), Confederate Dollar, Fourteenth Amendment, Freedman's Bureau, Jim Crow Laws, Sharecropping**

FURTHER READING

Belz, Herman. *Abraham Lincoln, Constitutionalism, and Equal Rights in the Civil War Era.* New York: Fordham University Press, 1998.

Franklin, John Hope. *Reconstruction After the Civil War.* Chicago: University of Chicago Press, 1994.

Harris, William C. *With Charity for All: Lincoln and the Restoration of the Union.* Lexington, KY: University Press of Kentucky, 1997.

Kennedy, Stetson. *After Appomattox: How the South Won the War.* Gainesville, FL: University Press of Florida, 1995.

Schmidt, James D. *Free to Work: Labor Law, Emancipation, and Reconstruction, 1815–1880.* Athens, GA: University of Georgia Press, 1998.

Simpson, Brooks D. *The Reconstruction Presidents.* Lawrence, KS: University Press of Kansas, 1998.

RECONSTRUCTION FINANCE CORP.

The Reconstruction Finance Corp. (RFC) was a U.S. government agency established by Congress on January 27, 1932, to provide financial aid to railroads, financial institutions, and business corporations during the Great Depression (1929–1939). In July 1932, with the passage of the Emergency Relief Act (ERA), the scope of the RFC was enlarged to include aid to agriculture and farms, and financing for state and local public employment works. The RFC, acting as a domestic federal bank, contributed greatly in the recovery effort to climb out of the Depression. During World War II (1939–1945), the RFC was expanded greatly to finance the construction and operation of war plants and to make loans to foreign governments.

The RFC was intended to be an independent, nonpolitical agency. As years passed, RFC funding grew. It began to assume the responsibility for disbursing huge sums of money, and began to become involved in politics. By 1948 congressional investigations of the RFC revealed widespread corruption; in 1952 it was reorganized. As a result of Eisenhower's efforts to limit government involvement in the economy, the RFC was dismantled under President Dwight D. Eisenhower (1953–1961). The RFC Liquidation Act terminated all of its lending powers. By 1957 its remaining functions had been transferred to other agencies.

The RFC was a useful agency during the Great Depression and World War II, as well as during post-World War II recovery in the United States, but by the late 1940s the RFC had outlived its financial stabilization function.

See also: **Great Depression**

RECYCLING PROGRAMS

Recycling programs comprise three elements in a continuum represented by the "chasing arrows" symbol: collection of recyclable materials from the waste stream, processing the commodities into new products, and purchasing products containing recycled materials. It has been estimated that each office worker in America produces from one-half to one and one-half pounds of solid waste each day, of which 70 to 90 percent is paper. Paper comprises at least 40 percent of American waste, and businesses contribute one-third of the nation's solid waste, For that reason, recycling programs in the business world commonly focus on waste paper. However, corporate recycling programs have come to include other types of waste, including glass, chemicals, oils, plastics, and metals.

Although the word "recycle" was not coined until the late 1960s, recycling has been a trash disposal option for centuries. Native Americans and early settlers routinely reused resources and avoided waste. Materials recovery was also a significant contributor to the United States' World War II effort, when businesses and citizens alike salvaged metal, paper, rubber, and other scarce commodities for military use. But the emergence of the "throwaway society" of the 1950s helped extinguish the recycling impetus. With seemingly unlimited landfill space, disposable and single-use products and packaging became the norm in the ensuing decades. Recycling did not regain popularity until the late 1960s and early 1970s, when environmental concerns became prominent in the "green revolution." The first national Earth Day celebration in 1970 heralded anti-litter campaigns, the creation of the Federal Environmental Protection Agency (EPA), and some municipal and corporate recycling programs.

See also: **Environmentalism**

REGRESSIVE TAX

A tax is a compulsory payment imposed by a government for public purposes. There are two major forms of tax assessment; direct taxes, which are imposed on an individual directly, and indirect taxes, which are imposed on a privilege or right which a person exercises. For example, the right to buy or sell real estate involves estate and inheritance taxes, or the right to make gifts of property involves gift taxes. In general, all taxes may be classified as proportional, imposing proportional rates on all incomes or property values, whether large or small; progressive, where taxes are graduated to impose the highest rates on the highest incomes, based on ability to pay; and the regressive tax, which that takes a smaller percentage from higher income individuals than from lower income individuals.

A regressive tax is a tax that is graduated so as to impose the highest rates on the lowest incomes and property value. For instance, overall, Social Security is a regressive tax because there is a maximum income limit beyond which no further taxes are paid. Therefore, very wealthy individuals pay a lower percentage of their total income to Social Security than do lower income individuals. Throughout the U.S. tax code there are many examples of regressive taxes, despite efforts to use more proportional or progressive taxes to create a fairer system.

See also: **Progressive Tax, Proportional Tax**

REGULATION

The regulation of industries in the United States is based largely on a concern for the public interest. Industries, especially those with a high potential for monopoly (such as water, gas, and telephone service), will often be regulated by agencies of government for the benefit of the public, so that consumers can be assured of quality services and products at reasonable rates. The rationale for the regulation of all or part of an industry is that if a monopoly exists, and competition is inappropriate, then monopolies should be regulated to avoid possible abuses of uncontrolled monopoly power. Regulation is a public sector (government) guarantee that consumers should benefit from the built-in economies of any monopoly. Regulators seek to establish customer rates that cover production costs and yield a "fair" or "reasonable" return to the enterprise.

There are problems associated with the regulation of business by the public sector. First, a regulated firm may resort to accounting manipulation to overstate its costs to obtain higher unjustified profits. Second, some regulatory commissions of the government function inadequately, sometimes even making "deals" with the industries they are regulating. Third, it is often uncertain which industries should be regulated. The trucking and airline industries both claim that if they were less regulated, they would be more competitive. In addition to the regulation of near monopoly industries and natural monopolies (like water and electricity), since the early 1960s, the public sector also regulates the conditions under which goods and services are produced, as well as the impact of production on society, and the physical quality of goods. This kind of social regulation is applied across the board to virtually all industries. Examples of social regulation includes the efforts of the Occupational Safety and Health Administration (OSHA), which regulates industries to protect workers against occupational injuries and illnesses, and the efforts of the Consumer Products Safety Commission (CPSC) which regulates minimum standards for potentially unsafe products. Though regulation itself can be controversial, few question whether it should exist. The primary question that any public sector regulation imposes is how and when it should be used.

See also: **Monopolies, Monopoly**

REINFORCED CONCRETE

Reinforced concrete is a composite building material that consists of concrete (a mix of cement, aggregates, and water that when hardened resembles stone) and steel rods, bars, or mesh. The material possesses the best qualities of concrete, which is able to withstand compressive (latitudinal) forces, and iron, which is able to withstand tensile (longitudinal) forces. Reinforced concrete was patented in 1867 by French gardener Joseph Monier (1823–1906), who used iron to strengthen concrete for tubs for his nursery. During the second half of the nineteenth century the material was used in the construction of bridges and buildings. In the early twentieth century concrete reinforced with steel came into widespread use. In the United States, the first building made entirely of reinforced concrete was the William E. Ward House, built in 1876, in Port Chester, New York. In 1903 Cincinnati's sixteen-story Ingalls Building (called the Transit Building after 1959) became the world's first skyscraper with a reinforced concrete framework. The success of the building project revolutionized the construction industry. Skyscrapers—many of steel-cage construction, but others built with reinforced concrete—transformed the appearance of the American city and were the country's contribution to twentieth century architecture.

Reinforced concrete was predominately used in the construction of factories. In the early 1900s, German-American architect Albert Kahn (1869–1942) expanded the Packard Motor Company plant in Detroit, Michigan, designing what became a series of factories using reinforced concrete and steel. Kahn's innovative designs enclosed large spaces, often all on one floor and with ample windows for natural lighting, ideal for manufacturing operations.

REPORT ON MANUFACTURES

In 1791 Alexander Hamilton (1755–1804), the first U.S. Secretary of the Treasury, submitted the third of three historic reports he had written which outlined a national fiscal (monetary) and economic system. The first two reports had been the Report on Public Credit (presented to Congress January 1790) and the Report on a National Bank (December 1790). On December 5, 1791, Hamilton presented the Report on Manufactures to Congress. The report outlined a plan for stimulating trade in the new republic and listed 17 viable industries that should be pursued by private citizens and encouraged by the federal government. As the leader of the Federalist Party, Hamilton advocated a strong central government. His party's position opposed that of Thomas Jefferson's (1743–1826) Democratic-Republicans, who favored a strict adherence to the U.S. Constitution (1788); the report, therefore, stressed the protection of personal liberties by a limited federal government.

In his Report on Manufactures, Hamilton argued that Congress should adopt certain measures that would help move the nation's economy away from its dependency on agriculture (which required importing most finished goods from other countries) and toward an economy that was diverse and balanced. To support the development of American industry, Hamilton advocated charging duties on or prohibiting the import of rival products. Domestic manufactured goods, however, would be exempted from export duties and new inventions would be encouraged, "particularly those which relate to machinery." Hamilton maintained that by enlarging the nation's manufacturing sector the United States would achieve true independence by decreasing its reliance on other nations for military and essential supplies. Further, he foresaw the tremendous growth in population that would occur in the nineteenth century as more and more European immigrants arrived in American ports to make their homes in the new nation. Believing the only way to support a burgeoning population was to diversify the economy, Hamilton asserted that the government ought to promote manufacturing.

Hamilton's vision of the nation's future (which turned out to be highly accurate) and his recommendations for developing and stimulating the economy were not well received in Congress. Many felt the Secretary of the Treasury was promoting his own personal interests at the expense of agriculture. His plan was never put to a vote.

See also: **Alexander Hamilton, Thomas Jefferson**

RESEARCH AND DEVELOPMENT

Research and development (R&D) is the process by which scientific and technological breakthroughs are used to create new or improved products or technologies. R&D generally involves three basic processes. The first is "basic" or "pure" research, which is the kind of exploration scientists and other researchers perform when they are motivated not by a specific goal or end product but by the desire to advance scientific knowledge wherever it leads. "Applied research" is research that takes the findings of basic research and modifies or elaborates them for a specific purpose. Finally, "development" is the process by which the insights of basic and applied research are transformed into an actual product or new process. For example, basic research into the properties of light and silica-based materials might be applied toward developing fiber optics, which in turn might be developed into fiber-optic cables for carrying digital data. Basic and applied research is conducted in government, academic, and industrial research laboratories, and today most product development is performed in company-run development laboratories.

The first U.S. industrial laboratories were modest affairs set up in the 1860s and 1870s by companies like Cambria Iron Co. and the Pennsylvania Railroad. In the 1870s Thomas Edison's (1847–1931) Edison Electric Light Company became the first company to devote a substantial portion of its revenues to industrial laboratory research. In the years before World War I (1914–1918) such companies as General Electric, AT&T, Standard Oil, and Eastman Kodak also established R&D labs. World War I opened the eyes of many Western governments to the need for industrial research, a process that was hastened by the requirement for new technologies to fight World War II (1939–1945). After 1945 the United States was the preeminent technological power, and the federal government's R&D spending in the 1950s and 1960s was used by government, academic, and industrial laboratories to fuel an explosion of new electronics, computer, aeronautical, defense, and space technologies.

When the U.S. government cut back on R&D funding at the end of the Cold War in the early 1990s, private industry filled the gap. By 1997, for example, total R&D investments reached an all-time high of more than $200 billion, two-thirds of which was conducted by private industry. The primary factors for this intensified industrial R&D were advances in biotechnology, electronics, and software; global competition; and years of strong profit growth. By 1996, 25 U.S. firms—led by General Motors, Ford Motor Company, and IBM—were spending more than $1 billion annually on R&D.

RETAIL INDUSTRY

The major trend in the history of the retail industry has been the transfer of sales from individual, independent, single-product merchants to chain stores, department stores, supermarkets, malls, and catalogs. (The chain store actually dates back as early as 700 B.C. in China.) Modern retailing began in the United States in 1859, when The Great Atlantic and Pacific Tea Company (A&P) became the first chain store in the country, selling tea in New York City. Soon afterward department stores and catalog stores appeared, the latter making use of the first direct mail lists to reach customers in rural areas. By the early 1900s the beginnings of retail industry in the United States were well established.

The A&P tea emporiums were typical of early food stores which specialized in one type of item. A&P purchased tea in New York dockyards and sold it at substantially lower prices (50 percent) than competitors. A&P was sophisticated in promoting its single product. Their tea emporiums were unlike the typical general store of the nineteenth century, for they tried to create the atmosphere of an oriental palace, evoking the Asian origins of their product. A&P also brought a new concept into food trade when it assigned brand names to bulk teas. It popularized these teas even further by organizing tea clubs in various cities. Tea club members received special discount rates on A&P products. The stores also printed colorful advertising pamphlets listing tea prices and delivery dates along with literary flourishes like poetry and essays. A&P offered money-back guarantees and it advertised in big national publications like *Harper's Weekly* as well as smaller religious publications, hoping to win the teetotaler market. When coffee became popular in the 1880s, A&P offered its own brand, Eight O'Clock breakfast coffee, which was sold in signature red bags. Though A&P would eventually expand into a chain of supermarkets, its tea emporium beginnings contributed much to the basic understanding of how a successful chain store should promote itself and its product.

During the same period early versions of department stores (Woolworths, 1879) and catalog retail stores (Sears, Roebuck & Company, and Montgomery Ward and Company, in the late 1800s) radically changed the look of sales for non-food products. These stores became institutions virtually synonymous with U.S. culture. Woolworths had great success with over 1,000 stores only 40 years after its founding. Sears, Roebuck & Company and Montgomery Ward grew to be the largest catalog retailers in the world. They began by selling only by mail order and they thus helped people in more rural areas keep up with home improvements.

The catalog sales were no doubt helped by direct mailing lists, which appeared as early as 1903. Multi-Mailing Company of New York gathered lists from phone books around the region—from New England to Ohio—with a total of 600,000 names. This was valuable information because farmers in rural areas installed their own telephone lines which were used by entire communities with as many as 100 people serviced by one line. Companies like Multi-Mailing sought out these telephone-line owners, believing that the rural telephone system identified prominent community members who held influence over their fellow villagers.

Around 1900 retailers owned either small general stores or grand downtown department stores. By World War I (1914–1918) the department stores were prominent. In the 1920s Sears, Roebuck & Company and Montgomery Ward opted to add retail stores to their catalog operations. As the number of stores spread, reaching even the more rural areas that had come to rely on catalog shopping, people increasingly opted to shop in the department stores themselves. A century after their beginnings, Sears and Montgomery Ward earned over three-fourths of their profits in their retail stores.

In the 1930s supermarkets appeared, imitating the department stores by offering the customer one-stop shopping. They quickly dampened business for individual merchants or single-item shops like A&P's tea emporiums. It was far easier to go to one place and pay once, than to make individual trips to the butcher, various produce stands, the bakery, and dry goods store. In 1930 the King Kullen supermarket was founded in New York City. Boasting that it was the first U.S. supermarket (a claim viewed skeptically by some industry historians), it was nevertheless a pioneer in that type of store. Its decision to outsource, or hire out, warehouse work led to a three-month labor strike. But the company maintained that the outsourcing decision was good because it allowed King Kullen to be more competitive by opening more new stores and by selling more products. In the years after World War II (1939–1945), the supermarket growth rate had peaked and small independent food retailers were driven out of business by tens of thousands of newly-opened supermarkets. Many remaining independent, individual, or small-chain retailers survived by pulling together into retail cooperatives.

For two decades after World War II, discount warehouses were the new trend in retail. These companies offered substantial discounts and they often managed to sell below manufacturer listed prices. Products were pushed out in high numbers with little overhead cost. This was possible because the stores greatly reduced services, and because they were usually located in the unfashionable shopping districts, which meant that they paid low rent for their retail space. These stores focused particularly on household electrical appliances. Later, the concept changed for discount stores—they became scaled-down department stores with lower prices and minimal services.

In the later part of the twentieth century the retail industry continued to experiment with new ways of reaching customers. Catalogs experienced a revival, especially for smaller companies that focused on a single product line with limited appeal such as Victoria's Secret's lingerie catalogs or Crate & Barrel's household items. These new-look catalogs were sized like magazines and introduced with high-quality design and paper. Other trends in the same period included shopping via television (viewing products on the screen and then purchasing over the phone with a credit card) and shopping over the Internet.

The retail industry grew up with the grandchildren of the Industrial Revolution, whose lives were increasingly complicated by work schedules and the urban pace, and who sought as much convenience as could be found in all aspects of living. This, and the highly competitive race for the biggest share of the market, pushed retailers to be ever more creative in finding ways to reach customers and dazzle them with store interiors, new products, or shockingly low prices. It made economic sense to put as much as possible under one roof because the customers seemed to want it and overhead costs were greatly minimized in relation to profit. But the retail giants—supermarkets, department stores, and malls alike—were not entirely invulnerable to the whims of the market, as seen in 1998, when the last of the once-mammoth Woolworth empire of general stores was slated to be closed.

See also: **Chain Stores, Department Stores, Mail Order House, Montgomery Ward and Company, Richard Warren Sears, Sears Roebuck and Company**

FURTHER READING

''A&P Homepage,'' [cited April 14, 1999] available from the World Wide Web @ www.aptea.com/.

Benson, John and Gareth Shaw, eds. *The Retailing Industry*. MA: IB Taurus & Co., Ltd., 1999.

Schultz, Ray. ''History Lesson.'' *Direct*, February 1998.

''Sears: About Our Company,'' [cited April 14, 1999] available from the World Wide Web @ www.sears.com/company/pubaff/history1.htm/.

Wholesale and Retail Trade USA: Industry Analyses, Statistics, and Leading Companies. Detroit: The Gale Group, 1998.

REVENUE

Revenue is a term commonly used in business. A company's revenue is all of the money it takes in as a result of its operations. Another way of defining a company's revenue is as a monetary measure of outputs, or goods sold and services rendered, with expense being a monetary measure of inputs or resources used in the production of goods or services. On the other hand, a company's net income or profit is determined by subtracting its expenses from its revenues. Thus, revenues are the opposite of expenses, and income equals revenues minus expenses.

For accounting purposes, income is distinguished from revenues. Income is an important concept in economics as well as accounting. Accountants prepare an income statement to measure a company's income for a given accounting period. Economists are concerned with measuring and defining such concepts as national income, personal income, disposable personal income, and money income versus real income. In each field the concept of income is defined in slightly different terms.

An example of revenue is when a store sells $300 worth of merchandise, for which it originally paid $200. In this example the company's revenue is $300, its expense is $200, and its net income or profit is $100. Other expenses that are typically deducted from sales or revenues include salaries, rent, utilities, depreciation, and interest expense.

See also: **Income**

REVERE, PAUL

Paul Revere (1735–1818) is best known as an American patriot during the American Revolution (1775–1783). He is the man who helped carry news of the approach of British troops to Lexington, Massachusetts, in what became known as Paul Revere's midnight ride. When Revere wasn't fighting for American independence, he was a creative and successful silversmith.

Paul Revere was born January 1, 1735 in Boston, Massachusetts. He was the third of twelve children born to Apollos De Revoire, a Frenchman. De Revoire changed the family name to Revere to make it easier for Americans to pronounce. Apollos De Revoire was a silversmith and he taught the trade to his son.

Paul Revere married Sarah Orne in 1756 after serving for a short time in the French and Indian War (1754–1763). At age twenty-one he began work in his father's silversmith business. Revere was a talented silversmith and an innovator in processing commercial-grade bronze and copper. His skills made him a success in his trade.

In his early years as a silversmith Revere developed an intense interest in the issue of American independence from England. He became involved in revolutionary activities and attracted wide public attention when he used his engraving skills to create a number of political cartoons aimed at the issue of independence.

> Listen my children and you shall hear / Of the midnight ride of Paul Revere, / On the eighteenth of April, in Seventy-five; / Hardly a man is now alive / Who remembers that famous day and year. / He said to his friend, "If the British march / By land or sea from the town to-night, / Hang a lantern aloft in the belfry arch / Of the North Church tower as a signal light,— / One if by land, and two if by sea; / And I on the opposite shore will be, Ready to ride and spread the alarm / Through every Middlesex village and farm, / For the country folk to be up and to arm."
>
> **Henry Wadsworth Longfellow, *Paul Revere's Ride***

Revere began to work closely with revolutionary leaders, such as Samuel Adams (1722–1803) and John Hancock (1737–1793). He also participated in the famous Boston Tea Party on December 16, 1773. He and other Boston protestors raided a British ship in Boston harbor and dumped the tea cargo into the ocean, dissenting against British taxes in the colonies. This protest was one of the crucial events leading up to the American Revolution (1775–1783).

In addition to his activities as a revolutionary, Revere directed his energies to a variety of areas. He pursued work on a wide-ranging field, from working with silver to the manufacture of gunpowder. In Massachusetts he created a mill that ground wheat and oats by using the swirling flow of river water to move grindstones. He designed and printed the first issue of U.S. paper money and was the first in the United States to discover the process of rolling sheet copper. In Canton, Massachusetts, he built the first copper-rolling mill in the country.

Revere was continually involved in the politics of his new nation. He served as an activist, a soldier, and a political thinker. He achieved great success as a silversmith and expanded his business efforts towards growing U.S. industries. Paul Revere was an entrepreneur and a patriot. He died in 1818.

See also: **American Revolution, Boston Massacre, Boston Tea Party**

FURTHER READING

American Antiquarian Society. *Paul Revere's Engravings, by Clarence S. Brigham.* Worcester: American Antiquarian Society, 1954.

Paul Revere on his famous ride.

Encyclopedia of American Biography. 2nd ed. New York: HarperCollins, 1996, s.v. ''Paul Revere.''

Forbes, Esther. *Paul Revere and the World He Lived In*. (1942; reprint), Peter Smith, 1992.

Goss, Elbridge Henry. *The Life of Colonel Paul Revere*. Boston: Gregg Press, 1972.

Taylor, Emerson G. *Paul Revere, by Emerson Taylor*. New York: E.V. Mitchell and Dodd, Mead & Co., 1930.

RHODE ISLAND

Rhode Island, the smallest state of the United States, has struggled to maintain its economic health. Born as a colony of dissenters and a haven for individual liberty, the state has not always matched its idealistic beginnings with its political and economic realities. It has experienced divisions between its old-line citizenry and the descendants of the immigrants who have staffed its factories. It reached an economic peak around the turn of the century but it has since fought competition from southern industries and has gone through periods of depression and recession. In the latter half of the twentieth century, however, Rhode Island achieved a significant economic recovery.

In 1524 the first European explorer of Rhode Island to arrive in the region was Italian Giovanni da Verrazano. In 1636 English clergyman Roger Williams established a colony at Providence seeking religious freedom for a group of nonconformists from the Massachusetts Bay Colony. As other towns developed in the area, Williams secured a charter from King Charles II for Rhode Island and Providence Plantations (which encompassed several towns), that guaranteed religious freedom and substantial local autonomy.

Rhode Island grew rapidly in agriculture and commerce, which included the slave trade. Its exports included naval stores, molasses, preserved meats, cider, and dairy products. Rhode Island was also a whaling center. As the colony with the highest degree of self-rule, Rhode Island was the first to declare its independence from England in 1776. Fearing too much federal power, however, it was the last state to ratify the U.S. Constitution (1790).

Rhode Island merchant ships in the early nineteenth century traded with China, India, the Baltics, and the East Indies, and later with the U.S. Pacific coast. The mid-nineteenth century in the state was marked by divisions between ordinary citizens and wealthy rural landowners who held nearly all the power in the legislature and who were the only ones allowed to vote. By 1843 a new constitution was formed which corrected some of the inequalities.

Meanwhile, the economy of the state had shifted from commerce to industry, with textile manufacturing as the most prominent. Samuel Slater established the first cotton mill in Pawtucket in 1790. Under the so-called ''Rhode Island System,'' company-built housing was established for the workers and their families. Oftentimes mill owners employed entire families that worked from sunup to sundown. Between 1830 and 1840 the number of mills in the state almost doubled. After 1830 steam power replaced water power in the mills and also provided the power for steamboats and newly emerging railroads.

Other products were being manufactured such as jewelry (represented best by Gorham Silver) and steam engines. By 1860 less than an estimated three percent of the state's workforce was in the maritime industry; 10 percent were employed in agriculture, and 50 percent in manufacturing. Between 1776 and 1860 Rhode Island's population had increased two and one-half times, mostly through foreign immigration.

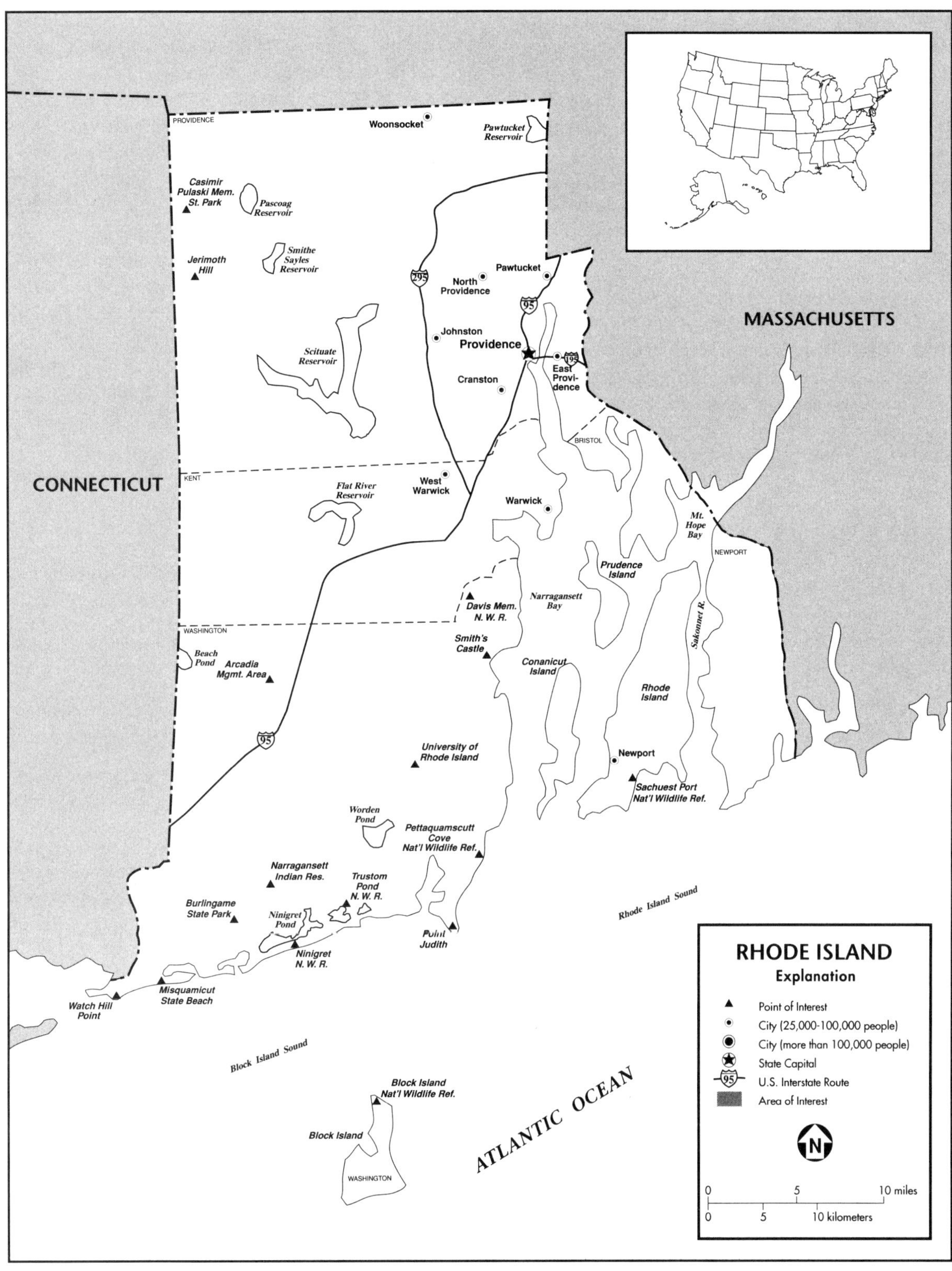

State of Rhode Island.

The port of Providence soon became the center for commerce in the region. With three rivers at the head of Narragansett Bay and a growing number of railroad termini, Providence boasted a large number of textile mills. It was also home to the metals industry, the banking and insurance sector, and the import-export business. Providence began to lose some of its prominence after 1845 when steamships found a more suitable port at Fall River, Massachusetts, and rail connections began to gravitate toward New York City.

As several southern states began seceding from the Union just before the American Civil War (1861–1865), Rhode Island still had some sympathies with the South because of its economic relationship with southern cotton planters. A slave-free state since 1807, Rhode Island even temporarily repealed its ''personal liberty law'' to make it easier for runaway slaves to be returned to their owners. Still, when the Union called for volunteers against the Confederacy, Rhode Island responded, exceeding its quota for troops. The state made great profits in the textile and other industries during the war. After the war, the town of Newport became a haven for newly rich Americans who built large mansions on its rocky shores Many of which still survive as tourist attractions.

According to historian William G. McLoughlin the decades following the war were Rhode Island's finest: ''Its manufacturers hobnobbed with the rich and powerful who controlled the nation. . . . (It) had reached the pinnacle of success. . . .'' Foremost among the rich and powerful people was Nelson W. Aldrich (whose daughter later married into the Rockefeller family) who, as a senator, controlled tariff schedules in the U.S. Congress. As chairman of the Finance Committee he was in a position to help protect businessmen against foreign competition and to encourage sound money policies. He also was instrumental in devising the Federal Reserve System.

The economic system in Rhode Island changed rapidly after World War I. French-Canadians, Irish, and Portuguese, encouraged to immigrate to provide cheap labor, began to outnumber people of the old Yankee stock. The state's industries continued to prosper and they were especially productive during World War I (1914–1918). After the war, however, decreased production caused labor unrest and a widespread strike of textile workers in 1922 crippled an industry that was already plagued by competition from textile mills in southern states. Bitter divisions in the state at this time, coupled with the onset of the Great Depression (1929–1939), helped to precipitate the 1934 Democratic overthrow of longtime Republican rule in the state.

Improvements in Rhode Island's economy have been slow in coming. Since the Depression years the state often had one of the highest rates of unemployment in the nation, reaching more than 15 percent by 1975. In the late 1990s about 30 percent of workers were still employed in manufacturing and many were working in low-paid jobs in the jewelry and textile industries. After a real estate boom in the 1980s the real estate market declined at the end of the decade. The state experienced a banking crisis in the early 1990s, which necessitated a government bailout of uninsured financial institutions. Rhode Island had slowly begun to recover from its economic doldrums, largely because of new jobs in the financial and electronic industries. Unemployment fell to around five percent by 1997.

See also: **Rhode Island System of Labor**

FURTHER READING

Conley, Patrick T. *Rhode Island Profile.* Providence: Rhode Island Publications Society, 1983.

James, Sydney V. *Colonial Rhode Island: A History.* White Plains, NY: Kraus International, 1975.

McLoughlin, William G. *Rhode Island: A Bicentennial History.* New York: Norton, 1978.

Rhode Island, Economic Research Division. *Rhode Island: Basic Economic Statistics 1982–1983.* Providence: Rhode Island, Department of Economic Development, Economic Research Division, 1983.

Steinberg, Sheila, and Cathleen McGuigan. *Rhode Island: An Historical Guide.* Providence: Rhode Island Bicentennial Commission, 1976.

RHODE ISLAND SYSTEM OF LABOR

The Rhode Island system of labor was initiated by English-born mechanist and businessman Samuel Slater (1768–1835), who built a water-powered cotton-spinning mill at Pawtucket, Rhode Island, in 1790. The machine, based on a mill invented by Englishman Richard Arkwright (1732–1792), was an immediate and unqualified success—introducing mechanization to manufacturing, which was previously done by hand. A few years after starting his mill, Slater began hiring whole families from the surrounding area, including children, to work the spinning machines. Child labor had long been used in Britain's textile factories and Slater himself had worked in them as a youth. In the Rhode Island mills, the families made up the workforce. Wages were low and the hours were long. But the Rhode Island system of labor worked, and by the 1820s it was firmly established in American industry. In 1832 an estimated 40 percent of all factory workers in New England were between the ages of seven and sixteen.

As the textiles industry grew, the supply of labor did not keep pace with the demands of the industry. Slater hired families who often relocated to be near the factory, giving rise to mill towns. By the late 1830s, factory conditions in New England deteriorated. Increased competition in the textile industry (which was the model for other industries of the day) forced factory owners to cut wages and lengthen hours to stay profitable and keep up with production demands.

The opening of new lands in the west shifted much of the nation's agriculture from New England's coastal states to the interior. As the farming population moved west, it became more difficult to recruit mill hands from the resident farming population. During the 1830s the mill owners turned to the steady stream of immigrants to supplement the factory workforce. Labor systems, such as Slater's and that of Francis Cabot Lowell (who hired farm girls to work in his factories but took care to ensure favorable working and living conditions), were no longer necessary. During the second half of the century, women and children continued to supply much of the factory labor, but without the paternalistic labor systems of Slater and Lowell.

See also: **Child Labor, Francis Cabot Lowell, Rhode Island, Samuel Slater Builds First Factory, Samuel Slater, Spinning Mills, Women in the Workplace**

RICARDO, DAVID

David Ricardo (1772–1823) was an English stockbroker who, working at the beginning of the nineteenth century, emerged as a major economic thinker during the early years of the industrial revolution. He is often referred to as the founder of scientific economics, because he used mathematics and abstract examples in his writing. His view of economics was ultimately a pessimistic one. Ricardo saw European economy torn into warring groups. He believed that in the long run the hardworking industrialist was bound to lose and that the benefits of the Industrial Revolution would end up in the hands of the already wealthy class of aristocratic landowners.

David Ricardo was born in April of 1772 in London, the third son of a wealthy Dutch-Jewish businessman. Ricardo's early passion for scholarship was delayed when he began to work in his father's investment business at age 14. He had a close relationship with his father and excelled in his work. At age 19, he married Abigail Delvalle, a Quaker, and eventually he left the family business to begin on his own, building a fortune by speculating in stock investing and other entrepreneurial ventures. In his late thirties, he began to write and published his first two books, *The High Price of Bullion* and *An Essay on the Influence of a Low Price of Corn on the Profits of Stock.*

In 1814, at age 42, David was wealthy enough to retire from his investment business. He could now give his full attention to intellectual pursuits, and by 1817 he had established his reputation as a leading thinker in England. His books by no means made him a cultural celebrity, but economically powerful, thoughtful people regarded him as one of the most influential intellectuals of his era. His life for the next 20 years centered largely around his continuing intellectual activity. He sat in parliament from 1819 to 1823, however, where he brought his knowledge about trade issues and finance to the British House of Commons and informed political debate of his day; thus, his writing had a role in rebuilding the English banking system after England's war with France ended in 1815.

Ricardo's approach to economics was new. Before him, economic writing was more literary than scientifically precise. It was a kind of loose-knit story involving many anecdotes. Ricardo chose to write about economics in a concise way, by eliminating numerous examples and instead explaining his ideas about the economy by using simple, easy-to-understand abstract models. Pursuing economic theory as a science, he explored economics by using basic principles and deductive reasoning to work toward his conclusions.

David Ricardo's notion of how the economics world worked was regarded as simple and elegant. He broke society into three parts: capitalists, landlords, and workers. The workers and the industrial capitalists, he argued, were in an impossible situation over the long run. The profits of hard-working creators of industry were eaten-up by the higher wage demands and by the costs of hiring additional help as business expanded. Ricardo maintained that ordinary workers wasted their income when their lives improved financially. For Ricardo the ordinary worker did not invest his money but only produced additional children to create larger burdens for the entire society.

Ricardo claimed that the only people who really improved under capitalism were the aristocratic landowners, who simply raised and lowered rents as they pleased. Thus they would absorb the extra profits made by the workers laboring for the capitalist industrialists. Ricardo also claimed that landlords, who produced nothing, served no useful purpose.

Ricardo was gloomy about the long term prospects of capitalism. He envisioned industrialists and common laborers "in the same boat." They were both being exploited by aristocrats who owned the land and who charged rent, based on the amount of money circulating in the economy. A situation he found unjust. But Ricardo's dire prophecies never came to pass. Wealth earned from industry was growing faster than that generated by the traditional agricultural-based society. With the cooperation of the British government, the industrial capitalists of Ricardo's era were able to reduce the power of the landowners, who were never able to dominate society as they had in the past.

Ricardo's approach to writing about economics made it more of a science and far more accessible to common readers. His gloomy attitude about capitalism alerted many of his optimistic friends and caused them to question the economic future. Some scholars have written that Ricardo's observations on capitalism led indirectly to the birth of a variety of socialist and progressive movements, all concerned with economic pathways that were not crowded with tax agents and Ricardo's nemesis, the landlords. He died in 1823.

See also: **Adam Smith, John Maynard Keynes**

FURTHER READING

Barber, William J. *A History of Economic Thought.* New York: Penguin Books, 1967.

Drabble, Margaret. *Oxford Companion to English Literature*, 5th ed. New York: Oxford University Press, 1985.

Heilbroner, Robert. *The Worldly Philosophers.* New York: Simon and Schuster, 1953.

Keynes, John M. *Essays in Biography.* London: MacMillan Press, 1937.

Straffe, Piero, ed. *David Ricardo, Works and Correspondence*, vol. 4. Cambridge: Cambridge University Press, 1965.

RICE

Rice is a cereal grass grown in warm, moist climates. The native inhabitants of Southeast Asia probably began cultivating rice for food seven thousand years ago. The crop spread northward into China and Japan, and westward into India, where it was observed in about 325 B.C. by Greek soldiers under the command of Alexander the Great (356–323 B.C.). Like sugar, which was also observed in India by the Greeks about 325 B.C., rice did not reach Europe until Moors (North African Muslims) invaded the Iberian Peninsula (present-day Spain and Portugal) in A.D. 711. When Spaniards colonized the islands of the West Indies and lands in South America in the late 1400s and throughout the 1500s, they introduced rice in the Western Hemisphere. There rice joined sugar, indigo, and tobacco as a profitable export item for the better part of the 1600s. Rice was among the enumerated articles in the British Parliament's Second Navigation Act (1660) which prevented colonies from exporting its products to anywhere except the British Isles. In 1671 rice was introduced into the North American mainland at South Carolina. By 1685 it became a commercial crop. Cultivation and production spread to North Carolina and Georgia. Because rice is a labor-intensive crop, rice plantations required numerous slaves for production. That way, along with tobacco and indigo, rice helped define the plantation economy of the South. After the American Civil War (1861–1865) and the abolition of slavery, southern growers could no longer support the crop. Production of rice moved westward. By 1900 Louisiana was supplying 70 percent of the U.S. rice production. In the early 1900s it was also introduced as a crop into California.

See also: **Agriculture, Georgia, Indigo, Navigation Acts, North Carolina, South Carolina, Slavery, Sugar, Tobacco**

RIGHT TO WORK

Right-to-work laws made it illegal for employees to be required to join a union as a precondition of employment. They were the opposite of closed-shop laws, which forbade workers from working for a firm unless they became union members.

Federal legislation passed during the New Deal of President Franklin D. Roosevelt (1933–1945) greatly strengthened the U.S. labor union movement. The

National Labor Relations Act of 1935 (also known as the Wagner Act) prevented companies from firing or unfairly treating workers who joined unions and required companies to bargain with duly elected labor representatives.

Although the number of unionized workers in the United States grew significantly because of the labor needs of World War II (1939–1945), in the postwar years an anti-labor climate emerged as a result of several major strikes, growing concern over communist infiltration of unions, and fears over the size and power of the unions. This environment resulted in the Labor-Management Relations Act of 1947 (usually called the Taft-Hartley Act). Surviving a veto by President Harry S. Truman (1945–1953), the law sharply curtailed union rights, though it did reaffirm the right of workers to organize and bargain as a group for higher wages and better working conditions. The law specifically gave workers the right not to join unions and outlawed closed shops.

The first U.S. state to ratify a right-to-work law was Florida, which in 1944—three years before Taft-Hartley—amended its constitution to ban closed shops. By 1998, when union representation was weakest, 21 states had right-to-work laws (mostly in the South and the West). Indiana, one of the few industrial states to adopt a right-to-work law, became the first state to repeal anti-closed shop legislation in 1965. In the same year President Lyndon B. Johnson (1963–1969) pushed hard to get the right-to-work clause of the Taft-Hartley Act repealed, but without success. In the mid-1990s, thirty U.S. states had some form of right-to-work provision for some state employees, and all employees of the federal government were covered by right-to-work protections.

Opponents of right-to-work laws argued that such laws enable non-union workers to enjoy the benefits unions secure for their members without bearing any of the costs and that union membership is generally beneficial. Among the arguments in favor of right-to-work laws is that forcing employees to join a union as a precondition of employment violates their civil rights.

***See also:* Closed Shop, Labor Movement, Labor Unionism, National Labor Relations Act, Taft-Hartley Act**

RIPPLE EFFECT

When someone drops a stone into a still pond of water, the water moves in ripples across the entire pond. A similar ripple effect occurs in economics. Economic ripples can be big or small, and the largest have an international impact. In 1998, when several of Asia's economies collapsed, primarily Japan, the effects came to the United States in both positive and negative ways. The negative ripple effect of the collapsed Asian economies was a sharp reduction in Asian demand for U.S. produced goods because of the sudden lack of disposable income. One area where the reduced Asian demand made itself felt was in the American Southeast, where the textile and apparel industries were weakened as overseas sales fell and foreign competition intensified. The U.S. automobile industry was also hurt because an increase in Asian demand for cheaper cars led Asian consumers back to purchasing cheaper Japanese-made vehicles rather than the often more expensive American-made imports.

The ripple effect in economics can have a positive side as well. The collapse of Asian economies led to an investment drain in the region. Investors pulled their money out of the now shaky Asian markets and back into the more stable U.S. market. With this increased investment in the United States, interest rates in the country dropped. Because of the Asian decline in 1998, the United States experienced a sharp bond rally and a drop in long-term interest rates, including mortgage rates. Many homeowners took advantage of the decrease in mortgage rates and refinanced their homes for a lower monthly payment.

The ripple effect, which occurs daily in many small ways throughout the world's economies, creates positive and negative effects which are largely unforeseeable. As world trade increases and nations work more closely together, the ripple effect's intensity increases. Asia's financial problems in 1998 were confined by International Monetary Fund (IMF) interventions, which kept the collapse contained to Asia. Without this intervention, the negative ripple effects could have wreaked more havoc in Latin America, where Brazil was vulnerable, and in Eastern Europe, creating a far deeper crisis for the U.S. economy.

ROBBER BARONS

The "robber barons" were industrial and financial tycoons of the late nineteenth century. They included banker and financier John Pierpont Morgan (1837–1913); oil industrialist John D. Rockefeller (1839–1937); steel mogul Andrew Carnegie (1835–1919); financiers James J. Hill (1838–1916), James

> The robber barons (especially the railroad men and the financiers who gained control of rail companies through stock buy-outs) hired lobbyists to work on their behalf to gain corporation subsidies, land grants, and even tax relief at both the federal and state levels. They converted their business prowess into political might.

Fisk (1834–1872), and Jay Gould (1836–1892); and rail magnates Cornelius Vanderbilt (1794–1877) and Collis Huntington (1821–1900). Hailed by some for expanding and modernizing the capitalist system, lauded by others for their philanthropic contributions to the arts and education, these businessmen were viewed by many more as opportunistic, exploitative, and unethical.

Many factors converged to make the robber baron businessman possible: the country was rich in natural resources, including iron, coal, and oil; technological advances steadily improved manufacturing machinery and processes; population growth, fed by an influx of immigrants, provided a steady workforce that was often willing to work for a low wage; the government turned over the building and operation of the nation's railways to private interests; and, adhering to the philosophy of laissez faire (non-interference in the private sector), the government also provided a favorable environment in which to conduct business. Shrewd businessmen turned these factors to their advantage, amassing great empires. They reinvested profits into their businesses and their fortunes grew. The robber barons (especially the railroad men and the financiers who gained control of rail companies through stock buy-outs) hired lobbyists to work on their behalf to gain corporation subsidies, land grants, and even tax relief at both the federal and state levels. They converted their business prowess into political might. In Washington, D.C., politicians grew tired of the advantage-seeking representatives of the nation's business leaders. Reform-minded progressives complained that the robber barons lived in opulent luxury while their workers barely eked out a living.

After a decades-long domination of the robber barons over the U.S. economy, changes around the turn of the century worked to curb their influence. In 1890 the federal government passed the Sherman Anti-Trust Act which made trusts illegal (trusts are combinations of firms or corporations formed to limit competition and monopolize a market). Workers continued to organize in labor unions with which corporations were increasingly compelled to negotiate. The Interstate Commerce Commission (ICC) was established in 1887 to prevent abusive practices. In 1913 the Sixteenth Amendment was ratified, allowing the federal government to collect a graduated income tax. Though many American businessmen and women would make great fortunes in the twentieth century, by the end of the 1920s the era of the robber barons had drawn to a close.

***See also:* Andrew Carnegie, Jay Gould, John P. Morgan, John D. Rockefeller, Sherman Anti-Trust Act, Sixteenth Amendment, Cornelius Vanderbilt**

ROCKEFELLER, JOHN DAVISON

The name Rockefeller has become synonymous with the idea of enormous personal wealth. In ordinary language one many hear the phrase "rich as Rockefeller," an enduring popular legacy for the man who built the largest fortune ever up to that time seen in the United States. John D. Rockefeller (1839–1932) created an oil empire that helped fuel the Industrial Revolution.

John Davison Rockefeller was born in 1839 in Richford, New York. His Baptist upbringing taught the young Rockefeller to be frugal, hard-working, and self-reliant. He despised waste and had a quiet disposition. Rockefeller's subdued character masked an aggressive ambition that would take him to the heights of success. In 1855, at age 16, he graduated from high school and began work as a bookkeeping clerk in Cleveland, Ohio. After four years Rockefeller left bookkeeping behind to start his own business in the new and rapidly growing oil industry.

As an entrepreneur, Rockefeller drew on the qualities instilled in him at childhood to run a successful and profitable business. He tried to save costs where possible and constantly reinvested his savings into his business. Rockefeller's business philosophy was akin to Charles Darwin's evolutionary theory of the "survival of the fittest." He could be a ruthless businessman, using harsh and even unethical methods to succeed, often driving his competition out of business.

By the 1870s Rockefeller's oil business grew to include refineries, lubrication plants, pipelines, cooperage plants, and other enterprises. The wide reach of his investments created an unwieldy and

John D. Rockefeller.

complicated business that Rockefeller controlled with an iron fist.

Rockefeller delegated management of his oil properties to 40 allied firms that, in 1882, centralized his operations under the Standard Oil Trust. The Standard Oil Trust monopolized 90 percent of all oil business in the United States and extended its influence into other parts of the world as well. It stifled competition in the oil industry.

While Rockefeller's business grew, the oil industry expanded. Rockefeller's increasing control over this important industry caused the United States government to examine more closely the fairness of trade and competition in the industry. The Ohio Supreme Court first asserted the illegality of Rockefeller's Trust in 1892. In 1870 Congress passed the Sherman Anti-Trust Act in part as a response against vast and powerful empires such as Rockefeller's. However it wasn't until 1911, under President Theodore Roosevelt (1901–1909), that the United States Supreme Court prosecuted the Standard Oil Trust for violation of anti-trust laws and dissolved its practices as "a monopoly in restraint of trade." By the time the Supreme Court completed its case against the Standard Oil Trust, John Rockefeller had pulled away from active involvement in his company's practices. He turned his attention to business ventures in minerals and ore in northwestern United States, and he developed ore operations in Colorado, Washington, and Minnesota.

John Rockefeller was one of the most successful U.S. entrepreneurs. He amassed a fortune of close to $1 billion, an outrageous sum for his day. Despite his enormous wealth Rockefeller did not forget his early upbringing. He regularly contributed to charity and created the Rockefeller Institute for Medical Research, the General Education Board, the Rockefeller Foundation, and the University of Chicago. John D. Rockefeller died at age 97 in Ormund Beach, Florida, on May 23, 1937.

See also: **Petroleum Industry, Robber Barons, Standard Oil Company**

FURTHER READING

Aiken, Edward N. *Flager: Rockefeller Partner and Florida Baron.* Gainesville, FL: University Press of Florida, 1991.

Carr, Albert H. *John D. Rockefeller's Secret Weapon.* New York: McGraw-Hill, 1962.

Chernow, Ron. *Titan: The Life of John D. Rockefeller, Sr.*. New York: Random House, 1998.

Gitelman, Howard M. *Legacy of the Ludlow Massacre: A Chapter in American Industrial Relations.* Philadelphia: University of Pennsylvania Press, 1988.

Hawkes, David F. *John D.: The Founding Father of the Rockefellers.* New York: Harper and Row, 1980.

ROEBLING, JOHN AUGUSTUS

John Augustus Roebling (1806–1869) came to the United States and created in New York what has become one of the nation's best-known and earliest examples of suspension bridges, the Brooklyn Bridge.

John Roebling was born in Prussia in 1806. He received an excellent formal education and graduated in 1826 with a degree in civil engineering from the Royal Polytechnic Institute in Berlin. As a practicing civil engineer, Roebling was dissatisfied with the simple road building projects available in his homeland at that time. He set his eyes elsewhere in search of more challenging work.

His search ended in the United States, where Roebling and his brother emigrated and established a 7,000-acre agricultural community in western Pennsylvania. Roebling was an unsuccessful farmer and found himself returning to his civil engineering interests and the building opportunities available in the United States.

IN PURSUIT OF HIS PHILOSOPHICAL IDEAL "TO BRING IN HARMONY ALL THAT SURROUNDS ME," JOHN AUGUSTUS ROEBLING BECAME A PIONEER OF SUSPENSION BRIDGES IN THE UNITED STATES.

He saw in his new country an opportunity to achieve the realization of his philosophical ideal of harmony. Creating order out of chaos was foremost in Roebling's life. The many bridge building projects he led, pioneering the design of the suspension bridge, were an extension of his desire "to bring in harmony all that surrounds me."

Drawn back into civil engineering, Roebling began his career in the United States first as a surveyor for the Pennsylvania Railroad. At the railroad he observed the thick, crude, and expensive rope used to haul heavy barges up hills to reach the canal systems and saw a way to improve the process. He invented and began manufacturing a smaller cable composed of many thin strands of wire twisted together to make a single cable, far stronger than the bulky rope then in use. Roebling was a leader in the manufacture of strong steel cables, and he later used their unique blend of strength and lightness in the construction of suspension bridges.

Roebling combined strength and lightness, extension-in-space and compactness, and the precision of steel cables with rolling Gothic arches in the stone towers of the bridges he created. His first suspension bridge was a highway bridge over the Monongahela River that runs through Pittsburgh, Pennsylvania. He then went on to construct a bridge across the Ohio River in Cincinnati, Ohio. Across the Niagara River in 1855, he built the first cable suspension bridge capable of handling human road traffic.

Roebling's last project, the design and construction of the Brooklyn Bridge, began in June 1869. The Brooklyn Bridge was the longest and most modern bridge ever attempted at that time. It spans New York's East River, connecting Manhattan and Brooklyn. Hanging from steel cables almost sixteen inches thick, the bridge boasts two Gothic towers along its 1,595 foot length.

During the first stages of construction, Roebling suffered an accident while inspecting the stone base-pilings of the bridge and his foot was crushed. An infection quickly set in and he died of tetanus complications on July 22, 1869.

The Brooklyn Bridge, finished in 1883, fourteen years after the death of its creator, is a symbol of American ingenuity as the nation emerged from a farming economy into an industrial nation. It was completed by Roebling's son, Washington, who carried out the realization of his father's dream.

See also: **Brooklyn Bridge**

FURTHER READING

Gimsing, Niels J. *Cable Supported Bridges: Concept and Design.* New York: J. Wiley, 1983.

Mann, Elizabeth. *The Brooklyn Bridge: A Wonder of the World Book.* New York: Mikaya Press, 1996.

McCullough, David G. *The Great Bridge.* New York: Simon and Schuster, 1972.

Placzek, Adolph K. *Architects.* New York: The Free Press, 1982.

Steinman, David B. *The Builders of the Bridge; the Story of John Roebling and His Son.* New York: Harcourt, Brace & Co., 1945.

ROOSEVELT, FRANKLIN DELANO

Franklin Delano Roosevelt (1882–1945), known as F.D.R., was the thirty-second president of the United States. He was the only president elected to four consecutive terms of office. According to polls of historians and political scientists, F.D.R. is consistently ranked with George Washington (1789–1797) and Abraham Lincoln (1861–1865) as one of the United States' three greatest presidents.

Roosevelt's politics in fighting both the Great Depression (1929–1939) and World War II (1939–1945) was always realistic: he stood for humanity and against rigid ideology. Roosevelt seemed to work against the abstract ideologies of fascism, communism, and European imperialism in an effort to find practical ways to help common people.

Some Roosevelt critics in the wealthy business community said he was leading the United States into communism. During the Great Depression he said to his business detractors: "The test of our progress is not

Franklin D. Roosevelt.

whether we add more to the abundance of those who have much; it is whether we provide enough for those who have too little.''

Roosevelt is known as the president who lifted the United States out of its deepest economic despair and revolutionized the country's way of life. While many businessmen opposed him, he understood that social security, unemployment compensation, stock securities regulation, farm price supports, minimum wages, and guarantees of collective bargaining were all ways in which capitalism could save itself, instead of surrendering to other systems and pulling itself apart.

Franklin Roosevelt was born into a prominent and wealthy family in Hyde Park, New York, in 1882. He received a traditional education at the respected Groton School and went on to graduate from Harvard University, then entering the Columbia University law school. Roosevelt became a lawyer without finishing law school, but his dreams seemed always to be about politics. He had great ambitions to become president, and as early as 1905 his fellow law clerks remarked how Roosevelt meant to enter politics and the White House.

In 1910 he was elected to the New York State Senate. From there, his career in public service went from the New York Senate to President Woodrow Wilson's (1913–1924) Assistant Secretary of the Navy, then to the governor of New York in 1928, and ultimately to the presidency of the United States in 1933. He was re-elected to the presidency three times before his death in 1945.

THE TEST OF OUR PROGRESS IS NOT WHETHER WE ADD MORE TO THE ABUNDANCE OF THOSE WHO HAVE MUCH; IT IS WHETHER WE PROVIDE ENOUGH FOR THOSE WHO HAVE TOO LITTLE.

Franklin D. Roosevelt

In 1921, at age 39, Roosevelt became seriously ill with polio, and he was almost completely paralyzed. Through exhausting courses of physical exercise, he fiercely struggled to cure himself. He made progress in recovery, but never regained the use of his legs. Prior to his illness, Roosevelt was seen by many as a spoiled rich man dabbling in politics. Little of his later political seriousness was apparent before his bout with polio. When asked how he could be so patient with a political opponent, he said: ''If you had spent two years in bed trying to wiggle your big toe, after that anything else would seem easy.''

Roosevelt ran for the presidency on the Democratic Party ticket in 1932, promising to balance the federal budget and provide direct aid to the needy. Though his Republican opponents saw Roosevelt as a dangerous ''socialist'' during the 1930s, they missed the point that Roosevelt's efforts were to save American capitalism from its worst traits. He also planned to break with ''foolish traditions'' in order to relieve the misery of one-third of the population, mired in the hard times of the Great Depression (1929–1939). Roosevelt won the election and began his first term of office in 1933.

On March 9, 1933, he convened a special session of Congress, which lasted 100 days. During that period more important legislation was passed than at any other comparable period in U.S. history. Roosevelt called his reform, recovery, and relief efforts the New Deal. To accomplish his social and economic goals he needed to overcome the deep-seated public prejudices against a strong federal government. Roosevelt went on the radio and talked informally to the public about what he wanted to do. This combination of decisive action and personal persuasion was effective. The most popular New Deal measures voted in were aimed at relieving the suffering of the unemployed, who made up about 30 percent of the country's workforce at the time. Roosevelt created federal jobs for the unemployed, assisted farmers ruined by the Depression, and protected citizens against loss of their homes by mortgage foreclosures. He also enacted the Social Security Act, which put in place an old-age pension system, as well as benefits to widows with children and the

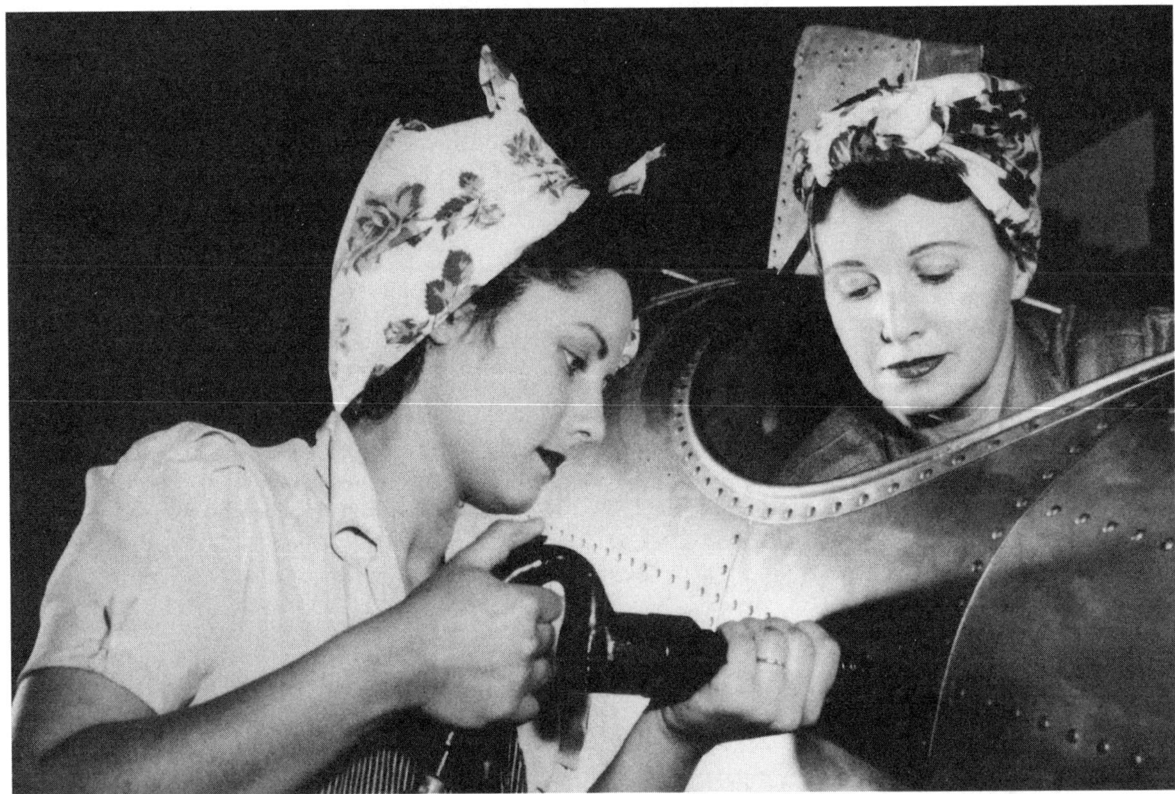

As the war stripped the workforce of men, women were hired to perform factory jobs, such as using this rivet gun to assemble aircraft for the war effort.

chronically disabled. A combination of New Deal legislation and World War II (1939–1945) worked to return the United States to prosperity.

By 1938 the Republicans and conservative Democrats had won enough seats in Congress to halt substantial increases in New Deal legislation, which was never without controversy. Regardless of the many perspectives held on Roosevelt and his terms in office, it is impossible to deny the central role he and his New Deal played in the shaping of the modern United States. F.D.R. died of a cerebral hemorrhage in Warm Springs, Georgia, on the morning of April 12, 1945. He died knowing World War II was won, and the economy repaired.

See also: **Great Depression, New Deal, Social Security Act, Unemployment, United Nations, World War II**

FURTHER READING

Davis, Kenneth S. *FDR: The New Deal Years, 1933–1937*. New York: Random House, 1979.

Larrabee, Eric. *Commander in Chief, Franklin Delano Roosevelt, His Lieutenants, and Their War*. New York: Harper and Row, 1987.

Morgan, Tom. *FDR: A Biography*. New York: Simon and Schuster, 1985.

Thomas, Henry. *Franklin Roosevelt*. New York: G. P. Putnam, 1962.

Zevin, B.D., ed. *Nothing to Fear: The Selected Addresses of Franklin Delano Roosevelt*. Boston: Houghton Mifflin Co., 1946.

ROSIE THE RIVETER

''Rosie the Riveter'' was the title of a song written in 1942, during World War II (1939–1945). The song quickly became a popular hit, and more importantly became the catch phrase that represented all women working in war-related industries.

The image of a woman war worker first appeared on the cover of the then-popular weekly magazine, *Saturday Evening Post*, on May 25, 1943. It was a painting by renowned artist Norman Rockwell of a woman worker; a muscular body, a cute saucy face, and very determined. She had a rivet gun, used for industrial assembly, resting across her lap, and the name ''Rosie'' painted on her lunchbox.

''Rosie the Riveter'' became the major symbol of the more than six million women who joined the workforce during World War II. The women worked in naval shipyards, lumber mills, steel mills, and foundries. They worked as welders, mechanics, electricians, and boilermakers. They operated buses, cranes, tractors, and worked as engineers, police officers, taxicab drivers, and members of federal government services.

When the war ended in 1945, so did the extraordinary job opportunities for women. ''Rosie the Riveter'' disappeared as quickly as she had been created. ''Rosie'' represented the superb skill, ability, and patriotism of all U.S. women working on behalf of the domestic, industrial efforts on the ''home front'' during World War II.

See also: **Women in the Workplace, World War II**

RUBBERMAID INCORPORATED

Rubbermaid Incorporated was the product of two founding businesses—one, a maker of toy balloons, and the other, the designer of a better dustpan. The Wooster Rubber Company started in May 1920, when nine Wooster, Ohio, investors pooled $26,800 to form a company to manufacture toy balloons, sold under the Sunshine brand name. Wooster Rubber was housed in a single building in Wooster—a small town 50 miles from Cleveland, Ohio. In 1927 Horatio B. Ebert and Errett M. Grable, two Aluminum Company of America executives, bought Wooster Rubber. By the late 1920s a new factory and office building had been constructed to house the prosperous business, but the fortunes of Wooster Rubber sunk during the Great Depression (1929–1939). In 1934 Ebert spotted Rubbermaid products in a New England department store, and he worked out a merger between the two firms.

Meanwhile, New Englander James R. Caldwell, who had first entered the rubber business as an employee of the Seamless Rubber Company in New Haven, Connecticut, looked around his kitchen during the depths of the Great Depression to see what he could improve. Caldwell and his wife conceptualized and developed 29 products, among them a red rubber dustpan. Although the rubber dustpan, designed and manufactured by Caldwell and his wife, cost $1.00—much more than the 39-cent metal pans then available in stores—Caldwell ''rang ten doorbells and sold nine dustpans,'' as he recalled in an interview published in the *New York Times* on May 19, 1974. Convinced there was a market for his products, Caldwell gave his enterprise a name—Rubbermaid—and expanded his line to include a soap dish, a sink plug, and a drainboard mat—products he sold in department stores throughout New England.

In 1934, Ebert spotted Rubbermaid products at a New England department store, and believing that such products could help his struggling Wooster Rubber, he engineered a merger of the two enterprises in July 1934. Still called the Wooster Rubber Company, the new group began to produce rubber household goods under the Rubbermaid brand name. With the merger, which was under Caldwell's leadership, Wooster Rubber had a happy reversal in fortunes; sales rose from $80,000 in 1935 to $450,000 in 1941. Of the 29 new products Caldwell and his wife thought up in their kitchen in 1933, the company had marketed 27 of them by 1941.

ALTHOUGH HIS RUBBER DUSTPAN COST $1.00—MUCH MORE THAN THE 39-CENT METAL PANS THEN AVAILABLE IN STORES, JAMES R. CALDWELL "RANG TEN DOORBELLS AND SOLD NINE DUSTPANS."

In 1942 however, U.S. involvement in World War II (1939–1945) caused the government to cut back on civilian use of rubber, which was also had important military uses. This eliminated Rubbermaid's housewares business, but the company was able to convert to military manufacturing. Beginning with rubber parts for a self-sealing fuel tank for warplanes, and moving on to other products such as life jackets and rubber tourniquets, the company manufactured military goods throughout the end of the war.

Following the war Wooster Rubber resumed its prewar production of rubber housewares. Because wartime shortages had not yet been completely redressed, no coloring agents were available and all Rubbermaid products were manufactured in black for several months. In 1947 the company introduced a line of rubber automotive accessories, including rubber floor mats and cup holders.

In 1955 the Wooster Rubber Company went public. This capital infusion allowed the company to branch into plastic products, and in 1956 a plastic dishpan was introduced. In 1957 the Wooster Rubber Company changed its name to Rubbermaid Incorporated to increase its association with its well-known brand name. The following year Rubbermaid began its first expansion beyond production of household goods when the company broadened its targeted market to include restaurants, hotels, and other institutions. Rubbermaid initially produced bathtub mats and doormats for these clients. By 1974 industrial and commercial products provided 25 percent of the company's sales.

Following the 1970s, during which the company made ill-fated ventures into motorboats and snow sleds, Rubbermaid refocused on home and commercial products in the early 1980s. Rubbermaid also expanded through acquisitions. The company added the Con-Tact brand of decorative plastic coverings in 1981; Little Tikes, a maker of plastic toys, in 1984; Empire Brushes, a leading U.S. maker of brooms, mops, and brushes, in 1994; the Graco brand of strollers, play yards, and infant swings in 1996; and Century Products, a manufacturer of car seats and strollers, in 1998. Then in March 1999, Newell, a housewares manufacturer based in Freeport, Illinois, purchased Rubbermaid for $6 billion. Newell then changed its own name to Newell Rubbermaid Inc. in tribute to the reputation of the Rubbermaid name.

FURTHER READING

Christensen, Jean. ''How Rubbermaid Invites Profits.'' *New York Times*, May 19, 1974.

Deutsch, Claudia H. ''A Giant Awakens, to Yawns: Is Rubbermaid Reacting Too Late.'' *New York Times*, December 22, 1996.

Farnham, Alan. ''America's Most Admired Company.'' *Fortune*, February 7, 1994.

Noble, Donald E. *Like Only Yesterday: The Memoirs of Donald E. Noble*. Wooster, OH: Wooster Book Co., 1996.

Ozanian, Michael K. and Alexandra Ourusoff. ''Never Let Them See You Sweat: Just Because Rubbermaid Is One of the Most Admired Companies in the Country Doesn't Mean Life Is Easy.'' *Financial World*, February 1, 1994.

Smith, Lee. ''Rubbermaid Goes Thump.'' *Fortune*, October 2, 1995.

Stevens, Tim. ''Where the Rubber Meets the Road.'' *Industry Week*, March 20, 1995.

RUDKIN, MARGARET FOGARTY

During an era when being a housewife was considered the appropriate goal of a woman, Margaret Rudkin (1897–1967) achieved acclaim as one of the most successful female entrepreneurs in the United States. Her concern for her son's health prompted this already wealthy housewife to begin baking her own ''health bread'' and within 10 years her Pepperidge Farm ovens were producing thousands of loaves a day at a baking facility she herself designed. Her business was later acquired by the Campbell Soup Company, which further expanded the successful brand of baked goods Rudkin had developed.

Margaret ''Peggy'' Rudkin was born Margaret Fogarty on September 14, 1897, in New York City, one of five children born to Joseph and Margaret Fogarty. Her father drove a truck, and the family lived with their grandmother until Margaret was 12, when her grandmother died. The family then moved to Flushing, New York, where Rudkin later graduated from Flushing's City High School as class valedictorian in 1915. Following graduation she went to work as a bookkeeper in a bank in Flushing and eventually became a bank teller.

At age 22 Rudkin began working on Wall Street at the brokerage firm of McClure, Jones, and Co. where she became a customer representative, helping people understand their investment choices more clearly. She met her husband, Henry Albert Rudkin, at the brokerage house, where he was one of the firm's partners. They were wed on April 8, 1923 and made their home in New York City.

The first years of the Rudkins' marriage were prosperous. They had three sons, and in 1928 they decided to build a house in nearby Fairfield, Connecticut, where they had purchased 125 acres of land. The Rudkins named their large Tudor-style house and the surrounding acreage ''Pepperidge Farm'' in 1931, after an old Pepperidge (black gum tree) that was on the property. Henry Rudkin sustained a serious injury while playing polo, making their activities afterward more limited.

In 1937 the Rudkins' youngest son, John, was diagnosed with asthma. The allergist said the additives in store-bought foods were probably aggravating the condition. Hearing this, Rudkin began to make all of her son's food from scratch, including bread.

Having never baked bread before, Rudkin used a recipe from her grandmother's cookbook. The recipe called for butter, whole milk, honey and whole-wheat flour, which Rudkin ground herself. Her son's health improved so much that the allergist requested she bake more loaves for his other asthma patients.

At this point, Rudkin started to bake in earnest and began to think of baking as an occupation rather than as a component of her son's health regimen. From this time on Rudkin, along with her husband and children, pursued the business.

Beginning in 1937 after she provided her son's allergist with some of the "health bread" she had made for her son, Rudkin began to explore the wider sales potential of her bread. She began by making bread for the upscale New York City market and before long her husband was delivering 24 loaves of bread a day to Charles and Co., a specialty food company in Manhattan.

By the end of her first year of baking, using ovens installed in one of the abandoned horse stables on their property, Rudkin was making and selling 4,000 loaves a week. Although the price was more than twice the price of a regular loaf of bread, people seemed drawn to the "old fashioned," homemade, and healthy image of Pepperidge Farm bread.

By 1940 Rudkin moved the bakery to a larger facility in Norwalk, Connecticut, where she was able to make 50,000 loaves a week. All this time, she was maintaining the high quality of all the ingredients. By 1947, launching a new bakery designed to Rudkin's own specifications, the Pepperidge Farm Co. was producing 4,000 loaves of bread per hour.

Growth and maintaining quality while expanding were Rudkin's main concerns. Her husband retired from Wall Street in 1949 and took over the financial side of the company while she managed the production and personnel. By this time, there were three bakeries: one in Connecticut, one near Chicago, and one near Philadelphia. Rudkin maintained quality control despite the massive expansion by specifying that her bread was not to be sold after two days on the shelf. When surplus bread was returned from the distributer, Rudkin used it to make poultry stuffing for a good profit.

In the 1950s Pepperidge Farm, under Rudkin's management, employed over 1,000 workers. By 1956 she introduced cookies that were "healthy," and in 1958 frozen pastries made their debut. By that time Pepperidge Farm (within 15 years of its inception) was a brand name recognized nationally; products were found in virtually every market. Among the growing list of products offered by the company during that period were rolls, coffee cake, Melba toast, stuffing, and Goldfish cocktail crackers.

By 1960 when Rudkin was 63, she and her husband decided to sell the Pepperidge Farm Company to the Campbell Soup Company for $28 million in Campbell stock. However the Rudkins kept a controlling interest in Pepperidge Farm itself, and for the next decade the company was run as an independent subsidiary of Campbell.

During the final years of her life Rudkin appeared in television commercials for Pepperidge Farm products and authored a cookbook in 1963. She also became a part-time public speaker as a kind of hobby. During this period the Rudkins divided their time between homes in Hobe Sound, Florida, and County Carlow, Ireland. Henry Rudkin died in 1966 and a year later Rudkin herself died of cancer in New Haven, Connecticut, at the age of 69.

Rudkin was clearly one of the most successful and nationally prominent businesswomen of her generation, a woman who started baking bread for her son and ended by making products with wide appeal among national consumers. During the 1950s and 1960s when the Pepperidge Farm product line was at the height of its popularity it is likely that the "homemade" quality of the products was the most appealing feature to the female shopper, who was likely making less homemade bread herself.

In the closing decades of the twentieth century Rudkin's legacy continued in the popularity of Pepperidge Farm products offered by the Campbell Soup Company, including garlic bread, gourmet cookies, fat-free croutons, stuffing, puff pastries, and Goldfish crackers. According to the 1997 Campbell annual report, the Pepperidge Farm line was considered one of the "jewels in [Campbell's] portfolio, delivering outstanding, double-digit sales growth." The report further stated that "a third of all American households with children now eat Goldfish" and singled out "Milano" as "the consumers' favorite Pepperidge Farm cookie."

Rudkin's managerial style allowed company growth in response to consumer demand while retaining quality control of Pepperidge Farm products as the production facilities grew. Rudkin made Pepperidge Farm a household name, largely by making an honest, high-quality product and not compromising quality to reduce price. She also succeeded in selling, with her bread, the idea of the store-bought "homemade" product. She did this just as fewer people were eating truly homemade foods in the 1940s and 1950s and as more and more foodstuff in the United States became commercially mass-produced.

FURTHER READING

Brendan, Gill. "Better Late than Never." *Sales and Marketing Management*, September 1996.

''Biscuits and Confectionery,'' [cited] available from the World Wide Web @ www.pepperidgefarm.com/financialcenter/1997AR/pages/bis_conf.html/.

Dictionary of American Biography. New York: Scribner's, 1988, s.v. ''Rudkin, Margaret.''

Rudkin, Margaret. *The Pepperidge Farm Cookbook*. New York: Grosset and Dunlap, 1965.

RURAL ELECTRIFICATION ADMINISTRATION

One of the most important New Deal programs for farmers was the Rural Electrification Administration (REA). This program, authorized by Congress in 1935, lent funds to rural cooperatives to generate and distribute electricity to areas not served by private utility companies. The impact of electrification in such isolated areas was enormous. In 1936, 90 percent of U.S. farms had no electricity. Without electric power, farm families had to perform back-breaking work by hand. They had to draw water from wells or pump it by hand, which made it impossible to have flush toilets. They lacked refrigerators, electric lights, and washing machines. All the farm chores, such as milking, also had to be done by hand. And without electricity, there was no access to radio or telephone. Life for farm families was exhausting and lonely, and lack of electric power was a major cause of poor health in rural areas. The REA, despite strong opposition from private utilities, made it possible for cooperatives to provide affordable electric power to the rural poor. By 1937, the program had enabled almost a quarter of a million farm households to obtain electricity; by 1945, that number had increased to 40 percent of the country's farms. Electricity brought farm families into the twentieth century. Not only did electric power make their work easier and more efficient, it brought them into closer contact, through telephones and radio, with other parts of the country. In addition, electrification made it possible for farmers to improve their businesses after World War II by diversifying operations.

See also: **New Deal, Tennessee Valley Authority**

RUST BELT

The term ''Rust Belt'' refers to an economic region in the northeast United States, roughly covering the states of Michigan, Wisconsin, Indiana, Illinois, Ohio, and Pennsylvania, a region known as the manufacturing heartland of the nation. Many of the factories and steel mills that produced the ''American economic miracle'' during and after World War II (1939–1945) were padlocking their gates by the 1970s. This was more than a downward phase in the business cycle. It was a structural crisis brought about by the aging of a generation of factories, the relative decline of the manufacturing sector, and increased global competition. The crisis brought unemployment to workers, and increased police and welfare costs to cities at the same time that it signaled a decline in tax revenues. When the factories shut down, the cities lost corporate and property tax revenues as workers followed jobs to the suburbs or to other parts of the country.

The term ''Rust Belt'' thus refers to a social crisis mostly affecting the cities. During the 1970s and 1980s, rust belt cities experienced deepening unemployment, out-migration of population, loss of electoral votes, and an overall decline in industry and the economy. Smaller industrial plants relocated to Mexico or to low-wage American Sun Belt states. Big steel companies dating from the nineteenth century, like Bethlehem Steel and U.S. Steel Co., became industrial dinosaurs in the mid-twentieth century, made obsolete by technological advances and competition from Japan and Germany (whose plants mostly dated from the post-World War II period).

One typical Rust Belt story is the Dodge Main plant in Hamtramck, Michigan, an older industrial suburb of Detroit. Built in 1910, Dodge Main for decades was the ''flag ship'' factory of Chrysler Motors Corporation. Because land was at a premium when the plant was built, it was six stories tall—a problem for assembly line production as the partially assembled units had to go from floor to floor. By the 1960s, as single story factories were being built in the suburbs or rural areas, the Dodge Main plant was obsolete. The plant was also the site of racial and union militancy, as African American workers formed the ''Dodge Revolutionary Union Movement'' (DRUM) to counter racial discrimination in the workplace and in the union.

By the early 1970s scores of factories that had once made up the Detroit skyline during the automotive boom were either razed or slated for destruction. The Chrysler Corporation in 1979 had to be bailed out of bankruptcy by the federal government and by concessions from its employees. The company revived, but Dodge Main went under the wrecker's ball in 1981.

By the mid-1980s, the Rust Belt began to recharge. Steel mills and factories retooled, making the transition from outdated, inefficient, and often unsafe facilities to innovative and progressive ones. This transformation was accompanied by downsizing and deregulation, which contributed to job insecurity for workers. Nevertheless, with these changes the name ''Rust Belt'' began to drop from common usage. By 1996, the double-digit unemployment rates of the 1970s had fallen to 4.4 percent. Some former Rust Belt states like Michigan began to experience lower average unemployment than the rest of the country. Part of this was due to low energy prices that favored energy-intensive manufacturing.

Several cities of the Rust Belt, such as Pittsburgh, Detroit, and Cleveland, have attempted to diversify their economies to escape the heavy dependence on manufacturing and have successfully made a transition to the ''service and information economy.'' The region must still avoid complacency and guard against a shortage in skilled labor. The Federal Reserve Bank of Chicago reported in 1997 that improved access to education and skills was required for continued growth in the region. Educational reforms and an increase in the market base of their products are only part of the measures planned by the former rust belt states to maintain a competitive edge. The economic fortunes of the Midwest—as is clear from the experience in the automobile and steel industries—is tied to a competitive global market. The rusting experience of the 1970s provided the region with the opportunity to retool for world competition.

See also: **Chrysler Motors Corporation, Sun Belt**

SAINT LAWRENCE SEAWAY

When Queen Elizabeth II, President Dwight D. Eisenhower (1953–1961), and other dignitaries gathered at the U.S. and Canadian border in June 1959 to officially open the St. Lawrence Seaway, it was the culmination of a project that had been discussed for almost 70 years. Ships could now travel along all of the Great Lakes, through the St. Lawrence River, and into the Atlantic Ocean. Along the way were such prominent U.S. port cities as Milwaukee, Chicago, Toledo, Cleveland, Detroit, and Buffalo. Following years of study and opposition by competing interests and in the U.S. Congress, joint Canadian and U.S construction on the final phase of the Seaway began in 1954. It would cost nearly $500 million and require the relocation of 6,500 citizens on both sides of the border before the Seaway officially opened in 1959. At over 2,300 miles the St. Lawrence Seaway linked North America's industrial heartland to the rest of the world's markets, serving as a boon to commercial shippers. However, both nations have lost money on the project over the years.

Canals had been built along the St. Lawrence River as far back as the 1680s (the river was named by explorer Jacques Cartier in honor of the saint on whose feast day Cartier discovered the waterway in 1535). These canals made it easier for fur traders centered in and around Montreal to ship their wares. In 1824 what is now known as the Lachine Canal was completed, linking Montreal with Lake St. Louis. Just a year later, however, New York's Erie Canal opened, attracting much of the region's shipping traffic, as it provided a shorter route between the Atlantic Ocean and the Great Lakes, as well as access to New York City through the Hudson River. Nonetheless the St. Lawrence River remained an important shipping route, especially to Great Britain.

In the 1890s Minnesota Congressman John Lind sponsored a resolution to look into a joint Canadian-American waterway which linked Lake Superior—the westernmost Great Lake, which extends to Duluth, Minnesota—with the Atlantic Ocean. The St. Lawrence River was deemed to be the most feasible route. By 1900 a network of shallow canals already made it possible to travel from Lake Superior all the way to Montreal. Between 1912 and 1932 the Welland Canal, which a century earlier linked Lake Erie to Lake Ontario (located north of Ohio and western New York) was rebuilt to support the heavy traffic.

[A]LONG WITH ITS BENEFITS TO NATIONAL DEFENSE (A GREAT LAKES SEAWAY) WILL CONTRIBUTE TO THE PEACETIME WELFARE OF A MULTITUDE OF LABORERS, SMALL BUSINESSMEN, HOMEOWNERS AND FARMERS.

Franklin D. Roosevelt, President (1933–1945), 1940

In 1921 a joint commission issued a report recommending that the United States and Canada enter into a treaty to improve passage through the St. Lawrence River between Montreal and Lake Ontario. The cost of building the Seaway, the report said, would be proportional according to each country's benefits. But interests such as railroads, which were in competition with the shipping industry, opposed the seaway project. In 1932 Canadian Prime Minister R. B. Bennett and U.S. President Herbert Hoover (1929–1933) signed a treaty which agreed to build a seaway to the Atlantic Ocean. Both nations would share the work and costs involved. The U.S. Senate, however, rejected the treaty in 1934.

The issue remained unsettled until the early 1950s, when vast fields of iron ore were discovered in Canada. A complete seaway along the St. Lawrence was supported as the best way to transport the ore to U.S. and Canadian steel mills. Others suggested such a passageway would also offer military advantages. As his predecessor Franklin D. Roosevelt (1933–1945) had been, President Harry S. Truman (1945–1953) was in favor of the seaway project. But both the U.S House of Representatives and the Senate resisted approval of St. Lawrence Seaway bills. Canada, it appeared, would move ahead with the project on its own. However, President Dwight D. Eisenhower, along with advocates in both houses of the U.S. Congress, successfully passed a bill to jointly build the St. Lawrence Seaway with Canada in 1954.

According to the original bill the Seaway would ultimately pay for itself through tolls paid by shippers. The project cost Canada $336.5 million and the United States $133.8 million. A separate project to harness the seaway for electrical power cost each nation an additional $300 million. The construction would ultimately require entire towns and villages to be relocated and about 40,000 acres of farmland in both countries was flooded. In early 1959 both countries agreed to share toll revenues roughly proportionate to the amount they spent on construction.

The St. Lawrence Seaway was officially opened on June 26, 1959, though the waterway had actually been operating for a full three months to assess any potential problems. In its first year almost 19 million metric tons of cargo passed through the Seaway, a figure that climbed to 30 million in 1964, 40 million in 1966, and 50 million in 1973. A high of over 57 million metric tons was reached in 1977. The one-billionth metric ton of cargo passed through the Seaway in June 1983, a year before the Seaway would celebrate its 25th anniversary.

The Seaway, however, has not been the revenue producer both countries thought it would be and, because it invested more money, Canada's losses have been higher. Supporters of the Seaway believed general and bulk cargo would be shipped along the route in large quantities. But the development of container ships whose cargo can be carried just as easily by train or truck has made the route primarily one for bulk cargo, such as grains and minerals, reducing potential business. Into the 1980s and 1990s different combinations of toll hikes and reductions were used to encourage use and increase revenue. Nonetheless, in the early 1990s the Seaway had created over 44,000 jobs and generated nearly $2 billion annually in personal income. Meanwhile, the Seaway's hydroelectric power project, at the Moses-Saunders Dam between Cornwall, Ontario and Massena, New York, supplied 1.6 million kilowatts of electricity to the surrounding area. In 1993 the Seaway registered its first total tonnage increase in five years, with almost 32 million metric tons floating through the Seaway. But this 2 percent increase was little more than half of the high achieved in 1977. However, into the mid-1990s annual tonnage shipped through the Seaway was increasing, moving closer to 40 million.

FURTHER READING

Canadian Encyclopedia, 2nd ed. Edmonton: Hurtig Publishers, s.v. ''Saint Lawrence Seaway.''

Dictionary of American History. New York: Scribner's, 1976, s.v. ''Saint Lawrence Seaway.''

Gibbons, Gail. *The Great St. Lawrence Seaway*. New York: William Morrow and Company, 1992.

''Great Lakes/St. Lawrence Seaway System,'' [cited May 25, 1999] available from the World Wide Web @ www.seaway.ca/english/features/history.html/.

Willis, Terri. *St. Lawrence River and Seaway*. New York: Raintree Steck-Vaughn Publishers, 1994.

SAMUEL SLATER BUILDS THE FIRST FACTORY

As a young British immigrant, Samuel Slater took credit for building the United States' first successful water-powered cotton mill in 1790. By producing replicas of innovative cotton-spinning machinery recently developed by the English, Slater was able to create a fully operational facility in Rhode Island. The construction of his factory represented a tremendous step forward for industry in the United States, which had been struggling to catch up to Great Britain in technological advancement. Slater became a textile entrepreneur whose style of factory construction and workforce management set the pattern for industrial development throughout New England. His contribution was so significant that President Andrew Jackson (1829–1837) once dubbed him the Father of American Manufacturers.

Prior to the Revolutionary War (1775–1783), England imposed many restrictions upon the colonial economy. Intent on maintaining an agrarian rather than an industrial economy in these regions, British legislators passed a series of acts to curb the development of industry in America. The first of these laws was enacted in 1719 and forbade the practice of metalworking. A 1750 law was more restrictive, explicitly prohibiting the use of a mill ''or other engine for slitting or rolling iron, or any plating forge to work with a tilt hammer, or any furnace for making steel.'' Before the enactment of this law some of this forbidden machinery had already been operational in the northern colonies.

Restrictions such as these, which expressed the common understanding of the subordinate role of the colonies in the mercantilist system , made up part of the complex set of motivations and complaints that eventually led to the separation of the colonies from England. Although the United States ultimately gained its independence, the British continued to hamper the new nation's industrial development by limiting the export of mechanical equipment. In response, the U.S. imposed protective tariffs on metalwork such as rolled iron, castings, and spikes, hoping to encourage a domestic capacity in these areas.

SLATER'S 1789 ARRIVAL MARKED THE UNFOLDING OF A FUTURE FOR INDUSTRY IN THE UNITED STATES: HE BROUGHT WITH HIM FROM ENGLAND A MENTAL BLUEPRINT OF THE STATE-OF-THE-ART MACHINERY USED FOR COTTON SPINNING.

The American Revolutionary War, the Embargo of 1807 (1807–1809), and, later, the War of 1812 (1812–1814), all of which involved blockades of American ports, impressed the U.S. political leadership with the necessity of fostering a domestic metalworking culture. For this reason, the United States Congress enacted patent law to provide incentive for industrial innovation although the patent process before 1836 was very lax and granted patents to ''inventors'' who were actually promoters. The same need to foster a metal-working culture led the new nation to found federal arsenals. The most famous one was in Springfield, Massachusetts, where in the last years of the eighteenth century inventors like Eli Whitney and Samuel Colt advanced and popularized the idea of standardizing machine parts. The United States endeavored to attain a degree of self-sufficiency in manufacturing and to move forward into industrial development, but it lacked both the workforce and the elements of technological know-how necessary to sustain industrial advancement. It continued to lag behind Western Europe, which had taken its first steps toward an industrial economy in the early eighteenth century.

This is what made Samuel Slater's 1789 arrival in New England so momentous. Slater brought with him from England a mental blueprint of the state-of-the-art machinery used for cotton spinning. British law sought to prevent the leakage of trade secrets, so Slater did not dare to carry written instructions or drawings on his passage overseas. Instead, he kept all of the information in his head, ''smuggling'' it into his new homeland.

Because England forbade the emigration of its skilled machinists, the 21 year-old Slater passed himself off as a farm laborer. In truth, he had already served as supervisor of machinery in a textile factory after completing an apprenticeship with Jedidiah Strutt, a successful British manufacturer of ribbed stockings. (Strutt's partner was Richard Arkwright, who had built world's first cotton-spinning mill in 1768.) Slater was about as skilled as a machinist could be, and in the United States he was to find fame and fortune in the application of his knowledge. Slater's contribution was not so much as an inventor. He made few if any breakthroughs in creating new machinery. His importance lay rather in the fact that his purloined knowledge of English technology filled in a number of blank spaces in the understanding of mechanical principles among inventors in the United States. It marked the unfolding of a direction and a future for industry in the new nation.

At the time of Slater's arrival, textile production in the United States was very crude. The work was labor-intensive and the result was of poor quality. He took a temporary position at the New York Manufacturing Company, a small textile business that had been struggling to replicate British yarn-spinning technology. But the New York facility lacked the waterpower that was necessary to run the new machinery, and Slater soon looked for opportunities elsewhere. He relocated to Pawtucket, Rhode Island where he joined the textile firm of Almy and Brown, who also aimed to imitate the British water-powered system. Slater offered the Pawtucket firm the expertise that it sought: He became a partner almost immediately and set out to erect the United States' first cotton-spinning mill.

Slater put his memory of the British technology to work, designing and constructing three machines for the carding of wool, several drawing and roving frames, and two spinning frames. Not long after the first mill's completion, Slater embarked on the construction of a larger facility, which was operational in 1793. The waterframe machinery was simple to use and did not require much manpower; in fact, the labor force consisted of 100 children who ranged in age from four to ten. Determined not to replicate the inhumane practices of some British manufacturers, Slater treated his little workers comparatively well and supplied them with good food. He eventually established a Sunday school for them, one of the first such schools in the nation.

Meanwhile Slater's wife Hannah, whom he had met and married in Rhode Island, turned out to be an inventor in her own right: she developed a method for making high-quality cotton sewing thread (previously, all thread had been made of linen). In 1798 Slater and his father-in-law went into partnership to manufacture the thread. Samuel Slater and Company, as their business became known, constructed its own machinery and erected mills near Pawtucket. Later the company expanded, opening mills in Smithfield, Rhode Island (later renamed Slatersville); Webster, Massachusetts; Jewett City, Connecticut; Amoskeag Falls, New Hampshire; and Manchester, New Hampshire. Slater had come a long way from introducing his first, modest-size facility. He had become one of several epicenters of industrial innovation in the United States. And with his good business and management sense he became something of a model for other U.S. manufacturers, who often emulated his practices.

Although Slater did not invent any new textile machinery, the construction of his first mill was often credited with launching the country's industrial revolution. Indeed, many other factories cropped up soon after his facility opened. Rhode Island's Blackwater River region, which surrounds the site of the original Slater mill in Pawtucket, became particularly dense with industry attracting immigrants and providing ample employment opportunities to whole families of mill workers. Around the country manufacturers of all kinds endeavored to construct their own machinery, promoting a trend that Slater had set in motion. The United States' transition from an agrarian to an industrial economy was underway.

See also: **Rhode Island System of Labor, Samuel Slater, Textile Industry**

FURTHER READING

Benes, James J. "An Industry Evolves: Lathes to Computers." *American Machinist.* August 1996.

Biographical Dictionary of American Business Leaders. Westport, CT: Greenwood Press, 1983, s.v. "Slater Family."

Gordon, John Steele. "Technology Transfer." *American Heritage*, February 1990.

Walton, Perry. *The Story of Textiles.* New York: Tudor Publishing Co., 1937.

Zimiles, Martha and Murray. *Early American Mills.* New York: Branhall House, 1973.

SANTA CLARA COUNTY V. SOUTHERN PACIFIC RAILROAD

In January 1886 a California circuit court heard the case of *Santa Clara County v. Southern Pacific Railroad Company*. The county government, the seat of which is San Jose, brought a complaint against the rail company over the issue of Southern Pacific's nonpayment of state taxes. The state had attempted to collect taxes for fences (which it assessed as "improvements") that Southern Pacific erected between the roadway and adjacent lands. The railroad company argued that California did not have the authority to assess taxes on the roadway or the fences because it had no jurisdiction to these lands or the improvements made to them. Southern Pacific's lawyers maintained that the corporation had been granted the lands through a federal act that was approved by the state of California. The declared object of the act was for "the construction of a railroad and telegraph line from the Missouri river to the Pacific, which, for all purposes of communication, travel, and transportation, so far as the public and the general government are concerned, should be operated 'as one connected, continuous line.'" Therefore, the assessment was judged void.

The favorable ruling that Southern Pacific received in this case stirred public outrage. Not only did the railroad control most of California's transportation, it exerted a powerful political influence. Among Southern Pacific's most vocal opponents was William Randolph Hearst (1863–1951), who, as publisher of the *San Francisco Examiner* newspaper, launched an attack on the monopolistic practices of the rail company. In 1901 the Southern Pacific became a bigger power when financier Edward Harriman (1848–1909) acquired it along with Central Pacific Railroad; Harriman thus dominated rail traffic in the West. Harriman's monopoly became the object of an investigation by the Interstate Commerce Commission (ICC) in 1906–1907.

Southern Pacific's undoing came partly at the hands of politician Hiram Johnson (1866–1945), the Progressive Republican candidate for California governor in 1910, who toured the state with his promise to "kick the Southern Pacific Railroad out of politics." Winning the election, Johnson and his fellow reformers gained control of both houses of the state legislature in 1911 and then they passed legislation to regulate the railroads and other public utilities. In 1913 the U.S. attorney general prosecuted Southern Pacific and Union railroads, claiming their merger violated the Sherman Anti-Trust Act of 1890.

See also: **Railroad Industry, Robber Barons**

SANTA FE

Santa Fe, New Mexico, is the oldest capital city in the United States. Situated in the north-central part of New Mexico, it was founded by the Spaniards in 1609–1610 as an outpost for their exploration and missionary activities in the Southwest. The original name given by the colonists was *La Villa Real de la Santa Fe*, which means the Royal City of the Holy Faith. Prior to the arrival of the Europeans, Santa Fe had been home to the Pueblo Indians, who were subjugated and converted to Christianity by the Spanish conquistadors. In a 1680 rebellion the Pueblo Indians reclaimed the city and occupied it again for the next twelve years, restoring native culture to the region. In 1692 the Spanish recaptured New Mexico and reestablished colonial rule. When Mexico gained independence from Spain in 1821, New Mexico became a province of the new country. Santa Fe flourished as a center for trade between the United States and Mexico. It prompted the establishment of a commercial route, the Santa Fe Trail, which ran from western Missouri, across the Plains, and along the Arkansas River to the Rocky Mountains, where the road turned south into Santa Fe. The wagon road was heavily used until 1880 when the railroad was completed, but the trains went through Albuquerque, not Santa Fe. By that time New Mexico had become a U.S. territory (1850). Santa Fe has remained New Mexico's capital city, although Albuquerque has far surpassed it as a commercial center.

See also: **New Mexico, Pueblo Indians, Santa Fe Trail**

SANTA FE TRAIL

The Santa Fe Trail was a major overland route for westward expansion during the 1800s. Like the Oregon Trail to the Pacific Northwest, it originated in Independence, Missouri. The Santa Fe Trail, whose terminus was Santa Fe in north-central New Mexico, proceeded westward along the prairie to Great Bend, Kansas. From there the route split into three branches. The western trail, also called the Taos Trail, followed the Arkansas River west to the Sangre de Cristo Range of the Rocky Mountains. Travelers then went due south through La Veta Pass (in south-central Colorado) into New Mexico. The middle trail also followed the Arkansas River westward into present day Colorado, traversing the grasslands in the southeastern corner of the state and following Raton Pass (south of present day Trinidad, Colorado) into New Mexico. The shortest route (and, due to Indian attacks, the most dangerous) cut southwest through Kansas, into the Cimarron Valley, and crossed the northwest corner of Oklahoma into New Mexico. From Santa Fe, another route, the Old Spanish Trail, extended westward to Los Angeles. After Mexico gained independence from Spain (1821), Santa Fe became the center of the country's trade with the United States. The Santa Fe Trail was about 1,200 miles (1,930 kilometers) long and took between 40 and 60 days to travel.

The Santa Fe Trail was first traversed in 1821 by Virginia-born trader William Becknell (1796?–1865), who in 1822 used wagons on the route. During the next two decades, less than one hundred wagons each year used the trail; by the late 1860s, the average number climbed to more than five thousand per year. The Santa Fe Trail remained a major commercial route until the 1880s, when the transcontinental railroad was completed.

See also: **California, Colorado, Kansas, New Mexico, Oklahoma, Oregon Trail, Santa Fe**

SAVINGS

Savings are the amount of income left after a consumer has finished making personal expenditures and paying taxes. People save to pay for retirement, education, or vacations. They usually put their savings into bank savings or checking accounts, invest them in securities like stocks or mutual funds, or keep savings as cash. The percentage of personal income that people save depends on how optimistic they are about their future income, their own personal inclination to spend now or "save for a rainy day," and the amount of interest or return they expect to get by saving or investing.

Economists generally regard saving as good because the economy can only grow if some consumers refrain from consuming and instead invest in the factories and equipment that enable companies to expand production. However, in a phenomenon called "the paradox of thrift," economists have also shown that when economic growth is threatened by weak demand, too much saving will actually result in slower economic growth because consumers will be buying less.

The amount of income that people in the United States save has varied significantly throughout the twentieth century. During the Great Depression (1929–1939) for example, consumers needed all their income for necessities—saving rates were consequently negative. During World War II (1939–1945), however, government rationing and savings bond drives encouraged people in the United States to save. By 1944 U.S. citizens were saving 25.7 percent of their incomes—the highest savings rate in the century. In the postwar years, U.S. citizens have saved less and less. By 1981 consumers were saving only 9.4 percent of their incomes; by 1989 only 5.1 percent, and by 1997 only 3.8

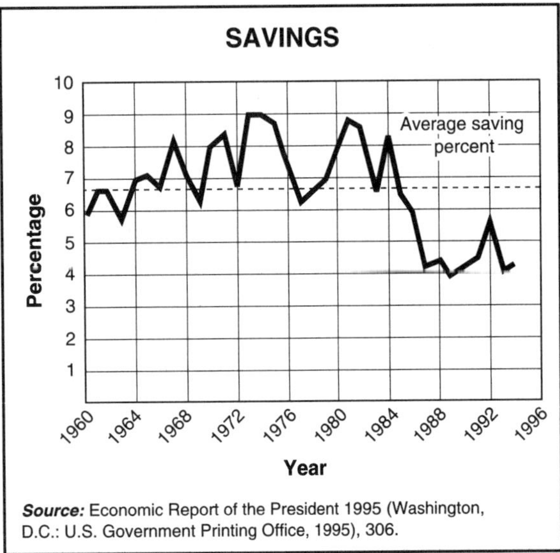

Source: Economic Report of the President 1995 (Washington, D.C.: U.S. Government Printing Office, 1995), 306.

The percentage of income saved by Americans has varied over the years, as demonstrated. Since the 1980s, saved income has generally declined.

percent—the lowest rate since the Depression. To encourage U.S. citizens to save more, Congress created Individual Retirement Accounts (IRAs) in 1982. IRAs did encourage consumers to invest more, but the savings rate continued to fall because easy-to-obtain credit cards and low home mortgage down payments enabled consumers to buy homes and other goods without first saving for them.

By the late 1990s some economists estimated that U.S. consumers were saving only a third of what they needed to maintain their standard of living in retirement. As the twentieth century ended, politicians debated several solutions for increasing national savings, including scrapping the income tax system in favor of a flat tax or a national sales tax and creating government-sponsored ''Universal Savings Accounts'' that would let U.S. citizens invest part of their taxes in mutual funds or bonds.

See also: **Investment**

SAVINGS & LOAN ASSOCIATIONS

Savings and loan associations (S&Ls), along with savings banks and credit unions, are known as thrift institutions. Thrifts and commercial banks are also known as depository institutions and are distinguished from non-depository institutions such as investment banks, insurance companies, and pension funds. S&Ls traditionally have taken savings, time, and demand deposits as their primary liability, and made most of their income from loaning deposits out as mortgages.

The first savings and loan association was organized in 1831 as the Oxford Provident Building Association of Philadelphia. Like the building societies of England and the credit cooperatives of Europe, it was a membership organization that took savings deposits from its members and in turn made home loans to them. S&Ls soon accepted deposits from the general public and became public depository institutions. They also became the primary source of credit for working individuals to purchase their own homes at a time when commercial banks did not offer mortgages. By the end of the nineteenth century there were nearly 6000 S&Ls in existence.

See also: **Savings and Loan (Failures of)**

SAVINGS AND LOAN FAILURES

Since the early 1930s savings institutions had enjoyed more than 50 years of economic success. However, the end of the 1970s threatened industrial prosperity with unprecedented high inflation and interest rates. The financial structure of the typical thrift was at the core of the problem. Most institutions borrowed for short terms, in the form of depositors' savings accounts, but lent for long terms through fixed-rate home mortgages. While interest rates remained stable, thrifts could earn acceptable profits. When market forces caused rates to soar, the delicate balance was threatened, as payments to depositors' rose without a corresponding increase in receipts from mortgages. In 1978 regulators allowed thrifts to pay higher interest rates on certificates of deposit. This checked disintermediation (savers going to other institutions), but the cost of funds rose. Profits, therefore, shrank or turned into losses.

Thrift executives knew that erosion of net worth jeopardized the industry's health. They sought relief from long-term, fixed-rate loans that tied them to low returns. The U.S. Congress was not prepared to back an industry-wide bailout. As a compromise, it passed the Depository Institutions Deregulation and Monetary Control Act (DIDMCA) in 1980, granting additional lending powers to thrifts. Most promising was the ability to originate short-term consumer loans and high-yield commercial real estate loans. Despite DIDMCA, about 36 percent of all thrifts were losing money by the end of 1980. Even worse, in 1981 about 80 percent of the industry lost money. Congress reacted with additional deregulation in 1982. It passed the Garn-St. Germain Act, giving thrifts even broader investment powers.

The government also allowed thrifts favorable reporting treatment. Purchasers of failing institutions were given special accounting privileges. In addition, thrifts were authorized by the Federal Home Loan Bank Board (FHLBB) to utilize lenient Regulatory Accounting Principles (RAP). The FHLBB allowed thrifts to reduce their capital requirements from five percent to three percent between 1980 and 1982. This leniency was allowed to keep troubled thrifts from being taken over by regulators.

After deregulation, and with interest rates subsiding in 1983, the industry appeared to be heading toward prosperity. Thrifts attempted to grow out of their problems by generating more high-yield investments. The real estate market was booming, so thrift managers were tempted to invest in risky commercial ventures. They often disregarded such factors as lack of expertise, unfamiliar geographic territories, and questionable appraisals and underwriting. Loan brokers and junk bond brokers also found an eager market in the thrift industry.

Depositors continued to patronize savings institutions despite growing losses and failures. DIDMCA had increased deposit insurance coverage to $100,000. With this level of insurance, depositors had little fear of losing their savings at faltering institutions. Indeed, the failing institutions often offered the highest rates.

In 1986 the Tax Reform Act repealed liberal depreciation and personal deduction provisions. Many commercial real estate deals were structured around such tax shelters. Without them, the enormous market for real-estate syndicates dried up. At the same time worldwide oil prices dropped, which negatively affected the economic health of states that relied on the oil industry. The real estate market in the Southwest went sour almost overnight, affecting real estate values throughout the country. The booming real estate market of 1983–1986 was transformed into an overbuilt market by 1987.

In 1988 the FHLBB committed nearly $40 billion in 1988 to take over failing institutions, merge them into marketable packages, and sell them to investors. But the program almost bankrupted the Federal Savings and Loan Insurance Corporation (FSLIC). FHLBB Chairman Danny C. Wall either concealed the depths of the FSLIC insolvency or did not recognize the extent of the problem. Matters were made worse by errors in judgment on the part of thrift managers, by the greed of investors, by weak examination and supervision practices by regulators, and by numerous alleged cases of fraud and misconduct on the part of thrift insiders, regulators, investors, and members of Congress.

When President George Bush (1989–1993) took over the presidency in 1989, he was extremely concerned about the unstable condition of the FSLIC and the accumulated losses at hundreds of thrifts. With the assistance of Richard C. Breeden, executive director of the White House Regulatory Task Force, Robert R. Glauber, undersecretary in the Treasury Department, and L. William Seidman, chairman of the Federal Deposit Insurance Corporation (FDIC), Bush drafted the Financial Institutions Rescue, Recovery, and Enforcement Act (FIRREA). In August, 1989, the act was approved by Congress and President Bush signed FIRREA into law a few days later.

FIRREA had four explicit goals. The first was to improve the ability of regulators to supervise savings institutions by strengthening industry capital and accounting standards. The second was to return the federal deposit insurance fund to a sound financial base. The third was to provide funds to deal with the disposal of failed institutions. The fourth was to strengthen the enforcement ability of regulators through reconfigured powers and a new organizational structure. An unstated goal of FIRREA was to return the emphasis of the business to its roots of home mortgage lending.

FIRREA featured several key provisions. It dissolved both the FSLIC and the FHLBB. The responsibility of insuring the thrift industry's deposits reverted to the FDIC. The duty of supervising the Federal Home Loan Bank (FHLB) system and individual thrifts was passed to a new organization, the Office of Thrift Supervision (OTS). Two new additional organizations were created. The Resolution Trust Corporation (RTC) was formed to dispose of the assets of failed thrifts. The Resolution Funding Corporation (RFC) was created as the fund-raiser for the RTC. The RFC was initially authorized to borrow up to $50 billion, through bonds, to fund RTC activities.

Numerous thrift powers were restructured. FIRREA banned investment in junk bonds, limited investment in nonresidential loans, set loan-to-one-borrower limits to national bank levels, and placed strict limitations on loans to affiliated parties. Most important, it mandated that thrifts hold at least 70 percent of their assets in mortgage-related investments. Penalties for failure to comply were tough at both the corporate and the individual level.

FIRREA directed the OTS to set capital requirements for thrifts at levels no less stringent than those of national banks. Core capital requirements were set at three percent of total assets, and tangible capital was set at 1.5 percent of total assets. Thus, the definition of capital itself was altered. The previous reliance on RAP standards of accounting was abolished.

President Bush's stated intention was to fix the thrift industry permanently by closing down or selling hundreds of thrifts. His method of ensuring that old problems would not resurface was to subject surviving thrifts to the capital and accounting rules applied to national banks.

FIRREA was a sharp response to the thrift crisis. Considerable controversy arose in the business community, especially among the thrifts that were directly affected. Some analysts believed that the capital requirements would bankrupt more institutions than necessary. There was a large group of thrifts working slowly to recover from their problems. They were not grossly insolvent but they would not be able to meet new capital requirements for years. Continued weaknesses within the real estate markets did not help. Imposing stringent standards on a weakened industry pushed hundreds of these thrifts over the brink. This presented the RTC with a larger, more expensive task than the government had expected.

The short-run impact of FIRREA on the business community extended further than the thrift industry. FIRREA caused all lending institutions to tighten credit practices, so businesses had to postpone or cancel worthy projects. Tight credit contributed to a declining economic climate. Banking regulators tightened oversight and enforcement in their industry. Although inflation and interest rates were in check, banking became more conservative. Many banks were satisfied to watch profit margins improve through lower costs of funds. The resulting "credit crunch" contributed to job losses throughout the economy. Closings and mergers within the thrift industry meant an additional dramatic drop in jobs.

By the end of September, 1991, the OTS estimated that 464 thrifts (21 percent of the industry) were on the brink of takeover. These institutions had not been seized because there was no money available to do so. The OTS intended to take over all failing institutions and have the RTC either sell them intact or liquidate them piecemeal. To dispose of a thrift intact, the RTC had to make up any negative net worth. The goal was to entice investors, especially commercial banks, to purchase failing thrifts through the financial backing of bonds issued by the RTC/RFC. Unfortunately, FIRREA stripped thrifts of many powers that had made them attractive investments. Unless a thrift could open new depository markets for a bank, it did not offer much advantage to the prospective purchaser.

FIRREA's objective of making depository insurance financially sound also failed to be met. FIRREA did not correct the problems that existed in the FSLIC; it merely pushed the problems onto the FDIC, jeopardizing its solvency. Because the $100,000 insurance coverage was not changed, depositors and institutions remained susceptible to risk-taking. Since fixed insurance premiums were not changed, risky institutions were afforded the same degree of protection at the same cost as safe institutions.

Resolving the thrift crisis involved huge federal payments to honor commitments made by the FSLIC and new ones resulting from FIRREA. A substantial amount of the borrowing was to be repaid from the sale of assets of failed thrifts. Unfortunately, asset sales could not cover the large borrowings. This shortfall became the responsibility of taxpayers. Like the national debt, the FIRREA debt will likely fall on future generations of taxpayers.

Several lessons emerged from FIRREA and the events that led to its passage. First, deregulation in the early 1980s seemed to hamper thrift industry efforts to reverse losses. More lenient rules and broadened powers were not accompanied by stricter supervision. Second, the deposit insurance system encouraged carelessness on the part of depositors and depository institutions. Fixed-price premiums ignored risk and transgressed the cardinal rules of insurance. Third, FIRREA may have been based on sound intentions, but the effect was similar to that of overmedication of a sickly patient. Good principles applied abruptly may have led the industry toward extinction. Fourth, an improperly funded program cannot expect success. FIRREA was more ambitious than its budget would allow. The final costs may not be known for generations.

FURTHER READING

Bush, Vanessa, and Katherine Morrall. "The Business Reviews a New Script." *Savings Institutions*, October 1989.

Lowy, Martin E. *High Rollers: Inside the Savings and Loan Debacle*. New York: Praeger, 1991.

Mayer, Martin. *The Greatest-Ever Bank Robbery: The Collapse of the Savings and Loan Industry*. New York: Charles Scribner's Sons, 1990.

Pilzer, Paul Z., and Robert Deitz. *Other People's Money: The Inside Story of the S and L Mess*. New York: Simon and Schuster, 1989.

United States Congressional Budget Office. *The Economic Effects of the Savings and Loan Crisis.* Washington, DC: United States Congressional Budget Office, 1992.

SCALAWAGS

"Scalawag" was a derogatory term used by recalcitrant white southerners after the Civil War and during the dozen years of Reconstruction (1865–1877). It was applied to those white southerners who cooperated with the Union troops and with the Reconstruction State legislatures. Many of these "Scalawags" came from small farm, non-slaveholding backgrounds and in fact had resented the southern planter class and its slave system even before the Civil War. They felt correctly that the existence of slavery hurt them too, because slave labor depressed the bargaining power of wage labor. They argued that slaves would always impoverish its non-slave-owning white neighbors. The Scalawags and many former slaves tried to join the Republican Party in the South to secure their status as full southern citizens. The majority of southern whites, however, looked at the Scalawags with contempt. In their eyes, the Scalawags were traitors to the southern cause and to their fellow whites. Some of these defeated members of the Confederacy joined paramilitary groups like the Ku Klux Klan and the Mississippi "Red Shirts" and others. They wanted to intimidate or, in some cases, to kill both the former slaves who were trying to secure their new rights and the Scalawags, who were trying to build an alliance with the ex-slaves in the southern Republican Party. The intimidation worked, for the most part, and the Republican Party never established itself in the post–Civil War South.

See also: **Carpetbaggers**

SCARCITY

Scarcity and its opposite, abundance, are relative and vague descriptions as to the availability of useful resources for human purposes. Resources that command a price in economic transactions, like fertile land, machines, or human talent, may be considered scarce. This market oriented definition of scarcity can be summed up in the following way: scarcity exists in a marketplace when a resource of any type commands a price in the market which make some producers forgo otherwise rewarding applications of the resource. The price of a resource in unrestricted economic transactions is a useful way to measure the scarcity of the resource. The more scarce a resource, the higher its price will tend to be. At times, when there is a limit to the availability of a resource, the resource will obviously be regarded as scarce in the marketplace. This scarcity will tend to drive prices up, or will cause the market to look elsewhere for more plentiful and less costly alternatives. Questions are always raised as to how human societies will respond to the depletion of resources, and how society will respond during times of acute general scarcity to avoid catastrophic suffering and mortality. Historically, scarcity has frequently caused changes in lifestyle, land migration, consumption-patterns, increased exploration for new material, development of general ecological awareness, and ecologically-oriented technology, so as to minimize the scarcity of resources needed for subsistence.

SCHUMPETER, JOSEPH ALOIS

Joseph Alois Schumpeter (1883–1950) was an Austrian economist who significantly shaped the development of economic theory in Europe. He taught economics at various universities in the Austro-Hungarian Empire and later at Harvard University in the United States. His many publications furthered the public's understanding of business cycles, the role of the entrepreneur, capitalist development, and the use of mathematics in economics.

Schumpeter was born in Triesch, Moravia (present-day Czech Republic), on February 8, 1883. He was the only son of Alois Schumpeter, a clothing manufacturer who died when Joseph was four years old. His mother, Joanna Gruner, later married an Austrian general. The family moved to Vienna and Joseph was raised in a traditional, aristocratic manner. In 1891 Schumpeter graduated with honors from the Theresianum, a distinguished boys' school. He then studied law and economics at the University of Vienna.

In 1906 Schumpeter completed his law degree and went to England where he spent a year doing research at the London School of Economics and the British Museum. He spent the following year in Cairo practicing law at the International Mixed Court of Egypt. It was there that he wrote his first book, a study of economic methodology entitled *The Nature and Essence of Theoretical Economics*. In this book Schumpeter tried to paint a picture of the field of theoretical economics for a German audience because he felt that they were not really familiar with the workings of ''pure economics.'' Economic theory was not even taught at German universities at the time.

Schumpeter obtained a position teaching economics at the University of Czernowitz (present-day Chernovtsy, Ukraine) in 1908 at the age of 26, making him the youngest professor in the Austro-Hungarian empire. In 1911 he joined the faculty at the University of Graz where he published *The Theory of Economic Development* (1912), which is often regarded as his most important work. In this book Schumpeter first argued that the entrepreneur was key to stimulating the business cycle, an idea that he would later expand.

During the 1913–1914 academic year Schumpeter went to Columbia University in New York as a visiting professor. Apart from that visit, Schumpeter remained at the University of Graz until 1918. His third major book was published in 1914 and was titled *Economic Doctrine and Method: A Historical Sketch*. This book was written as part of a handbook in economics and therefore was not as provocative as his first two publications. Nonetheless, the historical aspect of economics greatly interested Schumpeter and he would return to this topic later in life.

At the end of World War I (1914–1918) the Austro-Hungarian empire was broken up and Austria became a small republic. At this point Schumpeter left academic life to pursue a career in finance and to dabble in politics. Schumpeter briefly served as the secretary of finance in the new socialist government, but was forced to resign even before presenting his financial proposals to the parliament. Schumpeter's next career move was becoming president of a private bank in Vienna. When the bank failed in 1924, Schumpeter went bankrupt and returned to academic life.

The 1920s were a difficult decade for Schumpeter in all aspects of his life. His professional exploits outside of academia had failed. Though he was able to find employment again, he found it difficult to produce another book for quite a while. To make matters worse his mother, his new wife, and his newborn child all suddenly died, leaving Schumpeter depressed for many years.

In 1924 Schumpeter was appointed professor of public finance at the University of Bonn in Germany. He visited Harvard University in 1927 and again in 1930. At Harvard he helped found the Econometric Society, which focused on using statistics and mathematics in economic analyses. In the early 1930s Schumpeter was passed over for the position of economic theory department chair at the University of Berlin, Germany's most prestigious university. He was bitterly disappointed and decided to leave Europe. While this period had not been especially creative for Schumpeter, he did produce more than 70 articles between 1919 and 1932. In 1932 Schumpeter finally accepted a permanent position at Harvard as a professor of economics where he remained for the rest of his life, becoming a U.S. citizen in 1939.

In 1939 Schumpeter published his next book, *Business Cycles*, a theoretical, historical, and statistical analysis of the capitalist process. In this two-volume study Schumpeter argued that innovation was the chief agent of social change and that business cycles were a product of innovation. In 1942 Schumpeter published his next major work, *Capitalism, Socialism, and Democracy*, which was highly regarded by critics. In it Schumpeter maintained that capitalism would eventually become a victim of its own successes and die away. As business grew, it would become conservative in the worst sense of the word, thus eliminating risk-taking, innovative entrepreneurs from the decision-making process. Business would stagnate, and growing unrest among the people would lead to the triumph of socialism. In fact, his last book was on socialism, which he titled *Imperialism and Social Classes* (1951). When Schumpeter died of a cerebral hemorrhage in 1950, he left an unfinished manuscript behind him, *History of Economic Analysis*. This, his final work, was edited and published in 1954 by his third wife, Elizabeth Boody Schumpeter.

Schumpeter was a prolific writer; throughout his career he authored 15 books and pamphlets and over 200 articles, book reviews, and review articles. He also left hundreds of aphorisms in his private papers. Although he suffered from bouts of depression most of his life, Schumpeter was able to focus his energy on what he loved best and made a great contribution to the field of economics.

***See also:* Business Cycle, Capitalism, Entrepreneurship, Joseph Schumpeter, Socialism**

FURTHER READING

Allen, Robert Loring. *Opening Doors: The Life and Work of Joseph Schumpeter*. New Brunswick: Transaction Publishers, 1991.

Marz, Eduard. *Joseph Schumpeter: Scholar, Teacher, and Politician*. New Haven: Yale University Press, 1991.

Stolper, Wolfgang F. *Joseph Alois Schumpeter: The Public Life of a Private Man*. New Jersey: Princeton University Press, 1994.

Swedberg, Richard. *Schumpeter: A Biography*. New Jersey: Princeton University Press, 1991.

SCIENTIFIC MANAGEMENT

Scientific management, also known as Taylorism, is a system to gain maximum efficiency from workers and machinery. This system was developed by American industrial engineer Frederick Winslow Taylor (1856–1915). As foreman in a steel plant, Taylor undertook time and motion studies and conducted experiments to determine the "one best way" to do any given job. He developed detailed systems to yield the highest possible productivity levels. Taylor first presented his theories in 1903 to the American Academy of Mechanical Engineers. Efficiency was the cornerstone of Taylorism: production processes should not waste time or materials. He published his ideas in the landmark work, *The Principles of Scientific Management* (1911), and he became a well-known engineering consultant who was contracted by companies eager to maximize their output.

The doctrine of scientific management was soon embraced by U.S. industry. As transportation networks improved and U.S. population grew rapidly in the early 1900s, expansion of markets placed great demands on industry. Applying Taylor's scientific management, manufacturers were able to boost productivity by as much as 200 percent.

Because Taylorism broke production processes into individual tasks, each with its own best practice, new workers could be quickly and easily trained; adherents believed this was another benefit of the concept. Scientific management had many advocates, including engineers Frank Gilbreth (1868–1924) and Lillian Gilbreth (1878–1972). These two furthered Taylor's work by publishing volumes such as *Primer of Scientific Management* (1911), *Psychology of Management* (1912), and also studies on motion, fatigue, and time. Among those who applied scientific management were Ford Motor Company (in developing the assembly line for the Model T); Boston retailer Filene's (one of the first commercial enterprises to use the method); and Bethlehem Steel (which conducted experiments in the loading of pig iron).

Scientific management also had its detractors; Taylorism was criticized for having a dehumanizing effect on labor. In making every job routine, some charged, the system separated the minds of workers from their hands. The system was also criticized for eliminating the need for skilled workers and giving management absolute control over production processes. Theories concerning worker output were modified during the second half of the twentieth century. Nevertheless, principles of scientific management remained evident in the workplace in the late 1990s. The adoption of scientific management is credited with boosting American productivity and increasing stockholder profits.

See also: **William Edwards Deming, Peter Drucker, Frederick Winslow Taylor**

SEARS, RICHARD WARREN

Richard Warren Sears (1863–1914) and his partner A. C. Roebuck founded the first large-scale mail-order business in the United States and one of the world's largest retail stores. The company's extensive catalog eventually became a fixture in U.S. homes and changed the way people shopped. The company also helped foster the growth of the mail-order industry worldwide.

Richard Sears was born on December 7, 1863, in Stewartville, Minnesota, to Eliza A. Benton and James Warren Sears, a successful wagon maker. When Richard was 15, his father lost his substantial fortune in a stock farm venture; his father died two years later. Young Richard then took a job in the general offices of the Minneapolis and St. Paul Railroad to help support his widowed mother and his sisters.

Once he had qualified as a station agent Sears asked to be transferred to a smaller town in the belief that he could do better there financially than in the big city. Eventually he was made station agent in Redwood Falls, Minnesota, where he took advantage of every selling opportunities that came his way. He used his experience with railroad shipping and telegraph communications to develop his idea for a mail-order business.

In 1895 Sears married Anna Lydia Mechstroth of Minneapolis and they had three children. Sears retired from business in 1909 and lived his remaining years on his farm north of Chicago before his death on September 28, 1914.

The man who was known as the "P. T. Barnum of merchandising" had a humble and unremarkable start in business. As a railroad station agent in a small Minnesota town, Sears lived modestly, sleeping in a loft right at the station and doing chores to pay for his room and board. Since his official duties were not time consuming, Sears soon began to look for other ways to make money after working hours. He ended up selling coal and lumber and he also shipped venison purchased from Native American tribes.

In 1886 an unexpected opportunity came his way when a jeweler in town refused to accept a shipment of watches because no rail freight charges had been paid. Rather than having the railroad pay to return the shipment, Sears obtained permission to dispose of the watches himself. He then offered them to other station agents for $14 each, pointing out that they could resell the watches for a tidy profit. The strategy worked and before long Sears was buying more watches to sustain a flourishing business. Within just a few months after he began advertising in St. Paul, Sears quit his railroad job and set up a mail-order business in Minneapolis that he named the R. W. Sears Watch Company.

Offering goods by mail rather than in a retail store had the advantage of low operating costs. Sears had no employees and he was able to rent a small office for just $10 a month. His desk was a kitchen table and he sat on a chair he had bought for 50 cents. But the shabby surroundings did not discourage the energetic young entrepreneur. Hoping to expand his market, Sears advertised his watches in national magazines and newspapers. Low costs and a growing customer base enabled him to make enough money in his first year to move to Chicago and publish a catalog of his goods.

In Chicago Sears hired Alvah C. Roebuck to fix watches that had been returned to the company for adjustments or repairs. The men soon became business partners and they started handling jewelry as well as watches. A master salesman, Sears developed a number of notable advertising and promotional schemes, including the popular and lucrative "club plan." According to the rules of the club, 38 men placed one dollar each week into a pool and chose a weekly winner by lot. Thus, at the end of 38 weeks, each man in the club had his own new watch. Such strategies boosted revenues so much that by 1889 Sears decided to sell the business for $70,000 and move to Iowa to become a banker.

Sears soon grew bored with country life, however, and before long he had started a new mail-order business featuring watches and jewelry. Because he had agreed not to compete for the same business in the Chicago market for a period of three years after selling his company, Sears established his new enterprise in Minneapolis, Minnesota. He hired Roebuck again and this time he dubbed the product of their partnership A. C. Roebuck and Company. In 1893 Sears moved the business to Chicago and renamed it Sears, Roebuck and Company.

Once established in Chicago, the company grew rapidly. The first edition of the Sears catalog published in the mid-1880s had included a list of only 25 watches. By 1892, however, it had expanded to 140 pages offering "everything from wagons to baby carriages, shotguns to saddles." Sales soared to nearly $280,000. A mere two years later the catalog contained 507 pages worth of merchandise that average Americans could afford. Orders poured in steadily and the customer base continued to grow. By 1900 the number of Sears catalogs in circulation reached 853,000.

Sears was the architect of numerous innovative selling strategies that contributed to his company's development. In addition to his club plan, for example, he came up with what was known as the "Iowazation" project: the company asked each of its best customers in Iowa to distribute two dozen Sears catalogs. These customers would then receive premiums based on the amount of merchandise ordered by those to whom they had distributed the catalogs. The scheme proved to be spectacularly successful and it ended up being used in other states, too.

Such tremendous growth led to problems, however. While Sears was a brilliant marketer (he wrote all of the catalog material), he lacked solid organizational and management skills. He frequently offered merchandise in the catalog that he did not have available for shipment, and after the orders came in he had to scramble to find the means to fill them. Workdays were frequently 16 hours long; the partners themselves toiled seven days a week. Fulfilling orders accurately and efficiently also posed a challenge. One customer wrote, "For heaven's sake, quit sending me sewing machines. Every time I go to the station I find another one. You have shipped me five already." Roebuck became exhausted by the strain of dealing with these concerns and he sold his interest in the company to Sears in 1895 for $25,000.

With his partner out of the picture, Sears badly needed a manager. He eventually found one in Aaron Nussbaum, who bought into the company with his brother-in-law, Julius Rosenwald. By 1895 the company was grossing almost $800,000 a year. Five years later that figure had shot up to $11 million, surpassing sales at Montgomery Ward, a mail-order company that had been founded back in 1872. In 1901 Sears and Rosenwald bought out Nussbaum for $1.25 million.

According to John Steele Gordon's article published in *American Heritage*, it was Rosenwald, not

Sears, who transformed Sears, Roebuck "from a shapeless, inefficient, rapidly expanding corporate mess into the retailing titan of much of the twentieth century." He streamlined the system by which orders were processed, employing a color-coding scheme to track them and an assembly-line method of filling them. These efficient new techniques enabled the company to meet the challenge of handling an ever-increasing number of orders. By 1906, for example, Sears, Roebuck was averaging 20,000 orders a day. During the Christmas season the number jumped to 100,000 orders a day. That year the company moved into a brand-new facility with more than three million square feet of floor space. At the time it was the largest business building in the world.

In 1909 Sears resigned as president of the company he had founded. His health was poor and many of his extravagant promotional schemes had begun to run into opposition from his fellow executives, including Rosenwald. He turned the company over to his partner and retired to his farm north of Chicago. At the time of his death in 1914, Sears left behind an estate of $25 million and an enduring legacy of success in the highly competitive world of retailing.

Richard Sears had a genius for marketing and he exploited new technologies to reach customers nationwide via mail-order. At first he targeted rural areas: People had few retail options there and they appreciated the convenience of being able to shop from their homes. Sears made use of the telegraph as well as the mails for ordering and communicating. He relied on the country's expanding rail freight system to deliver goods quickly; passage of the Rural Free Delivery Act made servicing remote farms and villages even easier and less expensive.

However, the rapid growth of the mail-order business dominated by Sears, Roebuck had a negative impact on smaller retailers. Unable to compete with both the industry giant and its main competitor, Montgomery Ward, some merchants angrily began referring to the company as "Rears and Soreback" or "Shears and Rawbuck." They steadily lost customers to Sears' lower prices, wider selection, and aggressive promotional campaigns. But the growth of Sears, Roebuck had one positive impact nationwide. As residents of rural areas found themselves able to purchase the kinds of goods that had once been available only in big cities, they came to feel a greater sense of social connection with the rest of the country.

See also: **Chain Stores, Department Stores, Montgomery Ward, Sears Roebuck**

FURTHER READING

Bowman, John S., ed. *The Cambridge Dictionary of American Biography* . New York: Cambridge University Press, 1995, s.v. "Sears, Richard."

Emmett, Boris, and John E. Jeuck. *Catalogues and Counter: A History of Sears, Roebuck and Company.* Chicago: University of Chicago Press, 1950.

Gordon, John Steele. "No Respect: A Rule of Thumb on Executives' Salaries—They Aren't Overpaid If There'd Be No Company Without Them." *American Heritage*, September 1993.

Littell, Robert. "The Great American Salesman." *Fortune*, February 1932.

Weil, Gordon L. *Sears Roebuck U.S.A.* New York: Stein and Day, 1977.

SEARS, ROEBUCK AND CO.

Retail giant Sears, Roebuck and Co. can trace its roots to a shipment of unwanted pocket watches that Richard W. Sears (1863–1914) was able to sell to his fellow freight agents on the Minneapolis and St. Louis Railroad in 1886. After selling $5,000 worth of watches in six months, Sears quit the railroad and founded the R. W. Sears Watch Company in Minneapolis. Sears built his business by buying up discontinued lines from manufacturers and selling them at a discount to his customers. Business expanded so quickly that he moved to Chicago in 1887 and hired Alvah Roebuck as the company's watch repairer.

In 1888 Sears published its first mail order catalog, 80 pages of watches and jewelry. Within two years it had grown to 322 pages, and clothing and durable goods such as sewing machines and bicycles were added. The advent of the rural free delivery system in 1891 helped Sears reach its primary customer, the rural farmer, more easily. The 1894 catalog cover proclaimed Sears the "Cheapest Supply House on Earth." Much of the company's success was due to Richard Sears' innovative unconditional money-back guarantee, by which the company stood.

In 1893 Sears and Roebuck became partners and the firm changed its name to Sears, Roebuck and Co. A shrewd and aggressive salesperson, Richard Sears believed in continuous expansion and risk-taking. That made Alvah Roebuck uneasy and two years later he sold his interest to Sears, remaining on as a repairer. In 1895 the company reorganized with a capitalization of $150,000 split three ways among Richard Sears, local

> In fact, the cover of the May 1993 issue of *Fortune* featured the logos of Sears, IBM, and General Motors with the prominent headline, ''Dinosaurs!'' While normally I would not speak on behalf of other companies, my response to that headline paraphrases Mark Twain: ''reports of our deaths are greatly exaggerated.'' At Sears, we took that cover, that story, that entire experience, as a challenge. What could have been a serious setback to our progress and morale became quite the opposite and important rallying point in our ongoing re-invigoration and revitalization. The momentum was underway—our fire was lit. If that allusion to extinction hastened our pace, so much the better.
>
> **Arthur C. Martinez, CEO of Sears, Roebuck and Co., 1997**

entrepreneur Aaron Nusbaum, and Nusbaum's brother-in-law Julius Rosenwald. When Nusbaum was forced to sell out in 1901 after clashing with Sears, his one-third share in the company was worth $1.25 million.

The company went public in 1906, in part to raise money for a new headquarters on Chicago's West Side. Wall Street appeared leery of Sears's tactics so he resigned as president in 1908. He remained as chairman and retired in 1913, never having presided over a board meeting. He died in 1914.

Leadership of Sears, Roebuck fell to Julius Rosenwald and under his skillful direction sales increased sixfold from 1908 to 1920. In 1911 Sears began offering credit to its customers. At a time when banks would not consider extending credit to consumers, this move helped Sears to sell more big-ticket items. In 1913 the parcel post rate was introduced and Sears quickly became the parcel post's single largest customer. Rosenwald became one of the richest men in the world and also a noted philanthropist, donating more than $63 million in his lifetime, mainly to Jewish causes and to improve the education of Southern African Americans. He was named a trustee of the Tuskegee Institute and he became a good friend of its founder, Booker T. Washington (1856–1915).

Sears was exclusively a mail-order operation until 1925, when it opened its first retail outlet in Chicago. By the end of the decade it had 324 retail stores and in 1931 retail sales surpassed catalog sales. Sears's entry into retailing has been credited to Robert Wood, a former executive at rival cataloger Montgomery Ward and Company, who joined Sears in 1924. Wood, nicknamed ''The General,'' earned a reputation for genius through his long career in merchandising.

Wood became president of Sears in 1929 and he ran the company until 1954. Sears was becoming more involved in the affairs of its suppliers, many of whom depended solely on Sears for business. In 1929 two suppliers, Upton Machine and Nineteen Hundred Washer Company, merged with Sears's help to form Nineteen Hundred Corporation, which would become Whirlpool in 1950. In 1931 Sears diversified by creating its Allstate subsidiary to sell auto insurance.

In 1941 sales reached a new all-time high of $975 million, boosted by military spending and a consumer buying panic as U.S. involvement in World War II (1939–1945) appeared likely. During the war Sears supplied the military with a wide range of goods and some of the factories belonging to Sears suppliers were converted to munitions plants. Raw material shortages caused sales to suffer, however; the company refunded $250 million in orders that could not be filled. Around this time Sears began its first foreign ventures, opening a store in Havana, Cuba, in 1942 and several stores in Mexico in 1947.

Sales reached the one billion dollars mark in 1945 and doubled the next year. Correctly anticipating an economic boom after the war, Wood launched an aggressive expansion program that put Sears well ahead of its competition. New stores were located in the path of suburban expansion, which took off in the late 1940s and 1950s. By 1954 Sears's sales had grown to three billion dollars; Sears became a symbol of U.S. prosperity. During the 1950s Sears began to stock more clothing as sales of durable goods slackened. The company also strengthened ties to its suppliers and adopted a decentralized management structure.

The 1960s were another good decade for Sears. In 1960 the firm established its own shopping center development subsidiary, Homart Development. In 1963 sales were $5.1 billion and surveys showed that one in five U.S. consumers shopped at Sears regularly. In 1967 monthly sales topped one billion dollars for the first time.

As the 1970s began, Sears dominance of U.S. retailing was unchallenged. Construction of the Sears Tower in Chicago, the tallest building in the world for many years, was completed in 1974. At the same time skyrocketing oil prices led to nationwide recession, and a $170 million decline in profits for Sears. Sales remained flat for the next several years. Also during this period, competition in the form of specialty shops and discounters began to capture a greater share of the retail market. Within the company, decentralization introduced in the 1950s had resulted in widespread inefficiencies and rivalries among the different territories. As net income continued to decline from 1978 to 1980, it was clear that the company's poor financial performance required a solution.

Under the guidance of Edward Telling, who assumed control in 1978, Sears undertook a major reorganization in 1981. The company was organized into three major business groups: the Merchandise Group (buying and merchandise), Allstate Enterprises (insurance and financial services), and the Seraco Group (commercial and residential real estate). In addition, Sears became more involved in the growing financial services sector with the 1981 purchase of the nation's largest real estate brokerage Coldwell Banker Company, and securities firm Dean Witter Reynolds Inc. Further diversification took place in 1984 when Sears, along with IBM and CBS, launched Prodigy, an online service similar to America Online and Compuserve.

In 1985 Sears introduced the Discover Card, which combined credit and financial services and also offered savings accounts. In 1988 the company acquired Eye Care Centers of America, Pinstripes Petites, and Western Auto Supply. Its workforce swelled to an all-time high of 520,000. The company's stock continued to lag, however, and from 1986 to 1990 corporate profits slipped from $1.3 billion to $892 million. However, by 1991 Sears's financial services businesses began to contribute more earnings. Combining this with layoffs and other cost-cutting measures, Sears posted a profit of nearly $1.3 billion.

Following an unexpected loss of nearly $2.3 billion on sales of $53.1 billion in 1993, Sears began to sell off some of its non-core business assets. Eye Care Centers and Coldwell Banker's residential real estate operations were sold. Dean Witter and the Discover Card services were spun off. After a service fraud scandal and a 20 percent drop in sales, the Automotive Group stopped making repairs and then filled vacant bays through a deal with Pennzoil's Jiffy Lube. In 1994 the Homart division was sold, and Allstate was spun off.

Perhaps the most dramatic changes took place in the Merchandising Group. Under the direction of Arthur C. Martinez, who would become head of Sears in 1994, the company began to cater to female customers, who accounted for as much as 70 percent of merchandise sales. With an advertising campaign touting "the softer side of Sears," Martinez brought in more famous name clothing for women. The catalog was discontinued in 1989 after a 101-year run, although specialty catalogs were reinstated in 1994. The workforce was trimmed to 361,000, and unprofitable stores were closed while other stores were expanded.

In 1994, with the Sears Tower put in trust for transfer in 2003, company headquarters was moved to a 200-acre campus west of Chicago. During 1995 Martinez, now head of Sears, added 152 Circle of Beauty cosmetic boutiques, and Sears introduced its own line of denim sportswear, Canyon River Blues, which turned out to be a resounding success. In addition, Sears moved durable goods into their own free-standing buildings called Sears Hardware, Sears HomeLife, and Sears franchise stores. These stores would service customers who had previously ordered through the Sears catalog, especially in rural areas. Sears also began a new line of automotive after market stores called PartsAmerica, opening 30 stores in 1995 and another 60 stores in 1996. When the year was over Sears posted a solid profit of $1.8 billion on sales of $34.9 billion.

Having turned Sears around and put it back on the right track, Martinez was named *Financial World's* "CEO of the Year." From 1995 through 1997 Sears enjoyed rising sales, but the cost of spinning off divisions, reorganizations, and bad credit card debt cut into profits, which declined to $1.2 billion in 1997. Still a healthy retail giant, Sears had a network of 833 full-line mall-based department stores and 2,697 freestanding specialty stores in the United States in 1998. Having spun off many of its non-core businesses, the company was focused on selling apparel, furniture, hardware, and automotive merchandise.

See also: **Chain Stores, Department Store, Mail-Order House, Retail Industry, Richard Sears**

FURTHER READING

Emmet, Boris, and John E. Jeuck. *Catalogues and Counters: A History of Sears, Roebuck and Company*. Chicago: University of Chicago Press, 1965.

Katz, Donald R. *The Big Store*. New York: Viking, 1987.

Loomis, Carol J. "Dinosaurs." *Fortune*, May 3, 1993.

Martinez, Arthur C. "Transforming the Legacy of Sears." *Strategy and Leadership*, July/August 1997.

"Sears History," [cited January 28, 1999] available from the World Wide Web @ www.sears.com/company/pubaff/history1.htm/.

Sparks, Debra. "Arthur Martinez: Financial World's CEO of the Year." *Financial World*, March 25, 1996.

SEASONAL UNEMPLOYMENT

Individuals in the labor force searching for work may be subject to seasonal unemployment. Seasonal unemployment results from variations in employment patterns because of seasonal change. This is a common occurrence in the agricultural industry, where harvesting season naturally demands more workers than are needed during other months.

A similar situation occurs in the construction industry, which experiences a higher rate of unemployment in the winter months than during the spring or summer. This is not always the case. California is less likely to experience an intense employment fluctuation in its construction industry because of relatively mild seasonal change. Michigan, on the other hand, is much more apt to be affected with increased unemployment in its construction industry during the winter months.

Why do workers remain in such industries? Those employed in the construction industry are often attracted to the high wages. However, agricultural workers do not receive high compensation for their efforts. Harvesting work may often be completed by migrant workers. Migrant workers are individuals who move from region to region looking for employment. For instance, a worker from Latin America may migrate to California for harvesting work and then return home with his or her earnings at the end of the season.

Seasonal unemployment does not affect every part of the country. It varies from region to region.

See also: **Agriculture Industry, Migrant Workers, Structural Unemployment, Unemployment**

SECOND NEW DEAL

The Second New Deal was the name given to a series of federal programs passed by Congress between 1935 and 1938 to counteract the Great Depression. Several of the first New Deal programs proposed by President Franklin D. Roosevelt (1933–1945) had earlier been declared unconstitutional by the U.S. Supreme Court. Roosevelt's Second New Deal included higher taxes for the rich, stricter regulations for private utilities, and increased subsidies for rural electrification. Three federal acts formed the heart of the Second New Deal. The National Labor Relations Act of 1935, also known as the Wagner Act, established a set of fair employment standards and guaranteed the right of workers to organize and collectively bargain with management through union representatives. The Social Security Act of 1935 created a retirement fund, unemployment insurance, and welfare grants for local distribution, including aid for dependent children. The Fair Labor Standards Act of 1938 was the final significant piece of the Second New Deal. It prescribed the maximum hours employees could be required to work without being paid overtime and also prescribed the minimum wage they could earn.

Second New Deal programs fared better before the Supreme Court than did their predecessors. Fueled by his decisive victory in the 1936 presidential election, Roosevelt began his second term by proposing a ''court packing'' plan that would have allowed him to increase the size of the nation's high court by adding justices with a disposition favorable to his programs. Although Congress rejected the plan, the Supreme Court got the message, as the nine Justices began validating the constitutionality of more federal legislation. With the onset of World War II (1939–1945) America's attention turned from domestic policy to international affairs, and the president's New Deal programs faded into the background of an economy mobilizing for military production.

See also: **Fair Labor Standards Act, Great Depression, National Labor Relations Act, New Deal, Franklin D. Roosevelt, Social Security Act**

SECTIONALISM

Sectionalism is the belief in and support of political, social, and economic interests particular to a region or section of the country. By the mid-1800s the United States encompassed an enormous area of almost three million square miles following the addition of lands in the Louisiana Purchase, Texas, Florida, the Oregon Territory, and land ceded by Mexico. Although ruled by one government, people living thousands of miles apart developed their own political and economic interests and social causes, often not agreeing with other Americans on these issues. New leaders emerged who represented their own sections of the country rather than the country as a whole, increasing sectional conflict. The country seemed divided into three regions: the North, the South, and the West.

Economics is the major contributing factor to sectionalism. Consequently, well before the great expansion of the United States, the Constitution's framers were familiar with sectional differences. The North's cool climate and rocky soil proved unsuitable for large farms. Its economy soon depended on trade and the growth of industrial cities. The South's economy depended on farming and large plantations worked by black slaves from Africa. Sectional debate during the Constitutional Convention revolved around the slave trade, export taxes, and shipping.

By the 1850s sectionalism bitterly erupted over the issue of slavery and state's rights culminating in the American Civil War (1861–1865). American loyalties to their section overshadowed loyalty to the nation. Though the Civil War abolished slavery, sectionalism continued through Reconstruction and into the twentieth century with the Solid South acting as a political bloc into the 1960's. Another product of sectionalism was the Populist Party formed by farmers in the West and South in the late 1800s to compete against political groups led by Northeastern industrial interests. As the twentieth century came to a close, the North, South, and West still competed for federal money. Environmental issues consequently divided East and West. Many Easterners believed the vast Western lands needed protection while many Western economies relied on natural resource development. Despite the ongoing disputes, however, sectionalism will probably never again divide the United States as bitterly as it had in the mid-nineteenth century.

See also: **Civil War (Economic Causes of), Populist Movement, Slavery**

SECURITIES AND EXCHANGE COMMISSION

The Securities and Exchange Commission (SEC) is an independent, non-partisan regulatory agency. Created by Congress in 1934 under the Securities Exchange Act, the agency is tasked with regulating the United States investment industry. It ensures that U.S. securities markets operate fairly and honestly and can enforce punishments when violations are made.

SEC regulations are designed to hold publicly held entities, broker-dealers in securities, investment companies, and other securities market participants accountable to federal law. There are six main laws the SEC oversees: the Securities Act of 1933, the Securities Exchange Act of 1934, the Public Utility Holding Company Act of 1935, the Trust Indenture Act of 1939, the Investment Company Act of 1940, and the Investment Advisers Act of 1940.

The Securities Act of 1933, known also as the "truth in securities law," requires investors be provided with information concerning securities offered for public sale. This information often comes in the form of a "prospectus," a brochure detailing the security's history and performance. The act also set regulations to prevent fraud in securities sales.

The information disclosure statements established in the 1933 Securities Act were extended the next year under the Securities Exchange Act. This act extended the disclosure of information to all securities listed and registered for public trading on U.S. securities exchanges, such as the New York Stock Exchange. Disclosure law was further extended in 1964 with the Securities Act Amendments, which made similar provisions for equity securities in the over-the-counter market (securities markets where previously issued securities are re-traded).

The Public Utility Holding Company Act of 1935 regulates interstate holding companies involved in the electric utility industry or the retail distribution of natural or manufactured gas. These businesses are required to file detailed information concerning their operations and holdings.

Regarding bonds and other debt securities, the SEC has the power to regulate under the Trust Indenture Act of 1939. Debt securities offered for public sale and issued under trust agreements must adhere to guideline concerning trustees and capital, including high standards of conduct and responsibility on the part of the trustee.

In addition, the SEC monitors the principles set forth in the Investment Company Act of 1940, regulating the activity of companies engaged primarily in the securities industry—investing, trading in securities, and offering their own securities for public sale.

While the SEC oversees the application of all these laws and guidelines, it is a regulatory agency only and does not supervise any individual company's investment activities. It does have more supervision regarding investment advisers. The Investment Advisers Act of 1940 established a system requiring all persons or organizations who advise about securities investments (and receive compensation for this advisement) be registered with the SEC and conform to their established procedures of investor protection.

Because of SEC oversight, investors in U.S. securities markets are better protected from fraud, whether it be by investment advisers or companies engaged in criminal securities schemes.

See also: **New York Stock Exchange, Over-the-Counter Market**

SELECTIVE SERVICE ACT

The Selective Service Act was passed by Congress in May 1917; it required the registration of all American males between the ages of twenty-one and thirty for possible draft into military service. When the United States entered World War I (1914–18) on April 6, 1917, the U.S. armed forces were comprised of roughly 200,000 volunteers. In the weeks following Congress's declaration of war on Germany, not enough men signed up for service so Congress responded by enacting legislation to boost the number of enlisted men. Secretary of War Newton Baker (1871–1937) made clear that the registration could not be evaded. And George Creel, the head of the newly created Committee on Public Information, oversaw the production of an astounding output of propaganda including 75 million pamphlets and posters whose aim was to stimulate patriotism and hatred of anything German.

By June 5, 1917, more than nine million men had registered. Congress widened the registration requirement to include all men between the ages of eighteen and forty–five, and by the end of the war twenty–four million men had signed up. While 340,000 men failed to show up when called and four thousand were classified as conscientious objectors, nearly five million men served in the armed forces during World War I, two million of them in France alone. The typical soldier was a drafted man between the ages of twenty-one and twenty-three; he was white, single, and poorly educated. 400,000 soldiers were black and roughly 18 percent of the soldiers were foreign-born.

To ensure that the troops knew what they were fighting for, a copy of President Woodrow Wilson's (1913–1921) war message was included in every soldier's gear. Women volunteered in the navy as clerks and they joined the U.S. Signal Corps and Nurse Corps. Although defense-industry workers were able to receive deferments of service, the draft depleted the male labor force by 16 percent. Women stepped in to pick up the slack. When the fighting ended with Germany's surrender and the signing of the armistice on November 11, 1918, countries tallied their dead and wounded. Some 50,000 American soldiers died in battle; another 62,000 died from disease (a worldwide flu epidemic claimed many American soldiers' lives); and 200,000 were wounded.

Two decades later, in 1940 the United States braced itself for possible involvement in World War II (1939–1945). The first peacetime military draft in U.S. history began after the passage of the Selective Service Act of 1940. This system was in effect from 1940 to 1973. When the United States entered World War II in

This familiar Uncle Sam poster was placed near recruiting headquarters to inspire new recruits. The poster made its debut in WWI.

December 1941, the number of people on active duty was less than two million. In 1945 the number of men and women serving in the armed forces peaked at over twelve million. Both in 1942 and 1943, over three million men were inducted into the armed forces. Such numbers were required in fighting a war on two fronts—one in Europe and another in the Pacific.

At the end of World War II in 1945 the U.S. military had quickly demobilized almost 7 million soldiers. Only three years later, however, the Cold War extended the life of the Selective Service System. In 1948, in response to deteriorating relations between the Union of Soviet Socialist Republics (USSR)—and the United States, Congress restored the Selective Service System. It required the registration of all U.S. men between the ages of eighteen and twenty–five, with men between nineteen and twenty–five to be inducted for a twenty–one-month period of service. Registration began August 30, 1948; the program continued for twenty-five years.

During the Vietnam conflict, the numbers of soldiers peaked during the late 1960s. The Selective

Service System inducted 382,010 young men into the armed forces in the single year of 1966. As a result of criticism that the student deferment allowed the more affluent members of society to avoid the draft, President Richard Nixon instituted reforms in the way that the Selective Service System was run. First, in 1971, Nixon eliminated the student draft deferment. Rather than the local draft board determining who would be drafted, the system was nationalized through a draft "lottery." When a young man turned 19 years old, he immediately knew his likelihood of being drafted, depending on his birthdate in relation to a nationally run lottery drawing. This was a politically prudent move on President Nixon's part, because it was the *uncertainty* of being drafted that agitated the Vietnam generation. Eliminating this uncertainty went a long way towards containing the antiwar movement.

In 1973, as the U.S. shifted to the "all volunteer army," the draft ended. The Selective Service System remained in place, however, in case the U.S. ever gets involved in a big war.

See also: **Vietnam War, War and the Economy, World War I, World War II**

FURTHER READING

Johnson, R. Charles *Draft, Registration, and the Law.* Occidental, CA: Nolo Press, c1985.

United States. Congress. House. Committee on Education and Labor. Subcommittee on Post-secondary Education. Legislative Hearing. Washington: U.S. G.P.O., 1984.

SETTLEMENT AND ECONOMIC DEVELOPMENT: THE COLONIES TO 1763 (*OVERVIEW*)

In 1585, Richard Hakluyt the elder assured English readers of his pamphlet, *Inducements to the Liking of the Voyage Intended towards Virginia*, that North America held the economic potential to form the basis of a great English commercial empire. English colonization would open lucrative new American markets for "the Woollen clothes of England" and "sundry [of] our commodities upon the tract of that firme land." The "situation of the climate" and the "excellent soile" would in turn make North America an excellent source of "Oade [a blue dye], Oile, Wines, Hops, Salt," all of which English people could expect to obtain "better cheape than we now receive them." Hakluyt anticipated that the abundance of North American hides, whales, seals, and fish would all give England an edge in a market for these goods which was traditionally dominated by Russian merchants. The "excellent and fertile soile" on both sides of North America's "greate and deep" natural waterways promised "all things that the life of man doth require," and whatever settlers wanted to plant they could expect to harvest in abundance sufficient to "trafficke in."

Over the next 178 years, enterprising merchants and traders and hard-working Native Americans and settlers slowly made into reality Hakluyt's vision of North America as an integral part of a British North Atlantic commercial system. The first to feel the effects of this transformation were the Native Americans, who met English vessels at the shore with valuable furs which they readily exchanged for prized English goods such iron tools, glass beads, and woven cloth. Most early English settlements depended heavily on such trade to repay investors who had financed their voyages, and some economies such as New York's continued to rely significantly on the "Indian trade" through much of the colonial period. The fur trade also exerted a profound impact on Native American economic life as imported European goods began displacing traditional tools, weapons, utensils, apparel, and ornamentation. The historian James Axtell has termed this process "the first consumer revolution" in which Native Americans' appetite for European goods spurred the growth of a Native market for European products that extended rapidly into the interior of North America. Trade with Europeans altered nearly everything about Native life, disrupting and redirecting traditional trading patterns, producing a strain on the natural environment through over-hunting and over-trapping, and changing the way that American Indians clothed themselves, cooked their food, cultivated their soil, and hunted their game. Iron tools replaced implements of bone and stone, woolen garments replaced buckskin, muskets replaced arrows and spears. By 1700 many eastern woodland Indians had become permanently dependent on European commerce, and their participation in colonial commerce contributed greatly to North American economic growth.

Settlers of Jamestown, the first successful English settlement in North America, shared with the adventurers of the earlier, ill-fated Roanoake settlement of 1585 the hope of tapping into precious sources of New World mineral wealth. The founding settlers expected to exploit Virginia's game, fishing, and agriculture, and establishing a lucrative trade with the neighboring Powhattan empire. Nearly all these hopes were dashed

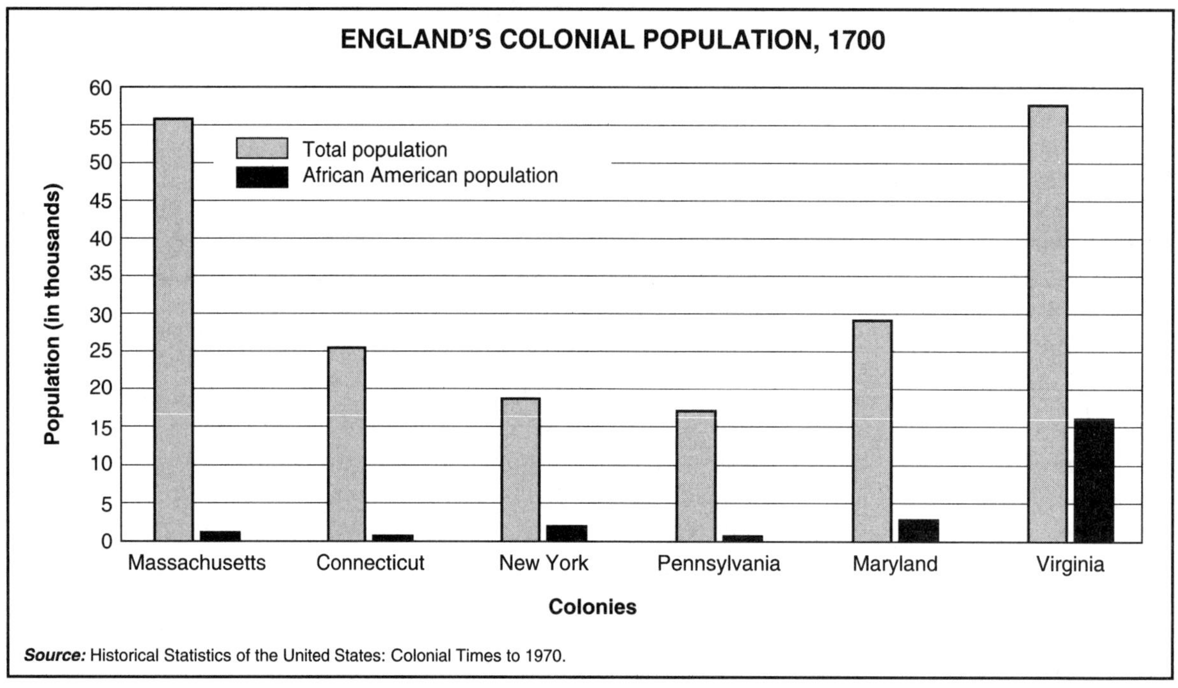

The English population in the American colonies was well established by 1700. The highest populations were in Massachusetts and Virginia.

as the Chesapeake colony teetered on the brink of failure for more than a decade. They found no gold or gems, manufacturing enterprises such as a glassworks failed, their Old World work habits ill-prepared them for the demanding task of tilling and planting virgin soil, they were continually racked by disease, and their repeated provocation resulted in perpetual strife with their Indian neighbors.

THE "EXCELLENT AND FERTILE SOILE" ON BOTH SIDES OF NORTH AMERICA'S "GREATE AND DEEP" NATURAL WATERWAYS PROMISED "ALL THINGS THAT THE LIFE OF MAN DOTH REQUIRE," AND WHATEVER SETTLERS WANTED TO PLANT THEY COULD EXPECT TO HARVEST IN ABUNDANCE SUFFICIENT TO "TRAFFICKE IN."

Adapted from Richard Hakluyt's *Inducements to the Liking of the Voyage Intended towards Virginia*, 1585

Tobacco, which the settler John Rolfe began cultivating in 1610, eventually became the staple crop that saved the colony. Europeans loved the crop in spite of the denunciations of smoking by prominent figures, including King James I himself. Jamestown planters were soon cultivating the "stinking weed" wherever they could find suitable land. Tobacco plantations began springing up along Chesapeake estuaries, creating a growing demand for labor and land as successful planters increased their holdings to put even more tobacco into cultivation. Settlers who founded the colony of Maryland in 1634 quickly began following the example of their Virginia neighbors. For much of the seventeenth century, Chesapeake planters relied mainly on the labor of indentured servants from England, occasionally supplementing that labor force with captive Indians or Africans whose status varied from person to person. English indentured servants bound themselves to work for a period of four to seven years, after which they were released. Many Africans brought to North America before 1660 shared that status, but a growing number came as slaves for life. Disease and malnutrition made life miserable for both European and African servants. When the supply of European servants began dwindling after 1660, planters turned increasingly to African slaves. By 1700, the economies of Virginia and Maryland had come to depend on the labor of lifetime slaves of African descent who cultivated the main export crop.

A very different economy emerged in the colonies of New England as families migrated to Plymouth, Massachusetts Bay, New Haven, Connecticut, Rhode Island, and New Hampshire to escape pressure to conform to the state-sanctioned ceremonies of the Church of England. The colder northern climate prevented the cultivation of staple crops common in England, but the land was suitable for traditional English farming methods. Significant equality in the size of family property was insured in many parts of

New England by an orderly process of land distribution. The New England governments granted large tracts to incorporated towns, which would in turn grant parcels to heads of households on the basis of present and future need. Commerce boomed during Massachusetts Bay's first decade of settlement as earlier settlers prospered by producing goods for sale to the thousands of new arrivals who took passage each year. Yet when the flow of migration ceased after the outbreak of the English Civil War in 1642, the nascent market economy dried up.

Massachusetts officials sought to compensate by developing overseas markets, successfully establishing a trading partnership with British colonies in the West Indies that continued throughout the colonial period. Yet the bulk of the New England economy rested on family farms. Their production was oriented toward achieving, not the exorbitant profits sought by great tobacco and sugar planters, but a "competence" in which members and heirs of each household could expect to enjoy an adequate diet, clothing, housing, and the modest comfort and enjoyment of family and community life.

Other seventeenth-century Anglo-American economies varied somewhat from these two early models. The Hudson River settlements, founded by the Dutch in 1613 and captured by the English in 1664, early centered on the fur trade but also developed a significant agricultural base. The New York agricultural economy was distinguished by the great Hudson River estates on which a few large landholding families such as the Livingstons achieved great wealth from the large numbers of tenant farmers who farmed their lands. The economies of Pennsylvania and the Jerseys rested on family farming by English, German, Scottish, and Scotch-Irish settlers. South Carolina, like Virginia, became a slave society which produced agricultural goods—in this case rice and indigo dye—for a lucrative European market. Many colonies, like North Carolina, also provided England with important sources of goods such as naval stores—white pine masts for ships, turpentine, pine tar, and hemp for rope.

By 1650 the commercial output of England's colonies had grown large enough to begin enriching many English planters as well as the Dutch merchants who transported tobacco and sugar from the English West Indian and Chesapeake markets to European ports. With the Restoration of Charles II to the throne of England in 1660, Parliament and royal officials began an energetic effort to shape a more consistent policy of colonial commerce that would favor English merchants and shippers while cutting the Dutch out of Anglo-American trade. The Navigation Act of 1660 restricted colonial trade to ships constructed in either England or English America which carried a crew at least 75 per cent English or Anglo-American. In addition, the act listed certain "enumerated goods"—tobacco, sugar, cotton, indigo, dyewoods, and ginger—that could be transported only to England or another colonial port. Over the next forty years Parliament refined its commercial policy by passing further Navigation Acts and developing the colonial administrative body that eventually became the Board of Trade. The system, never perfect, suffered from periodic abuse and neglect and was regularly circumvented by smugglers. Nevertheless, by the time the Act of Union united Scotland and England under one Parliament in 1707, a workable administrative framework for Anglo-American trade was in place, fostering the growth of a dynamic eighteenth-century empire of goods that benefited both Britain and her North American colonies.

Most historians agree that the colonial economy grew slowly but steadily during the first half of the eighteenth century, stimulating a corresponding rise in the volume of imported British goods. After 1740, however, the volume of cheap British imports to the colonies began an exponential rise in what some historians have termed an Anglo-American "commercial revolution." English manufacturers using traditional methods of production found ways to make more goods available at cheaper prices than ever before, and English merchants found ways to get these goods to prospective buyers through innovative marketing techniques such as paid newspaper advertisements and attractive shop displays. As the volume of imports rose and the prices dropped more colonists purchased more goods each year. In 1700, for example, only the wealthiest colonists could afford to drink tea regularly, and their homes alone were graced with elegant tea sets. Yet by 1760 tea, like the sugar that sweetened it, had become a "decency" enjoyed by the "middling sort" of colonist as well as the wealthy. The building of market roads and the clearing of river channels carried imported English goods a little further inland every year, and colonists found ways to acquire or reallocate the extra income needed to purchase a growing array of items. They could dress in a widening variety of European fabrics adorned with a growing selection of European lace and buttons, and complete their outfits with fashionable silk stockings, gloves, and wigs. They could pane their windows with imported glass, decorate their parlors with fashionable imported candlesticks, and set their tables with inexpensive ceramic tableware.

This growing participation in a transatlantic market of goods exerted a variety of pressures on eighteenth-century American life. The colonial appetite for imports produced a chronic trade imbalance between the colonies and England, resulting in a perpetual drain of hard currency from the colonies. Colonists responded in a variety of ways such as borrowing from European merchants against the value of future export crops and authorizing the issue of paper currency to expand the money supply. American Indians' increasing dependence on European goods began producing a backlash after 1740 as native prophets such as Neolin called upon Indians to purge themselves of European textiles, tools, and rum to reassert their native identity and regain their spiritual vitality. In contrast, the growing consumption of British goods contributed to a growing commonality of tastes, experiences, and identity among Anglo-American colonists who came to think of themselves increasingly as British Americans. Indeed, colonial protest and Revolution are almost inconceivable without this process. The Stamp Act and Townshend Duties that sparked the protest might not have been passed if the volume of colonial trade were not so great by the 1760s, and the protest might never have been so widespread or popular had not so many Anglo-Americans felt the sting of taxes on the British goods they wished to purchase.

FURTHER READING

Breen, T.H. "An Empire of Goods: The Anglicization of Colonial America." *The Journal of British Studies*, 25, 1986.

Egnall, Marc. *New World Economies*. New York: Oxford University Press, 1988.

Jones, Alice Hanson. *Wealth of a Nation to Be*. New York: Columbia University Press, 1980.

Mancall, Peter C. and Thomas Weiss. "Was Economic Growth Likely in Colonial British North America?" *Journal of Economic History*, 59, March 1999.

McCusker, John J. and Russell R. Menard. *The Economy of British America 1607-1789*. Chapel Hill and London: University of North Carolina Press, 1991.

SHARECROPPING

Sharecropping is a system of agriculture whereby the farmer who works the land receives proceeds of a portion of the crop harvest in return for his labor. After the American Civil War (1861–1865), the South was in ruins. Former plantation owners, now without slave

Poverty plagued the lives of many sharecroppers, who played a major role in the American agricultural system.

labor, also lacked the resources to hire wage laborers. Further, many freedmen disliked the idea of working for wages. Hearing of a rumored promise of "forty acres and a mule" at the end of the fighting, black men in the South wanted their own farms. Two systems of agriculture emerged: One was sharecropping and the other was tenant farming. Plantation owners divided up their land and arranged the tracts to be farmed by one of these two methods.

A sharecropper was furnished with a house and a plot of land. The landowner, however, retained ownership; the property was simply the sharecropper's to use to work the land. Often the house was nothing more than a shack, frequently the housing that had been supplied to the slaves. The sharecropper was provided with seed, fertilizer, tools, and other implements necessary to cultivate the land. Most, if not all, the labor in the fields was performed by the sharecropper and his family. If there were any wage laborers working under the sharecropper, they were under the supervision of (and were paid by) the landowner. At the end of the harvest, the yield was turned over to the landowner, who took it to market. Once the harvest was sold, the costs of the supplies were deducted from the proceeds, and the farmer was given between one-third and one-half of the remaining sum as payment for the sharecropper's labor. If the weather had been poor during the growing season or if the market price of the crop had dropped, the sharecropper often wound up in debt. As there would be little return on the harvest, the sharecropper would be unable to pay the landowner for the supplies. Most sharecroppers found themselves in this situation, particularly after the South's economy became based on a single crop—cotton. In the days following the Civil War, landowners were eager to make money. At the time cotton was the crop most easily converted to cash, since it was in high demand. But overproduction of cotton soon caused its price to plummet. In 1866 it sold for 43 cents a pound; between 1882 and 1902 the price never exceeded 10 cents a pound.

While the majority of sharecroppers were perpetually in debt to the landowners, some were able to turn a profit, which eventually afforded them increased independence as farmers. Some became tenant farmers (who rented the land from the landowner), while a few established their own farms.

See also: **Tenant Farming**

SHAYS' REBELLION

The years after the American Revolution (1775–1783) were very hard for most Americans. The former colonies, many of them saddled with large war debts, were struggling to find ways to pay their creditors. Soldiers from the Continental Army returned to their family farms to find their lands neglected, in need of extensive clearing and reworking before they were ready to produce a crop. A great postwar depression also meant that prices for farm produce in general were low. In the five years after the end of the Revolutionary War farmers sunk deeper and deeper into debt. Many of them had their lands and other property seized when they were forced to default on their debts. Such a tense environment erupted in a rebellion led by Daniel Shays in 1786–1787 as a protest against the Massachusetts government's refusal to provide economic relief to the struggling farmers of the state.

Daniel Shay led the violent protest against the Massachusetts government's refusal to provide relief to struggling farmers.

Conditions were especially bad in Shay's state of Massachusetts. The merchants and traders of colonial Massachusetts' seaports relied on trade with the British Empire for most of their income—especially England itself and the West Indies. The American Revolution had closed these imperial ports to American shipping, forcing merchants to pay for foreign goods and service with hard money, or specie—coined gold or silver—which was in short supply in the United States. The Massachusetts government, which also had to pay many of its creditors in specie, was similarly short of cash. In addition, the federal government (itself chronically short of cash) was defaulting on promises to pay wages and pensions owed to Revolutionary War veterans. Massachusetts responded to the crisis by raising revenue from taxes on land and other sources. Land taxes alone increased by over 60 percent in the three years between 1783 and 1786. Farmers who could not pay had their property seized. In severe cases, they were even sent to debtors' prison.

FOR GOD'S SAKE, HAVE MATTERS SETTLED PEACEABLY: IT WAS AGAINST MY INCLINATIONS I UNDERTOOK THIS BUSINESS; IMPORTUNITY WAS USED WHICH I COULD NOT WITHSTAND, BUT I HEARTILY WISH IT WAS WELL OVER.

Captain Daniel Shays, Letter to a friend, December, 1786

At first, the farmers tried remedies similar to those colonial leaders had tried with the British government in the decade before the American Revolution. Farmers petitioned government officials (including Massachusetts governor James Bowdoin) and the state legislature (then known as the General Court) to close the debtors' court and to print paper money so the farmers could make purchases and pay their taxes. Both Bowdoin and the General Court rejected the farmers' petitions, insisting that the power of the courts be respected. They also condemned the push for a paper currency on the grounds that it promoted inflation, making the money owed creditors worth even less. The General Court's new taxes for 1786 amounted to more than 30 percent of the average citizen's income, and it was payable only in cash.

When the General Court announced in the spring of 1786 its intention to again raise taxes throughout Massachusetts, several Continental Army veterans decided to take action. Former brevet major Luke Day led the resistance in Springfield, while Captain Job Shattuck provided leadership in Groton. The third leader in the struggle was Daniel Shays of Pelham in the western part of the state. Shays was, by all accounts, a reluctant leader. Although he had obtained a captain's commission in the Continental Army, by 1784 he had returned to farming and grown seriously in debt. During the summer of 1786 Shays emerged as a leader of the protestors in the western half of Massachusetts. By late August, armed groups of men numbering up to 1,500 were closing courthouses around the state.

Throughout the fall of 1786, the protestors organized themselves into an army. Calling themselves the Regulators, they continued to intimidate and threaten local and state officials. In response the General Court of Massachusetts authorized the raising of a 4,400-man militia and placed it under the command of Major General Benjamin Lincoln. Secretary of War Henry Knox even offered Governor Bowdoin a federal army if the state's resources proved inadequate. Despite efforts by Shays and others to negotiate a resolution to the growing problem, the Regulators continued to grow in numbers. By late January 1787, they had made plans to occupy the town of Springfield, Massachusetts and seize weapons stored at the arsenal there.

At 4:00 on the afternoon of January 25, 1787, Daniel Shays and 1,500 Regulators marched into Springfield headed for the arsenal. As they approached, they were fired upon by General William Shepard, who commanded the militia defense. When his warning shots were ignored, Shepard ordered his cannon to fire directly into the ranks of the Regulators. Four of the rebels were killed and another 20 were wounded. Shays' attack was driven off from such unexpected force. Over the next week and a half, General Lincoln drove the Regulators into the western half of the state. On the morning of February 4, he surprised Shays and the Regulators at Petersham, capturing a 10th of the force, and driving the others into the hills.

Lincoln's victory at Petersham ended the armed part of Shays' Rebellion. The General Court and local courts quickly took action to suppress the political aims of the rebels. Courts in Berkshire and Hampshire counties sentenced 14 men to die and fined or imprisoned hundreds more. The legislature met in mid-February to pass a special Disqualifying Act that pardoned former Regulators but disenfranchised them and barred them from jury duty and certain types of jobs for three years. A special commission led by General Lincoln offered pardons to many more of the former rebels. Shays himself sought refuge in Vermont until his pardon was granted, but he never returned to his Massachusetts farm and instead settled in New York, where he died in 1825.

The long-range effects of Shays' Rebellion were more positive for the poor farmers of rural Massachusetts. The state elections of April 1787 saw the defeat of Governor Bowdoin and better than half of the sitting legislators. The new General Court quickly began work to address the concerns of the rebels, eliminating the Disqualifying Act, distributing pardons, reducing taxes, and allowing persons to use property as well as specie to pay debts. Shays' Rebellion also helped convince thousands of Americans in Massachusetts and other states of the need for a strong national government, which could stabilize the currency, control and levy taxes, and maintain public order. The following year, Massachusetts ratified the U.S. Constitution.

See also: **Massachusetts, Whiskey Rebellion**

FURTHER READING

Feer, Robert A. *Shay's Rebellion.* New York: Garland, 1988.

Gross, Robert A., ed. *In Debt to Shays: The Bicentennial of an Agrarian Rebellion.* Charlottesville, VA: University Press of Virginia, 1993.

Kulikoff, Allan. *The Agrarian Origins of American Capitalism.* Charlottesville, VA: University Press of Virginia, 1992.

McGinty, Brian. ''Shays' Rebellion: A Black Cloud That Rose in the East.'' *American Heritage*, January 1987.

Szatmary, David. *Shays' Rebellion: The Making of an Agrarian Insurrection.* Amherst: University of Massachusetts Press, 1980.

SHEEP HERDERS

Sheep herders, workers in charge of tending sheep on the open range, proliferated in the last three decades of the 1800s. Following the end of the American Civil War (1861–1865), the open lands of the western United States saw an influx of ranchers. The U.S. government had fought a series of wars to put down rebellions staged by Native Americans, including the Sioux Uprising of 1862, and stockmen were encouraged to move onto the open range. By the end of the 1860s, the longhorn cattle industry, which originated in Texas, was flourishing. By the mid-1870s sheep ranchers appeared in significant numbers. In 1886, at the height of the open-range livestock boom, Montana alone had roughly a million sheep (and 664,000 head of cattle) grazing its lands.

Ranchers engaged in the practice of purchasing tracts of land adjacent to public lands, and then allowed their livestock to graze freely throughout the area. This method of open-range ranches allowed ranchers to control thousands of acres of land, but by 1890 sheep herders found themselves in conflict with the cattle raisers, as the seemingly endless open range became increasingly limited. Growth of the livestock industry meant that western lands were crowded with 26 million head of cattle and 20 million head of sheep. The industry continued to grow, and small ranchers and sheep herders were soon dominated by big business.

See also: **Open Range, Westward Expansion**

SHEPPARD-TOWNER ACT

The Sheppard-Towner Act, officially the National Maternity and Infancy Protection Act, was passed by Congress in April 1921. It provided matching funds to states for prenatal and children's health centers. The legislation was introduced in the House of Representatives in 1919 by Montana Representative Jeannette Rankin (1880–1973), the first woman elected to U.S. Congress. In December of that year, two similar bills were introduced in the Senate, one by Morris Sheppard, and the other by Horace Mann Towner. Women's advocacy groups joined the Children's Bureau (a federal statutory agency founded in 1912 and a leading force in the child welfare movement) to vigorously support passage of the legislation. In the wake of winning suffrage, American women proved a formidable lobbying force. Further, statistics provided a strong case for government support of a health program dedicated to the needs of women and children. At the time, childbirth was the second leading cause of death for women; one in five children died during their first year of life; and one in three died before the age of five. The Sheppard-Towner Act was passed into law sixteen months after it was introduced.

Under the legislation, using matching federal funds, states established health centers where nurses and physicians cared for pregnant women, infants, and children, and taught women prenatal, delivery, postnatal, and infant care. The program's objective was to reduce maternal and infant mortality rates, which, in studies carried out by the Children's Bureau, were revealed to be higher among lower income groups. Research showed that as family income doubled, the infant mortality rate dropped by 50 percent. Activists concluded that an outreach program was necessary to instruct all women, regardless of their circumstances, on proper health care for themselves and for their children. The health program set up by the Sheppard-Towner Act was formulated in 1917 in the Children's Bureau's annual report, authored by reformer Julia Lathrop (1858–1932), the head of the agency. Lathrop proposed a nationwide effort modeled on a New York City program, run by pediatrician Sarah Josephine Baker (1873–1945), that gave inner city mothers access to health care and provided routine physical examinations for children. Baker headed a New York City health care program that reduced the city's infant mortality rate to the lowest of all major cities worldwide. When the Sheppard-Towner legislation was passed, Lathrop became its administrator.

The Sheppard-Towner Act remained in force until 1929, when Congress failed to renew funding for the program. Critics charged that lawmakers had fallen prey to the influence of the American Medical Association (AMA) and others, who viewed the federally supported health care program as moving the nation one step closer to socialized medicine. This fear was shared by prominent physicians who exited AMA's Section on Pediatrics to found the American Academy of Pediatrics (AAP).

Though the program was relatively short-lived, its influence was lasting. The funding provided by the Sheppard-Towner Act helped countless women and children. The clinics also raised awareness of the importance of preventive health care in lowering mortality rates of expectant women and children. Another improvement was the introduction of the idea that state and local agencies could play an important role in personal health.

See also: **Family and Medical Leave Act, Nineteenth Amendment**

SHERMAN ANTI-TRUST ACT

The Sherman Anti-Trust Act was passed by Congress in 1890 in an attempt to break up corporate trusts (corporate trusts are combinations of firms or corporations formed to limit competition and monopolize a market). The legislation stated that "every contract, combination in the form of trust or otherwise, or conspiracy in the restraint of trade" was illegal. While the act made clear that anyone found to be in violation of restraining trade would face fines, jail terms, and the payment of damages, the language lacked clear definition of what exactly constituted restraint of trade. The nation's courts were left with the responsibility of interpreting the Sherman Anti-Trust Act; the Justices proved as reluctant to take on big business as was Congress.

The legislation was introduced in Congress by Senator John Sherman (1823–1900) of Ohio, in response to increasing outcry from state governments and the public for the passage of national anti-trust laws. Many states passed their own anti-trust bills or made constitutional provisions prohibiting trusts, but the statutes proved difficult to enforce, since big business found ways around them. When the legislation proposed by Sherman reached the Senate, conservative congressmen rewrote it; many charged the Senators with being deliberately vague. In the decade after the legislation's passage, the federal government prosecuted only eighteen anti-trust cases, and court decisions did little to break up monopolies. But after the turn of the century, reformers demanded that government regulate business.

In 1911 the U.S. Justice Department won key victories against monopolies, breaking up John D. Rockefeller's Standard Oil Company of New Jersey and James B. Duke's American Tobacco Company. The decisions set a precedent for how the Sherman Anti-Trust Act would be enforced, and they demonstrated a national intolerance toward monopolistic trade practices. In 1914 national anti-trust legislation was further strengthened by the passage of the Clayton Anti-Trust Act. This act outlawed price fixing (the practice of pricing below cost to eliminate a competitive product); it was also illegal for the same executives to manage two or more competing companies (a practice called interlocking directorates); and a corporation was prohibited from owning stock in another competing corporation. The creation of the Federal Trade Commission (FTC) that same year provided further insurance that U.S. corporations engaging in unfair practices would be investigated by the government.

See also: **Clayton Anti-Trust Act, Monopoly, Tobacco Trust**

FURTHER READING

Bryan, William Jennings, and Robert W. Cherny. *Cross of Gold: Speech Delivered Before the Democratic National Convention at Chicago, July 9, 1896*. Lincoln: University of Nebraska Press, 1996.

Calhoun, Catherine. *Winter with the Silver Queen*. American Heritage, November 1995.

Doty, Richard. *American Silver Coinage: 1794–1891*. New York: American Numismatic Society, 1987.

Eichengreen, Barry J., ed., and Marc Flandreau. *The Gold Standard in Theory and History*. New York: Routledge, 1997.

Dictionary of American History. New York: Charles Scribner's Sons, 1976, s.v. " Sherman Silver Purchase Act."

SHERMAN SILVER PURCHASE ACT

The free coinage of silver became a political debate in the United States following the Panic of 1873. The period of economic hardship between 1873 and 1878 motivated the demand for cheaper paper money. The market price of silver dropped sharply after 1873 because it was used less often in American and European currency, and it was becoming more expensive to mine.

Although there were still "Greenbackers" around who associated the Civil War paper money with the dynamic northern economy during the Civil War, most of those in favor of inflation did not support the trend toward paper-money and turned instead to silver, believing its free coinage would be as adequate as greenback cash. Silver miners obviously also supported silver coinage. This demand resulted in the 1878 passage of the Bland-Allison Act, which required the government to buy at least $2 million worth of silver bullion each month at market price to coin as legal tender silver dollars. While the act was a law, however, the country's presidential leaders weakened its effect by purchasing only the minimum amount of bullion. The Bland-Allison Act was never able to stop the decline of silver prices or to increase the circulation of money.

The nation's regional preferences for money lead to a clear divide in the country. In the eastern United States, businesses preferred the gold standard and opposed inflated money. In the West and South, however, indebted farmers needed inflation to boost the prices of their products, while owners of the silver mines prevalent in the western territories wanted free silver coinage to stimulate their own financial interests.

By 1890 the political influence of silver advocates in the West had grown so strong that on July 14, the Sherman Silver Purchase Act was passed as a compromise to appease all interests. Named after Ohio Senator John Sherman, it replaced the Bland-Allison Act as a measure to provide a greater government purchase of silver. The Sherman Silver Purchase Act required the U.S. treasury to more than double its monthly purchase of silver to 4.5 million ounces. The direct effect of the Sherman Act was a threat to the U.S. Treasury's gold reserves and a $156 million increase in the amount of paper money in circulation.

Ultimately, the Sherman Act did little to please anyone. Western farmers and silver miners remained dissatisfied with government compromise measures and felt threatened by the 1892 presidential election of Grover Cleveland (1893–1897), another supporter of the gold standard.

The U.S. Treasury's depleted gold reserves led to the Panic of 1893. To restrain public fear of the abandonment of the gold standard, President Cleveland called a special session of Congress, and the Sherman Silver Purchase Act was repealed in the autumn of that year.

See also: **William Jennings Bryan, Cross of Gold Speech, Currency, Free Silver, Gold Standard, Gold Resumption Act, Greenbacks**

FURTHER READING

Bryan, William Jennings, and Robert W. Cherny. *Cross of Gold: Speech Delivered Before the Democratic National Convention at Chicago, July 9, 1896*. Lincoln, Neb.: University of Nebraska Press, 1996.

Calhoun, Catherine. *Winter with the Silver Queen*. American Heritage, November 1995.

Doty, Richard. *American Silver Coinage: 1794–1891*. New York: American Numismatic Society, 1987.

Eichengreen, Barry J., ed., and Marc Flandreau. *The Gold Standard in Theory and History*. New York: Routledge, 1997.

Sherman Silver Purchase Act. *Dictionary of American History*. New York: Charles Scribner's Sons, 1976.

SHERMAN'S MARCH THROUGH GEORGIA

From mid-November to late December, 1864, General William Tecumseh Sherman led 62,000 Union soldiers on a march through Georgia towards the sea, leaving in their wake a trail of destruction sixty miles wide. During this Civil War (1861–1865) expedition, which started in Atlanta and ended in the port-city of Savannah, Sherman and his men sought to demolish not only the state's military resources but also its economic structure. The Union troops worked to cut off food supplies by setting fire to cities; stripping fields, barns, and houses; and raiding villages for food and livestock. The men laid waste to Georgia's commercial infrastructure city-by-city. Sherman's ultimate goal was to crush the Confederate states' will to fight, and his tactics were merciless and un-relenting. The war did not end here, however, though the general's campaign did accomplish nearly all of its objectives. The march was long remembered as an epic gesture of violence that swept the North toward its victory.

General Sherman, the son of a Supreme Court justice, hailed from Lancaster, Ohio. A graduate of the United States Military Academy at West Point, Sherman served as second lieutenant in the Second Seminole War (1835–1842) in Florida, then as first lieutenant on assignment in South Carolina. At the onset of the Mexican War in 1846, he was assigned to the Pacific Division in California. In 1853 he resigned from the military and set out for San Francisco, where he briefly pursued a banking career; economic unrest in California, however, put an end to that venture in 1857. After another short-lived career as a lawyer in Kansas, Sherman returned to his former vocation in the army accepting a superintendent post at the state military academy in Alexandria, Louisiana. Upon that state's secession from the Union in January 1861, Sherman went north out of loyalty. In May of that year he was appointed colonel of the 13th infantry, beginning a decorated Civil War career.

YOU CANNOT QUALIFY WAR IN HARSHER TERMS THAN I WILL. WAR IS CRUELTY, AND YOU CANNOT REFINE IT.

William Tecumseh Sherman, Letter to the Mayor of Atlanta, September 12, 1864

After fighting at Bull Run in July 1861, Sherman rose to the position of brigadier general of volunteers. His first campaign in Kentucky was unsuccessful, which earned him a reputation for being unstable and manic-depressive. In April 1862, he regained the confidence of his peers following a victory at the Battle of Shiloh. Promoted to major general, Sherman took charge of the Union troops that occupied Memphis, Tennessee, in 1862. The following year, after a victory under Lieutenant General (and post-war president) Ulysses S. Grant at Vicksburg, Mississippi, he rose again in the ranks, assuming command of the Army of Tennessee. But it was in Atlanta, Georgia, that Sherman secured his place as a key figure in the war. His 1864 campaign, which lasted from May to September, ultimately ravaged the metropolis—fire consumed numerous buildings, and the Union soldiers used brute force to demolish or disable the city's machinery. It was this destruction of the commercial infrastructure of the South for which Sherman became known and feared.

The general's march through Georgia represented a continuation of his "total war" strategy. Leaving the burning city of Atlanta behind, he led two massive columns of troops, which operated under Generals Oliver H. Howard and Henry W. Slocum, on an eastward course. Supplying his men only with bread, Sherman organized raiding parties that allowed them to live off the food and livestock of the land. In a December 16 letter to Lieutenant General Grant, Sherman described in explicit detail the way in which his troops weakened Georgia's cities while reinforcing themselves: "We started with about 5,000 head of cattle, and arrived with over 10,000; of course, consuming mostly turkeys, chickens, sheep, hogs, and the cattle of the country. As to mules and horses, we left Atlanta with about 2,500 wagons, and our transportation is now in superb condition."

After Atlanta Sherman set out for Milledgeville, where his high-spirited men held a mock court session in which they repealed Georgia's secession ordinance. From Milledgeville they went on to the state capital, then to Sandersville, Louisville, and Millen, ravaging and pillaging along the way. Wildly outnumbered by Sherman's men, the Confederate troops could do little to halt the trend of violence. Ultimately, on December 21, 1864, Sherman ended his hell-raising march just as he had planned: by nearly demolishing Savannah, the port city at the end of his route. The victory followed a campaign to cut-off food supplies to the city and to take possession of its rice fields and mills. After a 10-day siege Sherman forced out the Confederates and took control of the city, presenting it grandly to President Lincoln as a "Christmas present."

In the end Sherman estimated that his Georgia campaign amounted to $100 million in damages. A large portion of that sum represented the destruction of the state's economic resources, which crippled its cities and left them open to occupation by Union forces. Pleased with the success of his total-war campaign, Sherman went on to organize an equally devastating march through the Carolinas. Although the general found much of his strength in numbers, he refused to take on African American soldiers. Clearly racist, he disburdened his troops of freed slaves, issuing an order that allowed them to inhabit land rather than join the war. Nevertheless, the general succeeded in his campaigns. Sherman went on to vanquish Confederate troops under Generals Robert E. Lee and Joseph Johnston, and, in 1869, to succeed Lieutenant General Grant as commander of the U.S. Army.

***See also:* Civil War (Economic Impact of), War and the Economy**

FURTHER READING

Barrett, John Gilchrist. *Sherman's March Through the Carolinas.* Chapel Hill, N.C.: University of North Carolina Press, 1996.

Burke, Davis, Jeff Stone, ed., and Carolyn Reidy, ed. *Sherman's March.* New York: Vintage Books, 1988.

Dictionary of American History. New York: Charles Scribner's Sons, 1976, s.v. "Sherman's March to the Sea."

Marszlek, John F. *Sherman: A Soldier's Passion for Order.* New York: Vintage Books, 1994.

Royster, Charles. *The Destructive War: William Tecumseh Sherman, Stonewall Jackson, and the Americans.* New York: Vintage Books, 1993.

SHIPBUILDING INDUSTRY

From its earliest days the shipping industry was driven by the need to make contact with other people for migration, trade, and exploration. Many of the colonists arriving in what would become the United States brought a strong seafaring background with them. To facilitate transportation in the New World, they also settled along sea and river ports. These settlements invited participation in an already strong international sea trade. The abundance of forests on the coast offered easy access to materials for shipbuilders.

The shipbuilding industry was of such importance to the new nation that the first Congress in 1789 passed legislation to encourage the use of U.S.-made ships. The bill provided a 10 percent rebate on tariffs if the ship carrying the products was built in the United States. This incentive was important, because the young nation was bringing in a lot of finished goods and industrial products from Europe and sending back raw materials and agricultural products. But this was the last major legislation that Congress would pass for another 50 years to directly help the industry grow. The industry was already independently strong (ship-building was an important industry going back to colonial times) and the government wanted it to remain a private enterprise. However, the government did pass a Navigation Act of 1817 that protected coastal shipping from foreign competition.

It was significant that the government did not offer any subsidy, or government-funded bonus, to the industry until 1845, when the Postmaster General was authorized to subsidize steamships for transporting mail. These steamships were favored because they could be converted into warships. Nevertheless, the subsidy was soon revoked when, in 1858, it was considered to be a drain on national funds. By 1850, left mostly to itself, the U.S. shipbuilding industry soared to the enviable position of second in size behind England. By this time U.S.-manufactured "Clipper Ships" could be found in almost every port in the world. They were widely believed to be among the world's premier vessels.

During the American Civil War (1861–1865) the industry suffered. U.S. merchant ship owners faced the possibility of capture by privateers and they had to pay huge insurance rates due to the risks of sailing ships bearing the United States flag. It is not surprising that, in order to save their private enterprises (and ships), many ship owners transferred their vessels to foreign registries. The United States forbade these ships from ever returning to United States registries and consequently lost a great number of excellent ships to foreign competitors. In addition, the United States was lagging behind new technological advances. This gave foreign builders a substantial boost due to the new steel-hulled steam-propelled ships, which were considerably cheaper to produce. U.S. law prohibited the registration of foreign-built ships and the costs of building domestic ships made investment in U.S. shipbuilding quite unreasonable.

Various attempts by Congress to reinvigorate the industry were made between 1900 and 1914 but it was not until World War I (1914–1918) began that the United States was jolted into real action. U.S. ports were clogged with cargo and there were no ships to transport the exports. Faced with a potential economic disaster if export revenue disappeared, the government made the radical decision that foreign-built ships of any age could be registered with the United States fleet for use in foreign trade. The Shipping Act of 1916 established a Shipping Board of Directors that oversaw the acquisition and regulation of ships and the procedures of sale or disposal of these ships to U.S. citizens. The Act also called for a substantial boost in production of new ships and it provided funds to back the legislation. The government maintained that the industry would be privately owned and operated even though public funds were driving it. In 1920 the Merchant Marine Act addressed the transfer of publicly-owned vessels to private firms, as well as various issues surrounding maritime commerce, including regulation, federal aid, and claims settlements among carriers. Congress passed various bills aimed at providing financial incentives for private industry to take possession of publicly-owned ships. But investment in the shipping industry was still viewed with skepticism. Ultimately surplus ships were sold below cost.

With the opening of the Panama Canal, intercoastal shipping boomed. The Merchant Marine Act of 1936 provided subsidies to the shipping industry. The act also outlined policy on privately-owned ships, government production of ships when private industry was unable to keep up with demand, and regulations related to publicly-run ships.

The boom in production was at its height when World War II (1939–1945) broke out. The war boosted the industry and U.S. shipyards made many innovative contributions to shipbuilding, including the switch from rivets to welded seams and multiple production of standardized models. Once again, though, with the end of the war the government found itself with a surplus of ships. From the late 1940s to the early 1960s, demand for ships fluctuated widely, and the industry suffered. Shipyards had invested in modernizing their facilities, but the international competition, combined with the erratic character of demand, left shipbuilders drained.

The government tried to keep a quota of shipyards running by dividing its contracts among different shipyards in New England states, Louisiana, Florida, and on the Atlantic, Pacific, and Gulf Coasts. Ultimately the industry became dependent on government contracts and subsidies for its survival. The fact that other countries were also engaged in subsidizing their own shipping industries during the 1970s resulted in a glut of ships. It was a period of cut-throat competition among the ship-builders of different countries. Comparatively inexpensive ships brought lower shipping rates; thus foreign carriers won bigger freight contracts. The U.S. shipbuilders were still so far from making the transition to civilian markets that they had little chance of winning these contracts. The Reagan administration in the 1980s killed the last subsidies that were keeping the few remaining U.S. shipyards competitive and boosted Navy defense spending, further locking the U.S. industry into relying on the government for defense contracts.

The history of the shipbuilding industry in the United States appears to be a long change from the original hopes for a privately competitive industry to the complete opposite—an industry dependent on government contracts for survival. During periods of expanding demand the U.S. ship-building industry pioneered methods for using nuclear power on submarine and surface ships. It also developed fully submergible hydrofoils and applied the technology of missile systems to ships. Toward the end of the 1980s the U.S. approach was to convince foreign governments with highly-subsidized industries to minimize or withdraw their subsidies, but these attempts failed. The U.S. shipbuilding industry was caught between utilizing subsidies which had proven to be damaging in the long run and making an industry that was once privately operated into an entity utterly dependent on government contracts for its survival.

See also: **Clipper Ships, Steamboat Act of 1852**

FURTHER READING

Beazer, Cox, and Harvey Watkins. *U.S. Shipbuilding in the 1970s*. Lexington, MA: Lexington Books, D.C. Heath and Company, 1972.

Encyclopedia of American Industries. Detroit: Gale Research, Inc., 1998, s.v. ''Ship Building and Repairing.''

Heinrich, Thomas R. *Ships for the Seven Seas: Philadelphia Shipbuilding in the Age of Industrial Capitalism*. New York: Johns Hopkins Press, 1996.

''Longer Lives for Aging Cargo Ships.'' *New York Times*. January 1, 1990.

Shipbuilders Council of America. *Bringing Back America's Shipyards—A Major Step toward Bringing Back America's Independence*. Fairfax, VA: Shipbuilders Council of America, 1988.

SHORTAGE

A shortage exists when there is a greater demand for a product or service than there is a supply of the product or service. A shortage usually occurs when the price of a product or service in the marketplace is below its equilibrium price. The equilibrium price is the price at which there is neither an insufficient supply nor an over abundance of the product or service. When the price of a product or service is less than equilibrium, consumers will demand more of the product or service than the suppliers are willing to sell, which in turn creates a shortage. Consumers will then bid up the price of the product or service until it reaches its equilibrium. The equilibrium price is the one that brings the market into balance by equating supply and demand. If the government interferes with or takes control of a shortage situation, a black market may develop. A shortage may also be referred to as an excess demand.

See also: **Price, Surplus**

SINCLAIR, UPTON BEALL, JR.

Upton Sinclair (1878–1968) was a popular writer and social critic, a muckraker (exposing political and commercial corruption) writing during the first half of the twentieth century. During the sixty years of his life, Sinclair focused on subjects of ordinary American daily life, which he believed involved violations of decency and democracy. His most famous book, *The Jungle*, helped change the nature of the food processing industry in America by initiating a public outcry that led to strong government legislation regulating food processing and clean meat-packing. A socialist in his politics, he regularly took the side of the ordinary American consumers and he fought consistently for the civil liberties of working people.

Upton Beall Sinclair, Jr. was born on September 20, 1878, in Baltimore, Maryland, the only child of Upton and Priscilla Sinclair. He was born into a distinguished but impoverished Southern family. At age ten Sinclair went with his family to live in New York, where he rushed through eight years of school in just three, and at age fourteen entered City College of New York, where he majored in English literature. While in college, Sinclair began living on his own, supporting himself by writing regularly for comic papers, pulp magazines, and other adventure story magazines of the time.

In 1897, at age nineteen, he graduated from the college with a Bachelor of Arts and entered Columbia University for graduate work, where he studied French, German, and Italian. Sinclair continued to publish his writing while in school, supporting himself and, later, his mother.

YOU DON'T HAVE TO BE SATISFIED WITH AMERICA AS YOU FIND IT. YOU CAN CHANGE IT. I DIDN'T LIKE THE WAY I FOUND AMERICA 60 YEARS AGO, AND I'VE BEEN TRYING TO CHANGE IT EVER SINCE.

Upton Sinclair, Jr., ***San Francisco Sunday Chronicle*****, April 8, 1962**

Disillusioned by the materialistic atmosphere of New York at the beginning of the twentieth century, Sinclair abandoned the city in 1900 and went to live in a shack in the woods near Quebec, Canada. There he met and married his first wife, Meta Fuller, in 1901. His first and only son was born a year later.

From Canada Sinclair moved to Princeton, New Jersey, one of the intellectual and academic centers of the American Eastern seaboard. He continued writing but focused on socialist ideals and muckraking. His novel, *The Jungle*, made him famous, exposing in detail the appalling working conditions in the food packing industry. In this book he also graphically depicted the unsanitary conditions of the American meat-packing and meat-handling industry.

The publication of *The Jungle* awakened the American public to the dangerous practices of an unregulated food industry which was exploited for huge profits by careless businessmen. In 1906 President Theodore Roosevelt (1901–1909) invited Sinclair to the White House. After consulting with Sinclair the president ordered an investigation of the meat and food processing industries, which led to the passage of the first government regulated pure food laws in America.

During this time Sinclair continued to publish books exposing America's social problems and his writing continued to make a strong impact on his readers. In his muckraking style he exposed the shoddy and shallow lifestyles of New York's high society, as well as unethical and illegal practices of some Wall Street financiers.

Sinclair's political concerns were about the increasing problems of democracy trying to survive in the midst of the Industrial Revolution. This, combined with his moral sentiments, led Sinclair to take full advantage of the Progressive era. He aimed to educate Americans, many of them immigrants, as to how they were being cheated. Sinclair also encouraged his readers to join forces. He advocated forming guilds, organizations for democracy, and unions in order to combat those who pursued business merely as single-minded profiteers. Sinclair himself was one of the early founders, along with Clarence Darrow (1857–1938) and Helen Keller (1880–1968), of the American Civil Liberties Union (ACLU), an organization providing legal support in matters concerning civil liberties.

Sinclair's later years continued to be active. He was a vegetarian and maintained good health and vitality into advanced age. Sinclair remained involved with the Democratic Party, though he always regarded himself as a socialist and an anti-communist. Upton Sinclair died in 1968. His writings and advocacy live on in the society he believed he could change for the better.

See also: **Cattle Industry, Trust-Busting**

FURTHER READING

Bloodstone, William A. *Upton Sinclair.* Boston: Twayne Publishers, 1977.

Harris, Leon A. *Upton Sinclair, American Rebel.* New York: Crowell, 1975.

Kazin, Alfred. *On Native Grounds.* New York: Reynal and Hitchcock, 1942.

Mitchell, Gregg. *The Campaign of the Century: Upton Sinclair's Race for Governor of California and the Birth of Media Politics.* New York: Random House, 1992.

Sinclair, Upton. *Autobiography.* New York: Harcourt Brace, 1962.

SINGER, ISAAC MERRIT

In 1851 Isaac Singer (1811–1875), invented the first modern mass-produced sewing machine with an overhanging arm; this machine made it possible to sew any part of a garment. He also patented the foot treadle and the spring-equipped presser for holding down fabric while sewing with both hands.

Though people have been sewing for the last 20,000 years—joining pieces of material using bone needles, awls, and animal sinews for thread, or using iron needles which began in the fourteen century—it was not until the eighteenth century, when mechanical sewing machines were invented, that sewing and the textile industry could grow into one of the largest and most basic industries in the world.

Arguably, it was Isaac Singer who brought sewing out of the dark ages of crude stitching into the modern industrial age of mass-produced clothing and upholstered furniture. The French were the first to manufacture the sewing machine and used it to speed up the production of army uniforms in 1841. However, the innovations that Singer made in 1851 while repairing a clumsy Lerow and Blodgett sewing machine brought about what is now regarded as the first truly modern and mass-produced commercial and domestic sewing machine in the United States. This sewing machine, the Singer Sewing Machine, has been known to U.S. households for generations.

Isaac Singer left home at age 12 to work for the next seven years at a variety of unskilled jobs. He had little formal education but much real-life experience. At age 19 he took a job for a few months as an apprentice, but he left this shortly and began a 9-year period of wandering from state to state. He earned a

Isaac Singer.

living by mostly relying on his mechanical cleverness and experience. A lover of music and theatrics, as well, Singer spent part of his early adulthood as an actor, traveling the country with a theatrical troupe known as the Merritt Players. Plagued by money problems, the group eventually disbanded, leaving Singer destitute.

Singer officially became an inventor at age 28, while working in Illinois. He obtained his first patent from the government in 1839 for a rock-drilling machine. Singer, however, quickly spent the money he made from that invention; he also sold the patent rights and left himself with nothing. Ten years later, at age 38, he patented a wood and metal-carving machine. He then obtained financing to build a small factory in order to produce this device. Life and business were looking up for Singer, but then a boiler explosion occurred in the factory, destroying it. And again Singer was left penniless.

In Boston two years later, while working in a machine shop repairing a sewing machine, Singer again tried his hand at inventing. His employer told him that if he could make a practical, reliable, and mass-producable sewing machine, his fortune would be made. Within a few hours Singer drew a sketch of a new kind of sewing machine, and he built a prototype within 11 days.

Singer immediately applied for a patent on this machine, which he received on August 12, 1851. He then organized what became I. M. Singer and Company and began manufacturing sewing machines. Though he had some competition in the market, the fact that his machine could perform continuous stitching, put it in great demand almost immediately.

Singer fought off law suits from other sewing machine manufacturers, but he had achieved success. By 1854, despite losing some of the law suits, his company had reached and retained a commanding position in the industry. Singer created improvements on his original design and attached the improvements to his original patent, creating what is called a pooling of patents, where many patented ideas are brought together into a kind of giant and complicated product patent, making it difficult to steal.

Singer's greatest service to the consumer, both in the home and in industry, was that he had developed the first domestic sewing machine brought into general use. He made his machines available to many people by creating a time-payment program for buyers, possibly the first such program in U.S. business. Singer also aggressively fought the psychological barrier to mass consumer sales of sewing machines—the false belief that women of his era could not operate complicated machinery. Singer provided many demonstrations to manufacturers that anyone could use his sewing machine with a little training. Clearly the development of Singer's practical sewing machines and the ease with which they could be used contributed to the growth of the ready-made clothing industry in the nineteenth and twentieth centuries. Moreover, Singer contributed to the enhanced general employment of women.

Singer retired at age 51, a multi-millionaire. He lived a flamboyant life-style in New York City and throughout Europe, and left an estate of $13 million at his death in 1875.

FURTHER READING

Bissel, Don. *The First Conglomerate: 145 Years of the Singer Sewing Machine Company*. N.p., Don Bissel, 1999.

Brandon, Ruth. *Singer and the Sewing Machine: A Capitalist Romance*. New York: Lippincott, 1977.

Cooper, Grace R. *The Sewing Machine: Its Invention and Early Development*. Washington, DC: Smithsonian Institution Press, 1976.

Encyclopedia of World Biography, 2nd ed. Detroit: The Gale Group, 1998, s.v. "Isaac M. Singer."

Fucini, Joseph J. *Entrepreneurs*. Boston: G. K. Hall and Co., 1985.

SIT-DOWN STRIKE

Sit-down strikes began in 1936 as an aggressive method of calling attention to the needs of non-unionized workers in mass production industries. Because the American Federation of Labor (AFL) was not interested in organizing these workers, a handful of radical leaders rose to the challenge and began to push for the industry-wide unionization of unskilled labor. Workers in mass production industries, however, were reluctant to join unions because they were not convinced that labor had the power to mount successful strikes without the support of the majority of workers. Sit-down strikes showed that a minority of workers could effectively halt production and force management to pay attention to their demands.

The first sit-down strike occurred in 1936, when workers at three rubber plants in Akron, Ohio, went on an unauthorized strike as part of a campaign to force their employer to recognize the United Rubber Workers as their legitimate bargaining agent. Instead of setting up a picket line at the factory gates (which makes the strikers publicly visible but has little affect on production activities) they occupied the company buildings and refused to leave. This unprecedented and disruptive tactic, which stalled production and cut into company profits, shocked both industry and more moderate labor leaders but was extraordinarily effective. Sit-down strikes soon spread throughout other industries. The single most significant sit-down strike occurred in January and February 1937, when the United Auto Workers (UAW) confronted General Motors Corporation (GM) in the GM ''company town'' of Flint, Michigan. With only 122 members at the Flint strike plant, the UAW local was able to stop GM production. Strikers took over Fisher Body Number 1 plant, where GM kept the dies for all of its 1937 car models, making it impossible for the company to continue manufacturing. Crippled, GM was able to turn out only 150 cars per week, and by February agreed to accept the union. The Chrysler Corporation soon followed in March 1937.

Though sit-down tactics were nonviolent, management sometimes attempted to break the strikes by force and bloodshed was not an uncommon result. Sit-down strikes were highly effective in bringing unskilled labor into unions. After the strike against GM, UAW membership increased from 98,000 in February 1937, to 400,000 by that summer. By late 1937, federal laws to prohibit sit-down strikes and court decision upholding these laws eliminated the labor movement's ability to use this method. Though sit-down strikes could no longer be used by labor, it remained an effective means of protest. Sit-down tactics were later used effectively by Civil Rights activists and students protesting the Vietnam War (1964–1975).

See also: **American Federation of Labor, Labor Movement, Labor Unionism, Strike, United Auto Workers**

SIXTEENTH AMENDMENT

Proposed in Congress on July 12, 1909, and ratified February 3, 1913, the Sixteenth Amendment to the U.S. Constitution gives the federal government (specifically, the U.S. Congress) authority to levy and collect income taxes. The amendment states that incomes may be taxed ''from whatever sources derived'' and without regard to population. In other words, it is up to Congress to determine the level at which citizens of the country are taxed, and this may be done without apportionment among the individual states.

THE CONGRESS SHALL HAVE THE POWER TO LAY AND COLLECT TAXES ON INCOMES, FROM WHATEVER SOURCE DERIVED, WITHOUT APPORTIONMENT AMONG THE SEVERAL STATES, AND WITHOUT REGARD TO ANY CENSUS OR ENUMERATION.

Sixteenth Amendment, U.S. Constitution

One hundred years before the Sixteenth Amendment was approved, Congress had begun eyeing income tax as a way to collect funds for government use. Lawmakers first considered levying an income tax to help pay for the War of 1812 (1812–1814), which the new republic fought against Great Britain over shipping disputes. During the American Civil War (1861–1865) Congress imposed an income tax for the first time, charging workers and businessmen between three and five percent of their earnings and establishing (in 1862) a Bureau of Internal Revenue to administer the tax program. The war over, income taxes were phased out. In 1894, responding to increasing economic and political pressures, the legislature again passed an income tax law (two percent on all incomes over $4,000), as part of the Wilson-Gorman Tariff Ac, but the law was struck down by the U.S. Supreme Court, which declared it unconstitutional in the case of *Pollock v. Farmers' Loan and Trust Company* (1898). In the early 1900s the idea of an income tax received widespread political support for the first time. Progressive politicians could see that the nation's wealth was poorly distributed, as the gap between rich and poor was growing wider. Conservative politicians worried that the government would not be able to respond to a national emergency if it lacked resources. These political factions found a single voice in favor of a graduated income tax (a tax based on level of income those who earn more, pay higher taxes). To circumvent the U.S. Supreme Court it was necessary for Congress to propose an amendment to the Constitution. In ratifying the amendment the states gave Congress the authority to set rates and collect income tax.

Tax rates have fluctuated ever since the passage of the Sixteenth Amendment, reaching their highest mark during World War II (1939–1945), when the rate soared to 91 percent. The war effort also brought the innovation of automatic withholdings: Taxes were deducted directly from paychecks. In 1953 the Bureau of Internal Revenue was dramatically reorganized to create the Internal Revenue Service (IRS). Over the decades tax laws (collectively called the Tax Code) have become increasingly complex, prompting a recent movement in favor of a flat (versus the graduated) tax, where all taxpayers are charged at the same rate.

See also: **Flat Tax Provision, Pollock v. Farmers' Loan and Trust Company, Progressive Tax, Regressive Tax**

SLATER, SAMUEL

Samuel Slater (1768–1835) was an English-born manufacturer who introduced the first water-powered cotton mill to the United States. This invention revolutionized the textile industry and paved the way for the Industrial Revolution.

Samuel Slater was born in Derbyshire, England, on June 9, 1768. His father was a prosperous yeoman farmer who owned a farm near the Derwent River. Along the same river, in the town of Cromford, the first spinning mill driven by waterpower was built in 1771. This mill was owned by Jedediah Strutt and Richard Arkwright, the inventor of a revolutionary water-frame spinner. In 1776 Strutt and Arkwright dissolved their partnership, and Strutt started his own mill in Belper, where Slater lived. At the age of 14 Slater began an apprenticeship at the Strutt mill. Three years later he was promoted to supervisor of machinery and mill construction. In this position Slater learned everything about textile production, including the construction of machines.

In 1789 Slater began looking for other opportunities for advancement in the textile industry. He decided that the industry had reached its peak in England, but remained undeveloped in the United States, which was still largely agricultural and where handicraft methods of production still prevailed. No U.S. inventor had yet been successful in building a spinning machine, and British law prohibited the export of such machines. In an effort to preserve their dominance in industry, Britain also prohibited the emigration of skilled mechanics. In order to leave the country unnoticed Slater had to disguise himself as a farm laborer. He left England without notifying family and friends and only took his indenture with him to prove his familiarity with Strutt's cotton mills.

Slater sailed for 66 days to reach the United States, and upon his arrival he began working for the New York Manufacturing Company. Slater became dissatisfied with the mill, however, because it was poorly equipped and lacked sufficient water supply. Around that same time the owners of a machine-spinning mill in Pawtucket, Rhode Island, were looking for a mechanic familiar with the English system of production. Moses Brown and William Almy were impressed by Slater's experience and quickly hired him into their company. His primary role was to build a duplicate model of the Arkwright machine, for which he was paid one dollar a day.

[I]F I DO NOT MAKE AS GOOD YARN AS THEY DO IN ENGLAND, I WILL HAVE NOTHING FOR MY SERVICES, BUT WILL THROW THE WHOLE OF WHAT I HAVE ATTEMPTED OVER THE BRIDGE.

Samuel Slater, 1790

Although many Americans had attempted to copy the British machines prior to Slater's arrival, none had been successful. A cotton factory in Beverly, Massachusetts, built by John Cabot and Joshua Fisher, had the distinction of being the first textile mill in the United States. Due to imperfections in their machines, however, the mill produced products of poor quality, and it soon closed. On April 5, 1790, Slater signed an agreement with Almy and Brown to make equipment for the "spinning of cotton by water." Upon signing the agreement, Slater said, ". . . if I do not make as good yarn as they do in England, I will have nothing for my services, but will throw the whole of what I have attempted over the bridge." Despite the limited materials available in New England, Slater accomplished his mission in less than a year. On December 20, 1790, Slater's cotton mill began production with the Arkwright system.

Even though the new mill had Arkwright models it nonetheless experienced some initial problems. In particular there was difficulty securing good-quality raw cotton, and the equipment frequently broke down. Slater was especially disappointed in American cotton, which was poorly cleaned. Fortunately, just three years after Slater's first mill opened, Eli Whitney (1765–1825) invented the cotton gin, which properly cleaned the cotton in large enough quantities to satisfy Slater. Despite these initial setbacks the business quickly expanded. In 1793 Almy, Brown, and Slater constructed a new mill on the Blackstone River. It was called the Old Slater Mill and consisted of three carders and two spinning frames containing 72 spindles. In the same year Slater's wife, Hannah Wilkinson Slater, invented cotton-sewing thread. Prior to this time, linen thread was used for sewing. Hannah realized that twisting two strands of cotton yarn into one thread created a stronger and smoother thread than the linen. Slater was interested in this new invention, but did not develop machines for producing thread until much later.

Though Almy, Brown, and Slater became a successful company, Slater later disagreed with his partners over the management of the mill. Slater retained his interests in Almy, Brown, and Slater, and in 1798 organized a new firm called Samuel Slater and Company. In 1801 Slater built another mill based on the Arkwright system, this one in Massachusetts. He then helped build other cotton mills in Rhode Island, Connecticut, Massachusetts, and New Hampshire. By 1828 Slater was involved in 13 partnerships for processing cotton.

Not only did Slater mechanize the textile industry in the United States but he also introduced a new production system. Due to the fact that the family was such an important social institution in New England, Slater incorporated this into the production process. He introduced a family labor system where duties were divided according to age and gender. Men worked as laborers or skilled artisans, women cleaned raw cotton, and children worked in the mill. Slater's production system also featured a partnership or single-proprietorship form of ownership, personal management, small-scale production, and the use of waterpower. This production system is often referred to as the Slater system or Rhode Island system of manufactures.

Slater's system was facilitated by production villages. The families employed by Slater lived in company-owned housing near the mills; they shopped at company stores and went to company schools and churches. One of the first of these mill villages was called Slatersville and was located on the Branch River. By 1807 Slatersville consisted of the Slatersville Mill, two tenement houses for workers, the owner's house, and a company store.

Slater dedicated his entire life to building the textile industry and turned his company into a family business. By the 1830s Slater's health was declining. In 1833 while he was bedridden from rheumatism, President Andrew Jackson (1829–1937) visited New England to witness the growing textile industry. Upon meeting Slater, President Jackson named him the "Father of American Manufactures." Two years later, on April 20, 1835 Samuel Slater died in the mill village of Webster, Massachusetts.

See also: **Cotton, Rhode Island System of Labor, Samuel Slater Builds First Factory, Textile Industry**

FURTHER READING

Cameron, Edward Hugh. *Samuel Slater, Father of American Manufactures.* Freeport, ME: B. Wheelwright Co., 1960.

Gordon, John Steele. "Technology Transfer." *American Heritage,* February 1990.

Karwatka, Dennis. *Technology's Past: America's Industrial Revolution and the People Who Delivered the Goods.* Ann Arbor, MI: Prakken Publications, Inc., 1996.

Simonds, Christopher. *Samuel Slater's Mill and the Industrial Revolution.* Englewood Cliffs, NJ: Silver Burdett Press, 1990.

Tucker, Barbara M. *Samuel Slater and the Origins of the American Textile Industry, 1790–1860.* Ithaca, NY: Cornell University Press, 1984.

SLAVE CODES

Beginning in the mid-1600s, the American colonies began enacting slave codes into law. These laws enforced the system of bondage by depriving slaves of their civil rights, protecting the rights of the owners, and designating slaves as the property of their masters. Slaves were prohibited from owning weapons, receiving an education, meeting among themselves, moving about without their master's permission, and from testifying against white people in a court of law. Slaves were also treated differently than whites within the justice system: if a black man broke the law, he was punished more severely than was a white man who broke the same law; less severe punishments were given to white men who committed crimes against blacks.

After the American colonies fought for and won independence from Britain (in the American Revolution, 1775–83), slavery began to disappear from the northern states. Abolitionists (those who opposed slavery and lobbied for it to be abolished) grew in number and the economy of the North became increasingly industrial. The existence of northern ''free states'' and Great Britain's abolition of slavery throughout its empire (1833) gave rise to the ''underground railroad.'' Along this route, escaped slaves traveled from station to station where they were harbored until they reached freedom in a free state or in Canada. The escape of slaves threatened the South's economy, which had become increasingly dependent on agriculture and slave labor. Southerners complained the fugitive slave law passed by Congress in 1793 did not go far enough to protect their interests. In 1850, a second and more stringent fugitive slave law was passed. The law accompanied the Compromise of 1850, which dealt with the admission of Texas to the Union and the territories in the Southwest that were newly annexed from Mexico (in the Mexican War, 1846–48). The 1850 law required all citizens to obey the 1793 law; it also prohibited a jury trial for fugitives and denied them the right to testify.

In the 1800s southern lawmakers enacted legislation at the state level to further tighten the slave codes: Any action by a black or a white person that threatened the system of bondage was made into a serious crime. The slave codes, harsh and desperate attempts to preserve the South's agrarian lifestyle, fueled the abolitionist movement to end slavery. The American Civil War (1861–65) spelled the end of bondage but it would be another one hundred years before the civil rights of the nation's African American citizens were adequately protected by the legal and justice systems.

See also: **Abolition, Slavery, Underground Railroad**

SLAVERY *(ISSUE)*

The Portuguese were the first Europeans to enslave Africans. They began this practice during their explorations of the West African Coast in the fifteenth century. They usually acquired their slaves from other Africans and took them back to Europe where they were employed as servants or laborers.

Christopher Columbus opened the New World to Europeans in 1492, and soon Spain, Portugal, and other European states had established colonies. Regardless of whether the Europeans concentrated on mining precious metals (as the Spanish did), grew and refined sugar cane (as was true of virtually all the European powers), or settled down to grow staple agricultural exports (as in the English case), they soon had to confront the need for labor. The Spanish and, later, the English attempted to enslave American Indians, but that did not work well (in part because the lack of immunity to European diseases decimated the native populations), so they began to import laborers from Africa.

Actually, the English colonists turned first to their own poverty-stricken population of peasants who had been driven off the land by the conversion of crop land into sheep pasture during the sixteenth century. This displacement of the English peasantry was called the enclosure movement. It produced an army of desperate and angry peasants who wandered the English countryside looking for work, poaching game on the gentry's land, or engaging in robbery, for which many were hanged. Of the peasants who remained in England a good number would eventually make up the country's wage labor force as textile manufacturing changed England from an agricultural to an industrial economy. But tens of thousands of poor Britons also immigrated to the New World as indentured servants. Tobacco farming was profitable but labor-intensive and the Chesapeake colonies of Virginia, Carolina, and Maryland employed these bonded laborers. Until the late seventeenth century, most of the work force in the English mainland colonies were indentured servants, working an average of seven years to pay off the debt of ship passage. Some of these bonded servants eventually became prosperous in the America; many died from overwork, disease, and mistreatment, or else, after their debt was paid, migrated to the back country and lived as subsistence farmers.

By the last quarter of the seventeenth century, an improving employment picture in England dried up the stream of available indentured servants. The practice of many white servants of escaping and passing themselves off as independent laborers or small farmers as well as the fact that many of the popular protests and rebellions in the New World, like Bacon's Rebellion (1675–1676) involved poor former indentured servants, also led the colonial elite to consider an alternative labor source.

That source was African slaves. A lucrative system known as Triangular Trade provided this new labor source. Traders took rum, guns, powder, and

SLAVES AND SLAVEHOLDERS, 1860

States	Holders with 1-9 Slaves	Holders with 10-20 Slaves	Holders with 20-50 Slaves	Holders with 50-100 Slaves	Holders with 100-500 Slaves	Holders with 500-1000 Slaves	Holders with Over 1000 Slaves	Total Slave-Holders	Total Slaves
Alabama	21,793	5,906	4,344	1,341	346			33,730	435,080
Arkansas	941	142	56	10				1,149	111,115
Delaware	562	25						587	1,798
Florida	3,368	976	603	158	47			5,152	61,745
Georgia	27,191	7,530	5,049	1,102	211	1		41,084	462,198
Kentucky	31,819	5,271	1,485	63	7			38,645	225,483
Louisiana	14,886	3,222	2,349	1,029	543	4		22,033	331,726
Maryland	11,203	1,718	747	99	16			13,783	87,189
Mississippi	19,559	5,489	4,220	1,359	315	1		30,943	436,631
Missouri	21,380	2,400	502	34	4			24,320	114,931
North Carolina	24,520	6,073	3,321	611	133			34,658	331,059
South Carolina	16,199	5,210	3,646	1,197	441	7	1	26,701	402,406
Tennessee	28,389	5,523	2,550	335	47			36,844	275,719
Texas	16,292	3,423	1,827	282	54			21,878	182,566
Virginia	37,577	8,774	4,917	746	114			52,128	490,865
Total	275,679	61,682	35,616	8,366	2,278	13	1	383,635	3,950,511

Source: United States Census, Agriculture of the United States in 1860, p. 247.

Slavery was widespread in 1860, however the majority of slave holders owned less than 10 slaves.

trinkets to Africa where they were exchanged for slaves. The slaves were shipped below decks to the West Indies where they were sold. Then the traders hauled cargoes of sugar, and other products to North America, where the sugar was converted to rum, or else they sailed back to Europe. The trip to the New World was hideous for the slaves. They were packed into the slave ships like sardines and many died en route. This infamous leg of the Triangular Trade was known as the Middle Passage. In this fashion the slave trade continued for 300 years and millions of people were deported from Africa in the process.

Slavery may have been introduced in the English colonies as early as 1619 when a Dutch trading vessel brought 20 Africans to the Jamestown Colony. (Historians disagree on whether this particular group of Africans was enslaved or not.) At any rate, towards the end of the century as the settlers' tobacco plantations grew larger, their need for workers also grew and they found that Africans better served their needs. Africans could not pass themselves off as free men and their total subjugation meant that their exploitation was governed by cold calculation of how hard to work them.

In the Caribbean the cost of replacing slaves who died from overwork was low enough that it made economic sense to work the slave to death. That calculus of exploitation worked the other way in the mainland colonies. Slaves were sometimes worked to death, but the price of replacing slaves was high enough that they were often allowed enough food and just enough sleep to live an abbreviated life-span and even to replace their numbers through informal families in the slave quarters.

Between 1620 and 1670, through court decisions and legislative actions, African servitude was made permanent and the institution of slavery was born. It was based not only on the need for labor but also on the ideology of white supremacy. The British colonists clearly regarded the Africans as inferior.

By 1700 there were about 27,000 African slaves in British North America, a number which represented approximately 10 percent of the population. South Carolina had the greatest number of slaves, followed by Virginia. The number of slaves was relatively small in North Carolina, the Middle Colonies, and New England. The demand for slaves intensified in the eighteenth century because of the expansion of agriculture. In Virginia, for example, the number of slaves increased from 12,000 in 1708 to 120,000 in 1756. The slave trade also continued to expand and it was estimated that more than five million slaves were imported into all areas of the New World during the eighteenth century.

As the number of slaves increased, fear of uprisings intensified. By 1700 all the colonies had laws known as Slave Codes which governed the status of the slaves. Slaves were considered property, had no rights, and could be killed for misbehavior. There was no legal limit on lashings. These laws also restricted the movement for slaves, for example, under the Virginia Code, no slave could leave the plantation without permission.

Fear of resistance was not unfounded. There was an aborted slave revolt in Virginia in 1687, and a bloody uprising in New York in 1712. There were several outbreaks of violence in South Carolina in the 1720s and 1730s, and in 1741 panic swept New York

City when it was rumored that slaves and poor whites were conspiring to seize control of the city. The New York City conspiracy did not materialize but more than 150 people were arrested and many of them were executed.

Anti-slavery sentiment on the part of whites emerged in the late 1600s. The Pennsylvania Quakers issued a formal denunciation of slavery known as the "Germantown Statement" in 1687 and anti-slavery pamphlets began to appear during the eighteenth century. One of the best known of the early pamphleteers was John Woolman. And in 1775 Benjamin Franklin (1706–1790), Thomas Paine (1737–1809), and James Otis (1725–1783) founded the Pennsylvania Abolitionist Society.

The American Revolution (1775–1783) created a paradox with respect to slavery. The Declaration of Independence stated that "all men are created equal," but this was clearly not true in America where, in 1776, there were nearly 500,000 slaves. Moreover many Revolutionary leaders, including George Washington (1732–1799) and Thomas Jefferson (1743–1826), owned slaves. Even though they were critical of the institution of slavery they believed Africans to be inferior to whites and freed very few of their slaves during the struggle. Even so there were some changes after the war. Between 1777 and 1786 all of the northern states provided for either the immediate abolition, or gradual emancipation, of slaves. Moreover the Northwest Ordinance of 1787, prohibited slavery in the Northwest Territory (the area that eventually became the states of Ohio, Indiana, Illinois, Michigan, and Wisconsin). These changes resulted from a combination of economic and humanitarian forces. Slavery was not profitable in those areas where there were no large plantations and there were those who believed deeply that the practice was immoral.

But, at the same time cotton production was expanding in the South. When Eli Whitney invented the cotton gin in 1793, cotton farming became more profitable and the demand for slaves in that region suddenly increased. At the same time, southerners began to defend slavery as a virtuous institution rather than a necessary evil. As cotton culture expanded it came to be concentrated in the Lower South—South Carolina, Western Georgia, North Florida, Alabama, Mississippi, and Louisiana. By 1840 there were about 2.5 million slaves in the South, most of them concentrated in these states.

Cotton production continued to rise and by 1860 it represented 57 percent of all U.S. exports. This in turn led to an increased demand for slaves. Even though the importation of slaves was illegal after 1808, it is estimated that at least 300,000 were smuggled into the country between 1807 and 1860. Slaves were also bred, like cattle. A vigorous internal slave trade developed in which thousands of human beings were sold at auction.

Both the militant defense of slavery and militant opposition began to appear in the 1820s. Southerners argued that they had a constitutional right to hold property, including slaves. Southern pro-slavery advocates went on to quote Bible passages that mentioned the existence of slavery in Old Testament days. Others argued that a menial class was a requirement upon which to build civilized society—indeed, they held that slavery was the very condition of democracy in the South. And, of course, southern apologists for slavery also propounded the white supremacist doctrine that Blacks were perfectly suited to their subordinate role because they were physically strong and mentally inferior.

The anti-slavery movement evolved from the moderate pipe-dream of re-colonizing emancipated blacks in Liberia, in Africa. The American Colonization Society, founded in 1817, included prominent figures like James Madison and John Marshall. It proposed to free the slaves, compensate the owners, and return the freed slaves to Africa. But the size of the slave population even in 1830 precluded such a solution. Still, by publishing newspapers and pamphlets, the American Colonization Society at least began the process of education and advocacy of freeing the slaves.

A more radical solution was simply the immediate freeing of the slaves. This was the demand of the "abolitionist" movement that grew up around William Lloyd Garrison, of Massachusetts. Beginning in 1831, Garrison and his associates published *The Liberator* and broadcast the demand that slavery be ended immediately, by force if necessary, and without any compensation to the slave owners. In 1832 Garrison founded the New England Anti-Slavery Society and helped to found the American Anti-Slavery Society in 1833. These developments evoked fear and hatred in the South. Nonetheless, the abolitionist movement grew rapidly and was very active. It sponsored lectures on the subject. It sent the eloquent former slave, Frederick Douglass to England to spread the abolitionist message there.

Abolitionism was the culmination of a generation of reform movements: the temperance movement, the "asylum" movement for the humane treatment of the mentally ill, and the protest movement against the forcible relocation of the Cherokee Indian nation. The abolitionist movement was the biggest and most passionate of these reform movements. It was also uncompromising: at one point, Garrison publicly burned a copy of the Constitution because it had made provisions for slavery. By 1840 there were 250,000 abolitionists organized into 2,000 clubs or societies in fifteen states. Meanwhile, however, the institution of slavery continued to grow. By 1860 there were nearly four million slaves in North America.

If there was to be a resolution of the slavery issue, most people expected it to come through the political system. In the end, the political system failed to solve the problem or contain the explosive force of the slavery issue, but for a time it looked as though it might succeed. Political leaders like ''the Great Compromiser,'' Henry Clay, approached the slavery issue optimistically as a series of questions that might be balanced off against one another. Indeed, almost since the founding of the nation, the process of bringing new states into the union had been guided by the unwritten principle of balancing the admission of free and slave states. It was this spirit of patching together a compromise that animated the architects of the Missouri Compromise in 1820, the elements of which were that Missouri was brought in as a slave state; Maine was separated off from Massachusetts and admitted as a free state; and no more slave states were to be carved out of territory north of the southern boundary of Missouri.

The issue of slavery drove politics from 1820 to the Civil War. Throughout this period the pro-slavery southerners demanded that their ''property rights'' (to own slaves) be protected by the government through measures such as fugitive slave laws. This recalled the words of John Locke, the most influential philosopher for the generation that made the American Revolution. Locke declared that all men, as an essential condition of being human, had the ''inalienable'' right—in society as in the ''state of nature,''— to defend their ''life, liberty, and property.'' In drafting the ''Declaration of Independence'' in 1776, Thomas Jefferson had air-brushed that phrase to read ''life, liberty, and the pursuit of happiness.'' But, regardless of that cosmetic change, the slavery issue forced the nation to decide which was the more important ingredient of humanity—liberty or property. It was the controversy over Missouri's application to join the union as a slave state that led the aging Thomas Jefferson to declare that the slavery question was like a ''fire-bell in the night,'' waking the nation to the possibility of secession.

Slavery endured because it was profitable to the owners of slaves even though its presence inhibited the diversification of the Southern economy. Thus it was probably inevitable that the institution would be ended only by force. It was not until April 1865, when the Civil War ended, that slavery was declared dead. Its demise was finally promulgated in the U.S. Constitution with the ratification of the thirteenth Amendment in 1866.

See also: **Africans Arrive in Virginia, Henry Clay, Indentured Servants, Missouri Compromise,**

FURTHER READING

Curtin, Phillip D. *The Atlantic Slave Trade: A Census.* Madison, WI: University of Wisconsin Press, 1969.

Fogel, Robert William. *Without Consent or Contract: The Rise and Fall of American Slavery.* New York: New York, 1989.

Franklin, John Hope. *From Slavery to Freedom: A History of African Americans.* New York: Alfred A. Knopf, 1994.

Goode, Kenneth G. *From Africa to the United States and then . . . A Concise Afro-American History.* Glenview, IL: Scott, Foresman, 1969.

Robinson, Donald L. *Slavery in the Structure of American Politics, 1765–1820.* New York: Norton, 1979.

Sorin, Gerald. *Abolitionism; A New Perspective.* New York: Praeger, 1972.

Stevenson, Brenda E. *Life in Black and White: Family and Community in the Slave South.* New York: Oxford University Press, 1996.

SLOAN, ALFRED PRITCHARD, JR.

Alfred P. Sloan Jr. (1875–1966) was one of the most influential executives in twentieth century American manufacturing. As chief executive officer, president, and chairman of the board for the automaker General Motors (GM) over several important decades, Sloan was responsible for implementing strategies and practices that helped GM emerge as one of the most successful American companies of the century. In 1998, over thirty years after Sloan's death, GM still held the number one position in American business, leading *Fortune* magazine's list of the Top 500 American enterprises.

Sloan was born in New Haven, Connecticut in 1875, the son of Alfred P. Sloan Sr. and Katherine Mead Sloan. His father was a machinist with investments in a number of businesses, including a tea and coffee import company. When Alfred Jr. was five the family moved to Brooklyn, New York, where he excelled academically in its public schools. As a teen, he passed the entrance examination for Massachusetts Institute of Technology, but was denied admission because of his youth. He was allowed to enter at the age of seventeen and earned his degree in electrical engineering within three years.

Sloan married Irene Jackson and maintained a home on New York's Fifth Avenue. According to the profiles of him published during his lifetime in magazines like *Time* and *Forbes,* Sloan was the quintessential mid-century auto executive, with no interests or hobbies outside of the office. He and his wife had no children, but Sloan was close to a half-brother, Raymond, who was eighteen years his junior. When Raymond died in the 1940s, Sloan was deeply saddened, and increased the funding and time he gave to the Sloan-Kettering Institute for Cancer Research. His half-brother had been a hospital administrator and had drawn Sloan into medical philanthropy. Sloan was also known to be generous with his resources when he learned of a GM family in trouble; he once spent a Christmas holiday working toward finding the best medical care for the burned child of a plant manager, neither of whom he had ever met. He also refused to publish his autobiography, *My Years with General Motors*, until all of the people mentioned had passed away. Sloan himself died just two years later on February 17, 1966, and is buried in Cold Spring Harbor, New York.

Sloan's father was an investor in a New Jersey business called the Hyatt Roller Bearing Company, which made billiard balls. After Sloan Jr. received his degree from the Massachusetts Institute of Technology in 1895, he went to work at Hyatt as a draftsman. In just under a decade he had risen through the ranks to become its president. Part of the reason for both his and Hyatt's success came from Sloan's recognition of Hyatt's ability to expand its business by producing steel roller bearings for the auto industry. Through his sales to the executives who were usually the founders of their firms and pioneers in the auto industry, Sloan came to know many of the most important names in the business; Henry Ford (1863–1947) for example, was both a customer and a friend of Sloan's.

Hyatt Roller Bearing's success in making and marketing the anti-friction bearings used in the auto industry led to an investment involvement with one automaker, the United Motors Corporation. This company had originated a practice of linking to its parts suppliers in a mutually beneficial relationship. Sloan and Hyatt teamed with United in 1916 to become its only supplier of steel roller bearings. The investment of $13.5 million made Sloan a vice president when United Motors merged with General Motors two years later.

The General Motors Company had been founded in 1908 by William C. Durant (1861–1947), a promoter and salesman. Durant's erratic management style and his determination to expand the size of the company regardless of the business climate caused the company to go into receivership in 1910. A consortium of bankers ran the company until Durant regained control with financial backing from the chemical industry magnate, Pierre Du Pont. Durant hired Sloan as a vice president and director of the GM Corporation. Sloan's management style, in contrast to Durant, was methodical and organized. Sloan nearly quit in 1920. He was not the only member of GM's management who was frustrated with Durant. He encouraged his close friend Walter P. Chrysler (1875–1940), who was head of the Buick operations, to strike out on his own and launch what would become the number three auto maker, the Chrysler Corporation.

ACCORDING TO THE PROFILES OF HIM PUBLISHED DURING HIS LIFETIME IN MAGAZINES LIKE *TIME* AND *FORBES,* SLOAN WAS THE QUINTESSENTIAL MID-CENTURY AUTO EXECUTIVE, WITH NO INTERESTS OR HOBBIES OUTSIDE OF THE OFFICE.

In 1920 Sloan went on a trip to Europe with his wife and returned prepared to resign only to learn that Pierre Du Pont had helped to ease Durant into retirement. Du Pont took over as Chief Executive Officer. During this period Sloan developed a critique of the amorphous management culture at GM. When he became head of the company in 1923 he helped moved GM in the direction of rational and predictable growth. During his first years as president in the 1920s, GM doubled its manufacturing output and broke sales records. It also absorbed much of its competition, and some of the smaller carmakers either folded or were merged into General Motors during this time. Its biggest competitor was another Detroit–run operation, the Ford Motor Company, and under Sloan's direction GM surpassed Ford in just a few years.

Sloan's talent for running a thriving financial enterprise is one of the most significant success stories in twentieth century American business. GM was so financially sound that it was barely affected by the Great Depression; despite the Wall Street crash of 1929, its stock continued to pay shareholder dividends. In 1937 Sloan was elected board chair, and continued as both chair and CEO until 1946; he remained chairman of the board of directors until 1956, when he officially retired.

Sloan's restructuring of GM earned him a reputation for excellence both as a practical manager and as a management theorist. Automobile management theory before Sloan was most strongly influenced by Henry Ford. "Fordism" was dedicated to the mass production of a single product. Ford was reported to have said that the customer could have any color Model T that he wanted, as long as it was black. "Sloanism," on the other hand, paid attention to the customer as a choice–maker. Sloan encouraged diversity in product choices. But diversity did not mean chaos. His management accomplishments involved shaping the company rather than allowing the separate automobile companies that GM owned to go off in their own directions, guided by their own autonomous decisions in design, engineering, and production. Thus, Sloan transformed GM from a conglomerate of different companies overlapping each other in price range, technology, and product into a company guided by a single intelligence applied to five separate but interlocked divisions, each producing and marketing cars aimed at a particular segment of the market. On the low end was the affordable Chevrolet. In the middle range were Pontiac, Oldsmobile, and Buick. On the high end were the elegant Cadillacs. The divisions were able to share development, production, and engineering costs among themselves, which added greater profit to the higher-priced luxury models. And the design feature of automobile manufacture became an important generator of car sales through the institution of annual model changes.

When Sloan became chair of GM's board of directors in 1937, he was the highest-paid executive in the country. The mammoth size and economic success of General Motors led to labor unrest and the founding of the United Auto Workers union. Sloan's refusal in 1936 to meet with its representatives to address grievances over job security, wages, and safety resulted in a sit-down strike at GM plants, and the eventual legal recognition of the United Auto Workers a year later, a significant moment in American labor history. Not surprisingly, Sloan was a staunch supporter of Republican politics.

Sloan would also be remembered as a great philanthropist. At the height of the Great Depression in 1934, he founded the Alfred P. Sloan Foundation. It gave grants primarily for research into science and technology; in 1996 it bestowed $53 million. The auto executive also endowed the Sloan School of Management at his alma mater, the Massachusetts Institute of Technology. At its founding in 1931, it was one of the first graduate programs of its kind for executives already established in their careers. He also endowed the Sloan-Kettering Institute for Cancer Research at New York City's Memorial Hospital.

***See also:* Walter P. Chrysler, Chrysler Corporation, Ford Motor Company, Henry Ford, General Motors, United Auto Workers**

FURTHER READING

Drucker, Peter. "The Best Book on Management Ever." *Fortune*. April 23, 1990.

Flint, Jerry. "Alfred Sloan Spoken Here." *Forbes*. November 11, 1991.

Forbes, B.C. and O.D. Foster. *Automotive Giants of America: Men Who Are Making Our Motor Industry*. New York: B.C. Forbes Publishing Co., 1926.

Rae, John B. *Encyclopedia of American Business History and Biography; The Automobile Industry; 1920-1980*. New York: Facts on File, 1989, s.v. "Alfred Pritchard Sloan, Jr."

Sloan, Alfred P. *My Years With General Motors*. New York: Doubleday, 1964.

SLUMS

Slums are severely overcrowded urban areas characterized by the most extreme conditions of poverty, dilapidated housing, and crime.

Slums began appearing as immigration into the Northeastern cities increased following the War of 1812 (1812–1814). Within 35 years New York City grew from 100,000 to over half a million inhabitants as the result of immigration from England, Ireland, and Germany. To accommodate the massive influx of poor immigrants, large rooms of once fashionable dwellings were subdivided into smaller rooms with no light or ventilation and primitive sanitary facilities.

Housing structures, tenements, were hastily constructed on every available parcel of land in New York, Philadelphia, and Boston. Over 290,000 individuals per square mile packed New York's East Side. In 1832 filthy conditions spawned the spread of cholera. By the 1880's poverty, illiteracy, drunkenness, and crime thrived in frightfully overcrowded districts of Northeastern cities and Mid-Western cities, such as Chicago.

New York passed the first housing codes in 1867, 1879, and 1901, which established light, ventilation, and housing regulations for new construction. They did nothing, however, to improve existing buildings, and often tenements built according to code still had major defects. For example, the New York City code required that ''model'' tenements be built with air shafts for ventilation. But the shafts proved only to be a source of fowl odors, thus perpetuating the miserable conditions. (Jacob Riis raised public awareness with his photographs of New York slums published in 1890).

Between 1880 and 1920 the mix of immigrants shifted to predominantly eastern and southern Europeans. Slums were housing minorities whose assimilation into the mainstream of American life was often more difficult than the earlier northern European immigrants. Later immigrants came from the American South, East Asia, and Latin America.

The term ghetto, which originally was used to designate the Jewish area of Venice, Italy, now described the segregation of minorities in crowded sections of the inner cities. Between 1910 and 1970 approximately 6.5 million blacks moved to the North. Although most were underemployed and lived in the ghetto, many found good jobs in steel, rubber, and automobile industries. With the civil rights changes of the 1960's middle class blacks moved to the suburbs, but the ghettos remained as a home to the poor and a blight on the urban landscape. To help eliminate slums, the U.S. government focused on building public housing in the inner cities, but this effort was inadequate to counteract the endemic problems associated with poverty. By the end of the twentieth century, a self-perpetuating condition of despair created an underclass of individuals born in the slums and likely to remain there all their lives.

See also: **Ghetto, Tenements**

SMITH, ADAM

Adam Smith (1723–1790), a philosopher and lecturer at the University of Glasgow, taught Natural Theology—the search for design and order in the confusion of the cosmos—in eighteenth century Scotland. Smith became intrigued with economic theory, seeing economics as a largely ignored subject of philosophy. In 1776 he published an enormous book, a ''living picture'' of the economic circumstances of England, known as *The Wealth of Nations*, without promoting any social class, or advocating any ideology. The book had been called the ''bible of capitalism,'' but that was misleading. *The Wealth of Nations* was a profound effort to describe a ''system of perfect liberty,'' which was the way Smith referred to the small-business commercial capitalism of his era. His book, involving issues of personal self-interest, and competition, has become a classic economics text, and Smith was regarded as the seminal organizer of thoughts and ideas about the economics of capitalism.

Adam Smith was born in June 1723, in Kirkcaldy, Scotland. His father died prior to his birth, and Smith was raised by his mother, in comfortable circumstances in a home near Edinburgh. Smith's close relationship with his mother was life-long. She died at age 90, when Smith was in his 40s. He lived most of his life quietly in Scotland, reading, writing, and teaching. He was highly regarded as a teacher, and was considered to be a genius who was eccentric and absent-minded in most practical matters. Smith's education included three years at the University of Glasgow, Scotland, and seven years at Balliol College at Oxford University, England.

In 1751, not yet age 28, Smith was offered the Chair of Logic at the University of Glasgow, and shortly thereafter was given the Chair of Moral Philosophy. He gained considerable reputation and prestige in 1759, publishing a book called *The Theory of Moral Sentiments*, a work examining moral approval and disapproval.

In 1764, Smith went to France for 18 months. To relieve periods of boredom he felt there, Smith began work on a treatise of political economy, which formed the beginnings of his book, *The Wealth of Nations*. It was in France, working on his treatise, that he hit on one of his greatest insights: labor, not nature, was the source of what we call ''value''. He spent much time in his book elaborating this theme: labor as a source for all value. The book was published in 1776, a 900-page outpouring of a whole epoch. Smith had borrowed his ideas from many other philosophers—*The Wealth of Nations* mentions over 100 names specifically in his treatise. It is a brilliant synthesis of economic and philosophical thinking.

The Wealth of Nations was indeed a revolutionary book. Smith had no particular ideology and apologized for no particular class of people. He was concerned with the flow of goods and services consumed by everyone, constituting the ultimate aim and end of economic life. Smith's primary interest was in laying bare the mechanism by which society hangs together. He constructed a formulation of the laws of the marketplace, discovering what he called in Nature ''the invisible hand,'' whereby private interests and the passions of men are led in the direction most agreeable to the whole society.

Smith's laws of the market were simple. The drive of individual self-interest in a community of similarly motivated people results in competition. If left untampered by any deceitful means, competition among people will result in the provision of goods that society wants, in the amount society desires, at the price society is willing to pay.

Smith's explanation of free-market commerce was an excellent explanation for its era prior to the Industrial Revolution. Large problems arose when restraints of any kind came into play to eliminate Nature's "invisible hand" in matters of the economy. Adam Smith did not anticipate the intervention of governments with their regulations of commerce. In fact, he viewed such intervention as harmful to a free market economy. He did not, as well, anticipate huge industrial monopolies that owned entire areas of the economy, artificially rigged prices, and lowered worker wages. Since the eighteenth century, when Smith woke the world with his great explanation of general economics, the marketplace has changed vastly. Self-interest still plays the major hand, but it is more difficult to compete, since a variety of interests block much competition.

Despite the idea that Smith wrote largely as an apologist for capitalists and businessmen, nothing could be further from the truth. Smith wrote: "No society can surely be flourishing and happy if which by far the greater part of the numbers are poor and miserable," hardly the words of a corporate apologist. Yet, a capitalist class rising in the nineteenth century during the Industrial Revolution ignored much of Smith's work, and focused on his one remark—"let the market alone." Smith's bias, if he had one, was neither anti-labor nor anti-capital. Instead, he described a sensible economic analysis that, at bottom, favored the consumer. He said: "Consumption is the sole end and purpose of all production."

Adam Smith was a scholar and analyst of pre-industrial capitalism. *The Wealth of Nations* became a masterwork of political economy. More so, it was a rational classic guide to understanding the forces of competition and self-interest as the major conception of the human adventure in the Western world. Adam Smith died in 1790, but his economic theories have endured throughout the twentieth century.

See also: **Capitalism**

FURTHER READING

Heilbroner, Robert. *The Essential Adam Smith.* New York: W.H. Norton Co., 1986.

Muller, Jerry Z. *Adam Smith in His Time and Ours: Designing the Decent Society.* New York: Maxwell Macmillan International, 1993.

Nutter, G. Warren. *Adam Smith and the American Revolution.* Washington, DC: American Enterprise Institute, 1976.

Smith, Adam. *The Wealth of Nations.* Chicago: University of Chicago Press, 1976.

Werhane, Patricia H. *Adam Smith and His Legacy for Modern Capitalism.* New York: Oxford University Press, 1991.

SMOOT-HAWLEY TARIFF ACT

Reed Smoot and Willis Hawley were members of the U.S. Congress, who introduced a bill known as the Smoot-Hawley Tariff of 1930. This tariff (a tax on foreign imports) came to be synonymous with a major public policy blunder and failure. Smoot-Hawley was signed into law by President Herbert Hoover (1929–1933) after the stock market crash of 1929. Some historians argue that the tariff was so high that it created unprecedented foreign retaliation against the United States. According to this view, Smoot-Hawley helped convert what would have been a normal economic downturn in the U.S. economy into a major worldwide depression, the Great Depression (1929–1939).

The creation of the Smoot-Hawley Tariff presumably did the following: create the highest tariff rates in U.S. history, frighten the stock market, deepen the Great Depression (by reducing the foreign goods available to U.S. consumers), outrage foreign governments into retaliation, and create an open trade war in the midst of economic depression. On the other hand, there are scholars who argue that there is no compelling evidence that this tariff made the Depression worse. Several of them have even suggested that Smoot-Hawley has become a scapegoat for explaining the extended misery of the Depression. But, regardless of its effect in 1930, the Smoot-Hawley Tariff became a metaphor for underestimating the importance of the nation international trade policies.

See also: **Great Depression (Economic Causes of), Tariff**

SOCIAL GOSPEL

The Social Gospel was a Christian reform movement originating in the late nineteenth century. It was espoused by Protestants, who preached social responsibility as a means to salvation. Adherents believed that the social, economic, and political ills produced by unrestrained capitalism could be addressed by teaching religious values to the working class. They also believed that human nature could be improved by changing the conditions in which people lived and worked.

In addition to building churches in impoverished neighborhoods of American cities, Social Gospel reformers worked within the communities to urge businesses to adopt socially responsible practices. Movement leaders, including clergymen Washington Gladden (1836–1918) of Columbus, Ohio, and Walter Rauschenbusch (1861–1918) of Rochester, New York, acted as mediators between employees and employers. They also wrote books on applying Christian beliefs to alleviate social ills and they worked to lessen the effects of poverty.

The Social Gospel movement was one aspect of a greater progressivism of the late 1800s and early 1900s. Activists—including many young, middle-class individuals—were outraged by the living and working conditions of the urban poor. They argued that government needed to regulate big business—they argued that the doctrine of laissez faire, which opposes government interference in the economy, had only resulted in a capitalist society run amok. This view was at least partly responsible for government legislation imposing some regulations on U.S. industry. It also inspired a spirit of charitable works among many Americans. The reform movement resulted in the passage of building safety codes, enactment of anti-trust laws, approval of health safety standards for the food industry, establishment of settlement houses in inner cities (where residents could participate in educational and social activities), and urban beautification projects.

The legacy of the Social Gospel movement lasted well beyond the first three decades of the twentieth century. Protestant pastor Harry Emerson Fosdick (1878–1969) asserted that leaders such as Rauschenbusch had "ushered in a new era of Christian thought and action."

See also: **Muckrakers**

SOCIAL SECURITY ACT

As the Great Depression (1929–39) in the United States continued in the early 1930s, growing unemployment created widespread fear and insecurity. Between 1929 and 1933 the unemployment rate rose from 3.2 percent to 25.1 percent. Funds from charities and local government were almost completely drained. Many demands were placed on the federal government to design and implement economic and social reforms to help abate social tensions.

One of the groups that arose during this crisis was composed of senior citizens. Led by an elderly California physician by the name of Francis E. Townsend, the "Townsend Plan" involved a government program of monthly checks of $200 to citizens over the age of 60. The only way to stay on the program was to spend all of the money each month. According to Townsend, this requirement would put money in circulation and stimulate the economy. Beginning in 1933, the group formed a network of "Townsend Clubs" with a combined membership of over 5 million, mostly older, Americans who agitated for the reform.

President Franklin D. Roosevelt (1933–45) responded to these and other concerns by appointing the Special Committee on Social Security, chaired by Secretary of Labor Frances Perkins. The committee's recommendations became the foundation for one of the most significant federal social policies in U.S. history, the Social Security Act of 1935. The Social Security Administration provided unemployment insurance, aid to the poor, and pensions for the elderly.

The Social Security System acted as a non-profit insurance company, raising funds through taxes on employers and employees for old age insurance. The size of each pension was based on how much the worker contributed to the fund. Increased earnings resulted in increased pensions. In order to build up the fund, these social security pensions were not to be dispersed before 1942. Originally, this protection did not apply to non-workers who could not contribute to a pension fund. It also did not apply to family members of a deceased pensioner and to farmers and domestic laborers (who were usually poor).

Congress amended the Social Security Act in 1939 to authorize pension payments to survivors of deceased Social Security recipients. In 1965 Medicare was added to provide health care for eligible retirees. In 1989 Social Security covered 38 million people (nearly all the elderly), and it accounted for nearly a quarter of the one trillion-dollar federal budget. In the late 1980s the poverty rate among the elderly was just below that of the general population. In 1998 discussions began about shoring up the social security program. As the 76 million baby boomers reached retirement age, there would be fewer workers paying taxes compared to the number of people drawing benefits. Without revisions, experts predicted, funds would begin to run out early in the twenty-first century.

The Social Security Act included other programs as well. Unemployment insurance was developed to provide some security against joblessness; it was funded by employee and employer taxes. In 1938 minimum wage and child labor laws were implemented, while federal disability insurance was added in 1956. In the 1960s and 1970s government assistance programs grew significantly in response to demands of liberal activists. In 1965 Medicaid was added to help support health care for the poor. In the 1960s and 1970s the food stamp program was developed, which helped the poor buy food. In 1972 the Supplemental Security Income system was enacted to provide assistance for the elderly and disabled poor.

THE SOCIAL SECURITY SYSTEM ACTED AS A NON-PROFIT INSURANCE COMPANY, RAISING FUNDS THROUGH TAXES ON EMPLOYERS AND EMPLOYEES FOR OLD AGE INSURANCE. THE SIZE OF EACH PENSION WAS BASED ON HOW MUCH THE WORKER CONTRIBUTED TO THE FUND.

Another arm of the Social Security Act that significantly impacted the country's social structure and created much controversy was Aid to Dependent Children (ADC). Originally, ADC was designed to help widowed mothers who could not adequately support their families. In 1950 Congress amended ADC to provide grants not only to single parents but also to their children. The program was renamed Aid to Families of Dependent Children (AFDC). Additional amendments broadened coverage to include poor, two-parent families. By the late 1980s more than three million families were receiving AFDC benefits. The growth of this program over the years sparked debate about its role in creating an underclass. While most agreed that the program provided many families with temporary assistance, as was its original intent, critics charged that it stigmatized recipients and conveyed in them a sense of hopelessness, and that it in the same time caused resentment among taxpayers. In the 1980s the focus of anti-poverty programs turned to single mothers receiving AFDC. Initially, these programs provided work training and job placement and, as incentives, they also offered childcare assistance and Medicaid for a year after the recipient began to work. In 1988 the Family Support Act required mothers without children under three to work. In the early 1990s President Bill Clinton (1993–) allowed 42 states to change their AFDC programs in any way they saw fit. These states were not required to provide job training; they could impose time limits on adults receiving assistance and they could also withdraw assistance from those who did not comply with certain conditions. Because of these changes critics predicted a potential rise in single, working poor women who were not equipped to adequately support their children.

Over the years the Social Security Act was successful at protecting a large number of individuals from various forms of suffering. However, even though social security programs have grown and expanded to provide for the poor and disadvantaged, still in 1989 about 15 percent of Americans were poor and 37 million Americans had no medical insurance. In the late 1990s conservatives and liberals, as well as special interest groups on both sides, continued to debate the advantages of restricting or expanding social programs into the twenty-first century.

See also: **Great Depression, Medicare, Medicaid, Franklin D. Roosevelt, Townsend Clubs, Welfare Policy**

FURTHER READING

Albelda, Randy and Chris Tilly. "Once upon a Time: A Brief History of Welfare," *Dollars and Sense.* Boston: n.p., 1996.

Brinkley, Alan. *Voices of Protest: Huey Long, Father Coughlin, and the Great Depression.* New York: Random House, 1983.

Nash, Gerald, D. *The Crucial Era: The Great Depression and World War II 1929–1945.* New York: St. Martin's Press, 1998.

Patterson, James T. "Social Security." *The Reader's Companion to American History.*

Perkins, Frances. "A Dream Translated to Reality." *Public Welfare*, n.p., 1993.

Rose, Nancy E. "Work Relief in the 1930s and the Origins of the Social Security Act." *Social Service Review.* Chicago: The University of Chicago, 1989.

Stevenson, Richard W. "Squaring Off, at Last, on Social Security." *The New York Times*, November 29, 1998.

SOCIALISM

The word *socialism* was coined in 1832 by Pierre Leroux, editor of the Parisian journal, *Le Globe.* The doctrine of socialism took on many different meanings as it grew and expanded from western Europe to Russia, the United States, Asia, and Australia. In the days of the Soviet Union, it was a common popular misconception that Russians invented both socialism and communism and exported them, when in fact they borrowed these creeds from western Europe and developed their own versions.

All socialist theories are critical of wealth and the concentration of wealth in private hands; all of them advocate the elimination of poverty by equalizing the distribution of wealth, most often by some degree of collective (i.e., public) ownership. The most extreme socialist creeds have advocated the total elimination of private property. Because socialism also advocates some form of collective action, it can be defined not only as a theory but also as a movement.

The many varieties of socialism evolved in part from the disagreement on the means by which a more equitable distribution of wealth in society is to be achieved. Marxist socialism proposes the forceful establishment of a workers' dictatorship; conservative social democrats advocate parliamentary reform and trade unions; syndicalists favor a general strike of the workers; Christian socialists advocate a stringent application of the principles of the Bible.

SOD HOUSES

Sod houses were made of blocks of sod or layers of turf. Early settlers of the Great Plains constructed sod houses where there were no trees to supply lumber. The structures may have first appeared on the open prairie of Nebraska; as a building material, sod became known as ''Nebraska marble.'' Homesteaders cut sod with spades into square blocks which they piled up to build walls. Roofs were made of thatch or of sod blocks supported by a mat of branches, brush, and long grasses. The dwellings (called soddies) were less than ideal: though they remained cool in the hot summers and provided good insulation from the winter cold, they were prone to infestation by vermin. They were also full of dirt, which fell from the walls and ceiling in particles. Sod houses were improved or replaced with new dwellings around the turn of the century: Carrying building supplies such as timber, railroad lines reached into previously remote regions of the former frontier by 1900.

See also: **Homesteaders**

SOLE PROPRIETORSHIP

A sole proprietorship is a form of business organization owned and operated by one person. A proprietorship requires no formal legal process except appropriate licensing, if necessary, to begin providing goods or services for profit. The proprietor owns all assets and liabilities of the business. Although sole proprietorships are not limited in the number of workers employed, they generally are small in size. Sole proprietorships are a common form of organization with professionals, consultants, farmers, service businesses, small retail firms, and small local restaurants. The owner keeps records of revenues and costs that he must report on Schedule C of the personal federal income tax return.

Organizing a businesses as a sole proprietorship offers several advantages. In addition to their ease of formation, proprietorships afford the owner total flexibility and freedom in decision-making, management, and control since consultation with others is not required. The owner may retain all business profits as income, a strong incentive for doing well.

Economic disadvantages include the ability to raise capital. Most sole proprietors have limited personal financial resources, rarely sufficient for long term expansion. Specialization is also problematic. The proprietor may have an excellent talent or skill to start the business, but later must provide marketing and financial expertise that he may not possess. Sole proprietorships have limited life. If the owner dies or wants to quit, legally the business itself ceases to exist. Lastly, the largest risk in a sole proprietorship is unlimited liability. The owner is personally responsible for all the liabilities or debts of the business. If the business does poorly, both the firm's assets and the owner's personal assets may be taken to satisfy creditors.

Through the 1980s and 1990s, the percentage of total firms in the United States organized under sole proprietorships and their total sales remained relatively constant. In 1993approximately 75 percent of all firms were sole proprietorships, representing almost 16 million businesses. However, they accounted for less than six percent of total sales, or about $757 billion.

SONY CORPORATION

Since its post-World War II (1939–1945) founding in Japan, the Sony Corporation revolutionized the consumer electronics field. The Sony name became familiar throughout the world for such innovative products as the transistor radio, the Trinitron television, the Walkman cassette player, and the compact disk (CD). The company also joined in other diversified industries such as entertainment, battery manufacture, life insurance, and sports equipment. By the end of the twentieth century it cooperated with the People's Republic of China to produce television sets. Sony had become a major player on the international market.

After the devastation of World War II Japan was ripe for all kinds of business developments which would bring the country back to normal life, but at the same time, revolutionize its business practices and institutions. In 1946, with borrowed capital, Akio Morita and Masuri Ibuka set up the company known as Tokyo Tsushin Kogyo (Tokyo Telecommunications Engineering Corporation), the forerunner of Sony. They first developed a rice cooker, which was a failure, but they soon succeeded with a tape recorder. When Norio Ohga, a student of opera, wrote to complain about the tape recorder's sound quality, Morita and Ibuka invited him to present his critiques in person and later asked him to join the company, and he eventually became president and chairman.

In 1952 the two directors first heard of a tiny new capacitor called a transistor, which had been developed by Bell Laboratories and used by Western Electric to manufacture hearing aids. Ibuka obtained a patent license to begin producing the first transistor radios in 1954. They named the radio ''Sony,'' after the Latin word for ''sound'' and the word ''sonny,'' or little son. Prior to the Sony transistor radio portable radios were fairly large because of their vacuum tubes. Consumers were amazed at the compactness of Sony radios and were eager to buy them.

To market his product in the United States, Morita himself traveled to New York to meet with representatives of several large retail businesses. In 1958 Morita and Ibuka decided to change the whole name of the company to Sony Kabushiki Kaisha (Corporation). Within a year the company had developed a transistorized television.

Sony began to expand rapidly, establishing trade offices in Switzerland, the U.S., and England. A subsidiary was also set up to provide the adhesives and plastics needed for manufacturing. Other transistorized products were also developed such as the AM/FM radio and a videotape recorder. Sony's biggest gamble during the 1960s was the Trinitron television, which, at the time, used the most advanced color technology. Norio Ohga also headed a new venture called CBS/Sony, which became the largest manufacturer of phonograph records in Japan.

In the 1970s Sony was the pioneer in the development of Betamax video-cassette recorders (VCRs), yet by the end of the decade the Beta format had been superseded by the video home system (VHS) format introduced by Sony's competitors. A market war ensued between Sony and manufacturers of VHS systems—Sony refused to market a VHS line until the late 1980s and began to lose market share.

A more successful venture at Sony was the introduction of the Walkman compact cassette player in 1979. By using a small player and lightweight headphones a person was able to enjoy music while walking. The term ''Walkman'' soon became the generic name for similar products produced by Sony's competitors.

Norio Ohga became president of Sony in 1982 after Ibuka and Morita had begun to cut down on their duties. Ohga reached out to institutional markets as well as to individual consumers; he also focused attention on research and development. In partnership with the Dutch firm Phillips, Sony developed the first laser disk recorder, or compact disk (CD), which greatly improved sound quality. By the 1990s the CD format used by Sony and several competitors had virtually eliminated old phonograph systems.

From its bitter experience with the Beta-VHS conflict Sony officials had learned that a superior product alone would not guarantee sales. When the company developed a lightweight video camera in 1985 it did so in conjunction with over 100 competitors to ensure that future cameras would be compatible with its 8mm format. Sony also bought a company which manufactured the new digital audio tape (DAT), with hopes to ensure future compatibility among recording systems. Sony also sought to increase its institutional sales and to continue to diversify. It purchased Apple Computer's hard-disk technology operations, the Digital Audio Disk Corporation, CBS Records, and Columbia Pictures Entertainment. In 1990 Sony posted a 38.5 increase in earnings over 1989.

Like many other companies in the global economy Sony experienced a downturn in the 1990s. Appreciation in the value of the Japanese yen adversely affected the company's export sales in the mid-1990s. In 1995 Morita relinquished his chairmanship in favor of Ohga, and Nobuyuki Idei was named president. Despite setbacks the Morita era had led to Sony's great success. Sony occupied a pre-eminent place in a worldwide, consumer electronics industry—the company had 173,000 employees and annual sales of $51.2 billion in 1998. Morita had been the most visible spokesman for the company, as well as an effective purveyor of ideas. He created the Sony name and several of the product names—Walkman, Handycam, and Watchman. Under his leadership Sony engineers developed an astounding array of revolutionary electronic products which are now accepted as everyday necessities.

In 1998 Sony Electronics Inc. (SEL), the largest component of Sony America, became an independent company. Its president, Teruaki Aoki (responsible for Sony's entry into the digital video disk (DVD) market), told *Electronic Engineering Times* that SEL would be "an autonomous company now serving as a good partner for Sony Corporation." In the late 1990s Sony also began marketing an interactive video game console called PlayStation (and later PlayStation II), whose major competitor was the Sega Dreamcast system. In creating these practical luxuries the Sony Corporation has made their products essential to daily life as well as erasing the negative image once attached to products wearing the label "Made in Japan."

See also: **Akio Morita**

FURTHER READING

Fox, Barry. "A God of Japanese Electronics: Sony Corp. Founder and Chairman Akio Morita." *New Scientist*, July 11, 1992.

Kirkup, James. "Obituary: Masaru Ibuka." *Independent*, December 22, 1997.

Lyons, Nick. *The Sony Vision*. New York: Crown, 1976.

Morita, Akio. *Made in Japan: Akio Morita and Sony*. New York: Dutton, 1986.

Yoshida, Junko. "Sony Electronics Charts Independent Course." *Electronic Engineering Times*, August 3, 1998.

SOO LOCKS

Early settlers arriving in the upper peninsula of what became Michigan found only one way to get from Lake Superior to the other Great Lakes,the St. Mary's River. Because of its formidable rapids, the river was a challenge to travel and transportation. Settlers needing to cross the river were forced to carry their canoes around the rapids. As settlement and trade increased, boats arriving at the river had to unload their cargo, haul them around the rapids in wagons, and reload them in other boats before continuing on their journey.

The Northwest Fur Company constructed the first canal (called the "Soo Lock") in 1797. Based on the Canadian side of the river, the thirty-eight foot lock allowed small boats to navigate the St. Mary's rapids. A lock is a section of a canal that can be closed and opened to control water level, which is raised or lowered to transport a vessel from one level to another. This first lock was destroyed during the War of 1812 (1812–1814).

THE SOO LOCKS SERVE SMALL PASSENGER VESSELS AS WELL AS LARGE FREIGHTERS CARRYING OVER 72,000 TONS OF CARGO. IN THE LATE 1990S, THE LOCKS AVERAGED TRAFFIC OF 10,000 VESSELS PER YEAR.

For the next four decades the only way boats could pass between the Great Lakes was by a system of land rollers, which were used to circumvent the St. Mary's River rapids. In 1850 the railroad reached the region and improved transportation, but a traversable waterway was still necessary. Around the same time Michigan's Upper Peninsula was found to be rich in various ores including iron and copper. The U.S. mining industry pressed the government for a completed canal to facilitate shipment of these raw materials for use in the nation's growing manufacturing sector.

In the era when the federal and state governments were building roads and canals, and subsidizing privately owned transportation ventures (such as railroads), Congress granted 750,000 acres of Michigan public land (in lieu of monetary payment) to the Fairbanks Scale Company, which would construct the canal. The Fairbanks Company had extensive mining interests in the Upper Peninsula. Construction began in 1853 and was completed in 1855, meeting a two-year deadline set by the state. The company constructed a canal containing two locks (the State Locks), 350 feet in length, which would raise or lower sailing vessels to different water levels. The locks were turned over to the state of Michigan in May 1855.

Because of the expense of operating the locks, the state ceded management of the waterway system to the federal government in 1881. Managed by the Army Corps of Engineers, the State Locks were enlarged and an additional canal constructed (the North and South canals). In 1895, Canada built a canal on its side of the St. Mary's River which contains a single lock.

The Canadian canal, containing one lock, and the two Michigan canals, with four locks, are together known as the Sault or Soo locks (Soo is a phonetic version of Sault). They successfully allow commerce to flow between the Great Lakes and have supplied water-transported material to U.S. military forces in every major U.S. war and conflict since the 1800s. A variety of commodities pass through the locks, including grain and coal. The Soo Locks serve small passenger vessels as well as large freighters carrying over

72,000 tons of cargo. In the late 1990s, the locks averaged traffic of 10,000 vessels per year. A hydroelectric power plant supplies power to the Soo complex as well as to the power grid of Michigan's eastern Upper Peninsula.

SOUTH CAROLINA

South Carolina was carved out of a much larger piece of territory than other states, and it eventually became one of the most important states in the Old South. For good or ill, it is known for the most rabid opposition of any state to protective tariffs and northern antislavery movements, two issues that led the nation into a civil war. Its history has been marked by several divisions: between the English and other northern European patricians who settled the cosmopolitan city of Charleston and the less educated farmers of the interior, between whites and blacks, and between labor unions and anti-union advocates. In recent decades, however, the state has made the most of its resources by profiting from its important water ports, its good transportation networks, and an improving industrial climate.

Spanish and French explorers were the first Europeans to attempt settlements, all unsuccessful, in the present state of South Carolina. Under English King Charles I, the first permanent settlement was established as a proprietorship in 1670. The first colonists were ''adventurers'' from the English sugar cane producing island of Barbados. The first crop that was grown in the coastal swamps was rice, which was cultivated by imported black slaves. The agricultural know-how to construct the often elaborate system of channels and dams to irrigate the rice was contributed by the slaves who came from a similar rice-cultivation culture in western Africa. By the mid-1700s inland areas were beginning to develop. At first simply called ''Carolina,'' the colony included the future colonies of North Carolina and Georgia, as well as South Carolina, which broke apart from the north and became a royal colony in 1721. South Carolina supported the American Revolution (1775–1783) and ratified the U.S. Constitution in 1788.

Transportation networks soon grew from the port of Charleston, through the upcountry, and on to western territories. Several canals were constructed, and the first railroad, from Charleston to Hamburg, was the longest railroad in existence in 1833. South Carolina also boasted the first steam engine built for public railway service. However, in the mid-1800s constructing railroads through the mountains in the middle of the state proved impossible.

Any visitor to modern-day Charleston can sense the city's important history. Because it grew faster than any colonial city, historian Louis B. Wright called it ''a city-state ruled by an intelligent and cultivated oligarchy of great families who managed to monopolize control, generation after generation.'' The political and economic power naturally flowed to the city of Charleston, which controlled the colony (and later the state) for decades. Trade in products like rice, cotton, corn, pitch, and indigo flourished in the port of Charleston, as did the slave trade. Upcountry farmers were generally looked down upon by the elite of Charleston city.

SOUTH CAROLINIANS HAVE ALWAYS BEEN READY TO DECLARE THAT THEIR LAND WAS ONLY A LITTLE LESS DESIRABLE THAN EDEN.

Louis B. Wright, *South Carolina: A Bicentennial History*, 1976

Under the political leadership of Senator John C. Calhoun, in the mid-1800s South Carolina took the lead in congressional discussions on slavery and tariffs. The state greatly disliked the protective tariff which benefited northern manufacturers, raised the prices of manufactured goods, and reduced the ability of the British and the French to buy cotton from South Carolina and other southern states. In 1828 Calhoun outlined his argument for nullification (a rationale permitting a state to deny the viability of a federal regulation). The immediate issue was settled in the 1830s by a compromise devised by Henry Clay, but these divisions over the southern slave economy and the northern industrial system inevitably led to the American Civil War (1861–1865).

When South Carolina became the first state to secede from the Union in 1860, over than half the population of the state consisted of black slaves. When federal troops occupied the state during Reconstruction, South Carolinians blamed northern ''carpetbaggers'' for depleting the treasury of the state and running it into serious debt. They also blamed the economic chaos following the war on ex-slaves, thus reinforcing a legacy of racism which plagued the state for generation after generation.

After the war an economy based on slave labor had to reorient itself. The cultivation of rice in the state completely disappeared in a few decades following the war, but planters tried to keep producing cotton. A

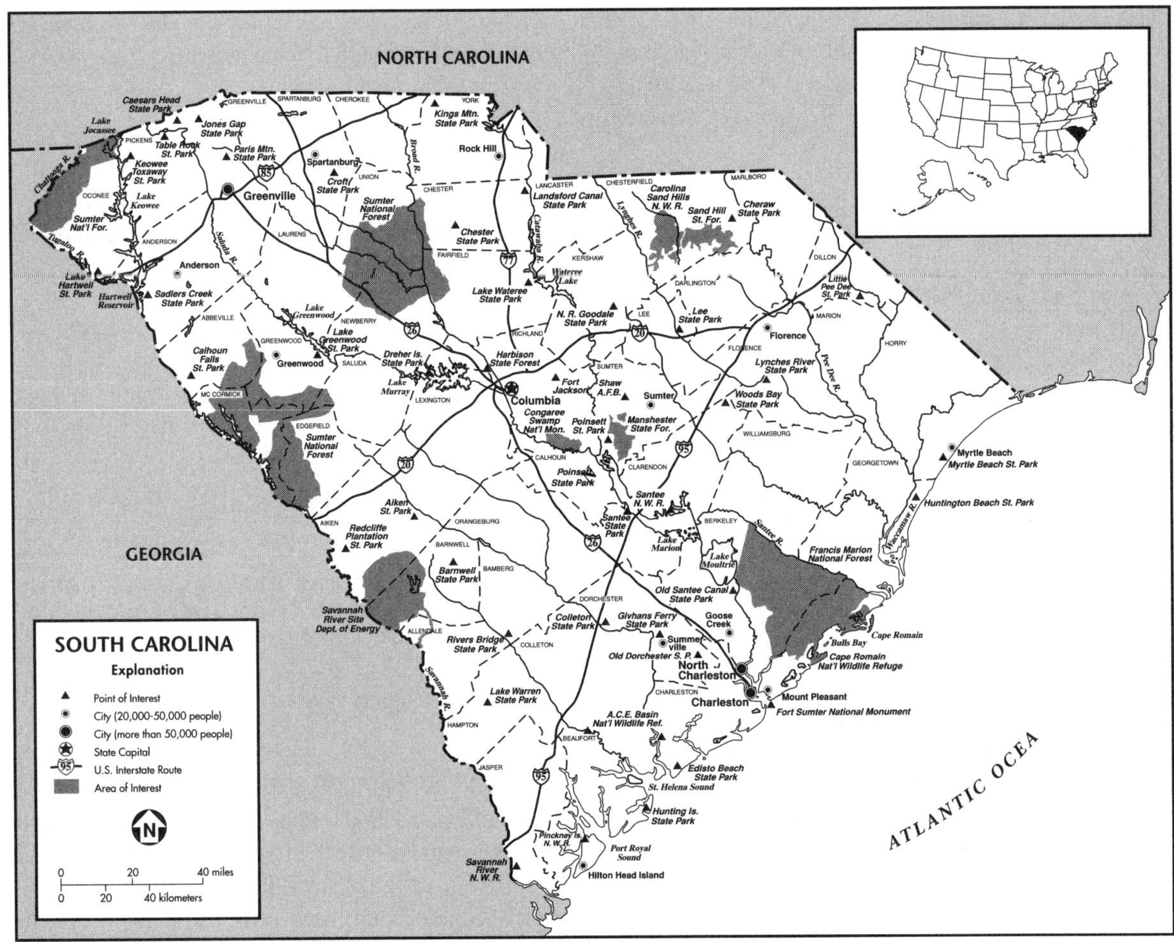

State of South Carolina.

system of tenancy and sharecropping developed, in which a small farmer would pay the landowner shares of his crop for renting the land. This system kept many small farmers in debt and perpetuated the class divisions between rich and poor. After much postwar political and economic turmoil the economy of the state gradually shifted from rice and cotton to tobacco, soybeans, and truck farming. Railroads devastated by the war were rebuilt, connecting most towns and cities. Tired of trying to make a living through sharecropping, poor farmers—both black and white—moved to the cities to find employment in textile mills, which after 1900 became the state's biggest industry.

Textiles dominated South Carolina's economy until after World War II (1939–1945), when attempts to diversify brought the chemical, paper, and other industries to the state. The harbors of Charleston, Port Royal, and Georgetown were also improved to facilitate commerce. After many textile mills closed in the 1970s and 1980s the textile industry dropped to second place in the state, behind chemical and allied products.

Although manufacturing industry is now the state's leading employer, agriculture is still important. Some of the major farm products in the 1990s included tobacco, cotton, food products, and soybean oil for newsprint ink. Along with forestry and forestry products, agriculture contributes about 25 percent to the state's economy.

A major blow to South Carolina's economy came in 1989 with Hurricane Hugo, the tenth strongest hurricane to ever hit the United States. The storm wreaked havoc, particularly in Charleston and other coastal towns, killing 37 people and causing over $700 million in property damage. In 1993 severe flooding and subsequent long-term drought were responsible for an estimated $226 million in crop loss.

After experiencing significant population loss from 1940 to 1970 the state rebounded, attracting a net gain of 210,000 between 1970 and 1980. In the late 1990s the state continued to suffer from a bad reputation as an industrial employer because of its low wage rates, its relatively untrained work force, and its anti-union climate. In fact only 3.3 percent of all South Carolina workers were unionized in 1996. Yet real per capita income increased faster than the national norm during the 1970s and early 1980s, reaching thirty-ninth in the nation by 1995. Increased investment from foreign and domestic sources and a growing tourist industry have aided the economy's continued growth.

South Carolina's Department of Commerce has been quite successful in attracting foreign companies, especially to the Piedmont region of the state. In the late 1990s the state government exempted all new industrial construction from local property taxes (excluding school taxes), and assessed industrial property very leniently. Moreover, local and regional authorities have cooperated in providing both low-interest industrial bonds and the infrastructure needed by new businesses. Business was also attracted by the state's conservative fiscal policies, its low pay scales, and its negative attitude toward labor unions.

See also: **Rice, Tariff of Abominations**

FURTHER READING

Jones, Lewis P. *South Carolina: A Synoptic History for Laymen*. Orangeburg, SC: Sandlapper Publishing, 1979.

Lander, Ernest M. *A History of South Carolina, 1856–1960*, 2nd ed. Columbia, SC: University of South Carolina Press, 1970.

Rogers, George C. *A South Carolina Chronology, 1497–1992*. Columbia: University of South Carolina Press, 1994.

Wallace, David Duncan. *History of South Carolina*. 4 vols. New York: American Historical Society, 1934.

Wright, Louis B. *South Carolina: A Bicentennial History*. New York, Norton, 1976.

SOUTH DAKOTA

In 1742 the first explorers traveled the area that is present day South Dakota, opening up the Upper Missouri Valley to French traders who bartered with the Indians by offering them metal pots, pans and tools for animal furs.

In 1762 France gave Louisiana to Spain during the French and Indian War. But when France was defeated in 1763, Britain gained control of French lands in Canada and east of the Mississippi. Later, in 1800, French emperor Napoleon Bonaparte forced Spain to return the land of Louisiana to France. And in turn Napoleon sold the Louisiana land to the U.S. for $15 million in order to finance his wars in Europe. The U.S. benefited greatly in this deal because its territory was doubled in size.

The next year President Thomas Jefferson (1801–1809) sent Captain Meriwether Lewis and Lieutenant William Clark (leaders of the Lewis and Clark expedition) to explore the region. In 1817 fur trading had begun to take place on the Missouri River at ''Fort Pierre.''

In the 1850s the fur trade was in decline. Fort Pierre was sold to the U.S. Army and soldiers took up the task of keeping peace between Indians and white settlers. Pierre would become the capital of South Dakota. Slowly over the years groups of Indians gave up their land and moved onto reservations. The land parcels they left behind were then purchased by land companies for farming, forestry, and building stone. These companies pressured the government to assign territorial status to the land, and in 1861 President James Buchanan (1857–1861) signed a bill which designated it as the Dakota Territory. The region included what is now North Dakota and South Dakota and most of the land in Montana and Wyoming.

During the 1860s and 1870s transportation networks opened up the Dakota Territory for additional markets making migration to the area much easier. Thus, when gold was discovered in Montana in the 1860s thousands of miners were able to travel from the east through Dakota. Federal money was also secured to begin building roads to Montana. When the Pacific Railroad to Sioux City, Iowa, was completed in 1868, farmers could transport wheat to eastern markets. Bridges were constructed over the Vermillion and James rivers which made it easier to reach the railroad at Sioux City. And when the Dakota Southern Railroad between Sioux City and Yankton opened in 1873 Yankton became an important stopover on the river which, in turn, helped attract more settlers to the area.

Immigrant farmers—Swedish, Danish, and Czech—entered the territory through Sioux City and settled in the territory to farm. These pioneers could purchase 160 acres for $1.25 per acre. The Homestead Act of 1862 allowed pioneers to claim the same amount of land for free if they worked the land for five years. (Farm crops often included corn, potatoes, onions, beets, beans, and other vegetables.) Life on the prairie was not easy for the pioneers; ever-present was the threat of blizzards in winter, fires in spring and fall, and drought in summer which could destroy homes, fields, and crops. Only the heartiest settlers could withstand the utter devastation possible in the difficult climate.

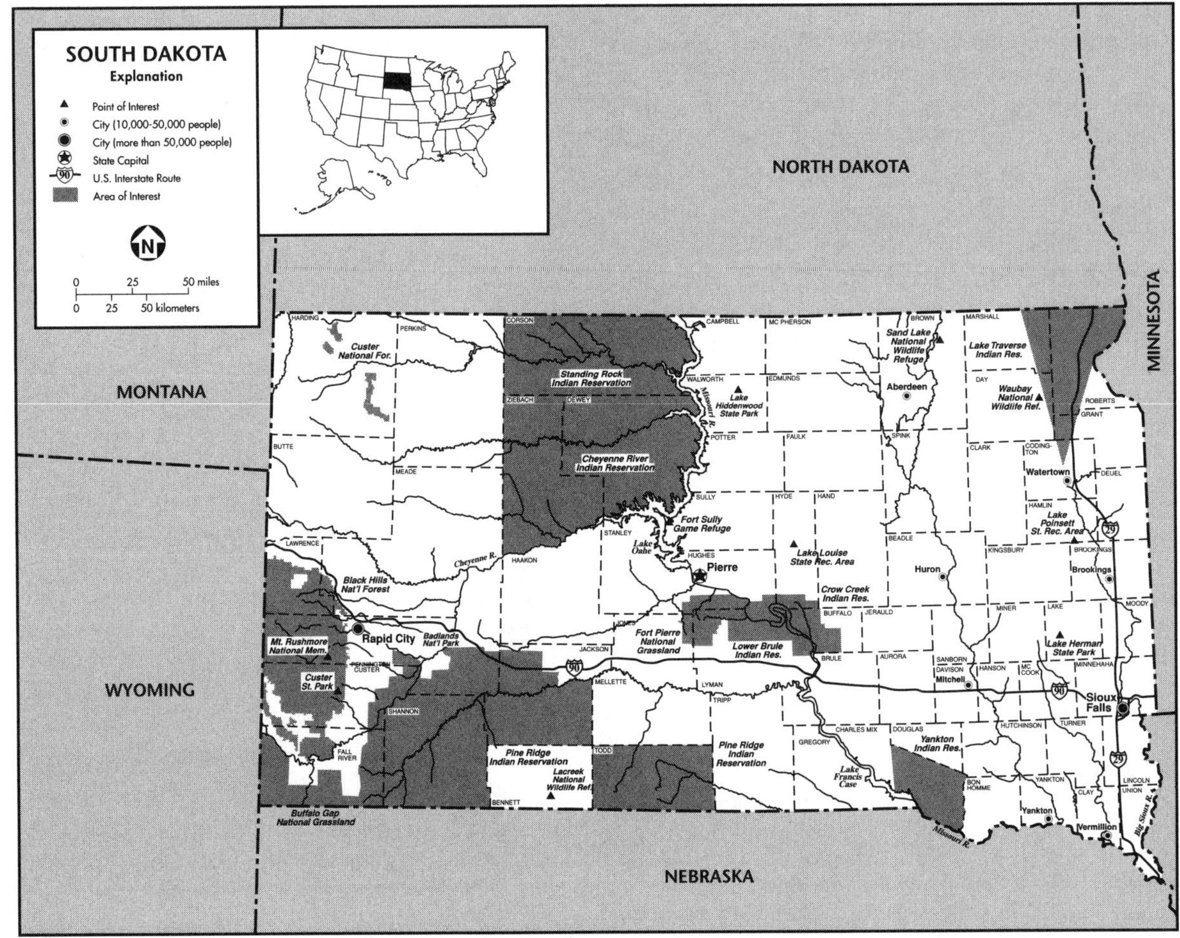

State of South Dakota.

In 1874 gold was discovered in the Black Hills. However, the Sioux Indians considered the Black Hills sacred ground. (Although most of Native Americans lived on reservations some still roamed the area.) The U.S. government was aware of this Native American belief and agreed in the Laramie Treaty (1868) to protect the area. However, when news spread that gold was discovered more than 800 miners flocked to the area to mine for gold illegally. When the government tried to buy the Black Hills from the Sioux for $6 million they refused, and instead attacked mining camps over the next few years in what was known as the Sioux War of 1876. The Sioux eventually agreed to surrender the Black Hills and most of the Native Americans settled in reservations. Miners settled in the area. At the height of the gold rush in 1877 more than 25,000 people lived in the Black Hills. The towns they populated included restaurants, laundries, grocery stores, saloons, and gambling houses.

At the same time as the Black Hills gold rush, cattle ranchers began to establish themselves in the area. Texas longhorn steers were driven from Texas to the lush range surrounding the Black Hills and the popularity of sheep ranching also grew. In 1884 more than 800,000 head of cattle and 85,000 sheep grazed the land. Not only did people in the Black Hills region purchase meat for food but as additional railroads were built ranchers were able to transport cattle and sheep to eastern cities for slaughter. In 1885 amid this period of heightened settlement and economic activity, South Dakota and North Dakota were approved for statehood.

When World War I (1914–1918) started prices of crops and livestock increased while the demand for farm products rose. This helped to bolster South Dakota's economy. However, after the war ended the price for these items fell. Because farmers received less income they couldn't repay debts; many lost their farms, and left the state. Soon after, The Great Depression (1929–1939) devastated many South Dakotans who were already affected by the state's economic crisis. In addition the 1930s brought drought, grasshopper plagues, dust storms, and crop failures which lasted for nearly ten years. Assistance arrived when President Franklin D. Roosevelt's (1933–1945) New Deal put 25,000 men to work planting trees for windbreaks and building recreational facilities. The government gave South Dakota $35 million to build schools and other public buildings, bridges, and roads. The federal government also purchased cattle and sheep and taught farmers to grow drought-resistant grass.

The start of World War II (1939–1945) helped lift South Dakota out of the depression because meat, dairy and grain products were needed for the war effort. The Sioux Falls Air Force Training Base and the Ellsworth Air Base outside Rapid City were built and machine shops and foundries were constructed all over the state.

After the war incomes from farming were on the upswing again. Many who had lost their farms were able to buy them back. Between 1945 and 1966 the government developed and implemented a plan that improved the state's economy and made it less dependent on farming for income. To control flooding and irrigation, dams were built on the Cheyenne, Grand, and Moreu rivers and on Rapid Creek. The Missouri River also was dammed in four locations to provide electric power, flood control, and irrigation. The Oahe, Francis Case, Sharpe, and Lewis and Clark lakes were created by damming the Missouri River, also known as the "Great Lakes of South Dakota," they have become a tourist attraction.

Severe weather continued to affect the state's economy. In the blizzards of 1966 and 1975 several people died and thousands of cattle were killed. The Rapid City Canyon Lake Dam burst in 1972, flooding the city, killing 238 people, and causing $100 million worth of property damage. In 1988 a drought in the state caused millions of dollars in damage to the wheat, rye, and corn crops. The drought also caused the Black Hills National Forest to catch fire; a lightening strike set $4.4 million worth of timber ablaze.

During the 1980s Native American unemployment on reservations reached 80 percent due to cuts in federal spending. Also, farm incomes fell as prices for farm products decreased while mortgages rose causing many people to lose their farms. In response to public suffering the state government provided $40 million in 1987 for low-interest loans to help new and expanding businesses. The state supported specific industries including plastic products, electronic components, women's clothing, surgical instruments, and life insurance, hoping that this initiative would create jobs for both Native American and non-Native American residents as well as attract other businesses.

In the 1990s Citicorp, the largest bank-holding company in the United States, set up a credit card operation in Sioux Falls. In the early 1990s manufacturing also expanded up to 10 percent each year, and in 1994 the state produced record corn and soybean crops. Casino gambling also became an important source of revenue after it was legalized in the state in 1989.

In 1995 the median household income was $29,578 with 14.5 percent of all South Dakotans below the federal poverty level.

See also: **Dry Farming, Native American Policy**

FURTHER READING

Grabowski, John F. *The Great Plains: Montana, Nebraska, North Dakota, South Dakota, Wyoming.* New York: Chelsea House Publishers, 1992.

Rezatto, Helen. *The Making of the Two Dakotas.* Lincoln, NE: Media Publishing, 1989.

Thompson, Kathleen. "South Dakota." *Portrait of America.* Austin TX: Steck-Vaughn Publishers, 1996.

Veglahn, Nancy. "South Dakota." *States of the Nation*, Dakota, SD: Wesleyan University, 1970.

Worldmark Encyclopedia of the States. Detroit: Gale Research, 1998, s.v. "South Dakota."

SOUTHWESTERN INDIANS

The pre-colonial Indians of the American Southwest included the Mogollon, Hohokam, Anasazi (or "Cliff Dwellers"), and the Anasazi's Pueblo descendents. Some historians refer collectively to their mutual forebearers as the Paleo-Indians. A few scholars also believe that the Paleo-Indians arrived in the area between 10,000 and 9,000 B.C..

The Southwestern Indians settled across present-day Arizona, New Mexico, northern Mexico, southern Utah, southern Colorado, and parts of Nevada. Their languages were classified as Aztec-Tanoan.

The Southwestern Indians began farming around 1500 B.C.. They grew corn, beans, and squash, and raised turkeys. Farming was difficult in the arid region, so they developed ways of irrigating the land. The Hohokam built a system of canals to carry water to their crops. The Anasazi developed techniques for dry farming. By 900 AD the various farming cultures were flourishing.

As settlers the Southwestern Indians crafted various conveniences for themselves—housewares, permanent homes, and roads. The Mogollon were skilled potters who made smooth clay pots and bowls, which they fired and painted with geometric designs and figures of animals and humans. The Hohokam were accomplished weavers of cotton cloth. The Anasazi produced various kinds of wicker containers and muralists. Southwestern Indians were also capable builders. They did not have beasts of burden; transportation was on foot, therefore, The Southwestern Indians built extensive road systems. They applied their construction skills to homebuilding as well. Living quarters were usually built above-ground using masonry techniques. Anasazi homes were carved out of the sides of cliffs and the walls of canyons.

The Apache and Navajo—descendants of the Anasazi—are also grouped as Southwestern Indians. These north woods groups arrived in the Southwest later and were very different from the earlier arrivals: they were predominately hunters and gatherers. They lived in tepees or brush shelters, and were fierce fighters who even raided the Pueblo settlements they encountered. By the time the Spaniards arrived (around 1540) both the Navajo and Apache were living in the Southwest. Unlike the Apache, Navajos adopted many Pueblo practices and also learned new ways from the Europeans.

When the Spaniards came to the region they unleashed drastic changes in the lives of Southwestern Indians. The Spaniards brought with them the first horses, mules, cattle, sheep, and hogs ever seen in the region. Intent on converting the native inhabitants to Christianity, the Spaniards established missions across the region. But the arrival of the Europeans also preceded the decline of Southwestern Indian culture. Combined with drought, the arrival of Europeans was responsible for the decline of the Southwestern Indian cultures by 1600. Many were killed in rebellions, others were subjugated, and some fled the region.

See also: **Anasazi, Arizona, Colorado, Nevada, New Mexico, Paleo-Indians, Pueblo Indians, Southwestern Indians, Utah**

SOVEREIGNTY

Sovereignty is the supreme power of an individual, country, or state to govern internal affairs without interference from any other comparable authority. Sovereign countries can conduct foreign affairs with other nations including negotiating treaties, engaging in international commerce, and making war and peace. Sovereignty defines political authority within the modern nation.

Sovereignty first applied to a king's divine right to rule his subjects. Unlimited power was believed to flow from God to the king enabling him to rule his kingdom. The term evolved through time to represent the power of a state to take every action necessary to regulate itself. In democratic countries, the ultimate source of sovereignty or government power lies with the people.

In 1777, the Second Continental Congress of the United States adopted the Articles of Confederation giving Congress a few powers typical of an independent sovereign nation. Congress alone had the power to conduct foreign affairs, negotiate treaties, control a national army, coin money, and operate a national postal system. The Articles did deliberately keep the central government weak by limiting sovereignty. Each state had its own state court to settle disputes. All important Congressional decisions required approval of at least nine states, and these resolutions were mere suggestions to the states. This limited sovereignty granted to Congress proved ineffective and ten years later the U.S. Constitution was ratified. It was followed by ratification of the Bill of Rights in 1791. The Tenth Amendment of the Bill of Rights states, "The powers not delegated to the United States by the Constitution, nor prohibited by it to the States, are reserved to the States respectively, or to the people." The United States is a sovereign nation in external affairs but the states do hold certain attributes of internal sovereignty, such as providing for public schools. The U.S. Constitution, the supreme law of the land, is the ultimate determinant of sovereignty powers in the nation.

"Popular sovereignty" is another variant of the term sovereignty in U.S. history, referring to the principle of allowing settlers to decide on their own a territory's slavery policy. The Kansas-Nebraska Bill of 1854 embraced popular sovereignty. Another use is sovereign rights of territorial waters. The United States has sovereign ocean rights extending 12 nautical miles from shore. These rights include fishing, shipping, navigation, and use of natural resources.

See also: **Article of Confederation, Continental Congress (Second), Kansas-Nebraska Act**

SPACE RACE

During World War II (1939–1945) Germany developed the world's first long-range guided missiles, firing warheads into English cities. Upon Germany's

On July 20, 1969 America won the space race when the crew of the Apollo landed on the moon. Edwin "Buzz" Aldrin, Jr. erected the American flag to serve as a permanent mark of the nation's accomplishment.

defeat and the end of the war, the United States recruited German rocket scientists, including Wernher von Braun (1912–1977), to help begin the U.S. missile program. The United States and Russia had become engaged in an intense military global rivalry, the Cold War. The resulting arms race between the two "superpowers" included the development and stockpiling of thermonuclear weapons and intercontinental ballistic missiles.

Under supervision of the U.S. Air Force, missile testing began at Florida's Cape Canaveral launch facilities in the early 1950s. However, the Soviet Union, known to excel in large missile development, shocked the United States when it became the first nation to place a satellite, *Sputnik 1*, in orbit around Earth in October 1957. A second Russian satellite went up the following month carrying a dog. Suddenly, the "space race" was on and the United States, in desperation, greatly accelerated its space program. Not only did Americans feel vulnerable to direct foreign attack but the U.S. claim to scientific superiority was shaken.

The United States attempted an orbiting satellite launch in December 1957, but the Vanguard missile embarrassingly exploded on lift-off. The following month *Explorer 1* blasted successfully into orbit. Through the 1950s the United States and Russia increasingly focused on manned space flight. The United States established the Project Mercury program with its original seven astronauts, a select group of daring Air Force test pilots. To oversee the civilian space program Congress created the National Aeronautics and Space Administration (NASA) in October 1958, taking over control from the military.

In April 1961, a second jolt rippled through the United States when Russia placed the first human, Yury Gagarin (1934–1968), in orbit around the Earth. The United States responded on May 5, 1961, as Alan Shephard (1923–) became the first American in space, riding the somewhat unreliable Redstone rocket into a suborbit trajectory.

With U.S. leadership clearly shaken by Russia's progress, President John F. Kennedy (1961–1963) on May 25, 1961 proclaimed a national goal to land an astronaut on the moon by the end of the decade and safely return him to earth. The pronouncement came as a surprise even to many in the space program. With the moon identified as the finish line for the space race, a clearly difficult goal was publicly set.

Later in 1961 John Glenn (1921–) became the first American to orbit the Earth. Four more manned Mercury flights were followed by Project Gemini in March 1965. Gemini, in its brief existence, introduced two-man space capsules, the first space walks, docking exercises, and more extended flight times. Project Apollo, the heart of the U.S. lunar program, followed in late 1966. A tragic capsule fire in January 1967, killed the first of three Apollo astronaut crews while sitting atop a missile on the launch pad. No further manned space flights occurred until October 1968. Then on Christmas Eve 1968, the first Apollo mission to orbit the moon sent back spectacular pictures to Earth, again captivating the public. Soon afterwards, on July 20, 1969, Apollo 11 astronauts Edwin "Buzz" Aldrin (1930–) and Neil Armstrong (1930–) became the first humans to walk on the moon. An estimated half a billion people around the world watched the event 240,000 miles away on live television. The space race was won.

ON JULY 20, 1969, APOLLO 11 ASTRONAUTS EDWIN "BUZZ" ALDRIN AND NEIL ARMSTRONG BECAME THE FIRST HUMANS TO WALK ON THE MOON. AN ESTIMATED HALF A BILLION PEOPLE AROUND THE WORLD WATCHED THE EVENT 240,000 MILES AWAY ON LIVE TELEVISION. THE SPACE RACE WAS WON.

Five more Apollo missions led to extended walks on the moon and the use of lunar roving vehicles. American society, however, had changed radically since the 1961 Kennedy pronouncement. The United States was in the throes of a highly controversial foreign war in Southeast Asia and domestic unrest was at a peak. Urban riots were tearing apart the national social fabric. Many questioned the billions of dollars spent on a program of debatable scientific value when there were such pressing social issues at home. After the Apollo 17 mission in December 1972, the program came to an abrupt end as funding was curtailed, canceling three more planned Apollo missions. With the space race over, the U.S. space program turned to unmanned exploration, the space shuttle program, and even collaboration with Russia on the *Mir* space station program and other related projects.

The United States' effort in the space race is recognized as one of the greatest peacetime national efforts in history involving government, the military, science, and industry. In 1966 the $6 billion space budget constituted over four percent of the entire federal budget, exceeding amounts spent on housing and community development. The Apollo program alone cost over $25 billion. At its peak, over 400,000 people were employed in the effort. With public relations a major facet of the space race, the astronauts became public heroes of almost mythological proportions.

However, accomplishments stemming from the space race were largely political. Geologic research objectives were only partially met with the 841 pounds of moon rock collected. The limited scientific benefits went largely to the medical field with advances in digital imaging, biomedical telemetry techniques, and other technological developments. In all, however, an amazing technological feat involving tremendous political and economic commitments had been accomplished within a decade's time.

See also: **Arms Race, Cold War**

FURTHER READING

Breuer, William B. *Race to the Moon: America's Duel with the Soviets*. Westport, CN: Praeger, 1993.

Heppenheimer, T. A. *Countdown: A History of Space Flight*. New York: John Wiley and Sons, 1997.

Kauffman, James L. *Selling Outer Space: Kennedy, the Media, and Funding for Project Apollo, 1961–1963*. Tuscaloosa: University of Alabama Press, 1994.

Lambright, W. Henry. *Powering Apollo: James E. Webb of NASA*. Baltimore: The John Hopkins University Press, 1995.

Reeves, Robert. *The Superpower Space Race: An Explosive Rivalry Through the Solar System*. New York: Plenum Press, 1994.

SPANISH-AMERICAN WAR

The 1898 war between the United States and Spain lasted only four months, yet its effects are still felt today. It ended in a relatively easy victory for the United States, which, just over a century after its birth as an independent nation, seemed eager to claim its place as a world power. In what Secretary of State John Hay (1898–1905) called "a splendid little war," the country demonstrated an intent to protect its economic interests abroad and to promote its own expansion. The brief conflict also marked an increased U.S. involvement in global affairs and a step away from the 1823

Monroe Doctrine, which suggested that the country would assert its power only within its own hemisphere. Significantly more far-reaching were the war's effects on Cuba, Puerto Rico, Hawaii, Guam, and the Philippines, whose destinies remained unalterably changed by the events that occurred between April and August of 1898.

The United States' initial impetus for going to war was its interest in Cuba—an interest that was primarily economic in nature. One of the last and largest remaining colonies of Spain, Cuba had been gearing up for a revolution throughout the nineteenth century. Its politically active population craved independence, and the United States sympathized with that plight. Already engaged in a guerrilla war with Spain, Cuban rebels looked to their country's larger neighbor for support. The United States supplied that support for reasons that were clearly apparent: It had $50 million invested in Cuba, and its annual trade with the sugar-producing island amounted to $100 million. Moreover, the United States had long opposed Spanish rule in Cuba for humanitarian reasons. The American press printed passionate coverage of Cuba's troubled relations with Spain: William Randolph Hearst and Joseph Pulitzer's national newspapers—the so-called yellow press—declared the situation ''intolerable.'' And the American public apparently agreed.

A tragic event ultimately motivated the country to take action: On February 15, 1898, the U.S. battleship *Maine* mysteriously exploded and sank in the Havana Harbor, where it apparently had been making a courtesy visit. Although the cause of the sinking, which claimed 266 lives, remains unexplained to this day, a naval investigation at the time surmised that the explosion was external in origin. The Spanish government approached the issue in a conciliatory manner, wishing to avoid conflict with the United States. But Madrid would not negotiate on the one issue that would have prevented war: the granting of independence to Cuba. Responding to an angered public, President William McKinley (1897–1901) and Congress took action, ordering the withdrawal of Spanish forces from Cuba on April 19 and officially declared war on April 25.

The war strategy of the United States included a blockade of Cuba; a naval campaign in the Philippines; an attack with ground forces in Santiago, Cuba; and a dispatch of troops to San Juan, Puerto Rico. The media reported that the blockade of Cuba, which involved the mobilization of hundreds of thousands of volunteer and army troops, was poorly organized. Soldiers lacked supplies; sanitary conditions were poor; and the food was unacceptable. Although by the war's end only 379 American men died in combat, thousands perished of disease. The Spanish military suffered from its own insufficiencies, particularly the decrepitude of its fleets, which remained vulnerable to U.S. naval power.

It did not take long for the United States to claim victory in the war, which ended on August 12 with the signing of a peace protocol. The final terms were set on December 10 with the negotiation and signing of the Treaty of Paris. Cuba was to gain its independence, while Puerto Rico, Guam, and the Philippines were to belong to the United States. The U.S. paid nothing for Puerto Rico and Guam, but it gave Spain $20 million for the Philippines. The Filipinos, however, continued to revolt and finally achieved independence in 1946. Eager for global expansion, President McKinley had already annexed Hawaii in July. Thus, the nation made the transition from hemispheric power to world power in one fell swoop.

The outcome of the war was an economic boon to the United States. The country was able to protect its interests in Cuba, and it even managed to gain potentially lucrative territory overseas. With the Hawaiian Islands the United States gained fruitful sugar plantations and a promising fishing industry. Of course, the United States paid dearly for its conquests: The war cost the country $250 million. Political unrest in the Philippines, which struggled for its own independence, was to be a source of grief for many years. But for the most part the American public wholeheartedly approved of the terms of its victory. Advocates of U.S. expansion and global prowess particularly exulted in their triumph, which secured the nation's place as a world power.

See also: **Imperialism, Philippines**

FURTHER READING

Dictionary of American History. New York: Charles Scribner's Sons, 1976, s.v. ''Spanish-American War.''

Gordon, John Steele. ''The Meaning of '98.'' *American Heritage*, May-June 1998.

Karp, Walter. *The Politics of War*. New York: Harper, 1980.

Millis, Walter. *The Martial Spirit*. Cambridge, MA: The Literary Guild of America, 1931.

Zimmerman, Warren. ''Jingoes, Goo-Goos, and the Rise of America's Empire.'' *Wilson Quarterly*, Spring 1998.

SPECIAL INTEREST GROUPS

Toward the end of the twentieth century, special interest groups exhibited several defining characteristics. First, special interest groups are associations joined voluntarily by individuals sharing at least one common interest or belief that defines the group's purpose. The National Education Association's (NEA) members teach. Members of the Sierra Club are interested in environmental issues. Members work together to focus and articulate issue positions and strategies designed to actively influence public policy.

A special interest group's key element is purposely influencing government policy, whereas Elks Clubs, university alumni associations, and Boy Scouts of America are apolitical groups primarily interested in service and social activities. Second, special interest groups have organizational structure whether formal or informal where persons routinely gather to assist their group. The NEA and Sierra Club are formal organizations with dues paying members. A neighborhood group may not have dues, officers, or bylaws, but meets regularly to support or oppose issues of local concern. Third, special interest groups are non-governmental, neither agencies nor political parties. Though interest groups often endorse candidates, they do not nominate candidates. Groups generally fall into one of two categories: trade associations or unions seeking economic betterment for their members; or, cause-related groups promoting some issue such as clean environment, gun control, or ban on abortions.

Although the pervasiveness of interest groups influencing politics is clearly a twentieth century phenomenon, discussion on the role of groups in the United States appeared in James Madison's *Federalist 10* (1787). Frenchman Alexis de Tocqueville described the United States as a nation of frequent joiners in his book *Democracy in America* (1835–1840). One of the earliest interest groups in the United States was the National Grange, founded in 1867, which advocated government railroad regulation. Interest group formation has occurred in a series of waves in U.S. history. The first arrived between 1830 and 1860 with groups such as the Grange and Abolitionist organizations. Next, in 1880 with intense industrialization, the American Federation of Labor (AFL), Knights of Labor, and various manufacturing associations sprang up. Between 1900 and 1920, many new organizations formed, such as the U.S. Chamber of Commerce, American Medical Association, and National Association for the Advancement of Colored People. The 1960's and 1970's witnessed a proliferation of cause-oriented and economic organizations including Common Cause and Ralph Nader's Public Citizen.

Near synonymous terms are pressure groups, public interest groups, lobbies, and vested groups.

See also: **Abolition, American Federation of Labor, Knights of Labor, Ralph Nader, National Grange**

SPECIE

Specie is metallic money in all of its forms, gold or silver traditionally, but including nickel and copper as well. Specie is distinguished from other forms of money such as paper money or credit instruments like checks, money order, credit cards and the like. The term specie is also occasionally applied to gold and silver bullion, which is ordinary gold and silver, as opposed to coins with collectible value. Since January of 1934, the gold coin is no longer routinely coined by the U.S. government, nor is it routinely in ordinary circulation in the United States. Public law 91-607, enacted in December of 1970, initiated the creation of non-silver dollars and half-dollars minted for general circulation. Coinage of the former 40 per cent silver half-dollar, pursuant to the *Coinage Act of 1965*, was discontinued in January of 1971. The Coinage Act also brought an end to the silver quarter and the dime, which are now coined with some silver and mostly baser metals, like copper and nickel. All coins in common circulation in the U.S., currently minted, are composed of baser metals, and specie is largely a form of metallic money of the past.

See also: **Money**

SPECULATION

Speculation is an economic term used to describe financial risk taking. For example, an individual investing money in a start-up business venture, where the outcome of profit or loss is unknown, is engaging in speculation. A speculator can calculate a variety of factors and forecast a possible result for an investment, but performance outcomes can never be definitively determined. To continue with the example of a start-up venture, the performance of the new business can be estimated through market studies regarding consumer demand for a product and how that demand is or is not presently being met in the marketplace. The start-up business may predict that its product is innovative and will quickly find a niche in the market, generating profit for the company. If this is true, the analysis proves accurate. However, if the economy experiences an economic downturn and enters into a depression as the business opens, the needs of the marketplace may change and the outcome may result in loss.

Speculation may be compared to gambling. However, the two are not the same. Gambling is an artificial form of risk taking and has no relation to business operations or market forces. Speculation relies on the marketplace and is subject to the whims of the economy. Speculation may also be confused with investment, which also takes place in the marketplace and is subject to the ups and downs of the economy, but these are also not the same. Investment involves a limited risk of capital and is usually designed to make a profit over the long-term. Speculation often involves larger amount of money and attempts to achieve a high profit in a short time frame.

See also: **Capital, Investment**

SPINNING MILLS

Spinning mills were introduced to the United States in 1790 by English-born mechinist and businessman Samuel Slater (1768–1835). The twenty-one year old had worked as a textile laborer for more than six years in an English mill, where he learned about the workings of a cotton-spinning machine invented (1783) by Richard Arkwright (1732–92). The British considered the Arkwright mill the cornerstone of their booming textile industry and laws prevented anyone with knowledge of the mill from leaving the country. Eager to seek his own fortune, Slater disguised himself in 1789 to evade the authorities and sailed from England to recreate the spinning mill in America.

Arriving in Providence, Rhode Island, Slater formed a partnership with the textile firm Almy and Brown. From memory Slater began building a spinning mill based on the Arkwright machine. The spinning mill debuted December 20, 1790, in the village of Pawtucket, Rhode Island, where the wheels of the mill were turned by the waters of the Blackstone River. The machine was a success and soon revolutionized the American textile industry, which had previously relied on cottage workers (the putting-out system) to manufacture thread and yarn.

Slater's innovation earned him the title "Father of American Manufactures" from President Andrew Jackson (1829–37), as well as the title "father of the American textile industry." He was credited with spawning the factory system in the United States. Within the first three decades of the 1800s, New England became the center of the nation's textile industry: the region's ample rivers and streams provided the necessary water power and the commercial centers of Boston and New York City readily received the finished products. Labor proved to be in ample supply as well: Because mill machinery was not complicated, children could operate it (and often did). Slater hired children ages seven to 14 to run the mill—a practice that other New England textile factories also adopted. The Jefferson Embargo of 1807, which prohibited importing textiles, also aided the industry. New England's mills provided the model for the American factory system. Slater had helped bring the Industrial Revolution to America.

Slater eventually broke away from Almy and Brown to open Samuel Slater & Company at Pawtucket, Rhode Island. He later operated mills in Connecticut and New Hampshire. The Pawtucket mill where he demonstrated his innovation is now the Slater Mill Historic Site and has been called the Cradle of American Industry.

See also: **Connecticut, Andrew Jackson, Napoleonic Wars (Economic Impact of), New Hampshire, Samuel Slater, Slater Builds First Factory, Samuel Slater, Textile Industry**

SPOILS SYSTEM

The spoils system is the political practice of playing favorites. Used throughout U.S. history, it commonly takes the form of filling appointive offices with loyal supporters. Among the nation's early presidents Thomas Jefferson (1801–1809) made particular use of the practice to place his allies in influential civil service posts.

By the time President Andrew Jackson (1829–1837) took office in 1829, this method of rewarding one's political allies was an integral part of the workings of government. Jackson's friend, Senator William Marcy (1786–1857) of New York, coined the phrase "spoils system" in 1832, when he stated, "to the victor belong the spoils of the enemy."

The spoils system grew in size as a result of the bitter competition that characterized the two party system during Jackson's presidency. During his first term of office (1829–1833) he assembled a group of unofficial advisers who reportedly met in the White House kitchen, earning them the nickname Kitchen Cabinet. Members included then-Secretary of State Martin Van Buren (1782–1862), who later served as

Jackson's vice president and then as president (1837–1841); Francis P. Blair (1791–1876), editor of the *Washington Post,* and an active participant in politics who would help Abraham Lincoln (1809–1865) during his presidential campaign (1860); and Amos Kendall (1789–1869), a journalist and Jackson administration speech writer who later became U.S. Postmaster General. The informality of the Kitchen Cabinet invited the mixing of politics and special interests. It operated outside the official institutions of government and yet was influential in formulating policy during the Jackson administration. Jackson drew harsh criticism for relying on his cronies in this way, and when he reorganized the federal Cabinet in 1831, the informal Kitchen Cabinet was disbanded.

ANDREW JACKSON'S FRIEND, SENATOR WILLIAM MARCY (1786–1857) OF NEW YORK, COINED THE PHRASE "SPOILS SYSTEM" IN 1832, WHEN HE STATED, "TO THE VICTOR BELONG THE SPOILS OF THE ENEMY."

The Kitchen Cabinet closed its doors, but the spoils system continued to influence policy when Martin Van Buren succeeded Jackson as president. Van Buren had been a leader of the Albany Regency which was the Democratic Party machine in New York state. This group of New York Democratic party leaders used the spoils systems to reward members and to maintain strict party discipline.

After the Civil War, the spoils system became an obstruction to good government. Placing political allies in important public service positions often failed to involve a determination of whether or not the person in question was qualified to hold the job. The practice bred corruption and inefficiency and reached staggering proportions by the time Ulysses Grant (1869–1877) became president. His administration was notoriously prone to graft-ridden awards of government contracts.

The failure of the spoils system brought on tragic consequences when in 1881 a frustrated office-seeker shot President James Garfield (1881) in a train station. Garfield's successor, Chester Arthur (1881–1885), though himself a creature of the spoils system, worked to dismantle it. The Pendleton Act of 1883 initiated reform of the system by establishing a federal Civil Service Commission and creating a class of government workers (14,000 out of a total of 100,000) who now had to take an examination to be awarded a government job. Though limited in size, the Civil Service Commission grew in later years.

The system was further refined in the twentieth century. To further separate civil service from politics, the Hatch Act (1940) forbid civil servants from political campaigning. The Hatch Act was revised in 1993 to allow most civil servants to participate in political activity on their personal time. Measures like the Civil Service Commission and the Hatch Act have been successful in limiting the use of the spoils system in the political process, but they haven't eradicated the practice. The spoils system is still (unofficially) practiced in some federal, state, and local government offices.

***See also:* Civil Service Act, Andrew Jackson, Thomas Jefferson**

SPRINGFIELD ARMORY

The southwestern Massachusetts town of Springfield, on the Connecticut River, first became an important weapons center during the American Revolution (1775–83) when a sizeable arsenal was built there in 1777. The town was considered to be ideally situated—close to two major overland routes and on a strategic waterway, but far enough inland from the Atlantic Ocean to be defensible. Springfield had been the site of a militia training field since the 1600s; during the war, the Continental Army added barracks and storehouses, which held muskets, cannons, and other weapons. The new republic continued to keep arms at the site after the war was over. In 1794 a U.S. Armory was established at Springfield; it was one of two federal arsenals personally selected by President George Washington (1789–96); the other was Harpers Ferry, in present-day West Virginia.

In 1795 musket manufacturing began at Springfield, with forty workers producing 245 muskets per month. Soon Springfield became a center for innovation in arms production. In 1819 American inventor Thomas Blanchard (1788–1864), who worked at the armory for five years, developed a lathe (a machine for shaping metal) that allowed for the mass production of rifle stocks. During the Industrial Revolution the Springfield Armory focused on mass production of interchangeable parts, which had the advantage of being replaceable (in case of malfunction) on the battlefield.

In 1903 the Springfield rifle was approved for production. Nicknamed the "Springfield Model '03" (the gun was marked with 'M1903'), it soon became standard issue for U.S. Army troops. The model was improved in 1906 to accommodate new ammunition; the resulting model, called the Springfield .30-06, was one of the most reliable and accurate military firearms in history. By the time World War I (1914–18) began, the armory had manufactured just over 840,000 Springfield rifles; during the war, it made another 265,000.

The Massachusetts city, which was incorporated in 1641, remained home to the weapons facility until 1974. Another milestone in the history of the armory was the 1786–87 siege by rebel leader Daniel Shays (1747?–1825) during the so-called Shays Rebellion. Just downstream from Springfield, American inventor Samuel Colt (1814–62) opened an armory in 1853 at Hartford, Connecticut, where he utilized 1,400 machine tools to revolutionize the manufacture of small arms.

See also: **American System of Manufactures, Colt's Manufacturing, Harpers Ferry Armory, Harpers Ferry Raid, Industrial Revolution, Massachusetts, Shays' Rebellion**

STAGFLATION

''Stagflation'' is a combination term, bringing together two words, ''stagnation'' and ''inflation.'' In economic terms, stagflation exists when there is slow or no growth in the real (inflation-adjusted) economy, accompanied by economic inflation (rising prices). A period of stagflation exists, for instance, when unemployment rates are high and the rates of inflation of products are also high. In 1982 the Council of Economic Advisers reported that there was no known reason to expect any regular or systematic association between the unemployment rate and the average rate of price-level change (inflation). The term came into existence during the 1970s, when the effort to reduce high inflation by trading inflation for increased employment actually resulted in both more inflation and rising unemployment: stagflation. Some economists argued that a permanent reduction in inflation brings about a permanent rise in the rate of unemployment, a famous economic tradeoff implied by the 'Phillips Curve,' developed by English economist A.W. Phillips. Phillips' theory was based on his study of English unemployment between 1862 and 1957, where it appeared that any economy would need to accept some growing rate of reasonable inflation in order to lower unemployment. The Phillips Curve data has never been proven to be accurate, according to data gathered in the United States, and the rare and episodic economic conditions of stagflation are still not clearly understood, except that the effort to reduce inflation by artificially increasing employment is by no means reliable, and may result in the paradoxical situation of stagflation, where prices on consumer items increase, but consumers are unable to afford the higher prices.

When both the rates of unemployment and inflation are high, a state of "stagflation" exists.

STAMP ACT (1765)

The Stamp Act, passed in March, 1765, was the first direct tax ever placed by the British government on the American colonies. The Act, which was to take effect November 1, 1765, required an official stamp on about 50 different types of documents, ranging from playing cards to newspapers and college diplomas. The stamp's cost depended on the value of the document. King George III's Prime Minister George Grenville, who led Parliament from 1763 to 1765, felt that such a tax was needed to help pay for the costs of the French and Indian War (1754–1763). Great Britain was deeply in debt from the expenses of winning the war against France, and the revenues it gathered from the colonies did not come close to paying the costs of collecting them. Because of the expenses of the war, the country's national debt had increased by more than 50 percent in the space of seven years, from 75 million pounds sterling to 137 million pounds sterling. In addition, Grenville wanted to keep the peace between Native Americans and settlers along the North American frontier and to crack down on colonial smuggling. The Stamp Act, which Grenville believed would raise about 100,000 pounds sterling per year, was meant to help pay the costs of these programs.

The colonists objected to the Stamp Act in part because it infringed on their rights as English citizens, but also because it put a tremendous financial burden on them. The colonies were in the middle of an economic depression which had its origins in the destruction caused by the French and Indian War, and

Angry mobs in other colonies followed Boston's example, using force to intimidate would-be stamp distributors. In Rhode Island the nominee for tax collector, Augustus Johnston, abandoned his duty before the end of August. Connecticut Sons of Liberty forced Jared Ingersoll out of office, while in Maryland Zachariah Hood had to leave the colony after anti-tax rioters burned his home.

cash was very scarce. The tax on stamps was payable only in hard cash—gold or silver. Paper colonial money (often devalued so much that it was practically worthless) was not accepted. Hard currency was also difficult to find in the colonies because English imports (including most manufactured goods) had to be paid for in cash, not colonial notes. In addition to setting colonists the problem of finding the money to pay their taxes, the act also threatened their material prosperity. The Stamp Act allowed officials to try accused lawbreakers in royal vice-admiralty courts, which did not use juries, as well as in regular criminal courts. These vice-admiralty courts, it was believed, would be less sympathetic to colonial viewpoints.

Local politics and class rivalry also played a role in resistance to the Stamp Act, particularly in Virginia and Massachusetts. Virginian lawyer Patrick Henry made the act the subject of his first speech in the colony's House of Burgesses in May, 1765. Henry's opinions on the Stamp Act were narrowly passed by the House and they, as the Virginia Resolutions, inspired open opposition to the Act in other colonies.

In Boston opposition to the Stamp Act was even more conspicuous. At that time a small clique of wealthy families, related by marriage, held most of the royal offices in the colony. These families included Governor Francis Bernard, Thomas Hutchinson (lieutenant governor and chief justice), and the brothers Andrew Oliver and Peter Oliver. This "royalist faction" was opposed by a coalition of poorer men known as the "popular faction," including the lawyer James Otis, Jr. and Boston politician Samuel Adams. The popular faction spread the idea that the royalist faction was behind the Stamp Act, and they were supported in this belief by two of Boston's largest gangs.

In the summer, 1765, Andrew Oliver was appointed distributor of stamps for the Boston area. On August 14 of that year, a dummy made up to look like Oliver was discovered, along with an old boot (a symbol for Lord Bute, George Grenville's predecessor as Prime Minister), hanging from an elm tree near Boylston Market in Boston. Despite the efforts of the town sheriff, until sundown, the objects remained on the elm, which became famous as the Liberty Tree. At that point a crowd, including members of the popular faction, gathered and removed the effigy. These "Sons of Liberty", led by shoemakers Ebenezer Macintosh and Henry Swift, paraded the effigy of Oliver to the waterfront, where they attacked and destroyed a warehouse the tax collector had built. The crowd—by this time a mob—then built a bonfire in front of Oliver's house and, when they ran low on firewood, began stripping the trees and buildings on his property. For over an hour, the Boston mob continued to dismantle Oliver's home, smashing his furniture and mirrors and scattering his valuables. Within a week another crowd confronted the tax collector and extorted from him a promise that he would resign his office. Later that month the Sons of Liberty attacked and destroyed the homes of Thomas Hutchinson and customs administrator Benjamin Hallowell in an effort to intimidate them as well.

Angry mobs in other colonies followed Boston's example, using force to intimidate would-be stamp distributors. In Rhode Island the nominee for tax collector, Augustus Johnston, abandoned his duty before the end of August. Connecticut Sons of Liberty forced Jared Ingersoll out of office, while in Maryland Zachariah Hood had to leave the colony after anti-tax rioters burned his home. More conservative protesters tried less violent means to express their dissent. In October, 1765, 27 delegates from nine colonies assembled in New York City to present their grievances as a united body: the Stamp Act Congress. Merchants in major port cities, such as New York, Philadelphia, and Boston, agreed to start an economic boycott of British goods with the goal of seeing the Stamp Act repealed.

On November 1, 1765, the day that the Stamp Act was to be put into effect, colonial government, communications, and commerce all came to a halt. In late November and December, however, the Sons of Liberty and other activists persuaded businesses, courts, and newspapers to begin work again in defiance of the Stamp Act. By this time, however, the government that had passed the Stamp Act had long since fallen. George III found Grenville distasteful and replaced him with Charles Watson-Wentworth, Marquis of Rockingham, in July, 1765. Rockingham, who was much more sympathetic to the American point of view than Grenville had been, launched a campaign to repeal the Stamp Act. On February 22, 1766, the House of Commons, led by William Pitt, repealed the Stamp Act. As an omen of things to come, however, they passed another law: the Declaratory Act (1766), which asserted Parliament's right to tax and make laws for the colonies.

See also: **American Revolution, Intolerable Acts, Sugar Act, Townshend Acts**

FURTHER READING

Bullion, John L. *A Great and Necessary Measure: George Grenville and the Genesis of the Stamp Act, 1763–1765.* Columbia, MO: University of Missouri Press, 1982.

Egnal, Marc M. *A Mighty Empire: The Origins of the American Revolution.* Ithaca, NY: Cornell University Press, 1988.

Fleming, Thomas. *Liberty! The American Revolution.* New York: Viking Penguin, 1997.

Morgan, Edmund Sears. *The Stamp Act Crisis: Prologue to Revolution.* Chapel Hill, NC: Institute of Early American History and Culture/University of North Carolina Press, 1995.

Thomas, Peter David Garner. *British Politics and the Stamp Act Crisis: The First Phase of the American Revolution, 1763–1767.* New York: Clarendon Press, 1975.

STANDARD & POOR'S

Standard & Poor's Corporation (S&P) is the largest statistical service organization in the United States. It specializes in the securities field and includes a range of corporate investments, like stocks, bonds, mortgages, notes, scrip, rights, options, etc. Standard & Poor's Corporation (a division of the McGraw-Hill Companies in the 1990s) is the result of a merger between the Standard Statistics Company and Poor's Publishing Company. The Standard & Poor's Corporation, known by its trademarks ''Standard & Poor's,'' ''S&P,'' and ''S&P 500, '' produces for investors useful collections of periodic reference publications containing financial statistics. S&P services include a weekly investment advisory service, a stock guide, a bond guide, industry surveys, and corporation records, as well as many other specifically targeted economic marketplace service sector guides. S&P has for many years produced its famous *S&P 500 Corporate Stock Index* in which 500 important companies, producing various large company or ''blue chip'' commodities, are averaged together with weights representing their importance in the total indexed selling value of their stocks. This index represents an aggregate view of the primary marketplace in the United States and illustrates statistical trends in both growth and weakness. The Index presents an ongoing series of statistical ''snapshots'' of the market to aid investors. The only real competitor of S&P as a leading publisher of investment data is Moody's Investor Service, Inc.

See also: **Stock Market**

STANDARD OF LIVING

Standard of living refers to the level of material well-being enjoyed by an individual or group. The standard of living is generally measured by the collective cost of goods and services that is considered to represent the essential consumption of any society's members. By some measures, the standard of living will also include certain publicly provided services, such as education, health services, transportation, and intangible quality of life factors like clean water and air, and cultural and leisure activities.

The term standard of living may also refer to the goals that individuals or groups obtain for themselves as consumers in terms of services, housing, furnishings, or automobiles. In the United States during the 1960s, the United States government's definition of poverty was developed as a variant of the general concept of the standard of living in the country. In 1996, for example, the average poverty line for a four-person family was a little over $16,000. The indexes used to measure poverty and create specific dollar amounts to define poverty are based on arguably variable statistics, but the fact that a poverty index has been established bears witness that U.S. society appears to recognize what seems to be a baseline financial standard of living and is able to approximate those who are living below the current indexed standard during any given year.

STANDARD OIL COMPANY

The origins of the Standard Oil Company date from 1863 when John D. Rockefeller (1839–1937), son of a modest businessman, and two others purchased a refinery in Cleveland, Ohio. Rockefeller foresaw the potential of refining Pennsylvania crude oil, which would revolutionize the way people lighted their homes, fueled their vehicles, and powered their industries. With easy access to railroads and the Great

Lakes, Rockefeller's home city of Cleveland, Ohio, soon became the hub for crude oil refining, thanks to the business acumen of Rockefeller and his partners.

After seven years of local success the company was incorporated in 1870. Rockefeller then began a series of shrewd business maneuvers, which included several mergers, the absorption of the next three largest refiners in the nation, and the use of favorable railroad rebates. (Rockefeller was such a hard-nosed negotiator that he talked the railroads not only into giving Standard Oil rebates; they even paid him rebates on his competitors' shipping!) In ten years, Rockefeller controlled $33 million of the $35 million annual refining capacity of the United States. By 1878 Rockefeller and partner Henry Flagler (1830–1913) had consolidated most of the oil refining in the nation, and Rockefeller became one of the five wealthiest men in the country.

The already gigantic company was growing at such an remarkable pace that it alarmed the "muckraker" exposé journalists of the late nineteenth century, like Ida Tarbell (1857–1944), who denounced Standard Oil as an "octopus," or a monopoly, strangling the forces of competitive capitalism, ruining the small businessman, and trampling on the rights of labor.

Standard Oil was, as the muckrakers said, a monopoly. Because it was able to establish dominance over its competitors in the field of refining, it was a "horizontal monopoly." And because it branched out from its original concentration on refining into the drilling of crude oil and the sale of petroleum products, it also became a "vertical monopoly."

One of Rockefeller's main contributions was in devising ways to structure this economic power. In 1882 Rockefeller and his associates established the first trust in the United States, which consolidated all of the company's assets under the New York Company, in which Rockefeller was the major shareholder. The 30 companies in the trust controlled 80 percent of the refineries and 90 percent of the oil pipelines in the country.

In an effort to check the monopolization of the economy, Congress passed the Sherman Anti-Trust Act in 1890. In 1892 the Ohio Supreme Court dissolved the Standard Oil Trust. The company, however, took advantage of the newly liberalized laws in New Jersey and incorporated there under a consolidated corporate structure. This maneuver enabled Standard Oil to continued to operate as a Trust.

Standard Oil accumulated $830 million in profits from 1899 to 1911. In 1906 a federal lawsuit against Standard Oil broke up the New Jersey trust. While Jersey Standard retained a number of smaller companies, it lost the largest refineries held in other states and its monopoly on production of oil and pipelines. Jersey Standard, still handling Rockefeller's trusts, acted quickly to acquire oil supplies in other states, particularly Texas. Although it eventually lost its domination of the oil market, the company was still huge and ripe for criticism.

In 1888 the first foreign affiliate of Standard Oil was created. The Anglo-American Oil Company Ltd. of London allowed Standard to begin securing interests outside the United States. It acquired companies in Latin America in the 1920s, particularly in Venezuela, and also expanded marketing companies abroad.

As more and more automobiles and trucks began to dominate transportation in the 1920s, Standard Oil's sales shifted from kerosene to gasoline. By 1950, however, the top-selling products were still fuel oils used as substitutes for coal to power ships and industrial plants; distillates used for home heating and diesel engines were also important products. The big profit earner, even in the early 1990s, remained crude oil, and not gasoline sales.

The legal confrontation finally came to a head in the United States Supreme Court in 1911. The Court ordered Standard Oil of New Jersey to divest itself of its 33 subsidiaries. Later the company changed its name to Esso, using the abbreviation from Standard Oil (S. O.). This caused protest from the companies that were still using the Standard Oil name, so the company officially changed its name to Exxon in 1972.

***See also:* Exxon, Monopoly**

FURTHER READING

Adelman, M. A. *The Genie Out of the Bottle: World Oil Since 1970*. Cambridge, MA: MIT Press, 1995.

Brown, Anthony Cave. *Oil, God and Gold: The Story of ARAMCO and the Saudi Kings*. Boston: Houghton Mifflin Co., 1999.

"Exxon Corporation," [cited April 14, 1999] available from the World Wide Web @ www.exxon.com/exxoncorp/index2.html/.

Henderson, Wayne. *Standard Oil: The First 125 Years*. Stillwater, MN: Motorbooks International, 1996.

Karl, Terry Lynn. *The Paradox of Plenty: Oil Booms and Petro-States*. Studies in International Political Economy, No 26. Berkeley and Los Angeles: University of California Press, 1997.

STANDARD TIME

Standard time was introduced in 1884; it was the outcome of an international conference held in Washington, DC, to consider a worldwide system of standard time. The international agreement divided the world into twenty-four different "standard" time zones; within each time zone, all clocks were to be set to the same time. The device of standardized time zones was necessitated by the expansion of industry: businesses, particularly those in the transportation industry, could not coordinate schedules when each community used its own solar time (the local time as determined by the position of the sun). Railroad schedules had been extremely complicated before the establishment of standard time zones, which the railroads readily adopted.

Each time zone spans 15 degrees of longitude, beginning at zero longitude (called the "prime meridian"), which passes through the observatory at Greenwich (a borough of London), England. Time zones are described by their distance east or west of Greenwich. The model also dictates that each time zone is one hour apart from the next. However, the borders of the time zones have been adjusted throughout the world to accommodate national, state, and provincial boundaries, further facilitating commercial activities. The contiguous United States has four time zones: Eastern, Central, Mountain, and Pacific. Waters off the Eastern seaboard are in the Atlantic time zone; Alaska, Hawaii, Samoa, Wake Island, and Guam each have their own time zones. Congress gave the Interstate Commerce Commission (ICC) authority to establish limits for U.S. time zones in 1918. This authority was transferred to the Department of Transportation in 1967. In navigation, ship operators typically use the local time (solar time) at Greenwich, which is called Greenwich mean time (GMT) or universal time (UT).

Standard time, while clearly borne out of necessity of the Industrial Revolution, has become only more critical in the decades since its adoption; the global business community relies on standard time to coordinate its activities.

STANFORD, LELAND

Leland Stanford (1824–93) was an industrialist and politician who amassed a large fortune from the development of the railroad industry in the west. He was one of the founders of the Central Pacific Railroad Company that helped build the first transcontinental railroad. He also served as governor of California and as a United States Senator. He donated a large portion of his fortune to found Stanford University in Palo Alto, California.

Leland Stanford.

Leland Stanford was born on March 9, 1824, in Watervliet, New York, the fifth of eight children. Stanford received a sound education; he first studied at the Clinton Liberal Institute and then at Cazenovia Seminary in New York. After finishing school he began working in a law office and he was admitted to the bar in 1848. He later established his own practice in Port Washington, Wisconsin but a fire destroyed it in 1852 and Stanford decided not to rebuild his practice. Instead he moved to California, where his brothers had already settled, to join their business of selling supplies to miners.

It was in California that Stanford first became involved in politics. He actively participated in the formation of the California Republican Party, and he ran unsuccessfully for State Treasurer in 1857. Despite this loss Stanford continued to pursue a career in politics and in 1859 he ran for governor of California but lost again. However, in 1861 Stanford won the gubernatorial election by a plurality, due to a split in the Democratic Party. His most important political act as governor was keeping California in the Union during the American Civil War (1861–65).

Around the time when Stanford was elected governor he also became interested in the possibility of building a transcontinental railroad. He joined forces with Collis P. Huntington (1821–1900), Charles Crocker (1822–88), and Mark Hopkins (1814–78) to form the Central Pacific Railroad Company in 1861. Stanford and his associates were referred to as the Big Four. They were eventually responsible for building the western half of the first transcontinental railroad. Stanford served as president of the company from its formation until his death.

The Big Four had little knowledge of the railroad industry and very little capital to invest in the venture so they relied on their political talents and connections to support the project. As governor of California Stanford approved several public grants for the railroad work done in his state. In addition he used his political contacts to acquire generous federal grants for the railroad, which included land grants for railroad construction and loans for financing the project. Stanford generated large sums of public money for a company in which he had a major personal interest as a stockholder.

When his term as governor ended in 1863 Stanford devoted all of his energy to the railroad industry. At that time the Central Pacific began building its part of the transcontinental railroad with construction of tracks eastward from Sacramento, California. The Union Pacific Railroad Company built the westward line from Omaha, Nebraska and the two lines met at Promontory Point, Utah, on May 10, 1869. The Central Pacific laid 1,086 miles of track, while the Union Pacific had built 689, which was advantageous for Central Pacific, because government subsidies were based on mileage. The Big Four profited nicely from this venture, however, great hardships were encountered before the project was accomplished; many lives were lost. Construction crews consisting mainly of Chinese immigrants worked through two harsh winters in the high Sierras. The goal was to complete the project as quickly as possible.

Once that rail line was completed Stanford and his associates developed other rail and water transportation systems in California. They bought out competing lines such as the California Pacific Railroad Company and the San Francisco and San Jose Railroad. They organized the Southern Pacific Railroad, of which Stanford served as director from 1882 to 1893. This company built a second transcontinental railroad from California to New Orleans.

The Big Four believed that their business could remain profitable only if they maintained their rail monopoly in California. Their policy was one of aggressive defense by which they would prevent competitors from forming other entry points into the state. They also purchased major river and ocean shipping lines. The Big Four dominated the railroad industry in the 1890s; their company was frequently criticized for being a "monopolistic octopus." Nonetheless Stanford personally remained popular among the public.

After 1870 Stanford became less involved in the daily activities of the railroad company and he retreated to his ranch in Palo Alto, California. In 1885 he returned to political life and was elected to the United States Senate. As a U.S. Senator, Stanford advocated private rights in business. He opposed the Interstate Commerce Act of 1887 because it allowed for government regulation of businesses. Stanford also served on minor congressional committees and supported popular legislation such as the exclusion of Chinese laborers, industrial co-operatives, and soft money. He represented California in the Senate until his death in 1893 at the age of 69.

Leland Stanford accumulated a fortune from his railroad interests. Stanford was not known for his philanthropy but he donated to particular charities to ensure his family name would become an institution. In 1885 Stanford's 15-year-old son died of typhoid fever while on vacation in Europe. Stanford was keenly interested in the boy's education and as a memorial to his son Stanford provided a 20 million-dollar endowment to found the Leland Stanford Junior University in Palo Alto. The school opened in 1891 and grew to become one of the country's most prestigious universities.

***See also:* California, Central Pacific Railroad, Monopolies, Railroad Industry, Transcontinental Railroad**

FURTHER READING

Clark, George Thomas. *Leland Stanford: War Governor of California, Railroad Builder and Founder of Stanford University.* Palo Alto: Stanford University Press, 1931.

Lewis, Oscar. *The Big Four: The Story of Huntington, Stanford, Hopkins, and Crocker, and of the Building of the Central Pacific.* New York: A.A. Knopf, 1938.

McGuire, William, and Leslie Wheeler. *American Social Leaders.* Santa Barbara: ABC-CLIO, 1993.

Snow, Richard F. "Biggest of the Four." *American Heritage*, December 1987.

Tutorow, Norman E. *Leland Stanford: Man of Many Careers.* Menlo Park, California: Pacific Coast Publishers, 1971.

STATES' RIGHTS *(ISSUE)*

Because of its fundamental relationship to the political and constitutional foundations of the United States, the issue of states' rights has been an enduring problem throughout the history of the United States. At its core, the matter raised questions of sovereignty and authority, and often overlapped other questions, like whether the country should have a centralized or decentralized government. Moreover, it had strong implications for the American economy, especially regarding trade, tariffs, banking, and labor, among others.

In the early eighteenth century the thirteen colonies of British North America had more in common with the Crown, especially economically, than they did with each other. But as that relationship slipped into acrimony—especially during the American Revolution (1775–1783)—the fight against a common foe, the forces of independence, the communication between the respective social classes in the different regions of the country and the evolution to statehood forged a greater sense of unity among the former thirteen colonies. Under the Articles of Confederation (adopted in 1777) the states retained political autonomy. The Confederation Congress had little authority and was unable to exert any effective control over the economic activity of individual states as well as the states' relations with foreign countries and with each other. The national government could not levy taxes, issue money, or enforce a uniform tariff on imports and exports. Congress could only ask the states for funds with which to fight the war and carry out the work of government.

When the framers of the Constitution assembled in the spring of 1787, they were faced with the sobering evidence of what independence had wrought. The machinery of government was clearly too cumbersome for the tasks that it had to accomplish. Yet they also remained dedicated to their revolutionary ideal of more liberty and less government. In the end, the Constitution that they produced reflected both realities. In the Tenth Amendment, the framers granted to the states a kind of states' bill of rights which specified that "... powers not delegated to the United States by the Constitution; nor prohibited by it to the States, are reserved to the States respectively. . . ." The Constitution did give the federal government the powers to tax, borrow, and coin money, regulate foreign and interstate commerce, establish a postal service, and issue patents and copyrights, but it also imposed constraints on the government's ability to regulate trade. The federal government could not impose duties on exports, could not discriminate against the ports of any state in its commercial regulations, could not restrict a carrier's freedom to enter or leave a state without stopping in another, and finally, could not extend any trade barriers between the states themselves.

When the First Bank of the United States (1791–1811) was chartered, the issue of states' rights was again raised. According to its charter, the First Bank was allowed to operate in all states, which gave it a considerable edge over state banks that could only operate in the states that chartered them. The First Bank maintained a large banking network in various parts of the country and it was also able to hold more notes than state banks. Proponents of states rights and advocates of free commerce, therefore, were instrumental in defeating legislation to re-charter the First Bank in 1812. They feared that it posed obstacles to the growth of state banks. This controversy continued when, years later, many critics blamed the Second Bank of the United States (1816–1836) for the panic (the word that was used for depression) of 1819. Maryland, Tennessee, Georgia, North Carolina, Kentucky and Ohio enacted laws to tax branches of the Second Bank out of existence. However, the Supreme Court handed down decisions in *McCulloch v. Maryland* (1819) and *Osborne v. United States Bank* (1824) which declared unconstitutional any state law that restricted the activities of the Second Bank of the United States.

During the 1820s and early 1830s, during heated Congressional debate over tariffs, the issue of states' rights again came to the fore. Southern states complained that the North was benefiting from tariffs at the expense of the South. Then Vice President John C. Calhoun (1782–1850), himself a southerner, put forth a states' rights constitutional doctrine called "Nullification". In what came to be known as the "nullification crisis" the legislature of South Carolina declared that the tariffs of 1828 and 1832 were "unauthorized by the Constitution" and therefore "null, void . . . [and] . . .not binding upon this State, its officers or citizens." The passage of that declaration of nullification, in the view of Calhoun and the legislature of South Carolina, automatically made the disputed law unconstitutional. Then the U.S. Congress was obliged to pass an amendment to the Constitution explicitly affirming the constitutionality of the law. At that point, the state had the option of either abiding by the law or else peacefully seceding from the Union.

Such a doctrine would have severely limited the central power of the federal government. Although the president at the time, Andrew Jackson, was on some issues friendly to states' rights, he was enraged over this challenge to the sovereignty of the national government. He threatened to have Vice President Calhoun hanged, he mobilized the U.S. Navy, and had the U.S. Congress pass a ''force bill'' to ensure the effective implementation of the disputed tariff laws.

The nullification crisis was only a part of the cause for Southern economic and political discontent. The episode represented growing sectional differences between North and South. Tariffs, which tended to favor manufactured goods over raw goods, reaffirmed the agrarian South's subordinate relationship to the North. After the Panic of 1837, Southern cotton went into a sustained decline while industrial commerce in the North continued to prosper. Moreover, because western expansion in the United States afforded Northeastern business interests other sources for raw goods, manufacturers became less dependent on the South as a supplier of raw materials.

Southerners believed that they were victims of a sinister conspiracy supported by Northern bankers, merchants, manufacturers, and their political agents. Southerners accused them of rigging prices, of manipulating the money market, and of causing much of the wealth of the South to flow steadily into the hands of the northern economic elite. On top of this, the South resented the Abolitionist Movement against slavery. In reaction to the anti-slavery movement, Southerners began to extol the differences between their agrarian economy and that of the industrialized North. Southerners characterized the institution of slavery as essential to their economy and their way of life. Slavery was a necessary labor regime, they argued, and the slaves themselves were almost like family members. Accordingly, they rooted their economic arguments in agrarian values and paternalistic notions of family and grounded their political voices in the rights of each individual state.

When the Southern vote against then-Presidential candidate Abraham Lincoln (1861–65) proved futile in the election of 1860, most South Atlantic states turned to what they believed was their only legal recourse—the right to secede from the Union. Secession was most popular in the deep South wherever the plantation system and slavery were well established. While many people in the upper South felt strong ties to the Union, they had a strong affinity for vested southern values, the southern agrarian economy, and the institution of slavery. Coupled with a strong belief in the rights of the states which dated back to Thomas Jefferson and James Madison, the issue of states' rights was never so strongly articulated as when the southern states exercised what they believe was a Constitutional right to secede. The outcome of that action, the Civil War and Reconstruction, resulted in settling the questions of precedence—the rights of states or the superior authority of a republican form of government.

***See also:* Bank of the United States (First National), Bank of the United States (Second National), Civil War (Economic Causes of)**

FURTHER READING

Baack, Bennett, and Ray, Edward. ''The Political Economy of Tariff Policy: A Case Study of the United States.'' *Explorations in Economic History*, 30, 1983.

Craven, Avery O. *The Growth of Southern Nationalism.* Baton Rouge: Louisiana State University Press, 1953.

Freehling, W.W. *Prelude to Civil War: The Nullification Crisis in South Carolina 1816–1836.* Reprint. Oxford University Press, 1992.

Nettels, Curtis P. *The Emergence of A National Economy, 1775–1815.* New York: Holt, Rhinehart and Winston, 1962.

Timberlake, Richard H., Jr. *The Origins of Central Banking in the United States.* Cambridge: Harvard University Press, 1978.

STEAMBOAT ACT OF 1852

The Steamboat Act of 1852 was the U.S. Congress' second attempt to ensure safety of the steamboats that dominated the nation's waterways, principally the Mississippi River, where ''packet'' steamboats regularly ferried passengers and freight between St. Louis and New Orleans. The legislation improved an earlier (1838) law that had proved a weak attempt to enforce vessel operators' compliance with certain safety standards and measures: vessels were required to undergo periodic hull and boiler inspections and to carry basic lifesaving and fire-fighting equipment. In the eight months preceding passage of the 1852 act, seven boiler explosions aboard steamboats claimed more than seven hundred lives. Congress responded to these maritime disasters by establishing precise standards for steamboat boiler construction, including rules about safety valves and operating pressures. It also set up a licensing system for all operators of passenger steamboats. Licensing came under the purview of the U.S. Department of Treasury, which hired civilian inspectors. The Steamboat Act of 1852 was the basis for the U.S. Steamboat Inspection Service, whose authority was steadily strengthened by subsequent acts of Congress—most of them in response to further disaster along American waterways. In 1865 the boiler blew up on the steamboat *Sultana,* which was en route between Memphis, Tennessee, and St. Louis, Missouri. The explosion and resulting fire claimed the lives of more than 1,500 of the 2,300 people on board—many of them Union soldiers recently released from Confederate prisons. Since the Steamboat Inspection Service had certified the *Sultana* to carry only 376 passengers, it was cleared of any blame; the vessel's operators were held responsible for the disaster. Nevertheless, Congress subsequently passed a series of steamboat safety laws to aid the Inspection Service's efforts to enforce safety. An 1871 act gave the service the authority to issue licenses to masters, pilots, and engineers. In 1903 the service was moved from the Treasury Department to the Department of Commerce and Labor. When that department split in 1913, the service came under the purview of the newly formed Department of Commerce. In 1932 the Steamboat Inspection Service was merged with the Bureau of Navigation (established 1844), which became known as the Bureau of Marine Inspection and Navigation.

See also: **Mississippi River, New Orleans**

STEAMBOATS

Steamboats were first developed in the late 1700s and became commercially viable in the early 1800s. There were two types of steam-driven vessels—those designed for the deep coastal waters along the eastern seaboard of the United States and those designed to navigate the shallower inland rivers of the nation's interior. Steamboats are propelled by steam engines, which drive paddle wheels (either along the boat's side or stern) to move the vessel through water.

The first workable steamboat was demonstrated by Connecticut-born inventor John Fitch (1743–98) on August 22, 1787, on the Delaware River. He launched two larger vessels in 1788 and 1790, receiving a patent for his design in 1791. But Fitch's fourth boat was ruined by a storm in 1792 and the innovator lost the support of his backers.

The first commercially viable steamboat was designed by Pennsylvania engineer and inventor Robert Fulton (1765–1815); the *Clermont* made its maiden voyage on August 17-22, 1807, when it sailed up the Hudson River from New York City to Albany in thirty hours, and then returned. The vessel was 133 feet long and had only a seven-foot (considered shallow) draft. The *Clermont* was the forerunner of the ''western'' steamboats that would soon dominate the interior waterways and Gulf Coast. In 1817 the stern paddle steamboat the *Washington* completed the first round-trip voyage between Louisville, Kentucky, and New Orleans, Louisiana—traveling along the Ohio and Mississippi rivers. By the end of that year dozens of steamboats were in operation on those two principle rivers and their tributaries; by 1840, there were more than two hundred on the Mississippi alone; by 1860, this number had swelled to more than one thousand. Mississippi steamboat traffic and trade had by 1850 pushed New Orleans to exceed New York City in volume of shipping, with New Orleans' outbound cargo accounting for more than half the nation's total exports.

Steamboat technology was put to use on many kinds of vessels. Packets were the most common kind of steamboat; they carried passengers and cargo from city to city. There were also towboats (which pushed cargo barges), showboats (outfitted for the entertainment of the paying public), ferries (which carried covered wagons and other vehicles across waterways in the absence of bridges), dredges (to deepen existing waterways), and light tenders (which conducted maintenance along rivers). This variety of steamboats made settlement possible by permitting travel from West Virginia in the East to the Rocky Mountains in the West, and from Minnesota in the North to Louisiana in the South.

The development of transcontinental railroads later in the 1800s caused steamboat use to decline. For decades more, however, they maintained a place in the nation's ever-expanding transportation network, particularly up and down the Mississippi River.

See also: **Robert Fulton, Steamboat Act of 1852**

STEEL INDUSTRY

Steel is an alloy of carbon and iron that is harder and stronger than iron. While the first ironworks were established in British North America in Jamestown, Virginia (1621), the U.S. steel industry did not develop on its own until after the American Civil War (1861–1865). Up until that time steel was too expensive to manufacture by the methods then available. Its use prior to the American Civil War was confined primarily to high-value products, and the United States imported nearly all of its steel until after the American Civil War.

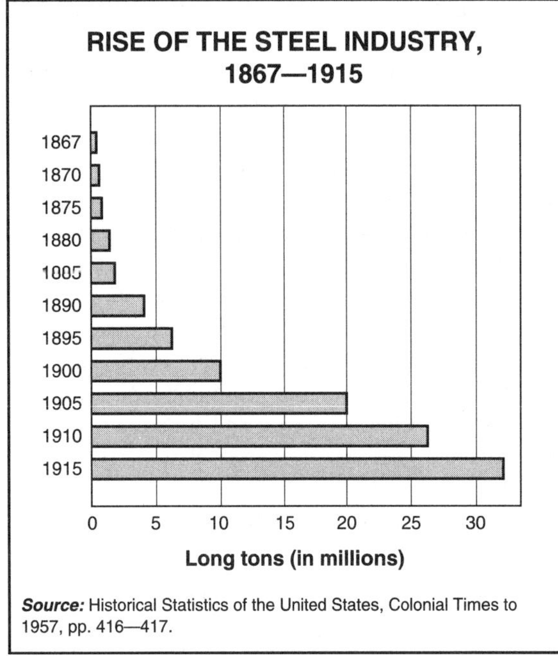

The growth of the steel industry is measured by the amount of steel produced. As illustrated, steel production skyrocketed in the 20th Century, making the U.S. the largest steel producing country in the world.

The coming of the steam age in the early part of the nineteenth century created a huge demand for iron. Up to this time most iron mines, forges, and blacksmiths were small operations. Steam created a demand for rolled iron to be used in making boilers. Using iron boilers, as the railroads and paddle-wheel river boats of the time did, was dangerous because the iron was not strong enough to contain the steam pressure and they often blew up, causing death and carnage. In addition, more than 30,000 miles of railroad track with iron rails were laid in the United States between 1830 and the beginning of the American Civil War. As a result iron mills became major enterprises, but the iron rails frequently warped because of temperature extremes, causing derailments.

Two inventions in the 1850s resulted in the rapid rise of the steel industry, which supplanted the iron industry by the end of the nineteenth century. One was the Bessemer process for making steel, developed by British engineer Henry Bessemer in 1856. The second was the Siemens-Martin open-hearth method, introduced in 1858. These processes, once perfected, greatly reduced the cost of producing steel. The first Bessemer converter in the United States was built in 1864, and the first open-hearth furnace, which was better suited to American iron ore, was built in 1868, and they both spurred steel production in the United States. By 1873 the United States was producing nearly 115,000 tons of steel rail, approximately one-eighth of all U.S. steel production. As the price of steel continued to drop, steel rails replaced iron rails. The ''iron age'' was over.

BY 1910 THE UNITED STATES WAS PRODUCING MORE THAN 24 MILLION TONS OF STEEL, BY FAR MORE THAN ANY OTHER COUNTRY. UNTIL WELL AFTER WORLD WAR II, THE STEEL INDUSTRY WOULD BE THE MEASURE OF THE NATION'S ECONOMY.

Between 1880 and 1900 U.S. steel production increased from 1.25 million tons to more than 10 million tons. The industry underwent consolidation as mill owners sought to benefit from economies of scale and to avoid what they called ''ruinous competition.'' Led by Andrew Carnegie, Henry Clay Frick, Charles Schwab, and others, the modern steel industry took shape. It was a period of violent labor disputes, most notably the Homestead strike of 1892. The companies managed to hold off unionization until the 1930s. In 1901 financiers J. Pierpont Morgan and Elbert H. Gary formed the United States Steel Corporation. With a capitalization of $1.4 billion, it was the largest industrial enterprise in the world. By 1910 the United States was producing more than 24 million tons of steel, far more than any other country. Until well after World War II (1939–1945), the steel industry would be the measure of the nation's economy.

In 1969 U.S. steel production peaked at more than 141 million tons. It was a time when international competition, led by newer and more efficient Japanese and European steel plants and by lower labor and transportation costs, began to challenge the U.S. domestic steel industry. The industry underwent a major shakeout in the early 1970s, and by 1975 U.S. steel production had fallen to 89 million tons. The industry suffered a major depression from 1982 to 1986. By 1988 production was up to more than 102 million tons, with greater efficiencies resulting in a smaller but more productive workforce. Then in 1991 it slipped to less than 90 million tons as an economic recession set in.

During the 1990s, restructuring, increased automation, new production techniques and upgraded facilities made U.S. steel-makers more productive. In the early 1990s approximately three-quarters of all U.S. steel production was accounted for by traditional integrated steel mills, which undertook every step of the steel making process, converting mixtures of iron ore, limestone, and coke (made from coal) into molten iron using a blast furnace. The molten iron was then converted into steel using basic oxygen furnaces (BOFs), after which the steel was cast into ingots and shaped. Some mills utilized a process called continuous casting that bypassed the production of ingots. The top six firms accounted for $25 billion worth of steel, or 40 percent of all shipments in 1992.

A second, fast-growing steel producer, known as ''minimills,'' accounted for one-quarter of U.S. steel production in the early 1990s. Minimills are non-integrated mills that feed scrap iron or steel into an electric arc furnace (EAF) rather than a blast or basic oxygen furnace. By 1997 minimills had the capacity to produce in excess of 50 million tons per year of carbon, alloy, and specialty steels—more than 40 percent of the total U.S. raw steelmaking capacity of 120 million annual tons. About 80 firms operated more than 100 scrap-fed electric steel plants in the U.S. in 1997. Minimills were projected to account for nearly half of all steel buyers' needs by 2000.

By the mid-1990s the U.S. steel industry was in good economic shape. From 1992 to 1998 it spent an aggregate of $50 billion to modernize its plants, and steel companies improved their financial position by reducing debt, underfunded pension plans, and other liabilities. After two strong years industry performance slackened slightly in 1996 as some plants suffered breakdowns after running at full capacity. Raw steel production during 1996 was 99.4 million tons, up from 97.1 million tons in 1995. Steel shipments rose in 1997 to 105.9 million net tons, then fell 3.5 percent in 1998 to 102.1 million tons.

Strong demand in the United States for steel in 1997 and 1998 resulted in a significant increase in imported steel of various kinds. Cheap imports from Russia, Japan, Brazil, and other countries forced the price of commodity grade steel down more than 10 percent in just a few weeks. To prevent other countries from dumping steel into the United States market, the U.S. steel industry could file antidumping petitions with the U.S. International Trade Commission, under the U.S. Department of Commerce, and the International Trade Administration. (''Dumping'' refers to the practice of one country selling commodities or finished products in another country at below cost or fair market value.)

Since 1980 the steel industry used antidumping complaints as a tool to curb imports, and in 1998 it filed complaints against Japan, Russia, and Brazil. However, the wave of imported steel, coupled with a projected slowdown in the growth rate of the U.S. economy and excess world steel producing capacity, signaled that 1999 would see a decline in the U.S. steel industry.

See also: **Bessemer Process, Andrew Carnegie**

FURTHER READING

Boselovic, Len. ''Tidal Wave of Cheap Steel Imports Sends Industry into Tailspin.'' *Knight-Ridder/Tribune News*, October 14, 1998.

Carter, Walter F. ''Steel Industry Facing Declines in '99.'' *American Metal Market*, January 20, 1999.

Hall, Christopher. *Steel Phoenix: The Fall and Rise of the U.S. Steel Industry*. New York: St. Martin's Press, 1997.

Livesay, Harold C. *Andrew Carnegie and the Rise of Big Business*. Boston: Little, Brown, 1975.

Misa, Thomas J. *A Nation of Steel: The Making of Modern America, 1865–1925*. Baltimore, MD: Johns Hopkins University Press, 1995.

Paskoff, Paul F., ed. *Iron and Steel in the Nineteenth Century*. New York: Facts on File, 1989.

STEEL PLOW

The steel plow was invented in 1837 by American John Deere (1804–1886). A blacksmith's apprentice for many years, Deere opened his own shop in Grand Decatur, Illinois, in 1836. Customers complained that their wood or iron plows proved ineffective in turning the prairie sod, which stuck to the implement's surface. Deere began tinkering with a smooth steel surface to make a plow that could successfully do the job. Using the steel from an old circular saw, he fashioned the first steel plow the next year. It worked as expected; the prairie grass fell away from the plow's smooth surface. The invention was a success and it proved to be a boon to corn farmers in the region. By the mid-1840s Deere and a business partner were manufacturing one thousand steel plows each year.

After the American Civil War (1861–1865) many farmers moved westward, encouraged by the land grants provided by the Homestead Act of 1862. Settling the Great Plains, these homesteaders created a growing demand for Deere's steel plow, the only implement capable of turning the prairie sod of the plains. By this time Deere had improved the quality of the steel he used and he had gone into business for himself, setting up John Deere and Company in 1868. The business he founded continues to manufacture steel plows and other agricultural machines, including tractors.

See also: **Agricultural Equipment Industry, John Deere, Homestead Act**

STEVENS, JOHN

John Stevens (1749–1838) was an engineer and inventor who was one of the earliest U.S. experimenters with steamboats. He built his career on promoting better transportation, not only with steamboats but also with railroads. Stevens built the first steam-powered locomotive in the United States. He firmly believed that efficient transportation on both land and water would be the main source of progress and prosperity for the country.

John Stevens was born to a wealthy family in New York in 1749. His father was a merchant and ship owner who was also politically active. Stevens was raised in Perth Amboy, New Jersey, and educated in small schools devoted to business training. He graduated from King's college (now Columbia University) in 1768 and then studied law. Three years later Stevens began working as a practicing attorney for the royal governor of New York. He soon discovered that he was more interested in politics than law and he became treasurer of New Jersey during the American Revolution (1775–1783). He rose to the rank of colonel through his fundraising efforts for the patriot cause.

In 1782 John Stevens married. Two years later the couple bought a large estate on the west side of the Hudson River, in what is now Hoboken, New Jersey. It was there that Stevens became fascinated with the idea of steam-powered transportation. Stevens bought a ferry service between Hoboken and New York and sought to improve it with steam-powered boats. He was inspired by John Fitch's steamboat, which ran along the Delaware River in 1788. At age forty Stevens taught himself the engineering science behind steam power. Soon he was able to draw his own designs for boilers and engines. Stevens then petitioned the New York legislature to grant him the exclusive privilege of steam navigation in the state, but he was unsuccessful. He was also unsuccessful in several other states, so he instead turned to his political connections in Congress and petitioned for the first federal patent laws in 1790. In August, 1791, Stevens was awarded a patent for improving steam machinery.

In 1797 Stevens joined his college friend Nicholas I. Roosevelt, and his brother-in-law Robert R. Livingston, in a partnership to build and operate steamboats. The partners disagreed over technical matters, such as the proper way to apply steam and they never built a successful boat together. In 1804 Stevens did manage to build a prototype, however, with the help of his sons. The boat, called *Little Juliana*, used a new high-pressure steam engine and two screw propellers. Meanwhile, Stevens' brother-in-law Livingston had purchased a temporary exclusive contract for steamboats on the Hudson River. Livingston believed that Stevens' boat did not meet the contract's speed requirements, so he instead convinced inventor Robert Fulton (1765–1815) to produce his five-mile-an-hour steamboat in the United States. Stevens was offended by Livingston's actions and he refused a place in the partnership of Fulton's future steamboat. In 1807 Fulton's boat, the *Clermont*, made its historical round trip voyage from New York to Albany.

Soon afterwards Stevens launched his first ocean-going, 100-foot steamboat called the *Phoenix*. In June of 1809 his son, Robert Livingston Stevens, captained the boat on its maiden voyage to Philadelphia. Because Fulton monopolized the use of the Hudson River, Stevens operated a ferry service on the Delaware River between Philadelphia and Trenton.

Stevens decided to pursue other transportation interests and around 1810 handed his steamboat interests over to his sons, who had also become capable and respected engineers. He turned his attention to adapting steam technology to the railroad, educating Congress on the advantages of the railroad over canals. Stevens succeeded in persuading Congress to pass the first U.S. railway act, which then led to the formation of companies to construct railroads, including a line from the Delaware to the Raritan River. Stevens also invented and constructed the first steam locomotive built in the United States. In 1825 he ran the experimental locomotive on a circular track on his estate in Hoboken.

Stevens dedicated his life to improving transportation and educating others about the benefits of efficient modes of transportation. He became a leader in promoting the utility of steam railroads in the United States. He also explored other transportation improvements before his death in 1838. For example, he designed a bridge and underwater tunnel from Hoboken to New York, and he also planned an elevated railroad system for New York City.

See also: **Baltimore and Ohio, Fulton, Robert, Steamboats**

FURTHER READING

Greene, Jack P., and J. R. Pole eds. *The Blackwell Encyclopedia of the American Revolution.* Malden, MA: Basil Blackwell, 1991.

Gregg, D. *Men in Business: Essays on the History of Entrepreneurship*. Cambridge, MA: Harvard University Press, 1952, s.v. ''John Stevens, General Entrepreneur, 1749–1838.''

Karwatka, Dennis. ''John Stevens: American Pioneer in Steam-Powered Transportation.'' *Tech Directions*, February, 1998.

Turnbull, Archibald Douglas. *John Stevens: An American Record*. New York: Century Co., 1928.

STOCK

Stock is a form of ownership interest in a company and a way for companies to fund their growth. A share of stock in a company represents a fraction of ownership or equity in that company's assets and growth. In exchange for giving the shareholder a piece of ownership, the shareholder takes the risk that the earnings of the company will decline, which could reduce the value of the shareholder's initial investment. The buyer of a company's stock is willing to take this risk because if the company's earnings grow rapidly the stockholder gets to share proportionately in that wealth. For example, an investor bought $1000 of stock in Digital Equipment Corporation in 1991 saw the investment fall in value to $651 by 1996. But an investor who invested $1000 in the stock of EMC Corporation in 1991 saw that investment increase to $18,700 five years later. Some investors prefer investing in bonds because bonds assure them of a specific return on their investment. No bond, however, can promise the eighteen-fold growth EMC gave its stockholders between 1991 and 1996.

There are two basic forms of stock: common and preferred. In addition to an ownership stake in the company, common stock, also called ''ordinary shares,'' entitles the shareholder to periodic payments of dividends, which are a share of the company's earnings, as well as a claim on the assets of the company if it goes bankrupt. Most common stock also gives the shareholder a right to vote on changes in the company's bylaws, on the election of corporate directors, and on any mergers with other companies. Holders of preferred stock usually do not have the same voting rights as common stockholders, but if the company goes bankrupt their share in its assets must be paid first before common stockholders receive their assets. Finally, the dividends that common stockholders are paid depend on the company's actual earnings, whereas preferred stockholders are always guaranteed a fixed dividend.

The practice of selling shares of stock arose as a way for companies to raise large amounts of capital for their projects. For example, the joint stock companies that took the financial risk of settling the New World did not need to rely only on banks or governments to raise funds—they could have raised the money they needed by selling shares to investors. Even in the late twentieth century many new companies started out as privately owned firms with a few owners and grew through bank loans or the investments of a few private investors. Many private firms reach a point in their growth where the only way to fund the massive investments they need to continue growing is by ''going public,'' that is, to sell a stake in their ownership of their company to the broad public. In 1995, 107 billion shares of stock changed hands, and by 1997 the total value of all the stock traded on the New York Stock Exchange alone was $7.6 trillion.

See also: **Bond, Capital, Investment, Joint Stock Company, Stock Market**

STOCK MARKET

Like a grocery market, a stock market is a place specifically designed to facilitate the purchase and sale of certain goods. Instead of selling food and supplies like a grocery, the stock market provides a venue for trade in companies, ventures, and other investments through the buying and selling of stocks, bonds, mutual funds, limited partnerships, and other securities. There are several regional stock exchanges throughout the United States, but the U.S. stock market is dominated by two exchanges: the New York Stock Exchange (NYSE) and the National Association of Dealers Automated Quotation (system), better known as NASDAQ-Amex. In 1996 investors could buy and sell the shares of about 3000 companies on the NYSE and some 5400 companies on the NASDAQ-Amex.

The NYSE was the first stock exchange established in the United States. It began operations on the island of Manhattan in New York, in 1792. The American Stock Exchange (Amex) started trading in the 1850s. At first the number of companies investors could buy shares in was quite small, but as the U.S.

Close up view of a ticker tape machine used to follow the stock markets.

economy exploded in the nineteenth century, businesses found it harder to fund ambitious new undertakings, like railroad construction, by relying only on their own resources or loans from banks. To raise the needed capital, companies turned to the stock market, where they sold stock (shares of which represents part ownership in the company) to the public.

THE STOCK MARKET ENTERED THE DAILY LIVES OF MILLIONS OF AMERICANS DURING THE 1920S, WHEN ECONOMIC GROWTH AND THE DESIRE TO STRIKE IT RICH QUICK DROVE STOCK PRICES TO AN ALL-TIME HIGH IN AUGUST 1929.

While individuals may invest in the stock market for a variety reasons, one of the primary motivators is to make a higher return on their money than may be available through a traditional, conservative bank savings account. The stock market, however, has more risk attached to it than does money in the bank. For instance, if a new telecommunications company offers its stock for sale on the market and performance outlooks for this company are promising, investors may rush to buy the stock, its value will go up, and the company will raise lots of capital. If, however, by the end of the year, the company has posted poor earnings and the performance outlook has turned sour, the same investors who rushed to buy stock in the company may now rush to sell, causing the value of the stock to drop.

The stock market entered the daily lives of millions of Americans during the 1920s, when economic growth and the desire to strike it rich quick drove stock prices to an all-time high in August 1929. Stock prices, however, were not in line with companies' actual earnings, and many people bought shares only through heavy borrowing, so at the first signs of uncertainty in the market in September 1929, the market collapsed, hitting rock bottom in July 1932. In the 1930s, the government took steps to reform the stock market and established the Securities and Exchange Commission to regulate stock trading. The 1950s and 1960s were periods of great growth in the number of companies selling shares on the stock market and in the number of investors buying stocks. In 1971 the NASDAQ was formed to provide a stock market for ''over-the-counter'' stocks, i.e., stocks not listed on the regular stock exchanges. One of the greatest bull markets in stock market history began in 1982, and 16 years later the NASDAQ and Amex merged to compete more effectively with the NYSE.

Trying to cover his Wall Street loses, this man attempts to sell his roadster on the streets of New York for $100 cash.

See also: **Bond, Capital, Investment, Stock, Stock Market Crash of 1929**

STOCK MARKET CRASH OF 1929

During the 1920s increasing numbers of Americans became interested in Wall Street and in buying stocks. A prospective buyer did not have to pay the full price of a stock in order to buy. Instead the practice of ''buying on margin'' allowed a person to acquire stock by expending in cash as little as ten percent of the price of a stock. The balance was covered by a loan from a broker, who was advanced the money by his bank, which, in turn, accepted the stock as collateral for the loan. Credit was easy, and the Federal Reserve System did little to restrict the availability of money for stock investment.

But mindful of the run of the bull market and the practice of buying on margin, pessimists kept insisting that all was not right with the speculative boom. Many newcomers to the market failed to realize that a stock certificate was only a piece of paper, and that its primary worth was essentially connected with the prosperity of the company that issued it. A strange and frightening fact was becoming apparent to some observers—the increase in the market value of most stocks often had little relationship to the profits or prospects of the issuing companies. The stock itself had taken on a life of its own, based on the circumstance that people were bidding for these equities (stocks) at ever-rising prices. Stock prices represented not corporate profit, but speculative buying of stock certificates.

In September 1929 confidence in the market's ability to continue its upward spiral began to weaken. Stock prices turned lower. Apparently investors were turning from ''bulls'' to ''bears'' in increasing numbers and were selling short. As the market was crowded with inexperienced but feverishly eager investors who lacked capital reserves, the falling prices produced a shock effect. For the small investor who had all of his/her money tied up in stocks, it became imperative to sell fast before the prices dropped lower. Since many people were in this situation, orders to sell flooded the market until the ticker tape could not keep pace with Exchange transactions. Chaos reigned as the figures listed on the "big board" became increasingly out of line with actual selling prices. Ignorance was an additional element in the panic.

To stem the crisis, a group of leading New York bankers decided to act. Meeting in the office of Thomas W. Lamont, a partner in J.P. Morgan and Company, the bankers pooled their resources and bought stock above the current market levels. Their purchases might be insignificant, but they reasoned that the well-known personalities involved might serve to restore the confidence of the small investor. Accordingly, on Thursday, October 24, 1929, Richard Whitney, vice-president of the New York Stock Exchange and broker for the House of Morgan, entered the market and attempted to stem the tide. Amazingly the tactic worked, but only temporarily—on the following Tuesday, October 29, 1929, the bottom fell out of the market. Within two weeks the value of stocks on the exchange had declined some 37.50 percent, and by early 1932, stocks were worth only 20 percent of their value at the 1929 peak.

As the debacle on Wall Street continued, the average New Yorker could still speak with scorn of the "numbers game." After all, the economy of the United States was apparently still in good shape. The railroads, the steel mills, communications facilities, and large segments of the citizenry stood untouched by the panic. Professor Irving Fisher of Yale University reassured the nation about the general state of the economy. The average citizen had little awareness that the figures on the "big board" at the New York Stock Exchange were indicative of forces which would have an impact upon how the majority of Americans lived or acted. They were soon made painfully aware of the situation. The Stock Market Crash of 1929 developed into the long-lasting Great Depression (1929–1939) and affected every aspect of American life.

See also: **Bear and Bull Markets, Great Depression, Great Depression (Causes of), Investment, New York Stock Exchange, Stock, Stock Market, Wall Street**

FURTHER READING

Galbraith, John Kenneth. *The Great Crash, 1929.* Boston, MA: Houghton Mifflin Co., 1954.

Hicks, John D. *Republican Ascendancy, 1921–1933.* New York: Harper and Row Publishers, 1960.

Leuchtenburg, William E. *The Perils of Prosperity, 1914–1932.* Chicago: University of Chicago Press, 1958.

Mitchell, Broadus. *Depression Decade, 1929–1941.* New York: Holt, Rinehart and Winston, Inc., 1947.

Robbins, Lionel. *The Great Depression.* New York: The Macmillan Company, 1934.

STREETCARS

Streetcars, also called trolleys, are power-driven vehicles that run on tracks through city streets. Prior to their invention, public or for-hire vehicles ran through urban areas: drawn by teams of horses or mules, the "horse railway" was of limited use, however, allowing only a few riders at a time. This method of transport was in use in eastern cities such as New York, Philadelphia, and Boston since the 1830s. It was substantially improved in 1852 when a grooved rail was developed, allowing the tracks to lay flush with the pavement. This improvement increased speed and capacity, and decreased interference with coach and wagon traffic. By the mid-1880s, more than four hundred horse-car companies operated in the United States, covering some six thousand miles of urban tracks and carrying close to 200 million passengers a year.

In 1871 American engineer and inventor Andrew Smith Hallidie (1836–1900) patented a street railway system, run by constantly moving underground cables or ropes, to which the cars were clamped. (The cables were powered by steam engines.) Hallidie's cable car system was introduced in San Francisco in 1874: the cars, which ably managed the city's hilly terrain, were a success. Soon other American cities, including Philadelphia, New York, and Chicago, installed cable cars. Chicago soon boasted the most extensive cable system in the world: By 1894, more than 1,500 cars operated on eighty-six miles of track. Cable car transportation peaked in the United States in 1890, when systems in twenty-three cities carried a total of 373 million passengers that year.

In the mid-1880s, the electric streetcar or trolley was invented in the United States by American engineer and inventor Frank Julian Sprague (1857–1934). An overhead electric wire provided the power and was capable of moving several cars at once. The cars

In 1893, just six years after the system's successful debut in Richmond, Virginia, there were more than 250 electric streetcar railways in the nation, operating on some 7,200 miles of track. By 1903 this number had climbed to more than 29,000 miles and represented 98 percent of the nation's urban rails.

resembled railroad cars and could travel as fast as twenty miles per hour. They ran along street tracks—just like the cable cars—but the trolleys were cleaner and cheaper to operate than either cable cars or horse drawn railcars. They reduced the average fare by as much as half (from ten cents to a nickel). The new technology was embraced at an impressive rate, making the electric streetcar one of the most widely accepted innovations in the history of technology (according to Kenneth T. Jackson, author of *Crabgrass Frontier: The Suburbanization of the United States*). In 1893, just six years after the system's successful debut in Richmond, Virginia, there were more than 250 electric streetcar railways in the nation, operating on some 7,200 miles of track. By 1903 this number had climbed to more than 29,000 miles and represented 98 percent of the nation's urban rails. Except for San Francisco, where the cable cars remained a nostalgic link to the city's past, cable cars had been replaced with the electric streetcar.

As city streets became congested, large urban centers undertook expensive public works projects to build elevated tracks to run ''els'' (elevated streetcars) or to dig tunnels to run subways. Boston opened the first American subway in 1897; New York's first subway line opened in 1904.

The advent of mass transit in the form of streetcars and subways had far-reaching effects: Cities were no longer defined by walking distances and began to expand outward. In many urban areas, including Chicago, streetcar lines were laid well beyond existing city boundaries. Outlying areas were quickly developed into residential neighborhoods. The country's burgeoning middle class, which could afford the typical streetcar or subway fare, was drawn to life in these quiet, tree-lined outskirts—far from the congestion of the inner city, which became increasingly devoted to business. Real estate development flourished, and a house in the suburbs became the goal for many working class families who remained, by necessity, in the cities. The trolley system, els, and subways had given rise to a population of commuters and began a cycle of urban sprawl that continued throughout the twentieth century. By the middle of the century, however, the automobile had largely overtaken public transportation. Between 1945 and 1981, 75 percent of government transportation dollars were allocated to building the nation's highways and a mere 1 percent was dedicated to public systems such as buses, trolleys, and subways.

STRIKE

A strike is a concentrated effort by a group of workers, to withhold their labor from their employer, for the purpose of creating favorable changes in wages, benefits, or working condition, or for winning employer recognition of labor union representation. There are different forms of strikes. A primary strike is a work stoppage aimed at an employer, directly. A sympathy strike is one where employees refuse to work in sympathy with others who are directly involved in a dispute. A sit-down strike happens when workers stop work and refuse to leave the employer's premises in order to prevent the hiring of replacements. A wildcat strike is one that occurs spontaneously, without formal union authorization. A general strike is an effort to stimulate a general work stoppage and has political overtones. All of these strikes have been common in the United States, with the possible exception of the general strike; a technique most often practiced in Europe, and Third World countries.

Strikes began to occur with some regularity in the United States in the nineteenth century and were regarded as illegal because they restrained trade. Any kind of strike is a test of economic strength and will. A union tries to prevent business operations and cause a loss of profits to the employer, in order to force changes. The employer tries to maintain profitability and maintain operations hoping pressures from loss of pay rise enough to force workers to return to work. During a strike the striking employees, often represented by a union, will attempt to prevent the employer form operations by picketing the employer's facilities. Picketing is the walking back and forth outside of the employer's premises by union members on strike, carrying picket signs with short statements on them relating to the issues of the strike. Picketing becomes a

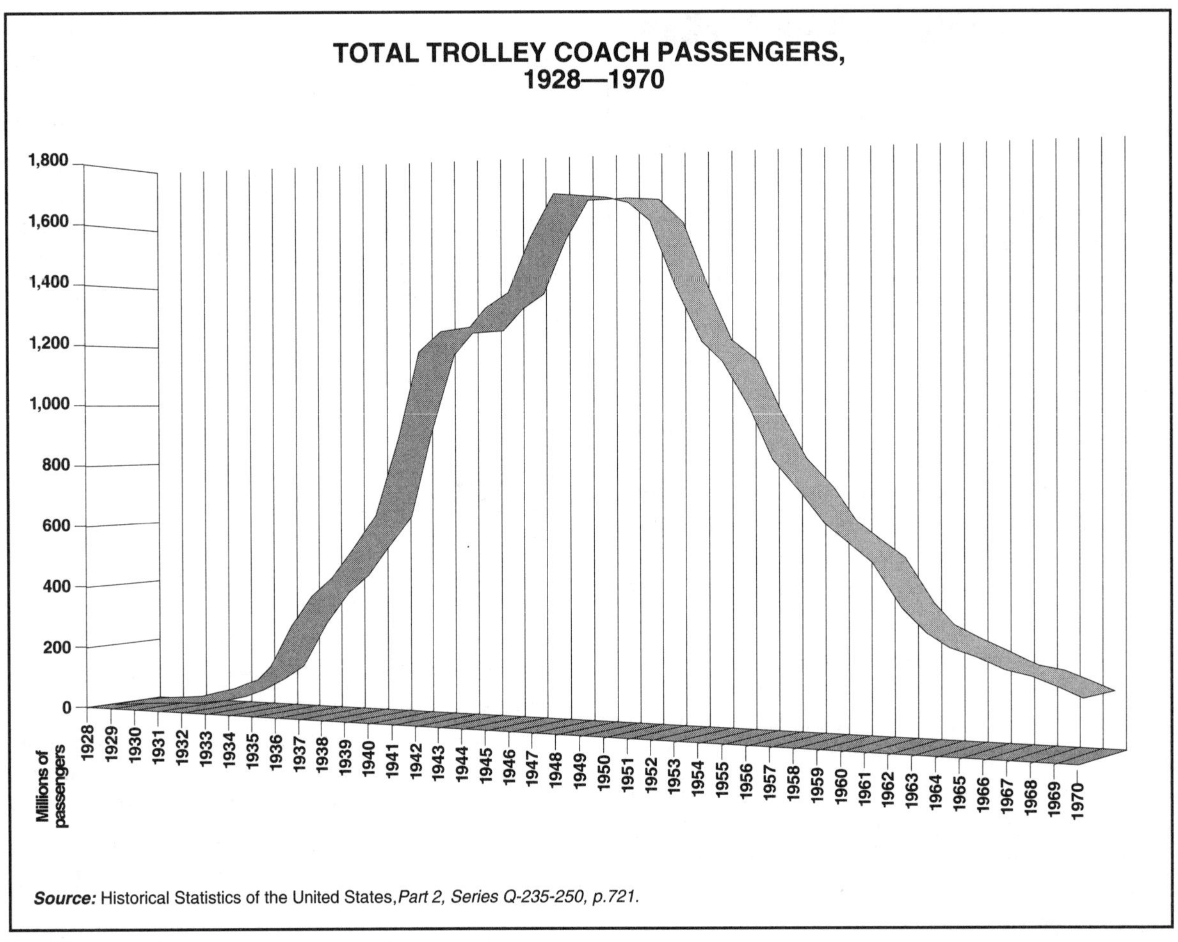

The rise and fall of passengers on trolley coaches is indicative of the effect of suburban growth upon mass transit systems.

public announcement of the existence of a labor dispute. It also serves the purpose of giving notice to other workers and the public, asking them in effect not to cross the picket line. While on strike workers generally receive "strike benefits" from their union, a small money stipend to help them with necessary expenses while remaining committed to continuing the strike until a settlement is reached. During the 1990s there were roughly 3000 to 5000 strikes per year, most of them a result of unsuccessful contract negotiations.

See also: **Collective Bargaining, Labor Unionism, Sit-Down Strike**

STRUCTURAL UNEMPLOYMENT

Structural unemployment is a type of unemployment that occurs to workers who are displaced by a change in marketplace needs. When the computer industry began its rapid rise, many workers were caught at a disadvantage. They did not learn the skills or did not already have them coming into the job market, which now demanded computer know-how. Unless these individuals learned the necessary new skills, they faced the possibility of structural unemployment.

Another instance where structural unemployment occurs concerns geography. During the 1970s, the automobile industry, concentrated in the Midwest, experienced a downturn. As a result, many in the auto labor force became unemployed. At the same time, the oil industry in Texas was experiencing a boom. Many workers unemployed in the Midwest and who also possessed skills that would benefit them in Texas chose to move West to take advantage of the economic opportunities available there.

The disparity between skills and/or labor may also be called mistmatch unemployment. Workers who are only familiar with word processing can not fill job vacancies for computer programmers. Technology and competition can also play a role in structural unemployment. The U.S. steel industry, which established itself during the nineteenth century, is at a disadvantage competing with the steel manufacturers in less developed nations, who benefit from the more recent development of their industry through the use of the latest technology.

Time spent learning the new skills demanded by the current job market can be consuming and, in addition, not all individuals are willing to pursue a job search in a new location. Thus, structural unemployment can be enduring.

See also: **Seasonal Unemployment, Unemployment**

STUDEBAKER

The Studebaker Corporation traced its business origins earlier than any other U.S. automobile manufacturer. It started in 1852 as a family operated blacksmith shop in South Bend, Indiana, and began manufacturing wagons five years later. During the American Civil War (1861–65) government contracts for wagons brought the firm new prosperity. In March 1868 brothers John, Clement, and Peter Studebaker each invested $25,000 and incorporated as the Studebaker Brothers Manufacturing Company.

In the highly competitive wagon industry, Studebaker became the world's largest manufacturer. With good management, technological innovation, and capital expansion, it pursued a strategy of large scale manufacturing of high quality products known for durability and beauty. Through a well-coordinated distribution system, its national marketing captured the dominant share of the large farm wagon market and a profitable share of the urban wagon and carriage markets. By 1870 it also became the government's largest supplier of wagons.

Studebaker became a modern corporation in 1893 through the efforts of John Studebaker's son-in-law, Frederick Fish, a Wall Street lawyer. The reorganization shifted power from the family to investors represented on a newly created board of directors. With additional capital and new leadership, the firm made a decisive change in its product line. Overcoming resistance from the surviving Studebaker brothers, Fish pushed the company into the new automobile industry. Studebaker started cautiously in 1897 by making bodies for the New York Electric Vehicle Company, and three years later it began manufacturing its own automobiles. Although Studebaker continued making carriages until 1910 and wagons until 1918, it was firmly committed to the automotive industry when the corporation reorganized again in 1911.

Under the leadership of president Albert Russell Erskine from 1915 to 1933, Studebaker attempted to become one of the dominant automobile manufacturers. Concentrating on producing trucks and cars for the competitive medium-priced market, it enjoyed its golden years immediately after World War I (1914–18), and it stood behind only the Ford Motor Company and General Motors in total assets. In 1924, however, it failed to buy out the Maxwell Motor Corporation, losing to Walter P. Chrysler, who then succeeded in building his own big, multi-model firm. Thereafter Studebaker remained one of the so-called ''Independents,'' relatively small automakers, in an industry dominated by the Big Three—General Motors, Ford Motor Company, and Chrysler Motors—all based in Detroit.

By March 1933 Studebaker was unable to pay its creditors because of president Erskine's high dividend policies despite an automobile market that was shrunken by the Great Depression (1929–39). Studebaker might have disappeared then, as many other Independents did during the Depression, however, it survived a court ordered bankruptcy and reorganized again in 1935 under the leadership of two former vice presidents. With president Paul G. Hoffman concentrating on sales and public relations and chairman Harold Vance concentrating on production, Studebaker recovered. From its headquarters still in South Bend, the firm produced cars (including the new low-priced Champion) with innovative engineering and design that distinguished them from Detroit products. By 1940 the firm was the largest of the Independents, with a market share of almost 2.5 percent. The national economy recovered from the Depression and the future looked bright.

World War II (1939–45) then significantly altered the automobile industry. When all civilian automobile production ceased by government order, automakers operated as defense contractors. Studebaker manufactured trucks and other products under government contracts that guaranteed profits without competitive pressures to control production costs.

After the war high consumer demand for new cars allowed all the Independent automakers to increase their market shares and total volume. Hoffman and Vance expressed optimism because Studebaker's distinctively designed cars attracted wide attention and increased sales. Studebaker reached its peak of prosperity in 1950, with record sales that brought it a four-percent market share. However in its rush to take

1947 Studebaker Champion Coupe.

advantage of the strong postwar market, the firm failed to modernize its plants, reduce high production costs, or correct worsening product quality. After the Korean War (1950–53) the loss of defense contracts and fierce competition between General Motors and Ford for industry leadership put all the Independent automakers at greater risk. Hoffman and Vance recognized that Studebaker was too small to survive alone and in 1954 they arranged a merger with the Packard Motor Company of Detroit.

Under the leadership of James J. Nance, formerly Packard's president, the new Studebaker Packard Corporation tried to imitate the Big Three. But Nance's efforts to cut production costs and improve quality led to labor strife in South Bend. Similarly, his efforts to imitate Detroit automakers' products failed to increase the company's declining sales. With losses mounting, Studebaker Packard survived only by merging in 1956 with Curtiss-Wright, the aeronautical firm. During the late 1950s it recovered somewhat by introducing a compact economy car, but the Big Three soon captured that market as well. In 1962 Studebaker made its last effort to find a niche in the automobile industry by launching the Avanti, a distinctive, streamlined sports type car with an all fiberglass body. However, small volume production of that car could not sustain the automaker. In December 1963 the South Bend plant closed, although car production continued on a reduced scale in Hamilton, Ontario, Canada until the fall of 1967. Then, the combination of its small size, inability to keep pace with competition, and managerial errors over a long period finally ended Studebaker's role as an automaker.

Nevertheless, the close of its automotive history did not mean the end of Studebaker. As it scaled down its automobile production during the early 1960s, it pursued a survival strategy of diversification. In November 1967 it arranged a new merger that created the Studebaker-Worthington Corporation. Producing a wide variety of products, some for the automotive industry, it operated for twelve years until it was absorbed by McGraw-Edison.

See also: **Automobile Industry**

FURTHER READING

Beatty, Michael, Patrick Furlong, and Loren Pennington. *Studebaker: Less Than They Promised.* South Bend, IN: And Books, 1984.

Critchlow, Donald T. *Studebaker: The Life and Death of an American Corporation.* Bloomington: Indiana University Press, 1996.

Langworth, Richard M. *Studebaker 1946–66: The Classic Postwar Years.* Osceola, WI: Motorbooks International, 1993.

Raucher, Alan R. *Paul G. Hoffman: Architect of Foreign Aid.* Lexington, KY: The University Press of Kentucky, 1985.

———. "Paul G. Hoffman, Studebaker, and the Car Culture," *Indiana Magazine of History*, 79, 1983.

SUBSIDIES

A subsidy is a government payment to individuals, businesses, other governments, and other domestic institutions and organizations. Unlike government purchases, for which the government receives goods or services, subsidies do not provide the government with any goods or services in return. The purpose of government subsidies is to ensure the availability of necessary goods and services.

A wide range of domestic businesses, individuals, and other organizations in the United States are eligible for government subsidies. A complete listing of all federal subsidies can be found in the government publication, *Catalog of Federal Domestic Assistance.* Among the areas receiving government subsidies are agriculture, maritime industries, and mass transportation.

SUBSISTENCE AGRICULTURE

Subsistence agriculture is a system of farming that provided the amount of crops the farmer needed to feed his family, with very little surplus to sell. During settlement of what became the United States, European immigrants were interested in securing land titles or renting lands so they could establish their families and begin to farm. Because shipment of produce was costly and time-consuming, only farmers near ports grew crops that would be sold for cash.

While southern plantations yielded bumper crops and grew richer on their exports, the typical settler of colonial times could afford neither vast land holdings nor slaves. The vast majority of farmers worked their own fields with the help of their families. They supplemented their harvest by raising a few heads of livestock and by hunting and fishing. In this way the early life of the settlers was not very much different from the lifestyle of the American Indians who had settled the land before them.

SUBURBS, RISE OF

The growth of U.S. cities in the nineteenth century was integrally linked with expanding industrialization and economic development. This process of urbanization led to the formation of a "classic" pattern for U.S. cities by the 1930s. Commercial centers that included banking districts and retail establishments were located in downtown areas. Enclaves of working-class neighborhoods were often distinguished by a predominance of ethnic or minority populations circling the downtown. There were industrial and manufacturing pockets, and a growing white middle class concentrated in residential developments toward the ever-expanding city boundaries. Bus and trolley lines radiated outward from the city center to provide a transportation network. The city was a socioeconomic mosaic.

Immediately following World War II (1939–1945), urbanization quickly transitioned into suburbanization. Suburbs are largely independent communities located in close proximity to large central cities. Many suburbs have their own local governments with mayors or city managers and police departments; county governments govern others. Federal investment in economic development immediately following the war included low-cost mortgages for veterans and highway construction programs. Reorganization of American life resulted. The average white middle class family moved to newly created communities on less expensive land outside the city boundaries. Suburbs offered yards, lower density single-family housing, less noise and air pollution, and relief from declining city neighborhoods with their escalating social ills. Millions of farmland acres were converted into bedroom communities. The exodus left cities with declining property values, significant loss of tax revenue, and diminished political and social importance.

Just as urban areas were experiencing a new wave of Southern African Americans migrating to cities in search of employment, white taxpayers, jobs, and capital were migrating in mass to the suburbs, leaving the cramped ghettos and industrial areas behind. Suburbs replaced cities as the place of upward class mobility and economic prosperity. In contrast to urban social mosaics of the early twentieth century city, suburbanites most valued racial, religious, and social class homogeneity. The African American middle class and other minorities ran into social barriers in this resettlement movement, spawned by racism.

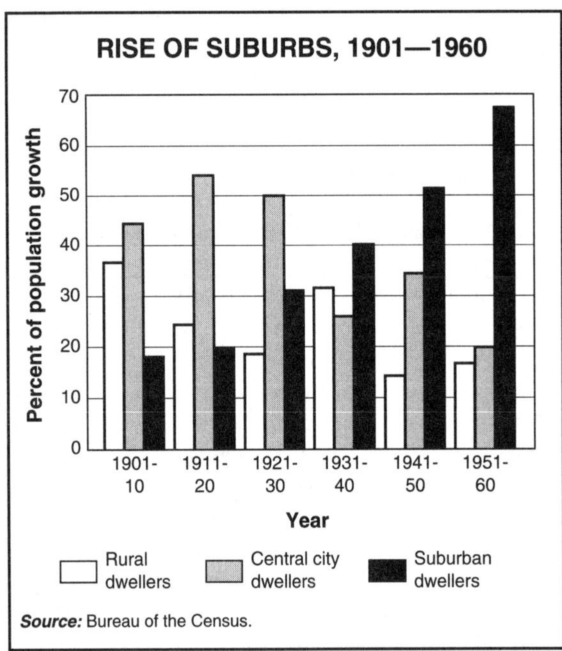

The shifting of the population from rural and city dwellers to the suburban areas began to shift in 1907, and by 1960 the majority of Americans were suburbanites.

By the late twentieth century the United States had fully transitioned from the urbanization of a century earlier to a suburbanized nation. By the 1960s urban factories, office complexes, and shopping centers had followed the population. Telecommunications developments in the 1980s further stimulated suburban growth. Businesses enjoyed more flexibility, locating in desirable settings as suburban business complexes increasingly linked to international economic markets. Suburbs developed their own economic bases independent of the earlier central-city business districts. Suburban ''downtowns,'' known as edge cities, developed on the fringes of metropolitan areas by the mid-1980s. New regional shopping malls replaced city center retail areas and neighborhood shopping centers. By the mid-1980s more Americans lived in suburbs than in central cities.

With the original inner cities in continuing socioeconomic crisis, efforts by cities to annex suburbs were normally resisted by suburban residents wishing to maintain their governmental independence. Planners also explored options of consolidating regional metropolitan tax bases and redistributing suburban revenues. Regional governments advocated ''fair share'' policies in proposing to locate industrial areas and low-income housing in suburban areas, rather than concentrating them in inner cities.

Suburban sprawl became a key issue with the proliferation and growth of suburbs. New suburbs ringed earlier ones. The rise of suburbia lead to the formation of metropolitan areas with the central city at their core. By the late 1980s about 75 percent of the U.S. population lived in metropolitan areas. Planners predicted the coming of the megalopolis representing the consolidation of multiple metropolitan areas spatially merging together.

As sprawl continued in the 1990s, the inner suburbs faced the same socioeconomic problems as the cities, including declining property values. In an endless cycle, lower values prompted higher property taxes, which forced more movement out to newer suburbs. With suburban residents frustrated over traffic congestion and sprawling commercial development, the growth of suburban populations began to slow in the 1980s. Rising gasoline prices and urban renewal attracted some back to the city. Urbanization of the suburbs was occurring, and urban renewal was becoming suburban renewal. Ever-expanding suburbs faced the same issues encountered earlier by cities. Revenue to provide water, sewer lines, fire protection, road maintenance, police, and new schools for the fast growing suburbs became issues as the cost of government services proved to be higher for low-density tract development.

Through the later decades of the twentieth century, areas of land development increased substantially faster than population growth. Regional governments in some areas adopted urban growth boundaries in an attempt to control the rapid loss of surrounding rural lands. Many attributed metropolitan air pollution problems to urban sprawl, low density housing patterns, and greater dependency on automobiles. The number of automobiles had grown several times faster during this time period than had the actual population. In total, the rise of suburbs in the late twentieth century was one of the more profound socioeconomic transformations in U.S. history.

See also: **Industrialization, Urban Renewal, Urbanization**

FURTHER READING

Angotti, Thomas. *Metropolis 2000: Planning, Poverty, and Politics*. New York: Routledge, 1993.

Dobriner, William M., ed. *The Suburban Community*. New York: Putnam, 1958.

Orfield, Myron. *Metropolitics: A Regional Agenda for Community and Stability*. Washington, DC: Brookings Institution Press, 1996.

Rusk, David. *Cities Without Suburbs*. Baltimore, MD: The Johns Hopkins University Press, 1993.

Whitehand, J.W.R. *The Making of the Urban Landscape*. Cambridge, MA: Blackwell, 1992.

SUGAR

Sugar is a crystallized material nutritionally important as a source of dietary carbohydrates and it can also be used as a sweetener and a preservative. It is predominately derived from sugarcane and sugar beets. Other sources are sorghum (a tropical grass), maple trees, and palms. Sugarcane was cultivated by South Pacific island natives as early as 6000 B.C.. During ancient times it was also grown in India, where it was noticed around 325 B.C. by Greek soldiers under the command of Alexander the Great (356–323 B.C.). While cultivation and refinement of sugarcane spread from India, it did not reach Europe until A.D. 711, when Moors (North African Muslims) invaded the Iberian Peninsula (present-day Spain and Portugal). In the 1490s Portuguese explorers carried sugarcane with them into the New World and planted it in Brazil. The Spanish colonists planted sugarcane in the Canary Islands at about the same time. Spanish explorer Christopher Columbus (1451–1506) took sugarcane cuttings to the island of Santo Domingo (present-day Dominican Republic) in 1493. About twenty years later the first sugar mill in the Western Hemisphere was built there. The Dutch introduced sugarcane cultivation and refining to Barbados. The French introduced it to Martinique; the British introduced it to the West Indies.

The crop became important to colonial economies throughout the Caribbean, where the Europeans used slave labor from Africa to work the fields. Sugar was the principle export of the region during the 1600s, but by the end of the century the economies of many Caribbean islands collapsed. Slaves were sold to growers on the North American mainland, where they were engaged in the production of other crops (such as rice, indigo, and tobacco). The sugarcane plant did not reach the North American mainland until 1751, when Jesuit (Catholic) missionaries brought sugarcane to Louisiana. A sugar mill was built there forty years later.

The cultivation of sugar beets dates back to ancient Babylonia (present-day Iraq), Egypt, and Greece. However, only as late as 1744 it was discovered that sugar beets are a source of the same sugar found in sugarcane. It was fifty years more before a practical method for removing the sugar from the beets was developed. In the early 1800s sugar mills were built across Europe and Russia. Sugar from beets was not introduced in the United States until 1838.

See also: **American Plants, Triangular Trade**

SUGAR ACT (1764)

The Sugar Act of 1764 was passed by the Parliament of Great Britain, in part, to cut down on smuggling between the West Indies and the American colonies and also to tighten England's grip on its empire. But mostly the Act was approved to raise money to pay England's national debt caused by the French and Indian War (1754–1763). It was for that reason that the law was also known as the Revenue Act. The Act had three major parts. First, the measure created a complicated system of loading and unloading cargo for merchant ships in order to make smuggling more difficult. Second, the Act made certain foreign goods (including sugar, coffee, indigo dye, and wines) more expensive in the colonies because the tax would boost the retail price. Third, it cut the importation duties on molasses in half, in an attempt to make the tax easier to collect.

FOR IF OUR TRADE MAY BE TAXED, WHY NOT OUR LANDS? WHY NOT THE PRODUCE OF OUR LANDS AND, IN SHORT, EVERYTHING WE POSSESS OR MAKE USE OF?

Samuel Adams, Boston town meeting, May 24, 1764

Parliament's motivation in passing the Sugar Act was to correct an earlier, failing piece of legislation. The 1733 Molasses Act tried to discourage colonists from buying molasses from French and Dutch West Indian planters by placing a high duty of sixpence per gallon on it. New England merchants, traders, and their agents had developed a thriving trade in rum, a popular alcoholic drink, which they distilled from molasses. They shipped the rum to ports in West Africa, where they exchanged it for African slaves. The same traders then carried the slaves to plantations in the Caribbean, where they were exchanged for molasses—the so-called ''Triangular Trade.'' Because the New England rum distilleries were generating so much business, colonial traders were scouring the West Indies for molasses; they often found French or Dutch molasses cheaper than that from British plantations. Parliamentary representatives believed that the steep tax on foreign molasses would help British sugar producers. (However, it could instead have ruined the New England rum industry had it been collected as planned.) In most cases, customs officials preferred not to collect the tax and allowed the colonial traders to import molasses from whatever areas they chose.

George Grenville, the author of the Sugar Act, wanted to use the estimated £40,000 per year he expected the tax to generate to help pay the costs of keeping 10,000 British soldiers on the American frontier. He did not anticipate the strong resistance he encountered from the colonists. They had never been expected to pay these kinds of taxes to this extent before, and they protested loudly. Bostonian Samuel Adams used the crisis to try to unite the merchants of the cities with the small farmers of the countryside. Lawyer James Otis Jr., in a pamphlet titled *Rights of the Colonies Asserted and Proved*, argued that Great Britain had no right to tax the colonists at all. Even solid Tories like Governor Francis Bernard protested the three pence tax, claiming that it would be difficult to collect and, if collected, would ruin colonial businesses. Similar protests were lodged in New York and Rhode Island. For the most part, however, complaints were limited to small special interest groups throughout the colonies. The Sugar Act was not the issue that would galvanize the colonists and turn them toward independence. It was an irritant in the relationship between the colonial officials of Great Britain and the colonists, but nowhere near as volatile an issue as the Stamp Act turned out to be a year later.

See also: **French and Indian War, Triangular Trade**

FURTHER READING

Barrow, Thomas C. *Trade and Empire: The British Customs Service in America, 1660–1775*. Cambridge, MA: Harvard University Press, 1967.

Becker, Robert A. *Revolution, Reform, and the Politics of American Taxation, 1763–1783*. Baton Rouge, LA: Louisiana State University Press, 1980.

Egnal, Marc M. *A Mighty Empire: The Origins of the American Revolution*. Ithaca, NY: Cornell University Press, 1988.

Ubbelohde, Carl. *The Vice-Admiralty Courts and the American Revolution*. Chapel Hill, NC: University of North Carolina Press for the Institute of Early American History and Culture (Williamsburg, VA), 1960.

Wells, William V. *The Life and Public Services of Samuel Adams*. Boston: Little, Brown, 1865.

SULLIVAN, LOUIS HENRY

Louis Henry Sullivan (1856–1924) inspired design and construction ideas for the most significant twentieth century American buildings, and for that he was called the ''Father of Modern Architecture.'' He was the inventor, and often the builder, of the uniquely American ''skyscraper,'' the tall buildings that created the great skylines of U.S. cities like New York and Chicago. His philosophy of building was also his philosophy of art. Sullivan designed the model for workplaces used by many modern businesses. He created the tall, densely-built downtown areas of the twentieth century U.S. metropolis; he created the visual reality of a kind of architecture in which design form followed the demands of functionality.

Louis Sullivan was born in Boston, Massachusetts, in September 1856, the only child of Patrick and Adrienne Sullivan. His father prospered in Boston as the owner/teacher of a music and dance academy. One of Sullivan's biographers suggested that at a young age Sullivan learned from his father the importance of gracefulness and symmetry, qualities that would later influence his thinking about architectural forms.

Sullivan attended public schools in Boston. In his autobiography, he praised a high school teacher, Moses Woolson, whom he greatly admired, saying that the instructor had instilled in him ''good methods of thinking, studying, and good work habits.'' Sullivan claimed to have relied upon such principles throughout his life.

At age 16 Sullivan passed the entrance examination at Massachusetts Institute of Technology (MIT) and entered the school in 1872. He studied architecture under the guidance of William Robert Ware. Sullivan was dissatisfied with MIT, however, and left after just one year. He cited his dislike of the school's strict focus on classical and academic architecture.

After leaving school Sullivan traveled throughout the country, briefly joining his parents in Chicago, Illinois. In the aftermath of the Chicago Fire of 1873, Sullivan saw the possibility of rebuilding the city with a modern and uniquely American vision. To learn his craft he left for Paris, France, to study at one of the great schools of architecture, the Ecole des Beaux Arts.

Sullivan studied long and hard in Paris, but the 18-hour days he spent studying were mentally exhausting. While in Europe, Sullivan also spent time traveling, specifically in Italy, where he saw first-hand the best of European architecture.

Returning to Chicago after just a year in Europe, Sullivan worked in an architect's office as a draftsman and soon developed a reputation for quick and skillful design. He rose in the ranks of Chicago's architects and displayed his great enthusiasm for building new kinds of American-style buildings in Chicago.

Sullivan's true architectural career started in 1880, when he began designing his own buildings to help rebuild Chicago. He started by concentrating on modern engineering techniques and advancements. His buildings were elegant and simple looking, with a focus on great height and safety. He also sought to accommodate the needs of twentieth century businessmen by creating buildings with highly concentrated office space.

Sullivan was a pioneer in designing the steel-framed skyscraper, which allowed him to create tall, structurally stable buildings. Through such building projects, Sullivan was able to articulate his main architectural idea: "form follows function." He voiced this in his 1924 autobiographical vision of architecture, *The Autobiography of an Idea.*

Sullivan worked hard to eliminate all traces of Greek and Roman architectural patchwork previously attached to the design of most American buildings. He was perhaps the first architect in the United States to develop a unique American style of architecture.

As Sullivan's architecture grew legendary, his personal life began splintering, and he devolved into an emotionally disturbed person. His behavior became erratic, he sought isolation, and at age 45, ill health forced him to work on only a series of small buildings and banks. Yet he continued as an architect, sharing his trade with others in the field. Most of Sullivan's innovative ideas were carried forth by his student, and later friend, Frank Lloyd Wright (1869–1959), whose own brilliant work would add new dimensions to architecture.

Though Sullivan's work had thoroughly penetrated the currents of modern twentieth century architecture, he died destitute and nearly alone. Frank Lloyd Wright visited his friend Louis Sullivan just three days before Sullivan's death, at the age of 68, in 1924.

The development of large, busy, complex urban centers of the early twentieth century was made possible by Sullivan's unique engineering innovations. His structures—safe yet often hundreds of floors high—combined functionality with beauty. Sullivan's impact on several major U.S. cities influenced much of the architectural design in the decades that followed.

See also: **Frank Lloyd Wright**

FURTHER READING

Kaufman, Mervyn. *Father of Skyscrapers: A Biography of Louis Sullivan.* Boston: Little, Brown and Co., 1969.

Menocal, Narciso. *Architecture as Nature, the Transcendental Idea of Louis Sullivan.* Madison: University of Wisconsin Press, 1981.

Paul, Sherman. *Louis Sullivan, an Architect in American Thought.* Englewood Cliffs, NJ: Prentice-Hall, 1962.

Sullivan, Louis. *The Autobiography of an Idea.* New York: Dover Publishing, Inc., 1956.

Wright, Frank Lloyd. *Genius and the Mobocracy.* New York: Duell, Sloan, and Pearce, 1949.

SUN BELT

The "Sun Belt" region of the United States comprises fifteen southern states, extending from Virginia to Florida in the Southeast, and westward through Nevada, including southern California. Because of the expansion of inexpensive residential retirement communities, the Sun Belt region has seen a 93 percent overall growth of population between 1970 and 1990, well above the national average. To many people in the United States, the Sun Belt offers inexpensive living, year-round recreational activities, mild climates, and an inexpensive non-union labor pool for the creation of new business enterprises. A large migration of people to the Sun Belt, as well as a high birth rate and a decline of migration from the region have all contributed to the rapid growth of the Sun Belt's population and manufacturing activities. Overall improvements in transportation, communications, living conditions, and services have all made the Sun Belt an attractive area for retirees, workers, and business.

SUPPLY AND DEMAND

"Supply and demand" refers to the idea that the price of a product is dependent on the amount of that product available to sell (the supply) and the desirability of the product to consumers (the demand). Sellers want high prices and buyers want low prices, and the strength of these conflicting desires will determine the price. In economic terms, supply refers to a schedule of quantities that people are willing to sell at different prices at a given time, and demand refers to a schedule of quantities people are willing to buy at different prices at a given time. The two terms in economics are linked together, like the terms "buyer" and "seller." The interaction between the supply of goods and services and the demand for them brings about a price, for each item and service, at which suppliers and demanders are willing and able to sell and buy the same quantity of goods. When the supply and demand are equal, the price of any product is said to be at an equilibrium price. The marketplace, the arena of business competition, is not only where the clash of interest between buyer and seller is worked out by the opposition of supply and demand, but it is also where buyers contend against buyers, and sellers against sellers. Supply and demand is always changing. Changes in willingness or ability to buy or sell are always occurring. The rise or fall of income alters the ability to buy. Fluctuations of desire or need alter the willingness to buy. On the seller's side, when the price of labor, land, or capital change, then the seller may alter his ability or willingness to offer his products on the markets at reduced or increased prices. Supply and demand in the marketplace is never a static phenomenon. The marketplace is always dynamic and changing, as supply changes, as demand changes, and as quantities of supplies and demands change.

SUPPLY-SIDE ECONOMICS

Reawakened in the United States in the late 1970s and early 1980s, the theory of supply-side economics looked at economic behavior by analyzing the supply of consumer items instead of the demand for them. This view of economics specifically focuses on the disincentive effects of taxes on private sector productivity, investment, and growth. Supply-side economists argues that reducing the tax rates on the supply-side would lead to greater economic growth, greater employment, and larger bottom-line tax revenues later.

Supply-side economics is not new in economic thought; its roots can be traced to Jean Baptiste Say's *Treatise on Political Economy and Taxation* (1817). The renewed interest in supply-side economics of the 1980s was stimulated by Dr. Arthur Laffer's Laffer's Curve and by the administration of President Ronald Reagan (1981–1989), which adopted this kind of economic thinking.

The Laffer Curve established to calculate the highest rates of tax the market would bear in various areas of the economy, always emphasizing tax reduction as the solution to economic issues. The supply-side theory of economics calls for a reduced government, reduced government spending, and a de-emphasis on any fiscal targets. Instead, great emphasis is placed on the free market and the de-regulation of private industry by the government. By the end of the supply-side era of the 1980s, the U.S. national debt was higher than at any other period of its history. The tax cuts did stimulate business and bring in more revenue, but government spending continued to grow in spite of the rhetoric.

SURPLUS

A surplus is the amount of money considered to be a profit in any general accounting period, which is available for carrying forward into the next accounting period. An economic surplus is similar to a net profit; it is the surplus resource in any business, household, or government after all cost, expenses, interest charges, and dividend payments have been made in any accounting period. A surplus should not be used synonymously with net profits, but rather should designate undivided profits, profits that have not, or do not need to be distributed in dividend payments to any investors or stockholders. A surplus, as well, may be accumulated profits of past periods which are left invested, and which continue to earn investment rates. This kind of surplus is known as an earned surplus. The American Institute of Certified Public Accountants has recommended that the term "surplus" be discontinued in favor of more specific and descriptive terms. Though surpluses continue to exist, the use of the term now rarely appears in balance sheet accounting presentations. More precise language is used, instead, such as "contribution in excess of par or stated value," or "additional paid-in capital." A surplus may arise for reasons other than having profits after all costs have been covered. A surplus might arise from a donation, or an appreciation of the value of owned business property, as well as other reasons. In banking, surplus refers to a portion of stockholders equity, and in economics, surplus refers to a situation in which at a given price, quantity supplied is greater then quantity demanded, and to alleviate this surplus prices must be lowered.

TAFT, WILLIAM HOWARD

Despite his imposing stature (six foot tall, three hundred pounds), William Howard Taft (1857–1930) was a reluctant President of the United States (1909–1913). To be leader of the nation was not Taft's first ambition, but his wife, brothers, and close-friend President Theodore Roosevelt (1901–1909) convinced Taft to run for the presidency in 1908. He won the election against Democratic candidate William Jennings Bryan. Taft's tenure as the twenty-seventh President was undistinguished. He was a man with little taste for politics, and he made many blunders throughout his term in office. Although he was a poor president, he was a fine Chief Justice of the U.S. Supreme Court, a position to which he was appointed in 1921, eight years after he left the White House. This appointment fulfilled a life-long ambition, and he performed his job with passion, competence, and enthusiasm.

William Howard Taft was born in Cincinnati, Ohio, on September 15, 1857 to a family that lived in comfortable circumstances. They had migrated to Ohio from New England. Since Taft's father and grandfather had both served as judges, he also aspired to a career on the bench. In preparation, he began his studies at Yale University, finishing second in his class, and he received a law degree from the Cincinnati Law School in 1880.

Determined to assist the citizens of his state, Taft held many public offices throughout his early career. In 1887 he served as an Ohio superior court judge. Three years later, Taft was named U.S. solicitor general by President Benjamin Harrison (1889–1893), a position he held successfully until 1892 when he returned to Ohio for a seat on the Circuit Court of Appeals.

Taft distinguished himself as a federal judge and developed an ambition to serve on the U.S. Supreme Court. That ambition would have to wait, however, as President William McKinley (1897–1901) requested

William Howard Taft.

in 1900 that Taft become president of the Philippine Commission. Working in the unstable and newly independent Philippine Islands, Taft established a civil government designed to serve the needs of its citizens, established an educational system, built roads and harbors, and pushed rapidly for limited self-government for the people whose islands were ''possessed legally'' by the United States during the Spanish-American War (1898).

Twice, in 1902 and in 1903, President Theodore Roosevelt offered Taft a seat on the U.S. Supreme Court. Taft regretfully turned it down to fulfill his commitment in the Philippines. A year later, however, Taft did accept Roosevelt's offer to become Secretary of War. This position still allowed him to be involved with matters in the Philippines and gave him responsibility for the construction of the Panama Canal. In addition to struggling with the problems and expenses of building the canal, Taft supported missions to Japan, hoping to create alliances for the U.S. in the Far East.

As President Roosevelt's term came to an end, he encouraged Taft to seek the presidency. Roosevelt and Taft had become good friends over the course of their careers and Roosevelt was convinced Taft was the best candidate for the job. With apprehension, Taft agreed to be the Republican presidential nominee in 1908, and in the election he defeated the Democratic candidate William Jennings Bryan. Even in victory, the new president still had misgivings, and said that he felt, "just like a fish out of water."

Taft's timid, conservative style alienated many in Congress. His attempt to reduce tariffs met with strong opposition from Republicans, while supporters of the measure were angered by what they perceived as Taft's lack of forcefulness. It was an inauspicious beginning.

The disagreements over tariff reductions set the tone for Taft's administration. Taft was denounced by many in Congress for what appeared to be weakness towards powerful business interests. His administration also seemed to reverse the strong conservationist policies of his predecessor by opening up much valuable government land for lumber and mining interests. He fired the head of the national Forest Service, Gifford Pinchot (1865–1946), who refused to cover up a scandal in the Interior Department.

Working against him in a coalition, Republicans and Democrats in Congress drove through a half dozen reform measures, most of which Taft opposed. The measures included the creation of a graduated income tax, the direct election of senators by the voters, and an increase in the powers of the Interstate Commerce Commission to control business. Taft was also faced with the uncertainties of social reform. Working people faced an increasingly volatile and shifting marketplace, and Taft paid little attention to making the necessary changes that would help stabilize the workplace by regulating relations between newly industrialized workers and growing industrial businesses.

Despite his discomfort in office and his difficulties with the legislative branch, Taft's administration was not without accomplishment. He oversaw the creation of the Postal Savings plan, a program to protect citizens' savings, and the admission of Arizona and New Mexico as new U.S. states. In addition, although Taft's predecessor Theodore Roosevelt had the reputation of a "trust buster," Taft's four years of leadership saw twice as many trust prosecutions as occurred throughout the eight years of Roosevelt's administration.

The tension between Taft and Congress eventually affected his friendship with Theodore Roosevelt. During the next presidential campaign in 1912, Taft and Roosevelt vied against each other for the Republican nomination. Taft was re-nominated, but in spite of that Roosevelt formed a new party, the Bull Moose Party. He ran against Taft in the election, and their competing campaigns split the Republican vote, giving the presidency to the Democratic candidate Woodrow Wilson (1913–1921).

Taft was relieved to leave White House. Over time, he and Roosevelt reconciled, and their friendship was restored. Taft taught law at Yale University until 1921, when President Warren Harding (1921–1923) named him Chief Justice of the Supreme Court. Taft's long-time ambition was fulfilled. He accepted the post. As Chief Justice, Taft was well respected and performed the functions of his position confidently and enthusiastically. He made no secret of his happiness to be out of the White House and back in the courthouse. Taft served eight years on the bench until his death in 1930, at age 78.

See also: **Interstate Commerce Commission, Spanish-American War, Tobacco Trust, Trust-Busting**

FURTHER READING

Anderson, Donald F. *William Howard Taft: A Conservative's Conception of the Presidency.* Ithaca: Cornell University Press, 1973.

Anderson, Judith I. *William Howard Taft: An Intimate History.* New York: Norton, 1981.

Burton, David H. *The Learned Presidency: Theodore Roosevelt, William Howard Taft, Woodrow Wilson.* Rutherford, N.J.: Fairleigh Dickinson University Press, 1988.

Coletta, Paolo E. *The Presidency of William Howard Taft.* Lawrence: University of Kansas Press, 1973.

Wilensky, Norman M. *Conservatism in the Progressive Era: The Taft Republicans of 1912.* Gainesville: University of Florida Press, 1965.

TAFT-HARTLEY ACT

The Taft-Hartley Act became law despite President Harry Truman's (1945–1953) veto. Also known as the Labor-Management Relations Act, it passed

Congress in 1947 and established guidelines to correct unions' unfair labor practices.

Taft-Hartley did several things to regulate labor practices in the United States. It prohibited secondary boycotts (in which the workers of a company convince employees of another organization to cease certain dealings with the company in order to pressure the employer to meet their needs) and authorized the payment of damages to parties injured by the boycotts. It abolished closed shops, which required all workers to be a member of a labor union, and did allow for union shops under specified conditions.

In addition, the Taft-Hartley Act established regulations for workers and employers regarding representation and bargaining. Workers now had the option of choosing to organize and bargain collectively or not. Workers gained the power to revoke a union from acting as their bargaining agent. Employers, employees, and unions received new guarantees of free speech. Employers could no longer hire an employee due to union affiliation or lack thereof. The National Labor Relations Board was given the authority to decide settlements for certain jurisdictional disputes. And, collective bargaining agreements became enforceable in federal district court.

The Taft-Hartley Act created a more neutral government stance on labor and unionism. Prior to the act, labor was regulated under a more pro-union policy established in the Wagner Act of 1935. Taft-Hartley allowed for more unbiased regulation of labor and unions while still protecting the rights of employees to be free from employer coercion.

It did, however, place a controversial requirement on unions. All union leaders had to take an oath declaring they were not members of the Communist party. Any union leader who did not take this oath was refused protection under the law. This provision was an early indicator of the "Red Scare" that swept the nation during the 1950s, when the government actively sought and tried citizens for alleged Communist beliefs.

See also: **Closed Shop, National Labor Relations Board**

TALLMADGE AMENDMENT

The Tallmadge Amendment of 1818 was a failed piece of legislation proposed by New York Representative James Tallmadge Jr. (1778–1853) in an attempt to resolve the question of how the Missouri Territory should be admitted to the Union. When the House of Representatives began deliberating the Missouri Territory's admission for statehood, the Union was comprised of equal numbers of free and slave states (eleven each). But Missouri threatened to throw off the balance: slavery was legal in the territory and ten thousand slaves lived there. The issue became a serious debate in the House, where the northern free states (due to their higher population of voters) held the majority. In his amendment to the bill granting Missouri statehood, Tallmadge proposed prohibiting the transport of any more slaves into the Missouri Territory. The measure would have let Missouri keep its slave status, but granted freedom to children born to slaves in the state after admission. By Tallmadge's proposal, Missouri's slave status would be temporary—lasting only until the slaves living there at the time of statehood died—because no slaves could be brought in and any offspring would be free. The measure passed in the House but was defeated in the Senate. The issue of Missouri's statehood remained unresolved at the end of the Congressional session. By the time Congress next convened, Maine had applied for statehood, giving lawmakers a neat, albeit temporary, way out of the dilemma of how to preserve balance between the free North and the slave South: By the Missouri Compromise of 1820, Missouri was admitted as a slave state, Maine as a free state.

See also: **Missouri Compromise, Slavery**

TARBELL, IDA MINERVA

Ida Tarbell (1857–1944) was a biographer and journalist who helped develop the form of journalism known as "muckraking." She exposed the corruption of big businesses, especially those that violated trust laws. She is most famous for contributing to the dissolution of the Standard Oil company, the biggest monopoly of her time.

Ida Tarbell was born on November 5, 1857 in Erie County, Pennsylvania. Her father was a farmer who switched careers with the discovery of oil in Erie County. He established a shop that made wooden oil tanks but was driven out of business by John D. Rockefeller's oil monopoly. Tarbell had a well-adjusted childhood despite this hardship; she was very well educated, graduating from Allegheny College in 1880 with a Bachelor of Arts degree in biology.

Tarbell never pursued a career in science instead she turned to writing. After teaching for two years at Poland Union Seminary in Ohio she became a staff member of *Chautauquan* magazine. The publication was dedicated to self-improvement through home study

Ida M. Tarbell.

and Tarbell eventually became the paper's managing editor. She left the job in 1891 to study in Paris where she pursued history at the Sorbonne and the University of Paris from 1891 to 1894. To support herself while she was abroad Tarbell wrote articles for magazines in the United States.

Tarbell's writing career took off when she met Samuel S. McClure (1857–1949), the creator of *McClure's*, a popular literary magazine. She began writing feature articles on important French figures, including Louis Pasteur (1822–95) and Napoleon Bonaparte (1769–1821). Her eight-part series on Napoleon was successful for both Tarbell and the magazine. The series was later published in 1895 as a book called *A Short Life of Napoleon Bonaparte*, and sold more than 100,000 copies.

Upon her return to the United States in 1894 Tarbell joined the staff of *McClure's* as a writer and associate editor. She wrote a series of articles on Abraham Lincoln (1809–65), which later became a respected book called *The Life of Abraham Lincoln* in 1900. McClure then began to restructure the format of the magazine to include contemporary social issues. Tarbell and other writers at *McClure's* began to write critical articles about important issues of the day such as corporate trusts. The goal of these articles was to expose corruption and the abuses of public power; these articles served as fuel for Progressivism, a reform movement of that time. President Theodore Roosevelt (1858–1919) was critical of this type of journalism and labeled it ''muckraking,'' a term which stayed with Tarbell for the rest of her career.

SHE LIVES SO WARMLY IN THE HEARTS OF HER FRIENDS THAT THEY TAKE NEW COURAGE IN A DISCORDANT UNIVERSE; ARE REESTABLISHED IN THEIR FAITH IN THE HUMAN RACE, LEARNING ANEW WHAT IT CAN BE, AT ITS BEST.

Ray Stannard Baker, personal diary, 1937

Tarbell's main contribution to this literary movement was her *History of the Standard Oil Company*, which originally appeared in *McClure's* in 19 installments in 1902 and was published as a book in 1904. Tarbell exposed the workings of John D. Rockefeller's oil monopoly. Her writings contributed to the company's prosecution under anti-trust laws and its eventual breakup in 1911. She claimed that she chose Standard Oil as the subject of her research because ''it satisfies most nearly the trust ideal of the entire control of the commodity in which it deals'' (*History of Standard Oil Company*, 1904). However it is no coincidence that Tarbell chose to write about the same monopoly that ran her father out of business. However, Tarbell's work was well researched and highly regarded despite this personal interest.

In 1906 Tarbell and some of her colleagues had a dispute with McClure and left the magazine to own and operate *American* magazine. Tarbell continued to expose corporate crimes and proclaim the need for honest government. As a result of her work, *The Tariff in Our Times* (1911), President Woodrow Wilson offered Tarbell a position on the Federal Tariff Commission in 1916. Tarbell refused but later participated in Wilson's Industrial Conference in 1919. She also participated in President Harding's Unemployment Conference in 1925. Another important series in *American* was on the history of the women's movement in the United States and her views on this subject were later published as *The Business of Being a Woman*.

American magazine was sold in 1915 and Tarbell spent the rest of her life as a lecturer and freelance writer. She continued writing books about business, but her later works were less critical than earlier ones. Tarbell toured a number of U.S. factories between 1912 and 1915 and was impressed by some of the latest business developments. She was particularly optimistic about the management techniques of Henry Ford. Tarbell also produced two friendly biographies of business leaders called *Life of Elbert H. Gary* (1923) and *Owen D. Young* (1932). She also published a history called *The Nationalizing of Business: 1878–98* (1936).

In 1939 Tarbell published her autobiography, *All in the Day's Work.* She then taught classes in biographical writing and worked as consulting editor of a Tucson magazine called *Letter* from 1943 to 1944. Tarbell died of pneumonia in 1944.

See also: **Henry Ford, Monopolies, Muckrakers, Pennsylvania, John D. Rockefeller, Standard Oil, Ida Tarbell, Woodrow Wilson**

FURTHER READING

Brady, Kathleen. *Ida Tarbell: Portrait of a Muckraker.* Pittsburgh, Pennsylvania: University of Pittsburgh Press, 1989.

Reitman, Janet. ''The Muckraker vs. the Millionaire.'' *Scholastic Update*, Teachers' Edition., 131, November 1998.

Tarbell, Ida M. *All in the Day's Work: An Autobiography.* New York: Macmillan, 1939.

———. *More than a Muckraker: Ida Tarbell's Lifetime in Journalism.* Edited by Robert C. Kochersberger. Knoxville, TN: University of Tennessee Press, 1994.

Tomkins, Mary E. *Ida M. Tarbell.* New York: Twayne Publishers, 1974.

TARIFF OF ABOMINATIONS

By the late 1820s the southeastern region of the United States was economically depressed. While the industrial northeast flourished, the agrarian south languished. Many historians now recognize that the soil of the older southern states was worn out and depleted, especially compared to the richer soil of the new Gulf states; at the time, however, many southerners blamed their fiscal ailments on tariffs. Leadership in the fight against the tariff fell to South Carolina, where the plantation aristocrats enjoyed political power and where the relative decline in prosperity was the greatest.

South Carolina's most eloquent spokesperson was John C. Calhoun (1782–1850), who by the late 1820s had completed his philosophical transformation from ardent nationalist to states' rights advocate. In fact, Calhoun then advocated the ultimate in states' rights thinking—a belief in, and support of, the doctrine of nullification, which Thomas Jefferson (1743–1826) and James Madison (1751–1836) first described in the Kentucky and Virginia Resolutions of 1798. In 1828, while running as a vice presidential candidate, Calhoun anonymously penned the ''South Carolina Exposition and Protest,'' an essay objecting to the Tariff of 1828, known to southerners as the Tariff of Abominations because of its high protective duties. The tariff was intended to protect the burgeoning industries of New England, where numerous factories had opened during the first three decades of the nineteenth century, but encountered much opposition from the south. Calhoun's authorship of the ''South Carolina Exposition and Protest'' remained secret, and for four years South Carolina did not act upon it, hoping that President Andrew Jackson (1829–1837) would fight for a lower tariff. In ''Exposition,'' and in a later paper called ''A Disquisition on Government,'' Calhoun explained his doctrine of nullification.

Contrary to popular belief, Calhoun did not advocate the secession of the southern states, an event which occurred during the American Civil War (1861–1865). Rather, he believed that nullification would prevent the disruption of the Union, and he saw nullification as an antidote to secession. The basic tenets of his argument were as follows. Each state was sovereign, and the Union was a contract between the states. Each individual state entered into an agreement with the others, and the U.S. Constitution outlined the terms of that covenant. The Constitution provided for a separation of powers between the states and the federal government, but not for a division of sovereignty. For sovereignty was not the sum of a number of governmental powers, but rather the will of the political community, which could not be divided without being destroyed. Prior to the Constitution, the states had been sovereign under the Articles of Confederation, and they had not given up their supreme authority when they joined the new Union. Since the Union had been created by the states, and not vice versa, it logically followed that the creator was more powerful than the created. As the federal government was not supreme, it could exercise only those powers given it by the states as embodied in the Constitution. Should it exceed these powers, the measures enacted would be unconstitutional.

After simmering for four years, the issue of nullification erupted in 1832 over a new tariff. In December 1831, President Jackson recommended to Congress a downward revision of the tariff and the elimination of the worst features of the Tariff of Abominations. Such a bill was finally pushed through in July 1832, but the new tariff was not low enough for the southern planters. Although some of the ''abominations'' were removed, the general level of the duties was only slightly lower. The greatest reductions were made on noncompetitive manufactured items, and the protective makeup of the tariff was hardly changed.

By mid-1832 South Carolina extremists were ready to put the nullification theory into action. Many denounced the Tariff of 1832 as unconstitutional and oppressive to the southern people. In the subsequent state election that fall the States' Rights and Unionist Parties made the tariff and nullification the chief issues, and when the States' Rights Party elected more than two-thirds of the legislature, it promptly called for a state convention. The convention met in November 1832, and by a vote of 136 to 26 the state adopted an Ordinance of Nullification, which declared the Tariffs of 1828 and 1832 null and void. After February 1, 1833, the tariffs would not be collected, and should the federal government forcibly attempt to collect them, South Carolina would secede.

Jackson met this challenge in typical fashion. He boldly proclaimed that the Constitution formed a government, not a league, and that the power of a single state to annul a federal law was ''incompatible with the existence of the Union, contradicted by the letter of the Constitution, unauthorized by its spirit, inconsistent with every principle on which it was founded, and destructive to the great object for which it was formed.'' Nullification he called an ''impractical absurdity,'' and concluded that ''disunion by armed force is treason.'' This proclamation received the enthusiastic support of nationalists. On January 16, 1833, Jackson sent a message to Congress reviewing the circumstances in South Carolina and recommending measures that would enable him to cope successfully with the situation. Tension mounted in February when the Senate passed the Force Bill, which authorized Jackson to use the United States Army and Navy if necessary to enforce the federal laws.

While the Senate was still debating the Force Bill, Henry Clay (1771–1852) brought forward a new compromise tariff bill calling for the gradual reduction of tariff duties over the next 10 years. By 1842 the tariff was not to exceed 20 percent. South Carolinians waited anxiously to see what would happen, for it was already apparent that no southern states were coming to her aid, and she would have to fight it out alone. Calhoun, who had resigned the vice presidency after the passage of the Tariff of 1832 and had been elected immediately to the Senate, objected to the Force Bill but feared that strong opposition might hurt the chances of reconciliation presented by Clay's Compromise Tariff. He and Clay worked to push the new tariff bill through Congress, and on March 2, 1833, the same day that the Force Bill was signed into law, Jackson also signed the Compromise Tariff.

Once the Compromise Tariff was passed, South Carolina repealed its Ordinance of Nullification; however, in a last gesture of defiance the convention declared the Force Bill null and void. Jackson ignored this final face-saving move on the part of South Carolina, for the Force Bill was irrelevant if the tariff duties were being collected.

Both sides claimed victory. Nationalists declared that the president and Congress had upheld the power of the federal government, while South Carolina asserted that nullification had proved an effective method of sustaining states' rights. However, the failure of any other southern state to rally to South Carolina's defense showed that the doctrine of nullification was unpopular, and from that time forward militant southerners looked to the doctrine of secession as their best redress against economic and political grievances.

***See also:* Andrew Jackson, South Carolina, States' Rights, Tariff**

FURTHER READING

Bancroft, Frederic. *Calhoun and the South Carolina Nullification Movement.* Baltimore: The Johns Hopkins University Press, 1928.

Coit, Margaret L. *John C. Calhoun.* Boston: Houghton Mifflin Co., 1950.

Freehling, William W. *Prelude to Civil War: The Nullification Controversy in South Carolina, 1816–1836.* New York: Harper & Row, 1965.

Taussig, Frank W. *The Tariff History of the United States.* New York: G. P. Putnam's Sons, 1923.

Wiltse, Charles M. *John C. Calhoun.* Indianapolis: Bobbs-Merrill Company, 1949.

TARIFFS

A tariff is a tax charged on imports either on the basis of quantity (for example, ''per ton;'' these are called specific tariffs) or on the basis of their value (called *ad valorem* tariffs). Tariffs are the primary means by which governments protect their industries from foreign competition. Tariffs can be levied directly, as goods cross the border, or indirectly, by requiring that a license or permit be purchased before the goods can be shipped. Tariffs generally serve two purposes: to generate tax revenues and to protect a domestic industry from foreign competition. If a government wants to encourage the growth of a newly emerging industry it can also use tariffs to free these ''infant'' industries from having to compete with established foreign producers on the basis of price. Because tariffs raise barriers to the free flow of international trade, however, in the long run they tend to impede global economic growth. As a temporary way of raising revenues or protecting an industry they can be effective—at least until other countries retaliate by raising their own tariffs.

The first U.S. tariff, of about 8.5 percent, was levied in 1789 on imports like molasses, hemp, steel, and nails in order to raise revenues for the young U.S. government. By the War of 1812 (1812–1814) the average tariff had risen to 25 percent and continued to rise to as high as 33 percent on imported cotton and wool during the 1820s. Under the Tariff of 1828 tariffs were raised to their highest level prior to the American Civil War (1861–1865). Since the Whig and then the Republican Parties represented the industrial Northeast, they favored raising tariffs, while the Democrats, the party of the slaveholding South, opposed them. When the South seceded in 1860, the Republicans seized power and raised tariffs by 10 percent. In 1882 Congress established a permanent Tariff Commission to recommend changes in tariffs and in 1897 the Dingley Tariff imposed the steepest tariffs rates ever (57 percent) on foreign imports.

When the federal government began to collect income taxes in 1913, tariffs began to lose their importance as a source of government revenue and the last great tariff law was the Smoot-Hawley Act of 1930. In 1934 the Reciprocal Trade Act gave the President independent authority to negotiate tariff reductions with foreign countries. In 1947 the United States joined 22 other countries in signing the General Agreement on Tariffs and Trade (replaced in 1995 by the World Trade Organization), which over the years has successfully worked to lower tariff barriers around the world.

See also: **Dingley Tariff, General Agreement on Tariffs and Trade, Smoot-Hawley Tariff**

TAYLOR, FREDERICK WINSTON

Frederick Winston Taylor (1856–1915), known as the ''Father of Scientific Management,'' pioneered the occupation of time study in industrial management. His love for perfection and control, carried arguably to extremes in the industrial workplace, led to his invention of hundreds of ways to increase worker productivity. He believed his efforts would promote harmony between management and labor. As an industrial engineer he introduced efficiency techniques in factory operations which Henry Ford (1863–1947) made famous on his assembly line. Taylor's ideas were welcomed by those seeking efficiency in production, but denounced by many, including unionists, who feared it would degenerate into a factory ''speed up'' system, where a worker's humanity would be diminished and the employee would become merely another cog in the wheel of the factory machine.

Frederick Taylor was born in Germantown, Pennsylvania, on March 3, 1856, the second of three children born to Franklin and Emily Taylor. Taylor's father was a lawyer and a poet who had inherited considerable wealth from the family's ownership of farms and other properties in the Philadelphia area. His mother was a staunch abolitionist, working to end slavery in the United States. She was a strict disciplinarian, and she worked to create an orderly environment around her. The young Taylor adopted much of his mother's thinking about order and control. An example of such desires to control his environment was demonstrated at age 12—he suffered from frequent nightmares, which he believed were caused by sleeping on his back. To prevent this he put together a harness device that would wake him up if he rolled onto his back.

Taylor attended the private Germantown Academy while living in Pennsylvania, and at age 13 he traveled with his parents to Europe. He spent three years there, studying under tutors in France and Germany. When Taylor returned to the United States in 1872, he was enrolled at the Phillips Exeter Academy, a private college-preparatory school in New Hampshire. He left the Academy in his senior year, claiming problems with his eyesight. He never went on to college but instead he began to work as a machinist; he embraced the work ethic vigorously and seemed to prefer working at a job rather than spending his time at college.

Taylor completed an apprenticeship as a machinist and began to work for Midvale Steel Co. in Philadelphia, Pennsylvania. While working at Midvale, he pursued a self-study program in mechanical engineering from the Stevens Institute and graduated with an engineering diploma in 1883 at age 27. He became the chief engineer at Midvale Steel and obtained a patent for his invention of the largest steam hammer ever built in the United States. Later, in 1898, while working at Bethlehem Steel Corp., Taylor and a colleague, J.M. White, invented the Taylor-White process—a method for the heat treatment of tool steel. This process yielded increased cutting and hardness capacities of 200 to 300 percent, and by the late 1990s was used in practically every machine shop in the world. Yet it was scientific industrial management that Taylor adopted as his primary occupation. In 1903 he started as a self-employed industrial consultant, specializing in managing businesses with the greatest time-cost efficiency.

Taylor promoted his ideas about efficiency engineering of both people and machine processes that would help speed up work. He likely did not realize his ideas would be used to claim management was making the employee into a kind of dehumanized robot. Such reforms in manufacturing as Taylor advocated became known as ''Taylorism.'' According to Taylorism, by scientific study (time-management study) of every step and operation in a manufacturing plant, data could be obtained as to the fair and reasonable production capacities of both man and machine. The application of that data in an effort to increase productivity would abolish the antagonism between employer and employee. For five years Taylor successfully applied his theory in a variety of establishments, administrative and sales departments, and shops.

Convinced of the correctness of his theory, Taylor devoted the remainder of his life to expounding those principles. He often gave his services free of cost, and wrote a book promoting his ideas on efficiency engineering titled *Principles of Scientific Management.* He also traveled extensively, lecturing about his theory.

Taylor's legacy has been controversial. In the early twentieth century he personified the efficiency movement of modern management. In the 1930s and 1940s he was known as the creator of modern industrial work methods, and by mid-century he became targeted by social scientists that said his methods were dehumanizing. (The 1970s regarded his methods often as ways to exploit employees.) Overall, Taylor and his supporters are likely best recalled for their work in publicizing the possibilities of a careful, systematic approach to industrial time-and-motion study to enhance industrial efficiency.

Frederick Taylor died in 1915, at age 59. He left an estate of over $1 million, all of which he earned in his lifetime.

***See also:* Productivity**

FURTHER READING

Haber, Samuel. *Efficiency and Uplift: Scientific Management in the Progressive Era, 1890–1920.* Chicago: University of Chicago Press, 1964.

Kaker, Sudhir. *Frederick Taylor: A Study in Personality and Innovation.* Cambridge, MA: MIT Press, 1970.

Kanigal, Robert. *The One Best Way: Frederick Winslow Taylor and the Enigma of Efficiency.* New York: Viking, 1997.

Nelson, Daniel. *Frederick W. Taylor and the Rise of Scientific Management.* Madison, WI: University of Wisconsin Press, 1985.

Schracter, Hindy L. *Frederick Taylor and the Public Administration Community.* Buffalo, NY: State University of New York Press, 1989.

TECUMSEH, DEATH OF

Tecumseh was born in a Shawnee village, Old Piqua, on the Mad River of Ohio, in 1768 near present-day Springfield, Ohio. He was the fifth of nine children; his father, a Shawnee warrior named Puckeshinewa, was killed in a 1774 battle, and his mother, Methoastaske, moved west of the Mississippi River with Creek relatives five years later. Tecumseh remained in Ohio country with an older sister, Tecumapease, and raised her in the tradition of his culture.

By age 14 Tecumseh found himself fighting Americans alongside his older brother, Chiksika, leading the Native American resistance to the continued spread of white settlement in the Ohio River valley. As he matured, Tecumseh became an acknowledged and respected leader. He also gained recognition arguing for humane treatment of American captives. During a series of raids against frontier settlements in Kentucky and Tennessee in the late 1780s and early 1790s, Chiksika was killed. Outnumbered, Tecumseh and his followers suffered a series of defeats in Ohio, leading to the Treaty of Greenville in 1795. The treaty ceded most of modern-day Ohio, leaving Native American control over the remaining parts of the Old Northwest Territory. Tecumseh, however, refused to participate in or recognize the treaty, asserting that those who participated did not have authority to sign away the

Tecumseh, Chief of the Shawnee.

land. He carried this traditional concept of communal land ownership with him into later days.

Following defeat in Ohio and after several moves within Ohio and Indiana, in 1798 Tecumseh settled in a village on the White River of eastern Indiana, near the modern-day town of Anderson. There, one of Tecumseh's younger brothers, Tenskwatawa, experienced a series of visions in 1805. Tenskwatawa became a powerful religious leader, especially after successfully predicting an eclipse in 1806. They relocated to a village near present-day Greenville, Ohio, where Tenskwatawa preached a native revitalization, offering to rescue Native American people from impending doom. Known as the Prophet, Tecumseh's brother espoused alcohol abstinence and the pursuit of a traditional way of life, which included repudiation of Western society's goods and customs. Many were receptive to the message, given the ongoing demise of their traditional economies, and his following increased. With many Native Americans coming to Tecumseh's village to see his famous brother, Tecumseh's political activism grew. He transformed the revitalization concept into a political movement that embraced the idea of communal property regarding native lands. In 1808 Tecumseh and Tenskwatawa again relocated their village, this time to the confluence of the Tippecanoe and Wabash Rivers, which became known as Prophetstown.

Tecumseh clashed with Indiana Territorial Governor William Henry Harrison (1773–1841) over the 1809 Treaty of Fort Wayne, which ceded yet more traditional lands. Meanwhile, Tecumseh's prominence rose to new heights. Relentlessly, he journeyed throughout much of the United States encouraging tribal groups to form a political confederacy, a pan-Native American federation, to stop the further loss of lands. An outstanding orator, Tecumseh argued that Native American land could not be given away without common consent of all Native American peoples. He took his message to the South where, though the Cherokee and three other Five Civilized Tribes rejected his call, the Creeks were responsive. While Tecumseh met with the Creeks in November 1811, the U.S. Army led by Harrison moved against Prophetstown. The resulting Battle of Tippecanoe destroyed the village and its food supply and sent Tecumseh's brother in flight to Canada.

While Tecumseh recovered from his terrible loss, the War of 1812 (1812–1814) broke out between the United States and Great Britain. He and his followers joined British troops in Michigan, where together they successfully captured Fort Detroit. Further engagements with U.S. troops followed in southern Michigan and northern Ohio. Tecumseh joined forces with British commander Henry Proctor, laying siege to Harrison's Fort Meigs. The siege failing, Tecumseh reluctantly accompanied Proctor in a retreat to Canada, where Harrison pursued them. Tecumseh was shot and killed at the Battle of the Thames in present-day southern Ontario in October 1813.

The death of Tecumseh marked the end of Native American resistance in the Ohio River valley and efforts at pan-tribal unity, a political concept alien to traditional Native American lifestyles. U.S. victories throughout the following year under the leadership of Andrew Jackson (1767–1845) broke the Native American hold on lands east of the Mississippi River. The following decades saw implementation of Jackson's removal policy, a plan to forcibly relocate Native Americans west of the Mississippi. Yet, the widespread admiration of Tecumseh's skills as a leader and orator, plus his bravery and humanitarianism, have established him as an American folk hero.

***See also:* Fallen Timbers (Battle of), Native American Policy**

FURTHER READING

Antal, Sandy. *A Wampum Denied: Procter's War of 1812*. East Lansing, Michigan: Carlton University Press, 1997.

Eckert, Allan W. *A Sorrow in Our Heart: The Life of Tecumseh*. New York: Bantam, 1992.

Edmunds, R. David. *The Shawnee Prophet*. Lincoln: University of Nebraska Press, 1983.

Hickey, Donald R. *The War of 1812: A Short History*. Urbana: University of Illinois Press, 1995.

Sudgen, John. *Tecumseh: A Life*. New York: Henry Holt, 1998.

———. *Tecumseh's Last Stand*. Norman: University of Oklahoma Press, 1985.

TELEGRAPH

The telegraph was the first communicational instrument that could send messages through wires via electricity. Though the invention was the result of several decades of research by many people, American inventor Samuel F.B. Morse (1791–1872) is credited with making the first practical telegraph in 1837. Morse was a portrait painter in New York City when he became interested in magnetic telegraphy in around 1832. With technical assistance from chemistry professor Leonard Gale (1800–1883) and the financial support of Alfred Vail (1807–1859), Morse conducted further experiments and finally developed a battery-powered instrument that provided the necessary steady source of electricity. He also developed Morse code, a system of variously arranged dots and dashes for transmitting messages. (For example, the most frequently used letter of the alphabet is *e*, which is rendered in Morse code by using one dot; the less frequently used *z* is rendered by two dashes followed by two dots.) By 1837 Morse had demonstrated the telegraph to the public in New York, Philadelphia, and Washington. He received a patent for his invention in the United States in 1840. In 1843 his telegraph was further promoted when the U.S. Congress approved construction of an experimental line between Washington, D.C., and Baltimore, Maryland. The following year, on May 24, 1844, Morse sent his first message across that line: "What hath God wrought!" Alfred Vail was on the receiving end of the wire.

By 1861 most major U.S. cities were linked by telegraph wires. The first successful trans-Atlantic cables were laid in 1866. Morse Code transmissions—called telegrams when transmitted via above-ground wires and cablegrams (or cables) when transmitted via underwater cables—were translated by operators or mechanical printers on both the sending and receiving ends of the message. The introduction of the telegraph marked the beginning of modern communications. When the first transcontinental telegraph line in the United States was completed on October 24, 1861, it eliminated overnight the need for the Pony Express, which had briefly enjoyed the status of the fastest way to transmit a message—about eight days from St. Louis, Missouri, to Sacramento, California, a distance that could be bridged by telegraph lines within minutes. The telegraph became the chief means of long distance communication. The telephone (invented 1875), which allows voice transmission over electrical wires, gradually replaced the telegraph. But for many decades the two technologies were in use together.

See also: **Samuel Finley Breese Morse, Pony Express, Transatlantic Cable**

TEMPERANCE MOVEMENT

With milk and water susceptible to contamination and spoilage in colonial times, many settlers turned to alcoholic beverages. Beer and wine were common on ships carrying colonists from Europe. Consequently, most colonists drank alcohol regularly beginning in childhood, and alcohol was key to almost every social gathering. Even church leaders commonly sanctioned moderate alcohol use. Following the American Revolution (1775–1783), distilled spirits such as whiskey became important commercial goods. With Americans drinking large quantities of liquor, concern about alcohol consumption existed from the nation's birth.

Predominantly led by evangelical Protestants, isolated pockets of opposition to the sale and consumption of distilled beverages began to coalesce by the 1810s. By the end of the War of 1812 (1812–1814), a radical temperance movement developed consisting of many denominations; Presbyterians, Quakers, Western Methodists, and people of other faiths united in a concerted effort to transform traditional social patterns. One such group, the Connecticut Society for the Reformation of Morals, formed in 1813. An early focus of the evangelical leaders was individual self-reform through abstinence to save the conscience and family harmony. In contrast, elite urban residents of property in the Northeast, who formed such groups as the Massachusetts Society for the Suppression of Intemperance, took a more conservative approach. They focused more on suppressing consumption by the lower economic classes to maintain social order and reduce crime.

The temperance movement blossomed nationally over the next decade, with the creation of the American Temperance Society in 1826. Auxiliary groups were established in every state with thousands of local organizations. The economic transition from an agrarian to an industrialized society more demanding of efficiency and scheduling very likely contributed to

> The standard view that abstinence was a response to industrialization and the growth of a market economy must be carefully qualified. Such developments undoubtedly contributed to the growing receptiveness of temperance in the 1820s, but they cannot account for the origins of the movement's ideology . . . In the future we must examine carefully the long-ignored moral societies that dotted the American landscape during the 1810s . . . and the hopes and fears of average evangelicals.
>
> **James R. Rohrer, "The Origins of the Temperance Movement: A Reinterpretation", *Journal of American Studies*, August 1990**

popularization of the movement. Transitioning from temperance to prohibition, the Society crusaded for complete abstinence from strong spirits. Under ''divine'' guidance, the national movement produced volumes of literature, including a number of journals dedicated to temperance. Through the 1830s total alcohol consumption plummeted from more than seven gallons per capita annually to slightly more than three. Dissension grew, however, with many favoring temperance rather than complete abstinence from wine, beer, and stronger spirits. Though momentum flagged in the 1840s, it was regained in part through the efforts of the Washington Temperance Society and the emotional lectures of John B. Gough and others. Marking a peak in the nineteenth century temperance movement, 13 of the 40 existing states had passed prohibition laws by the inception of the American Civil War (1861–1865).

The temperance movement shifted into national politics with the formation of the National Prohibition Party in 1869; in 1874 the Woman's Christian Temperance Union (WCTU) was founded. The Prohibition Party saw modest success in state elections through the 1870s and peaked in national popular support in 1892 with a presidential candidate. Its primary success was the influence of public policy to support temperance movement issues.

Following an 1888 U.S. Supreme Court ruling that key provisions of state prohibition measures violated federal interstate commerce laws, however, alcohol consumption burgeoned. The Anti-Saloon League, later considered by many to be the most effective temperance organization, was founded in 1893 by representatives of various temperance organizations and the evangelical Protestant churches. A powerful political lobby, the League worked within the existing political parties to support candidates sympathetic to governmental control of liquor.

The combined influence of the Anti-Saloon League, the WCTU, and the Prohibition Party in 1917 led to a wartime prohibition measure which quickly transformed into the Eighteenth Amendment of the Constitution. The amendment prohibited the manufacture, sale, transport, exporting, and importing of liquor in the United States. The states ratified the amendment by January 1919. Congress passed the Volstead Act, which provided for amendment enforcement, later in 1919 over the veto of President Woodrow Wilson (1913–1921). Prohibition went into effect January 1920, marking the twentieth century peak of the movement. For 13 years the nation was legally dry. Nevertheless, the demand for alcohol continued, giving rise to great disrespect for the law and extensive illegal activity, including smuggling, speakeasies, bootlegging, and a multibillion dollar criminal underworld. Widespread popular support did exist, however, and drinking habits altered substantially throughout the country, leading to a marked decline in alcohol-related accidents and deaths. Concerns grew through the 1920s about increasing police powers to enforce the amendment and intrusions into personal privacy.

In the end, legislators concluded that Prohibition was too oppressive and unenforceable. The Twenty-First Amendment, which repealed Prohibition and nullified the Eighteenth Amendment, quickly proceeded through ratification, becoming official in December 1933. The Volstead Act was rendered void, and individual states again became the arena for alcohol regulation. The renewed production and sale of alcohol served to bolster the depressed economy of the early 1930s by adding jobs and tax revenue.

Attitudes about alcohol consumption have fluctuated through time. Temperance again became an issue later in the twentieth century, as alcohol consumption peaked around 1980. New organizations, such as Mothers Against Drunk Driving, addressed alcohol-related topics such as traffic deaths, health problems, juvenile crime, and fetal alcohol syndrome.

See also: **Eighteenth Amendment, Prohibition, Twenty-First Amendment**

FURTHER READING

Epstein, Barbara L. *The Politics of Domesticity: Women, Evangelism, and Temperance in Nineteenth-Century America*. Irvington, New York: Columbia University Press, 1981.

Hamm, Richard F. *Shaping the Eighteenth Amendment: Temperance Reform, Legal Culture, and the Polity, 1880–1920*. Chapel Hill: University of North Carolina Press, 1995.

Kerr, K. Austin. *Organized for Prohibition: A New History of the Anti-Saloon League*. New Haven: Yale University Press, 1985.

Rorabaugh, William J. *The Alcoholic Republic: An American Tradition*. New York: Oxford University Press, 1979.

Tyrrell, Ian R. *Sobering Up: From Temperance to Prohibition in Antebellum America, 1800–1860*. Westport, Connecticut: Greenwood Press, 1979.

TENANT FARMING

Tenant farming is a system of agriculture whereby farmers cultivate crops or raise livestock on rented lands. It was one of two agricultural systems that emerged in the South following the American Civil War (1861–1865); the other system was sharecropping. The South in economic ruin, former plantation owners were now without slave labor and lacked resources to hire wage laborers. They began dividing up their land and arranging the tracts to be farmed by one of these two methods. In 1860 there were just under 700,000 farms in the South; in 1910 the division of the former plantations resulted in more than three million farms.

A tenant farmer typically could buy or owned all that he needed to cultivate crops; he lacked the land to farm. The farmer rented the land, paying the landlord in cash or crops. Rent was usually determined on a per-acre basis, which typically ran at about one-third the value of the crop. At the end of the harvest the landowner would be paid one-third the value of the crops or would receive one-third the crops directly from the farmer. While this system was superior to that of sharecropping and many sharecroppers aspired to being tenant farmers, the method also had its downfalls. Tenant farmers frequently found themselves in debt to the landowner. At the beginning of a planting season, the farmer would secure store credit based on the crop's expected yield. If conditions were poor or market prices for the crop decreased, the farmer became indebted to the storeowner and to the landowner (which was often the same person). Another consequence of tenant farming was the deterioration of the land; since it did not belong to them, many farmers were not motivated to do ample upkeep or make improvements, thus, farms tended to deteriorate. However some tenant farmers proved successful and ultimately moved off rented lands to purchase their own tracts. Generally, however, this was not the case and the system, along with sharecropping, proved to be a failure.

See also: **Reconstruction, Sharecropping**

TENEMENTS

Tenements (also called tenement houses) are urban dwellings occupied by impoverished families. They are apartment houses that barely meet or fail to meet the minimum standards of safety, sanitation, and comfort. Emerging in U.S. cities during the late 1800s, tenements took many shapes and forms: multistoried buildings, row houses, frame houses, and even converted slave quarters.

Between 1870 and into the early 1900s, U.S. population growth (buoyed by immigration in record numbers) outpaced construction. Housing was scarce, particularly for working-class families. In unprecedented numbers people crowded into the low-rent districts of cities, including New York, Baltimore, Philadelphia, Boston, Chicago, St. Louis, Charleston, and New Orleans.

Living conditions were deplorable: Built close together, tenements typically lacked adequate windows, rendering them poorly ventilated and dark, and they were frequently in disrepair. Vermin were a persistent problem as buildings lacked proper sanitation facilities.

The plight of tenement-dwellers became the object of reformers who waged campaigns with government to pass laws requiring landlords to meet certain standards of safety and sanitation. Legislation was passed (New York became the first state to adopt legislation in 1867, which was furthered in 1879 and 1901), but the laws did not require owners to retrofit existing buildings to comply with the new regulations.

Some improvements came as a result of scientific and technological advances, including water purification and sewage disposal systems; steel-frame construction, which made tall buildings (including skyscrapers) possible and allowed for a more efficient use of limited urban space; electric lighting; electric elevators; and steam heat. While the lives of many working class families improved with the expansion of the economy, many others remained in poverty. With their attendant problems of crowding, disrepair, lack of sanitation, and crime, tenements have continued to exist.

See also: **Slums, Urbanization**

TENNESSEE

Admitted to the Union as the sixteenth state on June 1, 1796, Tennessee is located in the eastern south central United States. It shares borders with Arkansas and Missouri in the west, Kentucky and Virginia in the north, North Carolina in the east, and Mississippi, Alabama, and Georgia in the south. Geographically, Tennessee is the country's thirty-fourth largest state, spreading across 42,000 square miles. Its population of approximately 5 million people ranks seventeenth among the 50 states. Memphis is the state's most populous city, and Nashville is its capital.

The eastern and western valleys of the Tennessee River separate the state into three regions: east Tennessee, middle Tennessee, and west Tennessee. Forming just east of Knoxville, the river loops 350 miles south into Alabama, and then streams north to join the Ohio River at Paducah, Kentucky. The Appalachian Mountains and its Blue Ridge range dominate the landscape of east Tennessee. Middle Tennessee is a broad and fertile area that covers about half the state, rolling gradually toward the rich bottomlands and hardwood forest of west Tennessee.

The most industrialized part of the state is east Tennessee, where motor vehicles, boats, and aircraft parts are manufactured by businesses that derive power from hydroelectric dams created by the Tennessee Valley Authority (TVA). The federal government's atomic energy research and development center is also located in east Tennessee at Oak Ridge. Middle Tennessee largely consists of farmland for the harvesting of tobacco, corn, and hay; the raising of cattle; and the production of dairy goods. Mining is also a major source of income for residents of both east and middle Tennessee. West Tennessee is home to some of the biggest cotton farms in the South.

Tennessee's early history was intertwined with that of the Cherokee peoples. In fact, the name "Tennessee" derives from the word *Tanasi*, a name the Cherokee gave to a village on the Little Tennessee River. In the eighteenth century the Cherokee allied themselves with Great Britain, fighting alongside British forces against the 13 colonies during the American Revolution (1775–1783). When America won its independence, most Cherokee settled in the area of what became modern-day Chattanooga. The Cherokee prospered in this area, owning plantations and developing an 85-character table of syllables that was used to print a weekly newspaper. But seven years after the 1828 gold rush in Tennessee, the Cherokee were coerced into signing a treaty under which they surrendered all legal claims to land in the region. In 1838 federal troops forcibly uprooted the Cherokee from their Tennessee homelands and drove them into the Arkansas Territory. Thousands of Cherokee were killed during the relocation, and thousands more suffered great hardship in what has been called the Trail of Tears.

The demise of the Cherokee in Tennessee coincided with the rise of Andrew Jackson (1829–1837) to the U.S. presidency. A former Democratic Congressman and Superior Court judge from Tennessee, Jackson served two full terms. In 1844 another former Democratic Congressman from Tennessee, James K. Polk (1845–1849), was elected president. Although Polk served only one term in office, his administration was responsible for increasing the amount of territory held by the United States by about 50 percent—acquiring the Oregon Territory from Britain and annexing Arizona, California, Nevada, New Mexico, Texas, Utah, and parts of Colorado, Kansas, Oklahoma, and Wyoming from Mexico.

A third former Tennessee Congressman, Andrew Johnson served as vice president in 1864. A year later he assumed the duties of chief executive following President Abraham Lincoln's (1861–1865) assassination. Johnson's first two years in office were consumed by the aftermath of the American Civil War (1861–1865). The war had left the South in ruins. Tennessee, which was the site of more Civil War battles than any other state except Virginia, was particularly devastated, and recovery was slow. Nonetheless, Tennessee was the first state to return to the Union when the war ended, and several northern investors fed capital into the state's industries and cities.

The Civil War ended slavery in the South, but it did not resolve race problems in Tennessee. Turmoil between African Americans and whites in the state continued well into the next century. In the 1860s six former Confederate Army officers from Pulaski, Tennessee, founded a terroristic white-supremacist organization called the Ku Klux Klan (KKK). In the 1870s the state adopted a constitutional provision requiring public schools to be segregated by race. Over the next 50 years the Tennessee legislature enacted a series of so-called Jim Crow laws that segregated the races in other sectors of society. Although the system of state-sponsored racial segregation would be dismantled by the U.S. Supreme Court's 1954 decision in *Brown v.*

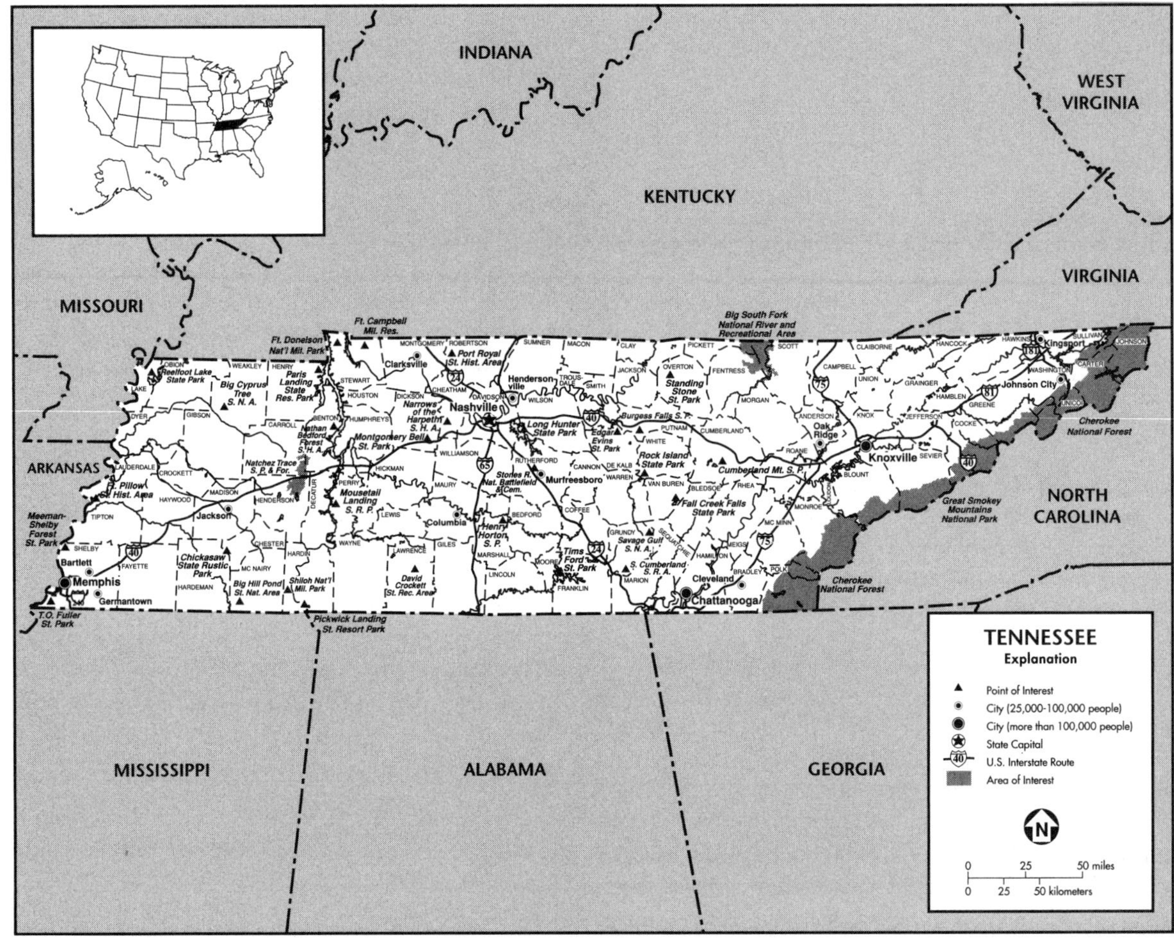

State of Tennessee.

the Board of Education and in the federal Civil Rights Act of 1964, white vigilantes continued terrorizing blacks in the South. The Reverend Dr. Martin Luther King, Jr. (1929–1968) was slain by one such gunman on April 4, 1968, while doing civil rights work in Memphis.

Although much of the history of the state is tragic, Tennessee had become a popular tourist attraction by the late twentieth century. Forty million tourists spent approximately $8 billion each year while visiting the state in the 1990s. Native American exhibits, Civil War battlefields, and a national civil rights museum are among the sites frequented by visitors to the state. Smokey Mountain National Park, the Graceland mansion of Elvis Presley, TVA recreational areas, and bluegrass music festivals are also popular. The Grand Ole Opry nationally broadcasts country-and-western music from Nashville.

Tennessee's unofficial nickname is the Volunteer State, which recognizes the many residents who have served in America's armed forces during times of war and international conflict. Tennessee has also been called the Monkey State, a reference to a 1925 trial. A high school biology teacher from Dayton was convicted and fined $100 for teaching Charles Darwin's theory of evolution in violation of a state law mandating that schools teach the *Bible*'s story of creation. The case attracted nationwide attention, featuring three-time presidential candidate and fundamentalist preacher William Jennings Bryan (1860–1925) as prosecutor against celebrated defense attorney and avowed atheist Clarence Darrow (1857–1938). During the 1990s Tennessee became widely known as the home of Vice President Albert Gore (1993–), whose family owns a farm in Carthage.

***See also:* Appalachain Mountains, Tennessee Valley Authority, Trail of Tears**

FURTHER READING

Dykeman, Wilma. *Tennessee: A Bicentennial History*. New York: Norton, 1975.

Patterson, Christine P. *Haunting Memories: Echoes and Images of Tennessee's Past.* Knoxville: University of Tennessee Press, 1996.

Smith, Samuel B., ed. *Tennessee History: A Bibliography.* Knoxville: University of Tennessee Press, 1974.

''State of Tennessee Home Page'' [cited May 1, 1999], available from the World Wide Web @ www.state.tn.us.

Worldmark Encyclopedia of the States. Detroit: The Gale Group, 1998, s.v. ''Tennessee.''

TENNESSEE VALLEY AUTHORITY

The Tennessee River, the largest tributary to the Ohio River, drains approximately 41,000 square miles of the eastern United States. With its headwaters in southwestern Virginia, the river flows southwesterly through Knoxville, Tennessee, dipping into northeastern Alabama before turning westward across the full length of the state then northward through western Tennessee into western Kentucky where its meets the Ohio River. The watershed also includes parts of North Carolina, Georgia, and Mississippi.

At the beginning of the twentieth century, the Tennessee River area was one of the poorest in the nation. Floods regularly inundated much of the region in late winter and early spring, logging had stripped the hills of forests, and poor farming techniques led to exceptional topsoil erosion rates. Many rural settlements had no electricity. The population was steadily dwindling as people left seeking employment.

During World War I (1914–1918) the U.S. government built two nitrite plants and a hydroelectric dam on the Tennessee River at Muscle Shoals, Alabama for munitions production. Following the war, the project was largely neglected. Nebraska Senator George Norris lobbied extensively for government operation of the unused facilities for local benefit. Congress twice passed legislation, in 1928 and 1931, only to be vetoed by Presidents Calvin Coolidge (1923–1929) and Herbert Hoover (1929–1933).

With newly-elected President Franklin D. Roosevelt (1933–1945) and Congress tackling a dramatic round of New Deal reform legislation early in 1933, known as the Hundred Days, Norris reintroduced his legislation. Opportunities for large-scale government planning projects offering employment relief keenly interested Roosevelt. The President took Norris' bill and dramatically enlarged the scope of it. The resulting Tennessee Valley Authority Act of 1933 created an unprecedented strategy of regional government planning and development. A novel concept, the newly created Tennessee Valley Authority (TVA) was conceived as an independent corporate agency, a federally owned corporation combining the power of government with the flexibility of private business. The act created a three-member board, appointed by the President, to oversee the autonomous program.

> The Tennessee Valley Authority is . . . the most ambitious regional development project ever undertaken by the United States government. . . . It encompassed dam construction, flood control, navigation, power generation and distribution, agricultural development, industrial development, resettlement, housing, community development, and indirectly, health and education. . . . Roosevelt regarded the TVA as the first step towards a system of national planning . . . Franklin Roosevelt had intended TVA to be the first of many regional authorities.
>
> **Higgins, Benjamin, "The American Frontier and the TVA,"** ***Society*****, March/April, 1995.**

The development of TVA was shaped to a substantial degree by its first administrative board. Arthur Morgan, Harcourt Morgan (no relation), and David Lilienthal argued about the focus and purpose of the agency while it faced court challenges from opponents. Arthur Morgan, the first chairman, wanted to emphasize planning and efforts to eliminate poverty and he wanted electric rates to be set at levels comparable to private industry. Lilienthal was a strong supporter of public ownership and he wanted the agency to compete aggressively with private power companies. Harcourt Morgan, who opposed government planning, allied with Lilienthal and thus TVA emphasized dams for flood control navigation and power generation. In 1936 the Supreme Court upheld the agency's authority to generate and sell electricity at Wilson Dam and in 1939 it held that the agency was constitutional. By then Roosevelt had dismissed Arthur Morgan as chair of the TVA board due to the feuding among the board members and he appointed Harcourt Morgan in his place. When Lilienthal became chairman in 1941, TVA was the leading producer of electricity in the entire nation; that position the agency has maintained.

Designed to be administered through integral regional management, the TVA began with the construction of multipurpose dams and reservoirs. Eventually, a system of forty-two dams affected the economies of seven states. With the increased demand for electrical power, the TVA began constructing steam-generating facilities in the 1940s. By the 1970s large steam plants, fed with coal from extensive strip mining operations, produced over 80 percent of TVA's power. In 1959 the TVA power program became self-financing, running at a profit in the 1960s as the nation's largest electricity producer. Since that time, the TVA paid dividends and repayments to the U.S. Treasury and made payments to states and counties in place of taxes.

During World War II (1939–1945) TVA completed additional dams to generate electricity for aluminum manufacture and the initially secret atomic facilities at Oak Ridge, Tennessee. In keeping with the agency's integral approach to problems, the completion of the dams also completed a 650 mile navigation channel that connected eastern Tennessee with the Ohio River and then down the Mississippi to the sea. The system today includes twenty-nine hydroelectric dams on the Tennessee River and its tributaries.

TVA's efforts led to electrification and a great deal of economic development of what had been a rural backward area during the 1930s and 1940s. By the 1950s demand for electricity in the region exceeded the capacity of the agency's hydroelectric dams. In 1959 Congress authorized TVA to issue bonds to fund the construction of coal-fired plants, using the extensive coal reserves of the region. In the late 1990s TVA operated eleven coal-fired power plants. TVA's power operations were also made self-supporting and federal funds were appropriated only for the non-power areas of the agency. The region continued to experience significant growth in industry and population.

The availability of abundant power at low rates attracted many businesses and industry to the region. To enhance commercial traffic and recreation, the TVA dredged the Tennessee River from its mouth upstream and created a navigation channel over 600 miles in length. The new system of inland waterways greatly facilitated the hauling of coal, construction materials, petroleum, forest products, and grain. By the 1960s per capita income had risen dramatically and population decline had ended due to hundreds of thousands of new jobs

Besides successfully bringing rural electrification and power for businesses to an area twice the size of the Tennessee Valley, other significant TVA programs included flood control, soil conservation, agriculture education through demonstration farms, fertilizer research and production, and recreational developments including the 170,000 acre ''Land Between the Lakes'' recreational area.

Through its early years, the TVA maintained a respected image promoting a popular image of progress. The TVA became a model for other nations, particularly developing Third World nations. However, increasing attacks over environmental issues grew in the 1960s. But TVA ran into problems in two areas: For one thing, the rise of the environmentalist movement brought a consciousness of the cost to the natural surroundings of such a large and ambitious project. Many considered the TVA a symbol of heavy-handed human conquest over the environment including initial population displacements and removal of thousands of acres of rich bottomlands from potential agricultural production through reservoir flooding. The Tellico Dam construction led to a highly publicized confrontation over environmental issues. A major violator of the Clean Air Act, the TVA spent $1 billion to remove sulfur dioxide emissions from its 12 coal-burning plants and for strip mine reclamation.

Another problem arose with the project to build nuclear facilities to produce electrical power. In the 1960s TVA began construction of several nuclear power plants to meet expected future growth in demand for power. These plants were plagued with problems and cost overruns, some due to the changes in the regulatory environment after the incident at Three Mile Island. Several of the plant projects were abandoned and not completed; three were completed and they remain in operation. The nuclear plants added significantly to TVA's debt and they also renewed opposition to the agency. Safety issues soon arose, triggering a Nuclear Regulatory Commission investigation in 1975. Back on track as a national pacesetter in nuclear plant construction, fourteen plants were under construction by the early 1980s at the cost of over $1 billion annually. Few actually became operational and the TVA was left in debt for billions of dollars by the 1990s.

In spite of these problems, in many ways the TVA was remarkably successful in achieving its original objectives of economic development in a severely depressed region. The TVA's electricity production was also useful as a ''yardstick'' gauge of the reasonableness of rate-requests charged to consumers by other utilities across the nation. Some observers note that this was the aspect of the system that earned it the enmity of the public utilities. Private utility companies saw the TVA as a threat and unsuccessfully challenged its constitutionality before the Supreme Court.

Roosevelt had envisioned similar authorities in many other river basins. However, the political climate was never again conducive to such projects. Congress was unwilling to grant such autonomy to a federally funded organization. A living legacy of the New Deal, TVA remained the most ambitious development project ever undertaken by the federal government.

See also: **New Deal**

FURTHER READING

Crease, Walter L. *TVA's Public Planning: The Vision, the Reality*. Knoxville, TN: University of Tennessee Press, 1990.

Durant, Robert F. *When Government Regulates Itself: EPA, TVA, and Pollution Control in the 1970s.* Knoxville: University of Tennessee Press, 1985.

Grant, Nancy L. *TVA and Black Americans: Planning for the Status Quo*. Philadelphia: Temple University Press, 1990.

Hargrove, Erwin C. *Prisoners of Myth: The Leadership of the Tennessee Valley Authority, 1933–1990.* Princeton: Princeton University Press, 1994.

Hubbard, Preston J. *Origins of the TVA: The Muscle Shoals Controversy*. Nashville: Vanderbilt University Press, 1961.

Miller, Barbara A., and Richard B. Reidinger, eds. *Comprehensive River Basin Development: The Tennessee Valley Authority*. Washington, DC: World Bank, 1998.

Neuse, Steven M. *David E. Lilienthal: The Journey of an American Liberal*. Knoxville, TN: University of Tennessee Press, 1996.

Selznick, Philip. *TVA and the Grass Roots: A Study in the Sociology of Formal Organization*. New York: Harper & Row, 1966.

TEXAS

Texas, or the Lone Star State, is known for the strength and character of its people, who have overcome various difficulties. As the economy has waxed and waned, Texans—very much dependent on ranching, farming, and oil production—have stood tall to overcome any adversity that has come their way.

In the 1600s the Spanish were the first to settle in Texas along the San Antonio River, where they established forts and churches. The Spanish taught the Native Americans who lived in the area about Christianity, and the Native Americans taught the Spanish how to farm the land and grow crops.

In 1689 a Spanish explorer named Captain Alonso de Leon left behind a cow and a calf at each river he came across during his expeditions through central and eastern Texas. When the Spanish left some of their missions, they left the cows to roam free on the land. These herds of cattle thrived on the Texas grasslands. Throughout Texas, the Spanish established large cattle ranches, each owned by a *hacendado*, who lived a privileged life. The *vaquero*, or cowboy, worked hard on the ranch for meager meals and a place to sleep. The Spanish established sheep ranches in Texas as well, and these rural estates have also had an impact on the state's economy.

Before the Louisiana Purchase in 1803, the United States took no interest in Texas land. When the Louisiana Territory became part of the United States, however, Texas became a next-door neighbor. In 1820 Moses Austin, a Missouri businessman, convinced the Spanish government to allow him to establish a colony in Texas. Austin's plan was to farm the rich soil along the Brazos River near what is now known as Houston. Upon their arrival in Texas, the colonists learned that Spain had been overthrown and a new government of Mexico ruled Texas. Over the next few years pioneers from Tennessee and other southern states migrated to Texas. They worked hard and fared well. As the number of such colonists grew, they demanded to have a greater influence on the policies and laws set forth by the Mexican government.

In 1835 war broke out as Texas successfully fought for independence from Mexico. After the war, the colonists of the new Republic of Texas faced the challenges of rebuilding their land and businesses. Because roads were not adequate, it was difficult to ship goods in and out of Texas. What's more, the Republic's government had no money. In order to attract newcomers, the government gave away huge tracts of land to settlers. The government also established the homestead-exemption law, which stated that those who fell delinquent on debt payments could not lose their land.

Between 1836 and 1847 the population of Texas quadrupled, with most of the new settlers coming from the United States. Many other settlers came from Germany, Belgium, France, England, Ireland, and Sweden to work on cattle ranches and cotton plantations. In

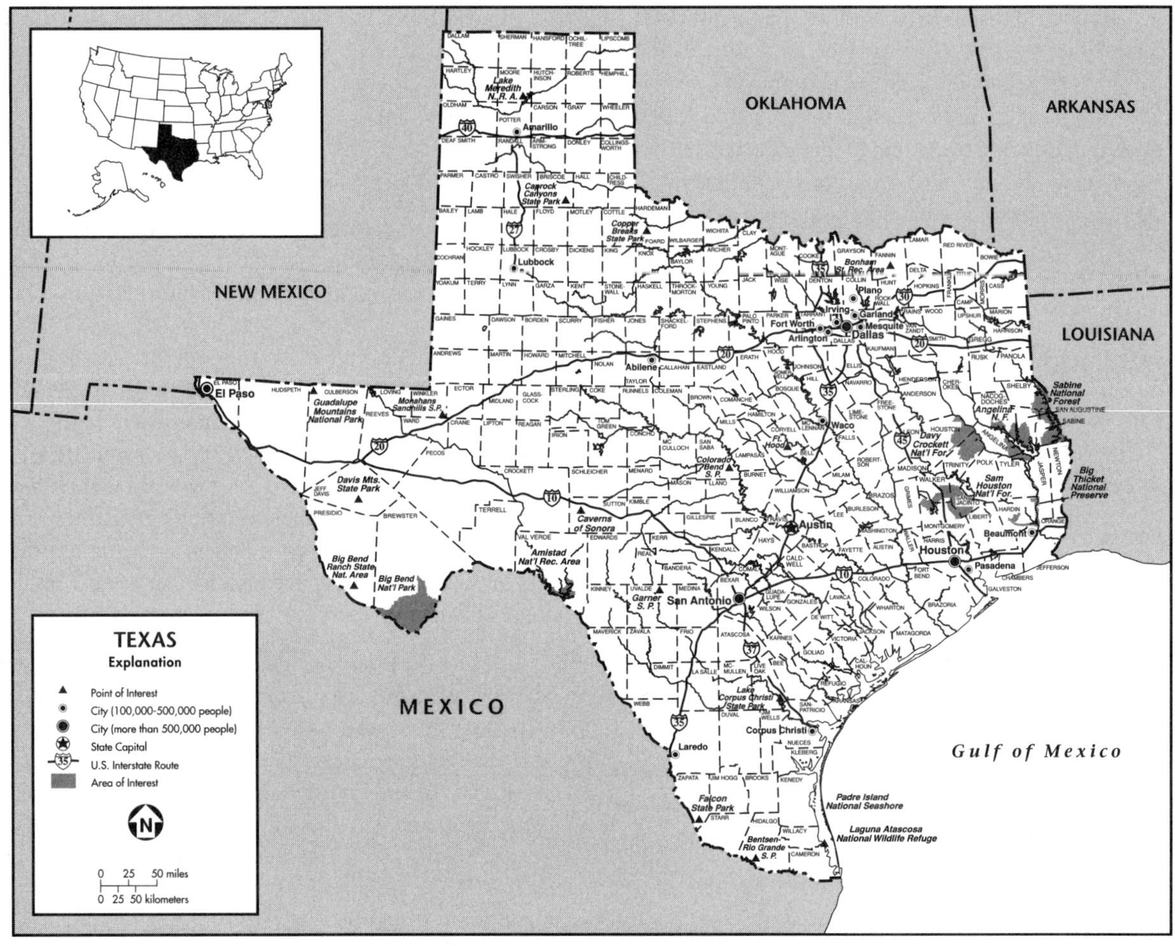

State of Texas.

1836 a few cities emerged in eastern and central Texas. San Antonio grew to become the largest town in Texas, and Galveston, founded in 1836, became the main port for shipping cotton.

Mexico still considered Texas a colony and threatened to declare war on the United States if it moved to allow Texas to become a state. Mexico held true to its words when, in 1845, the United States approved the statehood of Texas. The two-year war between the United States and Mexico (the Mexican War, 1846–1848) resulted in a peace treaty that forced Mexico to give up all claims on the American Southwest, as well as California.

During the years following the American Civil War (1861–1865) the state government's treasury was again depleted. The state's economy before the war depended on the land—and on the slaves who worked on the land. After the war, land prices dropped and, since slaves were free, labor was scarce. Nonetheless, the 4 million longhorn cattle roaming the ranges of Texas provided another source of income for the ailing economy. The cattle, a source of tallow, hide, and food, could be sold for $40 a head in the north. In 1866 large-scale cattle drives began in Texas, as more than 250,000 cattle were driven northward to market. For three to six months cowboys pushed the cattle toward their destination: railroad depots in Kansas or Missouri. The cattle-drive period lasted about 20 years. By the 1880s expanded railroads helped to transport the cattle, and such drives were no longer necessary.

IN TEXAS, OIL IS THE TAIL THAT WAGS THE WHOLE ECONOMY.

Professor Bernard Weinstein, Southern Methodist University

After the Civil War the U.S. population began to push westward, forcing Native Americans to move to reservations in Oklahoma. Within 30 years the population of the Texas Great Plains grew to exceed 500,000. Though rainfall was scarce, there were great reserves of underground water in Texas and a constant breeze.

These conditions led to the use of windmills for power and water.

By 1890 railroads crisscrossed the state. Three major railroads connected western and eastern Texas, the surrounding states, and the country's East and West Coasts. While the railroads provided efficient transportation, the costs remained relatively high for the ranchers and farmers until the Texas Railroad Commission was established to regulate freight rates.

Texas's economic base changed forever in 1901, when an oil gusher was discovered in Spindletop Hill just south of Dallas. News of the well traveled fast, and an influx of oil workers and engineers tripled the population almost overnight. From Spindletop, oil businessmen spread out to other cities looking for more. By the end of the year the government had issued more than five hundred charters to oil companies. In 1930 drillers discovered the biggest crude oil pool in the country in Rush County near Kilgore. At this site C.M. Joiner, who was drilling an exploratory well, founded the East Texas Oil Fields, an underground lake of crude oil that measured 40 miles long and between three and 10 miles wide.

Naturally, oil had a major impact on the state's economy. Farmers who discovered oil on their property became rich. Some laborers invested their savings on prospective wells only to turn up sand. Spin-off businesses developed to provide drilling equipment, tank cars, and pipelines. The industries brought people from the farms to the cities, leading to a more than 20 percent increase in city dwellers between 1900 and 1930. Other industries also flourished. During the 1920s new irrigation methods and farming equipment opened areas of the state for cotton growing, and production exploded. Texas produced more than a million bales of cotton in 1926, compared to only 50,000 bales in 1918.

The Great Depression (1929–1939) struck the country in the late 1920s, however, putting more than 300,000 Texans out of work. Many farmers suffered from drastically reduced cotton prices, and a drought in the Texas Panhandle caused farmers and ranchers to leave their homes. Attempts to establish relief programs for the poor and conservation programs for farmlands added to the state's financial difficulties.

World War II (1939–1945) helped to turn around the state's economy. Oil wells provided more than half of the petroleum for the nation during the war, and manufacturing jobs tripled as factories built aircraft, ships, and other goods for the war effort. After the war more than 60 percent of Texas's population lived in urban areas, and Texas remained a major ship and aircraft producer. These industries would remain important to the state's economy for years to come.

Another discovery made in Texas has led to the advancement of technology around the world. In 1958 Jack Kilby, an employee of Texas Instruments in Dallas, made a finding that led to the production of the silicon chip, enabling the development of handheld calculators, personal computers, and other miniaturized electronics.

Even though Texas's industry and agriculture were strong, the state's economy rose and fell according to the oil market during the 1970s and 1980s. When oil sold for more than $30 per barrel in the 1970s and early 1980s, the economy in Texas boomed, growing more than 6 percent a year—more than twice the national average. The high oil prices led to easy cash flow: Investors built high-rises in Dallas and Houston, and credit was easily extended. But in the late 1980s oil prices crashed to less than $14 per barrel due to overproduction. Construction stopped, several banks needed federal assistance to remain in business, and more than 20 percent of office space in Dallas and Houston stood vacant as thousands lost their jobs. As Professor Bernard Weinstein of Southern Methodist University stated, "[i]n Texas, oil is the tail that wags the whole economy."

In order to make up the $100 million in revenues that the government estimated it had lost for every $1 decline in the price of a barrel oil, the government raised fees on everything from vanity license plates to day-care centers. It also made efforts to attract new business to Texas, particularly high-tech companies. In 1986 oil prices again began to climb. The revived oil market, along with Texas's newly established high-tech businesses, helped to stabilize the state's economy by the 1990s.

From 1991 to 1996 total personal income grew in Texas by 20.2 percent, while the nation's growth was about 15 percent during the same period. In 1995 the median household income in Texas was $32,039. That same year, however, 17.4 percent of Texans were living below the federal poverty level.

***See also:* Cattle Drives, Longhorn Cattle, Petroleum Industry, Westward Expansion**

FURTHER READING

Frantz, Joe B. *Texas: A Bicentennial History*. New York: Norton, 1976.

Proctor, Ben and Archie P. McDonald. *The Texas Heritage*. Wheeling, Illinois: Harlan Davidson, 1998.

Richardson, Rupert, Ernest Wallace, and Adrian N. Anderson. *Texas, The Lone-Star State*. Englewood Cliffs, NJ: Prentice Hall, 1970.

Thompson, Kathleen. "Texas." In *Portrait of America*. New York: Steck-Vaughn Publishers, 1996.

Worldmark Encyclopedia of the States. Detroit: Gale Research, 1998, s.v. "Texas."

TEXAS ANNEXATION

> The annexation of Texas is but another name for the perpetuity of slavery; and we who now enjoy the rights and hold the soil of the Union, must bid farewell forever to the hope of relieving ourselves from the danger, the odium, and the disgrace inseparable from this pernicious institution.
>
> **Theodore Sedgwick, an opponent of Texas annexation**

During the early colonization of North America by European countries, Spain claimed a vast area of the Southwest including present-day Texas, New Mexico, Arizona, and California. However, few Spaniards actually settled in these areas and by 1820 only 3,500 non-Indian people occupied the entire region. San Antonio de Bexar, the Spanish capital of Texas, itself had only 800 residents. With the U.S. acquisition of the Louisiana territories from France in 1803, U.S. presence along the Mississippi River corridor posed a threat to the nearby Spanish claims. In an effort to hold off further U.S. expansion, Spain used the land of Texas as a buffer. Local Spanish authorities recruited some 300 U.S. citizens to accept low-priced land in exchange for maintaining loyalty to Spain. After some initial problems, the new settlers finally arrived in 1822 only to find that Mexico had gained independence from Spain (in 1821). However, the original land-grant agreement for the U.S. citizens was accepted by the new Mexican government.

Through the next several years more U.S. settlers filed into Texas than Mexico had anticipated and the buffer region was becoming a threat itself. By 1830 Mexican settlers were far out-numbered with over 15,000 white settlers and 1,000 black slaves living in Texas. The later settlers were generally disrespectful of the relatively ineffective Mexican rule. In an effort to discourage further settlement, Mexico attempted to abolish slavery and to stop further immigration from the United States. Mexico also boosted its military presence which further spurred a clamor for Texas independence.

Finally, open rebellion by Texas settlers occurred in October of 1835, with events escalating quickly. A siege of Texas volunteers by Mexican troops in the early San Antonio Spanish mission of the Alamo began in December, resulting in a climatic Mexican victory in March of 1836. While the Alamo was under siege, a group of Texas delegates drafted a Texas constitution patterned after the U.S. Constitution and proclaimed independence. Following other Mexican military victories in early 1836, the Texas volunteers struck back at San Jacinto in April, winning a stunning victory and capturing the Mexican head of state, General Antonio Lopez de Santa Anna. The Texans forced Santa Anna to grant independence, but the Mexican government later reneged, claiming that the act had been coerced. In addition, the United States was unwilling to annex Texas despite a referendum vote in 1836 among Texas settlers overwhelmingly favoring annexation. Consequently, for almost a decade Texas was an independent nation.

There were several reasons for the United States' unwillingness to accept Texas' request to be admitted to the Union. Most importantly, Texas was a slave state with its eastern portion heavily committed to cotton cultivation. Its annexation would upset the delicate balance of 13 slave states and 13 non-slave states currently making up the country. The United States, additionally, did not wish to further aggravate their political relationship with Mexico. Moreover, the common perception of U.S. citizens was that Texas' population largely consisted of undesirables. And again, in 1838 Congress defeated a bill to annex Texas.

As Texas was burdened by a huge debt following its independence and as it had no industry, Texas President Sam Houston implemented settlement policies encouraging immigration from the United States and Europe. Free land was offered, and consequently the immigrant population grew from 35,000 settlers in 1836 to 147,000 by 1846. An agrarian slave-based cotton economy flourished on the fertile soils along the rivers and it led to creation of a planter aristocracy concentrating economic wealth in the hands of a very small minority. Texas cotton attracted higher prices in Europe than Southern United States cotton. With the decline of slave-based agriculture in the U.S. border states such as Maryland and Kentucky, slavery-based economies were moving southwestward toward the deep South and Texas.

However, certain other economic and political developments began to catch the attention of the United States. Texas had established diplomatic relations with several nations, including Britain and France. Those two nations saw an independent Texas as an inhibitor to U.S. expansion. Mexico, who had thoughts of retaking the largely defenseless new nation, became convinced that the continued existence of the Texas Republic might actually serve as a buffer against U.S. expansionism as originally sought. The United States saw Texas' growing ties to European countries as a significant threat to its future expansion. In addition, despite its financially troubled status, Texas began expressing its own expansionist desires. While Texas already included parts of present-day New Mexico, Colorado, and Arkansas, in 1842 the Texas congress voted to extend Texas' boundaries all the way west to the Pacific Ocean to what was later California and some parts of northern Mexico.

Finally, with rising U.S. concern over Texas' future, lame-duck President John Tyler (1841–1845) submitted a treaty of annexation to Congress. The proposal immediately became an 1844 presidential election issue. An ardent proponent of annexation, James K. Polk (1845–1849) won the election, but before he could be inaugurated, Congress voted for annexation in 1845. Texas officially became part of the United States on December 29, 1845. Terms of the annexation agreement were generous to the new state, with Texas retaining all of its public lands and the United States paying $5 million to ease its debts.

Long term benefits to the United States for Texas annexation were significant. The annexation led quickly to war with Mexico in 1846. The victorious United States came away with control of the American Southwest and California through the Treaty of Guadalupe in 1848. The slave-based cotton production boomed as the number of slaves in Texas increased from 12,500 in 1840 to almost 170,000 in 1860. Besides the cotton trade, Texas became the king of the cattle industry in the nineteenth century and later a major oil producer. Texas annexation also rounded out the borders of a truly transcontinental United States.

FURTHER READING

Brack, Gene M. *Mexico Views Manifest Destiny, 1821–1846: An Essay on the Origins of the Mexican War.* Albuquerque, NM: University of New Mexico Press, 1975.

Hogan, William R. *The Texas Republic: A Social and Economic History.* Norman: University of Oklahoma Press, 1946.

McComb, David G. *Texas, a Modern History.* Austin, TX: University of Texas Press, 1989.

Merk, Frederick. *Slavery and the Annexation of Texas.* New York: Knopf, 1972.

Montejano, David. *Anglos and Mexicans in the Making of Texas, 1836–1986.* Austin, TX: University of Texas Press, 1987.

TEXAS COMPANY

The Texas Company was founded during the early boom years of the Texas oil industry. In 1901 a gusher at the Spindletop oil field sent hundreds of entrepreneurs into Beaumont, Texas. Pumping out as much as 100,000 barrels a day, the Spindletop wells led to the rapid establishment of over 200 oil companies. Among the entrepreneurs who came to Texas was Joseph S. ''Buckskin Joe'' Cullinan, an oilman who had begun his career working for Standard Oil Company in Pennsylvania. Cullinan saw an opportunity in purchasing the crude oil for resale to refineries. With the help of New York investment manager Arnold Schlaet, he formed the Texas Fuel Company with an initial stock of $50,000. Cullinan and Schlaet began soliciting additional investors in New York and Chicago. After raising three million dollars, they reorganized their venture as the Texas Company.

Cullinan immediately began construction on a pipeline between Spindletop and the gulf coast of Texas. He built a refinery at the Texas coastal city of Port Arthur, and from there the company shipped its oil to Louisiana sugar planters, who used it to heat their boilers. In the fall of 1902 salt water leaked into the Spindletop wells, ruining many of the companies based there. The Texas Company survived with a timely discovery of oil at Sour Lake, 20 miles northwest of Spindletop. Other oil strikes soon followed in Oklahoma and Louisiana.

With Cullinan's oil expertise and the financing of his New York backers, the Texas Company soon became one of the nation's most prominent oil companies. Cullinan continued to drill wells in the southwest region, building more pipelines to connect them with Port Arthur. By 1908 the company was selling oil to all but five western states, and by 1913 its assets were worth $60 million. The nickname ''Texaco'' came from the cable address of the company's New York offices. ''Texaco'' gained popularity as a product name and in 1906 the company registered it as a trademark. The well-known logo first appeared in 1909 as a red star with a green "T" in the center.

At the time of the Texas Company's founding, oil was used primarily for lighting and as fuel for factories and locomotives. The Texas Company met this demand with its first consumer product, Familylite Illuminating Oil, introduced in 1907. After 1910, however, the automobile revolutionized the oil industry. Demand for gasoline, formerly considered a waste byproduct of kerosene, expanded rapidly. The Texas Company followed this trend and by 1914 its gasoline production surpassed that of kerosene. The company went from distributing gasoline in barrels to underground tanks to curbside pumps, and in 1911 it opened its first filling station in Brooklyn, New York. By 1916 57 such stations were in operation across the country. Powered by the growth of the automobile industry and the high demand for petroleum created by World War I (1914–18), the Texas Company quadrupled its assets between 1914 and 1920.

After World War I the Texas Company continued to concentrate on its automotive gasoline and oil production by introducing new products and expanding its national sales network. In 1920 two researchers at the company's Port Arthur refinery developed the oil industry's first continuous thermal cracking process for making gasoline. Named after its founders, the Holmes-Manley process greatly increased the speed of the refining process as well as the amount of gasoline that could be refined from a barrel of crude. The Texas Company marketed this gasoline through its retail network, pushing into the Rocky Mountain region between 1920 and 1926 and into West Coast markets in 1928, with the acquisition of the California Petroleum Company.

Products introduced during the 1920s included the company's first premium gasoline as well as Texaco Aviation Gasoline and automobile motor oils. To market the lighter oils it refined from Texas crude, the Texas Company launched its first nationwide advertising campaign. The slogan "Clean, Clear, Golden" appeared at the company's filling stations, which displayed its motor oils in glass bottles. By 1928 the Texas Company owned or leased more than 4,000 stations in all 48 states.

The company's growth was also reflected in its corporate structure. Finding Texas's corporation laws too restrictive for doing business on such a large scale, the Texas Company decided to move its legal home. In 1926 it formed the Texas Corporation in Delaware, which then bought out the stock of the Texas Company and reorganized it as a subsidiary called the Texas Company of Delaware. The company also moved their headquarters from Houston to New York. The Texas Corporation acted as a holding company for the Texas Company of Delaware and the Texas Company of California—formerly the California Petroleum Company—until 1941, when it merged with both to form a single company known as the Texas Company.

The Texas Corporation's earnings reached an all-time high in 1929, but they dropped precipitously after the stock market crash in October of that same year. Overproduction, economic recession, and low prices plagued the oil industry in the early 1930s. The company embarked on a strategy of introducing new products to stimulate demand. Texaco Fire Chief Gasoline was launched in 1932 and the company advertised it by sponsoring a nationwide Ed Wynn radio program. Havoline Wax Free Motor Oil, developed after the acquisition of the Indiana Refining Company in 1931, followed two years later and by 1934 it halted the Texas Corporation's losses. In 1938 the Texas Corporation introduced Texaco Sky Chief premium gasoline and also began promoting its Registered Rest Rooms program, assuring motorists that their service stations were "Clean across the Country."

The entry of the United States into World War II (1939–45) brought dramatic changes for the Texas Company. About 30 percent of its wartime production went to the war effort, primarily in the form of aviation fuels, gasoline, and petrochemicals. The company worked closely with Harold L. Ickes, federal petroleum administrator for the war effort, who organized the nation's oil companies into several nonprofit operations. The Texas Pipe Line Company, a subsidiary, oversaw the completion of two federally sponsored pipelines from Texas to the East Coast. The Texas Company also joined War Emergency Tankers Inc., which operated a collective tanker fleet for the War Shipping Administration. Another such venture was the Neches Butane Products Company, which manufactured butadiene, an essential ingredient in synthetic rubber. This enterprise gave the Texas Company its start in the infant petrochemicals industry.

With the end of World War II the Texas Company faced renewed customer demand at home. In 1947 U.S. consumption of oil exceeded its production for the first time; the company reacted by tapping new foreign sources for its crude oil. The Texas Company formed the Trans-Arabian Pipe Line Company with three other oil companies to build a pipeline connecting Saudi Arabia's oil fields with the eastern Mediterranean.

In 1959 the Texas Company changed its name to Texaco Inc., formally taking on its longtime nickname. By the end of the twentieth century Texaco was one of the world's largest oil companies, with exploratory, manufacturing, and marketing operations located around the globe.

See also: **Exxon, Andrew Mellon, Petroleum Industry, Standard Oil**

FURTHER READING

Ackerman, Laurence D. "Texaco: One Brand, Many Markets." *Management Review*, September 1991.

Folmer, L. W. *Reaching for a Star: Experiences in the International Oil Business*. Austin, TX: L. W. Folmer, 1993.

James, Marquis. *The Texaco Story: The First Fifty Years, 1902–1952*. New York: Texas Company, 1953.

Shannon, James. *Texaco and the $10 Billion Jury*. Englewood Cliffs, NJ: Prentice Hall, 1988.

Texaco, Inc. *Texaco Today: The Spirit of the Star, 1902–1992*. White Plains, NY: Texaco Inc., 1992.

TEXTILE INDUSTRY

Although comprised of highly skilled craftsmanship the textile industry was essentially a cottage industry until the Industrial Revolution. The American textile industry was a direct product of the British factory system when Samuel Slater introduced the first cotton-spinning mill in 1790 in Pawtucket, Rhode Island. This change marked the beginning of New England's transformation from an agricultural region to a manufacturing one producing the modern forms of ownership, management, and big business. The factory system's emphasis on the individual worker was a major shift in the early U.S. labor system and it came to characterize U.S. industrial and social development.

In the 1790s Samuel Slater and his partner Moses Brown founded the firm of Almy, Brown, and Slater. Slater constructed machines based on the Arkwright model, a water-powered mill invented in the 1700s by Richard Arkwright. The business flourished and additional mills were constructed in Massachusetts, Rhode Island, and Connecticut. Slater altered the British system so that his firm would function effectively within the social and moral structure of the time. He focused on partnership and single proprietorship, on personal management, small-scale production, the use of water power, and the employment of family labor. From this system emerged a division of labor based on gender and age. Men were typically employed in supervisory capacities, as farm hands and laborers or as skilled artisans. Children and adolescents also worked in the mills while adult women remained at home. The children, often as young as seven or eight, would earn as little as 25 cents per week, and all wages would go directly to the head of the household. Hundreds of manufacturers throughout New England and the Mid-Atlantic states followed Slater's example and his mode of operation.

The Slater system was not the only factory form which developed during the early nineteenth century. In 1813 Francis Cabot Lowell introduced the use of power looms at his Boston Manufacturing Company in Waltham, Massachusetts. These operations combined the spinning of yarn and the weaving of cloth. Lowell employed women and girls who often lived in boarding houses built by the company. Historians have often labeled the Lowell style as the first form of big business in America. This was due to the large-scale, incorporated nature of these ventures, which were also characterized by professional management. The company operated from Waltham, Massachusetts, until 1823 when it relocated operations to Lowell, Massachusetts. The Lowell companies benefited from the tariff of 1816, which imposed a 25 percent tariff on imported cotton and woolen goods. This made them a financial success with profits reaching 20 to 24 percent annually.

A downturn occurred in the textile industry beginning in 1829 resulting in wage cuts. A labor strike ensued in 1834, which was one of the first forms of collective action taken by industrial workers. In response mill owners resorted to immigrant labor, hiring French, Canadian, Italian, and Irish workers to replace the native-born labor force. Strikes and riots in the 1840s reflected disputes between labor and management over the use of immigrant workers. Given these conditions in conjunction with the depression of 1836 through 1844, the textile industry struggled and labor won few victories during these years.

For much of the nineteenth century the Northeast remained the center of the textile production; cotton, woolen, linen, and thread output in this area was rising. In the 1880s, however, a major shift in location began to occur. Cotton mills became the symbol of the New South and mill towns sprang up in the Piedmont region from Virginia to Georgia and into Alabama. Small textile mills focused on small-scale production and

The textile industry was essentially a cottage industry until the Industrial Revolution and huge mills took over the bulk of textile manufacturing.

paternalistic practices by the owners. Mill agents and superintendents controlled these southern mill towns, with the company providing jobs, houses, food, clothing, and goods. The work force was drawn from the countryside and conditions were harsh. Attempts were made in the 1880s and 1890s to organize southern mill workers, but strikes were ineffective due to the generally poor conditions of the national economy.

In the early twentieth century conditions in the textile industry continued to be precarious, particularly in the North. The Industrial Workers of the World organized major strikes in 1912 and 1913 in Patterson, New Jersey, and Lawrence, Massachusetts. However, labor remained unable to make a major impact on management's long range operations. If labor grew too powerful in one area the firms simply moved to another location where cheaper labor could be hired. The introduction of synthetic fibers such as nylon and rayon also affected the industry. This greatly impacted the design of fashions and ultimately subjected textile producers to the whims of fashion designers and consumers. In addition, there was increasing international competition to be acknowledged—particularly from Japan. This led to many manufacturers shutting down production or moving south. By the 1920s New England textile towns had fallen into a depression.

While the textile industry struggled through this crisis the Great Depression (1929–39) effectively removed the industry from a central place in U.S. manufacturing. However, while many of the dominant textile companies of the early twentieth century went bankrupt, some thrived after World War I (1914–18). The most important of these, Burlington Mills, prospered remarkably during and after the Great Depression. Spencer Love founded the company in 1923 when it employed two hundred workers. In 1933 there were 6,900 employees and by 1962, at the time of Love's death, the company employed over sixty thousand people. These figures present a stark contrast to the fate of numerous other textile companies; the survival and growth of Burlington Mills can be attributed almost entirely to the management expertise of Spencer Love. The success of this company relied not only on the recurring theme of relocation of factories to areas of cheaper labor, but also on Love's understanding of the basic restructuring of the textile industry during his lifetime. When artificial and synthetic yarns started to displace the natural fibers of cotton, wool, and silk, Love protected his company by extensive diversification and the creation of a multidivisional infrastructure that linked manufacturing with sales. He also promoted greater control over his goods by integrating external services into his company. The most significant factor affecting the success of Burlington Mills was Love's aggressive management style, which was not bound to any particular tradition or plan. He kept the company profitable by experimenting with new products, new machinery, and progressive marketing strategies.

While other sectors of the manufacturing environment such as the steel, chemical, and automotive industries experienced significant expansion, the textile industry did not. The "managerial revolution" that occurred within high throughput companies such as DuPont or General Motors simply never happened in the textile industry. Spencer Love was an anomaly, attempting to transform the traditional textile industry via integration, diversification, and multidivisional structure. Unfortunately, many of the difficulties that had plagued this industry since its beginning were still in evidence in the late 1990s.

FURTHER READING

Blicksilver, Jack. "Cotton Manufacturing in the Southeast: An Historical Analysis." *Harvard Business Review*, 1959.

Chandler, Alfred D., Jr. "The Structure of American Industry in the Twentieth Century: A Historical Overview," *Business History Review*, Autumn 1969.

Forner, Eric and John A. Garraty, eds. *The Reader's Companion to American History*. Boston: Houghton Mifflin Company, 1991, s.v. "Textile Industry."

"Strategy and Structure in the Textile Industry: Spencer Love and Burlington Mills," [cited April 16, 1999] available from the World Wide Web @ http://web4.infortrac-custom.com/.

U.S. Industry Profiles. Detroit: The Gale Group, 1994, s.v. "Cotton Broadwoven Fabric Mills."

THIRTEENTH AMENDMENT

Proposed on January 31, 1865, and ratified on December 6, 1865, the Thirteenth Amendment abolished slavery throughout the United States. It stated that "neither slavery nor involuntary servitude, except as a punishment of crime whereof the party shall have been duly convicted, shall exist within the United States, or any place subject to their jurisdiction." On January 1, 1863, in the middle of the American Civil War (1861–1865), President Abraham Lincoln (1861–1865) issued the Emancipation Proclamation. It was an authority based on congressional acts, and it gave the president authority to confiscate rebel property and forbid the military from returning slaves of rebels to their owners. It therefore addressed only the rebelling southern states and did not resolve the issue of slavery for the nation as a whole. The Thirteenth Amendment (the first of the three so-called "Civil War Amendments") prohibited slavery throughout the country. The Fourteenth and Fifteenth Amendments extended the rights of citizenship to all people regardless of race or color.

See also: **Civil War (Economic Causes of), Civil War (Economic Impact of), Emancipation Proclamation, Slavery**

THOMAS, NORMAN MATTOON

Norman Mattoon Thomas (1884–1968) was the leader of the Socialist movement in the United States for more than four decades. He ran unsuccessfully for U.S. President on the socialist ticket six times. He also wrote numerous books, articles, and pamphlets touting the benefits of socialism and criticizing American capitalist society.

Norman Thomas was born on November 20, 1884 in Marion, Ohio, the son of a Presbyterian minister. He studied political science at Princeton University and then studied for the ministry at Union Theological Seminary. It was there that Thomas was introduced to the reform-minded Social Gospel Theology of Walter Rauschenbusch and the teachings of Christian Socialism. Thomas was ordained a minister in 1911 and became pastor of the East Harlem Presbyterian Church in New York.

During World War I (1914–1918), Thomas joined the Fellowship of Reconciliation, an organization of reformist and pacifist clergyman. He established a magazine for the group called *World Tomorrow*. In 1917 Thomas joined Roger Baldwin in founding the Civil Liberties Bureau—which later became the American Civil Liberties Union (ACLU)—to protect conscientious objectors who were trying to avoid military service.

In 1918 Thomas resigned from the church and became actively involved in the Socialist party. He served as associate editor of *The Nation* and became co-director of the League for Industrial Democracy, the educational branch of the Socialist party. When the head of the Socialist party, Eugene V. Debs (1855–1926), died in 1926, Thomas became his successor.

As leader of the Socialist party, Thomas spoke out in favor of public ownership and the democratic management of the country's industries, national resources, and transportation. He also supported a public employment system, unemployment insurance, a five-day workweek, and a minimum wage. Thomas ran for president on the socialist ticket six times between 1928 and 1948. His most successful campaign was in 1932, when he earned 884,781 votes.

Despite Thomas' enthusiasm and dedication, the Socialist party gradually lost supporters during his tenure. Many of the party's ideas had been incorporated into President Franklin D. Roosevelt's (1933–1945) New Deal, and there was mounting dissention within the Socialist Party over the proper role of the United States in foreign affairs. Thomas retired from politics in 1948, though he continued to publicly support causes such as world peace, nuclear disarmament, and crusade against poverty. Although many people did not agree with his views, Thomas was nonetheless a well-respected political figure until his death on December 19, 1968.

See also: **Socialism**

FURTHER READING

Duram, James C. *Norman Thomas.* New York: Twayne Publishers, 1974.

Fleischman, Harry. *Norman Thomas, A Biography: 1884–1968.* New York: Norton, 1969.

Gorham, Charles. *Leader at Large: The Long and Fighting Life of Norman Thomas.* New York: Farrar, Straus, and Giroux, 1970.

Johnpoll, Bernard K. *Pacifist's Progress: Norman Thomas and the Decline of American Socialism.* Chicago: Quadrangle Books, 1970.

Seidler, Murray Benjamin. *Norman Thomas: Respectable Rebel.* Syracuse, New York: Syracuse University Press, 1967.

Thomas, Norman. *The Norman Thomas Papers, 1904–1967.* Alexandria, Virginia: Chadwyck-Healey, 1983.

TIDEWATER

Virginia's Tidewater is in the eastern part of the state and consists of the low-lying region along the Atlantic Ocean which surrounds Chesapeake Bay. The area is roughly 100 miles (160 kilometers) wide and is crisscrossed by rivers and inlets which fill when the tide rises in the Atlantic. Salt marshes and swamps are also prevalent. The area includes the Eastern Shore, the peninsula that extends southward from Maryland and juts out between Chesapeake Bay (on the west) and the Atlantic (on the east). During colonial times an aristocratic culture emerged here that became highly influential in Virginia colonial politics between 1607 and 1710. The interests of the wealthy Eastern Shore families were often in direct opposition to those of the back country settlers. In 1676 these conflicting views resulted in Bacon's Rebellion, which pit frontiersmen headed by back country leader Nathaniel Bacon (1647–76) against the Virginia militia organized by English Colonial Governor William Berkeley (1606–77). The rebellion was put down after Bacon died of dysentary. Berkeley, who had always been favorable toward the Tidewater power-bloc, was recalled to England by the king for his action.

See also: **Back Country, Virginia**

TIMES MIRROR CO.

The Times Mirror Company was first incorporated in 1884 as the parent company of the *Los Angeles Times*; this collaboration was founded in 1881 by the *Los Angeles Daily Times* and its printer, the Mirror Printing and Binding House. The company was founded by Civil War veteran General Harrison Gray Otis—who had moved to California and made a fortune in real estate—and Colonel H. H. Boyce. Otis bought out Boyce two years later and then became the newspaper's president, general manager, and editor-in-chief.

Los Angeles was a small, sleepy town in the late nineteenth century, and the *Times's* circulation was less than 7,000 in 1890. In 1894 Henry Chandler became Otis's son-in-law. The two men would run the newspaper until Otis's death in 1917, whereupon Chandler would become president, general manager, and publisher of the *Times* for three decades. Descendants of Otis and Chandler would hold a controlling interest in the Times Mirror Company throughout the twentieth century.

At the beginning of the twentieth century the *Times* could boast it carried more advertising than any other newspaper in the world. By 1905 annual gross revenues topped $1 million. Throughout the century the newspaper grew with the city it served, publishing its first article on movie making in 1909 and its first movie review in 1913. (From 1922 to 1927 it even owned and operated the first commercial radio station in Los Angeles County.) The newspaper was known for its right wing, anti-union stance, and the company succeeded in keeping unions out of the *Times* in spite of a union-planted bomb that destroyed the *Times* building in 1910. The *Times* achieved notoriety in 1935, when it ran faked photos of pro-unionist author Upton Sinclair (1878–1968), who was running for governor of California.

Norman Chandler, Henry Chandler's son, became general manager in 1936, president and general manager in 1941, and assumed the title of publisher when his father died in 1944. That year the company also began publishing *The Mirror*, a tabloid-sized afternoon daily. In 1948 Times Mirror acquired its newsprint supplier, Publishers Paper Company, which was based in Lake Oswego, Oregon. Additionally, the newspaper company co-owned, along with CBS, television station KTTV, The station made its first telecast, the Rose Parade from Pasadena, California in 1949. The next year Times Mirror bought out CBS's interest in the station, and the *Times* began printing a daily television schedule.

At the end of the 1950s circulation of the *Times* stood at an average of 500,000 daily and 900,000 on Sundays. In addition to owning the *Times*, *The Mirror*, and KTTV, Times Mirror was active in paper manufacturing and commercial printing. As well, KTTV was renamed Times-Mirror Broadcasting Company once Times Mirror achieved full ownership in 1959.

In 1960 a period of acquisitions began for Times Mirror as Otis Chandler, grandson of Henry Chandler, succeeded Norman Chandler as the fourth publisher of the *Times*. The company ventured into book publishing when it acquired The New American Library in 1960. For the first time more than half of the company's net income came from non-newspaper sources. Annual revenues were more than $112 million, up from over $97 million the previous year.

Numerous acquisitions made in different areas of book and information publishing during the 1960s included Jeppensen and Co. (1961), a leading publisher of air navigation information (which became Jeppensen Sanderson in 1984); H. M. Goush Company (1961), a producer of travel maps; legal publisher, Matthew Bender and Co. (1963); The World Publishing Company (1963), publisher of *Webster's New World Dictionary*; The Sun Company (1964), publisher of the *San Bernardino Sun-Telegram*; Year Book Medical Publishers (1965); art book publisher Harry N. Abrams, Inc. (1966); and medical publisher The C. V. Mosby Company (1967). During the decade the company also purchased several lumber and pulp companies for its newsprint operations. In 1964 its stock became publicly traded on the New York and Pacific Exchanges.

By 1966 the *Los Angeles Times* was the nation's largest standard-size metropolitan newspaper in weekday circulation. In 1967 Times Mirror branched out into magazine publishing with the acquisition of *Popular Science* and *Outdoor Life*, followed by *Golf* and *Ski* magazines in 1972, all of which led to the creation of Times Mirror Magazines. In 1969 the company entered cable television with the purchase of CoAxial Systems Engineering Company in Palos Verdes, California, with a base of 5,700 subscribers and seven cable franchises.

As the *Los Angeles Times* passed the one million mark in weekday circulation in 1970, its parent company continued to acquire newspapers, magazines, television stations, cable companies, printing companies, publishers, and other businesses throughout the decade. In 1972 the Times Mirror became the largest publicly held publishing company in the United States, based on revenues and net income. By 1977 operating revenues exceeded $1 billion. Key acquisitions made during the 1970s included Long Island's suburban newspaper, *Newsday* (1970); the *Dallas Times Herald* (1970); Long Island Cablevision Corporation (1970); KDFW-TV in Dallas (1970); KTBC-TV in Austin, Texas (1973) (purchased from former First-Lady Lady Bird Johnson); The Sporting News Publishing Company (1977); *The (Stamford) Advocate* (1977); and, in 1979, the *Hartford Courant* (which was founded in 1764 and the nation's oldest continuously published newspaper.

Further acquisitions were made in the 1980s and included *The Denver Post* (1980); *The Morning Call* (1984), which served a nine-county region in eastern Pennsylvania and New Jersey; Xerox Learning Systems (1985); The A. S. Abell Co., publisher of *The Baltimore Sun*, for $600 million (1986); scientific, technical, and medical journal publisher CRC Press, Inc. (1986); and *National Journal* (1986), which published for government officials and decision-makers. In 1987 the Times Mirror Co. acquired the magazines *Field and Stream, Home Mechanix, Skiing*, and *Yachting* from Diamandis Communications Inc. In 1988 college textbook publisher Richard D. Irwin was purchased from Dow Jones and Co. for $135 million, and *Salt Water Sportsman* was added to the Times Mirror Magazine group.

Several properties were also sold during the 1980s, including the struggling *Dallas Times Herald* for $110 million in 1986, and *The Denver Post* in 1987. Times

Mirror divested 80 percent of its ownership in Publishers Paper Co. in 1986 and sold its directory printing company Times Mirror Press to GTE Directories Corporation in 1988.

Revenues continued to grow during the 1980s. Times Mirror reported more than $3 billion in revenues for the first time in 1987, while revenues for the *Los Angeles Times* exceeded $1 billion for the first time in 1988. Between 1986 and 1989 Times Mirror sold off more than $1 billion in assets and spent $750 million on acquisitions to refocus on its core print and electronic media businesses. For the entire decade the company spent $1.5 billion on acquisitions, and capital expenditures totaled $2.5 billion.

Despite its revenue growth, acquisitions, and capital expenditures, the company began to struggle financially in the 1990s. The decade began with a nationwide advertising slump that adversely affected revenues in the company's newspaper and magazine operations. *New York Newsday*, which was launched in 1985 to serve the city's Brooklyn and Queens boroughs, continued to lose money. The company posted a net loss of $66.6 million for 1992. After revenues fell to a five-year low of $3.36 billion in 1994 and the company's earnings per share fell by more than 15 percent, Mark Willes was brought in as president and chief executive officer (CEO). On January 1, 1996, he would succeed Robert Erburu as chairman of the board. In 1997 Willes also became publisher of the *Los Angeles Times*, where he oversaw drastic cuts in personnel. (Willes had earned a reputation for ruthless cost-cutting as vice chairman of General Mills, Inc., where he was known as "The Cereal Killer.")

Meanwhile, Times Mirror had agreed in 1994 to merge its cable television operations with Cox Communications Inc. for $2.3 billion, and that same year the company sold its four broadcast television stations. Within months of coming on board, Willes shut down the money-losing *New York Newsday* and the evening edition of *The Baltimore Sun*. One thousand jobs were cut, many of them at the *Los Angeles Times*, where certain sections of the newspaper were eliminated.

In 1996 Times Mirror exited the college textbook publishing business by exchanging Shepard's (a leading legal citation service), owned by McGraw-Hill Companies, for its Higher Education Group, which consisted of Richard D. Irwin, William C. Brown, Irwin Professional Publishing, Brown and Benchmark, and Mosby College. Shepard's then joined forces with medical and legal citation service Lexis-Nexis in a joint venture between Times Mirror and publisher Reed Elsevier. In 1998 Reed Elsevier would acquire Matthew Bender and the Times Mirror's remaining interest in the joint venture for $1.65 billion.

Other divestitures included selling Harry N. Abrams, Inc. and the *National Journal* in 1997 and Mosby Inc. in 1998. The sale of Mosby and Matthew Bender in 1998 occurred after Times Mirror attempted to merge the two companies, prompting several Mosby executives to resign. The sales were part of the company's strategy to exit professional book publishing. The sale of Mosby contributed to increases in earnings and revenues for 1998, with Times Mirror reporting a jump in net income to $1.42 billion from $250.3 million in 1997, while revenues rose from $2.9 billion in 1997 to $3 billion in 1998. Late in 1998 the company announced it would launch a new magazine, *Outdoor Explorer*, its first major publication launch since *New York Newsday* in 1986.

Since 1995 Times Mirror had executed a strategy of exiting non-core businesses, streamlining operations, and reinvigorating its existing businesses to achieve improved financial performance. That left the news and information company with three business segments: newspaper publishing, professional information and training, and magazine publishing.

***See also:* Publishing Industry**

FURTHER READING

Kreig, Andrew. *Spiked: How Chain Management Corrupted America's Oldest Newspaper.* Old Saybrook, CT: Peregrine Press, 1987.

Neuwirth, Robert. "LA Times Cuts 94." *Editor and Publisher*, January 2, 1999.

"Robust Competitors." *Advertising Age*, November 16, 1998.

Schwirlz, Mira. "Talk of the Town." *Brandweek*, March 8, 1999.

"Times Mirror History," [cited January 26, 1999] available from the World Wide Web @ www.tm.com/about/History/.

TIRE AND RUBBER INDUSTRY

Rubber is an unsaturated organic compound made of carbon and hydrogen. Natural rubber is collected from wild plants or plants cultivated on plantations. It is made from a secretion of certain plants that is called latex. It is tough, can stretch, and is a poor conductor of electricity, making it useful for a wide array of products, the most noteworthy of which are tires.

Rubber may have been used by the Maya Indians of Central and South America as far back as the eleventh century. Christopher Columbus (1451–1506) saw Native Americans playing with balls of tree gum on his second voyage to the New World about 1493. During the early nineteenth century, attempts were made to use rubber to treat clothes and footwear to make them water-resistant. In 1820 Charles Macintosh, a chemist from Scotland, created a way to bond two pieces of fabric, which made a waterproof cloak known as a ''mackintosh.'' Thomas Hancock, an English inventor, developed a machine which took scraps of rubber and caused them to be reusable. An American inventor, Charles Goodyear (1800–1860), created the process of vulcanization in 1839, a method to cure rubber, which increased its durability. This process was still used in almost the same way in the late twentieth century. By the early nineteenth century, the rubber industry in Europe was well established. After the development of vulcanization, rubber products began to be in great demand. Pneumatic carriage tires were invented around 1845, and Englishman John Boyd Dunlop (1840–1921) was responsible for founding the modern tire industry when he developed and patented pneumatic bicycle tires in 1888. By 1890 Charles Kingston Welsh and William Erskine Bartlett had made improvements to pneumatic tire design.

The early twentieth century saw an increase in the demand for tire and rubber products as automobiles increased in popularity. Soon tractor tires were replaced with rubber. Until 1940 all tires were from natural rubber that came from Asia. When World War II (1939–1945) made that source no longer available, the United States quickly had to develop ways to produce synthetic rubber to meet wartime demands. After the war ended, natural rubber became available again, and synthetic rubber was not in demand again until the 1960s. Both types of rubber, natural and synthetic, were in use throughout the end of the twentieth century.

Radial tires, an improvement that gave greater stability, were first developed by the Michelin company of France in the 1930s. This company, founded by two brothers in 1863, began to sell radial tires in the United States in the 1960s. By 1980, the company had four plants in the Unites States, and by the late twentieth century had become one of the world's biggest producers of automobile tires.

Bridgestone began as a company that sold clothes, but moved into rubber tire production in 1923. Bridgestone has operated plants in Singapore, Thailand, and Indonesia, and was for a time the leading supplier of tires to Japan. It purchased the Firestone company in 1988, which was the third leading tire producer in the United States at that time. Firestone suffered a number of losses in the 1990s, which have caused losses for Bridgestone.

The most important U. S. tire company has been the Goodyear Tire & Rubber Company, which began in 1898 and was named after Charles Goodyear, who invented vulcanization. It had produced more tires than any other company worldwide, and by 1991 had 41 plants in the United States alone, 43 in other countries, and over two thousand retail stores. Other important companies were Uniroyal–Goodrich, bought by Michelin in 1989, and the Cooper Tire & Rubber Company. Most companies in the tire industry had become multinational by the last part of the 1980s.

While tire products remain the predominant product of the rubber industry, there are many other products that use natural or synthetic rubber. These products include inner tubes, hoses, belts, rainwear, shoes, boots, insulation against sound or vibration, carpet backing, gaskets, seals, cables, steering wheels, bowling balls, latex gloves, and many other common products. The need for these products and their contribution to the U. S. economy is expected to continue well into the twenty-first century.

See also: **Rubbermaid, United States Rubber Company**

FURTHER READING

Hillstrom, Kevin, ed.*Encyclopedia ofAmerican Industries*. Volume 1, *Manufacturing Industries*. Detroit: Gale Research, Inc., 1995, s.v. ''Rubber & Miscellaneous Plastics Products.''

U. S. Industry Profiles: The Leading 100, 2d ed. Detroit: Gale Research, 1998, s.v., ''Rubber Products.''

French, Michael J. *The U. S. Tire Industry: A History*. Boston, Mass.: G. K. Hall & Co., 1991.

Rodengen, Jeffrey L. *The Legend of Goodyear: the First 100 Years*. Fort Lauderdale, Florida: Write Stuff Syndicate, 1997.

Blackford, Mansel G. *B. F. Goodrich: Tradition and Transformation, 1870–1995*. Columbus: Ohio State University Press, c 1996.

TOBACCO

Tobacco is an American plant, which is a member of the nightshade family. When Christopher Columbus

Tobacco plants are hung to dry after harvesting.

(1451–1506) arrived in the West Indies (islands in the Caribbean Ocean) in 1492, he found the native inhabitants smoking rolls of tobacco leaves, called taino. (The word tobacco is derived from the Spanish *tabaco,* which is probably from *taino.*) The practice of ''drinking smoke'' was observed to have a relaxing effect. Upon returning to Spain, Columbus took seeds of the plant with him. By 1531 tobacco was being cultivated on a commercial scale in the Spanish colonies of the West Indies. In 1565 English naval commander John Hawkins (1532–95) introduced tobacco to England, where smoking was ultimately condemned as a ''vile and stinking custom'' by King James I (1566–1625) decades later.

Tobacco was not commercially cultivated on the North American mainland until English colonist John Rolfe (1585–1622) carried seeds from the West Indies to Jamestown, Virginia, where he settled in 1610. By 1612 he had successfully cultivated tobacco and discovered a method of curing the plant, making it a viable export item. Jamestown, Virginia, became a boomtown and England's King James, who collected export duties, changed his mind about the habit of smoking. The coastal regions of Virginia, Maryland, and North Carolina were soon dominated by tobacco plantations, and the crop became the backbone of the economies in these colonies. Cultivation of tobacco did not require the same extent of land or slave labor as did other locally grown crops such as rice and indigo. But it depleted the nutrients of soil more rapidly, causing growers to expand their lands westward into the Piedmont region (the plain lying just east of the Blue Ridge and Appalachian mountains). In 1660 British Parliament passed the Second Navigation Act, declaring that tobacco and other articles from England's American colonies could only be exported to the British Isles. Tobacco prices dropped in response to the legislation and the colonial economies were weakened, causing political discontent with the mother country. But, despite the Second Navigation Act, European demand was not diminished and the colonists soon resumed exports. By 1765 colonial exports of tobacco were nearly twice the value of exports of bread and flour. The crop helped define the plantation economy of the South, which prevailed until the outbreak of the American Civil War (1861–65). During the 1800s companies such as R. J. Reynolds Tobacco and American Tobacco were founded. Tobacco has remained an important crop in the American south and the manufacture of tobacco continued to be an important industry.

***See also:* American Plants, American Tobacco Company, Columbian Exchange, Navigation Acts, Tobacco Trust**

TOBACCO INDUSTRY

The first permanent English settlement in the New World was a disaster for its early inhabitants. Times got so bad in the ''starving time'' of 1609–1610 that some of them resorted to cannibalism. Ten years later the Virginia colony exported 40,000 pounds of tobacco to England and the farmers were getting rich. The first successful commercial crop of tobacco was cultivated in Virginia in 1611 by Englishman John Rolfe and within seven years it had become the colony's leading export. By the 1630s the annual crop was 1.5 million pounds. People were planting tobacco everywhere, even in the roads. In spite of the fact that tobacco exhausted the land, over the next two centuries it was an important cash crop, though increasingly dwarfed during the nineteenth century by a much more important cash crop—cotton. After the Civil War and the abolition of slavery, most tobacco was grown by small, independent family-owned farms.

Initially tobacco was produced mainly for pipe smoking, chewing, and snuff. Cigars didn't become popular until the early 1800s. In 1847 the Phillip Morris Tobacco Company was established, which sold hand-rolled Turkish cigarettes. Two years later J.E. Liggett and Brother was formed in St. Louis. In the American West, chewing tobacco became so popular among cowboys and gold diggers that the R.J. Reynolds Tobacco Company built its operations around the product in 1875.

Cigarettes, which had been around in crude form since the early 1600s, didn't become widely popular in the United States until after the American Civil War (1861–1865). At that time, they were crudely made from scraps left over after the production of other tobacco products, primarily chewing tobacco. The invention of the first practical cigarette-making machine, sponsored by tobacco baron James Buchanan Duke (1856–1925) brought mechanically rolled cigarettes in the 1880s greatly increased the demand for cigarettes. One of the advertising ploys of the cigarette manufacturers was to point to the "sanitary" nature of mechanically rolled cigarettes. "No dirty immigrants hands" had rolled the cigarettes, in contrast to the cigar manufacturers in the immigrant ghettos of the north. Thus cigarettes became an expression of anti-immigrant sentiment as well as of the advent of science and modernity.

With the introduction of "Bright" tobacco, a uniquely cured yellow leaf grown in Virginia and North Carolina, cigarette sales steadily gained ground over other tobacco products. Cigarette sales surged again in the late 1880s with the introduction of the "White Burley" tobacco leaf. In 1901, six billion cigars were sold and only 3.6 billion cigarettes. With the emergence of the *Marlboro* brand, marketed from the newly established Philip Morris headquarters in New York, cigarettes soon became the major tobacco product. With the demand for cigarettes on the rise, R.J. Reynolds Company marketed a new cigarette brand called *Camel* in 1913.

By the early twentieth century, with the growth of cigarette sales and smoking, articles addressing the health effects of smoking began to appear in scientific and medical journals. In 1930, researchers in Cologne, Germany, made a statistical correlation between cancer and smoking. Eight years later, Dr. Raymond Pearl of Johns Hopkins University, reported that smokers did not live as long as non-smokers. By 1944, although admitting that "no definite evidence exists" linking smoking and lung cancer, the American Cancer Society began to warn about the possible health risks associated with smoking.

Despite these warnings cigarette sales sharply increased. During World War I (1914–1918), armed forces took up the "soldier's smoke." During the 1920s, the tobacco market soared, particularly among women, as cigarettes attracted a growing number of "flappers." The coincidence of the rise of cigarettes and the rise of feminism meant that the woman who smoked cigarettes, especially out of doors, was taking a stand in favor of women's rights. During the 1920s, the tobacco market soared, particularly among women. Popular brands of cigarettes included "Chesterfield," "Lucky Strike," "Old Gold," "Camel," "Raleigh," and "Marlboro." The Phillip Morris tobacco company began marketing the Marlboro in 1924 as a woman's cigarette that was as "Mild as May." Smoking rates among female teenagers tripled between 1925 and 1935.

With the introduction of the *Pall Mall* brand in 1939, the American Tobacco Company became the largest tobacco company in the United States. During World War II (1939–1945) the sale of cigarettes was at an all-time high. Tobacco companies sent millions of cigarettes to soldiers for free. Cigarettes were also included in a soldier's C-Rations. When the soldiers returned home from abroad, the tobacco industry had a steady stream of loyal customers. The cigarette culture was actively promoted. The main male movie stars of the age were smokers. Humphrey Bogart and John Wayne were smokers. (They also both developed lung cancer.) After World War II, the soldiers came home "hooked on cigarettes." One popular country-and-western song from the 1940s was "Smoke, Smoke, Smoke that Cigarette. . . ."

By the 1970s the two most influential tobacco companies were Philip Morris and R.J. Reynolds, with the popularity of their respective "Marlboro" and "Winston" brands. Another trend in the 1980s was the consumer interest in discount cigarettes, partly in response to the substantial increases in cigarette taxes. The 1990s saw an increasing support by the government to make tobacco companies liable for damages caused by their products exemplified in a 1992 U.S. Supreme Court decision. There also continued to be significant tax increases on cigarettes in many states, such as the 75 cents a pack tax levied by the state of Michigan. In addition, during the 1990s many businesses began to restrict or eliminate smoking in public places, in response to an Environmental Protection Agency (EPA) report in 1993 that categorized tobacco smoke as a class-A carcinogen. Increasing criticism of advertising strategies employed by tobacco companies also contributed to the decline in popularity of tobacco products.

The health risks associated with tobacco use resulted in a rise in lawsuits filed against tobacco companies in the late 1990s. Individuals sought compensation for poor health brought on by years of smoking and states asked for reimbursement on the large medical costs incurred by smoking-related illnesses. Both groups were successful and reforms were initiated. By the end of the twentieth century, the complexion of the tobacco industry in the United States was radically changed by shifting attitudes and regulations. Because of the unfavorable market conditions in the United States, companies sought to increase their sales in foreign markets, where attitudes about tobacco remained open and restrictions were more lenient.

Although tobacco had jump-started the American economy at a point when settlement was clearly costing more money than it was worth (except in the eyes of the religious dissidents of New England who merely wanted to be apart from England), and though it had helped to shape some of the fundamental characteristics of the emerging colonial American economy, the tobacco plant had also become a noxious but well entrenched part of the American culture.

See also: **American Tobacco Company, Tobacco, Tobacco Trust**

FURTHER READING

Breen, T.H.H. *Tobacco Culture: The Mentality of the Great Tidewater Planters on the Eve of Revolution.* Princeton: Princeton University Press, 1990.

Goodman, Jordan. *Tobacco in History: The Cultures of Dependence*. London: Routledge Press, 1994.

Hillstrom, Kevin, ed. *Encyclopedia of American Industries*, 2nd ed. Vol. 1: Manufacturing Industries. Detroit: Gale, 1997, s.v. "Tobacco Products."

Kluger, Richard. *Ashes to Ashes: America's Hundred-Year Cigarette War, the Public Health, and the Unabashed Triumph of Philip Morris.* New York: Alfred A. Knopf: Distributed by Random House, 1996.

U.S. Industry Profiles: The Leading 100, 2nd ed. Gale Research, 1998, s.v. "Tobacco Products."

TOBACCO TRUST

The American Tobacco Company was a huge holding company that monopolized the U.S. tobacco market between 1890 and 1910. Foundations for American Tobacco began in 1881 when James B. Duke (1856–1925) went into the cigarette business with his father, Washington Duke, founding W. Duke and Sons Company near Durham, North Carolina. The younger Duke led the company by aggressive, growth-oriented practices such as price-cutting (to undercut competitors) and spending up to 20 percent of sales on advertising and promotion. By the mid-1880s Duke expanded operations to take advantage of the cigarette markets in the North and West. Competition between his company and four other tobacco manufacturers intensified.

In 1889 New Jersey passed an incorporation law that allowed Duke to organize a merger with his competitors in 1890, thus founding the American Tobacco Company. Although it controlled almost 90 percent of the domestic cigarette market, American Tobacco continued to advertise extensively. Duke also increased profits by seeking an exclusive contract with a manufacturer of cigarette-machines. He integrated the company vertically (so that the company did everything from buying the tobacco leaves to selling finished tobacco products at its own retail chain, the United Cigar Store). Duke eliminated less profitable brands and also closed inefficient factories. The company employed non-union labor to keep costs low. As a result, American Tobacco could price competitively.

Duke continued his practice of buying competitors and by 1911 acquired 250 of them. By efficient management and strategic acquisitions American Tobacco was able to hold on to most of the tobacco market. In 1911 the company claimed 96 percent of domestic snuff sales, 85 percent of chewing tobacco and cigarette sales, and 75 percent of smoking tobacco.

On May 29, 1911, American Tobacco Company was dissolved in accordance with a ruling by the U.S. Supreme Court. The decision followed years of court challenges to Duke's monopoly that began in earnest in 1907; an American Tobacco subsidiary was indicted for price fixing (the practice of pricing below cost to eliminate a competitive product). This prompted the U.S. Justice Department to file a petition against the holding company. The Court charged American Tobacco Company with violating the Sherman Anti-Trust Act of 1890, which outlawed restraints on trade and attempts or conspiracy among competitors to monopolize a market. American Tobacco was condemned by the high court for its "unreasonable business practices." (The decision came just two weeks after a similar case against John D. Rockefeller's Standard Oil Company, which set the precedent for the enforcement of anti-trust laws.) Two decades after the passage of the first national anti-trust legislation (the Sherman Act), the federal government had finally voiced its determination to keep the U.S. marketplace competitive.

See also: **James Duke, Sherman Anti-Trust Act, Tobacco**

TORDESILLAS, TREATY OF

After early New World colonization efforts by the Vikings around A.D. 1000 several centuries passed before European explorations of the area were renewed. By 1450 political, economic, and technological changes were taking place, which made distant exploration more feasible and desirable. The Renaissance spawned interest in scientific inquiry and human control over the natural environment. Political centralization transformed the Middle Ages' small-localized principalities, ruled by rival noble families, into nation-states. Rulers gained great power following the decline of the Catholic Church's influence. Monarchs with centralized political power accumulated funds to finance exploration. Earlier overland exploration, highlighted by Marco Polo's journey to Cathay in the late thirteenth century, had whetted Europe's appetite for trade with the Orient. Wealthy fifteenth century Europeans desired goods available in the East, including jewels, porcelain, and spices.

The established overland routes came under control of other groups along the way, including Turkish Muslims, who gained control of the main route in the 1450s. The newly created nations of Western Europe, including England, Portugal, Spain, and France, became interested in seeking alternative routes for conducting trade with the East. With technological advances in shipbuilding and navigation, Portugal began exploration of trade routes by sea, and in 1487 charted an ocean route around Africa to India. Jewels and spices began arriving in Portugal, making Lisbon the new trade center for Europe.

With interest in overseas exploration heightened, explorer Christopher Columbus (1451–1506) sought a sponsor so that he might pursue a theory that contact with the East could be established by sailing west across the Atlantic Ocean. After Portugal refused to finance him, Spain provided financial support and ships, and Columbus set sail in late 1492. After ten weeks of sailing Columbus came to an island he named San Salvador. Though actually landing in what is now known as the Bahamas, Columbus proclaimed he had discovered the western route to the East. Excitedly, Spain claimed control over the discovery.

> Money and credit arrangements underlay the great expansion of trade. . . Spaniards brought back gold, pearls, jewels, and - above all - silver from their American colonies. . . Altogether it has been estimated that between 1500 and 1650 some 181 tons of gold and 16,000 tons of silver arrived in Europe from the Spanish colonies. . . The scope and the scale of long-distance trade changed greatly. . . (as) lines of credit and exchange had to be lengthened to accommodate the greater distances and times involved. . . (T)he European economy was poised to take advantage of the expanded trade.
>
> **William Phillips and Carla R. Phillips, *The Worlds of Christopher Columbus*, 1992.**

Portugal and Spain, the two leaders in fifteenth century exploration, had a short time earlier in 1479 and 1480 reached agreement that Spain would control the Atlantic region around the Canary Islands, and Portugal would hold rights to lands discovered south of the Canary Islands and west of Africa. In 1481 the Pope issued a charter called *Aeterni Regis* officially recognizing the agreement. Portugal, however, argued that the islands Columbus encountered were actually islands in the Atlantic Ocean previously claimed by their own explorers.

Because Spain and Portugal were the two primary Catholic powers, requests for resolution to the serious dispute went directly to Pope Alexander IV. The Pope issued a decree in May 1493, creating an imaginary north-south line separating the claims of Spain and Portugal. The line was drawn on maps 100 leagues west of the Cape Verde Islands, situated off the coast of Senegal on the West Coast of Africa. Spain was to assert exclusive control of lands west of the line, Portugal to the east. Excluded were lands already claimed by other European nations.

With further exploration, Portugal soon realized that Spain got the better of the deal and that the line's placement even threatened their exploration routes around Africa. Portugal returned to the Pope seeking a revision. In June 1494, Spanish and Portuguese ambassadors meeting at Tordesillas in northwestern Spain moved the line 270 leagues further west. The exact position of the line, however, was never very clear since the league unit of measure varied among countries at that time. Also, the Cape Verde Islands are 60 leagues wide, leaving doubt as to whether the distance to the line was to be measured from the east coast of the islands or the west. The Treaty of Tordesillas was later validated by Pope Julius II in 1506.

Columbus made three additional voyages between 1494 and 1502, exploring the Virgin Islands, Jamaica, Puerto Rico, and Trinidad. Not until later was it concluded that Columbus' findings were not in the East. Portugal maintained its interest in seeking a route around Africa, and navigator Vasco da Gama (1469–1525) reached India in 1498. Meanwhile, subsequent voyages by Portuguese explorer Pedro Alvares Cabral in 1500 east of the line established by the treaty led to the discovery of Brazil. Inland exploration westward from the Brazilian coast penetrated well beyond the line, but there was no opposition from Spain. As a result, Portugal established claim to a vast region of South America.

As the following century revealed, the Treaty of Tordesillas greatly favored Spain economically. West of the line Spain asserted claims over Mesoamerica, including the wealthy Aztec society, and Andean South America, containing the Inca. The Spanish colonies yielded incredible wealth with finds of silver and gold. Portuguese found very little such wealth. Other cultural implications of the division also extended far into the future with Latin America and the Caribbean being Spanish-speaking regions west of the line, and Brazil being the one nation with Portuguese as its official language. Treaty influences, however, were limited as other European countries never recognized the agreement and proceeded with their own explorations and claims of discovery in the western hemisphere.

See also: **Aztec, Inca, Mesoamerica**

FURTHER READING

Bell, Christopher R. V. *Portugal and the Quest for the Indies*. New York: Barnes and Noble, 1974.

Bulmer-Thomas, Victor, and Laurence Whitehead. *The Colonial and Post-colonial Experience: Five Centuries of Spanish and Portuguese America*. New York: Cambridge University Press, 1992.

Dos Passos, John. *The Portugal Story: Three Centuries of Exploration and Discovery*. Garden City, NY: Doubleday, 1969.

McAlister, Lyle N. *Spain and Portugal in the New World, 1492–1700*. Minneapolis: University of Minnesota Press, 1984.

Smith, Roger C. *Vanguard of Empire: Ships of Exploration in the Age of Columbus*. New York: Oxford University Press, 1993.

TOWNSEND CLUBS

Francis Everett Townsend (1867–1960) originated the "Townsend Plan" for old-age pensions in the United States during the Great Depression (1929–1939). Townsend became a doctor during the first decade of the twentieth century and practiced general medicine in a small community in South Dakota. His experience sensitized him to the problems of age and poverty. He eventually moved to California, and when he was 66, he lost his job as an assistant medical officer in Long Beach, California, in 1933. Townsend began to speak out actively about the hopeless conditions of the aged poor in the United States. He not only spoke about the problems of the aged poor, but he also proposed a partial solution in the *Long Beach Telegram* on September 20, 1933. He proposed that a pension of $150 per month (later $200) should be given to all U.S. citizens who retired at age 60 and who promised to spend the money within 30 days; he also proposed a national sales tax to finance the old age pension. This proposal was intended as a Depression recovery program as well as help for the elderly poor. The idea quickly became popular among older businessmen, professional people, and farmers. The "Townsend Movement," as it was called, was organized in local clubs and it claimed five million members at its peak in the 1930s. However, the increasing effectiveness of federal social security programs and dissension among members of the Townsend Clubs about who to support in 1936 for president contributed to the decline of the movement.

TOWNSHEND ACTS

The Townshend Acts, or Townshend Duties, tried to establish the British Parliament's right to tax the American colonies. Earlier attempts to impose duties, such as the Sugar Act (1764) and the Stamp Act (1765) had resulted in violent protests. In an attempt to avoid these controversies Chancellor of the Exchequer "Champagne Charlie," Charles Townshend, proposed a series of "indirect" taxes that would assert Parliament's right to tax the colonies. Townshend's duties made certain products that had to be imported from England, such as window glass, paper, lead, and artists' colors, more expensive for buyers. He also proposed a small three-pence tax on tea. Parliament passed the Townshend Duties in June 1767.

Since these items were considered luxury goods, purchased only by a small number of wealthy colonists, Townshend expected few, if any, protests from Americans. In order to ensure that the taxes were collected and smugglers were punished, however, the Chancellor appointed five new customs officials and dispatched them to Boston. He also created new Courts of Admiralty in the colonies, which could try accused smugglers without a jury, and established a Customs Board that could issue writs of assistance giving customs officers broad powers to search and seize colonists' property.

In advocating these measures, Townshend was acting on the advice of colonial representatives like Benjamin Franklin (1706–1790). Franklin, who was no longer in touch with the mood in the colonies, believed that Americans objected only to direct taxes, such as the Stamp Act. He told Parliament that Americans would not object to duties that were imposed to regulate trade throughout the empire. Franklin was mistaken. His views were refuted by a fellow Pennsylvanian, landowner and lawyer John Dickinson in a pamphlet entitled *Letters from a Farmer in Pennsylvania*. Dickinson declared that Parliament's attempt to impose duties solely for the purpose of generating income was a direct threat to the well being of all Americans. He urged colonial assemblies to petition Parliament to repeal the Townshend Acts.

Serious trouble erupted in Boston, where the new Customs Board had their offices, in 1768. Samuel Adams convinced the General Court of Massachusetts, the colonists' primary representative body, to write a Circular Letter for distribution to the other colonial assemblies, urging the representatives to petition Parliament for repeal of the Acts. The Massachusetts letter provoked a response from the new Secretary for American Affairs Wills Hill, Lord Hillsborough, who demanded that Massachusetts Governor Francis Bernard either force the General Court to apologize or dissolve the assembly. Adams and the Court refused, and reported back to Governor Bernard that the refusal had passed overwhelmingly. Hillsborough was angered again when a Boston mob attacked the customs officers who had seized merchant John Hancock's ship *Liberty* on suspicion of smuggling. The Secretary ordered four British regiments to be stationed in Boston—a decision that led directly to the Boston Massacre of March 5, 1770.

Despite the forceful actions of the British government, colonial opposition to British taxation stiffened throughout 1768 and 1769. On August 1, 1768, Samuel Adams convinced the General Court of Massachusetts to demand a boycott of British goods. Over the next year similar measures were adopted in New York, Pennsylvania, and South Carolina. The boycott put tremendous pressure on British manufacturers, who relied on the colonial markets to buy their goods. It also promoted, for the short term, some American industries, particularly the weaving of homespun cloth. On March 5, 1770 King George III's new Prime Minister, Lord Frederick North, asked Parliament to repeal most of the Townshend Acts, with the exception of the tax on tea. The issue of the tea tax would not be addressed until after the Boston Tea Party of 1773.

See also: **Boston Tea Party, Intolerable Acts, Stamp Act, Sugar Act**

FURTHER READING

Hosmer, James K. *Samuel Adams*. Boston: Houghton Mifflin, 1913.

Maier, Pauline R. *From Resistance to Revolution: Colonial Radicals and the Development of Opposition to Britain, 1765–1776*. New York: Knopf, 1972.

———. *The Old Revolutionaries: Political Lives in the Age of Samuel Adams*. New York: Knopf/Random House, 1980.

Thomas, Peter D.G. *The Townshend Duties Crisis: The Second Phase of the Revolution, 1767–1773*. New York: Oxford University Press, 1987.

Tyler, John W. *Smugglers and Patriots: Boston Merchants and the Advent of the American Revolution*. Boston: Northeastern University Press, 1986.

TRADE

Trade involves the exchange, purchase, or sale of goods and services. Whether international or domestic, trade makes possible the division and specialization of labor on which our productivity is based. If we could not exchange or trade the products of our specialized labor, each person would need to be entirely self-supporting. Trade is, in economic terms, a means of increasing productivity, as much as investment, or technological progress. Specialized production, followed by trade, makes it possible for everyone to have more commodities than they had before trading, even if some gain more by trading than others. Even though trading, including international trade, is an indirect means of enhancing all domestic productivity, there is frequently a bias of nationalism, which runs deep and causes countries to be suspicious of one another. Countries often discourage international trade to protect domestic industries and the jobs of people who work in them. Nations will place taxes called tariffs on imported goods to make them more expensive and discourage people from buying them. Some degree of protectionism seems inescapable in a world of intensified production and competition, although there is a movement to create large international trading blocks to improve the standard of living of all the member nations.

See also: **Standard of Living, Tariffs**

TRADE UNION

The transformation of economic enterprise that began after the American Revolution (1775–1783) was the major cause for the development of U.S. labor's most significant institution: permanent trade unions. With the rise of U.S. industry came the rise of a management class seeking to pay lower wages. During the late 1700s working men with trades (carpenters, shoemakers, typesetters, cabinetmakers, machinists, masons, coopers, tailors) created organizations to conduct their struggles, known often as "associations" or "societies." The membership of these early unions were confined to journeymen of a single craft, and they joined together not only to obtain better wages for themselves, but also to keep out of industry inferior untrained workmen known as "runaway apprentices" who worked for lower wages than the skilled tradesman or craftsman.

In 1886, a national organization, the American Federation of Labor (AFL) was created and rose to dominate the U.S. labor movement for the next 50 years. It was a federation of most of the early trade and craft unions scattered throughout the many states of the union, bringing together under the umbrella of the AFL most of the trade and craft unions. The AFL, a consolidation of separate trade unions, was first led by the father of the U.S. labor movement, Samuel Gompers (1850–1924). The focus of the AFL was largely aimed at short-term objectives, like higher pay and shorter hours of work. The AFL maintained that trade unions should restrict their membership to skilled and qualified craftsmen in specific trades, believing that a trade union composed of many different kinds of workers, including unskilled laborers, would lack the cohesiveness essential to hard-hitting business-like unionism. Trade unions ignored unskilled workers in the mass-production industries who eventually were unionized by the Congress of Industrial Organizations (CIO). In the 1960s, the AFL and the CIO pursued a cautious merger, under the name AFL-CIO.

See also: **American Federation of Labor, Congress of Industrial Organizations, Samuel Gompers, Labor Unionism**

TRADEMARK

A trademark is any work, name, device, or symbol, or any combination of them adopted and used by a manufacturer or businessman to distinguish or identify his goods or services from those goods manufactured or sold by others. Though patents and copyrights are specifically provided for in the U.S. Constitution, under Article 1, Section 8, the law of trademarks is not provided for in the Constitution. Federal trademark registration is based on the Interstate Commerce Clause in Section 8 of the Constitution, meaning that trademarks must be registered both federally, and in separate states of the union.

Applying for a trademark for federal registration entails processing by the U.S. Patent Office, a division of the Department of Commerce. Each state maintains trademark registers. In the United States all trademark rights require actual usage, not simply intended use. Trademarks are divided into strong (technical) trademarks, like Kodak (a coined expression), and weak (descriptive) trademarks, like Jucy (a phonetic variety of "juicy"). Trademarks must be renewed every 20 years, including a sixth year affidavit of use registration. A trademark is not the same as a trade name. Coca-Cola is a trademark, and Coca-Cola Co. is the trade name of the manufacturer. Trademark systems are used worldwide, and a U.S. trademark owner seeking to protect the use of his trademark in foreign countries must register it on a country-by-country basis. A trademark is a precious commodity for any flourishing business, and the use of trademarks is carefully monitored by business.

See also: **Brand Names**

TRAIL OF TEARS

By the 1780s war, disease, and starvation had killed most American Indians living along the eastern seaboard of North America. As white settlers pressed further inland in the early 1800s, many of the indigenous groups resisted further encroachment. Some seized on the opportunity to side with Britain in the American Revolutionary War (1775–1783) and again in the War of 1812 (1812–1814). But the Native Americans had picked the losing side, and after the latter war, General Andrew Jackson (1767–1845) devastated the settlements of the Creeks and other hostile Indian groups.

In contrast to the Creeks, the Cherokee had earlier accepted the U.S. presence as inevitable and adopted a peaceful policy of accommodation and coexistence. On the basis of a treaty signed with the United States in 1791, the Cherokee continued to live on their traditional lands in the hills of northwest Georgia and western North Carolina. During the early 1800s the Cherokee went through a remarkable period of cultural change. They adopted an agrarian economy in place of traditional hunting and gathering. Some Cherokee even became owners of plantations with slaves. Others became involved in commerce, managing stores, mills, and other businesses. Impressed with the benefits of reading and writing, a Cherokee silversmith, Sequoia, created a Cherokee alphabet that was quickly adopted. By the 1820s the Cherokee had established written laws and a constitution.

Between 1819 and 1829 the Cherokees developed an independent nation within U.S. boundaries. They adopted a constitution. As the Cherokees flourished, the white settlers grew resentful. The Georgia statehouse pressed the Cherokees to sell their land, which the Cherokee were reluctant to do. With the discovery of gold in Cherokee country in 1829 the State of Georgia increased the pressure on the Cherokee. President Andrew Jackson (1829–1837) signed the Indian Removal Act of 1830 that provided funds for removal of eastern Indians beyond the Mississippi River. The State of Georgia annulled the Cherokee constitution and ordered their lands seized.

DESPITE THE U.S. SUPREME COURT DECISION IN *CHEROKEE V. GEORGIA* (1831), ACKNOWLEDGING CHEROKEE'S RIGHT TO THEIR LANDS AND THEIR SOVEREIGNTY AS A NATION, JACKSON CONTINUED TO SUPPORT GEORGIA'S EFFORTS AT THEIR REMOVAL. AFTER MARSHALL'S RULING JACKSON REMARKED, "JOHN MARSHALL HAS MADE HIS DECISION; NOW LET HIM ENFORCE IT."

The Cherokee hired a lawyer who argued the case all the way to the Supreme Court. In his ruling, Chief Justice John Marshall agreed that the State of Georgia had no right to enter Cherokee lands and to displace the indigenous people. Despite the U.S. Supreme Court decision in *Cherokee v. Georgia* (1831), acknowledging Cherokee's right to their lands and their sovereignty as a nation, Jackson continued to support Georgia's efforts at their removal. After Marshall's ruling Jackson remarked, ''John Marshall has made his decision; now let him enforce it.''

Jackson persuaded Congress to grant the funds for the relocation of the Cherokee. Finally in 1835, after years of harassment and antagonism, a small group of Cherokee ceded by treaty all lands occupied by the Cherokee east of the Mississippi. The Cherokee peoples were given two years to vacate the transferred lands and move to a special Indian territory created by Congress in 1834 in what latter became Oklahoma.

Many Cherokee resisted removal. As the deadline approached in 1837, President Martin Van Buren (1837–1841) ordered federal authorities to force the Cherokee from their homes and place them in temporary detention camps. The Cherokee remained in the camps through the typically hot sweltering southeast summer and diseases began to spread. Suffering from dysentery, measles, and whooping cough, some two thousand died. Finally that October over fifteen thousand men, women, and children began a six-month, thousand-mile journey to the very unfamiliar country of Oklahoma. Most went overland from northwest Georgia, across central Tennessee, western Kentucky, southern Illinois, southern Missouri, and northern Arkansas, to Ft. Gibson in eastern Oklahoma. A smaller number were taken by flatboat down the Tennessee River to the Mississippi River and then up the Arkansas River. While en route, lacking adequate food, shelter, and clothing, another two thousand died from exposure, disease, and exhaustion. The Cherokee buried their dead along the route that became known as the ''Trail of Tears.'' The forced march became one of the most tragic and dishonorable chapters in U.S.-Indian relations.

The Cherokee reestablished their agrarian society in the hills of northeastern Oklahoma. They soon setup a new government and signed a constitution in 1839. Tahlequah, Oklahoma became the capital for the displaced population. During the 1837 roundup, rather than leave for Oklahoma, a thousand or more Cherokee had fled into remote areas of the East including the Great Smoky Mountains. They later received federal recognition, also, as the Cherokee of the North Carolina Qualla Reservation.

Departure of the Cherokee population left only scattered indigenous groups in the Southeast. By 1842 most of the Five Civilized Tribes—the Cherokee, Chickasaw, Choctaw, Creek, and Seminole—had been removed from their prosperous farms and plantations and resettled on the southeast to government-assigned lands in Oklahoma. The last of the Seminoles of Florida were removed in 1858.

The Cherokee's forced removal dramatized the fate of indigenous populations in the face of U.S. agricultural expansion. The tide of U.S. expansion eventually overwhelmed even those tribes with peaceful policies and firmly established economies. The Trail of Tears was later designated a National Historic Trail by Congress.

See also: **Georgia, Andrew Jackson, Oklahoma**

FURTHER READING

Anderson, William L., ed. *Cherokee Removal: Before and After.* Athens, GA: University of Georgia Press, 1991.

Gilbert, Joan. *The Trail of Tears Across Missouri.* Columbia, MO: University of Missouri Press, 1996.

Heidler, David S., and Jeanne T. Heidler. *Old Hickory's War: Andrew Jackson and the Quest for Empire.* Mechanicsburg, PA: Stackpole Books, 1996.

McLoughlin, William G. *After the Trail of Tears: The Cherokees' Struggle for Sovereignty, 1839–1880.* Chapel Hill, NC: University of North Carolina Press, 1993.

Remini, Robert V. *The Legacy of Andrew Jackson: Essays on Democracy, Indian Removal, and Slavery.* Baton Rouge, LA: Louisiana State University Press, 1988.

Rice, Horace R. *The Buffalo Ridge Cherokee: A Remnant of a Great Nation Divided.* Bowie, MD: Heritage Books, 1995.

Wilkins, Thurman. *Cherokee Tragedy: The Ridge Family and the Decimation of a People*, 2nd ed. Norman, OK: University of Oklahoma Press, 1986.

TRANSATLANTIC CABLE

In 1866 a transatlantic cable was laid along the ocean floor to carry telegraph messages from North America to Europe. But this success had been long-awaited: it followed four failed attempts to lay the wire. In 1854 American financier Cyrus W. Field (1819–1892) founded the New York, Newfoundland, and London Telegraph Company (two years later renamed the Atlantic Telegraph Company). He became determined to connect America and Europe with a submarine telegraph cable, which would greatly improve communication. Cables laid in 1857 and 1858 broke. A third cable was put down later in 1858 and it successfully carried messages across the Atlantic for a period of four weeks before it broke. A fourth wire was put down between Newfoundland (Canada), and Ireland in 1865, but before the project was completed, it too broke. The following year, aided by a cable developed by British mathematician and physicist William Thomson (1824–1907), the project was finally a success. Thomson, who had been a chief consultant during the laying of the first cable in 1857–1858, developed a theory on the mechanics of submarine cables, and a cable following his specifications was successfully laid, from east to west, between Valentia, Ireland, and Heart's Content, Newfoundland. The crewmen who worked on that project were also able to repair the cable laid in 1865. By 1900 there were fifteen telegraph cables lying on the floor of the Atlantic Ocean, enabling telegrams (called "cables" when they were intercontinental) to be transmitted between the United States or Canada and Europe. The development was a tremendous boom to communication. Prior to the transatlantic telegraph cable (1866), the fastest way to send a message across the ocean was aboard a ship. The telephone (invented 1875), which allows voice transmission over electrical wires, gradually replaced the telegraph. But for many decades the two technologies were both in use.

See also: **AT&T, Alexander Graham Bell, Telegraph**

TRANSCONTINENTAL RAILROAD

On May 10, 1869, the last tracks of the United States' first cross-country railroad were laid, making North America the first continent to be spanned from coast to coast by a rail line. The event was the fulfillment of a great national dream to knit the vast country closer together. Short-run rail lines had been in use since the 1840s, but the nation lacked a quick and reliable method for transporting people, raw materials, and finished goods between distant regions.

In the early 1860s, the U.S. Congress decided in favor of extending the railroad across the country. The

On May 10, 1869 the last spike of the world's first transcontinental was driven in Promontory, Utah. The celebration began by two locomotives traveling from either end of the railroad to meet in the middle where the tracks were finally connected.

federal government granted land and extended millions of dollars in loans to two companies to complete the project. After a long debate that had become increasingly sectional, Congress determined the railroad should run roughly along the 42nd parallel—from Omaha, Nebraska, to Sacramento, California. This route was chosen for its physical properties: the topography of the landscape would best allow the ambitious project. The Union Pacific Railroad was to begin work in Omaha and lay tracks westward; the Central Pacific Railroad was to begin in Sacramento and lay tracks eastward, crossing the Sierra Nevada Mountains.

Work began in 1863, and six years later the two projects met at Promontory in north-central Utah, northwest of Ogden. By the end of the 1800s, fifteen rail lines crossed the nation.

See also: **Oakes Ames, Oliver Ames, Central Pacific Railroad, Thomas Clark Durant, Robber Barons, Railroad Industry**

TRANSPORTATION ACT

The authority of the Interstate Commerce Commission (ICC), established 1887 by act of Congress, was later fortified by the Hepburn Act of 1906 and the Mann-Elkins Act of 1910. In 1920 Congress again increased the power of the regulatory agency by passing the Transportation Act. Among the provisions of the 1920 legislation was the rule, which allowed the ICC to establish rates at levels that were just high enough to yield a fair return on investment (ROI) for the railroad companies. Any returns to the railroads that were in excess of the established rate levels were to be "recaptured" by the government, placed in a fund, and from that fund, loans were to be made to struggling rail carriers. The act also empowered the ICC to override state regulatory statutes that fixed rate levels lower for intrastate carriers than they were for interstate carriers; Congress viewed such state regulations as discriminatory and, therefore, harmful to interstate commerce. Finally, the act loosened restrictions on railway pooling and railroad acquisitions, even directing the ICC to lead an initiative to consolidate the railroads into fewer, stronger systems.

After three decades of legislation, regulation, and antitrust litigation to curb the powerful railroads, the Transportation Act of 1920 was a double-edged sword: the recaptured earnings prevented any one railroad from becoming too big; but at the same time, the ICC was charged with overseeing the consolidation of the railroad industry. The stage was set for the decline of the nation's railroad systems: over the next two decades, competition for passenger and freight service was increased as automobiles, trucks, and airplanes proliferated. The railroads, limited by federal regulations, were unable to respond swiftly enough to remain competitive: rail companies could not adjust their rates or services without seeking state or federal approval first. Even those rail companies that remained solvent amidst the increased regulations had been weakened by the Transportation Act's policy of recaptured earnings, which prevented any accumulation of capital resources. Lack of reserves made it difficult for companies when the American transportation industry became more diverse and competitive. In the middle of the twentieth century, railroads foundered; many companies went into receivership pending their reorganization.

See also: **Interstate Commerce Commission Act, Hepburn Act, Mann-Elkins Act**

TRIANGLE SHIRTWAIST FIRE

Into the early twentieth century businesses operated free of government regulation and with few industry standards. No building codes existed and regular machinery or fire inspections were not performed. "Sweatshops" were common, where people worked for very low wages in crowded, unsafe conditions with poor ventilation or inadequate heat. No limit existed for the number of hours a person could be required to work, and child labor laws were non-existent. Fresh to the United States, speaking little English, and desperately seeking employment, immigrants were especially vulnerable to sweatshop employment. While seeking a better life in the United States immigrants instead often found exploitation and impoverishment. Children could be found routinely working in mills and factories under dismal conditions. Often women and their children worked side by side for over 15 hours a day.

Such a factory sweatshop operated in New York City's Greenwich Village section in 1911. It produced women's clothing and employing primarily women. Over 500 garment workers performed low-paying piecework for the Triangle Shirtwaist Company in the top three stories of the Asch Building, a ten-story building near Washington Square in New York City. Many of the women were recent Italian and Russian Jewish immigrants, mostly between 16 and 23 years of age, with some girls even younger. The building's structure was considered fire proof, but the interior on the upper three floors was packed with flammable objects including clothing products hanging from lines above workers' heads, rows of tightly-spaced sewing machines, cutting tables bearing bolts of cloth, and linen and cotton cuttings littering the floors.

Suddenly, a fire broke out near a corner of the eighth floor, spreading quickly to the two higher floors. With a door to the fire escape locked, workers anxiously waited at the windows for rescue. When fire crews arrived they discovered their fire ladders were several stories too short and water pressure was insufficient for water from the hoses to reach that height. Terrified, some workers clung to one another; many, to the horror of onlookers and rescue workers, began leaping to their deaths.

Few fire escapes were present, and company management had a policy of locking most exits, supposedly to guard against break-ins, but more accurately meant to contain the workers. The unlocked exits were only 20 inches wide, designed to restrict access by no more than one person at a time and to guard against employee theft. Though the company was a non-union shop, some of the workers had joined the International Ladies' Garment Workers' Union (ILGWU), formed in 1900. The building experienced several small fires, leading to complaints concerning insufficient exits from the building. In 1910 a general Cloakmakers' Strike to improve sanitation and safety conditions in New York City had been held. The strike led to the formation of the Joint Board of Sanitary Control to establish appropriate standards. Triangle's employees who had joined in the strike, however, had been replaced.

Late Saturday afternoon on March 25, 1911, at the conclusion of the six-day workweek, the Triangle Shirtwaist workers were shutting down operations for the night as quitting time was drawing close. Suddenly, a fire broke out near a corner of the eighth floor, spreading quickly to the two higher floors. With a door to the fire escape locked, workers anxiously waited at the windows for rescue. When fire crews arrived they discovered their fire ladders were several stories too short and water pressure was insufficient for water from the hoses to reach that height. Terrified, some workers clung to one another; many, to the horror of onlookers and rescue workers, began leaping to their deaths. Workers on the tenth floor were able to get to the roof of the building and escaped over ladders placed by students across to a nearby New York University building. Almost 100 employees died inside the structure, while 47 jumped to their deaths from the eighth and ninth floors to escape the flames. In total 146 workers died and 70 were seriously injured.

The company owners were indicted on charges of criminal negligence, but were acquitted eight months later in a jury trial and assessed only a small fine. They later received $65,000 in insurance payments for property damage. The fire, regarded as one of the worst industrial tragedies in U.S. history, aroused public anger over management and government indifference to worker safety. Women's unionization activity escalated as the ILGWU stepped up efforts to improve sweatshop conditions. Effects on local and national politics were profound, beginning a 20 year effort to introduce industry reforms.

One eyewitness to the catastrophe was Frances Perkins (1880–1965), at the time a lobbyist for the New York Consumers League. Perkins came away from the tragic scene with even more determination to help workers. The State of New York created a special commission with Perkins as its chief investigator to probe into factors surrounding the Triangle Shirtwaist fire and industrial working conditions in general throughout the state. Three years later, in 1914, the commission issued its report calling for widespread changes. One piece of legislation, passed over stiff opposition from business management in the state, limited the workweek for women and children to 54 hours. Perkins also served as executive secretary of New York City's Committee on Safety influencing the passage of more stringent city building codes and factory inspection requirements. Perkins ultimately became the first woman Presidential Cabinet member in the United States as the Secretary of Labor for President Franklin D. Roosevelt (1933–1945). The only Cabinet member to serve all four terms of Roosevelt's presidency, Perkins was a key person behind the New Deal's socio-economic reforms. The tragic event in New York had triggered more intensive efforts through protective legislation to gain the right of workers to safe working conditions.

See also: **Industrial Revolution, Women in the Workplace, Working Conditions in Factories**

FURTHER READING

Lehrer, Susan. *Origins of Protective Labor Legislation for Women, 1905–1925.* Albany, NY: State University of New York Press, 1987.

McClymer, John F. *The Triangle Strike and Fire.* Fort Worth, TX: Harcourt Brace College Publishers, 1998.

McEvoy, Arthur F. *The Triangle Shirtwaist Factory Fire of 1911: Social Change, Industrial Accidents, and the Evolution of Commonsense Causality.* Chicago: American Bar Association, 1994.

Stein, Leon. *The Triangle Fire.* New York: Carroll and Graf/Quicksilver Book, 1962.

———. *Out of the Sweatshop: The Struggle for Industrial Democracy.* New York: Quadrangle/New Times Book Company, 1977.

Tyler, Gus. *Look for the Union Label: A History of the International Ladies' Garment Workers' Union.* Armonk, NY: M. E. Sharpe, 1995.

TRIANGULAR TRADE

Triangular trade refers to the various navigation routes that emerged during the colonial period. There were numerous triangular paths that ships made to ferry people, goods (both raw and finished), and livestock. The most traveled triangular route began on Africa's west coast where ships picked up slaves. The second stop was the Caribbean islands—predominately the British and French West Indies—where slaves were sold to plantation owners; in turn, traders used the profits to purchase sugar, molasses, tobacco, and coffee. These raw materials were then transported north to the third stop, New England, where a rum industry was thriving. There ships were loaded with spirits. Traders made the last leg of their journey—back across the Atlantic to Africa's west coast, where the process began again.

On another route, manufactured goods were transported from Europe to the African coast, slaves were sent to the West Indies, and sugar, tobacco, and coffee were routed back to Europe, where the triangle began again. On yet another route, lumber, cotton, and meat were transported from the colonies to southern Europe, wine and fruits went to England and manufactured goods routed to the colonies, where the triangle began again. There were as many possible routes as there were ports and demands for goods.

The tragic result of the triangular trade was the transport of an estimated 10 million black Africans. Sold into slavery, these human beings were often chained below deck and allowed only brief, if any,

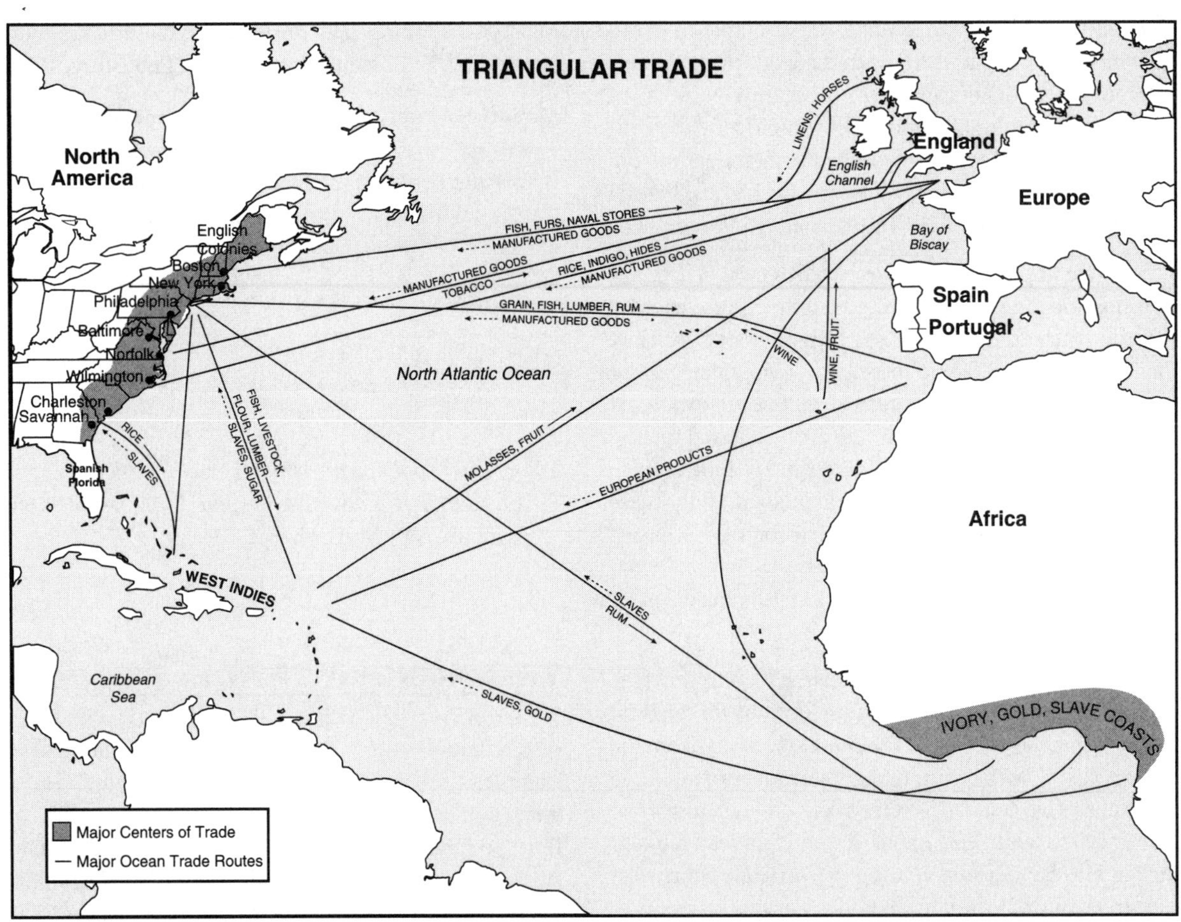

The various Atlantic Trade Routes of the 18th Century were triangular in design. Natural resources shipped from the colonies to England, manufactured goods from England shipped to the colonies and Africa, and slaves from Africa shipped back to the colonies.

periods of exercise during the Atlantic crossing (which came to be called the Middle Passage). Conditions for the slaves were brutal and improved only slightly when traders realized that if slaves perished during the long journey across the ocean, it would adversely affect their profits in the West Indies. After economies in the islands of the Caribbean crashed at the end of the 1600s, many slaves were sold to plantation owners on the North American mainland, thus initiating another tragic trade route. The slave trade was abolished during the 1800s, putting an end to the forced migration of Africans to the Western Hemisphere along these routes.

***See also:* Middle Passage, Molasses Act of 1733, Slavery, Sugar, Tobacco**

TRIBUTE

Tribute is payment made to a ruling or conquering nation by subjugated people in acknowledgment of submission or as a price for protection from other countries. Derived from the Latin word *tributum,* referring to property tax paid by Roman citizens, the term evolved to mean taxes levied on conquered peoples. Nations increased their wealth through these taxes.

After Cortez conquered the Aztec in 1521, the American Indians had to pay a special tax called a tribute to the Spaniards. Two slightly different perspectives on tribute existed in China for centuries. The Chinese used tribute to solidify political and trade ties with neighboring nations. China also received tribute from less powerful princes in Central and Southwest Asia and Korea, but returned to those countries gifts of equal value to the tribute.

In U.S. history, tribute is associated with U.S. shipping and the Barbary States of Northern Africa, including Morocco, Algiers, Tunis, and Tripoli. The Barbary States are part of modern-day Algeria, Libya, Morocco, and Tunisia. The Barbary Coast pirates had, since the 16th century, accepted payments or valuable presents in exchange for allowing merchant ships passage through the Mediterranean Sea. American ships ventured into the Barbary waters in the late eighteenth century. Refusing to comply with these demands, many U.S. ships were captured and their sailors enslaved. The U.S. government was too poor to buy its citizens' freedom and too weak to prevent such hostilities. The United States negotiated treaties with Morocco, Tripoli, and Tunis, and by 1802 had paid over $2 million in tributes. The piracy governments continued demanding higher tributes. Under President Thomas Jefferson (1801–1809) the United States fought against Tripoli in the Barbary Wars (1801–1805). In 1815 with warfare renewed against Algiers, a stronger United States demanded abandonment of all tribute claims. Although official payment of tribute ended in the mid-1810's, the United States occasionally paid tribute until the mid-nineteenth century.

See also: **Barbary States**

TRIPPE, JUAN TERRY

Juan Trippe (1899–1981), a pioneer of the jet age, made Pan American World Airways the world's largest airline in the mid-twentieth century. Trippe, who introduced commercial air service across the Atlantic and Pacific oceans in the 1930s, made Pan American Airways the first airline to offer affordable tourist class air travel. By the early 1960s Pan Am planes were flying into 86 countries on a route network covering some 80,000 miles.

The son of an investment banker, Trippe graduated from Yale University in 1921. He worked briefly as a bond salesman on Wall Street, intending to enter the family business, Trippe and Company. But his heart was set on planes and flying. Learning that some World War I (1914–1918) surplus single-engine pontoon Navy biplanes were available for sale, he used an inheritance and help from some wealthy Yale classmates to purchase seven of them. With his small fleet of planes he organized Long Island Airways, a sightseeing and charter service. In 1924 he put together Colonial Air Transport, which flew between Boston, Massachusetts, and New York City with the first U.S. air mail contract ever awarded.

When Trippe tried to expand the company's route beyond the Northeast to Florida and Havana, Cuba, Colonial's stockholders refused. He resigned from the company and, again with the financial help of friends, organized Pan American Airways, Inc. in 1927 from a merger of three rival flying services. He began airmail service from Florida to Puerto Rico, Cuba, and Central America. By 1929 Pan Am had 11,000 miles of routes, and passenger flights had been introduced.

After Charles Lindbergh (1902–1974) became an international hero as a result of his solo flight across the Atlantic Ocean in 1927, Trippe hired him as a consultant to advise Pan Am on creating ocean-going routes. The two men often traveled together over the proposed routes, with Lindbergh as the pilot. Trippe's first great success was the "China Clipper" route to China, inaugurated in the early 1930s. Atlantic routes to Europe followed. During World War II (1939–1945), the company acted as a contract carrier for the U.S. government, ferrying U.S. troops all over the globe.

After World War II, Trippe lobbied Congress unsuccessfully to establish Pan Am as the United States' exclusive international carrier. At the same time, believing that the future of air travel lay with the ordinary tourist, he introduced "tourist class" travel from New York City to London, England. In a 1944 speech he said, "The average man's holiday has been the prisoner of two grim keepers, money and time," and he sought to change that equation. He cut the usual round-trip fare in half and promoted his air travel campaign in a widely discussed article, "Now You Can Take That Trip Abroad." At first the major international air carriers resisted the idea of two classes of air service (first and tourist), and Great Britain even closed its airports to Pan Am flights with tourist seats. But the concept of low-cost airfares proved to be extremely popular, and, by 1952, all major airlines had posted competitive rates.

Trippe had the vision to see that the next advance in airline travel would be with the big 707 Boeing and the Douglas DC-8 jets. In 1958 Pan Am launched its first 707 route to Paris, France. The big jets flew almost twice as fast as the propeller-driven planes they replaced and carried many more passengers. Trippe ordered as many jets as the airplane manufacturers could produce, and, by the early 1960s, his airline dominated U.S. international air travel. In 1968 Pan Am had assets of over $1 billion.

Trippe, always the visionary, still wasn't satisfied. He became interested in development of the 747, the "jumbo jet" that would carry even more passengers than the 707. Pan Am ordered 25 of the huge planes, at a cost of $450 million and inaugurated their use in the 1960s. Unfortunately, Trippe, this time, was ahead of the curve. A world oil crisis in the early 1970s was particularly hard on airlines, and Pan Am, which had not streamlined its operations to meet increased competition at home and abroad, was no exception. Juan

Trippe died in 1981, as his company was still struggling to recovery from the oil crisis. Pan Am continued operations for ten years after its founders death, until it was dissolved in 1991.

See also: **Airline Industry**

FURTHER READING

Bender, Marilyn and Selig Altschul. *The Chosen Instrument: Pan Am, Juan Trippe, The Rise and Fall of an American Entrepreneur.* New York: Simon and Schuster, 1982.

Branson, Richard. ''Juan Trippe: Pilot of the Jet Age.'' *Time*, December 7, 1998.

Daley, Robert. *An American Saga: Juan Trippe and his Pan Am Empire.* New York: Random House, 1980.

Josephson, Matthew. *Empire of the Air: Juan Trippe and the Struggle for World Airways.* New York: Arno Press, 1972.

Newhouse, John. ''A Hole in the Market.'' *The New Yorker*, July 5, 1982.

Current Biography 1955. New York: H. W. Wilson, 1955, s.v. ''Juan Terry Trippe.''

TRUCKING INDUSTRY (COMMERCIAL)

Beginning in the early 1980s the trucking industry changed as deregulation and new technology brought new competitive pressures to the trucking industry. Information technologies and expanded services such as express delivery of light freight had become staples of the trade. Implementation of these new technologies and the promise of advantageous global trends insured the continued strength of an industry that experienced its worst years during the recession of the early 1980s.

Both state and federal governments had a tremendous impact on the revenues generated by the trucking industry. Although it experienced federal deregulation, the industry continued to deal with strict regulations in 28 states during the early 1990s. In an effort to make state regulations coincide with each other, Congress passed the Intermodal Surface Transportation Efficiency Act in 1991. The International Registration Plan would be passed in 1996 and the International Fuel Tax Agreement in 1998, legislating out repetitive registration requirements and fuel tax payments incurred by interstate truckers.

In addition to registration and tax costs, government programs such as the Motor Carrier Safety Assistance Program added an estimated $6,000 to $9,000 annually in maintenance work required to meet the standards of vehicle safety inspections that, like the International Registration Plan and Fuel Tax Agreement, were recognized by even the most strictly regulated states. The safety inspections, as well as a national Commercial Drivers License that may be obtained only after passing a competence exam, did lower insurance costs for the industry offsetting the initial expenses.

While Congress was legislating programs intended to make things less complicated for the trucking industry, the Environmental Protection Agency (EPA) mandated clean air laws making it necessary for trucking companies to find ways to utilize low sulfur fuels. Although the industry found it difficult to switch completely to the new fuels, advancements in exhaust purification and newly designed, highly efficient engines lowered emissions considerably.

Figures published during the early 1990s indicated that the trucking industry employed approximately eight million people, including part-time workers. The industry could be broken down into three main categories: those directly employed by trucking companies, those employed by employer groups, and those working for private carrier fleets. Although there was no real trucking union to speak of, a considerable number of truck drivers were members of the International Brotherhood of Teamsters (IBT). As was the case in most industries, union members tended to receive higher pay than non-union workers. Typically, large trucking companies that employed union workers put 60 to 65 percent of the company's profits aside for wages and benefits. Non-union drivers typically received 40 percent of the company's revenue in the form of wages and benefits. Annual salaries of long-distance drivers varied from $20,000 to $40,000 with a cap of approximately $60,000 for experienced drivers.

Other impacts on the trucking industry included advancements in communications technologies. The proliferation of fax and electronic mail were estimated to have cut nearly $75 million from the industry's annual profit margin. In order to compensate for the losses, the industry was able to carve out a new niche through the zero-inventory management policy used by many companies to reduce overhead costs during the early 1990s. A perfect fit for the trucking industry, this cost-saving policy called for same-day, warehouse-to-customer transportation of parts and manufacturing materials.

Because of competition from communications technologies, production efficiency technology became essential to the trucking industry's ability to compete. Computers mounted in truck dashboards and portable laptops became invaluable tools which freed truckers and company administrators from the tasks of monitoring fuel taxes and fuel management performance, engine performance, results and due dates for trailer inspections and so on. In addition to improvements in the efficiency of administrative duties, companies began utilizing safety applications including radar technology informing truckers when they followed behind another vehicle too closely, shipment planning software maximizing trailer time, and driver simulators.

Since the trucking industry relied on the health of the economy, it continued to be important for the trucking industry to expand into new, non-traditional markets and take advantage of progressing technologies. The trend toward a less restrictive international trade policy enhanced by the North American Free Trade Agreement (NAFTA) should ensure the industry's prosperity well into the next millennium.

FURTHER READING

American Trucking Association. *Profitable Trucking: A Guide for the Independent Contractor*. American Trucking Association, 1981.

Bumper to Bumper: The Complete Guide to Tractor-Trailer Operations, 3rd ed. Tempe, Arizona: Mike Byrnes and Associates, 1998.

Friedlaender, Ann Fetter. *Freight Transport Regulation: Equity, Efficiency, and Competition in the Rail and Trucking Industries*. Cambridge, MA: MIT Press, 1981.

Robyn, Dorothy L. *Braking the Special Interests: Trucking Deregulation and the Politics of Policy Reform*. Chicago: University of Chicago Press, 1987.

Teske, Eric Paul, Samuel Best, and Michael Mintorm. *Deregulating Freight Transportation: Delivering the Goods (AEI Studies in Regulation and Federalism)*. Washington, DC: AEI Press, 1995.

TRUMAN, HARRY S.

Like his most admired presidential hero, Woodrow Wilson (1913–1921), Harry Truman (1884–1972) spent two terms in the White House, and became far better known for his handling of war situations than for his progressive and protective post-war domestic policy efforts. Truman became the thirty-third president of the United States quite suddenly, on April 12, 1945, when President Franklin Roosevelt (1933–1945) died; Truman was thrust from vice president to president during the last days of World War II (1939–1945), at one of the most critical moments in U.S. history.

President Truman holds up a copy of the *Chicago Tribune*, published early election night with the headline "Dewey Defeats Truman."

Born in 1884., Harry S. Truman (the "S" does not stand for any name) was six years old, the eldest of three children, born to John and Ellen Truman, when the entire family moved from the family farm to Independence, Missouri. Truman grew up in Independence, read books a great deal, and at age 18, joined the Baptist church. He worked at a variety of odd jobs until 1918. After that, he went into the Missouri National Guard, became a lieutenant, and eventually went to France to fight in World War I (1914–1918), rising to the rank of colonel. Before and after World War I, Truman had gained much experience as a small businessman; he worked hard and believed in U.S. capitalism, but lightning never struck. Frustrated by his failures in business, Truman decided to enter politics in an effort to reduce much of the business corruption he saw around him.

He joined the Democratic Party, was elected county judge in Missouri, and won a reputation for scrupulous honesty, and straightforward talk. In 1934 he was elected to the United States Senate, and immediately began working on issues for the public good and those involving business corruption. The enactment of the Transportation Act of 1940 was a Truman program that greatly regulated railroad financing thereby reducing corrupt business practices and saving U.S. tax dollars.

Continuing in the spirit of watching for corruption in business, Truman involved himself as a senator by creating The Truman Committee in 1940, to oversee waste and corruption in defense spending. Corrupt business practices had a foothold in war-production efforts during World War II (1939–1945); Truman's efforts at uncovering waste and illegal business led to savings of $15 billion in tax dollars.

Truman's political career continued to rise, and he found himself serving as vice president under President Franklin Roosevelt. When Roosevelt died suddenly, Truman was thrust into the position of leader of the nation. World War II was ongoing, and there were many matters to challenge the new president (1945–1953). Thirteen days after Truman took office as president, the first United Nations conference met in San Francisco to plan for the post-war recovery. Days later, on May 7, 1945, Germany surrendered, and the war in Europe was over. The next day was Truman's sixty-first birthday. The United States was, however, still fighting a war with Japan, and preparing to deal with the communist Soviet Union and its dictator Joseph Stalin (1928–1953).

To end World War II completely, Truman made the profoundly controversial decision to drop two atomic bombs on Japan—one on Hiroshima, on August 6, 1945, and the next on the city of Nagasaki three days later. Japan surrendered on September 2, 1945. These events were stunning for the world, but more so for Truman, who had only learned of the atomic bomb's existence after becoming president months before. Truman's introduction into the U.S. presidency was likely the most dramatic and complex of any president.

Truman was a lifelong Democrat, and always a champion of Franklin Roosevelt's New Deal policies begun in the 1930s. As part of the post-war transition from a wartime economy to a peacetime economy, Truman sought to reconstruct the post-war United States in order to complete the New Deal. In September 1945, after barely five months as president, Truman requested that Congress create national health insurance for all U.S. citizens, and a permanent Federal Fair Employment Practices Commission (FEPC) to protect minority rights. Congress should also initiate an influx of money for scientific research and develop a large public power project on a variety of large U.S. rivers to provide clean and inexpensive electricity to U.S. residents with dam-generated power. The Republican Party, which controlled the Congress in 1946, blocked and stopped almost all of these measures. The Republicans believed that all of these plans would be bad for U.S. business and free enterprise.

Despite opposition from Republicans in Congress, Truman made consistent efforts to create a ''Fair Deal'' for the working post-World War II generation, and especially for veterans just back from the war. He fought to create civil rights legislation; repeal the Taft-Hartley Act which hindered union activities; create a new farm program stressing higher farmer incomes and lower consumer prices; provide federal aid to education; begin a federal housing program; and institute increases in the social security program. Conservative Democrats joined with Republicans to defeat most of Truman's domestic proposals.

Truman's legacy is largely that of a war president. He served the nation during World War II, the Korean War (1950–1953), and the Cold War with the Soviet Union. His progressive ideas of a ''Fair Deal'' were left for other generations of politicians to deal with.

Truman died of severe lung congestion on December 26, 1972, twenty years after leaving the White House.

See also: **Korean War, Franklin Roosevelt, United Nations, World War II**

FURTHER READING

Feinberg, Barbara S. *Harry S. Truman.* New York: Franklin Watts, Inc., 1994.

Fleming, Thomas. *Harry S. Truman, President.* New York: Walker and Co. Library, 1993.

Hamby, Alonzo. *Beyond the New Deal: Harry S. Truman and American Liberalism.* New York: Columbia University Press, 1973.

McCoy, Donald. *The Presidency of Harry S. Truman.* Kansas City, KS: University of Kansas Press, 1984.

McCullough, David. *Truman.* New York: Simon and Schuster, 1992.

TRUMP, DONALD JOHN

Billionaire real estate developer Donald Trump (1946–) showed the world that millions could be made in developing expensive commercial and residential properties. His intuitive sense of business and sharp eye for spotting a deal made Trump one of the most respected—and most hated—businesspersons of the 1980s. Without question, Trump became one of the most famous poster boys of an era known for its big-time financial wheeling and dealing and consumption.

Born Donald John Trump in 1946, he was the fourth of Frederick C. and Mary MacLeod Trump's five cildren. Trump was raised in Queens, New York, where his father was a builder and real estate developer who later specialized in constructing and operating middle-income apartments in Queens, Staten Island, and Brooklyn. Trump was a bright, energetic, and assertive child who grew up in a 23-room house with his siblings. By age 13 it was evident to his parents that he lacked discipline, so they sent him to the New York Military Academy. Trump did well there both socially and academically, and became a star athlete and student leader by the time he graduated in 1964.

While at the Academy Trump spent his spare time looking around at construction sites and renovating old houses. It seemed he would follow in his father's footsteps but on a much grander scale. He attended Fordham University, but later transferred to the University of Pennsylvania, where he obtained an undergraduate degree in finance from its Wharton School of Business in 1968. Following graduation he worked in his father's business, the Trump Organization. Soon Trump began putting his newly acquired business training to use; he was able to finance an expansion of the company's holdings by convincing his father to be more liberal in the use of loans based on the equity in the Trump apartment complexes. Eventually Trump bypassed his older brother and became president of his father's company, which concentrated on building houses and apartments. Though this was an important position it was not really fulfilling for Trump. He had bigger dreams of putting his signature on the Manhattan skyline.

Yearning for bigger, more profitable projects, Trump used $200,000 to move his residence to a small studio apartment in Manhattan in 1971. There he was closer to the affluent and influential set whom he felt could make dreams come true. ''If I ever wanted to be known as more than Fred Trump's son, I was eventually going to have to go out and make my own mark,'' Trump once said. In 1973, Trump persuaded his father to invest in the Manhattan real estate market. By then the company's worth had grown from $40 million when Donald Trump had joined the firm to a whopping $200 million.

Four years later Trump married New York fashion model Ivana Zelnickova Winklmayr, who had been an alternate on the 1968 Czech Ski Team. After their first child was born Trump named his wife vice president in charge of design for the Trump Organization. Ivana, an attractive and stylish woman, had a flair for design, and played a major role in supervising the renovation of the Commodore Hotel. She nicknamed her husband ''The Donald,'' and added a touch of style that he appreciated and welcomed. But later, as Trump's empire began to crumble, so too did his marriage.

In the mid-1990s Trump and Ivana, who had three children, divorced, and Trump married his second wife, Marla Maples, in 1994. The media lavished attention on Trump's second wedding, but for all the pomp and circumstance, the marriage was brief and ended in divorce. Trump and his second wife had a daughter together before their marriage ended.

Despite turmoil in his personal life, Trump's business ventures continued to thrive. His strategy was to buy dilapidated properties when prices were cheap, fix them up, and then make a huge profit when the economy picked up. He would either sell the real estate for a higher price than he paid or, more often than not, lease out space at steep prices. He made his first major deal in 1975, when he acquired the bankrupt Penn Central Railroad's Commodore Hotel and rail yards near the Hudson River. Trump then sold the rail yards to the city for a hefty commission, and won an unprecedented $120 million, 46-year tax abatement to tear down the Commodore and build the new Grand Hyatt Hotel in partnership with the Hyatt Corporation. To that amount he added $70 million in loans to construct the hotel. The deal incensed a number of community and political people in New York, who claimed that he used political connections to broker a deal with the city. Urban analysts, however, credit Trump with helping to ignite a building renaissance in a deteriorating part of town.

Ignoring naysayers and supporters alike, Trump continued to negotiate complex deals that made him the best-known and most controversial developer in New York. Against the wishes of New York City, Trump was able to convince the courts that he was entitled to a large amount of tax abatements, which the city was forced to pay. Trump used the abatements to help finance his flagship building, the posh Trump Tower on Fifth Avenue at Fifty-sixth Street, completed in 1980. The 58-story building featured a six-story atrium lined with pink marble and included an 80-foot waterfall. The luxurious building attracted well-known retail stores and celebrity renters. Residential condominiums sold for a pricey $10 million and higher. Of course all this overt show of opulence and wealth attracted national attention for Trump, and the Trump Tower became a major tourist attraction. As quoted in the *New York Times*, Trump dubbed the project ''the finest apartments in the top building in the best location in the hottest city in the world.''

Trump had a penchant for glitzy, controversial deals, and he maintained this interest throughout the 1970s and 1980s. In 1978 he bought the site of the Bonwit Teller department store and built a 68-story tower on Fifth Avenue, complete with a $2 million marble indoor waterfall. In the early 1980s he purchased a team in the upstart United States Football League, the New Jersey Generals, which sparked the league's antitrust lawsuit against the National Football League. Yet even Donald Trump could not make every deal golden. He once offered to construct a project, on the site that was later occupied by the Jacob Javits Convention Center, if New York City would name the building after Trump's father; the city declined. City officials also balked at Trump's plan to build a $5 billion complex on a strip of land running along the Hudson River from Fifty-ninth to Seventy-second streets.

Trump continued moving from one deal to another. He opened casinos and entered other real estate ventures. At times he ventured beyond the real estate market in hopes of making a mark in the high-stakes game of corporate raiding.

Early in his career Trump earned significant notoriety for artificially driving up real estate prices, and he drew similar criticism as he sought to acquire companies that were not looking for suitors. Beginning in 1986 he engaged in stock market deals that made him look like a corporate raider. He bought large stakes in a series of publicly traded companies, including MCI and Pillsbury, fueling takeover speculation that raised stock prices and allowed him to sell at a handsome profit. Though many criticized Trump's deals he was playing the game much like other speculators did. Extravagant speculation was rampant at that time and created a high-stakes climate. The process was simple: he would identify a company whose stock was undervalued, buy enough shares to take a noticeable position in the company, and make overtures of buying it. This would immediately attract the attention of other stock traders and drive the stock price higher. Trump, of course, was never really interested in buying, nor was the company interested in selling; but his actions prompted a significant increase in the value of his shares and enabled him to sell at a huge profit.

Some acquisitions, however, really did occur. In 1989 Trump acquired Eastern Airlines' shuttle operation for $365 million and renamed it the Trump Shuttle. In 1990 he was interested in acquiring American Airlines, bidding $7.5 billion for it, but the parent company was not interested in selling. Nonetheless, it seemed Trump was on a roll that would never end.

A genius at self-promotion, Trump named several huge projects after himself—making his name a household word by the end of the 1980s. He built or bought a succession of hotels and apartment houses in Manhattan, including the Plaza Hotel, Trump Plaza, and Trump Parc. He also became a major hotel and casino operator in Atlantic City, having astutely purchased property in the New Jersey seaside resort before the passage of a 1976 referendum legalizing gambling. This was where the Trump Princess Yacht was docked and where the Trump Shuttle airplane landed. Trump's Castle and the Trump Plaza and Taj Mahal casinos quickly became big moneymakers and helped raise Trump's profile nationally by sponsoring boxing championships. "The first time I did it, with Trump Tower, maybe it was ego," he once said. "But now it's economics. If somebody tells you you'll do a hundred million dollars more business if you call a building Trump Parc than if you call it Tower on the Park or some other name, you'd have to be some kind of masochist not to do it."

By 1990 many wondered how much Trump was really worth behind his complex financing schemes. His net worth had been estimated by some at as much as $3 billion, which Trump never confirmed or denied. But *Forbes* magazine decided to take a closer look, concluding that his property was worth just under $3.7 billion but his debts totaled $3.2 billion, for a net worth of only $1.5 billion. The magazine went on to predict that Trump could expect difficult times ahead.

This bleak prognosis proved accurate when the real estate market soured in 1990, and property values began to plummet. Trump's casinos suffered from over-saturation. Moreover, the credit market tightened, making it difficult for Trump to borrow additional money to cover his debts. Consequently, he missed $73 million in payments that were due in June 1990, and was extended an emergency $65 million loan, which the banks granted in order to save him from default and to protect their own investment. But that loan came at a hefty price: in return, Trump lost his freedom and was forced to relinquish much of his income and clear important business decisions with his creditors.

Trump was bitter about friends who turned on him during the bleak days. "I view these people as being born with garbage in their genes," he once said. But somehow Trump bounced back and was reported to be worth more than $2 billion by 1997. He also found some Chinese investors to help him build huge housing projects on Manhattan's West Side rail yards, a site which he had been trying fruitlessly to develop for years.

Donald Trump was noted in the business world primarily for his impact on the real estate and casino industries, yet he was perhaps best known to the public as a wealthy and eccentric celebrity. His businesses were major developing of real estate during the 1980s and he contributed to the rapid growth (and later, decline) of the real estate market. More recently, he focused on amassing a large entertainment and gambling concern that ranked as one of the largest in the United States in the late 1990s.

FURTHER READING

Byers, Paula K., and Suzanne M. Bourgoin, eds. *Encyclopedia of World Biography*. Detroit: Gale Research, 1998, s.v. "Trump, Donald."

Contemporary Authors. Detroit: Gale Research, 1990.

"I Am Donald, Hear Me Whine." *Forbes*, December 18, 1995.

"Married, Donald Trump and Marla Maples." *Time*, January 3, 1994.

Trump, Donald. *Surviving at the Top*. New York: Random House, 1990.

———. *The Art of the Deal*. New York: Random House, 1988.

TRUST-BUSTING

Prior to the birth of the United States, English common law provided few restrictions over business activities. By the mid-nineteenth century, U.S. courts had adopted a "rule of reason" in deciding cases involving accusations of restraint of competition. If the restraints applied broadly, they were often considered illegal. If more limited in time or geographic extent, restraints were allowed. Still, a laissez-faire approach to business persisted, meaning little governmental interference existed over business practices.

Following the American Civil War (1861–1865), industrialization grew at a brisk pace. With construction of a national railroad system, the cheaper transportation greatly expanded markets, and productivity grew. As competition heightened, the individually owned and managed companies sought means of protecting or expanding profits. State incorporation laws, however, strictly controlled mergers, forbidding companies to own stock in other companies. Therefore, one answer was to simply collaborate with competitors to set prices and control production. A form of such cooperation involved trusts in which one corporation would be created to oversee management of the stocks of cooperating corporations. Standard Oil became the first such trust in 1882. Trusts fixed prices and drove out new competition through price wars. Business consolidations in various industries, such as tobacco, beef, whiskey, and sugar, led to concentrations of capital and control by only a few people. Consumer protection was not the objective of what legislative and judicial oversight existed. Rather, the focus was on protection of new businesses trying to enter markets. The freedom to contract dominated all legal considerations. Eventually, trust became a general term applied to national monopolies.

Public demand for government intervention into trusts also rose dramatically through the 1880s. In response states adopted various laws, but these proved inconsistent and not applicable to interstate commerce. Congress responded in 1890 with passage of the Sherman Anti-Trust Act, the first major national legislation addressing business practices. The act prohibited trusts and other forms of group action potentially restraining interstate or international trade. Though strongly worded by considering all restraint of trade through cooperation unacceptable, the act was vague, leaving enforcement to the courts and executive branch of government. For example, President Grover Cleveland (1893–1897) was not inclined to enforce the act, believing trusts were a natural result of technological advances and stabilized the nation's economy by eliminating waste. The Supreme Court even ruled in 1895 that manufacturing was not considered interstate commerce, thus leaving many key industries free to continue operating under trusts.

By the time of President Theodore Roosevelt's (1901–1909) first term of office, a few hundred large companies controlled almost half of U.S. manufacturing and greatly influenced almost all key industries. The trust-busting movement began in 1904 with the Supreme Court's decision in *Northern Securities Co. v. U.S.* to break up a railroad trust. Over 40 antitrust lawsuits were filed under Roosevelt. Roosevelt, though becoming known as a "trustbuster," actually sought to reach a middle ground in government oversight of corporate activities. He, as did his successor William Howard Taft (1909–1913), provided the political resolve to use the Sherman Act to provide greater social accountability of businesses. But Roosevelt did not intend to end all corporate mergers, only regulate those considered grossly unresponsive to consumer needs.

Major Supreme Court decisions in 1911 ordered the break-up of Standard Oil, a corporate giant controlling railroads, sugar, and oil, and the American Tobacco Company. The decisions sanctioned the federal government's role to oversee marketplace economics. The rulings, however, reaffirmed the Court's use of the "rule of reason" to determine when trusts are anticompetitive. Such subjectiveness and unpredictability for future rulings led to public pressure for more

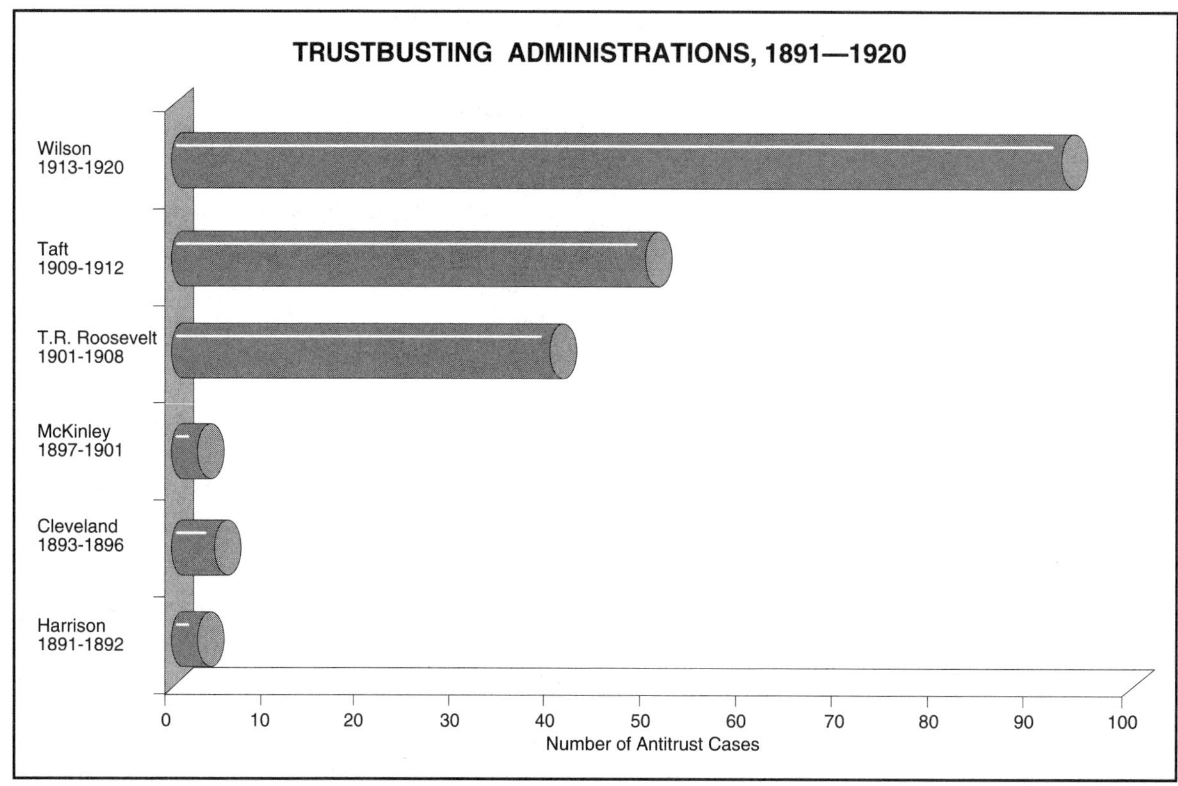

The number of antitrust lawsuits increased following the passage of the Sherman Anti-trust Act in 1890. President Wilson was credited with being the most aggressive toward "trust-busting."

effective trust-busting laws. Congress responded with the 1914 Clayton Anti-Trust Act prohibiting companies from charging different buyers different prices for the same products, contracts restricting business with competitors, mergers between competing companies, and companies buying stock in competing companies. These actions were to significantly lessen competition or lessen the creation of monopolies considered to be illegal. Importantly, the act exempted unions, by claiming human labor was not a commodity; certain farm organizations were also exempted. Associated with the Clayton Act was the 1914 Federal Trade Commission Act, creating the Federal Trade Commission (FTC) to tackle unfair business practices. Congress gave the FTC legal powers to issue cease-and-desist orders to combat unfair business activities.

With the economic boom years of World War I (1914–1918) and the 1920s, political interest in regulating business greatly diminished. The New Deal era of the early 1930s actually encouraged industrial collaboration to propel economic recovery from the Great Depression (1929–1939). Not until Congress passed the Robinson-Patman Act in 1936 and President Franklin D. Roosevelt's (1933–1945) attack on monopolies in the late 1930s was trust-busting reintroduced. The act strengthened price discrimination prohibitions designed to protect small businesses from larger competitors. Eighty trust suits were initiated in 1940. In 1950 Congress passed the last trust-busting law, called the Celler-Kefauver Antimerger Act, thereby closing some Clayton Act loopholes.

From the 1950s into the 1970s government aggressively pursued trust-busting. An example was the FTC's successful loosening of the Xerox Company's control of the photocopy industry. Trust-busting in the 1980s and 1990s, however, focused more on policing bad conduct rather than breaking up monopolies. Notable trust-busting included the break-up of American Telephone and Telegraph (AT&T). Accused of restricting competition in long-distance telephone service and telecommunications equipment, AT&T lost control over Western Electric, the manufacturing part of the company, and various regional operating telephone companies. President Ronald Reagan (1981–1989) reduced the FTC budget as a historic wave of corporate acquisitions occurred in the mid-1980s. By 1990 the states began to increasingly address illegal mergers, and soon federal interest grew again in examining competitive practices. President Bill Clinton (1993–) increased the budgets of the Justice Department's Antitrust Division as 33 lawsuits were filed in 1994. The most important antitrust case of the 1990s involved the Microsoft Corporation, accused of various monopolistic activities. As yet another wave of mergers swept the United States in the late 1990s, the age-old question persisted: does government have a legal right to limit commercial power? The U.S. public continued expressing largely conflicting attitudes over industrial combinations, as it had throughout much of history.

See also: **American Tobacco Company, Clayton Anti-Trust Act, Monopolies, Monopoly, Northern Securities Case, Sherman Anti-Trust Act, Standard Oil Company, Tobacco Trust, Trusts (Business)**

FURTHER READING

Freyer, Tony Allan. *Regulating Big Business: Antitrust in Great Britain and America, 1880–1990*. New York: Cambridge University Press, 1992.

Peritz, Rudolph J. R. *Competition Policy in America, 1888–1992: History, Rhetoric, Law*. New York: Oxford University Press, 1996.

Sklar, Martin J. *The Corporate Reconstruction of American Capitalism, 1890–1916: The Market, the Law, and Politics*. New York: Cambridge University Press, 1988.

Sullivan, E. Thomas, ed. *The Political Economy of the Sherman Act: The First One Hundred Years*. New York: Oxford University Press, 1991.

Wallace, James. *Overdrive: Bill Gates and the Race to Control Cyberspace*. New York: J. Wiley, 1997.

TRUSTS

A trust is a tool that an individual or institution uses to transfer property to a beneficiary. The party that grants the property is called the trustor. The trustor, in turn, gives the property to the trustee, who is charged with the task of disbursing the property to the beneficiary according to the instructions of the trustor. In the early 1990s, more than $1 trillion were held in U.S. trusts.

One important advantage that a trust has over a simple gift is that the trustor can exercise control over the disbursement of funds or property over time, even after his or her death (or dissolution, in the case of an institutional trustor). For example, a trustor may stipulate that funds periodically transferred to an all-male academy must be terminated if the school begins enrolling females. A second, and perhaps more important, advantage is that trusts can be used to minimize tax burdens incurred when wealth is transferred.

The two main categories of trusts are non-charitable and charitable, they are differentiated from one another primarily by tax status. Charitable trusts are organized for non-profit beneficiaries, such as educational, religious, and charitable organizations. Beneficiaries of noncharitable trusts typically include individuals or groups—particularly relatives or employees of the trustor—or profit seeking organizations.

Most trustees in the United States are banks' trust departments. However, other types of financial institutions act as trustees, and some companies specialize in trust management. Furthermore, a few trustees are separate entities that have been set up as foundations to manage large trust funds.

TRUSTS, BUSINESS

The word *trust* can be used to designate a group of companies that join together to control a domestic industry. The term was widely used in the late nineteenth century and early twentieth century. The American economy changed substantially following the American Civil War (1861–1865). Cottage industries, artisan production, and small-scale manufacturing declined, and a new, larger, factory-based manufacturing sector grew. Operating under relatively relaxed state business laws, financiers and manufacturing moguls became rich, often by suppressing the competition.

This led to a concentration of capital in just a few huge corporations, especially in transportation and heavy industry. The giant manufacturing and mining companies that survived the period of cutthroat competition soon folded into nationwide monopolies known as trusts. In a trust, the companies transferred their properties and stocks to a board of trustees who ran the companies in a way that avoided competition—for instance, by dividing the markets up to protect regional monopoly. Such business arrangements substantially restricted the opportunities for new competitors.

See also: **Standard Oil, Tobacco Trust, Trust-Busting, William Howard Taft,**

TUPPER, EARL SILAS

The story of Earl Tupper is one of American ingenuity, in which a young man with a basic high school education, an inventive genius, and a commercial eye was able to transform an ugly hunk of oil refinery waste known as "slag" into a form of plastic that could be made cheaply into many useful things. Tupper's new plastic and his methods of forming the plastic changed the shape and design of household objects, as well as commercial objects in the last half of the twentieth century. His marketing technique of hosting product demonstration parties in the home became extremely successful and has been imitated by other companies selling such items as underwear, home decorations, gardening supplies, and cooking utensils. Earl Tupper's Tupperware is one of the most recognized household names in the world.

Earl Tupper was born on July 28 1907, in Berlin, New Hampshire, and was the only child of Ernest and Lulu Tupper. His father, Ernest Leslie Tupper, ran a family farm and greenhouse. His mother, Lulu Clark Tupper, took in laundry to wash for neighbors and ran a boarding home. Earl's father was a person who loved to build and tinker, and he created several laborsaving gadgets. He was granted a patent for a device that facilitated the cleaning of chickens. Perhaps Earl Tupper developed his talent for inventions by watching his father.

Earl Tupper was energetic as a youngster, interested in business and in making money. He discovered he could sell a lot of the family's farm produce if he went door-to-door rather than just selling it at the farmer's market. By age 10, Earl learned that bringing the product to the customer was lucrative as well as enjoyable. He would reinvent this method years later in the form of the Tupperware party.

In 1925 Tupper graduated from high school in New Hampshire when he was 17 years old. After graduation he continued to work in the family businesses until he was nineteen. By then he had determined that somehow, as a businessman, he would make a million dollars by age 30. Tupper's early employment also included working as a mail clerk and as part of a railroad labor crew. In his spare time he took a course to learn tree surgery so he could start his own business tending trees and landscaping. In 1931, at age 24, Earl married and he and his wife later had five children, one daughter and four sons.

Although he started his landscaping business during the Great Depression (1929–1939), it was a modestly successful venture. His Tupper Tree-Doctors Company stayed open for six years. During this time, Tupper also kept himself busy conducting various experiments and writing a series of scientific papers that described his vast interests and numerous ideas for inventions. However, at age 30 he was forced into bankruptcy instead of having made his first million.

In 1936, after his bankruptcy, Earl met Bernard Doyle, an inventor working at the plastics manufacturing division of the Du Pont Corporation in Leominster, Massachusetts. Earl became intrigued with the possibilities of plastic and went to work at the plastics plant where he later said, according to the records of the National Museum of American History, "It was at Du Pont that my education really began." It was also where Tupper conducted his earliest experiments with plastics prior to World War II (1939–1945).

Earl Tupper worked for Du Pont for just one year and in 1938 he left the company to start the Earl S. Tupper Company, which advertised the design and engineering of industrial plastics. He wanted to experiment with plastic and asked Du Pont for some polyethylene slag, a waste product of the oil refining process. It was black, hard, putrid, and unworkable in that form. Tupper refined and cleaned the slag to produce a translucent, white, flexible, lightweight, odorless, and non-toxic plastic. This improved plastic, called Poly-T, became a revolutionary substance in the modern world. Tupper's modern plastic was made to withstand almost anything with the exception of sharp knife-cuts and near-boiling water. Tupper also designed injection-molding machines to create shaped objects out of his new plastic, and subsequently developed his famous, patented air-tight lid.

Most of the work during his company's first few years was performing subcontract work for Du Pont. The company made much of its money producing molded parts for gas masks and signal lamps for the U.S. Navy during World War II. After the war, along with hundreds of other manufacturers, Tupper turned his attention to the postwar consumer market. He made items such as plastic sandwich picks, unbreakable drinking tumblers, and plastic cigarette cases. These consumer products were often given away with other well-known products. The tumbler was offered with *Tek* toothbrushes and the cigarette cases were offered along with brand name cigarettes along with the cigarette company's logo imprinted on the case. Tupper then focused on creating a line of plastic food storage containers that would hold foods "air tight" in the refrigerator, sealing them against other odors and keeping foods fresh longer. These containers were known as "Tupperware," and were first distributed in department and hardware stores. Unfortunately, because of the bad reputation of other plastics, sales were dismal in stores. Consumers knew little of Tupper's new type of plastic and the ingeniousness of Tupper's air-tight seal needed to be demonstrated to customers.

Tupperware was also distributed through private household product companies, such as Stanley Home

Products. Some home product salespeople were selling fairly large quantities of Tupperware products, to the point where Tupper took notice, contacted them, and met with them to discuss possible new ways to market and distribute Tupperware. A Stanley Home Products saleswoman, Brownie Wise, suggested that Tupper develop a marketing strategy modeled after the Stanley Home Product Company's in-home selling parties. Thomas Damigella and several other Tupperware distributors also strongly urged Earl Tupper to pull his products out of department stores and to pursue direct marketing to the buyer using the ''home party.'' The idea was to demonstrate the products in the home of a person who sponsored a ''Tupperware party,'' where all questions could be answered in a social atmosphere. At one point small Tupperware products were given away to those who attended the parties. Brownie Wise was a very innovative, ambitious, and smart saleswoman and she went on to become vice president of the company Tupperware Home Parties in 1951 where she remained until 1958. Home demonstration parties have remained the primary outlet for Tupperware and have become an institution. By 1951, Tupper set up the Tupperware world headquarters in Orlando, Florida, on an 1,100-acre site chosen by Brownie Wise.

By the time he decided to retire, at age 51, Earl Tupper had created an enormously successful worldwide organization involved in the manufacture and direct sales of plastic containers—containers that were beautiful enough to be collected regularly by the Museum of Modern Art, in New York City, and displayed there, as early as 1947. Tupperware has also earned a place in the Musee des Arts Decoratifs in Montreal, the Philadelphia Museum of Art, and the Victoria and Albert Museum in London. The beauty and functionality of these products, and the direct face-to-face sales, became an unbeatable combination.

By the late 1940s Earl Tupper brought a clean, durable and attractive plastic into the world of commerce. Developing a high-quality plastic along with an ingenious method of production served as a catalyst for numerous plastic products that have since flooded the marketplace. The direct face-to-face selling technique of the company became extremely popular and the home party idea has continually evolved. Tupperware created literally millions of jobs for a sales force that has been mostly women. When Tupperware started to become popular household items the work force in the United States was going through major changes. During World War II, while so many of the country's men were in the armed forces, many women had entered the male-dominated job market, such as in factories. Women also worked at jobs created for the war effort and when the war ended so did the jobs. Upon the servicemen's return, women were pushed out of the job market. Also after World War II many children were born—the baby boom—and at that time many women who had children did not work outside the home. Selling Tupperware provided convenient part-time or full-time employment for many of these women who sought a career outside the home.

Tupper sold Tupperware to Rexall Corporation in 1958 for $16 million. In 1973 Early Tupper retired and moved to Costa Rica where he eventually became a citizen. At the age of 76, Tupper died of a heart attack in his adopted homeland on October 3, 1983, and was survived by a sister, five children, and 14 grandchildren. Although Tupper built an enormously successful company making numerous plastic products he never liked the term ''plastic.'' He used to insist on calling what he made ''Poly-T'' because ''a lot of plastic that is made is junk.''

Earl Tupper is remembered for more than quality children's toys, lettuce corers, orange peelers, tea strainers, gardening tools, and cake keepers, and other products he helped produce. The Earl S. Tupper Research and Conference Center is located at the Smithsonian Tropical Research Institute. The facility includes the Earl S. Tupper Tropical Sciences Library, laboratories for chemistry, plant physiology, histology, acoustic communication, entomology, and a scanning electron microscope.

FURTHER READING

Clarke, Alison J. *Tupperware: The Promise of Plastic in 1950s America.* Washington, DC: Smithsonian Institution Press, 1999.

National Museum of American History Exhibition *Earl S. Tupper Papers.*

The New York Times Biographical Service. Sanford, NC: Microfilming Corporation of America, 1993.

A Worldwide Success Story [cited June 30, 1999] available from the World Wide Web @ http://www.tupperware.com/.

TURNPIKES

Turnpikes are toll roads: the user pays a fee to travel the road. Only after the user paid the toll would the gatekeeper turn the ''pike'' or gate to allow the wagon or carriage on to the road. This practice, which was established in England in the 1700s, arrived in the

United States in the late 1700s when turnpike companies began surfacing roads and building bridges for a profit. The first American turnpike was built in 1785 in Virginia. The first major U.S. turnpike that was publicly financed was Pennsylvania's Lancaster Road: some 5,000 investors subscribed 30 dollars each to buy shares in the turnpike that was made of stone and gravel and connected Philadelphia to Lancaster. It opened in 1794 after two years of construction. The project inspired similar projects and around the turn of the century hundreds of turnpike companies emerged. They improved existing routes and established new ones; stagecoach travel increased as a result. As a transportation improvement, the toll roads were a big success for the developing nation. As a private business endeavor, however, toll roads proved a failure. Traveler's fees usually covered only maintenance. By 1825 turnpike companies' stocks had become worthless and most companies folded. Thereafter the government began operating toll roads as a way to finance pike projects: those who would use them had to pay fees. In this way, the taxpayer's burden was reduced.

See also: **National Road, Wilderness Road**

TWENTY-FIRST AMENDMENT

The year 1933 marked a benchmark in U.S. constitutional history. The Twenty-first Amendment was enacted. It is the only constitutional amendment to repeal another amendment. With its ratification, the Eighteenth Amendment's mandate to eliminate liquor consumption in the United States was repealed.

Fourteen years after it began, Prohibition ended. Although the Eighteenth Amendment did succeed in reducing the amount of alcohol consumed, it failed in its goal of eliminating the consumption of intoxicating liquors in the United States. Many people continued to imbibe. Taking advantage of the legal ban on alcohol, organized crime helped develop a black market in "bootleg" alcohol to meet continuing public demand. Criminals like Chicago gangster Al Capone (1899-1947) became multimillionaires. In the early 1930s, production and sales of "bootleg" liquor continued to rise and the Great Depression began. Prohibition was difficult to enforce in urban areas, and critics argued the increase in crime resulting from the ban offset reductions in consumption. In addition, millions of citizens were out of work and legalizing the liquor industry would create more jobs. Calls for the repeal of the Eighteenth Amendment were gaining ground.

During the 1932 Democratic national convention, the party platform included a call for the repeal of the

Due to public protest and increased crime, the Twenty-first Amendment repealed the Eighteenth Amendment, which was to prohibit the sale of intoxicating liquors.

Eighteenth Amendment. In the presidential election of that year, the Democrats won a landslide victory. In February 1933, the Twenty-first Amendment was proposed in Congress. It specified the amendment must be ratified by state conventions rather than state legislatures so that legislators (who were predominantly from rural areas that supported Prohibition) could not vote against ratification.

Before 1933 was over, the Twenty-first Amendment had passed. Prohibition was officially over. The amendment did give states the right to prohibit the importation or transportation of intoxicating liquors, and many states did enact their own prohibition laws in the 1930s. By 1966, however, all state prohibition laws were repealed.

See also: **Black Market, Eighteenth Amendment, Prohibition**

TYLER PREEMPTION ACT OF 1841

The Preemption Act, passed in 1841 during the administration of tenth president of the United States John Tyler (1790–1862), was a response to the widespread practice of squatting—illegally settling lands that had not been surveyed and were not yet for sale. During the first three decades of the 1800s the American West received an influx of settlers. The government's system of surveying lands before putting them on the market could not keep up with the demand for property. New arrivals on the frontier simply settled public lands, often building on them and working the land. The Preemption Act exonerated these trespassers by allowing any citizen or any immigrant who intended to become a citizen to purchase 160 acres (64.7 hectares) of public land at the minimum price as long as he had occupied and cultivated the land, and had built a cabin or other dwelling on the tract. This act, combined with Congressional legislation that offered less desirable surveyed tracts at gradually reduced rates, contributed to the settlement of the West and the Old Northwest (the present-day states of Ohio, Michigan, Indiana, Illinois, Wisconsin, and part of Minnesota).

See also: **Northwest Ordinance, Old Northwest**

TYSON FOODS

Tyson Foods, Inc. of Arkansas made news in the mid-1990s, not for its position as the largest poultry producer in the nation, but for its alleged political connections to the Clinton administration. As governor of Arkansas, Bill Clinton showed favoritism toward Tyson with tax breaks and personal services. In return Clinton accepted considerable presidential campaign funds from the company. Mike Espy, former secretary of agriculture during the first part of the Clinton administration, was accused, and later cleared, of accepting inappropriate gifts from Tyson. In 1998 Tyson accepted a settlement from the Office of Independent Counsel, agreeing to pay $6 million in penalties and costs for its alleged influence-buying. The unfavorable publicity, however, has not discouraged millions of consumers from buying Tyson products.

The history of Tyson Foods started with an Arkansas farmer, John Tyson, who hauled about 50 chickens to sell in Chicago during 1935. He named his business Tyson Feed & Hatchery and began making a profit buying and selling chickens prior to World War II (1939–45). Tyson eventually started raising chickens as well, and the company, incorporated in 1947, expanded significantly after the war.

Don Tyson joined his father in the business in 1952, and the company began to expand its production facilities. A large processing plant was built at the site of the company headquarters in Springdale, Arkansas. Tyson introduced an ice-pack processing line, which helped it to be more competitive. In an era when people were eating more and more chicken Tyson was in a good position to fulfill consumers' needs. In 1963 the company went public and changed its name to Tyson's Foods, Inc. Three years later Don Tyson took over as president following the accidental death of his father.

Improved methods for producing larger numbers of broiler chickens drove the prices of chicken down in the late 1960s. When Tyson lost more than a dollar per share in earnings in 1967 the firm began the process of acquiring smaller companies to increase its share of the market. In 1969 it purchased Prospect Farms, Inc., which became a precooked chicken division. In the same year Tyson successfully fended off a lawsuit from Arkansas chicken farmers who felt that the company had discriminated against them as suppliers.

In 1971, after a period of growth and diversification, the company's name was changed to Tyson Foods. The company acquired Ocoma Foods, Krispy Kitchens, and the poultry division of Wilson Foods. It also began to market the first breaded chicken breast patty and bought a hog operation in North Carolina. In the early 1970s, as Americans increasingly favored chicken over beef and pork, Tyson became a leader in introducing new chicken products. In addition to the chicken patty it sold chicken hot dogs and bologna, just a few of the 24 specialty products it had developed by 1979. A new chill process was used to produce fresh chickens and prolong shelf life.

Tyson bought the rest of Wilson Foods in 1978. In 1980 Tyson introduced a Chick 'n Quick line, which offered easy-to-prepare chicken portions. The company was also the largest producer of rock Cornish game hens and the biggest producer of hogs. Precooked chicken patties for restaurants also became big sellers during this period.

By the early 1980s the consumption of chicken had increased 30 percent since 1970. Tyson's ability to mass-produce chickens rapidly, as well as its introduction of prepared chicken products, had helped it to expand in this market. It continued to acquire other companies and by 1984 had expanded its operations into five other states besides Arkansas. Don Tyson won the gold award from the *Wall Street Transcript* in 1986 for his business successes.

A major coup for Tyson in 1988 was the takeover of Holly Farms Corporation, the national brand-name leader in chicken sales. Tyson battled for six months with the Nebraska firm ConAgra for control of Holly Farms and in 1989 Don Tyson finally agreed to pay $1.29 billion for Holly Farms. In 1990 Tyson's sales increased 50.7 percent as a result of the Holly Farms acquisition. Tyson's beef and pork operations also increased substantially after the merger.

Tyson next got into the seafood market in the early 1990s by acquiring Arctic Alaska Fisheries Corporation and Louis Kemp Seafood Company. Although the seafood market operations were not profitable at first, market activity was bolstered by the acquisition of the seafood division of International Multifoods Corporation.

Tyson continued to expand and to buy up competitors and suppliers. In 1994 the company decided to build four new poultry plants at a cost of $400 million and also bought a controlling interest in a Mexican chicken-processing company. In the same year it bought Culinary Foods, Inc., which manufactured specialty frozen foods, and Gorges Foodservice, Inc., a processor of beef for the food services industry. Tyson tried unsuccessfully to purchase WLR Foods Inc., a Virginia producer of turkey and chicken products. In 1995 Tyson purchased the chicken plants owned by Cargill, adding an additional output capacity of 2.5 million chickens per week. An equal increase in capacity was brought about with the acquisition of McCarty Farms Inc. of Mississippi. In 1997 Tyson took the very significant step of purchasing Hudson Foods, Inc., the fifth-largest producer of chickens in the U.S.

Don Tyson retired as chairman in 1995 and turned over control of operations to Leland E. Tollett. By the mid-1990s Tyson had reached the top position in chicken sales in the nation; by 1998 its sales had increased from $2.54 billion in 1989 to $6.4 billion. In the mid-1990s Tyson entered into a joint venture with the People's Republic of China, opened an office in Mexico, and established a resource office to help the company market goods on the international market. In 1998 the company exported its products to 43 countries.

Tyson Foods, in the words of its company philosophy, successfully sought to "segment, concentrate, and dominate." Tyson achieved all three goals through its many acquisitions; in the late 1990s Tyson also capitalized on the public's increasing desire for easily prepared chicken products.

FURTHER READING

Behar, Richard. "Arkansas Pecking Order." *Time*, October 26, 1992.

Buckler, Arthur. "Tyson Foods Isn't Chicken-Hearted About Expansion." *Wall Street Journal*, January 18, 1994.

McGraw, Dan. "The Birdman of Arkansas." *U.S. News & World Report*, July 18, 1994.

Tyson Foods, Inc. *Corporate Factbook*. Springdale, AR: Tyson Foods, 1996.

Warner, Melanie. "Tough Times for the Chicken King." *Fortune*, October 28, 1996.

UNDERGROUND RAILROAD

For the first few decades of the new nation, state after state in the North passed emancipation laws freeing slaves or future children of slaves. By the early 1800s the North had essentially abolished slavery. In the South, however, where slavery was much more crucial to the economy, emancipation was making little to no progress. By the 1830s Northern abolitionists, impatient with the very slow progress, adopted more radical tactics to end slavery. Evangelical Christian groups took the lead in demanding immediate emancipation of slaves without compensation to the slave owners. A newly formed American Anti-Slavery Society grew quickly to approximately 150,000 members by 1840. Abolitionism, however, remained largely unsupported by most Northern politicians. For instance, a major campaign to distribute anti-slavery literature in the South in the 1830s was stopped by proslavery interests with the help of President Andrew Jackson (1829–1837).

Meanwhile, slaves increasingly sought freedom by escaping to the North, often with assistance from Northern sympathizers. In a move that many saw as governmental sanction of slavery, Congress passed the Fugitive Slave Act in 1850. The act required Northern states to return runaway slaves and established harsh penalties for individuals assisting runaways.

In reaction, abolitionists fashioned the Underground Railroad. Neither a railroad nor underground, it was a hidden network composed primarily of people and places extending in all directions to help runaway slaves. Operating largely in darkness and disguise, free blacks with assistance from sympathetic Northerners provided direction, food, and shelter for those seeking freedom in the North or in Canada. The system, coded in railroad terminology for secrecy, consisted of various routes (lines), hiding places (stations), and assistants (conductors) who helped to transport escapees along the way. The escaped slaves were called packages or freight. The journey often required money for transportation, food, and bribes. The escapees used most anything for transportation, including travel by foot, small boat, covered wagon, and even in boxes shipped by rail or sea. Stations consisted of barns, cellars, attics, and secret rooms. The most heavily used routes were through Indiana, Ohio, and western Pennsylvania.

Due to the passage of the 1850 act, the desired destination for many runaway slaves became Canada, where they would be safe from U.S. lawmen and fugitive-slave hunters who could not cross the international border. A particularly common destination for many was Southern Ontario, with the Suspension Bridge at Niagara Falls serving as one well-used border crossing.

Through the Underground Railroad's years of operation until the conclusion of the American Civil War (1861–1865), an estimated 50,000 to 100,000 slaves sought freedom; because of the dire need for secrecy no records were kept. Because of the great danger in assisting slaves, no more than 3,000 people actually assisted, but the knowledge of the Underground Railroad's existence served to stir Northern sympathy toward the plight of the slaves. Some Northerners supported the effort for economic reasons as well. The industrial North was becoming increasingly agitated at the South's economy, which was based on unpaid slave labor, and the Railroad offered one means of undercutting the South's economy.

Many people associated with the Underground Railroad became well known, most notably Harriet Tubman (c1820–1913). A former slave herself who escaped through the system, Tubman traveled to the South on 19 occasions in the 1850s, recruiting those willing to take the chance of freedom. She reportedly helped 300 slaves directly through her own action. Harriet Beecher Stowe (1811–1896), who authored *Uncle Tom's Cabin* during this time, assisted fugitive slaves in Cincinnati, Ohio. Levi Coffin, a Quaker in Indiana, assisted more than 3,000 slaves from his

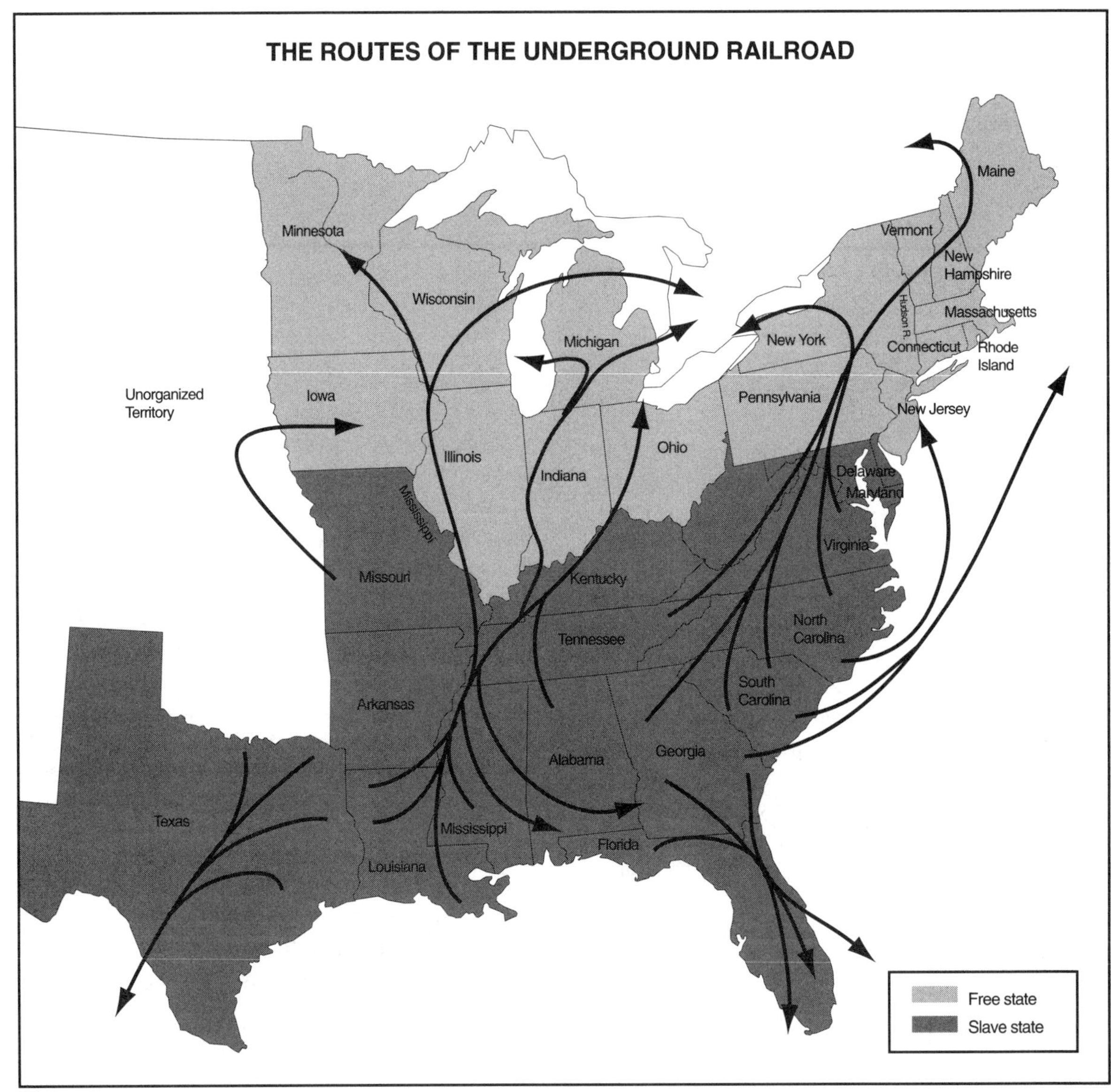

The Underground Railroad was used during the 1850s and 1860s to free 50,000–100,000 slaves with the help of 3000 individuals, over many routes, most ending in Canada.

home. Frederick Douglass (c1817–1895) was a fugitive slave who rose to prominence as an eloquent statesman for the abolitionists.

The Underground Railroad, impressive for its success, longevity, and complexity, was yet one more factor aggravating hostilities between the North and South. The Railroad has been noted as one of the more significant humanitarian efforts in U.S. history.

See also: **Fugitive Slave Act, Slavery**

FURTHER READING

Buckmaster, Henrietta. *Let My People Go: The Story of the Underground Railroad and the Growth of the Abolition Movement.* Columbia: University of South Carolina Press, 1992.

Mayer, Henry. *All on Fire: William Lloyd Garrison and the Abolition of Slavery.* New York: St. Martin's Press, 1998.

Rogers, William B. *We Are All Together Now: Frederick Douglass, William Lloyd Garrison, and the Prophetic Tradition.* New York: Garland Publishers, 1995.

Runyon, Randolph P. *Delia Webster and the Underground Railroad.* Lexington, KY: University Press of Kentucky, 1996.

Sprague, Stuart S., ed. *His Promised Land: The Autobiography of John P. Parker, Former Slave and Conductor on the Underground Railroad.* New York: Norton, 1996.

UNDERWOOD TARIFF ACT

Congress passed The Underwood Tariff Act in 1913. Its purpose was to reduce levies on manufactured and semi-manufactured goods and to eliminate duties on most raw materials. To compensate for the loss of revenue, the act also levied a graduated income tax (made legal by ratification of the Sixteenth Amendment earlier that year) on U.S. residents.

Protective tariffs had been the subject of political debate since they were first passed in 1828. After the American Civil War (1861–1865) the controversy over duties had become partisan, with Republicans, for the most part, favoring them, maintained duties were favorable to U.S. industry, and Democrats believed to the contrary. Republican administrations during the 1890s raised tariffs to unprecedented levels: The McKinley Tariff Act of 1890 was followed by the Dingley Tariff Act, which raised duties to as much as 57 percent and caused the cost of living to increase. Around the turn of the century, however, Republicans began to support opposition to high tariffs as well. As a result rates were reduced somewhat by the Payne-Aldrich Tariff Act of 1909, but prices remained artificially high and Democrats continued to press for a reduction in duties.

The election of 1912 proved a turning point for the Democrats: Woodrow Wilson (1856–1924) was voted into office and the party won control of Congress. In 1913 Wilson supported the Underwood Tariff Act, cutting or eliminating tariff rates. The legislation, sponsored by Representative Oscar Underwood (1862–1929), passed both houses of Congress. The reduced tariffs encouraged the import of foreign materials and manufactured goods, and prices of goods came down. The federal government now collecting less revenue in duties on foreign goods.

To offset the effect of less revenue from tariffs, the government levied an income tax for the first time. Incomes less than $4000 per year were exempt by the Underwood act, thus, nearly all factory workers and farmers were not required to pay the taxes. Those earning more than $4000 but less than $20,000 paid a mere one percent tax. Rates rose from there, but the highest tax was still just a scant six percent—on earnings exceeding $500,000.

The effect of the Underwood Tariff on foreign trade and on prices was limited: World War I (1914–1918) began the following year, curtailing imports. Protective tariffs became an issue again in the early 1920s, with the Emergency Tariff Act (1921) and the Fordney-McCumber Tariff Act (1922), which raised duties once again and gave the president authority to increase and decrease customs duties.

See also: **Dingley Tariff, Fordney-McCumber Tariff, Sixteenth Amendment, Tariff, Tariff of Abominations**

UNEMPLOYMENT

Reports on the economy often include information on unemployment to illustrate whether or not a nation's economy is doing well. Who is considered unemployed and what does the unemployment rate really represent?

The unemployed are individuals who do not currently have a job but are actively searching for one. These individuals, combined with those who are currently employed, make up the nation's labor force. A person who is not working and is not looking for a job is not considered unemployed.

The unemployment rate is usually described as a percentage. It is the percentage difference between the number of individuals in the labor force who are employed and those who are actively seeking work. In 1993 there were 129.5 million people in the U.S. labor force. Of that number, 8.7 million were unemployed, creating an unemployment rate of 6.7 percent for all workers.

There are two possible percentages for unemployment, the rate for all workers and the rate for civilian workers. All workers in the labor force include civilian workers and those in the U.S. armed forces. The civilian rate is considered to provide the clearest picture of the economy's strength because civilian workers are employed according to market forces. This is also the rate most often used by the media and in economic reports. The U.S. unemployment rate for civilian workers during 1993 was 6.8 percent.

Can a nation achieve full employment? Actually, a 6 percent unemployment rate is currently considered to be full employment. How can this be? The constant flux of the labor force, whether from seasonal variations or from a natural fluctuation of workers leaving one job and searching for another (for career advancement, skill demands, or some other motivation), makes it unrealistic to expect an unemployment rate of zero

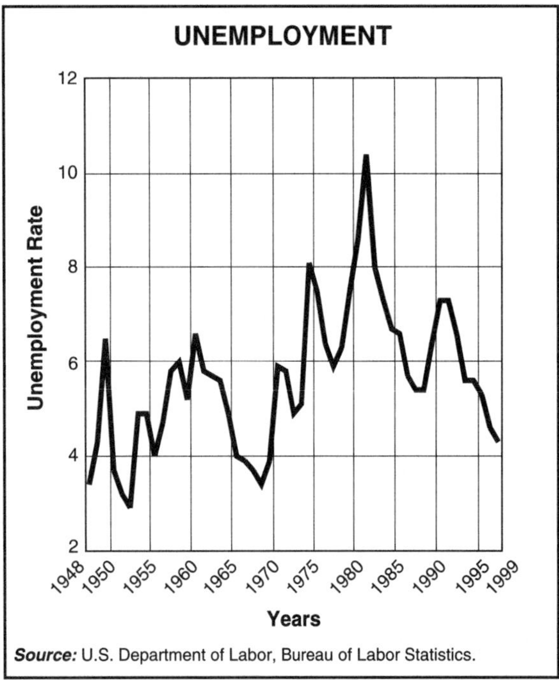

Source: U.S. Department of Labor, Bureau of Labor Statistics.

The Unemployment Rate represents the percentage of people who are able to work, but are currently seeking employment, as depicted in this graph for the last half of the 20th century.

will ever be achieved. The full employment rate has risen steadily over the years. From 1952 to 1958, full employment was considered to be a rate of 4 percent unemployment. The rate rose to 4.5 percent in 1970, increased to 4.9 percent in 1977, and held at 6 percent through 1998.

If the full employment rate is 6 percent unemployment and the 1993 unemployment rate for civilian workers was 6.8 percent, then the economy for that year was providing the jobs to meet the needs of employment seekers.

See also: **Seasonal Unemployment, Structural Unemployment**

UNION PACIFIC RAILROAD COMPANY

The Union Pacific Railroad Company (UP) came into existence in response to the widely held belief, fully formed by the 1850s, that the United States needed a rail link between its older, eastern states and the distant but rapidly growing states of the far west. Various proposals were made for northern, southern, and central routes but Congress could not agree on a plan. Following the southern states' secession from the United States in 1861, the remaining congressmen from the North quickly agreed on a route, and U.S. President Abraham Lincoln (1861–1865), urged on by military considerations as much as by those of economics, signed the Pacific Railroad Act of 1862.

The act called for the creation of a public corporation, called the Union Pacific Railroad Company, to build a railroad from Nebraska to the California-Nevada border and there to meet the Central Pacific rail line, building east from Sacramento, California, and later linked with San Francisco. The meeting place of the two railroads was eventually set at Promontory Summit, Utah Territory. As amended by a second piece of legislation, the act specified that the company would be supported by a loan of U.S. bonds from the federal government, to be paid back in 30 years, and by the issuance of its own bonds and capital stock. Further, the company would receive land grants in the amount of 6400 acres on alternating sides of every mile of track laid, a checkerboard swath of land across the middle of the country that would eventually total around 12 million acres of valuable minerals, grazing land, and metropolitan real estate.

While the logic and value of a railroad across the western United States seemed obvious in the late twentieth century, it was much less so in 1864. The men who became involved in the leadership of the UP—chiefly Thomas C. Durant (1820–1885) and brothers Oliver Ames (1807–1877) and Oakes Ames (1804–1873)—did so largely in order to make handsome profits off the railroad's hurried construction. Durant was the vice president and dominant figure in the company's early years; it was he and a handful of others who formed a construction company called Crédit Mobilier of America (CMA) to receive contracts from UP for the building of its vast railroad. Estimates vary as to precisely how inflated these contracts were, but later congressional investigations left no doubt that the backers of CMA intentionally siphoned off far more of the UP's capital than was fair to its investors or good for its future financial health. The investigations of the early 1870s also revealed that the CMA principals bribed members of Congress with company stock. The railroad that was built was a splendid success, and so vast a project might never have been undertaken without the promise of equally vast profits to be made.

In five years the UP crews laid more than 1000 miles of rail between Omaha, Nebraska, and Promontory Summit, Utah Territory, where on May 10, 1869, a golden spike completed the first transcontinental rail line. The railroad's completion supplied a critical impetus to the development of the western United States, which to that time had been settled only on the Pacific Coast and in areas of unusual mineral wealth, such as Colorado. With the arrival of the railroad, farmers, ranchers, and manufacturers were able to transport their goods to the great eastern metropolitan markets cheaply and quickly, and the West began to fill with pioneers. As the area's most significant railroad for almost 15 years, UP enjoyed rapid growth and excellent earnings for its scandal-ridden promoters, who were dominated from 1873 to the mid-1880s by financier Jay Gould (1836–1892).

Under Gould's direction UP expanded considerably during the 1870s, with its main route from Omaha, Nebraska to Ogden, Utah, joined by a host of feeder lines extending into neighboring territory. The most significant of these was a line running to the Pacific Ocean through Idaho and Oregon and a branch that progressed in the general direction of Los Angeles, California, which it reached in 1901. Unfortunately, Gould's tenure was also marked by mismanagement and an increasingly burdensome debt. After the financial panic of 1893 strained the U.S. economy to the utmost, UP was forced into bankruptcy.

Union Pacific was reorganized in 1895, with Edward H. Harriman acting as chairman. Under Harriman's leadership, UP became one of the best run, as well as one of the largest, U.S. railroads. Harriman first set about retrieving the various pieces of UP lost during bankruptcy and soon reassembled the company's three basic networks: those running between Omaha and Ogden, Ogden and the Pacific Northwest, and Ogden and Los Angeles. Seeking control of the Central Pacific run between Ogden and the San Francisco bay area, he gained control of Central's owner, Southern Pacific (SP) in 1901. Between 1898 and Harriman's death in 1909, the UP increased its track miles from 2000 to 6000.

An anti-trust case brought against UP resulted in a 1913 U.S. Supreme Court decision that the company was inhibiting competition and must divest itself of its SP holdings. Union Pacific was thus once again reduced to its three main routes—Omaha to Ogden, Ogden to Portland, and Ogden to Los Angeles—although new lines between Portland and Seattle were soon added.

In the 1930s an increasing portion of earnings were generated by UP's oil and gas holdings and industrial real estate, businesses that were an outgrowth of the generous land grants the railroad had received upon its formation. With the outbreak of World War II (1939–1945) Union Pacific had little to worry about in the financial realm. The need to shuttle huge amounts of personnel and heavy equipment around the United States gave UP all the business it could handle; company employment nearly doubling to 60,000 and revenue pushing to more than $500 million by war's end.

During the postwar period, UP restructured its holdings into three divisions: transportation, land development, and natural resources. In the mid-1960s the company began a concentrated program of mineral, oil, and gas exploration. To reflect its diversified nature, the company changed its name to Union Pacific Corporation (UP) in 1969. By the 1970s UP had moved into refining, thus completing the formation of a fully integrated oil and gas business. Eventually known as Union Pacific Resources Company, this subsidiary was spun off into a separate entity in 1995, enabling UP to once again concentrate on its core railroad business.

Beginning as far back as the 1930s and continuing through the end of the twentieth century, truck and automobile traffic eroded the railroad's share of both freight and passenger miles. This long-term trend, coupled with U.S. President Ronald Reagan's (1981–1989) deregulation of the railroad industry, led to a new era of railroad consolidation in the 1980s and 1990s. In 1982 Union Pacific acquired the Missouri Pacific and Western Pacific railroads, gaining a Chicago to Omaha line, three gateways to Mexico, and a route between Ogden and San Francisco. The original transcontinental railroad was again back under complete UP control. An even larger acquisition came in 1996, when Union Pacific paid $4 billion to once again join forces with Southern Pacific. The UP-SP marriage created the largest railroad in the United States, with 36,000 miles of track in 23 states, Canada, and Mexico.

***See also:* Oakes Ames, Oliver Ames, Thomas Durant, Jay Gould, Railroad Industry, Railroads (Federal Land Grants to), Robber Barons, Transcontinental Railroad**

FURTHER READING

Bailey, Edd H. *The Century of Progress; A Heritage of Service: Union Pacific, 1869–1969.* New York: Newcomen Society in North America, 1969.

Cook, William S. *Building the Modern Union Pacific.* New York: Newcomen Society of the United States, 1984.

Kenefick, John C. *Union Pacific and the Building of the West.* New York: Newcomen Society of the United States, 1985.

Klein, Maury. *Union Pacific: The Rebirth, 1894–1969.* New York: Doubleday, 1990.

———. *Union Pacific: Birth of a Railroad.* New York: Doubleday, 1987.

Willoughby, Jack. "The Rebuilding of Uncle Pete." *Forbes*, November 14, 1988.

UNITED AUTO WORKERS

The United Auto Workers (UAW) was created in 1936 to protect the rights of workers in America's largest industry, automobile manufacturing. Unionizing auto workers was a formidable task. Management was staunchly anti-union, harassing workers suspected of union activity and even employing spies to report on employee activities. Workers were subjected to capricious firings and bullying from foremen, and could not appeal management decisions. Because the American Federation of Labor (AFL) was not concerned with the needs of unskilled workers, a group of radical labor leaders emerged to advocate for their rights. John L. Lewis (1880–1969) of the United Mine Workers, David Dubinsky (1892–1982) of the International Ladies' Garment Workers, and Sidney Hillman (1887–1946) of the Amalgamated Clothing Workers formed the Committee of Industrial Organization (CIO), a committee within the AFL. The CIO worked on organizing unskilled labor into huge industry-wide unions. The UAW, with Homer Martin as its first president, became the auto workers' union.

Workers, intimidated by management's hostility, were reluctant at first to join the UAW. They needed proof that the union could succeed against the biggest and most powerful industry in the country. To confront these industry giants, organizers adopted a new tactic. They staged sit-down strikes at several plants, forcing companies to stop production. This strategy was so damaging to business that the auto companies were finally forced to accept the union as labor's legitimate bargaining agent.

The recognition of the UAW was a landmark in the struggle for labor rights. It signaled the emergence of a new generation of labor leaders who were ready to push hard for the rights of unskilled labor. And workers responded enthusiastically. UAW membership rose from 98,000 in early 1937 to 400,000 by mid-year. During the 1930s and 1940s, the UAW fought for and obtained significant improvements for its members, especially under the leadership of Walter Reuther (1907–1970), who served as UAW president from 1946 to 1970. The union successfully bargained for such measures as cost-of-living adjustments, wage increases, and pensions. In 1955, auto workers won a guaranteed annual wage. At the same time, however, the UAW grew increasingly bureaucratized in the years after World War II (1939–1945). Abandoning its more democratic roots, the UAW became a fiercely authoritarian and anti-Communist organization. Power was concentrated within the central administration, the autonomy of local chapters destroyed, and accusations or patronage abounded. Though the UAW continued to win concrete labor benefits, it imposed contracts on membership without their input and stifled internal debate. By the 1960s, workers grew increasingly alienated from the union, which had not brought a national strike against General Motors since 1945–1946. When disgruntled workers finally staged wildcat strikes in 1970, UAW officials broke up picket lines to force strikers back to work.

By the 1990s the UAW had modified many of its positions. Though power was still centrally concentrated, the UAW at the end of the twentieth century was one of the most democratic unions in the United States. Unlike many unions, such as the Teamsters, the UAW has been relatively free of corruption charges and maintains a good reputation for its efforts.

See also: **Automobile Industry, Labor Movement, Labor Unionism, Sit-Down Strikes**

UNITED FARM WORKERS

During the 1960s, the Civil Rights Movement prompted increasing political awareness and activity among several minority groups. Among these were the migrant farm workers, most of them Mexican, who traveled throughout California and the western states to take seasonal jobs in fields and orchards. Agricultural workers had never been covered by the National Labor Relations Board. They endured harsh conditions for meager pay, and had no job security or benefits. Often, families moved so frequently that their children were unable to attend school regularly. A transient lifestyle, lack of education, and language barriers created conditions that made it especially difficult for migrant workers to bargain effectively with agricultural businesses.

Cesar Chavez (1927–1993), a migrant worker from Yuma, Arizona, began organizing migrant workers in the 1950s. Chavez, who attended 36 elementary schools during his childhood and never finished high school, knew firsthand about the workers' needs. He could speak their language and relate to them as an insider. In 1962, Chavez formed the National Farm Workers Association to represent migrant Chicano and Filipino farmworkers. By 1965, his organization had 1,700 members and in 1966 it was chartered by the

American Federation of Labor and Congress of Industrial Organizations (AFL-CIO) as the United Farm Workers of America (UFW). Chavez was president of the UFW from its formation until his death in 1993. The UFW's first significant strike occured in 1965, when the union called for a national boycott of California grapes after growers refused to grant workers' demands for better pay and working conditions. In 1966, the DiGiorgio Corporation agreed to allow a union vote, but an investigation launched by California governor Edmund G. Brown, Sr., the first major politician to support the UFW, showed that the results had been rigged. Another election was held, which the UFW won. The grape boycott lasted five years, during which Chavez went on a hunger strike to publicize the exploitation of migrant workers. The grape boycott resulted in the first major victory for migrant workers in the United States. Later boycotts of lettuce and other produce met with similar success. In 1975, California passed legislation that required growers to bargain collectively with representatives elected by the workers, establishing the legal right of farm workers to unionize. Yet much work remained. In the 1970s, the UFW had to fight to maintain its autonomy against the Teamsters Union, which tried to take it over, while continuing its struggle for fair wages and safer conditions. Chavez went on two more hunger strikes, for 24 days in 1972 and for 36 days in 1988, to focus attention on the harmful effects of pesticides to which agricultural workers were routinely exposed. At the time of his death in 1993, he was leading another national boycott of grapes to protest pesticide use.

See also: **Cesar Chavez, Migrant Workers, Labor Movement, Labor Unionism**

UNITED MINE WORKERS (UMW)

Organized in 1890, the United Mine Workers (UMW) is a labor union founded as an affiliate of the American Federation of Labor (AFL). By the late 1880s, Midwestern mine owners were grossly exploiting workers, including numerous immigrants: conditions in the mines ranged from deplorable to dangerous, wages had dropped by as much as 20 percent, and mining families lived in squalor. During its first decade, the UMW came under the leadership of Illinois native John Mitchell (1870–1919). (Mitchell had begun working in coal mines at age twelve and was a member of the Knights of Labor (1885–1890), before joining the UMW and quickly ascending its ranks.) As president of the union after 1898, Mitchell undertook a massive organization drive, espousing the gospel of unionism and the dignity of man. Through Mitchell's efforts, diverse workers became the unified front of the UMW and a force to be reckoned with. In the early 1900s the UMW staged a series of successful strikes, calling attention to unfair labor practices and resulting in increased wages, reduced hours, and improved conditions. Mitchell became a national hero. He suffered health problems and was replaced as leader of the UMW in 1906.

For the next two decades, the coal industry was marked by increased competition; the UMW's tactics became radical. During the 1910s, a series of coal strikes were marked by violence, ending in the deaths of workers as well as government officials. In 1922 U.S. coal miners stages a six-month long strike to protest wage cuts. The massive demonstration paralyzed American industry and began a period of chronic depression in the coal mining industry. What resulted was cutthroat competition, which further hurt the cause of the workers.

The Great Depression (1929–1939), the severe economic downturn of the 1930s, saw the country's laborers joining unions in great numbers, particularly boosting the memberships of industrial (versus craft) unions such as the UMW. In 1935 dynamic UMW leader John Llewellyn Lewis (1880–1969) worked with other industrial unions to form an alliance, the Committee for Industrial Organization (CIO). The UMW's parent organization, the AFL, which was founded on the principles of craft unions, expelled the UMW and other CIO activists, who reorganized as the Congress of Industrial Organizations (CIO). In the 1940s the unions again became controversial: A UMW strike in 1946 stopped soft coal production, then the nation's primary source of energy. The strike severely impacted the steel and automotive industries, the rail service, and the average American, as people in twenty-two states were required to observe "dim-outs" to conserve coal. Consumers faulted the unions for shortages of consumer goods, suspension of services, and inflated prices.

Passage of the Taft-Hartley Act (1947) limited the impact of unions. The UMW has remained active on the national labor scene since its founding, though it struggled through controversy again in the 1970s when its leadership was found to be corrupt.

See also: **American Federation of Labor, Congress of Industrial Organizations, Labor Movement, Labor Unionism, John Llewellyn Lewis, John Mitchell**

UNITED NATIONS

At the end of World War I (1914–1918), President Woodrow Wilson (1913–1921) advocated the League of Nations to the American public. An international organization devised to foster international cooperation and the peaceful resolution of conflict, the League of Nations was a centrally weak but well-meaning organization. Its successor, the United Nations (UN), is substantially stronger. Created in 1945 after World War II (1939–1945), the UN began with 50 members. Among them were the United States, the Soviet Union, Great Britain, France, and China.

With a purpose to promote international harmony, peace, and cooperation between the world's nations, the United Nations is involved in many issues, including economic, social, cultural, health, and human rights matters. Its actions are divided between six main bodies: the General Assembly, a deliberative group to which all UN members belong; the Security Council, which attempts to maintain peace through economic sanctions or military action; the International Court of Justice, established to issue advice and settle disputes within its jurisdiction; the Economic and Social Council, to advise on economic and social issues; the Trusteeship Council, which administers non-self-governing territories; and the Secretariat.

The Secretariat is the UN's main administrative body and is headed by a secretary-general. It settles disputes, carries out peace-keeping activities, gathers information regarding political and economic trends, and oversees the activities of the organization's specialized agencies. The Secretariat is in charge of directing all bodies of the UN in fulfilling its goals.

There are many agencies within the organization that carry out specific tasks. The International Monetary Fund (IMF) is among them. It stabilizes the exchange rates between countries and may also play a role in lending money to nations. The World Bank lends funds for infrastructure projects. To deal with health problems on both an international and a local scale, the UN operates the World Health Organization. To specifically administer to the health and welfare of children worldwide, the UN directs projects through the United Nations' Children's Fund (UNICEF), one of its most well-known agencies.

While UNICEF may be the organization's most popular agency, the Security Council is one of the UN's most controversial. Through the Security Council, the UN deploys peacekeeping forces and administers economic sanctions. Since it was created in 1945, the UN has sent peacekeeping forces to India and Pakistan (1948, 1965), Korea (1950), Cyprus (1964), Israel and Syria (1974), Lebanon (1978), Angola (1988), Iraq and Kuwait (1991), Western Sahara (1991), and the former Yugoslavia (1993). Not all of these ventures were successful in keeping the peace. Support for actions like these is not always unanimous within the organization.

The United Nations is funded by member fees, which are based on per capita income, national income, and ability to meet obligations. Fifty years after its founding in 1945, the United Nations has grown to be a larger organization (184 members as of 1994), stronger than its predecessor, the League of Nations, and a prominent participant in world affairs.

UNITED PARCEL SERVICE OF AMERICA

Headquartered in Atlanta, Georgia, the United Parcel Service of America, Inc. (UPS) is the world's largest package delivery service. It serves over 200 countries and delivers to any address in the continental United States. The company had humble beginnings. In 1907, six years before the U.S. Postal Service began its parcel post system, teenagers Jim Casey and Claude Ryan of Seattle, Washington, borrowed money to expand their bicycle-delivery and messenger service. With the loan they established the American Messenger Company, the precursor to UPS. By 1913 their fleet, renamed Merchants Parcel Delivery, consisted of seven motorcycles. In 1918 the workers joined the International Brotherhood of Teamsters. When the company converted to truck delivery another partner, Charlie Soderstrom, elected to paint the trucks brown, a tradition still carried out by UPS. The company, whose name was changed to the United Parcel Service in the 1930s, pioneered the system of consolidated delivery whereby packages destined for one neighborhood would be delivered by one vehicle. UPS experimented with air service during the Great Depression (1929–1939). Until the late 1940s most of UPS's business was in department store deliveries.

UPS experienced a period of decline following World War II (1939–1945) because the increase in privately owned automobiles allowed people to carry their own packages. Due to the decline of contract service to retail stores, the company began to expand common-carrier parcel service. UPS began offering to pick up parcels (limited in weight and size) from any location and deliver them within a 150-mile radius. This initiative put UPS into direct competition with the U.S. Postal Service.

In the 1950s the need for fast and convenient package delivery in the United States and around the globe was growing. UPS spent several years fighting for federal authority to operate in all of the 48 contiguous states. In 1953 the company resumed air service, which it called Blue Label Air. Between 1964 and 1969 UPS doubled its sales and had expanded into the majority of the U.S. states, making it appear as if UPS would become the only parcel shipping company in the country. Its management team was tightly controlled, and stock was held by its own employees.

SERVICE IS ALL WE HAVE TO OFFER.

Charles Soderstrom, UPS executive, c1930

In 1976 unrest occurred among UPS package processing employees. The company announced plans to replace them eventually with part-time workers, which prompted a number of local Teamsters unions to go on strike. East coast businesses were disturbed by this, particularly as it came during their Christmas rush. Although the strikes were settled, relations between labor and management at UPS remained strained.

UPS continued to expand during this period, establishing a service in Germany in 1976. In 1980 UPS profits were $189 million out of revenues of $4 billion. Competition was fierce by this time, particularly with the emergence of the Federal Express Corporation (Fed Ex), which offered one-day express delivery. UPS countered with Blue Label Air, promising two-day delivery at a lower cost. UPS also dropped its traditionally conservative promotional policies and ran television advertisements for the first time.

While other businesses suffered from the recession of the early 1980s, UPS actually saw an increase in business volume as companies began to ship smaller lots in order to save money. Relations with the Teamsters union suffered when the union discovered that UPS's net income rose 74 percent in 1981, at a time when union wage increases had been capped. UPS employees continued to be dissatisfied, as reports of increasing profits to the company surfaced over the next two years. In 1984 secret negotiations resulted in a three-year agreement which satisfied the union's demands for better wages and benefits, and a major strike was averted. In 1985 UPS was able to offer next-day air service in 48 contiguous states, as well as international air package and document service.

From 1984 to 1991 UPS was the most profitable U.S. product transportation company. UPS now offered both one-day and two-day service, and had increased its earnings to over $700 million in 1987. Though it lagged behind Federal Express in the overnight package delivery business it was working to improve its computer technology to keep up with the competition. By 1988 UPS had established its own airline (UPS Airline), was delivering almost one billion more packages than the U.S. Postal service, and had begun expanding its European operations.

Kent C. Nelson became chairman and chief executive officer of UPS in 1989, initiating a major transformation of the company. New services such as less expensive two-day and three-day deliveries, inventory management, and warehousing were offered to clients. Technical innovations also increased efficiency, and more money was spent on advertising. UPS increased its global recognition by its sponsorship of the 1996 Olympics in Atlanta, and began to step up the profitability of its European and Asian operations, winning over considerable market share from Federal Express. Though profit margins decreased significantly during this time of expansion, the first six years of Nelson's leadership at UPS resulted in a 69 percent increase in sales. UPS was not as profitable abroad as in the United States, but it continued to develop overseas services. In the late 1990s it beat out Federal Express for a major air hub in Taiwan, and it also planned to expand its services to Latin America.

In 1998 UPS was capable of reaching over four billion people worldwide. Its high-technology data communications network tracked over 820,000 packages daily. UPS supplemented the efficiency and reliability of its operations with customer service improvements such as implementing instant tracking systems, order processing, and inventory control. The company operated on a hub system in which packages from a particular region were processed at a central location prior to shipping, which was located in Louisville, Kentucky. UPS in the late 1990s was still privately owned, its stock exclusively held by its managers, employees, retirees, and their families.

FURTHER READING

Batchelor, C. ''Forward to New Frontiers.'' *Financial Times*, June 13, 1997.

Duffy, Caroline A. ''UPS Toes the Line with Its Package-Tracking Technologies.'' *PC Week*, June 28, 1993.

Greenwald, John. ''Hauling UPS's Freight.'' *Time*, January 29, 1996.

Mitchell, C. ''New UPS Chief Sees Continuing Steady, Long-Term Strategy.'' *Knight-Ridder/Tribune Business News*, January 27, 1998.

"The UPS Story," [cited July 27, 1999] Available from the World Wide Web @ www.ups.com/about/story.html/.

UNITED STATES RUBBER COMPANY

In the years leading up to the formation of the United States Rubber Company, the rubber industry was marked by intense competition. Rubber footwear firms, then the industry's largest and most profitable operations, were competing through price wars. Rubber footwear turned an easy profit, and many new companies developed. The increasing number of companies influencing prices caused them to fluctuate dramatically. At the same time, a business financier named Charles Ranlett Flint (1850–1934) was involving himself in the rubber trade between Brazil and the United States. Flint was also involved in a wide range of industries, and he was famous for consolidating numerous firms into single, large industrial units. Numerous footwear firm owners thought that a major consolidation of companies, orchestrated by Flint, would stabilize the industry. In 1892 Flint joined 11 firms and created the United States Rubber Company. The new company immediately controlled half of the nation's footwear sales.

The United States Rubber Company's member firms made shoes that were commissioned by a central sales unit. A board of directors supervised the central selling organization, and the manufacturers operated with virtual autonomy. The new company shifted its assets early on, closing two small factories and acquiring two of its biggest rivals. By 1898 the United States Rubber Company increased its market share from 50 to 75 percent. The company, however, was turning only modest profits, due primarily to the financial strain of absorbing its competitors. As the 1800s ended the rubber industry was rapidly shifting its focus to tire manufacturing for the automobile industry. But U.S. Rubber ignored the industry changes and chose to remain solely a footwear company.

The new tire market turned high profits and companies competed heavily for top market shares. One of the industry's leading firms, Rubber Goods Manufacturing (RGM), saw its position in the industry gradually decline. In 1905 U.S. Rubber bought RGM as a means of entering the tire market. Immediately, the former footwear company was the top tire producer. As treasurer of U.S. Rubber, Charles Flint went to Brussels, Belgium, in 1906 to secure the entire rubber output of the Belgian Congo from King Leopold. U.S. Rubber was seen as one of the tire industry's most significant newcomers.

Rubber pressing machine.

The Du Pont family took control of U.S. Rubber in 1927. That same year, Du Pont and other elite industrialists wanted to consolidate U.S. Rubber, Goodyear, and Seiberling companies in order to establish a powerful industry leader. The idea failed to win support from financial institutions and shareholders that were unsatisfied with the industry's performance during the 1920s. With the onset of the Great Depression (1929–1939) in 1929, tire sales dropped by two-thirds and suppliers lowered prices for car manufacturers in order to maximize sales. In spite of these industry setbacks, U.S. Rubber thrived. It increased its market share from 6.9 percent in 1929 to 30 percent in 1931. The company's success was linked to Du Pont's interest in both U.S. Rubber and General Motors Corporation. U.S. Rubber's manufacturing base was in Detroit, Michigan, and General Motors' nearby location gave U.S. Rubber half of the carmaker's business in 1931. U.S. Rubber was simultaneously boosting its sales to Ford Motor Company.

The company held a key position in the tire and rubber industry for four decades. In 1966 U.S. Rubber changed its name to Uniroyal. In the 1970s, due to the recession and to the development of radial tires which required totally new production equipment and processes, the industry began to shift. Uniroyal was among the companies hardest hit. Though it was ensured a good market share with its General Motors contracts, the overall depression of the car industry and the expensive switch to radials overwhelmed the company finances. Adding to that, Uniroyal's sales on replacement tires were low. The company's losses in 1979 were heavy enough to lead to drastic cuts in capacity in 1980. In the mid-1980s Uniroyal sold many of its divisions and organized a buy-out by Clayton and Dubilier. In 1986 Uniroyal and Goodrich merged their tire operations to form a jointly owned Uniroyal Goodrich Tire Company (UGTC). The new company would combine Uniroyal's strong supplier business with Goodrich's large replacement business. But the venture wasn't successful. Debts, losses, and conflicting management styles brought the company down. In 1987 Dublilier and Clayton bought out Goodrich's holdings in the venture.

As the decade ended, more U.S. tire companies were taken over by foreign firms. The French company Michelin purchased UGTC in 1990. The Uniroyal brand, however, continued. In the late 1990s the Tiger Paw NailGard tire was issued, boasting the capacity to seal 90 percent of tread punctures up to diameters of three-sixteenths of an inch.

The competition that gave rise to the formation of the footwear trust, which came to be known as the United States Rubber Company, followed the rubber industry throughout the twentieth century. As the century ended, the competition that had marked the industry's history shifted to a global scale. Even U.S. Rubber—or Uniroyal—the longtime industry leader, had trouble staying afloat in the face of foreign competition.

See also: **Charles Ranlett Flint, Tire and Rubber Industry**

FURTHER READING

Blackford, Mansel G. and K. Austin Kerr. *B.F. Goodrich: Tradition and Transformation, 1870–1995*. Columbus: Ohio State University Press, 1996.

French, Michael J. *U.S. Tire Industry: A History*. Boston: Twayne Publishers, 1991.

Gent, Alan N., ed. *Engineering With Rubber: How to Design Rubber Components*. New York: Hanser Gardener Publications, 1992.

''Get to Know Us,'' [cited April 28, 1999] available from the World Wide Web @www.uniroyal.com/knowus_cov.htm/.

Ingham, John N. *Biographical Dictionary of American Business Leaders*. Greenwood, CT: Greenwood Press, 1983, s.v. ''Flint, Charles Ranlett.''

UNITED STATES STEEL

An important transaction occurred in New Jersey on February 25, 1901. Carnegie Steel—first owned by Andrew Carnegie (1835–1919)—was purchased by J. Pierpont Morgan (1837–1913), for $480 million. That day became stamped in history as the U.S. Steel Company was born.

Before the creation of U.S. Steel, Carnegie Steel had already been very successful. Carnegie's first exposure to steel came when he landed a job as a secretary and telegrapher for Tom Scott, a powerful overlord for the Pennsylvania Railroad (known familiarly as Pennsy's). By the age of 23, Carnegie was head of Pennsy's Railroad division and was making large sums of money with outside investments in oil, iron bridges, and other commodities. By the time he was 33, Carnegie's drive for success had become more innovative and efficient. He began modernizing older steel plants, then brought in a technology called Bessemer processing. This method reduced the cost of production in the steel industry from $160 per ton in 1875 to only $17 per ton in 1900. However by 1901 Carnegie decided to sell his business to Morgan and pursue a life devoted to philanthropic deeds such as making contributions to large corporate foundations and opening over 2,800 free libraries worldwide. At the time of his death, Carnegie had given away nearly all of his $350 million dollar empire.

The powerful U.S. Steel was not just one company. It was formed from a merger of 10 other companies: American Bridge Company; American Sheet Steel Company; American Steel Hoop Company; American Steel and Wire; American Tin Plate Company; Carnegie Steel Company; Federal Steel Company; Lake Superior Consolidated Iron Mines; National Steel Company; and the National Tube Company. U.S. Steel became the first billion-dollar company in the world, producing 67 percent of country's steel. By April 11, 1901, companies such as the Shelby Steel Tube Company and Bessemer Steamship Company were added to this industrial giant. U.S. Steel controlled massive iron deposits on the Mesabi Range in Minnesota and the coal reserves in western Pennsylvania. The company also controlled the largest shipping line on the Great Lakes, 80 blast furnaces, and 149 steel plants and mills. At the time, U.S. Steel's market share of finished steel products stood slightly over 50 percent. The mills of

U.S. Steel had the capacity to produce 60 percent of the nation's Bessemer steel, 75 percent of the pipe, 70 percent of the sheet metal, 68 percent of the nails, and 77 percent of the wire rod.

With such a massive company in operation, an important decision had yet to be addressed: Who was to run U.S. Steel? There were three main candidates for the job. Charles M. Schwab was a very bright veteran of the steel industry. He had worked his way through the Carnegie organization to become president of Carnegie Steel. Then there was Elbert Henry Gary, who was a lawyer and former judge, and the director of the Illinois Steel Company that had co-opted into Federal Steel, of which he had been president. Finally, there was J. P. Morgan, who had arranged the financing for the purchase. Morgan urged Schwab to become president of U.S. Steel and wanted Gary as chairman.

Schwab and Gary could not easily share the control of the company. In 1903 Schwab resigned and soon gained control over Bethlehem Steel Corporation, which he eventually made into the second largest steel producer in the country. Gary stayed as chief executive officer and led the U.S. Steel Company until he died in August, 1927. Before his death, Gary's goal for U.S. Steel was to avoid its becoming a monopoly. Gary was firm in attempting to uphold trade and encourage competition by using the basis of efficiency and price.

Following Elbert Gary's death, J. P. Morgan Jr., took over the position of chairman of the board of directors from 1927 to 1932. Essentially the leadership of the company came from Myron C. Taylor, chairman of the finance committee from 1927 to 1934, and chairman of the board from 1932 until his resignation in 1938.

The market shares for U.S. Steel dropped significantly in the following years due to competition, falling from 66 percent in 1901, to about 33 percent from the 1930s to the 1950s. One of the most noticeable growth spurts for U.S. Steel occurred during World War I (1914–1918) when sales doubled to $2 billion between the years 1915 and 1918. Sales remained at $2 billion annually through the 1920s. Significant drops in sales occurred in 1933 and 1934 during the Great Depression (1929–1939). Sales then climbed to $1 billion in 1940, and $3 billion in 1950. Wall Street's confidence in U.S. Steel had disappeared prior to the depression. Although product shares suffered the least, light rolled sheet fell dramatically because of hesitation to take on hot-strip mills.

Myron Taylor continued his efforts toward keeping U.S. Steel alive. One significant breakthrough came with the hiring of an engineering consulting firm of Ford, Davis, and Bacon in 1935. A complete study of the corporation produced more than 200 reports. The consultants criticized the lack of a rational management structure, and excessiveness due to two separate raw-steel operations—Carnegie Steel and Illinois Steel. Based on the consultants' suggestions, Taylor created Carnegie-Illinois Steel. In 1936 American Sheet and Tin Plate joined Carnegie-Illinois Steel, making it the largest steel company in the world.

Taylor then restructured the corporation's management as well, making Benjamin Fairless, from Republic Steel, the new president of Carnegie-Illinois Steel. Another management company was also created to stand between the holding corporation and the operating subsidiaries. The United States Steel Corporation of Delaware formed in 1938. This ended the firm control of the finance committee and gave operating officials freedom while coordinating their efforts. A final suggestion from consultants was to expand the development of more hot-strip mills. Therefore, in 1935, two more modern plants were constructed.

During the 1950s emphasis was placed on expansion. More hot-strip mills, pipe mills, and open hearths were built. In the 1960s there were inadequate profits, which forced restructuring. By 1969 U.S. Steel had borrowed $1.4 billion to finance expansion. During the 1970s, long-term growth in steel became hopeless in light of rising costs, foreign competition, and competitive pricing. The late 1970s saw the shutdown of 13 plants at a loss of $809 million. In 1982 U.S. Steel acquired Marathon Oil Company—a company holding reserves in oil and gas with revenue essentially equal to U.S. Steel's. Texas Oil and Gas Corporation, was also acquired by U.S. Steel in February 1986, for $3.6 billion.

In July 1986 United States Steel Corporation changed its name to USX Corporation. Then, in 1991, the company split into two separate entities: U.S. Steel and Marathon. The creation of a third group, the USX-Delhi Group, came about in 1992. During the early 1990s, USX-U.S. Steel was able to reduce fixed costs and increase productivity by cutting its raw steel capacity in half. USX closed four of its seven plants and reduced employees by 56 percent. This heralded a change in direction for the company. During 1992 USX-U.S. Steel diversified into the world of power technology. In the late 1990s, USX operated as two separate entities. The Marathon Oil Group specialized in natural gas exploration, research, domestic refining, marketing, and transportation of crude oil. The U.S. Steel Group remained a leading manufacturer of steel products.

FURTHER READING

Boucher, John Newton. *William Kelly: A True History of the So-Called Bessemer Process*. Greensburg, PA: Self-published, 1924.

Carnegie, Andrew. *The Empire of Business*. New York: Doubleday Page, 1913.

International Directory of Company Histories, Vol. 4. Detroit: The Gale Group, 1991, s.v. ''USX Corporation.''

Livesay, Harold C. *Andrew Carnegie and the Rise of Big Business*. New York: Harper Collins, 1975.

Urofsky, Melvin I. *Big Steel and the Wilson Administration*. Columbus, OH: Ohio State Univ. Press, 1969.

UNITED STATES V. E.C. KNIGHT COMPANY

In 1895 the Supreme Court decision in the case of *United States v. E.C. Knight Company* severely undermined the Sherman Anti-Trust Act of 1890. In an eight-to-one ruling, the high court determined that, although a monopoly in manufacturing, the American Sugar Company and its subsidiary, the E.C. Knight Company, had not monopolized trade. The government had prosecuted the sugar company for owning 98 percent of the nation's sugar-refining capacity, seeing this as a clear violation of the Sherman Anti-Trust Act's pronouncement that ''every contract, combination in the form of trust or otherwise, or conspiracy in the restraint of trade'' is illegal. But according to the Supreme Court justices, the Sherman act had given Congress the right to regulate interstate commerce only; since the Knight Company's manufacturing operations were all located within Pennsylvania, the federal government had no jurisdiction.

The court's narrow interpretation of the Sherman Anti-Trust Act delivered a painful blow to those who wanted government to break up or at least limit the powerful monopolies. Though the Sherman legislation provided the basis for trust-busting, its might would not be used until the first decade of the 1900s, when, after a change in political climate, Standard Oil Company and American Tobacco Company would be charged with, and (in 1911) found guilty of violating the Sherman Act. In 1913, antitrust cases were also brought against the Union and Southern Pacific Railroad merger, International Harvester Corporation, American Telephone and Telegraph (AT&T), and the New York, New Haven, and Hartford Railroad.

In 1914, national anti-trust legislation was strengthened by the passage of the Clayton Anti-Trust Act, which outlawed price fixing (the practice of pricing below cost to eliminate a competitive product). The Clayton Act also made it illegal for the same executives to manage two or more competing companies (a practice called interlocking directorates), and prohibited any corporation from owning stock in a competing corporation.

See also: **American Tobacco Company, Clayton Anti-Trust Act, Sherman Anti-Trust Act, Tobacco Trust**

UPJOHN COMPANY

In the Victorian era promoting and marketing early pharmaceutical products required talent, skill, and ingenuity. From the very beginning research and development played a major role in the development of modern pharmaceutical production. William Erastus Upjohn (commonly referred to as W.E.) was raised with his twelve brothers and sisters in an environment of medicine and pharmacia. His father and two uncles, all of whom were medical practitioners, nurtured this environment. W.E. Upjohn became a physician in 1875. While practicing medicine in Hastings, Michigan, he set up his own pharmaceutical laboratory. He began to experiment with formulas to develop a pill that would dissolve easily in the stomach. Upjohn revolutionized the drug industry in 1885, when he worked out problems and crushed a pill under his thumb to symbolize the achievement. This image became the trademark for the founding of the Upjohn Pill and Granule Company in 1886. The name was shortened to the Upjohn Company in 1903.

Dr. W.E. Upjohn's concern with the working conditions of his employees was evident, as he implemented a soup lunch program in 1911 and a group life insurance and benefit program in 1915. Having had a passion for horticulture, Upjohn donated a 17-acre park to the city of Kalamazoo, Michigan, and reduced the workday to seven hours in the summer so employees would have time to water their own lawns. Upjohn was a member of the commission that established the charter for the city of Kalamazoo in 1914, and served as the first mayor to administer the plan. Upon his death in 1932, W.E. Upjohn was in the process of trying to develop a form of employment insurance for the people of Kalamazoo. The Upjohn Company had over 1000 employees and net sales of $8.5 million.

Through the turn of the century souvenirs promoting Upjohn products were available at the Chicago's World Fair; the exhibit itself was an enormous bottle filled with colored pills. The Upjohn principle that medicine should have a pleasant taste was exemplified in flavored laxative wafers, alkalizers, and cherry-flavored cough syrup. Marketing through physicians became a method of promoting Upjohn products such as Kaopectate, an antidiarrheal. Eventually Upjohn became a leader in the development of medicines for treating the central nervous system, heart conditions, arthritis and cancer.

In 1913 Upjohn continued its emphasis on research and development by hiring its first research scientist, Dr. Frederick W. Heyl. Heyl developed an effervescent antacid in 1926 and patented a tablet named Digitora (developed from digitalis) for the treatment of heart disease. By 1940 the company had expanded and added twelve more research scientists. Upjohn was selected by the armed forces to process human serum albumin and penicillin. Upjohn became a major manufacturer of antibiotics, and by 1958 antibiotic sales had reached $22.6 million. International expansion during the 1950s enabled Upjohn to compete in foreign markets and advance their research. In 1985 thirty percent of their total sales were from the foreign market share which increased to 33 percent by the 1990s.

A swarm of publicity surrounded Upjohn in the late 1980s when the company applied for a new drug application for male baldness known as Rogaine. After three years of disappointing sales Upjohn changed marketing strategies by taking the product directly to the consumer. Investing $50 million to promote Rogaine the company become one of the world's top three advertisers. In the early 1990s Upjohn was quickly trying to develop a treatment for Acquired Immune Deficiency Syndrome (AIDS) as well as a group of steroids designed to treat spinal and head injuries, which would replace some products being lost to the generic market.

In the face of the changing global market Upjohn sought to consolidate its position in the ethical pharmaceutical industry. There was speculation that Upjohn was too small to compete with its larger rivals. In response to the challenge Upjohn reorganized and merged with Pharmacia AB of Stockholm, Sweden. Pharmacia & Upjohn became one of the world's largest pharmaceutical firms, with annual sales of $7 billion, a research budget of $1 billion, and over 30,000 employees.

See also: **Pharmaceutical Industry**

FURTHER READING

Carlisle, Robert D.B. *A Century of Caring: The Upjohn Story.* Elmsford, NY: Benjamin Co., 1987.

Dryer, Bernard V. *The Torch Bearers.* New York: Simon and Schuster, 1967.

Engel, Leonard. *Medicine Makers of Kalamazoo.* New York: McGraw Hill, 1961.

International Directory of Company Histories. Farmington Hills, MI: St James Press, 1999, s.v. "Upjohn Company."

Novotny, Ann and Carter Smith. *Images of Healing. A Portfolio of American Medical and Pharmaceutical Practice in the 18th, 19th, and early 20th Centuries.* New York: MacMillan Publishing Co., 1980.

URBAN RENEWAL

Urbanization of a society occurs when city population growth rates exceed that of rural areas. Urbanization was a hallmark of U.S. economic development throughout the nineteenth century and the first half of the twentieth century. Increasing industrialization lured multiple waves of immigrants into primarily Northern urban settings seeking employment. Initially, rural peoples arrived from farms at the beginning of the nineteenth century. Foreign immigrants followed from northern and western Europe in the mid-1800s and eastern and southern Europe in the 1890s through the early part of the twentieth century. Finally, African Americans came from the American South in two major migration waves during the first half of the twentieth century. Ethnic and racial enclaves and neighborhoods came to comprise the socioeconomic mosaics of cities.

Sanitation, poverty, and overcrowding were persistent urban problems from the beginning, and became a national problem toward the end of the nineteenth century. Enhancement of urban life was a key element of the 1930s New Deal programs. Congress created the U.S. Housing Authority in 1937 to clear slums and provide public housing for low-income residents. Employment programs funded the construction of public buildings such as schools, hospitals, and urban parks.

Economic prosperity characterized the United States after World War II (1939–1945). Transportation advances including urban freeway systems and low-cost government mortgages for war veterans fueled the great movement of white middle class city dwellers to the suburbs. With the exodus from cities taking away tax revenue and jobs, American cities began a steep downward spiral in quality of life and socioeconomic stability. Poverty, dilapidated housing, and high crime rates characterized inner city neighborhoods, largely populated by minorities. The urban black ghetto riots of the 1960s led to greater white migration to the suburbs, which became known as the "white flight." A pattern of urban de-industrialization followed, with manufacturing businesses moving out of inner city areas creating edge cities in the suburbs. Americans' attitudes toward the cities radically declined and racism became an urban problem rather than a Southern problem.

To counter these growing trends of declining inner cities, the first broad program of urban renewal was initiated in the 1950s. Congress funneled substantial amounts of federal financial aid to cities aimed at eliminating slums and ghettos and replacing them with improved housing and industrial and commercial areas. The Housing Act of 1954 provided "categorical" grants to restore older housing, directing public funds to specifically proposed actions. However, new high-rise housing projects of the 1950s and early 1960s soon represented the worst of black ghetto life.

The lack of success of categorical grants led to the Community Development Act of 1974. The act introduced block grants giving cities greater flexibility to address their specific needs through locally developed renewal plans. City plans required approval from the Department of Housing and Urban Development before qualifying for funding. Using block grants, cities would purchase slum areas, sometimes exercising eminent domain, to force the sale of private property to the government. The city would then demolish the buildings, clear the lots, and sell the land to private developers, or put it to public use. Highly toxic remains of abandoned industry often littered these inner city areas leading to costly environmental clean-up efforts. Prices for the cleared land were frequently set low and sometimes supplemented with tax breaks to attract private developers. Thus, the program operated at marked deficits for both city and federal governments. Housing developments, shopping centers, and office complexes were built in the newly cleared areas.

Although federal law required cities to assist displaced residents and businesses in finding new affordable locations, the dislocations often resulted in economic hardships. Urban renewal essentially became black removal. Cities typically built new public housing away from the renewal areas and traditional work sources while reserving renewal areas for the middle and upper income residents to stimulate economic growth.

The 1970s also saw other urban renewal programs including urban homesteading. Old abandoned houses that had fallen into city ownership were sold at low cost to individuals interested in restoring and living in them. The 1980s saw several states implement urban enterprise zones, attempting to attract new businesses to inner city areas. The zones provided tax cuts and relief from regulations including zoning laws and rent controls. These programs were largely ineffective, however, given the extent of city problems.

The results of federally funded urban renewal programs were mixed. A number of declining downtown areas were economically revitalized by introducing new industrial and commercial developments. Thousands of families found improved urban housing and new schools, parks, hospitals, museums, and libraries were erected in cleared slum areas. In some cases neighborhoods became integrated as a result. Many areas cleared under the federal programs, however, remained vacant. The high-rise low income public housing projects attracted poverty, crime, and disease. Consequently, many housing projects experienced high vacancy rates. Critics of urban renewal policies claimed cities' efforts to attract new business and higher-income residents caused cities that were already established to deteriorate.

The height of concerted urban renewal efforts at a national level ended after the 1970s. Under President Ronald Reagan (1981–1989), the U.S. government substantially reduced financial aid for urban development and housing. Through the remainder of the twentieth century, urban renewal became more the responsibility of city and state governments and renewal activity declined significantly. The 1990s brought concepts of empowerment zones, in which distressed urban areas received tax breaks, federal investment for creating new businesses, and job retraining programs. Other urban renewal concepts involved home ownership zones for affordable housing, and education opportunity zones to assist the most needy schools.

***See also:* De-Industrialization, Ghetto, Industrialization, Slums, Suburbs (Rise of), Tenements, Urbanization**

FURTHER READING

Ambrose, Peter J. *Urban Process and Power.* New York: Routledge, 1994.

Greenberg, Michael R., and Dona Schneider. *Environmentally Devastated Neighborhoods: Perceptions, Policies, and Realities.* New Brunswick, NJ: Rutgers University Press, 1996.

Kearns, Gerry and Chris Philo, ed. *Selling Places: The City as Cultural Capital, Past and Present.* New York: Pergamon Press, 1993.

King, Anthony D., ed. *Re-presenting the City: Ethnicity, Capital and Culture in the 21st-Century Metropolis.* New York: New York University Press, 1996.

Widner, Ralph R., and Marvin E. Wolfgang, eds. *Revitalizing the Industrial City.* Newbury Park, CA: Sage Publications, 1986.

> Another measure of the contrasts appearing in the nation's cities at the end of the nineteenth century was the differentiation of urban space. Since the 1850s lower Manhattan had been the province of commercial buildings, warehouses and tenements. However, by the 1880s the island had fragmented into a series of discrete neighborhoods increasingly divided by economic use, race, class, and ethnic origin. Wealthy and white-collar workers followed streetcar lines or elevated railroads uptown or to the urban periphery.
>
> **David Schuyler, *The New Urban Landscape: The Redefinition of City Form in Nineteenth-Century America*, 1986**

URBANIZATION

At the time of the American Revolution (1775–1783), communities within the capitals of the thirteen colonies were very small. Ninety-five percent of the country's population lived rurally, participating in the predominant agrarian economy. The nation's first census in 1790 found only five cities with more than 10,000 people and no city as large as 50,000. The process of urbanization soon took hold, however, and city populations grew rapidly. The close tie between economic development and urbanization became a hallmark of U.S. economic history. Where some nations evolved with a singular large urban center, the form of urbanization in the United States was far more regional. Urban networks grew with large cities supporting a network of smaller cities and the smaller cities supporting surrounding agricultural areas. Racing to develop transportation networks such as railroads and canals, competitive regions made investments into urban infrastructures, including cultural institutions such as museums, opera houses, parks, colleges, and theaters.

The nation's first cities were seaports such as Boston, New York, and Philadelphia. Harbor areas formed the hub of economic activity. Through the early nineteenth century, modes of transportation evolved slowly; a person's needs could be met within a comfortable framework of one or two miles. A diverse mixture of economic activities and social classes including warehouses, artisan shops, and homes of the wealthy merchants could be found around the harbor area. Residential and business districts were intertwined. Little differentiation between social classes and ethnicities was common.

By the mid-nineteenth century a transportation and communication revolution emerged. Railway growth and the introduction of the steam engine dramatically influenced urbanization. Commercial centers transformed into industrial cities. Factory production expanded, bringing greater numbers of people to the cities with foreign immigration serving to satisfy escalating demands for workers. Cities, however, had difficulty accommodating the increased numbers of people. Considerable crowding occurred because buildings could not extend above five stories due to insufficient elevator technologies and the inability to supply water above that height.

By 1870 almost 170 cities had populations over 10,000 and 15 cities had more than 100,000 people. Transportation by horse-drawn street railcars allowed greater mobility. Cities became less centered around their harbor areas. New commercial districts grew somewhat distant from the ports containing key financial institutions, retail shops, and entertainment facilities. The traditional apprenticeship system gave way to a wage-earning working class that sought inexpensive housing. Residential areas became more detached from businesses and fast-growing industrial areas. The continued industrial growth also lead to unprecedented crowding of laborers in congested industrial areas. The wealthy class began creating their own, more lavish residential areas.

Westward extension of the railroads spurred migration. Commercial agricultural production and trade grew away from the coastal cities. Urbanization moved westward as well. Urban markets served agricultural economies as transportation hubs and banking centers facilitated a cohesive, regional economic system.

Major technological advances spurred increased urbanization in the 1870s. Elevators significantly altered urban area economics. The rental value of upper-story office building floors became relatively equal to street level floors, greatly raising city center land values. After 1870 central business districts with clusters of tall buildings began to surface. The buildings contained offices, department stores, entertainment establishments, and government agencies. Administrative and financial centers evolved, anchoring corporate activities that were distributed among outlying smaller cities. By the late 1880s electric streetcars were introduced which greatly enhanced transportation. A classic American urban pattern appeared in cities of over 100,000 residents. The pattern included a central business district, immediately surrounded by slums and working class residential areas, with more prosperous suburbs further outward. By 1918 most Americans lived in urban settings, and the classic downtown era persisted through World War II (1939–1945).

In the 1890s immigration from eastern and southern Europe grew dramatically. These groups were more socially distinct than earlier immigrants from northern and western Europe. During the two world wars of the twentieth century, African American migration from the American South escalated in the cities. The various ethnic groups established distinct neighborhoods with their own commercial activities.

Urbanization led to complex socioeconomic problems following World War II. The emergence of suburbs detracted from the quality of life in city centers by relocating many jobs and desperately needed tax revenue. The population of some cities declined. The process of urbanization had largely run its course. Cities of the late twentieth century presented contrasts between complexes of office towers, convention centers, and lavish hotels, surrounded by pockets of homeless people, poorly supported schools, low income housing, and crime. A new immigration wave entered the cities, primarily from Asia, Latin America, Africa, and the Caribbean, establishing new middle class non-white neighborhoods. The combination of international corporate office buildings and multi-ethnic neighborhoods introduced a new era of American urban centers.

See also: **Industrial Revolution, Industrialization, Slums, Suburbs (Rise of), Tenements, Urban Renewal**

FURTHER READING

Andrews, Anthony P. *First Cities*. Washington, DC: Smithsonian Books, 1995.

Angotti, Thomas. *Metropolis 2000: Planning, Poverty, and Politics*. New York: Routledge, 1993.

Bookchin, Murray. *From Urbanization to Cities: Toward a New Politics of Citizenship.*. New York: Cassell, 1995.

Gottdiener, Mark. *The Social Production of Urban Space*, 2nd ed. Austin: University of Texas Press, 1994.

Kasinitz, Philip, ed. *Metropolis: Center and Symbol of Our Time*. New York: New York University Press, 1995.

Marshall, John U. *The Structure of Urban Systems*. Toronto: University of Toronto Press, 1989.

UTAH

Utah, like the early Massachusetts colonies, developed as a theocracy, in which church leaders controlled both spiritual and secular life. The Church of Latter-day Saints has dominated Utah's social, political, and economic life since the first Mormon pioneers traversed the desert to set up their earthly paradise in Salt Lake City. According to Utah historian Charles S. Peterson, "To the spiritual goals of salvation and world reform they added the temporal objectives of growth and survival." After much wrangling with the federal government, both the territory and (later) the state of Utah reluctantly decided to cooperate with the rest of the nation and managed to become economically successful in the social context of the United States.

Spanish and Mexican explorers were the first non-Indians to explore Utah. By the early 1800s, trade was common between the Indians of Utah and the Spanish provincial capital of Santa Fe. The main route through the old Southwest, the Spanish Trail, traversed Utah, at first bringing fur traders and later settlers bound for California. In 1847, following the death of the Church of Latter-day Saints (Mormon) leader Joseph Smith by lynching in Illinois, Brigham Young and a band of Mormon pioneers set out for Utah's Great Basin, seeking refuge from persecution in the East. Upon arrival, they established Salt Lake City and set about cultivating the arid environment by planting crops and establishing irrigation systems.

During four decades of the colonization of Utah, 450 towns and hamlets were set up, all located near a source of water, a precious commodity in the arid territory. From the beginning, the church was involved in all aspects of the settlers' lives, and all natural resources were considered communal. In the Great

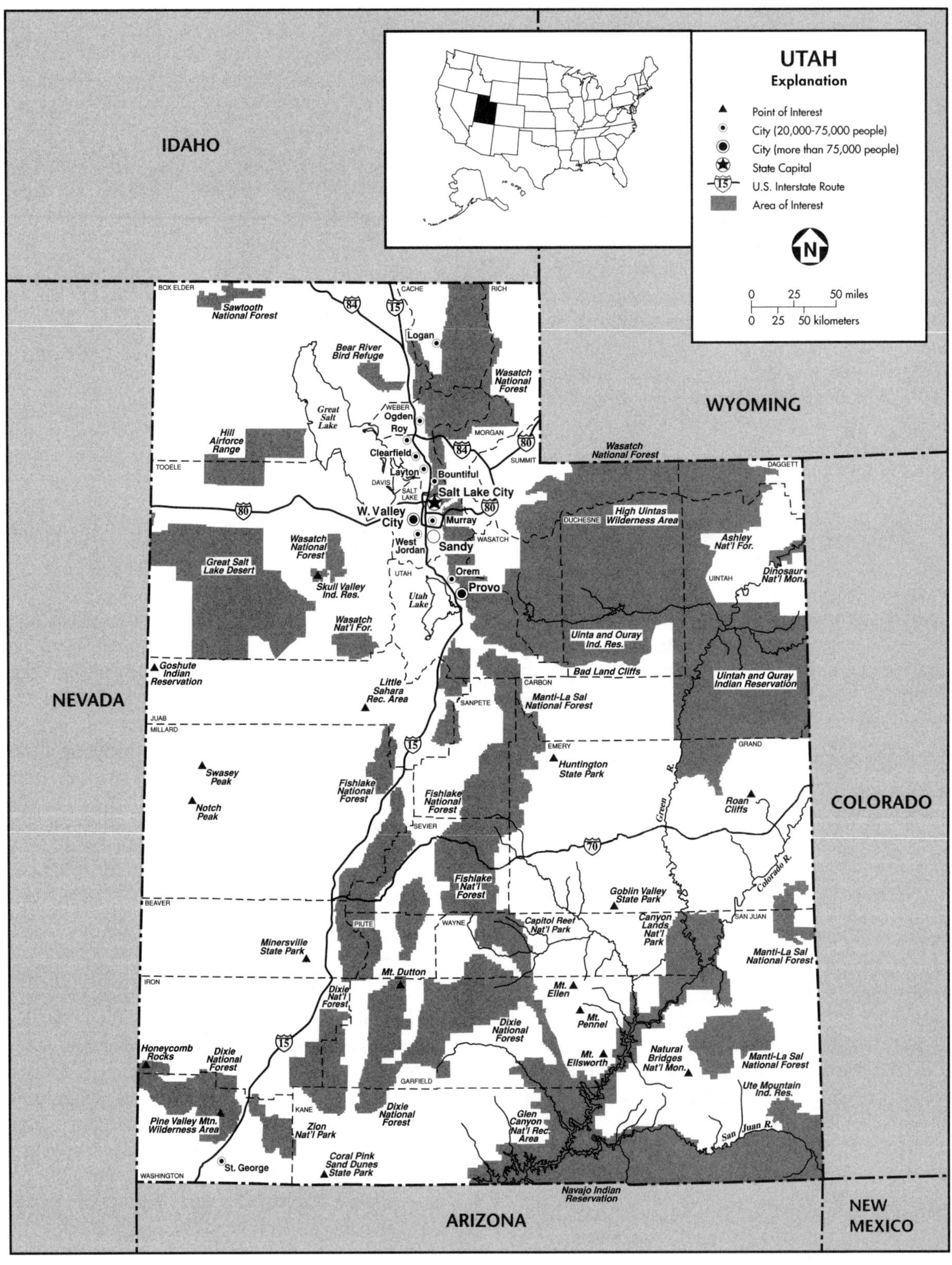

State of Utah.

Basin, the church leaders undertook to create a self-sufficient economy, planning and organizing various enterprises and using an "in kind," or barter, system to exchange goods and services. After the initial migration of U.S. Mormons, around 90,000 foreign converts arrived between 1850 and 1905.

The Treaty of Guadalupe-Hidalgo in 1848 gave the United States title to much of the land in the Southwest, and the Mormons set up a provisional state they called Deseret. Congress called it the Utah Territory; the area at that time encompassed most of Nevada and parts of Wyoming and Colorado, as well as the present state of Utah. The 46 years of territorial status were marked by a number of conflicts between Mormons and the federal government. Albert Cummings replaced Brigham Young as territorial governor in 1858, marking the beginning of a prolonged period of hostility against federal authorities.

Mormon traditions dominated the territory, since 70 percent of the population was of the Mormon faith, until 1870. Despite their desire to be self-sufficient, Mormons began to embrace economic opportunities as they presented themselves from outside the community. As president of the Church, Brigham Young had great economic as well as ecclesiastical and civic authority. He contracted with the Union Pacific Railroad in 1868 to lay part of the track in Utah. An historic day for Utah was the completion of the first transcontinental railroad, when the Central Pacific joined with the Union Pacific at Promontory Point, Utah, on May 10, 1869. New rail lines sprang up during the 1870s, making immigration to the state easier and creating a significant population growth in Salt Lake City. Agriculture dominated the economy until 1863, when silver was discovered in Bingham Canyon.

With mining of precious metals came the first influx of entrepreneurs. At first Mormons opposed mining but eventually came to see it as a natural way of developing the territory. Outside businessmen were suspicious of the Church's pervasive influence over all aspects of Utah's life, including the Mormons' practice of communitarian economics. The most hostility to Mormonism, however, was over the issue of polygamy, sanctioned by the Church until 1890. Many arrests were made by federal authorities among polygamous families.

Utah became a state in 1896. Mineral production increased in the new century. The mine owned by Utah Copper at Bingham was a prime example of the potential of mineral wealth in the state. Exploiting an entire mountain of copper, the company built mills, its own railroad, and a steam-generating plant. The considerable output of the mine, along with its gigantic open pit, was heralded as a wonder of modern industrialism. By 1930 Utah Copper was responsible for 50 percent of Salt Lake City's assessed valuation and 13 percent of the value of the whole state. With burgeoning mineral mining also came increased union activity. After an explosion that killed 200 miners at Scofield in 1900, radical union activity became commonplace. Joe Hill, a member of the Industrial Workers of the World (nicknamed the Wobblies), was executed in 1915 for the murder of two Salt Lake City citizens.

Modern cities began to grow in the new state, along with highways, power plants, and interurban railroads. In 1920 one-half of the population lived along the Wasatch Front. Although a number of ethnic groups were coming into the state and changing its demography, the Mormon population was still at 68 percent in 1920.

Prosperity marked the business sector of Utah in the 1920s, but agriculture and mining were depressed. In the 1930s union activity increased, mostly in the coal and copper industries. The Great Depression (1929–1939) was especially hard on Utah after severe droughts in both 1931 and 1934. High freight rates also hindered manufacturing. During World War II (1939–1945), however, wartime demands for food helped Utah's agricultural production; military installations and war-related industries brought about economic recovery.

Because of the high birthrate in Utah, the state's population more than doubled in the time since the war, while the per capita income decreased compared to the national average. In 1995 it was just over $18,000, ranking the state only forty-sixth in the nation. To ensure an adequate water supply for the future, in 1967 the state began work on the Central Utah Project, a dam and irrigation program which continued into the 1990s. Throughout the 1990s Utah's economy was one of the fastest growing in the nation, and the state boasted a low unemployment rate. The state had a budget surplus in 1994 and its population grew by 16.1 percent between 1990 and 1996.

Utah's leading industry is transport equipment manufacture, including aircraft parts and parts for missiles and rockets. A continuing source of controversy in the state is how to balance growth against the protection of the state's beautiful natural areas. On the Wasatch Front, air pollution is a problem, and the Division of Environmental Health is particularly concerned with the dumping of dangerous materials.

Trade has replaced the government as the largest employer in Utah. The federal government is still a major player in the state's economy, however, with around 14 percent of personal income derived from government sources. Since the government owns around 70 percent of all the land in the state and provides many jobs in the defense industry or the military, the federal presence is a rather controversial issue in the state today. Significant declines in military spending in the late 1980s and the 1990s have hurt Utah's economy. Though agriculture has declined in recent years, it is still a significant sector of the economy, with livestock and livestock products responsible for three-fourths of the agricultural income. Utah's mines are mostly noted for metal and coal extraction. In 1995 the state was the only producer of beryllium. Tourism is also a growing industry, focused on Utah's large number of national and state parks, as well as skiing, hunting, fishing, and other recreational activities. Economic development policy in the state is conservative, supporting business activities and opposing expansion of government social programs.

See also: **Santa Fe**

FURTHER READING

Alexander, Thomas. *Mormons and Gentiles: A History of Salt Lake City*. Boulder, CO: Pruett, 1984.

Arrington, Leonard J., and Davis Bitton. *The Mormon Experience: A History of the Latter-day Saints*, 2nd ed. Urbana: University of Illinois Press, 1992.

Ellsworth, Samuel G. *Utah's Heritage*. Salt Lake City: Peregrine Smith, 1984.

Peterson, Charles S. *Utah: A Bicentennial History*. New York: Norton, 1977.

Poll, Richard D., et al. *Utah's History*. Provo, UT: Brigham Young University Press, 1978.

UTILITIES INDUSTRY

Public and private utilities provide services such as electricity, gas, telephone, water, and sewerage treatment. Most of the utilities in the United States are privately owned, but are regulated by state and federal governments because of their monopolistic nature. In recent times, however, the government oversight that was demanded by the reformers of the Progressive period in American history (1900–1920) has been undermined by the proponents of deregulation.

Perhaps the most important utility in the United States during the late twentieth century was the electric utilities industry. Electricity could be generated in power plants using fuels such as coal, fuel oil, nuclear energy, and natural gas. The uses of electricity are seemingly endless and originate with the period of the great inventors of the nineteenth century. The electric light bulb was invented by Thomas Edison (1847–1931) in 1879, and the following year, he founded an electric power generating plant. Soon his company was challenged by George Westinghouse (1846–1914) and his United States Electric Light Company. Growth in the industry continued steadily through World War II (1939–1945). By 1951 nuclear energy was used to produce electricity, and the 1960s saw an increase in the use of nuclear reactors. These advances, however, were accompanied by occasional mishaps. A serious accident in 1979 at the Three Mile Island nuclear power plant in Pennsylvania created a credibility problem for the nuclear power industry, and new federal regulations in the 1970s focused on conservation. In the wake of escalating gasoline prices resulting from the OPEC oil embargo, alternative power sources such as water, wind, and solar energy were widely encouraged to produce electricity. Analysts predicted high output for the electric utilities in the twenty-first century, as the U.S. government was expected to continue deregulating the industry to stimulate competition and lower prices.

Coal gas (gas made from coal) was a popular source of energy until the mid-twentieth century. It is made by converting coal into combustible gases that can then be used as a fuel or as a component of chemicals and fertilizer. Coal provided the most common fuel gas for residential and commercial use for most of the nineteenth century through the 1940s, when consumers turned to cheaper natural gas.

Natural gas is primarily comprised of methane and used as fuel for homes and businesses. It was adopted as a cheap and clean fuel source. In the late nineteenth century natural gas was used for city streetlights and for cooking. In the period between World War II (1939–1945) and the 1960s, utility companies laid large grids of natural gas pipelines. The use of natural gas continued to grow during the late twentieth century, in part due to the deregulation of the industry which thereby resulted in lower prices.

Water systems are yet another important utility. Clean and healthy drinking water is among one of the most important elements in human society. Business and industry use large amounts of water to fight fires and irrigate crops. In the late twentieth century most water utilities were publicly owned. The beginnings of the modern water system in the United States date back to the late nineteenth century. As was the case with other utilities, population growth after World War II brought about an increased demand for water. Several federal regulations during the twentieth century, such as the Safe Drinking Water Act of 1974 (amended in 1996), helped set higher standards for the water supply. Two of the most notable water utilities in the United States during the late 1990s were the American Water Works—the largest water utility owned by investors—and the Metropolitan Water District of Southern California, which provided more drinking water than any other company in the United States at that time.

Wastewater and sewer systems are yet another component of public utilities. Wastewater treatment systems are primarily public, non-profit facilities that serve a local or regional area and may handle both residential and industrial wastes. Industrial wastewater is often treated at the point where it is generated and subsequently released into natural water systems or into the nearest public facility. Many homes in the United States still use small separate facilities such as septic tanks.

Sewer systems in the United States date back to the mid-nineteenth century. The importance of sanitary treatment and disposal of sewage was underscored by the deadly cholera epidemics that periodically plagued the country from 1832 through the 1850s. By the 1870s extensive construction of sewerage treatment plants was under way. The federal government imposed regulations on this industry from the mid to late twentieth century. There was renewed interest, as well, in the privatization of this industry, with some projections indicating that there may be one private company for each public facility by the year 2020.

Another utility was born with Claude Chappe's invention of the semaphor telegraph in 1792, which paved the way for the telecommunications industry. Telexes and telegrams were used to transmit messages in only one day. They remained popular until the 1970s, when they began to be replaced by facsimile machines and, in the 1990s, by electronic mail through the Internet. By 1994 only two telegraph carriers were still in operation. Telegraph industry leader Western Union Corporation began to add more modern methods of communications to its operations in an effort to remain competitive at the end of the twentieth century.

One of the most common aspects of the industry is the telephone. This 1870s invention by Alexander Graham Bell (1847–1922) profoundly changed the cultural and material complexion of the world. Based, in part, on technology spin-offs from the defense industry, the telephone eventually freed itself of telephone wires and evolved into the two-way radiotelephone. This category eventually included cellular phones, pagers, satellite and microwave facilities, and fiber optic lines. In the late 1990s the telecommunications industry was revolutionized by deregulation with the Telecommunications Act of 1996. While deregulation was designed to stimulate more competition, critics claimed that rather than improve service or drop rates the industry was moving in the direction of powerful monopolies.

The continued presence in some form of most of the components of the public utilities seems assured. Americans in the twenty-first century will undoubtedly continue to want all of the comforts and convenience that utilities provide. Deregulation of public utilities continued throughout the 1990s. It is, however, unclear whether this strategy will result in the positive outcomes of greater competition, cheaper prices, and environmentally safe management of our natural resources.

See also: **Alexander Graham Bell, Coal Industry, Thomas Edison, Nuclear Energy, Telegraph, George Westinghouse**

FURTHER READING

Creese, Walter L. *TVA's Public Planning: The Vision, The Reality.* Knoxville: University of Tennessee Press, 1990.

Keating, Ann Durkin. *Invisible Networks: Exploring the History of Local Utilities and Public Works.* Malabar, FL: Krieger Pub. Co., 1994.

Gruner, Alex. *The History of American Business and Industry.* New York: American Heritage, 1972.

Hammond, John Winthrop. *Men and Volts The Story of General Electric.* Phil Lippincott, 1941.

Heil, Scott, and Terrance W. Peck, eds. *Encyclopedia of American Industries* 2nd ed., vol 2. Detroit: Gale, 1997, s.v. "Electric Services," "Electric and Other Services Combined," "Radiotelephone Communications," "Telegraph and Other Message Communications," "Natural Gas Transmission and Distribution," "Gas and Other Services Combined," "Water Supply," "Sewage Systems," and "Refuse Systems."

Miller, Raymond C. *The Force of Energy: A Business History of Detroit Edison Co.* Michigan: Michigan State University Press, 1971.

Schurr, Sam H. *Electricity in the American Economy: Agent of Technological Progress.* New York: Greenwood Press, 1990.

UTOPIA

In the Greek language, "utopia" means: "no place," suggesting that utopia is never to be found on earth; that it is instead an eternally-empty ideal, or dream. In 1516, the famous English philosopher, Sir Thomas More, wrote extensively about utopia, where he depicted an 'ideal state' that has since given its name (Utopia) to all such later romantic visions of an ideal country, or a "heaven on earth" society. Typically, people who are known as Utopian writers criticize the present conditions of the world and outline vast revolutionary schemes without describing the concrete, specific steps necessary to achieve them. Some famous philosophers who were regarded as Utopian include Plato, who constructed an ideal society in his *Republic*, as well as Campanella, Bacon, and Rousseau. During the nineteenth century, Utopian thinking began to be taken more seriously, as technological advances associated with industrialization caused many people to believe that a Utopian world could be achieved with the help of technology and with a scientific system of economics. In particular, Engels, Saint-Simon, Fourier, Proudhon, and other nineteenth-century socialist philosophers began to write extensively about creating Utopian socialist communities. Utopian experiments were actually tried, both in the United States and in Europe, but they were all short-lived, and all failed. In the twentieth century, most people became more cynical about the prospects for Utopian societies, and at least two major satiric anti-Utopian books were written: Aldous Huxley's *Brave New World*, and George Orwell's *1984*.

See also: **Brook Farm**

UTOPIAN COMMUNITIES, COMMUNES *(ISSUE)*

During the seventeenth, eighteenth, and nineteenth centuries numerous European and American idealists sought to create examples of the perfect society in which everyone would benefit and there would be no conflict. Most of these experiments were set up in America where it was believed they would be relatively free from interference or persecution. That hope sometimes proved to be unfounded, but nevertheless many such communities did indeed experience a remarkable level of success and survived for many years.

There were two types of communitarian societies: sectarian and secular. The former were based upon a philosophy that was essentially religious, and the latter were not. Aside from religion, however, the two types shared many characteristics. They were usually small with seldom more than a few hundred people in a community. They all had charismatic leaders who were often very able, they all had developed some method of acquiring and maintaining land, they all developed some means of governing gender relations—ranging from celibacy to "communal marriage"—and they all developed a workable means of making a living for their members.

This couple chose to "drop out" of society and seek Utopia in commune life. Although often associated with the 1960s, the search for Utopia, via the commune system began in the United States as early as 1663.

The history of communitarian societies in America began in 1663 with the arrival of a group of Dutch Mennonites in Delaware. This settlement was destroyed when the British conquered New Netherlands in 1664. There was no similar attempt for several years until 1683 when settlers came to Maryland who were followers of Jean de Labadie, a German perfectionist thinker. Their community lasted for about twenty years before internal dissension caused it to split up and decline.

The first communal experiment to survive for a considerable period of time was founded by Johann Conrad Beissel, a German who had migrated to America in 1720. In 1732 Beissel founded a settlement in Pennsylvania which he called Ephrata. This community prospered until Beissel's death in 1768. After that it went into a period of decline until 1814 when the few remaining residents incorporated as the Seventh Day German Baptist Church which survived until 1934.

It was not until 1774 that an English-speaking group arrived who would exert significant influence on American society at large. These were the followers of "Mother" Ann Lee, who were commonly known as "The Shakers." This designation was assigned to them because of their habit of dancing during their religious services. "Mother" Ann and her people came from Manchester, England, and settled in upstate New York. Although "Mother" Ann died in 1784, the community survived under the able leadership of her American successors. They established their first fully communal town in Columbia County, New York, in 1787. From there they went on to establish twenty-two villages in seven states, continuing to expand until 1836. They were very good at attracting converts and, in fact, relied upon these skills for their survival because one tenet of their philosophy was strict adherence to celibacy. Their villages usually had an economy based on agriculture.

There was a surge in the appearance of communal societies in the early nineteenth century. By that time American nationalism had begun to develop; along with it came a growing interest in social reform. There was a widespread belief between 1820 and 1850 that American society could be improved or perfected in many ways. Thus the idea of perfectionist communities fit in very well with currently prevailing attitudes.

One of the first societies to develop in this era was headed by "Father" George Rapp who founded a community near Pittsburgh in 1804. He preached that the Second Coming of Christ was near and attracted many followers who believed that life in his community would prepare them for the millennial event. In 1814, the "Rappites" moved to Indiana where they remained for ten years. Then they returned to Pennsylvania and established a village (named Economy) near the site of their original community. They built woolen and cotton mills and a sawmill; they grew fruit, made wine, and produced silk. They were very successful and their community continued to operate at Economy until well into the 20th century.

Another perfectionist leader of this period was Robert Owen. Owen was a self-made businessman and for twenty-five years (1800–1825) was manager of New Lanark Mills, one of Scotland's largest cotton-spinning mills. During his career Owen became convinced that reforms in the factory system that would improve the standard of living of the workers were vital. He came to believe that improvements in human living conditions would lead to improved results in business. Eventually, he rejected the free enterprise philosophy entirely and adopted a pre-Marxian form of socialism. He called his idea the "New Moral World." In it everything would be accomplished by means of cooperation rather than competition. By 1824, he had decided to transform his dream into reality in America.

Owen purchased the Rappite property in Indiana for $150,000, renamed it New Harmony, and began his experiment in 1825. He did not have to start from scratch because the Rappites left him a ready-made community complete with houses, mills, shops, churches, factories, vineyards, and orchards.

Owen's idea was that New Harmony would be a fully communal society. There would be no private property, everyone would receive "credit" for their production, and all necessities would be supplied by the communal store. Unfortunately, the experiment did not work. The system was not well organized or managed, production lagged, there was no unity, morale collapsed, and by 1827, the experiment was over. Owen abandoned New Harmony and returned to England. It would be more than ten years before another experiment of this type was attempted.

Beginning in the 1840s new communal experiments began in America. These were based on the ideas of the French Socialist Charles Fourier as translated into English by his disciple Albert Brisbane. Many of Fourier's ideas were similar to those of Robert Owen. He declared that concern and cooperation were the secrets of social success. He argued that a cooperative society would lead to an immense increase in production. The fruits of all labor would be divided among all workers according to the contribution of each worker. Like Owen, Fourier believed that communities should be small and well-planned in all aspects. He called his ideal community a "phalanx."

Beginning in 1841, through 1848, there were 28 Fourierite phalanxes attempted in America. The first and most famous was Brook Farm in Suffolk County, Massachusetts. A number of famous Americans, including the author, Nathaniel Hawthorne, participated in this experiment which lasted until 1847. Other Fourier phalanxes were formed in New York, Pennsylvania, New Jersey, Indiana, Ohio, Michigan, Wisconsin, Illinois, and Texas. All but three were founded between 1841 and 1847, the period during which Brook Farm operated; most of them (thirteen) originated in 1844.

One of the most interesting and successful of the communitarian experiments in America was John Humphrey Noyes' Oneida Community. In 1834 Noyes announced that he had attained a state of perfection and was incapable of sin. He then formed the Perfectionist Church in Putney, Vermont, where he and his followers held all things, including marriage partners, in common. Such radical ideas caused the local authorities to charge Noyes with adultery whereupon he and his congregation fled to New York.

Noyes purchased forty acres of land near the town of Oneida in upstate New York where he began to build a Perfectionist Society. Not only were all things held in common, including marriage partners, but the group practiced ''scientific reproduction,'' which Noyes called ''stripiculture.'' This meant that partners who were ''morally perfect'' were selected to produce children who would inherit their parents' moral characteristics. The community would then educate the children and this process would eventually lead to the emergence of a superior class of people.

For several years the community made a successful living growing fruit, but later they added business and manufacturing to their activities and eventually began to concentrate on silverware. The community was well-planned, well-organized, and well-administered, and it prospered. People in surrounding communities, however, did not approve of the Oneida lifestyle. Threatened with legal action in 1879, for immorality, Noyes fled to Canada, and the colony soon broke up. It was converted to a joint stock company in 1881, and continued the successful manufacturing of silverware.

In the late nineteenth century the idea of perfecting society through the operation of small, socialized communities gave way to the idea of individual growth and development within a democratic system. Hence interest in communitarism declined, but that society is capable of improvement was an idea that never died.

See also: **Utopia**

FURTHER READING

Bestor, Arthur. *Backwoods Utopias: The Sectarian Origins and Owenite Phase of Communitarian Socialism in America, 1661–1829.* Philadelphia: University of Pennsylvania Press, 1970.

Hayden, Delores. *Seven American Utopias: The Architecture of Communitarian Societies, 1790–1875.* Cambridge, MA: M I T Press, 1976.

Holloway, Mark. *Heavens on Earth: Utopian Communities in America, 1680–1880.* New York: Dover, 1966.

Kern, Louis, J. *An Ordered Love: Sex Roles and Sexuality in Victorian Utopias-The Shakers, The Mormons, and The Oneida Community.* Chapel Hill, NC: University of North Carolina Press, 1981.

Rexroth, Kenneth. *Communalism: From Its Origins to the Twentieth Century.* New York: Seabury Press, 1974.

VANDERBILT, CORNELIUS

Cornelius ''Commodore'' Vanderbilt (1794–1877) was a shrewd businessman in the transportation industry. He built his fortune through freight and passenger boating lines, and later expanded to railroads. He was such a fierce and successful businessman that his competitors often paid him to vacate their markets. Vanderbilt left an estate of almost $100 million and founded Vanderbilt University.

Cornelius Vanderbilt was born on May 27, 1794, on Staten Island, New York. His father worked in boating, and Vanderbilt quit school at age 11 to join his father, working odd jobs on the waterfront. By the age of 16 young Vanderbilt was determined to become his own boatman. His choice of careers earned him the nickname ''Commodore.'' To finance his new career, Vanderbilt struck a deal with his mother. If he would plow and sow an uncultivated eight-acre field, his mother would loan him $100 to buy a boat. Vanderbilt earned the money and began a transport and freight service between New York City and Staten Island. Charging 18 cents a trip, Vanderbilt was able to repay the $100 loan in a year and earned an additional $1000 in profits.

Vanderbilt quickly developed a reputation for being capable, reliable, and honest. He charged reasonable prices and worked tirelessly. With the War of 1812 (1812–1814) he was given a chance to expand his enterprise. When the British threatened to invade New York, Vanderbilt arranged a three-month government contract to supply the island forts around New York. This profitable venture gave him enough money to buy a schooner that traveled over Long Island Sound and two more boats to engage in coastal trade. By the age of 24 Vanderbilt had saved $9000 and owned interests in several periaugers (a small two-masted, flat-bottomed vessel) and coasting schooners.

Vanderbilt was wise enough to recognize that steam was revolutionizing water transportation. The successes of steamboat inventors Robert Fulton and Robert R. Livingston persuaded Vanderbilt to sell all of his boating interests in 1818 and turn his attention to steamboats. Vanderbilt went to work for Thomas Gibbons, who owned one steamboat and operated a ferry between New Brunswick, New Jersey, and New York City. Vanderbilt started off working for $60 a month. In the 11 years that Vanderbilt worked for Gibbons, the line grew from one 25-ton steamboat to seven 200-ton boats. By 1828 Vanderbilt had saved more than $30,000.

Cornelius Vanderbilt.

A year later Vanderbilt moved his family to Manhattan, New York, and went into business for himself. He bought one of Gibbons' older steamboats and opened his own line running from New York to Philadelphia, Pennsylvania. He quickly slashed rates and sent his competitors into a panic. They responded by paying Vanderbilt generously not to run a line on their route. Vanderbilt then opened a line from New York to Peekskill, New York, and ran into competition from businessman Daniel Drew (1797–1879). Vanderbilt once again cut his rates immediately to increase business. When Drew followed suit, Vanderbilt purchased Drew's boat to eliminate the competition.

Vanderbilt's next venture was the New York-Albany route that brought him in direct competition with the powerful Hudson River Steamboat Association. Vanderbilt's line was so successful that once again he was paid off handsomely to not operate on that route. Vanderbilt quickly developed a successful business strategy: cut rates, drive away the competition or sell out, and then raise rates again. This approach was so successful that by the time he was 40, Vanderbilt was worth over $500,000 and operated over 1000 steamboats.

The Gold Rush of 1849 in California opened up new business possibilities for Vanderbilt. Most adventurers were traveling to California through Panama, but Vanderbilt opened a quicker and cheaper route through Nicaragua. The venture was a success and Vanderbilt's line carried 2000 passengers per month for nine years and made over $1 million in profits each year.

I HAVE BEEN INSANE ON THE SUBJECT OF MONEYMAKING ALL MY LIFE.

Cornelius Vanderbilt

In 1853 Vanderbilt took a small break from business. He commissioned a 270-foot steam yacht, the *North Star*, and set off for Europe with his family. He sold his controlling interest in the Nicaraguan line to his partners, Charles Morgan and Cornelius K. Garrison, who were supposed to pay Vanderbilt 20 percent of the gross receipts while he was away. The partners, however, refused to pay him. Rather than take them to court, Vanderbilt determined to ruin them financially. When he returned from his trip, he organized a new line to California via Panama and slashed his prices to only $35. He had driven Morgan and Garrison out of business by 1857. Vanderbilt then terminated the service when two Panamanian steamship lines agreed to pay him not to run that route.

Despite his successes in shipping, Vanderbilt was always looking for new business opportunities. At the age of 70 he became interested in the railroads. In 1857 Vanderbilt purchased a controlling interest in the Harlem Railroad, followed by the Hudson River Railroad in 1865, and New York Central in 1867. He then consolidated his holdings into one system that extended from New York City to Buffalo, New York. Vanderbilt tried to acquire the Erie Railroad from his old steamboat adversary, Daniel Drew, but failed. He did purchase several other lines and extended his service to Chicago, Illinois. By 1877 the New York Central Railroad System covered more than 4,500 miles.

Through his various business ventures Vanderbilt accumulated over $100 million. He was not known for philanthropy until his final years, when he donated $50,000 to the Church of the Strangers and $1 million to Central University, which then became Vanderbilt University. "The Commodore" died on January 4, 1877.

See also: **Daniel Drew, New York Central Railroad, Steamboat, War of 1812**

FURTHER READING

Auchincloss, Louis. *The Vanderbilt Era: Profiles of a Gilded Age*. New York: Scribner, 1990.

Conkin, Paul Keith. *Gone with the Ivy: A Biography of Vanderbilt University*. Knoxville: University of Tennessee Press, 1985.

Foreman, John. *The Vanderbilts and the Gilded Age: Architectural Aspirations*. New York: St. Martin's Press, 1991.

Patterson, Jerry E. *The Vanderbilts*. New York: Harry N. Abrams Pub., 1989.

Vanderbilt, Arthur T. *Fortune's Children: The Fall of the House of Vanderbilt*. Oklahoma City, OK: Quill Press, 1991.

VAUDEVILLE

Vaudeville, a light, comical theatrical entertainment, flourished at the end of the nineteenth century and beginning of the twentieth century. Its success, like that of organized baseball, was caused by the greater amounts of leisure time and money that industrialization afforded people. The word vaudeville is derived from an old French term for a satirical song, *vaudevire*, which is a reference to the Vire valley of France, where the songs originated. In the United States vaudeville acts performed variety shows, using music, comedy, dance, acrobatics, magic, puppets, and even trained animals. This form of stage entertainment was based on popular acts that could be seen in British music halls and bar rooms during the nineteenth century.

Vaudeville had made its way to the United States in the 1870s, when acts were performed in theaters in New York, Chicago, and other cities. Two early entrepreneurs in the entertainment form were American theater managers Benjamin Keith (1846–1914) and Edward Albee (1857–1930), who opened the Bijou Theatre in Boston in 1885. Eventually they operated almost four hundred theaters, including New York City's Palace Theater, the gem in the Keith-Albee crown. Troupes traveled the circuit of nearly one thousand theaters around the country. As many as two million U.S. citizens a day flocked to the shows to see headliners such as comedians Eddie Cantor (1892–1964) and W.C. Fields (1880–1946), singer Eva Tanguay (1878–1947), and French actress Sarah Bernhardt (1844–1923). Programs combined a variety of music, theater, and comedy to appeal to a wide audience. Scriptwriters attracted immigrant audiences by using ethnic humor, exaggerating dialects, and joking about the difficulties of daily immigrant life in the United States.

DURING THE FIRST TWO DECADES OF THE TWENTIETH CENTURY, VAUDEVILLE WAS THE MOST POPULAR FORM OF ENTERTAINMENT IN THE COUNTRY.

During the first two decades of the twentieth century, vaudeville was the most popular form of entertainment in the country. In the 1930s, just as New York opened the doors of its famous Radio City Music Hall, which was intended to be a theater for vaudeville, the entertainment form began a quick decline. Motion pictures, radio, and, later, television took its place; numerous vaudeville performers parlayed their success into these new media. Among those entertainers who had their origins in vaudeville acts were Rudolph Valentino, Cary Grant, Mae West, Jack Benny, George Burns, Gracie Allen, Ginger Rogers, Fred Astaire, Will Rogers, and Al Jolsen.

See also: **Amusement Parks, Baseball**

VEBLEN, THORSTEIN BONDE

Thorstein Veblen (1857–1929) had become widely known in the United States as the author of a book, *The Theory of the Leisure Class*, published in 1899. The book was an unexpected sensation. It remains as one of the most pungently written analyses of modern economics; it may be read as a satire on the ways of the aristocratic class, the follies and foibles of the robber barons and the rich. Veblen's analysis of modern commerce and economics did not include the traditional interplay of rationally calculated ''self-interest.'' Instead Veblen wrote of U.S. economic life as would an anthropologist. He regarded most economic activity, and specifically the accumulation of money, as a lavish modern-day counterpart of scalps hanging on a tribal tree. Veblen believed that the accumulation of wealth, well beyond the point of rational wants and needs, was evidence of deep-buried irrationalities. Veblen's second book, *The Theory of Business Enterprise*, published in 1904, was even more devastating than the first one, declaring that businessmen were needless saboteurs of any reasonable modern economic system. He made a credible case for the abolition of most businesses and of most government bureaucrats. He also made the first serious examination of the possibilities of using technology on all levels to establish within an economic system the conditions of freedom, security, and dignity for society as a whole.

Thorstein Bonde Veblen was born on July 30, 1857 in Manitowoc, Wisconsin. He was the sixth of 12 children born to Thomas and Kari Veblen, Norwegian immigrants who had settled in Minnesota, purchased a farm, and developed the farm with minimal contact with the outside community. Veblen's talent was already apparent in his early age, and his behavior was rather eccentric. His father enrolled him at a local college, Carleton College, hoping he might become a minister. Veblen graduated from Carleton in 1880 and went east to Yale University, where he studied philosophy. In three years he had his doctorate in philosophy, but his reputation as an eccentric inhibited his employment opportunities at universities where he applied for work. He ended up back at his parent's residence in Minnesota, where he eventually married. Veblen left Minnesota to live with his wealthy wife in Iowa for a time; he did little but reading until deciding to study economics at Cornell University in 1891.

A year after his study at Cornell, he was hired on to the staff at the University of Chicago. Veblen was a tutor and instructor at Chicago from 1892 to 1906. It was during this time that he published his books, *The Theory of the Leisure Class* and *The Theory of Business Enterprise*, which brought him much personal fame as an economic analyst. In his writing, Veblen put his finger on a central process of change that had been strangely overlooked by the investigations of other economists. The process was the emergence of technology and science as the major force of historic change. Veblen saw clearly, and uniquely, that the machine was the primary fact of economic life in the twentieth century.

Two major elements emerged out of Veblen's analysis and criticism: First, the importance of technology as the backbone of all commerce in the twentieth century. Second, that "economic man" can best be understood not by so-called economic laws but by looking at the irrational, untutored, and ritualistic behaviors of human beings while engaged in economic activity.

Veblen's view of businessmen in the twentieth century was like no other economist's. He saw the typical businessman as a predator draped in weird luxuries. Veblen introduced his famous phrase, "conspicuous consumption," to argue that the rich were not happy being rich and comfortable, but rather felt the urge to spend their lives buying wildly expensive and (frequently) bizarre things in order to indirectly brag to others about how wealthy they were. Their "consumption," Veblen contended, was irrationally raised to the level of being "conspicuous" to others: the purchase of 50 automobiles, for instance, or ten homes, and the conspicuous wearing of large items of gold and diamond jewelry.

Veblen was neither a socialist nor a capitalist; he seemed without economic ideology. He instead saw most economic behavior as psychological, often psychopathological. He concluded that businessmen were parasites and therefore unnecessary in a technological world which was capable of making consumer goods. He concluded that a class of engineers could take over the chaos of the business system and distribute to society the wealth created by machines and technology. It was an astonishing world-view for the first decade of the twentieth century, and his thinking along these lines has continued to resonate in economic thought.

Veblen lived to the age of 73. He died in 1929, just before the Great Depression (1929–1939) began. Veblen had a quiet, alienated, and profound vision for economists. He raised crucial questions related to the behavior of the economic man. In running down the robber barons of his era, as well as other businessmen, and in seeing the impact of technology as the major source of economic change in the modern era, Veblen arguably presented to his peers and to the public some of the most revolutionary modern thinking on the subject of business and commerce activities. Though his work was often idolized, his personal life was a lonely one. He lived his last years in an isolated cabin in California.

FURTHER READING

Coser, Lewis A. *Master of Sociological Thought.* New York: Harcourt Brace, 1977.

Diggins, Jack. *The Bard of Savagery.* New York: Seabury Press, 1978.

Heilbroner, Robert. *The Worldly Philosophers.* New York: Simon and Schuster, Touchstone Press, 1989.

Josephson, Matthew. *The Robber Barons.* New York: Harcourt Brace, 1962.

Lerner, Max. *The Portable Veblen.* New York: Viking Press, 1950.

VERMONT

The state of Vermont has retained its rural character throughout the history of a nation that has become increasingly urbanized and industrialized. Its quaint, natural beauty continues to attract thousands of tourists and summer residents who add greatly to the state's economy. Yet its manufacturing enterprises that make up over 50 percent of the state's revenues. Vermont has maintained its ties to the past, but has kept pace with the present.

The first European explorer of Vermont was Samuel de Champlain (1567–1635), who, in 1609, crossed the lake that now bears his name. From around 1650 through the 1760s, French, Dutch, English, and Iroquois Indians crossed Vermont, using trails between Montreal, Massachusetts, and New York. The first permanent settlement in the region was not established until 1724. For several decades both New York and New Hampshire claimed Vermont. Ethan Allen, a hero in the American Revolution (1775–1783), led a group that protested New York's claims. During the Revolution, Vermont adopted its own constitution and formed an independent republic; it was admitted to the Union in 1791.

Just before the War of 1812 (1812–1814) Vermonters engaged in smuggling to avoid the Embargo of 1808. The state continued trading with Canada during the war despite prohibitions on trade with Great Britain. By 1810 Vermont's population had reached 220,000, with most of the new settlers engaged in self-sufficient farming. After 1820, however, many began moving to the virgin lands of western New York, the Ohio Valley, and the trans-Mississippi region, which depleted Vermont's population. Despite an economic boost from newly built railroads, Vermont had simply run out of arable land and had overworked the available land. Vermont also had an insufficient number of manufacturing jobs, partly because the British had

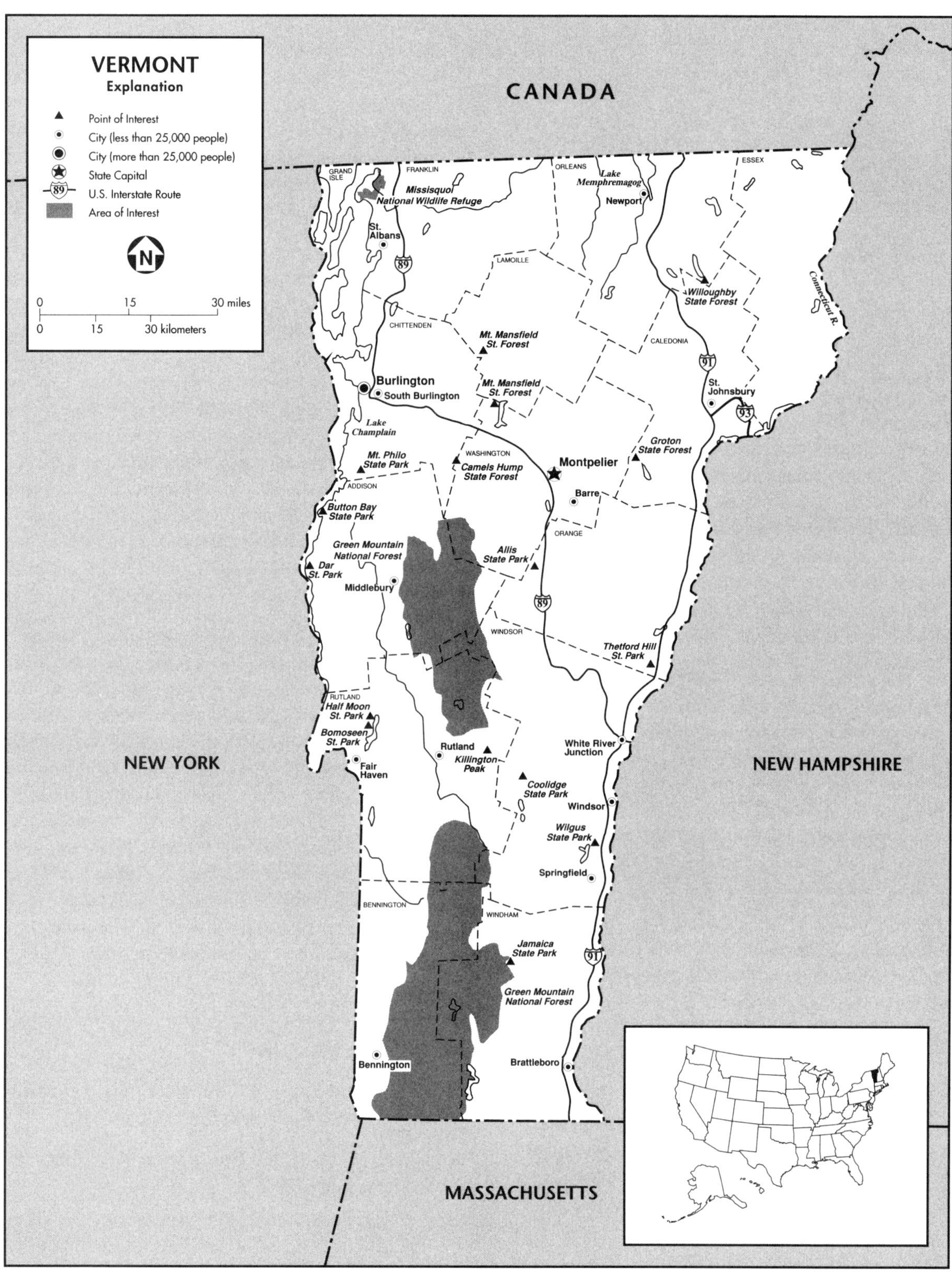

State of Vermont.

flooded the markets with cheaply produced cloth after the War of 1812.

VERMONT IS PART OF THE MODERN WORLD DESPITE ITS RURAL LANDSCAPE AND THE CURRIER AND IVES IMAGERY PROJECTED FROM THE GARISH SIDES OF MAPLE SYRUP TINS.

Charles D. Morrissey, *Vermont: A Bicentennial History*, 1981

The construction of the Champlain-Hudson Canal in 1823 and the railroads that were built in Vermont during the 1840s and 1850s did little to improve the state's economy, making it more vulnerable to competition from western territories. As emigration increased, however, those farmers remaining in the state were able to increase their prices for wool, butter, cheese, and milk. Irish and French-Canadian immigrants added to the population, and some light industry helped the economy to grow. By the late nineteenth century the well-known Vermont marble and granite quarries were being constructed, and the tourist industry began its steady rise into the twentieth century.

Vermonters seemed largely distant from many of the political and economic trends that gripped the nation after the American Civil War (1861–1865). They did not respond to the "free silver" message of presidential candidate William Jennings Bryan (1860–1925), nor to the Progressivism of the 1920s. The only U.S. President from Vermont, Calvin Coolidge (1923–1929), espoused rural conservatism. Though industrial growth occurred in towns such as Springfield, which manufactured the rifles named after the town; St. Johnsbury, where the famous St. Johnsbury scales were produced; Burlington, which boasted a number of textile mills; and quarry towns like Barre, Vermont remained primarily rural in character. In the early 1920s Vermont had the dubious honor of having more cows than people (a ratio which persisted until 1963).

The state was more forward-looking, however, in its approach to what would become a thriving tourist industry. Vermont established the first state publicity service in the nation. By 1911 it had produced its first publication, *Vermont, Designed by the Creator for the Playground of the Continent.* The state had recognized that its natural beauty was attracting many vacationers to its lakes, mountains, and, by the 1930s and 1940s, its ski resorts.

After World War II (1939–1945) both vacationers and second-home buyers flocked to Vermont over improved highways. A more suburban outlook began to pervade the state as professional people from New York and Massachusetts settled in the state. Native Vermonters wrestled with how to hold onto their rural heritage and, at the same time, embrace the economic benefits brought by the newcomers. A number of soil and water conservation measures were enacted by the state legislature, along with anti-litter and anti-billboard regulations.

Although manufacturing is the economic lifeblood of the state, Vermont remains the nation's most rural state, with two-thirds of its population living in towns of 2,500 or fewer. In the words of historian Charles T. Morrissey, "Vermont is not where Chicago or Pittsburgh or Detroit or other large cities grew. It is not where stockyards and slaughterhouses spread along the railroad tracks, or steel mills darkened the skies with smoke. . . .Vermont has been apart from the American mainstream." Modern Vermont's primary agricultural products are livestock and dairy products, followed by corn, hay, and apples. The state is also the nation's leading producer of maple syrup.

Mining is another profitable sector of Vermont's economy. It quarries granite and slate, is home to the world's largest marble reserve, and produces crushed stone, construction sand, and gravel. Dimension stone is the state's leading mineral commodity, making up slightly less than 50 percent of the state's total mineral production value. While these rural enterprises are important to the state, employment in recent decades has increased the most in manufacturing including such products as: electronics and machine parts. However, construction, wholesale and retail trade, and other service industries have also thrived. The state's per capita income in the mid-1990s was just over $22,000, which ranked thirtieth in the nation.

FURTHER READING

Bassett, T.D. S. *Vermont.* Hanover, NH: University Press of New England, 1983.

Crockett, Walter H. *History of Vermont.* 5 vols. New York: Century, 1921.

Hill, Ralph Nading. *Vermont: A Special World.* Montpelier: Vermont Life, 1969.

Morrissey, Charles T. *Vermont: A Bicentennial History.* New York: Norton, 1981.

Sherman, Micheal, and Jennie Versteeg, eds. *We Vermonters: Perspectives on the Past.* Montpelier: Vermont Historical Society, 1992.

VIETNAM WAR

The Vietnam War (1964–1975) was an eleven-year conflict in Southeast Asia between the American-backed government of South Vietnam and the Communist government of North Vietnam. The North Vietnamese sought to reunify the country following its partition in 1954, while the United States sought to contain Communist expansion by providing South Vietnam with economic and military aid. U.S. involvement reached its peak in 1968-1969, when over five hundred thousand U.S. troops were on the ground. The Pentagon spent $77.8 billion to finance the war. Approximately 58,000 U.S. citizens and over three million Vietnamese were killed during the conflict. Two years after the United States withdrew in 1973, North Vietnamese forces defeated the South Vietnamese and reunified the country.

Vietnam entered the twentieth century as a French colony. During World War II (1939—1945) the French evacuated the colony and the Japanese occupied it. An indigenous nationalist resistance movement to the Japanese invaders sprang up under the leadership of Ho Chi Minh (1892–1969). Ho Chi Minh was a member of both the Vietnamese and the French Communist Parties and the preeminent leader of national self-determination in Vietnam. When the Japanese were defeated in 1945 the French returned to Vietnam and tried to reestablish their colonial authority. For 56 days, the nationalist Vietnamese military force (called the *Viet Minh*, besieged the French fort at Dien Bien Phu where several thousand French troops were trapped. The French surrender led to peace talks in Geneva, Switzerland in 1954. The treaty required withdrawal of all French troops from Vietnam and a temporary partition of the country at the 17th parallel, with Communists retreating to the north and non-Communists moving to the south. National elections to unify Vietnam were scheduled for 1956.

U.S. President Dwight D. Eisenhower (1953–1961) feared that in a national election Ho Chi Minh would defeat the American-supported president of South Vietnam, Ngo Dinh Diem (1955–1963). As a result, elections were held only in South Vietnam. But the elections were rigged and Diem won an overwhelming majority of the vote, declared his country's independence from North Vietnam, and named Saigon as its capital. The decision whether to support Diem was a difficult one for U.S. policymakers. On one hand the United States was concerned that without U.S. support, the South Vietnam government would collapse and fall to the Communists. On the other hand

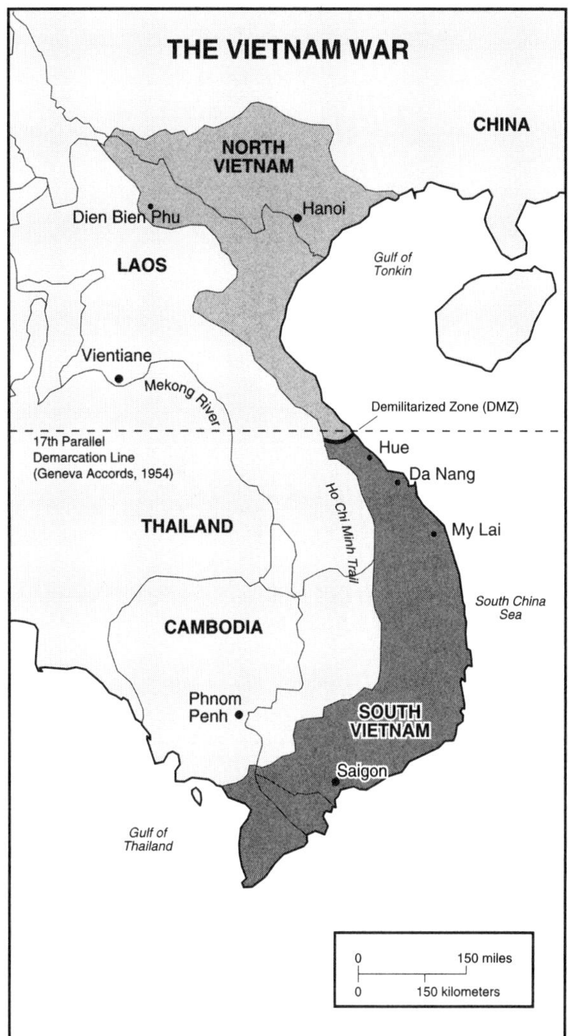

The 1954 treaty that ended French colonial control divided the country of Vietnam at the 17th parallel. The Communist government of North Vietnam waged war with the Southern, non-Communist government in order to unite the country. U.S. involvement came in an attempt to contain this Communist expansion.

President Eisenhower harbored reservations about getting U.S. troops mired in another Asian conflict so soon after the Korean War (1950–1953).

Diem's actions in office raised further concerns. His anti-Communist sympathies manifested themselves in harsh policies that alienated peasants and villagers. Diem, a Catholic, discriminated against Buddhists even though the Catholics made up only a small minority of the population that had played subordinate roles during the period of French colonialism. Opposition to Diem became widespread and in 1963 he was assassinated by elements in the Army. Diem's death was followed by ten successive South Vietnamese governments in 18 months.

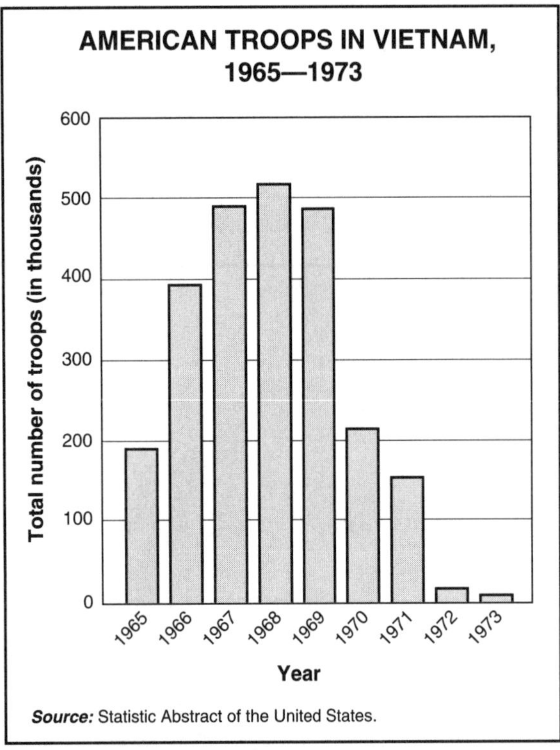

The total number of U.S. combat troops in Vietnam steadily increased until 1968, there was a significant withdrawal beginning in 1970 until 1973.

Taking advantage of this upheaval, the nationalist guerilla forces in South Vietnam (called the People's Liberation Armed Forces (PLAF) or, colloquially, the "Viet Cong") emerged under the political leadership of the National Liberation Front. The NLF was an organization of broad nationalist forces, led by the Communist Party of Vietnam. Their goal was the reunification of North and South Vietnam.

The United States responded to these developments by increasing the number of U.S. military, economic, and political advisers in Vietnam from 800 in 1961, when President John F. Kennedy took office, to 16,700 in 1963. During the 1964 presidential race Republican candidate Barry Goldwater charged President Lyndon B. Johnson (1963–1969), who took office following Kennedy's assassination, with not doing enough to win the war. Goldwater stated that Johnson would be responsible if Vietnam and its neighboring countries toppled like dominoes into the lap of the Communists.

Despite Goldwater's defeat, President Johnson was determined to not allow the so-called "domino theory" to become a reality. In August, 1964, U.S. ships off the coast of North Vietnam, in the Gulf of Tonkin, reported sonar indications of a torpedo attack. In response, Johnson ordered an air attack on North-Vietnamese ship bases and oil facilities. The next day the Senate granted the president's request for broad powers over the Southeast Asian conflict by passing the Gulf of Tonkin Resolution. The resolution gave the president authority to take all measures necessary to repel any further armed aggression against U.S. forces in the area.

Johnson relied on this "blank check" to commit the first U.S. combat troops to Vietnam on March 8, 1965. By the end of the year the initial commitment of 3,500 troops had increased to 80,000. These combat troops fought alongside the South Vietnamese armed forces, known as the Army of the Republic of Vietnam (ARVN). The ARVN was a poorly led group that lacked cohesion and motivation. In 1965 alone 113,000 ARVN troops were lost to desertion. Many U.S. soldiers disliked and mistrusted the ARVN and accused them of cowardice.

As the war dragged on in Vietnam, the anti-war movement picked up at home. Promises of victory by politicians and military commanders wore thin on an U.S. public confronted nightly by television images of bloody battles that accompanied mounting casualties. The credibility of U.S. government reports predicting imminent U.S. victory was further eroded by the 1968 Tet Offensive, an all-out assault on every major city in South Vietnam. The NLF forces suffered staggering losses during their offensive and made few strategic gains. The Viet Cong were virtually wiped out. But, though Tet was a military catastrophe for the NLF, it was a political victory. It took both U.S. and ARVN forces by surprise and had a resounding effect on the U.S. public.

The war had reached a stalemate and the Tet Offensive forced U.S. citizens to confront how deeply Communist resistance was entrenched throughout Vietnam. In 1969 opinion polls showed that for the first time in the war, a majority of respondents were opposed to the war. But, even though the war was becoming unpopular, most people were reluctant to pull out of Vietnam immediately. For a time, the American people were still willing to stand by the President in the struggle against Communism. Only between 20 and 40 percent of U.S. citizens polled in 1969 favored immediate withdrawal. But the protests were becoming larger and more frequent. And one-by-one, mainstream organizations and politicians began demanding peace in Vietnam. Inflation and higher taxes resulting from the war soured still other segments of society. It was no surprise that upon taking the oath of office in January, 1969, President Richard Nixon (1969–1974) promised to end the war with honor. But before he ended the war, President Nixon and his Secretary of State, Henry Kissinger, widened it.

In March of 1969 President Nixon ordered the secret bombing of Cambodia. His goal was to wipe out North Vietnamese and NLF bases along the South Vietnam border. The "Ho Chi Minh trail" went through this area, carrying provisions and troop convoys of the North Vietnamese Army (NVA). When U.S. troops invaded Cambodia the following year, college campuses erupted in protest. Four students at Kent State University in Ohio were killed by national guardsmen who had been called in to prevent rioting. Student protests were staged again in 1971 when the United States provided air support for an ARVN invasion of Laos and in 1972 when the United States began mining the Haiphong harbor. Nixon contended that these operations strengthened his hand at the bargaining table. He pointed to his program of "Vietnamizing" the war, which had reduced the number of U.S. troops in Southeast Asia to under 100,000 by 1972 and gave the South Vietnamese greater control of day-to-day tactical operations. In any event, during Christmas of 1972 the president ordered the final and most intense bombing of the war over Hanoi, the capital of North Vietnam.

On January 27, 1973, U.S. participation in the Vietnam War officially ended when the Treaty of Paris was signed by each of the parties to the conflict. The United States agreed to withdraw all of its forces from Vietnam and stop military operations in Laos and Cambodia. North and South Vietnam agreed to a cease-fire and all prisoners of war were to be released. U.S. military and economic aid to South Vietnam could continue.

Following the collapse of the South Vietnamese regime in 1975, the unified country of Vietnam collectivized the colonial rubber plantations, and some businesses were nationalized. Within ten years, however, elements of capitalism had crept into Vietnamese society. By the 1990s the Vietnam government began instituting policies to bring about a mixed economy involving state, collective, and private ownership. The opening of Vietnamese society improved relations with the United States, which ended a 20-year trade embargo against Vietnam in 1994. Full diplomatic relations between the two countries were established the next year.

See also: **Cold War, Richard Nixon**

FURTHER READING

Baily, Bernard, David Brion Davis, David Herbert Donald, John L. Thomas, Robert H. Wiebe, and Gordon S. Wood. *The Great Republic: A History of the American People*. Lexington, KY: D. C. Heath and Company, 1981.

Herring, George C. *America's Longest War: The United States and Vietnam 1950–1975*. New York: Alfred A. Knopf, 1986.

Karnow, Stanley. *Vietnam: A History The First Complete Account of the Vietnam War*. New York: The Vikings Press, 1983.

Powers, Thomas. *Vietnam: The War at Home*. Boston: G. K. Hall and Co., 1984.

Small, Melvin. *Johnson, Nixon, and the Doves*. New Brunswick, Rutgers University Press, 1989.

VIRGINIA

Virginia, home of presidents and cradle of American tradition, has a special place in the consciousness of the nation. Its economic history is perhaps less well-known than its political history. Supported, at first, by slave-owning plantations, the state depended for many years on tobacco and cotton crops. After the devastation brought about by the American Civil War (1861–1865), Virginia rebuilt its economy, adding industry to its agricultural base. Modern Virginia contains a healthy mix of farming, industrial, and service employment.

Virginia has claim to being the first permanent English settlement in America. The colonists who established Jamestown in 1607 named their colony Virginia in honor of the "Virgin Queen," Elizabeth I. The London Company, a joint-stock venture sponsored by King James I, claimed nearly all of the eastern coast of America, a great deal more land than now encompasses Virginia. Many in this expedition were gentlemen who had no clear idea of how to survive in the wilderness. Captain John Smith finally took matters into his own hands, declaring, "He that will not work neither shall he eat." As journalist Alistair Cooke wrote in his book, *Alistair Cooke's America*, this statement was "rooted . . . early and deep in the American consciousness." The colony weathered times of starvation, attacks by Indians, and the deaths of many people, but it somehow survived and even established its own form of representative government. After James I revoked the London Company's charter in 1624, Virginia became a royal colony.

The colony continued to grow along the James, York, Rappahannock, and Potomac rivers. It depended largely on the growing of tobacco (and later of cotton) with the help of indentured servants, both white and

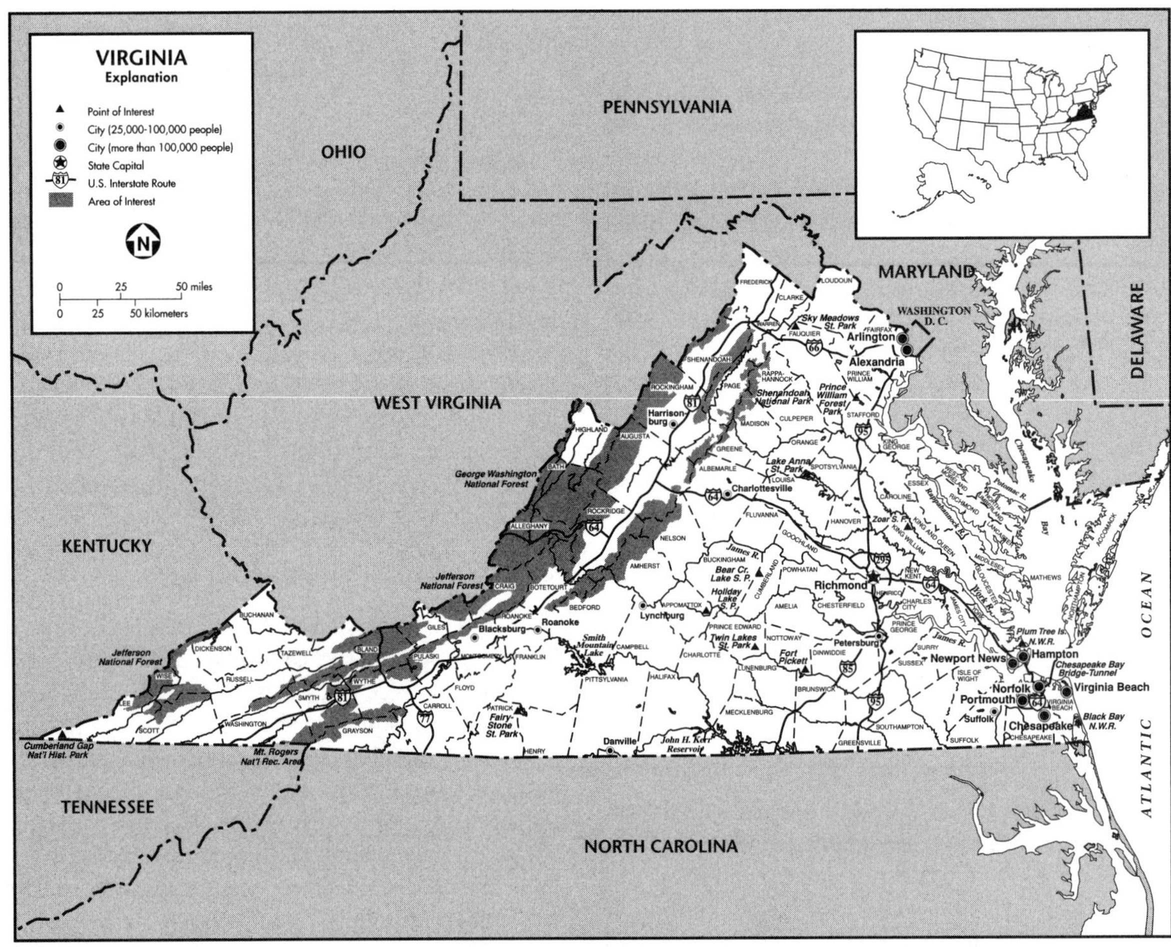

State of Virginia.

black. It is thought that the institution of slavery developed from the first black servants sent to Virginia. As eastern Virginians moved into the western part of the country, they began to lose much of their loyalty toward England, especially during the French and Indian War. The Virginia House of Burgesses engaged in repeated protests against British policy, which culminated in a boycott of British goods in response to the Townshend Acts. Virginia was the first colony to begin the move for independence from England in 1776 and it was a major player in the American Revolution (1775–1783). Virginia was so influential in this period that Virginians occupied the U.S. presidency for all but four of the nation's first 28 years.

In the early nineteenth century Virginia's influence began to decline. The eastern half of the state disputed constantly with the western half (later, the state of West Virginia), as eastern aristocrats held most of the political and economic power. Life all over the state remained largely rural and self-sufficient while roads were poor and mail delivery slow. Cities which did grow in the state, like Richmond and Norfolk, grew less rapidly than cities in other parts of the country.

By the mid-nineteenth century Virginia was entering another period of prosperity. The Valley Turnpike, completed in 1840, made transportation through the Shenandoah Valley easier. Agricultural experimentalists like Edmund Ruffin used new scientific methods to revitalize agricultural land worn out by years of tobacco farming. Land values rose with crop diversification, livestock production, and the use of new machinery. Industrial development was beginning too, as railroads began to form in a network across the state.

HE THAT WILL NOT WORK NEITHER SHALL HE EAT.

Captain John Smith, Jamestown Settlement

Closely tied to the economy of Virginia, especially on the eastern plantations, was the issue of slavery. In the 1830s the state was a major purveyor of the slave trade. Thus the growing antislavery movements of the

1850s were quite threatening to many Virginians. John Brown's raid on Harper's Ferry (then in Virginia) was a wake-up call to the state, which in the end reluctantly seceded from the Union in 1861.

As the main battlefront during the American Civil War (1861–1865), much of Virginia's countryside, as well as the city of Richmond, was left in ruins when the hostilities ended. The state also lost about half its territory when West Virginia seceded in 1863 to side with the North. A postwar debt of more than $45 million and corrupt Reconstruction leadership left Virginia in turmoil. After Reconstruction wealthy planters lost some of their political power. According to Louis D. Rubin, Jr., "Landed wealth, which had previously constituted a sufficient economic foundation for most Virginians, no longer sufficed." New leaders were rather "men who saw opportunity for themselves and their community in business, industrial development, railroading, [and] finance. . . ." This period was marked by significant expansion of railroads in the state, the most powerful being the Pennsylvania Central.

The state expanded greatly during this time, as suburbs of cities like Norfolk and Richmond developed and other towns like Hampton Roads and Roanoke grew rapidly due to their access to coal routes. Real estate boomed and manufacturing and mining companies sprang up. In 1893, however, a nationwide financial panic gripped the state. Small farmers in particular were devastated, with cash and credit in short supply. Blacks in the state were even worse off, lacking education and living with the legacy of slavery. In 1901 a state constitutional convention moved to eliminate black voting privileges, which had been in force since Reconstruction, thus reinforcing the continued segregation of society.

Conservative Democrats seemed destined to control the state after the turn of the century. In 1925, however, Harry Byrd, a liberal Democrat, won the governorship and embarked on an era of reform. During his tenure the state tax system was revised, along with a number of social reforms, and measures were taken to attract industry to the state.

After the Great Depression (1929–1939), Virginia entered a new era of prosperity, benefiting from defense contracts, manufacturing, and a growing tourist industry. Notable among the state's tourist attractions were the newly restored colonial capital city of Williamsburg and historic sites such as Jamestown, Monticello, and Civil War battlefields. Franklin D. Roosevelt's (1933–1945) New Deal, supported by Harry Byrd, was also responsible for the creation of Blue Ridge Parkway, part of the Shenandoah National Forest.

In the 1960s Virginia began to put its financial affairs in better order by enacting a sales tax and a multi-million-dollar bond issue which benefited the public school system. In the early 1980s the Virginia Beach/Norfolk area grew rapidly, largely as a result of federal jobs and new military spending. Between 1980 and 1990 the population of Virginia Beach grew by 50 percent. As non-agricultural employment increased, however, the economy of rural areas did not improve.

Virginia's economy experienced a recession in the late 1980s. Democratic governor Douglas Wilder responded by cutting state services and reducing budgets, thus creating significant hardships for education and less affluent counties. By the mid-1990s, however, Virginia's economy had rebounded, largely because of its diversified economy that included agriculture, manufacturing, as well as service industries—the latter mostly in federal government employment. In the late 1990s the port of Hampton Roads was one of the busiest in the country, with the largest amount of tonnage on the East Coast. In 1996 Virginia ranked fourteenth among the states in per capita income, at just under $25,000, and its unemployment rate in 1997 was just 4.5 percent, below the national average. The percentage of labor union membership in the state was only 6.8 percent of all workers. The state maintained a pro-business climate, which was aided by the state's conservative history, low wages, low tax rates, and weak labor movement. The Virginia Economic Development Corporation gave low-interest loans and other incentives to businesses, as did the Virginia Small Business Financing Authority.

See also: **Africans Arrive in Virginia, Civil War (Economic Impact of)**

FURTHER READING

Ashe, Dora J. Comp. *Four Hundred Years of Virginia, 1584–1984: An Anthology*. Lanham, MD: University Press of America, 1985.

Cooke, Alistair. *Alistair Cooke's America*. New York: Knopf, 1973.

Gottmann, Jean. *Virginia in Our Century*. Charlottesville, VA: University Press of Virginia, 1969.

Moger, Allen W. *Virginia: Bourbonism to Byrd*. Charlottesville: University Press of Virginia, 1968.

Rubin, Louis D., Jr. *Virginia: A Bicentennial History*. New York: Norton, 1977.

WABASH, ST. LOUIS AND PACIFIC RAILWAY COMPANY VS. ILLINOIS (1886)

In 1886 the U.S. Supreme Court decision in the case of *Wabash, St. Louis and Pacific Railway Company v. Illinois* declared that states could not regulate commerce that went beyond their boundaries. Instead, regulation had to come from the federal government. The decision provided the basis for the formation of the Interstate Commerce Commission in 1887.

With rail lines crisscrossing the nation, the question of who would control rail rates and monitor the practices of the railroads had become an increasingly difficult one to answer. Many states establish their own regulatory boards, but since the rail companies operated between states, enforcing state laws on them proved cumbersome and impractical. Meanwhile the railroads, operating without the oversight of any effective regulatory body, set their own standards and practices, which resulted in many abuses. When the Wabash, St. Louis and Pacific Railway Company challenged the intervention of the state of Illinois in its business, the case eventually went to the Supreme Court.

After the high court's ruling (1886), the federal government acted quickly to establish an independent U.S. government agency the following year, the Interstate Commerce Commission (ICC). The ICC was the first regulatory commission in the country. Originally charged with supervising the country's interstate rail operations, its authority was eventually expanded to include all forms of interstate commerce, including trucking, shipping, and even oil pipelines. In addition to controlling rates, the agency also enforced laws against discrimination.

See also: **Interstate Commerce Act, Interstate Commerce: Regulation and Deregulation, Munn vs. Illinois**

WAGE-PRICE CONTROLS

Wage and price controls were initiated by the U.S. government in 1942, in order to help win World War II (1939–1945), and maintain the general quality of life on the home front. In 1941 the Office of Price Administration (OPA) began a stormy career as an inflation fighter and food rationer. The mission of the OPA was to prevent profiteering and inflation as durable goods became scarcer in the United States because of the war. The Emergency Price Control Act of 1942 gave the OPA the ability to regulate prices in the marketplace, and brought 60 percent of all civilian food items under a form of control which froze prices at their store-by-store March 1942 levels. In a short time, 90 percent of the goods sold in more than 600 thousand retail stores in the United States were being price controlled and rationed by the federal government.

Wage-price controls disappeared with the end of World War II, as the domestic economy grew. Yet, it was only a few years later, after the outbreak of the Korean War in 1950, when President Harry Truman (1945–1953) obtained from Congress the authority to impose wage and price controls once again to deal with the inflationary domestic economy. Automobile prices were frozen, as were wages in the auto industry (until March 1951). Easy credit for new homes was restricted. The end of the Korean War ended wage-price controls, but did not end the government power to intervene during economic crises involving high inflation and scarcity of commodities. In 1962, a voluntary system of wage and price controls was adopted in order to avoid inflation. Known as ''Wage and Price Guideposts,'' as recommended by the Council of Economic Advisers to President John F. Kennedy (1961–1963), the price-wage controls would apply throughout the business sector and not aimed at single industries. The general guide for non-inflationary wage behavior was that the rate of increase in wages in each industry be equal to the trend rate of overall productivity increase. By contrast to the mandatory controls of World War II and Korea, this plan emphasized the voluntary compliance of business with the federal "guideposts."

The most extraordinary example of wage and price controls, the first attempted under peacetime conditions, was imposed by the Richard Nixon administration (1969–1974), beginning with the wage and price freeze of 1971, in an effort to deal with peacetime inflation. President Nixon designated his wage-price freeze policy as the Economic Stabilization Program of 1971–1974. The Council of Economic Advisers reviewed this policy and its usefulness after 1974, and concluded that the price and wage controls imposed by President Nixon in a peacetime economy "will be long debated and may never be resolved." During periods of high inflation in the U.S. economy, it is likely that the debate will re-emerge regarding the need for a period of wage-price controls.

See also: **Richard Nixon, Office of Price Administration, Harry S. Truman**

WAGES

The income given in exchange to those who supply their labor to any business is called "wages," and includes salaries, and various wage and salary supplements, such as bonuses, commissions, royalties, social insurance, pensions, and health plan benefits. About 75 per cent of all business costs are wages. At this level, wages have a very significant impact on all per unit production costs of any business. Wages differ widely among nations, regions, occupations, and individuals. Wage rates also differ by gender and race. Statistical data indicates that the general level of wages in the United States is among the highest in the world, with the explanation being that the United States demand for labor is great in relation to supply. Economists have also indicated that the labor demand is strong because the U.S. worker is highly productive, working in a country with an abundance of capital equipment, natural resources, advanced technology, better health and educational services, and the business and political support of a production oriented economy.

Evidence also suggests to economists that unionized labor is successful in raising the wages of its members. Union members typically receive a 10 to 15 percent wage advantage over non-union workers, without creating business obstructions. Why one person earns a high wage and another a lower wage is a matter of supply and demand. Even doing the same job, some workers bring superior abilities, skills, and commitment to the job, and frequently, such workers are rewarded with increased wages and job advancements. Geographic locations, market imperfections, and the differential in the work required can account for other differences in wages with similar groups of people in the workforce.

See also: **Labor Unionism, Trade Unions**

WAL-MART STORES

Wal-Mart Stores, Inc. was founded by Samuel Walton who graduated from the University of Missouri in 1940 with a degree in economics and went on to become a management trainee for J. C. Penney Company. After two years he went into the army, and upon his return three years later, he used his savings and a loan to open a Ben Franklin variety store in Newport, Arkansas. In 1950 he lost his lease, moved to Bentonville, Arkansas, and opened another store. By the late 1950s Sam and his brother J. L. (Bud) Walton owned nine Ben Franklin franchises.

In the early 1960s Sam Walton took what he had learned from studying mass merchandising techniques around the country and began to make his mark in the retail market. He decided that small-town populations would welcome, and make profitable, large discount shopping stores. He approached the Ben Franklin franchise owners with his proposal to slash prices significantly and operate at a high volume, but they were not willing to let him reduce merchandise as low as he insisted it had to go. The Walton brothers decided to go into that market themselves and opened their first Wal-Mart Discount City in Rogers, Arkansas, in 1962. The brothers typically opened their department-sized stores in towns with populations of 5,000 to 25,000, and the stores tended to draw from a large radius. "We discovered people would drive to a good concept," Walton said in *Financial World* on April 4, 1989.

Wal-Mart's "good concept" involved huge stores offering customers a wide variety of name-brand goods at deep discounts that were part of an everyday-low-prices strategy. Walton was able to keep prices low and still turn a profit through sales volume and an uncommon marketing strategy. Wal-Mart's advertising costs generally amounted to one-third that of other discount chains. Most competitors were putting on sales and running from 50 to one hundred advertising circulars per year, but Wal-Mart kept its prices low and only ran 12 promotions a year. By the end of the 1960s the brothers had opened 18 Wal-Mart stores and owned 15 Ben Franklin franchises throughout Arkansas, Missouri, Kansas, and Oklahoma. These ventures became incorporated as Wal-Mart Stores, Inc. in October 1969.

The 1970s held many milestones for the company. Early in the decade, Walton implemented his warehouse distribution strategy: the company built its own warehouses so it could buy in volume and store the merchandise, then proceeded to build stores throughout two hundred square mile areas around the distribution points. This cut Wal-Mart's costs and gave it more control over operations. It also meant that merchandise could be restocked as quickly as it was sold, and that advertising was specific to smaller regions and cost less to distribute.

Wal-Mart went public in 1970 to be listed on the New York Stock Exchange two years later. By 1976 the Waltons phased out their Ben Franklin stores so the company could put all of its expansion efforts into the Wal-Mart stores. By 1979 there were 276 Wal-Mart stores in 11 states. Sales had gone from $44 million in 1970 to $1.25 billion in 1979.

Sam's Clubs—100,000-square-foot, cash-and-carry discount membership warehouses—made their first appearance in 1983, proving so popular in the bigger markets that there were 148 of them by 1991. Overall the company had 1,500 stores in 29 states by 1990 with net sales of nearly $26 billion. Wal-Mart surpassed Sears as the number one retailer in the United States in 1991.

Wal-Mart came under much scrutiny for its impact on small towns—specifically, small retail businesses in those towns. Independent store owners often went out of business when Wal-Mart came to town, unable to compete with the superstore's economies of scale. In fact Iowa State University economist Kenneth Stone conducted a study on this phenomenon and told the *New York Times Magazine*, ''If you go into towns in Illinois where Wal-Mart has been for eight or 10 years, the downtowns are just ghost towns.'' He found that the businesses suffering most were drug, hardware, five-and-dime, sporting goods, clothing, and fabric stores, while major appliance and furniture businesses picked up, as did restaurants and gasoline stations, because of increased traffic. Wal-Mart did, however, develop a record of community service by awarding a $1,000 scholarship to a high school student in each community Wal-Mart operated in.

Wal-Mart continued to expand throughout the 1990s both in the United States and abroad. The U.S. growth was notable for the emergence of the new Wal-Mart Supercenter format, which was a Wal-Mart discount store with an integrated grocery store. The success of the Supercenters catapulted Wal-Mart into the top five U.S. food retailers. By the late 1990s Wal-Mart's domestic operations included more than 1,900 Wal-Mart discount stores (located in all 50 states), about 440 Wal-Mart Supercenters, and about 440 Sam's Clubs. Wal-Mart, whose revenue stood at $137.63 billion, had also become the largest retailer in the world, the fourth-largest company overall in the United States, and the nation's largest non-governmental employer with 825,000 employees.

See also: **Chain Stores**

FURTHER READING

Bowermaster, Jon. ''When Wal-Mart Comes to Town.'' *New York Times Magazine*, April 2, 1989.

Ortega, Bob. *In Sam We Trust: The Untold Story of Sam Walton and How Wal-Mart Is Devouring America.* New York: Times Business, 1998.

Trimble, Vance H. *Sam Walton: The Inside Story of America's Richest Man.* New York: Penguin, 1990.

Vance, Sandra S., and Roy V. Scott. *Wal-Mart: A History of Sam Walton's Retail Phenomenon.* New York: Twayne, 1994.

Walton, Sam, with John Huey. *Sam Walton, Made in America: My Story.* New York: Doubleday, 1992.

Zellner, Wendy, et. al. ''Wal-Mart Spoken Here.'' *Business Week*, June 23, 1997.

WALKER, FRANCIS AMASA

Amasa Walker (1799–1875) grew to prominence as a financial expert and economist in the United States after warning a group of distinguished New England businessmen during a financial recession in 1857 that the state-chartered banks of their region should suspend all cash (specie) payments in order to save the merchants from total ruin. Weeks later, many Boston banks stopped their specie payments, saving many businesses, and Walker's credentials as an expert were established. With the publication of his book, *The Science of Wealth*, in 1866, Walker's reputation grew as a U.S. economist working to free economic study from its reputation in that period as a mere extension of moral and theological philosophy. Walker was among the first economists to confront theory with statistical evidence. He pioneered in economics what is known as ''time series analysis,'' where economic variables were taken at different points in time and the results plotted on a graph so that economic changes could be visually assessed and compared to other changes in the society over a period of time.

Amasa Walker was born in May 1799, in Woodstock, Connecticut. He was the son of Walter Walker, a blacksmith, and Priscilla. Walker's poor health as an adolescent prevented him from going to college. In 1820, at age 21, he formed a business partnership in Brookfield, Massachusetts, to make shoes. After three years he left the shoe business and joined Methuen Manufacturing Co. as its agent. At age 26 he moved to Boston, where he pursued a variety of retail business ventures.

Walker's election to the Democratic National Convention in 1836 marked his entrance into public life. By 1839 he served as a director of the Franklin Bank in Boston and also as president of the Boston Temperance Society, and in 1848 he agitated for the abolition of U.S. slavery as a member of the Free Soil Party. In 1849 Walker was elected to the Massachusetts House of Representatives and a year later to the state Senate. He is remembered in his position as a congressman for his efforts to put copies of *Webster's Dictionary* in the public schools.

It was during the financial panic of 1857, however, that Walker emerged as an expert on finance, banking, and currency. He had published a series of articles for *Hunt's Merchant Magazine* that explained the nature of financial panics, especially those severe enough to call for the banks to suspend all specie payments. His advice to a group of New England merchants calling for a "suspension of specie payments" by the state-chartered banks to save the best merchants from financial ruin proved prophetic when the Boston banks stopped specie payments and saved many businesses.

Walker's fame as a financial expert helped his career as a college lecturer in political economy. He left his mark on Washington, D.C., by serving out a term as a Republican congressman between 1862 and 1863. Walker, as an economist and a congressman, advocated the elimination of the rights of state-chartered banks to create credit money. He argued that the practice was "prejudicial to the industrial and commercial interests of the nation," because of the unreliable fluctuations it caused in the economy. He held that the government should manage the nation's credit currency for the best interests of the population. Walker was against any bank-credit expansion. He believed it was unconstitutional and that bank-credit money destabilized the larger economy and helped cause what are now called "business cycles," periods of boom and bust.

In his effort to make his theories in economic thinking more credible, Walker pulled away from economics as a philosophy and insisted on using economics in a more scientific manner. He created his own scientific method of studying economics, which he discussed in his book *The Science of Wealth* in 1866. In his book Walker pioneered "time series analysis," where he measured specific economic variables at different points in time and plotted them on graphs so that the data could be compared and visually examined for information about the economy.

Walker argued against what he called "financial novelty" and he was a strong specie advocate, focusing on metallic money and remaining deeply suspicious of artificial credit creation. In his book Walker also described his opposition to legislation that fixed hours of work. He identified market forces bringing women's wages into equality with men's, and he advocated open immigration laws. He also emphasized the importance of labor unions as a necessary force to offset the advantages enjoyed by the owners of factories. As an economic thinker, Walker was less concerned with the production of physical objects than with the production and exchange of material that is useful and has exchange value.

Amasa Walker died in 1875, having pioneered a new era in economics ruled by science rather than philosophy. By using graphs and analysis in his economic proposals, Walker was arguably one of the first economists to be able to scientifically assess the subjective nature of market values and to statistically follow economic forces. His work was immensely popular, and it did much to develop an appreciation of economic questions among the general public.

See also: **Financial Panic, Specie**

FURTHER READING

Newton, Bernard. *The Economics of Francis Amasa Walker: American Economics in Transition.* New York: A.M. Kelley, 1968.

Sobel, Robert. *Machines and Morality: the 1850s.* New York: Crowell, 1973.

Spiegel, Henry W. *The Rise of American Economic Thought.* Philadelphia: Chilton Co., Book Division, 1960.

Temin, Peter. *Causal Factors in American Economic Growth in the 19th Century.* New York: Macmillan, 1975.

Vatter, Harold G. *The Drive to Industrial Maturity: the U.S. Economy, 1860–1914.* Westport, CT: Greenwood Press, 1975.

WALKER, SARAH BREEDLOVE

Sarah Breedlove Walker (1867–1919) was one of the first American women to become a millionaire, and she ran the largest business owned by an African American at the time. She made a prosperous business out of selling her self-made hair care products for African American women.

Walker was born December 23, 1867. Her father was a poor sharecropper, and former slave, in Delta, Louisiana. She was orphaned at the age of six and was thereafter raised by an older sister. She received very little formal education and at the age of 10 she began supporting herself. At 14 she married Moses McWilliams and in 1885 they had a daughter. Two years later her husband died and Walker was left a widow with a young child to support. She moved her family to St. Louis, Missouri, where she had relatives. There she worked as a hotel washerwoman for 18 years.

I GOT MY START BY GIVING MYSELF A START.

Sarah Breedlove Walker

Around 1904 Walker began to suffer from a scalp ailment called alopecia, which causes hair loss. At first she tried existing hair products to relieve her problem, before beginning to develop her own remedies. She started creating scalp treatments, then developed hair straighteners; next she began modifying existing hair techniques and tools until she developed the ''Walker Method'' of hair care. In 1906 Walker moved to Denver, Colorado, and married newspaperman Charles Joseph Walker. It was there that she founded the Madame C.J. Walker Manufacturing Company. She expanded her line of products to include hair growing tonic, strengtheners, toiletries, fragrances, and facial treatments.

In addition to expanding her product line, Walker developed new marketing techniques. At first she sold her products door to door by herself. Later she hired and trained other women to be ''Walker Agents'' and eventually she added a huge mail order department to her business. She also opened a beauty school that taught the Walker Method of hair straightening and hair growing. The business grew rapidly and in 1908 she opened a second office in Pittsburgh, Pennsylvania. Then in 1910 she opened her first factory in Indianapolis, Indiana.

Sarah Walker was also a social leader among the African American middle class. She was known as a good employer who sponsored philanthropic and educational projects initiated by her employees. She founded Lelia College, a hair care laboratory, and a chain of beauty salons in Harlem. She contributed generously to the National Association for the Advancement of Colored People (NAACP) and aided several local charities. She established scholarships for women at the Tuskegee Institute, Bethune-Cookman College, and Palmer Memorial Institute. In addition she supported black chapters of the Young Womens Christian Association (YWCA) and orphanages.

By 1917 the Madame C.J. Walker Manufacturing Company was the largest African American-owned business in the United States employing about 3,000 workers. Sarah Walker was one of the first American women to become an independent millionaire. She died in New York City on May 25, 1919.

See also: **Mary McLeod Bethune, Barbara Proctor**

FURTHER READING

Bundles, A'Lelia Perry. *Madam C.J. Walker*. New York: Chelsea House Publishers, 1991.

Eldred, Sheila Mulrooney. ''Inventing Dreams: Sarah Breedlove Walker (1867–1919).'' *New Moon*, January/February 1998.

Leavitt, Judith A. *American Women Managers and Administrators*. Westport, CT: Greenwood Press, 1985.

Snodgrass, Mary Ellen. *Late Achievers: Famous People Who Succeeded Late in Life*. Englewood, CO: Libraries Unlimited, 1992.

Vare, Ethlie Ann, and Gret Ptacek. *Mothers of Invention from the Bra to the Bomb: Forgotten Women and Their Unforgettable Ideas*. New York: Morrow, 1988.

WALL STREET

Wall Street, in the broadest sense, refers to the financial epicenter of all business and banking in the United States. Not only is Wall Street synonymous with U.S. financial interests, but also is an international symbol of financial power. Wall Street is an umbrella term encompassing the New York Stock Exchange (NYSE), the American Stock Exchange (Amex), the

The New York Stock Exchange, on Wall Street in New York City, in December, 1997. Despite the continuous changes in the market, the U.S. stock market, remains an international pulse of the world's economic status.

over-the-counter market called the National Association of Securities Dealers (NASD) and its automated quotation system (NASDAQ). It also includes bond markets, commodity futures markets, and various markets throughout the United States such as those in Chicago, Philadelphia, and Kansas City. In its physical sense, Wall Street, a street on the south tip of Manhattan Island in New York City, forms a triangular block with Broad and New streets, location of the nation's exchanges plus many commercial banks and business offices.

The name Wall Street derived from an early road located alongside a wall or stockade built across lower Manhattan in 1653 to protect a small Dutch colony. Local merchants and traders gathered on street corners and coffeehouses around Wall Street to buy and sell shares and loans (bonds), collectively known as securities. Although crude, this early trading set precedents which underlie American market practice for the next two hundred years.

In 1792, meeting under the famous buttonwood tree at 68 Wall Street, traders agreed to a formal organization or exchange for buying and selling shares and loans. In 1817 many of the same dealers agreed to organize into the New York Stock and Exchange Board. Early securities listed on the Exchange were U.S. government bonds and a few stocks of banks and insurance companies. Stocks and bonds not traded on the new Exchange were traded by curbstone brokers congregated outside the Exchange. These curbstone brokers were the predecessors of the American Stock Exchange and over-the-counter market. Industrial issues and railroad stocks and bonds appeared on the Exchange in the 1830s and 1840s. By the 1840s foreign capital became a major factor influencing American business expansion. Foreign bankers maintained offices on Wall Street as did domestic commercial banks, business corporations, insurance companies, and commodity exchanges for coffee, agricultural products, and metals.

Wall Street traders operated entirely free of regulation leading to unscrupulous practices by robber barons such as Jay Gould, Cornelius ''Commodore'' Vanderbilt, Andrew Carnegie, John D. Rockefeller, and J.P. Morgan. Consolidation of U.S. industry into immense trusts between 1880 and 1910 provided Wall Street's largest listed firms. Following the stock market crash of 1929, the Securities Exchange Act of 1934 established the Securities and Exchange Commission to protect people investing money in securities and to enforce federal laws governing trading practices. The modern era of Wall Street finance began in the 1950's. Individual investors began entering the market and all purpose securities firms serving all types of clients changed the face of Wall Street.

***See also:* Investment, New York Stock Exchange, Securities and Exchange Commission**

WALL STREET JOURNAL

The *Wall Street Journal,* published coast to coast, is the authoritative source for tracking business, financial, and economic news in the United States. With the largest daily circulation of any newspaper in the United States, the *Journal* is the nation's most influential newspaper. Dow Jones & Company owns and publishes the *Journal.*

The *Journal,* published daily on weekdays except holidays, is organized into three sections: Page One, Marketplace, and Money & Investing. On Friday a fourth section, Weekend Journal, is added. The *Journal*'s unique presentation is a six column style with no big headlines. Page One includes the legendary, ''What's News,'' in columns two and three. Under the subheadings of ''Business and Finance'' and ''World Wide'' are brief summaries of major economic news items and summaries of national and worldwide events. More in-depth coverage is found inside the section. Page One presents all the news in a tight, quick-read format with the same types of information found consistently in the same places. Section two, Marketplace, focuses on the impact of business on readers' careers and families, and keeps readers abreast of new product development. Section three, Money & Investing, contains all the economic statistical data and also provides columns offering explanations, insight, and perspective on the markets. The Weekend Journal, introduced in 1998, is devoted to leisure, art, and entertainment.

In 1882 Charles Dow (1851–1902) and Edward Jones (1856–1920) founded Dow, Jones & Company on the premise that business news could be reported in a lively but level-headed, unslanted style. Dow, Jones operations depended entirely on reporters daily touring brokerage houses, banks, and offices, listening and taking notes. On July 8, 1889 the *Wall Street Journal* was born. As the U.S. economy grew, the *Journal* provided stable commentary reporting market developments, general financial movement, and business interests. Clarence W. Barron purchased Dow Jones in 1902 and for twenty-six years was its dynamic force. ''Casey'' Hogate, entrusted with its management in 1933, began ''What's News.'' Refuting the idea the *Journal* must reach only a specific regional constituency, Hogate, perceiving all businessmen throughout the United States as a single community, provided a single reliable source of competent and comprehensive information to them. Barney Kilgore, president of Dow, Jones & Company beginning in 1945, creatively fashioned not only a thorough newspaper but added conciseness and even humor to business, Washington, and world wide news. By the 1970s the *Journal* was the United States' most trusted newspaper. In 1980 it overtook the *New York Daily News* to become number one in circulation.

See also: **Charles Dow**

WALLACE, HENRY

Henry Wallace (1836–1916) was a pastor, farmer, agricultural publicist and editor who acted as a leading spokesperson for Midwestern farmers. He sought to educate farmers in applied science in order to prepare them for the technological advancements of the nineteenth and twentieth centuries. This dramatically changed agricultural production in the United States, and Wallace's influence spread to the level of the federal government. He served on several commissions for President Theodore Roosevelt (1858–1919) and also impressed his views about agricultural development upon his family; his son and grandson continued his work in shaping U.S. agricultural policies.

According to biographer Richard S. Kirkendall, Henry Wallace ''was the first in an American line of Henry Wallaces who rose to prominence in Iowa and the United States'' (*Uncle Henry: A Documentary Profile of the First Henry Wallace*, 1993). Wallace was born on March 19, 1836, on a farm outside West Newton, Pennsylvania. His family was a hardworking, religious Scotch-Irish family of farmers. Wallace graduated from Jefferson College, Pennsylvania, in 1859. Although his roots were in agriculture Wallace chose to continue his education in theology at Allegheny Seminary in Pennsylvania, and Monmouth College in Illinois. He was ordained as a Presbyterian minister and served as a Union chaplain during the American Civil War (1861–1865). He then worked as a pastor for various churches in Illinois and Iowa until he retired from the ministry in 1877 due to health reasons.

In 1877 Wallace moved to Winterset, Iowa, and returned to the family farming business. He combined the skills he had learned as a preacher with his farming background and soon became the local spokesperson for farming issues. Though Wallace gave up the pulpit he found other ways to preach, namely through the press. He became involved in editorial work for local farm papers and eventually took partial ownership in the *Iowa Homestead*. In 1895 Wallace and his two sons established a family paper called *Wallaces' Farmer*. The paper became Wallace's forum to promote agricultural interests.

[T]HE VERY PERMANENCE OF OUR REPUBLIC WILL DEPEND ON THE DEVELOPMENT OF THE MANHOOD OF THE FARM.

Henry Wallace, presidential address to the National Conservation Congress, September 25, 1911

Henry Wallace was a man who respected traditions, especially religious and agrarian traditions. He also held a deep appreciation for modernization, above all in the form of applied science. Wallace saw agrarianism and scientific agriculture as complementary rather than contradictory. Other intellectuals of his time saw technology as a threat that would replace humans with machines. Wallace saw it as a means to improve the agrarian way of life; science would improve the quality of farming production rather than replace farmers. This would make farming a more rewarding and prestigious occupation. It would encourage farmers to remain on the land instead of fleeing to the cities. Wallace spent nearly four decades of his life attempting to persuade farmers to change their ways of thinking because he wanted them to see the advantages technology had to offer farming.

Wallace also believed that industrialization was a positive movement for farmers, but he argued that farmers would have to keep up with scientific advancements in order to survive in an industrial world. They had to learn how to work like business people. They also had to organize in order to protect their interests, just as the urban workers were organizing labor unions in the cities. To this end Wallace participated in agricultural organizations such as the Farmers' Protective Association, the Iowa State Improved Stock-Breeders' Association, and the Farmers' Alliance.

Wallace used his news writing and other publications to promote his ideas and to educate farmers. He wrote technical works about farming, such as *Clover Culture* (1892), *Clover Farming* (1898), and *The Skim Milk Calf* (1900). He also wrote two volumes on popular education, *Uncle Henry's Letters to the Farm Boy* (1897) and *Letters to the Farm Folks* (1915). He also wrote a memoir called *Uncle Henry's Own Story of His Life: Personal Reminiscences*, which was published after his death.

Wallace's views on U.S. agriculture reached the ears of politicians at the federal level. Wallace became a leader in the agricultural world. He represented the interests of the United States government on several occasions. In 1891 Wallace was asked to travel to Europe to investigate flax growing for the United States Department of Agriculture. In 1908 President Theodore Roosevelt appointed Wallace a member of the Country Life Commission, and two years later he became president of the National Conservation Commission. In 1913 Wallace returned to Europe on behalf of the government to study farm conditions in Britain. This was his final trip before his death in 1916.

Wallace's legacy in U.S. agricultural development continued for two generations after his death. His oldest son, Henry Cantwell Wallace, became President Warren Harding's (1921–1923) Secretary of Agriculture, and his oldest grandson, Henry Agard Wallace, became President Franklin D. Roosevelt's (1933–1945) first Secretary of Agriculture and second vice president. Both men were strongly influenced by the ideas of the first Henry Wallace, especially with respect to the importance of agricultural science in American farm life.

***See also:* Agricultural Equipment Industry, Agriculture Industry, Farmers' Alliance, Government Farm Policy**

FURTHER READING

Ferlegen, Lou, ed. *Agriculture and National Development: Views on the Nineteenth Century.* Ames: Iowa State University Press, 1990.

Kirkendall, Richard Stewart. *Uncle Henry: A Documentary Profile of the First Henry Wallace.* Ames: Iowa State University Press, 1993.

Lord, Russell. *The Wallaces of Iowa.* Boston: Houghton Mifflin, 1947.

Wallace, Henry Agard. *The Reminiscences of Henry Agard Wallace.* Glen Rock, NJ: Microfilming Corporation of America, 1977.

Winters, Donald L. *Henry Cantwell Wallace, as Secretary of Agriculture, 1921–1924.* Illinois: University of Illinois Press, 1970.

WALTON, SAM MOORE

Sam Walton (1918–1992) redefined the shopping experience for residents living in rural areas throughout the United States by opening a chain of Wal-Mart discount stores in towns previously served only by hardware and five-and-dime stores. His strategy of monopolizing the discount shopping market in rural areas made his stores the largest retail chain in the United States.

Sam Moore Walton was born to Thomas and Nancy Walton in Kingfisher, Oklahoma, on March 29, 1918, the eldest of two boys. His father, a farm-mortgage banker, moved his family to Missouri, where they lived in a succession of rural communities before settling in the medium-sized university town of Colombia. His father believed in saving money, so when the bottom fell out of the economy his family suffered less during the Great Depression (1929–1939) than did many of their neighbors.

Walton financed his education at the University of Missouri with money earned from a newspaper route. He graduated with a degree in economics in 1940. He took his first retailing job at a J.C. Penney store in Des Moines, Iowa, where he was a sales trainee. That job, however, was short-lived, as Walton was drafted in early 1942 as a communications officer in the Army Intelligence Corps, an assignment that enabled him to remain stateside for the duration of World War II (1939–1945). While in the service, he married Helen Robson on February 14, 1943. The couple had four children.

The retail industry seemed a natural place for Walton to make his mark, but he had no interest in being in someone's employ. In 1945, with a borrowed $25,000, he and his brother James opened a five-and-dime store called Ben Franklin in Newport, Arkansas. Walton was forced to move five years later when his landlord refused to renew the store's lease. He traveled across the state to Bentonville, which became headquarters to the Wal-Mart empire.

Walton started having doubts about the future of dime stores and, in the 1950s, started paying close attention to larger chains like K Mart and Zayre. These retailing giants avoided rural areas, preferring to place their stores in suburban or urban locations. In 1962 Walton and his brother opened the first Wal-Mart outlet in Rogers, Arkansas, about five miles from Bentonville. The two brothers thought large stores could be successful in small towns.

From the beginning the Wal-Mart concept was to join a friendly, general-store atmosphere with high-quality name brand merchandise at low prices. The idea slowly caught on. The stores were simple and basic, and many resembled barns, with merchandise overflowing from plastic bins or metal racks. Along with a top management team, Walton visited a half-dozen to a dozen Wal-Mart stores every week. At one store he might solicit suggestions on how yard goods could sell faster flat-folded than on bolts, or he might give advice on increasing deliveries of automotive supplies. At all of his stores he gave reassuring speeches that kept employees striving for improvement and higher sales.

By 1970, the year Walton took the company public, there were about 25 Wal-Mart stores. By 1972 the chain had more than doubled to 64 stores with sales of $125 million. The rate of growth was phenomenal and continued to improve under Walton's leadership. In 1983 *Forbes* magazine estimated Walton's net worth to be $2.1 billion, making him the second richest person in the United States behind oil magnate Gordon P. Getty. At that time Walton decided to explore another path, and he opened stores in medium-sized cities such as Little Rock, Arkansas; Springfield, Missouri; and Shreveport, Louisiana. He also opened stores in the suburbs of several large cities including Kansas City, Missouri, and Dallas, Texas. The strategy seemed to work, and by 1987 Wal-Mart had 1,108 stores located from Colorado to Virginia, with sales of over $20 billion. By 1989 there were 1,326 stores with sales of almost $26 billion.

Walton continued to try innovative ways to attract new customers. In April 1983 he launched the first Sam's Wholesale Club, which was aimed at small-business owners and others who wanted to buy bulk merchandise. The warehouses employed only a few laborers, and the goods were priced just eight to ten percent over cost. By 1991 there were over 200 Sam's Clubs in the United States. In December 1987 he introduced another new retailing concept with the opening of the first Hypermart USA store in Garland, Texas. Encompassing some 220,000 square feet of retail space, about four times the size of the standard Wal-Mart store, these "malls without walls" devote an almost equal amount of space to both food and non-food products. Wal-Mart Supercenters, another Walton innovation, have both a supermarket and a regular Wal-Mart under the same roof.

Wal-Mart is a success story that redefined the way retailers viewed growth markets. Walton showed the world that consumers, no matter where they lived, preferred the variety and discount pricing that his chain offered. Walton was constantly searching for ways to better serve his customers. He was always walking around competitor's stores to educate himself. He was not above getting down on his hands and knees to look under display cabinets. "Anyone willing to work hard, study the business, and apply the best principles can do well," Walton said in the *New York Times*.

Walton's business success has impacted Bentonville, Arkansas, home to the Wal-Mart Corporation. Walton and his wife have built tennis courts, a recreation hall for senior citizens, a day care center, a library, an athletic center, and a health club in Bentonville. Walton, or "Mr. Sam," as some called him, was unpretentious, and he did not believe in company perks like limousines.

Despite all of the success, Walton and his chain of discount stores were not without their detractors. Chief among them were the small town merchants who were ultimately driven out of business by the Wal-Mart stores. They knew they could not compete with the low prices and extensive variety of merchandise.

Regardless, Walton revolutionized the concept of discount stores in the United States and reshaped consumer shopping patterns. Without a doubt Walton was the epitome of modern retailing, adapting to contemporary demographic trends. He built his empire not in the large urban areas of the North, East, and West—the politically and economically dominant regions of the first two-thirds of the twentieth century—but in the South and Midwest and the former depressed and neglected regions of the nation. He pioneered retailing where others did not want to go, and because of his willingness to go to uncharted areas he reaped astounding financial benefits which propelled him to one of the world's richest and most respected businessmen of his time. Sam Walton's legacy continues. Five years after his death, Wal-Mart had grown to over 2,300 stores with annual revenues of $104.8 billion.

Among the honors Walton received in his lifetime were the Gold Winner in *Financial World*'s CEO rating, 1986; National Retail Merchants Association's gold medal for the most distinguished retailing performance of the year, 1988; *Financial World's* CEO of the Decade, 1989; *U.S. News and World Report's* Excellence Award in Business, 1990; and *Advertising Age's* Adman of the Year Award, 1991. The Presidential Medal of Freedom from President George Bush (1989–1993) in 1992 was the award that Walton deemed "the highlight of my entire career." Even though he was in a wheelchair Walton led his sales associates in a rousing Wal-Mart cheer. He died on March 29, 1992, of bone cancer at age 74, three weeks after receiving the medal from Bush.

See also: **Chain Store, Retail Industry, Wal-Mart**

FURTHER READING

Byers, Paula K., and Suzanne M. Bourgoin, eds. *Encyclopedia of World Biography*. Detroit: Gale Research, 1998, s.v. "Walton, Sam."

Ortega, Bob. *In Sam We Trust: The Untold Story of Sam Walton and How Wal-Mart is Devouring America*. New York: Times Business, 1998.

Trimble, Vance H. *Sam Walton*. New York: Dutton, 1990.

Walton, Sam. *The Inside Story of America's Richest Man*. New York: Dutton, 1990.

———. *Made in America*. New York: Doubleday, 1992.

WAMPUM

Wampum were beads or disks of polished mollusk shells that were used as money by the Native Americans. The word is a shortened form of *wampumpeag,* an Algonquin word meaning "white string of beads." Wampum was used primarily by the Eastern Woodlands Indians, who came into contact with the European settlers during the early 1600s. The colonists adopted wampum as money, and helped broaden its circulation. English fur traders, for example, sold their wares to coastal Indians in exchange for wampum; as the fur traders moved inland, they used wampum as exchange with other tribes, such as those of the Great Plains. Like gold or silver today, wampum was valued not only as a form of money but also as decoration. The white or purple shell beads were made into necklaces, woven into belts, and sewn to clothing. After treaties were signed, wampum belts were sometimes exchanged as a gesture of goodwill and continued peace. As foreign coinage and colonial coinage came into circulation, the use of wampum as money declined during the mid- to late-1600s.

See also: **New Netherlands, Pieces of Eight**

WAR AND COMMERCIAL INDEPENDENCE, 1790-1815 (*OVERVIEW*)

Between 1790 and 1815 the United States struggled to be taken seriously as an international political and economic power, even as rapid internal growth began to change the character of the nation. When George Washington (1789–1797) was inaugurated as the first U.S. president in 1789, the United States was still dealing with the tremendous economic problems left by the American Revolution (1775–1783). U.S. citizens were still trying to define what kind of nation theirs would be. Over the next 25 years economic changes enriched U.S. society, influenced domestic politics, and eventually led the country back into war with Great Britain.

In 1790 the United States was overwhelmingly a farming society. Small, independent family farms dominated New England and the Mid-Atlantic states, while cities like New York and Philadelphia were growing into large, important trade centers. Compared to the North an even greater proportion of the southern population lived on farms. One important difference between the North and South was that southern agriculture was marked by the institution of slavery, which was on its way to being outlawed in the northern states. Although the Constitution stipulated that the slave trade would come to an end in 1808, as that date came and went African slaves were becoming seemingly indispensable, especially for the cultivation of tobacco, rice, and cotton. Southern plantation owners used slavery to produce these staple commodities that sold at home and abroad for large profits. A majority of southern whites owned no slaves, but the entire southern economy and society were influenced by the institution of slavery.

By the end of the War of 1812 . . . Though the vast majority of U.S. citizens still lived on farms, they probably thought more about the economic world beyond their homes than their parents had. The people in the United States had witnessed the growth of a market economy over the previous 25 years. Although there were some ominous signs like increasing exploitation of slavery and the intractability of urban poverty, the country was poised to become a real economic and industrial power in the nineteenth century.

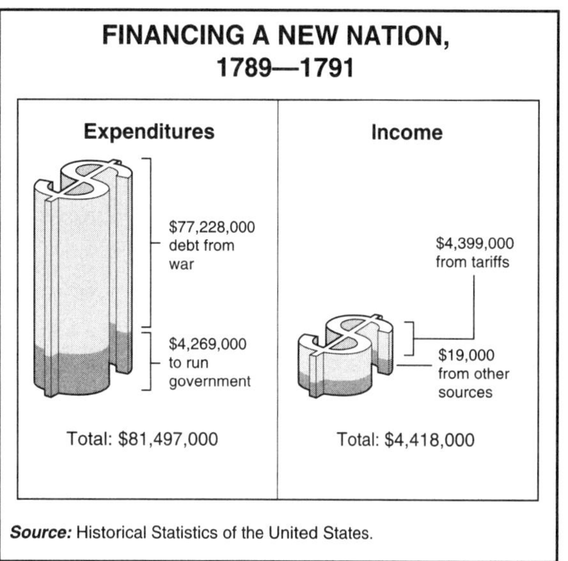

Upon becoming a new nation, the U.S. faced a serious financial crisis, the nation's expenditures far exceeding revenues.

When George Washington took office, one of his first tasks was to deal with economic problems that had plagued the country throughout the 1780s. The leading figure in the reconstruction of the national economy was Secretary of the Treasury Alexander Hamilton (1789–1795), who was a prominent New York lawyer and a brilliant adviser to Washington. Hamilton was an exponent of turning the agrarian U.S. into a modern commercial state. After Congress put the country on firmer financial footing in 1789 by passing a series of import taxes that would provide a steady stream of revenue and protect U.S.-made goods from foreign competition, Hamilton proposed a comprehensive package of financial measures to further develop the national economy.

In January 1790 Hamilton issued a ''Report on Public Credit,'' in which he proposed that the federal government assume the state debts left over from the Revolution and pay off all foreign and domestic national debts at face value. Congress agreed to pay $11 million in foreign debts and to repay all wartime investment certificates in full, despite the fact that many original investors had sold their certificates to financial speculators since the war. Following six months of debate in which the southern states had agreed to the deal even though they had already gone further towards paying off their debts, Congress approved the proposal to assume state debts.

In his Second Report on Public Credit, (December 1790) Hamilton also proposed the creation of the Bank of the United States. This proposal proved to be even more controversial than his First Report on Public Credit. The bank, which was to be backed by both public and private stockholders, faced opposition from Secretary of State Thomas Jefferson (1743–1826) and James Madison (1751–1836). The critics argued on the floor of Congress that the bank was an institution more in keeping with monarchy than U.S. democracy. Opponents of the bank claimed it would be an unconstitutional abuse of central government power and that the Constitution did not specifically give the federal government the power to create such an institution. Congress reluctantly passed authorization anyway, and the bank opened in 1791.

Hamilton's proposals exposed fundamental differences in how U.S. politicians perceived the national economy. Alexander Hamilton wanted to use federal government power to expand the economy. His ''Report on Manufactures,'' (December 1791) recommended that the economy be increasingly based on trade and manufacturing, and protected by high tariffs. Jefferson, Madison, and their supporters thought that a manufacturing economy was bound to expose U.S. society to moral and political decay and corruption—significant concerns for the new nation. Jefferson believed that farmers were ''the chosen people of God'' and that decentralized agriculture would provide the most ''virtuous'' basis for U.S. government. Jefferson envisioned a society led by independent land-owning farmers, and Hamilton placed his hopes in trade and finance. Though Congress accepted many of Hamilton's economic proposals in 1792, and though his programs restored the country to remarkable financial health, debate surrounding the role of central government, power, and the economy in the United States would continue for decades.

Beyond the political debates, the economic life of average U.S. citizens began to change during the 1790s. Pioneers were pushing westward and looking for new land, and by 1800 500,000 settlers were living west of the Appalachian Mountains. Congress supported integrating western lands into the United States—the Northwest Ordinance (re-authorized in 1789) outlined the process for the Northwest Territory to be broken down into states. In addition southern territories joined the Union: Kentucky and Tennessee became states in 1792 and 1796, respectively.

Since many westerners were looking for land and economic opportunity, their presence often brought them into hostile contact with Indian nations determined to resist the United States' westward encroachment. Though the Northwest Ordinance specified that Indian land treaties had to be respected, many U.S. migrants ignored this provision and violence was often the result. In the early 1790s Congress deployed the first "peacetime" U.S. army to battle against an Indian confederacy led by Miami chief Little Turtle, who fought to maintain native land rights. Little Turtle's forces were defeated in 1794 after several years of successful resistance. The pattern of conflict over land and natural resources was established.

Many of the U.S. citizens who moved to the west in the 1790s were becoming involved in the money economy. Rather than growing, trapping, shooting or fishing for food and other necessities, the sale of labor or goods gradually changed from within the previous frontier subsistence and barter economy. Instead of merely producing enough product to live on or to trade with neighboring farmers, U.S. farmers slowly began to produce surplus goods to sell for cash. The growing availability of paper money combined with a greater demand for "store-bought" goods. As the market opened up more cash and products were available. Homesteaders used surplus profits from their farming to buy non-essentials. Westerners raised extra livestock and produced whiskey that they hoped to trade back east. Mid-Atlantic farm women produced surplus butter and hen eggs that they sold to neighbors or at produce markets in Philadelphia, New York, or at country cross-roads for cash. Domestic trade was on the rise everywhere.

The increased commercial activity put pressure on the federal government to enforce tax laws and support trade. In 1794 the government cracked down on western Pennsylvanians who violently resisted paying taxes on whiskey (which they sometimes used as a form of currency, since distilled alcohol was more convenient and portable than the bushels of corn from which it was derived). The "Whiskey Rebellion" that ensued was repressed without loss of life by Washington, Hamilton, and 12,000 militia.

Western farmers caught up in the "market revolution" wanted to use the Mississippi River (which was then controlled by Spain) to establish water-trade routes to New Orleans—and, thence, to the world market. U.S. envoy Thomas Pinckney negotiated a treaty with Spain in 1795 that allowed U.S. citizens free access to the Mississippi River. Only about 20 percent of U.S. citizens were engaged in commercial farming by 1820, but their influence exceeded their numbers.

In addition to commercial farming, manufacturing was also on the rise during the 1790s. Urban artisans produced manufactured goods, like shoes, that appealed to farmers in the interior. Merchants who financed and organized this form of "putting out" production managed to increase their profits, even before mechanization took over. Artisan families in Lynn, Massachusetts, for example, produced 400,000 pairs of hand-sewn shoes in 1800. Though most manufacturing was still manual, waterpower fueled the beginnings of mechanization that would push industry forward in the nineteenth century. In 1790 Samuel Slater, Moses Brown, and William Almy harnessed the power of the Blackstone River and used stolen British industrial plans to open the first mechanized textile mill in the United States in Pawtucket, Rhode Island.

Increased agricultural production, manufacturing, and domestic trade characterized the Atlantic economies in the 1790s, not just the U.S. Foreign trade rose dramatically. In 1794, over the objections of Thomas Jefferson and his supporters (who were pro-French), George Washington declared the U.S. neutral in the French wars with the European monarchies. U.S. merchants could trade simultaneously with the French and British. U.S. neutrality during the French Revolution and the Napoleonic Wars initially boosted the shipping and export businesses. At first the U.S. merchant fleet could sail through French and British waters without coming under attack.

Political leaders in the U.S. were divided over whether the United States should remain neutral in the wars. Washington's successor, John Adams, threatened to engage the country in an undeclared war with France in 1798 but trade continued. As ship-building improved, merchants along the eastern seaboard ranged farther and even began to trade in China and North Africa. U.S. exports included both manufactured and agricultural goods, and cotton and cloth exports escalated after the invention of the cotton gin in 1793. Total U.S. export revenue rose from $33 million in 1794 to $94 million in 1801 and taxed imports increased even more sharply over the same period.

In 1800 Thomas Jefferson (1801–1809), then head of the Democratic Republican Party, was elected President. Though the campaign had been bitter, this peaceful transfer of power supposedly signaled an end to Hamiliton's "federalist" brand of centralized government and financial power. The agrarian Jefferson was less eager than Hamilton to encourage banking and manufacturing and more interested in paying off the national debt. However Jefferson did seem to put aside his scorn for government programs in 1803 when he negotiated the purchase of the Louisiana Territory from France for $15 million. In accomplishing this momentous act (which doubled the size of the U.S.), Jefferson did what he accused Hamilton of doing: he gave the central government powers (in this case the power to annex additional land) that were not mentioned in the Constitution.

And even Jefferson could not ignore the fact that increased foreign trade required military protection. The North African Barbary States were in the habit of preying upon foreign shipping. They would stop and board ships, demand tribute, and take sailors hostage for random. Although the Constitution specifically gave the power to make war to the Congress, Jefferson sent the American Navy to attack Tripoli and other North African states. Although it turned out to be a drawn-out affair, the United States triumphed in a series of naval engagements off the coast of Tripoli between 1801 and 1805 and kept the lines of trade open. The fact that he had to stretch the Constitution to do that does not make him a traitor to his earlier states' rights politics. It just means that Hamilton's vision of a powerful central government pursuing programs that enhanced the economic health of the country would prove to have an important place in the future of the nation

Far more difficult to solve were the problems caused by the Napoleonic wars. In 1803 the wars between France and England resumed with a vengeance, and U.S. citizens were increasingly pulled into the hostilities as they tried to trade with both sides and to profit from the re-export trade. The French and British imposed naval blockades on one another, meaning that they would try to block all goods from entering each other's countries by sea. U.S. shippers who ignored the blockades faced capture (especially in the West Indies). Since being a sailor in the British Navy was possibly the worst job that a free man could have in the nineteenth century, many seamen deserted the British Navy. When the British came upon a U.S. merchant vessel they frequently boarded the ship and "impressed" a portion of its crew into service. In the process, an estimated 6,000 sailors with U.S. citizenship were impressed (kidnapped) into the British Navy between 1803 and 1812.

The question facing the U.S. government was how to respond to the French and British aggression. Congress passed a Non-Importation Act in 1806 that imposed a boycott on British imports, a strategy of political resistance that had been tried before the American Revolution. That same year, Jefferson's ministers negotiated the Monroe-Pinckney Treaty with Great Britain that was supposed to solve trade problems and the impressment of U.S. sailors. However Jefferson refused to submit the treaty to Congress for ratification because he felt the final terms favored the British too much. The British raised the stakes in June, 1807, when the *H.M.S. Leopard* fired on the U.S. ship *Chesapeake* after the British unsuccessfully tried to impress some of the Chesapeake's U.S. sailors. The British did not back down from its policy of impressment, and they imposed even harsher trade restrictions on U.S. ships.

Despite the British hostility, Jefferson remained committed to solving the problems through commercial measures rather than military action. In 1807 he urged Congress to pass an embargo that would totally ban all French and British exports and imports. Congress repealed the Embargo in 1809, but followed it with other sanctions—the Non-Intercourse Act (1809) and Macon's Bill, Number Two (1810). James Madison (1809–1817), elected President in 1808, tried to stay true to Jefferson's vision of economic resistance, but these measures did nothing more than ruin the U.S. economy, especially in the Northeast which depended more on trade and shipbuilding. The French and British paid little attention to the embargoes and sanctions, and the huge drop in U.S. exports and imports sent the United States into an economic depression.

Finally in 1812 a group of western and southern Democratic Republicans in Congress convinced their colleagues that economic sanctions were not working, and the United States declared war on Great Britain. The War of 1812 (1812–1814) established that the United States would not allow trade interference, but its economic effects were mixed. The war raged for three years with few U.S. military successes, and Congress was hesitant to raise taxes to pay for militia, army, and navy forces. The British burned the capital at Washington DC in 1814. In the midst of the war with Great Britain, U.S. forces defeated the Creek Indians and killed Tecumseh, an Indian leader who had united many tribes in resistance to U.S. expansion. Both the defeat of the Creek and the death of Tecumseh signaled the likelihood that westward expansion would continue after the war.

The war also encouraged the growth of domestic manufacturing—new, larger textile mills and factories sprang up all over the Northeast to replace unavailable foreign goods. By the end of the War of 1812 the United States had proven that it was able to defend itself, even though it had few militarily memorable moments in the war. Though the vast majority of U.S. citizens still lived on farms, they probably thought more about the economic world beyond their homes than their parents had. The people in the United States had witnessed the growth of a market economy over the previous 25 years. Although there were some ominous signs like increasing exploitation of slavery and the intractability of urban poverty, the country was poised to become a real economic and industrial power in the nineteenth century. A U.S. economy, based both on farming and commerce, had been firmly established.

***See also:* Embargo, Alexander Hamilton, Thomas Jefferson, Louisiana Purchase, War of 1812**

FURTHER READING

Appleby, Joyce. *Capitalism and a New Social Order: The Republican Vision of the 1790s.* New York: New York University Press, 1984.

Hickey, Donald. *The War of 1812: A Forgotten Conflict.* Urbana, IL: University of Illinois Press, 1989.

Jensen, Joan. *Loosening the Bonds: Mid-Atlantic Farm Women, 1750–1850.* New Haven, CT: Yale University Press, 1986.

Kulikoff, Allan. *The Agrarian Origins of American Capitalism.* Charlottesville, VA: University Press of Virginia, 1992.

McCoy, Drew. *The Elusive Republic: Political Economy in Jeffersonian America.* Chapel Hill, NC: University of North Carolina Press, 1980.

WAR AND THE ECONOMY *(ISSUE)*

Perhaps no other single activity has had a greater impact on the economy of the United States than war. But how war affected the economy of the nation changed drastically between the nineteenth and twentieth centuries. During the late eighteenth and nineteenth century, war sometimes obstructed and other times invigorated the national economy. But in the twentieth century war provided a consistent impetus for prosperity, at the same time that it tied the U.S. economy closer and more intricately to a global market, a world alliance, and a defense industry.

For many U.S citizens independence from Britain didn't provide all the solutions it appeared to have promised. For some it only made things worse. The British Navigation Acts, although no longer restricting trade outside the Empire, were now applied against U.S. merchants who wished to trade inside the Empire. Moreover the mercantilist regulations of other European countries were often more stringent than the British laws had been. When the war ended the English proceeded to "dump" low-priced goods on the still infant American industries which had began to establish themselves during the years when the British Navy blockaded American ports. War-born industries found it impossible to compete against England's more mature industrial efficiency and economies of scale. Cheap British manufactured goods began reappearing on the U.S. market and the protection that U.S. industries had enjoyed due to trade disruptions during the war disappeared. Trade came to a standstill, domestic prices fell; farm produce also sold at the lower prices; consequently, unemployment rose sharply among urban and rural laborers.

In 1790 Secretary of the Treasury, Alexander Hamilton (1789–1795), convinced Congress to assume the debts incurred by the individual states during and after the American Revolution (1775–1783). According to Hamilton, this plan would bind wealthy citizens to the new federal government, establish it as a good credit risk internationally, and provide a compelling rationale for an immediate and effective federal tax system. The funding and assumption of this enormous debt would serve several purposes. If the debt were gathered together as the sole responsibility of the federal government, the credit of the nation would be restored at home and abroad. As capital came out of hiding, interest rates would be lowered. With lower interest rates investments in land, commerce, and industry would increase, and capital would multiply along with wages and jobs. All that would then be required was a national bank to provide internal control of finances and national programs to stimulate commerce and industry within the nation.

The outcome of the American Civil War (1861–1865) was determined in large part by the economic disparity between the two regions in their manpower and their industrial resources. In 1860 the North had a population of about 19.5 million to the South's 11 million, about four million of which were slaves. Estimates placed the size of the northern armies at about 1.5 million to the Confederacy's nine hundred thousand. But the system of volunteers, even with the offer of bounties, proved to be unreliable to furnish the

WAR AND THE U.S. ECONOMY
(in millions of dollars)

War	Estimated total war costs	Original war costs	Total costs to1970 of veterens' benefits	Total estimated interest payments on war loans
Vietnam Conflict	352,000	110,000	2,461	22,000
Korean Conflict	164,000	54,000	15,016	11,000
World War II	664,000	288,000	87,445	86,000
World War I	112,000	26,000	45,585	11,000
Spanish-American War	6,460	400	5,436	60
Civil War (Union only)	12,952	3,200	8,570	1,172
Mexican War	147	73	64	10
War of 1812	158	93	49	16
American Revolution	190	100	70	20

Source: Historical Statistics, pt. 2, series y849-903, p. 1140.

This table shows the cost of war to the U.S. Included are the benefits to veterans and interest payments. No other government act has had greater impact on the U.S. economy.

numbers needed to keep the armies up to strength and both the North and South were forced to use conscription.

An essential part of the war involved transportation of men and material. In 1859 the North had about 21,900 miles of railroads to the South's 6,600. In the North railroads connected the agricultural and manufacturing centers, but in the South railroads were inadequate in quality and lacked direct connections between major cities, thus there were problems getting supplies to where they were needed. The federal government also controlled the Navy and most of the merchant marine, which placed the South at a disadvantage in purchasing needed goods abroad and selling surplus agricultural products in foreign markets. While the North had 90 percent of the nation's industrial capacity, the South's lack of a developed industrial base created serious problems in acquiring sufficient supplies of arms and ammunition. Food supplies for the army were an even greater problem than equipment. The South's poor transportation system failed to get needed food to the armies in the field.

Perhaps one of the most telling reasons for the South's inability to win its independence was its inadequate financial system. There were no significant financial institutions in the Confederacy. At the close of the war the South would still depend upon banks in the North and in England for loans to rebuild the southern economy. The predominantly agricultural economy made it difficult to raise taxes or large sums of money. The devastation of a four-year war fought mainly in the South made this even harder. The provisional government finally resorted to printing paper money, but the currency came to have so little value that people eventually turned to barter. Ultimately the South was unable to raise the capital it needed to support the war effort. And its inability to amass capital continued well after the war was over. Some observers likened the post-Civil War South to a colony of the North: low-wage labor was there in abundance, but capital was lacking. Some historians note the attempt of the South to build a ''New South'' with developing industry over the next thirty years. But for much of the South the Civil War probably set things back a generation.

Statistics also tell the story of the effect of the Civil War on the economies of the South and of the North. From the South, 258,000 men died in the war. The North lost more—362,000. Those that survived were frequently maimed for life and rendered incapable of supporting themselves. In several southern states, the busiest manufacturing industries for several years after the war were producing prosthetic devices, such as wooden legs, for the wounded. The South also lost much of its livestock as well as its farm implements. Most significantly, the South lost its slave labor force, variously estimated at around 4 billion dollars (more expensive than all the land in the South).

Whereas the Southern economy had suffered a major set-back as a result of the war, the North had continued to advance. One important feature of this advance in the North was that, when the South seceded, the Northern Republicans, now in control of the 37th

Congress, in 1862 proceeded to pass the elements of the Republican program that the southern Democrats in Congress had been impeding. The Homestead Act of 1862 provided free government land to farm families in the north and west. The Morrill Land Grant Act of 1862 set aside new money to build colleges for agriculture and industrial sciences. Subsidies for the transcontinental rail lines were also voted in, as was a National Banking Act to standardize the national currency. All of these measures pointed in the direction of a post-war program for farming, industrial expansion, and wage labor (as opposed to slavery). It was only through the Civil War that these advances were possible.

In the case of both the Spanish-American War (1898) and World War I (1914–1918) war now became a stimulus to economic development. World War I initially cost the United States government about $33 billion plus interest. But rather than hurting the domestic economy, the war effort strengthened and improved the United State's competitive position in the world. Farmers enjoyed boom years as agricultural prices rose and the international market for their products expanded. Real wages for blue-collar workers increased modestly and all sectors profited from the war. Wartime demands for industrial products raised profits for many companies. The DuPont Company's stock multiplied by 1600 percent between 1914 and 1918 and DuPont grew from a debtor company to one with a surplus of $68 million at the end of the war. Steel production reached twice its prewar level by 1917. The standardization effort during the war led to greater postwar industrial efficiency and production.

President Woodrow Wilson (1913–1921) did much to encourage the United State's changing role in the world economy. In Wilson's view free trade promoted both universal prosperity and universal peace and democracy. International commerce led to a strong domestic economy and exports were essential for continued U.S. economic growth. Wilson felt that restrictions on trade, such as tariffs and trade agreements, hindered efficiency and denied the natural cycle of the international economy. Wilson firmly believed that goodwill flowed along with goods and that commercial contacts were effective guarantors of peaceful relations among states.

The war almost instantly reversed the credit standing of the United States. The nation, by the war's end, held billions of dollars in European debt obligations and was the globe's greatest creditor as well as its greatest economic power. By forcing the Europeans to accept goods instead of loans, the Wilson administration guaranteed that the country would be banker, arsenal, and breadbasket to the Allies. World War I set the foundation for the prosperity of the twenties and some economists argue, the background for the Great Depression (1929–1939) as well.

The outbreak of World War II (1939–1945) began the United State's climb out of the depths of the Depression. U.S. businesses profited from increased orders for military and non-military goods by European nations engaged in the conflict. Industries such as steel sold war goods to all parties and reaped a handsome profit. Later as the Europeans ran short of cash, President Franklin D. Roosevelt (1933–1945) developed a policy of U.S. funding for allied purchases. The policy was announced as a means whereby the United States would become the "arsenal of democracy," and was designed to advance U.S. political and economic interests without involving the nation in war. But even policy supporters within the Roosevelt administration doubted that the United States could stay out of the conflict and they began preparing the United States for war. The government increased its purchases of military goods from private industry, spurring production and creating jobs.

Despite the Roosevelt administration's friendly attitude toward big business, an unregulated marketplace approach to the war economy was impossible. Shortages and allocations of vital raw materials required economic oversight and coordination. By executive order Roosevelt created a variety of new agencies to oversee mobilization. Among these agencies were the War Production Board (WPB), which coordinated war-related industries, and the Office of Price Administration (OPA), which set prices on thousands of items to control inflation. There was also the National War Labor Board (NWLB), which set wages, monitored working conditions, and, if necessary, seized industrial plants in the event of labor strife. Roosevelt also converted older New Deal agencies into wartime organizations. The Reconstruction Finance Corporation (RFC) made loans to small businesses and homeowners during the Depression. During World War II the RFC loaned money at excellent terms to industries expanding to meet wartime demand.

The administration's combination of private capitalism and public stimulus accomplished exactly what the government intended: it made the United States the largest arms manufacturer in world history. U.S. labor built nearly 300,000 airplanes, nearly 400,000 pieces of artillery, 47 million tons of artillery ammunition, 44 billion rounds of small arms ammo, 86,000 tanks, and 6,500 ships. Many of these planes, tanks, and ships were used in the European and Pacific theaters of war, often with Russian, British, or other Allied soldiers using them. Frequently the infusion of U.S.-made material proved decisive in battle.

At the end of the war U.S. business and the economy were radically different than they were before Pearl Harbor. U.S. citizens enjoyed unprecedented prosperity. Corporate profits had skyrocketed. In 1943 alone earnings jumped $2.1 million over the prewar level. Workers' wages on average doubled; they increased from almost $25 a week to $50 a week and many people earned hefty overtime bonuses. Even farm income increased an incredible 250 percent, despite the loss of nearly 800,000 agricultural workers during the war.

The character of the economy also changed due to war. Despite administration attempts to distribute the benefits of government contracts broadly, 71 percent of all contracts went to the 100 largest U.S. corporations. By the end of 1942 there were 300,000 fewer small companies than there had been before the war, and fewer small farms. Labor also got bigger. The total labor force increased by 22 percent during the war, which along with the draft eliminated unemployment. Labor unions grew from 10.5 million members in 1939 to 14.75 million members in 1945 and they intended to make up for wages lost due to the "wage freeze" of the war years. As in the case of the post-World War I strike wave in 1919, there was a tremendous strike upheaval in 1945 and 1946.

An acknowledged power in the U.S. marketplace, big labor insured that many of the wage and benefit gains of the war years would continue into the next decades. Moreover because of wartime labor shortages the workforce was more diverse than before. Almost 60 percent of women in the United States were employed during the war. Industry, which for so long had closed its doors to African Americans, during the war employed 1.2 million. Sixty thousand African Americans migrated to Detroit alone during the war. The one problem with all this prosperity was that it was purchased with government deficits justified by the pressure of war.

The new administration under President Harry S. Truman (1945–1953) was faced with a significant economic problem: how to maintain wartime prosperity without a war. But the potential military confrontation with the Soviet Union not only cemented U.S. economic ties with Western Europe and increased U.S. trade, it also provided Truman with the perfect solution—a viable rationale for increased military expenditures. By the end of the 1940s, prosperity was insured by the twin forces of expansive U.S. trade and the growth of what President Dwight D. Eisenhower (1953–1961) would later term "the military industrial complex."

See also: **Civil War, (Economic Causes of), Civil War (Economic Impact of), Economic Development (Federal Involvement in), Military-Industrial Complex)**

FURTHER READING

Fearon, Peter. *War, Prosperity and Depression: The U.S. Economy 1917–1945*. Lawrence: University Press of Kansas, 1987.

Higgs, Robert, ed. *Arms, Politics, and the Economy: Historical and Contemporary Perspectives*. New York: Holmes and Meier, 1990.

Kennedy, David M. *Over Here: The First World War and American Society*. New York: Oxford University Press, 1980.

Nelson, Donald. *Arsenal of Democracy: The Story of American War Production*. New York: Harcourt, Brace, 1946.

Vatter, Harold G. *The U.S. Economy in World War II*. New York: Columbia University Press, 1985.

WAR INDUSTRIES BOARD (WIB)

Participation in World War I (1914–1918) required not only the mobilization of people, but of materials in the United States. The country entered the conflict on April 6, 1917, when Congress declared war on Germany, and the United States joined the Allied nations (France, Great Britain, Russia, Serbia, and twenty other nations, including Japan) to fight the Central Powers (Austria-Hungary, Germany, the Ottoman Empire, and Bulgaria). The U.S. war effort demanded that industry join with the federal government to ensure an adequate flow of supplies to the front and to keep things moving smoothly on the home front. President Woodrow Wilson (1913–1921) declared that "it is not an army that we must shape and train for war, it is a nation." Of all the committees and agencies that were established to advise and oversee the production and movement of materials, raw and finished, the most important was the War Industries Board (WIB), which, for the duration of the war, ran the nation's economy.

Formed in July 1917, the WIB was originally led by F.A. Scott (1873–1949); he resigned under the enormous pressure of the job. Succeeded by Daniel Willard (1861–1942), he too resigned, complaining of the War Industries Board's lack of power. In 1918 Wilson secured broader authority for the board when Congress passed the Overman Act. The president tapped American businessman Bernard Baruch (1870–1965), who was then serving on the Allied Purchasing Commission, to head the WIB.

IT IS NOT AN ARMY THAT WE MUST SHAPE AND TRAIN FOR WAR, IT IS A NATION.

President Woodrow Wilson, on U.S. mobilization for World War I

Under Baruch's leadership the WIB faced with the challenge of converting the nation's industry to wartime production. The wartime agency allocated supplies (war-related items received first priority on production lines), fixed prices (to ensure that manufacturers had a means to pay wages high enough that workers would not strike), ordered the standardization of goods (so resources would not be wasted), and made purchases, sending enough goods—about one quarter of all American production—to the European front. While the Selective Service Act (1917) and local draft boards had successfully mobilized the troops, the WIB mobilized the economy, ensuring the Allied nations' defeat of the Central Powers in November 1918. On December 31, President Wilson directed that the board be dissolved. It was officially disbanded in mid-1919. The war effort was a catalyst for U.S. economic growth: By the end of the decade, the gross national product (GNP) was 237 percent higher than it was in 1914, when fighting first broke out.

See also: **Bernard Baruch, Overman Act, Selective Service**

WAR LABOR BOARD

The War Labor Board (WLB) was a federal executive branch office that had authority to settle all labor disputes that could interfere with domestic industrial production during World War II (1939–1945). Established within the Office of Executive Management on January 12, 1942, WLB was a tripartite body consisting of twelve commissioners appointed by the president, with four commissioners representing management, four commissioners representing labor, and four commissioners representing the public. The chairman and vice-chairman were selected from the public's representatives. Labor and management representatives agreed there would be no strikes or lockouts for the duration of the war.

To resolve more quickly any disputes that might arise, WLB created ten regional offices, each with twelve commissioners who were vested with nearly the same powers as the national commissioners. Labor disputes were escalated according to a defined procedure. The parties were first required to negotiate pursuant to the provisions of the applicable collective bargaining agreement. If the dispute could not be settled in this manner, the Commissioners of conciliation at the Department of Labor would intervene. If their intervention failed to produce a satisfactory result, the Secretary of Labor was required to certify the matter to WLB, which would make a final determination via mediation, arbitration, or some other mutually acceptable process.

WLB was established in part to replace the Defense Mediation Board, which had been largely ineffective since its creation in 1941. On December 31, 1945, WLB itself was terminated and replaced by the National Wage Stabilization Board in the Labor Department.

See also: **War Labor Disputes Act, World War II**

WAR LABOR DISPUTES ACT

The Smith-Connally Anti-Strike Act of 1943, known more commonly as the War Labor Disputes Act (WLDA), was a measure enacted by the U.S. Congress, despite President Franklin D. Roosevelt's (1933–1945) veto. It gave the president the power to seize and operate privately owned industrial war plants, during World War II (1939–1945), when and if an actual or threatened strike interfered with war production efforts. Any strikes by unions or by employees in any of the designated war plants were prohibited. Any war-industry unions failing to give 30 days notice of intent to strike were held financially liable for all damages. This was one of the many efforts Congress initiated to bring order out of the chaos generated as U.S. industries converted to full-time war production. The general success of the WLDA, as well as other government-initiated controls of industry and production, enabled U.S. industry to produce twice as much as all enemy countries combined by 1944. The WLDA of 1943 expired after the end of World War II, and previous labor-dispute techniques used by American organized labor were gradually resumed.

See also: **Military-Industrial Complex, Strike, World War II**

WAR OF 1812

The War of 1812 (1812–1814) remains one of the least known of American wars. Some historians regard it as a minor sidelight to the Napoleonic Wars (1800–1814)in Europe. Others see it as a continuation of the struggle that began with the American Revolution (1775–1783). Most agree, however, that the war had its origins in the economic problems facing the young republic in the early nineteenth century. The war's end resolved some of these problems. But other problems raised by the war continued to plague the United States through the first half of the nineteenth century.

Contemporary sources suggest that the United States entered the War of 1812 partly to end British impressment (a kind of forced draft) of American sailors. This was undoubtedly the case. But the complete cause of the war was much more complex. The War of 1812 had just as much to do with American trading interests as it did with foreign powers respecting the rights of American citizens. Some of the war's fronts were opened to seize Canadian lands and to end British influence over Native Americans in the Great Lakes area. Historians have also suggested that the war was fought to enhance the prestige of the Republican (Anti-Federalist) Party, and to enhance the prestige of the United States. The end of the war is equally confusing. Although the United States has won most of its wars, the War of 1812 was a major exception. The Treaty of Ghent (1814) that ended the conflict simply restored the state of affairs that had existed before the war began.

The problem of European powers interfering with American trade was an old one, stretching back decades into the years following the American Revolution. They were rooted in the French Revolution (1789–1795) and the Napoleonic period (1799–1815). At the time, the British were trying to choke off foreign trade with France, while the French were denying the British access to Continental ports. The Orders in Council established Great Britain's intention to seize goods carried in neutral ships that were intended for French ports, while Napoleon's Berlin Decrees performed a similar service for ports in other mainland European nations. When the British warship HMS *Leopard* boarded the USS*Chesapeake* in 1807 and removed four sailors who had allegedly deserted from the British navy, the Americans responded with outrage. Following the example set by the thirteen American colonies in the 1760s, President Thomas Jefferson (1801–1809) guided an Embargo Act (1807) that ended almost all American foreign trade. However, the Embargo Act hurt the United States far more than it did the nation's trading partners. In 1809 Congress reopened trade with foreign nations (except for Britain and France) in the Non-Intercourse Act. This act also stated that trade with Britain and France would be resumed if the two countries agreed to respect U.S. shipping. Even this step did not help the faltering U.S. economy, and in 1810 Macon's Bill No. 2 opened trade with both countries with the stipulation that trade with either country would be cut off if the other agreed to drop its restrictions on U.S. trade. Napoleon quickly took advantage of the opportunity to hurt the British, and in 1811 President James Madison (1809–1817) cut off trade with England. In June of 1812 the British government finally repealed the Orders in Council. But by that time Madison had already asked Congress for a declaration of war.

The other major source of conflict between the British and the Americans was on the Great Lakes frontier. Since the conflict known as the Little Turtle's War (1791–1794), the territory known as the Old Northwest had been a place of constant conflict between Native Americans and U.S. settlers. After the Treaty of Greenville (1795) awarded most of what is now Ohio to the U.S. government, most Indians left the area. Among them were the Shawnee leader Tecumseh and his younger brother Tenkswatawa, sometimes known as the Shawnee Prophet. Tecumseh was determined to put together an inter-tribal confederacy to resist further American incursions into Indian lands. His dream was smashed at the battle of Tippecanoe (1811), when General William Henry Harrison confronted the Shawnee Prophet at Prophetstown and scattered Tecumseh's Native American confederation. Tecumseh promptly joined the British forces in Canada as a commander of auxiliaries. He helped seize Detroit from American general William Hull in 1812 before being killed at the Battle of the Thames (1813). Tecumseh's death marked the effective end of Indian resistance to white settlement in the Old Northwest.

The problem of how to pay for the war was also one that occupied the government of the young republic. One of the reasons that the United States lost most of its battles in the first year of the war was that Congress had made a declaration of war, increased pay for its soldiers and raised money to encourage enlistments, but it had also adjourned before voting taxes or appropriating funds. In March of 1813, Secretary of the Treasury Albert Gallatin was reduced to begging for money through subscribed loans. Gallatin had to call on financial lion Stephen Girard, who had made his money through a shipping business centered in Philadelphia, for help. Girard was probably the richest man in the United States at the time. The same Congress that had authorized war with Great Britain had also refused to renew the charter of the Bank of the United States—effectively killing off the government's primary financial institution. Girard himself, along with fur trader John Jacob Astor and a syndicate of wealthy businessmen, underwrote most of the needed loans. In less than two weeks he had sold $4,672,800 worth of loan subscriptions to the American public, and purchased a further $2,383,00 himself. Girard's efforts helped bring about U.S. victories in 1813, and contributed to Great Britain's willingness to negotiate an end to the war.

The War of 1812 came to an end when British and American negotiators signed the Treaty of Ghent on December 24, 1814. At the time the treaty was signed, events were going on at opposite ends of the country that dramatically affected the future of the United States. New Englanders had long objected to the restrictions placed on trade by Congress as war measures. From December 1814 to January 1815, the Hartford Convention met in Connecticut and published a list of New England grievances. These ranged from undue influence of southerners in Congress to a series of constitutional amendments designed to protect New England from the damaging effects of national actions. The Hartford Convention also established the principle of nullification—the right of a state to overturn a federal law in order to protect the interests of its citizens—a principle that would later be taken up by southern states. At the same time, on January 8, 1815, in Louisiana, General Andrew Jackson was beating the British army at the Battle of New Orleans. Jackson's victory, along with the news of the peace treaty, virtually destroyed the Federalist Party in the United States. Despite the fact that none of Madison's war aims had been achieved, many citizens regarded the War of 1812—and the "Era of Good Feelings" that followed it—as an unqualified success.

See also: **Embargo Act, Andrew Jackson, Tecumseh (Death of)**

FURTHER READING

Brown, Roger H. *The Republic in Peril: 1812*. New York: Columbia University Press, 1964.

Hickey, Donald R. *The War of 1812: A Forgotten Conflict*. Urbana: University of Illinois Press, 1989.

Horsman, Reginald. *The Causes of the War of 1812*. Philadelphia: University of Pennsylvania Press, 1962.

Stagg, J. C. A. *Mr. Madison's War: Politics, Diplomacy, and Warfare in the Early American Republic, 1783–1830*. Princeton: Princeton University Press, 1983.

Wilson, George. *Stephen Girard: America's First Tycoon*. Conshohocken, PA: Combined Books, 1995.

WAR PRODUCTION BOARD

Federal War Production Board (WPB) was an executive branch office in charge of mobilizing the U.S. economy for World War II (1939–1945). Established within the Office of Emergency Management on January 16, 1942, WPB had authority to obtain financing, enter contracts for procurement of industrial materials, and issue directives to private enterprises. With this authority WPB allocated resources between the military and civilian production sectors. Civilian production that was wasteful or unnecessary was stopped, while scarce or valuable goods were rationed. Quotas on consumer purchases were created for a host of commodities. Commercial automobile manufacturing plants were expanded under the WPB's direction, and then converted for the production of armored vehicles, jeeps, and bombers. Although WPB was effective at first, its authority eventually became diluted by other agencies with overlapping power, including the Office of War Mobilization. WPB was officially replaced by the Civilian Production Administration on October 4, 1945.

See also: **Office of Emergency Management, Rationing**

WARNER, JACK LEONARD

Pioneering motion picture executive and producer, Jack L. Warner (1892–1978), along with his three brothers, created Warner Brothers Pictures and turned it into one of the largest film studios in the United States. When Warner Brothers released *The Jazz Singer* in 1927, as the first "talking picture," it revolutionized the entertainment industry and initiated the movie's modern era. Aggressive, and at times crude and difficult, Warner epitomized the classic movie mogul during Hollywood's studio era.

Jack L. Warner was born in London, Ontario, on August 2, 1892, the ninth and youngest boy of the 12 Warner children. His Polish parents, Benjamin and Pearl Eichelbaum, emigrated from Poland in 1890 to live in Canada for a time before moving in 1894 to Youngstown, Ohio. Jack, whose original surname was Jacob, and his three brothers, Harry, Albert, and Sam, were expected to help at an early age with the family's finances. Harry worked as a cobbler's apprentice, then as a meat packer. Albert and Sam held a succession of odd jobs before they began exhibiting movies after they obtained a projector by pawning Sam's prized birthday gift from his father, a gold watch and chain.

A poor student, Jack Warner longed to be a stage performer. He took his middle name, Leonard, from a minstrel performer he admired. Warner's love of the limelight would continue throughout his career. At age 12 he had earned money as a singer in minstrel shows and operettas. In their fledgling movie business, Sam handled the projector, Harry and Albert supervised the advertising and tickets, and Jack Warner sang and danced before and after the picture.

From their humble start the Warner brothers would steadily mount their assault on the young motion picture business, incorporating their holdings as Warner Brothers Pictures, Inc. in 1923. During World War II (1939–1945) Jack Warner served as a lieutenant colonel in the Army Air Force where he organized the first motion picture unit.

The Warner brothers' family movie business started in Youngstown, Ohio, but it was moved to Newcastle, Pennsylvania, where the brothers opened their first theater. In 1903 they converted an empty store with a seating capacity of 99, one seat short of 100 to prevent the theater from being subject to local and state fire regulations. Distribution of films was a problem during these early years of the movie business, and theater owners could not depend on deliveries. To remedy this situation Harry Warner decided to form collaboration with exhibitors and theater owners to exchange films. This eventually became the Duquesne Amusement Supply Company, the first such organization in the country. It was short lived since film producers did everything possible to discourage the arrangement as a threat to their profits. The Warners finally sold the film supply company in 1912. The experience convinced the brothers that if they were to be sure of having movies to show they must make them themselves. They began to make what the trade called "Warner Features" at the old Vitagraph Studios in New York.

Their first blockbuster occurred when they bought the rights to the 1917 book by Ambassador James W. Gerard, *My Four Years in Germany*. The resulting film grossed almost a million dollars. The profits allowed the Warners to shift their operations to California, joining Jack who had earlier established a studio in Santa Paula, California. Now the brothers built a large studio on Sunset Boulevard in Hollywood and incorporated their business as the Warner Brothers Pictures, Inc. However, in 1923 they were still selling their pictures through independent distributors who advanced them money to make their films. The brothers set out to obtain control of a nationwide distributing system.

Jack Warner married Irma Solomon in 1914 and they had one son, Jack L. Warner, Jr. The couple divorced and Warner married actress Ann Page in 1936. Warner accepted her daughter from a previous marriage, Joy, as his own and the couple adopted a two-year-old girl whom they named Barbara.

In 1925 they borrowed enough money to buy the Vitagraph Company, which had a nationwide distribution system. Success was still precarious, however, and Warner Brothers was close to bankruptcy when the brothers decided to experiment with sound films. In 1926 they released *Don Juan*, starring John Barrymore with a completely synchronized musical score, although Barrymore's voice and that of the rest of the cast were not recorded. Its success encouraged Warner Brothers to make other sound films while improving the sound tracks. In 1927 *The Jazz Singer* became the first true "talking picture." The effect of film speech was electrifying to its first audience; the era of the silent film had reached its conclusion. By 1928 Warner Brothers was a $16 million corporation and within two years they were worth $230 million. In 1929 Warner Brothers acquired the Stanley Company with some 250 theater outlets nationwide, which insured audiences for Warner Brothers' movies.

With a head start over their competitors in sound, Warner Brothers became one of the dominant film studios during Hollywood's Golden Era. Warner Brothers' contract players included such stars as George Arliss, Leslie Howard, Paul Muni, James Cagney, Bette Davis, Humphrey Bogart, and Joan Crawford. Jack Warner, as production chief, oversaw such classic films as *Little Caesar* (1930), *A Midsummer Night's Dream* (1935), *The Adventures of Robin Hood* (1938), *Casablanca* (1942), *The Corn is Green* (1945), *Mildred Pierce* (1945), *A Streetcar Named Desire* (1952), *Rebel Without a Cause* (1955), and *My Fair Lady* (1964). Although it produced films in all the genres Warner Brothers' specialty became social issue films. During World War II Warner Brothers became the first studio to direct its resources toward the war effort.

One of the keys to Warner Brothers' success was Jack Warner's intimate and scrupulous attention to detail and his constant economizing. He looked upon the movie industry as any other kind of factory production. Every economy was employed, including repeated use of material, reassembled sets, and a minimum of wasted time and space. Warner personally supervised the selection of story material, the assignment and supervision of producers and directors, and the discovery and assignment of acting talent.

In the late 1940s Warner Brothers became the first of the Hollywood studios to go into television production. In 1956 the Warners relinquished financial control of their company, although Jack Warner remained President and largest single shareholder. In 1966, when Warner finally sold his interest in the studio, he received $25 million after taxes.

Warner lived the life of the stereotypical Hollywood movie mogul in great splendor in his Hollywood mansion. Difficult to work with and often rude, Warner had a reputation for arbitrary firings and feuds with his brothers and son. Like other movie titans such as Louis B. Mayer and Darryl F. Zanuck, Jack L. Warner defined the role of the movie executive during the studio era when individual personalities could dominate every aspect of the making and marketing of movies and their stars.

As the cofounder of Warner Brothers Pictures Jack Warner helped shape the direction of U.S. entertainment through the infancy of the film industry and into its Golden Age, creating some of most important and significant U.S. cultural exports. Images of our society have been so dramatically affected by film portrayals that it is difficult to imagine areas of modern life untouched by film's influence. By exploiting the technical innovation of sound recording, Warner Brothers' created film's modern era.

As studio production chief Jack Warner contributed significantly to the production of many film masterpieces and he helped define the studio system for the production of films that was directly related to their creation. His dominating personality and tight control also helped to set in motion the reaction against the studio system and the wrestling away of ultimate control over films to individual directors and actors, which has had both positive and negative impacts on the industry. In today's Hollywood it is difficult to imagine the power of a studio executive like Jack Warner, who was one of the last of his breed of visionary businessmen who helped create the influential mass entertainment industry. Jack L. Warner has contributed in significant ways to Hollywood legend and its unprecedented success as our culture's dominant artistic medium. Jack L. Warner died in Los Angeles on August 2, 1978.

See also: **Entertainment Industry, Movies**

FURTHER READING

Behlmer, Rudy, ed. *Inside Warner Bros. (1935–1951).* New York: Viking, 1985.

Spellng, Cass Warner. *Hollywood Be Thy Name: The Warner Brothers Story.* Rollin, CA: Prima, 1994.

Thomas, Bob. *Clown Prince of Hollywood: The Antic Life and Times of Jack L. Warner.* New York: McGraw-Hill, 1990.

Warner, Jack L. *Jack of All Trades: An Autobiography.* London: W.H. Allen, 1975.

Warner, Jack L. *My First Hundred Years in Hollywood.* New York: Random House, 1965.

WASHINGTON

According to Gordon V. Dodds in his 1986 history of the American Northwest, life in the states of Washington and Oregon has been marked by "the absence of severe class or cultural or economic or environmental conflict." It is a "pleasant, undemanding life for most residents. . . . It has been a place where people could start over by escaping from their constraints to carry on the old ways better in a new environment. It is perhaps most typically American in this characteristic of providing a chance to start over."

The Pacific Northwest must have seemed a very remote place indeed to anyone who wanted to "start over" during the nineteenth century. Because of its rugged coast, distant location, and impenetrable mountains, for centuries Europeans only sporadically visited the region. Sir Francis Drake (1540–96) and some Spanish explorers may have seen the Washington coast in the sixteenth century. The Spaniard Juan Perez explored the northwestern coast in 1774. Other Spanish explorers made the first known landing at the mouth of the Hoh River, but were ambushed by Native Americans. The Englishman Capt. James Cook (1728–79) followed the fur trade to the area in 1792. His fellow countryman George Vancouver (1757–98) later made maps of the Pacific coast and Puget Sound. Fur trading companies such as the Hudson's Bay Company eventually began to attract overland traders as well. Reports from the Lewis and Clark expedition, which first sighted the Pacific from the bank of the Columbia River in 1805, also inspired others to set out for the Northwest.

From the beginning of white settlement, the history of the area was characterized by disputes between Great Britain and the United States. Both countries wanted control of the land and the water ports. The

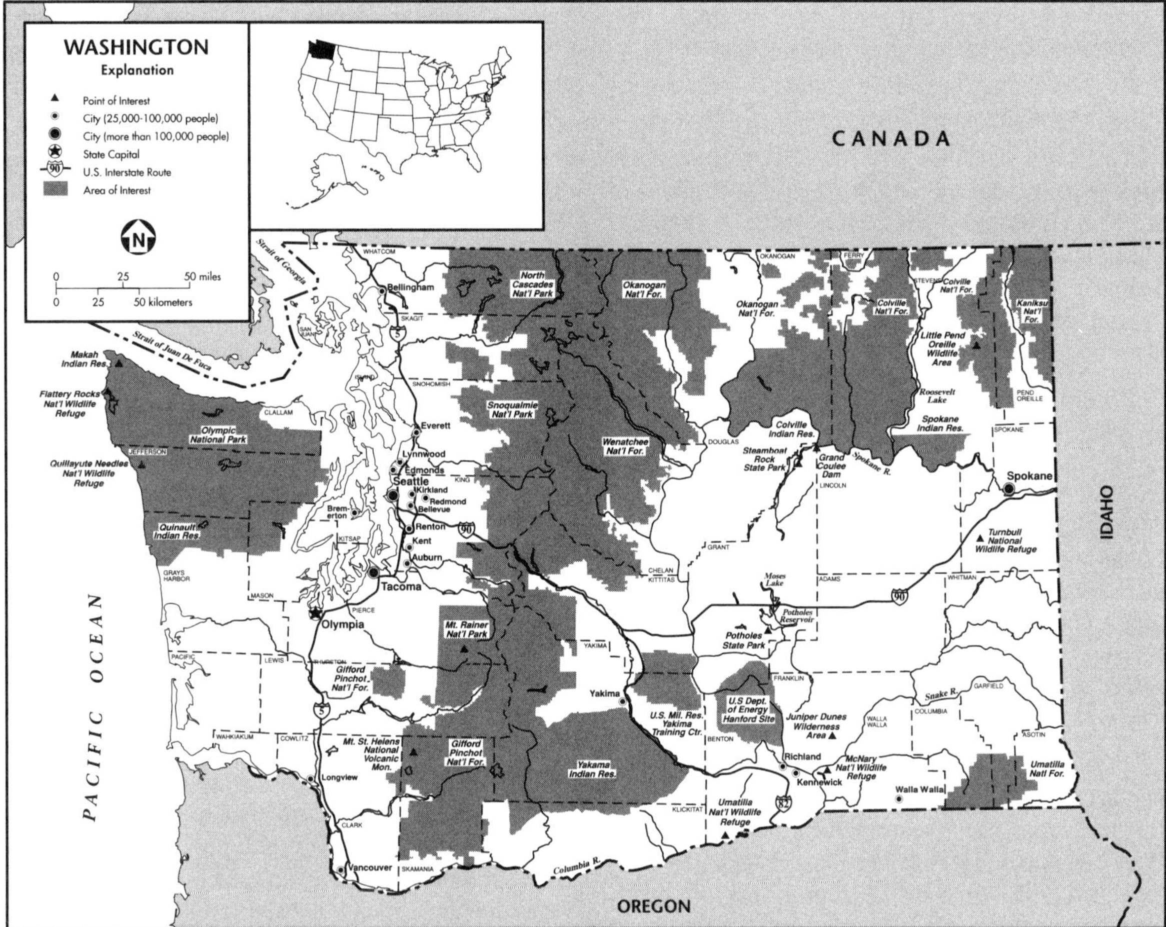

State of Washington.

border between the United States and Canada was settled in 1846, and the Oregon Territory was organized in 1848. It included the present state of Washington. About this time people were beginning to migrate from Missouri via the Oregon Trail to the present states of Oregon and southern Washington. A new Washington Territory was established in 1853. Most of the Indian uprisings which had hindered settlement in the territory were suppressed during the late 1850s.

Discoveries of gold in the Walla Walla area, in British Columbia, and in Idaho during the 1860s created a boom in the whole region. Immigration swelled following the completion of the Northern Pacific Railroad line to Puget Sound. By 1890 Washington's population had grown to over 357,000, up from just 24,000 in 1870. Lumbering, cattle farming, sheep raising, and agricultural farming were well established in Washington when the territory became a state in 1889. The city of Spokane literally boomed overnight when it became a hub for the Great Northern and the Northern Pacific railroads.

THERE HAS NOT BEEN MUCH TRAGEDY FOR WHITE PEOPLE IN THE HISTORY OF THE PACIFIC NORTHWEST.

Gordon B. Dodds, *The American Northwest: A History of Oregon and Washington*, 1986

The city of Seattle on the natural port of Puget Sound quickly became Washington's premier city. At first a center for coal shipments, it began to serve the lumber trade and expanded its commerce to Alaska, California, Europe, and other cities on Puget Sound. In 1909 Seattle hosted the Alaska-Yukon-Pacific Exposition, which celebrated both the Alaska gold rush and Seattle's own pride in its large seaport.

The era of railroads changed Washington significantly. It became much easier for raw materials to reach Puget Sound, and people were drawn from the eastern regions by promises of good land and unlimited opportunity. Manufactured goods from the East were now readily available to farmers and city-dwellers. In addition better waterways including canals along the

Columbia to bypass falls and rapids were helping lumber companies get their products to market.

Seattle in particular prospered during World War I (1914–18). Shipbuilding thrived during this period. Radical labor activities thrived as well, and Seattle became the headquarters of the Industrial Workers of the World (IWW). The first general strike in the United States, involving around 60,000 workers, was staged in Seattle in 1919 by the IWW. Centralia and Everett also experienced violent conflict between the IWW and conservative groups such as returning veterans.

Postwar readjustments followed during the 1920s as many farms were lost and the lumber business experienced a downturn. Apples, always a profitable crop for Washington, became even more important during this period as many wheat farms began to fail. By the middle of the 1920s, however, farm income was increasing. Lumbermen had to cope with an inadequate supply of timber because forests had been decimated to keep up with wartime demands, and the U.S. Congress passed several acts designed to provide better conservation of forests.

The Great Depression of the 1930s affected Washington much as it affected most of the country. Markets for field crops and forest products plummeted, and Washingtonians looked to President Franklin D. Roosevelt's (1933–45) New Deal programs for relief. Notable among those in the Northwest were the Grand Coulee and the Bonneville dam projects, which provided hydroelectric power and water for irrigation. More than one million acres were eventually reclaimed for farm production as a result of these projects.

World War II (1939–45) brought a new boom of economic activity, particularly to the Seattle area. The Boeing Corporation quickly established the aerospace industry as the state's primary employer. Boeing's rapid growth strained the housing facilities and infrastructure of the city; between 1939 and 1944 the number of workers employed at Boeing increased from 4,000 to 50,000. Shipyards also employed thousands in Seattle, Tacoma, Bremerton, and Vancouver. In addition, the federal government built the Hanford Reservation nuclear research center. This plant was instrumental in constructing the first atomic bomb and during peacetime was engaged in nuclear-powered electricity generation.

Postwar readjustments were inevitable in Washington as industries and farms began their transition from a wartime economy to a peacetime one. Small farms declined in favor of larger, technologically sophisticated ones; Boeing began its long reorientation to passenger aircraft after years of supplying military planes; fisheries declined because the salmon supply had rapidly been depleted; and large lumber concerns such as Weyerhaeuser in Tacoma solidified their operations while smaller firms went under.

In 1962 Seattle featured a world's fair, "Century 21," which showcased the city's assets. Rapid population growth marked the 1960s and 1970s, with concentration around Seattle and the Puget Sound area. This trend challenged both government and industry to balance economic needs with environmental protection. Both economic and environmental damage was suffered when an unexpected eruption of Mt. St. Helen's in May 1980 shocked the state and the nation with its destructive power.

A deep recession gripped Washington in the late 1970s. Logging was particularly hard hit. Between 1978 and 1982 employment in wood products industries dropped 30 percent. In the 1990s the economy was recovering after the 1980s expansion of Microsoft Corporation, Boeing, and Weyerhaeuser Paper. In the late 1990s the most important segments of the Washington economy were wholesale and retail trade, manufacturing (particularly aerospace equipment, shipbuilding, food processing, and wood products), agriculture, lumbering, and tourism. Another important segment in the 1980s and 1990s was film production. Many feature films, television movies, and documentaries used Washington locations and added millions of dollars to the economy. Washington ranked fifteenth among the states in per capita income in 1996. By the end of the decade unemployment in the state dropped to around five percent.

See also: **Boeing, Fishing Industry, Industrial Workers of the World, Lumber Industry, Microsoft, Weyerhaeuser**

FURTHER READING

Clark, Norman. *Washington: A Bicentennial History.* New York: Norton, 1976.

Dodds, Gordon B. *The American Northwest: A History of Oregon and Washington.* Arlington Heights, IL: Forum Press, 1986.

Johansen, Dorothy, and Charles Gates. *Empire of the Columbia: A History of the Pacific Northwest.* 2nd ed. New York: Harper and Row, 1967.

Meinig, D.W. *The Great Columbia Plain: A Historical Geography.* Seattle: University of Washington Press, 1968.

Stewart, Edgar I. *Washington: Northwest Frontier.* 4 vols. New York: Lewis, 1957.

WASHINGTON, BOOKER TALIAFERRO

Booker T. Washington (1856–1915) became one of the leading spokespeople for African Americans after the American Civil War (1861–1865). Washington strongly promoted the education of African Americans in practical skills and manual trades—he founded the Tuskegee Institute in Alabama to promote such goals. He became popular among white political leaders for his views on racial harmony, which emphasized economic opportunity over political protest.

Booker Taliaferro Washington was born in Franklin County, Virginia, on April 5, 1856. His mother was a slave who worked as a plantation cook. Washington's father was an unknown local white man who took no responsibility for his son. His mother later married another slave, but her husband escaped to West Virginia during the American Civil War, leaving his family behind. After the war ended in 1865, Booker's family was emancipated and the family was reunited in Malden, West Virginia. His stepfather had found a job at the salt furnaces and young Booker worked with him as a salt packer.

Booker desperately sought an education for himself, but his family needed him to work in order to support itself. His stepfather reluctantly agreed to let young Booker go to school on the condition that he continue to work in the salt mines before and after school. It was in school that Booker acquired his last name; he had only been called Booker until that time. When the pupils at school responded to roll call with two names, Booker named himself Washington. He later learned from his mother that he already had a last name, Taliaferro. So he became Booker Taliaferro Washington.

Washington continued his work at the salt furnaces, took another job at the coal mines, and still pursued his education. It was at the coal mines that Washington learned of the Hampton Institute in Virginia—this was a school dedicated solely to educating former slaves. It was suitable for Washington and his family because students could finance their education by working at the school.

Washington attended the Hampton Institute in 1872, and it proved to be a critical move for his future. It was at the institute that Washington learned of the educational philosophy that would shape his later beliefs and influence his writings. The Hampton Institute focused its program on practical skills and manual trades to improve the status of African Americans in the community. The institute emphasized industrial and agricultural education as well as teacher training.

Booker T. Washington.

Washington graduated with honors from the Hampton Institute in 1875 and went on to teach in rural schools in Malden. In 1878 he began his studies at the Wayland Seminary in Washington, D.C. He left the school, however, because he found the purely academic and theoretical atmosphere to be too superficial for his tastes. The world of books and ideas did not reflect the reality that most African Americans were living at that time. He appreciated the more practical approach of the Hampton Institute and returned there in 1879 as a teacher.

In 1881 the president of the Hampton Institute General Samuel Chapman Armstrong (1839–1893) recommended Washington for a new position. Washington would be the principal of a new school for African Americans to be built in Tuskegee, Alabama. The school had an annual legislative appropriation of $2000. It had no campus, buildings, pupils, or staff and Washington had to recruit pupils and teachers to the school himself. He also raised money for buildings and equipment, as the future site of the school was located on an abandoned plantation. Washington's first lessons to his students were practical ones. Students and faculty together planted crops and made the bricks for the new buildings.

At the Tuskegee Normal and Industrial Institute (later named the Tuskegee Institute, and now Tuskegee University), Washington taught the same self-help philosophy that he himself had learned at the Hampton Institute. Washington emphasized manual and industrial education, as well as practical trades such as carpentry, farming, mechanics, and teaching. He additionally emphasized discipline, cleanliness, and thrift among his students. Washington sought to impart to them a philosophy of African American self-sufficiency, and he urged his students to become capitalists. In 1900 Washington put his own teachings into practice and founded the National Negro Business League. The school, however was his real legacy, and he continued to watch his institute grow over the years. By 1888 Tuskegee Institute expanded to cover 549 acres and have over 400 enrolled students. By 1915 the school had 1500 students and a larger endowment than any other black institution.

Washington's influence and educational philosophy, however, extended outside of Tuskegee, Alabama. In 1895 he was asked to address the Cotton States and the International Exposition in Atlanta, Georgia. The event had an all-white audience of about 2000 people. Washington gave a speech at the exposition that was later dubbed the "Atlanta Compromise." The soon-to-be famous speech outlined Washington's proposal for racial harmony in the United States. He explained that self-improvement of African Americans in economic and educational matters would make them more law-abiding and less resentful toward white Americans. This would eventually, he asserted, promote racial harmony. Washington spoke out against the public protests occurring at that time and saw economic advancement as a more effective solution than political demonstrations to racial discord. Ultimately, he accepted racial segregation in exchange for economic opportunities. As he said in the speech: "In all things that are purely social we can be as separate as the fingers, yet one as the hand in all things essential to mutual progress."

Washington's speech was very popular among white Americans, and he soon became a spokesperson for his people. He developed strong ties with northern philanthropists such as Andrew Carnegie (1835–1919), George Eastman (1854–1932), Henry H. Rogers (1840–1909), and Julius Rosenwald (1862–1932). They appreciated Washington's entrepreneurial approach to race issues. Washington also became an advisor on racial matters to Presidents Theodore Roosevelt (1901–1909) and William H. Taft (1909–1913). His advice was sought as well by various governors and members of Congress.

The late 1800s were a difficult time for African Americans despite Washington's calls for racial harmony. Lynchings increased, Jim Crow laws enforcing racial segregation in public were passed, and there were threats of disfranchisement for African Americans in the South. These were clear signs that African Americans needed more than economic advancement to improve their social position in the United States. Other black intellectuals such as W.E.B. Du Bois (1868–1963) and William Monroe Trotter (1872–1934) began to speak out against the "accommodationism" that Washington supported. Du Bois in particular was critical of Washington's educational philosophy. He felt that it discouraged African Americans from striving for a higher education, instead Du Bois supported the opportunity for talented African Americans to attain a college education and serve as leaders of the black community. This opposition to Washington formed the Niagara Movement in 1905. It provided an alternative view to Washington's position of compromise and humility. In 1910 the same group founded the National Association for the Advancement of Colored People (NAACP).

Washington himself realized that economic opportunity alone was not enough to improve the conditions of African Americans. His public position never wavered, but Washington privately supported campaigns against injustice. He anonymously financed lawsuits against disfranchisement and segregation and secretly influenced other legal actions. Washington maintained a demanding public life until he became ill during a lecture series and died on November 14, 1915.

See also: **Civil Rights Movement, Jim Crow Laws**

FURTHER READING

Denton, Virginia Lantz. *Booker T. Washington and the Adult Education Movement.* Gainesville, FL: University Press of Florida, 1993.

Harlan, Louis R. *Booker T. Washington: The Wizard of Tuskegee, 1901–1915.* New York: Oxford University Press, 1983.

Miller, Jan. "Annotated Bibliography of the Washington-Du Bois Controversy." *Journal of Black Studies*, December 1994.

Riley, Jason L., "Return to Self-Reliance," *Wall Street Journal*, August 13, 1997.

Root, Nina J. "Portraits of Tuskegee." *Natural History*, February 1997.

WASHINGTON, GEORGE

George Washington (1732–1799) was commander-in-chief of the Continental forces during the American Revolution (1775–1783). He also served as the first President of the United States and was responsible for building much of the country's political and economic structure. Washington served two terms as president before retiring to his estate in Mount Vernon, Virginia.

George Washington was born at Bridges Creek in Westmoreland County, Virginia, on February 22, 1732. He was the first child of Augustine Washington and his second wife, Mary Ball. His father was a middling planter who owned about 10,000 acres of land. Augustine Washington was also very active in public life, serving as sheriff, church warden, and justice of the peace. George Washington received a basic education, studying math, surveying, and reading. In 1749, at the age of 17, he began working as the county surveyor. This job helped him become familiar with the frontier. With that knowledge and experience Washington was appointed major in the Virginia militia in 1752.

One year later Washington was faced with his first major military challenge. In 1753 the French were encroaching on British territory in the Ohio Valley, and the governor of Virginia sent Washington to dislodge them. This event was the beginning of the French and Indian War (1754–1763). Washington was then appointed as aide-de-camp to General Edward Braddock, who was ordered to oust the French in 1755. A year later Braddock died in combat and Washington was promoted to colonel and commander-in-chief of all Virginia troops; in 1758 he was promoted to brigadier.

When the French and Indian War ended, Washington resigned his commission and returned to Virginia to concentrate on his family. On January 6, 1759, he married Martha Dandridge Custis, a widow with two children. He was a dedicated stepfather and a skilled farmer. He also became actively involved in politics and was elected as representative from Frederick County to the Virginia House of Burgesses in 1758. He then served as justice of Fairfax county from 1760 to 1774.

In the late 1760s and early 1770s tension had begun to mount between Britain and the colonies, particularly over taxation and importation issues. As a legislator, Washington was very involved in colonial affairs. In 1774 he helped write and pass the Fairfax Resolves, which formed the Continental Association and the Continental Army. When the disputes with Britain turned into war, the Continental Congress on June 15, 1775, unanimously elected Washington to command the Continental Army. Throughout the American Revolution, from 1775 to 1783, Washington served as *de facto* chief executive of the United States. He proved to be a gifted leader with good administrative skills and political acumen. When the war was finally won, Washington handed over his powers to Congress at Annapolis, Maryland, and returned home to Mount Vernon to retire.

However, Washington was soon called back to serve his country. The Articles of Confederation proved too weak to hold the new country together, and in 1786 Washington described the situation as "anarchy and confusion." In an effort to revise the articles, Washington presided over the Constitutional Convention in 1787. In 1789 he was unanimously elected as the first President of the United States. He began his term by stating: "I walk on untrodden ground. There is scarcely any part of my conduct which may not hereafter be drawn into precedent."

Washington immediately became involved in the creation of the new government. He created the first Cabinet, establishing the departments of State, Treasury, and War. Alexander Hamilton (1755–1804) became the first Secretary of the Treasury, and together with Washington he developed the country's economic system. On July 4, 1789, Washington signed the first bill passed by Congress. It gave the government the right to tax and was used to pay the debt accumulated by the Revolution and establish American credit at home and abroad. Washington also approved the Federalist financial program and other proposals by Hamilton, including funding the national debt, assuming state debts, establishing a federal bank, creating a coinage system, and establishing an excise tax. In addition to these economic policies, Washington presided over the expansion of the country from 11 to 16 states.

After his first term as president ended in 1792, Washington had plans to retire from political life. His colleagues, however, persuaded him to serve one more term. On February 13, 1793, Washington was once again unanimously elected to the presidency. His second term focused on the young country's foreign policy. In 1793 Washington announced the Neutrality Proclamation to keep the United States out of all foreign disputes. Relations with France and Britain were tested during Washington's tenure, but he managed to keep peace. By 1796 Washington had grown tired of the demands of political life and once again decided to retire. This time he was able to have his way and pacify critics who called him a closet monarchist. On September 17, 1796, Washington published his

Farewell Address and returned home to Mount Vernon following the next presidential election.

His retirement was brief, as Washington was called again to public service in 1798. The United States was on the verge of war with France and President John Adams (1797–1801) asked Washington to raise an army for defense. Washington answered the call to duty, but the threat quickly subsided due to diplomatic negotiations. Once again he resigned his commission and returned to Mount Vernon. Soon after returning home, Washington, suffering from a serious throat infection, died on December 14, 1799. After George Washington's death, Congress unanimously agreed to erect a marble monument, called the Washington Monument, in the nation's capital to pay tribute to the country's first president.

***See also:* American Revolution, Articles of Confederation, French and Indian War, Alexander Hamilton**

FURTHER READING

Alden, John R. *George Washington: A Biography.* Louisiana: Louisiana State University Press, 1984.

Ferling, John E. *The First of Men: A Life of George Washington.* Tennessee: University of Tennessee Press, 1988.

Phelps, Glenn A. *George Washington and American Constitutionalism.* Lawrence: University Press of Kansas, 1993.

Schwartz, Barry. *George Washington: The Making of an American Symbol.* New York: Free Press, 1987.

Smith, Richard N. *Patriarch.* Boston, MA: Houghton Mifflin, 1993.

Wall, Charles Cecil. *George Washington: Citizen-Soldier.* Mt. Vernon, VA: Mount Vernon Ladies' Association, 1988.

WATSON, THOMAS JOHN

U.S. business executive Thomas J. Watson (1874–1956) assumed management of the International Business Machines Corporation (IBM) in 1924 and built it into one of the world's largest and most respected corporations. As a manufacturer of business machines and computers IBM, under Watson's innovative and inspired supervision, led a revolution in the business world that heralded the information age. By the end of 1955 Watson's last full year as IBM's chief executive officer, he had guided his company from debt to having total assets of $630 million and from fewer than 4,000 employees to 41,000. IBM was poised to dominate the emerging computer market and by the 1960s and 1970s it controlled 80 percent of the U.S. market. Due to Watson's effective leadership, IBM had become a model for corporate planning, research, and customer and employee loyalty.

Thomas John Watson was born February 17, 1874, in Campbell, New York. He was educated in New York at Addison Academy. His father urged him to study law when he graduated and offered to pay his college expenses, but Watson was anxious to pay his own way and to begin his business career. Watson took a year-long course at the Elmira School of Commerce and, at age 17, found a job as a bookkeeper in Clarence Risley's market in Painted Post, New York. Soon bored, he took a job as a peddler selling organs and sewing machines.

From such a modest start Watson would eventually emerge as one of greatest and most influential U.S. business executives. He married Jeanette Mary Kittridge of Dayton, Ohio in 1913, and they had two sons and two daughters. The sons, Thomas J. Watson, Jr. and Arthur K. Watson, followed their father to work for IBM.

In 1895 Watson joined the fast-growing National Cash Register (NCR) Company as a salesman. At first the company manager was uninterested in hiring him but Watson persisted, making numerous trips to the company's Buffalo office. After several months he was finally offered a position. The United States was in the midst of a depression and Watson sometimes went many weeks without a single sale. He sustained himself by quoting the tried-and-true slogans and homilies that he later would use at IBM. Despite his early lack of success he received encouragement from his superiors, and within two years Watson had become the top salesman in the Buffalo office. He moved steadily up the corporate ladder to become general sales manager and was given a position in NCR's Dayton home office in 1903. This period was marked by Watson's aggressive assault on NCR's competition, namely the creation of a company to undercut competitor's prices on second-hand cash registers, which proved to be illegal; however, it is unclear whether Watson was aware of this. Watson, along with NCR's president and 28 others, was indicted and convicted for the scheme. An appeals court later ordered a new trial but it was never held. In 1913, in a dispute over an anti-trust legal issue, Watson was fired from NCR though he was presented with a $50,000 parting gift.

Watson was selected to head the Computing-Tabulating-Recording Company of Elmira, New York, a small holding company that controlled four small firms that produced punch-card tabulators, time clocks, and other business machines. As company president, Watson acted to secure loans to finance expansion. The move helped the company's gross sales increase from $2 million in 1914 to more than $33 million by 1949. Personnel increased from 235 to 12,000 during the same period. Watson was committed to research and development and much of the borrowed funds went into engineering laboratories that produced new machines such as the keypunch, card sorters, tabulators, and eventually the computer. In 1924 the firm merged with International Business Machines Corporation taking its name. By then the business he had taken over had more than doubled in terms of plant size, number of employees, and volumes of sales. As the head of IBM, Watson helped those figures double yet again about every five years during his reign.

In the 1930s a new engineering laboratory was built in Endicott, New York, and IBM entered the electrical typewriter business with the purchase of Electromatic Typewriters, Inc. of Rochester, New York. As the holder of more than 1,400 patents as of 1941, IBM held a virtual monopoly in the field of business machines. IBM would maintain its dominance through Watson's inspired leadership. Having been a salesman Watson devoted considerable effort in training his sales force, insisting that IBM salesmen should know how to install, operate, and repair all the equipment they sold. Working out the three basic steps in the selling technique, the approach, the demonstration, and the closing, Watson insisted that his salesmen stress that IBM sold not machines but service.

Watson's personality and manner defined the IBM corporate identity that extended to its severely conservative dress code and the ever-present stimulating signs that graced IBM offices such as "Aim High and Think in Big Figures," "Serve and Sell," and IBM's trademark, a Watson creation: "Think." Dignified and conservative in his dress and manner, Watson neither smoked nor drank, nor did he take vacations. He worked 16-hour days and spent most of his evenings at the functions of his many employees' clubs. Watson was extremely concerned about IBM's corporate image, and was rigid in his hiring and personnel practices. Before World War II (1939–1945), employees at IBM were exclusively male and white Anglo-Saxon Protestants. Jews, Catholics, blacks, and women were unacceptable to him.

All employees were expected to have a copy of *Men, Minutes and Money*, a collection of Watson's speeches and essays and to be freshly shaved. They were also to wear daily shined shoes, and to follow their chairman's dress style—dark suits, quiet ties, and white shirts—whether in the main New York office or in the Endicott factory. The IBM image virtually defined the corporate concept of the "organization man." Yet the benefits of conforming to IBM's image were many. *Forbes* magazine declared in a 1948 article that Watson had created "the nearest to ideal working conditions." Watson paid higher wages than did his competition. There were few firings and benefits included health and life insurance, a rarity at the time. IBM workers were made to feel that they were members of a special group who were encouraged for their innovations and originality and they were expected to carry a THINK notebook to record their inspirations.

By 1955, Watson's last full year as IBM's chief executive, the company's total assets were $630 million, with a domestic work force of 41,000 employed in branch offices in 189 cities and plants in six cities. The IBM World Trade Corporation had 19,000 employees, 11 plants, and 208 branch offices in 82 countries. Watson had seen his struggling company grow into a world giant that would continue, under the direction of his son, Thomas, Jr., to dominate the business machine market and the rapidly developing computer industry.

Watson's principal interest outside of business was as a patron of the arts. He began acquiring paintings when he was only 24, and he was an outspoken advocate of the mutual benefit in joining the world of art with business. At the 1939 New York World's Fair he exhibited paintings by artists from 75 countries and a collection by U.S. artists that IBM had acquired. For many years he served as a trustee at Columbia University and as the president of the International Chamber of Commerce. An adviser to several U.S. presidents, Watson, who never graduated from college, was the recipient of 32 honorary degrees. For offering IBM's considerable research and production capacity to the war effort during World War II (1939–1945), Watson was given the U.S. Medal of Merit. He also received numerous decorations from several foreign countries including the Merit Cross of the German Eagle, which Watson returned to German leader Adolph Hitler (1889–1945) in 1940, stating that the policies of the Nazis were contrary to the causes for which he worked.

Thomas Watson died in 1956, one year after his retirement from IBM. During his tenure as head of IBM, Watson created one of the world's largest and most influential corporations. Dominating its markets IBM supplied the business machines upon which U.S. business depended by creating new products to meet customers' needs. Through the development of data processing equipment and a successful computer line IBM changed the very nature of modern business itself.

Watson also forged the dominating principles of the corporate culture with its emphasis on company loyalty and team spirit, accomplishing the difficult task of simultaneously encouraging employee uniformity and innovation and individuality.

See also: **Computer Industry, International Business Machines**

FURTHER READING

Belden, Thomas Graham, and Marva Robins. *The Lengthening Shadow: The Life of Thomas J. Watson.* Boston: Little, Brown, 1962.

Engelbourg, Saul. *International Business Machines: A Business History.* New York: Armo Press, 1976.

Rodgers, William. *Think: A Biography of the Watsons and IBM.* New York: Stein and Day, 1969.

Simmons, W. W. *Inside IBM: The Watson Years: A Personal Memoir.* Bryn Mawr, PA: Dorrance, 1988.

Watson, Thomas J., Jr. *A Business and Its Beliefs: The Ideas that Helped Build IBM.* New York: McGraw-Hill, 1963.

WELFARE POLICY *(ISSUE)*

There is no one single date that can be assigned as the beginning of the welfare system in the United States. Instead, both the ideology and the institutions of the welfare state have grown like weeds, cut back occasionally, only to reappear and to establish themselves again. There are, for instance, elements of the welfare ethic in the notion that people have an obligation to look out for one another's welfare going all the way back to the Puritan communities of New England. The "covenant" that each person had with God and with his or her immediate family also extended in some measure to all the inhabitants of the village. This is not to deny that the Puritans expressed the Protestant fixation with individual salvation, and that in this important sense they would make their peace with the competitive individualism of capitalism. But, especially before the rise of a systematic ideology of competitive capitalism in the eighteenth and nineteenth century, the social solidarity of the medieval village also informed the way that people looked at each other. It prompted the expectation that they could look forward to a certain helpfulness from each other. Even when this village world-view was in decline with the rise of the cities, there were still back-water religious communities—the Shakers, the Quakers, the Moravians, the Amish, and the Utopian communities—and the general frontier neighborliness of cooperative labor exchanges—the barn-raisings, corn husking, or quilting parties—that represented a much older tradition. This older, cooperative heritage, mediated by the labor movement and by the socialist tradition, contributed an alternative ethic that formed part of the welfare system in modern U.S. history.

The strength of the dominant ideology of competitive capitalism in the United States has meant that welfare policy has had countless critics. In spite of these attacks, in the twentieth century this welfare movement has been sustained by the great reform movements of the age: the Progressive Movement (1900–1920), the New Deal (1933–1940) and the Great Society (1964–1968). Each of these reform movements looked to the government as the instrument of reform. The cornerstone of the welfare tradition in the twentieth century was the Social Security Act of 1935. This reform came out of popular demands for a national pension system for the elderly. The "Townsend Plan" was the brainchild of Dr. Francis E. Townsend, a retired California physician. The essence of the plan was that the federal government would make monthly payments of $200 to all citizens over the age of sixty. The sole stipulation was that the money had to be spent within one month. This would stimulate the demand for goods and pull the country out of depression. Five million mostly elderly citizens joined the Townsend Clubs in support of the plan. Although it was unrealistic in its approach to funding the proposed system, the Townsend Plan prompted President Franklin Roosevelt's administration—especially Secretary of Labor Francis Perkins—to consider the plight of the elderly and the Social Security System was the result. This mandatory system of government administered pensions (paid for by contributions from both the worker and the employer) expanded to include a program for unemployment insurance (funded solely by the employer) as well as aid to disabled people and to children.

President Lyndon B. Johnson's (1963–1969) Great Society and his War on Povertywent on from there in its expansion of the welfare system. The War on Poverty set out to reduce unemployment by helping the poor to improve their education, skills, work efficiency, and in general, equip themselves for success in the modern economy. In an effort to get local citizens to involved themselves in the programs, local governments or private nonprofit organizations were required to prepare plans, administer them, and pay 10 to 25 percent of their cost. In the ensuing years, the Job Corps, the Neighborhood Youth Corps, the College

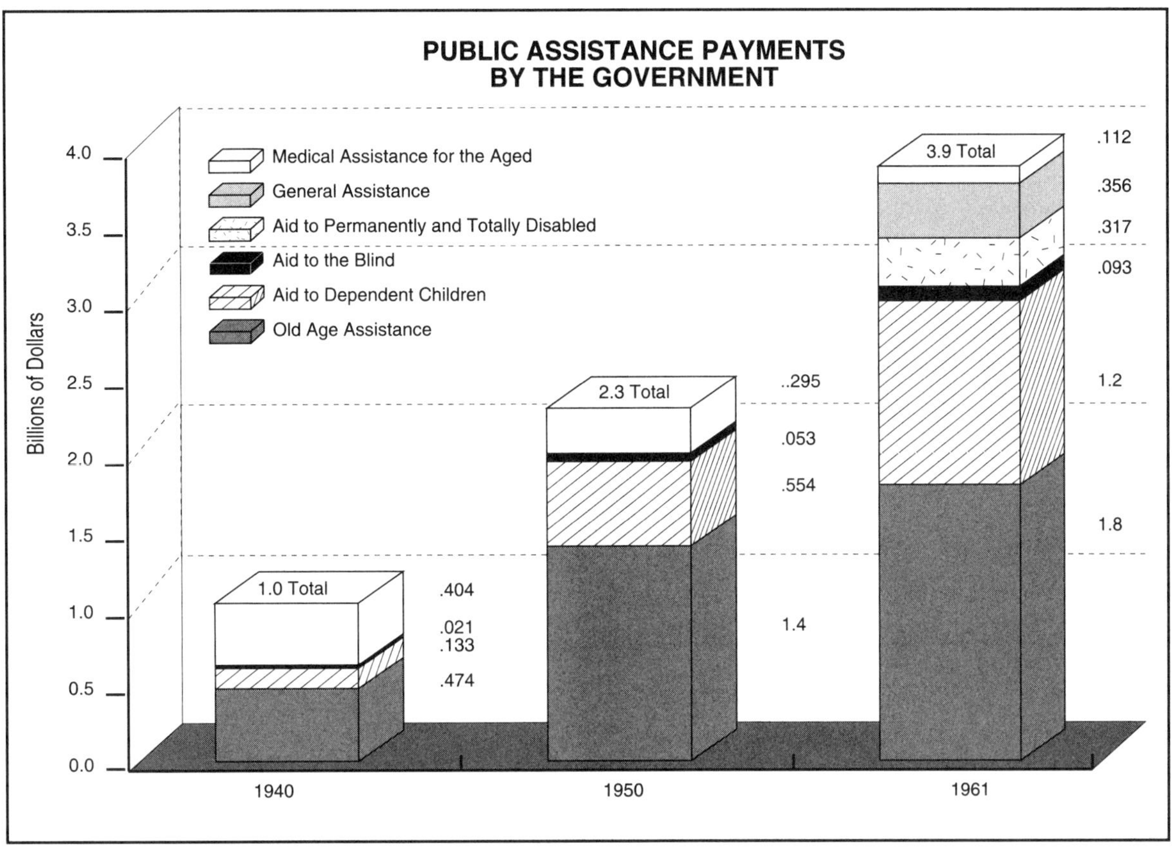

Shown by this graph is the growth of Public Assistance payments by amount and programs from 1940 to 1961.

Work-Study Program, Project Head Start, Foster Grandparents, Upward Bound, Volunteers in Service to America (VISTA), and the Office of Legal Services were all initiated as the War on Poverty's arsenal.

Almost as soon as the programs began, they were met with open opposition. Critics claimed that training costs for VISTA programs averaged more than $8,000 per graduate, and that nearly half of the graduates failed to find jobs. Others claimed that only a fraction of the poor ever received any benefits. Senator Walter Mondale once chided that the War on Poverty ''authorized dreams and appropriated peanuts.'' Defenders claimed that the policies were stifled by the war in Vietnam.

During President Richard M. Nixon's (1969–1974) administration, the welfare system, partly federal and partly local in character, posed especially difficult problems. Throughout the 1960s there had been a marked expansion of relief rolls, especially in the category of Aid to Families with Dependent Children (AFDC). Between 1961 and 1970 the AFDC caseload rose from 921,000 to 2.2 million families, with an increase of almost 30 percent in 1970 alone. The federal welfare bill grew from $2.1 billion in 1960 to nearly $18 billion in 1972, while the number of persons on welfare rolls increased from 7.3 million in 1961 to 14.9 million in 1972. Fifteen percent of the population of New York, 25 percent of the population of Newark, NJ, and about six percent of all U.S. citizens were on welfare. Of those families receiving welfare in 1971, 49 percent were white while 46 percent were black; 55.5 percent were children, 15.6 elderly, 9.4 percent were blind or disabled, and less than one percent were employable males.

The welfare explosion was attributed to several factors. The poor were becoming more visible as they moved from isolated rural areas into cities. Rising violence and rioting in ghettos convinced many people of the necessity to do something to improve opportunities. VISTA workers, poverty lawyers, and the National Welfare Rights Organization made the poor more aware of their rights and instructed them how to get welfare payments. The Supreme Court overruled state laws that denied benefits to newcomers. And finally the growing productivity of the national economy made the continued existence of abject poverty a less defensible blot on the U.S. way of life.

The existing welfare system buckled under the new burdens thrust upon it. Critics everywhere condemned it because it required employed fathers to leave the household so that their families could qualify for public assistance. Its procedures were degrading and it helped only about a fourth of the poor. Some reformers proposed that the federal government pay the entire cost of all welfare programs. Some sociologists recommended a system of federal family allowances in which every family, rich or poor, would receive a monthly government payment for each child in the family. But critics of this system pointed to the cost (approximately $14 billion annually) and charged that it would give poor families an incentive to have more children. Moreover, they claimed that because it wasn't based on need, more than 70 percent of the money would go to families above the poverty line. Other reformers sought to reduce taxation of the poor, arguing that taxes could be brought more in line with ability to pay by reducing sales and social security taxes, and collecting more of the needed revenue through income taxes. But opponents of tax reforms argued that the poor should be made to pay taxes to make them aware of the costs of government, give them a sense of contributing to their country, and make them better citizens.

In 1969, Nixon called for the replacement of the AFDC with a Family Assistance Plan (FAP) that would give every family of four on welfare with no outside income a basic federal payment of $1,600 a year. There was also a "work requirement" in which recipients with school-age children could be referred to work or training on penalty of forfeiting a part of their FAP payments. Supporters of this path-breaking concept argued that a guaranteed annual income would stimulate economic growth. They claimed that putting money into the hands of the poor would raise consumer spending, stimulate production, and create new jobs, which would take many of the poor off welfare. Between 1968 and 1972, the Office of Economic Opportunity quietly conducted a test of the idea with seven hundred families in five communities in New Jersey and Pennsylvania. The results showed that nearly all of the families with guaranteed incomes worked at least as hard to add to their incomes as other families.

But the idea of a guaranteed income also had many critics. Some Democrats opposed it for partisan reasons (not wanting Nixon to take credit for the program), some because they deemed the benefits were too low and the work requirement too coercive. Some conservative Republicans opposed guaranteed income for being too liberal. Those already a part of the social welfare establishment opposed it because they had a vested interest in maintaining the existing system. After passing the House of Representatives in 1970, the proposed FAP legislation failed in the Senate. From that point on the Nixon Administration backed off from it, but the idea of a guaranteed income remained on the agenda for the future.

In 1974 a new Supplementary Security Income (SSI) replaced existing federal-state programs for needy aged, blind, and disabled who did not qualify for adequate Social Security benefits. Application of federal standards of eligibility doubled the number of persons eligible to 6.2 million. The federal government assumed responsibility for guaranteeing persons in these categories a minimum income from all sources.

During the 1990s increased pressures to reform the welfare system resulted in the federal government relinquishing a good portion of its administrative, regulative, and enforcement responsibilities to individual states. State legislatures, however, frequently implemented what some liberals claimed were draconian changes in the system—cutting benefits and squeezing the welfare system to the point where welfare recipients were allowed far fewer months of benefits and were pressed to get jobs even if the jobs were so low-paying or so lacking in other necessary features, such as day-care provisions, that incentive to get the jobs was limited.

See also: **Townsend Clubs, Social Security Act**

FURTHER READING

Aaron, Henry J. *Why is Welfare so Hard to Reform.* Washington, DC: Brookings Institute, 1973.

Harrington, Michael. *The Other America: Poverty in the United States.* New York: Penguin Books, 1963.

Lens, Sidney. *Poverty Yesterday and Today.* New York: Crowell, 1974.

Levitan, Sar A. *Progress in Aid of the Poor for the 1970s.* Baltimore: Johns Hopkins University Press, 1969.

Wogaman, Philip. *Guaranteed Annual Income: The Moral Issues.* Nashville, TN: Abington Press, 1969.

WELLAND CANAL

The Welland Canal connects Lakes Ontario and Erie. Because of the difference in elevation between the Atlantic and the Great Lakes, a system of canals and locks was required to allow large boats to navigate the connected waterways. (A lock is a section of a canal that can be closed to control the water level and it is then used to either raise or lower a vessel to another body of water). The Welland Ship Canal is part of this system. It lies entirely within the Canadian province of Ontario, extending 27 miles (43 kilometers) from Port Weller on Lake Ontario (the eastern-most of the Great Lakes) to Port Colborne on Lake Erie. The natural waterway that connects these two bodies is the Niagara River. The height difference of the two lakes (Lake Erie is 326 feet or 99 meters higher than Lake Ontario) makes Niagara's spectacular waterway of falls and rapids unnavigable. The original Welland Canal was completed in 1829. Built by a private company that had secured government loans, the project cost nearly 8 million dollars. In 1833 an extension to the canal was completed. Six years later, Upper Canada (today the province of Ontario) took over the Welland to enlarge the canal to accommodate bigger ships. That project was completed by 1845; a second enlargement was undertaken in 1887. The Canadian government has continued to improve the waterway since. It remains the vital link for shipping between the nation's interior and the Atlantic Ocean.

See also: **Erie Canal, Soo Locks**

WELLS, FARGO AND COMPANY

On the morning of January 24, 1848, a construction foreman working for California land baron John Sutter, discovered something shining in the bottom of a ditch. Though Sutter attempted to keep this discovery secret, word soon spread across the country that gold had been found in California. To meet the needs of the every increasing number of Gold Rush pioneers, Henry Wells, William G. Fargo, and other investors formed Wells, Fargo and Company. Initially the company provided three services: banking, expressing (high-speed delivery services), and mail delivery. Five years later, Wells, Fargo and Company added overland stagecoach services. From these humble, yet inspired, beginnings rose a financial giant.

Wells Fargo opened for business in San Francisco on July 13, 1852. The company's banking department, run by banker Reuben W. Washburn, purchased gold from transitory miners, paying for it with standard-issue gold coins and bills of exchange that could be shipped back east. The company provided extensive communications and shipping services as well. To support these new services offices were built in Sacramento and Placer County to express the gold. Wells Fargo also contracted small banking and express firms to service other areas.

In 1855 a bank crisis felled two of California's largest banking houses causing a financial crisis from which Wells Fargo emerged as the primary bank and express company in the California region. The company continued to expand and it soon had over sixty agencies on the West Coast. The 1860s confirmed the dynamic nature of Wells Fargo. The California economy had expanded to include not only placer mining (which extracts material from deposits by hand, dredging, or with hydraulic nozzles) but also agriculture, manufacturing, and hard rock mining; industries of this type required long-term investment. Wells Fargo survived this economic shift while their express and communications services expanded. In 1861 Wells Fargo's growing express service would take over the famed Pony Express, and in 1864 the company provided the first electronic transaction by telegraph.

In 1866 Wells Fargo purchased the Overland Mail and Express Company. This strategic move placed Wells Fargo in control of essentially all express services west of the Mississippi River. However, in 1869 the new transcontinental railroad effectively brought an end to Wells Fargo's stagecoach empire. However, the "iron horse" became a great asset to the company, because it allowed for faster express delivery. Utilizing this faster mode of transportation as well as the new, expanded economy, Wells Fargo began to market agricultural products nationally. The company became the first express company to provide ocean-to-ocean delivery service. Thanks to this service, the earnings of Wells, Fargo, and Company topped one million dollars annually from 1890 to 1892.

Even the economic panic of 1893 could not damage Wells Fargo's financial earnings. By 1899 company earnings were once again over one million dollars. Earnings increased to almost five million dollars by 1909, with profitability soaring to $27 million in that same year. Soon afterward express business for the company decreased because of railroad disruptions, competition from the U.S. Postal Service, and regulation brought about by the Interstate Commerce Commission. However, by July 1, 1918, Wells Fargo employed 35,000 people in 10,000 domestic offices. This considerable workforce was merged with the American Railway Express during World War I (1914-1918). The express division of Wells Fargo became a subsidiary of American Express, providing secured transportation of funds via armored cars.

The company's banking business merged with the Nevada National Bank in 1905. This move proved to be wise, as Wells Fargo maintained a strong banking presence throughout the Great Depression (1929-1939) and into the 1940s. The company continued to grow.

This growth can be partially attributed to the dramatic increase in the population of California after World War II (1939-1945). However, it is easier to understand the company's expansion by taking a brief look at the many strategic mergers and purchases made by Wells Fargo from 1960s to the late 1990s. In 1960 it merged with the American Trust Company. In 1986 Wells Fargo's purchased Crocker National Corporation and Crocker Bank, increasing the company's assets by $19.2 billion. Other acquisitions in the 1980s included the personal trust business of the Bank of America (1987) and Barclays Bank of California (1988). A cooperative agreement with The Hong Kong and Shanghai Banking Corporation Limited in 1989 led to the establishment of the Wells Fargo HSBC Trade Bank.

Wells Fargo continued to grow ever larger and stronger throughout the 1990s. In 1990 alone the company acquired four California-based organizations: Valley National Bank, Central Pacific Corporation, Torrey Pines Group (totaling over $1.5 billion in assets), and Citizen Holdings (with $207 million in deposits). Wells Fargo merged with First Interstate Bankcorp in 1996. A merger with Norwest Corporation vaulted Wells Fargo to the seventh largest U.S. bank holding company in the United States with a total of $92.8 billion in assets as of September, 1998.

See also: **Gold Rush of 1849**

FURTHER READING

Beebe, Lucius. *U.S. West: The Saga of Wells Fargo.* New York: Dutton, 1949.

Dictionary of American History. New York: C. Scribner's Sons, 1976, s.v. ''Wells Fargo.''

Dillon, Richard H. *Wells, Fargo Detective: The Biography of James B. Hume.* Reno, NV: University of Nevada Press, 1986.

Loomis, Noel M. *Wells Fargo.* New York: Clarkson N. Potter, 1968.

Ward, Geoffrey C. *The West: An Illustrated History.* New York: Little, Brown, and Company, 1996.

WEST VIRGINIA

West Virginia is a state full of natural beauty yet it is plagued by economic difficulties. Its rugged terrain has made communication and transportation difficult. Though blessed with coal and timber resources, it has gone through many periods of economic depression. Although the economy improved throughout the 1990s, West Virginia is still one of the nation's poorest states

In the 1640s, before European settlers reached the land, Iroquois and Cherokee Indians inhabited the area which later became West Virginia. When Europeans did arrive, Shawnees, Delawares, and Tuscaroras disputed their claims. Early explorers were fur traders, two of whom, Robert Fallam and Thomas Batts, claimed the Ohio valley for England in 1671. The French also claimed the area, not surrendered until after the French and Indian War. Several thousand settlers inhabited the eastern panhandle area of the territory by 1750. More settlement in interior sections occurred through the time of the American Revolution (1775–1783), though periodic skirmishes with Indians slowed the pioneers' progress. West Virginia was originally part of Virginia, which was instrumental in forming the Union in 1788.

After the War of 1812 (1812–1814), conflicts developed between eastern and western Virginia. Slaveholding planters dominated the eastern section while the westerners were mostly small farmers or workers in small industries. The east controlled most of the state leaving the west with unequal representation, poor roads, unfair taxes, and other evidence of economic deprivation. In addition, according to one historian, ''Most parts of western Virginia were like the Shenandoah region, a true borderland between the North and the South.'' (John Alexander Williams) Two constitutional conventions failed to settle the differences and it was not until Virginia seceded from the Union in 1861 that West Virginia decided to side with the North and separate from Virginia, entering the Union in 1863 as the 35th state. The state did not gain control of the upper panhandle area until 1871.

Trade developed naturally along the state's rivers in towns such as Wheeling and Harpers Ferry, but traversing the mountainous terrain of West Virginia has always been a challenge. Although Wheeling was the western terminus of the National Road, other roads were slow in coming and often almost impassable. The first successful railroad to be built was the Baltimore and Ohio (B&O), completed to Wheeling in 1852. Later railroads enabled the state to gain access to its timber and coal resources and opened up areas of the interior. The Chesapeake and Ohio, completed in 1873, extended westward from the old Virginia Central to the Ohio River. At its terminus was a new town called Huntington, after the railroad magnate who had financed the line. The two panhandles at the northwestern and eastern ends of the state can be seen as West Virginia's successful attempts to hold on to two important railroad corridors.

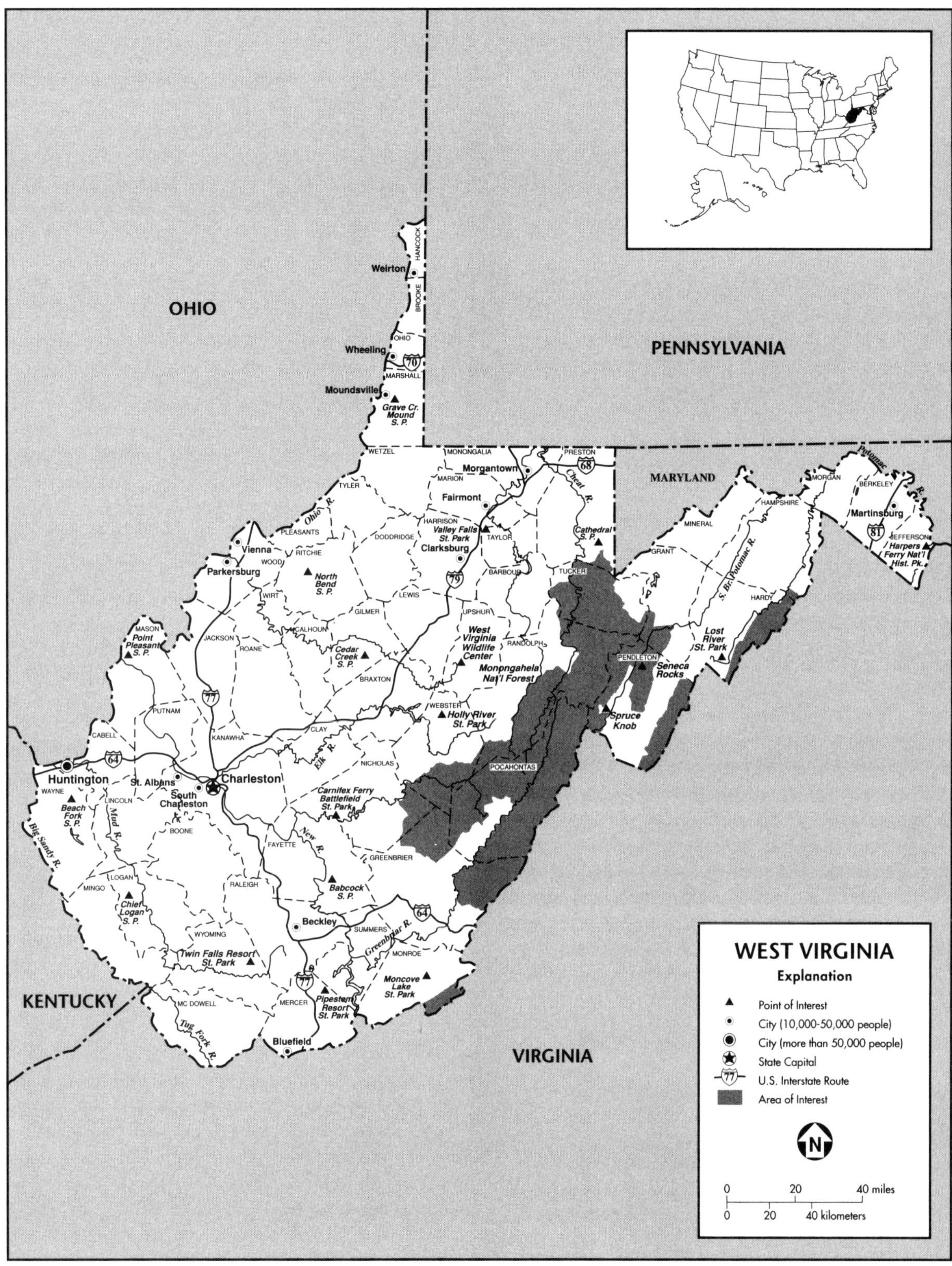

State of West Virginia.

The rapid changes brought about by the American Civil War (1861–1865) and by the formation of a new state had some important consequences. Industrialism moved southward and eastward along the expanding railroads and new kinds of communities arose. Lingering rivalries between unionists and secessionists, along with the difficult transitions from an agricultural to an industrial economy, often caused open conflict. In the backward mountain areas, these sometimes erupted into the legendary ''mountain feuds.''

After the Civil War governors of both Republican and Democratic parties worked to improve transportation, encourage immigration, and change the tax structure to encourage business. Several powerful senators from West Virginia who had made large fortunes in coal, oil, timber, and railroads held sway over party politics in the state for many years. West Virginia industrialists often cooperated with businessmen from other states, giving the state an almost colonial economy dominated by outside interests. Republican governors of the early twentieth century, notably Stephen B. Elkins, supported progressive legislation such as safety regulations for coal mines, revised corporate tax laws, and highway improvements.

The exploitation of the state's vast coal resources after 1890 would not have been possible without the state's network of railroads, especially after the completion of the Norfolk and Western. The same could be said of timber resources: From 1908 to 1911, 1,500 mills produced up to 1.5 billion board feet of lumber annually. Technological improvements in the industry, such as the band saw and the geared locomotive, helped to increase production of lumber and transportation of logs. An unfortunate consequence of this boom period was the destruction of millions of acres of virgin forest. After the 1920s a decline occurred and lumbering was again an important sector of modern West Virginia's economy.

Since 1890 the United Mine Workers of America (UMHA) had been attempting to unionize West Virginia miners, often with violent consequences. One of the most dramatic episodes in United States labor history occurred in West Virginia in 1920–1921. In Mingo and Logan counties, federal troops were called in to quell miners' unrest at the Baldwin-Felts mine in 1920. The so-called ''Matewan Massacre'' involved the deaths of ten men when the conflict got out of hand. When a union member was gunned down in 1921 by a company guard, 3,000 angry miners marched along the Kanawha River, fighting for five days on Blair Mountain with a sheriff's posse until the violence was quelled by federal authorities, who threatened to use howitzers and poison gas dropped from several U.S. Army bombers which were deployed at the Charleston airport.

The Great Depression (1929–1939) of the 1930s was devastating to West Virginia, with the greatest effects felt in the coal industry. Volunteer relief workers had difficulty keeping up with the needs of unemployed miners. President Franklin D. Roosevelt's (1933–1945) New Deal programs, in combination with private philanthropy, brought a measure of economic stability to the state and helped to make the West Virginia Democratic Party the majority party. Later political developments also increased the power of labor unions in the state, particularly the UMWA, under the leadership of the dynamic John L. Lewis.

World War I (1914–1918) and World War II (1939–1945) brought several economic changes to the state as chemical, steel, and textile industries grew up in the Kanawha and Ohio river valleys and the eastern panhandle. Decreasing the state's reliance on mining, these industries added new economic dimensions to the state and gave it a more diverse character.

After World War II, however, West Virginia's coal industry went into a state of decline. Mechanization and strip-mining caused many mineworkers to lose their jobs, and many began to immigrate to other states. In 1960 West Virginia was one of the most economically depressed states. Though antipoverty programs in the John F. Kennedy (1961–1963) and Lyndon B. Johnson (1963–1969) administrations brought some measure of relief, the state's manufacturing and mining industries had declined dramatically. In the early 1980s West Virginia experienced a serious recession, particularly in the steel, glass, chemical, and mining industries. In 1985 West Virginia had the highest unemployment rate in the nation. In 1995 the per capita personal income was still only $18,444, the second lowest in the U.S., and 16.7 percent of the population lived below the federal poverty level.

In the 1990s things improved for the state in several ways. Industrial production is still strong in the Kanawha, Ohio, and Monongahela valleys. Coal and timber production increased and the state gained a number of federal projects under the tenure of Senator Robert C. Byrd, chairman of the Senate Appropriations Committee. After the completion of Interstate Highway 64, tourism has also become an important sector of the economy. West Virginia's numerous, well-maintained state parks, glassmaking centers, and historic sites such as Harpers Ferry and the Cass Scenic Railroad have attracted approximately two million visitors a year.

See also: **Coal Industry, Virginia**

FURTHER READING

Conley, Phil, and William Thomas Doherty. *West Virginia History*. Charleston, SC: Education Foundation, 1974.

Rice, Otis K. *West Virginia: The State and Its People*. Parsons, WV: McClain, 1972.

———. *West Virginia: A History*, 2nd ed. Lexington, KY: University of Kentucky Press, 1993.

Williams, John Alexander. *West Virginia: A Bicentennial History*. New York: Norton, 1976.

Willis, Todd C., ed. *West Virginia Blue Book, 1984*. Charleston, SC: Jarrett, 1984.

WESTERN UNION CORPORATION

The first electromagnetic communication that revolutionized the world's economic and social life was transmitted on May 24, 1844, by Samuel Finley Breese Morse (1791–1872). At the Capitol building in Washington D.C., in the presence of Dolly Madison, Henry Clay, and other officials, Morse tapped out his famous message, ''What hath God wrought?'' This telegraphed message, transmitted in Morse Code, traveled 40 miles to a Baltimore, Maryland, train depot and was received in seconds by Alfred Vail (1807–1859), the financier of Morse's telegraph. The era of telecommunication had begun.

When Congress declined Morse's proposal for the government to purchase his telegraph patent, Morse and several partners formed the Magnetic Telegraph Company. Competition among telegraph rivals across the country was fierce. Prepared to compete with 50 other telegraph companies in operation throughout the United States, the New York and Mississippi Valley Telegraph Company (NYMVTC) was formed on April 8, 1851, in Rochester, New York. Five years later the growing NYMVTC was renamed the Western Union Telegraph Company. In 1857 Morse and his Magnetic Telegraph Company teamed up with businessman and financier Cyrus Field (1819–1892) in a project to lay a transatlantic telegraph cable. In the meantime, Western Union had begun the almost impossible task of stringing the first transcontinental telegraph poles to enable coast-to-coast communication. This rapid mode of communication heralded the end of the U.S. government's pony express service. It also saw the end of Morse's Magnetic Telegraph Company. In 1866 Morse recognized that his company could not compete against such a big rival, and in 1866 the Magnetic Telegraph Company merged with Western Union Telegraph Company. Along with the introduction of the commercial telegraphic machine, Western Union was successful in developing its own transatlantic cable technology. The company was well on its way to becoming the fastest messenger service in the country.

The social and economic impact of the telegraph resounded across the country. As the telegraph lines followed the westward expansion of the railroad, ordinary people paid the expensive fees for communicating quickly across vast regions. Big business and governments experienced the advantages of communication as new services were offered to keep pace with the changing needs of the American people. After Western Union moved its headquarters from Rochester to New York City in 1866, it introduced stock tickers as a method to speed New York Stock Exchange quotes to brokerage firms. One of Western Union's key services was the Money Transfer. Introduced in 1871, this service was still used in the late 1990s.

Time was not yet standardized across the country, so in 1870 Western Union developed its own time service. The nation's tallest building in 1877, built by Western Union, had a time ball at the top, which dropped at noon on a signal telegraphed from the U.S. Naval Observatory. The need for a standardized time schedule was becoming apparent for safety factors and to avoid confusion as communication across the country became more immediate. Generally acknowledged by the public as the most reliable regulation of time, the official start of Standard Railway Time was signaled in 1883 from the descent of the Western Union time ball. With clocks that rang school bells, blew factory whistles, and flashed signal lights Western Union became known as ''The Nation's Time Keeper.''

The technology of communication advanced rapidly. Western Union began using radiotelegraph to reach people on ships. Telegrams became extremely popular. The key and sounder had been replaced by the teletypewriter, only to be replaced by Western Union's introduction of the telex, a direct dial customer-to-customer teleprinter service in 1958. The telex would go on to serve as Western Union's second chief source of revenue. Mailgram messages began in 1970, becoming very popular for social and commercial use due to overnight delivery. The operation of the first domestic satellite communication system, Westar, was launched in 1974. By 1982 Western Union became the first U.S. company to have five satellites in orbit. For many years Western Union up-linked messages, data, and graphics to Westar satellites from major publishers, broadcasters, and corporations, and delivered the information across the country at the speed of light.

As early as the American Civil War (1861–1865) Western Union was contracted by the U.S. government to provide direct messaging to the White House communications room. Services included the filling of special money transfers, ensuring messaging needs were met and delivered to the troops during wartime, and delivering military orders of condolence for the armed forces. The services provided by Western Union to the government grew widely in the years following the Civil War. The company was chosen to provide communication for the Department of Defense, linking agency offices and supplying microwave communications for defense and intelligence agencies. A Western Union network connected the Federal Reserve member banks to a central computer center. Through Western Unions networks, law enforcement agencies exchanged data, and the Federal Aviation Administration provided flight and weather information to pilots.

Generations of people associated Western Union with hand delivered messages announcing births, deaths, homecomings, and even proposals of marriage. Western Union's telex business experienced success as the company continued to focus on other innovative business ideas. By the 1960s, however, telegraph use was waning as the telephone became the preferred method of communication. When it became cheaper to send data by telephone, the telex business began to suffer. Western Union was on the decline.

Since 1987 Western Union experienced many corporate and business changes. Despite its many past successes, the company found itself on the verge of bankruptcy in the early 1990s. On April 18, 1991, Western Union Corporation shareholders changed the name of the company to the New Valley Corporation in an effort to distance the failing enterprise from its successful subsidiary, Western Union Financial Services. New Valley assumed existing debts, but these soon skyrocketed to $800 million. In 1994 a bankrupt New Valley sold Western Union Financial Services Incorporated, all the Western Union money transfer trademarks, and trade names associated with the Western Union name, totaling $1.19 million. Utilizing this capital, New Valley continued to function, posting significant financial losses well into the late 1990s.

See also: **Samuel Finley Breese Morse, Standardization of Time, Telegraph, Utilities Industry, Westward Expansion**

FURTHER READING

Brewer, A.R. *Western Union Telegraph Company, 1851–1901.* New York: The Company, 1901.

Gallagher, Edward A. *Getting the Message Across; The Story of Western Union.* New York: Newcomen Society in North America, 1971.

International Directory of Company Histories, vol. 17. Farmington Hills, MI: Gale Group, 1988–1998, s.v. ''New Valley Corporation.''

McFall, Russell W. *Making History by Responding to its Forces.* New York: Newcomen Society in North America, 1971.

Rivise, Maurice Joseph. *Inside Western Union.* New York: Sterling Pub. Co., 1950.

WESTINGHOUSE, GEORGE

George Westinghouse (1846–1914) was an inventor who applied his talents to the railroad and electrical industries. He was a prolific inventor who obtained more than 400 patents during his career, best known for developing and promoting the alternating current power system as a substitute for direct current.

George Westinghouse was born in Central Bridge, New York, on October 6, 1846, the eighth of ten children. When Westinghouse was ten years old, his father moved the family to Schenectady, New York, where he opened a machine shop. Westinghouse worked in his father's factory as a child and gained experience and skill using a variety of machinery. In 1863 he enlisted in the Union Army as a private, serving during the American Civil War (1861–1865). One year later he became a third assistant engineer in the Navy.

After his military service ended, Westinghouse briefly attended Union College and continued to help in his father's factory. In 1865 Westinghouse received his first patent for a rotary steam engine. That particular product was not successful, but it was the first of many patents for Westinghouse. He next became interested in the workings of the railroad.

Westinghouse's first big success as an inventor came in 1869 when he patented an air brake for railroad cars—until that time, trains were stopped with manually-operated brakes. Westinghouse developed a compressed air brake, which was later improved through 20 additional patents. This invention led to the organization of the Westinghouse Air Brake Company in 1869 in Allegheny, Pennsylvania. He continued to improve the brake system and developed a revolutionary automatic train brake in 1872. His inventions greatly improved the railroad industry by allowing trains to operate safely at higher speeds.

In addition to brakes, Westinghouse was interested in other aspects of the railroad. With the increasing volume of rail traffic he saw the need to improve the signaling devices and interlocking switches of railroads. He studied European signaling systems and worked on signaling improvements using the combination of compressed air and electricity. In 1881 Westinghouse formed the Union Switch and Signal Company. Once again, his ideas made the railroads safer and more efficient.

Westinghouse's inventions, however, were not limited to the railroad industry. In the early 1880s Westinghouse applied some of his ideas about compressed air to the new natural gas industry. A well drilled in the yard of his home served as the source of several dozen inventions for controlling and distributing natural gas. Westinghouse invented a reduction valve for natural gas which allowed the gas to be transmitted at high pressure but distributed at low pressure.

This interest in natural gas then led Westinghouse toward involvement in the control and distribution of electricity. Westinghouse believed that a device similar to the reduction valve could be applied to electricity. Once again he studied European systems to see what could be applied to his new project. In 1886 he formed the Westinghouse Electric Company to develop and promote the use of alternating current electricity. A researcher for his company, Nikola Tesla (1856–1943), designed a polyphase system of alternating current and applied it to motors and lights. Westinghouse was one of the first inventors to understand that cheap, long-distance electrical power could come from transformers that would convert high alternating voltages to lower voltages at the point of use.

Westinghouse's revolutionary idea was initially tough to sell to the public. His main opposition came from Thomas Edison (1847–1931) and his company, which supported direct current rather than alternating current. Westinghouse slowly established a foothold in the electrical industry. By 1890 his company had installed more than 300 central power stations. The first big test for the system came in 1893 when Westinghouse won the contract to supply electricity for the World Columbian Exposition in Chicago. Westinghouse produced an impressive show of a quarter of a million lights. This success led to a new contract to build three generators to harness the power of Niagara Falls. The success of that project established the effectiveness and efficiency of alternating current power. In less than ten years Westinghouse had been able to convince the public of the value of alternating current power. Soon afterwards 95 percent of all electrical power produced was alternating current.

Despite the success of this invention, the Westinghouse company ran into some financial troubles in the early 1900s. In 1907 the company went bankrupt due to the general business crisis and financial panic of the time. Westinghouse regained control of the company a year later, but could not quickly recover its prosperity. In 1911 he retired from active management of the company, though he continued to experiment with new products.

George Westinghouse died in New York City on March 12, 1914. The Westinghouse Company continued to market the alternating current system as well as electrical devices that worked well with the new system. To this end the company developed many new innovations during Westinghouse's lifetime and afterwards. Among these were the first steam turbine for an electric utility, the first mail roll drive for a steel mill, the first American-built tungsten lamp, the first commercial radio station, and the first television camera tube.

See also: **Patent, Railroad Industry, Utilities Industry**

FURTHER READING

Berger, Joseph. *The Young Scientists: America's Future and the Winning of the Westinghouse.* Reading, MA: Addison-Wesley, 1994.

Leupp, Francis Ellington. *George Westinghouse: His Life and Achievements.* Boston: Little, Brown, and Company, 1919.

Prout, Henry G. *A Life of George Westinghouse.* New York: The American Society of Mechanical Engineers, 1921.

Ravage, Barbara. *George Westinghouse: A Genius for Invention.* Austin, TX: Raintree Steck-Vaughn, 1997.

Steck, Robert N. ''George Westinghouse Meets the Wizard.'' *D&B Reports.* September-October 1990.

WESTWARD EXPANSION

The United States inherited, in essence, the British empire's imperialistic tradition and it eventually became a global power that surpassed Great Britain. In 1790, however, the United States held less than 900,000

The expansion generated major socio-political and economic issues. Should American Indian tribes be treated as conquered subjects or as sovereign nations? How could the then-limited federal government defend ever-expanding boundaries, provide safety to its citizens, and ensure stable social order? How could a market economy develop where no infrastructure existed? How could the vast raw materials of the West be transported to the emerging eastern industrial centers?

square miles of territory. Much of the land was still claimed by indigenous societies, and the borders were contested by various European nations. Yet, the notion of national expansion was ingrained in the minds of the young nation's citizens.

The general unifying philosophy of manifest destiny propelled desires for national expansion. Use of the term first appeared in 1845 in the context of the impending Texas Annexation. Coming from a quasi-religious ideological base, manifest destiny was a belief that Americans were a chosen people who were ordained by a higher power to carry forward the ideas of liberty, civilization, and individual economic opportunity while assuming control over more and more lands. This belief grew partly from Charles Darwin's (1809–1882) biological theory that only the fit survive and prosper. Many believed the United States was a nation of destiny, an inevitable self-fulfilling prophesy.

In actuality, reasons for expansion continually varied with changing domestic politics, economics, and military needs. The strong desire for a substantial land base to support a free market society was an early major factor. In order to grow, the capitalistic economy and republican form of government needed surplus land and abundant natural resources such as wood, fossil fuels, minerals, and water. Many feared that without a surplus the parceling of limited resources to a growing population would eventually lead to class conflict. Not everyone embraced this philosophy. Some believed that conquest, particularly the continuing subjugation of Indian societies, was not in keeping with Christian or democratic ideals. Anti-expansionist sentiments heightened when a clearly imperialistic war broke out against Mexico in 1846.

Major events marked the geographic expansion to the West. The Louisiana Purchase in 1803 almost doubled the size of the United States with the addition of over 827,000 square miles. The lands included the future state of Louisiana and the entire Plains region between the Mississippi River and the Rocky Mountains north of Texas to the 49th parallel at the Canadian border. The Lewis and Clark Expedition (1804–1806) to the Pacific Northwest provided accounts of vast open spaces, rich soils, fast flowing rivers, and abundant game, and it thus gave impetus for further westward expansion. Driven by the prevailing Jacksonian populist ideals of economic equality, the country greatly expanded its borders in the 1840s under the policies of presidents John Tyler (1841–1845) and James Polk (1845–1849). The United States annexed the Republic of Texas in 1845, adding another 390,000 square miles. An 1846 treaty with Britain added the 286,000 square mile Oregon Territory stretching from the Rockies in Montana to the Pacific Ocean, including later Oregon, Washington, Idaho, and western Montana. Following the war with Mexico, the 1848 Treaty of Guadeloupe added another 529,000 square miles, including the future states of California, Arizona, New Mexico, and Utah.

As the growing slave-based cotton economy attracted new settlers into the Texas Republic, emigration over the Oregon Trail to the Pacific Northwest began in earnest in 1843. Also due to a serious economic depression in the early 1840s and declining living conditions in eastern communities, the emigrants annually leaving the United States on the Trail substantially increased in number by 1845. Discovery of gold in California in late 1848 led to the fabled Gold Rush of 1849. Within thirty years gold was found in almost every region of the West. Western agriculture that was first established in many areas to support local mining booms now expanded producing surplus for export elsewhere in the United States.

The expansion generated major socio-political and economic issues. Should American Indian tribes be treated as conquered subjects or as sovereign nations? How could the then-limited federal government defend ever-expanding boundaries, provide safety to its citizens, and ensure stable social order? How could a market economy develop where no infrastructure existed? How could the vast raw materials of the West be transported to the emerging eastern industrial centers?

American Indian sovereignty was recognized in the 1850s through numerous treaties in which Indian groups ceded property rights to vast tracts of western land. In exchange they retained lessor lands and various promises of governmental assistance. These initially sizable reservations were later commonly reduced through governmental coercion as settlers crowded in and gold was discovered.

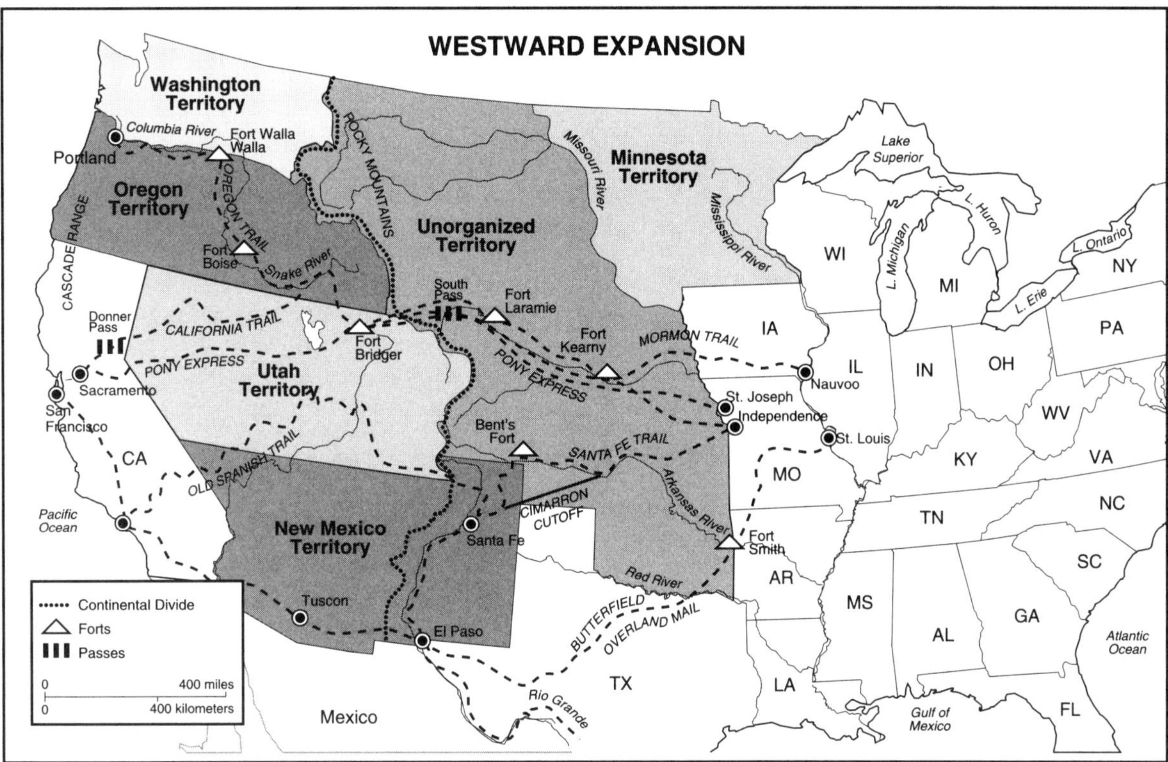

By the late 1840s, thousands of settlers had moved toward the West. They settled along many now famous trails.

During the 1850s and 1860s the United States underwent a revolutionary socio-economic transformation from a largely rural agrarian, slow-paced, fragmented society to much more closely integrated nationalistic society. In addressing socio-economic needs, the U.S. government adopted increasingly liberal land policies to facilitate settlement. By 1862 a person could obtain title to 160 acres of land for only a small filing fee and five years of working the land (a policy designed to also discourage land speculators). As the more productive lands filled, Congress passed revisions increasing the size of claims to foster economic self-sufficiency. These federal land laws promoted Jeffersonian ideals of widespread family ownership of farms; they also raised substantial revenue for the still young nation; and they supported infrastructure developments for transportation, education, and general economic development.

As for the infrastructure, most emigrants who sought new lives in the West brought their cultures with them. Starting anew with old ways, they replicated familiar churches, farms, house styles, and towns. The emigrants most often arrived in kinship clans and worked together in temporary labor pools and mutual interdependence to become economically viable; they also received considerable assistance from government subsidies.

Regarding the transportation dilemma, development of the West was closely tied to railroad construction. In 1862 Congress passed legislation authorizing construction of two railroads that eventually linked the Mississippi valley with the Pacific Coast in 1869. To promote settlement and economic development, the government provided generous subsidies in land grants and loans to railroad companies. Thus the railroad companies became the first big businesses of the United States. They held enormous power that was sometimes reflected in fixed prices and interference in state and local politics. The economic panic of 1873 and following depression slowed their expansion, but by 1877 railroad construction resumed. Three more transcontinental rail lines were completed by 1883: the Northern Pacific, Santa Fe, and Southern Pacific.

U.S. expansion in North America was essentially completed by 1867, when the United States purchased the 590,000 square mile territory of Alaska from Russia for $7.2 million. Over a century later, the midpoint for population distribution in the United States for the first time moved west of the Mississippi River.

See also: **Government Land Policy, Lewis and Clark Expedition, Louisiana Purchase, Manifest Destiny, Mexican Cession, Oregon Country Cession, Texas Annexation**

FURTHER READING

Billington, Ray A., and Martin Ridge. *Westward Expansion: A History of the American Frontier*, 5th ed. New York: Collier Macmillan Publishers, 1982.

Haynes, Sam W. *James K. Polk and the Expansionist Impulse*. New York: Longman, 1997.

Owsley, Frank L., Jr., and Gene A. Smith. *Filibusters and Expansionists: Jeffersonian Manifest Destiny, 1800–1821*. Tuscaloosa, AL: University of Alabama Press, 1997.

Robbins, William G. *Colony and Empire: The Capitalist Transformation of the American West*. Lawrence, KS: University Press of Kansas, 1994.

Stephanson, Anders. *Manifest Destiny: American Expansionism and the Empire of Right*. New York: Hill and Wang, 1995.

Weeks, William E. *Building the Continental Empire: American Expansion from the Revolution to the Civil War*. Chicago: Ivan R. Dee, 1996.

WEYERHAEUSER COMPANY

Weyerhaeuser Company, based in Washington state, was incorporated as Weyerhaeuser Timber Company in 1900. The company was a joint venture between railroad magnate James J. Hill of Pacific Northwest Timber, and Frederick Weyerhaeuser, joint owner of Weyerhaeuser and Denkmann—a Midwestern lumber company that relied on Wisconsin and Minnesota forests. Prior to World War I (1914–1918), the company was run by Frederick Weyerhaeuser, A German-born immigrant to the Midwest. His business philosophy evolved over his lifetime and became the operating philosophy for the new company. Weyerhaeuser felt that ''The way to make money is to let the other fellow make some too.''

Timber holdings doubled in the period preceding World War I. The company opened a sawmill to produce lumber and soon had the nation's first all-electric lumber mill in 1915. Although demand for lumber for railroad cars declined during World War I as steel was more heavily utilized, demand for lumber for military planes and other military uses increased.

John P. Weyerhaeuser, eldest son of the founder, led the company during the war and through the 1920s. He relied heavily, as his father had, on George Long, general manager from 1900 to 1930. Long, an early proponent of reforestation, approached the federal government before World War I to lobby for cooperative forest fire prevention and for lower property taxes for timberland to make reforestation economically viable. This lobbying led to the Clark-McNary Act in 1924, which addressed these issues and expanded the national forest. The act also encouraged changes in taxation policies at the state level to promote reforestation. Weyerhaeuser responded by creating the Logged Off Land Company in 1925 to handle the sale of ''logged off'' land, study reforestation, and lobby at the state level for lower timberland taxes. By the end of the 1920s Weyerhaeuser was the largest private owner of timber in the United States.

The Great Depression (1929–1939) produced hard times for the company, as few businesses or homes were being built. The depression in the lumber market would have been devastating if not offset by the company's 1931 diversification into pulp (a wood-derived raw material in the manufacture of paper, paperboard, and other products). By 1933 profits from pulp offset losses from lumber. In 1940 the company expanded its lumber business to include plywood and paneling. In 1941 the company started the first tree farm in the United States, near Gray's Harbor in Washington.

Rapid technological and commercial changes in the lumber industry following World War II (1939–1945) affected Weyerhaeuser. The hand-operated whipsaw was replaced by the power chain saw, and truck hauling replaced hauling by rail. Pent-up demand in construction, from the 1930s and early 1940s, led to greatly increased sales of lumber in this postwar era. Under the continued leadership of the Weyerhaeuser family, the company expanded into particle board production, ply-veneer, hardboard, and hardwood paneling in the 1950s. Timberland holdings expanded beyond the Pacific Northwest for the first time, as land was purchased in Mississippi, Alabama, and North Carolina. In 1959, with its increased diversification, the company dropped ''Timber'' from its official name to become Weyerhaeuser Company, and adopted its current trademark, a triangular tree over the word ''Weyerhaeuser.''

In 1960, and for the first time in company history, the presidency of Weyerhaeuser passed out of the family to Norton Clapp. Under Clapp the company went public in 1963 and expanded overseas, into Japan. George Weyerhaeuser succeeded Clapp as CEO in 1966, and served until 1988. The volcanic eruption of Mount Saint Helens in May 1980, was a setback for the company. Weyerhaeuser's Saint Helens Tree Farm was just below the mountain's dome and the company lost 68,000 acres of timberland. By 1983 the company had completed a timber salvage program and replanted 18 million seedlings in the volcanic area.

As part of a diversification program, Weyerhaeuser entered the insurance, home building, mortgage banking, garden products, pet supplies, and disposable diaper markets in the 1970s and 1980s. These new ventures added little to the company's profitability. Under John Creighton, who became president in 1988, Weyerhaeuser returned to a focus on forest products. Weyerhaeuser strengthened its core businesses through the purchase of two pulp mills, several sawmills, and approximately 175,000 acres of timberland in Georgia from the Proctor and Gamble Company in 1992 for $600 million. By the end of the twentieth century, Weyerhaeuser was the world's largest private owner of softwood timber and the world's largest producer of softwood lumber and market pulp. Weyerhaeuser had annual sales of nearly $11 billion and owned 5.3 million acres of timberland in the United States.

See also: **Lumber Industry, Environmentalism**

FURTHER READING

Taylor, John H. ''Rip Van Weyerhaeuser.'' *Forbes*, October 28, 1991.

Twining, Charles E. *F. K. Weyerhaeuser: A Biography*. St. Paul, MN: Minnesota Historical Society Press, 1997.

———. *Phil Weyerhaeuser: Lumberman*. Seattle: University of Washington Press, 1985.

Weyerhaeuser Corporation. *Where the Future Grows*. Tacoma, WA: Weyerhaeuser Corporation, 1989.

Weyerhaeuser, George H. *Forests for the Future: The Weyerhaeuser Story*. New York: Newcomen Society in North America, 1981.

WHALING INDUSTRY

Whaling is an ancient industry. There is evidence that whales were hunted along the coasts of Alaska and Siberia since 2000 B.C. The first mention of it in European sources dates from A.D. 875, but it is uncertain whether this is a reference to harvesting beached whales or to hunting them at sea. Although whaling in some form was conducted throughout the Middle Ages by the English, French, Icelanders and Norwegians, there is no clear proof that live whales were captured in Europe until 1575, when they were hunted in the Bay of Biscay. New England colonists brought the practice from Europe and made whale meat a part of their diet.

> A sailor's life is a hard life. (They) are exposed to many hardships, (of) which those of us who reside on land have no conception. Even when our ships are commanded by a pious man, the influence of the seaman is often very bad; and many are the young men who have left home with good habits, but when they have returned, they have become dissipated.
>
> **Reverend Daniel Lord, Pastor, Mariner's Church of Boston, July 30, 1841**

By the seventeenth century whale hunting was on the increase. Whale oil, which was produced when the animal's blubber (fat) was boiled down, was in great demand for lubrication and as a fuel for illumination. Realizing its commercial potential, the Massachusetts government encouraged the industry in 1639 by stipulating that whaling ships were exempt from taxation for seven years, and that members of the crew were free from their military obligations during the fishing season. The first organized whale fishery in North America was found on Long Island (an island near New York City) sometime after 1640, but Nantucket (an island off the coast of Massachusetts) had become the center of the industry by the late seventeenth century. These early whalers hunted the right whale, a forty-four foot mammal that migrated south to spend the winter off the American coast. The sailors slept in their own beds at night, since whales were spotted from lookout stations on land and caught near the shore by men in small boats. The animals would be dragged to the beach, where their blubber was removed and boiled down (the contemporary term was ''tried out'').

In the eighteenth century the growth in population and the beginnings of the Industrial Revolution increased the need for whale oil. It lubricated machines and fueled the lamps that illuminated the streets of major cities. It cleaned wool in textile mills and became a base for paint. By the middle of the century, spermaceti, a waxy solid that was extracted from the whale's head, was made into candles that were excellent sources of light and had a pleasant odor. It was also used for ointments and perfumes.

The increased demand for oil coincided with the hunting of the sperm whale, which began around 1812.

American commercial whaling was at its height in the 1840s and 1850s. Although whale's are still illegally hunted in various countries, the industry has been abandoned by America.

Its heads contained spermaceti and also a reservoir of oil that was known for its purity and lightness In general the oil from sperm whales burned more brightly than that from right whales, and it was marketed separately. Since sperm whales preferred deep water, whalers built large ships were built that were capable of sailing in the open ocean. These vessels contained tryworks, equipment that allowed the sailors to render the oil at sea. Since sailors no longer had to return to shore after each kill, the new technology completely changed the nature of the industry. Voyages could last four or five years, and American whaling slowly spread to all the oceans of the world. The industry began to have an influence on U.S. diplomatic policy, playing a role in the opening of Japan, the purchase of Alaska, and other important events.

Larger ships and long voyages meant that the crew could be divided according to their social standing. The officers, who were usually white and middle class, ate better food and lived in the rear part of the ship, where they had more space and privacy than the crew. The captain would have would have a parlor and bedroom. Many took their wives and sometimes their children to sea with them.

Ordinary sailors were usually poor whites, African or Native Americans. They were forced to live in cramped quarters in steerage or in the forward part of the ship. They ate food that was at best barely palatable and at times rancid. Fresh fruits or vegetables were rare, and death by scurvy, a disease caused by a lack of vitamin C, was relatively common. Nathaniel Robinson, a young man who went to sea in 1843, disliked the salt-cured horse and tar-like molasses he had to eat. He was particularly repelled by a pig's snout with bristles attached that he saw floating in a pan of food. Robinson became deathly ill on the voyage and died the day after he returned home.

Life aboard ship could be monotonous, but when a whale was sighted there was a flurry of excitement. The ship sailed near the creature and lowered whaleboats, which were about thirty feet in length and carried six men. The whale was approached carefully, so it would not become frightened, and so the harpooner could stand and steady himself. When he struck the animal, it would often dive to tremendous depths. The boat usually contained about 18,000 feet of line, which could be attached to the harpoon, and which whistled and burned as it spun out, following the diving whale. At times the whale would not dive, but swim along the surface at tremendous speed, taking the whaleboat on what was known as a ''Nantucket sleigh ride.'' Once the sailors survived the stricken beast's initial reaction, the long process of weakening the whale by tightening and slackening the rope began. It could take seven hours to exhaust the whale. When the animal became tired, the whaleboat would pull along side and an officer would kill it by plunging a six-foot razor-sharp lance into its lungs. The entire hunt was fraught with danger. Sailors had to avoid the whale's powerful fins and jaws, and the animals were known to attack the whaleboat, crushing or capsizing it. In 1820, the mother ship itself, the Essex, was rammed twice by sperm whale and sank, losing nearly half the crew.

The proceeds from the sale of the oil were divided between the owners of the vessel and the crew. Those who owned the ship or provided the capital investment took at least a quarter and usually much more of the profit. Often ownership was shared among a number of investors to lessen the risk. Captains could receive ten times as much as seamen. The rest of the crew's pay was proportionate to their tasks, and those who performed menial jobs obtained the least. The owners often lent the crew money to purchase their equipment, and often they charged 25 percent interest for their loans. In addition the ship usually had a company store, where the men could buy tobacco, clothes, and other sundries at high prices. After deducting their expenses, seamen might earn little for their hard and dangerous work. In 1844 John Murray returned from a voyage on the Milton for which the captain was paid nearly $6,000.00. Murray's wages after expenses amounted to ten cents, but the owners gave him an extra $10.00 on condition that he press no legal claim against them.

I WANT ONE MORE WHALE BAD. WE HAVE GOT BUT ONE MONTHS SALT MEET (MEAT) IN THE SHIP BUT I WOULD NOT MIND (STAYING) UNTILL THAT IS GON AND THIN LIVE ON FAITH UNTILL WE GET IN WHERE WE CAN GET SOME MORE.

Master of the *Roman*, His ship "intirly encircled with (Arctic) Ice", September 1853

American commercial whaling reached its height in the 1840s and 1850s, when at one point 700 of the 900 vessels engaged in the industry were registered in the United States. By that time New Bedford with its deeper harbor had surpassed Nantucket as the nation's whaling capital. Whaling began to decline after 1859, when oil was discovered in Pennsylvania, and kerosene, an oil derivative that burned more brightly, surpassed whale oil as a fuel for lamps. The Civil War (1861–1865) also damaged the industry, as Confederate raiders wreaked havoc on the largely defenseless whaling fleet. In addition, over-fishing made whales more difficult to find. By the late 1860s the business had contracted by 70 percent. It was saved by an increased demand for baleen, bony slats from the upper palate of certain whales that were used to strain food. It was excellent for making combs or umbrellas, providing support for corsets, and filling out Victorian skirts. Yet baleen could not prevent the eventual failure of the American whale industry, which declined by 20 percent every five years throughout the second half of the nineteenth century. With the development of spring steel in 1907, even the baleen market collapsed.

Whaling has continued in the twentieth century but not as an American industry. Indigenous peoples, many of whom live around the Arctic Circle, continued to hunt whales, and countries like Japan, Norway, Iceland, the Soviet Union (now Russia) and others engaged aggressively in the practice. The whale still provided many saleable products. Hydrogenated whale oil can be used for margarine, and bowhead whale oil is still the best lubricant for watches or clocks. Whale flesh is a valuable source of meat, and vitamins can be extracted from their inner organs. Whalebone can be ground for livestock feed.

The whaling nations built large factory ships that could drag the entire animal on deck for processing. They were so efficient was that in 1946 the International Whaling Commission (IWC) was established to save the creatures from extinction. In its first 40 years the commission made little progress, but in 1986, a moratorium went into effect that banned all commercial whaling. Canada left the IWC in 1982 in order to protect the hunting rights of its native people, and Norway resigned in 1992, maintaining that some types of whales could be harvested without endangering the species. Japan takes about 500 minke whales a year for "research" purposes. The fear however, that whales may become extinct have made them a symbol for the Conservation movement. Although the United Nations has banned all commercial whaling, Japan, Norway, and Canada continue to hunt these creatures.

See also: **Massachusetts**

FURTHER READING

Church, Albert Cook. *Whale Ships and Whaling*. New York: Bonanza Books, 1938.

Creighton, Margaret S. *Rites and Passages: The Experience of American Whaling, 1830–1870*. Cambridge: Cambridge University Press, 1995.

Ellis, Richard. *Whales and Men*. New York: Knopf, 1991.

Hohman, Elmo P. *The American Whaleman*. New York: Longmans, Green, 1928.

Sherman, Stuart C. *The Voice of the Whaleman*. Providence: Providence Public Library, 1965.

WHISKEY REBELLION

In June 1794, innkeeper John Lynn agreed to sublet part of his rented house in western Pennsylvania to John Neville. Neville was an excise inspector whose job it was to make sure that the federal tax on whiskey was collected from the backwoods frontiersmen. When the news circulated that Lynn was sheltering a tax collector in his home, however, a dozen armed men went to the inn. The men kidnapped Lynn, carried him into the woods, stripped him naked, shaved off his hair, and coated him with hot tar and feathers. After extracting a promise from Lynn not to allow his house to be used as a tax office and not to reveal their identities to the authorities, the men tied him to a tree and left him overnight in the middle of the forest. Although Lynn kept his promise, the notoriety he gained from his association with the tax ruined his business. Events like

Lynn's kidnapping threatened federal tax collectors all across western Pennsylvania during the summer of 1794. They marked the beginning of what became known as the Whiskey Rebellion—the largest and most serious challenge to federal authority yet faced by the new United States.

The Whiskey Rebellion had its roots in the period around the American Revolution (1775–1783). Before the war hundreds of families crossed the Appalachian Mountains, searching for better, cheaper land. They were accompanied by an equal number of land speculators, who were working for rich colonial interests. The speculators laid claim to hundreds of thousands of acres of the best farm land in the name of men who already owned thousands of acres in Virginia, Pennsylvania, New York, and elsewhere. George Washington (1789–1797), who had trained as a surveyor, was one of the largest buyers of land. He owned more than 63,000 acres in western Pennsylvania by the time he became president. Absentee landowners like Washington claimed most of the best land, and the poor farmers were forced to survive on the remnants.

A COMPETENT FORCE OF MILITIA SHOULD BE CALLED FORTH AND EMPLOYED TO SUPPRESS THE INSURRECTION AND SUPPORT THE CIVIL AUTHORITY IN EFFECTUATING OBEDIENCE TO THE LAWS AND PUNISHMENT OF OFFENDERS.

Alexander Hamilton to President George Washington, August 2, 1794

Separated from the older colonies by the mountains, the frontiersmen were forced to rely on themselves for protection and assistance. They were threatened by hostile Native Americans and hampered by lack of money, but they were especially frustrated by transportation problems. All the major colonial markets for their grain were on the other side of the Appalachians, and the costs of transporting their produce across the mountains were very high. The Spanish, who controlled the mouth of the Mississippi River, blocked an alternate route down the Ohio and Mississippi rivers. In order to turn a profit on their excess grain, the frontiersmen built private stills and converted it into whiskey. Whiskey was easier to sell than raw grain, and it held its value better.

When the U.S. Constitution was ratified in 1788 the new federal government agreed to assume the outstanding war debts of the former colonies. In order to pay these debts, President Washington's Secretary of the Treasury Alexander Hamilton (1755–1804) pushed a tax on whiskey and other alcoholic beverages through Congress in 1791. Many congressional delegates from the West were opposed to the whiskey tax. For his part, Hamilton believed that such a tax was the fairest way of spreading the costs of the American Revolution and the maintenance of the federal government across the population.

What Hamilton failed to consider was how strongly the settlers across the Appalachian Mountains felt about paying the tax. The western frontiersmen believed that they were maintaining their rights against the distant federal government in the same way their predecessors had done against the British government during the 1760s and 1770s. They felt betrayed by John Jay's (1745–1829) negotiations with the Spanish from 1785 to 1786 that kept them from shipping their grain down the Mississippi. Further, after two major defeats of federal troops by Miami and Shawnee tribesmen, the frontiersmen believed that the federal government was even unable to protect them.

During September 1791, representatives of the four westernmost Pennsylvania counties—Washington, Fayette, Allegheny, and Westmoreland—assembled at Pittsburgh, Pennsylvania, to discuss how to persuade Congress to repeal the whiskey tax. Although Hamilton would later portray them as radical anti-federalists, they held moderate views about the national government. Other westerners were not so tolerant. By the summer of 1794 what little patience they had was exhausted. Early in the morning of July 16, 1794, some 50 men armed with rifles approached the house where John Neville was staying. They demanded that Neville resign his position as excise inspector and turn over to them all the information he had collected on distilling in the area. Neville and the armed men exchanged shots; five of the besiegers were wounded, one of them fatally. The next day a mob of hundreds of local residents surrounded Neville's property. Neville, who had been reinforced by several soldiers from Fort Pitt, escaped without injury, but several soldiers were wounded and died, as did three or four of the attackers. The mob burned Neville's home and property to the ground.

The attack on John Neville marked the beginning of the Whiskey Rebellion. Throughout August and September threats of violence against tax collectors and inspectors spread out of the western districts of Pennsylvania and into Maryland, Virginia, Ohio, and Kentucky. In most cases, the rioters got their way through intimidation, and little blood was shed. The largest assembly came outside Pittsburgh on August 1, 1794, where about 7,000 frontiersmen gathered—mostly poor people who did not own property or even a still and were not directly affected by the tax. "Not surprisingly, then," wrote historian Thomas Slaughter in *The Whiskey Rebellion: Frontier Epilogue to the American Revolution* (1986), "their grievances were primarily economic in character; their victims were primarily members of wealthier commercial classes; and the property they envied was often the object of violence." However, the townspeople managed to defuse much of the threat by welcoming the frontiersmen into their houses and making whiskey freely available. They also convinced them not to burn property in the town and allowed them to expel some of the most obnoxious townsmen. The presence of the soldiers at nearby Fort Fayette also helped keep the rioters in check. Within a few weeks the whiskey rebels had dispersed and returned to their homes.

At the same time the Whiskey rebels near Philadelphia were beginning to disperse, the federal government was preparing to take action. President Washington called a meeting of his Cabinet to consider what action to take regarding the rebels. He found himself in agreement with Treasury Secretary Hamilton that the rebellion was a serious threat to the Constitution and the federal government. A proclamation was issued instructing the rebels to disperse by September 1. By that date, however, Hamilton had already begun to assemble a 12,950-man army that he believed would crush the rebellion and teach his political opponents a lesson. Although cooler heads had already prevailed among the leaders of the westerners, Hamilton's army marched at the end of September.

The Whiskey Rebellion trickled to a halt without much bloodshed. There were only two fatalities in western Pennsylvania, both of them accidental—one boy was shot by a soldier whose gun went off accidentally, and a drunken rebel supporter was stabbed with a bayonet while resisting arrest. By November 19 the federal army had managed to round up only 20 accused "leaders" of the Whiskey Rebellion. Eighteen of the accused were later acquitted in the courts; the other two were convicted of treason but were later given a presidential pardon.

The Whiskey Rebellion ended not because of the threat posed by Hamilton's army, but because many of the concerns of the frontiersmen were finally addressed. On August 20, 1794, an American army under General "Mad" Anthony Wayne decisively defeated a confederation of Native Americans at the battle of Fallen Timbers, outside modern Toledo, Ohio. The Treaty of Greenville (1795) that Wayne negotiated with the Native Americans opened the Ohio country to settlement. The Jay Treaty (1794) with Great Britain, and the Pinckney Treaty (1795) with Spain moved foreign troops away from western American borders and opened the Mississippi River to American shipping. Perhaps the most significant factor, however, was the fact that a political party with sympathies toward the frontier position, the Jeffersonian Republicans, came into power in the election of 1800. One of the first actions of President Thomas Jefferson's (1801–1809) administration was to strike down the Whiskey Tax and other internal taxes.

See also: **Appalachain Mountains, Jay Treaty, Pinckney Treaty**

FURTHER READING

Badwin, Leland Dewitt. *Whiskey Rebels: The Story of a Frontier Uprising*. Pittsburgh: University of Pittsburgh Press, 1976.

Boyd, Stephen R., ed. *The Whiskey Rebellion: Past and Present Perspectives*. Westport, CT: Greenwood Press, 1985.

Bruchey, Stuart. *The Roots of American Economic Growth, 1607–1861: An Essay in Social Causation*. New York: Harper and Row, 1965.

Porter, David. *The Whiskey Rebellion and the Trans-Appalachian Frontier*. Washington, PA: Washington and Jefferson College, 1994.

Slaughter, Thomas. *The Whiskey Rebellion: Frontier Epilogue to the American Revolution*. New York: Oxford University Press, 1986.

WILD AND SCENIC RIVER ACT

The federal government enacted protective legislation called the Wild and Scenic River Act (WSRA) in 1968 to preserve and protect wild and scenic rivers in America, including their immediate surrounding environment for the benefit of present and future generations. It was legislation to forbid all commercial development projects, along designated wild and scenic rivers, which might in any way affect the wilderness, the scenery, and the purely recreational use of the rivers. Some of the national Wild and Scenic Rivers include the Alagnak, Bluestone, Delaware, Donner and Blitzen, Great River, Missouri, Obed, and Rio. The Wild and Scenic Rivers are managed by different federal agencies, including the U.S. Forest Service, National Park Service, and the Fish and Wildlife Service. The designation of specific protected rivers near human communities has created the potential for significant conflict between resource and conservation management agencies and the commercial interests of local residents. Strategic efforts are made by managing federal agencies to incorporate local values with the planning and management of protected rivers to reduce conflict potential. According to the WSRA, a wild river is ''free of impoundment's and generally inaccessible except by trail, with watershed or shorelines essentially primitive and waters unpolluted. These represent vestiges of primitive America.''

See also: **Environmentalism**

WILDCAT BANKS

Wildcat banks were state-chartered financial institutions that operated in the United States from the early 1800s until the American Civil War (1861–1865). They were known as wildcat banks for their free lending policies and their issue of paper currency (called specie) that could not be backed up by gold or silver. A holder of the bank's paper currency could have it redeemed with specie by presenting the currency (bank notes) at the bank's office, which was located ''where the wildcats'' lived.

The Second National Bank of the United States (1816–1836), a federally controlled bank, was able to restrain the wildcat institutions, which predominated in the West and South, by requiring them to issue only the amount of currency they could convert to coin. But when the charter of the Second National Bank of the United States was allowed to expire (1836), the wildcat banks resumed their unsound banking practices. Paper currency issue and lending went unregulated amidst a rush to buy land on the frontier. The nation's currency wildly fluctuated as the renegade financial institutions loosened and tightened the money supply to suit their own needs. Furthermore, because there were so many banks issuing their own notes, another problem introduced itself: counterfeiting. No one could tell what was true bank currency and what was the product of a good counterfeiter. On July 11, 1836, President Andrew Jackson (1767–1845), intent on reining in the wildcat banks, issued the Specie Circular—an order that government agents accept nothing but gold or silver as payment for new land. When prospective land buyers (particularly in the West) took their paper bills to the state-chartered banks to be converted to coin, they found the banks' tills were empty. The holders were denied the face value of their notes. Bank after bank closed its doors, causing a financial panic in 1837. But many state banks remained in business and the issue of regulating paper currency continued to trouble the nation. During the American Civil War, Congress authorized the issue of 150 million dollars in national notes, called greenbacks. Through subsequent acts of Congress, including the creation of a national banking system (1863), the federal government eventually put the state banks out of business and replaced them with federally backed institutions. The nation's financial problems were not adequately addressed until 1913, when the Federal Reserve Act was passed to strengthen the federal control of the banking system and to bring about stabilization of currency.

See also: **Bank of the United States (Second National Bank), Currency, Federal Reserve Act of 1913, Greenbacks, National Bank Act of 1863**

WILDERNESS ROAD

The Wilderness Road was a trail blazed by American pioneer Daniel Boone (c. 1734–1820) as he led settlers westward across the Appalachian Mountains into present-day Kentucky between 1761 and 1771. By 1790 the road that passed through the Cumberland Gap (at the intersection of Tennessee, Kentucky, and North Carolina) had become a principal route westward. Settlers traveled Wilderness Road from Virginia, across the Appalachians, and into the Ohio River Valley. The route remained well traveled until about 1840. By that time the government–built National Road extended westward from Maryland, traversing the Appalachians, and descending into the fertile lands of Ohio, Indiana, and Illinois. Boone's westward route allowed for the early development of the nation's first frontier—the lands lying just west of the Appalachians. Wilderness Road later became part of U.S. Highway 25 and it is today part of the Dixie Highway.

See also: **Appalachian Mountains, Back Country, Daniel Boone, Cumberland Gap, Kentucky, National Road, North Carolina, Tennessee**

WILSON, THOMAS WOODROW

Woodrow Wilson (1856–1924), the twenty-eighth president of the United States, left a great legacy of domestic legislation that profoundly affected both American business and American workers. Most of that legacy was created during the first two years of his eight-year, two-term service in the White House.

Thomas Woodrow Wilson was born in Staunton, Virginia, in 1856, into the family of a Presbyterian minister. Wilson dropped the use of his first name after he graduated from college, and was known thereafter as Woodrow Wilson. Wilson grew up in an atmosphere

Woodrow Wilson.

of religious piety and scholarly interests. By the time he was two years old, the family had moved to Augusta, Georgia, where Wilson grew into young manhood. While he was growing up, his father took the young Wilson to many industrial and agricultural sites, where he learned directly about the conditions of ordinary working people.

Wilson began his professional life in a law office in Atlanta, Georgia, but by 1883, at age 27, he decided he wanted to be a college teacher instead of an attorney. He subsequently began to study history and politics at Johns Hopkins University in Baltimore, Maryland, where he obtained a Ph.D. in political science. Wilson thrived as a teacher and later as a professor and scholar. In 1902, at age 42, he was elected president of Princeton University.

His efforts and successes at Princeton University attracted wide public notice. Leaders in the Democratic Party of New Jersey sought him out as a candidate for governor. He was indeed elected governor of New Jersey in 1910. In that office, he enacted a primary election law, a corrupt-practices act, a public utilities act, employee liability law, and various school-reform laws. His work in New Jersey eased many of the burdens of the average working person and also began to reduce corrupt business operations.

Those who worked in national politics did not overlook Wilson's progressive work in New Jersey. He was encouraged to run for federal office, and in 1912, in a race against Republican William Howard Taft (1857–1930), and Progressive Theodore Roosevelt (1858–1919), Woodrow Wilson, a Democratic candidate, was elected to the presidency in a political landslide.

Beginning his presidency in 1913, Wilson quickly began to pursue his domestic political agenda. In October of his first year in office, Wilson's Congress passed the Underwood Tariff Act which lowered the unfair tax rates of imported items like wool, sugar, iron ore, steel rails, and many other important items.

Next he began his most crucial domestic reforms, including the creation of a Federal Reserve Board, later called the Federal Reserve System, to help control money policies in the United States and to insure fairness in all transactions. The creation of the Board is generally regarded as the most far-reaching piece of legislation covering banking and currency in the nation's history.

In 1914 Wilson had established the Federal Trade Commission (FTC) to halt unfair business trade practices. The Clayton Anti-Trust Act was also passed to police unfair practices in business. Wilson's Adamson Act established an eight-hour work day for railroad employees, while his Child Labor Act limited the work hours of children and began a new program of federal regulation in industry.

After two years of successful domestic legislation, Wilson ran into global problems with the start of World War I (1914–1918). Under his leadership, the United States declared war against Germany in 1917 in what he called an effort to keep "the world . . . safe for democracy." For the duration of his presidency Wilson worked on efforts dealing with international issues. Much of his important domestic legislation, which focused on controlling big business and easing the burdens of working people in America, was obscured by his interventions during World War I and his pioneering efforts in the creation of the League of Nations in the post-war era.

Though Wilson is largely regarded as the great war-president who led the United States in World War I (1914–1918) and whose efforts to create the international peace organization the League of Nations led later to its more-stable successor, the United Nations, it is arguable that Wilson's greatest achievements were made by his domestic policies. Such policies and programs began to effectively control the lopsided concentration of power in American business. Woodrow Wilson's first administration successfully enacted many of the progressive federal laws that controlled outrageously high tariffs, monopolistic and illegal industrial practices, and the federal control of the banking system. At the early stages of his presidency, Wilson was also successful in achieving progressive legislation to stabilize the balance between business interests and the interests of American workers, both industrial and agricultural.

Wilson, ''tired of swimming upstream,'' as he put it, died in his sleep in 1924. He suffered a series of strokes for many years before his death.

See also: **Clayton Anti-Trust Act, Federal Reserve System, Underwood Tariff, World War I**

FURTHER READING

Clements, Kendrick. *The Presidency of Woodrow Wilson.* Kansas City: University of Kansas Press, 1992.

Clements, Kendrick. *Woodrow Wilson, World Statesman.* New York: Twayne, 1987.

Heckscher, August. *Woodrow Wilson.* New York: Scribner, 1991.

Link, Arthur. *Wilson.* Princeton: Princeton University Press, 1947–1965.

Schulte Nordholt, J.W. *Woodrow Wilson: A Life of World Peace.* Berkley and Los Angeles: University of California Press, 1991.

WISCONSIN

The state of Wisconsin is located in mid-America between the Great Lakes and the Mississippi River. The land it encompasses had several built-in advantages for development. From the early fur traders to the modern industrialists, Wisconsin entrepreneurs used the state's waterways and water ports for transporting goods to markets elsewhere. Immigrants from northern, central, and eastern Europe created a prosperous farming region on the Wisconsin prairie. In modern times the area became known mostly for its dairy herds. Other industries have thrived in Wisconsin as well, particularly its breweries, lumber mills, and canning factories.

Native American tribes in Wisconsin first encountered Frenchmen in the 1630s, and became dependent on them for trading in furs. Father Jacques Marquette and Louis Jolliet traversed Wisconsin territory on their way to the Mississippi in 1673. Many other Frenchmen came during that period to establish missions or to trade in furs. Following the French and Indian War (1756–63), the British took control of Wisconsin. They ceded it to the United States in 1783. The Ordinance of 1787 included Wisconsin in the Northwest Territory; later parts of Wisconsin were included in the Indiana Territory, the Illinois Territory, and the Michigan Territory.

Lead mining originally brought white miners, called ''Badgers,'' to Wisconsin in the 1820s. They received their nickname because like badgers miners too must dig into the ground. The 1832 Black Hawk War drove out most of the remaining native Americans. White settlement began in earnest after that, and those indigenous people who stayed were eventually settled on reservations within the state. Wisconsin became a separate territory in 1836. New Englanders and southerners, lured by the lead mining in the southwestern part of the territory, flocked to the area during the 1830s. In 1848 Wisconsin became the thirtieth state of the Union.

Transportation and industry developed more slowly in the territory than some speculators had hoped. A canal was finally opened between the Fox and Wisconsin rivers in 1851. But it was not heavily traveled, despite millions of dollars in expenditures by the state and the federal government. The first rail line was built in the 1850s between Milwaukee and Prairie du Chien. Speculation reigned as farmers along the proposed route bought up railroad stock, often with disastrous economic consequences. Communities also competed fiercely to be included on the route. By the 1860s, the Chicago and Northwestern Railroad and the Chicago, Milwaukee, and St. Paul railroads dominated the state's transportation system. They helped foster the growth of Wisconsin's emerging lumber, dairy, and food processing industries.

CHEESE AND BEER—WHEN YOU THINK OF EITHER OF THE TWO, YOU THINK OF WISCONSIN.

Richard Nelson Current, *Wisconsin: A Bicentennial History*, 1977

The development of the state would not have occurred without a major influx of immigrants, primarily from northern Europe. In the 1820s these included mostly the Irish and the English, but by 1860 the predominance of German arrivals led some to call Wisconsin a ''German state.'' Yet, the area was attractive to many nationalities. In the 1880s the state lured as many Scandinavians as Germans, and later many immigrants from southern and eastern Europe settled there.

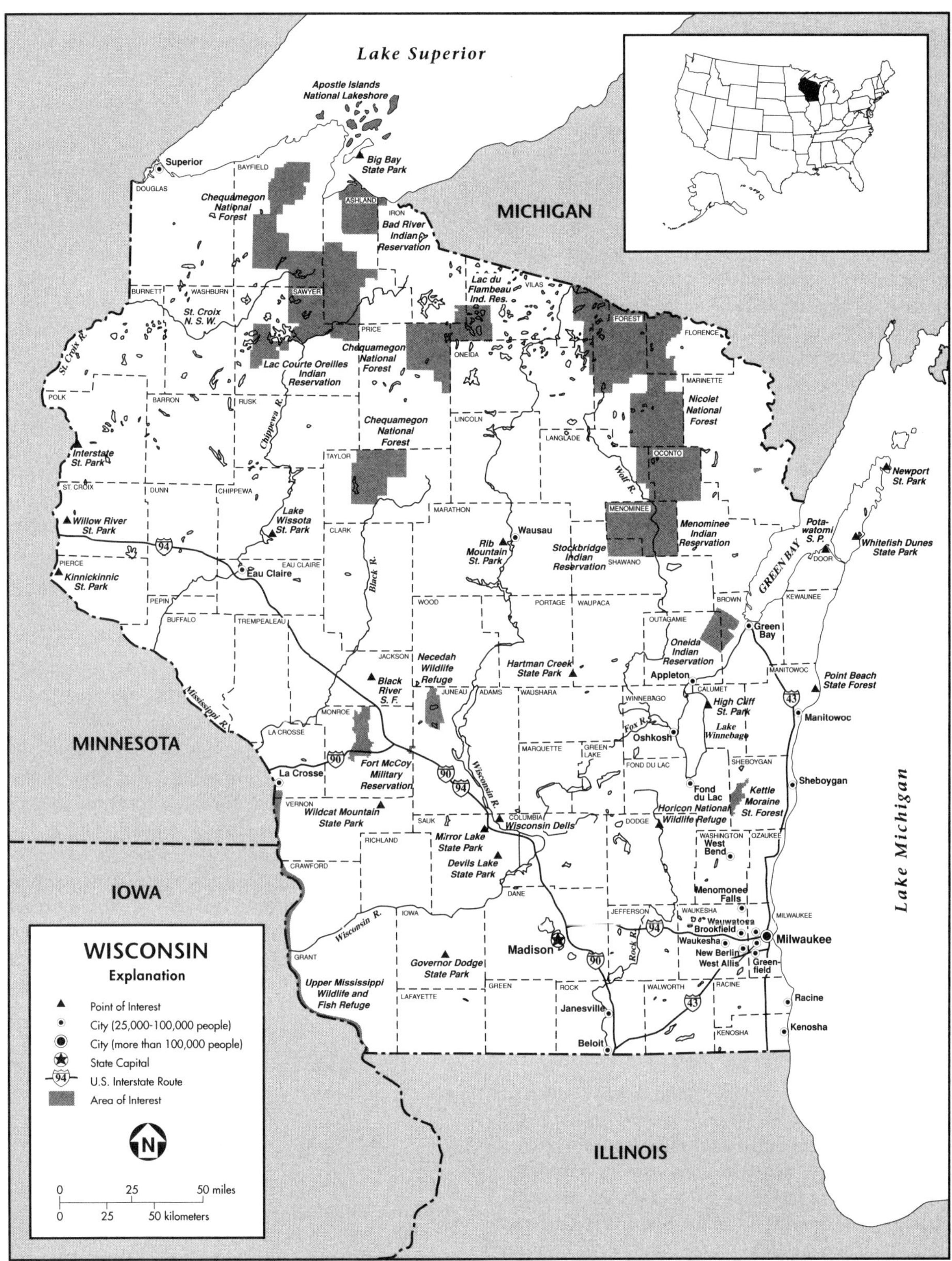

State of Wisconsin.

Many of these foreign-born Americans established farms across the entire state. At first they planted wheat, which was the biggest cash crop of the prairie because the McCormick reaper, first produced in Chicago in 1846, enabled farmers to harvest vast amounts of wheat in a short period of time. During the American Civil War (1861–65), sales of wheat to Great Britain provided the cash needed to finance the war effort. Usually departing from Milwaukee, the wheat shipments found their way through the Great Lakes and on to the eastern states and the rest of the world. After decades of wheat production, the soil began to be depleted of its resources. In response, Wisconsin farmers began to diversify, turning to the production of wool, sorghum, flax, sugar beets, tobacco, and hops.

Eventually dairy farming came to be identified with Wisconsin. The industry was established by New Yorkers and northern European immigrants who had brought their dairy-farming and cheese-making experience with them. By 1899 nearly 90 percent of the farms in Wisconsin had milk cows. Cheese factories proliferated, producing mostly "American" cheese or Cheddar, usually in a Wisconsin version that was called Colby. By 1919 Wisconsin was distributing almost two-thirds of the country's cheese.

Wisconsin also became a major producer of pork and pork products. A pioneer in that industry was Philip D. Armour (1832–1901). He made his reputation by supplying cured pork to soldiers in the American Civil War. Vegetable canning also became an important sector of Wisconsin's economy. In the infancy of the pressure-canning industry, Albert Landreth achieved significant success canning peas in Manitowoc. By 1918 Wisconsin canned as many peas as all the other states combined. Other vegetables such as sweet corn and beans also became important in the canning industry. The industry got a boost when large amounts of canned products were needed to supply soldiers in World War II (1939–45). Wisconsin remained a leader in the canning business thereafter.

Beer breweries are most prominently associated with Wisconsin in the public's mind. German immigrants had brought with them the technique for producing a lager beer that withstood storage better than earlier versions made in the region. Milwaukee became the center of brewing, with the Blatz, Schlitz, Pabst, and Miller families leading the industry. Many other cities produced beer, mostly for local consumption, but Milwaukee exported large amounts to other states and countries. The city became identified as the producer of the best brews. The bigger breweries survived the days of the Prohibition era by producing other products like soft drinks and candies.

Since the days of progressive Republican governor Robert La Follette (1855–1925) in the early twentieth century, Wisconsin has been known for its forward-looking approach to government and the economy. La Follette obtained legislative approval for increased taxation of railroads, the first state income tax in the nation (1911), and the first workmen's compensation program. La Follette's son Philip continued the reform tradition during the 1920s by supporting state regulation of electric power, labor disputes, and business practices. Philip La Follette's (1897–1965) so-called Little New Deal paralleled many of President Franklin D. Roosevelt's (1882–1945) national policies during the 1930s.

Although Wisconsin's economy diversified after World War II, the dairy industry remained its backbone into the 1990s. Cattle and calves in Wisconsin numbered 3.7 million in 1997 and were valued at 2.627 billion dollars. Dairy farming was also connected to two controversial environmental issues in the 1990s. The first linked agricultural runoff from animal wastes to contamination of Milwaukee's drinking water in 1993; the second involved a dispute over the use of bovine growth hormone to increase milk production.

Southeast Wisconsin, especially the Milwaukee area, was the cradle of industry by the late 1990s. Although some major breweries left the city, others continued to produce there and in other Wisconsin cities like La Crosse. Important paper and lumber products firms included Consolidated Paper in Wisconsin Rapids and Fort Howard Paper in Green Bay. Racine became home to Johnson & Son, a wax products company, and J.I. Case, a producer of agricultural equipment. Meat-packer Oscar Mayer located his operations in Madison. New and existing industries were assisted by the state Department of Development, as well as hundreds of local development corporations.

Wisconsin's water ports continued to be vital to the state's economy. In 1959 oceangoing vessels were first allowed access to Wisconsin via the Great Lakes through the St. Lawrence Seaway. Traffic to Wisconsin on the seaway, however, failed to meet expectations. In the 1990s, the busiest of all U.S. ports was Superior on Lake Superior; it handled mostly iron ore and coal. Important Lake Michigan ports, which also depended heavily on coal, included Milwaukee, Green Bay, Port Washington, Oak Creek, Manitowoc, and Sturgeon Bay. On the Mississippi River, Prairie du Chien and La Crosse processed the largest amount of cargo.

See also: **Brewing Industry, Robert LaFollette, Prohibition, Saint Lawrence Seaway**

FURTHER READING

Current, Richard N. *Wisconsin: A Bicentennial History.* New York: Norton, 1977.

Gara, Larry. *A Short History of Wisconsin.* Madison, WI: State Historical Society of Wisconsin, 1962.

Nesbit, Robert C. *Wisconsin: A History.* Madison: University of Wisconsin Press, 1973.

Risjord, Norman K. *Wisconsin: The Story of the Badger State.* Madison: Wisconsin Trails, 1995.

Smith, Alice E. *The History of Wisconsin.* Vol. 1, *From Exploration to Statehood.* Madison: State Historical Society of Wisconsin, 1973.

WOMEN IN THE WORKPLACE (ISSUE)

Over a 120-year period the identity of the woman worker has changed dramatically. From the 1820s, with the onset of industrialization in the United States, until 1940, the average female employee was young and single. If married, a woman working outside the home was likely poor and African American. From the 1940s to the 1970s, however, married women became the largest component of the female labor force. The number of gainfully employed, white middle-class women also rose rapidly.

In 1920 women composed 23.6 percent of the labor force and 8.3 million women older than the age of 15 worked outside the home. By 1930 the percentage of women in the work force rose to 27 and their numbers increased to 11 million. World War I (1914–1918) had expanded women's employment in new sectors of the economy and by 1920, 25.6 percent of employed women worked in white-collar office-staff jobs, 23.8 percent in manufacturing, 18.2 percent in domestic service, and 12.9 percent in agriculture. While the first generation of college-educated women entered professions in the 1920s, they found opportunities only in nurturing "women's professions" such as teaching and social work, and within medicine, nursing, and pediatrics. In factories, while male factory workers on federal contracts in 1920 started at 40 cents an hour, women started at 25 cents.

The Women's Bureau, a new federal agency approved by Congress in June 1920, was charged with reporting the conditions of women in industry and promoting the welfare of working women. The Women's Trade Union League (WTUL) also fought to improve women's labor conditions in the 1920s. The WTUL argued that protective legislation based on

> After World War II ended, a woman's average weekly pay fell from $50 to $37, a decline of 26 percent that contrasts sharply to an overall postwar decrease of four percent. Although three-quarters of women employed in war industries were still employed in 1946, 90 percent of them were earning less than they had earned during the war.

women's special position as child bearers should not be used against women workers by restricting their access to certain jobs.

Women laborers worked long hours and both the Women's Bureau and WTUL fought for shorter workdays. By the early 1920s all but five states upheld the 10-hour day/50-hour week work schedule; those five embraced the 54-hour workweek. Efforts to improve working conditions for women were consistently undermined by society's ambivalence about combining the roles of wife and mother with those of worker and professional.

The Great Depression (1929–1939) did little to alter the role of women in the U.S. workplace. According to the 1930 census almost eleven million women, or 24.3 percent of all women in the country, were gainfully employed. Three out of every ten of these working women were in domestic or personal service. Of professional women three-quarters were schoolteachers or nurses. The greatest numbers of women continued to work in domestic service with clerical workers just behind. Out of every ten women workers in 1940 three were in clerical or sales work, two were in factories, two in domestic service, one was a professional—a teacher or a nurse—and one was a service worker. During the Depression women entered the workforce at a rate twice that of men—primarily because employers were willing to hire them at reduced wages. In unionized industries, however, women fared better. Women constituted seven percent of all workers in the automobile industry and 25 percent of all workers in the electrical industry. The integrated International Ladies Garment Workers Union had 200,000 members and it secured for pressers in Harlem high wages of $45 to $50 per week. But such pay was the exception, not the rule.

Married women who worked faced particular hostility. They heard that they were taking jobs away from men, that the woman's place was in the home, and that children needed a mother at home full time. Both

Female switchboard operators connecting telephone calls in the 1940s.

private companies and the government dismissed large numbers of married women and made it difficult for married women to get high-paying professional or clerical jobs. Section 213 of the 1932 Federal Economy Act prohibited more than one family member from working for the government, barring many married women from federal employment. Even positions that were traditionally held by women, such as teacher and librarian, were affected.

New Deal legislation provided relief to both male and female workers in need although women often did not receive their full share of benefits. The 1933 National Recovery Administration (NRA) designed codes that improved women's wages, shortened their hours, and increased the number of women employed, but the codes did little for the two million women who lost their jobs and sought relief. Although the Works Progress Administration (WPA) launched successful projects for women's employment, women had difficulty getting such jobs. Only one member of a household was eligible to qualify for a relief job and women had to prove themselves economic heads of households. Women with physically able husbands could not qualify because men were considered heads of households, even if they were unable to find jobs.

Things quickly changed with World War II (1939–1945). Government posters featured women rolling up their sleeves and affirming ''We Can Do It.'' Radio stations sponsored contests for ''Working Women Win Wars Week.'' The number of workingwomen rose from 11.9 millions in 1940 to 18.6 millions in 1945. By the end of the war women comprised 36.1 percent of the civilian workforce and they were enjoying increases in income created by the wartime economy. Once women's employment became vital to the war effort it was applauded as patriotic. Between 1940 and 1945 women's presence in the labor force grew by more than 50 percent.

After the war, however, traditional gender assumptions about work retained their hold. The government position was that ''now, as in peacetime, a mother's primary duty is to her home and children.'' Although some 1.5 million mothers with small children worked, childcare remained inadequate. The government financed only 3,102 childcare centers to serve working mothers, providing for only a small fraction of the children in need of care. Most working mothers left their children with family members or left them to fend for themselves. The scarcity of institutional assistance for these women implied that while society approved of working women, it still expected them to take care of their children themselves. Moreover, most people considered women in the workplace a temporary phenomenon. Though women proved themselves the equal of men in many jobs, they were still being paid less. Because most of the working women had been trained primarily to be homemakers, they lacked the education and skills necessary to enter career paths leading to good pay, advancement, and security.

After World War II ended, a woman's average weekly pay fell from $50 to $37, a decline of 26 percent that contrasts sharply to an overall postwar decrease of four percent. Although three-quarters of women employed in war industries were still employed in 1946, 90 percent of them were earning less than they had earned during the war. Faced with a postwar decrease in the already inadequate number of childcare facilities many working mothers withdrew from the workforce. While the actual number of women in paid employment rose, they tended to be older women with no children to care for at home and were employed in an increasingly narrow range of jobs.

By 1960 over one-third of women were employed, while more and more married women went to work to obtain the many accoutrements of middle-class life. In 1963 Betty Friedan's best seller, *The Feminine Mystique*, argued that women were oppressed by a culture that consistently denied them opportunities outside the domestic sphere. Friedan went on to suggest that women should have the same freedom for self-fulfillment that men possessed. The book reawakened the feminist movement. In 1966 Friedan and others founded the National Organization of Women (NOW). By the late 1960s the government required that all institutions receiving federal funds use non-discriminatory hiring practices and by the early 1970s affirmative action laws were in place. In this atmosphere public opinion about women in the workplace began to change. But few women were able to break into the male-dominated professions and careers and the pay for women who worked full-time was less than 60 percent of the median for men.

The battle to gain rights for women in the workplace equal to the rights of men began before World War II and continued into the early 1990s. The specific legislative fight at the federal level to gain equal wages for equal work took about 17 years. Not until 1963, with the support of President John F. Kennedy (1961–1963), did such an act finally pass. The Equal Pay Act was intended to ensure that women would get paid the same wages as men for equal work. It was carefully written to raise women's wages, not to lower men's. Women filing suit under the Equal Pay Act could win up to two years of the wages they would have earned had they been paid equally with men. Discriminating employers could also be required to pay that same amount again as punishment, in addition to reimbursing successful claimants for the costs of hiring an attorney and court charges. Unfortunately, the act contained loopholes. The Equal Pay Act stipulated that the jobs of men and women must require equal skill, equal effort, and equal responsibility, each factor to be examined separately, for the jobs to be covered by the act. There was no provision that women must have access to the same jobs as men.

In subsequent years several other actions bolstered the rights of female workers. In 1964 the Civil Rights Act was passed and its broader language helped close some of the loopholes of the Equal Pay Act and further advance the rights of female workers. Title VII of the Civil Rights Act did not allow employers to deny jobs to women because of their sex. Thus it became illegal to manipulate jobs so that women would be excluded from those with higher pay. The Equal Employment Opportunity Commission (EEOC) was created to enforce this new employment right.

See also: **Home Front, National Recovery Administration, Rosie the Riveter, Women's Movement, Works Progress Administration**

FURTHER READING

Banner, Lois. *Women in Modern America: A Brief History*. New York: Harcourt Brace Jovanovich, 1984.

Chafe, William. *The American Woman: Her Changing Social, Economic, and Political Roles, 1920–1970*. New York: Oxford University Press, 1972.

Hartmann, Susan M. *The Home Front and Beyond: American Women in the 1940s*. Boston: Twayne, 1982.

Kanowitz, Leo. *Women and the Law: The Unfinished Revolution*. Albuquerque: University of New Mexico Press, 1969.

Rosenberg, Rosalind. *Divided Lives: American Women in the Twentieth Century*. New York: Hill and Wang, 1992.

WOMEN'S MOVEMENT

As the United States approached the age of industrial expansion in the 1800s, an increased awareness of social problems began to arise. Advocacy groups rallied for the abolition of slavery, reform in mental institutions and prisons, and equal rights for women. While these social issues gained attention, the roles of men and women began to change. The industrial age brought about a shift in family life as more married men worked in factories, which kept them away from home for 10 to 12 hours each day. Because women could not own property and were not allowed equal access to education and employment as were men, a married woman's life was limited to staying home and caring for the children, tending to household chores, and working at menial jobs. Single women were allowed to work in factories, but their wages were only half that of their male counterparts.

The movement toward equal rights was lead by Elizabeth Cady Stanton (1815–1902) who was born in 1815 in Johnstown, New York. Cady Stanton and her husband, Henry Brewster Stanton, a lawyer and abolitionist, attended the World Antislavery Conference in London, England, where they met other reformists such as Lucretia Mott (1793–1880), a Hicksite Quaker. The women, however, were not allowed to participate in the conference because they were female. On July 19–20, 1848, in Seneca Falls, New York, the two women organized the first public political meeting in the United States that focused on women's rights. The meeting was attended by 240 people, 40 of them men. The Seneca Falls Convention focused on the "Seneca Falls Declaration of Sentiments," which was modeled after the *Declaration of Independence*. The document was written by Cady Stanton, Mott, Martha Wright, Mary Ann McClintock, and Jane Hunt; it included a detailed list of female oppression by men, specifically citing depriving women of the rights to vote, to own property, and to equal employment and education. The "Resolutions" included in the "Declaration of Sentiments" were approved.

In 1865 the Fourteenth Amendment was introduced to Congress which allowed African American males the right to vote but specifically excluded females. Cady Stanton and Susan B. Anthony 1820–1906), who began campaigning for women's rights with Cady Stanton in 1951, reviewed an early draft of the proposal and took issue with the term "male citizen" which had never been used before in the U.S. *Constitution*. While they were sympathetic to the fact that former slaves needed this ballot to protect their rights, Cady Stanton and Anthony did not support it. Despite their opposition, Congress passed the Fourteenth Amendment in July 1868.

Over the next 20 years additional women's rights groups were formed and some success was attained at local levels. In 1870 women were given the right of citizenship in the Wyoming and Utah Territories and in the Washington Territory in 1883. In Michigan and Minnesota, widowed mothers of school children were given the right to vote on school issues in 1875. The same was afforded to widows in Vermont and New York in 1880.

In 1882 the U.S. Senate and the House of Representatives appointed Select Committees on Woman Suffrage and, for the first time in 1886, the "Susan B. Anthony Amendment," or the woman's suffrage amendment, was debated on the Senate floor. Gradually women won the right to own property and to have professional careers but it wasn't until 1920 that the Nineteenth Amendment was passed, giving women the right to vote.

The women's movement gained momentum and made important strides toward equality during the social unrest of the 1960s when civil rights groups and Vietnam War (1964–1975) protesters were demanding change. In 1963 author Betty Freidan wrote the best-seller "The Feminine Mystique," which described the unhappiness of the majority of middle-class women who wanted more out of life than to be housewives. At the same time, the Presidential Commission on the Status of Women (chaired by Eleanor Roosevelt) issued a report titled *American Women*, which documented discrimination against women in education, employment, taxes, and the law. As a result, the Equal Pay Act (1963) was passed that required employers to provide equal wages for equal work for men and women. President John F. Kennedy (1961–1963) further mandated that the federal government hire "solely on the basis of ability to meet the requirements of the position, and without regard to sex." This was the government's first attempt to address women's issues since 1920.

In 1964 the Equal Employment Opportunity Commission (EEOC), an organization developed to defend employment rights of minorities, also began to work toward securing rights for women. The Civil Rights Act of 1964 was broadened to include not only discrimination in jobs based on race, creed and natural origin but also sex.

Women rallied all over the country advocating for equal rights.

In 1966 Betty Freidan and others founded the National Organization for Women (NOW). NOW's statement of purpose was "to take action to bring women into full participation in the mainstream of American Society NOW, assuming all privileges and responsibilities thereof in truly equal partnership with men." The group focused on increasing the number of women in government jobs, legalizing abortion and increasing the number of day-care centers, and most of their goals were accomplished. In 1969 Betty Freidan, with author and feminist, Gloria Steinem (1934–), and U.S. representatives from New York Bella Abzug (1971–1976) and Shirley Chisholm (1969–1983) formed the National Women's Political Caucus (NWPC). The group worked to increase the number of females holding political office; they were very successful in this mission during President Jimmy Carter's (1977–1981) administration. Smaller radical groups formed over the next 10 years that advocated for various women's rights. These groups encouraged Congress in 1974 to pass the Equal Credit Opportunity Act (ECOA), which made it illegal to deny anyone credit based on gender.

Challenging the barriers to women's rights over the years led to more opportunity and economic power for women during the latter half of the twentieth century. In the early 1990s women received 54 percent of university Bachelor's degrees and 53 percent of all Master's degrees. By the mid-1990s women continued to advance in politics as well as the workforce. In 1997 there was still a difference in pay between men and women in the same positions—women holding mid-level jobs were still paid an average of 26-cents less per hour than their male counterparts.

See also: **Fourteenth Amendment, Nineteenth Amendment, Women in the Workplace**

FURTHER READING

Davis, Flora. *Moving the Mountain.* New York: Crowell, 1979.

Dubois, Ellen Carol, ed. *Woman Suffrage and Women's Rights.* New York: New York University Press, 1998.

Epstein, Cynthia Fuchs. *Woman's Place: Options and Limits in Professional Careers.* Berkeley and Los Angeles: University of California Press, 1970.

Flexner, Eleanor and Ellen Fitzpatrick. *Century of Struggle: The Woman's Rights Movement in the United States.* Cambridge, MA: Belknap Press, 1996.

Newman, James L. "Becoming the Birthplace of Women's Rights: The Transformation of Seneca Falls, New York." *Focus,* Fall 1992.

Wheeler, Marjorie Spruill, ed. *One Woman One Vote: Rediscovering the Woman Suffrage Movement.* Troutdale, OR: NewSage Press, 1995.

WOMEN'S TRADE UNION LEAGUE (WTUL)

Founded in 1903, the Women's Trade Union League (WTUL) sought to represent the cause of working-class women to middle- and upper-class reformers. Women were openly excluded from other labor organizations, which maintained that women simply did not have a place in the workforce. Male laborers were wary that including women in the labor cause would lower their own wages, and most felt that the woman's place was in the home. Whatever the prevailing sentiment among working-class men, the fact was that women were in the workplace in numbers. In 1903, the year the WTUL organized, there were 6.3 million women in the American workforce. The organization sought to secure state and federal legislation to protect female laborers, sponsor educational programs, and campaign for woman suffrage (the right to vote). By 1906 Jewish cap-maker Rose Schneiderman (1882–1972) rose to a position of leadership within the WUTL. In 1909, the Schneiderman-led WTUL joined forces with the International Ladies Garment Workers Union (ILGWU) and staged a strike against sweatshops (exploitative garment factories) in New York City. After a three-month strike, called the ''Uprising of the 20,000,'' tens of thousands of garment workers won wage increases, shorter hours, and somewhat safer work conditions. In 1911 Schneiderman was among those who turned out to join an April 5 procession to mourn the victims of the infamous Triangle Shirtwaist Factory fire. One hundred and forty-six workers, most of them Jewish immigrant women, had perished in the March 25, blaze in a building that failed to meet required safety standards. In the wake of the tragedy, Schneiderman resolved that workers would never again be forced to risk their lives to earn a living. Public outrage was now on the side of the movement to increase worker safety. The WUTL eventually became dominated by middle-class leaders who steered the organization away from union activities (including strikes), alienating its working-class membership. In the early 1920s the organization rallied against passage of an equal rights amendment to the U.S. Constitution, asserting that women workers needed protection from exploitation, not equal opportunities. By 1930 the WTUL had dissolved.

See also: **American Federation of Labor (AFL), Triangle Shirtwaist Factory Fire**

WORK ETHIC

The work ethic is characterized by the desire to work hard and efficiently. Significant aspects of the work ethic include frugality, accumulation of wealth, organized and systematic ways of life, and approval of diligence and disapproval of indulgence.

Early Greeks and Romans believed manual work to be a curse and left it to slaves. Aristocratic disdain for work continued throughout the Middle Ages except in monasteries, where work was of the ways by which a monk was sanctified. In early modern times, with the rise of capitalism and the middle class, the monastic respect for work was spread to the laity. In 1903, the sociologist Max Weber (1869–1920) proposed in *The Protestant Ethic and the Spirit of Capitalism.* that the modern work ethic developed from grew out of the thought of the Protestant reformer John Calvin (1509–1564). Calvin taught predestination, a belief that a person's eternal destiny (Heaven or Hell) is independent of one's actions on earth. It has been predetermined ahead of time. Yet, one may have a hint of God's plan by observing whether certain signs of election are present in one's life. Calvin's followers suggested that material success was one of these. In other words, success in this world, which is usually attained through hard work, means that you have been chosen to go to heaven. Scholars have long debated whether the Weber thesis is true. Nonetheless, a belief in the moral value of work, whatever its origin, has been an important facet of the West's material progress.

Largely because of a productivity rate decrease in the 1970s, questions arose regarding viability of the work ethic in the United States. The productivity drop off apparently resulted from an increased proportion of young inexperienced workers in the labor force. By 1979 an upward trend resumed. At the end of the twentieth century time spent working, attitudes toward work, and economic indicators point to a continued presence of a strong work ethic. Increasingly, studies showed that workers believed work rather than leisure yields not only material goods but self-fulfillment. With increases in education, technology, life expectancy, and with the need to balance family care with work, the logistics of work continue to evolve but the work ethic remains constant.

WORKING CONDITIONS IN FACTORIES *(ISSUE)*

During the late nineteenth century the U.S. economy underwent a spectacular increase in industrial growth. Abundant resources, an expanding labor force, government policy, and skilled entrepreneurs facilitated this shift to the large-scale production of manufactured goods. For many U.S. citizens industrialization resulted in an unprecedented prosperity but others did not benefit as greatly from the process. The expansion of manufacturing created a need for large numbers of factory workers. Although the average standard of living for workers increased steadily during the last decades of the nineteenth century, many workers struggled to make ends meet. At the turn of the century it took an annual income of at least $600 to live comfortably but the average worker made between $400 and $500 per year.

Factory workers had to face long hours, poor working conditions, and job instability. During economic recessions many workers lost their jobs or faced sharp pay cuts. New employees found the discipline and regulation of factory work to be very different from other types of work. Work was often monotonous because workers performed one task over and over. It was also strictly regulated. Working hours were long averaging at least ten hours a day and six days a week for most workers, even longer for others. For men and women from agricultural backgrounds these new conditions proved challenging because farm work tended to be more flexible and offered a variety of work tasks. Factory work was also different for skilled artisans, who had once hand-crafted goods on their own schedule.

Factory conditions were also poor and, in some cases, deplorable. Lack of effective government regulation led to unsafe and unhealthy work sites. In the late nineteenth century more industrial accidents occurred in the United States than in any other industrial country. Rarely did an employer offer payment if a worker was hurt or killed on the job. As industries consolidated at the turn of the century factories grew larger and more dangerous. By 1900 industrial accidents killed thirty-five thousand workers each year and maimed five hundred thousand others, and the numbers continued to rise. The general public became concerned with industrial accidents only when scores of workers were killed in a single widely reported incident, such as the many coal-mine explosions or the tragic Triangle Shirtwaist Company fire in 1911. In one year alone 195 workers in steel and iron mills were killed in Pittsburgh, Pennsylvania.

In order to save money many employers hired women and children to work in factories because these workers would work for lower wages than men. Some women were paid as little as six dollars per week, a sum much lower than a male would have received. Most female workers performed unskilled or semi-skilled machine work but some worked in industries that demanded heavy labor. Some women, for instance, worked on railroads, while others were employed as machinists.

IN THE LATE NINETEENTH CENTURY MORE INDUSTRIAL ACCIDENTS OCCURRED IN THE UNITED STATES THAN IN ANY OTHER INDUSTRIAL COUNTRY . . . . BY 1900 INDUSTRIAL ACCIDENTS KILLED THIRTY-FIVE THOUSAND WORKERS EACH YEAR AND MAIMED FIVE HUNDRED THOUSAND OTHERS, AND THE NUMBERS CONTINUED TO RISE.

Children also worked long hours for low wages. The number of children employed in factories rose steadily over the last three decades of the nineteenth century. By 1900 roughly 1.7 million children under the age of 16 worked in factories; less than half that many children had been employed 30 years before. Under pressure from the public many state legislatures passed child labor laws, which limited the hours children could work to ten hours per day, but employers often disregarded such laws. In southern cotton mills children who operated looms throughout the night had cold water thrown in their faces to keep them awake. Long working hours for children also meant that accidents were more likely to occur; like adult workers, many children were injured or killed on the job.

Worker responses to poor factory conditions and low wages were varied. Some employees intentionally decreased their production rate or broke their machines, while others quit their jobs and sought work in other factories. Other workers resorted to a more organized means of protest by joining labor unions although most industrial workers were not union members. Most workers, having few alternatives, simply endured the hardship of factory work.

In response to the problem of poor working conditions and the apparent indifference of industrial barons, membership in the American Federation of Labor (AFL), a union for skilled workers formed in 1886, grew rapidly from 256,000 members in 1897 to 1,676,000 in 1904. More radical and politically active trade unions often had even larger memberships, mostly because they were not as exclusionary as the AFL and because they welcomed unskilled labor, like those who worked in factories. One of the most radical, the Industrial Workers of the World (IWW), founded in 1905 and popularly known as the Wobblies, recruited primarily among the unskilled immigrants but also competed with the AFL to attract skilled laborers. Less radical than the Wobblies and more successful at recruiting supporters were the socialists, who gained political strength because of the growing numbers of immigrants and disenchanted unskilled laborers. The lack of real class conflict in the United States and the electoral reforms of the era undercut the socialists' efforts on a national level. Despite growing union activism the vast majority of workers remained unorganized throughout the first decade of the twentieth century.

Trying to prevent legislation to provide job security, guarantee a minimum wage, or ensure the safety of the workplace, most businessmen and conservatives argued that wages were set by the marketplace and that higher wages and worker protection would lead to higher prices for consumers. Government had long supported business using court injunctions and armed troops to put down strikes and break unions. In the 1890s, ruling that unions operated as "combinations in restraint of trade," the federal government used the Sherman Antitrust Act against unions more often than against businesses.

During the Progressive era several states passed legislation helpful to labor, such as laws establishing a minimum wage for women, maximum work hours, and workmen's compensation, and abolishing child labor and convict leasing. Groups such as the National Child Labor Committee, the Woman's Trade Union League, and the National Consumers League spearheaded the drives for many of these measures. Ironically, organized labor opposed minimum-wage laws for women because it preferred to win such measures through collective bargaining or strikes rather than through legislation. Business had to persuade labor to accept workmen's compensation plans, which unions opposed because the benefits were not very generous and many sorts of workers were excluded. Businessmen wanted the plans to protect themselves against the large payments that courts sometimes awarded in injury cases.

In 1904 a group of reformers established the National Child Labor Committee, an organization that dedicated to investigating the problem of child labor and lobbying state-by-state for legislation to end the abuse. It was, however, not effective because each state feared restrictive legislation could give other states a competitive advantage in recruiting industry. In 1907 a federal law against child labor, sponsored by Senator Alan Beveridge (1899–1911) of Ohio, went down to defeat and three years later in 1910 there were still an estimated two million children employed in factories. Only when the loopholes in state laws become apparent to reformers did they lobby for federal legislation, most of which did not come until the end of the 1920s.

In 1912 a Children's Bureau was established as an agency of the Department of Commerce and Labor. Its mandate was to examine "all matters pertaining to the welfare of children," which included child labor, and it was led by Julia C. Lathrop, the first woman to head a federal agency. Progress, however, was still slow. In 1916 senators Robert L. Owen and Edward Keating sponsored a bill that restricted child labor; the bill passed both houses of Congress with the strong support of President Woodrow Wilson (1913–1921). The law was based on a recommendation of the National Child Welfare Committee but it only prevented the interstate shipment of goods produced in factories by children under 14 and materials processed in mines by children under 16. It also limited children's workday to eight hours. In 1918 the Supreme Court declared this law unconstitutional because it was directed toward the regulation of working conditions not the control of interstate commerce. In 1919 Congress passed the Child Labor Act, which placed a tax on companies that used child labor, but the court again overturned the law. In 1924 there was an attempt to amend the Constitution to prohibit child labor but it never received approval from the required number of states.

***See also:* American Federation of Labor, Child Labor, Industrial Workers of the World, Mass Production, Frederick Winslow Taylor, Women in the Workplace**

FURTHER READING

Banner, Louis. *Women in Modern America: A Brief History*. New York: Harcourt Brace Jovanovich, 1984.

Dubofsky, Melvin. *Industrialism and the American Worker, 1865–1920*. Arlington Heights, IL: AHM, 1975.

Gutman, Herbert G. *Work, Culture, and Society in Industrializing America*. New York: Knopf, 1976.

Kanowitz, Leo. *Women and the Law: The Unfinished Revolution*. Albuquerque: University of New Mexico Press, 1969.

Rodgers, Daniel T. *The Work Ethic in Industrial America, 1850–1920*. Chicago: University of Chicago Press, 1978.

WORKS PROGRESS ADMINISTRATION

The Works Progress Administration (WPA) was the first major unemployment program of the New Deal and one of the most successful of the public works programs authorized by the Emergency Relief Appropriation Act in April 1935. The program, under the leadership of Harry Hopkins (1890–1946), provided about 3 million public sector jobs per year to unemployed heads of families. Most WPA workers built libraries, schools, hospitals, playgrounds, airports, bridges, and roads, but the program also employed writers, actors, musicians, and visual artists at jobs in their fields. The concept that the federal government, and not private industry, should create jobs was a sharp departure from conventional policy, and aroused significant controversy. Many objected that the WPA was a handout, joking that its initials really meant "We Putter Around." Some charged that WPA writers and artists were Communist sympathizers who did not deserve a government paycheck. Despite such criticisms, the WPA was a well-managed program that funneled almost 85 percent of its total budget into wages and salaries. From 1935 to its end in 1943, the WPA employed more than 8.5 million people and instituted almost 1.5 million projects, including sewer and road construction, murals in public buildings, written guides to each state, and the Historical Records Survey. Equally important, the program improved morale for millions of jobless Americans.

See also: **Harry Hopkins, New Deal**

WORLD WAR I

When the United States entered World War I (1914–1918) by declaring war on Germany on April 6, 1917, the global conflict had been underway for more than two and a half years. Also known as the Great War, World War I started as a result of the assassination of Archduke Franz Ferdinand, heir to the Austro-Hungarian throne. What began as a skirmish between Austria-Hungary and Serbia (the archduke was killed in the Serbian city of Sarajevo) quickly snowballed into a massive conflict when these nations' more powerful allies joined the dispute. Europe's existing alliance structure pitted the Central Powers—Germany, Austria-Hungary, and Turkey—against the Triple Entente—France, Britain, and Russia. After provocation from Germany, whose naval fleets had begun to sink American merchant ships in British waters, President Woodrow Wilson (1913–1921) made the decision to mobilize U.S. troops.

Wilson's decision had immediate economic repercussions, as the U.S. government faced the task of raising money for the war effort. Analysts determined that the country would need upwards of $33.5 billion to finance its participation in the war, plus money for loans to European allies. With the War Loan Act (1917), Congress proposed that the U.S. would provide $3 billion in such loans, though the sum was later increased. Now it fell upon President Wilson and Congress to determine where the necessary money would come from. They offered a solution by passing the War Revenue Act (1917), which stated that 74 percent of funding for the war would come from taxation imposed on the highest individual and corporate incomes. With this bill Wilson and Congress demonstrated an intent to place the financial burden on the wealthy and to give a break to middle- and low-income individuals and families. A year later Congress passed another revenue act, which increased this burden on the nation's wealthiest, who were now called upon to provide 80 percent of funding for the war.

In another move designed to raise money, the U.S. Treasury Department issued a series of bonds called liberty loans. These were long-term bonds that promised to earn the holder 3.5 to 4.25 percent in interest. The campaign to sell the bonds was massive in scope. Liberty loan committees formed in all regions of the country, and spokespersons appeared in theaters, hotels, restaurants, and other public gathering places. Even clergymen contributed to the marketing effort, urging members of their congregations to support the country through liberty loan purchase. Banks stepped forward to lend money for liberty loans at rates lower than the interest on the bonds. The campaign was a tremendous success. Of the five bonds issued between May 1917 and April 1919 (the last of these was called a victory loan), all of them were oversubscribed.

Although participation in World War I required vast government spending, the country's domestic economy benefited greatly from the effort. Established in July 1917, a War Industries Board endeavored to tap the nation's industrial resources while protecting its basic economic infrastructure. A demand for supplies, weaponry, food, and other materials resulted in increased productivity among manufacturers and farmers. It was a boom time not only for large corporations, many of whose profits wildly multiplied, but also for farmers, who saw a rise in agricultural prices, and for blue-collar workers, whose wages increased. Businesses expanded their international markets by exporting

American troops advancing in France on May 20, 1918. The soldier without a mask (*left*) is overwhelmed by mustard gas fumes.

goods to European ally countries. All in all, American industry profited enormously from increasing its production, exploiting its resources, and mobilizing its workforce.

Other participating nations, however, suffered more losses than gains during the course of the war. After the defeat of the Central Powers and the signing of an armistice in 1918, the Triple Entente and its allies pressed for reparations from Germany, which more than any other nation was held responsible for the war. The Treaty of Versailles, signed on June 28, 1919, placed the bulk of financial responsibility on Germany, and a Reparations Commission was established to determine the amount that the defeated Country would pay in damages to property and civilians. When the U.S. Senate refused to ratify the 1919 treaty, the United States forfeited its place on the commission, which decided in June 1920 that Germany would pay upwards of three billion gold marks a year for 35 years. The committee increased this amount in the following year, demanding a sum that Germany simply could not produce (indeed, in 1933 then-German leader Adolf Hitler (1889–1945) announced Germany's refusal to make further payments). Although the United States did not receive compensation for damages directly from Germany, it did collect payment on loans from its European allies, who derived these sums from German reparations.

American participation in World War I resulted in the loss of lives and a tremendous output of its financial resources. In addition to the $33 billion the U.S. government initially spent on the war, interest rates and veterans' benefits increased this sum to $112 billion. Yet the economic gains that were achieved during wartime far outweighed such losses. Between 1914 and the end of the decade, average annual incomes rose from $580 to $1,300. Moreover, the increase in international trade continued to raise profits for various industries. Propelled by the economic boost of war, America ushered in a new decade—the prosperous 1920s.

See also: **War and the Economy, War Industries Board**

FURTHER READING

Churchill, Allen. *Over Here!: An Informal Re-Creation of the Home Front in World War I.* New York: Dodd Mead, 1968.

Dictionary of American History. New York: Charles Scribner's Sons, 1976, s.v. ''Liberty Loans'' and ''Reparation Commission.''

O'Brien, Patrick. ''The Economic Effects of the Great War,''*History Today*, December 1994.

Tompkins, Vincent, ed., *American Decades: 1910–1919*. TK CITY: Gale Research, 1980–1989.

The Oxford Companion to American History. New York: Oxford University Press, 1966, s.v. ''Liberty Loans.''

WORLD WAR II

World War II (1939–1945) was an international conflict involving 61 countries that mobilized over 100 million people for military service in four geographic regions: Europe, Asia, Africa, and the South Pacific. The war left 55 million people dead (30 million civilian and 25 million military), cost over one trillion dollars, and resulted in more material destruction than any other armed conflict in history. The United States emerged from the war as the most powerful nation in the world, while the Soviet Union gained a stronghold over Eastern Europe.

The war pitted the Allied Powers (the United States, Canada, Australia, Great Britain, France, Russia, and China, among others) against the Axis Powers (Germany, Italy, Japan, Hungary, Bulgaria, Romania, and others). The leading figures for the Allies were U.S. President Franklin D. Roosevelt (1933–1945), British Prime Minister Winston Churchill (1940–1945, 1951–1955), and Soviet Premier Joseph Stalin (1928–1953). The Axis was led by German dictator Adolph Hitler (1933–1945), Italian dictator Benito Mussolini (1922–1943), and Japanese Prime Minister Hideki Tojo (1941–1944).

World War II began on September 1, 1939, when 1.5 million German troops invaded Poland. Germany's superior air power and technologically advanced armored and motorized divisions overwhelmed Polish forces that were often fighting on horseback with obsolete equipment. By September 20, Poland had been overrun by the German *blitzkreig* (lightening war).

England and France declared war on Germany in response to the invasion. Undeterred, German forces swept through Western Europe in the spring of 1940, taking Norway, Denmark, Belgium, Luxembourg, and the Netherlands. In June France was overtaken. The German war machine was not stymied until that fall when Hitler attempted to subdue Britain by air and sea. Aided by the development of radar, Britain handed Germany its first significant defeat of the war, forcing Hitler to indefinitely postpone a land invasion of England.

Despite its proclaimed neutrality, the United States was preparing for war. Congress approved the sale of surplus war material to Britain in June 1940, and it passed the first peace-time-draft legislation in September. In March 1941, Congress appropriated $7 billion in Lend-Lease aid to countries fighting against the Axis. Four months later the United States stationed Marines in Iceland and authorized the Navy to escort convoys in the area. In August President Roosevelt and Prime Minister Churchill signed the Atlantic Charter, outlining joint national policies for the postwar period.

> Soldiers, Sailors, and Airmen of the Allied Expeditionary Force! You are about to embark upon the Great Crusade, toward which we have striven these many months. The eyes of the world are upon you. The hopes and prayers of liberty-loving people everywhere march with you . . . I have full confidence in your courage, devotion to duty, and skill in battle. We will accept nothing less than full victory!
>
> **Dwight D. Eisenhower, Supreme Commander, Allied Expeditionary Force, D-Day, June 5, 1944**

U.S. relations with Japan were also deteriorating. In September 1940, the United States prohibited the exportation of steel, scrap iron, and aviation gasoline to Japan after Japanese troops entered northern Indochina. When Japanese troops occupied southern Indochina in July 1941, President Roosevelt retaliated by freezing Japanese assets in the United States. Diplomatic efforts between the two countries ended when Japan bombed the U.S. naval base at Pearl Harbor, Hawaii, on December 7, 1941. The next day Congress declared war on Japan.

Axis military conquests continued in 1942. In January Japan invaded New Guinea, the Solomon Islands, the East Indies, Burma, and the Philippines. In February Germany invaded North Africa and two months later sent troops into Greece and Yugoslavia. On June 22, 1941, Hitler ordered three million troops into Russia. Dubbed Operation "Barbarossa," Germany's invasion took the Soviet Red Army by surprise. More than a million Soviet troops were taken prisoner during the first three months of battle, and by the end of the year, German soldiers had advanced several hundred miles, camping outside of Moscow and fighting in Stalingrad.

Hitler's drive into Russia marked the peak of territorial expansion for Axis powers during World War II. It also marked a turning point. German advances were slowed by autumn rains, and then halted by the Russian winter. Most German soldiers in Russia lacked warm clothing and sufficient supplies. A number of German divisions retreated, while others were taken prisoner by the better-outfitted Russians. Reinforcements and resources sent to bolster German troops on the Eastern Front in 1942 did so at the expense of Axis

The attack on Pearl Harbor, Hawaii, on December 7, 1941, thus causing the U.S. to declare war on Japan the following day.

campaigns on the Western Front and in Africa during 1943.

The Allies began 1943 with a string of victories in North Africa, ultimately leading to the surrender of all Axis forces on the continent by May. From North Africa the Allies invaded Sicily, where they routed enemy troops and proceeded onto the Italian mainland. Hitler's attempt to invigorate the Russian invasion during the summer of 1943 only further depleted Axis resources. As 1943 ended the Soviets were on the offensive, driving German forces back across Poland. At the same time the Allies were on the offensive in the South Pacific where U.S. troops captured the Solomon, Aleutian, and Gilbert Islands.

At the outset of 1944 the Allies drafted plans for an invasion to end the war in Europe. U.S. General Dwight D. Eisenhower (1890–1969) headed "Operation Overlord," the largest amphibious assault in history. In the early morning hours of D-Day, June 5, 1944, 5,000 ships, 10,000 planes, and 176,000 soldiers crossed the English Channel and pounded the beaches at Normandy, France. Despite suffering heavy casualties against well-armed, concrete-fortified German defenses known as pillboxes, the Allies opened a 60-mile beachhead through which a million troops would pass during the next month. Paris was liberated by August. The Germans made a desperate Nazi counterattack at the German-Belgian border in December 1944, which is called the "Battle of the Bulge" for the deep bulge it created in Allied lines. After its failure, the German army collapsed inside the Allied vise. U.S. forces from the west and Russian forces from the east converged at the Elbe River in April, and Germany unconditionally surrendered the next month, on May 7, 1945.

Following victory in Europe, the Allies turned their attention to the South Pacific. After securing control of Iwo Jima, the Philippines, and Okinawa, the Allies made plans for invading Japan. To avoid the heavy casualties predicted to result from such an invasion, President Harry S. Truman (1945–1953), who took office following President Roosevelt's death, authorized the dropping of two atomic bombs. On August 6, 1945, the first bomb was dropped on Hiroshima, and three days later the second bomb was dropped on Nagasaki. Japan unconditionally surrendered on September 2.

Prior to his death Roosevelt met with Churchill and Stalin in February 1945, at the Yalta Conference, where the three leaders agreed to separate postwar Germany into four zones that would be occupied by the United States, Great Britain, France, and the Soviet Union. During the period of occupation Germany would be disarmed and its economy rebuilt. The Red Army's occupation of its postwar zone, however, gave way to the creation of Communist governments in Eastern Europe under Soviet control. The Yalta Conference also established the groundwork for an international war crimes tribunal at Nuremberg for the prosecution of Nazi leaders. Finally, the Yalta Conference finalized details for the creation of the United Nations.

World War II also brought greater unity to the U.S. home front. Over 16 million U.S. citizens served in the armed forces during the war, so just about everyone knew a relative, friend, or acquaintance that was fighting in some part of the world. Families pulled together through food shortages, increased taxes, and lines at the gas station. An unprecedented number of women went to work, particularly in factories. Not surprisingly, the troops' return home in 1945 precipitated the postwar Baby Boom.

See also: **Baby Boom, Home Front, Lend-Lease Act, Postwar Prosperity, United Nations, War and the Economy**

FURTHER READING

Ambrose, Stephen E. *Citizen Soldiers: The U.S. Army from the Normandy Beaches to the Bulge to the Surrender of Germany, June 7, 1944 to May 7, 1945.* New York: Touchstone Books, 1998.

———. *Eisenhower: Soldier and President.* New York: Simon and Schuster, 1990.

———. *The Victors: Eisenhower and His Boys: the Men of World War II.* New York: Simon and Schuster, 1998.

Baily, Bernard, David Brion Davis, David Herbert Donald, John L. Thomas, Robert H. Wiebe, and Gordon S. Wood. *The Great Republic: A History of the American People.* Lexington, KY: D.C. Heath and Company, 1981.

Morris, Herman C. and Harry B. Henderson. *World War II in Pictures (2 vols.).* World Cleveland, 1945.

WOZNIAK, STEPHEN GARY

The technical genius behind the Apple I and II microcomputers that launched Apple Computer, Inc., Stephen Wozniak (1950–) revolutionized computer design. By creating machines that were easy to use and relatively low in price, he helped launch the era of the personal computer. With Apple cofounder Steven Jobs (1955–), Wozniak worked out of his garage to develop Apple's breakthrough computers. Within 10 years he was running a company with 1,000 employees and annual sales of $500 million.

Stephen Gary Wozniak was born on August 11, 1950, in San Jose, California. Wozniak was the eldest of three children. His father, Jerry, was an engineer at Lockheed. Wozniak's interest in science and engineering came early. His father gave him a crystal radio kit when he was seven and an electronics kit a year later. Around fourth grade Wozniak recalls reading Tom Swift books about "this young guy who was an engineer, and he owned his own company. . . . It was just the most intriguing world, like the first TV shows you ever watched." His father also helped with various science fair projects on electronics. By sixth grade Wozniak had designed a computer that played tic-tac-toe. Wozniak continued to design computers through high school and college, without taking a course or even buying a book on how to do it. He just pieced things together with a group of like-minded friends. At age 14 Wozniak won an award for building a binary adding and subtracting machine, one of hundreds of small computers he designed before Apple.

Growing up in Sunnyvale in the Silicon Valley, the area between San Francisco and San Jose that is studded with electronics firms, Wozniak felt right at home. Something of a math and science prodigy, Wozniak was also a cutup and a practical joker. As his mother, Margaret, recalls, "I knew my son would either be rich or wind up in jail." Although Wozniak scored a perfect 800 on his math SAT, he lacked social skills and shunned parties, preferring technical magazines. In 1968 Wozniak attended the University of Colorado, having been rejected by Cal Tech. His second year was spent at De Anza College before he transferred to the University of California at Berkeley to study electrical engineering. Dropping out of Berkeley after his junior year, Wozniak became a designer of calculator chips at Hewlett-Packard. He also began to attend meetings of the Homebrew Computer Club, a group of Silicon Valley high-tech enthusiasts that set him on the course of designing inexpensive personal computers.

Wozniak met the younger Steven P. Jobs, another Homestead High alumnus, in 1968. In 1971 the pair started their first business venture: making "blue boxes" that allowed people to make free long-distance phone calls. They built the devices and sold them for $150 each to Wozniak's fellow students. He and Jobs continued to build microcomputers for the Homebrew Computer Club and in 1976 Jobs proposed starting a computer company, Apple Computer. He was 22 and Wozniak was 26. After several high-tech names were rejected, Jobs, who had worked in an orchard, proposed the name Apple. With Jobs concentrating on marketing and sales, Wozniak began to build the first Apple computer.

The Apple I was assembled in Jobs' family garage. Wozniak's design stressed simplicity and ease of use. Microcomputers prior to Apple were mainly for electronic hobbyists; Wozniak had constructed a machine that was affordable, useful, fun, and simple. Within a month of assembling the Apple I, they landed a $50,000 order. Wozniak's later design of a flexible disc (a ''floppy disc'') to replace the clumsy magnetic tape that all small computers then used for information storage was a revolutionary breakthrough. It was incorporated into the Apple II, a computer that made the company's fortune and transformed the personal computer business. The Apple II was the first small computer with a plastic case, the first with high-resolution color graphics, the first with so few chips for a complete system, and the first with a built-in speaker port for sound. Wozniak had designed a small but effective personal computer that could be used by ordinary people without complex training and commands that had been essential in microcomputers up to this time. Apple, therefore, had extended computer use to a much wider audience and pioneered the personal computer market. In subsequent refinements Apple marketed the IIe, III, and the IIc, as well as Lisa and Macintosh in the early 1980s. Wozniak's technical genius was behind each of these projects.

Wozniak married three times. He met his first wife, Alice Robertson, over a Dial-a-Joke line that he had started and sometimes manned as ''Stanley Zeber Zenskanitsky.'' They divorced in 1980. Wozniak's second wife, Candi Clark, was an Apple financial analyst who made the 1976 Olympics as a kayaker. The couple had three children. In 1981 the two were aboard Wozniak's Beechcraft Bonanza on a flight to San Diego to purchase their wedding rings when the plane crashed on takeoff. Candi suffered a skull fracture and numerous broken bones in her face. Wozniak was afflicted with short-term amnesia for five weeks. The accident, Apple's growing bureaucracy, and management hassles precipitated Wozniak taking a leave of absence from the company. While away from Apple, he resumed studying for his computer science degree at Berkeley, which he received in 1987. In the late 1990s Wozniak married Suzanne Mulkern, who also had three children from a former marriage. Mulkern, a lawyer, had been a seventh-grade classmate of Wozniak.

Wozniak gave away about half his shares in Apple before it went public in 1980, including $40 million in stock to his first wife, $4 million to his parents, brother and sister, and $2 million to friends. However, Wozniak's remaining 3.7 million shares were worth around $100 million. In 1982 and 1983 Wozniak, a rock music enthusiast, organized two U.S. Festivals of rock music and in 1987 the first U.S.-Soviet stadium rock concerts in Moscow, Russia. He has donated over $7 million to various charities, particularly in the San Jose area.

Wozniak remained devoted to his family in the late 1990s; he said that he would rather be remembered as a good father than as an icon of the computer era. His leisure activities included attending Golden State Warrior games, playing Tetris on his GameBoy, and going through manuals on new computer programs. He also collected uncut sheets of two dollar bills

Wozniak, who continued to see himself as an engineer and programmer rather than as a business executive, became less and less involved in the running of Apple in the late 1990s; he continued to offer design ideas, maintain an office, and earn a small salary from the company. In 1991 he embarked on a new career as a grade-school teacher. Inspired by his son Jesse's growing interest in computers, Wozniak began an ad-hoc class for him and his fifth-grade classmates in 1992. He later expanded Jesse's class, started a new one of 20 fifth-graders, and taught a class for teachers at the local middle school. Wozniak intended to complete his teacher certification and maintain his teaching at the elementary school level. He said, ''I was born to teach—I have always had this gift with children.''

Wozniak is one of the true pioneers of the computer age. By designing a simple-to-use and relatively inexpensive microcomputer, he helped to create the personal computer business that has transformed modern life. More of an inventive engineer than a businessman, Wozniak's computer designs have become standard in the technological revolution that he helped to start. The multibillion-dollar personal computer industries can trace its origins in part to Wozniak's innovations. Wozniak helped initiate the continuing development of smaller, faster, and easier to use computers that could reach more users. The world following the appearance of the first Apple computer has changed remarkably, and Wozniak's innovations have contributed greatly to those changes.

Wozniak has used the fortune he gained from his inventions to make a difference in his community and in the world. He has brought people together for rock music, accelerated the thaw in U.S.-Soviet relations by offering computer expertise and arranging exchanges, and served in his local community as a teacher of the next generation of computer wizards. Wozniak has predicted that computers will eventually reach the physical limit of their hardware, which will allow programmers to create what he has called ''something like a Ten Commandments of Software.'' For example, computers shall not crash, and error messages shall be understandable. Wozniak foresees future computers becoming more like real people, moving away from menu-driven controls. At the very end of the twentieth century, despite his withdrawal from active work at Apple, Wozniak remained on the cutting edge of computer design.

See also: **Paul Allen, Computer Industry, William Gates III, Steven Jobs**

FURTHER READING

Friesberger, Paul, and Michael Swaine. *Fire in the Valley: The Making of the Personal Computer.* Berkeley and Los Angeles: Osborne/McGraw-Hill, 1984.

Garr, Doug. *Woz: The Prodigal Son of Silicon Valley.* New York: Avon, 1984.

Linzmayer, Owen W. *Apple Confidential: The Real Story of Apple Computer, Inc.* San Francisco: No Starch Press, 1999.

Moritz, Michael. *The Little Kingdom: The Private Story of Apple Computer.* New York: William Morrow, 1984.

Rose, Frank. *West of Eden.* New York: Penguin, 1990.

WRIGHT, FRANK LLOYD

Frank Lloyd Wright (1869–1959) was considered one of the most influential and most important twentieth century U.S. architects. His buildings—more than 400—possessed the quality and feel of genius at work. His designs, his unique ideas about homes, seemed eternally futuristic, enormously functional, and have influenced every sphere of twentieth century architecture.

Frank Lloyd Wright was one of the most dramatic and eccentric U.S. geniuses. He was born on June 8, 1867, the eldest of three children born to William and Anna Lloyd Wright in the small town of Richland Center, Wisconsin, on the American prairie. Wright's mother had emigrated from Wales with her family. Her brothers and her father, who was a Unitarian minister, became skilled carpenters and built themselves homes in the Wisconsin River Valley. Wright's relationship with his mother was very close throughout his life. When he was very young his mother, who was a schoolteacher, used the Froebel Kindergarten Method at home, which introduced children to pure geometric forms and their patterns on grids. Scholars have speculated that Wright's later use of so much sophisticated geometric design in his work was an outgrowth of his early integrated exposure to geometric design as a learning tool.

His father, William Carey Wright, was a Baptist minister and musician. When Wright was three years old, his family moved to Massachusetts, where his father worked as a minister. Around 1880 the family moved back to Wisconsin. His father opened a music conservatory and Wright went to school and worked on his uncle's farm. When Wright was 18, his father divorced his wife, leaving him with his mother and two younger siblings. After his parents' divorce in 1885, Wright sought part-time employment in Madison, Wisconsin. He also had plans to study at the University of Wisconsin. Wright took a job with a Madison contractor as a draftsman's apprentice, and he took engineering and graphics courses for a year at the university. That was the end of his formal education. To further his architectural training, Wright left Madison in 1887 for Chicago, Illinois, where he obtained employment as a draftsman with Joseph Silsbee, an architect.

Chicago in the late 1880s was booming and Wright was there to take advantage of the wealth of opportunities available. Architects from all over the world had come to Chicago to rebuild the city after it was destroyed in a devastating fire in 1871. Wright, having learned the architectural basics from Silsbee, began to undertake his own commissions and projects for private residential home design. In 1888 he joined the firm of Adler and Sullivan, where he primarily designed homes.

He landed a job with Dankmar Adler and Louis Sullivan, one of the most progressive architectural firms in the country. Here Wright developed a very close relationship with Louis Sullivan (1856–1924), who was known for his "form follows function" ideology. By the time Wright was in his early 20s, he had worked on some of the most impressive buildings in Chicago.

Wright left Sullivan in 1893 and established his own business. From 1893 to 1910 he built approximately 273 houses, many of which were the "Prairie-house style"—a combination of Japanese design elements and American influences.

In 1889 Wright married Catherine Lee Clark Tobin. Frank and Catherine had six children, two of whom became architects. To support his wife and children in the manner to which he was accustomed, Wright took

Frank Lloyd Wright with a model of a museum, the first New York building of the architect.

on extra work designing houses. Wright ''bootlegged'' designs from Sullivan's firm, adding his own ideas—Sullivan subsequently severed his contract with Wright. In 1893 Wright started his own architectural business. In 1909 he abandoned his wife and children, running off to Europe with Mamah Borthwick Cheney, the wife of a former client. The couple stayed away from the United States for a year, returning in 1911 to settle in Spring Green, Wisconsin, where Wright built his well-known residence Taliesin (''shining brow'' in Welsh). In 1914 a servant at the Taliesin residence set fire to the house and murdered Mamah, two of her children, and four other occupants as they tried to escape the flames. The house was almost completely destroyed. Wright rebuilt Taliesin and later traveled to Tokyo, where he was commissioned to build the Imperial Hotel.

During the 1920s Wright developed a new construction method using pre-cast concrete blocks that were reinforced with metal. Several houses were built with this new method, of which the most notable is the Mallard house in Pasadena, California. Wright's personal life was in a shambles during this decade and his professional life was greatly affected: Commissions were not as numerous and many commissions that Wright did have were postponed or cancelled due to the Great Depression (1929–1939).

In 1922 Wright married the sculptress Miriam Noel. In 1925 Taliesin burned down again. Wright's career suffered because of continual scandal in his personal life, which was continually unraveling. Wright's finances and emotions were depleted. His life was filled with lawsuits, bad publicity, bankruptcy, and bitterness. In 1928 Wright married his fourth wife, Olgivanna Milanoff, a Montenegrin aristocrat, who was at one time a student of G.I. Gurdjieff, a Russian-born esoteric thinker and mystic. This marriage lasted for the rest of Wright's life.

During the early 1930s Wright devoted his time to writing and lecturing. In 1931 Wright set up the Taliesin Fellowship and turned his residence into a studio-workshop for apprentices who would pay to study with him and work on Wright's commissions. As the economy in the country stabilized, building resumed and Wright designed two well known buildings: the Kaufman House, which was cantilevered over a waterfall at Bear Run, Pennsylvania, and an administration building for the S.C. Johnson and Son Company in

Racine, Wisconsin. Wright also kept himself busy designing houses and communities that he thought were the perfect answer to modern society; for example, Broadacre City was a decentralized community with no distinction between town and country. He designed homes that would reflect an ideal, democratic America—Usonia. In 1938 he built Taliesin West, a permanent desert camp made of stone, wood and canvas, near Phoenix Arizona.

Wright began to lecture and teach. Although his designs continued to be built at a steady pace for more than two decades, he was not to see fame re-emerge in his life until the 1950s. He was in his eighties then, but he had survived into old age with good energy and a burning passion about his beliefs in radical architecture. Wright wrote several books about architecture. He was idolized in the 1950s as a daring, individualistic genius. The eccentricities for which he was once scorned had helped to make him popular. Clearly, before he died, Frank Lloyd Wright had secured a position in the public imagination as a uniquely American icon; a brilliant, loner, "cowboy"-architect—a genius to architecture, as Albert Einstein was a genius to physics.

During the 1940s and 1950s Wright continued to design and build innovative and impressive structures. During this time his designs were perhaps more varied and radical than previous decades—college campuses, crescent-shaped houses, circular houses, and lastly, the unprecedented concrete, spiral-shaped Guggenheim Museum, his last major work. Although his work has been criticized as impractical and expensive, none of his structures have sustained damages due to faulty engineering.

Wright believed that U.S. architecture should reflect the environment in which it was built, the environment of the frontier and of the abundance of land. Wright described his work as "organic architecture, that which proceeds, persists, creates, according to the nature of man and his circumstances as they both change." He created homes with strong horizontal lines and shapes, with roofs that were low pitched with large overhangs, and with flourishes that created a sense of the horizon and of spaciousness. The inside of his homes, influenced by Japanese designs, had large open spaces, huge central rooms, few closed corners, many large windows, and a geometric emphasis in the room's decor. His homes were unadorned; nothing "fancy" or "fake" or unnecessary was present. His ceilings were built high—cathedral ceilings—and many of his houses were heated with radiant heat (coils built into the concrete slab floors which circulated warm water through the coils to radiate heat into the home evenly). And since automobiles had become easier to start, he stopped building garages and instead attached simple carports that would protect the car from heavy snow but retain the open feel of the total design.

Frank Lloyd Wright's designs of homes and buildings have inspired generations of architects, including much of what is called "modern architecture." His influence has been international—many other countries have considered Frank Lloyd Wright's designs to be a major influence on their contemporary styles. More than 30 states in the United States possess Frank Lloyd Wright structures, and most architectural critics agree that every state in the country has buildings that reflect Wright's style. His many imitators constitute Wright's greatest success. Even if his more severe designs are changed and distorted, the general horizontal style of Wright's prairie architecture created a distinct shape of architectural content that has influenced the way Americans see modern architecture. His brilliant designs of Taliesin West, his Arizona headquarters; the inexpensive Usonian homes; the great Kaufman House, built over a waterfall in Pennsylvania; his designs for the Imperial Hotel in Tokyo, and the Guggenheim Museum in New York City are all breath-taking examples of his great success as an architect and an artist. Frank Lloyd Wright died in 1959.

See also: **Louis Sullivan**

FURTHER READING

Blake, Peter. *Frank Lloyd Wright: Architecture and Space*. Baltimore: Penguin Books, 1964.

Brooks, H. Allen. *The Prairie School: Frank Lloyd Wright and His Midwestern Contemporaries*. Toronto: University of Toronto Press, 1971.

Brooks, H. Allen, ed. *The Writings of Wright*. Cambridge: MIT Press, 1983.

Gill, Brendan. *Many Masks*. Putnam, 1987.

Wright, Frank Lloyd. *An Autobiography*. New York: Duell, Sloan and Pearce, 1943.

WRIGLEY, WILLIAM, JR.

William Wrigley, Jr. (1861–1932) was a salesman and industrialist. He started his career as a soap salesman and ended it as the owner of the largest chewing gum company in the United States. Wrigley was also the owner of the Chicago Cubs baseball team and had a baseball stadium in Chicago, Illinois, named after him.

William Wrigley, Jr. was born on September 30, 1861 in Philadelphia, Pennsylvania. His father, William Wrigley, Sr., was a soap maker who had founded his own company, the Wrigley Manufacturing Company, in 1870. Wrigley worked for his father's company as a child, selling soap from a basket on the streets of Philadelphia. At the age of 11, Wrigley went to work in the soap factory. He stirred vats of liquid soap and earned $1.50 a week. When Wrigley was 13, he returned to sales. He traveled by train or wagon from town to town selling his father's soap. This early sales experience would prove to be useful for his later career as a businessman in his own right.

In 1891 Wrigley left his father's company with hopes of starting his own business. He left Philadelphia for Chicago with only $32 to his name, but an abundance of ambition and enthusiasm. In Chicago his uncle, William Scotchard, loaned him $5,000 to start his own business on the condition that his cousin become his partner. In April 1891, at the age of 29, Wrigley started his business selling Wrigley's scouring soap. He offered premiums to merchants as an incentive to buy his product. Wrigley gave merchants baking powder as a premium, but baking powder soon became a more popular product than soap, so Wrigley switched his main product. In 1892 he began to offer two packages of chewing gum as a premium in place of the baking powder. When demand for the chewing gum surpassed that for the baking powder, Wrigley once again switched products.

At that time there were about a dozen other companies selling chewing gum, but the industry was not developed. In 1892 Wrigley hired the Zero Manufacturing Company to produce chewing gum for him. That same year he introduced his first two brands of gum called Lotta and Vassar. In 1893 he introduced Juicy Fruit and Spearmint gums.

Initially Wrigley had to work hard to break into the chewing gum business because established companies offered products already popular with the public. Wrigley relied on his sales and advertising skills to promote his products and distinguish them from other brands of chewing gum. He continued to offer retailers premiums for carrying his product. The premiums included a variety of products, such as lamps, razors, and scales. In addition, he saw the advantage of familiarizing the public with his products through newspaper, magazine, and poster advertising.

In 1899 six of the largest gum manufacturers merged to form a "chewing gum trust." Wrigley was offered the opportunity to join the merger, but he refused. As he explained, "We propose to keep our identity . . . and if we cannot do business by fair and square methods, we prefer not to do business at all." The Wrigley Company still prides itself on this legacy of independence and integrity.

Though the company struggled during its early years, Wrigley's persistence and dedication paid off. In 1906 he put his advertising philosophy to the test. Wrigley had introduced Spearmint gum to the public several years earlier, but it was not initially very popular. In 1906 Wrigley began a limited advertising campaign in Buffalo, Rochester, and Syracuse, New York, to specifically promote Spearmint. The campaign was so successful that in 1907 Wrigley spent $284,000 to continue to promote this product across the country. As a result of this effort, Spearmint sales rose dramatically and reached over $1.3 million in 1909. By 1910 Wrigley's Spearmint was the most popular gum in the country.

The success of Spearmint made Wrigley the world's largest chewing gum maker. In 1911 Wrigley bought the Zero Manufacturing Company and established the William Wrigley, Jr. Company. He also began to expand his interests abroad. In 1910 he opened a factory in Canada, followed by factories in Australia in 1915, and Great Britain in 1927. Before Wrigley's death, his company had factories in Chicago, Manhattan, Brooklyn, Toronto, London, Berlin, Frankfurt, and Sydney. The company's expansion into international markets led to the creation of new products and flavors as well as new marketing techniques. Wrigley advertised in more than 30 languages and taught the world how to chew gum.

Wrigley retired as company president in 1915, though he continued to serve as chairman of the board. His son, Philip Knight Wrigley, took over the family business and Wrigley explored his other business and leisure interests. By 1921 Wrigley became principal owner of the Chicago Cubs and later acquired two other baseball teams. He also purchased Santa Catalina Island off the coast of California and turned it into a popular resort. When William Wrigley, Jr. died on January 26, 1932, his family business had already become one of the most popular brand names in the United States.

See also: **Baseball**

FURTHER READING

Allen, Michael Patrick. *The Founding Fortunes of a New Anatomy of the Super-Rich Families in America*. New York : Truman Talley Books, 1987.

Darby, Edwin. *The Fortune Builders.* Garden City, NY: Doubleday, 1986.

Ingham, John N. *Biographical Dictionary of American Business Leaders.* Westport, CT: Greenwood Press, 1983, s.v. "Wrigley William, Jr."

Olsen, Frank H. *Inventors Who Left Their Brands on America.* New York: Bantam Books, 1991.

WYOMING

The state of Wyoming has been bypassed by the sweeping changes which affected a majority of the United States in the nineteenth and twentieth centuries. It is ranching country with little population and many open spaces. Wyoming has small cities and it has, in recent years, prospered from its abundant energy resources. But a large portion of the state remains much as it was when pioneer wagon trains crossed it in the mid-nineteenth century.

French Canadian traders were the first Europeans to enter Wyoming, but an American fur trader, John Colter, was the first to do any important exploration. After he reported on the natural wonders of the northwestern part of Wyoming, other traders and trappers crossed the territory. The old Oregon Trail crossed Wyoming, and between 1840 and 1867 thousands traversed the territory on their way to Oregon, California, or other points west. Some were travelling to the California, Idaho, and Colorado gold countries; others were escaping from the American Civil War (1860–1865) and its aftermath; still others simply hoped for good land on which to build new homes. They stopped at landmarks like Devil's Gate and Split Rock and at supply points like Fort Laramie, but few chose to stay in the arid land of Wyoming permanently. The economy of the area at that time was largely based on trading posts which served the travelling wagon trains, most establishments were run by mountain men. Other enterprises, such as blacksmith shops and ferries or toll bridges across rivers, also sprang up to serve the needs of the pioneers.

The Union Pacific Railroad eventually brought permanent settlers to Wyoming. It was the first time a railroad had been built before the creation of a new territory. Cheyenne, Laramie, Rawlins, Rock Springs, and other towns sprang up as the railroad made its way across the country in 1866 and 1867. Each experienced a boom and then a decline as the railroad workers moved from town to town. Wyoming officially became a territory in 1868, but growth was slow. In 1869 it had a population of barely nine thousand.

After the quelling of Indian uprisings in the late 1870s, Wyoming soon became cattle country. The cattlemen and some foreign investors hoped to get rich because the grass was free and the price of cattle was high. Texas longhorns were driven to the southeastern part of the territory, and later Hereford cattle were introduced. Although sheep were also raised on the ranches, Wyoming came to depend on cattle more than any other territory. The American myth of the cowboy was especially strong in Wyoming. According to T. A. Larson's bicentennial history of Wyoming, the image of a strong, lonely figure in open cattle country appealed to a nation in which the grips of growing industrialization and urbanization appeared as signs of "a complex civilization in which the individual felt he counted for very little."

Small ranchers and cowboys had difficulty competing with big "cattle barons," who not only bought up much of the land but also held the most important influence in local and state politics. Though profiting from the land, many cattlemen lived in towns and visited their ranches only occasionally. Unfortunately for the cattle speculators, in addition to overgrazing and low cattle prices, a drought in the summer of 1886 and a harsh winter that same year had disastrous results. Shortly after Wyoming became a state in 1890, the so-called Johnson County War of 1891–1892 pitted large against small landowners and culminated in the arrest of large landowners for practicing vigilante justice.

Life in Wyoming proceeded at a slow pace throughout the early decades of the twentieth century. Stockmen suffered greatly during the Great Depression (1929–1939) of the 1930s. A long period of drought destroyed hay and grass and many animals had to be destroyed. Cattlemen were forced to accept government subsidies in order to survive. During World War I (1914–1918) and World War II (1939–1945), however, despite some grumbling among cattlemen about beef rationing, cattle ranches prospered. In the decades following World War II, Wyoming's economy came to depend more and more on cattle, and very large ranches became the norm.

Wyoming's growth was minimal throughout most of its history because the land was mostly unsuitable for traditional farming. It is still sparsely populated state, ranking last in population in the 1990 census. The development of coal, oil, and natural gas resources brought some growth in the 1970s during the nationwide energy crisis; but this growth too slowed during the 1980s. The 1990s saw some improvement in the oil and coal industry; in the late 1990s Wyoming ranked first in the nation in coal production. In addition to

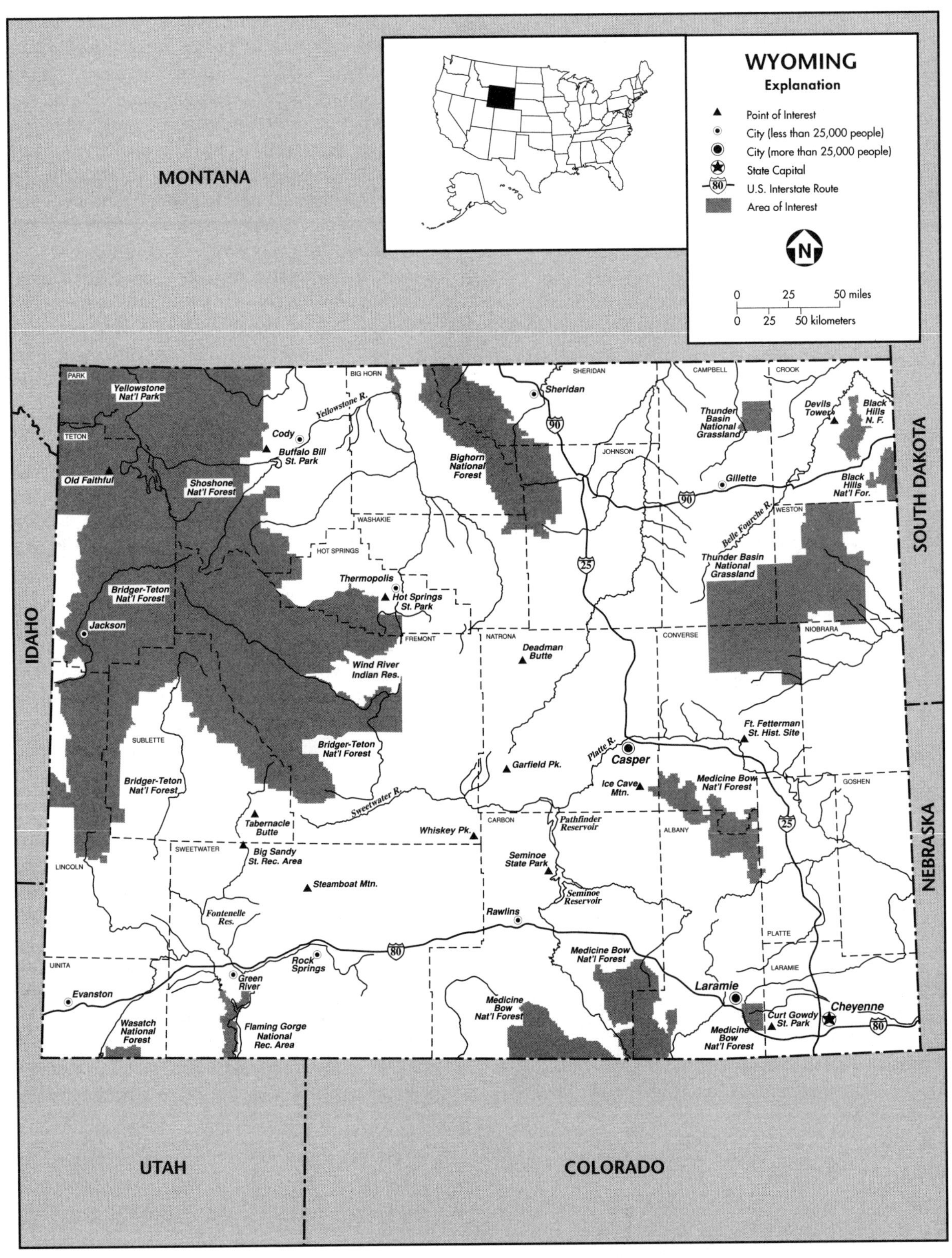

State of Wyoming

energy production, the economy of Wyoming is based largely on feed grains and livestock, with the timber industry also an important sector. Tourism is becoming an important industry in the state, especially at the state's two national parks, Yellowstone and Grand Teton. In addition, urban dwellers are increasingly seeking seasonal or permanent havens in Wyoming's mountains and open spaces. With no personal or corporate income taxes, the state is favorable to business. It ranked 35th among the 50 states in per capita personal income in 1996.

See also: **Cattle Industry, Cowboy, Cow Towns, Native American Policy**

FURTHER READING

Athearn, Robert G. *Union Pacific Country*. New York: Rand McNally, 1971.

Larson, T. A. *Wyoming: A Bicentennial History*. New York: Norton, 1977.

———. *Wyoming: A History*. New York: Norton, 1984.

Mead, Jean. *Wyoming in Profile*. Boulder, CO: Pruett, 1982.

Woods, L. Milton. *The Wyoming Country Before Statehood*. Worland, WY: Worland Press, 1971.

YELLOW DOG CONTRACTS

A yellow dog contract is a labor contract in which workers are required to refrain from joining a union in exchange for being hired. It emerged in the nineteenth century as one of many tactics companies used to discourage workers from organizing to win wage increases and improved working conditions.

During rapid industrialization of the United States in the years after the American Civil War (1861–1865), many workers endured seven-day workweeks, minimal pay, and inhumane working conditions. As a result, the U.S. labor movement successfully organized many new unions. As unions pushed for eight-hour days, pro-business legislators and sympathetic judges passed laws to prevent labor unions from recruiting new members. Across the country legislatures passed laws outlawing ''combinations'' of workers that, in the words of one such law, ''willfully or maliciously injured another in his . . . business.'' Because unionizing a company's labor force could be viewed as ''injuring'' that business, union activism was successfully thwarted.

In the famous Pullman Strike of 1894 which was led by socialist Eugene V. Debs (1855–1926), members of the American Railway Union went on strike against the Pullman Palace Car Company of Chicago when it cut wages by 25 percent. Refusing to work on any train that pulled a Pullman railcar, the union looked like it could prevail because almost every train passing through Chicago carried Pullman cars. When the striking workers began attacking the trains, however, President Grover Cleveland (1885–1889) called in the U.S. Army to end the strike. When Pullman reopened its plant later that year, it required all new employees to sign yellow dog contracts.

In 1898 Congress passed the Erdman Act, which prevented railroads that were engaged in interstate commerce from forcing their employees to sign yellow dog contracts. In *Adair v. the United States*, however, the U.S. Supreme Court ruled that the Erdman Act was unconstitutional. Throughout the 1920s many U.S. businesses continued to require workers to reject union membership as a precondition of employment, but the onset of Great Depression (1929–1939) finally shifted the law to the side of labor. The Norris-LaGuardia Act of 1932, the National Industrial Recovery Act of 1933, and the Wagner Act of 1935 formally recognized the rights of labor unions to organize and explicitly outlawed yellow dog contracts.

***See also:* Closed Shop, Labor Movement, Labor Unionism, National Industrial Recovery Act, Norris-LaGuardia Act**

ZENITH ELECTRONICS CORPORATION

Zenith Electronics Corporation's beginnings were very modest. In 1918 two ham radio operators, Karl E. Hassel and R. H. G. Mathews, began manufacturing radio equipment at a kitchen table under the name Chicago Radio Laboratory. Hassel ran an amateur radio station with the call letters 9ZN, from which they named their first product Zenith. In 1921 these two men were joined by Eugene F. McDonald Jr. McDonald, already a self-made millionaire when he joined the company, was pivotal to Zenith's growth. He was much more than a financial backer. McDonald's flamboyant style was echoed in the company's dramatic advertising methods. This style, coupled with innovative genius and an ability to sense changes in public tastes, meant that for more than three decades McDonald was Zenith in the public perception. The company was incorporated as Zenith Radio Corporation in 1923 and it officially began to manufacture under the Zenith name.

Zenith's inventors and technicians kept the company at the forefront of the infant radio industry. In 1924 Zenith introduced the world's first portable radio. Two years later Zenith introduced the first home radio receiver that operated directly from regular AC electric current. Another early accomplishment was the first automatic push-button radio tuner, which was introduced in 1927. That same year saw the first use of the famous Zenith slogan, "The Quality Goes In Before The Name Goes On." By the late 1920s Zenith was in 12th place in a $400 million industry.

During the Great Depression (1929–1939) Zenith's sales dropped from $10 million in 1929 to less than two million dollars in 1932, but the company managed to stay afloat. Just prior to U.S. involvement in World War II (1939–1945) Zenith became a pioneer in television and FM radio broadcasting. In 1939 Zenith's station W9XZV went on the air as the first all-electronic television station. This was followed the next year by W9XEN, one of the first FM stations in the United States and the first in the Midwest. By 1941 Zenith had risen to second place in a $600 million industry, behind only RCA. Although World War II caused a decline in normal consumer business, this decline was more than offset by war production. Zenith manufactured radar, communications equipment, and high-sensitivity frequency meters.

Following World War II Zenith concentrated on improving television. The company introduced its first line of black-and-white television receivers in 1948. While experimenting with color television in its laboratories until the quality was up to the company standard, Zenith continued to work on its black-and-white televisions. The company invented the first wireless remote control in 1956 which revolutionized television tuning, and it held the leading position in black-and-white television production from 1959 on.

The color television breakthrough came in 1961, when Zenith introduced a ten-receiver line of color sets. Demand for these sets grew so quickly that the company had to expand its facilities. Also that year Zenith's experimental stereophonic FM broadcasting system was approved by the FCC as the national standard. Color television improvements continued steadily. In 1969 Zenith introduced the patented Chromacolor picture tube, which set the standard for brightness in the color television industry for many years. By 1972, the year it introduced a line of 25-inch televisions, Zenith was number one in production of color television sets. Between 1972 and 1978 Zenith was able to maintain the leading position in the fiercely competitive U.S. color television market, but the company was overtaken by RCA in 1979.

Starting in the 1970s the entire U.S. electronic consumer goods industry was under increasing competitive pressure from Asian manufacturers. Manufacturers from Japan, Taiwan, and Korea began selling great numbers of electronics products in the United States at prices below what U.S. companies could afford to offer. As a result, Zenith's share of the television-set market fell steadily in the 1970s and

1980s. Searching for a turnaround, the company entered the personal computer field in 1979 but exited that sector in 1989, finding it to be just as competitive as that of television. Zenith marketed its last radio in 1982 and changed its long out-dated name to Zenith Electronics Corporation in 1985. In 1988, continuing its long tradition of innovation, Zenith became one of the earliest proponents of high-definition television, the super-sharp digital television technology that was supposed to replace the standard analog television.

From the mid-1980s into the late 1990s Zenith lost money every year except for 1988, when it reported a modest $12 million profit. By the mid-1990s the company had shifted most of its manufacturing to Mexico in order to cut costs. By that time the company was also the last of the American-controlled television manufacturers. That changed in 1995 when LG Group, based in South Korea, purchased a fifty-eight percent stake in Zenith. The company's financial condition continued to worsen. In May 1998 Zenith announced that it planned to restructure under the protection of bankruptcy laws, intending to emerge from bankruptcy as a wholly owned subsidiary of LG Group.

See also: **RCA-Victor**

FURTHER READING

Cahill, Joseph B. "Zenith's Quest for Recovery." *Crain's Chicago Business*, January 13, 1997.

Cones, Harold N. and John H. Bryant. *Zenith Radio: The Early Years, 1919–1935.* Atglen, PA: Schiffer, 1997.

Curtis, Philip J. *The Fall of the U.S. Consumer Electronics Industry: An American Trade Tragedy.* Westport, CT: Quorum Books, 1994.

Kartus, Lisa. "The Strange Folks Picking on Zenith." *Fortune*, December 19, 1998.

Oloroso, Arsenio, Jr. "Zenith's Revamp on High Wire." *Crain's Chicago Business*, September 14, 1998.

Zenith Radio Corporation. *Zenith: Highlights of the First 60 Years.* Glenview, IL: Zenith Radio Corporation, 1978.

Index

A

B

D

E

F

G

H

J

K

M

N

O

P

S

T

U

V

W

X

Y

Z